The British Boxing
Board of Control
BOXING
YEARBOOK
2005

Edited and compiled by
Barry J. Hugman

Queen Anne Press

First published in Great Britain in 2004 by
Queen Anne Press
a division of Lennard Associates Ltd
Mackerye End, Harpenden
Hertfordshire, AL5 5DR

A CIP catalogue record for this book
is available from the British Library

ISBN 1 85291 659 1

Typeset and designed by
Typecast (Artwork & Design)
Labrador Way, Northfield Lane
Watergore, South Petherton
Somerset, TA13 5LH

Printed and bound in Great Britain by
Biddles Ltd

Front cover
Scott Harrison retaining his WBO World Featherweight title
against William Abelyan of USA at Braehaed Arena, Glasgow
(Christopher Furlong/Getty Images)
Inset: Amir Khan with his Olympic silver medal
(Getty Images)

Back cover:
Amir Khan in the Olympic lightweight final
against Mario Cesar Kindelan Mesa of Cuba
(Omar Torres/AFP/Getty Images)

Contents

ST. ANDREW'S SPORTING CLUB

Est. 1973

THE HOME OF SCOTTISH BOXING

Holiday Inn Glasgow City West, Bothwell Street, Glasgow, G2 7EN
Tel: 0141 248 5461   Fax: 0141 248 5922
E-Mail: STANDREWSSPORT@AOL.COM

SEASON DATES 2004/5

Monday 20th September 2004
Monday 11th October
Monday 15th November
Saturday 4th December
(Ladies Night - Dinner Dance Cabaret)

Monday 31st January 2005
Monday 21st February
Monday 21st March
Monday 25th April
Saturday 14th May
(May Ball - Dinner Dance Cabaret)

Director: Tommy Gilmour

Acknowledgements

For the past 21 years this has been a considerable team effort, with many of the original members still participating, and I would like to take time out and thank all those who have helped to establish the *British Boxing Yearbook* as the 'Wisden' of British boxing. We think that it is an essential work of reference for the sport and one that, in its own way, is just as important to the boxing public as is the weekly *Boxing News*.

As in previous years, I am indebted to the BBBoC's General Secretary, Simon Block, along with Lynne Conway, Helen Oakley and Donna Streeter, for their continued help and support in placing information at my disposal and being of assistance when required. Simon's assistant, Robert Smith, who is also the Southern Area Secretary and a former pro fighter of note, was again extremely helpful, as was another former well-known boxer, Dai Corp, the Welsh and Western Area Secretary who now works out of the Board's Cardiff office.

On a business front, I would like to thank the BBBoC for their support and Bernard Hart, the Managing Director of the Lonsdale International Sporting Club, for his efforts in organising the annual British Boxing Board of Control Awards Luncheon where the book will be launched. The Awards Luncheon has been an ongoing function since 1984, when it was established by myself and the Board to coincide with the launch of the first Yearbook and Bernard, ably backed up by Kymberley and Chas Taylor, make sure the standard remains top class. At the same time, I would like to thank all of those who advertised within these pages for their support.

Ron Olver has been with the *Yearbook* from day one and, as ever, remains a tower of strength with his help and support. Once again, despite it being another difficult year and suffering continued ill-health, Ron has produced the Directory of Ex-Boxers' Associations. A former Assistant Editor of both *Boxing News* and *Boxing World*, he is also well known as the British correspondent of the *Ring*; the author of *The Professionals*; for producing the boxing section within *Encyclopedia Britannica*; his work on *Boxing*, Foyles' library service; and as the former co-editor of the *Boxing News Annual*. His honorary work, which included being the Chairman of the BBBoC Charity Grants' Committee; the Vice-President of many ex-boxers' associations; the Public Relations Officer of the London Ex-Boxers' Association; membership of the Commonwealth Boxing Council as New Zealand's representative; and the International Hall of Fame has, in recent years, seen him honoured by the Boxing Writers' Club, the BBBoC, and the Commonwealth Boxing Council. He has been further honoured by the Boxing Writers' Club, who have made him an Honorary Life Member. It was due to Ron's promptings that the ex-boxers' associations came into being as we now know them, and he will always be remembered by the *Boxing News'* readership as the man responsible for the 'Old Timers' page, now in its 37th year.

Members of the *Yearbook* 'team' who wrote articles for this year's edition and who have recently been published, or are in the process of publishing their own books are: John Jarrett (*Gene Tunney: The Golden Guy Who Licked Jack Dempsey*); Bob Lonkhurst (*Fen Tiger: The Success of Dave 'Boy' Green*); Ralph Oates (*The Heavyweight Boxing Quizbook*); Tony Gee (*Up To Scratch*. At this moment in time, Tony is preparing a book on the history of bareknuckle fighting in Scotland); Melanie Lloyd (Currently working on *Sweet Fighting Man – Volume11*) and Tracey Pollard (who continues to work on a book about the life and times of Brian London, the former British heavyweight champion). Also, we welcome Keith Robinson, who is looking to publish an in-depth work on Bob Fitzsimmons.

I am also indebted to Patrick Myler, who has long been associated with the Yearbook, for allowing me to reproduce a well-written piece on Johnny Caldwell and Freddie Gilroy from his excellent book, *The Fighting Irish*. At a time when I was boxing as a young amateur bantamweight, these were the men I looked up to. They were star quality. Yet again, Wynford Jones, the Class 'A' referee, came to my rescue when travelling to the Board's offices on a regular basis in order to collate vital data required for this publication, and also produced an article titled: Eddie Thomas: Champion and Maker of Champions. Other members of the Yearbook 'team' are Bob Yalen, who has covered boxing with ABC across the world and looks after the World Title Bouts' section; Harold Alderman, an unsung hero who has spent over 40 years researching the early days of boxing through to modern times, has extended the Early Gloved Championship Boxing section from 152 to 170lbs; Chris Kempson, who produces Highlights from the Amateur Season, is our man in the world of amateur boxing; Eric Armit, who is a leading authority on boxers' records throughout the world, is responsible for the A-Z of Current World Champions; and Derek O'Dell, a former amateur boxer and Chairman of Croydon EBA, produces the Obituaries' section.

Regarding photographs, as in previous years the great majority were produced by Les Clark (Les also writes the Boxing Quiz with a Few Below the Belt within these pages), who has possibly the largest library of both action and poses from British rings. If anyone requires a copy of a photo that has appeared in the *Yearbook* credited to Les, or requires a list, he can be reached at 352 Trelawney Avenue, Langley, Berks SL3 7TS. Other photos were supplied by my good friends, Paul Speak and Philip Sharkey. More help came in the shape of Larry Braysher, a well-known collector, who supplied several photos for the Obituaries' section and the Gilroy v Caldwell and Eddie Thomas articles.

Also, additional input came from Neil Blackburn (who yet again provided information to make the Obituaries' section as complete as possible); Mrs Enza Jacoponi, the Secretary of the European Boxing Union (EBU Championship data covering the past 12 months); Simon Block (Commonwealth and British Championship data); Patrick Myler (Irish amateur boxing); Malcolm Collins (Welsh amateur boxing); Moira, John McKay and Brian Donald (Scottish amateur boxing); Peter Foley, Dave Cockell, Saphire Lee, Jenny Peake and Dave Norman (English amateur boxing); and Dai Corp, John Jarrett, Brian McAllister, Ken Morton, Les Potts, and Robert Smith (Area title data). Although the research on world title bouts since gloves continues to wind down, I would again like to praise the efforts of men such as Tracy Callis, Luckett Davis and John Hogg, who are always available to help track down old-time fighters' records from abroad.

Finally, my thanks go to Jean Bastin, who continued to produce a high standard of typesetting and design, and my wife, Jennifer, who looks after the proof reading.

TARA BOXING PROMOTIONS & MANAGEMENT

Doughty's Gym, Princess Road, Shaw, Oldham OL2 7AZ
Tel/Fax: 01706-845753 (Office) Tel: 01706-846762 (Gym)
07932-085865 (Mobile)

Trainer/Manager: Jack Doughty
Trainers: Eamon Vickers, Ray Ashton,
Maurice Core, Andy Jessiman
Matchmaker: Richard Poxon M.C: Michael Pass

BOXERS
Shinny Bayaar - Flyweight
Gary Ford - Bantamweight
Choi Tseveenpurev - British Masters
Featherweight Champion
Charles Shepherd - Former British, Commonwealth & IBO
World Super-Featherweight Champion
Bobby Vanzie - Former British & Commonwealth
Lightweight Champion
Tom Hogan - Light-Welterweight
Gary Hadwin - Welterweight
Wayne Shepherd - Light-Middleweight
Gary Dixon - Super-Middleweight
Darren Stubbs - Super-Middleweight

Introduction

by Barry J. Hugman

It gives me great pleasure to welcome you to the 21st edition of the *British Boxing Yearbook*. The format hasn't changed too much over the years, certainly not since the 1993 edition, as myself and the team continue to monitor and update the current goings on, while also continuing to research the past and pass on our findings.

Beginning with the modern era, once again we have decided to stay with the way we produce Current British Based-Boxers: Complete Records. The decision to have one alphabet, instead of separating champions, being taken on the grounds that because there are so many champions these days – British, Commonwealth, European, IBF, WBA, WBC, WBO, and more recently WBU, IBO, WBF, etc, etc, and a whole host of Inter-Continental and International titles – it would cause confusion rather than what was really intended. If you wish to quickly locate whether or not a boxer fought during the past season (1 July 2003 to 30 June 2004) then the Boxers' Record Index at the back of the *Yearbook* is the place to look. Also, as in the very first edition, we chart the promotions in Britain throughout the season, thus enabling one to refer to the exact venue within a boxer's record.

Regarding our records, if a fighter is counted out standing up we have continued to show it as a stoppage rather than that of a kayo or technical kayo, as in fights where the referee dispenses with the count. Thus fights are recorded as count outs (the count being tolled with the fighter still on the canvas), retirements (where a fighter is retired on his stool or by his corner during a contest) and referee stopped contest. Of course, other types of decisions would take in draws, no contests, and no decisions. In these days of health and safety fears, more and more boxers are being counted out either standing up or when initially floored, especially when a referee feels that the man on the receiving end is unable to defend himself adequately or requires immediate medical attention. One of the reasons that we have yet to discriminate between cut-eye stoppages and other types of endings, is because a fighter who is stopped because of cuts is often on his way to a defeat in the first place. Thus, if you want to get a true reflection on the fight it is probably better to consult the trade paper, Boxing News, rather than rely on a referee's decision to tell you all you want to know; the recorded result merely being a guide.

Continuing the trend, there are always new articles to match the old favourites. Regular features such as Home and Away with British Boxers (John Jarrett), World Title Bouts During the Season (Bob Yalen), A-Z of Current World Champions (Eric Armit), Highlights from the Amateur Season (Chris Kempson), Directory of Ex-Boxers' Associations (Ron Olver), Obituaries (Derek O'Dell) and two regular quizzes (Ralph Oates and Les Clark), etc, being supported this year with interesting articles such as Andy Smith: An Appreciation (Bob Lonkhurst); Steve Holdsworth: A Man for all Boxing Seasons (Ralph Oates); Jane Couch: The Fleetwood

Assassin (Melanie Lloyd); Eddie Thomas: Champion and Maker of Champions (Wynford Jones); Jack Bates: Boxing's Quiet Genius (Tracey Pollard); Pugilists and the Britannia: Fistic Entertainments at a Glasgow Music Hall (Tony Gee) and Lanky Bob: How Good Was Bob Fitzsimmons (Keith R. Robinson).

Elsewhere, hopefully, you will find all you want to know about English, British Area, British, Commonwealth, European and world title bouts that took place in 2003-2004, along with the amateur championships that were held in England, Scotland, Wales and Ireland, as well as being able to access details on champions from the past, both amateur and professional.

Historically, what was started several years ago under the heading of Early Gloved Boxing, has now been extended from 152lbs to 170lbs in this edition. Much of this work was due to Harold Alderman painstakingly piecing together results for the pre-Lonsdale Belt and named-weight division period. There are still many who believe as gospel much of what was reported down the ages by 'respected' men such as Nat Fleischer, the owner of *The Ring* Magazine and the *Ring Record Book*, and then copied by numerous historians who failed to grasp what the sport was really like before the First World War. Hopefully, we will complete the exercise, with just the heavyweight (all those above 170lbs) class left, in the 2006 edition.

Basically, boxing prior to the period in question was a shambles, following bare fists with an assortment of driving gloves, knuckle gloves, and two-ounce gloves, etc, until it arrived at what we recognise today. There were no commissions, newspapermen becoming all-powerful by naming their own champions at all kinds of weights, and in much of America the sport was illegal, no-decision contests rescuing it from being abolished. If you thought today was dire, then boxing prior to that period was almost impossible in all divisions bar the heavyweights. Because travel was difficult and news travelled slowly, fighters were able to move from town to town proclaiming themselves to be the best and 'ringers' constantly prevailed. With today's research being aided by access to early newspapers, and the use of computers, it is becoming clear that men like Fleischer 'took' the best fighters of the day and then 'fitted' them into the named-weight divisions we now know so well. If that is still as clear as mud, then turn to the pages in question.

Abbreviations and Definitions used in the record sections of the Yearbook:
PTS (Points), CO (Count Out), RSC (Referee Stopped Contest), RTD (Retired), DIS (Disqualification), NC (No Contest), ND (No Decision).

British Boxing Board of Control Ltd: Structure

(Members of the Commonwealth Boxing Council and European Boxing Union)

PRESIDENT	Lord Brooks of Tremorfa DL
CHAIRMAN	His Honour Alan Simpson MA, Oxon
VICE CHAIRMAN	Charles Giles
GENERAL SECRETARY	Simon Block
ADMINISTRATIVE STEWARDS	Baroness Golding* John Handelaar Sir Geoffrey Inkin OBE Dennis Lockton Nicky Piper Leonard Read QPM Andrew Vanzie* Billy Walker*
REPRESENTATIVE STEWARDS	Geoff Boulter Bernard Connolly Paul Gooding* Ken Honniball Kevin Leafe* Phil Lundgren Ron Pavett* Fred Potter John Ratnage* Brian Renney Dave Roden Tony Behan* Derry Treanor* John Williamson
STEWARDS OF APPEAL*	Robin Simpson QC (Chairman) His Honour Brian Capstick QC Geoffrey Finn William Tudor John Robert Kidby Prof. Andrew Lees Timothy Langdale QC John Mathew QC Colin Ross-Munroe QC Peter Richards FRCS Nicholas Valios QC
HONORARY STEWARDS*	Frank Butler OBE Sir Henry Cooper OBE, KSG Capt. Robert Graham BEM Mary Peters DBE Dr Oswald Ross Bill Sheeran
HONORARY MEDICAL CONSULTANT*	Dr Roger C. Evans FRCP
HONARARY PARLIAMENTARY CONSULTANT*	Jimmy Wray MP
LEGAL ADVISOR*	Michael Boyce
HEAD OFFICE	The Old Library Trinity Street Cardiff CF10 1BH Tel: 02920 367000 Fax: 02920 367019 E-mail: sblock@bbbofc.com Website: www.bbbofc.com

* Not directors of the company

AREA COUNCILS - AREA SECRETARIES

AREA NO 1 (SCOTLAND)
Brian McAllister
11 Woodside Crescent, Glasgow G3 7UL
Telephone 0141 3320392. Fax 0141 3312029
E-Mail bmacallister@mcallisters-ca.com

AREA NO 2 (NORTHERN IRELAND)
John Campbell
8 Mount Eden Park, Belfast, Northern Ireland BT9 6RA
Telephone 02890 683310. Fax 02890 683310
Mobile 07715 044061

AREA NO 3 (WALES)
Dai Corp
The Old Library, Trinity Street
Cardiff CF10 1BH
Telephone 02920 367000. Fax 02920 367019
E-Mail sblock@bbbofc.com

AREA NO 4 (NORTHERN)
(Northumberland, Cumbria, Durham, Cleveland, Tyne and Wear, North Yorkshire [north of a line drawn from Whitby to Northallerton to Richmond, including these towns].)
John Jarrett
5 Beechwood Avenue, Gosforth, Newcastle upon Tyne NE3 5DH
Telephone/Fax 01912 856556
E-Mail john.jarrett5@btopenworld.com

AREA NO 5 (CENTRAL)
(North Yorkshire [with the exception of the part included in the Northern Area - see above], Lancashire, West and South Yorkshire, Greater Manchester, Merseyside and Cheshire, Isle of Man, North Humberside.)
Richard Jones
1 Churchfields, Croft, Warrington, Cheshire WA3 7JR
Telephone/Fax 01925 768132
E-Mail r.m.jones@mmu.ac.uk

AREA NO 6 (SOUTHERN)
(Bedfordshire, Berkshire, Buckinghamshire, Cambridgeshire, Channel Islands, Isle of Wight, Essex, Hampshire, Kent, Hertfordshire, Greater London, Norfolk, Suffolk, Oxfordshire, East and West Sussex.)
Robert W. Smith
The Old Library, Trinity Street, Cardiff CF10 1BH
Telephone 02920 367000. Fax 02920 367019
E-Mail rsmith@bbbofc.com

AREA NO 7 (WESTERN)
(Cornwall, Devon, Somerset, Dorset, Wiltshire, Avon, Gloucestershire.)
Dai Corp
The Old Library, Trinity Street
Cardiff CF10 1BH
Telephone 02920 367000. Fax 02920 367019
E-Mail sblock@bbbofc.com

AREA NO 8 (MIDLANDS)
(Derbyshire, Nottinghamshire, Lincolnshire, Salop, Staffordshire, Herefordshire and Worcestershire, Warwickshire, West Midlands, Leicestershire, South Humberside, Northamptonshire.)
Les Potts
1 Sunnyside Villas, Gnosall, Staffordshire
Telephone 01785 823641. Mobile 07973 533835
E-Mail lezpotts@hotmail.com

Foreword

by Simon Block *(General Secretary, British Boxing Board of Control)*

My optimism about the number of tournaments in last year's Foreword was slightly misplaced.

Despite a busy start to the season there was a drop in the overall number of tournaments from the period 1st July to 30th June from 198 to 183 (see "Facts and Figures" 2003 to 2004).

With the revision of Sky Sport dates and a question mark over the future of BBC TV coverage of boxing there is a good chance that the numbers will drop even further this year. The figures do fluctuate, as a look through all the Yearbooks since the first one in 1986 will confirm, and there is no cause for alarm but, nevertheless, none of us in boxing can afford to be complacent. Boxing has no divine right to exist. Despite a long and noble history stretching back to the 1700s and all the great champions who have formed a part of the fabric of British life, both participation in and enjoyment of, the sport faces great competition. Coverage of football now swamps all other sports in the media, the development of new sports, particularly in the martial arts, and the appeal of WWF wrestling to younger people all mitigate to knock boxing from its perch as one of the major spectator sports. Traditional sports such as tennis, cricket and golf are seeking to make themselves more accessible to the sections of society that traditionally came into boxing and with a variety of different forms of entertainment including computer games into which young people channel their energies these days, these are issues to be faced.

Lennox Lewis CBE, arguably our most successful boxer ever, has now retired to enjoy family life and despite rumours of a comeback the career of the exciting Naseem Hamed MBE must surely have drawn to a close. For the current stars, Richard Hatton and Joe Calzaghe, the public awaits the career defining contests that have so far eluded even the acknowledged negotiating skills of Frank Warren and genuine talents such as Scott Harrison, Johnny Nelson and Howard Eastman may not be as familiar to the greater British public than was the case with their predecessors a few decades ago.

So what is to be done? Well, we here at the Board are still intent on setting up a Joint Consultative Forum with our amateur counterparts in England, Wales and Scotland and, although the process splutters along in fits and starts, we are slowly getting there with the encouragement of the Minister for Sport and the support of the All Party Parliamentary Group on Boxing and UK Sport. Many senior Government figures now recognise the social and health benefits of getting our young people into boxing gymnasia, particularly in some of the more deprived areas of the country, and we hope that a Joint Consultative Forum can secure the necessary funding to encourage grass roots development, the breeding ground for both participants and spectators. Some of the future amateur stars will almost certainly turn professional and bring with them their supporters into the professional game.

A great responsibility lies with the promoters who promote the matches that people pay to see. Although we have witnessed some truly wonderful contests over the last 12 months, making the job of our Awards Committee very difficult in selecting the nominations for 'Contest of the Year', let alone the winner, we have noted over the last few years some excellent potential matches that have failed to be made. I refer in particular to the flyweight and light-middleweight divisions of a year or two back and, in the absence of a major world title challenge for Richard Hatton at the time of writing, all boxing fans will want to see him against Junior Witter, the current British and European Champion.

Then we can look at the proliferation of 'world' and 'international' titles that we have become so used to over here. Whilst these have proved of immense value to both boxers and promoters in the furtherance of their careers (some of the best contests over the last 12 months have been not only for British titles but for WBU and IBO titles as well), there is no doubt that they enable boxers to develop careers along parallel lines without the best meeting the best. Professional boxing must be just about the only sport in the world where this can happen. Arsenal could not have won the Premier Championship last season without somewhere along the way meeting Chelsea, Manchester United and Liverpool. Greece could not have won Euro 2004 without the knockout competition and Jonny Wilkinson had to kick the winning shot over the bar against Australia before England could call themselves the rugby world champs. It surely would not be cricket if England could claim to have won the 'Ashes' without actually having to beat Australia!

Demand from promoters, TV companies and, to some extent, boxers, has encouraged the situation in boxing and regrettably I doubt whether it will change significantly by the time I am called upon to write next year's Foreword. In 2004, the Board celebrated its 75th Anniversary with a wonderful evening at the grand City Hall in Cardiff, attended by so many of our current and former champions. I started work for the Board at the time of the 50th Anniversary celebrations with a similarly wonderful evening at the Cafe Royal in London in 1979. It is unlikely, I suspect, that I will still be General Secretary by the time we celebrate our 100th Anniversary, but I hope I am still around and sound in mind and body enough to enable me to accept an invitation to attend, wherever it might be held. Dare I hope that by then having the gloves on at sometime will be the norm rather than the exception for our youngsters, as well five figure gates for our major boxing tournaments and boxing events topping the TV viewing figures.

The silver medal success of Amir Khan in the Athens Olympics demonstrates how quickly the media and public react to the emergence of a new boxing star and, for the first time in years, amateur boxing is back on the back pages of the national newspapers.

The General Secretary of the British Boxing Board of Control, a position more concerned with regulation than promotion, has only limited powers in this respect but such as they exist I will be doing all I can during the remainder of my tenure to keep boxing where it should be - on top, wearing a crown.

EVANS-WATERMAN PROMOTIONS

Licensed to the British Boxing Board of Control

Members of the Professional Boxing Promoters' Association

**88 WINDSOR ROAD
BRAY, MAIDENHEAD
BERKS SL6 2DJ**

Tel: 01628 623640   Fax: 01628 684633   Mobile: 07768 954643

e-mail: jimbox@tinyworld.co.uk

CURRENT LIST

HEAVYWEIGHTS
Roman Greenberg	–	8-10 Rounds
Jacklord Jacobs	–	6-8 Rounds
James Gilbert	–	4-6 Rounds

CRUISERWEIGHTS
Tommy Eastwood	–	8-10 Rounds
Keith Fletcher	–	6-8 Rounds
Shpetim Hoti	–	4-6 Rounds

LIGHT-HEAVYWEIGHT
Nick Okoth	–	4-6 Rounds

SUPER-MIDDLEWEIGHTS
Jamie Hearn	–	6-8 Rounds
Matthew Barney (WBU Champion)	–	10-12 Rounds
Geard Ajetovic	–	6-8 Rounds

LIGHT-MIDDLEWEIGHTS
Clint Smith	–	4-6 Rounds
Neil Jarmonski	–	4-6 Rounds

WELTERWEIGHTS
Robert Lloyd-Taylor	–	6-8 Rounds
Rocky Muscus	–	4-6 Rounds

LIGHT-WELTERWEIGHT
Chris McDonagh	–	6-8 Rounds

LIGHTWEIGHTS
Peter McDonagh (Southern Area Champion)	–	8-10 Rounds
Jon Honney	–	8-10 Rounds

SUPER-FEATHERWEIGHT
Mickey Bowden	–	8-10 Rounds

SUPER-BANTAMWEIGHT
Gary Davis	–	6-8 Rounds

WEST LONDON'S FASTEST RISING STABLE
Trainers: Johnny Bloomfield - Johnny Eames - Darren Whitman

British Boxing Board of Control Awards

The Awards, inaugurated in 1984 in the form of statuettes of boxers, and designed by Morton T. Colver, are supplied by Len Fowler Trophies of Holborn. Len was an early post-war light-heavyweight favourite. As in 2003, the Awards Ceremony, which has reverted back to a luncheon format, is due to be held this coming Autumn in London and will again be co-hosted by the Lonsdale International Sporting Club's Bernard Hart.

British Boxer of the Year: The outstanding British Boxer at any weight. 1984: Barrry McGuigan. 1985: Barry McGuigan. 1986: Dennis Andries. 1987: Lloyd Honeyghan. 1988: Lloyd Honeyghan. 1989: Dennis Andries. 1990: Dennis Andries. 1991: Dave McAuley. 1992: Colin McMillan. 1993: Lennox Lewis. 1994: Steve Robinson. 1995: Nigel Benn. 1996: Prince Naseem Hamed. 1997: Robin Reid. 1998: Carl Thompson. 1999: Billy Schwer. 2000: Glenn Catley. 2001: Joe Calzaghe. 2002: Lennox Lewis. 2003: Ricky Hatton.

British Contest of the Year: Although a fight that took place in Europe won the 1984 Award, since that date, the Award, presented to both participants, has applied to the best all-action contest featuring a British boxer in a British ring. 1984: Jimmy Cable v Said Skouma. 1985: Barry McGuigan v Eusebio Pedroza. 1986: Mark Kaylor v Errol Christie. 1987: Dave McAuley v Fidel Bassa. 1988: Tom Collins v Mark Kaylor. 1989: Michael Watson v Nigel Benn. 1990: Orlando Canizales v Billy Hardy. 1991: Chris Eubank v Nigel Benn. 1992: Dennis Andries v Jeff Harding. 1993: Andy Till v Wally Swift Jnr. 1994: Steve Robinson v Paul Hodkinson. 1995: Steve Collins v Chris Eubank. 1996: P. J. Gallagher v Charles Shepherd. 1997: Spencer Oliver v Patrick Mullings. 1998: Carl Thompson v Chris Eubank. 1999: Shea Neary v Naas Scheepers. 2000: Simon Ramoni v Patrick Mullings. 2001: Colin Dunne v Billy Schwer. 2002: Ezra Sellers v Carl Thompson. 2003: David Barnes v Jimmy Vincent.

Overseas Boxer of the Year: For the best performance by an overseas boxer in a British ring. 1984: Buster Drayton. 1985: Don Curry. 1986: Azumah Nelson. 1987: Maurice Blocker. 1988: Fidel Bassa. 1989: Brian Mitchell. 1990: Mike McCallum. 1991: Donovan Boucher. 1992: Jeff Harding. 1993: Crisanto Espana. 1994: Juan Molina. 1995: Mike McCallum. 1996: Jacob Matlala. 1997: Ronald Wright. 1998: Tim Austin. 1999: Vitali Klitschko. 2000: Keith Holmes. 2001: Harry Simon. 2002: Jacob Matlala. 2003: Manuel Medina.

Special Award: Covers a wide spectrum, and is an appreciation for services to boxing. 1984: Doctor Adrian Whiteson. 1985: Harry Gibbs. 1986: Ray Clarke. 1987: Hon. Colin Moynihan. 1988: Tom Powell. 1989: Winston Burnett. 1990: Frank Bruno. 1991: Muhammad Ali. 1992: Doctor Oswald Ross. 1993: Phil Martin. 1994: Ron Olver. 1995: Gary Davidson. 1996: Reg Gutteridge and Harry Carpenter. 1997: Miguel Matthews and Pete Buckley. 1998: Mickey Duff and Tommy Miller. 1999: Jim Evans and Jack Lindsey. 2000: Henry Cooper. 2001: John Morris and Leonard 'Nipper' Read. 2002: Roy Francis and Richie Woodhall. 2003: Michael Watson.

Sportsmanship Award: This Award recognises boxers who set a fine example, both in-and-out of the ring. 1986: Frank Bruno. 1987: Terry Marsh. 1988: Pat Cowdell. 1989: Horace Notice. 1990: Rocky Kelly. 1991: Wally Swift Jnr. 1992: Duke McKenzie. 1993: Nicky Piper. 1994: Francis Ampofo. 1995: Paul Wesley. 1996: Frank Bruno. 1997: Lennox Lewis. 1998: Johnny Williams. 1999: Brian Coleman. 2000: Michael Ayers and Wayne Rigby. 2001: Billy Schwer. 2002: Mickey Cantwell. 2003: Francis Ampofo.

Ricky Hatton, the 2003 'British Boxer of the Year', receives his award from Lord Brooks of Tremorfa, the new President of the BBBoC　　　　　Les Clark

Andy Smith: An Appreciation

by Bob Lonkhurst

Few men involved in boxing possessed the knowledge and skills Andy Smith did. Apart from being a first class manager and trainer who knew the game inside out, he was also an astute businessman who used his skills to the benefit of his fighters. Referred to as Mr Smith by all the boys he trained, he had the respect of everyone who knew him.

"I was a very lucky man to have been with Mr Smith", remarked Dave 'Boy' Green one day during 2003, whilst preparing his biography. "We had a great relationship. He was a father-figure to me in a lot of ways. If every manager was like Andy Smith you wouldn't need a Boxing Board of Control".

Green's words reflected the feelings of every boxer handled by Andy, a man who refused to take his cut from boys until they were earning good money. Dave never forgot that, and is as close to his former trainer and manager now as when he was fighting almost 30 years ago.

Andy was born at Johnstone in Renfrewshire on 16 October 1925. His father, Andrew senior, had plenty of ring experience and had loved the game ever since he had his first boxing lesson whilst in the Boy Scouts. Although he was small, he developed into one of the best amateurs in the district and turned professional in 1922 at the age of 18. He also earned extra money fighting in the boxing booths.

Because his family weren't keen on boxing, Smith took the name of 'Young Hawker' because he had built up a good business selling fruit and vegetables from a barrow. Yet he always made himself available for a fight at short notice and had the reputation of being able to give a good account of himself.

In 1932, Tommy Watson, a Glasgow booth promoter, called upon him to top a show in a ten rounder against 19-year-old Benny Lynch. Although Benny was still relatively unknown, he had taken part in about 30 official fights and many others in the booths. Lynch was awarded the decision, but from that day the two became close friends. By this time, Smith had his own boxing club at Johnstone and invited Benny to visit him. With his parents constantly involved in drunken rows, Lynch jumped at the chance, and frequently stayed at the Smith's house. Apart from training together, the two boxers often travelled to England and joined up with either the Len Johnson or Battling Sullivan Booths.

Andy Smith learned all the rudiments of boxing at his father's club. Although he had barely a dozen amateur contests, he succeeded in winning a Western District championship. Yet his father, who reportedly took part in over 400 contests, considered he was not good enough to go very far and ordered him to give up boxing. He had completed an engineering apprenticeship and got a good job as a tool maker, so a career away from boxing was more attractive and much safer.

Andy joined the Fleet Air Arm in January 1944 and saw service during the final 18 months of the second world war.

He reached the rank of Chief Petty Officer, but was discharged on medical grounds in May 1947 following a horrific accident in the Middle East. He was one of a group of 20 servicemen being transported in the back of a truck which became involved in a collision and spun off the road. As it hurtled down a ravine, Andy and the others were thrown out, but the vehicle landed on his legs trapping him for several hours. Many of his mates lying alongside him were dead, and he later discovered that he was one of only two survivors.

Within three months of his discharge, Andy joined Wimpey and went into lodgings at Carmarthen. He became a mechanical engineer, travelling throughout south and west Wales looking after plant equipment on road constructions. He learned to speak fluent Welsh, and whilst at Briton Ferry near Swansea, met the lady who would become his wife.

Andy and Valerie were married in 1950, and in 1954 he was promoted to plant manager and transferred to St Ives, where he built a detached bungalow the following year. He left Wimpey in 1964 and joined the St Ives Sand & Gravel company. When that company sold out to A.R.C., his new employers appointed him director in charge of mechanical equipment for the whole region. He also became a full member of the Institute of Quarrying in December 1965.

Following his move to St Ives, Andy formed a local boxing club at Crown Yard above some lock-up garages. It developed well and in 1965 was awarded the Tony Noble trophy for being the best amateur club in Britain. It was a tremendous achievement and it was the first time the award had gone to a club outside London.

By this time, Andy was involved in training professionals and had a gym at Bluntisham. The first men he looked after were the Laud brothers from St Ives – Mickey, Monty and Winston, and trained them throughout their careers. Mickey started fighting for pay in 1963 and his brothers a year later. All developed into sound professionals, Monty winning the Southern Area bantam and featherweight championships, and Winston the Southern Area lightweight title. Their careers were, however, much shorter than Mickey's. He boxed on a regular basis until 1973, amassing a record of 28 wins, six draws and 28 defeats. Mickey also challenged for the Southern Area lightweight title, but was disqualified in the sixth round against Brian Brazier in 1965.

During his time in Wales, Andy got to know Brian Curvis and the people who handled him, particularly Dicky Dobbs. There was tremendous mutual respect between the parties and when Curvis was at the peak of his professional career Andy was engaged to help him. He was in his corner for the fight with Dave Charnley in March 1964 and the Welshman also trained at his Bluntisham gym for his world welterweight title fight against Emile Griffith, six months later. The following year, Andy accompanied Brian to Johannesburg for his losing fight with Willie Ludick.

It was at about this time that Joe Bugner first came on the scene. By virtue of his work with St Ives Sand & Gravel, Andy travelled the region extensively and one day somebody told him about a big strapping lad who excelled at athletics and was also a useful young boxer.

Although he was only 15, Joe was a tremendous javelin and discus thrower, and also boxed for his local club, Bedford Boys. Andy took a great interest in him, especially after Joe won the London North-West Divisional heavyweight championship in sensational style at RAF Stanmore in March 1967.

The following month, Andy was even more impressed when the young heavyweight stopped experienced, Dave Hallinan, in the opening round on a club show at Chatteris. Another future star also scored an emphatic first round victory on the same bill. In only his fifth schoolboy contest, Dave 'Boy' Green beat Ray McLean from the London-based Lynn Club in the first 42 seconds.

Bugner was just a small boy when his mother brought him to England from Hungary, together with his elder brother, Bill, and sister, Margaret. He was only 17 when he signed professional terms with Andy, but, despite the high hopes the manager had for him, he was knocked out in three rounds by Paul Brown on his debut at the Anglo American Sporting Club in London.

Although it was a disastrous start in the paid ranks, his astute manager instilled massive confidence into the youngster. Having a fight almost every month during 1968, Joe progressed well, winning all 11 contests, ten inside the distance, including a stoppage victory over Paul Brown.

Tall and handsome, Bugner was a young man with an adonis profile. By working with leading promoters, Harry Levene, Mickey Duff and Mike Barrett, Andy ensured that he not only got maximum exposure, but was also carefully eased up the heavyweight ladder. Boxing regularly at the big London venues, the Royal Albert Hall and Wembley, he took on and beat a series of American opponents.

Although he suffered a minor set-back when outpointed by Dick Hall at Manchester in August 1969, he continued to progress steadily under Andy's guidance. Victories over solid opponents, Johnny Prescott, Roberto Davila, Manuel Ramos, Ray Patterson, Brian London, Chuck Wepner, Eduardo Corletti and others steered him towards a triple championship contest with champion Henry Cooper at Wembley on 16 March 1971.

At a press conference after contracts were signed, Andy remarked: "Joseph is a dedicated boxer. I did promise him this title fight by his 21st birthday. That is on March 13, so it wasn't a bad estimate".

Their plans, however, very nearly came unstuck because, on 10 February 1971, Bugner took a fight against Bill Drover of Canada at York Hall, Bethnal Green, shown live on BBC television and for which he was paid about £3,000. The result was a draw, but the fact was Joe struggled against a man he was expected to overwhelm. Andy, however, was unconcerned and told the press not to pay too much attention to Bugner's performance or the result.

"Joe was under instructions not to get involved with this fellow," he insisted. "Caution was the watchword.

Personally I am overjoyed that he came through the fight without a mark. It proved I was right taking a calculated risk in accepting the match and was ideal preparation before meeting Cooper. Joe will be all the better for it".

Wembley was sold out weeks before the fight, which was shown on close-circuit TV at cinemas across the nation. The critics were divided as to the likely outcome, but were in general agreement that Andy had done a wonderful job with Bugner, who was not a born fighter. He had to be taught to box, but wanted to do it for the chance to earn big money.

Although Andy always had strong relationships with all his boxers, that with Joe was special because he was so young when they first met. Not having a father in Britain, he took it upon himself to become a father-figure as the young fighter's career developed. It wasn't just about business because Andy wasn't like that. He was a special breed who genuinely cared for the men he trained. He took them into his home for a week or more before important fights in order that he could keep a close eye on them and monitor their moods and diets.

As is well documented, Bugner beat Cooper to become British, European and Commonwealth champion, but lost the titles to Jack Bodell six months later. Although he was also beaten by the American, Larry Middleton, Andy picked him up brilliantly and steered him to further success and a position high in the world rankings. After regaining the European title, which he held for three years before relinquishing it, Joe was manoeuvred into consecutive big money non-title fights with Muhammed Ali and Joe Frazier. Despite losing both on points, he came out of those fights with enormous credit.

Bugner was originally scheduled to defend his European title against British and Commonwealth champion, Danny McAlinden, at Earls Court on 2 July 1973, the night he faced Frazier. Despite the importance of the contest, McAlinden's manager, Jack Solomons, foolishly allowed him to go ahead with a contest against Morris Jackson of America in May, very much against the wishes of Andy Smith. When Danny was beaten inside three rounds the £100,000 triple championship fight fell through and Frazier was brought in as a high profile replacement.

Bugner put on his best-ever display that night and was then unbeaten for two years, which included three successful defences of his European championship. Yet, despite his considerable success, he was often extremely frustrating. "Why do we bother?" a despairing Andy Smith was often heard to remark late at night after fights in London. "I know the talent is there somewhere – we've just got to get it out". One of Joe's most disappointing displays was in the searing heat of Kuala Lumpur on 1 July 1975, when he erred on the side of caution in a world title fight against Muhammed Ali. Whilst he displayed great courage, he took no chances and was beaten widely on points.

Bugner's success did, however, highlight the immense talent of Andy Smith both as a manager and trainer. Although his gymnasiums were situated in Cambridgeshire, an area not noted for producing top class professional fighters, he received massive national publicity.

Knowledgeable fight fans soon acknowledged him as one of the finest in the business.

Des Morrison, a schoolmate of Bugner, joined the camp in 1970 and stayed with Smith throughout his professional career, spanning 50 contests over 13 years. During that time, he became the first man to win the British light-welterweight championship when he beat Joe Tetteh in November 1973. He also held the Southern Area welter and light-welter titles and challenged unsuccessfully on four occasions for British and Commonwealth championships.

Andy moved his gymnasium from Bluntisham to Huntington and then in January 1974 opened a new training camp at St Ives in a former school which he had converted.

He called it Andy's Boxing Academy. The Mayor of St Ives conducted the opening ceremony, while Joe Bugner and Des Morrison proudly displayed their European and British championship belts to a packed house.

In the years that followed, Joe and Des were joined in the camp by a succession of good fighters including Jeff Gale, Harry Watson, Steve Hopkin, Jimmy Harrington, John Bibby, Joey Joynson and Andy 's younger son, Robert. Gale and Hopkin won Southern Area championships, the latter also challenging unsuccessfully for the British light-middleweight title. The man who created the most interest, however, was Dave 'Boy' Green, a young farm worker from Chatteris.

Andy (right) and the man he led to a world title shot – Dave 'Boy' Green

A good amateur, Green was strongly fancied to win an ABA championship in 1974, but was having great difficulty getting sparring at his local club. His trainer therefore suggested that he went to Andy Smith's gym one Sunday morning in November 1973. Andy was very receptive and, on discovering Dave's status, invited him to return the following week and train with his boxers.

It was a wonderful experience for Green because apart from giving him an insight into the serious business of professional boxing, it also provided him with much needed sparring. Des Morrison was in full training for his title fight with Joe Tetteh and being about the same weight, Andy invited the Chatteris youngster to spar with him.

Andy was impressed by his attitude and determination, and invited him to train at the gym on a regular basis. By working with professionals, Dave's punching power and style improved dramatically and he ran up a string of impressive inside-the-distance victories. Although his heart was set on winning an ABA championship, he was somewhat surprised when Andy took him aside one day and asked if he had considered turning professional.

Smith was an astute judge of fighters and quickly recognised that Green's aggressive style would be well suited to the professional ranks. Mutual respect had quickly developed between the two and after some discussion it was agreed that win or lose in the ABA's, Dave would turn professional under Andy. It was one of the best decisions he made in his entire life.

Green reached the light-welterweight semi-finals of the ABA championships, but was outpointed by Terry Waller in what BBC television commentator, Harry Carpenter, described as: "one of the outstanding amateur contests of not only this year, but any other year". Dave was a new star in the making and fight fans across the nation eagerly awaited his move into the pro ranks.

At the time, Dave was earning £15 a week working as a carrot packer on a farm at Southery, Norfolk. He got married in October that year and before making his pro debut two months later, Andy advised him to carry on with his job, live on his wages, and put all the money from his fights into a bank account to save up for a deposit on a house. It was the first of many pieces of business advice Andy gave Dave, which helped him become a very rich man.

Andy brought Dave along carefully but steadily, matching him with opponents of widely contrasting styles at both welter and light-welterweight. He beat everyone put in front of him and, in doing so, built up a massive following with his exciting style. Within 18 months he had won all 15 contests, 12 inside schedule, and faced Joey Singleton for the British light-welterweight championship at the Royal Albert Hall on 1 June 1976.

The great arena was packed, but Green brought to boxing a new breed of fans. Country folk from the Fens flocked to London in their thousands, dressed in farm attire and wearing boots splattered with imitation cows muck. They blew horns and bugles, played banjos and yelled "Tally Ho" from the galleries. The Londoners lapped it up, just as they did Dave's performance as he ripped the championship from Singleton in six rounds.

As he did with Bugner, Andy got Green maximum exposure by working with Levene, Duff and Barrett. He also ensured that he was well paid as his career steadily progressed, with well made yet attractive matches. Six months later Dave beat Jean-Baptiste Piedvache for the European title and, in March 1977, stopped John H. Stracey in a final elimination for the WBC welterweight championship.

Again Andy bargained hard on behalf of his fighter, insisting that Dave received as much as Stracey because, in his words: "Green was the trump card". He told Dave they had a choice of a flat rate or a percentage of the gate. Knowing Wembley would be a sell-out, the astute Scot advised his man to go for the percentage and trusting his judgement, Dave agreed. He has always maintained that by doing so he earned at least £5,000 more than John who took the flat rate.

Green was always appreciative of his manager's guidance. "I would never have got where I am if it hadn't been for Mr Smith", he told local reporters one day at the St Ives gym. "He has taught me to box and control myself in my punching, and brought me on a bomb. You cannot do half a job. What you need is natural ability, dedication, and the right coach".

Green's first set-back came when he challenged Carlos Palomino for the world title at Wembley in June 1977. In what the WBC made their 'fight of the year', Dave was knocked out in round 11 with the fight in the balance. He put up a fantastic display and, despite Andy's tireless efforts to secure a return, the champion showed little interest. A fight with Wilfredo Benitez was set for 1979, but never took place because Green was obviously considered too dangerous. They could have gone to Puerto Rico, but Andy refused because of what the heat did to Bugner at Kuala Lumpur.

After Green had won and lost the European

Dave 'Boy' Green, Andy and Joe Bugner (right)

welterweight title, Andy and the promoters skilfully manoeuvred him into a big money fight with Sugar Ray Leonard at Maryland, USA, in 1980. Dave was knocked out in four rounds, and, although he fought on for another 18 months, was never the same fighter. The sparkle had gone and his career was brought to an abrupt end by Andy in emotional fashion at the Royal Albert Hall on 3 November 1981.

The relationship between Andy and Green was like father and son, and the manager was not prepared to see him hurt or humilated. At the end of the fifth round of a fight with substitute, Reg Ford, of Guyana, Andy climbed into the ring, put his hand on Dave's shoulder and said: "That's it son – I'm pulling you out". After calling referee, Harry Gibbs, to the corner, he went to the centre of the ring, took the MC's microphone and uttered the chilling words: "Ladies and gentlemen, that is the last time you will see the Fen Tiger".

Andy knew that Green was likely to win the fight in the next couple of rounds, after which it would have been impossible to persuade him to retire. Dave would have claimed it was just an off night and insisted on continuing. Apart from being his manager, Andy was also his greatest friend, business and financial advisor. He had already set him up in a lucrative business, of which he is now the joint owner 23 years after leaving the ring.

A passionate and eloquent speaker, Andy Smith did so much to promote the careers of his fighters, particularly Bugner and Green. He extended warmth and compassion to them, gave them shrewd business advice and helped both become very rich men. More importantly, his boxers left the ring in good health.

Andy knew Green better than anyone and was the only person who could demand that he quit whilst still on his feet. Despite Dave's protests, there was never any talk of a comeback, because he knew the manager would not entertain it. "There are not many Dave 'Boy' Greens in this world, so we have to look after him", Andy told the press after Dave's career was over.

Despite his commitment to boxing, Andy never gave up work. Even when Joe Bugner was at his peak he was still selling plant equipment through his company, Andy Smith

Robert Smith with Dave 'Boy' Green in his corner

Enterprises, which he operated from his home address. He set up Aqua Sports, a prominent fishing and leisure interest at Chatteris Marina, and was part-owner of Tony Powell Sports, a sportswear and leisure company. With an eye to the future, he introduced Dave 'Boy' Green into the company in 1977, but refused to allow him to invest any of his own money. He later became an Associate Director of Renoak Limited, owned by Green and his business partner.

During the mid-1980s, Andy became disillusioned with boxing. Like many people before him he was convinced that the sport was in decline, so he gradually drifted away and involved himself in other things. It was fitting therefore that his younger son, Robert, remained in the sport in differing capacities.

Robert virtually grew up in his father's St Ives gym, watching the professionals train. When he was old enough he was given the job of checking opponents records and frequently telephoned Eric Armit, an historian, who still writes a regular column in *Boxing News*.

He developed into a fine boxer, gaining great experience from sparring with men such as Mickey Laud, Des Morrison and Green. He won a national schoolboy championship in 1978 and was a losing finalist in 1977 and 1979. He also won a Home Counties title, boxed for Young England against Hungary before turning professional in 1981 as R.W. Smith. In an eight-year pro career, dogged by shoulder injuries, he won 16 of 21 contests. He then took out a trainers licence and among those he coached was Joe Bugner's son.

Away from boxing, Robert attended an engineering college, did an apprenticeship and became a tool-maker by trade. After being made redundant he used his money to go to college and obtain a degree in business studies. In 1994, he was appointed Southern Area Secretary of the British Boxing Board of Control and is now Assistant General Secretary. When he was a boy, his father always explained about boxer's contracts, something which held him in good stead for contentious situations which lay ahead.

Andy had two other sons, Andrew and Alan, and a daughter, Marie, who is his youngest child. He always encouraged his sons to go to the gym because he wanted them to be able to look after themselves. He told them that if they ever walked into a pub and a fight occurred, they would always be able to get out without any problem.

Although Andrew and Alan did not progress as much as Robert, both boxed in the services. Andrew, who is now a helicopter engineer, won a navy championship, whilst Alan, who lives in California and owns a video production company, won a Combined Services title. He had joined the Marines and had two postings in Northern Ireland.

Andy was extremely proud of his family and what they achieved. Yet tremendous credit must go to him because, apart from being a good provider, he was a strong disciplinarian. He had the philosophy that provided a boy trained hard and was properly looked after, there was no reason why he shouldn't box. He did, however, maintain that if a boy wasn't good enough he shouldn't be allowed to participate, something he learned from his father.

Whenever asked if he would let his own sons box, he replied: "Of course. I look after other people's sons, so it would be hypocritical of me to say I wouldn't let my sons do so".

Andy Smith was an absolute credit to boxing and those he trained and managed were extremely fortunate because their well-being was always his priority. Despite being very successful in boxing and business, he can be considered unfortunate never to have had at least one world champion.

The problem was he had good quality fighters, but in good quality times. Joe Bugner was around at the same time as Ali, Frazier, Foreman and others, whilst Dave 'Boy' Green was at his peak at the time of Palomino, the most under-estimated world champion, Benitez, Pipino Cuevas, Harold Weston, Pete Ranzany, Armando Muniz and Angel Espada. "Dave is so unfortunate to have been born when he was", he once remarked. "At any other time he would have become world champion".

Green has always expressed his gratitude for the support and guidance given to him by Andy and never hesitates to say so whenever called upon to give a talk about his career. He has kept in close contact throughout the years since he left boxing and in the early 1990s drove Andy to Darlington for a reunion with Brian Curvis, whom he had not seen for many years.

Although Andy has been in poor health during recent years, Dave has continued to visit him on a regular basis. He has never forgotten everything his former manager did for him. Emotional at seeing his great friend unwell, he often remarks: "I owe nearly everything to Mr Smith. I would never have got where I did in boxing and business without him".

Jane Couch: The Fleetwood Assassin

by Melanie Lloyd

Women's boxing will always be a subject of healthy debate. These days girls are very gradually breaking down the barriers to train in amateur clubs as times are changing. But there is one woman whose face springs to mind as soon as you mention the female side of our sport, and that is Jane Couch. She became the pioneer of licensed female boxing in this country. This interview was a first for me as I have never written about a woman before and was curious about how things would go. The day I got to know Jane Couch, talk to her and spend time with her, left me bursting with a feeling of admiration. Not only for what she has achieved and what she stands for, but for who she is. Despite all the hardships along the way, Jane has emerged with a sunny personality. 'Boxing News' often call her 'Charismatic', and they've got it right. Thanks to her warmth and kindness, I immediately felt as if I had known her for years and I drove back up the M4 with a smile on my face, delighted that I had found myself a new friend.

Jane lives at Spaniorum Farm, near Bristol, with her trainer, Tex, and his wife Pat. I arrived there on a Saturday morning in July and got out of my car to be surrounded by horses, chickens and friendly faces. Tex met me at the door of his gym and showed me around the impressive facilities that he has built up over the years, which houses not only three boxing rings but extensive fitness facilities, including a mass of punch bags, weights, exercise machines and a sauna. And then Jane appeared from the office. We crossed the courtyard to her cosy living quarters and she made me a nice cup of tea.

Jane is a pretty woman. She looks younger than her 36 years and has a bright smile that lights up her face and makes her green eyes twinkle. She has a Mickey Mouse tattoo that she had done as a dare as a girl and had boxing gloves added later on. And then there are the trade-mark corkscrew curls that we've all come to identify her with. Her Northern accent is spoken with a soft voice. She has a highly active, fast-moving mind. She's tough, of course she is, she has to be. In her chosen profession, being hard is a mandatory requirement on the job description. But, at the same time, I found her to be a gentle and kind lady.

Jane Couch was born in the front bedroom of a house in Albert Street, in the close-knit fishing community of Fleetwood on 14 August 1968. Her tough background has been well documented during her ten-year boxing career, but for those who are not aware she was a wild child who spent some of her formative years travelling around with her brother and his punk band, One Way System. She survived a bus running over her head at the age of 15 and as a young woman it once took five policemen to put her into their van. She was smashed in the face with a baseball bat by a man she was evicting from a London pub and even got thrown off a two-storey roof and lived to tell the tale. Out of control she might have been, but nobody could question her resilience and determination, qualities that would go on to serve her well in her boxing life. At the age of 24, Jane found herself serving six weeks in Drake Hall Open Prison after being sentenced to three months for various offences. It was during this time that she began to wonder about her life and where she was going.

When Jane was released from Drake Hall she saw a 'Cutting Edge' documentary on women's boxing. It changed her life. She decided there and then that she would become a boxer. She had her first fight lined up before she had even started to box. Anxious to learn her knew-found trade she turned up at a local boxing gym in Fleetwood and it was here that she was christened with her ring name. "I used to walk in and all the lads used to shout, 'Here she is, the Fleetwood Assassin', and it just stuck".

Jane's trainer and manager, Tex Woodward, is also an unusual character. Tex cuts a tall, elegant figure. He has white hair, a wise and knowing face and his concise words are spoken with cultured accent. He boxed for the RAF in the mid 1950s and was also an RAF PT Instructor, before having 20 professional fights at welterweight between 1956 and 1964. To my mind, Jane and Tex share one of those classic relationships between boxer and trainer. I asked Jane to describe their bond. "It's love, hate really isn't it? It's like really hard with a trainer. I call him granddad, because that's what he's like. He's like me best friend. Like me soul mate. And other days I hate him. But I tend to be on the side where if they're a bit older they know so much more about the game. And he does. Tex has been coaching for about 50 years. He's a good trainer and he's really helped me. He's the only one who has helped me, out of the whole boxing world. When I first started he's the only one that was there. But I don't know, it's a weird one. You'll have to ask him". So I did. Tex told me: "Love, hate I would think. More hate than love"! His eyes were laughing as he said these words.

Jane continued: "It reminds me of Mike Tyson and Cus D'Amato. It's like the same sort of relationship, because Tyson was from the street as well. I don't think I was too bad early on. I wasn't really educated, in life or anything. You know what it's like when you're young, you think you know it all. You think you're clever, and you're not. I think someone older teaches you that as well. When you realise what he's done. And I think he was the only one who could have controlled me, because I was a bit of a handful. I still am a bit of a handful, but I'm more humble now. I've got a lot more respect now".

I asked Tex if Jane has been his first boxing protégé. "Well she's not exactly a protégé anymore is she? She's an accomplished female fighter. She's won a world title. I haven't had anybody else win a world title. I've had a few British Area champions like Gary McConnell, a heavyweight, who was the Western Area champion. But Jane's the only real champion I've had. I've had more success squash coaching. I've had five junior internationals.

None of the boxers have beaten me [at squash] yet. Not even Jane".

Another very important person in Jane's life is Sandra 'the Midget' Rouse. For many years Sandra has been a part of Jane's boxing career in the form of friend (first and foremost), sparring partner and corner woman. Jane affectionately refers to Sandra as 'Midge'. "She lives just down the road. Midge has been doing boxing training longer than me. Not to compete, she doesn't like to compete, but she likes it for fitness training. And she's an artist, she draws and paints fighters and things, she did all those pictures up there". Jane points to a wall in her abode that is decorated with an array of colourful and eye-catching paintings that were created by her friend. "And she helps me with all the promotions and stuff".

So what makes a woman want to step into a boxing ring and take punches in the face for a living? Jane certainly doesn't do it for the money – she recently won two world title belts in America and she told me, "I got paid $2,000 but by the time we converted the money, £700.00 is what I came home with. Twenty-two million viewers they had! But there you go, I don't do it for the money and it's a good job I don't, isn't it? I couldn't believe it when they told me what the television audience was. And the main event, the men's fight, 400,000 they got there and it was crap. People were walking out. They paid for two of us to fly over, but the rest of me team paid their own way out. The Midget, Stewart and Jumbo, they booked flights on the internet and bought rooms when they got out there". I found this information absolutely shocking. Jane shook her head ruefully, "That's what people don't get. They all think I'm loaded doing all these fights, I've had 30 fights now, but I've still got to work hard. And then I went into promoting, and that's even harder. I had to do it really, to get fights in this country and to keep myself busy while I was waiting. Because the big fights always do come for me as I'm a big enough name in the world now. So I know that it will come, but they always try and catch you when you haven't had a fight for a bit, or short notice and stuff".

Jane's first boxing match was a Women's International Boxing Federation (WIBF) promotion and her opponent was London policewoman, Kalpna Shah. The fight took place in Wigan on 30 October 1994 and Jane literally battered Kalpna into submission within two, two-minute rounds. Having had so many spur-of-the-moment fights out in the big, wide world Jane was now entering a different world. This was her first organized boxing match. "It's different to street fighting. Anyone can street fight. With boxing, you've got to think about it every day. It just changes you as a person. I think, if anything, it stops you from street fighting because you've got more about you then and you know it's just not the way to do it. I wouldn't fight in the street or anything now. I don't even go out". Jane was promised a purse of £150 to fight Kalpna which she never received, she was told that the promoter had lost too much money on the show. This was a sign of things to come.

Jane's second fight came three months later and this time she topped the bill on a WIBF show at the Marine Hall in Fleetwood. Her opponent, Fosteres Joseph was a social worker from London's East End. It was a war that Jane won on points over six rounds. More importantly, this was the night that she connected with Tex for the first time. It was after the fight and celebrations were the order of the day. Tex remembers it well, even though drink had been taken at the time! "Jane, Steve [Presnail], who was her manager at the time, and myself were the only three left standing and I said to Jane, look, you're a great personality, lovely girl and all the rest of it. What a pity you can't box. Come to me and I'll teach you how to box and she said: 'Yes, we'll go to America and I'll become a world champion'. So anyway, she came to the farm for the weekend and every time she stayed a bit longer and a bit longer, and eventually she sort of moved in". Jane laughed: "Now he can't get rid of me"!

Jane had two more fights in the Fleetwood area. She stopped Jane Johnson in four and beat Julia Shirley on points. Her next five fights would be abroad. Meanwhile, because of the novelty value, fame was beckoning. She got invited on shows such Michael Barrymore and Frank Skinner and during the later she met the former British heavyweight champion, Brian London, and legend, Marvin Hagler. Mind blowing stuff for the girl from Fleetwood, but she took it all in her stride. And then it was back to business, back to the gym, back to Tex's gruelling circuit training.

In May 1996, Jane, Tex and the team travelled to Copenhagen to box Frenchwoman, Sandra Geiger. Sandra was a former Karate Champion and when Jane fought her she was the WIBF light-welterweight champion. Jane won the fight on points over ten rounds and took Sandra's title. "She was really hard! I thought I was going to *die* in that fight. That was the closest I've ever been to death. We had no idea, we was so naïve". Tex says: "But after that we knew what Jane could do". After the fight something terribly sad happened. Sandra had disappeared and Tex went to find her. When he located her he found her in her dressing room in the dark, all alone. Sandra cut a tragic figure as she lay shivering on a massage couch, covered by a towel, whimpering. Jane angrily told me: "Her trainer, everybody, they just *left* her! The Commissioner came out, he'd been in to see her, and he said, 'Can you be a bit quiet? This is serious'". Tex explained: "The trouble was I couldn't speak to her because she couldn't speak English and I couldn't speak French, so I just held her hand".

Jane's next fight was in March 1997 in New Orleans. In the other corner was the tough Andrea DeShong. Jane stopped her in the seventh round, but again she didn't get paid. She was so hard up financially after this match that she had to return to Fleetwood and borrow £200 off the loan man to get by. Five months later Jane returned to America to box Leah Mellinger at the Foxwoods Casino. Leah was announced as a black-belt in karate and undefeated FFKA world champion kick-boxer. On top of the bill was Roy Jones, who took less than a round to blow away Montel Griffin in their re-match. Jane won her fight with Leah on points over ten hard rounds. After the fight, George Foreman remarked to Tex: "You've got a good girl there". Jane was certainly getting noticed in America, even though she was forbidden from boxing in her own country under the Board of Control licensed rules. Another admirer that she collected along the way was Angelo Dundee, who once sent her a good luck letter and a pair of shorts. Jane told me: "They were Mickey Mouse shorts, they were. His wife got them for me".

In January 1998 Jane travelled out to America again, this time to Lula in Mississippi. She fought the veteran American, Dora 'The Destroyer' Webber, at the Lady Luck Rhythm and Blues Casino. Jane lost the fight on points. Dora was a spoiler and a seasoned brawler and this fight was billed as 'Female Fistic Frenzy'. Jane returned to America in January 1998 to fight Dora Webber again, this time to Atlantic City. Again she lost on points. "Jane was absolutely robbed against her", said Tex. "Yeah, that's right. I boxed her head off. I had to change my style for America, you've got to be more the aggressor, whereas here you can box. They don't appreciate that over there, they don't even score the jab. You could be landing like ten shots, and if they land one heavy shot, that's it. It cancels it all out. You learn that though with experience, don't you?" After the fight was over Jane visited all four sides of the ring and waved triumphantly to the crowd. The fact that she didn't get the decision was something that she took in her stride, and the American fans loved her. "They were all going mad, yeah".

In June 1997 Jane's biggest fight began. She applied to The British Boxing Board of Control for a licence to box in this country. I spoke to General Secretary, Simon Block (BBBofC), who told me: "I wasn't General Secretary at the time but I remember the Board's position clearly. Jane was never refused a licence. She applied for a licence to box in this country and the Board replied, stating that we were not in a position to consider taking responsibility for women boxing in this country at that time". Jane was not satisfied with the reply so she took The Board to an industrial tribunal for sexual discrimination, and won. The court case, which was heard at Montague Court Building in Croydon, took six months in total and when all the evidence had been presented, Jane had to wait another six weeks for a decision, which came in March 1998. The battle reached such newsworthy status that Jane found herself on all the TV news programs, being interviewed outside the courtroom as she fought for her right to fight. She also made all the papers, tabloids and broadsheets, including 'The Times', 'The Guardian' and 'The Independent'.

The Board's reasons for not accepting women boxers was rejected by the tribunal. The only point that I questioned was the risk to an unborn baby. I asked Jane what she thought. "Well there *is* a risk to an unborn baby. But there again, you wouldn't go in the ring pregnant. You've got to be professional enough to know that. You get pregnancy tests 30 days before, 20 days before, 10 days before, so there's no way you *would* be. And there was actually a case (in America) where a woman *was* pregnant and because of the testing it showed up, so there's *no risk*. In America they already had these really stringent rules in place. You have to use protection, and the other thing is to abstain. That's what most people would do. That's what *I* would do anyway. And I mean, God, you really wouldn't want to do that would you? It would be really bad for the sport. I mean, what you gonna' say? You can't run the 100

metres sprint because you might be pregnant? In any sport, not just boxing, but rugby, football, the women have got to be professional enough to know, haven't they?" Simon Block told me, "A female boxer applying to appear on a show in this country would need to produce a negative pregnancy test result that had been certified by a medically qualified person. The test must have been done within seven days of the contest".

During the court case, Jane developed the greatest respect for her solicitor, Sarah Leslie (Irwin Mitchell, London), and her barrister, Dinah Rose. Dinah was certainly not a lady who minced her words. She was quoted in 'The Independent' as saying: "*This is one of the crudest forms of gender stereotyping. It is an attempt to protect the last bastion of male-only sport against the participation of women*". I was surprised when Jane informed me that Dinah was only 26 years old at the time. "If I ever got to be a quarter as clever as her... What a diamond. It was unbelievable what she did. She says to the doctor, 'Excuse me doctor but if you were going on holiday and you found out the pilot was a woman, would you get on the plane and fly'? And he went: 'Not if she was due on her period'. She asked [the doctor]: 'Why's that'? And he said: 'Because women are unstable at that time', to which Dinah replied: 'Well God forbid they should ever look after children if they're unstable'. They just hung themselves, they just hung themselves in the court. These days the Board are brilliant with me. Honestly. We're on first-name terms". Simon Block endorsed this point of view. "I see Jane Couch as a classic boxing success story. She has used boxing to turn her life around and I think she handles herself very well. In fact, I'm a guest of hers in a couple of weeks at a Nigel Benn dinner". Jane described the day her boxing licence finally arrived. "It was wicked. It was all I ever wanted".

On 25 November 1998, Jane Couch made boxing history when she stepped through the ropes at Caesar's Nightclub in Streatham to become the first woman to ever box on a Board of Control licensed show in Britain. Her opponent was Simone Lukic. It was a complete mismatch and Jane stopped the German in two rounds. At the time, Jane felt totally unmoved by the fact that she was making history. She remembers that Tex was arguing with the promoters about the music that would accompany her into the ring. "Oh yeah, and he didn't want me to come out to it so we was having an argument about it, because there was swearing on it. But I didn't really feel any different because like I said before, when you're doing it you don't realize you are making history. And even now, I don't realize that I have. When I retire, I'll sit back and realize but at the time I didn't look at it like that. That fight wasn't any different to any other. You feel built up, and ready to go, and scared, but I didn't think about making history. It just didn't even register. And I was thinking why are all these photographers here? It's only a boxing match. What about all the other people on the bill'? That's what really annoys me. Boxing is boxing and they shouldn't just give one boxer on the bill all the recognition. They all should get it".

"I think with me though, over the years it's been overkill with journalists and photographers and that. I don't even do anything now, interviews, anything. I just took a step back from it because it was overkill. It was like, every newspaper you picked up, every time you turned on the TV, I was there. And it got to the point that I said to him [Tex] I can't cope with it. I don't like it. It's not my way. And people see you as something different, that you're craving the publicity. So I've took a step back this past few years, just stepped right back out of it. Because I don't like that world. I don't like what it brings with it".

On 20 February 1999, Jane took on Marischa Sjauw on a WSO promotion at the Thornaby Pavilion in Middlesborough. It was a good fight and Jane won it on points, having knocked the Dutchwoman down in the first round. After that fight, Jane had to have stitches in her head, a hazard of her chosen profession. For her pains, she retained her WIBF Title and somewhere along the line the WBF title had come into the mix too.

After a points win against Heike Noller in Birmingham in April 1999, the following October Jane went on to fight Australian, Sharon Anyos, at the David Lloyd Tennis Centre in Raynes Park. For the record, they fought on Halloween. This was a first fight for Jane at Lightweight (9st 9lb). When Anyos entered the ring it was discovered she had not been wearing her groin or breast protectors. She was sent back to the dressing room to get properly dressed. The fight was for the vacant WBF and WIBF Lightweight titles and battle commenced. Jane won on points.

In March the following year, Jane stopped Michelle Strauss in three rounds at York Hall. The following July she stopped Galina Gumliiska in six at the Elephant and Castle. Then it was back across the Atlantic to fight Liz Mueller at the Foxwoods Casino, Jane losing the points decision over six rounds. It was nearly a year later, in June 2001, that Jane fought Viktoria Oleynik at the Wembley Conference Centre, winning a four rounder on points. Continuing with the 'have gloves – will travel' philosophy it was off to Jamaica next to do battle with Shakurah Witherspoon at Montego Bay. Jane won on points over four rounds.

Jane ended the year 2001 in fine style with a dazzling performance against Tzanka Kurova at Bristol's Marriott Hotel in December. There was a big weight difference – Jane weighed in at 9st 10lbs, whereas her Bulgarian opponent's weight was officially recorded as 10st 7lbs. Tzanka was rumoured to weigh more like 11 stone. Jane stopped her in three rounds anyway.

On 21 June 2002, Jane travelled to Waco in Texas to fight the tough, switch-hitter, Sumya Anani. The 'Fleetwood Assassin' was stopped for the first and only time in her career when Sumya caught Jane with a rocking left cross to the face in the fourth round and then leapt on her. As the crowd shouted and screamed for blood, Jane found herself trapped on the ropes, her left arm partially caught between the ropes, and she was unable to defend herself. As Sumya waded in and unleashed a barrage of shots that knocked Jane's head back and forth referee, Jerry McKenzie, finally intervened. "Yeah, she was a good fighter, but I don't really know what happened to be honest, because I've never been stopped, in the gym or anything. But as I went back like, she pushed me and me hand caught in the ropes. I couldn't get

me hand out, like even to defend meself and he [the referee] was right to stop it. But he should have stopped it and let me get me hand out". Tex was quick to inform me that, in his opinion, Jane was ahead on points at the time of the stoppage. Jane remembered: "We had a hell of a trip to Texas that week. That flight was like, a 30-odd hour trip and we got stuck in New York for eight hours. You either get a good trip to America, or a bad one. Even when we landed at Texas we still had another three-hour drive to the event. I was absolutely knackered. She's a good fighter, don't get me wrong, but Sumya is more of a strong brawler rather than a skilful fighter. But the ref definitely should have let me get me hand out and carry on. But then it's fate isn't it? Because you probably wouldn't get any fights if you won everything, would you? And that's why when I fought Jaime Clampitt for the two titles it meant even more".

Six weeks later Jane was back in action at the Norbreck in Blackpool. She won a six-round points decision against Borislava Goranova. She then had a re-match with Borislava the following December at the Thistle Hotel in Bristol and again won on points, this time over ten rounds. Incidentally, this was Jane's first promotion with her company, Jane Couch Promotions. In February the following year, Jane fought Borislava again and this time she stopped her in seven rounds at Bristol's Marriott Hotel.

As Jane's career grew, so did her army of admirers. In May 2003 she fought the Ukrainian champion, Larisa Berezenko, at the Hand Stadium Indoor Arena in Clevedon. Jane knew little of Larisa's style before she met her in the ring, but she was reported to be a seasoned Thai and kick-boxer with 59 wins out of 60 amateur fights. Jane won the fight on points over eight rounds. And there would be no doubt as to the pedigree of Jane's next opponent.

Five weeks later, on 21 June 2003, Jane was back to work, the venue being the Staples Centre in Los Angeles, and her opponent, billed as the 'The Most Dangerous Woman in the World', was the Dutch phenomenon, Lucia Rijker. This formidable female had led a life of sporting prowess, beginning when she was six years old and became interested in judo. When Jane fought Lucia, 'The Dutch Destroyer' had a perfect record of 15-0, with 14 of those wins by KO. Jane, however, was more experienced with a record of 19-4 with eight KOs. Jane lost the points decision that night but she put up the bravest of showings, forcing Lucia to go the distance for only the second time in her career as the girls boxed for eight gruelling rounds.

Jane returned to Spaniorum Farm to recover from her match with Lucia and on 21 September 2003 stepped through the ropes once more at Bristol's Mariott Hotel to fight Brenda Bell-Drexel, aka 'The Texan Tiger'. Jane won the fight on points over ten rounds, but Brenda was not averse to the odd low blow here and there and afterwards Jane remarked: "It just made me grateful that I don't have a willy"! The following December, exactly three months after their previous meeting, Jane fought Brenda again at the same venue. This time Jane won on points, again over eight rounds.

Then, in February 2004, came Jane's fourth and final

fight with the durable Borislava Goranova, again at the Bristol Mariott. Jane won it on points over six rounds and with a career record of two stoppage wins and seven losses at the time she fought Jane, Borislava had worked herself into the category of journeywoman. Jane remains the only person to have stopped the brave Bulgarian and you have to take your hat off to her for her bravery.

Two months later, on 13 April 2004, Jane travelled to Visé in Belgium to fight Nathalie Toro for the vacant Women's European (EBU) light-welterweight title, Jane losing on points over ten rounds. Nathalie was the home fighter and Jane knew that she was taking the fight as the opponent once again. This was something that she has become used to over the years and she has never let it bother her.

On 12 June 2004, Jane travelled across the water one more time, to the Foxwood's Casino. Her opponent was Canada's Jaime Clampitt, who was seven years younger than Jane and this would be her 15th professional fight. And, as the reigning IWBF world light-welterweight champion, her title was on the line. Also, rather suspiciously, another world title belt had been thrown into the pot – The North American Boxing Association. Jane laughed: "The North! They just made that up for her I think. It was the IWBF one that I wanted". Jane arrived in Connecticut just two days before the fight and she soon discovered that once more she was expected to play very much the supporting role, but there again she knew that would be the case before she left England. "Yeah, always. And it's really obvious as well when you get there. They just didn't expect us to win. Or maybe they expected us to win a close fight and then get ripped off. The Foxwood's Casino, it's a massive casino, it's like a mint place, but we was in the overflow hotel, just opposite. And then you get to the press conference and they just want to talk to their fighters and you're just sat there. But I'm used to it. That's what they didn't get. They was like building her up and I was just sat being quiet and I'm used to all that, so it didn't bother me at all". Jane played me the video of the fight. As the camera focused on Jane and her corner, which consisted of Tex, Sandra 'The Midget' Rouse and Stewart McKenzie, the first thing that jumped out at me was how much the consummate professional Jane has blossomed into over the years. As soon as her boots touched the canvas she put on a sharp display of shadow boxing for the crowd. She cut an impressive figure, garbed in classy black trimmed with gold, her hair intricately plaited close to her head, Alicia Keys style. - the look really suits her. "Yeah, I always do, because it comes out and it looks so unprofessional when you're hair keeps coming out. She came out to '*I am the World's Greatest*' [R.Kelly]. I mean, how egotistical is that?" I asked Jane what music she came out to. "Usually, as the opponent, you don't get asked, they just put any music on. But I just said: 'Oh, put owt on'. I wasn't too nervous for this fight, but I was nervous because it was my last chance, at top level. I was well aware of that. Just because you've been to the top of the world once, you can't keep going". And, of the fight, I found it a thrilling affair. It was toe to toe all the way, with Jaime coming forward,

head on for most of the rounds and Jane putting far superior boxing skills into play. She used her height and reach advantage beautifully and her upper-cuts, in particular, were delivered with natural style and finesse. In the tenth and final round, Jane knew she had won the fight, but from past experience, because Jaime was still on her feet Jane felt sure that she would be robbed of the decision. She couldn't resist a bit of showboating as she finished the fight on top. "Because I hadn't knocked her out I didn't think I was going to get the decision. I knew I'd won the fight and I was doing all that". She raises her fist in the air to demonstrate. "I never do that but it was just thinking, I know you're going to rob me so I'm going to tell you I know that I've won. And then when they give it me, I thought, oh no"! It was a very tough night's work, with both ladies finishing the final round cut and bleeding. The scores were 96-94, 96-94 and 96-95, much closer than they should have been. Jane said: "They made it close but at least they didn't rob me. Because that's rubbish when that happens". As we watched the decision being announced on the tape, Jane laughed happily. "I loved that. When they said, 'And the new…' It was wicked"! Tex is obviously and justifiably immensely proud of his charge's performance that night. "That was Jane's best fight, ever! She's never boxed like that before. Ten years of coaching finally clicked". After her win, Jane faxed the England football team who were in Portugal at the time, competing in the 2004 European Championship. '*Follow that*', she wrote. '*You'd better be there at the final*'. One thing is for sure, having witnessed this fight from beginning to end, I cannot see how anybody, male or female, could have put any more into it than these two women. It makes the paltry £700 that Jane got paid even more atrocious.

As our interview drew to a close I asked Jane who is the toughest women she has ever fought. "Sandra Geiger, without doubt. I didn't want to box again after fighting her. I was hurting for months". And who is her favourite woman she has ever fought, personality wise? "Probably Brenda Bell-Drexel. She was nice. She went out of her way to do everything. You know how strict medicals and that are here. She went out of her way, and she travels. I respect boxers who travel, because I have to do it and I know how hard it is".

I know that Jane is a great Rocky Marciano fan, but I was interested to know who her favourite fighters are today? "I love Mickey Ward, and Arturo Gatti. I boxed on the same bill as Mickey. And in England I like all the Manchester fighters. I like Ricky Hatton and Michael Gomez. And I like Joe Calzaghe. I like all of them. They're all great. But I think Mickey Ward's just great. And he's a nice guy as well, a really nice guy. And Gatti, he's wicked".

Jane is now 36 years old and she has been boxing professionally for ten years. I asked her how much longer she intends to go on? "I don't know. Before I went to America this last time I thought, if I can't pull this off it's time to go, or box at a lower level. I wasn't sure if I was still world class because I've been doing it for 11 years and I was a little bit, like doubting myself really. But I have a good training camp and then I just pulled that out of the bag. I've never boxed like that before in my life. So I don't know, it's hard to say. Like all fighters, I think I'll know when the time comes. Everyone's got a shelf life, haven't they? But I think I'm alright yet. I feel good. I'm never over me fighting weight. I've been at ten stone for 11 years. And, like I say, I'm getting into the promoting side of it now and am enjoying that. I'm also enjoying working with all the lads as well. And I'm enjoying promoting the lads in our gym that are not really big names yet".

Thanks to the determination of Jane Couch, women's boxing in this country is a much safer place to be now, rather than in the past when women were only boxing on unlicensed shows and were so much more vulnerable and open to exploitation. Although Jane's crusade to obtain her boxing licence was never really about women's rights in her mind, she was very much an icon for her contemporaries. "When I took the Board of Control to court, I stood outside the court room and said: 'Look I'm not some sort of lesbian, left-wing boxer and I'm not doing this for women's rights, I'm doing it for me. I'm doing it because I want a licence. It's not about what the other women want. Like with me, I've been striving to achieve, achieve, achieve all the time. And even now, after five world titles, you don't realise what you've done. I think when it's all over and it's gone, because it's a short career, that's when it will hit home. What you did for the women, what you did for the sport. I mean, alright it didn't take off in this country, and to be honest I never really expected it to because we haven't got the grounding. We've got no amateurs coming through. Even if the girls want to take it up the amateurs don't show any interest anyway. So how are you going to get good women boxers unless they don't get put through the proper amateur structure? They shouldn't be allowed to come out of kick-boxing or Thai boxing and just be allowed to turn pro because pro boxing is different. So if I had a young girl now I'd want her to be put through the amateurs, because that's what I would have wanted. To learn with the head-guards and the big gloves, because the boys have to do it". I put it to Jane that there are some girls coming through in the amateur clubs now. "But what are the ABA doing for them? I mean, we've just had a girl over from Northern Ireland, who represented Belfast in the Milan Games. Won a silver medal. And the girl from Dublin won the gold. Well, where were the English reps? Them girls came from Ireland to me, to train here with me, and the next thing they've won gold and silver. Don't tell me there's no girls in our gyms that couldn't have gone, that couldn't have been representing this country. And that's where they're going wrong. That's why women's boxing won't progress here, because in Belfast and in Dublin they get the girls work. They get them representing their country. There must be girls here. We had a girl train with us as an amateur. She had four fights and she couldn't get any more. They [the amateur authorities in England] are not interested. They're just not interested".

At the time I submitted this article, Jane's record was 24-6(8), which makes her one of the most experienced female boxers in the world today.

Jane seen here at a recent charity evening she organised in Bristol   Les Clark

Eddie Thomas: Champion and Maker of Champions

by Wynford Jones

Eddie Thomas first saw the light of day at Colliers' Row, near Heolgerrig, Merthyr Tydfil on 27 July, 1926 and was the third of six sons born to Mary and Urias Thomas.

As a young boy he attended Georgetown School and the brothers sang in the Cyfarthfa Church Choir. When Eddie left school he worked briefly at a gent's outfitters in Merthyr High Street, but this experience was shortlived and it was not long before he succumbed to the teasing of his brothers, soon following his father and older brothers into the mining industry. And so it was that mining became one of the strands which permeated the whole of his life. The other strand was boxing.

Mary came from a farming family, but Urias came from a fighting family and this undoubtedly influenced the young Eddie, who became attracted to boxing. As a junior he won a Welsh ABA title in 1943 at Penarth and went on to win the British bantamweight title. By 1944 he was representing Wales in his first season as a senior and was based at Ephraim Hamer's boxing gymnasium at the Servicemens' Club in Merthyr.

His amateur career was packed with contests and Eddie often boxed as many as five times per week. In 1946 he won the Welsh and ABA lightweight titles and represented Britain against France in Paris against the American 'Golden Gloves' team, winning his own contest, while the team gained a 5-3 victory, before turning professional with the London manager, Sam Burns, after over 135 amateur contests.

Sam Burns worked as a general manager for promoter Jack Solomons, a fishmonger who began promoting at the Devonshire Club and who later went on to become Britain's leading fight figure in the post-war years. Jack was a larger than life character, the ultimate showman with his bow tie and ever present cigar, and he was particularly successful in staging many high profile outdoor shows.

In his first professional fight, Eddie outpointed Ivor Simpson over four rounds on the undercard of the first encounter between Freddie Mills and Bruce Woodcock at Harringay Arena. Woodcock was the winner on points over 12 rounds in a tough battle and it was already clear that Eddie was guaranteed high profile exposure by being in the Burns/Solomons camp.

After wins over Reg Quinlan in Aberdare and Don Chiswell in Merthyr, Eddie's fourth appearance as a professional came on 4 September at Ninian Park, Cardiff on the undercard of the clash between the American, Ike Williams, and Ronnie James of Swansea for the lightweight championship of the world. The show was beset by problems, with Wales having had almost constant rain during the fortnight leading up to the fight. On fight day itself, Solomons pronounced to journalists, awaiting news of a postponement, that he would be placing a bucket on the balcony of his room at the Angel Hotel. He insisted that when the bucket was almost full the rain would stop and that the sun would come out! When the bucket was almost full the rain did in fact stop and, as the fans began to arrive, the venue was bathed in evening sunshine!

When the show got underway, Eddie defeated Bob Ramsey on points over six rounds, but fortune did not favour Ronnie James. At Cardiff Arms Park in August 1944 he had knocked out another Solomons protégé, namely Eric Boon, to win the British lightweight title, but Williams was an exceptional boxer who had perfected the 'bolo' punch and it was his devastating body punching which sealed his victory with a ninth-round knockout.

Eddie had made a good start to his professional career before he lost his 11th contest when he was stopped in three rounds by Vrjoe Pitulainen at Harringay, the famous north London venue at which he was to appear many times.

On 26 July 1948, Eddie appeared on the undercard of one of British boxing's great nights. Freddie Mills was matched in a return with Gus Lesnevich at London's White City, and duly won the light-heavyweight championship of the world on points over 15 rounds. Freddie had achieved his ambition at last, having been stopped by Lesnevich in ten rounds in their first encounter at Harringay in May 1946. Eddie was matched with Ernie Roderick from Liverpool, the man who had dominated the British welterweight scene for more than nine years.

Roderick had won the British title by knocking out Jake Kilrain at Liverpool on 23 March 1939 and had won his first Lonsdale Belt outright, beating Arthur Danahar on points. He later went on to defend successfully against Gwyn Williams and Eric Boon before losing his title on points to Henry Hall on 8 November 1948 in his fifth defence of the title, thus depriving him of outright possession of a second Lonsdale Belt.

Soon after winning the British welterweight title, Ernie Roderick was beaten in a challenge for the world title by the legendary Henry Armstrong. The contest took place on 25 May 1939 and Roderick lost on points over 15 rounds.

Such was the calibre of Ernie Roderick, but Eddie, in only his 18th professional contest, emerged as the winner on points over eight rounds. This victory was hugely significant and clearly showed that Thomas was a champion in the making.

Even as an ex-champion, Roderick was still a force to be reckoned with and they were matched again in a British title eliminator on 6 September 1949. Eddie once again confirmed his superiority with a points win over 12 rounds.

Thomas won his first title as a professional when he beat Gwyn Williams on points at Harringay over 12 rounds on 2 September 1948 to become welterweight champion of Wales and, on 15 November 1949, he became welterweight champion of Great Britain when outpointing Henry Hall of Sheffield over 15 rounds, again at Harringay. At the end of the contest, Eddie took the microphone and sang the song 'Bless This House' to the fans and this developed into something of a tradition.

Eddie had previously beaten Henry Hall on 26 January 1948 at the Royal Albert Hall. It had been a gruelling battle, with both boxers giving and taking heavy punishment. In fact, Eddie once suggested to me that neither he nor Hall could have been the same men after that fight and he admitted to experiencing abdominal pains for several months following the contest.

When asked by the Press what his plans were after his title win over Hall, Eddie replied that he was returning home and wanted to give a tea-party for the people in his street. This is indicative of the way in which Welsh boxers have appreciated the support and encouragement of their fellow-countrymen from the youngest to the oldest members of the community.

His first defence of the title brought him face to face with fellow Welshman, Cliff Curvis, at St Helen's Rugby and Cricket Ground, Swansea. This was a close contest and the referee, Jack Hart, the man who chaired the meeting at which I was accepted as a referee some 26 years later, awarded the decision to Thomas after 15 rounds. In many ways this was a disappointing contest, with the referee frequently having to call for more action, but it must be remembered that there was much at stake with two Welshmen contesting a title on their native soil.

Eddie made a superb start to 1951 and, for him, it was both a make and break year. On 27 January he knocked out Pat Patrick in 13 rounds in Johannesburg to win the Empire title. Vivian Grainger wrote in the *Johannesburg Sunday Express*: "Thomas dictated the fight almost throughout with

one of the finest left hands ever seen in this country" and Paul Irwin, writing in the *Johannesburg Sunday Times*, described the ending thus: "(Patrick) was suddenly straightened with a right and then smashed down with a perfect left hook to the point of the jaw. Patrick went down as though pole-axed and stayed down long beyond the ten second count".

Eddie was now British and Empire champion, but there was little time to savour his latest victory for just over two weeks later he was in the ring at the Market Hall, Carmarthen to relieve the Italian, Michele Palermo, of the European title. This contest saw Eddie using his outstanding left hand to full advantage and displaying first-class counterpunching.

Thomas was now a triple champion, but at this point things started to turn sour. In June he lost his European title to the Frenchman, Charles Humez, at Coney Beach Arena, Porthcawl, a place often described as the graveyard of champions. Having trained in Brighton, it was clear from the first bell that his usual spark was missing and, in October, disaster struck once more when he lost his British and Empire titles to Wally Thom on an extremely controversial points decision. Thom was to prove a thorn in the flesh of Thomas, for in later years, as a star referee, he was to deprive Thomas' highly talented protégé, Howard Winstone, of victory in his world title battle with the Mexican, Vicente Saldivar, at Ninian Park, Cardiff.

During his career, Eddie had trouble with his hands which often needed painkilling injections and, although he enjoyed playing football and cricket, this led to the need for a cartilage operation which kept him out of the ring for virtually two years. He also experienced weight problems and even though he came back in 1953-54 he was not the same boxer. It was a matter of great pride to Eddie that he was never knocked down in his entire career, a record which few can boast.

In 1951, Eddie was ranked as number one contender for the world title, but Jack Solomons was unable to match him with the immortal 'Sugar' Ray Robinson and the opportunity to meet the latter fell to Randolph Turpin when the American moved up to middleweight after having weight-making problems himself at welter. It is interesting to note that not only did Turpin and Thomas box in the same team for Britain as amateurs, but they appeared on a number of professional bills together, with their careers moving almost in parallel under the Solomons banner. Randolph Turpin ensured a place for himself in the history books by taking the world title from Robinson at London's Earls Court Arena on 10 July 1951, but one wonders what Thomas might have achieved had there been a light-middleweight division at this time.

The true calibre of Eddie Thomas can be judged from his contest with Billy Graham, Eddie beating the American on points over ten rounds at Harringay, in what was his 23rd professional contest, in February 1949. Graham, at that time, was a veteran of 77 contests and following this he engaged in a four-fight series with the great 'Cuban Hawk', Kid Gavilan. In February 1950, Graham beat Gavilan on points over ten rounds in New York, before losing a subsequent ten rounder on points to the Cuban and twice challenging him for his world title. Graham's second challenge took place in Havana and it seems certain that he was the victim of a home-town decision. His battles with the 'Kid' place Graham at the pinnacle of the welterweight division, so the significance of the Thomas/Graham result can be readily appreciated. One can only speculate as to what might have happened had Eddie been given the opportunity to box for the world title.

In the Graham contest, Thomas won at least eight of the ten rounds, with his left hand dictating the pattern of the fight, and by the halfway stage the American's left eye was almost closed. The right uppercut to the heart was a key weapon in Eddie's armoury and he took an immense amount out of Graham by throwing this punch time and again during the contest. At the end, Graham acknowledge Thomas' superiority and presented Eddie with his kit after the fight. Eddie's delighted fans greeted his victory by singing 'Mae Hen Wlad Fy Nhadau' and 'Sosban Fach'.

When Eddie returned to the ring at the latter end of his career he was unable to rediscover the momentum of times past and there were a few mediocre performances. After losing on points over eight rounds to Ron Duncombe in Manchester on 10 December 1954, Eddie realised that now was a sensible time to retire. Retirement, however, merely marked the end of his boxing career and the beginning of an even more remarkable career as trainer, manager, promoter and cut-man of extraordinary repute.

Much of the money Eddie had earned in the ring was invested in small mines and this was a constant thread throughout his working life, with periods of success followed by heavy financial loss. Having turned his attention to training boxers, a couple of gyms were started

Eddie, right, seen on his way to a points win over the American, Billy Graham, in what was possibly his best-ever victory

in local pubs in Dowlais before he settled in the much-loved gym in High Street, Penydarren and the Dowlais Amateur Boxing Club saw the emergence of some amazingly talented young boxers.

The high point came when Howard Winstone won a gold medal for Wales at the 1958 Empire Games held in Cardiff, but there was success also for Gerald Jones, Don James, John Gamble and Malcolm Price. They accumulated titles galore and there were many international vests in what became one of Britain's most successful gyms.

After his success at the Empire Games, Howard turned to the professional ranks and the others gradually followed. As the partnership between Howard and Eddie became so successful so too the achievements of the gym snowballed. Howard and the others were joined by Carl Gizzi, the heavyweight from Rhyl, Eddie Avoth from Cardiff, Roger Tighe, a Commonwealth Games medallist from Hull, and Ken Buchanan from Scotland, already a boxer of immense talent.

The triumphs are almost too numerous to mention. Winstone and Buchanan were both steered to world title victories, while Avoth became British and Commonwealth light-heavyweight champion and Gizzi challenged Chris Finnegan for the titles he had taken from Avoth. During this time the reputation of Eddie and his stable was attracting boxers from all over the country. Middleweight, Phil Matthews, was trained in Merthyr and boxed Bunny Sterling for the British title, while Eddie was also involved in the career of Tim Wood and, at the request of Jack Solomons, took Danny McAlinden to the British heavyweight title, having first worked his corner on the Ali/Frazier bill at Madison Square Garden in March 1971, when McAlinden beat Ali's brother, Rahman, on points over six rounds.

As the years passed, Eddie developed an enviable reputation as a cut man and his skills were often in demand. The story of how he saved Ken Buchanan's title against Ismael Laguna by nicking with a razor blade the base of the swelling that was closing Ken's eye is now the stuff of legend. Such was the esteem in which he was held, when Henry Cooper parted company with his long-time cut man, Danny Holland, Eddie Thomas was called in to handle the corner and he did this for Cooper's last three championship fights, earning the praise of the British Boxing Board of Control's chief medical adviser, Dr Adrian Whiteson, in the process. Eddie was often asked what he used in the treatment of eye injuries and his replies often added to the mystique. He sometimes said that he used duff (coal waste) from the Merthyr Vale Colliery and, at other times, claimed to have bought some magical potion at Dowlais market. In truth, of course, he was only able to use the adrenaline solution permitted by the Board, namely vaseline and pressure.

As the 70s ran their course, Eddie became the manager of Colin Jones and steered him to British, Commonwealth and European welterweight titles, thus emulating his own achievements as a boxer. He also secured three world title fights for Colin, but after the latter retired Eddie drifted from the scene.

When Eddie started out as a manager it was not possible to hold a promoter's licence at the same time and he overcame the problem by persuading his friend, Billy Long, to take out a licence. Billy was subsequently followed by Eddie's brother, Cyril, as the promoter and thus he was able to guarantee work for his successful stable. His boxers worked for Jack Solomons and Harry Levene, two intense promotional rivals, and he also worked closely with Les Roberts, matchmaker at the National Sporting Club in London's Piccadilly. Eddie steadfastly refused to align himself with one promoter or promotional group and this principled approach obviously cost him a great deal of money. He also had a disagreement with Mike Barrett and Mickey Duff following Howard Winstone's world title win over Mitsunori Seki and this denied his boxers access to major London promotions for a few years. Eddie invested heavily in shows in Wales and for many years he was the one man who kept boxing going in the principality.

When the British Boxing Board of Control celebrated its 50th anniversary in 1979, Eddie Thomas was honoured at the banquet at Cardiff's City Hall as the man who had contributed most to Welsh boxing over the previous half century, his achievements towering above all others.

As the years passed he received a variety of honours. He was inducted into the Welsh Sports Hall of Fame, was honoured by the Boxing Writers' Club, an honour that was important to him because it came from within the sport, was awarded the Freedom of Merthyr as well as an MBE, and,

finally, he became Mayor of his beloved Merthyr Tydfil, the town of which he always talked with such knowledge and passion. This, for him, was the honour which capped all others.

He was immensely proud of his home town and spoke eloquently of its industrial, cultural and sporting heritage. He was a true product of his 'filltir sgwar' (square mile) as we say in Welsh, never wanting to leave the town. He loved the people of Merthyr and they loved him. Even though he made and lost large sums of money in his mining ventures, he always provided old-age pensioners with cheap coal and he did a great deal of charity work. His love of soccer also shone through in his generous support of Merthyr Tydfil AFC over many years. He cared about so many aspects of community life and never missed an opportunity of raising the profile of the town. In truth, Merthyr could not have wished for a finer ambassador.

Eddie Thomas died on 2 June 1997 after a long battle against cancer, his funeral at Tabernacle Chapel, Merthyr Tydfil being an amazing experience. The singing would have pleased him, especially the old Welsh funeral favourite, 'O fryniau Caersalem', and later at the crematorium, 'Bless This House', the song he first sang to the crowd at Harringay all those years ago. Ultimately, the service was a celebration of the life of a great man. Rarely have so many people been reduced to tears of laughter as we listened to speaker after speaker share their memories of Eddie, a true champion and maker of champions.

The statue of Eddie Thomas at Bethesda Memorial Gardens, Merthyr Tydfil

Freddie Gilroy v Johnny Caldwell: The Epic Encounter

by Patrick Myler

Great home-grown ringmen are rare enough in Ireland, but when two come along together and in the same weight division as did bantamweight rivals Freddie Gilroy and Johnny Caldwell, it is fair reason for the fans to get excited. These two Belfast-men blazed a trail together as amateurs, won bronze medals in the 1956 Olympics at Melbourne (Gilroy at bantamweight and Caldwell at flyweight) and moved on to further success as professionals. When increasing weight forced Caldwell into the bantamweight division, the prospect of him meeting Gilroy in the ring was inevitable. Sometimes expected classic encounters between local rivals turn out to be damp squibs, but not the 1962 showdown between Gilroy and Caldwell at the King's Hall. It remains indelibly etched in the memories of those lucky enough to be there as one of the most exciting ring battles ever waged in Ireland, or anywhere else.

Gilroy, from the Ardoyne district of Belfast, was a southpaw with a wicked punch in either hand. Pound for pound, there has never been a harder hitter in Irish boxing history. Caldwell, nicknamed 'the Cold-eyed Killer' because of his icy stare, was from Cyprus Street, just off the city's Falls Road. He was probably a better box-fighter than Gilroy, but it is a matter of personal preference as to which was the superior fighter. Caldwell was British champion at flyweight and bantamweight and held a version of the world title. He won 29 of his 35 fights, 15 inside the distance, lost five and drew one. Gilroy won 28 out of 31, with three losses. Eighteen of his wins were scored inside the distance, with ten of them on count-outs, a remarkably high knockout total for a man weighing around 8st 6lbs (118lbs).

Gilroy turned professional in 1957 after an honour-laden amateur career. Resisting the tempting offers from cross-Channel managers to sign with them, he remained faithful to his amateur trainer, Jimmy McAree, who guided him throughout his professional campaign. The baby-faced destroyer swept through the bantamweight ranks to earn a shot at Peter Keenan's British and Empire titles after only 13 contests. Keenan went the way of all the others, floored seven times before being rescued by the referee in the 11th round. A fine points win over former world champion Mario D'Agata in London led to a crack at another Italian, Piero Rollo, for the European championship. "Win this one", promoter Jack Solomons told Gilroy, "and I'll do everything in my power to get you a world title fight". The Irishman duly obliged, although he had a hard tussle with the tough veteran before emerging the winner on points. World title-holder Joe Becerra, however, was in no hurry to accommodate Gilroy or Solomons. Freddie kept busy by defending his British Empire title in Belfast against South African Bernie Taylor, who was counted out in the fifth round, and then putting his three titles at stake against Glaswegian Billy Rafferty. The Scot gave him an unexpectedly hard battle, absorbing everything the Belfastman threw at him and closing Gilroy's right eye with

the fury of his counter attacks. But Rafferty was surviving on sheer grit when the referee called a halt because of the Scot's badly cut eye in the 13th round.

While waiting for Becerra to make up his mind about defending his world title, Gilroy took on a 'warm up' bout against a little-known Mexican, Ignacio Pina. As sometimes happens, the 'sacrificial lamb' decided he was nothing of the kind and proceeded to hand the Irishman a boxing lesson. Not only did Gilroy suffer his first loss in 22 outings, but he was put on the floor for the first time by a sharp right in the opening round. His disappointment was quickly forgotten when Joe Becerra announced his retirement and the world bantamweight scene was thrown into confusion. The National Boxing Association of America paired Eloy Sanchez of Mexico, whose knockout defeat of Becerra in a non-title fight had prompted his abdication, with Eder Jofre of Brazil for the vacant title. The European Boxing Union and the British Boxing Board of Control disagreed with the NBA and chose to recognise the winner of a match between Gilroy and Alphonse Halimi of France as the world title-holder.

The record books show that Halimi outpointed Gilroy over 15 rounds at the Empire Pool, Wembley, on 25 October 1960. The cold statistic does not reveal that there was hardly a person in the arena, outside of the French party, who agreed with the verdict of the Belgian referee Philippe de Backer. Though floored in the 13th round (the bell rang at three) Gilroy seemed to have been in command most of the way. He constantly slipped under the Frenchman's guard to pound away at his mid-section and trapped him on the ropes time after time. Halimi had more success when he stayed in the centre of the ring and scored with jabs and hooks. The Irishman was in some trouble in the 14th round, but he threw everything into the last round and appeared to be a clear winner. It was the first time a neutral referee had handled a world title fight in Britain (at Halimi's insistence), although this is now standard practice. The ringside pressmen were unanimous in their opinion that Gilroy was the better man. *Boxing News*, the British trade paper, devoted its front page to a picture of the contest under the heading, 'Shock verdict robs Gilroy of world title'.

Perhaps it was the depression following his unlucky 'world title' setback that caused Freddie to lose again next time out, a shock stoppage in nine rounds by Pierre Cossemyns in Brussels. The Irishman had already knocked out Cossemyns in four rounds on his way to the top and may have dismissed his rival too lightly. He should have remembered what happened to another Belfast idol, John Kelly, when he tangled with the dangerous Belgian. Gilroy was floored three times in the fourth round of the return encounter, but fought his way back and had Cossemyns in trouble in the eighth. As he attempted to apply the finisher, he walked straight into a smashing right that dropped him for eight. Down three more times before the bell saved him, he was battered to the canvas again in the next round and his seconds threw in the towel. It was the only time he lost inside the course. Gilroy took ten months off, then beat Scotland's Billy Rafferty for the second time. His successful defence of the British title earned him the Lonsdale Belt outright, the first Irishman to achieve that distinction. The stage was now set for the local showdown with John Caldwell.

Caldwell had turned professional in 1958, a year after Gilroy, with a fine amateur record of only seven defeats in 250 contests. Ever since he first pulled on a pair of boxing gloves at the age of ten, the tiny youngster's natural ability to jab, hook and uppercut with the skill of a veteran had onlookers enraptured. His capture of the Ulster junior and senior titles, plus the national junior and senior honours, in the 1955-56 season was the first time any boxer had won that cluster of crowns in one period. Clearly an exceptional talent, Caldwell was snapped up by Scottish promoter/manager Sammy Docherty. Most of his early professional appearances were reserved for Glasgow and London audiences, who saw him brilliantly outscore the British Empire flyweight champion Dennis Adams in only his fifth contest and chop down former European title-holder Young Martin of Spain seven times on the way to a great third round knockout. After 17 straight victories, John's hometown fans, who had seen only three of those bouts, were adequately compensated when his challenge for Frankie Jones' British flyweight title was arranged for the King's Hall on 8 October 1960. The Scot's three-year reign came to an abrupt halt in the third round as he lay crumpled, face downwards, on the canvas after taking two precision rights to the jaw.

Increasing weight forced Caldwell to give up his flyweight title. But after only three outings as a bantamweight, all inside-the-distance wins, he found himself in with Alphonse Halimi, Gilroy's 'conqueror', for the European version of the world championship. He reached the peak of his career that 1961 night at the Wembley Pool, London, to trounce the Frenchman over 15 rounds. Halimi was never in with a chance and he was very nearly knocked out in the last round. Caldwell, as cool as ice, scored repeatedly with sharp jabs, hooks and crosses and neatly ducked or skipped away from his rival's desperate attempts to nail him. Halimi's left eye, nicked in the second round, spurted blood after a hard exchange in the seventh. He brought out every trick he knew to try to turn the tide, but the Belfastman trumped everything. Halimi knew as he emerged from his corner for the last round that only a knockout could save his title. He threw everything he had at his opponent, only to find it returned with vigour. Caldwell's cornermen almost choked with fright as they watched him engaging the still threatening Frenchman in a final punch-up. All John had to do was stay on his feet to win, but here he was risking all in a crazy late attack. Their fears were dispelled when Caldwell dug a left to the body, followed up with a right to the jaw, a left and another right and Halimi was down. It was nearly impossible to hear the count, such was the crowd's din, but the champion crawled up at five. Caldwell rushed in to finish the job, but the

referee restrained him and continued to count to eight. Only by clinging on like a limpet did Halimi survive until the final bell. In notching up his 22nd consecutive victory, Caldwell was now bantamweight champion of the world, at least according to the European Boxing Union and the British Board of Control. He gave Halimi a chance to regain the honour five months later, again in London, but the Hallowe'en night clash failed to produce any fireworks. Caldwell was a clear points winner, but it was a boring affair punctuated with outbreaks of slow hand-clapping from the disappointed crowd.

The Brazilian Eder Jofre was recognised as world champion by the National Boxing Association of America and the eagerly awaited showdown with Caldwell for the undisputed title was finally set for 18 January 1962. It was unfortunate for the Irishman that he had to enter enemy territory and face a hostile crowd of 20,000 wildly enthusiastic Jofre supporters who booed and jeered Caldwell all the way to the ring at the Ibirapuera Stadium in Sao Paulo. As if that was not enough to tear at his confidence, he had to face the fact that he was meeting one of boxing's all-time greats. In a magnificent 20-year career, Jofre was world champion at bantamweight and featherweight and only lost two contests, each to the same man, Fighting Harada of Japan. Going into the Caldwell fight he boasted an unbeaten run of 43 bouts, with 30 wins by the short route. He had drawn three times. Caldwell had won all his 25 contests, 13 inside schedule. But records count for little in the ring. As Sammy Docherty hammered frantically on the ring apron to signal his man's retirement, referee Willie Pep, himself a former ring great, threw his arms around the gallant Irishman and led him to his corner. The little Belfastman had fought with commendable bravery, but he was on a mission without hope. Downed by a body blow in the fifth round for a count of nine, Caldwell already knew who was the real world champion; and it wasn't him. Reg Gutteridge, reporting for the London *Evening News*, wrote:

> Caldwell, at times, boxed intelligently and always defiantly, yet the harsh and sad truth is that he looked a dainty pretender to the throne in comparison with the Brazilian. Before Pep finally acted in two minutes, 45 seconds of the tenth round, Caldwell's only challenge lay in raw courage, fitness and Irish pride, but these, historically, are the possession of losers.

Nine months later Caldwell climbed into a Belfast ring for the first time in two years, to meet Freddie Gilroy in one of the most natural pairings in Irish boxing history. Local promoter George Connell teamed up with his big-time London counterpart, Jack Solomons, to put on the fight, in which Gilroy's British and Empire bantamweight titles were at stake. The Fleet Street boys had to dig deep into their dictionaries to lavish the superlatives on two boxers who fought the fight of their lives. Frank McGhee wrote in the *Daily Mirror*:

> Whenever men meet to argue about the great fights of all time, the night Freddie Gilroy, the baby-faced

bantamweight, kept his British and Empire titles against the pale-eyed little challenger, John Caldwell, will be lived again. This is how murderously, memorably wonderful it was to be in Belfast on Saturday night – this battle of two local boys who never pretended to like each other and who proceeded to make that the understatement of any year in the nine bitter, bruising, bloodstained rounds of raw hate it lasted. Not that the arguments are over. Caldwell's retirement, forced by a cut the length of his right eyebrow, has left him still unconvinced that but for this he would have won against a man who was weakening visibly. Gilroy, slamming the suggestions that if he made the weight he would be a burnt-out shell of a man, is equally certain he could have kept and increased a desperately slender points lead.

The fight began at a tremendous pace and never faltered. The punch-for-punch exchanges in the opening three minutes set the pattern for the rest of the bout and even though Caldwell was on the floor within the sound of the first bell, he stormed back to win the second round with lightning-fast, strength-sapping hooks to the body. It was Gilroy ripping in punches with little regard for his personal safety, then Caldwell swinging the fight his way with bewildering clusters of blows, and all the time the crowd roaring itself hoarse with excitement. First blood to Caldwell in the sixth round, when a red trickle appeared by the champion's eye. Gilroy's seconds did an excellent job of patching up the injury. In the eighth, two searing left hooks to the body had Caldwell doubled over in pain. His mouth hung open as he gasped for air. Gilroy showed him no mercy. "Before a fight I go into a church and pray", Caldwell had once said. "I pray for myself and I pray that my opponent will not be seriously injured. Then I go into the ring and try to hurt him as much as I can". The man they called 'the Cold-eyed Killer' was giving an honest assessment of what boxing is all about. He gave no quarter and expected none. In a torrid ninth round both boxers were covered in blood, most of it coming from Caldwell's eyebrows. He looked dejected as he went back to his corner. His chief second, Danny Holland, an expert 'cuts man' who looked after Henry Cooper in many such crises, had a brief consultation with Sammy Docherty and then called over the referee, Belfastman Andy Smyth, to tell him Caldwell could not go on.

Inevitably, there was public demand for a return match, but it was not to be. Gilroy, in fact, never fought again. He did sign a contract with Jack Solomons for another bout with Caldwell, but a dispute over the terms caused long delays and ended in Gilroy and his manager being fined £1,000 for breach of contract. They were given six months to pay by the British Board of Control. When the time expired and the fine had not been paid, the board withdrew the licences of Gilroy and Jimmy McAree. It was a sad way to end what had been a short but memorable career. But Gilroy seemed content to spend more time with his family and, from his ring earnings, he bought the Tivoli bar in Donaghadee, County Down, as well as a nice house in the hills overlooking his native city. Life was good until the violence of the early 1970s reached the normally peaceful fishing port. Gilroy's pub was bombed and anti-Catholic slogans were daubed on the walls. He sold out and took his family to Australia. Three years later, after a short sojourn as a barman in Dublin, he returned to Belfast to work for a furniture firm along with Jimmy McAree, the man who had 'discovered' him as an eager nine-year-old and who had guided him throughout his amateur and professional careers. But even that job was not to last.

Gilroy's disappearance from the boxing scene gave Caldwell a clear run at the now vacant British and Empire bantamweight titles, which he duly collected at the expense of England's George Bowes, who was outboxed, outfought and forced to retire with a badly cut eye in the seventh round. History was made in that 1964 contest, as Caldwell became the first Irishman to win British championships at two different weights. But recurring rows with his manager and an obviously growing disenchantment with the fight game spoiled any hopes his fans cherished of his renewing his world title quest. Though still only 27, he looked like a battle-weary veteran as he lost his titles at the first defence to Liverpudlian Alan Rudkin. Under pressure from the start, Caldwell was bleeding heavily from the nose by the sixth round and his eye was cut in the ninth. Rudkin's body blows were taking a further toll. When the Irishman fell against the ropes in the tenth round after another sustained attack, Scottish referee George Smith called off the action. John blamed his defeat on his nose injury, claiming he could not breathe properly from the third round. An operation, the second on his nose, seemed to correct the trouble, but he suffered further complications in his comeback bout against Monty Laud. He looked impressive at the start as he scored with good combinations, but his performance deteriorated as the bout progressed. He suffered a cut on his nose in the ninth round and lost the points verdict to a strong, bustling opponent. He saw there was no point in carrying on boxing.

Sadly, little remained of the substantial purses he earned during his seven-year campaign (he was reckoned to have received £10,000 for each of his world title fights with Halimi and Jofre) and he drove a taxi around Belfast for some time after his retirement. After an unrewarding spell in Canada, he returned to join the lengthy dole queues that haunt his home town.

FOOTNOTE: Gilroy is keeping well and is an officer of the Northern Ireland Ex-Boxers Association. The first Irishman to win a Lonsdale Belt outright, he lost the belt some years ago and has made repeated, so far unsuccessful, appeals for its return. Caldwell has fought a long battle with cancer.

This extract from *The Fighting Irish* (published by Brandon Books, Dingle, Co. Kerry, in 1987) is by permission of the author, Patrick Myler, whose other books include *A Century of Boxing Greats* (1997) and *Gentleman Jim Corbett: the truth behind a boxing legend* (1998), both published by Robson Books.

Gilroy (left) tears in two-fistedly as Caldwell looks to get his punches off at the same time

Jack Bates: Boxing's Quiet Genius

by Tracey Pollard

Manchester fighters are making the headlines but not for the first time. Currently home to the biggest name in British boxing, Ricky Hatton, and also world title holders, British champions and some of the country's hottest prospects, the area can also boast some of our most successful trainers. The names of trainers, Brian Hughes, Billy Graham, Bob Shannon and Jack Doughty, have become as familiar as those of their fighters. Phil Martin is another and he put Manchester back on the map in the early '90s with his full camp of champs, but ask about the golden era of Manchester boxing and the same three names will inevitably come up – McAvoy, Brown and King. Local heroes and national boxing legends.

The legendary trio became a celebrated quartet with the addition of Johnny 'Nipper' Cusick, but one name that is rarely heard is that of Jack Bates. All four Manchester champions emerged from the same stable, all trained by the same man – Bates. To that list add British champions, Frankie Johnson and Brian London and the talented Tommy Proffitt. Most people will know the name of Ricky Hatton's trainer, but few have heard of Jack Bates! How many people are even aware that Brian London had a trainer other than his father, Jack!

It is rare to find a photograph of Bates in the typical pose with his fighters after a victory and he obviously preferred to work quietly behind the scenes, but this was a man described by sports writers as 'Trainer of champions', 'Champion maker' and 'One of the finest trainers in the boxing business'. When he died he was hailed as 'One of the most knowledgeable men in the game' and 'One of the most respected and well-liked men in boxing' and he was perhaps best summed up by one journalist as 'Boxing's quiet genius'.

So who was this sad faced little man? Jack was born on 21 April 1907, in Collyhurst, a suburb of Manchester. His mother, Isabella, was a widow who had lost her husband during the South African war at the turn of the century. She was a tailoress who made cavalry uniforms and his father, Ernest, her second husband, was a tailor's presser. Unfortunately, his father was also a ladies man who frequently went missing from the family home for long periods. He was missing when Isabella died, leaving Jack, who was just 16, and his younger sister, Elizabeth, to fend for themselves. Jack had been working in a mill from the age of 14, by which time he was already boxing and had to take a fight to raise the extra money for his mother's funeral. Ernest also died a few months later from illness caused by his exposure to mustard gas during the war. The two youngsters were not only orphaned but homeless too, as the landlord would not let them stay in their house.

Elizabeth was taken in by her mother's sister and Jack was left literally on the street. As he stood in the rain a neighbour asked him why he didn't go home and he replied, "I would if I had a home to go to". Not surprisingly, especially considering his naturally melancholy features,

she took him in. Later he went to live with John and Anne Fleming, neighbours who had taken him under their wing. John's brother was Harry Fleming, who trained amateur boxers, and, in a pivotal moment in British boxing history, suggested that Jack train at Harry's Corpus Christie club and let Harry manage him.

It was the start of a beautiful relationship. Jack came to regard Harry as a father figure and from these first seeds the famous Collyhurst stable would grow. Harry continued to train his amateurs and Jack brought his professional experience of over 100 fights, many on the Kid Furness boxing booth on fairgrounds all over the North. He would take his boxing kit to work and could find fights every week and sometimes twice on Sundays on local shows. He continued to box until he was 25, meeting many leading boxers of the time and reputedly having around 400 contests before retiring. Even on the day of his wedding his wife, Sara, walked him to the station where he caught a train to Blackpool to box as part of 'Geo Black's Troup', a touring variety show. He was very proud of the fact that he had 52 fights in 1929, which was thought to be a record at the time (and possibly to this day).

Jack boxed at fly and bantamweight, but his habit of turning up at whatever show was on in the area after he finished work meant that he frequently faced featherweights or more often, lightweights. His son, Derek, remembers that his dad always told him that this was how he became such an accomplished 'in-fighter'. He learnt to avoid too much punishment by keeping in close.

There was a shortage of suitable sparring partners among Harry's amateurs, but he was soon joined by his

Jack as a fighter

friend, Henry Fitzsimmons, and later, Jackie Brown. His rather unpolished style of fighting has often been compared to that of his idol, Harry Greb (not known for his gentlemanly technique), and is described by Denis Fleming, Henry's son, in his book, *'Manchester Fighters'*: "He could take a punch himself and he could throw one and, moreover, he was sharp enough to capitalise on the mysteries of in-fighting instilled in him by his manager. Had Bates been able to control his aggressive nature and his perverse delight in 'mixing it' (as in his no-holds-barred encounter with the Durham miner, Douglas Parker, in what was an unofficial eliminator for the title), there is no doubt that he would have proved a serious threat to the champion, Harry Corbett." Parker won that contest, having been beaten in their previous meeting, but it wasn't Jack's only brush with the title. His battle with Alf 'Kid' Pattenden in April of '29 was a characteristic crowd-pleaser. Pattenden was the British bantamweight champion, but was not defending his title on this occasion. By the ninth round, Jack was slightly in front when Pattenden threw the punch that won him the fight. But, as the newspapers were quick to point out, this was the first time Jack had been put on the canvas in over 100 contests. Victory would have given Jack a shot at the title, but his performance left his reputation untarnished and earned him a share of what could have been the 'Fight of the Year'.

Jack was also sought out as a sparring partner. He never forgot the time he was offered an all-expenses trip to London, where his services would be required for about three weeks as a sparring partner for Teddy Baldock (British bantamweight champion 1929-31). He was to be paid £3 per round, which would be terrific wages to Jack. Imagine his disappointment when he was sent home after just one day. Years later, Jack was at a London dog track with his son, Derek, when Derek spotted someone waving and shouting to get Jack's attention. It was Teddy Baldock and they were delighted to see each other and spent some time reminiscing over a cup of tea. Baldock apologised for that earlier incident and said, "I'm sorry Jack but you were just too good". My dad forgave him of course, but he never forgot how disappointed he'd been at the time.

A succession of truly exciting, gutsy fighters have emerged over the years who have been labelled 'Manchester Warriors' during their careers. They thrill fight fans with their fight-anybody, throw-caution-to-the-wind, never-say-die approach, which has resulted in some memorable slug-fests. They include Michael Brodie, Michael Gomez, Wayne Rigby, Najib Daho, and Jock McAvoy and, possibly, one of the earliest was Jack Bates.

In later years there would be an element of rivalry and jealousy between the champions of the Collyhurst stable, but in the early days there was a great camaraderie. Fleming often sent his lads on tour with the boxing booths and would try to book them onto the local shows in groups. For his services he received two shillings and sixpence in the £1. Jack was still boxing when his regular sparring partner, Jackie Brown, asked him to become his trainer. In fact, he later recalled taking Brown along when he fought in Wales. "I remember taking Jackie once when he was about 16 to box in Wales and I seconded him in a ten rounder. I fought

and beat Danny Dando, the Welsh bantamweight champion over 15 rounds. I was paid £10 and Jackie £3. We got it in silver in packets and counted it on the dressing room floor. Jackie, after that fight, gave up work in a cap factory and wisely became a full-time boxer. It was Jackie Brown who got me to turn trainer. 'Chuck boxing and look after me and the others,' he pleaded. And I did. I was in charge of all Harry Fleming's boys".

Jack coached his charges to box in exactly the opposite style to his own, with the emphasis on defence. "It's not what you're going to do to him, but what you're going to stop him doing to you," he preached. He continued to spar with Brown and with his other boxers, now as their trainer. The gym had moved by this time to new headquarters over an old coalyard on Paley Street in Collyhurst. The conditions were primitive with precious little by way of equipment in a room, having bare stone walls and a wooden floor (Although, strange as it may sound, this is where Jack held his sister's wedding reception!). The shower facilities consisted of buckets of icy water thrown by Jack. The meagre facilities were extended somewhat by Jack's habit of erecting a ring in his own garden! To the delight of his neighbours, and his young son, Derek, the popular fighters used to spar in the unbordered garden of his Collyhurst home. Despite his melancholy visage, Jack was cheerful, well-liked, and greatly respected by his fighters. After 12 months, Brown was joined by Johnny King and Jock McAvoy and even after their retirement they all spoke fondly of their trainer.

With so many of the country's best boxers in his care, Jack was often asked which one was the best. "Best boxer, Nipper Cusick, best boxer-fighter, Jackie Brown, particularly with his speed, best schemers, Johnny King and Jock McAvoy, because they could walk around and almost coax a man to take their best right-hand punches." He categorized all his fighters in this way and coached them accordingly. He thought that schemers were the hardest men to fight, as they watched for mistakes and took advantage of them as he felt Pattenden had done with him years earlier. Jack had a subconscious habit of rolling his gloves on his pants and Pattenden picked up on it, waited and caught Jack. In early '56, Jack had a new protege, Brian London, and he named him as the best heavyweight prospect he had ever seen. "He has everything, punch, boxing ability and, above all, the killer instinct". Jack correctly predicted, "Brian London will be British heavyweight champion in two years time".

Jack's career as a trainer was split into two parts – before and after the war. Long before the arrival of Brian London, came the period of domination by the Collyhurst stable, the 'golden era' of Manchester boxing. Shortly before his death, Jack enjoyed a reunion with his famous trio and a journalist, who was present, reported that they all paid glowing tributes to the sad faced and gentle mannered little man who was a credit to boxing. There is no doubt that Jack enjoyed strong and lasting friendships with his fighters but, as in any relationship, and certainly in any boxing stable, there were occasional rifts. Rivalries developed between the four champions, which is not surprising as they were matched with each other on several occasions, and

Jack had to mediate between them. He also had to placate the volatile McAvoy.

By 1939 the Collyhurst stable had champions at flyweight, bantamweight, featherweight and middleweight and this at a time when there were only eight divisions in all. After the war, Jack added a lightweight and a heavyweight to that list. Jackie Brown became his first champion in October 1929, when he defeated Bert Kirby in a match that was originally scheduled to be an eliminator. It unexpectedly became a title fight with the sudden and tragic death of the reigning champion, 23-year-old Johnny Hill. Brown then lost the title in the return in 1930 and regained it when he again defeated Kirby in their third fight in '31. That same year, Brown took the European title from an overweight Rumanian, Lucien Popescu, and defended it successfully three times before his world title fight in October '32. In uncharacteristic style, Brown battered Victor 'Young' Perez before the towel was thrown in. Sadly, the little Tunisian only had 11 years to live before he met a tragic end in Auschwitz.

The dilapidated Collyhurst gym over the top of a run-down coal yard could now boast a world champion. Brown's last three title fights had been at Manchester's Belle Vue, which was fortunate as Bates' wife would never agree to his travelling abroad. If he was enjoying professional success by 1939 it was a different story on the personal front. His marriage was over and he was back in

the home of the woman who had treated him like her own son, Anne Fleming, whose husband, John, had since died. Jack's sister had not been treated well by her uncle and Jack had taken her to live with him and Sara. She stayed with them for three years until her own marriage to Sara's brother. After the separation, Jack's six children lived with their mother, but young Derek was always closest to his father and was a constant visitor to the gym. He was also aware of his father's poor health. From a young age, Jack had been plagued with stomach disorders, later found to be ulcers. "He used to always send me for medicine and I would take bottles of this white liquid to the gym. It said to take one or two spoonfuls, but he just used to drink it from the bottle". Jack and Sara were later reconciled and had another child, their fifth daughter.

In 1934 Fleming moved his Collyhurst stable to different premises in Collyhurst. Obviously charmed by the glamour of the previous premises, the gym was once again situated over a coalyard. By this time they had three champions with first, King and then McAvoy winning titles. They were both area champions, but in October 1932 King took Dick Corbett's British bantamweight title, which Corbett had won in their previous encounter for the vacant title. King and Corbett were destined to continue their competition for the right to the Lonsdale Belt over the next two years, with Corbett regaining the title in their return, by

A group photo, taken in the gym shows (from left to right) Jock McAvoy, Jack, Harry Fleming, Johnny King and Jackie Brown with their 'mascot' seated

which time King had also won the British Empire title. They would fight two draws before King eventually became champion again in 1935, with a points victory over Len Hampston, Corbett having been stripped of the title earlier.

King longed to emulate Brown's world title success, but failed to take the title from Panama Al Brown in '32, losing on points over 15 rounds. He also lasted 15 rounds in his failed attempt at the British featherweight title against Nel Tarleton. But he would not lose his bantamweight title so easily. He defended it twice successfully before the war and the fight that finally lost him his title nine years later would be his last.

The first of those defences was against his stablemate, Jackie Brown. If McAvoy was one of the Manchester warriors, Brown and King would provide one of the great Manchester wars. It was their second meeting and King also climbed in with his other stablemate, Johnny Cusick, on two occasions. This must have been difficult for Jack Bates, having worked so hard with Fleming to bring his fighters to this standard, only to see them pitted against each other. They may not have wanted the Brown v King fight, but the Manchester fans were clamouring for it and the two fighters were eager to settle their rivalries once and for all. The two had been kept apart for some time, forbidden to spar with each other and training separately. Brown had lost his world title in his fourth defence to Benny Lynch, in what was their second meeting. He then moved up to bantamweight, but in this first fight with Brown, King's title was not at stake. Jack supervised King's training, while Fleming watched over Brown. Jack was in King's corner, but Tom Hurst and Harry Levene stepped in for Brown, while Fleming promised to stay away from Belle Vue altogether on the night. He would not regret that decision.

King stopped Brown in six rounds. The referee finally pulled him off as he savagely beat Brown unconscious as he floundered helplessly on the ropes. But the animosity dissolved when he saw the condition of his old friend and he wept. After the fight, Jack and King went to see Brown in his dressing room. He came out to see them and the two fighters embraced. Jack didn't believe in bombarding a fighter with too much information in the corner, he thought that a trainer should pick out a couple of useful things only. After the fight he said, "Johnny won because he followed instructions". Brown still believed he was capable of beating King, but he was stopped again when they met a second time for King's title. This time he was knocked out in the 13th round. It was a sickening defeat for Brown, but he would still produce 100 more wins before he retired in 1939. But, unlike Brown, King could never better Cusick, although both of their hard-fought contests lasted the full 12 rounds. Brown and Cusick also met twice, resulting in one victory each. The three were so equally skilled and so evenly matched that four of the six contests went the distance and one lasted 13 rounds.

Little wonder that the public had wanted to see these matches between three of the country's top fighters. Six thrilling battles, but what an awkward situation for Jack and Fleming. Jack used to have his fighters living with him for two or three weeks before a fight as his son, Derek, remembers, "They all lived with us from time to time. My mum talks about one time when Johnny King was staying and they had a break-in during the night. She believes that they were after King's Lonsdale Belt, but they didn't get it – he was sleeping with it under his pillow! Another time, Jackie Brown was sleeping in our back bedroom and, according to mum, he said, 'I don't know how anybody can sleep in there, there are icicles hanging from the ceiling'".

For the first King v Cusick encounter, Fleming was in King's corner and it was Jack this time who chose to stay neutral. He was undoubtedly grateful that McAvoy was a middleweight! Jack had always maintained that a good defensive boxer with a punch could beat a good attacking fighter and, remembering his summing-up of his fighters' skills, he always believed that Cusick was the most skilled boxer of them all. Few would argue. 'Nipper' was poetry in motion, an artist of the ring – but only, Jack knew when he was 'up' for the fight. He recalled having to encourage Cusick to go back out during the fight with Freddie Miller. Cusick returned to the corner a disheartened man, but Jack said, "Let's see how the next round goes". Cusick won the next round easily, but his enthusiasm waned after that. The attitude of one of his most talented fighters frustrated Jack and the two fell out briefly, but he could never stay angry for long. Jack always had a particular interest in Cusick and, although he never claimed to have a favourite among his fighters, he devoted a lot of time to 'Nipper'. The two were also neighbours.

Jack was involved with Cusick from the age of 16 and spent months working with him solidly, moulding him into a master of his craft. But his son, Derek, recalls that his dad used to say he'd made a mistake with Cusick. "He always said, 'I spoilt Cusick'. He spent all that time teaching him how to avoid getting hurt and blamed himself because Cusick was so good that he didn't think he should have to take any punishment. Cusick could be absolutely brilliant and certainly didn't lack courage, but dad wondered if sometimes his heart wasn't in it. He told me that when Cusick fought King he got caught on the chin and went down. Dad was in Cusick's corner this time and said that his biggest surprise was that Cusick got up! But then he went on to win". More often than not, Cusick was on form and could run rings around his opponents. He defeated Jim 'Spider' Kelly for the third time in Belfast for the British and Empire featherweight title in 1939. The 12th-round stoppage gave Collyhurst its fourth British champion. One of those champions (Brown) had now lost his crown and the stable's third title had been delivered by Jack McAvoy.

McAvoy was the last of the three to join the Collyhurst stable, in 1931. Jack may have believed that Cusick had skill and courage and bags of heart, but didn't always have his heart in the fight. With McAvoy there was no question about it – this man loved to fight. His greatest strength was his strength. His sheer aggression saw him win roughly 88 of at least 132 victories inside the distance, knocking 53 of those opponents clean out. It may have made him difficult to work with in the gym, but he was a formidable force in the ring and campaigned at three separate weights. He won his middleweight crown in a return with Len Harvey in 1933. Both fights had lasted the full 15 rounds, but this time McAvoy got the verdict. It was a title he would successfully defend five times before voluntarily relinquishing it six years later. In the three years after winning the title he not only defended it twice, but made attempts at three other titles. He went up against boxing greats like Marcel Thil (for the European light-heavyweight title), John Henry Lewis (for the world light-heavyweight title) and Jack Petersen (for the British heavyweight title). All of those fights went the distance, with McAvoy losing on points, and the crowd at the Madison Square Garden world title fight with Lewis voiced their disapproval at the verdict. McAvoy also managed to knock out the reigning world middleweight champion, Ed 'Babe' Risko, less than three minutes into their fight at the Garden just three months earlier. Jock had the champion down six times before the final KO. Fortunately for Risko it was a non-title fight and he made sure there was never a return.

McAvoy defeated Eddie Phillips in 1937 to claim the British light-heavyweight title. Phillips had taken the title from Jock's old middleweight foe, Len Harvey, and Harvey wanted it back. This resulted in two encounters in '38 and '39. Tough distance fights once again with points verdicts going to Harvey as he first reclaimed the title and then held on to it. As his record shows, only the very best lasted with Jock, the others were put away early. He was still winning more fights than he lost when he called it a day in 1945.

The careers of all four of Jack's champions and Jack himself were curtailed by the most devastating opponent of them all – World War 2. It would be insulting to simply say that there was relatively little boxing during the next six years. Only those who were there can imagine the horrors and sadness experienced by those who were involved. Fortunately, our Collyhurst heroes all returned safely, but, inevitably, they lost many friends and fellow boxers. Jack was deeply saddened by the death of his friend, Johnny Grimshaw, a promising lightweight from Jack's stable who died in Burma in 1943 without seeing his baby son. Also, his former opponent, Jack Davies, an All-England open lightweight champion and a very young and exceptionally talented boxer, nicknamed 'The Boy Wonder', who often travelled to his professional contests still in his school uniform. Young Jack died in a Japanese POW camp.

Johnny King was incredibly lucky to survive the war. His battleship, 'The Prince of Wales', was sunk by Japanese aircraft and he spent three hours in icy, oil-filled waters before being rescued. Unfortunately, his relief was short-lived as he was taken to Singapore which was almost immediately under enemy attack. He managed to escape on a minesweeper, which deposited him in Batavia just as the Japanese were being deposited by parachute! After a frantic journey back to the now deserted dock, Johnny and a friend managed to row out to a tramp steamer. An arduous journey followed, via Calcutta and Ceylon, but at least he was on his way home.

Jack Bates enlisted in the RAF and, after his basic training, was unsurprisingly selected to go on a PTE course. He was singularly unimpressed with the RAF methods of fitness training and clashed with his superiors. His son, Derek, got the impression that it was actually a serious matter at the time. "My dad angered the officer in charge by saying that the exercises were a complete waste of time and I got the impression that there was some sort of altercation which led to an ultimatum; leave or be court marshalled", Jack ending up on ground crew at Biggin Hill. It was here that he was first confronted with the realities of war during an air raid. He later told his son: "I witnessed the most sickening thing I had ever seen when a young man of only 20 or so was blown apart in front of me in an air raid". His feelings of helplessness prompted him to apply for another transfer to the gunnery training course in Lincolnshire. From there he moved to Bomber Command at a base in Norfolk and life as a rear gunner in Wellington and Halifax bombers. He would later tell Derek: "I wonder if I would have applied for such a job if I'd realised what a hair-raising experience it was to be, sat in the rear of a plane wondering what was going to happen next". It was indeed one of the more hazardous occupations of the war (if there was such a thing).

Jack was one of the fortunate few who managed to complete his full quota of 30 missions, many did not and the tragic average was only five or six. He completed his tour of duty in Lancasters which, as he used to say, was a completely different proposition from the Halifax. But, as Derek points out. "It was none-the-less hair-raising. After all a rear gunner is a rear gunner no matter what he sits in". His final posting was to Rudlow Manor, the secret base at Box Hill, near Bath. He used to run into other sportsmen while he was there. Stan Mortenson and Stanley Matthews ended up playing in the Bath team which, unsurprisingly, never seemed to lose. He also used to see heavyweight boxer, Jack London, and they became good friends.

For some time after the war Jack was not involved with boxing. In 1947 he was approached by Harry Fleming, who was preparing Johnny King for his forthcoming fight with Jackie Paterson for King's bantamweight title. Jack was acknowledged for his ability to get a fighter's weight down, although his methods included some old tricks that would be considered antiquated today. He always made his boxers climb on the scales backwards so that he could exaggerate their weight and make them work harder to get it off. Also, as his charges would usually live with him in the run-up to their fight, he would wrap them in layers of pullovers and such like and pile on the heat. Now, Fleming wanted his old friend to step in and get Johnny's weight down at the 11th hour. Jack said he would be glad to help with Johnny's preparations, but with only two weeks to go he must postpone the fight or he wouldn't stand a chance. Fleming refused and it was widely believed that King needed the money. There was no ill feeling between Jack and Harry about the decision. Derek Bates knows how much affection they had for each other: "I remember one time my dad had his arm around Harry's shoulders. He looked at me and said, 'I love this man', I'll never forget it". He also remembers seeing his dad in the gym with Johnny before the fight: "My dad was really worried for Johnny and he was giving him advice but Johnny just smiled. He said that after what he'd gone through, expecting to die in the shark-infested sea, this was nothing". In fact, some of Johnny's fellow sailors on that terrible day were in the crowd for the fight.

Jack was right to be concerned. Paterson was a tremendous champion in the making, but Johnny had not won three in a row since 1938 and had lost his last four. He gave the appreciative crowd value for money and when the end came in round seven they all rose to sing 'For he's a jolly good fellow'. But Johnny was inconsolable and wept as he announced his retirement.

The careers of McAvoy, Brown and King have been well documented over the years, particularly in the excellent biographies by Brian Hughes and Jack Doughty. This brief summary of their achievements is probably all that is required to familiarise the reader with their achievements, which are, of course, also the achievements of Bates. Harry Fleming had died shortly after King's last fight and the careers of the big three and that of Johnny Cusick were now as good as over, but Jack's was about to begin again.

Derek Bates remembers that his dad had been invited to a local boxing show: "Len Steele had invited my dad to watch Tommy Proffitt box at Islington Baths. I remember that they introduced Tommy as the ABA champion. Shortly afterwards my dad started helping at Len's gym". Steele had a successful gym in Ashton-Under-Lyne, a small town just outside Manchester, where he managed around 30 fighters. Those training alongside Tommy included Harry Warner, an Ashton-based boxer (managed by Tommy Miller), who went on to become a renowned referee, and Ken Daniels, who later trained his own Manchester champions, Najib Daho, Phil Martin and countless others. Johnny Cusick and the former Welsh welterweight champion, Gwyn Williams, were also there, both hoping to regain their titles.

Jack and Len worked together and Proffitt developed into an outstanding professional. When Jack decided it was time to move into premises of his own he bought Tommy's contract. Jack had taken out a manager's licence just before the war and also a matchmaker's licence. Now his ambition was to bring another British title to Manchester and observers fully believed that Tommy was the man to do it. "Tommy Proffitt is my bet to be the next bantamweight champ", wrote one journalist, "Jack Bates is his manager – let us admit this, all managers are not like Jack Bates. All cannot weigh up a fighter as quickly as Jack and appreciate fully that in a certain boy there is the making of a champion".

It was October 1950 and Bates had found his gym, right on his doorstep in Collyhurst. He was training Proffitt for his eliminator with Peter Keenan and Ray Fitton for his London fight against Theo Medina, the former French bantamweight champion, and within the next few years he had built up a new and thriving stable. Derek was now doing National Service and spent the next two years in Khartoum with the 1st Battalion of the East Lancashire Regiment. He eagerly looked forward to his father's regular letters with news of the gym. But it was not all good news. Derek's sister, Irene, one of twin girls, had died of pernicious anaemia, aged 22. It was a condition which later affected Derek and some of Jack's other children, but they were able to receive treatment. The vaccine which could have saved Irene was developed just two years too late.

Jack's stable was swelling. Other members included heavyweight, Dennis Lockton, now a steward for the BBB of C and Stan Skinkiss, later a well-known Manchester trainer. Also Neville Tetlow, Tom Reddington, Phil Milligan

and two brothers called Williamson. Many of Jack's post-war fighters had one thing in common – an impressive amateur career, like Skinkiss, who only lost eight of his 60 amateur contests and Frank Williamson, who had 350 amateur fights. Tetlow was a brilliant amateur bantam-weight who, in one highly successful run as a professional, knocked out Vernon Sollas in three rounds, Ron Perry in five and stopped Chic Brogan. All of these members of Jack's stable were to become successful, highly-rated fighters in the Manchester area. Tommy Proffitt, who was a member of the 1948 British Olympic team, was soon being tipped to be Jack's next champion. Jack claimed that Tommy would be the best of them all. "Tommy will be a better bantam champion than Johnny King", he said, "he can box, has a great left and punches harder than anyone of his weight". As proof he cited Tommy's unbeaten record so far that year against Jimmy Gill, Ron Bissell, Charles Savard and Fernando Gagnon, the bantamweight champion of Canada. All won inside the distance. Jack was preparing Tommy for his next fight, but he was not going to be able to be there as he was going in hospital for an operation on his ulcers. Tommy told reporters that he wanted to win to cheer Jack up. "Jack has done everything for me, now I hope to repay him a little". He did win, this time with a fifth-round stoppage. He also scored wins over the Scottish champ, Eddie Carson, and the Belgian champ, Michel Dicky. Jack probably wasn't very popular in Belgium because Tommy's stablemate, Ray Fitton, also derailed their featherweight champion, Jean Machtelinck. The Belgian held a previous victory over Ronnie Clayton, who had failed to defeat him three times, and he was favourite to defeat Fitton. Fitton also held a victory over the bantamweight champion, Danny O'Sullivan.

Jack had been involved with a Plymouth lightweight called Tommy Shaw during his time in the south of England and Shaw now signed Jack as his manager. Reporter, Rupert Rice, observed Jack's activities with interest. "Ray Fitton, the Manchester featherweight, shocked the boxing world, especially the London end, by his recent victory over the reigning bantam champion, Danny O'Sullivan. Yet how many realise that much of the credit is due to Jack Bates, the veteran northern trainer? When the O'Sullivan v Fitton contest was first mooted, Fitton approached Bates to take charge of his training. There is no finer man in England for conditioning a fighter than Bates, for in the past he has trained such fistic stars as McAvoy, King, Brown and Cusick, bringing them from six-round preliminary boys to British, European and world champions. In several letters to me, Bates promised that he would so remodel the style of Fitton that he would become a puncher as well as a boxer. Fitton showed his punching prowess by almost knocking out the British bantam champ in the last round. Last year, Bates became manager to Tommy Proffitt. Tommy had previously been an ABA champion, but his entry into the paid ranks was as disastrous as it could have been, losing his first three fights. With patience and the ready co-operation and confidence of his charge, Bates gradually altered the style of Proffitt from that of an ordinary, clever boxer into a dynamic punching machine. So much so that Proffitt, today, is well up in the ranks of world bantams. In addition, he is considered the most improved boxer, weight for weight, in the country and a hot tip to succeed Danny O'Sullivan as bantam champion. Having done so much for Proffitt, Bates has now taken under his wing the Plymouth lightweight, Tommy Shaw. Bates has struck a mighty blow for the prestige of the much neglected trainer. He has shown the boxing public, and the boxer himself, how really valuable are the services of a first-class trainer".

Tommy's next contest was an eliminator for the title against an old foe, Scotland's Bobby Boland. Boland lost their first fight on a disqualification, won the second and this time, once again, was disqualified, taking Tommy a step closer to the title. Unfortunately, he didn't get any nearer because he was beaten in the final eliminator by another Scot, Peter Kennan, in a contest for the right to meet champion, Danny O'Sullivan.

The two Williamson brothers decided to fight under different names. Jackie (Braddock) was extremely talented, but his brother, Frankie (Johnson) was exceptional. They hardly lost a fight in the first few years of their careers, and, by early 1952, Jackie had become the Central Area welterweight champion, but his impressive record had developed a number of blemishes. Frankie was still winning, mostly inside the distance, and, soon after, he scored one of his less frequent points victories to give Jack his fifth British champion. Frank defeated Tommy McGovern to become the British lightweight champion and added the Empire title six months later by beating Frank Flannery, stopping him in the tenth. Frankie had never travelled further than Ireland for his fights, but he had to go all the way to Melbourne, Australia to face Flannery. Undaunted, he returned there for two more contests involving the Empire title against Pat Ford. He lost his title in the first on points and unluckily was stopped in the 13th round of the return two months later. He soon returned to form back in England and successfully defended his British title against Joe Lucy in April '55, but he lost it to the same man 12 months later. A run of victories in '56 gave him the confidence to challenge Peter Waterman for his British welterweight crown, but he was again unsuccessful. (One of the reasons Jackie Braddock may not have emulated his brother's success could have been his habit, unknown to Jack of course, of going out on a run from the gym and detouring into the pub!)

The stable now also included Brian and Jack, the fighting sons of Bates' old war-time buddy, Jack London. In January 1956, journalist, Frank Taylor, finally managed to catch up with Bates, who had come through a typically busy week. "Jack is now a sprightly 48-year-old who still moves fast", he reported. "On Tuesday night he was in Frank Johnson's corner for the Sammy McCarthy fight; he caught the midnight train to Manchester, moved on to Blackpool in the afternoon to see the London brothers, Brian and Jack, then returned to Manchester to superintend the boys, among them Jackie Braddock". Jack told Taylor that he believed the game had improved in some ways since his day. "There are more cagey fighters these days, we have learned a lot, particularly on how to stop the other fellow. However, referees spoil too many fights. They want to be the central figures. Above all they step in and stop the boys as soon as they go into a clinch. That's what's killing in-fighting in this country". He also criticised fighters who he believed prance about too much. "You waste energy that way", he said. "The great ones just stalk around, conserving energy, walking into their opponent, while they are balanced to punch with their full weight".

He told Tom Phillips of the *Daily Herald* (forerunner to *The Sun*): "People who say the good old days were the best are magnifying the skill of the old-time fighters in their memories. Many of them have forgotten that all sports have improved in the last 50 years. They're faster, the styles are better, that's generally accepted. The cry, 'Be first' is wrong. Today the boy who learns the art of making his man come to him has the advantage, especially if he learns proper footwork". So, what did make a perfect boxer? Jack thought he'd found it in Brian London. "Brian is a tutor's delight. He has everything, knows how to get on top of a man, fights like heck, has a heart as big as himself, punches at a terrifically quick rate and his footwork is grand. He's got the 'killer' instinct".

Brian had one other quality that made him a tutor's delight – he loved to train, still does in fact, even today, and Jack expected his boys to train hard. Derek is always surprised to see boxers use 20 minutes of skipping to wind down. "My dad always insisted that knees were kept high and he felt that a sign of good skipping was when he couldn't hear the rope touch the floor. It certainly wasn't something you could do for 20 minutes". Derek would know, as he flirted very briefly with boxing, fighting at featherweight like his dad, but without the success. He said, "Jack believed that no boy need take any harm if he disciplined himself while he was in boxing and left his enjoyment until after he has retired – like Gene Tunney did!"

Brian fulfilled Jack's prophecy by becoming British heavyweight champion two years later as predicted. He fought the best heavyweights in the world at the time, indeed, many of the best ever. Like McAvoy, he travelled to America and fought the world champion without getting a title. He actually fought three world champions during his career and was involved in some of British boxing's most memorable fights. It was another British champion for a delighted Jack, but by this time he had already achieved his real ambition – to bring another British title to Manchester.

Jack didn't get to see the second half of Brian's career, which included many memorable victories and some unforgettable defeats. In the film of one of those rather sensational defeats, the infamous 'Brawl In Porthcawl', the quiet, mild-mannered little trainer can be seen wading in along with just about everybody else in that near-riot. Jack had certainly been involved in televised fights before, including Jock McAvoy's 1938 British light-heavyweight title fight with Len Harvey, which was thought to be the first televised bout, although it was not seen by the general public.

After years of illness caused mainly by stomach ulcers, Jack had one final operation in June 1962. He couldn't believe the difference it made, he had never felt so well in all his life. He had never been able to keep his food down and now he found he could eat whatever he liked. On one memorable evening he met Derek and his wife and some friends in the local pub and was asked how he was feeling. Derek says, "I'll never forget, he said 'I've got my friends around me and my son and his wife beside me, if I died tomorrow I'd be happy'. And a few weeks later he did die". Jack was found dead at his home in Collyhurst on 19 December. He was just 55 years old and had died of heart failure.

Tributes appeared in every newspaper after his death and people still want to pay tribute to the quiet genius all these years later. In a gym that is very basic by today's leisure club standards, Brian Hughes is also training champions and once again a little stable in Collyhurst is one of the most successful in the country. Brian has seen his fair share of boxers, fighters and schemers, but he actually saw the originals too, because as a young boy he used to sweep up and do odd jobs at Jack Bates' gym. Like Jack, Brian didn't really have a father around and he saw Jack as a father figure, just as Jack had felt the same bond with Fleming. Not surprisingly, he has been compared to his idol and mentor, Bates. "I wasn't fit to lace his shoes", says Brian, "I didn't know who my father was and Jack was brilliant to me, giving me half a crown to sweep up and such. He was a good judge of a fighter and knew I wasn't too good, not that he said so. I knew I wasn't good enough myself really, but he used to send me to Tommy Proffitt's amateur gym. He was a beautiful man. Even at a young age I used to watch him coach Frank Johnson, the first Manchester champion since Cusick. There were no pads then and he used to put an old horse-hair glove on back-to-front and get in the ring, dressed in a suit ready to go out after. He was brilliant to watch and used to say: 'You don't want cauliflower ears and all that. Look after your face. Don't go like a bull at a gate', which was the opposite of how he'd fought himself. He used to be on the door at the Cromford Club in Manchester and if I went there he'd say: 'Get on home, son' and he'd put me in a taxi. He was a lovely, lovely man, being one of the best, if not *the* best. You couldn't compare me to Bates and Fleming. No disrespect to my lads, but in those days, with only eight weight divisions, championships really meant something. I knew his fighters, I used to take old McAvoy to shows and they all spoke highly of him. Tommy Proffitt used to tell me he would have been a champion if he'd met Jack when he was a kid. Tommy does indeed still think highly of Jack. "He was a great man as well as a great trainer, treating everyone the same, irrespective of how good they were and was a thorough gentleman. What he didn't know about boxing wasn't worth knowing. He gave you confidence in the corner. Cusick was training for his comeback at Len Steele's and was a great influence on me, being such a skilled boxer. I knew I could punch, but I wanted his technique. I used to train too hard, but Jack showed me the right way to train. Ron Olver once asked me if I had any regrets and I told him that I just wish I'd met Jack earlier".

In the years just before his death, Jack had been less actively involved with boxing and worked on reception at the Cromford club. Jack London also worked there for a short time. Despite his short stature and quiet manner, Jack was quite capable of turning people away if necessary. The club had many celebrity patrons and Dennis Lockton remembers Jack refusing entry to the singer, Alma Cogan, and her entourage one evening, undeterred by her minder, who demanded: "Don't you realise who this is?" Jack did know, but it didn't make any difference, as Tommy said, Jack treated everybody the same. "He also had to ask Patrick McGoohan, the star of the television series, 'The Prisoner', to leave one night", Dennis recalls. But mostly Dennis remembers Jack from his days training alongside Johnson, Braddock and Skinkiss. He not only sparred with the London brothers, but he fought them both too. "Yes, I think that's enough about that", he jokes. "Jack was a great untrained psychologist, not just in boxing, but in every direction – he was a great little thinker. He had me weighed up from the start!"

Brian London is the only one of Jack's champions who is still with us today to share his views on Jack. Sadly, Johnny King died very shortly after Jack. Both died penniless. Jack had been disillusioned with the low wages when he boxed and Derek believes that he was also underpaid as a trainer. McAvoy and Brown both died in 1971, not long after Frank Johnson, and Johnny Cusick died in 1990. Coincidentally, Brian's father, Jack, died exactly one year to the day after Bates. The normally taciturn, Brian, can't say enough in praise of his old trainer: "He was a great, fantastic trainer. Jack didn't over-train you, he taught you how to punch properly, a real cracker, probably the best trainer in the country. He was a real class fella".

So, praise indeed, but the last word should go to Jack himself, speaking in the mid-1950s: "I won't knock boxing. It's a grand sport. It's up to the people in it to make it so".

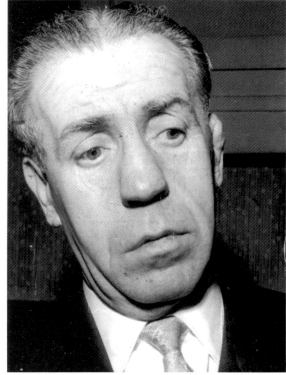

Jack in his latter years

Steve Holdsworth: A Man for all Boxing Seasons

by Ralph Oates

In the 1989 edition of the *Boxing Yearbook*, Derek O'Dell wrote an excellent article, titled: *The Advent of the Video in Boxing*. The said item touched upon his chance meeting (when duly accompanied by Barry Hugman and the late Fred Snelling) with Steve Holdsworth, who was at the time recording fights at a west-London venue. It was very clear from the article that Mr Holdsworth spoke his mind. It was also equally apparent that Steve knew the boxing game inside out and hence, in so doing, had a great deal to offer the sport.

Future events have, of course, shown this fact to be so very true. For if you watch boxing on Eurosport you will be more than aware that the very same Steve Holdsworth is the excellent, no-nonsense commentator. Steve gives viewers the run down on both fighters before they go into action and then further proceeds to explain what is happening during the course of the fight. He does not sugar-coat his opinions, which is refreshing, and he calls it as to how he's seeing it, giving his opinion about the value of the victory and the worth of the championship should there be one on the line during the contest. The man takes no prisoners and that, in truth, is the way it should be. Steve loves the sport and is more than aware that the anti-boxing brigade will take every opportunity to have a go at the game, hence he wants it to be seen at its very best – fighters taking part in bouts which mean something and not contesting second-rate championships, which at the end of the day mean very little except both insult and confusion to those who have watched the event. It is so very easy to go with the flow and say what people want you to say, give praise when its not warranted, and say little when constructive criticism is really the requirement.

In this day and age, it takes a brave man to stand up and speak his mind – it takes a fighter. Well, Steve fits the bill, having been both an amateur and professional boxer, and his words are well worth listening to. Steve is able to understand and appreciate exactly what is taking place in that roped arena in a way only an ex-fighter can. He knows the feelings that go on inside the boxer's mind, while waiting for that bell to sound the start of the first round. The self doubts that may emerge and hence have to be quickly overcome before the first punch is thrown. In turn, this vital ring experience helps Steve to relay what is taking place in an expert way through the eyes of a boxer, who knows exactly what it is like to deliver a punch and thus take one in return, and accept the joy of winning and the despair of losing. Boxing is not about robots performing, but men who are flesh and blood and feel pain just like the rest of us do. Fighters have good days, they have bad days, they have worries, they have concerns and we could say boxers, on occasion, have a bad day at the office. Steve is so very aware of this and often takes this into consideration when expressing his views on their respective performances. It's also worth remembering that Steve has also played several other roles in boxing, so is well versed on the many other aspects of the game. All of this makes him a first-class boxing commentator. On behalf of the *Yearbook*, I contacted Steve to ask about his career to date and his general views on the sport.

(Ralph Oates) When were you born?
(Steve Holdsworth) I was born on 17 April 1956.
(RO) How old were you when you first started to box?
(SH) I was 16 years of age when I first started to learn.
(RO) Have any other members of your family ever boxed?
(SH) My father Geoff was an ex-pro, I believe he is still Britain's youngest ever LICENSED professional, having been granted his boxing license on his 16th birthday. His brother, Heckie, was a hard-punching featherweight who, before turning professional, won the ABA tournament, as the ABAs were known during the war years, in 1941.
(RO) What made you take up boxing?
(SH) My father. I was getting into fights at school and he felt I could do so much better if trained properly. Let me add that I was not doing too badly in my fistic endeavours at school.
(RO) Which amateur club did you box for?
(SH) My first amateur club was Callowland ABC in Watford. I moved thereafter to Markyate ABC in Hemel Hempstead, before joining the Army and boxing for them.
(RO) How many amateur bouts did you have?
(SH) I had about 35 to 40 amateur bouts.
(RO) In which stance did you box?
(SH) I was orthodox.
(RO) Many fighters do not like boxing southpaws. How did you feel about meeting them in combat?
(SH) I only (to my recollection) lost to one southpaw, Cornelius Boza-Edwards, who, in the course of time, went on to become a most successful fighter in the professional ranks, winning both European and WBC world super-featherweight titles. I never really had trouble with southpaws, but did have problems with punchers and Boza was a banger.
(RO) Who was your most difficult opponent in the amateur ranks?
(SH) Boza was tough. I also fought Vernon Vanreil, who gave me a boxing lesson, and a guy in Crawley, who had a great pro style. I lost on points to him and just could not get near him. Unfortunately, I don't remember his name. I also fought Connell Tannion four times; he was always tough. It should have been two each, but he got the nod three times in our four meetings. I fought Sylvester Mittee in the 1976 ABA semis, but he hit too hard for me and stopped me in the last round. Mittee, of course, went on to win the British and Commonwealth welterweight titles in the professional ranks.
(RO) What made you decide to turn professional?
(SH) It was my dad's idea. I never really gave it much thought and turned pro under him as my manager and

trainer. I think he was living vicariously, but, on reflection, I have no regrets.

(RO) Who was your most difficult opponent in the professional ranks?

(SH) My most difficult opponent in the pro ranks was another big (and busy) puncher in Ricky Beaumont from Hull. Ricky, like Boza, was twice an ABA champion and a decent pro who fought in an eliminator for the British title. Ricky battered me, but I went the distance of six rounds with him. Liverpool's Dave Taylor also outpointed me over the six-round distance, however, I had to get off the floor in the first round in that bout. In my opinion, Dave should have gone places, but was chucked in with decent fighters far too soon.

(RO) In which weight division did you box when in the professional ranks?

(SH) The lightweight division.

(RO) How many professional bouts did you have?

(SH) I only had 12 professional fights.

(RO) How many of your bouts did you win?

(SH) I won five, lost four, and drew three of my respective contests.

Steve pictured with Randy Turpin's light-heavyweight Lonsdale Belt

(RO) What made you decide to retire from the ring when you did?

(SH) My dad was taken ill and contacted a disease that would take his life within three years. Coupled with persistent hand trouble, I felt I had no choice but to pack it in.

(RO) What career did you decide to embark upon once you retired from boxing?

(SH) When I retired from the ring I was a little lost. I had a poor education and no long-term training for anything worthwhile. The trade paper, *Boxing News*, ran an advertisement looking for a member of staff so I applied and, unbelievably, got the job. Since I had no formal training, I did not last too long. I then bummed around doing a myriad of temporary jobs, including driving and warehouse work and the occasional office job.

(RO) How do you feel about female involvement in the sport?

(SH) I am not a great fan of women in boxing in any capacity, but I support their right to do what they like. It will never really take off around the world. I think in this country, at this moment there are only three licensed female professional fighters – Jane Couch, Cathy Brown and Juliette Winter.

(RO) Who is your favourite old-time fighter?

(SH) My favourite is the one and only 'Sugar' Ray Robinson, who, of course, won the world welterweight title and the world middleweight crown five times. I also have a huge regard for Henry Armstrong (real name Henry Jackson) as he won world titles at three different weights – featherweight, welterweight and lightweight, and held them simultaneously. Henry also drew over ten rounds with Ceferino Garcia, when challenging for the world middleweight championship in 1940. I also liked Dwight Braxton (later Dwight Muhammad Qawi), who won the WBC world title at light-heavyweight and the WBA world crown at cruiserweight. He was tiny, his official height being 5ft 6¾ ins, but he gave all the big men murder. Ray Mancini, the former WBA lightweight champion, was also my kind of fighter.

(RO) How do you feel about title fights being held over the duration of 12 rounds rather than that of 15?

(SH) I would prefer to see title fights held over the old 15-round distance as it separated the men from the boys. All of these so-called inter this and inter that should be cut to ten or even eight rounds. They have polluted the sport.

(RO) How do you feel boxers of today compare with past boxers with regard to both their skill and tehnique?

(SH) It is said that it is impossible to compare today's fighters with those of yesteryear. I say nonsense. Not much has changed with the skill and technique factor, but today's men at heavyweight are that much bigger. As the saying goes though, "It's not the size of the dog in the fight, it's the size of the fight in the dog".

(RO) Who is your favourite modern-day fighter?

(SH) These days, I admire the likes of Marco Antonio Barrera and Erik Morales.

(RO) Based on what you have read and seen over the years, who would you consider to be the greatest boxer to be produced by Britain?

(SH) The greatest boxer to be produced by Britain must have been Ted 'Kid' Lewis, who, of course, won the world welterweight title. Plus there are many others I admire like John Conteh (light-heavyweight), John H. Stracey (welterweight), Randolph Turpin (middleweight) and Ken Buchanan (lightweight). However, considering what Lewis achieved, winning not only the world welterweight crown but also the British and European featherweight titles, British, European and British Empire welterweight titles, along with the British, European and British Empire middleweight crowns must be the best and his record is a clear indication of this.

(RO) Which is your favourite weight division?

(SH) My favourite weight division depends on the characters in it at the time. One year it may be the middleweights, another year the featherweights or welterweights.

(RO) Who in your opinion is the best world heavyweight champion in the history of the sport?

(SH) Joe Louis must be the best heavyweight champion. that's not to say he would have beaten everyone around today, but he did make 25 successful defences of the title. Rocky Marciano is another favourite and, believe it or not, I have a sneaking regard for Riddick Bowe and Evander Holyfield. Ali also features highly on my list, but Lennox Lewis leaves me cold.

(RO) Which is your favourite world heavyweight title fight?

(SH) I have two, these being the two bouts which Riddick Bowe and Evander Holyfield engaged in. They were classics and even their non-championship encounter rates highly with me.

(RO) How do you feel about fighters who continue to box on even when middle aged?

(SH) I have no problems with that, providing they can satisfy the various commissions that they are fit to fight and not just turning up for the money.

(RO) What changes if any would you like to see made in the sport?

(SH) There have been several changes made to the sport in this country. We now have the full-point scoring system. In the old days it was a quarter of a point, then the half-point margin. I think it is unfair for anyone to lose on an injury. If a single round has been completed, there must be a way of coming to a decision. The no-contest rule should be invoked if a match should last less than a round and it will not be long, I feel, before we have three judges at ringside to score instead of a referee.

(RO) What annoys you most in boxing?

(SH) What annoys me most in boxing is principally the anarchic situation we have with about 16 men being able to call themselves a world champion in the same weight division. This is ridiculous. Bad decisions also irk the life out of me and I would like to see even more co-operation between the BBB of C and the ABA.

(RO) How do you feel about the vast number of governing bodies in the sport at the moment?

(SH) I absolutely hate the amount of so-called world governing bodies, they are ruining the sport. Good for business? Do me a favour.

(RO) How do you feel about there being so many weight divisions in the sport today?

(SH) I have no real problem with the split weight division if it makes the sport safer, but I have my doubts.

(RO) Have you ever had any awkward moments in the sport?

(SH) I have had many awkward moments in the sport, but none spring to mind.

(RO) When boxing what would you say was your proudest moment?

(SH) My proudest moment as a boxer was winning the Army lightweight title (for my dad) and I followed that by winning the Combined Service title shortly after. As a novice, I got a win over the Home Counties champion, Dave Laxen (we are mates), and I was dead chuffed as he was a hot favourite. I also went the distance with the Swedish Olympic captain, Ove Lundby, in Sweden and, before that, I beat the triple Hungarian champion, Laszlo Fodor. Very satisfying. Another moment springs to mind when I was awarded the best loser trophy after fighting my way to the semi-finals of the BAOR championships in Berlin in 1974.

(RO) I understand that you once managed boxers. Did you enjoy this role?

(SH) Yes I did manage boxers for a time, but I cannot say I enjoyed it. Unless you have major connections so to speak, you are wasting your time.

(RO) You also promoted fights. Did you enjoy that role?

(SH) It was a miserable time for me as you have to get bums on seats and that is not easy. You really can lose a lot of money being a promoter, make no mistake.

(RO) You also attempted match-making. Did you find this rewarding?

(SH) I am not being negative, but I have to say no I did not find it rewarding at all. It is the most difficult of boxing tasks, believe me. It is really difficult attempting to get certain boxers to meet. It's just one long headache.

(RO) You have also been an MC. How did you find this?

(SH) Loved it. I found it a very easy and a most enjoyable job.

(RO) Do you still keep fit?

(SH) No, I am terribly unfit and have not done any training since I quit the sport in 1979.

(RO) What would you say to those who would like to ban boxing?

(SH) I would tell them to mind their own business.

(RO) There have been a number of films made about boxing over the years. Do you have a favourite?

(SH) Not really, but I must say the first Rocky film with Sylvester Stallone was pretty well done. The rest were a rip off, but the first, like the first Rambo film, 'First Blood', was a cracker.

(RO) What is your favourite sport apart from boxing?

(SH) I am not really a sporty type of person. I don't support a football team and hate the American sports. I watch a bit of snooker and some horse racing but sport, apart from boxing, doesn't do much for me.

(RO) What was the best advice you were given when boxing?

(SH) The best advice I was given when boxing was probably: "pack it in son".

(RO) How long have you been married?

(SH) I have never been married, but have lived with my partner, Elaine, for almost 23 years. We have two sons, Joe, 21, and Max, 18. They are good, well-adjusted kids and Elaine did a great job of bringing them up.

(RO) Do you have a hobby?

(SH) As far as hobbies are concerned, I don't get a lot of time. I am lucky since I turned my hobby (boxing) into my living. When I get the time I build, fix, and maintain computers for friends.

(RO) What advice would you give to anyone embarking on a career in boxing?

(SH) My advice to anyone considering a career in boxing is FORGET IT, unless you sell tickets, can box and fight and have a manager and promoter with your interests at heart. You must also dedicate yourself to the sport, as it should be all-consuming to get the best out of it.

(RO) How long have you been a boxing commentator for Eurosport?

(SH) I have been the Eurosport boxing commentator for 13 years, since May of 1991.

(RO) Have you ever considered writing a book about boxing?

(SH) Yes I have, and will one day sit down to write it. At the moment it's a matter of finding the time to put the required material together.

(RO) Looking back at your career in boxing, if you had your time over again would you do anything different?

(SH) I probably wouldn't change much if I could have my time over again. Everything we do make us the people we are today. I am not everyone's cup of tea and wouldn't want to be.

After talking to Steve it came across loud and clear that he was a man devoted to the sport of boxing. It was also very evident that he was most modest about his own achievements and contribution to the sport. Being both a professional and amateur exponent of the noble art and then a manager, promoter, matchmaker, MC, and now a TV commentator for Eurosport is indeed an impressive list and one to be proud of; no, one to be very proud of. There can surely be no argument when I say that Steve Holdsworth is a man for all boxing seasons. On behalf of the *Yearbook*, I wish Steve and his family the very best for the future.

Steve (right) and Colin Hart (left), the Sun boxing writer, seen here with Alan Shaw, a former vocalist with the pop group, Unit Four Plus Two

Lanky Bob : How Good Was Bob Fitzsimmons?

by Keith R. Robinson

'The cave-men of the ring are extinct.
Champions of the future will be as children
compared to the rough and ready battlers of
twenty or more years ago'. Bob Fitzsimmons 1914.

As eyewitnesses to the exploits of Bob Fitzsimmons have faded from the fight scene so too has his reputation as a fighter drifted into the realm of myth and legend. Those who saw him, with a few notable exceptions, recognised his stature as a great champion. However, it might be argued that years of praise – little short of idolatry – have served to obscure his qualities as a fighter and fistic innovator. And as a man he has become mired in accounts of his quaint and eccentric behaviour, characterised as a freakish buffoon.

Whatever his limitations as an intellectual or a social lion, Bob bowed to none as a fistic oracle. The opening quote describes perfectly the transitional fighter who thrived between the end of the prize-ring and the rise of the Queensberry code. Many fighters of the period failed to adapt to the new code of gloved combat and fell by the wayside. Others capitalised on their prize-ring skills, tailored them to limited rounds and developed tactics more suited to points scoring.

It is becoming quite acceptable to praise fighters of the modern era as the very epitome of speed, skill and awesome power and to mock the pioneers as little more than sluggers scarcely able to adopt a proper stance, slow as treacle and lacking in skills. Bob Fitzsimmons' career gives the lie to this misconception.

* * *

Fitz was a scrappy Cornish-Kiwi kid when first he entered the ring as a 14 year old, winning three bare-knuckle bouts cia. 1877, which by his own account were fought under time limited rounds. The facial damage inflicted on his opponents caused the youngster to forsake knuckle fighting for amateur action with gloves. Though he seems to have enjoyed some success in competitions he was also a regular performer in sporting saloons and in the alley at the side of the family smithy in his adopted home town of Timaru, on the south island of New Zealand.

A first visit to Sydney, Australia in 1883 resulted in three quick wins. He moved there as a journeyman blacksmith in 1885 and stayed five years, engaging in about 14 bouts, losing two, and many exhibitions under the auspices of long-time Australian prize-ring champion, Larry Foley. Though printed records have not yet come to light it is certain that Fitz travelled with boxing booths on the Sydney – Melbourne circuit, taking on all-comers. The Sydney of the 1880s was a breeding ground of great fighters such as Peter Jackson, Mick Dooley, Frank Slavin, Billy McCarthy, Jim Hall, Billy Murphy and Young Griffo who were all in action and well known to the young smith. Bob sparred the top pros and amateurs, attended all the shows and studied closely local and visiting fighters. Fitz claimed that he had never taken instruction until he went to America in 1890. This is not strictly true as he spent two seasons under the tutelage of Dan Lea in Timaru and while not on good terms with Foley, trainer of all those greats previously mentioned, he did exercise at Larry's gym and no doubt observed him in action. Bob further claimed that he had never trained while in Australasia; if he meant fulltime training he was certainly correct.

Legend has it that Fitz was a roaring success in Sydney, carrying all before him. The truth is that he suffered knockouts at the hands of Dooley and Hall, though the last was very suspect, could never find a backer and rarely attracted a purse. Almost six feet tall, weighing in the region of 150lbs and of a distinctly unhealthy appearance, Bob did not inspire the confidence of local sportsmen. What is now clear is that he was asthmatic and poorly conditioned. He was, however, a clean living, married man and rarely missed an opportunity to further his fistic education.

Fitz upped stakes and sailed off to the US in 1890. Without a reputation, but with confidence to spare, he immediately issued a challenge to all the middleweights of America. Granted a trial against the club stalwart, Frank Allen, at the California Amateur Club, the newcomer so impressed the committee that he was matched as a substitute against Australian Billy McCarthy.

After eight months and three fights stateside Fitz was world's middleweight champion, having displayed the kind of skill and grit that would endear him to American fans. Against McCarthy he refused to accept the bout on a foul, insisting on fighting through to victory. Against Arthur Upham he showed a cruelty which, though unwarranted against so limited an opponent, showed that he was a master of the seamier side of the sweet science, destroying Arthur with rabbit punches. Against middleweight champion 'Nonpareil' Jack Dempsey, Fitz outboxed and outpunched the foremost ring general of his day – a man considered unbeatable – ruthlessly cutting him down in 13 rounds with power punches to head and kidneys. Bob's tactics in America would have amazed the Sydney crowd – he was considered a gentlemanly character downunder – and one can only assume that he had been advised by his handlers to get tough.

By this stage of his career, Bob was already a very accomplished boxer, being a stylist in the mould of Peter Jackson or Jim Corbett, but with a mastery of punches and tactics now outlawed or forgotten by the majority of modern boxers. The pivot blow, kidney punch, back handers and rabbit punches were then only illegal under the Queensberry code if specifically barred by the fight articles agreed by negotiation before the bout. Such articles often prohibited hitting in clinches and hitting on the break. So confident was he that Fitz usually agreed to the other man's terms however restrictive. Bob had learned these skills in Australasia, from impromptu street fights, his booth fighting and exhibitions at Foley's. The young blacksmith enjoyed the danger of meeting all comers – miners, lumberjacks, steelworkers, local champs and small town bullies – and revelled in the unexpected. Bob was never one to pass up the chance of expert advice. Close Aussie pal, George Dawson, was the master of kidney punching – which destroyed Dempsey and Jimmy Carroll and Bob's first US manager, was notorious as having taught the pivot blow to George La Blanche. The kidney punch was a deadly weapon, but the pivot blow was as dangerous to the user as the the victim.

During the transitional period, championship bouts were usually to a finish and the referee ruled the roost – his verdict was final. If he didn't agree with the articles he would ignore them. The police were present at big fights and were liable to interfere if things got too rough. In the small halls and on the road mob law often ruled, with the hometown fighter having all the advantages. Bob knew all the tricks and was not adverse to using them if he came upon a tartar. In his memoirs he tells of warning rough guys to mend their ways – low blows, hitting after the bell, biting, etc. – and giving them a dose of their own medicine if they failed to heed his warnings. Outside the ring Fitz was an amiable individual, inside he was out to win. Later fighters such as Harry Greb were renowned for their dirty tactics used as a matter of course. Not so Fitz, he had the punch to finish any fighter without resorting to dirty tricks unless provoked.

An argument often used to discredit old-timers is to disparage their training methods. Fitz for one was very enlightened, usually training in the country or by the sea and adhering strictly to his dictum that training should never be boring. Running, sparring, bagwork, floor exercises, swimming, cycling and regular hunting trips kept him busy and interested. Bob used his sparring sessions to perfect his side-stepping, feinting and parrying skills. Wrestling was a regular part of his training routine, having once been an essential element of fighting under London Prize Ring rules. It was the leading combat sport amongst the Cornish community of Timaru and Bob's elder brother Jarrett is said to have been a skilled 'wrassler'. Fitz met top grappler, Joe Acton, in November 1891, gaining the first fall in 45 minutes before losing by two falls to one.

Once in America Bob never again had to work in the debilitating atmosphere of the forge, trained fulltime and was able to live in more wholesome accommodation. Being an assiduous trainer at a time when many boxers lacked dedication, he ate well but not to excess and rarely drank alcohol because of his low tolerance. The unhealthy, weak-winded, Sydney beanpole was transformed into a canny, rock-hard competitor attracting fans and backers alike.

After defeating Jim Hall and Dan Creedon with outstanding displays of hard punching, Bob had run out of credible middleweight challengers. He is often criticised for not regularly defending his title. However, championship contests against Jim Hall, Ted Pritchard (twice), John O'Brien, Alex Greggains and Dan Creedon were not brought off because of being banned by State authorities, or due to problems with the health or finance of his challengers. Fitz had become middleweight champion after only 20 fights, but his rough fistic upbringing had given him a breadth of experience which was invaluable.

Fitz dominated the middleweight ranks from 1891, refusing his claims to the championship until his eventual 'retirement' in 1910. The immediate pretenders to his title, Kid McCoy and Tommy Ryan, were never considered viable challengers – McCoy was too erratic in his behavior and often accused of lacking 'bottle', while Ryan was too small – and neither could find backers. When Fitz was matched with Stan Ketchel in 1908 ringsiders deplored the prospect, but experienced boxing writer Otto Floto wrote:

> 'there is no denying that with Fitz at his best, and Ketchel at his best we would have to [place] our [bets], on the red topped slugger'.

Fitz never faced a middleweight who gave him trouble. The legendary fight to a finish in Sydney against the Guyanan, 'Starlight', during which he was said to have been floored and his opponent having retired with a broken hand, was in fact a waltz. Dempsey was methodically dismantled. Hall and Creedon, both effective punchers, were clinically dispatched with power punches to the head. Like his successors, Ketchel, Harry Greb and Mickey Walker, Fitz relished a tear up and occasionally his enthusiasm let him down. Against Peter Maher and Joe Choynski he was badly hurt, and floored by Joe, but when hurt Fitz was a very dangerous animal as both found to their cost. Bob's talents as a puncher are unquestioned. Most fistic experts who saw him in action were of the opinion that he was most certainly the hardest ever middleweight hitter and pound for pound the heaviest hitter of them all. He did not need to set himself for a delivery, his heavy punches were launched, with either hand, from any angle, at any stage of an encounter. When hurt or wasted he was at his most dangerous.

Bob was unbeaten between February 1890 and June 1899. A disqualification loss to Tom Sharkey in 1896 should be dismissed as a setup engineered by Sharkey, a promoter and the referee, Wyatt Earp. The longevity of Fitz's dominance at around 158lbs commends him as perhaps the greatest middleweight of all.

After his win over Creedon in September 1894, Bob set his sights on a challenge for the heavyweight championship. James J. Corbett had been champion since 1892 and had a reputation as the fastest and most skilled heavyweight ever, a claim boosted by a 62-rounds draw with Peter Jackson.

Many prize-ring champions weighed within the 158lbs limit, Tom Sayers and Jem Mace to name but two. Charlie Mitchell challenged John L. Sullivan for the prize-ring crown at 166lbs and Corbett for the Queensberry title at 159lbs. Although a few eyebrows were raised when Fitz challenged the latter, it was a perceived gulf in skills which caused comment rather than weight. Corbett underestimated Fitz and considered winning a foregone conclusion. He had the advantage of having fought the long fight with Jackson and Fitz's claim to having taken a dive in his loss to Jim Hall in Sydney convinced Gentleman Jim that Bob would quit under pressure.

Few now give Fitz credit as being a thinking fighter, but as a 'small' heavyweight he radically adapted his style to take on bigger men. He stripped out all the pettier moves and concentrated on perfecting an aggressive style which took him inside where he could use his short-arm punching to advantage, this at a time when infighting was often barred. Bob was renowned for his short punches, never pulling his first back and always punching through his target. Fitz's footwork was admired by his contemporaries. Never up on his toes, he conserved his strength, advancing flat-footed manoeuvring into position for his 'solar plexus' punch. Bob preferred the term 'fatal shift', as a more accurate description of the move which brought him many victories. It began with a straight left and following right aimed for the jaw, which were sometimes feints or deliberate misses. From his orthodox stance, Fitz shifted his right foot forward beyond the left foot, which allowed maximum leverage for a left hook to his opponent's body. A following left or right to the jaw finished the job, if required. So famous was this move that all Bob's opponents were well aware of it and on their guard. However, Bob was so well practiced in the shift that when the chance occurred he executed the move in one flowing action, his opponent taken by surprise and powerless to resist the inevitable.

Fitz's transformation into a 'heavyweight' fighter was truly remarkable for a man in his 30s. His invention of the fatal shift, a true innovation for which, despite his modest dismissal of the move as a hit to the wind, deserves all credit.

While aggression is a valid form of defence he did not neglect any of his skills. Kid McCoy, who sparred with Bob on many occasions, opined that 99 times out of a hundred swings (hooks) thrown at Bob were taken on his shoulders.

At Carson City, Nevada on 17 March 1897, when he assumed the mantle of heavyweight champion, Fitz is said to have been heavily punished by Corbett – a boxer with greater speed of hand and foot – floored, cut and bloodied. Bob had calculated that Jim would never be tempted to aggress unless convinced that his opponent was sorely weakened. Fitz advanced doggedly taking all but the hardest punches and countering wildly. The Cornishman was credited with landing a lucky punch while engaged in crude and wild work – a critique subscribed to by Corbett himself. In truth, Fitz's amateurish tactics were designed to draw Jim into position for the 'fatal shift', the long-headed smith believing that Jim's chin was too elusive a target. This was not a new tactic in Bob's game, there being evidence that he had used similar wiles in Australia. And he had bluffed the taller Jim Hall by falling short with his punches and drawing his opponent into the danger zone before felling him with one of the hardest punches ever seen in New Orleans. Both Corbett and Hall screamed fluke and pleaded for a rematch.

Bob was a tough, skilled and tenacious fighter who outthought and outfought the fastest and most skilled heavyweights of his time, while, by his own contention, still able to make the middleweight limit. In heavyweight competition, Fitz occasionally weighed 172lbs, but, like Archie Moore, he could move happily up and down the weights without perceptible effect on his form.

With possible title defences against Corbett, McCoy and Sharkey having fallen through, Fitz signed to meet 12-fight novice, James J. Jeffries, in June 1899. Whether drugged, as he claimed, over confident or beaten on merit, Bob lost his championship to Jeffries at the age of 36. After toying with retirement, Fitz mounted a comeback in 1900, beating top contenders, Gus Ruhlin on 10 August and Tom Sharkey on 24 August, both by knockout, on the promise of a title challenge on 31 August. Fitz had engaged in toe-to-toe slugging matches with the two top contenders within 14 days and was victorious. He had whipped himself into great physical condition and was ready to face the champion and seek revenge. On 27 August, Jeffries' manager, Bill Brady, announced that Jeff was unfit and had stopped training. The fight was off and Fitz 'retired'. It could be argued that Brady took fright at Bob's form and pulled the plug.

The match finally took place during July 1902 and Fitz, now aged 39 and outweighed by 47lbs, was beaten in eight torrid rounds. Having, literally, smashed both hands on Jeff's skull, Fitz had reached the end of his career as a heavyweight. As a final hurrah he demoralised and outclassed young gun, George Gardner, to relieve him of his world's light-heavyweight championship in November 1903, thus becoming boxing's first triple world's champion.

Only five middleweights since Fitz have harboured serious pretentions towards the heavyweight title. Kid McCoy followed Bob up the weight ladder beating Joe Choynski, Peter Maher and Gus Ruhlin, but failing against Tom Sharkey and Corbett – all men decisively beaten by Fitz.

Stan Ketchel, who was tipped as early as 1907 as a threat to Jack Johnson, faced only one name heavyweight before challenging Johnson, that being Porky Flynn, at best a man of the second rank. The Ketchel – Johnson bout was a mysterious affair that was rumoured to have had a 'no-knockout' agreement. After 11 rounds, Stan scored a knockout blow and Lil' Arthur iced the Michigan Assassin with his next shot.

Two non-champions of middleweight poundage who were bonafide heavyweight contenders were Sam Langford, whose qualifications were beyond dispute, and Jack 'The Giant Killer' Dillon, who, at 5'7½" and 158lbs, was the leading contender to Jess Willard and was given more than an even chance of winning.

Harry Greb had wins over Gunboat Smith, Tommy Gibbons, Tommy Loughran and Gene Tunney and outsped and outpunched Jack Dempsey in a gym spar, but couldn't get the 'Manassa Mauler' into a public ring. One man, who we should consider an honourary middleweight who challenged for the big one was Billy Conn and he nearly made it against Joe Louis.

Since Greb, no middleweight has been seriously considered as a threat to a heavyweight champion, not Ray Robinson, nor Carlos Monzon, nor Marvin Hagler, nor Roy Jones, nor Bernard Hopkins. If such luminaries could not be ceded a chance against recent heavyweights, how could the lightest heavyweight champion of them all be taken seriously and compared with Louis, Ali, Tyson or Lewis?

Middleweights have naturally stayed the same size, but, just as naturally, heavyweights have got bigger. The big heavyweights of today are the result of a better standard of living, or, more precisely, a higher standard of nutrition. Few leading heavyweights born prior to World War II exceeded 200lbs in condition and those that did rarely displayed speed or skills much above the average. A 200 pounder today might be considered a little too light for top class competition.

For the sake of argument, and historical fairness, what if Fitz had been born in 1963 rather than 1863?

The average height and weight of 28 top heavyweights from the original George Godfrey to Luther McCarty was 6'0¼" and 192.5lbs. The same statistics for a similar group of heavies from 'Bonecrusher' Smith and Vitali Klitschko, show 6'3¼" in height and 228.25lbs in weight. By applying these statistics proportionately to Bob on the day that he fought Corbett, the late 20th-century Fitz would be 6'2¾" tall and 199lbs in weight.

Four men have risen from the light-heavyweight and cruiserweight divisions to claim bits of the heavyweight championship – Michael Spinks (199¾lbs), Evander Holyfield (208lbs), Michael Moorer (217lbs) and Roy Jones (196lbs). Each man built up with modern nutritional methods, weight training and the possible use of bulk inducing preparations. Our 20th century Bob Fitzsimmons would be a natural 199 pounder, retaining all the skill, speed and power of the 1890s competitor. Surely this truly pound-for-pound Fitz would be a match for any of today's super heavyweights?

He would be better trained. Fitz was never known to tire, he would not be exhausted after four rounds praying for his second wind. He fought his first and only 20-round fight at the age of 40, outlasting a 26-year-old, 12 or 15-round fights would be in his own words, "Pie".

Tactically Bob was never at a loss. If one ploy failed

another was tried. He didn't have plan A or B, his fertile boxing brain being ever active and he didn't go into the ring with a set plan. "How do I know what the other man will do?"

He was indefatigable, accepting pain and using it as a spur to greater endeavour. He didn't suffer from a bully's insecurity, nor did he fear defeat – it was not an option. Fitz, like the second Jack Dempsey, couldn't be psyched out of a match, he was impervious to stares or windups.

* * *

Bob Fitzsimmons finally retired in March 1914 after 37 years of ring activity. He was the first triple world champion, winning all the titles open to a man of his weight. He won the middleweight championship weighing 150½ lbs and in modern times he would have been eligible for six divisions. Henry Armstrong equalled Bob's feat in March 1938 when adding the lightweight championship to the feather and welter titles he already held and holding all three concurrently for three months.

Fitz was the oldest man to win the premier championship when beating Corbett aged 34, holding this distinction until 1951 when Jersey Joe Walcott turned the same trick at age 37. Bob was the lightest man ever to win the heavyweight championship at 168lbs, an accomplishment unlikely ever to be equalled.

These achievements are beyond dispute. More difficult to evaluate is Fitz's quality as a fighter. Certainly his courage was never seriously in doubt, nor his determination. Stilted, faded and silent films tell little of his skills. The testimony of ringsiders and boxing writers who saw him in the flesh is massively in agreement that Fitz was the outstanding fighter of his time. Contemporaries of such diverse skills and talents as Kid McCoy, Battling Nelson and Joe Gans lauded him, while only Joe Choynski and Jim Hall remained unconvinced of his greatness.

Few fighters graced the ring as long as Bob and fewer maintained their reputation for so long a time. The standing of Corbett and Jeffries waxed and waned, while that of Fitz was maintained. When Jeffries retired undefeated in May 1905, Fitz was, by some, awarded the title by reversion. Crippled in hand and foot he lost his claim in 13 rounds to 'Philadelphia' Jack O'Brien. Jeffries returned to be humiliated by champion Jack Johnson, a man whose title claims Fitz had championed. The 'White Hope' era bloomed bright and blousey and boxing's wiseacres prayed for a fistic saviour. The *Boston Post's* Bill Baily mused;

> 'Fighters come and go, but the downright lovers of the Queensberry sport will always keep Lanky Bob on a pedestal all by his lonesome'. (1911)

Robert Fitzsimmons was a remarkable man and a more remarkable fighter. Though wide of shoulder, his lean and aged look, knock-kneed and ungainly stance and strangely vacant countenance seemed to breed disdain in his opponents. Each was convinced that old Fitz was ripe for picking. In his prime none but the giant Jeffries made good that conviction.

Pugilists and the Britannia: Fistic Entertainments at a Glasgow Music Hall

by Tony Gee

Around the end of the prize-ring era, through the transitional period between knuckles and gloves, and into the gloved era of boxing the music hall/variety theatre provided an often lucrative and undemanding route for pugilists with celebrity standing to capitalize on their fame. (This was usually in sparring exhibitions, whilst on occasions more versatile entertainment abilities were displayed.) However, very little has previously been written on the subject and the topic is clearly far too large for sufficient justice to be done to it in a mere article. Perhaps a widespread in-depth study will be undertaken in the future; in the meantime, this piece concentrates on just one particular establishment in Glasgow with solid fistic performance ties and details some of the boxers who featured on its bills.

It should be pointed out that the music hall selection was not determined by any logical process. There are more obvious candidates, such as the Washington Music Hall in Battersea, London. (This was for a time managed by renowned pugilist Charlie Mitchell for his father-in-law, the celebrated minstrel George Washington 'Pony' Moore, and was said in 1896 by the *Sporting Life*, when referred to as the Washington Palace of Varieties, to supply a "strong connecting link in the history of English, American, and Australian boxers".) Instead the choice of place evolved from information found during several years' research through Glasgow newspapers, part of extensive work undertaken for my forthcoming book on bareknuckle fighting in Scotland. (Hence all the papers named in this article were published in Glasgow, with the exception of three London ones – the *Music Hall and Theatre Review*, the *Sporting Life* and *The Sportsman*.)

The Britannia Music Hall in Trongate will be familiar to television viewers of the first series of *Restoration*, shown in 2003, highlighting Britain's endangered architectural heritage. It was one of 30 buildings on which the programmes focused. However unfortunately, despite being described at the time as the "most complete and unaltered early Victorian music hall in the UK" and thus an "important piece of theatrical and social history", it did not even feature amongst the final ten buildings from which the one deemed by voters the most deserving of restoration (Manchester's Victoria Baths) was selected. The Britannia had a strong Irish clientele (not surprising given the contingent from the Emerald Isle living in the surrounding area), a fact which certainly did not discourage the booking of fistic celebrities. The golden period for pugilistic acts at the Britannia seems to have been the 1890s, and consequently this article primarily limits itself to that decade. The principal performers therefore included in the piece had either competed with both knuckles and gloves or limited themselves to the latter.

Jem Mace is ironically, given his stated preference for bareknuckle fighting, often regarded as the father of the modern scientific school of boxing. A legendary fistic figure

(some questionable conduct notwithstanding), he can be considered the most celebrated of the pugilists appearing at the Britannia during its early years, and indeed probably throughout its entire history. Astonishingly, Mace exhibited in Scotland at least once in each of five different decades. His engagement in August 1869 at the Britannia, then being advertised as the "*Pre-Eminently Popular Place of Amusement in Glasgow*", was with his cousin and favourite exhibition partner, Po(o)ley Mace. (The Britannia, following extensive renovations, had reopened just a month before, when it was described by the *Glasgow Weekly Mail* as "one of the handsomest of such establishments in the kingdom".) The *Glasgow Saturday Post, And Weekly Journal* related that as well as the fistic entertainment provided by the Maces, Jem's many cups and belts were displayed. The engagement, so stated the *Weekly Mail* when commenting in complimentary fashion on the final evening's performance, was a very successful one.

Whilst Jem's appearances then were when he was a relatively young man, he also featured at the Trongate establishment at the end of his life – actually in the year of his death. In January 1910 the *Daily Record & Mail* reported that A E Pickard, the proprietor of what was by

A debonair Jem Mace (reproduced by kind permission of Antiquities of the Prize Ring)

now known as the Panopticon, had secured Mace's services "at great expense". In fact Mace told an *Evening Times* reporter whilst in Glasgow that he had not as yet received his old-age pension, probably because "they think I am making too much". The *Evening Citizen* regarded his appearance in a sparring act on the opening night as a "marvellous performance" for someone of his age (he was 78 years old at the time), and the Panopticon's proprietor must have been delighted at the interest the elderly pugilist excited. The engagement would definitely have been extended for a further week but for Pickard having already engaged Mace at his Clydebank venue and thus been reluctant to disappointment his customers there.

Another fighter who, like Mace, attained champion status under bareknuckle rules, Jem Smith featured at the Britannia in March 1893 in what was stated to be his first Scottish appearance. However, whilst the *Sporting Life* reported that his three round display with Jem Young (described by the newspaper as an "old sparring partner") on the opening night of his engagement was thoroughly enjoyed by the audience, the Glasgow press apparently failed to show much enthusiasm, the *North British Daily Mail* especially being more impressed with a four round one, between Jack Smith and Bill Murray, on the undercard.

The same bill also included a boxing display in which the participants were Abe Daltr(e)y, Josh Higgins and Selena Seaforth. According to the famous referee Bernard John Angle, Daltrey was as a fistic teacher almost of the calibre of the renowned Ned Donnelly (the 'Royal Professor'), and Seaforth under Abe's tuition "obtained a knowledge of boxing that put some of the sterner sex to shame". This comment regarding Seaforth may not have been an exaggerated one, particularly as it was made by such a recognised authority as Angle. Certainly when Daltrey, Higgins and Seaforth returned to the Britannia in August 1894 and appeared in a sketch entitled 'Fisto, or the Rival Maidens', both the *Glasgow Evening News* and the *Music Hall and Theatre Review* emphasized that the piece included a pugilistic exhibition in which the female performer took part. This boxing was, in turn, described by the *North British Daily Mail* as "being the fastest and most telling seen on the Britannia stage for a long time past".

A two-time opponent of Jem Smith with the gloves, Ted Pritchard was one of several prominent fighters who exhibited at the Britannia on more than one occasion during the 1890s. When he appeared with the clever and determined Scottish pugilist Lachie Thomson in January 1893, on the first night the Britannia was crowded to overflowing despite prices having been doubled. (Although Pritchard was the more famous name, Thomson was obviously a big draw in Glasgow too; when he was the headliner at what was then beginning to be advertised as the Britannia Variety Theatre – although subsequently not always so – in December 1891, the *Music Hall and Theatre Review* mentioned that "as a natural sequence, the house is packed".) Pritchard and Thomson's three round spar was considered by the *North British Daily Mail* to have been "exceedingly clever on both sides" and "conducted with the greatest good feeling".

In February of 1894 Pritchard returned to the Trongate establishment. The *Music Hall and Theatre Review* noted he and Jem Young were the main attraction and described their boxing as "pretty". The *Glasgow Evening News* elaborated, commenting that the sparring styles of the men (Pritchard's defensive adeptness and Young's purposeful albeit unimaginative approach) were worthy of comparison. There followed a further engagement for Pritchard at the Britannia in October of the same year, this time with the well-known Harry Nickless. According to the *Music Hall and Theatre Review*, their salary, as "principal artistes" of what it described as a "very good all-round company", was a large one. The financial rewards, so the paper stated, had been negotiated for them by Tom Prichard, an apparently successful London variety and dramatic agent.

A further fistic celebrity to feature more than once at the Britannia in the last decade of the 19th century was the aforementioned Charlie Mitchell, whose excellent record included a drawn bareknuckle contest of over three hours with the legendary John L Sullivan. At the end of January and the beginning of February 1895 he appeared at the Britannia, along with the respected Bill 'Chesterfield' Goode, in what was advertised as a "SPECIAL ENGAGEMENT AT ENORMOUS OUTLAY". ('Pony' Moore was also mentioned as accompanying the pugilists, but the *Sporting Life*, on reporting the opening night, stated that commitments in London had detained him.) Back in 1890 Mitchell had been charged with violently assaulting Goode, being subsequently acquitted, but presumably any residual bad feeling had either evaporated or else was allayed by the financial inducements. According to the *Sporting Life*, although prices were increased for the engagement, the Britannia was "crammed to the doors each evening", whilst on the last night, despite entrance fees being "exactly doubled, many undred [sic] were unable to obtain admission". Incidentally, prior to the event certain Glasgow newspapers had billed Mitchell as appearing with Ted Pritchard, but the *Sporting Life* of the same date made no reference to the latter with regard to the Britannia, noting that it was Goode who had been engaged with Mitchell, and the former sources thereafter concurred.

When Mitchell returned to the Britannia in the May of the same year his partner was redoubtable Australian Frank Slavin, best remembered for the unfair treatment he experienced in an infamous bareknuckle affair against Jem Smith and his celebrated glove contest with Peter Jackson. The engagement was also a successful one; indeed, the *Evening Times* related that "Mr Kean [the proprietor and manager] had by special request to retain them one night longer".

Frank Craig was yet another noted pugilist who appeared more than once at the Britannia in the 1890s. The 'Coffee Cooler', as he was commonly known, was certainly an interesting character; Eugene Corri, who refereed him many times, later recalled that his "intelligence was marked, his knowledge of languages really remarkable, and his fighting style distinctly unorthodox". In December 1894, only one week after having swiftly conquered the man *The Sportsman* wrote of as "long looked upon as the best middle-weight in the country [Ted Pritchard]", Craig began an engagement at the Britannia. This, according to the *Music Hall and Theatre Review*, featured him not only sparring three rounds nightly but also then playing a selection of tunes on the mouth organ and giving a rendition of an old plantation dance.

Britannia audiences were given further evidence of Craig's versatility when in May 1896 he again performed at the Trongate venue. A report of the opening night in the *Evening Times* said that he was "accompanied by his clever Picaninnies [sic] – smart knockabout artistes of colour", and the combination sang plantation songs and danced extremely well. Particular mention was made of Craig's expertise with the mouth organ but it does not seem as though he felt it necessary to include any demonstration whatsoever of his fistic prowess.

Irishman Peter Maher, who could boast a victory over Craig (knocking him out inside two rounds at Boston in July 1894), was, the *Sporting Life* wrote, a "much-talked-of pugilist" when he graced the Britannia stage in August 1895. The same newspaper reported that on the opening night Mr Kean had high expectations with regard to the attendance and was far from disappointed; the *Glasgow Evening News* observed that good boxing entertainment was

"always a sure draw in the Britannia, and the hall was literally packed". According to the former source, Maher had as his "sparring partner Patsy Gregan, the ex-heavyweight champion of Ireland", and the four rounds in which they engaged provided a "lively exhibition of sparring". However, the *Glasgow Evening News* considered that Gregan was "too far out-classed to make the exhibition of very great interest". Neither report, as can be seen from the quotations given above, backs up the claim made by some record books and compilers that the event (on the 26th) resulted in Maher knocking out one Patsy Gregson. The *Evening Times*, though, did state that he "somewhat easily gained a victory over his opponent", whom it named as Cregan, and the *North British Daily Mail* declared that Maher had the "fight in hand from start to finish [against Creagan]".

This article, as mentioned at the start, merely details some of the fistic exponents who appeared at the Britannia, whilst the establishment itself was just one of several music hall/variety theatres in Glasgow to feature boxers on its bills. It can be seen, therefore, given the likelihood of the same pattern having been repeated throughout at least a good proportion of the major cities and towns in Britain, that the music hall stage did indeed provide ample opportunities for pugilists with box-office appeal to enhance their financial position in circumstances generally requiring comparatively little effort.

Frank Craig, the versatile 'Coffee Cooler'

TBS SPORT MANAGEMENT LTD
TBS Gym, Woodford, Essex
Boxing Training • Management • Promotions

Tony Burns	office:	020 8550 8911
Tony Sims	mobile:	07739 617830
Jim McDonnell	fax:	020 8550 8915
Terry Steward	e-mail:	t.burns@tbs.ltd.uk

Managed Boxers

Steve Spartcus	Light-Heavyweight	16-1-0	English Champion
Andrew Lowe	Light-Heavyweight	13-1-0	Southern Area Champion
Dave Stewart	Lightweight	13-0-0	British Masters Champion
Daniel Cadman	Middleweight	5-0-0	
Darren Barker	Light-Middleweight		2002 Commonwealth Games Gold Medal Winner
Lloyd Otte	Super-Bantamweight		England International

Trained Boxers

Danny Williams	Heavyweight	32-3-0	WBU Inter-Continental Champion
Takaloo	Light-Middleweight	22-4-0	
Steve Murray	Lightweight	23-3-0	
Brett James	Welterweight	14-3-2	
Alex Arthur	Super-Featherweight	17-1-0	IBF Inter-Continental Champion

Licensed by The British Boxing Board of Control Ltd
Registered Office: Abacus House, 68a North Street, Romford RM1 1DA
Incorporated in England: 4765859 / VAT Number: 815 1039 61

Home and Away with British Boxers During 2003-2004

by John Jarrett

JULY

It was a bad night for the 'V boys' at the Goresbrook Arena in Dagenham, with Birmingham's Jimmy Vincent and Bradford's Bobby Vanzie losing their fights for the vacant British welterweight and British lightweight titles, respectively. After 12 excellent rounds between Vincent and the Manchester southpaw, David Barnes, referee John Keane raised the glove of Barnes as winner and new champion, the signal for a crescendo of booing that shook the building.

To the majority in a sweltering arena it looked as though the 34-year-old one-time journeyman had finally hit the jackpot, but the verdict and the title went to the unbeaten 22-year-old (12-0) by a single point. It was later revealed that Barnes had broken a knuckle in his right hand, possibly in round three, according to his trainer, Brian Hughes.

Lightweight champion Vanzie, late in getting to the arena after being stuck in traffic in the Blackwall Tunnel, probably wished he had stayed in the tunnel after seeing

There were many who thought Jimmy Vincent had won the vacant British welterweight title at the end of 12 hard-fought rounds, but it was not to be as David Barnes (right) was given the verdict   Les Clark

53

young Graham Earl take referee Paul Thomas' decision and his British championship along with it. This one was also a disputed decision, although closer than Barnes-Vincent, but the undefeated kid got it, much to Vanzie's disgust. And, as if that wasn't bad enough, Frank Warren said he didn't want to promote Bobby any more!

Mr Warren was pleased with the performance of Bedford heavyweight, Matt Skelton, having his first outing under the Sports Network umbrella. A former Muay-Thai fighter, the 30-something Skelton is an 18-stone wrecking ball and the French veteran, Antoine Palatis, was happy when it was stopped in the fourth of a six-rounder.

Confidence is something a fighter needs as he climbs into the ring to do battle with his opponent, but depending on who is in the opposite corner could well make him over-confident. And that can be bad! Take this fight at the Braehead Arena in Renfrew with Scott Harrison defending his WBO featherweight title against Manuel Medina, the 34-year-old Mexican. On the cover of the fight programme, Harrison is holding four aces in his hands, cards bearing photos of Marco Antonio Barrera, Johnny Tapia, Erik Morales, and Prince Naseem Hamed. These are the guys he wants next, after taking care of Medina.

That night, everything went pear-shaped as Medina took the title with a split decision and Harrison's dreams assumed nightmare proportions. Was Scott over-confident, thinking he just had to turn up? Was he over-trained, was he under-trained, was he weight-weakened? He is a big fighter for a nine-stone man, but whatever Scott Harrison was, when he went to bed that night he was no longer the WBO featherweight champion. That title now belonged to Manuel Medina.

It was a bad night for Glasgow. In the chief supporting bout, Willie Limond lost his long-awaited challenge to British super-featherweight champion, Alex Arthur, the Edinburgh man winning in round eight when the referee stopped it. Willie had gone 18 fights without defeat, but this was a fight too far against the champion, who retained his unbeaten record, 16 wins, 14 inside.

It was a bad night for Scotland altogether as another favourite in Brian Carr failed in his challenge to Commonwealth super-bantamweight champion, Esham Pickering, who also picked up the vacant British title when he stopped Carr inside four rounds. It is all coming together for Pickering now, he's boxing well and even starting to punch harder. He had only seven early wins in 22, but there was nothing wrong with the right that dropped Brian in the fourth. Although getting up he was in trouble and it was stopped. In the dressing room, the 34-year-old Carr announced his retirement.

Howard Eastman (right) remained supreme in Europe when the challenger for his middleweight title, Hacine Cherifi, retired at the end of the eighth round
Les Clark

The Battersea boys, Howard and Gilbert Eastman, notched a family double at Norwich. The European middleweight champion, Howard, retained his title when Frenchman, Hacine Cherifi, retired on his stool after eight painful rounds, while younger brother Gilbert punched Jason Collins full of holes in just 24 seconds of the opening round. Don't mess with these boys!

Saved by the bell! A classic moment in boxing saw a young Cassius Clay dropped by a Henry Cooper left hook back in 1963. At the Norwich Sports Village, the Southern Area light-middleweight champion, David Walker, was saved by the timekeeper twice in the first two rounds of his defence against Forest Hill's Spencer Fearon. Seconds before round one ended, a Fearon left hook sent Walker crashing to the canvas. He beat the count and made it back to his stool. Come the end of round two, another booming left hook lands and Walker is down again, right on the bell and at the end of the third round it was Fearon who was on the deck and happy to hear the bell. Walker figured that was enough thrills for one night and turned it on in the fourth to bring the referee's intervention, but it had been a close call.

At Playboy publisher Hugh Hefner's Beverly Hills mansion, London pin-up boy, David Haye, stood out against the Playboy pin-ups when his flashing fists took care of Kansas City journeyman, Vance Wynn, in just 54 seconds of round one. It looked like the end of the road for the 34-year-old Chatham warrior, John Armour, when Australia's Nathan Sting forced his retirement in round 11 of their fight for Armour's WBU bantamweight title. John was struggling all the way in this all-southpaw battle but his corner waited until round 11 was almost over before throwing the towel in. It was John's second loss in 32 fights (1 draw).

The chief support on that Brentwood bill saw the former WBU lightweight champion, Colin Dunne, reach the end of the road when 'Hartlepool Bulldog', Kevin Bennett, knocked him down twice inside two rounds to force an upset stoppage.

A regular visitor to German rings as a fixture in the corner of Sven Ottke, the veteran London cut-man, Dennie Mancini, was able to secure a crack at the NBA middleweight title for his Southern Area champion, Allan Gray. On paper it looked a tough assignment for the Putney puncher (16-6-2), as the champion, Dirk Dzemski, was unbeaten in 19 bouts and the fight was in Dessau, in the old East Germany, an hour's drive from Berlin.

In the ring it looked a tough assignment as Gray was decked three times in the first three rounds and again in the final round. But in between the knockdowns Allan boxed a canny fight, following the shrewd advice from Mancini and his trainer, Brian Lawrence, and at the end the champion looked like the loser, cut eye, bloody nose, facial bruises. Dzemski was the winner, but Gray came home thinking maybe he would renew his licence. Hell, he's only 31.

Brixton barber, Ted Bami, figured to trim the South African, Samuel Malinga, at the Plymouth Pavilion and retain his WBF light-welterweight title before moving up to better things. But it was the barber who got clipped in round three, courtesy of a Malinga right hand, and when Ted got up the referee, John Coyle, considered he was not able to fight on and counted him out.

The story is as old as boxing itself, the old champ trying to come back and the hand-picked opponent seizing his chance to make his name. On the Plymouth show it was Michael Ayers, the former British and IBO lightweight champion and WBO title challenger, at 38, trying to get it all back against the Basingstoke southpaw, Jon Honney, who had lost nine of his 14 fights. It was only a six-threes, which was just as well for the former champion as he dropped a 59-56 decision. "I feel I have more to offer," Ayers said ruefully as he came out of the ring. Sadly, he doesn't.

AUGUST

Southampton's Matthew Barney entered the ring at York Hall as British super-middleweight champion, fully expecting to add the vacant Commonwealth title to his collection by beating Charles Adamu. But the strong Ghanaian, with a mere five pro fights behind him, took the decision and the title after 12 dreary rounds that saw Barney let the fight drift away from him when he should have outboxed his sometimes crude opponent and come out a winner.

To his credit, Adamu was prepared to work for 12 rounds while Barney was far too negative. Adamu threw him to the canvas twice as they tangled in clinches and Matthew twice fouled the African without penalty, low punches dropping Adamu in round seven and in the ninth. Barney stuck his head in Adamu's face and forced him back into a corner. It was a lousy fight, but the right man won it.

Colin Kenna came to town from Southampton to challenge the Southern Area heavyweight champion, Michael Sprott, for his title, but was no match once the bell got them away. Sprott, although only two pounds heavier, looked much bigger and stronger and so it turned out. Two big left hooks sent Kenna crashing on his back and it was all over at 1.28 of round one. "Michael is the best heavyweight in Britain", said his cornerman, Dennie Mancini, adding: "He'd beat any of them".

The vacant Southern Area welterweight championship went to Brett James of St Pancras after a gruelling battle with Slough's Sammy Smith. The better boxer of the two, James floored Sammy with a right hand in the second round, but he was soon on his feet and back in the fight. By the final bell both men were bloodied but unbowed.

Former amateur star David Haye had no trouble with the 41-fight veteran, Greg Scott-Briggs, knocking out the Chesterfield cruiser at 2.04 of round one to notch his sixth win as a money fighter. But Haye needs tougher opposition than this.

The road back for Gary Thornhill started at the Everton Park Sports Centre in Liverpool with a four-threes against Jason Nesbitt. Now 35, the local man hadn't boxed in almost a year, in fact Gary hadn't boxed a lot in his nine-year career, putting only 27 fights in the book (22-4-1), but he had boxed some good'uns. Names like Nicky Cook,

Scott Harrison, Richie Wenton, Michael Gomez, Dean Pithie, and Justin Juuko studded his record. Gary stopped Wenton and knocked out Pithie and was a champion, winning the Central Area and WBO Inter-Continental titles at super-featherweight. He also reigned briefly as British featherweight champion after stopping Wenton, but was stripped when he tested positive for amphetamine.

Now he was trying again, although it didn't figure to be much of a test. Birmingham's Jason Nesbitt had only won a couple of fights and had lost more times than Thornhill had boxed. He lost again this night as Gary hammered him down and out inside 2.16 of round one. While it lasted the former champ looked good.

Another former champ, Prince Naseem Hamed, won a fight without taking his clothes off. Hamed's opponent was a Greek Cypriot from London who had conned Naz out of 50 grand for two limited edition Mercedes. He was sentenced to a year in the slammer, time enough to reflect upon the error of his ways. It could have been worse - he could have been sentenced to ten rounds in the ring with the former world champ!

David Starie was another ex-champ in the news, announcing his retirement at 29 with a pro log of 31-4.

From Bury St Edmunds, Starie won two ABA titles, (light-middle 1993; middle 1994) before turning pro and becoming British and Commonwealth super-middleweight champion and winning a Lonsdale Belt outright. He couldn't quite make the top rung, losing to Joe Calzaghe (WBO) and Sven Ottke in Germany for the WBA and IBF titles.

SEPTEMBER

Heavyweights were the flavour of the month as the indoor season got under way. At the Rivermead Leisure Centre in Reading, the local big boy, Michael Sprott, challenged the British and Commonwealth heavyweight champion, Danny Williams, for his titles, but finished on his face in round five. It was a pity, because Michael hadn't done too badly up to that point.

Stopped in seven in their previous fight (February 2002), Sprott came in a stone lighter and eight wins better, five inside. And for the best part of four rounds he was winning the fight, boxing well. Then the champion struck with a left to the body that was low, causing Sprott to drop his hands and look at the referee. Bad move. Williams slammed a right to the jaw and Sprott fell on his face.

After surviving a seventh-round knockdown, England's Jason Booth (left) came on strong to nick the IBO super-flyweight title from the defending champion, Lunga Ntontela

Les Clark

The bell rang and Sprott somehow got to his feet in time to return to his corner. He was still shaken coming out for the fifth and Danny seized his chance, blasting in more punches, one of which again landed below the belt. Terry O'Connor, the referee, once again ignored Sprott's appealing glance and once again Williams felled the local man, this time with a booming left hook.

It was all over, much to the disgust of Sprott's corner team and his supporters, who booed long and loud. Coming out for that fifth round, Michael should have remembered what happened at the end of the fourth. He should have remembered what happened to Jack Sharkey when he turned to complain to the referee. Jack Dempsey knocked him out! Protect yourself at all times, the man said.

One big guy to keep an eye on was Matt Skelton, the 'Bedford Bomber', who blasted the former British champion, Mike Holden, into a sixth-round stoppage defeat in their Dagenham fight. It was Skelton's eighth straight win, all inside the distance and victory gave him the inaugural English heavyweight title, with the promise of more to come.

Another 30-something heavyweight is Audley Harrison, the Sydney Olympics super-heavyweight gold medallist, who racked up his 12th straight pro victory when knocking over trialhorse, Quinn Navarre, in round three in Miami. It was Harrison's American debut and he didn't impress anyone, apart from Navarre, that is.

Like most of our top heavyweights, Julius Francis is the wrong side of 30, but he is still pushing leather, looking to get his British title back. He took a short-notice fight in Kiev against the unbeaten Ukrainian, Vladimir Virchis, for something called the IBF Inter-Continental interim title and was not disgraced in losing the decision.

Shifting to the other end of the scale, little Damaen Kelly stepped into the lion's den and got badly mauled. The brave Belfast boxer made the long haul to Colombia to fight the local hero, Irene Pacheco, for his IBF flyweight title and retired in his corner after six painful rounds. Kelly's fine skills were no match for the champion, unbeaten in ten years and 29 fights, 22 inside, and Pacheco gradually increased the pressure to drop the Irishman three times in the sixth to prompt Damaen's withdrawal.

Like Kelly in Colombia, Argentine Aldo Rios was never going to beat Ricky Hatton in his Manchester backyard, although he did last three rounds longer, sitting it out at the end of the ninth round of his WBU light-welterweight title challenge. Rios, really just a lightweight, couldn't hurt Hatton, who dropped his man in the first and the ninth before it was over. Still unbeaten after 33 fights (25 inside), Hatton is ready for the top men in the division, if politics allow.

One fighter British fans would love to see in with Hatton is Junior Witter, the Commonwealth champion, who retained his title on the MEN Arena bill with a two-rounds stoppage of Aussie-based Kenyan, Fred Kinuthia. The Bradford switch-hitter took his pro log to 27-1-2, his only loss coming in a late substitute challenge to Zab Judah for his IBF title in June 2000.

There were mixed fortunes for the Booth brothers at Nottingham, with Jason winning the IBO super-flyweight title, being awarded a split decision over the champion from South Africa, Lunga Ntontela, while Nicky, the British bantamweight boss, struggled against Australian southpaw, Nathan Sting, who retained his WBU belt with a unanimous decision.

Jason was a good winner after surviving a seventh round knockdown and Nicky did well to come through a rough fifth round to battle through to the finish.

On the same bill, Jawaid Khaliq repeated a previous victory over the tough Russian, Maxim Nesterenko, to keep his IBO welterweight title when gaining a clear decision over the former European champion to take his record to a respectable 22-1-1.

Nothing excites a fight crowd like a knockout puncher and Enzo Maccarinelli is building a fan base in Wales with his dynamic punching. He won the WBU cruiserweight title with a left-hook demolition of Bruce Scott and in the Newport ring he destroyed the Estonian challenger, Andrei Kiarsten, in just 70 seconds with a big right hand. That made the stats 15-1, 11 inside. Next?

Maybe not next, but sometime in the future, David Haye will answer the bell against Maccarinelli. The former World Amateur Championship silver medallist is an exciting talent as he proved in his battle with Lolenga Mock, a toughie from the Congo fighting out of Denmark. Haye took his record to 7-0, all inside, but had to climb off the deck in round two to stop his man in the fourth.

Yorkshire has a winner in James Hare, the WBF welterweight champion, who ran his unbeaten log to 27 (1 draw) with a second round stoppage of experienced South African, Jan Bergman, at Huddersfield. Dropped three times by left hooks, the former WBU champion at the weight was rescued by the third man 55 seconds into round two. James can box and he can punch and it will take a good tortoise to catch this Hare!

OCTOBER

National feeling was running high at the Meadowbank Stadium in Edinburgh as the local hero, Alex Arthur, prepared to defend his British super-featherweight title against former champion, Michael Gomez. Arthur was Scotland's new 'Golden Boy', undefeated in 16 fights, 14 inside the distance being testimony to his power. Victory would give him the Lonsdale Belt in his first pro fight before his hometown fans.

Across the ring, Gomez had his own agenda. He'd been to hell and back in his private life and he'd experienced the highs and lows of the professional ring in a 28-5 career that saw him win the British title now held by Arthur and challenge for the vacant WBU crown. Kevin Lear stopped him in that fight, but Gomez had bounced back with three wins under his new trainer, Billy Graham. He was hungry again and ate Alex Arthur up inside five thrilling rounds in a sensational upset. The Manchester man edged the opening round, letting Arthur feel his favourite left hook, but the champion outboxed his man in round two. Gomez stormed out for the third round and the Scot did well to last the three minutes, yet he battled back in the fourth and both showed facial damage at the bell. Round five saw the dramatic finish. A thudding left hook started the rot and the champion was down. He beat the count but two savage rights felled him again. Up too soon, he was smashed by left hooks and a final right and it was over.

There was a sensational fight at Manchester, where Michael Brodie battled 12 glorious rounds with the tough South Korean, In-Jin Chi, for the vacant WBC featherweight title. After the fight, the farce! Chi was announced as the majority winner, before a later check of the scorecards showed the correct result to be a draw. With both eyes closing fast and bleeding from a scalp wound, Brodie, robbed in a WBC super-bantam title bout three years previously, had become boxing's 'Nearly Man'! He deserved better.

By contrast, there was a lousy fight at Portsmouth where Tony Oakey lost his unbeaten record and his WBU light-heavyweight title to British super-middleweight champion, Matthew Barney, the Southampton man winning a split decision after taking the job on a couple of days notice. Oakey's supporters reacted badly to the decision and there were some ugly scenes before the new champion was able to leave the ring. On the same card, another late sub in Jon Honney gave the British lightweight champion, Graham Earl, fits before losing this non-title bout on points.

After just 22 fights (two losses, one draw), the Sidcup light-middleweight, David Walker, reached for the moon and fell flat on his face, being hopelessly outmatched against the European champion, Roman Karmazin, as the tall Russian retained his title inside three rounds at Alexandra Palace in London. Walker was floored three times before the finish. Carl Froch took another step up the ladder on this bill when he outpointed Russian southpaw, Vage Kocharyan, over eight rounds to take his pro log to 9-0. Carl looked good.

Heavyweight Herbie Hide made it 2-1 over Russia when he stopped Alex Vasiliev in five rounds, but the 'Queensberry Rules' took a bashing as well as the visitor, Hide hitting his man after the bell, then hitting him After knocking him down in rounds four and five. Black marks for the referee, Lee Cook, who ignored the fouls.

James Hare (right) found Jozsef Matolcsi a tough customer before getting to his Hungarian rival in the tenth round

Les Clark

Over in Las Vegas, Audley Harrison made it 13-0 as he stopped brawling Lisandro Diaz in the fourth round, taking his time before finishing it with a blazing combination that showed what he can do. He just needs to do it more often! One man looming in his future is big Matt Skelton, who improved on Harrison's performance when becoming the first man to stop Ratko Draskovic. The Serbian had gone eight rounds (decision) with Harrison in his last fight, but three rounds was more than enough against Skelton, who had previously hammered Costi Marin into submission in Portsmouth two weeks earlier in just 1.46 of round one. Big man, big punch!

James Hare hung on to his WBF welterweight title at the MEN Arena in Manchester, but found it tough going against the stubborn Hungarian, Jozsef Matolcsi, before a thudding right to the body knocked all the fight out of the visitor in the tenth round. He was under pressure when the third man stopped it, with Hare still champion and still undefeated in 29 fights (1 draw) and happy his night's work was done.

On the same bill, British and Commonwealth light-middleweight champion, Jamie Moore, turned in a superb performance to knock out Gary Logan in round five, with the Croydon man announcing his retirement when he came out of the ring. The Salford southpaw, 24 to Logan's 35, took his record to 18-1, while Gary leaves the game with a 33-8-1 log.

At the venerable York Hall, Commonwealth champions, Esham Pickering and Nicky Cook, retained their titles with impressive showings against tough opposition. Super-bantamweight Pickering found a brilliant right uppercut to take out Ghana's Alfred Tetteh in round seven, while featherweight Cook had to go all the way to defeat another Ghana entry in Aneytei Laryea. On that card, WBF super-middleweight champion, Robin Reid, warmed up for his coming challenge against Sven Ottke by knocking out Dmitri Adamovich of Belarus in the fourth round.

Over in Belfast, the Ulster Hall was packed to see the local favourite, Brian Magee, extend his winning streak to 20-0, as he retained his IBO super-middleweight title for the fifth time with a first-round knockout of Argentina's Omar Eduardo Gonzalez. The Belfast southpaw was delighted, although there was some doubt as to the power of the finishing shot, a right hook high on the head. Gonzalez protested but he was still shaky going back to his stool.

Former British and Commonwealth heavyweight champion, Julius Francis, dropped an eight-rounds decision to the ex-European champ, Luan Krasniqi, in Hamburg.

NOVEMBER

It was sweet revenge for Scott Harrison as he went straight back in with the man who lifted his WBO featherweight title four months previously, Manuel Medina, and crushed the Mexican in 11 rounds to stamp his presence once more in a tough division. Scott nearly got the job done in the opening round, heavy punches sending Medina to the canvas. He got up and made it to the bell, then got more of the same in round two. But Manuel, a five-time title claimant with 76 fights behind him, had boxed his way back into the fight and by halfway Harrison was cut over the left eye with blood seeping from his scalp following head clashes.

It was a rough, tough fight through the middle rounds and in the tenth it swung in favour of the Scot. The 32-year-old veteran suddenly looked tired and Harrison dropped him twice with ripping punches and the Mexican was glad to hear the bell. Gamely he came out for round 11, but he was running on empty and after being dumped on the canvas once more his trainer-manager signalled the referee to stop it. Harrison was a champion again and, at 26, was looking for the top men.

Another fighter looking to make some money was Scotland's Lawrence Murphy, who gave his career a shot in the arm and WBU middleweight champion, Wayne Elcock, a shot on the chin that draped him dramatically over the bottom rope. Time, two minutes, 28 seconds and a new champion!

Belfast southpaw, Brian Magee, showed continued improvement as he punched his way to an eighth-round stoppage win over veteran Frenchman, Hacine Cherifi, to send a packed Kings Hall crowd wild with delight. Shades of Barry McGuigan! Magee took his unbeaten tally to 21 fights, 16 inside, as he took the former WBC middleweight champion apart. And after eight rounds Cherifi was pulled out, his face a red mask from cuts on his forehead and right eye.

In a nip-and-tuck contest for the British featherweight title on the Belfast show, the champion, Roy Rutherford, was edged out of it by Dazzo Williams 115-114 and returned home to Coventry without his Lonsdale belt, but still believing he had done enough to win, as did many in the crowd. But it was Williams who caught the eye of the referee, Paul Thomas, and his name goes in the book alongside Jim Driscoll, Nel Tarleton and Howard Winstone, after only 11 professional fights, 2 defeats. That's boxing, 2003 style!!

Still in Belfast, the British and Commonwealth light-middleweight champion, Jamie Moore, had too much of everything for Andrew Facey, dropping his challenger five times before it was halted in round seven. At super-middleweight, the vacant British title found a new home after Tony Dodson handed Scot Allan Foster his first defeat, the fight being stopped in round 11.

Sheffield's stylist, Johnny Nelson, got back in the groove when defending his WBO cruiserweight title in the little town of Bayreuth in Germany. Coming out of the opposite corner was his leading contender, Alexander Petkovic, undefeated in 31 fights (3 draws) and, at 23, 13 years younger than the champion.

Nelson had been through a bad time, with a kidnap threat hanging over his family that involved police protection, and his last two fights had been less than sensational. But this young upstart, Petkovic, was still some way from being a champion and Nelson was rarely troubled in taking a majority decision, retaining his belt for the 11th time.

Johnny's fight was one leg of a British hat-trick, with Matt Skelton blasting out Patriche Costel in 2.58 of round one at heavyweight and the young Welsh lightweight, Jamie Arthur, taking out Andrei Mircea in round three.

Fighting his way back to a hoped-for title shot, former British welterweight champion, Harry Dhami, shook off two years of ring rust to outclass Central Area champion, Lee Armstrong, in a six rounder in Glasgow. "Two more fights and I'll be ready", said Harry.

Clinton Woods was getting a shot at the vacant IBF light-heavyweight title in his own Sheffield backyard and the cards looked stacked against the veteran Jamaican-American, Glengoffe Johnson. The visitor was used to being the underdog and coming out on the short end, money and decisions, in his 50-fight career. Stopped only once, by world middleweight supreme, Bernard Hopkins, and beaten by Sven Ottke in an IBF super-middle title bid, Johnson was hoping his luck would change in Sheffield.

Woods, stopped in six rounds by then world champion, Roy Jones, had won British, Commonwealth and European titles in his 35-2 pro career and, at 31, was three years the younger man. The punches flew for 12 rounds, back and forth, and when it was over neither man had won, a draw being announced. Each man had his backers, but the general view with pundits and punters alike was that Johnson had done enough to win. Now they would have to do it all over again.

The undercard saw a couple of former champions out for a run, with one-time WBO cruiserweight king, Carl Thompson, coasting to a points win in a six over oft-beaten Paul Bonson, while former British lightweight champion, Bobby Vanzie, eased to a decision over the Welsh southpaw, Keith Jones.

Fortunately for Kevin Bennett, the Commonwealth lightweight champion, Michael Muya, is a boxer rather than a puncher, otherwise the Hartlepool challenger would never have lasted the distance. Having built a points lead, Kevin was utterly exhausted through the last two rounds, when it looked like he would go over if someone had opened a window in the Bridgend Sports Centre and let in a breath of air. At the final bell, Bennett was the new champion, victory lining him up for a crack at Jason Cook, who won the vacant IBO title with a seventh-round stoppage over Argentina's Ariel Olveira in the main event that night.

DECEMBER

Going to Germany to challenge Sven Ottke for his IBF/WBA super-middleweight titles just a couple of weeks before Christmas, you had to figure Robin Reid still believed in Santa Claus. Coming home from the fight, Robin had another legendary name on his mind, telling a reporter: "At least Dick Turpin wore a mask when he robbed people"!

As expected, of course, the rugged German retained for the 20th time on a unanimous decision after an untidy 12 rounds. What Robin Reid did not expect that night in Nuremberg was that he had TWO men to beat, the champion and the referee! For long after the final bell, fair-minded fans were still talking about his performance. Not

An untidy fight saw Eamonn Magee (left) pick up the vacant WBU welter title after outscoring Jimmy Vincent   Les Clark

Reid's, not Ottke's, but the Belgian referee, Roger Tilleman's!

Looking like someone out of a Poirot movie, with his handlebar moustache, Monsieur Tilleman was a throwback to those amateur referees of years ago who inhabited rings in Continental Europe, stopping the action every few seconds for perceived petty infringements and forgetting the fact that they were only in there because the rules stated there had to be three men in the ring, one in long pants.

Whether Sven Ottke would have won the fight without the blatant assistance of Tilleman is a moot point. The champion was cagey, crafty, clever, and he knew just what to do to keep his titles. Robin Reid knew what he had to do, but the referee wouldn't allow him to do it! "I was almost afraid to hit him", complained Reid afterwards. Robin did hit Ottke in round six and knocked him down, but the third man called it a slip much to Reid's disgust. When things got messy and untidy, with heads bumping in the clinches, Ottke played to the referee and Reid was usually admonished, whether guilty or not. At the final bell, Ottke was still undefeated (officially) as a professional after 33 fights, leaving Robin Reid as sick as a parrot!

Ricky Hatton didn't put a glove wrong when taking a unanimous decision from Ghana tough man, Ben Tackie, at the MEN Arena in Manchester to retain his WBU light-welterweight championship for the 11th time and take his record to 34-0. Tackie had lost his last two fights, to Sharmba Mitchell and world champ Kostya Tszyu, and Hatton looked ready for either of those two as he turned loose a brilliant performance, outboxing and outpunching the teak-tough Ghanaian. Ricky has rarely looked better and is ready for fights with the top men. Whether these fights will happen is something else again.

Down the bill, Ricky's younger brother, Matthew, had a much tougher evening when held to a six rounds draw with unbeaten Darlington welterweight, Franny Jones. This was a cracking contest, with Jones (6-0-2) impressing against the more experienced house fighter. Hatton took his log to 17-2-1.

Also on the Manchester bill, David Barnes retained his British welterweight title with an emphatic eighth-round stoppage of fellow southpaw, Kevin McIntyre. Usually when a fighter wins a title he improves 50 percent next time out and so it was with the 22-year-old Barnes, whose championship win over Jimmy Vincent was controversial. Against McIntyre, David put it all together and when he dropped his man twice in round eight, the towel came in and was accepted by the referee. The young champion is still undefeated after 14 fights, eight inside.

If you go to see Enzo Maccarinelli fight, get there early and don't take your eyes off the ring. You might miss it! The Swansea puncher did it again, blasting South African champion, Earl Morais, into submission after just 1.30 of round one to retain his WBU cruiserweight title. That was 20 seconds longer than his last defence against Andrei Kiarsten! Right hands did the damage this night, putting the chill on the South African at the National Ice Rink in Cardiff.

Former Commonwealth light-welterweight champion, Eamonn Magee, controlled the forward rushes of Jimmy Vincent in a somewhat messy and untidy contest for the vacant WBU welterweight title, coming out with a unanimous decision on the Cardiff bill. And it was not a good night for another former champion, Wayne Alexander, who was well beaten by Delroy Mellis. The former British and European light-middleweight champion had nothing left when Mellis smashed him down in the eighth with a right, then a left hook. Wayne got up but it was all over.

There was also a shock for WBF welterweight champion, James Hare, in the Huddersfield ring when he was outboxed and finally outpunched by the lanky Mexican, Cosme Rivera, who brought the fight to an end in round ten, dumping Hare on the canvas with a left hook. Back to the drawing board for James.

It's not over till the fat lady sings! The West Ham southpaw, Steve Roberts, looked a points winner going into the sixth and final round against Darren Rhodes and was already tentatively matched with IBO light-middle champ, Sergio Martinez. But, at one minute of the final three, Roberts failed to beat the count after being knocked down. That's the fight business for you!

The Audley Harrison road show moved into the town of Laughlin in Nevada, where the Sydney gold medallist was due to meet Brian Nix in a ten-round fight. It wasn't ten rounds and it certainly wasn't a fight, Harrison ending it in round three with a fast combination to take his pro log to 14-0 in his second American appearance.

Like 'em or not, the ladies are here to stay and two of our better female fighters were in action, with Jane Couch beating Brenda Bell-Drexel in Bristol and Cathy Brown

Howard Eastman (left) was not at his best for his European middleweight title defence against the Russian, Sergei Tatevosyan, but did enough   Les Clark

losing to Womens' European flyweight champion, Stefania Bianchini, in Italy.

JANUARY

Climbing into the Wembley ring for a defence of his British and Commonwealth heavyweight titles against Michael Sprott, Danny Williams figured to rack up his hat-trick over the Reading man, take him home, and stick him on the (reinforced) mantlepiece along with his other boxing trophies. The champion had already stopped Sprott twice, even if the last time (September) was controversial.

Well, you never can tell in this business. The boys went 12 rounds and, at the final bell, Dave Parris, the referee, pointed to Michael Sprott as the winner and new champion. It was a 115-114 verdict that drew a mixed reception. It wasn't a great fight, but it was a gruelling affair, Williams being rocked in rounds seven and eight and bleeding from the nose and mouth, while Sprott's left eye was almost closed at the finish. They'll probably do it again someday, somewhere…

Brixton's Keith Long had gone 12 rounds with Williams for the titles in 2002 and now he was fighting Denis Bakhtov for his WBC International title on the Wembley bill. Again Keith went the full route, but the Russian had the better skills and came out with the decision to keep his crown. WBU light-middleweight champion, Takaloo, got a shock when Eugenio Monteiro, a Portugese based in Manchester, dropped him in the opening round and went on to take the points over eight rounds in a non-title affair. Former ABA champion, Kevin Mitchell, looks one to watch, but not in knock-over jobs like he had against Peterborough's Jaz Virdee. The stats had Mitchell at 3-0, all inside, Virdee 0-3, two inside, and it was all over in 73 seconds after the latter had been sent crashing from a left hook. Harlow's Steve Murray had twice challenged for the British lightweight title and come up short. Now he was coming back and looked good stopping Walsall's Jimmy Beech inside four rounds, the left hand still working well, jabbing and hooking, until it was stopped with Jimmy in trouble.

Esham Pickering, enjoying his time in the sun, added the vacant European super-bantamweight title to his British and Commonwealth championships with a fine performance against Vincenzo Gigliotti at Bradford. After a shaky start, the 31-year-old Italian got into the fight through the middle rounds and Esham had his hands full. But by round nine, it was Pickering back in charge as Vincenzo lost steam and the Newark man turned it on, dropping his man for the full count in the tenth to become a triple champ.

It was not vintage stuff from British, Commonwealth, and European middleweight champion, Howard Eastman, as he defended the latter title at Goresbrook Leisure Centre in Dagenham against the cagey Russian challenger, Sergei Tatevosyan, but it was enough to keep the title and take Eastman to 39-1 as a pro, his sole defeat coming in a world title challenge against William Joppy. That was a fight many figured Howard could have won with more effort, but that's his style and he hasn't done badly with it.

His younger brother, Gilbert, is a champion too as the Southern Area light-middleweight boss, but his title was not on the line against the tough Scot, Craig Lynch, a loser 60-56 in a cracking six rounder.

On the Dagenham bill, Carl Froch continued his march to a shot at British champion, Tony Dodson, with a two-rounds stoppage win over southpaw, Dmitri Adamovich. Froch, already the English champion, took his unbeaten log to 11-0 as he dumped the man from Belarus three times before it was halted. Carl looks the goods!

Steven Spartacus was unbeaten in 15 fights coming in, English and British Masters light-heavyweight titleholder, and Ovill McKenzie looked to have a tough job on his hands with the flashy champion. But Ovill jabbed away, stayed clear of the big punches, and by the end of the six rounds was a shock points winner. Steven, his right eye and left cheek swollen, congratulated McKenzie on a smart fight.

Stockwell stylist, Richard Williams, was back in the ring, fighting for the Common-wealth light-middleweight title vacated by the Salford southpaw, Jamie Moore, who hung on to his British crown. Williams was in against Ayittey Powers of Ghana and, at 32, couldn't afford to blow this one. Richard had promised so much in a career adding up to 17-2-1 (14 inside), winning the Commonwealth title and going on to take the IBO championship, but, troubled with illness and injury, he blew the IBO title in a hard fight with Sergio Martinez. Now it was seven months later and he was back in the groove and Mr Powers couldn't stay with him, being under heavy pressure when the referee stopped it in round seven. With a bit of luck, Richard might just go on and do something special.

Ted Bami, a London barber, came back after losing his WBF light-welterweight belt in a three-rounds shocker to Samuel Malinga and showed that he could box as well as bang when taking a six rounds decision from Jozsef Matolcsi, the tough Hungarian who had floored James Hare before being stopped in ten in a WBF welterweight title bout.

Bad news for Bobby Vanzie. He lost his prized Lonsdale Belt while he was at the gym! Actually, the belt Bobby won outright was stolen in a flash burglary at his home, while his wife and children were upstairs. Relieved that they were safe, the former British lightweight champion was understandably upset at the theft.

Leading Glasgow promoter, Tommy Gilmour, staged his usual 'Burns Night' boxing dinner at the St Andrews Sporting Club, with a difference. It was Tommy's 250th show and he pulled out all the stops with a pipe band marching in off the street and a liberal sprinkling of celebrities from both sides of the ropes. Top of the bill, after the haggis and 'neeps, saw the local favourite, Craig Dickson, stop Dean Nicholas in round five of a welterweight bout.

FEBRUARY

If at first you don't succeed…Glengoffe Johnson lives by those half-dozen words. It is a belief that has taken him through his 35 years, through his 50 professional fights, through five fights for one title or another, and on this night in Sheffield, the other guy's hometown, it carried him through 12 gruelling rounds against big local favourite, Clinton Woods, to land the unanimous decision. At the end, the man with the mike told the capacity crowd at the Ponds Forge Leisure Centre that Johnson was the new world light-heavyweight champion of the International Boxing Federation.

Johnson's belief in himself even brought him back to Clinton's hometown, where four months previously many thought the Miami-based Jamaican unlucky when a draw was announced. This time he made no mistake. Woods once again fought out of his skin, but Johnson was just that little bit better, having learned in a tougher school and it finally paid off. He was the champ!

Another veteran to show he still had gas in his tank was Manchester's Carl Thompson, who weathered what looked like a career-ending beating against Sebastiaan Rothmann to knock out the IBO cruiserweight champion in the ninth round with a devastating right hand. At 39, Thompson was past his sell-by date, but they say a puncher always has a chance and he had always been a puncher! Dropped himself at the end of the fourth, he then knocked the South African into the ropes as the fifth ended. But going into round nine, Carl had a swollen left eye and Rothmann couldn't miss him with the left and Thompson looked ready to go. Then it happened! Carl smashed a right to the jaw and the champion fell on his face. The crowd were on their feet and somehow Rothmann was on his as the count reached eight. But he was still out of it and Thompson had snatched victory from the jaws of defeat.

Former British and Commonwealth lightweight champion, Bobby Vanzie, needed to look good, with a crack at his old title already lined up. Well if you need to look good you don't fight Tony Montana! You have a job hitting this fellow with a handful of rice. In a lousy fight, Vanzie at least tried to land some punches, which is why the referee gave him the verdict after six rounds against Brendan Ingle's Kosovan refugee.

Castleford southpaw, Noel Wilders, had a brisk workout, beating Vladimir Borov in a four on the big Sheffield show. The former European champion dropped the Bulgarian in the opener and Borov did well to finish on his feet.

Matt Skelton and Julius Francis had talked a good fight and York Hall was packed to see what promised to be a good fight. But all the hot air failed to produce hot action in the ring and Francis, at 39, was happy to go the limit as Skelton retained his English heavyweight title. At least Julius snapped Matt's knockout streak, standing at 11.

In Nottingham, the local boy, Jawaid Khaliq, turned back the challenge of Ener Julio for his IBO welterweight title with a competent display that failed to ignite the crowd in the Harvey Hadden Leisure Centre. The Colombian was a former WBO and IBO champion at light-welter, but those days were behind him and he was never going well against Khaliq, who was defending for the seventh time. Boxing for the inaugural English super-featherweight title, Roy Rutherford beat Stephen Chinnock on an injury stoppage, an unfortunate clash of heads putting the Rugely man out of action in the fourth with a nasty cut over his left eye. Steve had started well, with Roy coming into the fight in the fourth and final round.

At Bridgend, Dazzo Williams, the man who took the British featherweight title off Rutherford in a thriller, retained it for the first time when turning back the challenge of former champion, Jamie McKeever. This was another cracker and Dazzo stamped his authority with a fine performance.

At the Ice Rink in Cardiff, Joe Calzaghe kept his fans happy as he retained his WBO super-middleweight belt for the 14th time, equalling the record set by Chris Eubank, the man he beat for the title all of six years ago. The Armenian challenger, Mger Mkrtchian (I don't know how to pronounce that so don't ask), proved a stubborn foe before Joe got him down and out in round seven. Still unbeaten in 37 fights (30 inside), Joe was stepping up to light-heavy next time out.

Veteran Londoner, Garry Delaney, had probably his last shot at the brass ring when going in with 23-year-old bomber, Enzo Maccarinelli, for the Swansea man's WBU cruiserweight title, and did himself proud. Garry took the champion into unknown territory before being stopped in round eight. Enzo damaged a knuckle on his left hand in the opening round, yet still managed to floor his man seven times to force a stoppage. The Welshman had never gone beyond four rounds in winning 16 of his 17 fights.

Sunderland-based Scot, Ryan Kerr, won the vacant Northern Area super-middleweight title when the South Shields veteran, Eddie Haley, was stopped in round five with a nasty left eye that was almost closed. These two had fought a cracker four months previously that trade paper Boxing News tabbed number eight on its list of best domestic fights of 2003, and this one was shaping up as a repeat. Still, Eddie hung on to his Northern Area middleweight title as Kerr moved to 10-0.

Newark's WBF super-featherweight champion, Carl Greaves, warmed up for a coming title defence with a comfortable points victory over Nuneaton journeyman, Jason Nesbitt, at the Robin Hood Executive Sporting Club in Nottingham. At Dudley, the West Bromwich southpaw, Marcus Portman, lifted the British Masters welterweight title from champion, Richard Swallow, over ten hard rounds. Marcus was banged up around both eyes, but went home with the belt.

MARCH

Two guys named Harrison made the news this month. WBO featherweight champion, Scott, due to fight his number-one contender, William Abelyan, at the Braehead Arena in Renfrew, instead found himself facing the lanky Colombian, Walter Estrada, who came in at a week's notice. The visitor didn't do too badly for three rounds before Harrison stepped up a gear and Estrada was floored as the fourth round ended.

Coming out for round five, the Colombian threw his gloves as though he didn't want to see them again, but

Harrison had the bit between his teeth now and body punches dropped the challenger. When Estrada got up his ambition was gone and after a minute of the round so was he. Harrison took his pro log to 21-2-1 (11 inside) and was looking for bigger fish to fry.

The heavyweight Harrison picked up his first title since turning pro after the Sydney Olympics, when he knocked out Richel Hersisia, ambitiously billed as 'The Dutch Sonny Liston' (please!), in four rounds at Wembley to become WBF champion. The big fellow admitted it was a minor league title and he was right. And up until the finish it was a minor league performance from Harrison against a smaller man, who, although unbeaten in 21 fights, had fought nobody of note.

As usual, Audley dwarfed his opponent, keeping him at arm's length, prodding tentative right jabs and covering whenever Hersisia even thought about throwing a punch. But in the fourth round, Harrison showed what he could do with a blazing combination of punches that sent the Dutchman down on his face. He rolled on to his back and was still there at the count of ten. All over!

In winning his 15th money fight (11 inside), the 32-year-old Harrison is still giving this type of opponent too much respect before doing later what he could well be doing sooner. Hopefully, one of these days he will get it right and win a proper title.

One heavyweight who would love to have a crack at Harrison is the former champion, Herbie Hide. They have

In a contest between two good British fighters, Jason Booth (right) retained his IBO super-fly title at the expense of Dale Robinson, who lost his unbeaten record into the bargain
Les Clark

exchanged words about exchanging punches, but so far it has been all verbal. Herbie kept his hand in with a fight against Lithuanian southpaw, Mendauga Kulikauskas, at Nottingham and was doing okay for three rounds, well, almost three rounds, before a clash of heads opened a nasty gash over his left eye. Coming up for the fourth, the referee called in the doctor who advised a stoppage and Herbie was back on the shelf.

On that Nottingham bill, local hot-shot, Carl Froch, added the Commonwealth super-middleweight title to his English championship when taking a decision from Ghana's Charles Adamu. But for five rounds, Carl was less than sensational as the champion caught him with jabs and right hands and he needed a driving finish over the last half of the fight, with an eighth round knockdown, to clinch his victory. Now unbeaten in 12 fights, Carl looks the goods but is still learning.

British super-featherweight champion and unbeaten in 16 fights (14 inside) Edinburgh's Alex Arthur looked the goods before he ran into the hammering fists of Michael Gomez and his brilliant future dissolved in five rounds. Now he was coming back in the same Meadowbank ring in his hometown against Uganda's Michael Kizza. Alex won,

in two minutes, 58 seconds of the opening round, but I could have given him a better fight than did Kizza, who threw maybe one punch before collapsing from a left hook for the full count. The bout had the obligatory title for television, this one the IBF Inter-Continental championship. These 'Inter' titles are the most perishable things in the punch business; they're always conveniently vacant!

Gateshead light-middleweight, Danny Moir, fights better away from his home patch. At the Heathrow Thistle Hotel, Danny battled ten good rounds to shade Kevin Phelan and collect the British Masters championship. Well done that man!

Good matches do get made and you usually get a good fight. Like the one between IBO super-flyweight champion, Jason Booth, and the undefeated (15-0) Dale Robinson of Huddersfield. Fighting in his hometown, Dale boxed a treat, but the tough little champion always looked to have that little bit extra and he needed it to keep his title over the long haul, an 11th round knockdown sealing his points win.

They figured that the Liverpool cruiserweight, Tony Moran, was ready for the top after winning 11 of his 13

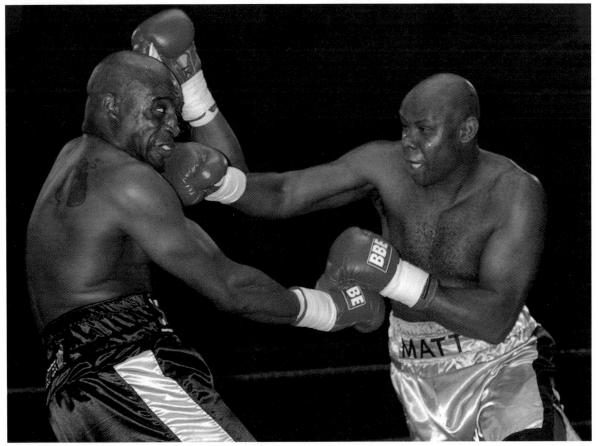

After just 19 months as a pro, the 30-something Matt Skelton (right) won the British and Commonwealth heavyweight titles when knocking out Michael Sprott

Les Clark

fights, but British and Commonwealth champion, Mark Hobson, proved them all wrong when he took Moran apart, downing him in rounds one and two and knocking him spark out in round three.

By contrast, Dagenham featherweight, Nicky Cook, was ready when his big chance came, a crack at the European championship held by the unbeaten Frenchman, Cyril Thomas. Commonwealth champion, Cook, was also undefeated, in 22 fights, and he had more stuff in his locker than Thomas. Nicky was ruthless as he floored his man twice in the seventh before knocking him out with a sizzling left hook to the body in the ninth round.

Carl 'Ingemar' Johanneson learned the pro game in American gyms and rings before coming home with a 15-1 record to show us his stuff. The Leeds-born battler hammered Carl Greaves to defeat inside three rounds to win the WBF super-featherweight title and show he was a man to be reckoned with.

David Haye stuck another victory on his record when Hastings Rasani decided he had had enough after just 2.17 of round one. The man from Zimbabwe had won only one of his last 12 fights and he was never going to win this one as Haye's power punches knocked the stuffing out of him. Now 11-0, all inside, David is a talent who needs something tough to get his teeth into.

APRIL

After two fights and three verdicts, the Korean hard man, In-Jin Chi, finally got his hands on the WBC featherweight belt, knocking out Michael Brodie in seven rounds at the MEN Arena in Manchester. Six months previously in this same ring, Chi was announced the majority points winner of a gruelling 12 rounder with Brodie in verdict number one. Half an hour later, the bungling WBC officials led by their president, Jose Sulaiman, did their sums again and discovered that the decision was a majority draw! Verdict Number Two! They were duly rematched, with Chi having no qualms about returning to Manchester, this time knowing what he had to do.

Their first bout had been brutal and after a fight like that the men are rarely the same. As an old boxing friend would say, they had their soul case knocked out of them. In the rematch, this certainly seemed to apply to Michael Brodie, whilst the Korean looked a division bigger and fought like it, marching straight through the Manchester man and dumping him on the canvas in the very first round!

Michael was never in the fight after that. Whatever he tried, Chi took it and gave it back, in spades! And in the seventh round, a terrific left uppercut smashed into Brodie's nose and he dropped in agony to take the full count. "I got beaten by the better fighter", he admitted after only his second loss in 37 fights. "I'll be back." He will be back, but he may never be the same.

Excellent fighter though is, Brodie runs a poor second at the box office to his fellow Mancunian, Ricky Hatton. The week before Brodie v Chi, Hatton drew almost a sellout crowd to the same arena, although most of the ticket buyers were disappointed when the feared Brazilian, Kelson Pinto, pulled out three days before the fight, for whatever reason. Enter Dennis Holbaek Pedersen of Denmark.

Hatton-Pinto was a fight, Hatton-Pedersen was a mismatch. The not-so-great Dane was brave but hopelessly outmatched as the WBU light-welterweight champion took his unbeaten record to 35, 25 inside and retained his title for the 12th time with a sixth -round stoppage. Ricky won as he pleased, dropped Pedersen twice in round four with his favourite body shot, hammered him through the fifth and forced the referee's intervention in the sixth. The fans are not daft and it's clear that Hatton needs a big fight, a meaningful fight.

Hartlepool's former heavyweight contender, Dave Garside, is to be congratulated in bringing local boy, Michael Hunter, through 18 unbeaten fights (1 draw) to win the vacant British super-bantamweight title at the Borough Hall without the backing of television. And the cameras would love this kid! Michael thrashed Mark Payne all over the ring before the referee, Mickey Vann, stopped it in round seven. A former WBF titleholder at the weight, Hunter was a credit to his trainer, Neil Fannan, and to himself.

Darlington's Northern Area welterweight champion, Oscar Hall, should have appeared on that Hartlepool show but was pulled off as he had landed a shot at previous victim, Alan Bosworth, for his English title. So Oscar was in Bradford to have his picture taken with Bosworth and watch Junior Witter box Salvatore Battaglia for the vacant European light-welterweight title. The Italian cried off sick, a possible opponent, Gavin Down, was denied a bout with Witter by the Board and John Ingle told Hall to get kitted up. He was in the main event! Witter was no stranger to Oscar, as they had sparred often when both were handled by the Ingles and Hall had actually beaten Junior three times as amateur. But this was to be Witter's first professional appearance in his hometown and he didn't mess about, stopping Oscar in round three.

There may be some doubt about Matt Skelton's age but there is no doubt about his ability to fight, and no doubt at all about his power. Ask Michael Sprott. Defending his British and Commonwealth heavyweight titles in his hometown (Reading), Sprott was hammered into the canvas in the final round and when he got up it was too late. Matt Skelton was the new champion, setting a record for the division by winning in the shortest time, 19 months, in only his 13th fight. Only one of his fights has gone the distance. Meet the 'Bedford Bomber'!

The International Boxing Organisation recognised Brian Magee as their super-middle-weight champion, a title he had defended six times. Yet the Belfast southpaw had still only had 21 fights as a professional! They grow up so fast these days. At the King's Hall, Brian did it again, turning back the challenge of Nigeria's Jerry Elliott to win a unanimous decision in a disappointing fight, but he had to get off the floor in the opening round to do it.

The promising career of Stockwell light-middleweight, Richard Williams, took a nosedive when he was pulled out by his corner after nine rounds with Sergio Martinez, the Argentine southpaw who had taken Richard's IBO title from him ten months previously. That was a close fight, this one no contest - Martinez all the way.

Little Damaen Kelly was back in the Belfast ring after a four-year absence, having his first fight since losing to world champion, Irene Pacheco, in Columbia. First minute, first round, with Andrei Kostin of Russia, and Kelly is cut. So what, he fights better when he bleeds! A blazing attack dropped the Russian and when he got up a right hand like an arrow put him down again, the referee stopping it at 2.43 of round one.

It was the end of the road for the Leeds welterweight, Derek Roche, who announced his retirement at 31, following his defeat by Mihaly Kotai in Manchester. As British champion, Derek won a Lonsdale Belt outright and twice boxed for 'world' titles.

MAY

The town of Hartlepool is carrying the flag for north-east boxing with Michael Hunter winning the British super-bantamweight title and his gym pal, Kevin Bennett, lifting the Commonwealth lightweight title. Bennett was out again this month in a gruelling IBO challenge against Jason Cook at Bridgend, the place he had won his belt six months previously. Bennett was not so lucky this time, losing a unanimous decision to the tough Welshman, who claimed a shoulder injury hampered his performance. The fight was scrappy at times, but the champion did enough to win.

The exploits of Hunter and Bennett probably inspired the latest comeback of Hartlepool lightweight, Alan Temple, at the age of 31. The southpaw finally won himself a title when he beat Silence Saheed by an eighth-round disqualification to win the vacant British Masters championship at Gravesend. Saheed, a Nigerian fighting out of the Peacock Gym in London, threatened to sweep Temple out of the ring with his wild attack, but Alan had seen it all before and boxed his way into a comfortable lead after seven rounds. In the eighth, the African finally got home a long left hook and Temple went down. That is when Saheed blew it. He continued punching the Hartlepool man on the deck, bringing an instant disqualification. Temple deserved his victory, although it was not how he wanted it to end.

Audley Harrison showed he could go 12 rounds when he defended his WBF heavyweight title against former British and Commonwealth champion, Julius Francis, coming out with a unanimous decision. Once again it was a case of Harrison showing Francis too much respect for what he was, not what he was now, a 39-year-old ex-champ. It was not until the dying seconds of the contest that Audley opened up and Francis went down. He got up again and finished the course. Harrison should have done that a helluva lot earlier instead of playing safe in what was a boring contest.

On that Bristol undercard, Young Muttley gave the fans what they didn't get in the main event – action. Fighting Sammy Smith for the vacant English light-welterweight title, the West Bromwich lad steamed into Smith and

dumped him on the canvas four times in just 1.50 of round one, the third man stopping it. Champion stuff.

The former British and Commonwealth heavyweight champion, Danny Williams, picked up the vacant WBU International title with a three rounds win over Augustin N'Gou, a big African from the Ivory Coast, who surrendered on his stool claiming a shoulder injury. Williams loafed through two rounds before throwing a few punches in the third, convincing N'Gou he was out of his depth. The fight was a short-notice job when first Wayne Alexander and then Ossie Duran pulled out of a WBU title fight with Takaloo.

An injury stoppage also ended the European super-bantamweight title defence of Esham Pickering against Juan Garcia Martin at Reading, the Spaniard retiring in the eighth round claiming an injury to his right elbow. It hadn't been a bad fight until then, with Pickering building a lead against a man with a dangerous right hand. Martin lost for the first time as a money fighter.

Bermondsey cruiserweight, David Haye, did well to destroy the former IBF champion, Arthur Williams, in three rounds on the Reading bill, even if the American had seen better days and was 39. He had missed none of the big names in the division in a 49-fight career, yet Haye walked through him with powerful shots until the referee had seen enough. David took his log to 10-0, all inside and could go all the way.

A pro for 11 years, Peter Oboh is enjoying his time in the sun. The British and Commonwealth light-heavyweight champion retained his titles with a one-sided beating of his challenger, Andrew Lowe, who was pulled out by his corner after ten painful rounds. Peter also has the WBA International belt, which he uses to keep his pants up.

On paper Justin Juuko looked a good match for Michael Gomez, who was defending his WBU super-featherweight title at Widnes. At 31, the Ugandan had fought at top level in the States in compiling a 39-7-1 record. That was the good news. The bad news was that Juuko took the fight on ten days notice, had weight problems and hadn't boxed in a year in what were meaningless fights back home.

It got worse! In the ring with a fired-up Gomez, Juuko had nothing and was rescued by Mickey Vann, the referee, at 2.05 of round two. Bad enough and, fortunately for the Ugandan and everyone else concerned with this so-called world championship fight, it didn't get any worse.

Boxing in the UK held no fears for Pablo Sarmiento. The Spanish-based Argentinian had won his IBO light-welterweight title here almost three years ago with a stoppage of Billy Schwer and came back to beat Michael Ayers and Gary Ryder in title bouts. So Pablo wasn't too worried about giving Colin Lynes a title shot in Dagenham, just up the road from Colin's home in Hornchurch. He should have been! The fight was nothing sensational, it was the verdict, two American judges giving it to Lynes by lop-sided scores, while Britain's John Coyle gave it to the visitor. Colin Lynes was happy, his people were happy, Sarmiento, less than happy. Win some, lose some.

There were mixed fortunes for three former champions.

Gary Thornhill, the ex-British featherweight and WBO Inter-Continental super-feather titleholder, continued his comeback with an impressive fourth-round stoppage of Sheffield southpaw, Daniel Thorpe, while the former British lightweight and WBF light-welter champ, Wayne Rigby, couldn't even win the vacant Central Area ten stone title as Tony Montana gave him the run-around for ten rounds and in Glasgow Charles Shepherd, the ex-super-feather champ at IBO, British and Commonwealth levels, could only draw with Barry Hughes for the vacant WBU International lightweight title.

JUNE

Britain's light-welterweight rivals were in action this month but not against each other, which is the fight the whole country is keyed up for. When will Ricky Hatton stop defending his WBU title against foreign imports and heavy lightweights and sign for a fight against Junior Witter? At least if Ricky beats the Bradford switch-hitter we'll know he's the best in Britain, then he can try and get the top men in the division. And on their showings this month, a lot of people will be putting their money on Witter to beat the Manchester marauder.

At Nottingham, Witter was devastating as he annihilated Italy's Salvatore Battaglia in less than two rounds to add the vacant European championship to the British and Commonwealth titles he already held. Battaglia was dumped on the canvas three times before the referee spread his arms, having seen enough, and it was over. It was an impressive display by Junior and surely they should be calling him 'Senior' by now!

Ten days later, at the MEN Arena in Manchester, Hatton was less than sensational in making his 13th defence of the WBU title against the stubborn Argentinian, Wilfredo Carlos Vilches. Ricky won all right, the scores were unanimous and lop-sided, but even he admitted: "After four or five rounds I lost my strength and I even thought to myself, am I going to make this"!

Several factors appear to have caused Hatton's listless display, including a lack of motivation in preparing for opponents who didn't pose a genuine challenge to his ranking and an admitted lack of training and excess weight to shift in a short time. "You wouldn't believe what weight I was", he told Boxing News. And there was also a hand injury referred to from his fight two months previously against the Dane, Pedersen, which had given trouble in

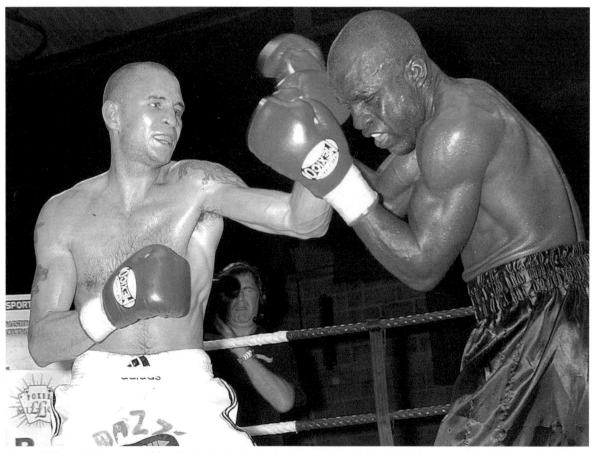

Dazza Williams (left) outscored Roy Rutherford twice during the season with the British featherweight title being the prize and now stands just one defence away from owning a Lonsdale Belt

Les Clark

training. In hindsight, maybe Vilches was the right opponent after all. Maybe it's just as well Ricky wasn't in with Kostya Tszyu, Vivien Harris or Sharmba Mitchell.

At Renfrew's Braehead Arena, Scott Harrison crushed his mandatory challenger, William Abelyan, in three rounds to retain his WBO featherweight title and announced that he was ready for the big boys, meaning the likes of In-Jin Chi, Marco Antonio Barrera, Juan Manuel Marquez and the relentless Manny Pacquiao. Unfortunately, Scott is in a similar situation as Joe Calzaghe found himself and Ricky Hatton now finds himself. They are ready for the big fights. But the big fights aren't ready for them. Money! Boxing politics! Different sanctioning bodies! Opposing television networks! Promoters protecting their investments! Is it any wonder the big fights rarely get made?

The other Harrison on the British boxing scene, Audley, defended his WBF heavyweight title against the undefeated Pole, Tomasz Bonin, at London's Alexandra Palace, the referee, John Keane, making what many considered a premature stoppage in round nine after Bonin had been rocked into the ropes. Harrison's performance was, as usual, cautious against a smaller, lighter man, with too few flashes of what he could do. One of these days he will do it all. We hope so, anyway!

Harrison's biggest domestic rival is Matt Skelton, the British and Commonwealth champion, and if the latter has many more fights like his four-rounds demolition of Australia's Bob Mirovic at York Hall, fans will soon be asking "Audley Who?" The 'Bedford Bomber' is everything Harrison is not and it was too much for the big man from 'Down Under'. Mirovic was floored in the opening round by a heavy right uppercut, beat the count and smashed a right to Skelton's head that worried Matt. In round two Skelton blasted away with both hands, doing some damage, but in doing so left himself open and the Aussie landed a big left hook and at the bell the champion's right eye was seen to be closing. In the third, a desperate Skelton smashed away and a right and left hook dropped big Bob again. The pace was tremendous for big men and, after four rounds, Mirovic had had enough and a relieved Skelton was still the champ!

After the disappointing debacle with Sven Ottke in Germany, Robin Reid got his hands on another title when beating Brian Magee in Belfast for the Irishman's IBO super-middleweight championship, a unanimous decision but a lousy fight by all accounts. Magee suffered his first defeat in 23 fights when making the eighth defence of his bauble against the 33-year-old Runcorn man.

On the Skelton bill at York Hall, Graham Earl and Bobby Vanzie renewed their rivalry, this time for the British lightweight title stripped from the Luton man for not meeting Bobby earlier in a mandatory defence of the belt he won in their first controversial meeting. Many figured that Vanzie was robbed in the first match and again this time around, but Earl boxed better as the champion and he took it by one point. But the fight was good enough to go on again. No doubt it will.

Like Vanzie and Earl, Dazzo Williams and Roy Rutherford will always give you a good fight. The Welshman had relieved Roy of the British featherweight title in a Belfast thriller, but this time around he was a clearer winner in hometown Hereford. Building an early lead, Williams flagged in the middle rounds, but turned it on through the closing stretch to keep his title.

The Hatton bill in Manchester saw an upset, as Anthony Farnell was hammered into submission in the tenth round by unsung Eugenio Monteiro, following up on his great wins over Takaloo and Gilbert Eastman. The locally-based Portugese puncher outfought Farnell and in the tenth outpunched him, a vicious right sending him to the canvas. He beat the count but was gone and it was stopped. Worse was to follow for the Mancunian. Ordered to hospital, the ambulance driver didn't know the way, didn't know where the switch was for his siren and was stopped by the police as the lights were not flashing. Fortunately, Anthony was okay when they did, eventually, reach the hospital.

Facts and Figures, 2003-2004

There were 594 (601 in 2002-2003) British-based boxers who were active between 1 July 2003 and 30 June 2004, spread over 183 promotions (198 in 2002-2003) held in Britain, not including the Republic of Ireland, during the same period. The 594 boxers active during 2003-2004 comprised 482 men already holding licenses, or having been re-licensed, and 112 (131 in 2002-2003) new professionals. These figures include three women, Cathy Brown, Jane Couch and Juliette Winter, and seven foreign-born boxers, listed in the 'Active British-Based Boxers: Career Records' introduction, who began their careers elsewhere but are now domiciled in Britain.

Unbeaten During Season (Minimum Qualification: 6 Contests)

8: Kevin Mitchell, Matt Skelton. 7: Kevin Anderson, Ali Nuumembe, Chas Symonds, Gary Woolcombe. 6: Femi Fehintola, Audley Harrison, David Haye, Carl Johanneson,

Amer Khan, Barrie Lee, Michael Lomax, Barry Morrison, John Murray, Nadeem Siddique, John Simpson, Paul Smith, Isaac Ward (1 draw), Gary Young.

Longest Unbeaten Sequence (Minimum Qualification: 10 Contests)

37: Joe Calzaghe. 36: Ricky Hatton. 26: Thomas McDonagh (2 draws). 23: Nicky Cook, Michael Jennings. 21: Steven Bendall, Graham Earl. 20: Michael Hunter (1 draw). 19: Johnny Nelson (1 draw). 18: Jason Cook, Jawaid Khaliq. 17: Audley Harrison, Lee Meager (1 draw). 15: David Barnes, Steve Foster, Roman Greenberg. 14: Enzo Maccarinelli, Martin Power, Matt Skelton, Junior Witter. 13: Carl Froch, Young Muttley, Dave Stewart. 12: Danny Hunt. 11: Dean Hickman (1 draw), Jason McKay, Danny Smith (1 draw). 10: Kevin Anderson, Scott Gammer (1 draw), David Haye, Ryan Kerr, Nadeem Siddique, Chas Symonds, Gary Young.

Most Wins During Season (Minimum Qualification: 6 Contests)

8: Kevin Mitchell, Matt Skelton. 7: Kevin Anderson, Lee McAllister, Ali Nuumembe, Chas Symonds, Gary Woolcombe. 6: Femi Fehintola, Audley Harrison, David Haye, Carl Johanneson, Amer Khan, Barrie Lee, Michael Lomax, Barry Morrison, John Murray, Nadeem Siddique, John Simpson, Paul Smith, Gary Young.

Most Contests During Season (Minimum Qualification: 10 Contests)

24: Pete Buckley. 17: Brian Coleman, Jason Nesbitt. 15: Daniel Thorpe. 14: Patrick Cito, Lee Williamson. 12: Ojay Abrahams, Peter Dunn. 11: Simeon Cover, Anthony Hanna, Henry Janes, Ernie Smith. 10: Howard Clarke, Dave Hinds, Hastings Rasani, Nigel Senior, William Webster.

Most Contests During Career (Minimum Qualification: 50 Contests)

227: Pete Buckley. 162: Brian Coleman. 130: Tony Booth. 99: Keith Jones. 97: Paul Bonson. 96: Nigel Senior. 95: Karl Taylor. 93: Anthony Hanna. 92: Arv Mittoo. 83: Leigh Wicks. 80: Ojay Abrahams, Michael Pinnock. 79: Harry Butler. 77: Howard Clarke. 75: Darren Ashton. 74: Ernie Smith. 73: Wayne Shepherd. 71: Paul Wesley. 67: Dave Hinds. 64: David Kirk. 60: Lee Williamson. 59: Carl Allen. 57: Johnny Nelson. 52: Chris Woollas. 50: Richard Inquieti.

Stop Press: Results for July/August 2004

Empress Ballroom, Winter Gardens, Blackpool - 3 July (Promoter: Ellis)

Jeff Thomas w pts 6 Anthony Hanna. Daniel Thorpe w rsc 1 Joel Viney. Isaac Ward w pts 6 Dave Hinds. Oscar Hall w pts 6 Peter Dunn.

The Sports Centre, Newport – 3 July (Promoter: Sports Network)

Enzo Maccarrinelli w pts 12 Ismail Abdoul (WBU Cruiserweight Title). Bradley Pryce w rsc 8 Keith Jones (Welsh Welterweight Title). Gavin Rees w rsc 2 Michael Muya. Jamie Arthur w pts 6 Frederic Bonifai. Tony Doherty w pts 4 David Kirk. Darren McDermott w pts 4 Neil Addis. Nathan King w pts 6 Nick Okoth. Barrie Jones w pts 4 Pete Buckley.

The Football Ground, Ashton Gate, Bristol – 3 July (Promoter: Chris/Jamie Sanigar)

Lee Haskins w rsc 5 Sergei Tasimov. Michael Graydon drew 6 Henry Jones. Leigh Alliss w pts 4 Carl Wheeler. Gavin Tait w rsc 5 Justin Hicks. Tommy Marshall w pts 6 Arv Mittoo.

Savoy Hotel, The Strand, London – 8 July (Promoter: Evans-Waterman Promotions)

Eric Teymour w rsc 2 Lee Woodruff. David Kehoe w pts 6 Rocky Muscus. Robert Lloyd-Taylor w pts 4 Ivor Bonavic.

Aston Villa Leisure Centre, Birmingham – 8 July (Promoter: Bradley)

Steve Brumant w pts 8 Ernie Smith. Terry Adams w rsc 6 Geraint Harvey. Darren Gethin drew 6 Joe Mitchell. David Davies w pts 6 Neil Marston. Jonjo Finnegan w pts 6 Paul Billington.

Sky Blue Connexion, Coventry – 10 July (Promoter: Shakespeare Promotions)

Andy Halder w pts 10 Conroy McIntosh (Midlands Area Middleweight Title). Choi Tseveenpurev w rtd 6 Harry Ramogoadi. Robert Norton w rsc 4 Chris Woollas. Scott Lansdowne w rsc 4 David Ingleby. Brian Coleman w rsc 7 Richard Swallow. Richard Mazarek w rsc 1 Richard Inquieti. Joe McCluskey w rsc 4 Declan English.

York Hall, Bethnal Green, London – 30 July (Promoter: Sports Network)

Graham Earl w rsc 6 Steve Murray (British Lightweight Title). Steve Foster w pts 8 Jean-Marie Codet. John McDermott w co 7 Suren Kalachyan. Martin Power w co 2 Delroy Spencer. Neil Sinclair w pts 6 Craig Lynch. Tony Doherty w pts 6 Ernie Smith. Lee Beavis w pts 4 Jason Nesbitt. Chris Hooper w pts 4 Steve Gethin. Gokhan Kazaz w rsc 2 Dean Powell. Martin Concepcion w rsc 1 Brian Coleman.

Louisville, Kentucky, USA – 30 July

Danny Williams w co 4 Mike Tyson.

Stuttgart, Germany – 31 July

Alexander Dimitrenko w pts 8 Julius Francis.

Hammanskraal, South Africa – 7 August

Silence Mabuza w co 5 Noel Wilders (IBO Bantamweight Title)

Lagos, Nigeria – 15 August

Bash Ali w rsc 4 Tony Booth (WBF Cruiserweight Title)

Diary of British Boxing Tournaments, 2003-2004

Tournaments are listed by date, town, venue and promoter, and cover the period 1 July 2003 – 30 June 2004

Code: SC = Sporting Club

Date	Town	Venue	Promoters
05.07.03	Brentwood	International Centre	Matchroom/Prince Promotions
11.07.02	Darlington	Dolphin Leisure Centre	Garside
12.07.03	Renfrew	Braehead Arena	Sports Network
17.07.03	Walsall	Bescot Stadium	Bradley
17.07.03	Dagenham	Goresbrook Leisure Centre	Sports Network
22.07.03	Bethnal Green	York Hall	Eugene Maloney
25.07.03	Norwich	Sports Village	Hennessy Sports
26.07.03	Plymouth	The Pavilions	Matchroom/Prince Promotions
31.07.03	Sheffield	Octagon Centre	Dennis Hobson
01.08.03	Bethnal Green	York Hall	Lion Promotions
03.08.03	Stalybridge	Copley Centre	Ingle
29.08.03	Liverpool	Everton Park Sports Centre	Vaughan
05.09.03	Doncaster	The Dome	Rushton
05.09.03	Sheffield	Ponds Forge Arena	Dennis Hobson/Evans-Waterman Promotions
06.09.03	Huddersfield	Leisure Centre	Matchroom/Prince Promotions
06.09.03	Aberdeen	Beach Ballrooms	John Ingle
07.09.03	Shrewsbury	Butter Market Club	Bradley
13.09.03	Newport	Sports Centre	Sports Network
13.09.03	Coventry	At7 Centre	Capitol Promotions
13.09.03	Wakefield	Light Waves Leisure Centre	Sheppard
15.09.03	Leeds	Paramount Queens Hotel	Walker
18.09.03	Dagenham	Goresbrook Leisure Centre	Sports Network
18.09.03	Mayfair	Marriott Hotel	Helliet
18.09.03	Mayfair	Millenium Hotel	Evans-Waterman Promotions
20.09.03	Nottingham	Harvey Hadden Leisure Centre	Matchroom/Prince Promotions
21.09.03	Bristol	Marriott Hotel	Couch
22.09.03	Cleethorpes	Winter Gardens	Dalton
25.09.03	Hull	Willerby Manor	Pollard
25.09.03	Bethnal Green	York Hall	Eugene Maloney
26.09.03	Millwall	Britannia International Hotel	John Merton Promotions
26.09.03	Reading	Rivermead Leisure Centre	Lion Promotions
27.09.03	Manchester	MEN Arena	Sports Network
02.10.03	Liverpool	Everton Park Sports Centre	Sports Network
02.10.03	Sunderland	Marriott Hotel	North-East SC
04.10.03	Muswell Hill	Alexandra Palace Grand Hall	Hennessy Sports
04.10.03	Belfast	Ulster Hall	Matchroom/Prince Promotions
05.10.03	Bradford	Pennington's Nightclub	John Ingle
06.10.03	Barnsley	Metrodome	Koncrete Promotions
06.10.03	Birmingham	Burlington Hotel	Cowdell
09.10.03	Bristol	Whitchurch Leisure Centre	Matchroom/Prince Promotions
10.10.03	Darlington	Dolphin Leisure Centre	Garside
11.10.03	Portsmouth	Mountbatten Centre	Sports Network
12.10.03	Sheffield	Grosvenor House Hotel	DVSA Promotions
17.10.03	Glasgow	Thistle Hotel	Morrison
18.10.03	Manchester	MEN Arena	Matchroom/Prince Promotions
19.10.03	Shaw	Tara Leisure Centre	Tara Promotions
20.10.03	Glasgow	Holiday Inn Hotel	St Andrew's SC
20.10.03	Bradford	Hilton Hotel	Yorkshire Executive SC
24.10.03	Bethnal Green	York Hall	Harding
25.10.03	Edinburgh	Meadowbank Stadium	Sports Network

26.10.03	Longford	Heathrow Thistle Hotel	Currivan/Carmen
27.10.03	Glasgow	Hilton Hotel	Evans-Waterman Promotions
29.10.03	Leicester Square	Equinox Nightclub	Holland
30.10.03	Belfast	Ulster Hall	Callahan & Breen Promotions
30.10.03	Dudley	Town Hall	Bradley
01.11.03	Glasgow	Bellahouston Sports Centre	Matchroom/Prince Promotions/St Andrew's SC
06.11.03	Dagenham	Goresbrook Leisure Centre	Sports Network
07.11.03	Sheffield	Hillsborough Leisure Centre	Dennis Hobson/Evans-Waterman Promotions
08.11.03	Bridgend	Recreation Centre	Matchroom/Prince Promotions
08.11.03	Coventry	Leofric Hotel	Capitol Promotions
11.11.03	Leeds	Elland Road (Leeds FC)	Spratt
14.11.03	Bethnal Green	York Hall	Lion Promotions
14.11.03	Hull	KC Stadium	Pollard
15.11.03	Coventry	Leofric Hotel	Coventry SC
17.11.03	Glasgow	Holiday Inn Hotel	St Andrew's SC
18.11.03	Bethnal Green	York Hall	Eugene Maloney
21.11.03	Millwall	Britannia International Hotel	John Merton Promotions
22.11.03	Belfast	King's Hall	Matchroom/Prince Promotions
23.11.03	Rotherham	Magna Centre	Koncrete Promotions
26.11.03	Mayfair	Hilton Hotel	Evans-Waterman Promotions
27.11.03	Longford	Heathrow Thistle Hotel	Currivan/Carmen
28.11.03	Hull	KC Stadium	Hull & District SC
28.11.03	Derby	Storm Arena	Hennessy Sports
29.11.03	Renfrew	Braehead Arena	Sports Network
30.11.03	Swansea	Brangwyn Hall	Geraldine Williams
01.12.03	Barnsley	Keresforth Hall	Dalton
01.12.03	Leeds	Paramount Queens Hotel	Walker
01.12.03	Bradford	Hilton Hotel	Yorkshire Executive SC
04.12.03	Huddersfield	Leisure Centre	Matchroom/Prince Promotions
04.12.03	Sunderland	Marriott Hotel	North-East SC
05.12.03	Bristol	Dolman Exhibition Hall	Jamie Sanigar
06.12.03	Cardiff	Ice Rink	Sports Network
07.12.03	Bradford	Pennington's Nightclub	John Ingle
07.12.03	Glasgow	Thistle Hotel	Morrison
08.12.03	Barnsley	Brooklands Hotel	Koncrete Promotions
08.12.03	Birmingham	Burlington Hotel	Cowdell
10.12.03	Sheffield	Moat House Hotel	Dennis Hobson
11.12.03	Bethnal Green	York Hall	Hennessy Sports
13.12.03	Manchester	MEN Arena	Sports Network
15.12.03	Cleethorpes	Winter Gardens	Dalton
21.12.03	Bolton	Reebok Stadium Premier Suite	Wood
21.12.03	Bristol	Marriott Hotel	Couch
16.01.04	Bradford	Pennington's Nightclub	Harding
19.01.04	Glasgow	Holiday Inn Hotel	St Andrew's SC
24.01.04	Wembley	Conference Centre	Sports Network
30.01.04	Dagenham	Goresbrook Leisure Centre	Hennessy Sports
31.01.04	Bethnal Green	York Hall	Matchroom/Prince Promotions
06.02.04	Sheffield	Ponds Forge Leisure Centre	Dennis Hobson/Evans-Waterman Promotions
07.02.04	Bethnal Green	York Hall	Sports Network
10.02.04	Barnsley	Metrodome	Koncrete Promotions
13.02.04	Bristol	Dolman Exhibition Hall	Jamie Sanigar
14.02.04	Nottingham	Harvey Hadden Leisure Centre	Matchroom/Prince Promotions
14.02.04	Holborn	Connaught Rooms	Eugene Maloney
16.02.04	Scunthorpe	Glandford Park (Scunthorpe UFC)	Shinfield
19.02.04	Dudley	Town Hall	Bradley
20.02.04	Bethnal Green	York Hall	Eugene Maloney

20.02.04	Southampton	St Mary's Stadium Mike Channon Suite	John Merton Promotions
20.02.04	Doncaster	The Dome	Rushton
21.02.04	Cardiff	Ice Rink	Sports Network
21.02.04	Brighton	Hove Town Hall	Pyle
21.02.04	Norwich	Sports Village	John Ingle/Featherby
23.02.04	Nottingham	Holiday Inn Hotel	Scriven
26.02.04	Widnes	Kingsway Leisure Centre	Sports Network
26.02.04	Sunderland	Marriott Hotel	North-East SC
28.02.04	Manchester	Midland Hotel	Dixon
28.02.04	Bridgend	Recreation Centre	Matchroom/Prince Promotions
29.02.04	Shaw	Tara Leisure Centre	Tara Promotions
29.02.04	Bristol	Marriott Hotel	Couch
05.03.04	Darlington	Dolphin Leisure Centre	Garside
06.03.04	Renfrew	Braehead Arena	Sports Network
08.03.04	Birmingham	Burlington Hotel	Cowdell
12.03.04	Nottingham	Ice Arena	Hennessy Sports
12.03.04	Millwall	Britannia Hotel	John Merton Promotions
12.03.04	Irvine	Volunteer Rooms	St Andrew's SC
13.03.04	Huddersfield	Leisure Centre	Matchroom/Prince Promotions
15.03.04	Glasgow	Holiday Inn Hotel	St Andrew's SC
15.03.04	Bradford	Hilton Hotel	Yorkshire Executive SC
20.03.04	Wembley	The Arena	Lion Promotions
25.03.04	Longford	Heathrow Thistle Hotel	Currivan/Carmen
27.03.04	Edinburgh	Meadowbank Arena	Sports Network
30.03.04	Southampton	The Guildhall	Bishop
01.04.04	Bethnal Green	York Hall	Sports Network
02.04.04	Plymouth	College of St Mark & St John Main Hall	Jamie Sanigar
03.04.04	Manchester	MEN Arena	Sports Network
03.04.04	Sheffield	Waltheof Sports Centre	John Ingle
07.04.04	Leicester Square	Equinox Nightclub	Baker
08.04.04	Peterborough	Moat House Hotel	Sanders
09.04.04	Rugby	Benn Hall	Shakespeare Promotions
10.04.04	Manchester	MEN Arena	Matchroom/Prince Promotions
15.04.04	Dudley	Town Hall	Bradley
16.04.04	Bradford	Pennington's Nightclub	Hennessy Sports
16.04.04	Hartlepool	Borough Hall	Garside
17.04.04	Belfast	King's Hall	Matchroom/Prince Promotions
19.04.04	Glasgow	Holiday Inn Hotel	St Andrew's SC
20.04.04	Sheffield	Octagon Centre	Dennis Hobson
22.04.04	Glasgow	Kelvin Hall	Matchroom/Prince Promotions/St Andrew's SC
23.04.04	Glasgow	Thistle Hotel	Morrison
23.04.04	Leicester	Ramada Jarvis Hotel	Griffin
24.04.04	Reading	Rivermead Leisure Centre	Sports Network
25.04.04	Nottingham	Sport Nottingham Arena	Scriven
26.04.04	Cleethorpes	Winter Gardens	Frater
27.04.04	Leeds	Elland Road (Leeds UFC)	Spratt
01.05.04	Coventry	Leofric Hotel	Coventry SC
01.05.04	Bridgend	Recreation Centre	Matchroom/Prince Promotions
01.05.04	Gravesend	Woodville Halls	Roe
06.05.04	Barnsley	The Metrodome	Sports Network
07.05.04	Doncaster	The Dome	Rushton
07.05.04	Bethnal Green	York Hall	Frank Maloney
08.05.04	Dagenham	Goresbrook Leisure Centre	Matchroom/Prince Promotions
08.05.04	Bristol	Whitchurch Leisure Centre	Chris Sanigar/Harding
10.05.04	Birmingham	Burlington Hotel	Cowdell
12.05.04	Reading	Rivermead Leisure Centre	Evans-Waterman Promotions/Dennis Hobson

13.05.04	Bethnal Green	York Hall	Sports Network
14.05.04	Sunderland	Marriott Hotel	North-East SC
15.05.04	Aberdeen	Beach Ballrooms	John Ingle
22.05.04	Manchester	Midland Hotel	Dixon
22.05.04	Widnes	Kingsway Sports Centre	Sports Network
27.05.04	Huddersfield	Leisure Centre	Matchroom/Prince Promotions
28.05.04	Glasgow	Thistle Hotel	Morrison
02.06.04	Nottingham	Ice Arena	Hennessy Sports
02.06.04	Hereford	Leisure Centre	Matchroom/Prince Promotions
04.06.04	Dudley	Town Hall	Bradley
04.06.04	Hull	Willerby Manor Hotel	Hull & District SC
05.06.04	Bethnal Green	York Hall	Sports Network
07.06.04	Glasgow	Holiday Inn Hotel	St Andrew's SC
08.06.04	Sheffield	Institute of Sport	Koncrete Promotions
12.06.04	Manchester	MEN Arena	Sports Network
14.06.04	Cleethorpes	Winter Gardens	Dalton
17.06.04	Sheffield	Octagon Centre	Dennis Hobson
19.06.04	Renfrew	Braehead Arena	Sports Network
19.06.04	Muswell Hill	Alexandra Palace Grand Hall	Chris Sanigar/Harding
25.06.04	Bethnal Green	York Hall	Eugene Maloney
26.06.04	Belfast	King's Hall	Matchroom/Prince Promotions

Despite taking a right to the jaw, Chas Symonds (left) stopped Dave Wakefield, the son of the 1960s fighter, in the fifth round at the York Hall on 20 February 2004   Les Clark

Active British-Based Boxers: Career Records

Shows the complete record for all British-based boxers who have been active between 1 July 2003 and 30 June 2004. Names in brackets are real names, where they differ from ring names, and the first place name given is the boxer's domicile. Boxers are either shown as being self-managed or with a named manager, the information being supplied by the BBBoC shortly before going to press. Also included are foreign-born fighters who made their pro debuts in Britain, along with others like Patrick Cito (Congo), Varuzhan Davtyan (Armenia), Eugenio Monteiro (Portugal), Farai Musiiwa (Zimbabwe), Hastings Rasani (Zimbabwe), Harry Ramogoadi (South Africa) and Choi Tseveenpurev (Mongolia), who, although starting their careers elsewhere, now hold BBBoC licenses.

Ojay Abrahams

Watford. *Born* Lambeth, 17 December, 1964
Middleweight. Former British Masters Middleweight Champion. Ht. 5'8½"
Manager A. Ayling

21.09.91	Gordon Webster W RSC 3 Tottenham
26.10.91	Mick Reid W RSC 5 Brentwood
26.11.91	John Corcoran W PTS 6 Bethnal Green
21.01.92	Dave Andrews DREW 6 Norwich
31.03.92	Marty Duke W RSC 2 Norwich
19.05.92	Michael Smyth L PTS 6 Cardiff
16.06.92	Ricky Mabbett W PTS 6 Dagenham
13.10.92	Vince Rose L RSC 3 Mayfair
30.01.93	Vince Rose DREW 6 Brentwood
19.05.93	Ricky Mabbett L RSC 4 Leicester
18.09.93	Ricky Mabbett L PTS 6 Leicester
09.12.93	Nick Appiah W PTS 6 Watford
24.01.94	Errol McDonald W RSC 2 Glasgow
09.02.94	Vince Rose W PTS 6 Brentwood
23.05.94	Spencer McCracken L PTS 6 Walsall
11.06.94	Darren Dyer W RSC 1 Bethnal Green
29.09.94	Gary Logan L PTS 10 Bethnal Green *(Southern Area Welterweight Title Challenge)*
13.12.94	Geoff McCreesh L PTS 6 Potters Bar
11.02.95	Gary Murray L PTS 8 Hamanskraal, South Africa
17.07.95	Andreas Panayi L PTS 8 Mayfair
02.10.95	Larbi Mohammed L RTD 5 Mayfair
08.12.95	Jason Beard W CO 2 Bethnal Green
09.04.96	Kevin Thompson W RSC 3 Stevenage
07.05.96	Harry Dhami L RSC 5 Mayfair *(Vacant Southern Area Welterweight Title)*
12.11.96	Spencer McCracken L PTS 8 Dudley
22.04.97	Paul King W RSC 4 Bethnal Green
29.05.97	Paul Ryan L RSC 3 Mayfair
30.06.97	Ahmet Dottuev L RSC 4 Bethnal Green
08.11.97	Anthony McFadden L PTS 8 Southwark
24.03.98	Leigh Wicks W PTS 6 Bethnal Green
28.04.98	Jim Webb W RSC 2 Belfast
10.09.98	Delroy Leslie L PTS 10 Acton *(Vacant Southern Area L. Middleweight Title)*
19.12.98	Michael Jones L PTS 6 Liverpool
23.01.99	Wayne Alexander L DIS 1 Cheshunt *(Vacant Southern Area L. Middleweight Title)*
01.05.99	Wayne Alexander L RSC 3 Crystal Palace
26.06.99	Geoff McCreesh L PTS 8 Millwall
05.10.99	Hussain Osman L PTS 4 Bloomsbury
23.10.99	Paul Samuels L PTS 8 Telford
18.01.00	Howard Eastman L RSC 2 Mansfield
23.03.00	Pedro Thompson DREW 6 Bloomsbury
08.04.00	Anthony Farnell L PTS 8 Bethnal Green
16.05.00	Ryan Rhodes L PTS 6 Warrington
23.05.00	Alexandru Andrei L PTS 6 Paris, France
04.07.00	Lester Jacobs L PTS 4 Tooting
21.09.00	Harry Butler W PTS 6 Bloomsbury
07.10.00	Kofi Jantuah L RTD 3 Doncaster
25.11.00	Donovan Smillie W RSC 2 Manchester
16.12.00	Marlon Hayes L RTD 6 Sheffield
15.01.01	Gordon Behan DREW 6 Manchester
24.02.01	Ruben Groenewald L PTS 6 Bethnal Green
22.04.01	Harry Butler W PTS 6 Streatham
17.05.01	Lee Murtagh W RSC 2 Leeds *(Vacant British Masters L. Middleweight Title)*
21.06.01	Charden Ansoula L PTS 4 Earls Court
28.07.01	Gary Logan L RSC 4 Wembley
10.12.01	Jimmy Vincent L PTS 10 Birmingham *(British Masters L. Middleweight Title Challenge)*
28.01.02	Ian Cooper W PTS 6 Barnsley
16.03.02	John Humphrey L PTS 10 Bethnal Green *(Vacant Southern Area L.Middleweight Title)*
13.04.02	Mihaly Kotai L PTS 6 Liverpool
20.04.02	Freeman Barr L PTS 8 Cardiff
10.05.02	Carl Froch L RSC 1 Bethnal Green
15.06.02	Sam Soliman L PTS 4 Tottenham
17.08.02	Wayne Elcock L PTS 4 Cardiff
17.09.02	David Starie L RSC 4 Bethnal Green
25.10.02	Gilbert Eastman L PTS 4 Bethnal Green
12.12.02	Allan Gray L PTS 10 Leicester Square *(Southern Area Middleweight Title Challenge. Vacant WBF International Middleweight Title)*
05.03.03	David Walker L PTS 6 Bethnal Green
19.04.03	Geard Ajetovic L PTS 4 Liverpool
12.05.03	Jason Collins L PTS 10 Birmingham *(Vacant British Masters S.Middleweight Title)*
05.07.03	Allan Foster L PTS 4 Brentwood
18.09.03	Steve Roache W CO 2 Mayfair
18.10.03	Michael Jones L PTS 6 Manchester
22.11.03	Jason McKay L PTS 4 Belfast
01.12.03	Omar Gumati L PTS 6 Leeds
10.02.04	Daniel Teasdale L PTS 6 Barnsley
23.02.04	Matt Galer L PTS 4 Nottingham
08.03.04	Hamid Jamali L PTS 8 Birmingham
02.04.04	Scott Dann L RSC 6 Plymouth
06.05.04	Daniel Teasdale L PTS 4 Barnsley
13.05.04	Conroy McIntosh L RSC 2 Bethnal Green
12.06.04	Matthew Macklin L PTS 4 Manchester

Career: 80 contests, won 20, drew 4, lost 56.

Terry Adams

Birmingham. *Born* Birmingham, 1 November, 1978
Welterweight. Ht. 5'8"
Manager T. Nerwal

19.02.04	Neil Addis W CO 2 Dudley
15.04.04	Geraint Harvey W PTS 6 Dudley

Career: 2 contests, won 2.

Neil Addis

Ferndale. *Born* Church Village, 7 July, 1980
Middleweight. Ht. 5'11"
Manager D. Davies

15.11.03	Richard Mazurek L PTS 6 Coventry
22.11.03	Ciaran Healy L RSC 2 Belfast
10.02.04	Dean Walker L PTS 6 Barnsley
19.02.04	Tony Adams L CO 2 Dudley
27.03.04	Scott Forsyth L RSC 3 Edinburgh

Career: 5 contests, lost 5.

Geard Ajetovic   Les Clark

Geard Ajetovic

Liverpool. *Born* Beocin, Yugoslavia, 28 February, 1981
Middleweight. Ht. 5'8½"
Manager G. Storey

19.04.03	Ojay Abrahams W PTS 4 Liverpool
17.05.03	Jason Samuels W PTS 4 Liverpool

26.09.03 Gary Beardsley W RSC 3 Reading
07.11.03 Joel Ani W RTD 1 Sheffield
06.02.04 Tomas da Silva W RSC 4 Sheffield
12.05.04 Dmitry Donetskiy W PTS 6 Reading
Career: 6 contests, won 6.

Henry Akinwande

Dulwich. *Born* London, 12 October, 1965
IBF Inter-Continental Heavyweight
Champion. Former Undefeated WBN &
WBC FeCarBox Heavyweight Champion.
Former Undefeated WBO, European &
Commonwealth Heavyweight Champion.
Ht. 6'7"
Manager Self

04.10.89 Carlton Headley W CO 1 Kensington
08.11.89 Dennis Bailey W RSC 2 Wembley
06.12.89 Paul Neilson W RSC 1 Wembley
10.01.90 John Fairbairn W RSC 1 Kensington
14.03.90 Warren Thompson W PTS 6
Kensington
09.05.90 Mike Robinson W CO 1 Wembley
10.10.90 Tracy Thomas W PTS 6 Kensington
12.12.90 Francois Yrius W RSC 1 Kensington
06.03.91 J. B. Williamson W RSC 2 Wembley
06.06.91 Ramon Voorn W PTS 8 Barking
28.06.91 Marshall Tillman W PTS 8 Nice,
France
09.10.91 Gypsy John Fury W CO 3 Manchester
(*Elim. British Heavyweight Title*)
06.12.91 Tim Bullock W CO 3 Dussledorf,
Germany
28.02.92 Young Joe Louis W RSC 3 Issy les
Moulineaux, France
26.03.92 Tucker Richards W RSC 2 Telford
10.04.92 Lumbala Tshimba W PTS 8 Carquefou,
France
05.06.92 Kimmuel Odum W DIS 6 Marseille,
France
18.07.92 Steve Garber W RTD 2 Manchester
19.12.92 Axel Schulz DREW 12 Berlin,
Germany
(*Vacant European Heavyweight Title*)
18.03.93 Jimmy Thunder W PTS 12 Lewisham
(*Vacant Commonwealth Heavyweight
Title*)
01.05.93 Axel Schulz W PTS 12 Berlin, Germany
(*Vacant European Heavyweight Title*)
06.11.93 Frankie Swindell W PTS 10 Sun City,
South Africa
01.12.93 Biagio Chianese W RSC 4 Kensington
(*European Heavyweight Title Defence*)
05.04.94 Johnny Nelson W PTS 10 Bethnal
Green
23.07.94 Mario Schiesser W CO 7 Berlin,
Germany
(*European Heavyweight Title Defence*)
08.04.95 Calvin Jones W CO 2 Las Vegas,
Nevada, USA
22.07.95 Stanley Wright W RSC 2 Millwall
16.12.95 Tony Tucker W PTS 10 Philadelphia,
Pennsylvania, USA
27.01.96 Brian Sergeant W RSC 1 Phoenix,
Arizona, USA
23.03.96 Gerard Jones W DIS 7 Miami, Florida,
USA
29.06.96 Jeremy Williams W CO 3 Indio,
California, USA
(*Vacant WBO Heavyweight Title*)
09.11.96 Alexander Zolkin W RSC 10 Las
Vegas, Nevada, USA
(*WBO Heavyweight Title Defence*)

11.01.97 Scott Welch W PTS 12 Nashville,
Tennessee, USA
(*WBO Heavyweight Title Defence*)
12.07.97 Lennox Lewis L DIS 5 Stateline,
Nevada, USA
(*WBC Heavyweight Title Challenge*)
13.12.97 Orlin Norris W PTS 12 Pompano
Beach, Florida, USA
(*Final Elim. WBA Heavyweight Title*)
06.03.99 Reynaldo Minus W RSC 2 St Paul,
Minnesota, USA
15.05.99 Najeed Shaheed W RSC 9 Miami,
Florida, USA
22.02.00 Chris Serengo W RSC 1 Capetown,
South Africa
25.05.00 Russull Chasteen W CO 5 Tunica,
Mississippi, USA
08.12.00 Ken Craven W CO 1 Tallahassee,
Florida, USA
(*Vacant WBC FeCarBox Heavyweight
Title*)
17.03.01 Peter McNeeley W CO 2 Tallahassee,
Florida, USA
16.06.01 Maurice Harris W CO 1 Cincinnati,
USA
17.11.01 Oliver McCall L CO 10 Las Vegas,
Nevada, USA
08.03.02 Curt Paige W RSC 1 Kissimmee,
Florida, USA
29.10.02 Sam Ubokane W RSC 7 Capetown,
South Africa
10.12.02 Roman Sukhoterin W PTS 12
Constanta, Romania
(*WBN Inter-Continental Heavyweight
Title Challenge*)
31.05.03 Timo Hoffmann W PTS 12 Frankfurt,
Germany
(*IBF Inter-Continental Heavyweight
Title Challenge*)
10.04.04 Anton Nel W RSC 10 Carabas, Nigeria
(*IBF Inter-Continental Heavyweight
Title Defence*)
Career: 48 contests, won 45, drew 1, lost 2.

Mark Alexander   Les Clark

Mark Alexander

Hackney. *Born* Hackney, 18 November,
1975
Featherweight. Ht. 5'9½"
Manager T. Sims

10.04.01 Steve Hanley W PTS 4 Wembley
31.07.01 Damien Dunnion W PTS 4 Bethnal
Green
19.12.01 Dazzo Williams L PTS 6 Coventry
15.05.03 Buster Dennis W PTS 4 Mayfair
01.08.03 Arv Mittoo W PTS 4 Bethnal Green
25.09.03 Henry Castle L PTS 6 Bethnal Green
01.11.03 John Simpson L PTS 4 Glasgow
Career: 7 contests, won 4, lost 3.

Wayne Alexander

Croydon. *Born* Tooting, 17 July, 1973
L.Middleweight. Former Undefeated
British & European L.Middleweight
Champion. Former Undefeated Southern
Area L.Middleweight Champion. Ht. 5'8¾"
Manager F. Warren

10.11.95 Andrew Jervis W RTD 3 Derby
13.02.96 Paul Murray W PTS 4 Bethnal Green
11.05.96 Jim Webb W RSC 2 Bethnal Green
13.07.96 John Janes W RSC 3 Bethnal Green
05.06.97 Prince Kasi Kaihau W CO 4 Bristol
29.11.97 John Janes W RSC 1 Norwich
21.03.98 Darren Covill W RSC 2 Bethnal Green
09.05.98 Pedro Carragher W CO 2 Sheffield
14.07.98 Lindon Scarlett W RSC 5 Reading
05.12.98 Jimmy Vincent W RSC 3 Bristol
23.01.99 Ojay Abrahams W DIS 1 Cheshunt
(*Vacant Southern Area
L. Middleweight Title*)
01.05.99 Ojay Abrahams W RSC 3 Crystal
Palace
07.08.99 George Richards W RSC 2 Dagenham
19.02.00 Paul Samuels W RSC 3 Dagenham
(*Vacant British L. Middleweight Title*)
12.08.00 Paul Denton W RSC 1 Wembley
10.02.01 Harry Simon L RSC 5 Widnes
(*WBO L. Middleweight Title Challenge*)
28.07.01 Viktor Fesetchko W PTS 8 Wembley
17.11.01 Joe Townsley W RSC 2 Glasgow
(*British L. Middleweight Title Defence*)
19.01.02 Paolo Pizzamiglio W RSC 3 Bethnal
Green
(*Vacant European L. Middleweight
Title*)
18.01.03 Viktor Fesetchko W PTS 6 Preston
06.12.03 Delroy Mellis L RSC 8 Cardiff
07.02.04 Howard Clarke W RSC 2 Bethnal
Green
Career: 22 contests, won 20, lost 2.

Amir Ali

Sheffield. *Born* Sheffield, 10 January, 1985
L. Welterweight. Ht. 5'10"
Manager D. Coldwell

23.11.03 Jason Nesbitt W PTS 6 Rotherham
06.05.04 Pete Buckley W PTS 4 Barnsley
08.06.04 Nigel Senior W PTS 6 Sheffield
Career: 3 contests, won 3.

Haider Ali

Shadwell. *Born* Quetta, Pakistan, 12
November, 1979
S. Featherweight. Ht. 5'8½"
Manager F. Warren

24.05.03 Buster Dennis W PTS 4 Bethnal Green
17.07.03 Jason Nesbitt W PTS 4 Dagenham
29.11.03 Jus Wallie W PTS 4 Renfrew
22.05.04 Steve Bell L PTS 6 Widnes
Career: 4 contests, won 3, lost 1.

Wayne Alexander   Les Clark

John Alldis

Crawley. *Born* London, 21 February, 1970
Lightweight. Ht. 5'8"
Manager J. Pyle

21.02.04 Junior Anderson W CO 1 Brighton
07.04.04 Keith Jones W PTS 6 Leicester Square
12.05.04 Jon Honey L PTS 6 Reading
Career: 3 contests, won 2, lost 1.

John Alldis   Les Clark

Carl Allen

Wolverhampton. *Born* Wolverhampton, 20
November, 1969
Lightweight. Former Undefeated Midlands
Area S. Bantamweight Champion.
Ht. 5'7¹/₄"
Manager P. Bowen

26.11.95 Gary Jenkinson W PTS 6 Birmingham
29.11.95 Jason Squire L PTS 6 Solihull
17.01.96 Andy Robinson L PTS 6 Solihull
13.02.96 Ervine Blake W RSC 5
         Wolverhampton
21.02.96 Ady Benton L PTS 6 Batley
29.02.96 Chris Jickells W PTS 6 Scunthorpe
27.03.96 Jason Squire DREW 6 Whitwick
26.04.96 Paul Griffin L RSC 3 Cardiff
30.05.96 Roger Brotherhood W RSC 5 Lincoln
26.09.96 Matthew Harris W PTS 10 Walsall
         *(Midlands Area S. Bantamweight Title
         Challenge)*
07.10.96 Emmanuel Clottey L RTD 3 Lewisham
21.11.96 Miguel Matthews W PTS 8 Solihull
30.11.96 Floyd Havard L RTD 3 Tylorstown
29.01.97 Pete Buckley W PTS 8 Stoke
11.02.97 David Morris DREW 8
         Wolverhampton
28.02.97 Ian McLeod L RTD 3 Kilmarnock
21.05.97 David Burke L PTS 4 Liverpool

30.06.97 Duke McKenzie L PTS 8 Bethnal
         Green
12.09.97 Brian Carr L PTS 8 Glasgow
04.10.97 Sergei Devakov L PTS 6 Muswell Hill
03.12.97 Chris Lyons W PTS 8 Stoke
21.05.98 Roy Rutherford L PTS 6 Solihull
09.06.98 Scott Harrison L RSC 6 Hull
30.11.98 Gary Hibbert L PTS 4 Manchester
09.12.98 Chris Jickells W RSC 3 Stoke
04.02.99 Mat Zegan L PTS 4 Lewisham
17.03.99 Craig Spacie W PTS 8 Stoke
08.05.99 Phillip Ndou L RSC 2 Bethnal Green
14.06.99 Pete Buckley W PTS 6 Birmingham
22.06.99 David Lowry L PTS 4 Ipswich
11.10.99 Lee Williamson L PTS 6 Birmingham
19.10.99 Tontcho Tontchev L CO 2 Bethnal
         Green
20.12.99 Nicky Cook L CO 3 Bethnal Green
08.02.00 Lee Williamson W PTS 8
         Wolverhampton
29.02.00 Bradley Pryce L PTS 4 Widnes
28.03.00 Lee Williamson W PTS 8
         Wolverhampton
16.05.00 Bradley Pryce L RSC 3 Warrington
24.06.00 Michael Gomez L CO 2 Glasgow
10.10.00 Steve Hanley W PTS 8 Brierley Hill
05.02.01 Lee Meager DREW 6 Hull
12.03.01 Pete Buckley W PTS 6 Birmingham
27.03.01 Pete Buckley W PTS 8 Brierley Hill
15.09.01 Esham Pickering L PTS 6 Derby
17.11.01 Steve Conway L PTS 8 Dewsbury
08.12.01 Esham Pickering L PTS 8 Chesterfield
07.02.02 Mark Bowen L PTS 6 Stoke
20.04.02 Esham Pickering L PTS 6 Derby
21.07.02 Eddie Nevins L PTS 4 Salford
07.09.02 Colin Toohey DREW 6 Liverpool
26.10.02 Dazzo Williams W RSC 2 Maesteg
02.12.02 Esham Pickering L PTS 6 Leicester
28.01.03 Lee Meager L PTS 8 Nottingham
09.05.03 Jeff Thomas DREW 6 Doncaster
08.11.03 Baz Carey W RSC 2 Coventry
28.11.03 Carl Greaves L PTS 4 Derby
28.02.04 Michael Kelly L PTS 4 Bridgend
03.04.04 Andy Morris L PTS 4 Manchester
16.04.04 Dave Stewart L PTS 6 Bradford
17.06.04 Scott Lawton L PTS 10 Sheffield
         *(Vacant Midlands Area Lightweight
         Title)*

Career: 59 contests, won 18, drew 5, lost 36.

Carl Allen   Les Clark

77

Mike Allen

Rhyl. *Born* St Asaph, 12 September, 1980
S. Middleweight. Ht. 5'10"
Manager T. Gilmour

08.11.03 Freddie Yemofio W RSC 4 Bridgend
28.02.04 Gary Ojuederie L RSC 1 Bridgend
01.05.04 William Webster W CO 2 Bridgend
Career: 3 contests, won 2, lost 1.

Peter Allen

Birkenhead. *Born* Birkenhead, 13 August, 1978
Lightweight. Ht. 5'5"
Manager T. Miller

30.04.98 Sean Grant L PTS 6 Pentre Halkyn
21.06.98 Garry Burrell W PTS 6 Liverpool
20.09.98 Simon Chambers L PTS 6 Sheffield
16.11.98 Stevie Kane W PTS 6 Glasgow
07.12.98 Simon Chambers L PTS 6 Bradford
28.02.99 Amjid Mahmood L PTS 6 Shaw
12.03.99 Marc Callaghan L PTS 4 Bethnal Green
15.09.99 Steve Brook L PTS 6 Harrogate
07.10.99 Nicky Wilders L PTS 6 Sunderland
18.10.99 Mark Hudson L PTS 6 Bradford
15.11.99 Craig Docherty L RSC 1 Glasgow
09.12.01 Jeff Thomas L PTS 6 Blackpool
01.03.02 Andrew Ferrans L PTS 8 Irvine
15.03.02 Ricky Burns L PTS 6 Glasgow
17.04.02 Andrew Smith W PTS 6 Stoke
24.06.02 Tasawar Khan L PTS 6 Bradford
14.09.02 Carl Greaves L PTS 6 Newark
08.10.02 Andrew Ferrans L PTS 8 Glasgow
21.10.02 Tony McPake L PTS 6 Glasgow
17.11.02 Choi Tseveenpurev L RSC 4 Shaw
16.02.03 Darryn Walton L PTS 6 Salford
31.05.03 Mally McIver L PTS 6 Barnsley
29.08.03 Steve Mullin L PTS 6 Liverpool
25.04.04 Craig Johnson L PTS 6 Nottingham
08.05.04 Michael Graydon L PTS 6 Bristol
30.05.04 Willie Valentine W PTS 4 Dublin
Career: 26 contests, won 4, lost 22.

Leigh Alliss   Les Clark

Leigh Alliss

Stroud. *Born* Stroud, 11 September, 1975
L. Heavyweight. Ht. 5'9½"
Manager C. Sanigar

06.03.03 Ovill McKenzie L PTS 4 Bristol
12.05.03 Mark Phillips W PTS 6 Southampton
13.06.03 Egbui Ikeagbu W PTS 6 Bristol
09.10.03 Mark Phillips W PTS 4 Bristol
05.12.03 Dale Nixon W RSC 2 Bristol
13.02.04 Hastings Rasani W PTS 6 Bristol
08.05.04 Michael Pinnock W PTS 4 Bristol
Career: 7 contests, won 6, lost 1.

Adnan Amar

Nottingham. *Born* Nottingham, 17 February, 1983
L. Welterweight. Ht. 5'9"
Manager J. Ingle

11.06.01 Steve Hanley W PTS 4 Nottingham
13.11.01 Duncan Armstrong W PTS 6 Leeds
21.10.02 Jason Gonzales W PTS 6 Cleethorpes
23.02.03 Arv Mittoo W PTS 6 Shrewsbury
16.03.03 Gareth Wiltshaw W PTS 6 Nottingham
16.04.03 Dave Cotterill W PTS 4 Nottingham
28.04.03 Ernie Smith W PTS 6 Cleethorpes
12.05.03 Pedro Thompson W RSC 4 Birmingham
08.06.03 David Kirk W PTS 6 Nottingham
06.09.03 Chris Duggan W PTS 4 Aberdeen
23.02.04 Wayne Shepherd W RSC 5 Nottingham
10.05.04 Ernie Smith W PTS 6 Birmingham
04.06.04 Dean Hickman L RSC 8 Dudley
(Vacant Midlands Area L.Welterweight Title)
Career: 13 contests, won 12, lost 1.

(Terry) Junior Anderson

Southampton. *Born* Leeds, 23 May, 1974
Featherweight. Ht. 5'8"
Manager Self

17.03.03 Neil Read L CO 2 Southampton
21.02.04 John Alldis L CO 1 Brighton
01.05.04 John Mackay L CO 2 Gravesend
Career: 3 contests, lost 3.

Kevin Anderson   Les Clark

Kevin Anderson

Buckhaven. *Born* Kirkcaldy, 26 April, 1980
Welterweight. Ht. 5'8"
Manager T. Gilmour

12.04.03 Paul McIlwaine W RSC 2 Bethnal Green
19.04.03 Piotr Bartnicki W RSC 2 Liverpool
17.05.03 Georges Dujardin W RSC 1 Liverpool

05.07.03 Mohamed Bourhis W CO 2 Brentwood
06.09.03 Sergei Starkov W PTS 6 Huddersfield
01.11.03 Alban Mothie W PTS 8 Glasgow
14.02.04 Andrei Napolskikh W PTS 8 Nottingham
13.03.04 Lance Hall W RSC 1 Huddersfield
22.04.04 Dmitri Yanushevich W RSC 2 Glasgow
27.05.04 Danny Moir W RSC 1 Huddersfield
Career: 10 contests, won 10.

Joel Ani

Tottenham. *Born* Nigeria, 6 February, 1972
Middleweight. Ht. 5'8"
Manager B. Lawrence

22.10.92 Danny Quacoe W CO 1 Bethnal Green
03.02.93 Kevin Adamson L RSC 6 Earls Court
29.03.93 George Wilson W PTS 6 Mayfair
06.05.93 Korso Aleain W RSC 2 Bayswater
23.06.93 Steve McGovern L PTS 6 Edmonton
02.10.98 Gareth Lovell DREW 6 Cheshunt
11.12.98 Mark Richards L DIS 3 Cheshunt
26.02.99 David Baptiste L RSC 5 Longford
26.09.02 Harry Butler W PTS 4 Fulham
25.10.02 Craig Lynch L PTS 6 Millwall
01.02.03 Mickey Quinn L PTS 4 Belfast
23.02.03 Michael Thompson W DIS 1 Streatham
17.05.03 Graham Delehedy L RSC 4 Liverpool
17.07.03 Gokhan Kazaz L PTS 4 Dagenham
26.09.03 Kreshnik Qato L PTS 6 Millwall
04.10.03 Ciaran Healy L PTS 4 Belfast
29.10.03 Bobby Banghar L PTS 4 Leicester Square
07.11.03 Geard Ajetovic L RTD 1 Sheffield
13.12.03 Paul Smith L PTS 4 Manchester
27.03.04 Martin Concepcion L RTD 3 Edinburgh
02.06.04 Daniel Cadman L CO 2 Nottingham
Career: 21 contests, won 5, drew 1, lost 15.

John Armour

Chatham. *Born* Chatham, 26 October, 1968
Bantamweight. Former WBU Bantamweight Champion. Former Undefeated European & Commonwealth Bantamweight Champion. Ht. 5'4¾"
Manager Self

24.09.90 Lupe Castro W PTS 6 Lewisham
31.10.90 Juan Camero W RSC 4 Crystal Palace
21.01.91 Elijro Mejia W RSC 1 Crystal Palace
30.09.91 Pat Maher W CO 1 Kensington
29.10.91 Pete Buckley W PTS 6 Kensington
14.12.91 Gary Hickman W RSC 6 Bexleyheath
25.03.92 Miguel Matthews W PTS 6 Dagenham
30.04.92 Ndabe Dube W RSC 12 Kensington
(Vacant Commonwealth Bantamweight Title)
17.10.92 Mauricio Bernal W PTS 8 Wembley
03.12.92 Albert Musankabala W RSC 5 Lewisham
(Commonwealth Bantamweight Title Defence)
28.01.93 Ricky Romero W CO 1 Southwark
10.02.93 Morgan Mpande W PTS 12 Lewisham
(Commonwealth Bantamweight Title Defence)
09.06.93 Boualem Belkif W PTS 10 Lewisham
01.12.93 Karl Morling W CO 3 Kensington
14.01.94 Rufus Adebayo W RSC 7 Bethnal Green
(Commonwealth Bantamweight Title Defence)

23.09.94	Shaun Anderson W RSC 11 Bethnal Green

(Commonwealth Bantamweight Title Defence)

14.02.95   Tsitsi Sokutu W RSC 7 Bethnal Green
(Commonwealth Bantamweight Title Defence)

19.04.95   Antonio Picardi W RSC 8 Bethnal Green
(Vacant European Bantamweight Title)

19.05.95   Matthew Harris W RSC 3 Southwark

29.11.95   Redha Abbas W CO 5 Bethnal Green
(European Bantamweight Title Defence)

17.12.96   Lyndon Kershaw W RSC 8 Bethnal Green

29.01.97   Petrica Paraschiv W PTS 12 Bethnal Green
(Vacant Interim WBC International Bantamweight Title)

20.05.97   Anatoly Kvitko W RSC 8 Gillingham

28.11.97   Ervine Blake W PTS 10 Bethnal Green

12.12.98   Carlos Navarro L RSC 4 Southwark
(WBU S. Bantamweight Title Challenge)

19.06.99   Mohamed Ouzid W RSC 5 Dublin

25.07.00   Alexander Tiranov W PTS 8 Southwark

09.12.00   Francis Ampofo W PTS 12 Southwark
(Vacant WBU Bantamweight Title)

01.12.01   Ian Turner W PTS 8 Bethnal Green

11.05.02   Francis Ampofo W PTS 12 Dagenham
(WBU Bantamweight Title Defence)

21.09.02   Francis Ampofo W PTS 12 Brentwood
(WBU Bantamweight Title Defence)

05.07.03   Nathan Sting L RTD 11 Brentwood
(WBU Bantamweight Title Defence)

Career: 32 contests, won 30, lost 2.

(Shaun) Lee Armstrong

Huddersfield. *Born* Hartlepool, 18 October, 1972
Central Area L. Middleweight Champion. Former Undefeated Central Area S.Featherweight Champion. Ht. 5'8"
Manager C. Aston

26.04.96   Daryl McKenzie W RSC 4 Glasgow
10.05.96   Charlie Rumbol W PTS 6 Wembley
23.05.96   Ian Richardson W PTS 6 Queensferry
04.10.96   Michael Gibbons L RSC 3 Wakefield
18.11.96   Garry Burrell W PTS 6 Glasgow
20.02.97   Carl Greaves W RSC 4 Mansfield
10.04.97   Chris Lyons W PTS 6 Sheffield
28.04.97   Hugh Collins W RTD 5 Glasgow
26.06.97   Garry Burrell W PTS 6 Sheffield
06.10.97   Roger Sampson L PTS 6 Bradford
13.11.97   Graeme Williams W PTS 6 Bradford
30.11.97   Gary Jenkinson W PTS 6 Shaw
06.02.98   Nigel Leake W PTS 6 Wakefield
05.04.98   John T. Kelly W PTS 4 Shaw
21.05.98   Pete Buckley W PTS 6 Bradford
14.06.98   Pete Buckley W PTS 6 Shaw
23.10.98   Nigel Leake W RSC 3 Wakefield
(Vacant Central Area S. Featherweight Title)
11.12.98   Ian McLeod L RSC 8 Prestwick
(IBO Inter-Continental S. Featherweight Title Challenge)
21.02.99   Bobby Lyndon W RSC 5 Bradford
03.04.99   John T. Kelly L PTS 6 Carlisle
25.04.99   Chris Lyons W PTS 8 Leeds
02.10.99   Jamie McKeever DREW 6 Cardiff

14.11.99   Keith Jones W PTS 6 Bradford
11.12.99   Jason Dee L RSC 4 Merthyr
21.02.00   Gary Flear W PTS 8 Glasgow
27.03.00   Sebastian Hart L CO 4 Barnsley
24.09.00   Dave Travers W PTS 6 Shaw
23.10.00   Craig Docherty DREW 8 Glasgow
10.12.01   Arv Mittoo W PTS 6 Bradford
27.04.02   Keith Jones W PTS 6 Huddersfield
09.05.02   Richard Inquieti L RSC 5 Sunderland
22.02.03   Gavin Wake W PTS 10 Huddersfield
(Vacant Central Area L. Middleweight Title)
17.11.03   Harry Dhami L PTS 6 Glasgow
Career: 33 contests, won 23, drew 2, lost 8.

Alex Arthur

Edinburgh. *Born* Edinburgh, 26 June, 1978
IBF Inter-Continental S.Featherweight Champion. Former Undefeated WBA Inter-Continental S.Featherweight Champion. Former British S.Featherweight Champion. Former Undefeated IBF & WBO Inter-Continental S. Featherweight Champion. Ht. 5'9"
Manager F. Warren

25.11.00   Richmond Asante W RSC 1 Manchester
10.02.01   Eddie Nevins W RSC 1 Widnes
26.03.01   Woody Greenaway W RTD 2 Wembley

28.04.01   Dafydd Carlin W PTS 4 Cardiff
21.07.01   Rakhim Mingaleev W PTS 4 Sheffield
15.09.01   Dimitri Gorodetsky W RSC 1 Manchester
27.10.01   Alexei Slyautchin W RSC 1 Manchester
17.11.01   Laszlo Bognar W RSC 3 Glasgow
19.01.02   Vladimir Borov W RSC 2 Bethnal Green
11.03.02   Dariusz Snarski W RSC 10 Glasgow
(Vacant IBF Inter-Continental S.Featherweight Title)
08.06.02   Nikolai Eremeev W RTD 5 Renfrew
(Vacant WBO Inter-Continental S.Featherweight Title)
17.08.02   Pavel Potipko W CO 1 Cardiff
19.10.02   Steve Conway W CO 4 Renfrew
(Vacant British S. Featherweight Title)
14.12.02   Carl Greaves W RSC 6 Newcastle
(British S.Featherweight Title Defence)
22.03.03   Patrick Malinga W RSC 6 Renfrew
(Vacant WBA Inter-Continental S.Featherweight Title)
12.07.03   Willie Limond W RSC 8 Renfrew
(British S.Featherweight Title Defence)
25.10.03   Michael Gomez L RSC 5 Edinburgh
(British S.Featherweight Title Defence)
27.03.04   Michael Kizza W CO 1 Edinburgh
(Vacant IBF Inter-Continental S.Featherweight Title)

Career: 18 contests, won 17, lost 1.

Alex Arthur   Les Clark

Jamie Arthur

Cwmbran. *Born* Aberdeen, 17 December, 1979
S. Featherweight. Ht. 5'9"
Manager F. Warren/F. Maloney

22.03.03	Daniel Thorpe W PTS 4 Renfrew
28.06.03	James Gorman W PTS 4 Cardiff
13.09.03	Dave Hinds W RTD 1 Newport
11.10.03	Dafydd Carlin W RSC 4 Portsmouth
15.11.03	Andrei Mircea W RSC 3 Bayreuth, Germany
06.12.03	Jus Wallie W PTS 6 Cardiff
27.03.04	Karl Taylor W PTS 6 Edinburgh

Career: 7 contests, won 7.

Jamie Arthur   Les Clark

Darren Ashton

Stoke. *Born* Stoke, 26 February, 1969
Cruiserweight. Former Undefeated
Midlands Area L. Heavyweight &
S. Middleweight Champion. Ht. 6'1"
Manager Self

13.10.93	Tony Colclough W RSC 1 Stoke
08.12.93	Nigel Rafferty W PTS 6 Stoke
23.03.94	L. A. Williams W PTS 6 Stoke
23.05.94	Nigel Rafferty W PTS 6 Walsall
30.11.94	Carlos Christie L PTS 6 Solihull
04.03.95	John Wilson NC 3 Livingston
06.05.95	Dale Nixon W RSC 4 Shepton Mallet
13.05.95	Stefan Wright W PTS 6 Glasgow
11.10.95	Neil Simpson L RSC 3 Solihull
17.11.95	Mark Baker L RSC 1 Bethnal Green
12.01.96	Frederic Alvarez L PTS 6 Copenhagen, Denmark
27.05.96	Harri Hakulinen L PTS 4 Helsinki, Finland
09.07.96	Chris Johnson L RSC 1 Bethnal Green
08.02.97	Paul Bowen L PTS 4 Millwall
04.04.97	Mark Snipe W RSC 2 Brighton
26.06.97	Clinton Woods L PTS 6 Sheffield
02.09.97	Adrian Strachan W PTS 4 Southwark
15.09.97	Darren Dorrington W DIS 2 Bristol
21.11.97	Stuart Fleet W RSC 4 Hull
	(Vacant Midlands Area S. Middleweight Title)
07.02.98	Sven Hamer L RSC 6 Cheshunt
27.03.98	Toks Owoh L RSC 2 Telford

16.05.98	Ali Forbes L PTS 6 Chigwell
23.05.98	Howard Eastman L RSC 4 Bethnal Green
23.09.98	Bobby Banghar L RSC 2 Bloomsbury
13.11.98	Graham Townsend L DIS 6 Brighton
30.11.98	Mervyn Penniston-John L PTS 4 Manchester
19.12.98	Ole Klemetsen L RSC 2 Liverpool
11.02.99	Alex Mason W PTS 10 Dudley
	(Vacant Midlands Area L. Heavyweight Title)
13.03.99	Glenn Williams L PTS 4 Manchester
17.05.99	Tony Booth L PTS 6 Cleethorpes
04.06.99	Lee Osie Manuel L RSC 5 Vigo, Spain
	(Transcontinental L. Heavyweight Title Challenge)
31.07.99	Darren Corbett L RSC 2 Carlisle
09.10.99	Glenn Williams L PTS 6 Manchester
28.10.99	Warren Stowe W PTS 6 Burnley
04.12.99	Mike Gormley L PTS 4 Manchester
21.02.00	Tony Oakey L PTS 4 Southwark
04.03.00	Neil Linford L PTS 6 Peterborough
20.03.00	Brian Magee L RTD 5 Mansfield
29.05.00	Roy Finlay L PTS 4 Manchester
21.10.00	Tony Oakey L PTS 4 Wembley
31.10.00	Konstantin Schvets L RSC 1 Hammersmith
30.11.00	Neil Linford L PTS 4 Peterborough
08.12.00	Delroy Leslie L RTD 3 Crystal Palace
27.01.01	Peter Haymer L PTS 4 Bethnal Green
17.02.01	Faisal Mohammed L RSC 1 Bethnal Green
28.03.01	Michael Pinnock DREW 6 Piccadilly
20.04.01	Tony Griffiths W PTS 4 Millwall
28.04.01	Enzo Maccaranelli L CO 1 Cardiff
27.05.01	Lee Whitehead W RSC 2 Manchester
15.06.01	Garry Delaney L RTD 4 Millwall
	(Vacant British Masters Cruiserweight Title)
13.09.01	Mark Brookes L PTS 4 Sheffield
20.09.01	Tony Strong W PTS 4 Blackfriars
09.10.01	Nathan King L PTS 6 Cardiff
27.10.01	Steven Spartacus L PTS 4 Manchester
19.11.01	Billy McClung L PTS 6 Glasgow
19.01.02	Steven Spartacus L PTS 4 Bethnal Green
10.02.02	Blue Stevens L PTS 4 Southwark
02.03.02	Pinky Burton L PTS 6 Wakefield
18.03.02	Paul Bowen L PTS 6 Crawley
20.04.02	Andrew Facey L PTS 6 Derby
28.04.02	Scott Baker L RSC 6 Southwark
13.06.02	John Killian L PTS 4 Leicester Square
05.10.02	Mark Brookes L PTS 4 Chesterfield
30.10.02	John Killian L PTS 4 Leicester Square
16.11.02	Phill Day DREW 4 Coventry
14.12.02	Michael Thompson L PTS 4 Newcastle
08.01.03	Gareth Hogg L RSC 2 Aberdare
16.02.03	Alan Page L PTS 4 Salford
16.03.03	Carl Wright DREW 6 Nottingham
03.04.03	Jamie Warters L PTS 6 Hull
09.05.03	Ryan Walls L PTS 6 Longford
31.05.03	Courtney Fry L PTS 4 Bethnal Green
01.08.03	Ryan Walls L PTS 4 Bethnal Green
13.09.03	Carl Wright W PTS 4 Coventry
26.10.03	Colin Kenna L CO 1 Longford

Career: 75 contests, won 16, drew 3, lost 55, no contest 1.

Michael Ayers

Tooting. *Born* London, 26 January, 1965
L.Welterweight. Former Undefeated
British, IBO, WBC International &

Southern Area Lightweight Champion.
Ht. 5'8"
Manager Self

16.05.89	Young Joe Rafiu W RSC 5 Wandsworth
27.06.89	Greg Egbuniwe W CO 1 Kensington
15.11.89	Mille Markovic W RSC 2 Lewisham
05.12.89	Darren Mount W RSC 2 Catford
26.04.90	Nick Hall W CO 3 Wandsworth
04.06.91	Stuart Rimmer W CO 1 Bethnal Green
22.06.91	Wayne Weekes W RSC 6 Earls Court
	(Vacant Southern Area Lightweight Title)
21.09.91	Peter Till W RSC 5 Tottenham
	(Elim. British Lightweight Title)
28.01.92	Jorge Pompey W PTS 8 Hamburg, Germany
19.02.92	Rudy Valentino W RSC 7 Muswell Hill
	(Southern Area Lightweight Title Defence. Elim. British Lightweight Title)
27.06.92	Sugar Gibiliru W RSC 6 Quinta do Lago, Portugal
13.10.92	Scott Brouwer W RSC 4 Mayfair
	(Vacant WBC International Lightweight Title)
20.02.93	Danny Myburgh W RSC 5 Earls Court
	(WBC International Lightweight Title Defence)
16.04.93	Giovanni Parisi L PTS 12 Rome, Italy
	(WBO Lightweight Title Challenge)
24.05.94	Karl Taylor DREW 8 Sunderland
30.09.94	John O. Johnson W RSC 3 Bethnal Green
07.11.94	Bamana Dibateza W PTS 6 Bethnal Green
17.02.95	Paul Burke W RSC 6 Crawley
	(Vacant British Lightweight Title)
31.03.95	Karl Taylor W RSC 8 Crystal Palace
	(British Lightweight Title Defence)
23.05.95	Charles Shepherd W RSC 3 Potters Bar
	(British Lightweight Title Defence)
30.09.95	Dave Anderson W RTD 7 Basildon
	(British Lightweight Title Defence)
27.09.96	Tony Swift W RSC 5 Stevenage
20.11.96	Colin Dunne W RSC 9 Wembley
	(British Lightweight Title Defence)
21.03.98	Alan Temple W RSC 2 Bethnal Green
30.05.98	Anthony Maynard L PTS 8 Bristol
06.11.98	Steve Tuckett W RSC 5 Mayfair
03.12.98	Roger Sampson L PTS 6 Mayfair
12.01.99	Jean Gomis W RTD 5 Bethnal Green
12.03.99	Luis Flores W RSC 4 Bethnal Green
	(Vacant IBO Lightweight Title)
25.05.99	Mkhuseli Kondile W CO 3 Mayfair
	(IBO Lightweight Title Defence)
02.10.99	Pablo Sarmiento W RSC 6 Cardiff
	(IBO Lightweight Title Defence)
20.12.99	Tony Miller W RSC 10 Bethnal Green
	(IBO Lightweight Title Defence)
01.07.00	Wayne Rigby W RSC 10 Manchester
	(IBO Lightweight Title Defence)
19.08.00	Mehdi Labdouni W CO 1 Brentwood
	(IBO Lightweight Title Defence)
03.03.01	Wayne Rigby W PTS 12 Wembley
	(IBO Lightweight Title Defence)
10.11.01	Pablo Sarmiento L PTS 12 Wembley
	(IBO L.Welterweight Title Challenge)
26.07.03	Jon Honney L PTS 6 Plymouth

Career: 37 contests, won 31, drew 1, lost 5.

B

David Bailey

Pimlico. *Born* London, 23 August, 1980
S. Featherweight. Ht. 5'5"
Manager A. Urry

07.05.04 Dean Ward W PTS 6 Bethnal Green
25.06.04 Mickey Coveney L PTS 4 Bethnal
Green
Career: 2 contests, won 1, lost 1.

David Bailey   Les Clark

Martyn Bailey

Wrexham. *Born* Wrexham, 16 January,
1976
British Masters Middleweight Champion.
Ht. 5'8"
Manager Self

07.10.99 John Marsden W PTS 6 Sunderland
27.11.99 Lee Molloy L RSC 2 Liverpool
18.02.00 Donovan Davey W PTS 6 Pentre
Halkyn
06.03.00 Richard Inquieti L RSC 5 Bradford
05.05.00 Richard Inquieti W PTS 6 Pentre
Halkyn
22.09.00 David Smales W RSC 3 Wrexham
28.11.00 Paul Martin W PTS 6 Brierley Hill
04.02.01 Pedro Thompson W PTS 6 Queensferry
08.04.01 Peter Dunn W PTS 6 Wrexham
10.06.01 Robert Burton DREW 6 Ellesmere Port
08.10.01 Reagan Denton L PTS 4 Barnsley
21.10.01 Wayne Shepherd W PTS 6 Pentre
Halkyn
16.11.01 Robert Burton DREW 4 Preston
08.03.02 Danny Moir W PTS 6 Ellesmere Port
29.04.02 Paul Lomax DREW 6 Bradford
01.11.02 Tony Byrne W PTS 6 Preston
02.12.02 Lee Murtagh W RSC 6 Leeds
(*British Masters Middleweight Title
Challenge*)
07.05.03 Paul Lomax W RTD 3 Ellesmere Port
(*British Masters Middleweight Title
Defence*)
05.12.03 Darren Dorrington W RSC 6 Bristol
(*British Masters Middleweight Title
Defence*)
Career: 19 contests, won 13, drew 3, lost 3.

Colin Bain

Glasgow. *Born* Hawick, 10 August, 1978
Lightweight. Ht. 5'8"
Manager K. Morrison

14.03.03 Dafydd Carlin W PTS 6 Glasgow
16.05.03 Martin Hardcastle W PTS 6 Glasgow
12.07.03 Gareth Wiltshaw W PTS 4 Renfrew
25.10.03 Dave Hinds W PTS 4 Edinburgh
27.03.04 Dave Hinds W PTS 4 Edinburgh
23.04.04 Pete Buckley W PTS 6 Glasgow
19.06.04 Henry Jones W PTS 4 Renfrew
Career: 7 contests, won 7.

Carl Baker

Sheffield. *Born* Sheffield, 3 January, 1982
Heavyweight. Ht. 6'4"
Manager J. Ingle

06.09.03 Dave Clarke W RSC 1 Aberdeen
15.09.03 Billy Wilson W RSC 2 Leeds
28.11.03 Slick Miller W CO 1 Hull
03.04.04 Paul King L PTS 6 Sheffield
Career: 4 contests, won 3, lost 1.

Scott Baker

Walthamstow. *Born* Londonderry, 29
August, 1977
Cruiserweight. Ht. 6'2"
Manager Self

22.06.99 Adam Cale W PTS 4 Ipswich
13.09.99 Georgie Stevens L PTS 4 Bethnal
Green
01.10.99 Jason Brewster W RTD 5 Cleethorpes
16.06.00 Adam Cale W PTS 4 Bloomsbury
08.09.00 Mark Dawson L RSC 3 Hammersmith
03.02.01 Slick Miller L RSC 4 Brighton
16.12.01 Jimmy Steel W PTS 4 Southwark
28.04.02 Darren Ashton W RSC 6 Southwark
03.06.03 Marcus Lee L RSC 3 Bethnal Green
01.05.04 Shpetim Hoti L PTS 4 Gravesend
Career: 10 contests, won 5, lost 5.

Vince Baldassara

Clydebank. *Born* Clydebank, 6 November,
1978
L. Middleweight. Ht. 5'11"
Manager B. Winter

14.03.03 George Telfer L PTS 4 Glasgow
28.02.04 Rob MacDonald W PTS 6 Manchester
Career: 2 contests, won 1, lost 1.

Ted Bami (Minsende)

Brixton. *Born* Zaire, 2 March, 1978
L.Welterweight. Former WBF L.
Welterweight Champion. Ht. 5'7"
Manager B. Hearn

26.09.98 Des Sowden W RSC 1 Southwark
11.02.99 Gary Reid W RSC 2 Dudley
10.03.00 David Kehoe W PTS 4 Bethnal Green
08.09.00 Jacek Bielski L RSC 4 Hammersmith
29.03.01 Keith Jones W PTS 4 Hammersmith
05.05.01 Francis Barrett W PTS 6 Edmonton
31.07.01 Lance Crosby W PTS 6 Bethnal Green
19.03.02 Michael Smyth W CO 4 Slough
23.06.02 Keith Jones W RSC 4 Southwark
17.08.02 Bradley Pryce W RSC 6 Cardiff

Colin Bain (continued)

26.10.02 Adam Zadworny W PTS 4 Maesteg
07.12.02 Sergei Starkov W PTS 4 Brentwood
08.03.03 Andrei Devyataykin W RSC 1 Bethnal
Green
12.04.03 Laszlo Herczeg W RSC 9 Bethnal
Green
(*Vacant WBF L.Welterweight Title*)
26.07.03 Samuel Malinga L RSC 3 Plymouth
(*WBF L.Welterweight Title Defence*)
09.10.03 Zoltan Surman W RSC 3 Bristol
31.01.04 Jozsef Matolcsi W PTS 6 Bethnal
Green
08.05.04 Viktor Baranov W RSC 2 Dagenham
Career: 18 contests, won 16, lost 2.

(Ratesh) Bobby Banghar

Bedford. *Born* Bedford, 30 June, 1977
L. Middleweight. Ht. 5'10¾"
Manager Self

02.01.97 Mark Dawson W PTS 4 Swansea
27.01.98 Neville Smith DREW 4 Piccadilly
06.02.98 Carl Nicholson W RSC 3 Wakefield
26.03.98 Robert Peel W PTS 4 Piccadilly
30.04.98 Michael Pinnock W PTS 6 Purfleet
14.06.98 Paul Carr W PTS 6 Golders Green
23.09.98 Darren Ashton W RSC 2 Bloomsbury
21.11.98 Errol McDonald L CO 6 Southwark
26.02.99 Graham Townsend L PTS 6 Bethnal
Green
20.05.99 Matthew Barney L RSC 5 Kensington
(*Vacant British Masters
S. Middleweight Title*)
30.09.00 Leigh Wicks W PTS 4 Peterborough
24.03.01 Ernie Smith W PTS 4 Chigwell
16.06.01 Ernie Smith W PTS 4 Dagenham
22.07.03 Karim Hussine W PTS 6 Bethnal Green
29.10.03 Joel Ani W PTS 4 Leicester Square
26.02.04 Thomas McDonagh L CO 2 Widnes
(*WBU Inter-Continental
L.Middleweight Title Challenge*)
Career: 16 contests, won 11, drew 1, lost 4.

David Barnes (Smith)

Manchester. *Born* Manchester, 16 January,
1981
British Welterweight Champion. Ht. 5'8½"
Manager F. Warren/B. Hughes

07.07.01 Trevor Smith W RSC 2 Manchester
15.09.01 Karl Taylor W PTS 4 Manchester
27.10.01 Mark Sawyers W RSC 2 Manchester
15.12.01 James Paisley W RTD 2 Wembley
09.02.02 David Kirk W RTD 1 Manchester
04.05.02 David Baptiste W CO 3 Bethnal Green
01.06.02 Dimitri Protkunas W RSC 1
Manchester
28.09.02 Sergei Starkov W PTS 6 Manchester
12.10.02 Rusian Ashirov W PTS 6 Bethnal
Green
14.12.02 Rozalin Nasibulin W RSC 3 Newcastle
18.01.03 Brice Faradji W PTS 6 Preston
05.04.03 Viktor Fesetchko W PTS 8 Manchester
17.07.03 Jimmy Vincent W PTS 12 Dagenham
(*Vacant British Welterweight Title*)
13.12.03 Kevin McIntyre W RTD 8 Manchester
(*British Welterweight Title Defence*)
03.04.04 Glenn McClarnon W PTS 12
Manchester
(*British Welterweight Title Defence*)
Career: 15 contests, won 15.

David Barnes   Les Clark

Matthew Barney

Southampton. *Born* Fareham, 25 June, 1974
WBU L.Heavyweight Champion. Former
Undefeated British, IBO Inter-Continental,
Southern Area & British Masters
S.Middleweight Champion. Ht. 5'10³/₄"
Manager Self

04.06.98	Adam Cale W PTS 6 Barking
23.07.98	Adam Cale W PTS 6 Barking
02.10.98	Dennis Doyley W PTS 4 Cheshunt
22.10.98	Kevin Burton W PTS 6 Barking
07.12.98	Freddie Yemofio W PTS 4 Acton
17.03.99	Simon Andrews W RTD 4 Kensington
09.05.99	Gareth Hogg W PTS 4 Bracknell
20.05.99	Bobby Banghar W RSC 5 Kensington
	(British Masters S. Middleweight Final)
05.06.99	Paul Bowen DREW 10 Cardiff
	(Southern Area S. Middleweight Title Challenge)
20.08.99	Adam Cale W PTS 4 Bloomsbury
05.10.99	Delroy Leslie L PTS 10 Bloomsbury
	(Vacant Southern Area Middleweight Title)
15.04.00	Mark Dawson W PTS 6 Bethnal Green
06.05.00	Jason Hart W PTS 10 Southwark
	(Vacant Southern Area S. Middleweight Title)
30.09.00	Neil Linford L PTS 10 Peterborough
	(Elim. British S. Middleweight Title)
02.02.01	Darren Covill W PTS 6 Portsmouth
16.03.01	Matt Mowatt W RSC 1 Portsmouth
	(British Masters S. Middleweight Title Defence)
14.07.01	Robert Milewics W PTS 8 Wembley
20.10.01	Jon Penn W RSC 4 Portsmouth
26.01.02	Hussain Osman L RTD 9 Dagenham
	(Vacant IBO Inter-Continental S.Middleweight Title. Southern Area S.Middleweight Title Defence)
08.04.02	Hussain Osman W PTS 12 Southampton
	(IBO Inter-Continental & Southern Area S. Middleweight Title Challenges)
22.09.02	Paul Owen W CO 7 Southwark
	(Vacant British Masters S.Middleweight Title)
20.10.02	Chris Nembhard W PTS 10 Southwark
	(Southern Area S. Middleweight Title Defence)
29.03.03	Dean Francis W PTS 12 Wembley
	(Vacant British S.Middleweight Title)
01.08.03	Charles Adamu L PTS 12 Bethnal Green
	(Vacant Commonwealth S.Middleweight Title)
11.10.03	Tony Oakey W PTS 12 Portsmouth
	(WBU L.Heavyweight Title Challenge)

Career: 25 contests, won 20, drew 1, lost 4.

Matthew Barr

Walton. *Born* Kingston, 22 May, 1977
Middleweight. Ht. 5'11"
Manager Self

02.12.97	Keith Palmer L RSC 3 Windsor
23.02.98	Martin Cavey W RSC 1 Windsor
14.05.98	Gerard Lawrence L RSC 1 Acton
29.10.98	Sonny Thind W RSC 2 Bayswater

20.05.99	Paul Knights L RSC 1 Barking
31.10.99	Allan Gray W PTS 4 Raynes Park
25.02.00	John Humphrey W RSC 1 Newmarket
06.05.00	Ernie Smith W PTS 4 Southwark
22.10.00	Ernie Smith W PTS 4 Streatham
23.11.00	Harry Butler W PTS 4 Bayswater
23.11.01	John Humphrey L RSC 2 Bethnal Green
13.09.02	Brian Knudsen W PTS 6 Randers, Denmark
29.03.03	Lee Hodgson W RSC 1 Wembley
29.10.03	Jimi Hendricks W RSC 4 Leicester Square
27.11.03	Leigh Wicks W PTS 4 Longford

Career: 15 contests, won 11, lost 4.

Coleman Barrett

Wembley. *Born* Galway, 10 November, 1982
Cruiserweight. Ht. 6'1"
Manager R. McCracken

11.12.03	Marcus Lee W PTS 4 Bethnal Green
12.03.04	Dave Clarke W PTS 6 Nottingham
02.06.04	Terry Morrill W PTS 4 Nottingham

Career: 3 contests, won 3.

Coleman Barrett   Les Clark

Francis Barrett

Wembley. *Born* Galway, 7 February, 1977
European Union & Southern Area
L.Welterweight Champion. Ht. 5'7"
Manager Self

12.08.00	Mohamed Helel W PTS 4 Wembley
23.09.00	Trevor Smith W RSC 1 Bethnal Green
21.10.00	Keith Jones W PTS 4 Wembley
24.02.01	David White W PTS 4 Bethnal Green
10.03.01	Karl Taylor W RSC 3 Bethnal Green
26.03.01	Tony Montana W PTS 4 Wembley
05.05.01	Ted Bami L PTS 6 Edmonton
22.09.01	Gary Reid W PTS 4 Bethnal Green
19.01.02	Dafydd Carlin W PTS 4 Bethnal Green
25.05.02	David Kirk W PTS 6 Portsmouth
25.10.02	Darren Covill W PTS 4 Bethnal Green
21.12.02	Keith Jones W PTS 6 Dagenham
05.03.03	Jon Honney W PTS 10 Bethnal Green
	(Vacant Southern Area L.Welterweight Title)
27.05.03	Silence Saheed L RSC 1 Dagenham

04.10.03 David Kirk W PTS 6 Muswell Hill
11.12.03 Oscar Hall W PTS 10 Bethnal Green
02.06.04 Gavin Down W PTS 10 Nottingham
*(Vacant European Union
L.Welterweight Title)*
Career: 17 contests, won 15, lost 2.

Francis Barrett   Les Clark

Ryan Barrett
Thamesmead. *Born* London, 27 December,
1982
Lightweight. Ht. 5'10"
Manager M. Roe

13.06.02 Gareth Wiltshaw W PTS 4 Leicester
Square
06.09.02 Jason Gonzales W PTS 4 Bethnal
Green
12.12.02 Martin Turner W RSC 1 Leicester
Square
08.03.03 David Vaughan DREW 4 Bethnal
Green
04.10.03 Dafydd Carlin L PTS 4 Belfast
01.05.04 Marty Kayes W RSC 2 Gravesend
19.06.04 Kristian Laight W PTS 4 Muswell Hill
Career: 7 contests, won 5, drew 1, lost 1.

(Alex) Sandy Bartlett
Inverness. *Born* Dingwall, 20 April, 1976
S. Bantamweight. Ht. 5'7"
Manager T. Gilmour

15.03.04 Marty Kayes W PTS 6 Glasgow
19.04.04 Abdul Mougharbel L PTS 6 Glasgow
Career: 2 contests, won 1, lost 1.

(Shinebayer) Shinny Bayaar
(Sukhbaatar)
Carlisle. *Born* Mongolia, 27 August, 1977
Flyweight. Ht. 5'0"
Manager J. Doughty

10.10.01 Damien Dunnion L PTS 8 Stoke
09.12.01 Delroy Spencer W PTS 4 Shaw
17.11.02 Anthony Hanna W PTS 6 Shaw

20.03.03 Sunkanmi Ogunbiyi L PTS 4
Queensway
08.06.03 Darren Cleary W RSC 2 Shaw
19.10.03 Delroy Spencer W PTS 6 Shaw
21.02.04 Reidar Walstad W RSC 1 Cardiff
Career: 7 contests, won 5, lost 2.

Gary Beardsley
Belper. *Born* Belper, 18 July, 1968
Middleweight. Former Undefeated British
Masters L.Middleweight Champion.
Former Undefeated British Masters
Middleweight Champion. Ht. 5'10"
Manager Self

09.02.95 Shaun Stokes W RSC 3 Doncaster
01.03.95 Eddie Haley W RSC 1 Glasgow
06.03.95 Stefan Scriggins L PTS 6 Leicester
15.03.95 Jamie Gallagher W PTS 6 Stoke
20.10.95 Dewi Roberts W PTS 6 Mansfield
22.11.95 Richard Swallow DREW 6 Sheffield
06.12.95 John Smith W PTS 8 Stoke
06.02.96 Georgie Smith L RSC 1 Basildon
22.03.96 Mark Legg W PTS 6 Mansfield
09.12.96 Derek Roche L RSC 2 Bradford
16.01.97 Steve Levene L PTS 6 Solihull
29.01.97 Howard Clarke L PTS 6 Stoke
20.11.99 William Webster W PTS 6 Grantham
18.01.00 Mike Duffield W RTD 2 Mansfield
09.04.00 Matt Mowatt W PTS 6 Alfreton
01.07.00 Wayne Pinder L PTS 4 Manchester
19.11.00 Matt Mowatt W PTS 10 Chesterfield
*(Vacant British Masters Middleweight
Title)*
08.12.00 Cornelius Carr L PTS 4 Crystal Palace
25.02.01 William Webster W PTS 6 Derby
30.11.02 Michael Monaghan L PTS 6 Newark
28.01.03 Matthew Thirlwall W PTS 6
Nottingham
05.03.03 Howard Eastman L RSC 2 Bethnal
Green
16.04.03 Matthew Thirlwall L PTS 6
Nottingham
31.05.03 Hussain Osman L RSC 5 Bethnal
Green
26.09.03 Geard Ajetovic L RSC 3 Reading
01.12.03 Lee Murtagh W RSC 6 Leeds
*(British Masters L.Middleweight Title
Challenge)*
Career: 26 contests, won 13, drew 1, lost 12.

Lee Beavis
Northolt. *Born* Isleworth, 9 April, 1982
L.Welterweight. Ht. 5'8"
Manager F. Warren/F. Maloney

11.10.03 James Gorman W PTS 4 Portsmouth
06.11.03 Daniel Thorpe W PTS 4 Dagenham
01.04.04 James Gorman W RTD 2 Bethnal
Green
24.04.04 Anthony Hanna W PTS 4 Reading
13.05.04 Pete Buckley W PTS 4 Bethnal Green
Career: 5 contests, won 5.

Jimmy Beech
Walsall. *Born* Walsall, 19 January, 1979
Lightweight. Ht. 5'7"
Manager Self

23.06.99 Ike Halls W RTD 2 West Bromwich
03.09.99 Tom Wood W PTS 6 West Bromwich
07.04.00 Willie Limond L RSC 2 Glasgow

28.01.01 Lenny Hodgkins W PTS 6
Wolverhampton
16.11.01 Pete Buckley W PTS 6 West
Bromwich
23.11.01 Henry Castle L PTS 4 Bethnal Green
07.02.02 Dave Cotterill W PTS 6 Stoke
25.02.02 Mickey Bowden W PTS 4 Slough
09.03.02 Tony Mulholland L PTS 6 Manchester
05.05.02 James Rooney W RSC 5 Hartlepool
25.05.02 Henry Castle L PTS 4 Portsmouth
07.09.02 Ricky Eccleston W RSC 3 Liverpool
28.09.02 Michael Gomez L RSC 4 Manchester
14.12.02 Gavin Rees L PTS 4 Newcastle
22.03.03 Willie Limond L CO 4 Renfrew
28.04.03 Tony McPake L PTS 6 Nottingham
27.05.03 Billy Corcoran W PTS 6 Dagenham
26.09.03 Jimmy Beech L RTD 2 Reading
14.11.03 Scott Lawton L RSC 5 Bethnal Green
24.01.04 Steve Murray L RSC 4 Wembley
Career: 20 contests, won 9, lost 11.

Jimmy Beech   Les Clark

Steve Bell
Manchester. *Born* Manchester, 11 June,
1975
S. Featherweight. Ht. 5'10"
Manager F. Warren/T. Jones

08.05.03 Jus Wallie DREW 4 Widnes
27.09.03 Jaz Virdee W RSC 1 Manchester
13.12.03 Fred Janes W PTS 4 Manchester
03.04.04 Pete Buckley W PTS 4 Manchester
22.05.04 Haider Ali W PTS 6 Widnes
Career: 5 contests, won 4, drew 1.

Steven Bendall
Coventry. *Born* Coventry, 1 December,
1973
IBO Inter-Continental Middleweight
Champion. Former Undefeated WBU Inter-
Continental Middleweight Champion.
Ht. 6'0"
Manager Self

15.05.97 Dennis Doyley W RSC 2 Reading
13.09.97 Gary Reyniers W PTS 4 Millwall
27.02.99 Israel Khumalo W PTS 4 Oldham

02.07.99 Darren Covill W RTD 3 Bristol
24.09.99 Sean Pritchard W PTS 6 Merthyr
03.12.99 Ian Toby W PTS 6 Peterborough
07.04.00 Des Sowden W RSC 3 Bristol
02.06.00 Simon Andrews W RSC 5 Ashford
08.09.00 Jason Barker W PTS 6 Bristol
03.11.00 Eddie Haley W RSC 1 Ebbw Vale
01.12.00 Peter Mitchell W PTS 8 Peterborough
22.08.01 Bert Bado W RSC 1 Hammanskraal, South Africa
29.09.01 Alan Gilbert W RTD 3 Southwark
08.12.01 Jason Collins W PTS 12 Dagenham
(Vacant WBU Inter-Continental Middleweight Title)
02.03.02 Ahmet Dottouev W RTD 4 Brakpan, South Africa
(WBU Inter-Continental Middleweight Title Defence)
26.04.02 Viktor Fesetchko W RSC 10 Coventry
(Vacant IBO Inter-Continental Middleweight Title)
13.07.02 Phillip Bystrikov W RSC 5 Coventry
06.09.02 Tomas da Silva W RSC 8 Bethnal Green
24.01.03 Lee Blundell W RSC 2 Sheffield
(IBO Inter-Continental Middleweight Title Defence)

26.04.03 Mike Algoet W PTS 12 Brentford
(IBO Inter-Continental Middleweight Title Defence)
14.11.03 Kreshnik Qato W PTS 8 Bethnal Green
Career: 21 contests, won 21.

Kevin Bennett

Hartlepool. *Born* Birmingham, 15 August, 1975
Lightweight. Former Undefeated Commonwealth Lightweight Champion.
Ht. 5'7"
Manager M. Marsden

01.12.99 Karim Bouali W PTS 4 Yarm
28.03.00 Les Frost W RSC 2 Hartlepool
25.06.00 Steve Hanley W PTS 6 Wakefield
23.07.00 Gary Reid W RSC 4 Hartlepool
28.10.00 Gary Harrison W RTD 2 Coventry
27.11.00 Keith Jones W PTS 4 Birmingham
23.01.01 Tommy Peacock W RSC 5 Crawley
03.03.01 Iain Eldridge W PTS 6 Wembley
08.05.01 Keith Jones W PTS 6 Barnsley
04.06.01 Gary Ryder L RSC 6 Hartlepool
20.10.01 Paul Denton W PTS 4 Portsmouth
03.11.01 Mark Ramsey W PTS 6 Glasgow
26.01.02 Glenn McClarnon L PTS 8 Dagenham

18.05.02 Colin Lynes L RSC 4 Millwall
21.03.03 Keith Jones W PTS 4 West Bromwich
21.06.03 Zoltan Surman W RSC 4 Manchester
05.07.03 Colin Dunne W RSC 2 Brentwood
08.11.03 Michael Muya W PTS 12 Bridgend
(Commonwealth Lightweight Title Challenge)
01.05.04 Jason Cook L PTS 12 Bridgend
(IBO Lightweight Title Challenge)
Career: 19 contests, won 15, lost 4.

Danny Berwick

Kettering. *Born* Market Harborough, 4 November, 1974
Cruiserweight. Ht. 5'11"
Manager J. Weaver

13.09.03 Stewart West L RSC 3 Coventry
Career: 1 contest, lost 1.

Jim Betts

Scunthorpe. *Born* Tickhill, 6 October, 1977
Lightweight. Former Undefeated British Masters Flyweight Champion. Ht. 5'6½"
Manager M. Marsden

26.03.98 Des Gargano W PTS 6 Scunthorpe
13.05.98 David Jeffrey W RSC 3 Scunthorpe
05.06.98 Chris Price W PTS 6 Hull
11.09.98 Marty Chestnut W PTS 6 Newark
16.10.98 Marty Chestnut W PTS 6 Salford
28.11.98 Ola Dali W PTS 4 Sheffield
17.05.99 Dave Travers W RTD 4 Cleethorpes
17.07.99 Ross Cassidy W RSC 1 Doncaster
27.09.99 Graham McGrath W PTS 6 Cleethorpes
19.02.00 Chris Price W PTS 6 Newark
19.06.00 Chris Price W PTS 4 Burton
30.08.00 David Coldwell W RSC 2 Scunthorpe
(Vacant British Masters Flyweight Title. Elim. British Flyweight Title)
26.02.01 Chris Emanuele L PTS 6 Nottingham
08.05.01 Sean Grant W RSC 3 Barnsley
11.06.01 Daniel Ring W PTS 6 Nottingham
15.09.01 Nicky Booth L RSC 7 Nottingham
(British & Commonwealth Bantamweight Title Challenges)
18.03.02 Ian Turner W RTD 4 Crawley
18.05.02 Gareth Payne W PTS 6 Millwall
27.07.02 Colin Moffett W RSC 3 Nottingham
27.04.04 Jason Nesbitt W PTS 6 Leeds
Career: 20 contests, won 18, lost 2.

Paul Billington

Warrington. *Born* Billinge, 1 March, 1972
L. Heavyweight. Ht. 5'10"
Manager T. Miller

14.09.02 Michael Monaghan L RSC 4 Newark
29.05.03 Karl Wheeler L PTS 6 Sunderland
21.09.03 Shane White DREW 6 Bristol
12.10.03 Danny Grainger L PTS 6 Sheffield
01.12.03 Mark Flatt W RSC 2 Bradford
21.12.03 Shane White L RSC 2 Bristol
22.04.04 Steve McGuire L RTD 3 Glasgow
Career: 7 contests, won 1, drew 1, lost 5.

Wayne Bloy

Grimsby. *Born* Grimsby, 30 November, 1982
Bantamweight. Ht. 5'5"
Manager S. Fleet

14.06.04 Neil Read DREW 6 Cleethorpes
Career: 1 contest, drew 1.

Kevin Bennett   Les Clark

(Aivaras) Ivor Bonavic (Urbonavicius)

Canning Town. *Born* Jonava, Russia, 22 April, 1982
Welterweight. Ht. 5'8"
Manager J. Bowers

12.03.04 Chris Long L PTS 6 Millwall
08.05.04 Arek Malek L PTS 4 Dagenham
05.06.04 Gary Woolcombe L PTS 4 Bethnal Green

Career: 3 contests, lost 3.

Paul Bonson

Featherstone. *Born* Castleford, 18 October, 1971
Cruiserweight. Former Central Area L. Heavyweight Champion. Ht. 5'10"
Manager Self

04.10.96 Michael Pinnock W PTS 6 Wakefield
14.11.96 Michael Pinnock DREW 6 Sheffield
22.12.96 Pele Lawrence DREW 6 Salford
20.04.97 Shamus Casey W PTS 6 Leeds
26.06.97 Andy Manning L PTS 6 Sheffield
19.09.97 Mike Gormley W PTS 6 Salford
03.10.97 Rudi Marcussen L PTS 4 Copenhagen, Denmark
03.12.97 Alex Mason DREW 6 Stoke
14.12.97 Willie Quinn L RSC 4 Glasgow
15.01.98 Alex Mason L PTS 6 Solihull
13.02.98 Peter Mason L PTS 4 Seaham
23.02.98 Martin McDonough W PTS 6 Windsor
07.03.98 Michael Bowen L PTS 6 Reading
14.03.98 Alain Simon L PTS 6 Pont St Maxence, France
08.04.98 Tim Brown DREW 4 Liverpool
21.05.98 Mark Hobson L PTS 6 Bradford
21.06.98 Kenny Rainford L PTS 6 Liverpool
01.09.98 Roberto Dominguez L PTS 8 Vigo, Spain
23.10.98 Rob Galloway W PTS 6 Wakefield
16.11.98 Chris P. Bacon L PTS 8 Glasgow
11.12.98 Robert Zlotkowski L PTS 4 Prestwick
20.12.98 Glenn Williams L PTS 6 Salford
24.04.99 Kenny Gayle DREW 4 Peterborough
29.05.99 Dave Johnson L PTS 6 South Shields
19.06.99 Sebastiaan Rothmann L PTS 8 Dublin
12.07.99 Jim Twite L PTS 4 Coventry
07.08.99 Juan Perez Nelongo L PTS 8 Arona, Tenerife
11.09.99 Mark Hobson L PTS 4 Sheffield
02.10.99 Enzo Maccarinelli L PTS 4 Cardiff
16.10.99 Robert Zlotkowski L PTS 6 Bethnal Green
27.10.99 Peter McCormack W PTS 6 Birmingham
04.12.99 Glenn Williams W PTS 4 Manchester
11.12.99 Chris Davies L PTS 4 Merthyr
05.02.00 Paul Maskell L PTS 4 Bethnal Green
11.03.00 Tony Dodson L PTS 4 Kensington
26.03.00 Wayne Buck L PTS 8 Nottingham
29.04.00 Cathal O'Grady L PTS 4 Wembley
13.05.00 Mark Hobson L PTS 4 Barnsley
25.06.00 Andy Manning W PTS 10 Wakefield
(Vacant Central L. Heavyweight Title)
08.09.00 Robert Milewicz L PTS 4 Hammersmith
21.10.00 Jon Penn L PTS 6 Sheffield
12.11.00 Glenn Williams L PTS 10 Manchester
(Central Area L.Heavyweight Title Defence)
24.11.00 Alex Mason L PTS 6 Darlington

09.12.00 Mark Baker L PTS 6 Southwark
23.01.01 Calvin Stonestreet W PTS 4 Crawley
03.02.01 Tony Dodson L PTS 4 Manchester
18.02.01 Butch Lesley L PTS 6 Southwark
13.03.01 Konstantin Schvets L PTS 6 Plymouth
07.04.01 Rob Hayes-Scott L PTS 4 Wembley
26.04.01 Mike White L PTS 6 Gateshead
17.05.01 Clint Johnson W PTS 6 Leeds
24.05.01 Sven Hamer L PTS 4 Kensington
04.06.01 Joe Gillon DREW 6 Glasgow
11.06.01 Darren Chubbs L PTS 4 Nottingham
21.06.01 Michael Pinnock W PTS 6 Sheffield
27.07.01 Clinton Woods L PTS 6 Sheffield
09.09.01 Eamonn Glennon W PTS 6 Hartlepool
28.09.01 Elvis Michailenko L PTS 6 Millwall
13.11.01 Tony Moran W PTS 6 Leeds
23.11.01 Elvis Michailenko L PTS 6 Bethnal Green

06.12.01 Shaun Bowes W RSC 5 Sunderland
16.12.01 Tommy Eastwood L PTS 4 Southwark
26.01.02 Dominic Negus L PTS 4 Bethnal Green
10.02.02 Butch Lesley L PTS 4 Southwark
25.02.02 Roman Greenberg L PTS 6 Slough
15.03.02 Michael Thompson L PTS 6 Spennymoor
22.03.02 Mark Smallwood L PTS 6 Coventry
19.04.02 Michael Thompson L PTS 6 Darlington
11.05.02 Mark Brookes L PTS 4 Chesterfield
15.06.02 Peter Haymer L PTS 4 Tottenham
23.06.02 Scott Lansdowne W PTS 4 Southwark
13.07.02 Jason Brewster W PTS 6 Wolverhampton
27.07.02 Albert Sosnowski L PTS 4 Nottingham
08.09.02 Varuzhan Davtyan L PTS 4 Wolverhampton
22.09.02 Neil Linford L PTS 6 Southwark

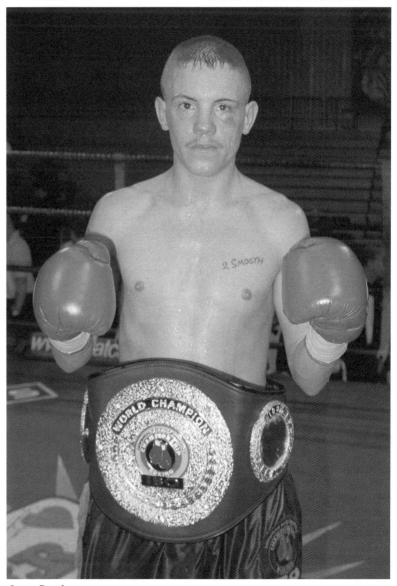

Jason Booth   Les Clark

85

29.09.02 Tony Dowling L PTS 6 Shrewsbury
12.10.02 Andrew Lowe L PTS 4 Bethnal Green
25.10.02 Carl Froch L PTS 6 Bethnal Green
30.11.02 Robert Norton L PTS 6 Coventry
14.12.02 Nathan King W PTS 4 Newcastle
18.01.03 Enzo Maccarinelli L PTS 4 Preston
08.02.03 Steven Spartacus L PTS 6 Norwich
05.03.03 Marcus Lee W PTS 4 Bethnal Green
18.03.03 Mark Krence L PTS 4 Reading
28.03.03 Eric Teymour L PTS 6 Millwall
19.04.03 Tony Moran L PTS 4 Liverpool
12.05.03 Colin Kenna L PTS 6 Southampton
10.06.03 Lee Swaby L PTS 4 Sheffield
26.09.03 Garry Delaney L PTS 6 Reading
06.10.03 Pinky Burton L PTS 6 Barnsley
07.11.03 Carl Thompson L PTS 6 Sheffield
14.11.03 Tony Booth L PTS 6 Hull
01.12.03 David Ingleby W PTS 6 Leeds
20.02.04 Colin Kenna L PTS 6 Southampton
13.03.04 Neil Dawson L PTS 4 Huddersfield
16.04.04 John Keeton L PTS 4 Bradford
01.05.04 Carl Wright L PTS 6 Coventry
Career: 97 contests, won 19, drew 6, lost 72.

Jason Booth

Nottingham. *Born* Nottingham, 7 November, 1977
IBO S.Flyweight Champion. Former Undefeated British Flyweight Champion. Former Undefeated Commonwealth Flyweight Champion. Ht. 5'4"
Manager M. Shinfield

13.06.96 Darren Noble W RSC 3 Sheffield
24.10.96 Marty Chestnut W PTS 6 Lincoln
27.11.96 Jason Thomas W PTS 4 Swansea
18.01.97 David Coldwell W PTS 4 Swadlincote
07.03.97 Pete Buckley W PTS 6 Northampton
20.03.97 Danny Lawson W RSC 3 Newark
10.05.97 Anthony Hanna W PTS 6 Nottingham
19.05.97 Chris Lyons W PTS 6 Cleethorpes
31.10.97 Mark Reynolds W PTS 6 Ilkeston
31.01.98 Anthony Hanna W PTS 6 Edmonton
20.03.98 Louis Veitch W CO 2 Ilkeston
　　　　　(Elim. British Flyweight Title)
09.06.98 Dimitar Alipiev W RSC 2 Hull
17.10.98 Graham McGrath W RSC 4 Manchester
07.12.98 Louis Veitch W RSC 5 Cleethorpes
08.05.99 David Guerault L PTS 12 Grande Synthe, France
　　　　　(European Flyweight Title Challenge)
12.07.99 Mark Reynolds W RSC 3 Coventry
16.10.99 Keith Knox W RSC 10 Belfast
　　　　　(British & Commonwealth Flyweight Title Challenges)
22.01.00 Abie Mnisi W PTS 12 Birmingham
　　　　　(Commonwealth Flyweight Title Defence)
01.07.00 John Barnes W PTS 6 Manchester
13.11.00 Ian Napa W PTS 12 Bethnal Green
　　　　　(British & Commonwealth Flyweight Title Defences)
26.02.01 Nokuthula Tshabangu W CO 2 Nottingham
　　　　　(Commonwealth Flyweight Title Defence)
30.06.01 Alexander Mahmutov L PTS 12 Madrid, Spain
　　　　　(European Flyweight Title Challenge)
23.02.02 Jason Thomas W PTS 6 Nottingham

01.06.02 Mimoun Chent L TD 8 Le Havre, France
　　　　　(Vacant European Flyweight Title)
16.11.02 Kakhar Sabitov W RSC 6 Nottingham
28.04.03 Lindi Memani W PTS 8 Nottingham
20.09.03 Lunga Ntontela W PTS 12 Nottingham
　　　　　(IBO S.Flyweight Title Challenge)
13.03.04 Dale Robinson W PTS 12 Huddersfield
　　　　　(IBO S.Flyweight Title Defence)
Career: 28 contests, won 25, lost 3.

Nicky Booth

Nottingham. *Born* Nottingham, 21 January, 1980
Former Undefeated British Bantamweight Champion. Former Commonwealth Bantamweight Champion. Ht. 5'5"
Manager Self

26.02.98 Shane Mallon W RSC 4 Hull
15.05.98 Marty Chestnut W PTS 6 Nottingham
14.07.98 Ian Napa L PTS 6 Reading
11.09.98 Anthony Hanna DREW 6 Cleethorpes
25.11.98 Anthony Hanna L PTS 6 Clydach
30.04.99 Delroy Spencer W PTS 6 Scunthorpe
06.06.99 Delroy Spencer W PTS 4 Nottingham
20.09.99 Russell Laing W PTS 8 Glasgow
03.12.99 David Jeffrey W PTS 4 Peterborough
03.03.00 Shaun Anderson W PTS 6 Irvine
22.05.00 Gareth Payne W PTS 4 Coventry
24.09.00 Gary Ford W PTS 6 Shaw
09.10.00 Tommy Waite W PTS 12 Liverpool
　　　　　(British & Commonwealth Bantamweight Title Challenges)
26.02.01 Ady Lewis W RSC 7 Nottingham
　　　　　(British & Commonwealth Bantamweight Title Defences)
11.06.01 Kevin Gerowski W RSC 4 Nottingham
14.07.01 Jose Sanjuanelo L RSC 9 Wembley
　　　　　(Vacant IBO Bantamweight Title)
15.09.01 Jim Betts W RSC 7 Nottingham
　　　　　(British & Commonwealth Bantamweight Title Defences)
23.02.02 Stephen Oates W RSC 7 Nottingham
　　　　　(British & Commonwealth Bantamweight Title Defences)
27.07.02 Moses Kinyua W CO 5 Nottingham
　　　　　(Commonwealth Bantamweight Title Defence)
21.09.02 Steve Molitor L PTS 12 Brentwood
　　　　　(Commonwealth Bantamweight Title Defence)
16.11.02 Sergei Tasimov W RSC 3 Nottingham
28.04.03 Jamie Yelland W PTS 12 Nottingham
　　　　　(British Bantamweight Title Defence)
20.09.03 Nathan Sting L PTS 12 Nottingham
　　　　　(WBU Bantamweight Title Challenge)
Career: 23 contests, won 17, drew 1, lost 5.

Tony Booth

Hull. *Born* Hull, 30 January, 1970
Cruiserweight. Former Undefeated British Masters L. Heavyweight Champion. Former Undefeated British Central Area Cruiserweight Champion. Ht. 5'11¾"
Manager Self

08.03.90 Paul Lynch L PTS 6 Watford
11.04.90 Mick Duncan W PTS 6 Dewsbury
26.04.90 Colin Manners W PTS 6 Halifax
16.05.90 Tommy Warde W PTS 6 Hull
05.06.90 Gary Dyson W PTS 6 Liverpool

05.09.90 Shaun McCrory L PTS 6 Stoke
08.10.90 Bullit Andrews W RSC 3 Cleethorpes
23.01.91 Darron Griffiths DREW 6 Stoke
06.02.91 Shaun McCrory L PTS 6 Liverpool
06.03.91 Billy Brough L PTS 6 Glasgow
18.03.91 Billy Brough W PTS 6 Glasgow
28.03.91 Neville Brown L PTS 6 Alfreton
17.05.91 Glenn Campbell L RSC 2 Bury
　　　　　(Central Area S. Middleweight Title Challenge)
25.07.91 Paul Murray W PTS 6 Dudley
01.08.91 Nick Manners DREW 8 Dewsbury
11.09.91 Jim Peters L PTS 8 Hammersmith
28.10.91 Eddie Smulders L RSC 6 Arnhem, Holland
09.12.91 Steve Lewsam L PTS 8 Cleethorpes
30.01.92 Serg Fame W PTS 6 Southampton
12.02.92 Tenko Ernie W RSC 4 Wembley
05.03.92 John Beckles W RSC 6 Battersea
26.03.92 Dave Owens W PTS 6 Hull
08.04.92 Michael Gale L PTS 8 Leeds
13.05.92 Phil Soundy W PTS 6 Kensington
02.06.92 Eddie Smulders L RSC 1 Rotterdam, Holland
18.07.92 Maurice Core L PTS 6 Manchester
07.09.92 James Cook L PTS 8 Bethnal Green
30.10.92 Roy Richie DREW 6 Istrees, France
18.11.92 Tony Wilson DREW 8 Solihull
25.12.92 Francis Wanyama L PTS 6 Izegem, Belgium
09.02.93 Tony Wilson W PTS 8 Wolverhampton
01.05.93 Ralf Rocchigiani DREW 8 Berlin, Germany
03.06.93 Victor Cordoba L PTS 8 Marseille, France
23.06.93 Tony Behan W PTS 6 Gorleston
01.07.93 Michael Gale L PTS 8 York
17.09.93 Ole Klemetsen W PTS 8 Copenhagen, Denmark
07.10.93 Denzil Browne DREW 8 York
02.11.93 James Cook L PTS 8 Southwark
12.11.93 Carlos Christie W PTS 6 Hull
28.01.94 Francis Wanyama L RSC 2 Waregem, Belgium
　　　　　(Vacant Commonwealth Cruiserweight Title)
26.03.94 Torsten May L PTS 6 Dortmund, Germany
21.07.94 Mark Prince L RSC 3 Battersea
24.09.94 Johnny Held L PTS 8 Rotterdam, Holland
07.10.94 Dirk Wallyn L PTS 6 Waregem, Belgium
27.10.94 Dean Francis L CO 1 Bayswater
23.01.95 Jan Lefeber L PTS 8 Rotterdam, Holland
07.03.95 John Foreman L PTS 6 Edgbaston
27.04.95 Art Stacey W PTS 10 Hull
　　　　　(Vacant Central Area Cruiserweight Title)
04.06.95 Montell Griffin L RSC 2 Bethnal Green
06.07.95 Nigel Rafferty W RSC 7 Hull
22.07.95 Mark Prince L RSC 2 Millwall
06.09.95 Leif Keiski L PTS 8 Helsinki, Finland
25.09.95 Neil Simpson W PTS 8 Cleethorpes
06.10.95 Don Diego Poeder L RSC 2 Waregem, Belgium
11.11.95 Bruce Scott L RSC 3 Halifax
16.12.95 John Marceta L RSC 2 Cardiff
20.01.96 Johnny Nelson L RSC 2 Mansfield
15.03.96 Slick Miller W PTS 6 Hull
27.03.96 Neil Simpson L PTS 6 Whitwick

17.05.96 Mark Richardson W RSC 2 Hull
13.07.96 Bruce Scott L PTS 8 Bethnal Green
03.09.96 Paul Douglas L PTS 4 Belfast
14.09.96 Kelly Oliver L RSC 2 Sheffield
06.11.96 Martin Jolley W PTS 4 Hull
22.11.96 Slick Miller W RSC 5 Hull
11.12.96 Crawford Ashley L RSC 1 Southwark
18.01.97 Kelly Oliver L RSC 4 Swadlincote
27.02.97 Kevin Morton L PTS 6 Hull
25.03.97 Nigel Rafferty DREW 8 Wolverhampton
04.04.97 John Wilson L PTS 6 Glasgow
16.04.97 Robert Norton L RSC 4 Bethnal Green
15.05.97 Phill Day W PTS 4 Reading
11.09.97 Steve Bristow L PTS 4 Widnes
22.09.97 Martin Langtry W PTS 6 Cleethorpes
04.10.97 Bruce Scott W PTS 8 Muswell Hill
28.11.97 Martin Jolley W PTS 6 Hull
15.12.97 Nigel Rafferty W PTS 6 Cleethorpes
06.03.98 Peter Mason W RSC 3 Hull
09.06.98 Crawford Ashley L RSC 6 Hull
  (British L. Heavyweight Title Challenge. Vacant Commonwealth L. Heavyweight Title)
18.07.98 Omar Sheika W PTS 8 Sheffield
26.09.98 Toks Owoh L PTS 6 Norwich
29.10.98 Nigel Rafferty W PTS 8 Bayswater
14.12.98 Sven Hamer W PTS 6 Cleethorpes
05.01.99 Ali Saidi W RSC 4 Epernay, France
17.05.99 Darren Ashton W PTS 6 Cleethorpes
12.07.99 Neil Simpson L PTS 10 Coventry
  (Elim. British L. Heavyweight Title)
27.09.99 Adam Cale W PTS 6 Cleethorpes
16.10.99 Cathal O'Grady L CO 4 Belfast
18.01.00 Michael Sprott L PTS 6 Mansfield
12.02.00 Thomas Hansvoll L PTS 6 Sheffield
29.02.00 John Keeton L RSC 2 Widnes
09.04.00 Greg Scott-Briggs W PTS 10 Alfreton
  (Vacant British Masters L. Heavyweight Title)
15.05.00 Michael Pinnock W PTS 6 Cleethorpes
19.06.00 Toks Owoh L RSC 3 Burton
08.09.00 Dominic Negus W PTS 6 Bristol
30.09.00 Robert Norton L RSC 3 Peterborough
31.10.00 Firat Aslan L RSC 2 Hammersmith
11.12.00 Mark Krence L PTS 6 Sheffield
05.02.01 Denzil Browne L RSC 5 Hull
  (Vacant Central Area Cruiserweight Title)
01.04.01 Kenny Gayle DREW 4 Southwark
10.04.01 Mark Baker L PTS 4 Wembley
16.06.01 Butch Lesley L RSC 3 Dagenham
09.09.01 Tommy Eastwood L PTS 4 Southwark
22.09.01 Peter Haymer L PTS 4 Bethnal Green
15.10.01 Colin Kenna L PTS 6 Southampton
01.11.01 Terry Morrill W RSC 7 Hull
24.11.01 Matt Legg L PTS 4 Bethnal Green
16.12.01 Blue Stevens L PTS 4 Southwark
19.01.02 John McDermott L RSC 1 Bethnal Green
20.04.02 Enzo Maccarinelli L PTS 4 Cardiff
28.04.02 Scott Lansdowne L PTS 4 Southwark
10.05.02 Paul Buttery L PTS 4 Preston
23.06.02 Neil Linford L RSC 5 Southwark
03.08.02 Mark Krence L PTS 4 Derby
17.08.02 Enzo Maccarinelli L RTD 2 Cardiff
23.09.02 Slick Miller W PTS 6 Cleethorpes
05.10.02 Phill Day W PTS 4 Coventry
19.10.02 James Zikic L PTS 4 Norwich
27.10.02 Hughie Doherty L PTS 4 Southwark
21.11.02 Jamie Warters W PTS 8 Hull
28.11.02 Roman Greenberg L PTS 4 Finchley

08.12.02 David Haye L RTD 2 Bethnal Green
30.01.03 Mohammed Benguesmia L RTD 4 Algiers, Algeria
05.04.03 Jason Callum L PTS 6 Coventry
17.05.03 Tony Moran L PTS 6 Liverpool
26.07.03 Kelly Oliver L PTS 4 Plymouth
26.09.03 Radcliffe Green W PTS 6 Millwall
14.11.03 Paul Bonson W PTS 6 Hull
14.02.04 Oneal Murray W PTS 8 Holborn
01.05.04 Elvis Michailenko L RTD 4 Gravesend
Career: 130 contests, won 44, drew 8, lost 78.

Alan Bosworth   Les Clark

Alan Bosworth

Northampton. *Born* Northampton, 31 December, 1967
L.Welterweight. Former Undefeated English Lightweight Champion. Former Undefeated British Masters L.Welterweight Champion. Ht. 5'7"
Manager Self

17.10.95 Simon Hamblett W RSC 2 Wolverhampton
29.10.95 Shaun Gledhill W PTS 6 Shaw
16.11.95 Brian Coleman W PTS 6 Evesham
23.11.95 David Thompson W RSC 4 Tynemouth
13.01.96 Jason Blanche W PTS 6 Halifax
31.01.96 Arv Mittoo W PTS 6 Stoke
16.02.96 John Docherty W PTS 6 Irvine
24.03.96 Scott Walker DREW 6 Shaw
16.05.96 Yifru Retta W PTS 6 Dunstable
07.03.97 Wayne Rigby L RSC 5 Northampton
09.09.97 Colin Dunne L RSC 8 Bethnal Green
31.10.98 Alan Temple L PTS 6 Basingstoke
26.02.99 Des Sowden W PTS 6 Longford
13.03.99 Paul Burke L PTS 6 Manchester
24.04.99 Jan Bergman L RSC 6 Munich, Germany
02.07.99 Keith Jones W PTS 6 Bristol
24.09.99 Woody Greenaway L PTS 6 Merthyr
03.12.99 Darren Underwood W CO 5 Peterborough
20.01.00 Brian Coleman W PTS 6 Piccadilly
24.03.00 Allan Vester L PTS 12 Aarhus, Denmark

  (IBF Inter-Continental L. Welterweight Title Challenge)
28.04.00 George Scott L PTS 8 Copenhagen, Denmark
02.06.00 Mohamed Helel W PTS 6 Ashford
25.07.00 Shea Neary L PTS 10 Southwark
01.12.00 David Kirk DREW 8 Peterborough
13.03.01 Eamonn Magee L RSC 5 Plymouth
23.06.01 Keith Jones W PTS 6 Peterborough
23.11.01 Daniel James W RSC 7 Bethnal Green
  (Elim. British L.Welterweight Title)
16.03.02 Junior Witter L RSC 3 Northampton
  (Vacant British L.Welterweight Title)
28.09.02 Eamonn Magee L RSC 5 Manchester
28.01.03 Oscar Hall L PTS 10 Nottingham
  (Elim. British L. Welterweight Title)
25.07.03 Gavin Down W RSC 5 Norwich
  (British Masters L.Welterweight Title Challenge. Elim. British L.Welterweight Title)
11.12.03 Stephen Smith W PTS 10 Bethnal Green
  (Vacant English L.Welterweight Title)
Career: 32 contests, won 17, drew 2, lost 13.

John Bothwell

Ballieston. *Born* Glasgow, 8 August, 1981
Featherweight. Ht. 5'5"
Manager A. Morrison

17.10.03 Marty Kayes W PTS 6 Glasgow
30.10.03 Colin Moffett DREW 4 Belfast
07.12.03 Ian Reid W PTS 6 Glasgow
06.03.04 Fred Janes DREW 4 Renfrew
08.04.04 Chris Hooper L CO 2 Peterborough
28.05.04 Jason Nesbitt L RSC 3 Glasgow
Career: 6 contests, won 2, drew 2, lost 2.

Mickey Bowden

Forest Hill. *Born* Lewisham, 30 June, 1975
Featherweight. Ht. 5'8"
Manager Self

25.02.99 Kevin Gerowski W PTS 4 Kentish Town
09.05.99 Graham McGrath W RSC 4 Bracknell
07.08.99 Brendan Bryce W PTS 4 Dagenham
26.05.01 Anthony Hanna W PTS 4 Bethnal Green
25.02.02 Jimmy Beech L PTS 4 Slough
25.04.02 Nelson Valez L PTS 4 Las Vegas, Nevada, USA
30.10.02 Anthony Hanna W PTS 4 Leicester Square
12.12.02 Richmond Asante W PTS 6 Leicester Square
20.09.03 Stephen Chinnock L PTS 8 Nottingham
14.11.03 Anthony Hanna W PTS 4 Bethnal Green
19.06.04 John Mackay L PTS 8 Muswell Hill
Career: 11 contests, won 7, lost 4.

Jason Brewster

Coseley. *Born* Wolverhampton, 6 February, 1971
Heavyweight. Ht. 6'1"
Manager Self

23.06.99 Mark Williams DREW 6 West Bromwich
03.09.99 Adam Cale W PTS 6 West Bromwich
01.10.99 Scott Baker L RTD 5 Cleethorpes

18.02.00 Nigel Rafferty L PTS 6 West Bromwich
11.05.00 Tony Dowling L RSC 2 Newark
09.06.00 Paul Richardson L PTS 6 Blackpool
10.09.00 Adam Cale W PTS 4 Walsall
06.11.00 Nigel Rafferty W PTS 8 Wolverhampton
13.11.00 Mark McManus L RTD 2 Bethnal Green
01.04.01 Paul Richardson L RSC 4 Wolverhampton
20.05.01 Kevin Burton W PTS 6 Wolverhampton
07.09.01 Slick Miller W PTS 6 West Bromwich
24.09.01 Lee Nicholson W PTS 6 Cleethorpes
15.12.01 Butch Lesley L RSC 1 Chigwell
17.02.02 Lee Nicholson W PTS 6 Wolverhampton
13.07.02 Paul Bonson L PTS 6 Wolverhampton
05.10.02 Tony Moran L PTS 4 Liverpool
14.12.02 John McDermott L RSC 1 Newcastle
15.02.03 Phill Day L PTS 6 Wolverhampton
05.07.03 Albert Sosnowski L RSC 2 Brentwood
Career: 20 contests, won 7, drew 1, lost 12.

Michael Brodie

Manchester. *Born* Manchester, 10 May, 1974
Featherweight. Former Undefeated IBO & WBF Featherweight Champion. Former Undefeated British, European & Commonwealth S. Bantamweight Champion. Ht. 5'6"
Manager Self

03.10.94 Graham McGrath W RSC 5 Manchester
20.10.94 Chip O'Neill W CO 3 Middleton
28.11.94 Muhammad Shaffique W CO 2 Manchester
13.12.94 Pete Buckley W PTS 6 Potters Bar
16.02.95 G. G. Goddard W PTS 6 Bury
03.04.95 Garry Burrell W RSC 4 Manchester
05.05.95 G. G. Goddard W PTS 6 Swansea
17.05.95 Ian Reid W RSC 3 Ipswich
10.06.95 Chris Clarkson W PTS 6 Manchester
14.11.95 Niel Leggett W CO 1 Bury
25.11.95 Karl Morling W RSC 1 Dagenham
18.12.95 Marty Chestnut W RTD 3 Mayfair
26.02.96 Bamana Dibateza W PTS 6 Manchester
13.04.96 John Sillo W CO 1 Liverpool
07.05.96 Elvis Parsley W RSC 1 Mayfair
06.07.96 Colin Innes W RSC 2 Manchester
19.09.96 Ervine Blake W RSC 4 Manchester
09.11.96 Miguel Matthews W PTS 6 Manchester
22.03.97 Neil Swain W RSC 10 Wythenshawe
(Vacant British S. Bantamweight Title)
30.08.97 Pete Buckley W PTS 8 Cheshunt
01.11.97 Wilson Docherty W CO 4 Glasgow
(British S. Bantamweight Title Defence. Vacant Commonwealth S. Bantamweight Title)
31.01.98 Brian Carr W RSC 10 Edmonton
(British & Commonwealth S. Bantamweight Title Defences)
23.05.98 Simon Ramoni W PTS 12 Bethnal Green
(Commonwealth S. Bantamweight Title Defence)
17.10.98 Sergei Devakov W PTS 12 Manchester
(European S. Bantamweight Title Challenge)

13.03.99 Salim Medjkoune W RSC 9 Manchester
(European S. Bantamweight Title Defence)
31.07.99 Serge Poilblan W RSC 12 Carlisle
(European S. Bantamweight Title Defence)
01.10.99 Drew Docherty W RSC 6 Bethnal Green
(European S. Bantamweight Title Defence)
26.02.00 Salim Medjkoune W RSC 9 Carlisle
(European S. Bantamweight Title Defence)
01.07.00 Mustapha Hame W CO 4 Manchester
(European S.Bantamweight Title Defence)
09.09.00 Willie Jorrin L PTS 12 Manchester
(Vacant WBC S.Bantamweight Title)
03.02.01 Sergio Aguila W RSC 4 Manchester
06.10.01 Frederic Bonifai W RSC 5 Manchester
26.11.01 Sean Fletcher W CO 2 Manchester
18.05.02 Pastor Maurin W PTS 12 Millwall
(Vacant WBF Featherweight Title)
09.11.02 Luis Fuente W PTS 12 Altrincham
(WBF Featherweight Title Defence)
21.06.03 Juan Cabrera W PTS 12 Manchester
(Vacant IBO Featherweight Title)
18.10.03 In-Jin Chi DREW 12 Manchester
(Vacant WBC Featherweight Title)
10.04.04 In-Jin Chi L CO 7 Manchester
(Vacant WBC Featherweight Title)
Career: 38 contests, won 35, drew 1, lost 2.

Casey Brooke

Great Wyrley. *Born* Birmingham, 8 July, 1971
Welterweight. Ht. 5'11"
Manager T. Nerwal

06.06.00 Arv Mittoo L PTS 6 Brierley Hill
07.07.00 John Tiftik L RSC 2 Chigwell
10.10.00 Rene Grayel L PTS 6 Brierley Hill
28.11.00 Rene Grayel L PTS 6 Brierley Hill
03.02.01 Gary Harrison L PTS 6 Brighton
12.03.01 Tony Smith L PTS 6 Birmingham
26.09.03 Nathan Ward L RSC 1 Reading
26.10.03 Danny Cooper L PTS 6 Longford
30.11.03 Chris Brophy L PTS 6 Swansea
20.02.04 Tony Smith L PTS 6 Doncaster
30.03.04 Jay Morris L RSC 1 Southampton
Career: 11 contests, lost 11.

Mark Brookes

Swinton. *Born* Doncaster, 1 December, 1979
L. Heavyweight. Ht. 6'0"
Manager D. Hobson

21.10.00 Rob Galloway W RSC 5 Sheffield
11.12.00 Jimmy Steel W PTS 6 Sheffield
24.03.01 Matthew Pepper W RSC 1 Sheffield
18.06.01 Clint Johnson W PTS 6 Bradford
27.07.01 Michael Pinnock W PTS 4 Sheffield
13.09.01 Darren Ashton W PTS 4 Sheffield
22.09.01 Valery Odin L PTS 4 Canning Town
15.12.01 Clint Johnson W PTS 4 Sheffield
11.05.02 Paul Bonson W PTS 4 Chesterfield
05.10.02 Darren Ashton W PTS 4 Chesterfield
05.12.02 Simeon Cover W RSC 3 Sheffield
18.03.03 Peter Haymer L PTS 6 Reading
10.06.03 Michael Pinnock W PTS 4 Sheffield
31.07.03 Hastings Rasani W PTS 6 Sheffield

10.12.03 Peter Haymer DREW 6 Sheffield
06.02.04 Simeon Cover W RSC 4 Sheffield
20.04.04 Neil Simpson W PTS 10 Sheffield
(Elim. British L.Heavyweight Title)
Career: 17 contests, won 14, drew 1, lost 2.

Mark Brookes   Les Clark

Chris Brophy

Swansea. *Born* Preston, 28 January, 1979
Welterweight. Ht. 5'10"
Manager N. Hodges

29.10.03 Aidan Mooney L RSC 5 Leicester Square
30.11.03 Casey Brooke W PTS 6 Swansea
21.12.03 Gary O'Connor L PTS 6 Bolton
21.02.04 Tony Doherty L RSC 2 Cardiff
02.04.04 Tommy Marshall DREW 6 Plymouth
26.04.04 Scott Haywood L RSC 5 Cleethorpes
05.06.04 Ashley Theophane L RSC 3 Bethnal Green
Career: 7 contests, won 1, drew 1, lost 5.

Cathy Brown

Peckham. *Born* Leeds, 28 July, 1970
Former WBF European Flyweight Champion. Ht. 5'2"
Manager A. Booth

31.10.99 Veerle Braspenningsx W PTS 5 Raynes Park
05.02.00 Veerle Braspenningsx W RSC 6 Sint-Truiden, Belgium
01.07.00 Jan Wild W PTS 6 Southwark
(Vacant WBF European Flyweight Title)
31.10.00 Viktoria Vargal W RSC 3 Hammersmith
28.02.01 Marietta Ivanova W PTS 4 Kensington
26.04.01 Oksana Vasilieva L PTS 4 Kensington
16.06.01 Romona Gughie W RSC 3 Wembley
22.11.01 Audrey Guthrie W PTS 6 Mayfair
(WBF European Flyweight Title Defence)
13.12.01 Ilina Boneva W RSC 5 Leicester Square
13.03.02 Svetla Taskova W PTS 4 Mayfair
13.06.02 Alina Shaternikova L PTS 10 Leicester Square
(Vacant WBF Womens Flyweight Title)

30.10.02 Monica Petrova W PTS 6 Leicester Square
20.03.03 Juliette Winter L PTS 4 Queensway
26.04.03 Regina Halmich L PTS 10 Schwerin, Germany
          (WIBF Flyweight Title Challenge)
17.12.03 Stefania Bianchini L PTS 10 Bergamo, Italy
          (European Flyweight Title Challenge)
Career: 15 contests, won 10, lost 5.

Denzil Browne

Leeds. *Born* Leeds, 21 January, 1969
Central Area Cruiserweight Champion.
Ht. 6'2½"
Manager D. Hobson

18.10.90 Mark Bowen W PTS 6 Dewsbury
29.11.90 R. F. McKenzie L PTS 6 Sunderland
13.12.90 Gary Railton W RSC 2 Dewsbury
21.02.91 Mark Bowen W PTS 6 Walsall
21.03.91 R. F. McKenzie W PTS 6 Dewsbury
09.05.91 Darren McKenna W PTS 6 Leeds
27.06.91 Steve Yorath W PTS 6 Leeds
01.08.91 Tony Colclough W RSC 1 Dewsbury
09.10.91 R. F. McKenzie L PTS 6 Manchester
30.10.91 Gus Mendes W RSC 6 Leeds
23.01.92 Darren McKenna W PTS 6 York
19.03.92 Ian Bulloch W PTS 8 York
23.09.92 Steve Yorath W PTS 8 Leeds
29.10.92 Sean O'Phoenix W RSC 4 Leeds
25.02.93 Cordwell Hylton W PTS 8 Bradford
22.04.93 Dave Muhammed W PTS 8 Mayfair
01.07.93 Steve Osborne W RSC 1 York
07.10.93 Tony Booth DREW 8 York
01.12.93 Lennie Howard W RSC 6 Kensington
26.10.94 Steve Lewsam W CO 2 Leeds
21.01.95 Dennis Andries L RSC 11 Glasgow
          (Vacant British Cruiserweight Title)
08.07.95 Bobbi Joe Edwards L PTS 8 York
11.11.95 John Keeton L RSC 4 Halifax
13.01.96 Albert Call W PTS 6 Halifax
04.06.96 Bobbi Joe Edwards W PTS 10 York
          (Vacant Central Area Cruiserweight Title)
25.03.97 Chris Okoh L PTS 12 Lewisham
          (Commonwealth Cruiserweight Title Challenge)
05.02.01 Tony Booth W RSC 5 Hull
          (Vacant Central Area Cruiserweight Title)
02.06.01 Lee Swaby DREW 8 Wakefield
31.07.03 Phill Day W RSC 6 Sheffield
05.09.03 Tony Dowling L PTS 6 Sheffield
11.11.03 Hastings Rasani W PTS 6 Leeds
Career: 31 contests, won 22, drew 2, lost 7.

Darren Bruce

Grays. *Born* Orsett, 1 December, 1972
Welterweight. Former Undefeated IBO
Inter-Continental Welterweight Champion.
Ht. 5'11"
Manager B. Hearn

28.11.97 Noel Henry W RSC 1 Bethnal Green
27.01.98 Darren McInulty W PTS 4 Bethnal Green
11.03.98 Kevin Lang W RSC 6 Bethnal Green
02.05.98 Harry Butler W RSC 6 Kensington
05.06.98 Leigh Wicks W PTS 6 Southend
08.09.98 Darren McInulty W CO 1 Bethnal Green
31.10.98 Shaun O'Neill W RSC 1 Southend
06.11.98 Delroy Mellis W RTD 3 Mayfair
11.12.98 John Green W RSC 1 Cheshunt
26.02.99 George Richards W PTS 6 Coventry
27.04.99 Dennis Berry W RSC 3 Bethnal Green
29.06.99 Frederic Noto L PTS 10 Bethnal Green
16.10.99 Charlie Kane W RTD 5 Bethnal Green
          (Vacant IBO Inter-Continental Welterweight Title)
05.02.00 Michael Smyth W CO 5 Bethnal Green
          (IBO Inter-Continental Welterweight Title Defence)
11.03.00 Mark Ramsey DREW 6 Kensington
02.12.00 Willy Wise L PTS 12 Bethnal Green
          (Vacant IBO Welterweight Title)
14.07.01 Mark Ramsey L PTS 6 Wembley
29.06.02 Peter Dunn W PTS 6 Brentwood
21.09.02 Derek Roche L PTS 8 Brentwood
07.12.02 Piotr Bartnicki L RSC 3 Brentwood
19.04.03 Andrzej Butowicz W PTS 6 Liverpool
05.07.03 Darren Rhodes L RSC 3 Brentwood
Career: 22 contests, won 15, drew 1, lost 6.

Steve Brumant

Birmingham. *Born* Birmingham, 18 May, 1971
L. Middleweight. Ht. 5'7"
Manager T. Nerwal

18.09.97 Gerard Lawrence W CO 1 Alfreton
24.01.98 Anthony Farnell L PTS 4 Cardiff
28.04.98 Nicky Bardle W RSC 5 Brentford
24.03.99 Paul Dyer L PTS 4 Bayswater
20.05.99 David Kirk L PTS 4 Kensington
30.09.99 Delroy Mellis W PTS 6 Kensington
26.11.99 Scott Garrett W RSC 4 Bayswater
19.12.99 Wahid Fats L PTS 8 Salford
19.04.00 Karim Hussine L PTS 4 Kensington
24.06.00 Gerard Murphy L PTS 4 Glasgow
10.10.00 Jason Samuels L PTS 6 Brierley Hill
22.09.03 Davey Jones W PTS 6 Cleethorpes
31.01.04 Michael Lomax L PTS 6 Bethnal Green
13.03.04 Reggie Robshaw W PTS 4 Huddersfield
Career: 14 contests, won 6, lost 8.

Paul Buchanan

West Denton. *Born* Newcastle, 23 October, 1981
Middleweight. Ht. 5'10"
Manager G. Robinson

31.01.01 Gary Jones W RTD 1 Piccadilly
26.04.01 Lee Woodruff W PTS 6 Gateshead
08.03.02 Neil Bonner W PTS 6 Ellesmere Port
25.03.02 Dean Cockburn W PTS 6 Sunderland
06.03.04 Davey Jones W PTS 4 Renfrew
01.05.04 Gareth Lawrence W PTS 4 Gravesend
Career: 6 contests, won 6.

Pete Buckley

Birmingham. *Born* Birmingham, 9 March, 1969
L. Welterweight. Former Undefeated Midlands Area S. Featherweight Champion. Former Midlands Area S. Bantamweight Champion. Ht. 5'8"
Manager Self

04.10.89 Alan Baldwin DREW 6 Stafford
10.10.89 Ronnie Stephenson L PTS 6 Wolverhampton
30.10.89 Robert Braddock W PTS 6 Birmingham
14.11.89 Neil Leitch W PTS 6 Evesham
22.11.89 Peter Judson W PTS 6 Stafford
11.12.89 Stevie Woods W PTS 6 Bradford
21.12.89 Wayne Taylor W PTS 6 Kings Heath
10.01.90 John O'Meara W PTS 6 Kensington
19.02.90 Ian McGirr L PTS 6 Birmingham
27.02.90 Miguel Matthews DREW 6 Evesham
14.03.90 Ronnie Stephenson DREW 6 Stoke
04.04.90 Ronnie Stephenson L PTS 8 Stafford
23.04.90 Ronnie Stephenson W PTS 6 Birmingham
30.04.90 Chris Clarkson L PTS 8 Mayfair
17.05.90 Johnny Bredahl L PTS 6 Aars, Denmark
04.06.90 Ronnie Stephenson W PTS 8 Birmingham
28.06.90 Robert Braddock W RSC 5 Birmingham
01.10.90 Miguel Matthews W PTS 8 Cleethorpes
09.10.90 Miguel Matthews L PTS 8 Wolverhampton
17.10.90 Tony Smith W PTS 6 Stoke
29.10.90 Miguel Matthews W PTS 8 Birmingham
21.11.90 Drew Docherty L PTS 8 Solihull
10.12.90 Neil Leitch W PTS 8 Wolverhampton
10.01.91 Duke McKenzie L RSC 5 Wandsworth
18.02.91 Jamie McBride L PTS 8 Glasgow
04.03.91 Brian Robb W RSC 7 Birmingham
26.03.91 Neil Leitch DREW 8 Wolverhampton
01.05.91 Mark Geraghty W PTS 8 Solihull
05.06.91 Brian Robb W PTS 10 Wolverhampton
          (Vacant Midlands Area S. Featherweight Title)
09.09.91 Mike Deveney L PTS 8 Glasgow
24.09.91 Mark Bates W RTD 5 Basildon
29.10.91 John Armour L PTS 6 Kensington
14.11.91 Mike Deveney L PTS 6 Edinburgh
28.11.91 Craig Dermody L PTS 6 Liverpool
19.12.91 Craig Dermody L PTS 6 Oldham
18.01.92 Alan McKay DREW 8 Kensington
20.02.92 Brian Robb W RSC 10 Oakengates
          (Midlands Area S. Featherweight Title Defence)
27.04.92 Drew Docherty L PTS 8 Glasgow
15.05.92 Ruben Condori L PTS 10 Augsburg, Germany
29.05.92 Donnie Hood L PTS 8 Glasgow
07.09.92 Duke McKenzie L RTD 3 Bethnal Green
12.11.92 Prince Naseem Hamed L PTS 6 Liverpool
19.02.93 Harald Geier L PTS 12 Vienna, Austria
          (Vacant WBA Penta-Continental S. Bantamweight Title)
26.04.93 Bradley Stone L PTS 8 Lewisham
18.06.93 Eamonn McAuley L PTS 6 Belfast
01.07.93 Tony Silkstone L PTS 8 York
06.10.93 Jonjo Irwin L PTS 8 Solihull
25.10.93 Drew Docherty L PTS 8 Glasgow
06.11.93 Michael Alldis L PTS 8 Bethnal Green
30.11.93 Barry Jones L PTS 4 Cardiff
19.12.93 Shaun Anderson L PTS 6 Glasgow
22.01.94 Barry Jones L PTS 6 Cardiff
29.01.94 Prince Naseem Hamed L RSC 4 Cardiff
10.03.94 Tony Falcone L PTS 4 Bristol
29.03.94 Conn McMullen W PTS 6 Bethnal Green
05.04.94 Mark Bowers L PTS 6 Bethnal Green
13.04.94 James Murray L PTS 6 Glasgow
06.05.94 Paul Lloyd L RTD 4 Liverpool
03.08.94 Greg Upton L PTS 6 Bristol

89

26.09.94	John Sillo L PTS 6 Liverpool
05.10.94	Matthew Harris L PTS 6 Wolverhampton
07.11.94	Marlon Ward L PTS 4 Piccadilly
23.11.94	Justin Murphy L PTS 4 Piccadilly
29.11.94	Neil Swain L PTS Cardiff
13.12.94	Michael Brodie L PTS 6 Potters Bar
20.12.94	Michael Alldis L PTS 6 Bethnal Green
10.02.95	Matthew Harris W RSC 6 Birmingham *(Midlands Area S. Bantamweight Title Challenge)*
23.02.95	Paul Ingle L PTS 8 Southwark
20.04.95	John Sillo L PTS 6 Liverpool
27.04.95	Paul Ingle L PTS 8 Bethnal Green
09.05.95	Ady Lewis L PTS 4 Basildon
23.05.95	Spencer Oliver L PTS 4 Potters Bar
01.07.95	Dean Pithie L PTS 4 Kensington
21.09.95	Patrick Mullings L PTS 6 Battersea
29.09.95	Marlon Ward L PTS 4 Bethnal Green
25.10.95	Matthew Harris L PTS 10 Telford *(Midlands Area S. Bantamweight Title Defence)*
08.11.95	Vince Feeney L PTS 8 Bethnal Green
28.11.95	Barry Jones L PTS 6 Cardiff
15.12.95	Patrick Mullings L PTS 4 Bethnal Green
05.02.96	Patrick Mullings L PTS 8 Bexleyheath
09.03.96	Paul Griffin L PTS 4 Millstreet
21.03.96	Colin McMillan L RSC 3 Southwark
14.05.96	Venkatesan Deverajan L PTS 4 Dagenham
29.06.96	Matt Brown W RSC 1 Erith
03.09.96	Vince Feeney L PTS 4 Bethnal Green
28.09.96	Fabrice Benichou L PTS 8 Barking
09.10.96	Gary Marston DREW 8 Stoke
06.11.96	Neil Swain L PTS 4 Tylorstown
29.11.96	Alston Buchanan L PTS 8 Glasgow
22.12.96	Brian Carr L PTS 6 Glasgow
11.01.97	Scott Harrison L PTS 4 Bethnal Green
29.01.97	Carl Allen L PTS 8 Stoke
12.02.97	Ronnie McPhee L PTS 6 Glasgow
25.02.97	Dean Pithie L PTS 4 Sheffield
07.03.97	Jason Booth L PTS 6 Northampton
20.03.97	Thomas Bradley W PTS 6 Newark
08.04.97	Sergei Devakov L PTS 6 Bethnal Green
25.04.97	Matthew Harris L PTS 6 Cleethorpes
08.05.97	Gregorio Medina L RTD 2 Mansfield
13.06.97	Mike Deveney L PTS 6 Paisley
19.07.97	Richard Evatt L PTS 4 Wembley
30.08.97	Michael Brodie L PTS 8 Cheshunt
06.10.97	Brendan Bryce W PTS 6 Piccadilly
20.10.97	Kelton McKenzie L PTS 6 Leicester
20.11.97	Ervine Blake L PTS 8 Solihull
06.12.97	Danny Adams L PTS 4 Wembley
13.12.97	Gary Thornhill L PTS 6 Sheffield
31.01.98	Scott Harrison L PTS 6 Edmonton
05.03.98	Steve Conway L PTS 6 Leeds
18.03.98	Ervine Blake L PTS 8 Stoke
26.03.98	Graham McGrath W RTD 4 Solihull
11.04.98	Salim Medjkoune L PTS 6 Southwark
18.04.98	Tony Mulholland L PTS 4 Manchester
27.04.98	Alston Buchanan L PTS 8 Glasgow
11.05.98	Jason Squire W RTD 2 Leicester
21.05.98	Lee Armstrong L PTS 6 Bradford
06.06.98	Tony Mulholland L PTS 6 Liverpool
14.06.98	Lee Armstrong L PTS 6 Shaw
21.07.98	David Burke L PTS 6 Widnes
05.09.98	Michael Gomez L PTS 6 Telford
17.09.98	Brian Carr L PTS 6 Glasgow
03.10.98	Justin Murphy L PTS 6 Crawley
05.12.98	Lehlohonolo Ledwaba L PTS 8 Bristol
19.12.98	Acelino Freitas L RTD 3 Liverpool
09.02.99	Chris Jickells L PTS 6 Wolverhampton

16.02.99	Franny Hogg L PTS 6 Leeds
26.02.99	Richard Evatt L RSC 5 Coventry
17.04.99	Martin O'Malley L RSC 3 Dublin
29.05.99	Richie Wenton L PTS 6 Halifax
14.06.99	Carl Allen L PTS 6 Birmingham
26.06.99	Paul Halpin L PTS 4 Millwall
15.07.99	Salim Medjkoune L PTS 6 Peterborough
07.08.99	Steve Murray L PTS 6 Dagenham
12.09.99	Kevin Gerowski L PTS 6 Nottingham
20.09.99	Mat Zegan L PTS 6 Peterborough
02.10.99	Jason Cook L PTS 4 Cardiff
09.10.99	Brian Carr L PTS 6 Manchester
19.10.99	Gary Steadman L PTS 4 Bethnal Green
27.10.99	Miguel Matthews W PTS 8 Birmingham
20.11.99	Carl Greaves L PTS 10 Grantham *(British Masters S. Featherweight Title Challenge)*
11.12.99	Gary Thornhill L PTS 6 Liverpool
29.01.00	Bradley Pryce L PTS 4 Manchester
19.02.00	Gavin Rees L PTS 4 Dagenham
29.02.00	Tony Mulholland L PTS 4 Widnes
20.03.00	Carl Greaves L PTS 4 Mansfield
27.03.00	James Rooney L PTS 4 Barnsley
08.04.00	Delroy Pryce L PTS 4 Bethnal Green
17.04.00	Franny Hogg L PTS 8 Glasgow
11.05.00	Craig Spacie L PTS 4 Newark
25.05.00	Jimmy Phelan DREW 6 Hull
19.06.00	Delroy Pryce L PTS 4 Burton
01.07.00	Richard Evatt L PTS 4 Manchester
16.09.00	Lee Meager L PTS 4 Bethnal Green
23.09.00	Gavin Rees L PTS 4 Bethnal Green
02.10.00	Brian Carr L PTS 4 Glasgow
14.10.00	Gareth Jordan L PTS 4 Wembley
13.11.00	Kevin Lear L PTS 6 Bethnal Green
24.11.00	Lee Williamson L PTS 6 Hull
09.12.00	Leo O'Reilly L PTS 4 Southwark
15.01.01	Eddie Nevins L PTS 4 Manchester
23.01.01	David Burke L PTS 4 Crawley
31.01.01	Tony Montana L PTS 6 Piccadilly
19.02.01	Kevin England W PTS 6 Glasgow
12.03.01	Carl Allen L PTS 6 Birmingham
19.03.01	Duncan Armstrong L PTS 6 Glasgow
27.03.01	Carl Allen L PTS 8 Brierley Hill
05.05.01	Danny Hunt L PTS 4 Edmonton
09.06.01	Gary Thornhill L PTS 4 Bethnal Green
21.07.01	Scott Miller L PTS 4 Sheffield
28.07.01	Kevin Lear L PTS 4 Wembley
25.09.01	Ricky Eccleston L PTS 4 Liverpool
07.10.01	Nigel Senior L PTS 6 Wolverhampton
31.10.01	Woody Greenaway L PTS 6 Birmingham
16.11.01	Jimmy Beech L PTS 6 West Bromwich
01.12.01	Chill John L PTS 4 Bethnal Green
09.12.01	Nigel Senior L PTS 6 Shaw
26.01.02	Scott Lawton L PTS 4 Bethnal Green
09.02.02	Sam Gorman L PTS 6 Coventry
23.02.02	Alex Moon L PTS 4 Nottingham
04.03.02	Leo Turner L PTS 6 Bradford
11.03.02	Martin Watson L PTS 4 Glasgow
26.04.02	Scott Lawton L PTS 4 Coventry
10.05.02	Lee Meager L PTS 6 Bethnal Green
08.06.02	Bradley Pryce L RSC 1 Renfrew
20.07.02	Jeff Thomas L PTS 4 Bethnal Green
23.08.02	Ben Hudson DREW 4 Bethnal Green
06.09.02	Dave Stewart L PTS 6 Bethnal Green
14.09.02	Peter McDonagh L PTS 4 Bethnal Green
20.10.02	James Paisley L PTS 4 Southwark
12.11.02	Martin Hardcastle DREW 6 Leeds
29.11.02	Daniel Thorpe L PTS 6 Hull
09.12.02	Nicky Leech L PTS 6 Nottingham

16.12.02	Joel Viney L PTS 6 Cleethorpes
28.01.03	Billy Corcoran L PTS 6 Nottingham
08.02.03	Colin Toohey L PTS 6 Liverpool
15.02.03	Terry Fletcher L PTS 4 Wembley
22.02.03	Dean Lambert L PTS 4 Huddersfield
05.03.03	Billy Corcoran L PTS 6 Bethnal Green
18.03.03	Nathan Ward L PTS 4 Reading
05.04.03	Baz Carey L PTS 4 Manchester
15.05.03	Mike Harrington W PTS 4 Clevedon
27.05.03	Dave Stewart L PTS 4 Dagenham
07.06.03	Rimell Taylor DREW 6 Coventry
12.07.03	George Telfer L PTS 4 Renfrew
22.07.03	Chas Symonds L PTS 6 Bethnal Green
01.08.03	Jas Malik W PTS 4 Bethnal Green
06.09.03	John Murray L PTS 4 Huddersfield
13.09.03	Isaac Ward L PTS 6 Wakefield
25.09.03	Gary Woolcombe L PTS 6 Bethnal Green
06.10.03	Scott Haywood L PTS 6 Barnsley
20.10.03	Joel Viney W PTS 6 Bradford
29.10.03	David Kehoe L PTS 6 Leicester Square
07.11.03	Femi Fehintola L PTS 6 Sheffield
14.11.03	Dave Stewart L PTS 4 Bethnal Green
21.11.03	Henry Castle L PTS 4 Millwall
28.11.03	Lee Meager L PTS 4 Derby
13.12.03	Derry Matthews L PTS 4 Manchester
21.12.03	Daniel Thorpe L PTS 6 Bolton
16.01.04	Nadeem Siddique L PTS 4 Bradford
16.02.04	Scott Haywood L PTS 6 Scunthorpe
29.02.04	Gary O'Connor L PTS 6 Shaw
03.04.04	Steve Bell L PTS 4 Manchester
16.04.04	Isaac Ward L PTS 6 Hartlepool
23.04.04	Colin Bain L PTS 6 Glasgow
06.05.04	Amir Ali L PTS 4 Barnsley
13.05.04	Lee Beavis L PTS 4 Bethnal Green
04.06.04	Tristan Davies L PTS 6 Dudley

Career: 227 contests, won 31, drew 10, lost 186.

(Andrew) Stefy Bull (Bullcroft)

Doncaster. *Born* Doncaster, 10 May, 1977
Central Area Lightweight Champion.
Former Undefeated Central Area
Featherweight Champion. Ht. 5'10"
Manager J. Rushton

30.06.95	Andy Roberts W PTS 4 Doncaster
11.10.95	Michael Edwards W PTS 6 Stoke
18.10.95	Alan Hagan W RSC 1 Batley
28.11.95	Kevin Sheil W PTS 6 Wolverhampton
26.01.96	Robert Grubb W PTS 6 Doncaster
12.09.96	Benny Jones W PTS 6 Doncaster
15.10.96	Kevin Sheil DREW 6 Wolverhampton
24.10.96	Graham McGrath W PTS 6 Birmingham
17.12.96	Robert Braddock W RSC 4 Doncaster *(Vacant Central Area Featherweight Title)*
10.07.97	Carl Greaves W PTS 6 Doncaster
11.10.97	Dean Pithie L RSC 11 Sheffield *(Vacant WBO Inter-Continental S. Featherweight Title)*
19.03.98	Chris Lyons W RSC 4 Doncaster
08.04.98	Alex Moon L RSC 3 Liverpool
31.07.99	Jason Dee L RSC 4 Carlisle
09.05.03	Joel Viney W RTD 3 Doncaster
02.06.03	Jason Nesbitt W PTS 6 Cleethorpes
05.09.03	Dave Hinds W PTS 6 Doncaster
20.02.04	Anthony Christopher W PTS 6 Doncaster
07.05.04	Daniel Thorpe W PTS 10 Doncaster *(Central Area Lightweight Title Challenge)*

Career: 19 contests, won 15, drew 1, lost 3.

Matthew Burke

Stratford. *Born* London, 7 October, 1980
S.Featherweight. Ht. 5'11¼"
Manager B. Hearn

29.06.02 Joel Viney W PTS 4 Brentwood
21.09.02 Andy Robinson W PTS 4 Brentwood
07.12.02 John Simpson L PTS 4 Brentwood
18.10.03 John Murray L RSC 1 Manchester
Career: 4 contests, won 2, lost 2.

Pinky Burton

Selby. *Born* Perth, 13 December, 1979
British Masters Cruiserweight Champion.
Ht. 5'11½"
Manager T. Gilmour/C. Aston

28.04.01 Nathan King L PTS 4 Cardiff
28.01.02 Rob Galloway W RSC 4 Barnsley
02.03.02 Darren Ashton W PTS 4 Barnsley
17.02.03 Eamonn Glennon W PTS 6 Glasgow
24.03.03 Michael Pinnock W PTS 4 Barnsley
02.06.03 Ovill McKenzie W PTS 8 Glasgow
06.10.03 Paul Bonson W PTS 6 Barnsley
25.03.04 Ryan Walls W PTS 10 Longford
(*British Masters Cruiserweight Title Challenge*)
Career: 8 contests, won 7, lost 1.

Robert Burton   Les Clark

Robert Burton

Barnsley. *Born* Barnsley, 1 April, 1971
Central Area L.Middleweight Champion.
Former Central Area Welterweight
Champion. Ht. 5'9"
Manager Self

05.02.01 Gavin Pearson W RSC 3 Bradford
23.02.01 Scott Millar W CO 5 Irvine
20.03.01 Peter Dunn W PTS 6 Leeds
08.05.01 Arv Mittoo W PTS 4 Barnsley
10.06.01 Martyn Bailey DREW 6 Ellesmere Port
08.10.01 Gavin Pearson W RSC 2 Barnsley
16.11.01 Martyn Bailey DREW 4 Preston
24.11.01 Peter Dunn L PTS 6 Wakefield
28.01.02 Peter Dunn W RSC 8 Barnsley
(*Vacant Central Area Welterweight Title*)
23.08.02 David Walker L RSC 2 Bethnal Green
19.10.02 John Humphrey L RTD 4 Norwich

09.02.03 Donovan Smillie L PTS 6 Bradford
24.03.03 Andy Halder L PTS 6 Barnsley
31.05.03 David Keir W RSC 9 Barnsley
(*Central Area Welterweight Title Defence*)
01.11.03 Scott Dixon L PTS 6 Glasgow
08.12.03 Jed Tytler W PTS 6 Barnsley
10.02.04 Paul Lomax W PTS 6 Barnsley
06.05.04 Matthew Hatton L PTS 10 Barnsley
(*Central Area Welterweight Title Defence*)
08.06.04 Lee Murtagh W CO 3 Sheffield
(*Vacant Central Area L.Middleweight Title*)
Career: 19 contests, won 10, drew 2, lost 7.

Harry Butler

Worcester. *Born* Wisbech, 12 August, 1977
L.Heavyweight. Ht. 5'8"
Manager Self

19.07.97 Takaloo L RSC 1 Wembley
30.08.97 Patrick Pasi L PTS 4 Cheshunt
26.09.97 Darren Williams L PTS 6 Port Talbot
21.10.97 John Green L PTS 6 Yarm
15.11.97 Michael Jones L PTS 4 Bristol
02.12.97 Ross McCord W RSC 3 Swansea
13.12.97 Hercules Kyvelos L PTS 4 Sheffield
06.01.98 Alan Gilbert L PTS 4 Brighton
13.02.98 Gareth Hogg L RSC 3 Weston super Mare
14.03.98 Sonny Thind L PTS 4 Bethnal Green
03.04.98 Jon Foster L PTS 6 Ebbw Vale
18.04.98 Anthony Farnell L PTS 6 Manchester
02.05.98 Darren Bruce L RSC 6 Kensington
04.06.98 Adrian Houldey L PTS 6 Dudley
14.06.98 Gerard Lawrence L PTS 6 Golders Green
08.08.98 Sonny Pollard W RSC 4 Scarborough
05.09.98 Jawaid Khaliq L PTS 4 Telford
26.09.98 James Lowther L RSC 6 York
21.11.98 Brian Knudsen L RSC 4 Southwark
18.02.99 Clive Johnson L PTS 6 Barking
05.03.99 Paul Burns L RSC 5 Liverpool
23.04.99 Jason Williams L RSC 7 Clydach
26.06.99 Lawrence Murphy L RSC 1 Glasgow
19.09.99 Mick Mulcahy L PTS 6 Shaw
14.10.99 Lester Jacobs L PTS 6 Bloomsbury
06.11.99 Junior Witter L PTS 6 Widnes
06.12.99 Malcolm Melvin L PTS 8 Birmingham
20.12.99 Richard Williams L RSC 1 Bethnal Green
26.02.00 Jason Cook L PTS 6 Swansea
13.03.00 Christian Brady L PTS 6 Birmingham
20.03.00 Jamie Moore L RSC 2 Mansfield
15.05.00 Ernie Smith W PTS 6 Birmingham
26.05.00 Barry Connell L PTS 4 Glasgow
21.09.00 Ojay Abrahams L PTS 6 Bloomsbury
07.10.00 Michael Alexander L PTS 6 Doncaster
26.10.00 Matthew Ashmole W PTS 6 Clydach
23.11.00 Matthew Barr L PTS 4 Bayswater
30.11.00 Shpetim Hoti W PTS 4 Bloomsbury
11.12.00 Jimmy Vincent L PTS 6 Birmingham
28.01.01 Peter Jackson L PTS 6 Wolverhampton
10.02.01 Thomas McDonagh L PTS 6 Widnes
24.02.01 Spencer Fearon L PTS 4 Bethnal Green
09.03.01 John Humphrey L RSC 1 Millwall
22.04.01 Ojay Abrahams L PTS 6 Streatham
05.05.01 Liam Lathbury L PTS 6 Brighton
19.05.01 Delroy Leslie L PTS 6 Wembley
21.06.01 Shpetim Hoti W PTS 4 Earls Court
04.07.01 Darren Covill W RSC 4 Bloomsbury
26.07.01 Lee Blundell L RSC 4 Blackpool

20.09.01 Ruben Groenewald L PTS 4 Blackfriars
08.10.01 Roddy Doran L PTS 6 Birmingham
20.10.01 Ty Browne L PTS 4 Portsmouth
31.10.01 Roddy Doran DREW 6 Birmingham
16.11.01 Mark Richards L PTS 6 West Bromwich
23.11.01 Erik Teymour L RSC 2 Bethnal Green
26.01.02 Jamie Moore L RSC 3 Dagenham
04.03.02 Malcolm Melvin L PTS 8 Birmingham
15.03.02 Tom Cannon L PTS 6 Glasgow
24.04.02 Jim Rock L PTS 6 Dublin
11.05.02 Jason McKay L PTS 4 Dagenham
01.06.02 Mickey Quinn L PTS 4 Manchester
15.06.02 Darren Rhodes L PTS 4 Leeds
23.08.02 Matthew Thirlwall L RSC 3 Bethnal Green
26.09.02 Joel Ani L PTS 4 Fulham
06.10.02 Craig Winter L PTS 6 Rhyl
20.11.02 Dean Cockburn L PTS 6 Leeds
03.12.02 Roddy Doran L PTS 6 Shrewsbury
22.12.02 Alan Page L RSC 1 Salford
24.02.03 Hamid Jamali L PTS 6 Birmingham
21.03.03 Sam Price L PTS 4 Longford
29.03.03 Courtney Fry L RSC 3 Wembley
05.09.03 Jason Rushton L PTS 4 Doncaster
30.10.03 Darren McDermott L PTS 4 Dudley
07.11.03 Paul Owen L PTS 4 Sheffield
14.11.03 Jamie Hearn L PTS 4 Bethnal Green
28.11.03 Daniel Cadman L PTS 4 Derby
11.12.03 Matthew Thirlwall L PTS 6 Bethnal Green
29.02.04 Shane White L PTS 6 Bristol
12.03.04 Ovill McKenzie L RSC 2 Millwall
Career: 79 contests, won 7, drew 1, lost 71.

John Butler

Worcester. *Born* Hereford, 18 April, 1982
L.Middleweight. Ht. 6'3"
Manager D. Gardiner

05.09.03 Raz Harrison L RSC 2 Doncaster
18.11.03 Gary Woolcombe L PTS 4 Bethnal Green
Career: 2 contests, lost 2.

Paul Butlin

Oakham. *Born* Oakham, 16 March, 1976
Heavyweight. Ht. 6'1½"
Manager A. Phillips

05.10.02 Dave Clarke W PTS 4 Coventry
16.11.02 Gary Williams W RSC 1 Coventry
09.12.02 Slick Miller W PTS 6 Nottingham
08.03.03 Dave Clarke W PTS 6 Coventry
19.04.03 Paul Buttery L RSC 3 Liverpool
27.04.04 Ebrima Secka W PTS 6 Leeds
Career: 6 contests, won 5, lost 1.

Paul Buttery

Preston. *Born* Preston, 12 May, 1977
Heavyweight. Ht. 6'2½"
Manager T. Gilmour

03.02.01 Luke Simpkin L RSC 1 Manchester
24.04.01 Dave Faulkner W CO 1 Liverpool
16.11.01 Eamonn Glennon W RSC 1 Preston
10.05.02 Tony Booth W PTS 4 Preston
01.11.02 Colin Kenna DREW 6 Preston
19.04.03 Paul Butlin W RSC 3 Liverpool
17.05.03 Collice Mutizwa W RSC 1 Liverpool
01.05.04 Scott Gammer L CO 1 Bridgend
Career: 8 contests, won 5, drew 1, lost 2.

Daniel Cadman

Waltham Abbey. *Born* Harlow, 25 June, 1980
S.Middleweight. Ht. 5'10"
Manager T. Sims

25.07.03	Leigh Wicks W PTS 4 Norwich
04.10.03	Patrick Cito W PTS 6 Muswell Hill
28.11.03	Harry Butler W PTS 4 Derby
30.01.04	Mike Duffield W RSC 1 Dagenham
02.06.04	Joel Ani W CO 2 Nottingham

Career: 5 contests, won 5.

Daniel Cadman   Les Clark

Marc Callaghan

Barking. *Born* Barking, 13 November, 1977
S. Bantamweight. Ht. 5'6"
Manager B. Hearn

08.09.98	Kevin Sheil W PTS 4 Bethnal Green
31.10.98	Nicky Wilders W RSC 1 Southend
12.01.99	Nicky Wilders W RTD 2 Bethnal Green
12.03.99	Peter Allen W PTS 4 Bethnal Green
25.05.99	Simon Chambers L RSC 1 Mayfair
16.10.99	Nigel Leake W PTS 4 Bethnal Green
20.12.99	Marc Smith W PTS 4 Bethnal Green
05.02.00	Steve Brook W RSC 2 Bethnal Green
01.04.00	John Barnes W PTS 4 Bethnal Green
19.08.00	Anthony Hanna W PTS 4 Brentwood
09.10.00	Jamie McKeever L PTS 6 Liverpool
04.11.00	Nigel Senior W RSC 4 Bethnal Green
03.03.01	Anthony Hanna W PTS 6 Wembley
26.05.01	Roy Rutherford L RSC 3 Bethnal Green
01.12.01	Nigel Senior L CO 1 Bethnal Green
26.01.02	Richmond Asante W PTS 4 Dagenham
18.03.02	Michael Hunter DREW 6 Crawley
11.05.02	Andrew Ferrans W PTS 6 Dagenham
21.09.02	Steve Gethin W PTS 6 Brentwood
07.12.02	Stevie Quinn L PTS 4 Brentwood
08.03.03	Dazzo Williams L PTS 8 Bethnal Green
05.07.03	Mark Payne L PTS 6 Brentwood
08.05.04	Baz Carey W PTS 6 Dagenham
27.05.04	Steve Gethin W PTS 6 Huddersfield

Career: 24 contests, won 16, drew 1, lost 7.

Marc Callaghan   Philip Sharkey

Jason Callum

Coventry. *Born* Coventry, 5 April, 1977
Heavyweight. Ht. 6'3"
Manager O. Delargy

05.04.03	Tony Booth W PTS 6 Coventry
15.11.03	Slick Miller W PTS 4 Coventry
01.05.04	David Ingleby W PTS 6 Coventry

Career: 3 contests, won 3.

Joe Calzaghe

Newbridge. *Born* Hammersmith, 23 March, 1972
WBO S. Middleweight Champion. Former Undefeated British S. Middleweight Champion. Ht. 5'11"
Manager F. Warren

01.10.93	Paul Hanlon W RSC 1 Cardiff
10.11.93	Stinger Mason W RSC 1 Watford
16.12.93	Spencer Alton W RSC 2 Newport
22.01.94	Martin Rosamond W RSC 1 Cardiff
01.03.94	Darren Littlewood W RSC 1 Dudley
04.06.94	Karl Barwise W RSC 1 Cardiff
01.10.94	Mark Dawson W RSC 1 Cardiff
30.11.94	Trevor Ambrose W RSC 2 Wolverhampton
14.02.95	Frank Minton W CO 1 Bethnal Green
22.02.95	Bobbi Joe Edwards W PTS 8 Telford
19.05.95	Robert Curry W RSC 1 Southwark
08.07.95	Tyrone Jackson W RSC 4 York
30.09.95	Nick Manners W RSC 4 Basildon
28.10.95	Stephen Wilson W RSC 8 Kensington *(Vacant British S. Middleweight Title)*
13.02.96	Guy Stanford W RSC 1 Cardiff
13.03.96	Anthony Brooks W RSC 2 Wembley
20.04.96	Mark Delaney W RSC 5 Brentwood *(British S. Middleweight Title Defence)*

Joe Calzaghe   Les Clark

04.05.96	Warren Stowe W RTD 2 Dagenham
15.05.96	Pat Lawlor W RSC 2 Cardiff
21.01.97	Carlos Christie W CO 2 Bristol
22.03.97	Tyler Hughes W CO 1 Wythenshawe
05.06.97	Luciano Torres W RSC 3 Bristol
11.10.97	Chris Eubank W PTS 12 Sheffield
	(Vacant WBO S. Middleweight Title)
24.01.98	Branco Sobot W RSC 3 Cardiff
	(WBO S. Middleweight Title Defence)
25.04.98	Juan Carlos Gimenez W RTD 9 Cardiff
	(WBO S. Middleweight Title Defence)
13.02.99	Robin Reid W PTS 12 Newcastle
	(WBO S. Middleweight Title Defence)
05.06.99	Rick Thornberry W PTS 12 Cardiff
	(WBO S. Middleweight Title Defence)
29.01.00	David Starie W PTS 12 Manchester
	(WBO S. Middleweight Title Defence)
12.08.00	Omar Sheika W RSC 5 Wembley
	(WBO S. Middleweight Title Defence)
16.12.00	Richie Woodhall W RSC 10 Sheffield
	(WBO S. Middleweight Title Defence)
28.04.01	Mario Veit W RSC 1 Cardiff
	(WBO S. Middleweight Title Defence)
13.10.01	Will McIntyre W RSC 4 Copenhagen, Denmark
	(WBO S. Middleweight Title Defence)
20.04.02	Charles Brewer W PTS 12 Cardiff
	(WBO S. Middleweight Title Defence)
17.08.02	Miguel Jimenez W PTS 12 Cardiff
	(WBO S.Middleweight Title Defence)
14.12.02	Tocker Pudwill W RSC 2 Newcastle
	(WBO S. Middleweight Title Defence)
28.06.03	Byron Mitchell W RSC 2 Cardiff
	(WBO S.Middleweight Title Defence)
21.02.04	Mger Mkrtchian W RSC 7 Cardiff
	(WBO S.Middleweight Title Defence)

Career: 37 contests, won 37.

Alan Campbell

Kirkham. *Born* Greenock, 5 April, 1974
L. Middleweight. Ht. 5'11"
Manager Self

08.03.01	Richard Inquieti W PTS 6 Blackpool
26.07.01	Brian Gifford W PTS 6 Blackpool
28.02.04	Jon Hilton L RSC 3 Manchester
15.05.04	Dave Wakefield DREW 6 Aberdeen

Career: 4 contests, won 2, drew 1, lost 1.

Tom Cannon

Coatbridge. *Born* Bellshill, 18 March, 1980
S.Middleweight. Ht. 5'11½"
Manager R. Bannon/K. Morrison

15.06.01	Valery Odin L PTS 4 Millwall
20.10.01	Andrew Lowe L PTS 4 Glasgow
26.01.02	Arthur Shekhmurzov DREW 4 Bethnal Green
15.03.02	Harry Butler W PTS 6 Glasgow
08.06.02	Ty Browne W PTS 4 Renfrew
06.09.02	Gary Dixon W PTS 6 Glasgow
21.10.02	Dean Cockburn DREW 4 Glasgow
19.06.04	Lee Woodruff W PTS 4 Renfrew

Career: 8 contests, won 4, drew 2, lost 2.

(Barry) Baz Carey

Coventry. *Born* Coventry, 11 March, 1971
Lightweight. Ht. 5'4½"
Manager A. Phillips

19.12.01	J.J. Moore L PTS 4 Coventry
18.01.02	J.J. Moore DREW 4 Coventry
25.02.02	Chris McDonagh L PTS 6 Slough

19.03.02	Ilias Miah W PTS 6 Slough
21.09.02	Jackson Williams L PTS 6 Norwich
10.10.02	Dean Scott W RSC 2 Stoke
19.10.02	Lee McAllister L PTS 4 Renfrew
21.11.02	Chris Hooper L RTD 3 Hull
22.03.03	Dave Hinds W PTS 6 Coventry
05.04.03	Pete Buckley W PTS 4 Manchester
12.05.03	Matthew Marshall L PTS 6 Southampton
07.06.03	Joel Viney W PTS 6 Coventry
26.07.03	Andrew Ferrans DREW 4 Plymouth
13.09.03	Paul McIlwaine W RTD 2 Coventry
12.10.03	Daniel Thorpe DREW 6 Sheffield
08.11.03	Carl Allen L RSC 2 Coventry
15.03.04	Andrew Ferrans L PTS 10 Glasgow
	(Vacant British Masters S.Featherweight Title)
17.04.04	Michael Kelly L PTS 4 Belfast
26.04.04	Rendall Munroe L PTS 6 Cleethorpes
08.05.04	Marc Callaghan L PTS 6 Dagenham

Career: 20 contests, won 6, drew 3, lost 11.

Baz Carey   Les Clark

Dafydd Carlin

Belfast. *Born* Brecon, 2 August, 1978
Northern Ireland Lightweight Champion.
Ht. 5'6"
Manager Self

01.04.01	Paddy Folan W PTS 4 Southwark
28.04.01	Alex Arthur L PTS 4 Cardiff
03.06.01	Dave Hinds W PTS 4 Southwark
22.09.01	Danny Hunt L PTS 4 Bethnal Green
15.12.01	Matthew Hatton L PTS 6 Wembley
19.01.02	Francis Barrett L PTS 4 Bethnal Green
12.02.02	Scott Miller L PTS 4 Bethnal Green
20.04.02	Bradley Pryce L RSC 8 Cardiff
12.10.02	Ross Minter L RSC 1 Bethnal Green
08.12.02	Ben Hudson L PTS 4 Bethnal Green
01.02.03	Robbie Murray L PTS 4 Belfast
18.02.03	Peter McDonagh W PTS 4 Bethnal Green
14.03.03	Colin Bain L PTS 6 Glasgow
05.04.03	Gary Hamilton W PTS 10 Belfast
	(Vacant Northern Ireland Lightweight Title)
04.10.03	Ryan Barrett W PTS 4 Belfast
11.10.03	Jamie Arthur L RSC 4 Portsmouth
06.03.04	Willie Limond L RSC 1 Renfrew

Career: 17 contests, won 5, lost 12.

Brian Carr

Moodiesburn. *Born* Glasgow, 20 June, 1969
Scottish Featherweight Champion. Former Commonwealth S. Bantamweight Champion. Ht. 5'6"
Manager K. Morrison

18.12.94	Fred Reeve W CO 2 Glasgow
21.01.95	Shaun Anderson W PTS 6 Glasgow
04.03.95	G. G. Goddard W PTS 8 Livingston
13.05.95	Paul Wynn W RTD 2 Glasgow
08.06.95	Abdul Manna W PTS 6 Glasgow
13.10.95	Muhammad Shaffique W PTS 6 Glasgow
17.12.95	Abdul Mannon W PTS 8 Glasgow
16.03.96	Chip O'Neill W PTS 4 Glasgow
26.04.96	Mike Deveney W PTS 10 Glasgow
	(Vacant Scottish Featherweight Title)
20.09.96	Fred Reeve W RSC 3 Glasgow
06.11.96	Mike Deveney W PTS 10 Glasgow
	(Scottish Featherweight Title Defence)
22.12.96	Pete Buckley W PTS 6 Glasgow
04.04.97	Lyndon Kershaw W PTS 10 Glasgow
	(Elim. British S. Bantamweight Title)
05.07.97	Kevin Sheil W RSC 5 Glasgow
12.09.97	Carl Allen W PTS 8 Glasgow
01.11.97	Steve Conway W PTS 6 Glasgow
31.01.98	Michael Brodie L RSC 10 Edmonton
	(British & Commonwealth S. Bantamweight Title Challenges)
17.09.98	Pete Buckley W PTS 6 Glasgow
06.02.99	Patrick Mullings L PTS 12 Halifax
	(Vacant British S. Bantamweight Title)
27.02.99	Fondil Madani W CO 3 Bethnal Green
09.04.99	Keith Jones W PTS 8 Glasgow
26.06.99	Cassius Baloyi L RTD 9 Glasgow
	(WBU Featherweight Title Challenge)
09.10.99	Pete Buckley W PTS 6 Manchester
12.11.99	Harry Woods W PTS 6 Glasgow
11.12.99	Lee Williamson DREW 6 Liverpool
18.03.00	Nedal Hussein L PTS 12 Glasgow
	(Vacant Commonwealth S. Bantamweight Title)
26.05.00	Ian Turner W PTS 6 Glasgow
24.06.00	Dave Hinds W PTS 4 Glasgow
02.10.00	Pete Buckley W PTS 4 Glasgow
03.11.01	Mishek Kondwani W PTS 12 Glasgow
	(Vacant Commonwealth S.Bantamweight Title)
18.03.02	Michael Alldis L PTS 12 Crawley
	(Vacant British S. Bantamweight Title. Commonwealth S. Bantamweight Title Defence)
22.03.03	John Mackay L PTS 8 Renfrew
12.07.03	Esham Pickering L RSC 4 Renfrew
	(Vacant British S.Bantamweight Title. Commonwealth S.Bantamweight Title Challenge)

Career: 33 contests, won 25, drew 1, lost 7.

Henry Castle

Salisbury. *Born* Southampton, 7 February, 1979
Featherweight. Ht. 5'6¾"
Manager K. Sanders/E. Maloney

29.01.01	Jason Nesbitt W CO 6 Peterborough
26.03.01	Eddie Nevins W RSC 2 Peterborough
23.11.01	Jimmy Beech W PTS 4 Bethnal Green
11.03.02	David Lowry W RSC 1 Glasgow
20.04.02	Jason Nesbitt W PTS 4 Cardiff
25.05.02	Jimmy Beech W PTS 4 Portsmouth

17.08.02 Joel Viney W RSC 1 Cardiff
23.11.02 John Mackay L RTD 8 Derby
29.03.03 Jus Wallie L RSC 2 Portsmouth
25.09.03 Mark Alexander W PTS 6 Bethnal Green
21.11.03 Pete Buckley W PTS 4 Millwall
20.02.04 Daleboy Rees W RSC 4 Bethnal Green
Career: 12 contests, won 10, lost 2.

Stephen Chinnock

Rugeley. *Born* Lichfield, 4 December, 1975
Midlands Area Featherweight Champion.
Ht. 5'10"
Manager Self

10.09.00 Neil Read W RSC 5 Walsall
06.11.00 Jason Nesbitt W PTS 6 Wolverhampton
27.11.00 Jason White W PTS 4 Birmingham
20.05.01 Gareth Wiltshaw W PTS 6 Wolverhampton
07.10.01 Kevin Gerowski W PTS 10 Wolverhampton
(Vacant Midlands Area Featherweight Title)
18.01.02 John Mackay W PTS 4 Coventry
13.04.02 Neil Read W CO 3 Wolverhampton
(Midlands Area Featherweight Title Defence)
08.09.02 Nigel Senior W PTS 6 Wolverhampton
17.05.03 Dazzo Williams L PTS 10 Liverpool
(Elim. British Featherweight Title)
20.09.03 Mickey Bowden W PTS 8 Nottingham
14.02.04 Roy Rutherford L RSC 4 Nottingham
(Vacant English S.Featherweight Title)
Career: 11 contests, won 9, lost 2.

Stephen Chinnock   Les Clark

Anthony Christopher

Aberystwyth. *Born* Aberystwyth, 18 August, 1981
Welterweight. Ht. 5'8¼"
Manager Self

23.09.01 Arv Mittoo DREW 6 Shaw
29.09.02 Ernie Smith W PTS 6 Shrewsbury
03.12.02 Ernie Smith L PTS 6 Shrewsbury
23.02.03 Dean Larter L PTS 6 Aberystwyth
20.02.04 Stefy Bull L PTS 6 Doncaster
06.03.04 Gary Young L CO 1 Renfrew
Career: 6 contests, won 1, drew 1, lost 4.

(Patoma) Patrick Cito (Sitho)

Birmingham. *Born* Congo, 15 September, 1976
S. Middleweight. Ht. 5'9"
Manager N. Nobbs

11.02.94 Maneno Oswald L CO 6 Dar-es-Salaam, Tanzania
29.06.96 Shadrack Kipruto W PTS 6 Nairobi, Kenya
13.07.96 Joe John L RSC 8 Nairobi, Kenya
22.02.97 Rashid Matumla L PTS 10 Tanga, Tanzania
07.12.97 Joseph Marwa L PTS 10 Dar-es-Salaam, Tanzania
12.09.98 Jong-Myung Kim W CO 3 Nairobi, Kenya
28.04.99 Mondi Mbonambi L RSC 3 Benoni, South Africa
03.10.99 John Tshabalala L PTS 6 Johannesburg, South Africa
29.10.99 Johan Sinden DREW 6 Guateng, South Africa
28.11.99 Johnson Tshuma L PTS 8 Peddie, South Africa
25.06.00 Mack Rarzar W CO 1 Johannesburg, South Africa
05.10.00 Tyrone Churchill W RSC 2 Johannesburg, South Africa
12.11.00 Renier Dorfling L RSC 1 Mpumalanga, South Africa
29.08.01 William Gare L PTS 8 Gaborone, South Africa
08.05.03 Matthew Hall L PTS 4 Widnes
31.05.03 Ryan Kasprzycki W RSC 2 Barnsley
08.06.03 Alan Page L RSC 3 Shaw
31.07.03 Paul Owen L PTS 6 Sheffield
29.08.03 Paul Smith L PTS 4 Liverpool
18.09.03 Ciaran Healy L PTS 4 Mayfair
25.09.03 Sonny Pollard L PTS 6 Hull
04.10.03 Daniel Cadman L PTS 6 Muswell Hill
23.11.03 Daniel Teasdale NC 1 Rotherham
07.12.03 Donovan Smillie L PTS 6 Bradford
07.02.04 Gokhan Kazaz L PTS 4 Bethnal Green
19.02.04 Peter Jackson DREW 4 Dudley
29.02.04 Darren Stubbs L PTS 6 Shaw
12.03.04 Matthew Thirlwall L RSC 3 Nottingham
16.04.04 Donovan Smillie L RSC 3 Bradford
22.05.04 Tony Quigley L PTS 4 Widnes
04.06.04 Danny Grainger L PTS 6 Hull
Career: 31 contests, won 5, drew 2, lost 23, no contest 1.

Patrick Cito   Les Clark

Dave Clarke

Blackpool. *Born* Dover, 20 June, 1976
Heavyweight. Ht. 6'1"
Manager L. Veitch

22.11.01 Roman Greenberg L RSC 5 Paddington
11.02.02 Colin Kenna L RSC 4 Southampton
15.03.02 Shaun Bowes L PTS 6 Spennymoor
24.03.02 Tommy Eastwood L PTS 6 Streatham
11.05.02 Ivan Botton L PTS 6 Newark
03.06.02 Tony Moran L PTS 6 Glasgow
25.06.02 Carl Wright L PTS 6 Rugby
20.07.02 Matt Legg L RSC 2 Bethnal Green
05.10.02 Paul Butlin L PTS 4 Coventry
12.10.02 Enzo Maccarinelli L RSC 2 Bethnal Green
20.11.02 Costi Marin W RSC 2 Leeds
30.11.02 Ahmad Cheleh W RSC 1 Liverpool
05.12.02 Roman Greenberg L RSC 1 Sheffield
08.01.03 Scott Gammer L PTS 4 Aberdare
08.03.03 Paul Butlin L PTS 6 Coventry
17.03.03 Costi Marin W PTS 6 Glasgow
24.03.03 Neil Dawson L PTS 4 Barnsley
13.04.03 Oneal Murray W PTS 4 Streatham
28.04.03 Shane Woollas L PTS 6 Cleethorpes
15.05.03 Matt Skelton L RSC 1 Mayfair
28.06.03 Scott Gammer L RSC 1 Cardiff
06.09.03 Carl Baker L RSC 1 Aberdeen
06.10.03 Neil Dawson L PTS 6 Barnsley
01.12.03 Lee Mountford L PTS 6 Bradford
24.01.04 Augustin N'Gou L PTS 6 Wembley
16.02.04 Chris Woollas L PTS 6 Scunthorpe
12.03.04 Coleman Barrett L PTS 6 Nottingham
25.04.04 Luke Simpkin L RSC 2 Nottingham
07.06.04 Dave McKenna L PTS 6 Glasgow
Career: 29 contests, won 4, lost 25.

Dave Clarke   Les Clark

Howard Clarke

Warley. *Born* London, 23 September, 1967
Middleweight. Ht. 5'10"
Manager Self

15.10.91 Chris Mylan W PTS 4 Dudley
09.12.91 Claude Rossi W RSC 3 Brierley Hill
04.02.92 Julian Eavis W PTS 4 Alfreton
03.03.92 Dave Andrews W RSC 3 Cradley Heath

21.05.92   Richard O'Brien W CO 1 Cradley
            Heath
29.09.92   Paul King W PTS 6 Stoke
27.10.92   Gordon Blair L RSC 4 Cradley Heath
16.03.93   Paul King W PTS 6 Edgbaston
07.06.93   Dean Bramhald W RTD 2 Walsall
29.06.93   Paul King W PTS 6 Edgbaston
06.10.93   Julian Eavis L PTS 8 Solihull
30.11.93   Julian Eavis W PTS 8 Wolverhampton
08.02.94   Nigel Bradley W RTD 6
            Wolverhampton
18.04.94   Andy Peach W PTS 6 Walsall
28.06.94   Dennis Berry L RSC 3 Edgbaston
12.10.94   Julian Eavis W PTS 8 Stoke
25.10.94   Andy Peach W RSC 3 Edgbaston
02.11.94   Julian Eavis L PTS 8 Birmingham
29.11.94   Julian Eavis W PTS 6 Cannock
07.12.94   Peter Reid W PTS 8 Stoke
25.01.95   Dennis Berry L PTS 8 Stoke
08.03.95   Andrew Jervis W PTS 6 Solihull
11.05.95   David Bain W RSC 1 Dudley
20.09.95   Michael Smyth DREW 6 Ystrad
02.10.95   Nigel Wenton L PTS 6 Mayfair
02.12.96   Martin Smith L PTS 8 Birmingham
29.01.97   Gary Beardsley W PTS 6 Stoke
11.02.97   Prince Kasi Kaihau L RSC 4
            Wolverhampton
19.03.97   Mark Cichocki W PTS 6 Stoke
15.04.97   Prince Kasi Kaihau W PTS 6
            Edgbaston
30.04.97   Allan Gray W PTS 8 Acton
22.05.97   Michael Alexander W RSC 3 Solihull
21.06.97   Paul Samuels L PTS 8 Cardiff
09.09.97   Harry Dhami L PTS 8 Bethnal Green
05.11.97   Andras Galfi W PTS 8 Tenerife
27.01.98   Mack Razor L PTS 8 Hammanskraal,
            South Africa
23.03.98   Lindon Scarlett DREW 6 Crystal
            Palace
18.07.98   Jason Papillion W PTS 8 Sheffield
13.03.99   Fernando Vargas L RSC 4 NYC, New
            York, USA
            (IBF L. Middleweight Title Challenge)
05.11.99   Michael Rask L PTS 12 Aalberg,
            Denmark
            (WBA Inter-Continental
            L. Middleweight Title Challenge)
29.05.00   Anthony Farnell L PTS 12 Manchester
            (WBO Inter-Continental
            L. Middleweight Title Challenge)
12.08.00   Takaloo L PTS 12 Wembley
            (Vacant IBF Inter-Continental
            L.Middleweight Title)
04.11.00   Richard Williams L CO 4 Bethnal
            Green
16.12.00   Ryan Rhodes L PTS 6 Sheffield
03.02.01   Michael Jones L PTS 4 Manchester
26.02.01   Jawaid Khaliq L PTS 6 Nottingham
07.04.01   Gary Lockett L RSC 2 Wembley
06.05.01   Ian Cooper L PTS 6 Hartlepool
04.06.01   James Docherty L PTS 6 Hartlepool
14.07.01   Gary Lockett L CO 1 Wembley
15.09.01   Thomas McDonagh L PTS 6
            Manchester
10.11.01   Ossie Duran L PTS 6 Wembley
26.11.01   Wayne Pinder L PTS 6 Manchester
16.12.01   Erik Teymour L PTS 6 Southwark
27.01.02   Paul Samuels L PTS 6 Streatham
03.03.02   Lee Murtagh NC 2 Shaw
20.04.01   Wayne Elcock L PTS 4 Cardiff
25.05.02   Ross Minter W RSC 2 Portsmouth
08.06.02   Alexander Vetoux L RSC 4 Renfrew
27.07.02   Mihaly Kotai L RSC 1 Nottingham

08.12.02   Matthew Tait L PTS 6 Bethnal Green
21.12.02   Matthew Thirlwall L PTS 6 Dagenham
25.01.03   Paul Samuels L PTS 6 Bridgend
08.02.03   Michael Jones L PTS 6 Liverpool
05.03.03   Gilbert Eastman L PTS 6 Bethnal
            Green
05.04.03   Paul Smith L PTS 4 Manchester
21.06.03   Wayne Pinder L PTS 4 Manchester
01.08.03   Arthur Shekhmurzov L PTS 6 Bethnal
            Green
17.10.03   Scott Dixon L PTS 6 Glasgow
25.10.03   Lawrence Murphy L PTS 6 Edinburgh
14.11.03   Sonny Pollard L PTS 6 Hull
07.02.04   Wayne Alexander L RSC 2 Bethnal
            Green
03.04.04   Paul Smith L PTS 4 Manchester
10.04.04   Wayne Pinder L PTS 4 Manchester
08.05.04   Allan Foster L PTS 4 Dagenham
04.06.04   Andrew Facey L PTS 6 Hull
17.06.04   P.J.Maxwell L RSC 1 Sheffield
Career: 77 contests, won 27, drew 2, lost 47, no
         contest, 1.

Darren Cleary

Salford. *Born* Salford, 28 February, 1980
Bantamweight. Ht. 5'5"
Manager Self

27.05.01   Marty Kayes W PTS 4 Manchester
07.07.01   Marty Kayes W PTS 4 Manchester
18.03.02   Jamil Hussain DREW 4 Crawley
27.04.02   Jamil Hussain DREW 4 Huddersfield
11.05.02   Jimbo Rooney W PTS 4 Dagenham
08.07.02   Martin Power L PTS 4 Mayfair
21.12.02   Rocky Dean L PTS 4 Millwall
08.06.03   Shinny Bayaar L RSC 2 Shaw
17.07.03   Martin Power L PTS 6 Dagenham
26.02.04   Mark Moran L PTS 4 Widnes
22.05.04   Mark Moran DREW 4 Widnes
Career: 11 contests, won 3, drew 3, lost 5.

Edwin Cleary

Leamington. *Born* Leamington, 8 January,
1973
L. Heavyweight. Ht. 5'10½"
Manager J. Harding/J. Griffin

20.03.97   Gary Reyniers W PTS 6 Newark
16.05.97   Slick Miller DREW 6 Hull
10.07.97   Kevin Burton W RSC 1 Doncaster
18.08.97   Kevin Burton W PTS 6 Nottingham
30.09.97   Gary Reyniers DREW 6 Edgbaston
30.10.97   Jon Rees W PTS 6 Newark
27.03.98   Israel Khumalo W CO 2 Telford
04.06.98   Martin McDonough W PTS 6 Dudley
11.09.98   Peter Mason L PTS 6 Newark
15.08.99   William Webster W PTS 6 Derby
22.05.00   Dean Ashton DREW 4 Coventry
15.11.03   Ovill McKenzie L PTS 4 Coventry
Career: 12 contests, won 7, drew 3, lost 2.

(Adrian) Ady Clegg

Pontefract. *Born* Pontefract, 30 May, 1984
L.Middleweight. Ht. 5'10"
Manager C. Aston

13.09.03   Brian Coleman W PTS 6 Wakefield
06.10.03   Richard Inquieti W PTS 6 Barnsley
15.03.04   Richard Inquieti W PTS 6 Bradford
19.04.04   Keith Ellwood W CO 5 Glasgow
27.05.04   Jon Harrison L PTS 4 Huddersfield
Career: 5 contests, won 4, lost 1.

Dean Cockburn

Doncaster. *Born* Doncaster, 28 March, 1979
S. Middleweight. Ht. 5'9½"
Manager Self

17.09.01   Mark Chesters W RSC 4 Glasgow
17.11.01   Paul Wesley W PTS 4 Glasgow
25.03.02   Paul Buchanan L PTS 6 Sunderland
21.06.02   Darren Stubbs W RSC 1 Leeds
08.10.02   Jason McKay L PTS 6 Glasgow
21.10.02   Tom Cannon DREW 4 Glasgow
01.11.02   Neil Bonner W RSC 2 Preston
20.11.02   Harry Butler W PTS 6 Leeds
17.03.03   Barry Thorogood W PTS 4
            Southampton
10.05.03   George Robshaw L PTS 6 Huddersfield
07.05.04   Simeon Cover W PTS 6 Doncaster
14.06.04   Terry Morrill W RTD 4 Cleethorpes
Career: 12 contests, won 8, drew 1, lost 3.

Brian Coleman

Birmingham. *Born* Birmingham, 27 July,
1969
L. Middleweight. Ht. 5'11"
Manager Self

21.11.91   Jamie Morris DREW 6 Stafford
11.12.91   Craig Hartwell DREW 6 Leicester
22.01.92   John O. Johnson L PTS 6 Stoke
20.02.92   Davy Robb L PTS 6 Oakengates
31.03.92   Blue Butterworth L PTS 6 Stockport
17.05.92   Korso Aleain L RSC 5 Harringay
17.09.92   Nicky Bardle L PTS 4 Watford
21.10.92   Jason Barker W PTS 6 Stoke
10.12.92   A. M. Milton DREW 4 Bethnal Green
31.03.93   A. M. Milton L PTS 4 Bethnal Green
26.04.93   Jason Beard L PTS 6 Lewisham
06.05.93   Mark Allen W PTS 6 Walsall
18.05.93   Sean Metherell DREW 6 Kettering
27.05.93   Blue Butterworth L PTS 6 Burnley
23.06.93   Jonathan Thaxton L PTS 8 Gorleston
11.08.93   Steve Howden L RSC 4 Mansfield
13.09.93   Mick Hoban L PTS 6 Middleton
01.12.93   A. M. Milton L PTS 4 Bethnal Green
08.12.93   Chris Pollock W PTS 6 Stoke
16.12.93   Mark Newton L PTS 6 Newport
11.01.94   Paul Knights L RSC 4 Bethnal Green
08.02.94   Andy Peach W PTS 6 Wolverhampton
18.02.94   Cam Raeside L PTS 6 Leicester
08.03.94   Chris Pollock L PTS 6 Edgbaston
29.03.94   P. J. Gallagher L PTS 6 Bethnal Green
14.04.94   Cham Joof L CO 3 Battersea
02.06.94   Scott Walker L CO 1 Middleton
12.09.94   Shabba Edwards L PTS 6 Mayfair
19.09.94   Mark Breslin L CO 1 Glasgow
09.11.94   Kenny Scott L PTS 6 Stafford
23.11.94   Billy McDougall W PTS 4 Piccadilly
29.11.94   Warren Stephens W PTS 6
            Wolverhampton
09.12.94   Danny Stevens L RTD 2 Bethnal Green
24.01.95   Wayne Jones L PTS 6 Piccadilly
07.02.95   Alan Temple L PTS 6 Ipswich
23.02.95   Darren Covill L PTS 6 Southwark
16.03.95   Paul Knights L RSC 2 Basildon
02.07.95   Tommy Lawler L PTS 4 Dublin
08.09.95   George Naylor L PTS 6 Liverpool
27.09.95   Allan Gray L PTS 6 Bethnal Green
20.10.95   Mikael Nilsson L PTS 4 Ipswich
02.11.95   Marco Fattore W PTS 6 Mayfair
16.11.95   Alan Bosworth L PTS 6 Evesham
24.11.95   Chris Barnett L PTS 6 Manchester
02.12.95   Neil Sinclair L RTD 1 Belfast
20.01.96   James Hare L PTS 6 Mansfield

95

29.01.96 Dave Fallon L PTS 6 Piccadilly
13.02.96 Martin Holgate L PTS 4 Bethnal Green
21.02.96 Marco Fattore W PTS 6 Piccadilly
13.03.96 Paul Samuels L PTS 6 Wembley
03.04.96 Ian Honeywood L PTS 6 Bethnal Green
20.04.96 Ray Robinson L PTS 6 Brentwood
24.05.96 Scott Dixon L PTS 8 Glasgow
08.06.96 Mark Winters L PTS 4 Newcastle
06.07.96 Nick Boyd L PTS 4 Manchester
16.08.96 Charlie Paine W PTS 6 Liverpool
27.08.96 Dave Brazil L PTS 6 Windsor
19.09.96 Ricky Sackfield W RSC 3 Manchester
27.09.96 Nicky Bardle L PTS 4 Stevenage
08.10.96 Marcus McCrae W PTS 6 Battersea
09.11.96 Mark Haslam L PTS 6 Manchester
27.11.96 Bernard Paul L PTS 6 Bethnal Green
09.12.96 Wayne Windle L PTS 6 Chesterfield
18.01.97 Paul Burke L PTS 6 Manchester
19.02.97 Anthony Campbell L PTS 6 Acton
25.03.97 Craig Stanley DREW 4 Lewisham
03.04.97 Kevin McCarthy L PTS 6 Wembley
22.04.97 Georgie Smith L PTS 6 Bethnal Green
19.05.97 John O.Johnson DREW 6 Cleethorpes
02.06.97 Steve McLevy W RSC 5 Glasgow
02.08.97 Junior Witter L PTS 4 Barnsley
13.09.97 Jason Rowland L PTS 8 Millwall
04.10.97 Everald Williams L PTS 4 Muswell Hill
24.10.97 Anthony Maynard L CO 1 Birmingham
27.01.98 Kevin McCarthy L PTS 6 Streatham
23.02.98 Kevin McKillan L PTS 6 Salford
05.03.98 Junior Witter L PTS 6 Leeds
24.03.98 Jon Harrison DREW 6 Wolverhampton
03.04.98 Peter Nightingale L PTS 6 West Bromwich
23.04.98 Marc Smith W PTS 6 Edgbaston
06.05.98 Stuart Rimmer L PTS 6 Blackpool
18.05.98 Steve Conway L PTS 6 Cleethorpes
26.05.98 Rimvidas Billius L PTS 4 Mayfair
06.06.98 Jamie McKeever L PTS 4 Liverpool
18.06.98 Shaun Stokes L PTS 6 Sheffield
12.09.98 Graham Earl L PTS 4 Bethnal Green
03.10.98 Peter Nightingale L PTS 6 West Bromwich
12.10.98 Christian Brady L PTS 6 Birmingham
22.10.98 Colin Lynes L RSC 2 Barking
25.11.98 Arv Mittoo W PTS 6 Clydach
07.12.98 Gavin Down L PTS 6 Manchester
21.01.99 Dennis Griffin W PTS 6 Piccadilly
06.02.99 Tontcho Tontchev L PTS 6 Halifax
26.02.99 Peter Nightingale L PTS 6 West Bromwich
08.03.99 Sammy Smith W PTS 8 Birmingham
25.03.99 Ernie Smith W PTS 6 Edgbaston
03.04.99 Ricky Hatton L CO 2 Kensington
27.05.99 Ernie Smith L PTS 6 Edgbaston
04.06.99 Steve Conway L PTS 6 Hull
26.06.99 Steve Murray L PTS 6 Millwall
07.08.99 Jonathan Thaxton L PTS 6 Dagenham
13.09.99 Bobby Vanzie L PTS 8 Bethnal Green
27.09.99 Steve Conway L PTS 6 Leeds
24.10.99 Peter Nightingale L PTS 10 Wolverhampton
  (Midlands Area Welterweight Title Challenge)
06.11.99 Jacek Bielski L PTS 4 Bethnal Green
22.11.99 Sonny Thind W RSC 5 Piccadilly
30.11.99 Ernie Smith W PTS 8 Wolverhampton
11.12.99 Oscar Hall L PTS 6 Liverpool
20.01.00 Alan Bosworth L PTS 6 Piccadilly
12.02.00 Shaun Stokes W PTS 4 Sheffield
24.02.00 Ernie Smith W PTS 6 Edgbaston
09.03.00 Paul Burns L PTS 6 Liverpool

25.03.00 Michael Jennings L PTS 6 Liverpool
16.05.00 Michael Jennings L PTS 6 Warrington
25.05.00 Lee Molyneux L PTS 6 Peterborough
19.06.00 Gavin Down L PTS 4 Burton
19.08.00 Glenn McClarnon L PTS 6 Brentwood
25.09.00 Derek Roche L PTS 6 Barnsley
14.10.00 Colin Lynes L PTS 6 Wembley
31.10.00 Ivan Kirpa L RSC 3 Hammersmith
02.12.00 John Tiftik L PTS 4 Chigwell
11.12.00 Lee Bird W CO 4 Cleethorpes
23.01.01 Paul Knights L PTS 6 Crawley
03.02.01 Darren Spencer L PTS 6 Manchester
10.02.01 Carl Wall L RSC 1 Widnes
17.03.01 Bradley Pryce L PTS 4 Manchester
26.03.01 Ross Minter L PTS 6 Wembley
28.04.01 Ismail Khalil L PTS 4 Cardiff
08.05.01 Gavin Wake L PTS 4 Barnsley
21.05.01 Ernie Smith L PTS 6 Birmingham
09.06.01 Matthew Hatton L RTD 2 Bethnal Green
08.12.01 Gavin Down L RSC 1 Chesterfield
23.02.02 Young Muttley L PTS 4 Nottingham
22.03.02 Sam Gorman L PTS 6 Coventry
26.04.02 Andy Egan L PTS 6 Coventry
08.06.02 Ronnie Nailen L PTS 4 Renfrew
23.08.02 Brett James L PTS 6 Bethnal Green
28.09.02 Thomas McDonagh L RSC 1 Manchester
18.02.03 Ben Hudson L PTS 6 Bethnal Green
09.03.03 Wayne Shepherd L PTS 6 Shaw
22.03.03 Andy Egan L PTS 6 Coventry
05.04.03 Matthew Hall L RSC 1 Manchester
09.05.03 Sammy Smith L PTS 6 Longford
31.05.03 Terry Fletcher L PTS 4 Barnsley
15.06.03 Lee McAllister L PTS 6 Bradford
22.07.03 Ashley Theophane L PTS 6 Bethnal Green
03.08.03 Lee McAllister L PTS 4 Stalybridge
13.09.03 Ady Clegg L PTS 6 Wakefield
25.09.03 Elvis Mbwakongo L PTS 6 Bethnal Green
05.10.03 Steve Conway L PTS 6 Bradford
18.10.03 Colin Lynes L PTS 4 Manchester
26.10.03 Kevin Phelan L PTS 6 Longford
18.11.03 Mark Stupple L PTS 6 Bethnal Green
29.11.03 Barrie Lee L PTS 4 Renfrew
07.12.03 Ali Nuumembe L RTD 2 Bradford
16.02.04 Dave Pearson W PTS 6 Scunthorpe
29.02.04 Mark Paxford L PTS 6 Shaw
16.04.04 Franny Jones L PTS 6 Hartlepool
23.04.04 Barry Hughes L PTS 8 Glasgow
01.05.04 Richard Mazurek L PTS 6 Coventry
08.05.04 Michael Rennie L PTS 4 Dagenham
28.05.04 Barrie Lee L PTS 6 Glasgow
Career: 162 contests, won 23, drew 7, lost 132.

Jason Collins

Walsall. *Born* Walsall, 5 December, 1972
Middleweight. Former Undefeated British Masters S. Middleweight Champion.
Ht. 5'9"
Manager Self

18.02.99 Biagio Falcone L PTS 6 Glasgow
17.03.99 Stuart Harper W RSC 2 Stoke
06.06.99 Jon Foster DREW 6 Nottingham
15.08.99 Matt Galer W PTS 6 Derby
28.10.99 Lee Blundell DREW 6 Burnley
20.11.99 Dennis Berry L PTS 6 Grantham
14.12.99 Jorge Araujo L PTS 6 Telde, Gran Canaria, Spain
15.01.00 Martin Jolley W RTD 1 Doncaster
18.02.00 Oscar Hall DREW 6 West Bromwich

27.02.00 Jawaid Khaliq L PTS 6 Leeds
05.03.00 Wayne Shepherd W PTS 6 Shaw
21.03.00 Sharden Ansoula W PTS 6 Telde, Gran Canaria
21.05.00 Neville Brown L RSC 2 Derby
08.07.00 Darren Rhodes DREW 4 Widnes
04.09.00 Darren Rhodes W PTS 4 Manchester
01.10.00 Juergen Braehmer L CO 1 Hamburg, Germany
13.11.00 Takaloo L RSC 2 Bethnal Green
16.12.00 Louis Swales DREW 4 Sheffield
27.01.01 Spencer Fearon W PTS 4 Bethnal Green
26.03.01 P.J. Maxwell W PTS 4 Wembley
20.04.01 Jim Rock L PTS 6 Dublin
08.06.01 Leigh Wicks W PTS 4 Hull
21.06.01 Lester Jacobs L CO 9 Earls Court
  (WBF Middleweight Title Challenge)
07.09.01 Delroy Mellis W DIS 5 Bethnal Green
22.09.01 Ian Cooper L PTS 10 Newcastle
  (Vacant British Masters Middleweight Title)
27.10.01 Ryan Rhodes L PTS 4 Manchester
17.11.01 Gerard Murphy L PTS 4 Glasgow
08.12.01 Steven Bendall L PTS 12 Dagenham
  (Vacant WBU Inter-Continental Middleweight Title)
12.02.02 Delroy Leslie L RSC 1 Bethnal Green
18.03.02 Andrew Buchanan W PTS 4 Crawley
01.06.02 Wayne Elcock L RSC 2 Manchester
17.08.02 Jeff Lacy L CO 1 Cardiff
21.09.02 Wayne Asker DREW 6 Norwich
10.10.02 Mike Duffield W PTS 4 Piccadilly
25.10.02 Matthew Thirlwall L RSC 5 Bethnal Green
23.11.02 Wayne Elcock L RSC 1 Derby
24.02.03 Michael Monaghan L PTS 8 Birmingham
20.03.03 Kreshnik Qato L PTS 4 Queensway
29.03.03 Gary Lockett L CO 1 Portsmouth
12.05.03 Ojay Abrahams W PTS 10 Birmingham
  (Vacant British Masters S.Middleweight Title)
06.06.03 Danny Thornton L PTS 10 Hull
  (Vacant Central Area Middleweight Title)
12.07.03 Lawrence Murphy L PTS 4 Renfrew
25.07.03 Gilbert Eastman L RSC 1 Norwich
06.10.03 Alan Jones L PTS 8 Birmingham
28.11.03 Danny Thornton L PTS 10 Hull
  (Central Area Middleweight Title Challenge)
25.04.04 Michael Monaghan L PTS 6 Nottingham
10.05.04 Hamid Jamali L PTS 8 Birmingham
02.06.04 Alan Jones L PTS 6 Hereford
Career: 48 contests, won 13, drew 6, lost 29.

Ricky Colquhoun

Castleford. *Born* Pontefract, 26 November, 1974
Middleweight. Ht. 5'9"
Manager S. Butler

10.10.03 Jimi Hendricks L RSC 1 Darlington
Career: 1 contest, lost 1.

Martin Concepcion

Leicester. *Born* Leicester, 11 August, 1981
L. Middleweight. Ht. 5'9"
Manager F. Warren/F. Maloney

Martin Concepcion   Les Clark

06.12.03	Danny Gwilym W RSC 2 Cardiff
07.02.04	Jed Tytler W RSC 2 Bethnal Green
27.03.04	Joel Ani W RTD 3 Edinburgh
05.06.04	William Webster W RSC 1 Bethnal Green

Career: 4 contests, won 4.

Barry Connell

Glasgow. *Born* Glasgow, 25 July, 1979
S. Middleweight. Ht. 6'1"
Manager K. Morrison

24.02.00	Colin Vidler W PTS 6 Glasgow
07.04.00	Ernie Smith W PTS 6 Glasgow
26.05.00	Harry Butler W PTS 4 Glasgow
14.03.03	Paul Owen W PTS 6 Glasgow
22.03.03	Simeon Cover W PTS 4 Renfrew
16.05.03	Martin Thompson DREW 4 Glasgow
17.10.03	Simeon Cover W PTS 6 Glasgow
07.12.03	Paul Owen W PTS 6 Glasgow
29.02.04	Gary Dixon L RTD 3 Shaw

Career: 9 contests, won 7, drew 1, lost 1.

Steve Conway

Dewsbury. *Born* Hartlepool, 6 October, 1977
Lightweight. Ht. 5'8"
Manager Self

21.02.96	Robert Grubb W PTS 6 Batley
24.04.96	Ervine Blake W PTS 6 Solihull
20.05.96	Chris Lyons W PTS 6 Cleethorpes
30.05.96	Ram Singh W PTS 6 Lincoln
03.02.97	Jason Squire W PTS 6 Leicester
11.04.97	Marc Smith W PTS 4 Barnsley
22.09.97	Arv Mittoo W PTS 6 Cleethorpes
09.10.97	Arv Mittoo W PTS 6 Leeds
01.11.97	Brian Carr L PTS 6 Glasgow
14.11.97	Brendan Bryce W PTS 6 Mere
04.12.97	Kid McAuley W RSC 5 Doncaster
15.12.97	Nicky Wilders W PTS 6 Cleethorpes
05.03.98	Pete Buckley W PTS 6 Leeds
25.04.98	Dean Phillips W PTS 6 Cardiff
09.05.98	Gary Flear W PTS 4 Sheffield
18.05.98	Brian Coleman W PTS 6 Cleethorpes
05.09.98	Benny Jones W PTS 4 Telford
19.12.98	Gary Thornhill L RSC 9 Liverpool
	(WBO Inter-Continental S. Featherweight Title Challenge)
04.06.99	Brian Coleman W PTS 6 Hull
27.09.99	Brian Coleman W PTS 6 Leeds
27.02.00	Chris Price W RTD 3 Leeds
21.03.00	Pedro Miranda L RSC 3 Telde, Gran Canaria
15.07.00	Arv Mittoo W PTS 6 Norwich
20.10.00	Junior Witter L RTD 4 Belfast
25.02.01	Ram Singh W RSC 2 Derby
02.06.01	Jimmy Phelan W PTS 4 Wakefield
18.08.01	Keith Jones W PTS 8 Dewsbury
17.11.01	Carl Allen W PTS 8 Dewsbury
27.04.02	Steve Robinson W PTS 8 Huddersfield
05.10.02	Rakheem Mingaleev W RSC 4 Huddersfield
19.10.02	Alex Arthur L CO 4 Renfrew
	(Vacant British S. Featherweight Title)
05.07.03	Dariusz Snarski W RSC 4 Brentwood
05.10.03	Brian Coleman W PTS 6 Bradford
06.11.03	Yuri Romanov L PTS 8 Dagenham
23.11.03	Gareth Wiltshaw W RSC 5 Rotherham
16.04.04	Norman Dhalie W CO 3 Hartlepool

Career: 36 contests, won 30, lost 6.

Jason Cook

Maesteg. *Born* Maesteg, 27 February, 1975
IBO Lightweight Champion. Former Undefeated Welsh L.Welterweight Champion. Former Undefeated European Lightweight Champion. Ht. 5'9"
Manager B. Hearn

11.10.96	Brian Robb W RSC 2 Mayfair
27.11.96	Andrew Reed W RSC 3 Bethnal Green
27.05.97	Marc Smith W PTS 4 Mayfair
31.10.97	Marc Smith W PTS 4 Mayfair
24.01.98	David Kirk W RSC 3 Cardiff
26.05.98	Trevor Smith L RSC 1 Mayfair
23.02.99	Darren Woodley W RSC 4 Cardiff
28.05.99	Dave Hinds W RSC 1 Liverpool
02.10.99	Pete Buckley W PTS 4 Cardiff
11.12.99	Woody Greenaway W RSC 1 Merthyr
	(Vacant Welsh L. Welterweight Title)
26.02.00	Harry Butler W PTS 6 Swansea
17.04.00	Andrei Sinepupov W RTD 3 Birmingham
12.05.00	Keith Jones W PTS 10 Swansea
	(Welsh L. Welterweight Title Defence)
09.10.00	Assen Vasilev W PTS 6 Liverpool
17.02.01	Dariusz Snarski W PTS 8 Kolbrzeg, Poland
18.03.02	Nono Junior W RSC 1 Crawley
11.05.02	Andrei Devyataykin W PTS 6 Dagenham
29.06.02	Viktor Baranov W PTS 6 Brentwood
03.08.02	Sandro Casamonica W RSC 3 San Mango D'Aquino, Italy
	(Vacant European Lightweight Title)
26.10.02	Nasser Lakrib W RSC 5 Maesteg
	(European Lightweight Title Defence)
25.01.03	Stefano Zoff W PTS 12 Bridgend
06.09.03	Vincent Howard W RTD 3 Huddersfield
08.11.03	Ariel Olveira W RSC 7 Bridgend
	(Vacant IBO Lightweight Title)
01.05.04	Kevin Bennett W PTS 12 Bridgend
	(IBO Lightweight Title Defence)

Career: 24 contests, won 23, lost 1.

Nicky Cook

Dagenham. *Born* Stepney, 13 September, 1979
European & Commonwealth Featherweight Champion. Former Undefeated WBF Inter-Continental S. Featherweight Champion. Ht. 5'6½"
Manager J. Harding

11.12.98	Sean Grant W CO 1 Cheshunt
26.02.99	Graham McGrath W CO 2 Coventry
27.04.99	Vasil Paskelev W CO 1 Bethnal Green
25.05.99	Wilson Acuna W PTS 4 Mayfair
12.07.99	Igor Sakhatarov W PTS 4 Coventry
20.08.99	Vlado Varhegyi W PTS 4 Bloomsbury
27.11.99	John Barnes W PTS 6 Liverpool
20.12.99	Carl Allen W CO 3 Bethnal Green
10.03.00	Chris Jickells W RSC 1 Bethnal Green
27.05.00	Anthony Hanna W PTS 6 Mayfair
16.06.00	Salem Bouaita W PTS 6 Bloomsbury
04.11.00	Vladimir Borov W RSC 1 Bethnal Green
08.12.00	Rakhim Mingaleev W PTS 8 Crystal Palace
19.05.01	Foudil Madani W RSC 1 Wembley
28.11.01	Woody Greenaway W RSC 3 Bethnal Green

97

19.12.01 Marcelo Ackermann W RSC 3
Coventry
*(Vacant WBF Inter-Continental
S.Featherweight Title)*
20.04.02 Jackie Gunguluza W RTD 4 Wembley
*(WBF Inter-Continental
S.Featherweight Title Defence)*
10.07.02 Andrei Devyataykin W PTS 8
Wembley
05.10.02 Gary Thornhill W RSC 7 Liverpool
*(WBF Inter-Continental
S.Featherweight Title Defence)*
08.02.03 Mishek Kondwani W RSC 12
Brentford
*(Vacant Commonwealth Featherweight
Title)*
31.05.03 David Kiilu W CO 2 Bethnal Green
*(Commonwealth Featherweight Title
Defence)*
24.10.03 Anyetei Laryea W PTS 12 Bethnal
Green
(Commonwealth Featherweight Title)
20.03.04 Cyril Thomas W CO 9 Wembley
*(European Featherweight Title
Challenge)*
Career: 23 contests, won 23.

Gary Coombes
Birmingham. *Born* Solihull, 10 August,
1978
L. Welterweight. Ht. 5'8"
Manager T. Nerwal

15.04.04 Justin Hicks DREW 6 Dudley
10.05.04 Andy Cosnett W RSC 3 Birmingham
04.06.04 Kristian Laight DREW 6 Dudley
Career: 3 contests, won 1, drew 2.

Danny Cooper
Southampton. *Born* Southampton, 11 July,
1967
Welterweight. Ht. 5'6¹/₂"
Manager Self

12.04.86 Barry Bacon W PTS 6 Isle of Man
30.04.86 Mark Broome W CO 6 Edmonton
02.12.86 Tony Ekubia L RSC 4 Southend
14.03.88 Tony Whitehouse W RSC 1 Mayfair
18.05.88 Young Gully W RSC 4 Portsmouth
24.11.88 Steve Phillips W PTS 6 Southampton
02.03.89 Glyn Mitchell L PTS 6 Southampton
09.05.89 Eamonn Payne W PTS 6 Southend
25.10.90 B.F. Williams W PTS 6 Battersea
16.12.91 Ron Shinkwin W PTS 6 Southampton
17.03.03 Danny Gwilym W PTS 6 Southampton
12.05.03 Rocky Muscas W PTS 6 Southampton
26.10.03 Casey Brooke W PTS 6 Longford
Career: 13 contests, won 11, lost 2.

Danny Cooper   Philip Sharkey

Darren Corbett
Belfast. *Born* Belfast, 8 July, 1972
L.Heavyweight. Former Undefeated IBO
Inter-Continental L.Heavyweight
Champion. Former Commonwealth, IBO
Inter-Continental & All-Ireland
Cruiserweight Champion. Ht. 5'11"
Manager Self

10.12.94 David Jules W RSC 1 Manchester
13.12.94 Carl Gaffney W RSC 1 Potters Bar
21.02.95 Steve Garber W PTS 6 Sunderland
18.03.95 Gary Williams DREW 6 Millstreet
14.04.95 Dennis Bailey W RSC 2 Belfast
27.05.95 R. F. McKenzie L PTS 6 Belfast
26.08.95 Nigel Rafferty W PTS 6 Belfast
07.10.95 Nigel Rafferty W PTS 6 Belfast
02.12.95 Bobbi Joe Edwards W PTS 6 Belfast
07.05.96 Cliff Elden W RSC 1 Mayfair
28.05.96 Darren Fearn W RSC 1 Belfast
03.09.96 Chris Woollas W RSC 7 Belfast
05.11.96 Ray Kane W RSC 5 Belfast
*(Vacant All-Ireland Cruiserweight
Title)*
17.12.96 Chris Woollas W RSC 1 Doncaster
28.01.97 Nigel Rafferty W PTS 10 Belfast
*(All-Ireland Cruiserweight Title
Defence)*
29.04.97 Noel Magee W CO 2 Belfast
*(All-Ireland Cruiserweight Title
Defence)*
02.06.97 Chris Okoh W RSC 3 Belfast
*(Commonwealth Cruiserweight Title
Challenge)*
17.10.97 Hector Sanjuro W PTS 6 Ledyard,
Connecticut, USA
20.12.97 Robert Norton W PTS 12 Belfast
*(Commonwealth Cruiserweight Title
Defence)*
21.02.98 Dirk Wallyn W PTS 10 Belfast
28.04.98 Konstantin Ochrej W RSC 4 Belfast
*(Vacant IBO Inter-Continental
Cruiserweight Title)*
26.05.98 Roberto Dominguez W CO 1 Mayfair
*(IBO Inter-Continental Cruiserweight
Title Defence)*

Nicky Cook   Les Clark

28.11.98 Bruce Scott L RSC 10 Belfast
(Commonwealth Cruiserweight Title Defence. Vacant British Cruiserweight Title)
10.04.99 Stephane Allouane L RSC 9 Manchester
(Vacant IBO Inter-Continental Cruiserweight Title)
31.07.99 Darren Ashton W RSC 2 Carlisle
14.12.99 Neil Simpson W PTS 12 Coventry
(Vacant IBO Inter-Continental L. Heavyweight Title)
25.03.00 Lennox Lewis W RSC 2 Liverpool
(IBO Inter-Continental L. Heavyweight Title Defence)
16.06.01 Tyler Hughes W RSC 1 NYC, New York, USA
16.11.01 Radcliffe Green W PTS 8 Dublin
05.04.03 Clint Johnson W RSC 4 Belfast
17.04.04 Karim Bennama L RSC 6 Belfast
Career: 31 contests, won 26, drew 1, lost 4.

Darren Corbett　　　　　Les Clark

Billy Corcoran

Wembley. *Born* Galway, 18 November, 1980
Lightweight. Ht. 5'7³/₄"
Manager R. McCracken

23.08.02 Jason Nesbitt W PTS 4 Bethnal Green
25.10.02 Jason Nesbitt W RSC 2 Bethnal Green
21.12.02 Daniel Thorpe W CO 2 Dagenham
28.01.03 Pete Buckley W PTS 6 Nottingham
05.03.03 Pete Buckley W PTS 6 Bethnal Green
16.04.03 Mark Payne DREW 4 Nottingham
27.05.03 Jimmy Beech L PTS 6 Dagenham
04.10.03 Martin Hardcastle W PTS 6 Muswell Hill
28.11.03 Haroon Din W RSC 3 Derby
30.01.04 Rakhim Mingaleev W PTS 6 Dagenham
16.04.04 Anthony Hanna W PTS 4 Bradford
Career: 11 contests, won 9, drew 1, lost 1.

Andy Cosnett

Warley. *Born* Birmingham, 22 November, 1977
L.Welterweight. Ht. 5'9"
Manager P. Cowdell

10.05.04 Gary Coombes L RSC 3 Birmingham
Career: 1 contest, lost 1.

Danny Costello

Norwood. *Born* Lambeth, 21 August, 1975
S. Bantamweight. Ht. 5'6¹/₂"
Manager Self

26.10.96 Henry Jones W RSC 3 Liverpool
24.10.98 Ross Cassidy W PTS 4 Liverpool
10.03.00 Lennie Hodgkins W PTS 4 Chigwell
14.10.00 Anthony Hanna DREW 4 Wembley
02.12.00 Sean Green W PTS 4 Chigwell
16.06.01 Sean Green L RSC 3 Dagenham
08.05.04 Ian Napa L PTS 4 Dagenham
Career: 7 contests, won 4, drew 1, lost 2.

Jane Couch

Fleetwood. *Born* Fleetwood, 12 August, 1968
WBF & NABFW L.Welterweight Champion. Former Undefeated WBF Lightweight Champion. Former Undefeated WIBF & WBF Welterweight Champion. Ht. 5'7"
Manager Tex Woodward

30.10.94 Kalpna Shah W RSC 2 Wigan
29.01.95 Fosteres Joseph W PTS 6 Fleetwood
18.04.95 Jane Johnson W RSC 4 Fleetwood
01.07.95 Julia Shirley W PTS 6 Fleetwood
24.05.96 Sandra Geiger W PTS 10 Copenhagen, Denmark
(WIBF Welterweight Title Challenge)
01.03.97 Andrea Deshong W RSC 7 New Orleans, Louisiana, USA
(WIBF Welterweight Title Defence)
24.08.97 Leah Mellinger W PTS 10 Ledyard, Connecticut, USA
(WIBF Welterweight Title Defence)
24.10.97 Dora Webber L PTS 6 Lula, Mississippi, USA
10.01.98 Dora Webber L PTS 10 Atlantic City, New Jersey, USA
25.11.98 Simone Lukic W RSC 2 Streatham
20.02.99 Marisch Sjauw W PTS 10 Thornaby
(WIBF Welterweight Title Defence. Vacant WBF Welterweight Title)
01.04.99 Heike Noller W PTS 8 Birmingham
31.10.99 Sharon Anyos W PTS 10 Raynes Park
(Vacant WBF Lightweight Title)
09.03.00 Michelle Straus W RSC 3 Bethnal Green
01.07.00 Galina Gumliska W RSC 6 Southwark
(WBF Lightweight Title Defence)
19.08.00 Liz Mueller L PTS 6 Mashantucket, Connecticut, USA
16.06.01 Viktoria Oleynikov W PTS 4 Wembley
31.07.01 Shakurah Witherspoon W PTS 4 Montego Bay, Jamaica
16.12.01 Tzanka Karova W RSC 3 Bristol
21.06.02 Sumya Anani L RSC 4 Waco, Texas, USA
(Vacant WIBA L. Welterweight Title)
03.08.02 Borislava Goranova W PTS 6 Blackpool
08.12.02 Borislava Goranova W PTS 10 Bristol
(Vacant WBF L.Welterweight Title)
26.02.03 Borislava Goranova W RSC 7 Bristol
15.05.03 Larisa Berezenko W PTS 8 Clevedon
21.06.03 Lucia Rijker L PTS 8 Los Angeles, California, USA
21.09.03 Brenda Bell-Drexel W PTS 10 Bristol
21.12.03 Brenda Bell-Drexel W PTS 8 Bristol
29.02.04 Borislava Goranova W PTS 6 Bristol

03.04.04 Nathalie Toro L PTS 10 Vise, Belgium
(Vacant European L.Welterweight Title)
12.06.04 Jaime Clampitt W PTS 10 Mashantucket, Connecticut, USA
(Vacant WBF & NABFW L.Welterweight Titles)
Career: 30 contests, won 24, lost 6.

Mickey Coveney

West Ham. *Born* London, 26 November, 1981
Featherweight. Ht. 5'4"
Manager Self

12.06.00 Stevie Quinn W PTS 4 Belfast
30.11.00 Gareth Wiltshaw W PTS 4 Peterborough
24.02.01 Dazzo Williams L CO 1 Bethnal Green
03.06.01 Gareth Wiltshaw W PTS 4 Southwark
09.09.01 Richmond Asante W PTS 4 Southwark
28.11.01 Steve Gethin W PTS 4 Bethnal Green
24.03.02 Anthony Hanna W PTS 4 Streatham
25.06.04 David Bailey W PTS 4 Bethnal Green
Career: 8 contests, won 7, lost 1.

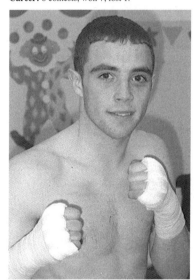

Mickey Coveney　　　　　Les Clark

Simeon Cover

Worksop. *Born* Clapton, 12 March, 1978
L. Heavyweight. Ht. 5'11"
Manager Self

28.03.01 Danny Smith L PTS 6 Piccadilly
18.08.01 Rob Stevenson W PTS 6 Dewsbury
24.09.01 Colin McCash L PTS 6 Cleethorpes
01.11.01 Rob Stevenson L PTS 6 Hull
16.11.01 Jon O'Brien L PTS 6 Dublin
24.11.01 Darren Rhodes L RSC 5 Wakefield
31.01.02 Shpetim Hoti W PTS 6 Piccadilly
13.04.02 Earl Ling L CO 4 Norwich
13.05.02 Roddy Doran DREW 8 Birmingham
02.06.02 Gary Dixon W PTS 6 Shaw
03.08.02 Mike Duffield W RSC 2 Derby
14.09.02 Ivan Botton L PTS 6 Newark
05.12.02 Mark Brookes L RSC 3 Sheffield
15.02.03 Peter Jackson W RSC 2

Wolverhampton
23.02.03 Roddy Doran L PTS 10 Shrewsbury
*(Vacant British Masters
S.Middleweight Title)*
22.03.03 Barry Connell L PTS 4 Renfrew
12.04.03 Danny Smith L CO 5 Norwich
08.06.03 Ivan Botton W PTS 6 Nottingham
25.07.03 Steven Spartacus L CO 3 Norwich
*(Vacant British Masters L.Heavyweight
Title)*
06.10.03 Hamid Jamali L PTS 6 Birmingham
17.10.03 Barry Connell L PTS 6 Glasgow
14.11.03 Terry Morrill W PTS 6 Hull
01.12.03 Clint Johnson L PTS 6 Leeds
15.12.03 Lee Nicholson W RSC 4 Cleethorpes
06.02.04 Mark Brookes L RSC 4 Sheffield
12.03.04 Hastings Rasani L CO 6 Irvine
07.05.04 Dean Cockburn L PTS 6 Doncaster
15.05.04 Gary Thompson W PTS 6 Aberdeen
04.06.04 Danny Norton L RSC 3 Dudley
Career: 29 contests, won 9, drew 1, lost 19.

Simeon Cover   Les Clark

Darren Covill

Welling. *Born* Welling, 11 April, 1970
Middleweight. Ht. 5'8"
Manager Self

23.02.95 Brian Coleman W PTS 4 Southwark
19.05.95 Allan Gray L PTS 6 Southwark
04.06.95 Dick Hanns-Kat W RSC 3 Bethnal
Green
14.09.95 Gavin Barker W CO 1 Battersea
21.09.95 Shaun Stokes L PTS 6 Sheffield
22.11.95 Jason Barker L PTS 4 Sheffield
05.02.96 Jason Barker W RSC 1 Bexleyheath
21.03.96 Paul Miles L PTS 4 Southwark
11.07.97 Leigh Wicks W RSC 2 Brighton
26.09.97 Jason Williams L PTS 6 Port Talbot
08.10.97 Steve Roberts L PTS 6 Poplar
08.11.97 David Baptiste W PTS 4 Southwark
06.12.97 Ali Khattab L PTS 4 Wembley
31.01.98 Paolo Roberto L PTS 6 Edmonton
13.02.98 John Docherty W RSC 1 Barrhead
21.03.98 Wayne Alexander L RSC 2 Bethnal
Green
04.06.98 Darren McInulty DREW 6 Barking
10.09.98 Cornelius Carr L RTD 2 Acton
25.11.98 Leigh Wicks L PTS 4 Streatham

16.01.99 Anthony McFadden L RSC 2 Bethnal
Green
18.02.99 Adrian Stone L RSC 2 Barking
24.03.99 Lester Jacobs L RSC 2 Bayswater
02.07.99 Steven Bendall L RTD 3 Bristol
27.02.00 Gareth Hogg L RSC 3 Plymouth
02.02.01 Matthew Barney L PTS 6 Portsmouth
24.03.01 Allan Foster L RTD 3 Sheffield
12.05.01 Hughie Doherty L PTS 4 Plymouth
04.07.01 Harry Butler L RSC 4 Bloomsbury
20.09.01 Lester Jacobs L CO 2 Blackfriars
22.11.01 Dean Powell L PTS 4 Mayfair
08.12.01 Tomas da Silva L PTS 4 Millwall
15.12.01 Reagan Denton L PTS 4 Sheffield
27.03.02 John Tiftik W RSC 2 Mayfair
25.04.02 Brendan Rollinson L PTS 4 Hull
21.05.02 Elroy Edwards L PTS 4 Custom House
13.07.02 Conroy McIntosh L PTS 4
Wolverhampton
21.07.02 Wayne Pinder L CO 2 Salford
23.08.02 Carl Froch L RSC 1 Bethnal Green
10.10.02 Freddie Yemofio L PTS 4 Piccadilly
25.10.02 Francis Barrett L PTS 4 Bethnal Green
21.12.02 William Webster L PTS 4 Dagenham
13.09.03 Tony Doherty L PTS 4 Newport
26.09.03 Danny Gwilym L PTS 6 Millwall
29.10.03 Geraint Harvey L PTS 4 Leicester
Square
21.11.03 Lee Williamson L PTS 6 Millwall
Career: 45 contests, won 8, drew 1, lost 36.

Ben Coward

Swinton. *Born* Barnsley, 16 November,
1976
Middleweight. Ht. 5'9"
Manager H. Rainey

26.11.97 Pete Stanway W PTS 6 Sheffield
06.02.98 Brian Stanway L RSC 1 Wakefield
15.12.98 Shaun O'Neill L RSC 5 Sheffield
02.06.03 Steve Scott DREW 6 Cleethorpes
11.07.03 Dave Pearson W PTS 6 Darlington
20.02.04 Lance Hall L RSC 2 Doncaster
Career: 6 contests, won 2, drew 1, lost 3.

Jamie Coyle

Stirling. *Born* Stirling, 24 August, 1976
L. Middleweight. Ht. 6'0"
Manager T. Gilmour

02.06.03 Richard Inquieti W RSC 2 Glasgow
20.10.03 Jed Tytler W RSC 2 Glasgow
04.12.03 George Robshaw DREW 6
Huddersfield
28.02.04 Geraint Harvey W PTS 4 Bridgend
22.04.04 Peter Dunn W PTS 6 Glasgow
Career: 5 contests, won 4, drew 1.

Michael Crossan

Glasgow. *Born* Glasgow, 21 June, 1975
S. Bantamweight. Ht. 5'6"
Manager A. Morrison

17.10.03 Hussain Nasser W PTS 6 Glasgow
07.12.03 Rocky Dean W PTS 6 Glasgow
23.04.04 Dean Ward W PTS 6 Glasgow
19.06.04 Colin Moffett DREW 4 Renfrew
Career: 4 contests, won 3, drew 1.

Peter Culshaw

Liverpool. *Born* Liverpool, 15 May, 1973
Flyweight. Former Undefeated WBF &

WBU Inter-Continental S. Flyweight
Champion. Former Commonwealth
Flyweight Champion. Former Undefeated
WBU & Central Area Flyweight
Champion. Ht. 5'6"
Manager T. Gilmour

02.07.93 Graham McGrath W PTS 6 Liverpool
28.09.93 Vince Feeney W PTS 6 Liverpool
11.12.93 Nick Tooley W RSC 1 Liverpool
25.02.94 Des Gargano W PTS 6 Chester
06.05.94 Neil Swain W PTS 6 Liverpool
26.09.94 Daryl McKenzie W PTS 6 Liverpool
20.04.95 Rowan Williams W CO 6 Liverpool
29.09.95 Maxim Pougatchev DREW 8 Liverpool
05.03.96 Louis Veitch W RSC 3 Barrow
*(Central Area Flyweight Title
Challenge)*
13.04.96 Lyndon Kershaw W RSC 3 Liverpool
25.06.96 Danny Ward W RSC 3 Stevenage
*(Commonwealth Flyweight Title
Challenge)*
27.09.96 James Wanene W RSC 7 Stevenage
*(Commonwealth Flyweight Title
Defence)*
02.08.97 Jason Thomas W PTS 8 Barnsley
11.09.97 Ady Lewis L RSC 8 Widnes
*(Commonwealth Flyweight Title
Defence. British Flyweight Title
Challenge)*
12.03.98 Foudil Madani W RSC 4 Liverpool
*(Vacant WBU Inter-Continental
S. Flyweight Title)*
24.10.98 Mzukisi Marali W RSC 7 Liverpool
(Vacant WBU Flyweight Title)
05.03.99 Zolile Mbityi W PTS 12 Liverpool
(WBU Flyweight Title Defence)
15.05.99 Adrian Ochoa W RSC 9 Blackpool
(WBU Flyweight Title Defence)
09.03.00 Oscar Andrade W PTS 12 Liverpool
(WBU Flyweight Title Defence)
24.05.00 Jake Matlala W PTS 12 Carnival City,
South Africa
(WBU Flyweight Title Defence)
11.11.00 Dimitar Alipiev W CO 1 Belfast
(WBU Flyweight Title Defence)
09.06.01 Ian Napa W RSC 8 Bethnal Green
(WBU Flyweight Title Defence)
06.04.02 Sergei Tasimov W RSC 2 Copenhagen,
Denmark
05.10.02 Celso Dangud W PTS 8 Liverpool
29.11.02 Ncedo Cecane W PTS 12 Liverpool
(Vacant WBF S. Flyweight Title)
29.03.03 Wandee Chareon W PTS 12 Wembley
(WBF S. Flyweight Title Defence)
02.06.04 Andrei Kostin L PTS 8 Hereford
Career: 27 contests, won 24, drew 1, lost 2.

Gary Cummings

Sheffield. *Born* Sheffield, 11 November,
1972
Welterweight. Ht. 5'9"
Manager J. Ingle

13.04.03 Wasim Hussain W RSC 2 Bradford
17.04.03 Dave Hill W CO 5 Hull
06.06.03 Danny Smith L PTS 6 Norwich
11.07.03 Franny Jones L RSC 2 Darlington
13.09.03 Gwyn Wale W PTS 6 Wakefield
01.12.03 Graham Delehedy L RSC 1 Bradford
Career: 6 contest, won 3, lost 3.

Scott Dann

Plymouth. *Born* Plymouth, 23 July, 1974
English Middleweight Champion. Former
Undefeated IBO Inter-Continental
Middleweight Champion. Ht. 5'10½"
Manager C. Sanigar

15.11.97	Jon Rees W RSC 1 Bristol
25.04.98	Israel Khumalo W RSC 3 Cardiff
30.05.98	Michael Alexander W PTS 4 Bristol
14.07.98	Richard Glaysher W RSC 1 Reading
24.10.98	James Donoghue W PTS 6 Bristol
27.02.00	James Donoghue W RSC 1 Plymouth
07.04.00	Martin Jolley W RSC 2 Bristol
08.09.00	Sean Pritchard W RSC 5 Bristol
06.10.00	Peter Mitchell W RSC 3 Maidstone
03.11.00	Anthony Ivory W PTS 8 Ebbw Vale
13.03.01	Jason Hart W RSC 2 Plymouth
12.05.01	Elvis Adonesi W CO 7 Plymouth
	(Vacant IBO Inter-Continental
	Middleweight Title)
13.09.01	Jon Penn L RSC 5 Sheffield
10.05.02	Mark Phillips W PTS 6 Bethnal Green
10.07.02	Mark Phillips W PTS 4 Wembley
29.11.02	Delroy Leslie W RSC 1 Liverpool
	(Final Elim. British Middleweight
	Title)
16.04.03	Howard Eastman L RSC 3 Nottingham
	(British, Commonwealth & European
	Middleweight Title Challenges)
26.07.03	Kreshkik Qato W RSC 2 Plymouth
09.10.03	Hussain Osman W PTS 8 Bristol
02.04.04	Ojay Abrahams W RSC 6 Plymouth
08.05.04	Danny Thornton W RSC 3 Bristol
	(Vacant English Middleweight Title)

Career: 21 contests, won 19, lost 2.

Scott Dann   Les Clark

Tomas da Silva

Canning Town. *Born* Sao Luiz Maranhao,
Brazil, 19 May, 1976
L. Middleweight. Ht. 5'11"
Manager A. Bowers

22.09.01	Conroy McIntosh W PTS 4 Canning Town
03.11.01	Ryan Kerr L PTS 4 Glasgow
16.11.01	Tommy Tolan W RSC 6 Dublin
08.12.01	Darren Covill W PTS 4 Millwall
16.12.01	Duje Postenjak L PTS 6 Glasgow
09.02.02	Thomas McDonagh DREW 4 Manchester
18.02.02	Biagio Falcone W RSC 3 Glasgow
19.04.02	Mark Graversen L PTS 6 Aarhus, Denmark
06.09.02	Steven Bendall L RSC 8 Bethnal Green
27.10.02	Matthew Tait L PTS 6 Southwark
03.12.02	Dean Powell L PTS 4 Bethnal Green
18.01.03	Thomas McDonagh L PTS 4 Preston
05.04.03	Ciaran Healy L PTS 4 Belfast
13.09.03	Michael Monaghan L PTS 6 Newport
02.10.03	Carl Wall DREW 4 Liverpool
06.11.03	Gokhan Kazaz L PTS 4 Dagenham
18.11.03	Matthew Tait L PTS 8 Bethnal Green
13.12.03	Anthony Farnell L PTS 6 Manchester
06.02.04	Geard Ajetovic L RSC 4 Sheffield
01.04.04	Daniel Teasdale L PTS 4 Bethnal Green
16.04.04	Ryan Rhodes L RSC 4 Bradford

Career: 21 contests, won 4, drew 2, lost 15.

Tristan Davies

Telford. *Born* Shrewsbury, 13 October, 1978
L. Welterweight. Ht. 5'10"
Manager E. Johnson/D. Bradley

04.06.04	Pete Buckley W PTS 6 Dudley

Career: 1 contest, won 1.

Varuzhan Davtyan

Birmingham. *Born* Armenia, 11 August, 1972
L. Heavyweight. Ht. 5'8½"
Manager Self

Previous record unknown

09.03.02	Tony Dodson W PTS 6 Manchester
09.05.02	Rasmus Ojemaye W RSC 3 Leicester Square
29.06.02	Elvis Michailenko L PTS 6 Brentwood
08.09.02	Paul Bonson W PTS 4 Wolverhampton
05.10.02	Mark Hobson L RSC 3 Huddersfield
30.11.02	Eric Teymour L PTS 6 Liverpool
14.12.02	Tomasz Adamek L RTD 4 Newcastle
05.03.03	Carl Froch L RSC 5 Bethnal Green
17.05.03	Jason McKay L PTS 6 Liverpool
24.05.03	Eric Teymour L PTS 4 Bethnal Green
28.06.03	Nathan King L PTS 4 Cardiff
26.07.03	Tony Dodson L RTD 3 Plymouth
20.09.03	Adrian Dodson W PTS 4 Nottingham
20.03.04	Andrew Lowe L PTS 6 Wembley
30.03.04	Jamie Hearn W PTS 4 Southampton
02.06.04	Steven Spartacus L RSC 1 Nottingham

Career: 16 contests, won 5, lost 11.

Lenny Daws

Morden. *Born* Carshalton, 29 December, 1978
L. Welterweight. Ht. 5'10½"
Manager R. McCracken

16.04.03	Danny Gwilym W RSC 2 Nottingham
27.05.03	Ben Hudson W RSC 2 Dagenham
25.07.03	Karl Taylor W RTD 2 Norwich
04.10.03	Ernie Smith W PTS 4 Muswell Hill
28.11.03	Tony Montana W PTS 6 Derby
11.12.03	Keith Jones W PTS 6 Bethnal Green
30.01.04	Denis Alekseev W CO 3 Dagenham

Career: 7 contests, won 7.

Lenny Daws   Les Clark

Neil Dawson

Rotherham. *Born* Rotherham, 1 July, 1980
Cruiserweight. Ht. 6'4"
Manager T. Gilmour/C. Aston

12.11.02	Eamonn Glennon W PTS 6 Leeds
24.03.03	Dave Clarke W PTS 4 Barnsley
06.10.03	Dave Clarke W PTS 6 Barnsley
04.12.03	Wlodek Kopec W PTS 4 Huddersfield
13.03.04	Paul Bonson W PTS 4 Huddersfield
08.06.04	Greg Scott-Briggs W RSC 3 Sheffield

Career: 6 contests, won 6.

Phill Day

Swindon. *Born* Swindon, 5 November, 1974
Cruiserweight. Ht. 5'11½"
Manager A. Phillips

07.07.95	Tim Redman L RSC 2 Cardiff
21.09.95	John Pettersson L RSC 4 Battersea
10.11.95	L. A. Williams W PTS 6 Bristol
21.02.96	Carl Heath L PTS 6 Piccadilly
18.10.96	David Jules W RSC 1 Barnstaple
09.12.96	Naveed Anwar W PTS 6 Bristol
24.03.97	Jim Pallatt W CO 1 Bristol
15.05.97	Tony Booth L PTS 4 Reading
17.01.98	Richie Chapman W PTS 4 Bristol
07.03.98	Lee Swaby W PTS 4 Reading
16.04.98	Cliff Elden W RSC 3 Mayfair
30.05.98	Chris P. Bacon L RSC 4 Bristol
05.10.02	Tony Booth L PTS 4 Coventry
16.11.02	Darren Ashton DREW 4 Coventry
15.02.03	Jason Brewster W PTS 6 Wolverhampton
18.03.03	David Haye L RSC 2 Reading
17.04.03	Jamie Warters DREW 6 Hull
10.06.03	Carl Thompson L CO 4 Sheffield
31.07.03	Denzil Browne L RSC 6 Sheffield

Career: 19 contests, won 8, drew 2, lost 9.

Rocky Dean

Thetford. *Born* Bury St Edmonds, 17 June, 1978
S. Bantamweight. Ht. 5'5"
Manager Self

14.10.99	Lennie Hodgkins W PTS 6 Bloomsbury
30.10.99	Lennie Hodgkins W PTS 6 Southwark
18.05.00	Danny Lawson W RSC 1 Bethnal Green
29.09.00	Anthony Hanna W PTS 4 Bethnal Green
10.11.00	Chris Jickells L RSC 1 Mayfair
19.04.02	Peter Svendsen W PTS 6 Aarhus, Denmark
19.10.02	Sean Grant W RSC 3 Norwich
21.12.02	Darren Cleary W PTS 4 Millwall
08.02.03	Steve Gethin DREW 4 Norwich
11.07.03	Isaac Ward DREW 4 Darlington
26.07.03	Michael Hunter L RSC 1 Plymouth
10.10.03	Isaac Ward L PTS 6 Darlington
06.11.03	Martin Power L PTS 6 Dagenham
07.12.03	Michael Crossan L PTS 6 Glasgow

Career: 14 contests, won 7, drew 2, lost 5.

Garry Delaney

West Ham. *Born* Newham, 12 August, 1970
Southern Area Cruiserweight Champion. Former Undefeated British Masters Cruiserweight Champion. Former Commonwealth, WBO Inter-Continental & Southern Area L. Heavyweight Champion. Ht. 6'3"
Manager Self

02.10.91	Gus Mendes W RSC 1 Barking
23.10.91	Joe Frater W RSC 1 Bethnal Green
13.11.91	John Kaighin W PTS 6 Bethnal Green
11.12.91	Randy B. Powell W RSC 1 Basildon
11.02.92	Simon Harris DREW 8 Barking
12.05.92	John Williams W PTS 6 Crystal Palace
16.06.92	Nigel Rafferty W CO 5 Dagenham
15.09.92	Gil Lewis W CO 2 Crystal Palace
06.10.92	Simon McDougall W PTS 8 Antwerp, Belgium
10.11.92	John Oxenham W CO 5 Dagenham
12.12.92	Simon McDougall W PTS 8 Muswell Hill
30.01.93	Simon Collins W PTS 8 Brentwood
28.09.93	Glazz Campbell W CO 6 Bethnal Green
	(Southern Area L. Heavyweight Title Challenge)
06.11.93	John Kaighin W CO 1 Bethnal Green
21.12.93	Ray Albert W RSC 3 Mayfair
	(Vacant WBO Inter-Continental L. Heavyweight Title)
11.01.94	Jim Murray W RSC 7 Bethnal Green
	(WBO Inter-Continental L. Heavyweight Title Defence)
09.04.94	Simon Harris W CO 6 Bethnal Green
	(WBO Inter-Continental & Southern Area L. Heavyweight Title Defences)
09.07.94	Sergio Merani W PTS 12 Earls Court
	(WBO Inter-Continental L. Heavyweight Title)
30.09.94	Arigoma Chiponda W CO 2 Bethnal Green
	(Vacant Commonwealth L. Heavyweight Title)
18.03.95	Ernest Mateen W RTD 7 Millstreet

	(Vacant WBO Inter-Continental L. Heavyweight Title)
09.05.95	Noel Magee L RTD 7 Basildon
	(Commonwealth L. Heavyweight Title Defence)
06.02.96	Francis Wanyama W PTS 6 Basildon
09.04.96	Joey Paladino W RSC 1 Stevenage
07.02.97	John Kiser W PTS 6 Las Vegas, Nevada, USA
04.03.97	Peter Oboh W DIS 8 Southwark
27.09.97	Julius Francis L RSC 6 Belfast
	(Vacant British Heavyweight Title. Commonwealth Heavyweight Title Challenge)
05.06.98	Darron Griffiths W PTS 6 Southend
23.01.99	John Keeton L PTS 12 Cheshunt
	(Vacant WBO Inter-Continental Cruiserweight Title)
01.05.99	Tim Brown W PTS 8 Crystal Palace
04.09.99	Lee Swaby W PTS 8 Bethnal Green
29.04.00	Jesper Kristiansen L RTD 10 Varde, Denmark
	(Vacant WBO Inter-Continental Cruiserweight Title)
06.10.00	Dominic Negus W PTS 10 Maidstone
	(Southern Area Cruiserweight Title Challenge)
10.03.01	Bruce Scott L RTD 3 Bethnal Green
	(British Cruiserweight Title Challenge. Vacant Commonwealth Cruiserweight Title)
15.06.01	Darren Ashton W RTD 4 Millwall
	(Vacant British Masters Cruiserweight Title)
14.07.01	Chris P. Bacon W RSC 10 Liverpool
	(British Masters Cruiserweight Title Defence)
20.10.01	Tony Dowling W RSC 6 Glasgow
02.03.02	Sebastiaan Rothmann L PTS 12 Brakpan, South Africa
	(WBU Cruiserweight Title Challenge)
26.09.03	Paul Bonson W PTS 6 Reading
21.02.04	Enzo Maccarinelli L RSC 8 Cardiff
	(WBU Cruiserweight Title Challenge)

Career: 39 contests, won 31, drew 1, lost 7.

Graham Delehedy

Liverpool. *Born* Liverpool, 7 October, 1978
Welterweight. Ht. 5'8"
Manager T. Gilmour

17.05.03	Joel Ani W RSC 4 Liverpool
27.10.03	Rocky Muscus W RSC 2 Glasgow
01.12.03	Gary Cummings W RSC 1 Bradford
27.05.04	Ernie Smith W RSC 3 Huddersfield

Career: 4 contests, won 4.

(Dennis) Buster Dennis (Mwanze)

Canning Town. *Born* Mawokota, Uganda, 31 December, 1981
Featherweight. Ht. 5'0"
Manager A. Bowers

28.03.03	Vitali Makarov W RSC 2 Millwall
03.04.03	Chris Hooper L RSC 1 Hull
15.05.03	Mark Alexander L PTS 4 Mayfair
24.05.03	Haider Ali L PTS 4 Bethnal Green
21.11.03	Anthony Hanna W PTS 6 Millwall
30.11.03	Daleboy Rees W PTS 6 Swansea
20.02.04	Chris Hooper W RSC 2 Bethnal Green
01.04.04	Kevin O'Hara L PTS 4 Bethnal Green
19.06.04	Riaz Durgahed L PTS 4 Muswell Hill

Career: 9 contests, won 4, lost 5.

Paul Denton (Ramsey)

Birmingham. *Born* Birmingham, 12 April, 1970
L. Middleweight. Ht. 5'10"
Manager Self

18.03.93	Mark O'Callaghan W RSC 4 Lewisham
29.04.93	Dave Maj DREW 6 Mayfair
11.08.93	Billy McDougall W PTS 6 Mansfield
01.10.93	Ferid Bennecer W CO 3 Waregem, Belgium
01.12.93	Brian Hickey W CO 1 Kensington
28.01.94	Youssef Bakhouche L PTS 6 Waregem, Belgium
07.05.94	Viktor Fesetchko L PTS 6 Dnepropetrousk, Ukraine
23.09.94	Roy Rowland W RSC 5 Bethnal Green
03.01.95	Patrick Charpentier L RSC 4 Epernay, France
25.02.95	Paul Ryan L RSC 4 Millwall
25.11.95	Michael Carruth L PTS 8 Dublin
03.02.96	George Naylor W RSC 3 Liverpool
26.04.96	Ross Hale W RSC 4 Cardiff
15.11.96	Frank Olsen L RSC 4 Nestved, Denmark
14.03.97	Mark Winters L PTS 8 Reading
13.06.97	Alan McDowall DREW 6 Paisley
21.03.98	Naas Scheepers L PTS 8 Hammanskraal, South Africa
19.09.98	Neil Sinclair L RSC 1 Dublin
19.12.98	Ricky Hatton L RSC 6 Liverpool
16.02.99	Steve Tuckett L PTS 6 Leeds
27.02.99	Michael Carruth L RSC 5 Bethnal Green
27.05.00	Jacek Bielski L PTS 6 Mayfair
19.06.00	Oscar Hall L PTS 4 Burton
08.07.00	Michael Jennings L PTS 6 Widnes
12.08.00	Wayne Alexander L RSC 1 Wembley
02.10.00	Kevin McIntyre L PTS 6 Glasgow
18.11.00	Pavel Melnikov L PTS 4 Dagenham
01.12.00	Paul Dyer L PTS 4 Peterborough
11.12.00	Michael Jennings L PTS 4 Widnes
17.02.01	David Walker L PTS 4 Bethnal Green
26.02.01	James Hare L PTS 4 Nottingham
07.04.01	Brett James L PTS 4 Wembley
24.04.01	Paul Burns L PTS 4 Liverpool
08.05.01	Derek Roche L PTS 6 Barnsley
27.05.01	Jamie Moore L RSC 3 Manchester
07.07.01	Thomas McDonagh L PTS 6 Manchester
20.10.01	Kevin Bennett L PTS 4 Portsmouth
26.11.01	James Hare L RTD 4 Manchester
09.02.02	Matthew Hatton L PTS 6 Manchester
02.03.02	Ross Minter L PTS 6 Bethnal Green
10.05.02	Leo O'Reilly L PTS 6 Bethnal Green
14.12.02	Matthew Hatton L PTS 6 Newcastle
05.03.03	Costas Katsantonis L PTS 6 Bethnal Green
08.04.03	Jason Rowland L PTS 6 Bethnal Green
24.05.03	Matthew Macklin L PTS 6 Bethnal Green
12.07.03	Kevin McIntyre L PTS 4 Renfrew
16.01.04	Gavin Down L RSC 4 Bradford

Career: 47 contests, won 7, drew 2, lost 38.

Reagan Denton

Sheffield. *Born* Sheffield, 26 June, 1978
S. Middleweight. Ht. 5'11"
Manager Self

15.05.99	Pedro Thompson W PTS 4 Sheffield
15.11.99	Colin Vidler W PTS 4 Bethnal Green

25.09.00	William Webster W PTS 4 Barnsley
08.10.01	Martyn Bailey W PTS 4 Barnsley
15.12.01	Darren Covill W PTS 4 Sheffield
24.03.03	Dave Pearson W PTS 6 Barnsley
06.10.03	Michael Pinnock W PTS 6 Barnsley
23.11.03	Gary Dixon L PTS 4 Rotherham
08.12.03	William Webster W RSC 6 Barnsley

Career: 9 contests, won 8, lost 1.

Norman Dhalie   Les Clark

Norman Dhalie

Birmingham. *Born* Birmingham, 24 March, 1971
Welterweight. Ht. 5'7"
Manager Self

06.04.92	Karl Morling L PTS 6 Northampton
27.04.92	Wilson Docherty L RSC 2 Glasgow
02.07.92	John White L RSC 6 Middleton
29.09.92	Gary Marston DREW 6 Stoke
07.10.92	Jacob Smith W PTS 6 Sunderland
03.12.92	Bradley Stone L CO 4 Lewisham
26.01.93	Neil Smith L PTS 4 Leicester
13.02.93	John White L CO 2 Manchester
20.04.93	Bobby Guynan L PTS 6 Brentwood
29.04.93	Kevin Toomey L PTS 6 Hull
23.05.93	Mike Anthony Brown W PTS 4 Brockley
09.06.93	Joey Moffat L RTD 4 Liverpool
30.09.93	Simon Frailing W PTS 6 Hayes
06.10.93	Kevin McKillan L RSC 1 Solihull
06.12.93	Colin Innes W PTS 6 Bradford
16.12.93	Peter Till L PTS 8 Walsall
19.01.94	John Naylor L RSC 3 Stoke
21.02.94	Hugh Collins L RTD 4 Glasgow
14.04.94	Mike Anthony Brown L PTS 6 Battersea
28.04.94	John Stovin DREW 6 Hull
06.05.94	Sugar Gibiliru L RTD 5 Liverpool
02.09.94	Dave Fallon L DIS 4 Spitalfields
28.09.94	Tanveer Ahmed L CO 5 Glasgow
24.11.94	Tony Foster L RTD 7 Hull
17.02.95	Paul Knights L RTD 5 Crawley
16.06.95	George Naylor L PTS 6 Liverpool
25.10.95	Joe Donohoe W PTS 6 Stoke
20.12.95	J. T. Williams L CO 2 Usk
16.03.96	Robbie Sivyer L CO 4 Barnstaple
15.10.96	Wayne Windle W PTS 6 Wolverhampton
02.12.96	Andy Robinson W PTS 6 Birmingham
06.10.97	Vic Broomhead W PTS 6 Birmingham
14.10.97	Chris Pegg W RSC 5 Wolverhampton
11.11.97	Vic Broomhead W PTS 6 Edgbaston
02.03.98	Wayne Windle W PTS 6 Birmingham
23.04.98	Thomas Bradley L CO 5 Edgbaston
27.05.99	Carl Tilley W RSC 1 Edgbaston
04.03.02	Nicky Leech L PTS 6 Birmingham
23.11.02	Terry Fletcher L CO 2 Derby
09.02.03	Nadeem Siddique L PTS 4 Bradford
08.06.03	Jeff Thomas L PTS 6 Shaw
01.08.03	Dave Stewart L RTD 2 Bethnal Green
20.10.03	George McIlroy L PTS 6 Glasgow
30.01.04	John Murray L CO 2 Dagenham
16.04.04	Steve Conway L CO 3 Hartlepool

Career: 45 contests, won 12, drew 2, lost 31.

(Hardip) Harry Dhami

Gravesend. *Born* Gravesend, 17 April, 1972
Welterweight. Former British Welterweight Champion. Former Undefeated Southern Area Welterweight Champion. Ht. 5'10"
Manager T. Gilmour

29.10.92	Johnny Pinnock W PTS 6 Hayes
20.05.94	Nick Appiah W RSC 4 Acton
27.05.94	Chris Vassiliou W RSC 5 Ashford
11.10.94	Steve McNess DREW 6 Bethnal Green
09.11.94	Clay O'Shea L PTS 6 Millwall
30.11.94	Robert Wright L PTS 8 Wolverhampton
17.11.95	John Bosco L PTS 6 Bethnal Green
08.12.95	Nicky Thurbin L PTS 8 Bethnal Green
25.04.96	Chris Pollock W PTS 6 Mayfair
07.05.96	Ojay Abrahams W RSC 5 Mayfair
	(*Vacant Southern Area Welterweight Title*)
20.11.96	Andy Peach W RTD 3 Wembley
14.03.97	Paul Dyer W PTS 10 Reading
	(*Southern Area Welterweight Title Defence*)
20.05.97	Paul Miles W RTD 2 Gillingham
	(*Southern Area Welterweight Title Defence*)
09.09.97	Howard Clarke W PTS 8 Bethnal Green
26.09.98	Allan Gray W PTS 10 Southwark
	(*Southern Area Welterweight Title Defence*)
12.12.98	Kevin McCarthy W PTS 10 Southwark
	(*Southern Area Welterweight Title Defence*)
15.05.99	Paul Burns W PTS 8 Blackpool
12.12.99	Lee Bird W PTS 6 Chigwell
27.03.00	Derek Roche W PTS 12 Barnsley
	(*British Welterweight Title Challenge*)
14.10.00	Malcolm Melvin W PTS 12 Wembley
	(*British Welterweight Title Defence*)
27.11.00	Spencer McCracken W PTS 12 Birmingham
	(*British Welterweight Title Defence*)
19.11.01	Neil Sinclair L RSC 5 Glasgow
	(*British Welterweight Title Defence*)
17.11.03	Lee Armstrong W PTS 6 Glasgow

Career: 23 contests, won 17, drew 1, lost 5.

Craig Dickson

Glasgow. *Born* Glasgow, 6 March, 1979
Welterweight. Ht. 5'11"
Manager T. Gilmour

21.10.02	Paul Rushton W RSC 2 Glasgow
18.11.02	Ernie Smith W PTS 6 Glasgow
17.02.03	Jon Hilton W RSC 2 Glasgow
14.04.03	Richard Inquieti W PTS 4 Glasgow
20.10.03	Danny Moir W RSC 3 Glasgow
19.01.04	Dean Nicholas W RSC 5 Glasgow
19.04.04	Ernie Smith W PTS 6 Glasgow

Career: 7 contests, won 7.

Haroon Din

Sheffield. *Born* Middlesbrough, 21 May, 1978
British Masters L.Welterweight Champion. Ht. 5'8"
Manager Self

21.09.98	Les Frost L PTS 6 Cleethorpes
14.12.98	Les Frost L RSC 1 Cleethorpes
02.05.99	Amjid Mahmood W PTS 6 Shaw
20.05.00	Dave Travers W PTS 6 Leicester
24.06.00	Willie Limond L PTS 4 Glasgow
30.08.00	Leon Dobbs W CO 1 Scunthorpe
19.11.00	Carl Greaves L RSC 4 Chesterfield
24.09.01	Nigel Senior W PTS 6 Cleethorpes
17.12.01	Nigel Senior W PTS 6 Cleethorpes
31.01.02	Ilias Miah W RSC 3 Piccadilly
20.04.02	Gareth Wiltshaw W PTS 6 Derby
17.11.02	Gareth Wiltshaw W PTS 6 Bradford
05.04.03	Andy Morris L RSC 1 Manchester
28.11.03	Billy Corcoran L RSC 3 Derby
05.03.04	Jason Nesbitt W PTS 6 Darlington
14.05.04	Jackson Williams W RSC 5 Sunderland
	(*Vacant British Masters L.Welterweight Title*)

Career: 16 contests, won 10, lost 6.

Gary Dixon   Les Clark

Gary Dixon

Carlisle. *Born* Carlisle, 2 November, 1974
S. Middleweight. Ht. 5'10½"
Manager Self

18.03.01	Jamie Logan W PTS 6 Shaw
10.05.01	Paul Owen L RSC 3 Sunderland
26.07.01	Michael Thompson W PTS 6 Blackpool

23.09.01	Mark Sawyers DREW 6 Shaw	
09.12.01	Danny Wray W RSC 4 Shaw	
03.03.02	William Webster W PTS 6 Shaw	
02.06.02	Simeon Cover L PTS 6 Shaw	
06.09.02	Tom Cannon L PTS 6 Glasgow	
17.11.02	Conroy McIntosh L RSC 2 Shaw	
09.03.03	Mike Duffield W PTS 6 Shaw	
19.10.03	Farai Musiiwa L PTS 6 Shaw	
23.11.03	Reagan Denton W PTS 4 Rotherham	
29.02.04	Barry Connell W RTD 3 Shaw	

Career: 13 contests, won 7, drew 1, lost 5.

Scott Dixon

Hamilton. *Born* Hamilton, 28 September, 1976

L. Middleweight. Former Undefeated WBO Inter-Continental L. Middleweight Champion. Former Undefeated Commonwealth Welterweight Champion. Former Undefeated WBB & Scottish Welterweight Champion. Ht. 5'9"
Manager Self

13.10.95	Andrew Smith W PTS 4 Glasgow	
17.12.95	Martin Evans W RSC 4 Glasgow	
12.02.96	Colin Innes W PTS 6 Glasgow	
16.03.96	Ian Richardson W PTS 4 Glasgow	
26.04.96	Andy Green W RSC 5 Glasgow	
24.05.96	Brian Coleman W PTS 8 Glasgow	
20.09.96	Alan Temple W PTS 6 Glasgow	
06.11.96	Rocky Ferrari DREW 6 Glasgow	
22.12.96	Marc Smith W PTS 6 Glasgow	
04.04.97	Jimmy Phelan W PTS 6 Glasgow	
16.05.97	Dean Bramhald W PTS 6 Glasgow	
13.06.97	Chris Price W PTS 6 Paisley	
05.07.97	Mark McGowan W PTS 4 Glasgow	
12.09.97	Gerard Murphy W PTS 8 Glasgow	
01.11.97	Nigel Bradley W PTS 4 Glasgow	
12.11.97	John Green DREW 8 Glasgow	
14.12.97	Tony Walton W PTS 6 Glasgow	
27.02.98	Chris Saunders W PTS 10 Glasgow	
	(Elim. British Welterweight Title)	
19.09.98	Michael Carruth L PTS 12 Dublin	
	(Vacant WAA Welterweight Title)	
13.11.98	Lee Molyneux W PTS 4 Brighton	
26.02.99	Edwin Murillo W CO 6 Bethnal Green	
	(WBB Welterweight Title Challenge)	
07.06.99	Mark Ramsey W PTS 8 Glasgow	
22.10.99	Derek Roche L PTS 12 Coventry	
	(British Welterweight Title Challenge)	
05.02.00	Sean Sullivan W PTS 12 Bethnal Green	
	(Vacant Commonwealth Welterweight Title)	
06.06.00	Charlie Kane W RSC 6 Motherwell	
	(Commonwealth Welterweight Title Defence. Vacant Scottish Welterweight Title)	
24.06.00	Leith Wicks W PTS 4 Glasgow	
19.08.00	Steve Roberts L RSC 9 Brentwood	
	(Vacant WBF L. Middleweight Title)	
25.11.00	Anthony Farnell L RSC 7 Manchester	
	(WBO Inter-Continental L. Middleweight Title Challenge)	
20.03.01	Wayne Shepherd W PTS 6 Glasgow	
27.04.01	Anders Styve L PTS 4 Aalborg, Denmark	
18.05.01	Ruben Varon W RSC 5 Guadalajara, Spain	
07.07.01	Jamie Moore W CO 5 Manchester	
	(Vacant WBO Inter-Continental L.Middleweight Title)	
22.09.01	Takaloo L CO 1 Bethnal Green	

	(WBU L.Middleweight Title Challenge)	
15.03.02	Michael Rask L PTS 8 Vilborg, Denmark	
17.05.03	Marcus Portman L PTS 6 Liverpool	
06.09.03	Darren Rhodes DREW 6 Huddersfield	
17.10.03	Howard Clarke W PTS 6 Glasgow	
01.11.03	Robert Burton W PTS 6 Glasgow	
12.03.04	Ryan Rhodes L PTS 8 Nottingham	
24.04.04	Matthew Macklin L RTD 5 Reading	

Career: 40 contests, won 27, drew 3, lost 10.

Craig Docherty

Glasgow. *Born* Glasgow, 27 September, 1979

Commonwealth S. Featherweight Champion. Ht. 5'7"
Manager T. Gilmour

16.11.98	Kevin Gerowski W PTS 6 Glasgow	
22.02.99	Des Gargano W PTS 6 Glasgow	
19.04.99	Paul Quarmby W RSC 4 Glasgow	
07.06.99	Simon Chambers W PTS 6 Glasgow	
20.09.99	John Barnes W PTS 6 Glasgow	
15.11.99	Peter Allen W RSC 1 Glasgow	
24.01.00	Lee Williamson W PTS 6 Glasgow	
19.02.00	Steve Hanley W PTS 6 Prestwick	
05.06.00	Sebastian Hart W RSC 1 Glasgow	
23.10.00	Lee Armstrong DREW 8 Glasgow	
22.01.01	Nigel Senior W RSC 4 Glasgow	
20.03.01	Jamie McKeever W RSC 3 Glasgow	
11.06.01	Rakhim Mingaleev W PTS 8 Nottingham	
27.10.01	Michael Gomez L RSC 2 Manchester	
	(British S.Featherweight Title Challenge)	
18.03.02	Joel Viney W CO 1 Glasgow	
13.07.02	Dariusz Snarski W PTS 6 Coventry	
25.01.03	Nikolai Eremeev W PTS 6 Bridgend	
12.04.03	Dean Pithie W CO 8 Bethnal Green	
	(Commonwealth S. Featherweight Title Challenge)	
01.11.03	Abdul Malik Jabir W PTS 12 Glasgow	
	(Commonwealth S.Featherweight Title Defence)	
22.04.04	Kpakpo Allotey W RSC 6 Glasgow	
	(Commonwealth S.Featherweight Title Defence)	

Career: 20 contests, won 18, drew 1, lost 1.

Adrian Dodson

Islington. *Born* Georgetown, Guyana, 20 September, 1970

S. Middleweight. Former IBO S. Middleweight Champion. Former Undefeated WBO Inter-Continental L. Middleweight Champion. Ht. 5'10"
Manager Self

31.03.93	Chris Mulcahy W RSC 1 Bethnal Green	
14.04.93	Rick North W RTD 1 Kensington	
06.05.93	Greg Wallace W RSC 3 Las Vegas, Nevada, USA	
23.06.93	Russell Washer W PTS 6 Edmonton	
22.09.93	Robert Peel W CO 1 Bethnal Green	
23.10.93	Julian Eavis W RSC 4 Cardiff	
26.02.94	Shamus Casey W CO 1 Earls Court	
12.03.94	Danny Juma W PTS 6 Cardiff	
09.04.94	Stuart Dunn W RSC 1 Mansfield	
04.06.94	Andrew Jervis W RSC 2 Cardiff	
10.09.94	Colin Pitters W PTS 6 Birmingham	
25.02.95	Lloyd Honeyghan W RSC 3 Millwall	

07.10.95	Hughes Daigneault W RSC 4 Belfast	
	(Vacant WBO Inter-Continental L. Middleweight Title)	
02.12.95	Craig Snyder W RSC 8 Belfast	
	(WBO Inter-Continental L. Middleweight Title Defence)	
04.05.96	John Bosco W RSC 7 Dagenham	
	(WBO Inter-Continental L. Middleweight Title Defence)	
27.11.96	Anthony Joseph W CO 1 Bethnal Green	
	(WBO Inter-Continental L. Middleweight Title Defence)	
29.01.97	Rachid Serdjane W DIS 5 Bethnal Green	
29.04.97	Viktor Fessetchko W RSC 3 Belfast	
19.12.97	Ronald Wright L RTD 6 Millwall	
	(WBO L. Middleweight Title Challenge)	
24.03.98	Nestor Tobias W RSC 4 Bethnal Green	
28.08.98	Israel Ponce W RSC 2 Atlantic City, New Jersey, USA	
08.09.98	Mpush Makambi L CO 11 Bethnal Green	
	(Vacant IBO Middleweight Title)	
11.12.98	Mpush Makambi L RSC 8 Prestwick	
	(IBO Middleweight Title Challenge)	
27.04.99	Orlando Wiet W PTS 10 Bethnal Green	
29.06.99	Derek Wormald W PTS 6 Bethnal Green	
20.08.99	Lorant Szabo W PTS 8 Bloomsbury	
05.10.99	Alain Bonnamie L DIS 12 Bloomsbury	
	(Vacant Commonwealth Middleweight Title)	
19.08.00	Paul Wesley W PTS 4 Brentwood	
03.03.01	Paul Jones W CO 3 Wembley	
	(Vacant IBO S.Middleweight Title)	
07.04.01	Ramon Britez L CO 5 Wembley	
	(IBO S. Middleweight Title Defence)	
20.09.03	Varuzhan Davtyan L PTS 4 Nottingham	

Career: 31 contests, won 25, lost 6.

Tony Dodson

Liverpool. *Born* Liverpool, 2 July, 1980

British S.Middleweight Champion. Former Undefeated Central Area S.Middleweight Champion. Former WBF Inter-Continental S.Middleweight Champion. Ht. 6'0¹/₂"
Manager B. Hearn

31.07.99	Michael McDermott W RTD 1 Carlisle	
02.10.99	Sean Pritchard W RSC 3 Cardiff	
22.01.00	Mark Dawson W PTS 4 Birmingham	
11.03.00	Paul Bonson W PTS 4 Kensington	
19.08.00	Jimmy Steel W RSC 3 Brentwood	
09.09.00	Danny Southam W RSC 2 Manchester	
09.10.00	Elvis Michailenko DREW 6 Liverpool	
03.02.01	Paul Bonson W PTS 4 Manchester	
25.09.01	Paul Wesley W PTS 6 Liverpool	
13.10.01	Roman Divisek W CO 1 Budapest, Hungary	
10.11.01	Valery Odin W RSC 4 Wembley	
10.12.01	Jon Penn W RSC 2 Liverpool	
	(Vacant Central Area S.Middleweight Title)	
23.02.02	Jason Hart W RSC 2 Nottingham	
09.03.02	Varuzhan Davtyan L PTS 6 Manchester	
13.04.02	Brian Barbosa W PTS 8 Liverpool	
07.09.02	Mike Algoet W PTS 10 Liverpool	
	(Vacant WBF Inter-Continental S.Middleweight Title)	

26.10.02   Albert Rybacki L RSC 9 Maesteg
     (WBF Inter-Continental
     S.Middleweight Title Defence)
19.04.03   Pierre Moreno L RSC 9 Liverpool
     (Vacant WBF Inter-Continental
     S.Middleweight Title)
26.07.03   Varuzhan Davtyan W RTD 3 Plymouth
22.11.03   Allan Foster W RSC 11 Belfast
     (Vacant British S.Middleweight Title)

Career: 20 contests, won 16, drew 1, lost 3.

Tony Doherty

Pontypool. *Born* London, 8 April, 1983
Welterweight. Ht. 5'8"
Manager F. Warren/B. Hughes

08.05.03   Karl Taylor W PTS 4 Widnes

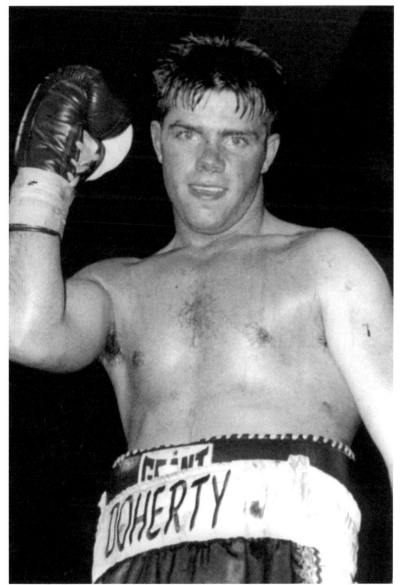

Tony Doherty   Les Clark

28.06.03   Paul McIlwaine W RSC 1 Cardiff
13.09.03   Darren Covill W PTS 4 Newport
06.12.03   James Paisley W RSC 3 Cardiff
21.02.04   Chris Brophy W RSC 2 Cardiff
24.04.04   Keith Jones W PTS 6 Reading
22.05.04   Karl Taylor W RTD 2 Widnes

Career: 7 contests, won 7.

Dmitry Donetskiy

Southampton. *Born* Russia, 21 January, 1978
Middleweight. Ht. 5'9"
Manager J. Bishop

20.02.04   Isidro Gonzalez W RSC 6
     Southampton
30.03.04   Steve Russell W PTS 6 Southampton

12.05.04   Geard Ajetovic L PTS 6 Reading

Career: 3 contests, won 2, lost 1.

Roddy Doran

Shrewsbury. *Born* Shrewsbury, 15 March, 1972
Middleweight. Former Undefeated Midlands Area Middleweight Champion. Former Undefeated British Masters S.Middleweight Champion. Ht. 5'11"
Manager Self

08.10.01   Harry Butler W PTS 6 Birmingham
31.10.01   Harry Butler DREW 6 Birmingham
11.02.02   Freddie Yemofio W PTS 8 Shrewsbury
15.04.02   William Webster W PTS 8 Shrewsbury
13.05.02   Simeon Cover DREW 8 Birmingham
29.09.02   Simon Andrews W PTS 6 Shrewsbury
03.12.02   Harry Butler W PTS 6 Shrewsbury
23.02.03   Simeon Cover W PTS 10 Shrewsbury
     (Vacant British Masters
     S.Middleweight Title)
30.06.03   Mark Phillips W PTS 6 Shrewsbury
07.09.03   Conroy McIntosh W PTS 10
     Shrewsbury
     (Vacant Midlands Area Middleweight
     Title)
28.11.03   Damon Hague W PTS 10 Derby
     (Elim. WBF S.Middleweight Title)
12.03.04   Damon Hague L PTS 12 Nottingham
     (Vacant WBF S.Middleweight Title)

Career: 12 contests, won 9, drew 2, lost 1.

Darren Dorrington

Bristol. *Born* Bristol, 24 July, 1968
Middleweight. Western Area S. Middleweight Champion. Ht. 5'11"
Manager C. Sanigar

13.09.93   Justin Smart DREW 4 Bristol
03.11.93   Russell Washer W PTS 4 Bristol
20.01.94   Shamus Casey W PTS 6 Battersea
29.01.94   Barry Thorogood DREW 6 Cardiff
10.03.94   Ray Price W RSC 6 Bristol
25.05.94   Steve Thomas W PTS 4 Bristol
02.07.94   Paul Murray W RSC 3 Keynsham
03.08.94   Gary Pemberton W CO 4 Bristol
07.10.94   Peter Vosper W RSC 6 Taunton
     (Vacant Western Area S. Middleweight
     Title)
27.10.94   Russell Washer W PTS 8 Bayswater
22.11.94   Robert Allen L RSC 5 Bristol
21.03.95   Lee Crocker L PTS 6 Swansea
19.10.96   Peter Vosper W RSC 3 Bristol
09.12.96   Ernie Loveridge W PTS 6 Bristol
21.01.97   Peter Mitchell W RSC 5 Bristol
24.03.96   Peter Mitchell W RSC 7 Bristol
05.06.97   Paul Carr W PTS 6 Bristol
15.09.97   Darren Ashton L DIS 2 Bristol
11.10.97   Jason Matthews L RSC 7 Sheffield
     (WBO Inter-Continental Middleweight
     Title Challenge)
17.01.98   Rob Stevenson W RSC 3 Bristol
30.03.98   Bruno Girard L PTS 8 Tenerife
30.05.98   Jason Hart W RTD 2 Bristol
14.07.98   Adrian Riley W RTD 2 Reading
24.10.98   Jimmy Vincent DREW 6 Bristol
02.07.99   Elvis Adonesi L RTD 11 Bristol
     (Vacant WBU Inter-Continental
     L. Middleweight Title)
07.04.00   Elvis Adonesi L PTS 12 Bristol
     (Vacant WBU Inter-Continental
     Middleweight Title)

30.09.01 Simon Andrews W RSC 4 Bristol
(Western Area S.Middleweight Title Defence)
16.12.01 Viktor Fesetchko L PTS 10 Bristol
(Vacant WBF European Middleweight Title)
06.03.03 Mark Phillips W PTS 8 Bristol
13.06.03 Dale Nixon W RSC 5 Bristol
05.12.03 Martyn Bailey L RSC 6 Bristol
(British Masters Middleweight Title Challenge)
Career: 31 contests, won 19, drew 3, lost 9.

Tony Dowling

Lincoln. *Born* Lincoln, 5 January, 1976
Cruiserweight. Ht. 6'2"
Manager Self

22.03.96 Slick Miller W RSC 4 Mansfield
30.05.96 Nigel Rafferty W PTS 6 Lincoln
29.07.96 Albert Call L RSC 4 Skegness
12.02.00 Adam Cale W PTS 4 Sheffield
20.03.00 Danny Southam W PTS 4 Mansfield
11.05.00 Jason Brewster W RSC 2 Newark
08.07.00 Slick Miller W PTS 4 Widnes
09.09.00 Lee Swaby L RSC 9 Newark
(Vacant British Masters Cruiserweight Title)
20.04.01 Cathal O'Grady L RSC 1 Dublin
15.09.01 Michael Pinnock W PTS 6 Derby
20.10.01 Garry Delaney L RSC 6 Glasgow
11.05.02 Gary Thompson W RSC 3 Newark
29.09.02 Paul Bonson W PTS 6 Shrewsbury
30.11.02 Scott Lansdowne L RSC 2 Newark
(Vacant Midlands Area Cruiserweight Title)
05.09.03 Denzil Browne W PTS 6 Sheffield
14.11.03 David Haye L RSC 1 Bethnal Green
(Vacant English Cruiserweight Title)
25.04.04 Slick Miller W RSC 2 Nottingham
Career: 17 contests, won 11, lost 6.

Gavin Down

Chesterfield. *Born* Chesterfield, 2 February, 1977
L.Welterweight. Former British Masters L.Welterweight Champion. Former Undefeated Midlands Area L.Welterweight Champion. Ht. 5'9"
Manager Self

21.09.98 Peter Lennon W RSC 1 Cleethorpes
27.11.98 Trevor Tacy L PTS 6 Nottingham
07.12.98 Brian Coleman W PTS 6 Manchester
26.02.99 Brian Gifford W PTS 6 West Bromwich
27.03.99 Lee Molyneux W PTS 4 Derby
15.05.99 Les Frost W RSC 1 Sheffield
27.06.99 Lee Molyneux W PTS 6 Alfreton
03.10.99 Ernie Smith W RSC 1 Chesterfield
28.11.99 Dave Gibson W PTS 6 Chesterfield
09.04.00 Sammy Smith W PTS 6 Alfreton
21.05.00 Arv Mittoo W PTS 6 Derby
19.06.00 Brian Coleman W PTS 4 Burton
13.08.00 Lee Bird W PTS 6 Nottingham
30.08.00 Ram Singh W PTS 6 Scunthorpe
04.11.00 Sebastian Hart W RSC 4 Derby
19.11.00 David Kirk W PTS 10 Chesterfield
(Vacant British Masters L.Welterweight Title)
11.12.00 Dave Gibson W RSC 5 Cleethorpes
25.02.01 Jay Mahoney W RSC 1 Derby

01.04.01 Steve Saville W RSC 3 Alfreton
(Vacant Midlands Area L.Welterweight Title)
16.06.01 Arv Mittoo W PTS 6 Derby
21.07.01 Tommy Peacock W RSC 1 Sheffield
15.09.01 Lee Williamson W PTS 6 Derby
08.12.01 Brian Coleman W RSC 1 Chesterfield
12.02.02 Bradley Pryce L RSC 9 Bethnal Green
(Vacant IBF Inter-Continental L.Welterweight Title)
11.05.02 Woody Greenaway W RSC 3 Chesterfield
05.10.02 Daniel Thorpe W RSC 2 Chesterfield
19.10.02 Daniel James W RTD 5 Norwich
28.01.03 Tony Montana W PTS 4 Nottingham
25.07.03 Alan Bosworth L RSC 5 Norwich
(British Masters L.Welterweight Title Defence. Elim. British L.Welterweight Title)
16.01.04 Paul Denton W RSC 4 Bradford
12.03.04 Jon Hilton W RTD 1 Nottingham
02.06.04 Francis Barrett L PTS 10 Nottingham
(Vacant European Union L.Welterweight Title)
Career: 32 contests, won 28, lost 4.

Gavin Down   Les Clark

Mike Duffield

Cleethorpes. *Born* Cleethorpes, 9 April, 1969
S.Middleweight. Former Midlands Area S.Middleweight Champion. Ht. 6'2½"
Manager Self

22.09.97 Ian Toby L PTS 6 Cleethorpes
21.10.97 Ian Toby W PTS 6 Yarm
14.11.97 Mike Gormley L RSC 2 Mere
15.12.97 Jon Penn L RSC 2 Cleethorpes
16.03.98 Matt Galer L PTS 6 Nottingham
28.04.98 Gary Reyniers DREW 6 Brentford
18.05.98 Carlton Williams W PTS 6 Cleethorpes
17.07.98 Mike White W PTS 6 Mere
21.09.98 Phil Ball W RSC 2 Cleethorpes
26.11.98 Gordon Behan L RSC 3 Edgbaston
(Vacant Midlands Area Middleweight Title)
18.02.99 Lawrence Murphy L RSC 2 Glasgow
29.05.99 Eddie Haley L RSC 6 South Shields
28.11.99 Martin Jolley W PTS 6 Chesterfield
18.01.00 Gary Beardsley L RTD 2 Mansfield
15.05.00 William Webster L PTS 6 Birmingham

15.07.00 Earl Ling L PTS 6 Norwich
30.08.00 Matthew Pepper W RSC 4 Scunthorpe
04.11.00 Damon Hague L RSC 3 Derby
(Vacant WBF European S. Middleweight Title)
20.04.02 Donovan Smillie W PTS 4 Derby
31.05.02 Jamie Wilson W PTS 6 Hull
03.08.02 Simeon Cover L RSC 2 Derby
08.09.02 Peter Jackson L PTS 4 Wolverhampton
21.09.02 Danny Smith L PTS 6 Norwich
10.10.02 Jason Collins L PTS 4 Piccadilly
02.11.02 Peter Jackson W PTS 10 Wolverhampton
(Vacant Midlands Area S.Middleweight Title)
21.12.02 Carl Froch L RSC 1 Dagenham
09.03.03 Gary Dixon L PTS 6 Shaw
17.04.03 Mark Ellwood L PTS 10 Hull
(Vacant British Masters L.Heavyweight Title)
15.06.03 Donovan Smillie L RSC 3 Bradford
(Vacant British Masters S.Middleweight Title)
17.07.03 Peter Jackson L PTS 10 Walsall
(Midlands Area S.Middleweight Title Defence)
02.10.03 Paul Smith L RSC 1 Liverpool
14.11.03 Mark Ellwood L PTS 6 Hull
01.12.03 Lee Nicholson L PTS 6 Barnsley
30.01.04 Daniel Cadman L RSC 1 Dagenham
Career: 34 contests, won 9, drew 1, lost 24.

Mike Duffield   Les Clark

Chris Duggan

Coatbridge. *Born* Glasgow, 26 May, 1981
Welterweight. Ht. 5'10½"
Manager Self

03.02.01 Ty Browne L RSC 1 Brighton
27.07.01 Dean Walker L RSC 4 Sheffield
10.12.01 Carl Walton L PTS 6 Birmingham
15.04.02 Arv Mittoo W PTS 6 Shrewsbury
13.05.02 Lee Williamson L RSC 3 Birmingham
09.06.03 Mally McIver L RSC 3 Bradford
03.08.03 Jonathan Woollins L RSC 1 Stalybridge
06.09.03 Adnan Amar L PTS 4 Aberdeen
07.12.03 Nadeem Siddique L RSC 2 Bradford
Career: 9 contests, won 2, lost 7.

Peter Dunn

Pontefract. *Born* Doncaster, 15 February, 1975
Middleweight. Ht. 5'8"
Manager Self

08.12.97	Leigh Daniels W PTS 6 Bradford
15.05.98	Peter Lennon W PTS 6 Nottingham
18.09.98	Jan Cree L RSC 5 Belfast
23.10.98	Bobby Lyndon W PTS 6 Wakefield
03.12.98	Craig Smith L RSC 3 Sunderland
17.03.99	Des Sowden W PTS 6 Kensington
15.05.99	Ray Wood DREW 4 Blackpool
29.05.99	Dean Nicholas L PTS 6 South Shields
01.10.99	Jon Honney L PTS 4 Bethnal Green
18.10.99	Jan Cree W PTS 6 Glasgow
26.11.99	Gavin Pearson DREW 6 Wakefield
18.02.00	John T. Kelly L PTS 6 Pentre Halkyn
11.03.00	Iain Eldridge L RSC 2 Kensington
18.09.00	Joe Miller L PTS 6 Glasgow
26.10.00	Ram Singh W PTS 6 Stoke
27.11.00	Young Muttley L RSC 3 Birmingham
22.02.01	Darren Spencer W PTS 6 Sunderland
03.03.01	Glenn McClarnon L PTS 4 Wembley
20.03.01	Robert Burton L PTS 6 Leeds
08.04.01	Martyn Bailey L PTS 6 Wrexham
17.05.01	Gavin Pearson L PTS 6 Leeds
25.09.01	Darren Spencer L PTS 4 Liverpool
06.10.01	Lee Byrne L RSC 4 Manchester
13.11.01	Richard Inquieti DREW 6 Leeds
24.11.01	Robert Burton W PTS 6 Wakefield
28.01.02	Robert Burton L RSC 8 Barnsley
	(Vacant Central Area Welterweight Title)
23.03.02	Colin Lynes L PTS 4 Southwark
19.04.02	Oscar Hall L PTS 6 Darlington
28.05.02	Matt Scriven L PTS 8 Leeds
29.06.02	Darren Bruce L PTS 6 Brentwood
28.09.02	Surinder Sekhon L PTS 6 Wakefield
13.09.03	Wayne Shepherd W PTS 6 Wakefield
20.09.03	Michael Lomax L PTS 4 Nottingham
04.10.03	Andy Gibson L PTS 6 Belfast
25.10.03	Gary Young L PTS 6 Edinburgh
13.12.03	Michael Jennings L PTS 6 Manchester
19.02.04	Young Muttley L PTS 4 Dudley
26.02.04	Matthew Hatton L PTS 6 Widnes
06.03.04	Jason Rushton L PTS 6 Renfrew
10.04.04	Ali Nuumembe L PTS 6 Manchester
22.04.04	Jamie Coyle L PTS 6 Glasgow
06.05.04	Jason Rushton L PTS 4 Barnsley
19.06.04	Chris Saunders L PTS 4 Muswell Hill

Career: 43 contests, won 9, drew 3, lost 31.

Colin Dunne

Holloway. *Born* Liverpool, 19 September, 1970
Lightweight. Former WBU Lightweight Champion. Former Undefeated WBF & Southern Area Lightweight Champion. Ht. 5'6"
Manager T. Toole

07.12.93	Mark O'Callaghan W RSC 1 Bethnal Green
14.01.94	Wayne Jones W RSC 3 Bethnal Green
04.03.94	Malcolm Thomas W CO 1 Bethnal Green
26.04.94	Steve Burton W CO 2 Bethnal Green
17.05.94	Phil Found W PTS 6 Kettering
23.09.94	Steve Howden W CO 1 Bethnal Green
11.10.94	Jimmy Phelan W PTS 6 Bethnal Green
09.11.94	Mark O'Callaghan W RSC 2 Millwall
09.12.94	David Thompson W RSC 3 Bethnal Green
20.01.95	Chris Aston W RSC 4 Bethnal Green

03.03.95	Marco Fattore W RSC 3 Bethnal Green
19.04.95	Rudy Valentino W PTS 6 Bethnal Green
12.05.95	Chris Aston W RSC 4 Bethnal Green
27.09.95	Steve Howden W RSC 4 Bethnal Green
28.10.95	Chris Clarkson W RSC 4 Kensington
08.12.95	Jonathan Thaxton W RSC 5 Bethnal Green
	(Vacant Southern Area Lightweight Title)
05.03.96	Rudy Valentino W RSC 4 Bethnal Green
03.04.96	Kino Rodriguez W RSC 2 Bethnal Green
10.05.96	Lajos Nagy W RSC 5 Wembley
03.07.96	Marian Stoica W PTS 8 Wembley
24.10.96	Bamana Dibateza W PTS 8 Wembley
20.11.96	Michael Ayers L RSC 9 Wembley
	(British Lightweight Title Challenge)
24.04.97	Lewis Reynolds W CO 4 Mayfair
	(Southern Area Lightweight Title Defence)
30.06.97	Demir Nanev W RSC 8 Bethnal Green
09.09.97	Alan Bosworth W RSC 8 Bethnal Green
28.11.97	Zoltan Kalocsai W PTS 12 Bethnal Green
	(Vacant WBU Lightweight Title)
23.05.98	Emmanuel Clottey W PTS 12 Bethnal Green
	(WBU Lightweight Title Defence)
21.07.98	Affif Djelti W PTS 12 Widnes
	(WBU Lightweight Title Defence)
12.12.98	Sedat Puskullu W RSC 3 Southwark

27.02.99	Phillip Holiday W PTS 12 Bethnal Green
	(WBU Lightweight Title Defence)
13.07.00	Leonti Voronchuk W CO 4 Bethnal Green
25.07.00	Rakhim Mingaleev W RTD 5 Southwark
14.10.00	Billy Schwer W PTS 12 Wembley
	(WBU Lightweight Title Defence)
16.06.01	Barrie Kelley W CO 3 Dagenham
07.09.01	Sergei Starkov W RSC 3 Bethnal Green
10.11.01	Alan Temple W RSC 7 Wembley
26.01.02	Martin Jacobs W PTS 12 Dagenham
	(WBU Lightweight Title Defence)
18.05.02	Wayne Rigby W RTD 10 Millwall
	(WBU Lightweight Title Defence. Vacant WBF Lightweight Title)
21.09.02	Esteban Morales W PTS 12 Brentwood
	(WBU Lightweight Title Defence)
07.12.02	David Burke L PTS 12 Brentwood
	(WBU Lightweight Title Defence)
05.07.03	Kevin Bennett L RSC 2 Brentwood

Career: 41 contests, won 38, lost 3.

Riaz Durgahed

Bristol. *Born* Mauritius, 4 May, 1977
Featherweight. Ht. 5'6"
Manager C. Sanigar

29.02.04	Jason Thomas W RSC 1 Bristol
19.06.04	Buster Dennis W PTS 4 Muswell Hill

Career: 2 contests, won 2.

Colin Dunne Les Clark

Graham Earl

Luton. *Born* Luton, 26 August, 1978
British Lightweight Champion. Former
Undefeated Southern Area Lightweight
Champion. Ht. 5'5¾"
Manager F. Maloney

02.09.97	Mark O'Callaghan W RSC 2 Southwark
06.12.97	Mark McGowan W PTS 4 Wembley
11.04.98	Danny Lutaaya W RSC 2 Southwark
23.05.98	David Kirk W PTS 4 Bethnal Green
12.09.98	Brian Coleman W PTS 4 Bethnal Green
10.12.98	Marc Smith W RSC 1 Barking
16.01.99	Lee Williamson W RSC 4 Bethnal Green
08.05.99	Benny Jones W PTS 6 Bethnal Green
15.07.99	Simon Chambers W CO 6 Peterborough
04.03.00	Ivo Golakov W RSC 1 Peterborough
29.04.00	Marco Fattore W PTS 6 Wembley
21.10.00	Lee Williamson W RSC 3 Wembley
10.03.01	Brian Gentry W RSC 8 Bethnal Green *(Vacant Southern Area Lightweight Title)*
22.09.01	Liam Maltby W CO 1 Bethnal Green *(Southern Area Lightweight Title Defence)*
15.12.01	Mark Winters W PTS 10 Wembley *(Elim. British Lightweight Title)*
12.10.02	Chill John W PTS 10 Bethnal Green *(Southern Area Lightweight Title Defence)*
15.02.03	Steve Murray W RSC 2 Wembley *(Southern Area Lightweight Title Defence. Final Elim. British Lightweight Title)*
24.05.03	Nikolai Eremeev W PTS 8 Bethnal Green
17.07.03	Bobby Vanzie W PTS 12 Dagenham *(British Lightweight Title Challenge)*
11.10.03	Jon Honney W PTS 8 Portsmouth
05.06.04	Bobby Vanzie W PTS 12 Bethnal Green *(Vacant British Lightweight Title)*

Career: 21 contests, won 21.

Gilbert Eastman

Battersea. *Born* Guyana, 16 November, 1972
Southern Area L Middleweight Champion.
Ht. 5'10"
Manager Self

22.04.96	Wayne Shepherd W PTS 4 Crystal Palace
09.07.96	Costas Katsantonis W RSC 1 Bethnal Green
11.01.97	Mike Watson W RSC 1 Bethnal Green
25.03.97	Danny Quacoe W RSC 3 Lewisham
30.08.97	Karl Taylor W PTS 4 Cheshunt
08.11.97	Ray Newby W PTS 6 Southwark
14.02.98	Cam Raeside W RSC 5 Southwark
21.04.98	Dennis Berry W RSC 6 Edmonton
23.05.98	Shaun O'Neill W RSC 1 Bethnal Green
12.09.98	Everald Williams W RTD 5 Bethnal Green
21.11.98	Lindon Scarlett W RTD 3 Southwark
06.03.99	Kofi Jantuah L RSC 11 Southwark *(Commonwealth Welterweight Title Challenge)*

25.10.02	Ojay Abrahams W PTS 4 Bethnal Green
21.12.02	Pedro Thompson W RSC 2 Dagenham
05.03.03	Howard Clarke W PTS 6 Bethnal Green
16.04.03	Andrew Facey L RSC 3 Nottingham
25.07.03	Jason Collins W RSC 1 Norwich
04.10.03	Spencer Fearon W RSC 4 Muswell Hill *(Vacant Southern Area L.Middleweight Title)*
28.11.03	Eugenio Monteiro L PTS 8 Derby
30.01.04	Craig Lynch W PTS 6 Dagenham
16.04.04	Delroy Mellis W RSC 5 Bradford *(Southern Area L.Middleweight Title Defence)*

Career: 21 contests, won 18, lost 3.

Howard Eastman

Battersea. *Born* New Amsterdam, Guyana,
8 December, 1970
European Middleweight Champion. Former
Undefeated British, Commonwealth, IBO
Inter-Continental, WBA Inter-Continental
& Southern Area Middleweight Champion.
Ht. 5'11"
Manager Self

06.03.94	John Rice W RSC 1 Southwark
14.03.94	Andy Peach W PTS 6 Mayfair
22.03.94	Steve Phillips W RSC 5 Bethnal Green
17.10.94	Barry Thorogood W RSC 6 Mayfair
06.03.95	Marty Duke W RSC 1 Mayfair
20.04.95	Stuart Dunn W RSC 2 Mayfair
23.06.95	Peter Vosper W RSC 1 Bethnal Green
16.10.95	Carlo Colarusso W RSC 1 Mayfair
29.11.95	Brendan Ryan W RSC 2 Bethnal Green

31.01.96	Paul Wesley W RSC 1 Birmingham
13.03.96	Steve Goodwin W RSC 5 Wembley
29.04.96	John Duckworth W RSC 5 Mayfair
11.12.96	Sven Hamer W RSC 10 Southwark *(Vacant Southern Area Middleweight Title)*
18.02.97	John Duckworth W CO 7 Cheshunt
25.03.97	Rachid Serdjane W RSC 7 Lewisham
14.02.98	Vitali Kopitko W PTS 8 Southwark
28.03.98	Terry Morrill W RTD 4 Hull
23.05.98	Darren Ashton W RSC 4 Bethnal Green
30.11.98	Steve Foster W RSC 7 Manchester *(Vacant British Middleweight Title)*
04.02.99	Jason Barker W RSC 6 Lewisham
06.03.99	Jon Penn W RSC 3 Southwark *(Vacant IBO Inter-Continental S. Middleweight Title)*
22.05.99	Roman Babaev W RSC 6 Belfast *(WBA Inter-Continental Middleweight Title Challenge)*
10.07.99	Teimouraz Kikelidze W RSC 6 Southwark *(WBA Inter-Continental Middleweight Title Defence)*
13.09.99	Derek Wormald W RSC 3 Bethnal Green *(British Middleweight Title Defence)*
13.11.99	Mike Algoet W RSC 8 Hull *(WBA Inter-Continental Middleweight Title Defence)*
18.01.00	Ojay Abrahams W RSC 2 Mansfield
04.03.00	Viktor Fesetchko W RTD 4 Peterborough
29.04.00	Anthony Ivory W RTD 6 Wembley

Gilbert Eastman   Les Clark

25.07.00 Ahmet Dottouev W RTD 5 Southwark
(WBA Inter-Continental Middleweight Title Defence)
16.09.00 Sam Soliman W PTS 12 Bethnal Green
(Commonwealth Middleweight Title Challenge)
05.02.01 Mark Baker W RTD 5 Hull
10.04.01 Robert McCracken W RSC 10 Wembley
(British & Commonwealth Middleweight Title Defences. Vacant European Middleweight Title)
17.11.01 William Joppy L PTS 12 Las Vegas, Nevada, USA
(Vacant WBA Interim Middleweight Title)
25.10.02 Chardan Ansoula W RSC 1 Bethnal Green
21.12.02 Hussain Osman W RTD 4 Dagenham
28.01.03 Christophe Tendil W RTD 4 Nottingham
(Vacant European Middleweight Title)
05.03.03 Gary Beardsley W RSC 2 Bethnal Green
16.04.03 Scott Dann W RSC 3 Nottingham
(British, Commonwealth & European Middleweight Title Defences)
25.07.03 Hacine Cherifi W RTD 8 Norwich
(European Middleweight Title Defence)
30.01.04 Sergei Tatevosyan W PTS 12 Dagenham
(European Middleweight Title Defence)
Career: 40 contests, won 39, lost 1.

Tommy Eastwood

Epsom. *Born* Epsom, 16 May, 1979
Cruiserweight. Ht. 5'11½"
Manager F. Maloney

09.09.01 Tony Booth W PTS 4 Southwark
16.12.01 Paul Bonson W PTS 4 Southwark
12.02.02 Adam Cale W PTS 4 Bethnal Green
24.03.02 Dave Clarke W PTS 6 Streatham
23.06.02 Brodie Pearmaine W PTS 4 Southwark
24.01.03 Lee Swaby L PTS 6 Sheffield
26.11.03 Brian Gascoigne W RSC 2 Mayfair
Career: 7 contests, won 6, lost 1.

Tommy Eastwood   Les Clark

Chris Edwards

Stoke. *Born* Stoke, 6 May, 1976
Flyweight. Ht. 5'3"
Manager P. Dykes

03.04.98 Chris Thomas W RSC 2 Ebbw Vale
21.09.98 Russell Laing L PTS 6 Glasgow

26.02.99 Delroy Spencer L PTS 6 West Bromwich
17.04.99 Stevie Quinn L RSC 4 Dublin
19.10.99 Lee Georgiou L RSC 2 Bethnal Green
03.12.99 Daniel Ring L PTS 4 Peterborough
15.05.00 Paddy Folan L PTS 6 Bradford
07.10.00 Andy Roberts W PTS 4 Doncaster
27.11.00 Levi Pattison W PTS 4 Birmingham
16.03.01 Jamie Evans L PTS 6 Portsmouth
03.06.01 Darren Taylor DREW 6 Hanley
08.10.01 Levi Pattison L PTS 4 Barnsley
06.12.01 Neil Read W PTS 8 Stoke
10.10.02 Neil Read W PTS 6 Stoke
13.06.03 Lee Haskins L PTS 6 Bristol
23.04.04 Delroy Spencer DREW 6 Leicester
Career: 16 contests, won 5, drew 2, lost 9.

Wayne Elcock

Birmingham. *Born* Birmingham, 12 February, 1974
Middleweight. Former WBU Middleweight Champion. Ht. 5'9½"
Manager F. Maloney

02.12.99 William Webster W PTS 6 Peterborough
04.03.00 Sonny Pollard W RSC 3 Peterborough
07.07.01 Darren Rhodes W PTS 4 Manchester
09.10.01 Valery Odin W PTS 4 Cardiff
02.03.02 Charles Shodiya W RSC 1 Bethnal Green
20.04.02 Howard Clarke W PTS 4 Cardiff
01.06.02 Jason Collins W RSC 2 Manchester
17.08.02 Ojay Abrahams W PTS 4 Cardiff
23.11.02 Jason Collins W RSC 1 Derby
15.02.03 Yuri Tsarenko W PTS 10 Wembley
05.04.03 Anthony Farnell W PTS 12 Manchester
(WBU Middleweight Title Challenge)
29.11.03 Lawrence Murphy L CO 1 Renfrew
(WBU Middleweight Title Defence)
07.02.04 Farai Musiiwa W PTS 6 Bethnal Green
05.06.04 Michael Monaghan W PTS 4 Bethnal Green
Career: 14 contests, won 13, lost 1.

Iain Eldridge

Watford. *Born* Watford, 26 February, 1975
Welterweight. Ht. 5'8"
Manager P. Rees

18.11.99 Des Sowden W RSC 4 Mayfair
21.02.00 Lee Sharp L PTS 6 Glasgow
11.03.00 Peter Dunn W RSC 2 Kensington
22.07.00 Ross McCord W RSC 2 Watford
19.08.00 Karl Taylor W PTS 4 Brentwood
03.03.01 Kevin Bennett L PTS 6 Wembley
23.11.01 Costas Katsantonis L RSC 1 Bethnal Green
(Vacant Southern Area L.Welterweight Title)
15.10.02 Wayne Wheeler DREW 4 Bethnal Green
25.10.02 Lee Meager L RSC 5 Bethnal Green
03.12.02 Cristian Hodorogea L PTS 4 Bethnal Green
18.11.03 Brett James L PTS 10 Bethnal Green
(Southern Area Welterweight Title Challenge)
Career: 11 contests, won 4, drew 1, lost 6.

Matthew Ellis

Blackpool. *Born* Oldham, 12 April, 1974
Heavyweight. Ht. 5'11¾"
Manager Self

03.02.96 Laurent Rouze W CO 1 Liverpool
01.04.96 Ladislav Husarik W RTD 4 Den Bosch, Holland
06.09.96 Darren Fearn W RSC 6 Liverpool
26.10.96 Daniel Beun W RSC 1 Liverpool
01.03.97 Yuri Yelistratov L RSC 5 Liverpool
20.07.97 Ricardo Phillips W PTS 4 Indio, California, USA
26.09.97 Albert Call DREW 6 Liverpool
12.03.98 Yuri Yelistratov W RSC 1 Liverpool
21.07.98 Chris Woollas W RSC 5 Widnes
24.10.98 Peter Hrivnak W RSC 1 Liverpool
12.12.98 Harry Senior W PTS 8 Southwark
27.02.99 Michael Murray W PTS 8 Bethnal Green
15.05.99 Biko Botowamungu W PTS 8 Blackpool
27.05.00 Alex Vasiliev W CO 4 Southwark
16.09.00 Dimitri Bakhtov W PTS 4 Bethnal Green
18.11.00 Chris Woollas W PTS 4 Dagenham
17.02.01 Alexei Osokin W PTS 8 Bethnal Green
12.07.01 Ronnie Smith W PTS 6 Houston, Texas, USA
22.09.01 Colin Abelson W CO 1 Bethnal Green
02.03.02 Dennis Bakhtov L RSC 5 Bethnal Green
(WBC International Heavyweight Title Challenge)
29.03.03 Derek McCafferty W PTS 4 Wembley
31.05.03 Audley Harrison L RSC 2 Bethnal Green
27.10.03 Tony Moran L RSC 4 Glasgow
Career: 23 contests, won 18, drew 1, lost 4.

Keith Ellwood

Edinburgh. *Born* Edinburgh, 14 December, 1979
L. Middleweight. Ht. 6'1"
Manager T. Gilmour

02.10.00 Pedro Thompson W RSC 3 Glasgow
15.02.01 Chris Nembhard L RSC 2 Glasgow
19.04.04 Ady Clegg L CO 5 Glasgow
Career: 3 contests, won 1, lost 2.

Mark Ellwood

Hull. *Born* Hull, 13 June, 1963
L.Heavyweight. Former Undefeated British Masters L.Heavyweight Champion. Ht. 5'9½"
Manager Self

01.11.01 Adam Cale W PTS 6 Hull
25.04.02 Mark Phillips W PTS 6 Hull
26.09.02 Shpetim Hoti W PTS 6 Hull
21.11.02 Martin Thompson W PTS 6 Hull
11.12.02 William Webster W PTS 6 Hull
17.04.03 Mike Duffield W PTS 10 Hull
(Vacant British Masters L.Heavyweight Title)
14.11.03 Mike Duffield W PTS 6 Hull
Career: 7 contests, won 7.

Declan English

Burton. *Born* Burton, 28 March, 1981
Lightweight. Ht. 5'7"
Manager N. Nobbs

17.06.04 David Pereira L PTS 6 Sheffield
25.06.04 Rob Jeffries L PTS 6 Bethnal Green
Career: 2 contests, lost 2.

Andrew Facey

Sheffield. *Born* Wolverhampton, 20 May, 1972
English L.Middleweight Champion. Former Undefeated Central Area Middleweight Champion. Ht. 6'0"
Manager J. Ingle

06.12.99	Peter McCormack W CO 2 Birmingham
09.06.00	Matthew Pepper W RSC 1 Hull
04.11.00	Earl Ling W PTS 6 Derby
11.12.00	Gary Jones W PTS 6 Cleethorpes
10.02.01	Louis Swales W RSC 3 Widnes
17.03.01	Darren Rhodes L PTS 4 Manchester
24.03.01	Matthew Tait W PTS 4 Chigwell
16.06.01	Earl Ling DREW 6 Derby
09.12.01	Michael Pinnock W PTS 6 Shaw
02.03.02	Darren Rhodes W RSC 6 Wakefield
	(Vacant Central Area Middleweight Title)
20.04.02	Darren Ashton W PTS 6 Derby
13.04.02	Leigh Wicks W PTS 6 Norwich
03.08.02	Damon Hague L CO 5 Derby
	(Final Elim. WBF Middleweight Title)
25.10.02	William Webster W PTS 4 Cotgrave
16.04.03	Gilbert Eastman W RSC 3 Nottingham
06.11.03	Matthew Macklin W PTS 10 Dagenham
	(Vacant English L.Middleweight Title)
22.11.03	Jamie Moore L RSC 7 Belfast
	(British & Commonwealth L.Middleweight Title Challenges)
04.06.04	Howard Clarke W PTS 6 Hull

Career: 18 contests, won 14, drew 1, lost 3.

Andrew Facey Les Clark

Anthony Farnell

Manchester. *Born* Manchester, 1 July, 1978
Middleweight. Former WBU Middleweight Champion. Former Undefeated WBO Inter-Continental L. Middleweight Champion. Ht. 5'10"
Manager F. Warren/T. Jones

03.05.97	Lee Molyneux W PTS 4 Manchester
02.08.97	Martin Renaghan W RSC 3 Barnsley
20.09.97	Dominique van der Steene W CO 1 Aachen, Germany
13.12.97	Paul Scott W RSC 3 Sheffield
24.01.98	Steve Brumant W PTS 4 Cardiff
21.03.98	Hughie Davey W PTS 6 Bethnal Green
18.04.98	Harry Butler W PTS 6 Manchester
09.05.98	David Thompson W CO 1 Sheffield
18.07.98	Lee Molyneux W CO 3 Sheffield
05.09.98	Darren Williams W RTD 4 Telford
31.10.98	Mark Richardson W PTS 6 Atlantic City, New Jersey, USA
28.11.98	George Richards W RSC 7 Sheffield
19.12.98	Koba Kulu W RTD 5 Liverpool
27.02.99	Koba Kulu W RSC 1 Oldham
01.05.99	Alan Gilbert W RSC 8 Crystal Palace
29.05.99	John Long W RSC 6 Halifax
	(Vacant WBO Inter-Continental L. Middleweight Title)
07.08.99	Israel Ponce W RSC 3 Atlantic City, New Jersey, USA
09.10.99	Javier Santibanez W CO 1 Manchester
	(WBO Inter-Continental L. Middleweight Title Defence)
27.11.99	Marino Monteyne W CO 6 Lubeck, Germany
29.01.00	Ian Toby W RSC 3 Manchester
08.04.00	Ojay Abrahams W PTS 8 Bethnal Green
29.05.00	Howard Clarke W PTS 12 Manchester
	(WBO Inter-Continental L. Middleweight Title Defence)
04.09.00	Juan Carlos Sanchez W PTS 12 Manchester
	(WBO Inter-Continental L. Middleweight Title Defence)
25.11.00	Scott Dixon W RSC 7 Manchester
	(WBO Inter-Continental L. Middleweight Title Defence)
15.01.01	Sergio Acuna W PTS 12 Manchester
	(WBO Inter-Continental L. Middleweight Title Defence)
17.03.01	Shakir Ashanti W RSC 2 Manchester
	(WBO Inter-Continental L. Middleweight Title Defence)
07.07.01	Takaloo L RSC 1 Manchester
	(Vacant WBU L.Middleweight Title)
15.09.01	Lee Blundell W RSC 2 Manchester
	(Vacant WBO Inter-Continental L.Middleweight Title)
27.10.01	Pavel Melnikov W RSC 12 Manchester
	(WBO Inter-Continental L. Middleweight Title Defence)
09.02.02	Matt Galer W RSC 3 Manchester
01.06.02	Ruben Groenewald L PTS 12 Manchester
	(Vacant WBU Middleweight Title)
28.09.02	Ruben Groenewald W PTS 12 Manchester
	(WBU Middleweight Title Challenge)
18.01.03	Nikolai Talalakin W RTD 10 Preston
	(WBU Middleweight Title Defence)
05.04.03	Wayne Elcock L PTS 12 Manchester
	(WBU Middleweight Title Defence)
13.12.03	Tomas da Silva W PTS 6 Manchester
06.03.04	Lawrence Murphy W RSC 3 Renfrew
	(WBU Middleweight Title Challenge)
12.06.04	Eugenio Monteiro L RSC 10 Manchester
	(WBU Middleweight Title Defence)

Career: 37 contests, won 33, lost 4.

Spencer Fearon

Forest Hill. *Born* London, 20 December, 1973
L. Middleweight. Ht. 6'0"
Manager Self

28.06.97	Mark Sawyers W PTS 4 Norwich
13.09.97	Danny Quacoe W PTS 4 Millwall
21.03.98	Perry Ayres W PTS 4 Bethnal Green
16.05.98	Danny Quacoe W PTS 4 Bethnal Green
26.09.98	Rob Stevenson W CO 2 Norwich
14.11.98	Prince Kasi Kaihau W CO 5 Cheshunt
23.01.99	George Richards L PTS 6 Cheshunt
08.04.00	Leigh Wicks W PTS 4 Bethnal Green
12.08.00	Freddie Yemofio W RSC 4 Wembley
23.09.00	Matthew Bowers W RSC 2 Bethnal Green
27.01.01	Jason Collins L PTS 4 Bethnal Green
24.02.01	Harry Butler W PTS 4 Bethnal Green
03.04.01	Lee Blundell L PTS 6 Bethnal Green
03.06.01	Gary Logan L RSC 2 Southwark
	(Vacant Southern Area Middleweight Title)
08.02.03	Leigh Wicks W PTS 6 Brentford
25.07.03	David Walker L RSC 4 Norwich
	(Southern Area L.Middleweight Title Challenge)
04.10.03	Gilbert Eastman L RSC 4 Muswell Hill
	(Vacant Southern Area L.Middleweight Title)

Career: 17 contests, won 11, lost 6.

Femi Fehintola

Bradford. *Born* Bradford, 1 July, 1982
S. Featherweight. Ht. 5'7"
Manager D. Hobson

26.09.03	John-Paul Ryan W PTS 6 Reading
07.11.03	Pete Buckley W PTS 6 Sheffield
10.12.03	Jason Nesbitt W PTS 6 Sheffield
06.02.04	Jason Nesbitt W PTS 6 Sheffield
20.04.04	Kristian Laight W PTS 6 Sheffield
17.06.04	Anthony Hanna W PTS 6 Sheffield

Career: 6 contests, won 6.

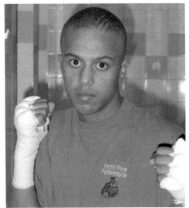

Femi Fehintola Les Clark

Andrew Ferrans

New Cumnock. *Born* Irvine, 4 February, 1981
British Master S.Featherweight Champion. Ht. 5'9"
Manager T. Gilmour

19.02.00	Chris Lyons W PTS 6 Prestwick
03.03.00	Gary Groves W RSC 1 Irvine
20.03.00	John Barnes DREW 6 Glasgow
06.06.00	Duncan Armstrong W PTS 6 Motherwell
18.09.00	Steve Brook W PTS 6 Glasgow
20.11.00	Duncan Armstrong W PTS 6 Glasgow
23.02.01	Dave Cotterill L RSC 2 Irvine
30.04.01	Dave Cotterill W RSC 1 Glasgow
04.06.01	Jason Nesbitt W RSC 2 Glasgow
17.09.01	Gary Flear W PTS 8 Glasgow
10.12.01	Jamie McKeever L PTS 6 Liverpool
21.01.02	Joel Viney W PTS 8 Glasgow
01.03.02	Peter Allen W PTS 8 Irvine
13.04.02	Tony Mulholland L PTS 4 Liverpool
11.05.02	Marc Callaghan L PTS 6 Dagenham
23.09.02	Greg Edwards W RTD 4 Glasgow
08.10.02	Peter Allen W PTS 8 Glasgow
18.11.02	Joel Viney W PTS 6 Glasgow
30.11.02	Colin Toohey L PTS 6 Liverpool
28.02.03	Simon Chambers W RSC 7 Irvine
28.04.03	Craig Spacie L PTS 6 Nottingham
26.07.03	Baz Carey W PTS 6 Plymouth
01.11.03	Anthony Hanna W PTS 4 Glasgow
19.01.04	Dariusz Snarski W PTS 6 Glasgow
15.03.04	Baz Carey W PTS 10 Glasgow *(Vacant British Masters S.Featherweight Title)*
08.05.04	Carl Johanneson L RSC 6 Bristol *(WBF S.Featherweight Title Challenge)*

Career: 26 contests, won 17, drew 2, lost 7.

Andrew Ferrans Les Clark

Mark Flatt

Hemel Hempstead. *Born* Hemel Hempstead, 24 April, 1974
L. Heavyweight. Ht. 6'4"
Manager P. Rees

01.12.03	Paul Billington L RSC 2 Bradford

Career: 1 contest, lost 1.

Wes Fleming

Liverpool. *Born* Birkenhead, 27 October, 1979
L. Middleweight. Ht. 5'10"
Manager G. Storey

22.11.03	Tommy Tolan L RSC 2 Belfast

Career: 1 contest, lost 1.

Scott Flynn

Edinburgh. *Born* Edinburgh, 27 March, 1984
S. Bantamweight. Ht. 5'8"
Manager F. Warren/D. Powell

19.06.04	Henry Janes L RSC 4 Renfrew

Career: 1 contest, lost 1.

(Patrick) Paddy Folan (Powders)

Huddersfield. *Born* Birmingham, 25 June, 1972
Featherweight. Ht. 5'7"
Manager C. Aston

25.10.98	Waj Khan W PTS 6 Shaw
26.11.98	Daniel Ring DREW 6 Bradford
07.12.98	Kevin Gerowski L PTS 6 Bradford
21.02.99	Chris Emanuele DREW 6 Bradford
19.04.99	Gary Groves L CO 1 Bradford
19.09.99	Gary Ford L PTS 6 Shaw
14.11.99	Shane Mallon W PTS 6 Bradford
26.11.99	Chris Emanuele L RSC 5 Wakefield
05.03.00	Gary Ford L PTS 6 Shaw
15.05.00	Chris Edwards W PTS 6 Bradford
25.06.00	Levi Pattison L PTS 6 Wakefield
30.11.00	Neil Read W PTS 6 Blackpool
07.12.00	John-Paul Ryan L PTS 6 Stoke
11.02.01	Michael Hunter L RSC 6 Hartlepool
20.03.01	Sean Grant DREW 6 Leeds
01.04.01	Dafydd Carlin L PTS 4 Southwark
09.04.01	Sean Grant L PTS 6 Bradford
10.06.01	Lee Holmes L PTS 6 Ellesmere Port
31.07.01	Jamie Yelland L RSC 5 Bethnal Green
22.10.01	Sean Grant L PTS 6 Glasgow
19.11.01	Gary Groves W PTS 6 Glasgow
09.12.01	Joel Viney L PTS 6 Blackpool
21.02.02	Gypsy Boy Mario W PTS 6 Sunderland
02.03.02	Sean Hughes L PTS 6 Wakefield
28.05.02	John Paul Ryan L PTS 6 Leeds
24.06.02	Gary Groves W RSC 2 Bradford
20.07.02	Steve Foster L CO 1 Bethnal Green
05.10.02	Sean Hughes L PTS 4 Huddersfield
05.10.03	Sean Hughes L RSC 4 Bradford *(Vacant Central Area S.Bantamweight Title)*
23.11.03	Fred Janes L RSC 5 Rotherham
19.04.04	Furhan Rafiq L PTS 6 Glasgow

Career: 31 contests, won 7, drew 3, lost 21.

Scott Forsyth

Edinburgh. *Born* Edinburgh, 23 July, 1982
Middleweight. Ht. 6'0"
Manager A., Morrison

27.03.04	Neil Addis W RSC 3 Edinburgh

Career: 1 contest, won 1.

Allan Foster

Northampton. *Born* Kilmarnock, 8 November, 1973
S. Middleweight. Ht. 5'11"
Manager T. Gilmour

03.12.99	Steve Timms W RSC 4 Peterborough
05.03.00	Richie Jenkins W PTS 6 Peterborough
02.06.00	Leigh Wicks W PTS 4 Ashford
06.10.00	Paul Johnson W PTS 4 Maidstone
01.12.00	Michael Pinnock W PTS 4 Peterborough
17.02.01	Tommy Matthews W PTS 4 Bethnal Green

24.03.01	Darren Covill W RTD 3 Sheffield
31.07.01	Mark Snipe W PTS 6 Bethnal Green
16.03.02	Alan Jones DREW 6 Northampton
08.10.02	Clint Johnson W PTS 6 Glasgow
05.07.03	Ojay Abrahams W PTS 4 Brentwood
22.11.03	Tony Dodson L RSC 11 Belfast *(Vacant British S.Middleweight Title)*
08.05.04	Howard Clarke W PTS 4 Dagenham

Career: 13 contests, won 11, drew 1, lost 1.

Steve Foster

Salford. *Born* Salford, 16 September, 1980
English Featherweight Champion. Ht. 5'6"
Manager S.Foster/S.Wood/F.Warren

15.09.01	Andy Greenaway W PTS 4 Manchester
27.10.01	Gareth Wiltshaw W PTS 4 Manchester
02.03.02	Andy Greenaway W RSC 1 Bethnal Green
04.05.02	Gareth Wiltshaw W PTS 4 Bethnal Green
08.07.02	Ian Turner W RSC 1 Mayfair
20.07.02	Paddy Folan W CO 1 Bethnal Green
28.09.02	Jason White W RSC 3 Manchester
14.12.02	Sean Green W RSC 3 Newcastle
22.03.03	David McIntyre W PTS 4 Renfrew
24.05.03	Henry Janes W PTS 6 Bethnal Green
12.07.03	David McIntyre W RTD 3 Renfrew
18.09.03	Alexander Abramenko W RTD 4 Dagenham
06.11.03	Vladimir Borov W RSC 8 Dagenham
13.12.03	Steve Gethin W RTD 3 Manchester
26.02.04	Sean Hughes W RSC 6 Widnes *(Vacant English Featherweight Title)*

Career: 15 contests, won 15.

Julius Francis

Woolwich. *Born* Peckham, 8 December, 1964
Heavyweight. Former Undefeated Commonwealth Heavyweight Champion. Former British Heavyweight Champion. Former Undefeated Southern Area Heavyweight Champion. Ht. 6'2"
Manager Self

23.05.93	Graham Arnold W RSC 5 Brockley
23.06.93	Joey Paladino W CO 4 Edmonton
24.07.93	Andre Tisdale W PTS 4 Atlantic City, New Jersey, USA
28.08.93	Don Sargent W RSC 2 Bismark, USA
01.12.93	John Keeton W RSC 4 Bethnal Green
27.04.94	Manny Burgo W PTS 4 Bethnal Green
25.05.94	John Ruiz L CO 4 Bristol
12.11.94	Conroy Nelson W RSC 4 Dublin
23.11.94	Gary Charlton W RSC 1 Piccadilly
23.02.05	Damien Caesar W RSC 8 Southwark *(Vacant Southern Area Heavyweight Title)*
27.04.95	Keith Fletcher W PTS 10 Bethnal Green *(Southern Area Heavyweight Title Defence)*
25.05.95	Steve Garber W PTS 8 Reading
01.07.95	Scott Welch L RSC 10 Kensington *(Southern Area Heavyweight Title Defence. Final Elim. British Heavyweight Title)*
24.10.95	Neil Kirkwood W RSC 7 Southwark
30.11.95	Nikolai Kulpin L PTS 10 Saratov, Russia

111

05.02.96 Michael Murray L PTS 10 Bexleyheath
(Elim. British Heavyweight Title)
09.04.96 Damien Caesar W CO 1 Stevenage
(Vacant Southern Area Heavyweight Title)
07.05.96 Darren Fearn W PTS 8 Mayfair
09.07.96 Mike Holden W PTS 10 Bethnal Green
28.09.96 James Oyebola W RSC 5 Barking
(Southern Area Heavyweight Title Defence)
15.02.97 Zeljko Mavrovic L RSC 8 Vienna, Austria
(European Heavyweight Title Challenge)
30.06.97 Joseph Chingangu W PTS 12 Bethnal Green
(Vacant Commonwealth Heavyweight Title)
27.09.97 Garry Delaney W RSC 6 Belfast
(Commonwealth Heavyweight Title Defence. Vacant British Heavyweight Title)
28.02.98 Axel Schulz L PTS 12 Dortmund, Germany
18.04.98 Vitali Klitschko L RSC 2 Aachen, Germany
30.01.99 Pele Reid W RSC 3 Bethnal Green
(British & Commonwealth Heavyweight Title Defences)
03.04.99 Danny Williams W PTS 12 Kensington
(British & Commonwealth Heavyweight Title Defences)
26.06.99 Scott Welch W PTS 12 Millwall
(British & Commonwealth Heavyweight Title Defences)
29.01.00 Mike Tyson L RSC 2 Manchester
13.03.00 Mike Holden L PTS 12 Bethnal Green
(British Heavyweight Title Defence)
03.04.01 Mike Holden W PTS 12 Bethnal Green
(Final Elim. British Heavyweight Title)
28.07.01 Danny Williams L CO 4 Wembley
(British & Commonwealth Heavyweight Title Challenges)
10.05.02 Luke Simpkin DREW 6 Millwall
13.09.02 Steffen Nielsen W CO 6 Randers, Denmark
26.04.03 Sinan Samil Sam L RSC 7 Schwerin, Germany
(European Heavyweight Title Challenge)
13.06.03 Steffen Nielsen L PTS 10 Aalborg, Denmark
(Vacant European Union Heavyweight Title)
06.09.03 Vladimir Virchis L PTS 12 Kiev, Ukraine
(Vacant IBF Inter-Continental Interim Heavyweight Title)
18.10.03 Luan Krasniqi L PTS 8 Hamburg, Germany
27.11.03 Oleg Maskaev L RSC 2 Moscow, Russia
07.02.04 Matt Skelton L PTS 10 Bethnal Green
(English Heavyweight Title Challenge)
08.05.04 Audley Harrison L PTS 12 Bristol
(WBF Heavyweight Title Challenge)
Career: 41 contests, won 23, drew 1, lost 17.

Simon Francis

Sheffield. *Born* Sheffield, 2 October, 1981
Cruiserweight. Ht. 6'2"
Manager D. Coldwell

06.05.04 Gary Thompson W PTS 4 Barnsley
08.06.04 Gary Thompson W RTD 2 Sheffield
24.06.04 Slick Miller W PTS 6 Gibralter
Career: 3 contests, won 3.

Carl Froch

Nottingham. *Born* Nottingham, 2 July, 1977
Commonwealth S.Middleweight Champion. Former Undefeated English S.Middleweight Champion. Ht. 6'4"
Manager Self

16.03.02 Michael Pinnock W RSC 4 Bethnal Green
10.05.02 Ojay Abrahams W RSC 1 Bethnal Green
23.08.02 Darren Covill W RSC 1 Bethnal Green
25.10.02 Paul Bonson W PTS 6 Bethnal Green
21.12.02 Mike Duffield W RSC 1 Dagenham
28.01.03 Valery Odin W RSC 6 Nottingham
05.03.03 Varuzhan Davtyan W RSC 5 Bethnal Green
16.04.03 Michael Monaghan W RSC 3 Nottingham
04.10.03 Vage Kocharyan W PTS 8 Muswell Hill
28.11.03 Alan Page W RSC 7 Derby

(Vacant English S.Middleweight Title. Elim. British S.Middleweight Title)
30.01.04 Dmitri Adamovich W RSC 2 Dagenham
12.03.04 Charles Adamu W PTS 12 Nottingham
(Commonwealth S.Middleweight Title Challenge)
02.06.04 Mark Woolnough W RSC 11 Nottingham
(Commonwealth S.Middleweight Title Defence)
Career: 13 contests, won 13.

Courtney Fry

Wood Green. *Born* Enfield, 19 May, 1975
L. Heavyweight. Ht. 6'1¹/₂"
Manager H. Holland

29.03.03 Harry Butler W RSC 3 Wembley
31.05.03 Darren Ashton W PTS 4 Bethnal Green
24.10.03 Ovill McKenzie W PTS 4 Bethnal Green
20.03.04 Clint Johnson W RSC 2 Wembley
02.04.04 Paulie Silva W PTS 4 Plymouth
08.05.04 Radcliffe Green W PTS 6 Bristol
19.06.04 Valery Odin W PTS 8 Muswell Hill
Career: 7 contests, won 7.

Carl Froch   Les Clark

Matt Galer

Burton. *Born* Burton, 15 December, 1973
Middleweight. Ht. 5'8"
Manager Self

30.09.97	Martin Cavey W CO 1 Edgbaston
18.11.97	Chris Pollock W PTS 6 Mansfield
16.03.98	Mike Duffield W PTS 6 Nottingham
14.05.98	Freddie Yemofio W RSC 4 Acton
14.10.98	Carlton Williams L PTS 6 Stoke
25.03.99	Gordon Behan L RSC 9 Edgbaston
	(Midlands Area Middleweight Title
	Challenge)
15.08.99	Jason Collins L PTS 6 Derby
13.11.01	Danny Thornton W RSC 4 Leeds
09.02.02	Anthony Farnell L RSC 3 Manchester
23.02.04	Ojay Abrahams W PTS 4 Nottingham
12.06.04	Gary Lockett L RSC 4 Manchester

Career: 11 contests, won 6, lost 5.

Scott Gammer

Pembroke Dock. *Born* Pembroke Dock, 24
October, 1976
Heavyweight. Ht. 6'2"
Manager P. Boyce

15.09.02	Leighton Morgan W RSC 1 Swansea
26.10.02	James Gilbert W RSC 1 Maesteg
08.01.03	Dave Clarke W PTS 4 Aberdare
25.01.03	Ahmad Cheleh W CO 1 Bridgend
28.06.03	Dave Clarke W RSC 1 Cardiff
13.09.03	Derek McCafferty W PTS 6 Newport
08.11.03	Mendauga Kulikauskas DREW 6
	Bridgend
28.02.04	James Zikic W PTS 6 Bridgend
01.05.04	Paul Buttery W CO 1 Bridgend
02.06.04	Paul King W RSC 3 Hereford

Career: 10 contests, won 9, drew 1.

Brian Gascoigne

Kirkby in Ashfield. *Born* Kirkby in
Ashfield, 4 June, 1970
Cruiserweight. Ht. 6'5"
Manager M. Shinfield

23.11.98	Lennox Williams W RSC 3 Piccadilly
30.04.99	Shane Woollas DREW 6 Scunthorpe
03.10.99	Lee Swaby DREW 6 Chesterfield
06.12.99	Mark Hobson L RSC 3 Bradford
09.04.00	Nigel Rafferty W PTS 6 Alfreton
25.06.00	Danny Southam L RSC 4 Wakefield
04.12.00	Huggy Osman L PTS 6 Bradford
10.04.01	Kevin Barrett L RSC 1 Wembley
26.09.02	Adam Cale W PTS 4 Fulham
17.02.03	Tony Moran L RSC 1 Glasgow
31.05.03	Nate Joseph W RTD 1 Barnsley
02.06.03	Costi Marin W PTS 6 Glasgow
26.11.03	Tommy Eastwood L RSC 2 Mayfair

Career: 13 contests, won 5, drew 2, lost 6.

Steve Gethin

Walsall. *Born* Walsall, 30 July, 1978
Featherweight. Ht. 5'9"
Manager Self

| 03.09.99 | Ike Halls W RSC 3 West Bromwich |

24.10.99	Ricky Bishop W RSC 4
	Wolverhampton
22.01.00	Sebastian Hart L PTS 4 Birmingham
10.09.00	Nigel Senior DREW 6 Walsall
03.06.01	Richmond Asante L PTS 4 Southwark
28.11.01	Mickey Coveney L PTS 4 Bethnal Green
09.12.01	Gary Groves W PTS 6 Shaw
17.02.02	Gary Groves W PTS 6 Wolverhampton
01.06.02	Gary Davis W RSC 2 Manchester
21.09.02	Marc Callaghan L PTS 6 Brentwood
02.12.02	Neil Read W RTD 3 Leicester
14.12.02	Isaac Ward L PTS 4 Newcastle
08.02.03	Rocky Dean DREW 4 Norwich
15.02.03	Anthony Hanna W PTS 6
	Wolverhampton
08.05.03	Derry Matthews L RSC 3 Widnes
07.09.03	Henry Janes L PTS 4 Shrewsbury
02.10.03	Mark Moran L PTS 4 Liverpool
20.10.03	John Simpson L PTS 8 Glasgow
30.10.03	Gareth Payne W PTS 6 Dudley
13.12.03	Steve Foster L RTD 3 Manchester
05.03.04	Isaac Ward L PTS 6 Darlington
27.05.04	Marc Callaghan L PTS 6 Huddersfield

Career: 22 contests, won 8, drew 2, lost 12.

Andy Gibson

Larne. *Born* Larne, 6 June, 1979
L. Middleweight. Ht. 5'11"
Manager T. Gilmour

23.09.02	Jason Samuels W PTS 4 Glasgow
03.10.02	Danny Moir W RTD 4 Sunderland
18.11.02	Andy Halder W PTS 4 Glasgow
20.01.03	Richard Inquieti W RSC 5 Glasgow
04.10.03	Peter Dunn W PTS 6 Belfast
17.04.04	Taz Jones L PTS 6 Belfast

Career: 6 contests, won 5, lost 1.

Alan Gilbert

Crawley. *Born* Bromley, 17 November,
1970
Middleweight. Ht. 5'11"
Manager Self

02.12.97	Martin Cavey W RSC 1 Windsor
06.01.98	Harry Butler W PTS 4 Brighton
23.02.98	Jon Harrison W PTS 6 Windsor
21.04.98	Paul Henry L PTS 4 Edmonton
08.08.98	Lee Murtagh L PTS 4 Scarborough
03.10.98	C. J. Jackson W RSC 3 Crawley
25.02.99	Justin Simmons W RSC 5 Kentish
	Town
01.05.99	Anthony Farnell L RSC 8 Crystal
	Palace
07.08.99	Wayne Shepherd DREW 8 Dagenham
	(Vacant British Masters
	L. Middleweight Title)
11.03.00	Michael Jones L RTD 3 Kensington
12.06.00	Jim Rock L PTS 6 Belfast
22.07.00	Delroy Mellis L RSC 3 Watford
	(Vacant Southern Area L.Middleweight
	Title)
23.01.01	Delroy Mellis L RSC 3 Crawley
	(Southern Area L. Middleweight Title
	Challenge)
29.09.01	Steven Bendall L RTD 3 Southwark
10.02.02	Allan Gray DREW 4 Southwark
28.04.02	Allan Gray L PTS 10 Southwark
	(Vacant Southern Area Middleweight
	Title)
03.08.02	Lee Blundell L RSC 6 Blackpool
	(IBF Inter-Continental Middleweight
	Title Challenge)

15.10.02	Dean Powell W PTS 4 Bethnal Green
28.04.03	Ben Ogden L RSC 1 Nottingham
20.06.03	Leigh Wicks W PTS 4 Gatwick
25.07.03	Ryan Rhodes L RSC 5 Norwich
21.02.04	Leigh Wicks W PTS 4 Brighton
17.04.04	Jason McKay L PTS 6 Belfast
13.05.04	Gokhan Kazaz L PTS 4 Bethnal Green

Career: 24 contests, won 8, drew 2, lost 14.

Michael Gomez (Armstrong)

Manchester. *Born* Dublin, 21 June, 1977
WBU S.Featherweight Champion. Former
Undefeated WBO Inter-Continental &
British S.Featherweight Champion. Former
WBO Inter-Continental S.Featherweight
Champion. Former Undefeated Central
Area & IBF Inter-Continental
Featherweight Champion. Ht. 5'5"
Manager F. Warren/T. Jones

10.06.95	Danny Ruegg W PTS 6 Manchester
15.09.95	Greg Upton L PTS 6 Mansfield
24.11.95	Danny Ruegg L PTS 4 Manchester
19.09.96	Martin Evans W RSC 1 Manchester
09.11.96	David Morris W PTS 4 Manchester
22.03.97	John Farrell W RSC 2 Wythenshawe
03.05.97	Chris Williams L PTS 4 Manchester
11.09.97	Wayne Jones W RSC 2 Widnes
18.04.98	Benny Jones W PTS 4 Manchester
16.05.98	Craig Spacie W RSC 3 Bethnal Green
05.09.98	Pete Buckley W PTS 6 Telford
14.11.98	David Jeffrey W RSC 1 Cheshunt
19.12.98	Kevin Sheil W RSC 4 Liverpool
13.02.99	Dave Hinds W RSC 6 Newcastle
27.02.99	Chris Jickells W RSC 5 Oldham
	(Vacant Central Area Featherweight
	Title)
29.05.99	Nigel Leake W RSC 2 Halifax
	(Vacant IBF Inter-Continental
	Featherweight Title)
07.08.99	William Alverzo W PTS 6 Atlantic
	City, New Jersey, USA
04.09.99	Gary Thornhill W RSC 2 Bethnal
	Green
	(Vacant British S. Featherweight Title)
06.11.99	Jose Juan Manjarrez W PTS 12 Widnes
	(WBO Inter-Continental
	S. Featherweight Title Defence)
11.12.99	Oscar Galindo W RSC 11 Liverpool
	(WBO Inter-Continental
	S. Featherweight Title Defence)
29.01.00	Chris Jickells W RSC 4 Manchester
29.02.00	Dean Pithie W PTS 12 Widnes
	(British S. Featherweight Title
	Defence)
24.06.00	Carl Allen W CO 2 Glasgow
08.07.00	Carl Greaves W CO 2 Widnes
	(British S. Featherweight Title
	Defence)
19.10.00	Awel Abdulai W PTS 8 Harrisburg,
	USA
11.12.00	Ian McLeod W PTS 12 Widnes
	(British S.Featherweight Title Defence)
10.02.01	Laszlo Bognar L RSC 9 Widnes
	(WBO Inter-Continental
	S. Featherweight Title Defence)
07.07.01	Laszlo Bognar W RSC 3 Manchester
	(WBO Inter-Continental
	S. Featherweight Title Challenge)
27.10.01	Craig Docherty W RSC 2 Manchester
	(British S.Featherweight Title Defence)
01.06.02	Kevin Lear L RTD 8 Manchester
	(Vacant WBU S. Featherweight Title)

28.09.02 Jimmy Beech W RSC 4 Manchester
18.01.03 Rakhim Mingaleev W RTD 4 Preston
05.04.03 Vladimir Borov W RSC 3 Manchester
25.10.03 Alex Arthur W RSC 5 Edinburgh
(*British S.Featherweight Title Challenge*)
03.04.04 Ben Odamattey W RSC 3 Manchester
(*Vacant WBU S.Featherweight Title*)
22.05.04 Justin Juuko W RSC 2 Widnes
(*WBU S.Featherweight Title Defence*)
Career: 36 contests, won 31, lost 5.

Isidro Gonzalez

Brixton. *Born* Spain, 30 November, 1978
Middleweight. Ht. 5'9"
Manager B. Baker

05.09.03 P.J.Maxwell L RSC 6 Sheffield
20.02.04 Dmitry Donetskiy L RSC 6 Southampton
12.06.04 Matthew Hall L RSC 3 Manchester
Career: 3 contests, lost 3.

Simon Goodwin

Cambridge. *Born* Cambridge, 13 January, 1979
Cruiserweight. Ht. 6'2"
Manager J. McDonnell

28.07.03 Marcus Lee L PTS 4 Plymouth
Career: 1 contest, lost 1.

James Gorman

Belfast. *Born* Belfast, 1 August, 1979
L. Welterweight. Ht. 5'8"
Manager A. Wilton

28.06.03 Jamie Arthur L PTS 4 Cardiff
11.10.03 Lee Beavis L PTS 4 Portsmouth
25.10.03 George Telfer L PTS 4 Edinburgh
22.11.03 Peter McDonagh W PTS 4 Belfast
28.02.04 Ceri Hall L PTS 6 Bridgend
01.04.04 Lee Beavis L RTD 2 Bethnal Green
Career: 6 contests, won 1, lost 5.

Jimmy Gould

Coseley. *Born* Wolverhampton, 8 July, 1977
Welterweight. Ht. 5'10"
Manager Self

23.06.99 Benny Jones W PTS 6 West Bromwich
03.09.99 Dave Travers W PTS 6 West Bromwich
06.11.00 Jon Honney W PTS 6 Wolverhampton
28.01.01 David White W PTS 6 Wolverhampton
20.05.01 Keith Jones W PTS 6 Wolverhampton
07.09.01 Woody Greenaway W PTS 6 West Bromwich
07.10.01 Steve Hanley W PTS 6 Wolverhampton
13.04.02 Keith Jones W PTS 8 Wolverhampton
25.05.02 Raymond Narh L RSC 3 Portsmouth
08.09.02 Tony Montana L PTS 8 Wolverhampton
08.03.03 Tony Conroy W PTS 4 Coventry
08.05.03 Michael Jennings L RTD 6 Widnes
(*Vacant WBU Inter-Continental Welterweight Title*)
30.10.03 Richard Swallow L PTS 10 Dudley
(*Vacant British Masters Welterweight Title*)
Career: 13 contests, won 9, lost 4.

Michael Gomez   Paul Speak

Nathan Graham   Les Clark

Nathan Graham

Aylesbury. *Born* Aylesbury, 21 September, 1982
Welterweight. Ht. 5'9"
Manager D. Williams

24.04.04 Tom Price W RSC 2 Reading
Career: 1 contest, won 1.

Danny Grainger

Chesterfield. *Born* Chesterfield, 1 September, 1979
L. Heavyweight. Ht. 5'11"
Manager J. Ingle

05.10.02 Jamie Wilson W PTS 6 Chesterfield
21.10.02 Jamie Wilson W PTS 6 Cleethorpes
29.11.02 Gary Jones W PTS 6 Hull
08.06.03 Darren Stubbs W RSC 2 Shaw
12.10.03 Paul Billington W PTS 6 Sheffield
03.04.04 Terry Morrill W RSC 5 Sheffield
04.06.04 Patrick Cito W PTS 6 Hull
Career: 7 contests, won 7.

Allan Gray

Putney. *Born* Roehampton, 4 August, 1971
Southern Area Middleweight Champion.
Former Undefeated WBF Inter-Continental
Southern Area Middleweight Champion.
Ht. 5'9"
Manager Self

19.05.95 Darren Covill W PTS 6 Southwark
23.06.95 Wayne Jones W PTS 6 Bethnal Green
27.09.95 Brian Coleman W PTS 6 Bethnal Green
28.10.95 John O. Johnson W PTS 6 Kensington
29.11.95 Justin Simmons L PTS 6 Bethnal Green
08.12.95 Mike Watson W PTS 8 Bethnal Green
15.03.96 Mike Watson DREW 6 Dunstable
29.04.96 Mike Watson W PTS 6 Mayfair
03.07.96 Jon Harrison W PTS 6 Wembley
24.10.96 Costas Katsantonis W PTS 6 Mayfair
29.01.97 Gary Hiscox W PTS 6 Bethnal Green
19.02.97 Costas Katsantonis W PTS 6 Acton
30.04.97 Howard Clarke L PTS 8 Acton
27.01.98 Peter Nightingale W PTS 6 Streatham
26.09.98 Harry Dhami L PTS 10 Southwark
(Southern Area Welterweight Title Challenge)
16.02.99 Lee Bird W PTS 6 Brentford
31.10.99 Matthew Barr L PTS 4 Raynes Park
15.04.00 Jim Rock L PTS 10 Bethnal Green
(Vacant All-Ireland L. Middleweight Title)
22.10.00 Delroy Mellis L RSC 6 Streatham
(Southern Area L.Middleweight Title Challenge)
28.10.01 Leigh Wicks W PTS 4 Southwark
16.12.01 Leigh Wicks W PTS 4 Southwark
10.02.02 Alan Gilbert DREW 4 Southwark
28.04.02 Alan Gilbert W PTS 10 Southwark
(Vacant Southern Area Middleweight Title)
12.12.02 Ojay Abrahams W PTS 10 Leicester Square
(Southern Area Middleweight Title Defence. Vacant WBF Inter-Continental Middleweight Title)
05.07.03 Dirk Dzemski L PTS 12 Dessau, Germany
(NBA Middleweight Title Challenge)

20.02.04 Matthew Tait W PTS 10 Bethnal Green
(Southern Area Middleweight Title Defence)
Career: 26 contests, won 17, drew 2, lost 7.

Allan Gray   Les Clark

Michael Graydon

Bristol. *Born* Bristol, 30 October, 1985
S. Featherweight. Ht. 5'9"
Manager C. Sanigar

13.02.04 Fred Janes DREW 6 Bristol
08.05.04 Peter Allen W PTS 6 Bristol
Career: 2 contest, won 1, drew 1.

Michael Graydon   Les Clark

Carl Greaves

Newark. *Born* Nottingham, 12 June, 1976
S.Featherweight. Former WBF
S.Featherweight Champion. Former
Undefeated British Masters & Midlands
Area S. Featherweight Champion. Ht. 5'7"
Manager Self

22.03.96 Paul Hamilton W PTS 6 Mansfield
30.05.96 Kevin Sheil W PTS 6 Lincoln
02.10.96 Robert Grubb W PTS 8 Stoke
01.11.96 Benny Jones W PTS 6 Mansfield
26.11.96 Danny Ruegg W RTD 4 Sheffield
04.12.96 Des Gargano W PTS 6 Stoke
20.02.97 Lee Armstrong L RSC 4 Mansfield
10.04.97 Kevin Sheil W PTS 6 Sheffield
08.05.97 Benny Jones L RSC 4 Mansfield
10.07.97 Stefy Bull L PTS 6 Doncaster
18.08.97 Graham McGrath W PTS 6 Nottingham
06.10.97 Ervine Blake L PTS 10 Birmingham
(Vacant Midlands Area S. Featherweight Title)
30.10.97 Graham McGrath W PTS 6 Newark
18.11.97 Garry Burrell W CO 4 Mansfield
07.05.98 John T. Kelly W PTS 6 Sunderland
14.10.98 Andy Robinson W PTS 6 Stoke
02.12.98 Graham McGrath W PTS 6 Stoke
18.03.99 Ernie Smith W PTS 6 Doncaster
27.06.99 Chris Jickells W PTS 10 Alfreton
(British Masters S. Featherweight Final)
20.11.99 Pete Buckley W PTS 10 Grantham
(British Masters S. Featherweight Title Defence)
18.01.00 Keith Jones W PTS 6 Mansfield
19.02.00 Marc Smith W PTS 6 Newark
20.03.00 Pete Buckley W PTS 4 Mansfield
11.05.00 Marco Fattore W PTS 8 Newark
08.07.00 Michael Gomez L CO 2 Widnes
(British S. Featherweight Title Challenge)
09.09.00 Dave Hinds W PTS 6 Newark
19.11.00 Haroon Din W RSC 4 Chesterfield
24.03.01 Nigel Senior W CO 6 Newark
(Vacant Midlands Area S. Featherweight Title)
16.06.01 Dave Hinds W PTS 6 Derby
11.05.02 Wayne Wheeler W RSC 1 Newark
14.09.02 Peter Allen W PTS 6 Newark
14.12.02 Alex Arthur L RSC 6 Newcastle
(British S. Featherweight Title Challenge)
16.04.03 Ben Odamattey W PTS 12 Nottingham
(Vacant WBF S.Featherweight Title)
24.10.03 Keith Jones W PTS 6 Bethnal Green
28.11.03 Carl Allen W PTS 4 Derby
23.02.04 Jason Nesbitt W PTS 6 Nottingham
20.03.04 Carl Johanneson L RTD 3 Wembley
(WBF S.Featherweight Title Defence)
24.06.04 Rakhim Mingaleev W PTS 6 Gibralter
Career: 38 contests, won 31, lost 7.

(Roger) Radcliffe Green

Balham. *Born* Jamaica, 24 November, 1973
Cruiserweight. Ht. 5'9½"
Manager Self

26.03.01 Peter Haymer L PTS 4 Wembley
22.04.01 Adam Cale W CO 5 Streatham
03.06.01 Rob Hayes-Scott W RSC 4 Southwark
21.07.01 John Keeton L PTS 4 Sheffield
28.10.01 Michael Pinnock W PTS 4 Southwark
16.11.01 Darren Corbett L PTS 8 Dublin
10.02.02 Valery Odin L PTS 6 Southwark
20.04.02 Nathan King L PTS 6 Cardiff
04.05.02 Andrew Lowe L PTS 4 Bethnal Green
22.09.02 Mark Baker L PTS 6 Southwark
27.10.02 Neil Linford DREW 10 Southwark
(Vacant British Masters L.Heavyweight Title)
08.02.03 Eric Teymour L RTD 1 Norwich
29.03.03 Andrew Lowe L PTS 10 Wembley
(Vacant Southern Area L. Heavyweight Title)
26.09.03 Tony Booth L PTS 6 Millwall
07.11.03 Andrew Lowe L PTS 6 Sheffield
07.02.04 Bruce Scott L PTS 6 Bethnal Green
08.05.04 Courtney Fry L PTS 6 Bristol
Career: 17 contests, won 3, drew 1, lost 13.

Stuart Green

Glenrothes. *Born* Kirkcaldy, 13 December, 1984
L. Welterweight. Ht. 5'6"
Manager T. Gilmour

17.11.03	Chris Long W PTS 6 Glasgow
12.03.04	Jason Nesbitt W PTS 8 Irvine
07.06.04	Gavin Tait W PTS 6 Glasgow

Career: 3 contests, won 3.

Roman Greenberg

Maidenhead. *Born* Russia, 18 May, 1982
Heavyweight. Ht. 6'2½"
Manager J. Evans

22.11.01	Dave Clarke W RSC 5 Paddington
25.02.02	Paul Bonson W PTS 6 Slough
25.04.02	Jakarta Nakyru W RSC 4 Las Vegas, Nevada, USA
28.11.02	Tony Booth W PTS 4 Finchley
05.12.02	Dave Clarke W RSC 1 Sheffield
20.12.02	Derek McCafferty W PTS 4 Bracknell
24.01.03	Piotr Jurczk W CO 1 Sheffield
04.03.03	Calvin Miller W RSC 2 Miami, Florida, USA
18.03.03	Gary Williams W RSC 1 Reading
15.05.03	Tracy Williams W RTD 2 Miami, Florida, USA
29.05.03	Troy Beets W RSC 3 Miami, Florida, USA
05.09.03	Luke Simpkin W RTD 4 Sheffield
18.09.03	Konstanin Prizyuk W RSC 1 Mayfair
26.11.03	Mendauga Kulikauskas W RSC 5 Mayfair

15.04.04	Jason Gethers W RSC 6 NYC, New York, USA

Career: 15 contests, won 15.

Gary Greenwood

Hinckley. *Born* Leicester, 9 December, 1974
Lightweight. Ht. 5'8"
Manager Self

09.03.00	Ray Wood W PTS 4 Liverpool
03.12.00	Tony Montana DREW 6 Shaw
13.02.01	Dave Travers W PTS 6 Brierley Hill
10.05.01	Brian Gifford W PTS 6 Sunderland
23.06.01	Jay Mahoney L PTS 4 Peterborough
17.11.01	Nigel Senior W PTS 6 Coventry
09.02.02	Jason Gonzales W PTS 6 Coventry
22.03.02	Dave Cotterill W PTS 6 Coventry
02.06.02	Mally McIver W RSC 1 Shaw
13.07.02	Gary Reid W RSC 5 Coventry
10.10.02	Stuart Rimmer W RSC 1 Stoke
30.11.02	Nigel Senior W PTS 4 Coventry
23.02.03	Ernie Smith W PTS 4 Shrewsbury
05.04.03	Keith Jones DREW 8 Coventry
15.11.03	Silence Saheed L RTD 1 Coventry

Career: 15 contests, won 11, drew 2, lost 2.

Omar Gumati

Chester. *Born* Chester, 18 May, 1984
L. Middleweight. Ht. 5'9"
Manager M. Goodall

07.05.03	Craig Goodman W PTS 6 Ellesmere Port
02.10.03	Danny Moir L PTS 6 Sunderland
01.12.03	Ojay Abrahams W PTS 6 Leeds

Career: 3 contests, won 2, lost 1.

Jake Guntert

Abingdon. *Born* Oxford, 14 January, 1983
Middleweight. Ht. 5'10"
Manager F. Maloney

07.05.04	Lee Williamson W PTS 6 Bethnal Green
25.06.04	Mark Wall W CO 1 Bethnal Green

Career: 2 contests, won 2.

Jake Guntert   Les Clark

Danny Gwilym

Bristol. *Born* Bristol, 15 January, 1975
L. Middleweight. Ht. 5'7"
Manager T. Woodward

16.12.01	Wayne Wheeler L RSC 2 Bristol
11.02.02	James Lee L PTS 6 Southampton
12.07.02	Mo W PTS 6 Southampton
26.02.03	Wasim Hussain W PTS 6 Bristol
17.03.03	Danny Cooper L PTS 6 Southampton
16.04.03	Lenny Daws L RSC 2 Nottingham
26.09.03	Darren Covill W PTS 6 Millwall
12.10.03	Mo L PTS 6 Sheffield
06.12.03	Martin Concepcion L RSC 2 Cardiff

Career: 9 contests, won 3, lost 6.

Roman Greenberg   Les Clark

Danny Gwilym   Les Clark

Gary Hadwin

Carlisle. *Born* Carlisle, 10 February, 1969
Welterweight. Ht. 5'9"
Manager J. Doughty

02.06.02	Andrei Ivanov L PTS 6 Shaw
08.11.02	Jason Rushton L CO 4 Doncaster
25.09.03	Dave Hill L PTS 6 Hull

Career: 3 contests, lost 3.

Damon Hague (Wheatley)

Derby. *Born* Derby, 29 October, 1970
WBF S.Middleweight Champion. Former
Undefeated WBF Middleweight Champion.
Former Undefeated WBF European &
Midlands Area S.Middleweight Champion.
Ht. 6'0"
Manager D. Ingle

27.11.98	Jimmy Steel DREW 6 Nottingham
14.12.98	Dean Ashton W PTS 6 Cleethorpes
26.02.99	Adrian Houldey W RSC 5 West Bromwich
27.03.99	Mark Owens W RSC 2 Derby
15.05.99	Michael Pinnock W PTS 4 Sheffield
27.06.99	Mark Owens W RSC 5 Alfreton
15.08.99	Ian Toby W PTS 6 Derby
03.10.99	Simon Andrews W PTS 6 Chesterfield
20.11.99	Simon Andrews W RSC 4 Grantham
15.01.00	Matthew Pepper W CO 1 Doncaster
09.04.00	Matthew Pepper W RSC 3 Alfreton
21.05.00	Martin Jolley W PTS 6 Derby
19.06.00	William Webster W PTS 4 Burton
13.08.00	Martin Jolley W RTD 1 Nottingham
04.11.00	Mike Duffield W RSC 3 Derby
	(Vacant WBF European S. Middleweight Title)
25.02.01	Rob Stevenson W PTS 8 Derby
16.06.01	Dean Ashton L DIS 1 Derby
21.07.01	Leigh Wicks W PTS 4 Sheffield
15.09.01	Dean Ashton W RTD 2 Derby
	(Vacant Midlands Area S.Middleweight Title)
08.12.01	Rob Stevenson W RSC 7 Chesterfield
20.04.02	Jimmy Steel W PTS 6 Derby
03.08.02	Andrew Facey W CO 5 Derby
	(Final Elim. WBF Middleweight Title)
23.11.02	Leigh Wicks W PTS 6 Derby
28.01.03	Wayne Pinder L RSC 7 Nottingham
	(Vacant WBF Middleweight Title)
16.04.03	Wayne Pinder W RSC 2 Nottingham
	(WBF Middleweight Title Challenge)
28.11.03	Roddy Doran L PTS 10 Derby
	(Elim. WBF S.Middleweight Title)
12.03.04	Roddy Doran W PTS 12 Nottingham
	(Vacant WBF S.Middleweight Title)

Career: 27 contests, won 23, drew 1, lost 3.

Andy Halder

Coventry. *Born* Coventry, 22 August, 1973
Middleweight. Ht. 5'11"
Manager J. Weaver

13.07.02	Martin Scotland W PTS 4 Coventry
05.10.02	Andrei Ivanov W PTS 6 Coventry
25.10.02	Jon Hilton W PTS 6 Cotgrave

18.11.02	Andy Gibson L PTS 4 Glasgow
30.11.02	Conroy McIntosh W PTS 4 Coventry
24.01.03	Chris Steele W PTS 4 Sheffield
08.03.03	Conroy McIntosh W PTS 4 Coventry
24.03.03	Robert Burton W PTS 6 Barnsley
10.06.03	P.J.Maxwell L RSC 1 Sheffield
13.09.03	Lee Williamson W PTS 6 Coventry
08.11.03	Lee Williamson W PTS 6 Coventry
21.02.04	Michael Thomas W RSC 3 Brighton

Career: 12 contests, won 10, lost 2.

Eddie Haley

South Shields. *Born* South Shields, 25
August, 1965
Northern Area Middleweight Champion.
Ht. 5'9"
Manager T. Conroy

06.06.94	Brian Dunn W PTS 6 Glasgow
25.10.94	Sven Hamer L RSC 4 Southwark
30.11.94	Roy Chipperfield W RSC 3 Solihull
23.01.95	Billy Collins L RSC 4 Glasgow
01.03.95	Gary Beardsley L RSC 1 Glasgow
27.04.95	Gary Silvester W RSC 2 Hull
19.05.95	James Lowther L RSC 5 Leeds
21.05.98	Jon Penn L RSC 2 Bradford
29.10.98	Ian Toby W PTS 10 Newcastle
	(Vacant Northern Area Middleweight Title)
13.02.99	Ian Toby W RSC 6 Newcastle
	(Northern Area Middleweight Title Defence)
29.05.99	Mike Duffield W RSC 6 South Shields
23.10.99	Toks Owoh L RSC 3 Telford
15.01.00	Ryan Rhodes L RSC 5 Doncaster
17.04.00	Dave Johnson W RSC 6 Glasgow
	(Northern Area Middleweight Title Defence)
03.11.00	Steven Bendall L RSC 1 Ebbw Vale
02.10.03	Ryan Kerr L PTS 8 Sunderland
26.02.04	Ryan Kerr L RSC 5 Sunderland
	(Vacant Northern Area S.Middleweight Title)

Career: 17 contests, won 7, lost 10.

Ceri Hall

Loughor. *Born* Swansea, 25 March, 1980
L. Welterweight. Ht. 5'10"
Manager P. Boyce

15.09.02	Martin Turner W RSC 1 Swansea
10.04.03	Silence Saheed DREW 4 Clydach
08.11.03	Peter McDonagh W PTS 4 Bridgend
28.02.04	James Gorman W PTS 4 Bridgend
19.06.04	Chris Long W PTS 4 Muswell Hill

Career: 5 contests, won 4, drew 1.

Jason Hall

Hanwell. *Born* Perivale, 19 November,
1975
L. Welterweight. Ht. 5'8 1/2"
Manager Self

19.04.97	Johannes Musa W RSC 3 Las Vegas, USA
06.06.97	Raul Basulto L RSC 10 Las Vegas, USA
30.07.97	Mark Chang w pts 4 Las Vegas, USA
27.06.98	Andrew Poulos W PTS 4 Vancouver, Canada
29.06.99	Brendan Ahearne W PTS 6 Bethnal Green
20.08.99	Keith Jones W PTS 6 Bloomsbury

05.10.99	John Paul Temple W PTS 6 Bloomsbury
06.11.99	Woody Greenaway W RSC 5 Bethnal Green
10.03.00	Arv Mittoo L RSC 3 Bethnal Green
18.02.01	Marco Fattore W PTS 6 Southwark
01.04.01	Gary Flear W PTS 8 Southwark
28.04.01	Bradley Pryce L PTS 12 Cardiff
	(Vacant WBO Inter-Continental Lightweight Title)
15.12.01	Steve Murray L RSC 4 Wembley
	(Elim. British Lightweight Title)
22.09.02	Chill John W PTS 6 Southwark
29.11.03	Nigel Wright L PTS 6 Renfrew

Career: 15 contests, won 10, lost 5.

Jason Hall   Philip Sharkey

Lance Hall

Birmingham. *Born* Sutton Coldfield, 16
March, 1976
Welterweight. Ht. 5'5"
Manager T. Nerwal

22.09.03	Luke Teague L RSC 1 Cleethorpes
24.10.03	Jas Malik W RSC 1 Bethnal Green
08.11.03	Stuart Phillips L PTS 4 Bridgend
26.11.03	Nathan Ward W PTS 4 Mayfair
20.02.04	Ben Coward W RSC 2 Doncaster
13.03.04	Kevin Anderson L RSC 1 Huddersfield
12.05.04	Anthony Small L RSC 1 Reading

Career: 7 contests, won 3, lost 4.

Matthew Hall

Manchester. *Born* Manchester, 5 July, 1984
L. Middleweight. Ht. 5'7 3/4"
Manager F. Warren/B. Hughes

28.09.02	Pedro Thompson W RSC 1 Manchester
14.12.02	Pedro Thompson W PTS 4 Newcastle
18.01.03	Clive Johnson W PTS 4 Preston
05.04.03	Brian Coleman W RSC 1 Manchester
08.05.03	Patrick Cito W PTS 4 Widnes
06.05.04	Craig Lynch W PTS 6 Barnsley
12.06.04	Isidro Gonzalez W RSC 3 Manchester

Career: 7 contests, won 7.

(Michael) Oscar Hall

Darlington. *Born* Darlington, 8 November, 1974
L. Welterweight. Northern Area Welterweight Champion. Ht. 5'9"
Manager J. Ingle

09.05.98	Trevor Smith W PTS 4 Sheffield
27.02.99	Lee Molyneux W PTS 4 Oldham
15.05.99	Chris Price W PTS 4 Sheffield
29.05.99	Brian Gifford W RSC 1 Halifax
04.06.99	Arv Mittoo W PTS 6 Hull
27.09.99	Dave Gibson W PTS 6 Leeds
11.12.99	Brian Coleman W PTS 6 Liverpool
18.02.00	Jason Collins DREW 6 West Bromwich
02.03.00	Ernie Smith W PTS 6 Birkenhead
09.06.00	Dave Gibson W PTS 6 Hull
19.06.00	Paul Denton W PTS 4 Burton
13.08.00	Lee Molyneux W PTS 6 Nottingham
04.11.00	Ram Singh W PTS 6 Derby
24.11.00	Dean Nicholas W PTS 6 Darlington
11.12.00	Ram Singh W CO 4 Cleethorpes
16.06.01	David Kirk W PTS 6 Derby
18.08.01	David White W PTS 6 Dewsbury
22.09.01	Dean Nicholas W DIS 9 Newcastle
	(Vacant Northern Area Welterweight Title)
17.11.01	Paul Lomax W PTS 4 Dewsbury
15.03.02	Stuart Rimmer W RSC 4 Spennymoor
19.04.02	Peter Dunn W PTS 6 Darlington
10.05.02	Arv Mittoo W PTS 4 Bethnal Green
28.01.03	Alan Bosworth W PTS 10 Nottingham
	(Elim. British L.Welterweight Title)
11.07.03	William Webster W PTS 8 Darlington
10.10.03	Gary Reid L RSC 2 Darlington
11.12.03	Francis Barrett L PTS 10 Bethnal Green
05.03.04	Karl Taylor W PTS 6 Darlington
16.04.04	Junior Witter L RSC 3 Bradford
04.06.04	Lee Williamson W PTS 6 Hull

Career: 29 contests, won 25, drew 1, lost 3.

Anthony Hanna

Birmingham. *Born* Birmingham, 22 September, 1974
Lightweight. Former Undefeated Midlands Area Flyweight Champion. Ht. 5'6"
Manager Self

19.11.92	Nick Tooley L PTS 6 Evesham
10.12.92	Daren Fifield L RSC 6 Bethnal Green
11.05.93	Tiger Singh W PTS 6 Norwich
24.05.93	Lyndon Kershaw L PTS 6 Bradford
16.09.93	Chris Lyons W PTS 6 Southwark
06.10.93	Tiger Singh W PTS 6 Solihull
03.11.93	Mickey Cantwell L PTS 8 Bristol
25.01.94	Marty Chestnut W PTS 6 Picaddilly
10.02.94	Allan Mooney W RTD 1 Glasgow
13.04.94	Allan Mooney L PTS 6 Glasgow
22.04.94	Jesper Jensen L PTS 6 Aalborg, Denmark
03.08.94	Paul Ingle L PTS 6 Bristol
01.10.94	Mark Hughes L PTS 4 Cardiff
30.11.94	Shaun Norman W PTS 10 Solihull
	(Vacant Midlands Area Flyweight Title)
24.02.95	Darren Greaves W RSC 5 Weston super Mare
06.03.95	Mark Hughes L PTS 6 Mayfair
27.04.95	Mickey Cantwell L PTS 6 Bethnal Green
05.05.95	Mark Cokely W RSC 4 Swansea
04.06.95	Mark Reynolds L PTS 10 Bethnal Green
	(Elim. British Flyweight Title)
02.07.95	Mickey Cantwell L PTS 6 Dublin
02.11.95	Shaun Norman DREW 10 Mayfair
	(Midlands Area Flyweight Title Defence)
31.01.96	Marty Chestnut DREW 6 Stoke
20.03.96	Harry Woods L PTS 6 Cardiff
22.04.96	Neil Parry W PTS 6 Manchester
14.05.96	Dharmendra Singh Yadav L PTS 4 Dagenham
08.10.96	Marty Chestnut W PTS 6 Battersea
11.12.96	Mark Reynolds DREW 8 Southwark
28.01.97	Colin Moffett L PTS 4 Belfast
28.02.97	Paul Weir L PTS 8 Kilmarnock
14.03.97	Jesper Jensen L PTS 6 Odense, Denmark
30.04.97	Clinton Beeby DREW 6 Acton
10.05.97	Jason Booth L PTS 6 Nottingham
02.06.97	Keith Knox L PTS 6 Glasgow
14.10.97	Louis Veitch L PTS 6 Kilmarnock
27.10.97	Russell Laing W PTS 4 Musselburgh
13.11.97	Noel Wilders L PTS 6 Bradford
24.11.97	Shaun Anderson L PTS 8 Glasgow
20.12.97	Damaen Kelly L PTS 4 Belfast
31.01.98	Jason Booth L PTS 6 Edmonton
23.02.98	David Coldwell L PTS 6 Salford
19.03.98	Andy Roberts L PTS 6 Doncaster
18.05.98	Chris Emanuele W RSC 3 Cleethorpes
11.09.98	Nicky Booth DREW 6 Cleethorpes
18.09.98	Colin Moffett DREW 4 Belfast
29.10.98	Nick Tooley W RTD 6 Bayswater
25.11.98	Nicky Booth W PTS 6 Clydach
21.01.99	Ola Dali W PTS 6 Piccadilly
13.03.99	Damaen Kelly L PTS 12 Manchester
	(Vacant British Flyweight Title. Commonwealth Flyweight Title Challenge)
24.04.99	Noel Wilders L PTS 6 Peterborough
07.06.99	Alston Buchanan W RSC 3 Glasgow
29.06.99	Tommy Waite L PTS 4 Bethnal Green
16.10.99	Stevie Quinn W PTS 4 Belfast
22.11.99	Frankie DeMilo L PTS 6 Piccadilly
04.12.99	Ady Lewis L PTS 6 Manchester
19.02.00	Ian Napa L PTS 6 Dagenham
13.03.00	Mzukisi Sikali L PTS 6 Bethnal Green
27.05.00	Nicky Cook L PTS 6 Mayfair
25.07.00	David Lowry L PTS 4 Southwark
19.08.00	Marc Callaghan L PTS 4 Brentwood
29.09.00	Rocky Dean L PTS 4 Bethnal Green
07.10.00	Oleg Kiryukhin L PTS 6 Doncaster
14.10.00	Danny Costello DREW 4 Wembley
31.10.00	Dmitri Kirilov L PTS 6 Hammersmith
10.02.01	Tony Mulholland L PTS 4 Widnes
19.02.01	Alex Moon L PTS 6 Glasgow
03.03.01	Marc Callaghan L PTS 6 Wembley
24.04.01	Silence Mabuza L PTS 6 Liverpool
06.05.01	Michael Hunter L PTS 4 Hartlepool
26.05.01	Mickey Bowden L PTS 4 Bethnal Green
04.06.01	Michael Hunter L PTS 4 Hartlepool
01.11.01	Nigel Senior L PTS 6 Hull
24.11.01	Martin Power L PTS 4 Bethnal Green
08.12.01	Faprakob Rakkiatgym L PTS 8 Dagenham
24.03.02	Mickey Coveney L PTS 4 Streatham
23.06.02	Johannes Maisa L PTS 4 Southwark
30.10.02	Mickey Bowden L PTS 4 Leicester Square
08.11.02	Sean Green L PTS 6 Doncaster
17.11.02	Shinny Bayaar L PTS 6 Shaw
14.12.02	Michael Hunter L PTS 8 Newcastle
15.02.03	Steve Gethin L PTS 6 Wolverhampton
24.02.03	Jackson Williams W PTS 6 Birmingham
08.06.03	Darryn Walton L PTS 6 Shaw
25.09.03	Rob Jeffries L PTS 6 Bethnal Green
01.11.03	Andrew Ferrans L PTS 4 Glasgow
14.11.03	Mickey Bowden L PTS 4 Bethnal Green
21.11.03	Buster Dennis L PTS 6 Millwall
29.11.03	Willie Limond L PTS 4 Renfrew
09.04.04	Rendall Munroe L PTS 6 Rugby
16.04.04	Billy Corcoran L PTS 4 Bradford
24.04.04	Lee Beavis L PTS 4 Reading
12.05.04	Chris McDonagh L PTS 4 Reading
02.06.04	John Murray L PTS 4 Nottingham
17.06.04	Femi Fehintola L PTS 6 Sheffield

Career: 93 contests, won 19, drew 7, lost 67.

Martin Hardcastle

Leeds. *Born* Pontefract, 27 August, 1976
S.Featherweight. Former Undefeated British Masters S.Featherweight Champion. Ht. 5'6"
Manager T. O'Neill

02.03.02	Mick McPhilbin W RSC 4 Wakefield
28.05.02	Dave Curran W RSC 3 Leeds
05.10.02	Gwyn Wale L PTS 4 Huddersfield
12.11.02	Pete Buckley DREW 6 Leeds
20.12.02	Jon Honney L PTS 4 Bracknell
28.03.03	Silence Saheed L PTS 4 Millwall
17.04.03	Matt Teague W PTS 6 Hull
16.05.03	Colin Bain L PTS 6 Glasgow
24.05.03	Simon Chambers W RSC 2 Sheffield
15.06.03	Paul Rushton W RTD 2 Bradford
15.09.03	Nigel Senior W PTS 6 Leeds
04.10.03	Billy Corcoran L PTS 6 Muswell Hill
07.12.03	Jeff Thomas W PTS 10 Bradford
	(Vacant British Masters S.Featherweight Title)
15.05.04	Lee McAllister L PTS 8 Aberdeen

Career: 14 contests, won 7, drew 1, lost 6.

James Hare

Robertown. *Born* Dewsbury, 16 July, 1976
Welterweight. Former WBF Welterweight Champion. Former Undefeated Commonwealth & European Union Welterweight Champion. Ht. 5'6"
Manager T. Gilmour/C. Aston

20.01.96	Brian Coleman W PTS 6 Mansfield
25.06.96	Mike Watson W PTS 4 Mansfield
13.07.96	Dennis Griffin W RSC 4 Bethnal Green
14.09.96	Paul Salmon W RSC 4 Sheffield
14.12.96	Jon Harrison W PTS 4 Sheffield
25.02.97	Kid McAuley W PTS 4 Sheffield
12.04.97	Andy Peach W RSC 1 Sheffield
13.12.97	Costas Katsantonis W RSC 3 Sheffield
09.05.98	Peter Nightingale W PTS 4 Sheffield
18.07.98	Karl Taylor W PTS 4 Sheffield
28.11.98	Peter Nightingale W PTS 6 Sheffield
15.05.99	Lee Williamson W RSC 2 Sheffield
23.10.99	Mark Winters DREW 6 Telford
23.10.00	Dean Nicholas W RSC 1 Glasgow
23.01.01	Mark Ramsey W PTS 6 Crawley
26.02.01	Paul Denton W PTS 4 Nottingham
08.05.01	Jessy Moreaux W RSC 3 Barnsley
26.05.01	John Humphrey W RSC 7 Bethnal Green

(Elim. British Welterweight Title)

08.10.01	John Ameline W PTS 8 Barnsley
26.11.01	Paul Denton W RTD 4 Manchester
28.01.02	Monney Seka W PTS 10 Barnsley

(Vacant European Union Welterweight Title)

27.04.02	Julian Holland W RSC 6 Huddersfield

(Commonwealth Welterweight Title Challenge)

15.06.02	Abdel Mehidi W PTS 8 Leeds
05.10.02	Farai Musiiwa W RSC 8 Huddersfield

(Commonwealth Welterweight Title Defence)

30.11.02	Earl Foskin W RSC 1 Liverpool

(Commonwealth Welterweight Title Defence)

22.02.03	Frans Hantindi W RSC 1 Huddersfield

(Commonwealth Welterweight Title Defence)

21.06.03	Roman Dzuman W PTS 12 Manchester

(Vacant WBF Welterweight Title)

06.09.03	Jan Bergman W RSC 2 Huddersfield

(WBF Welterweight Title Defence)

18.10.03	Jozsef Matolcsi W RSC 10 Manchester

(WBF Welterweight Title Defence)

04.12.03	Cosme Rivera L RSC 10 Huddersfield

(WBF Welterweight Title Defence)

01.05.04	Jason Williams W RSC 2 Bridgend
27.05.04	Moise Cherni W RSC 5 Huddersfield

Career: 32 contests, won 30, drew 1, lost 1.

Audley Harrison

Wembley. *Born* Park Royal, 26 October, 1971
WBF Heavyweight Champion. Ht. 6'4³/₄"
Manager Self

19.05.01	Michael Middleton W RSC 1 Wembley
22.09.01	Derek McCafferty W PTS 6 Newcastle
20.10.01	Piotr Jurczyk W RSC 2 Glasgow
20.04.02	Julius Long W CO 2 Wembley
21.05.02	Mark Krence W PTS 6 Custom House
10.07.02	Dominic Negus W PTS 6 Wembley
05.10.02	Wade Lewis W RSC 2 Liverpool
23.11.02	Shawn Robinson W RSC 1 Atlantic City, New Jersey, USA
08.02.03	Rob Calloway W RSC 5 Brentford
29.03.03	Ratko Draskovic W PTS 8 Wembley
31.05.03	Matthew Ellis W RSC 2 Bethnal Green
09.09.03	Quinn Navarre W RSC 3 Miami, Florida, USA
03.10.03	Lisandro Diaz W RSC 4 Las Vegas, Nevada, USA
12.12.03	Brian Nix W RSC 3 Laughlin, Nevada, USA
20.03.04	Richel Hersisia W CO 4 Wembley

(WBF Heavyweight Title Challenge)

08.05.04	Julius Francis W PTS 12 Bristol

(WBF Heavyweight Title Defence)

19.06.04	Tomasz Bonin W RSC 9 Muswell Hill

(WBF Heavyweight Title Defence)

Career: 17 contests, won 17.

Jon Harrison

Plymouth. *Born* Scunthorpe, 18 March, 1977
Welterweight. Ht. 5'11¹/₂"
Manager Self

13.01.96	Mark Haslam L PTS 6 Manchester
13.02.96	Paul Samuels L CO 1 Cardiff
16.05.96	Dave Fallon W RSC 4 Dunstable
03.07.96	Allan Gray L PTS 6 Wembley
01.10.96	Cam Raeside L PTS 6 Birmingham
07.11.96	Nicky Bardle L PTS 6 Battersea
14.12.96	James Hare L PTS 4 Sheffield
19.04.97	Jason Williams W PTS 6 Plymouth
11.07.97	Pat Larner L PTS 6 Brighton
07.10.97	Paul Salmon L PTS 6 Plymouth
23.02.98	Alan Gilbert L PTS 6 Windsor
24.03.98	Brian Coleman DREW 6 Wolverhampton
14.07.98	Jason Williams L RTD 2 Reading
12.05.01	Ernie Smith W PTS 4 Plymouth
15.09.01	Darren Williams L PTS 6 Swansea
02.04.04	Nathan Wyatt W PTS 6 Plymouth
27.05.04	Ady Clegg W PTS 4 Huddersfield

Career: 17 contests, won 5, drew 1, lost 11.

(Ryan) Raz Harrison

Doncaster. *Born* Doncaster, 23 October, 1984
L. Middleweight. Ht. 6'0"
Manager J. Rushton

05.09.03	John Butler W RSC 2 Doncaster
07.05.04	Andrei Ivanov W RSC 2 Doncaster

Career: 2 contests, won 2.

Scott Harrison

Cambuslang. *Born* Bellshill, 19 August, 1977
WBO Featherweight Champion. Former Undefeated British, Commonwealth & IBO Inter-Continental Featherweight Champion. Ht. 5'7"
Manager F. Maloney

07.10.96	Eddie Sica W RSC 2 Lewisham
11.01.97	Pete Buckley W PTS 4 Bethnal Green
25.03.97	David Morris W PTS 4 Lewisham
04.10.97	Miguel Matthews L RSC 4 Muswell Hill
16.12.97	Stephane Fernandez DREW 6 Grand Synthe, France
31.01.98	Pete Buckley W PTS 4 Edmonton
09.06.98	Carl Allen W RSC 6 Hull
17.10.98	Rakhim Mingaleev W PTS 8 Manchester
06.03.99	John Matthews W RSC 4 Southwark
10.07.99	Smith Odoom W PTS 12 Southwark

(IBO Inter-Continental Featherweight Title Challenge)

24.01.00	Patrick Mullings W PTS 12 Glasgow

(Commonwealth Featherweight Title Challenge)

29.04.00	Tracy Harris Patterson W PTS 10 NYC, New York, USA
15.07.00	Tom Johnson W PTS 12 Millwall

(IBO Inter-Continental Featherweight Title Defence)

11.11.00	Eric Odumasi W RSC 12 Belfast

(Commonwealth Featherweight Title Defence)

24.03.01	Richie Wenton W RSC 4 Sheffield

Audley Harrison   Les Clark

(Vacant British Featherweight Title. Commonwealth Featherweight Title Defence)

15.09.01 Gary Thornhill W RSC 5 Manchester
(British & Commonwealth Featherweight Title Defences)
17.11.01 Steve Robinson W RSC 3 Glasgow
(British & Commonwealth Featherweight Title Defences)
11.03.02 Tony Wehbee W RSC 3 Glasgow
(Commonwealth Featherweight Title Defence)
08.06.02 Victor Santiago W RSC 6 Renfrew
(Vacant WBO Interim Featherweight Title)
19.10.02 Julio Pablo Chacon W PTS 12 Renfrew
(WBO Featherweight Title Challenge)
22.03.03 Wayne McCullough W PTS 12 Renfrew
(WBO Featherweight Title Defence)
12.07.03 Manuel Medina L PTS 12 Renfrew
(WBO Featherweight Title Defence)
29.11.03 Manuel Medina W RSC 11 Renfrew
(WBO Featherweight Title Challenge)
06.03.04 Walter Estrada W RSC 5 Renfrew
(WBO Featherweight Title Defence)
19.06.04 William Abelyan W RSC 3 Renfrew
(WBO Featherweight Title Defence)
Career: 25 contests, won 22, drew 1, lost 2.

Geraint Harvey

Pontypridd. *Born* Pontypridd, 1 September, 1979
Welterweight. Ht. 5'9"
Manager D. Davies

22.09.03 Steve Scott W PTS 6 Cleethorpes
29.10.03 Darren Covill W PTS 4 Leicester Square
21.12.03 Danny Moir L PTS 6 Bolton
14.02.04 Arek Malek L PTS 4 Nottingham
28.02.04 Jamie Coyle L PTS 4 Bridgend
15.04.04 Terry Adams L PTS 6 Dudley
24.04.04 Chas Symonds L PTS 4 Reading
Career: 7 contests. won 2, lost 5.

Geraint Harvey   Les Clark

Lee Haskins

Bristol. *Born* Bristol, 29 November, 1983
Flyweight. Ht. 5'5"
Manager C. Sanigar

06.03.03 Ankar Miah W RSC 1 Bristol
13.06.03 Chris Edwards W PTS 6 Bristol
09.10.03 Neil Read W PTS 4 Bristol
05.12.03 Jason Thomas W PTS 6 Bristol
13.02.04 Marty Kayes W PTS 6 Bristol
08.05.04 Colin Moffett W RSC 2 Bristol
Career: 6 contests, won 6.

Lee Haskins   Les Clark

Matthew Hatton

Manchester. *Born* Stockport, 15 May, 1981
Central Area Welterweight Champion.
Ht. 5'8¹/₂"
Manager F. Warren

23.09.00 David White W PTS 4 Bethnal Green
25.11.00 David White W PTS 4 Manchester
11.12.00 Danny Connelly W PTS 4 Widnes
15.01.01 Keith Jones W PTS 4 Manchester
10.02.01 Karl Taylor W PTS 4 Widnes
17.03.01 Assen Vassilev W RSC 5 Manchester
09.06.01 Brian Coleman W RTD 2 Bethnal Green
21.07.01 Ram Singh W RSC 2 Sheffield
15.09.01 Marcus Portman W RSC 3 Manchester
15.12.01 Dafydd Carlin W PTS 6 Wembley
09.02.02 Paul Denton W PTS 4 Bethnal Green
04.05.02 Karl Taylor W RSC 3 Bethnal Green
20.07.02 Karl Taylor W RTD 2 Bethnal Green
28.09.02 David Kirk L PTS 6 Manchester
14.12.02 Paul Denton W PTS 6 Newcastle
15.02.03 David Keir L RSC 4 Wembley
08.05.03 Jay Mahoney W PTS 6 Widnes
17.07.03 Jay Mahoney W RSC 1 Dagenham
27.09.03 Taz Jones W PTS 6 Manchester
13.12.03 Franny Jones DREW 6 Manchester
26.02.04 Peter Dunn W PTS 6 Widnes
06.05.04 Robert Burton W PTS 10 Barnsley
(Central Area Welterweight Title Challenge)
12.06.04 Matt Scriven W RSC 4 Manchester
Career: 23 contests, won 20, drew 1, lost 2.

Ricky Hatton

Manchester. *Born* Stockport, 6 October, 1978
WBU L.Welterweight Champion. Former Undefeated British, WBO Inter-Continental & Central Area L.Welterweight Champion. Ht. 5'7¹/₂"
Manager F. Warren

11.09.97 Kid McAuley W RTD 1 Widnes
19.12.97 Robert Alvarez W PTS 4 NYC, New York, USA
17.01.98 David Thompson W RSC 1 Bristol
27.03.98 Paul Salmon W RSC 1 Telford
18.04.98 Karl Taylor W RSC 1 Manchester
30.05.98 Mark Ramsey W PTS 6 Bristol
18.07.98 Anthony Campbell W PTS 6 Sheffield
19.09.98 Pascal Montulet W CO 2 Oberhausen, Germany
31.10.98 Kevin Carter W RSC 1 Atlantic City, New Jersey, USA
19.12.98 Paul Denton W RSC 6 Liverpool
27.02.99 Tommy Peacock W RSC 2 Oldham
(Vacant Central Area L. Welterweight Title)
03.04.99 Brian Coleman W CO 2 Kensington
29.05.99 Dillon Carew W RSC 5 Halifax
(Vacant WBO Inter-Continental L. Welterweight Title)
17.07.99 Mark Ramsey W PTS 6 Doncaster
09.10.99 Bernard Paul W RTD 4 Manchester
(WBO Inter-Continental L. Welterweight Title Defence)
11.12.99 Mark Winters W RSC 4 Liverpool
(WBO Inter-Continental L. Welterweight Title Defence)
29.01.00 Leoncio Garces W RSC 3 Manchester
25.03.00 Pedro Teran W RSC 4 Liverpool
(WBO Inter-Continental L. Welterweight Title Defence)
16.05.00 Ambioris Figuero W RSC 4 Warrington
(WBO Inter-Continental L. Welterweight Title Defence)
10.06.00 Gilbert Quiros W CO 2 Detroit, Michigan, USA
(WBO Inter-Continental L. Welterweight Title Defence)
23.09.00 Giuseppe Lauri W RSC 5 Bethnal Green
(WBO Inter-Continental L.Welterweight Title Defence. WBA Inter-Continental L. Welterweight Title Challenge)
21.10.00 Jonathan Thaxton W PTS 12 Wembley
(Vacant British L.Welterweight Title)
26.03.01 Tony Pep W CO 4 Wembley
(Vacant WBU L. Welterweight Title)
07.07.01 Jason Rowland W CO 4 Manchester
(WBU L.Welterweight Title Defence)
15.09.01 John Bailey W RSC 5 Manchester
(WBU L.Welterweight Title Defence)
27.10.01 Fred Pendleton W CO 2 Manchester
(WBU L.Welterweight Title Defence)
15.12.01 Justin Rowsell W RSC 2 Wembley
(WBU L.Welterweight Title Defence)
09.02.02 Mikhail Krivolapov W RSC 9 Manchester
(WBU L. Welterweight Title Defence)
01.06.02 Eamonn Magee W PTS 12 Manchester
(WBU L. Welterweight Title Defence)
28.09.02 Stephen Smith W DIS 2 Manchester

(WBU L.Welterweight Title Defence)
14.12.02 Joe Hutchinson W CO 4 Newcastle
(WBU L. Welterweight Title Defence)
05.04.03 Vince Phillips W PTS 12 Manchester
(WBU L.Welterweight Title Defence)
27.09.03 Aldi Rios W RTD 9 Manchester
(WBU L.Welterweight Title Defence)
13.12.03 Ben Tackie W PTS 12 Manchester
(WBU L.Welterweight Title Defence)
03.04.04 Dennis Holbaek Pedersen W RSC 6
Manchester
(WBU L.Welterweight Title Defence)
12.06.04 Wilfredo Carlos Vilches W PTS 12
Manchester
(WBU L.Welterweight Title Defence)
Career: 36 contests, won 36.

Barry Hawthorne

Port Glasgow. *Born* Greenock, 21 July, 1978
Lightweight. Ht. 5'9"
Manager Self

18.10.99 Paul Quarmby W PTS 6 Glasgow
15.11.99 Jason Edwards W PTS 6 Glasgow
24.01.00 Steve Brook DREW 4 Glasgow
19.02.00 Stevie Quinn L RSC 5 Prestwick
06.06.00 Nigel Senior W PTS 6 Motherwell
18.09.00 Nigel Leake W RSC 4 Glasgow
20.11.00 John Barnes W PTS 6 Glasgow
04.06.01 Joel Viney W PTS 8 Glasgow
13.04.02 Jamie McKeever L PTS 6 Liverpool
27.10.03 Joel Viney W RSC 1 Glasgow
13.03.04 Dariusz Snarski W PTS 6 Huddersfield

22.04.04 Henry Janes W PTS 6 Glasgow
Career: 12 contests, won 9, drew 1, lost 2.

David Haye

Bermondsey. *Born* London, 13 October, 1980
Cruiserweight. Former Undefeated English
Cruiserweight Champion. Ht. 6'3"
Manager A. Booth

08.12.02 Tony Booth W RTD 2 Bethnal Green
24.01.03 Saber Zairi W RSC 4 Sheffield
04.03.03 Roger Bowden W RSC 2 Miami,
Florida, USA
18.03.03 Phill Day W RSC 2 Reading
15.07.03 Vance Wynn W RSC 1 Los Angeles,
California, USA
01.08.03 Greg Scott-Briggs W CO 1 Bethnal
Green
26.09.03 Lolenga Mock W RSC 4 Reading
14.11.03 Tony Dowling W RSC 1 Bethnal
Green
(Vacant English Cruiserweight Title)
20.03.04 Hastings Rasani W RSC 1 Wembley
12.05.04 Arthur Williams W RSC 3 Reading
Career: 10 contests, won 10.

David Haye   Les Clark

Peter Haymer

Enfield. *Born* London, 10 July, 1978
L. Heavyweight. Ht. 6'1¼"
Manager Self

25.11.00 Adam Cale W RSC 1 Manchester
27.01.01 Darren Ashton W PTS 4 Bethnal Green
10.03.01 Daniel Ivanov W CO 2 Bethnal Green
26.03.01 Radcliffe Green W PTS 4 Wembley
05.05.01 Terry Morrill W PTS 4 Edmonton
22.09.01 Tony Booth W PTS 4 Bethnal Green
24.11.01 Nathan King L PTS 4 Bethnal Green
12.02.02 Nathan King L PTS 4 Bethnal Green
09.05.02 Mark Snipe W PTS 4 Leicester Square
15.06.02 Paul Bonson W PTS 4 Tottenham
30.10.02 Jimmy Steel W PTS 4 Leicester Square

Ricky Hatton   Paul Speak

18.03.03   Mark Brookes W PTS 6 Reading
18.09.03   Ovill McKenzie W PTS 4 Mayfair
10.12.03   Mark Brookes DREW 6 Sheffield
Career: 14 contests, won 11, drew 1, lost 2.

Scott Haywood

Derby. *Born* Derby, 5 June, 1981
L. Welterweight. Ht. 6'0"
Manager M. Shinfield

06.10.03   Pete Buckley W PTS 6 Barnsley
23.11.03   Arv Mittoo W PTS 6 Rotherham
16.02.04   Pete Buckley W PTS 6 Scunthorpe
26.04.04   Chris Brophy W RSC 5 Cleethorpes
Career: 4 contests, won 4.

Ciaran Healy

Belfast. *Born* Belfast, 25 December, 1974
Middleweight. Ht. 5'11"
Manager J. Rooney

05.04.03   Tomas da Silva W PTS 4 Belfast
18.09.03   Patrick Cito W PTS 4 Mayfair
04.10.03   Joel Ani W PTS 4 Belfast
22.11.03   Neil Addis W RSC 1 Belfast
26.06.04   Jason McKay L PTS 6 Belfast
Career: 5 contests, won 4, lost 1.

Jamie Hearn

Colnbrook. *Born* Taplow, 4 June, 1982
L. Heavyweight. Ht. 5'11¹/₂"
Manager J. Evans

27.09.02   Jimmy Steel W PTS 4 Bracknell
03.12.02   Mark Phillips W PTS 4 Bethnal Green
20.12.02   Danny Norton W PTS 4 Bracknell
18.03.03   Darren Stubbs L RSC 3 Reading
13.06.03   Liam Lathbury W RSC 4 Bristol
04.10.03   Jason McKay L PTS 8 Belfast
14.11.03   Harry Butler W PTS 4 Bethnal Green
30.03.04   Varuzhan Davtyan L PTS 4 Southampton
12.05.04   Hastings Rasani W RSC 4 Reading
Career: 9 contests, won 6, lost 3.

Jamie Hearn   Les Clark

(Donvill) Jimi Hendricks

Birmingham. *Born* Birmingham, 2 April, 1973
S. Middleweight. Ht. 5'10"
Manager J. Gill

21.02.03   Davey Jones L PTS 6 Doncaster

21.03.03   Kevin Phelan L RSC 6 Longford
09.05.03   Steve Scott W PTS 6 Doncaster
06.06.03   Steve Russell W PTS 6 Norwich
29.08.03   Carl Wall L PTS 6 Liverpool
18.09.03   Gokhan Kazaz L PTS 4 Dagenham
27.09.03   Jason Rushton L PTS 4 Manchester
10.10.03   Ricky Colquhoun W RSC 1 Darlington
29.10.03   Matthew Barr L RSC 4 Leicester Square
30.11.03   Mark Phillips L PTS 6 Swansea
Career: 10 contests, won 3, lost 7.

Gary Hibbert

Oldham. *Born* Oldham, 5 February, 1975
Lightweight. Former Undefeated Central Area Lightweight Champion. Ht. 5'8½"
Manager Self

02.06.96   John T. Kelly W PTS 6 Shaw
13.10.96   Sean Morrison W RSC 2 Shaw
16.03.97   David Kirk W PTS 6 Shaw
08.06.97   Bamana Dibateza W PTS 4 Shaw
18.09.98   Jimmy Phelan W PTS 6 Manchester
17.10.98   Dennis Griffin W RSC 4 Manchester
30.11.98   Carl Allen W PTS 4 Manchester
13.03.99   Mark Haslam W PTS 10 Manchester
    (Vacant Central Area Lightweight Title)
01.07.00   Marco Fattore W PTS 4 Manchester
09.09.00   Woody Greenaway W RSC 2 Manchester
03.02.01   Franck Benoni L PTS 6 Manchester
04.06.01   Alan Temple L PTS 6 Hartlepool
07.07.01   Gaeten Trovato W RSC 1 Amsterdam, Holland
06.10.01   Yannick Paget W RSC 2 Manchester
26.11.01   Rosalin Nasibulin W RSC 3 Manchester
09.03.02   Alan Temple W RSC 1 Manchester
23.03.02   Andrei Devyataykin L RSC 4 Southwark
07.09.02   David Burke L RSC 10 Liverpool
    (Vacant Commonwealth Lightweight Title)
08.02.03   Anthony Maynard DREW 6 Liverpool
19.04.03   Chris Barnett W RSC 7 Liverpool
18.10.03   Anthony Maynard W PTS 6 Manchester
14.02.04   Tony Montana L PTS 6 Nottingham
28.02.04   Dean Phillips L RSC 5 Bridgend
Career: 23 contests, won 16, drew 1, lost 6.

Dean Hickman

West Bromwich. *Born* West Bromwich, 24 November, 1979
Midlands Area L.Welterweight Champion. Ht. 5'7"
Manager Self

17.02.02   Wayne Wheeler DREW 6 Wolverhampton
13.04.02   Wayne Wheeler W PTS 6 Wolverhampton
13.07.02   Dai Bando W RSC 1 Wolverhampton
02.11.02   Darren Goode W RSC 2 Wolverhampton
15.02.03   Gareth Wiltshaw W PTS 6 Wolverhampton
21.03.03   David Vaughan W PTS 6 West Bromwich
30.06.03   Dave Hinds W RSC 4 Shrewsbury
17.07.03   Lee McAllister W PTS 6 Walsall
30.10.03   John-Paul Ryan W PTS 6 Dudley

15.04.04   Tony Montana W PTS 6 Dudley
04.06.04   Adnan Amar W RSC 8 Dudley
    (Vacant Midlands Area L.Welterweight Title)
Career: 11 contests, won 10, drew 1.

Justin Hicks

Yeovil. *Born* Yeovil, 15 July, 1976
L. Welterweight. Ht. 6'0"
Manager C. Sanigar

05.12.03   Kristian Laight W PTS 6 Bristol
13.02.04   Chris Long L RSC 4 Bristol
15.04.04   Gary Coombes DREW 6 Dudley
Career: 3 contests, won 1, drew 1, lost 1.

Justin Hicks   Les Clark

Herbie Hide

Norwich. *Born* Nigeria, 27 August, 1971
Heavyweight. Former WBO Heavyweight Champion. Former Undefeated British, WBC International & Penta-Continental Heavyweight Champion. Ht. 6'1½"
Manager Self

24.10.89   L. A. Williams W CO 2 Bethnal Green
05.11.89   Gary McCrory W RTD 1 Kensington
19.12.89   Steve Osborne W RSC 6 Bethnal Green
27.06.90   Alek Penarski W RSC 3 Kensington
05.09.90   Steve Lewsam W RSC 4 Brighton
26.09.90   Jonjo Greene W RSC 1 Manchester
17.10.90   Gus Mendes W RSC 2 Bethnal Green
18.11.90   Steve Lewsam W RSC 1 Birmingham
29.01.91   Lennie Howard W RSC 1 Wisbech
09.04.91   David Jules W RSC 1 Mayfair
14.05.91   John Westgarth W RTD 4 Dudley
03.07.91   Tucker Richards W RSC 3 Brentwood
15.10.91   Eddie Gonzalez W CO 2 Hamburg, Germany
29.10.91   Chris Jacobs W RSC 1 Cardiff
21.01.92   Conroy Nelson W RSC 2 Norwich
    (Vacant WBC International Heavyweight Title)
03.03.92   Percell Davis W CO 1 Amsterdam, Holland
08.09.92   Jean Chanet W RSC 7 Norwich
06.10.92   Craig Peterson W RSC 7 Antwerp, Belgium
    (WBC International Heavyweight Title Defence)
12.12.92   James Pritchard W RSC 2 Muswell Hill

30.01.93	Juan Antonio Diaz W RSC 3 Brentwood	

(Vacant Penta-Continental Heavyweight Title)

27.02.93 Michael Murray W RSC 5 Dagenham
(Vacant British Heavyweight Title)
11.05.93 Jerry Halstead W RSC 4 Norwich
(Penta-Continental Heavyweight Title Defence)
18.09.93 Everett Martin W PTS 10 Leicester
06.11.93 Mike Dixon W RSC 9 Bethnal Green
(Penta-Continental Heavyweight Title Defence)
04.12.93 Jeff Lampkin W RSC 2 Sun City, South Africa
(WBC International Heavyweight Title Defence)
19.03.94 Michael Bentt W CO 7 Millwall
(WBO Heavyweight Title Challenge)
11.03.95 Riddick Bowe L CO 6 Las Vegas, Nevada, USA
(WBO Heavyweight Title Defence)
06.07.96 Michael Murray W RSC 6 Manchester
09.11.96 Frankie Swindell W CO 1 Manchester
28.06.97 Tony Tucker W RSC 2 Norwich
(Vacant WBO Heavyweight Title)
18.04.98 Damon Reed W RSC 1 Manchester
(WBO Heavyweight Title Defence)
26.09.98 Willi Fischer W RSC 2 Norwich
(WBO Heavyweight Title Defence)
26.06.99 Vitali Klitschko L CO 2 Millwall
(WBO Heavyweight Title Defence)
14.07.01 Alexei Osokin W RSC 3 Liverpool
22.09.01 Joseph Chingangu L RSC 2 Newcastle
16.04.03 Derek McCafferty W RSC 7 Nottingham
27.05.03 Joseph Chingangu W CO 1 Dagenham
04.10.03 Alex Vasiliev W RSC 5 Muswell Hill
12.03.04 Mendauga Kulikauskas L RSC 4 Nottingham

Career: 39 contests, won 35, lost 4.

Dave Hill

Hull. *Born* Hull, 14 May, 1974
Welterweight. Ht. 5'9¾"
Manager S. Pollard

17.04.03 Gary Cummings L CO 5 Hull
25.09.03 Gary Hadwin W PTS 6 Hull
07.12.03 George Telfer L RSC 4 Glasgow

Career: 3 contests, won 1, lost 2.

Jamie Hill

Blackpool. *Born* Blackpool, 8 May, 1974
L. Welterweight. Ht. 5'6"
Manager L. Veitch

24.05.03 Lee Bedell L RSC 3 Sheffield
17.11.03 Darren Johnstone L PTS 6 Glasgow

Career: 2 contests, lost 2.

Jon Hilton

Manchester. *Born* Pendleton, 25 March, 1982
L. Middleweight. Ht. 6'1"
Manager W. Barker

10.10.02 Ian Thomas L PTS 6 Stoke
25.10.02 Andy Halder L PTS 6 Cotgrave
02.12.02 Jimmy White W RSC 5 Leicester
09.12.02 Richard Swallow L PTS 6 Nottingham
17.02.03 Craig Dickson L RSC 2 Glasgow

13.04.03 Dave Wakefield L PTS 4 Streatham
28.02.04 Alan Campbell W RSC 3 Manchester
12.03.04 Gavin Down L RTD 1 Nottingham

Career: 8 contests, won 2, lost 6.

Dave Hinds

Birmingham. *Born* Leicester, 5 January, 1971
L. Welterweight. Ht. 5'5"
Manager Self

19.09.95 Martin Evans W RSC 5 Plymouth
08.11.95 Wayne Pardoe L CO 4 Walsall
04.04.96 Paul Salmon L RTD 5 Plymouth
06.10.97 Eddie Sica L RSC 1 Piccadilly
25.11.97 Graham McGrath W PTS 6 Wolverhampton
06.12.97 Adam Spelling W RSC 1 Wembley
27.01.98 Malcolm Thomas L PTS 6 Piccadilly
06.03.98 Jon Dodsworth W RSC 1 Hull
12.03.98 Jamie McKeever L PTS 4 Liverpool
20.03.98 John O'Johnson L PTS 6 Ilkeston
23.04.98 Roy Rutherford L RSC 5 Edgbaston
26.05.98 David Kehoe L RSC 5 Mayfair
07.10.98 Steve Saville L PTS 6 Stoke
26.10.98 Eddie Nevins L PTS 6 Manchester
26.11.98 Steve Saville L PTS 6 Edgbaston
07.12.98 Danny Bell L PTS 6 Nottingham
13.02.99 Michael Gomez L PTS 6 Newcastle
23.04.99 Mark Ramsey L PTS 6 Clydach
17.05.99 Jesse James Daniel L PTS 6 Cleethorpes
28.05.99 Jason Cook L RSC 1 Liverpool
17.07.99 Bradley Pryce L PTS 4 Doncaster
03.09.99 Young Muttley L RSC 4 West Bromwich
13.11.99 Humberto Soto L PTS 6 Hull
11.12.99 Gavin Rees L RSC 2 Liverpool
07.02.00 Liam Maltby L PTS 4 Peterborough
13.03.00 Danny Hunt L PTS 4 Bethnal Green
23.03.00 Marco Fattore L PTS 6 Bloomsbury
13.05.00 Alan Kershaw L PTS 6 Barnsley
22.05.00 Tony Conroy L PTS 4 Coventry
09.06.00 Elias Boswell W RSC 5 Blackpool
24.06.00 Brian Carr L PTS 4 Glasgow
01.07.00 Ricky Eccleston L PTS 4 Manchester
25.07.00 Kevin Lear L PTS 6 Southwark
09.09.00 Carl Greaves L PTS 6 Newark
16.09.00 Leo O'Reilly L RSC 2 Bethnal Green
27.11.00 Ricky Eccleston L PTS 4 Birmingham
04.12.00 Gavin Pearson L PTS 6 Bradford
11.12.00 Miguel Matthews W PTS 6 Birmingham
11.02.01 James Rooney L PTS 6 Hartlepool
26.03.01 Kevin Lear L CO 1 Wembley
03.06.01 Dafydd Carlin L PTS 4 Southwark
16.06.01 Carl Greaves L PTS 6 Derby
29.09.01 Scott Lawton L RSC 2 Southwark
15.12.01 Danny Hunt L PTS 4 Wembley
26.01.02 Chris McDonagh L PTS 4 Bethnal Green
03.03.02 Mally McIver L PTS 6 Shaw
11.03.02 Willie Limond L PTS 6 Glasgow
11.05.02 Craig Spacie L PTS 6 Chesterfield
15.06.02 Dave Stewart L PTS 6 Tottenham
23.06.02 Peter McDonagh L PTS 6 Southwark
13.07.02 Tony McPake L RSC 3 Coventry
22.03.03 Baz Carey L PTS 6 Coventry
29.03.03 Martin Power L PTS 4 Portsmouth
13.04.03 Nadeem Siddique L PTS 4 Bradford
06.06.03 Paul Rushton W PTS 6 Hull
20.06.03 Steve Mullin L PTS 4 Liverpool
30.06.03 Dean Hickman L RSC 4 Shrewsbury

05.09.03 Stefy Bull L PTS 6 Doncaster
13.09.03 Jamie Arthur L RTD 1 Newport
25.10.03 Colin Bain L PTS 4 Edinburgh
06.11.03 Andy Morris L PTS 4 Dagenham
18.11.03 Rob Jeffries L PTS 6 Bethnal Green
15.12.03 Matt Teague L PTS 6 Cleethorpes
27.03.04 Colin Bain L PTS 4 Edinburgh
23.04.04 Daniel Thorpe L PTS 6 Leicester
12.05.04 Nathan Ward L PTS 4 Reading
02.06.04 John O'Donnell L PTS 4 Nottingham

Career: 67 contests, won 7, lost 60.

Mark Hobson   Les Clark

Mark Hobson

Huddersfield. *Born* Workington, 7 May, 1976
British & Commonwealth Cruiserweight Champion. Ht. 6'5"
Manager C. Aston/T. Gilmour

09.06.97 Michael Pinnock W PTS 6 Bradford
06.10.97 P. R. Mason W PTS 6 Bradford
13.11.97 P. R. Mason W PTS 6 Bradford
27.02.98 Colin Brown DREW 6 Irvine
21.05.98 Paul Bonson W PTS 6 Bradford
15.06.98 Martin Jolley W RSC 3 Bradford
25.10.98 Mark Snipe W RSC 3 Shaw
26.11.98 Danny Southam W RSC 5 Bradford
19.04.99 Mark Levy L PTS 8 Bradford
11.09.99 Paul Bonson W PTS 4 Sheffield
06.12.99 Brian Gascoigne W RSC 3 Bradford
11.03.00 Nikolai Ermenkov W RSC 3 Kensington
27.03.00 Luke Simpkin W PTS 4 Barnsley
13.05.00 Paul Bonson W PTS 4 Barnsley
25.09.00 Mark Dawson W CO 1 Barnsley
26.02.01 Billy Bessey W PTS 4 Nottingham
24.04.01 Sebastiaan Rothmann L RTD 9 Liverpool
(WBU Cruiserweight Title Challenge)
08.10.01 Firat Arslan L RSC 7 Barnsley
10.12.01 Luke Simpkin W RTD 3 Liverpool
23.02.02 Valery Semishkur W PTS 6 Nottingham
27.04.02 Lee Swaby W PTS 10 Huddersfield

123

(Final Elim. British Cruiserweight Title)
05.10.02 Varuzhan Davtyan W RSC 3 Huddersfield
25.01.03 Abdul Kaddu W RSC 4 Bridgend
(Vacant Commonwealth Cruiserweight Title)
10.05.03 Muslim Biarslanov W RSC 2 Huddersfield
05.09.03 Robert Norton W PTS 12 Sheffield
(Commonwealth Cruiserweight Title Defence. Vacant British Cruiserweight Title)
13.03.04 Tony Moran W RSC 3 Huddersfield
(British & Commonwealth Cruiserweight Title Defences)
27.05.04 Lee Swaby W RSC 6 Huddersfield
(British & Commonwealth Cruiserweight Title Defences)
Career: 27 contests, won 23, drew 1, lost 3.

Lee Hodgson   Les Clark

Lee Hodgson

Hayes. *Born* Hammersmith, 28 June, 1973
Middleweight. Ht. 5'9¹/₂"
Manager D. Currivan

27.09.02 Kevin Phelan W RSC 1 Bracknell
03.12.02 Leigh Wicks W PTS 4 Bethnal Green
08.02.03 Dean Powell W PTS 4 Brentford
21.03.03 Elroy Edwards W RSC 3 Longford
29.03.03 Matthew Barr L RSC 1 Wembley
20.03.04 Rob MacDonald W RSC 3 Wembley
07.04.04 Conroy McIntosh L RSC 3 Leicester Square
Career: 7 contests, won 5, lost 2.

Gareth Hogg

Torquay. *Born* Newton Abbott, 21 October, 1977
L. Heavyweight. Ht. 6'2"
Manager C. Sanigar

13.02.98 Harry Butler W RSC 3 Weston super Mare
09.05.99 Matthew Barney L PTS 4 Bracknell
07.08.99 Clive Johnson W PTS 4 Dagenham
27.02.00 Darren Covill W RSC 3 Plymouth
29.03.00 Simon Andrews W RSC 5 Piccadilly
12.05.01 Oddy Papantoniou W RSC 2 Plymouth
10.07.01 Kevin Rainey W RSC 1 Montreal, Canada

23.06.02 Mark Phillips W PTS 4 Southwark
08.01.03 Darren Ashton W RSC 2 Aberdare
13.02.04 Dale Nixon W RTD 4 Bristol
Career: 10 contests, won 9, lost 1.

Mike Holden

Manchester. *Born* Ashton under Lyme, 13 March, 1968
Heavyweight. Former Undefeated British Heavyweight Champion. Ht. 6'4"
Manager Self

04.10.94 Gary Williams W RSC 4 Mayfair
20.12.94 Pat Passley L RTD 3 Bethnal Green
07.10.95 R. F. McKenzie W RSC 2 Belfast
14.11.95 Michael Murray L PTS 6 Bury
09.07.96 Julius Francis L PTS 10 Bethnal Green
28.09.96 Mikael Lindblad W PTS 6 Barking
26.06.97 Israel Ajose W RSC 1 Salford
02.09.97 Mika Kihlstrom W RSC 1 Southwark
12.12.98 Nigel Rafferty W RTD 2 Chester
08.05.99 Harry Senior L PTS 8 Bethnal Green
15.07.99 Derek McCafferty W RSC 1 Peterborough
13.03.00 Julius Francis W PTS 12 Bethnal Green
(British Heavyweight Title Challenge)
03.04.01 Julius Francis L PTS 10 Bethnal Green
(Final Elim. British Heavyweight Title)
13.09.01 Keith Long L PTS 10 Sheffield
(Elim.British Heavyweight Title)
15.03.02 Luke Simpkin W PTS 6 Millwall
15.10.02 Antoine Palatis W PTS 6 Bethnal Green
24.01.03 Michael Sprott L RSC 4 Sheffield
12.04.03 Albert Sosnowski L PTS 6 Bethnal Green
18.09.03 Matt Skelton L RSC 6 Dagenham
(Vacant English Heavyweight Title)
Career: 19 contests, won 10, lost 9.

Jon Honney

Basingstoke. *Born* Basingstoke, 6 August, 1975
Lightweight. Ht. 5'7"
Manager Self

01.10.99 Peter Dunn W PTS 4 Bethnal Green
18.12.99 Marco Fattore W PTS 4 Southwark
21.02.00 Costas Katsantonis L RSC 1 Southwark
13.07.00 Mickey Yikealo L PTS 4 Bethnal Green
29.09.00 Manzo Smith L PTS 4 Bethnal Green
06.11.00 Jimmy Gould L PTS 6 Wolverhampton
16.03.01 Woody Greenaway W PTS 6 Portsmouth
07.09.01 Young Muttley L RSC 1 West Bromwich
20.10.01 Martin Watson L RSC 3 Glasgow
23.02.02 Darrell Grafton L RTD 1 Nottingham
28.11.02 Henry Jones W PTS 4 Finchley
20.12.02 Martin Hardcastle W PTS 4 Bracknell
05.03.03 Francis Barrett L PTS 10 Bethnal Green
(Vacant Southern Area L.Welterweight Title)
27.05.03 Stephen Smith L PTS 8 Dagenham
26.07.03 Michael Ayers W PTS 6 Plymouth
11.10.03 Graham Earl L PTS 8 Portsmouth
07.04.04 Peter McDonagh L PTS 10 Leicester Square
(Vacant Southern Area Lightweight Title)

12.05.04 John Alldis W PTS 6 Reading
22.05.04 Nigel Wright L RSC 2 Widnes
Career: 19 contests, won 7, lost 12.

Chris Hooper

Scarborough. *Born* Barking, 28 September, 1977
Featherweight. Ht. 5'9"
Manager E. Maloney

01.11.01 Jason Nesbitt W RSC 6 Hull
28.01.02 Greg Edwards W RSC 2 Barnsley
27.07.02 John Mackay L PTS 4 Nottingham
26.09.02 Sid Razak W PTS 6 Hull
21.11.02 Baz Carey W RTD 3 Hull
03.04.03 Buster Dennis W RSC 1 Hull
20.02.04 Buster Dennis L RSC 2 Bethnal Green
08.04.04 John Bothwell W CO 2 Peterborough
Career: 8 contests, won 6, lost 2.

Chris Hooper   Les Clark

Simon Hopkins

Brighton. *Born* Crawley, 7 June, 1979
Middleweight. Ht. 5'6"
Manager J. Pyle

15.12.03 Luke Teague DREW 6 Cleethorpes
21.02.04 Richard Mazurek L RSC 3 Brighton
Career: 2 contests, drew 1, lost 1.

Shpetim Hoti

New Cross. *Born* Montenegro, 29 November, 1974
L. Heavyweight. Ht. 5'11¹/₂"
Manager Self

21.09.00 Elvis Michailenko L PTS 4 Bloomsbury
30.11.00 Harry Butler L PTS 4 Bloomsbury
21.06.01 Harry Butler L PTS 4 Earls Court
31.01.02 Simeon Cover L PTS 6 Piccadilly
26.09.02 Mark Ellwood L PTS 6 Hull
17.11.02 Darren Stubbs L RTD 2 Shaw
20.06.03 David Louzan W RSC 5 Gatwick
05.09.03 Amer Khan L RTD 4 Sheffield
19.02.04 Danny Norton L PTS 4 Dudley
01.05.04 Scott Baker W PTS 4 Gravesend
Career: 10 contests, won 2, lost 8.

Ben Hudson

Cambridge. *Born* Cambridge, 29 March, 1973
L. Welterweight. Ht. 5'6"
Manager T. Sims

23.08.02	Pete Buckley DREW 4 Bethnal Green
06.09.02	Scott Lawton L PTS 4 Bethnal Green
26.09.02	Jas Malik W CO 3 Fulham
27.10.02	Peter McDonagh W PTS 6 Southwark
08.12.02	Daffyd Carlin W PTS 6 Bethnal Green
18.02.03	Brian Coleman W PTS 6 Bethnal Green
08.04.03	Peter McDonagh L PTS 4 Bethnal Green
26.04.03	Robert Lloyd-Taylor W PTS 4 Brentford
27.05.03	Lenny Daws L RSC 2 Dagenham
25.09.03	Chas Symonds L PTS 6 Bethnal Green

Career: 10 contests, won 5, drew 1, lost 4.

Justin Hudson

Bexleyheath. *Born* Maidstone, 13 March, 1971
L. Middleweight. Ht. 5'9"
Manager E. Maloney

27.10.02	Elroy Edwards L RSC 3 Southwark
08.04.03	Arv Mittoo W PTS 4 Bethnal Green
03.06.03	Dave Wakefield W PTS 4 Bethnal Green
20.02.04	James Paisley L PTS 4 Bethnal Green

Career: 4 contests, won 2, lost 2.

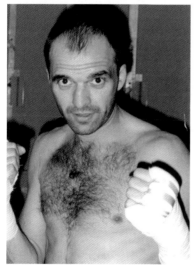

Justin Hudson   Les Clark

Barry Hughes

Glasgow. *Born* Glasgow, 18 November, 1978
Lightweight. Ht. 5'8"
Manager Self

07.12.98	Woody Greenaway L PTS 6 Acton
18.02.99	Leon Dobbs W RSC 1 Glasgow
09.04.99	Gareth Dooley W PTS 6 Glasgow
26.06.99	Des Sowden W CO 1 Glasgow
04.10.99	Tony Smith W RSC 5 Glasgow
12.11.99	Brendan Ahearne W RSC 5 Glasgow
13.12.99	Jason Vlasman W RSC 2 Glasgow
24.02.00	No No Junior W RSC 1 Glasgow
18.03.00	Gary Flear W RSC 4 Glasgow
07.04.00	Billy Smith W PTS 6 Glasgow
12.08.00	Dave Travers W PTS 4 Wembley
15.03.02	Woody Greenaway W PTS 8 Glasgow

19.10.02	Arsen Vassilev W CO 3 Renfrew
08.12.02	Paul McIlwaine W RSC 2 Glasgow
16.05.03	Martin Watson L RTD 8 Glasgow
	(Vacant Scottish Lightweight Title)
06.03.04	Peter McDonagh W PTS 6 Renfrew
23.04.04	Brian Coleman W PTS 8 Glasgow
28.05.04	Charles Shepherd DREW 12 Glasgow
	(Vacant WBU Inter-Continental Lightweight Title)
19.06.04	Nigel Senior W RSC 3 Renfrew

Career: 19 contests, won 16, drew 1, lost 2.

Sean Hughes

Pontefract. *Born* Pontefract, 5 June, 1982
Central Area S. Bantamweight Champion.
Ht. 5'9"
Manager M. Marsden

02.03.02	Paddy Folan W PTS 6 Wakefield
25.06.02	John Paul Ryan W PTS 6 Rugby
05.10.02	Paddy Folan W PTS 6 Huddersfield
10.02.03	Neil Read W PTS 6 Sheffield
24.05.03	John-Paul Ryan W PTS 6 Sheffield
13.09.03	Daniel Thorpe W PTS 6 Wakefield
05.10.03	Paddy Folan W RSC 4 Bradford
	(Vacant Central Area S.Bantamweight Title)
07.12.03	Marty Kayes W PTS 6 Bradford
26.02.04	Steve Foster L RSC 6 Widnes
	(Vacant English Featherweight Title)

Career: 9 contests, won 8, lost 1.

Danny Hunt

Southend. *Born* Rochford, 1 May, 1981
English Lightweight Champion. Ht. 5'7"
Manager F. Maloney

29.11.99	Chris Lyons W PTS 4 Wembley
13.03.00	Dave Hinds W PTS 4 Bethnal Green
13.04.00	Steve Hanley W PTS 4 Holborn
13.07.00	Dave Travers W PTS 4 Bethnal Green
27.01.01	Lee Williamson L RSC 2 Bethnal Green
03.04.01	Lee Williamson W PTS 4 Bethnal Green
05.05.01	Pete Buckley W PTS 4 Edmonton
22.09.01	Dafydd Carlin W PTS 4 Bethnal Green
15.12.01	Dave Hinds W PTS 4 Wembley
02.03.02	Gary Flear W PTS 4 Bethnal Green
04.05.02	Jason Nesbitt W PTS 4 Bethnal Green
14.09.02	David Kehoe W RSC 3 Bethnal Green
15.02.03	Mark Bowen W RSC 1 Wembley
29.03.03	Daniel Thorpe W PTS 6 Portsmouth
02.10.03	Chill John W PTS 10 Liverpool
	(Vacant English Lightweight Title)
07.02.04	Anthony Maynard W PTS 10 Bethnal Green
	(English Lightweight Title Defence)
05.06.04	Chris McDonagh W CO 3 Bethnal Green

Career: 17 contests, won 16, lost 1.

Michael Hunter

Hartlepool. *Born* Hartlepool, 5 May, 1978
British S.Bantamweight Champion. Former
Undefeated WBF & Northern Area
S.Bantamweight Champion. Ht. 5'7¹/₂"
Manager D. Garside

23.07.00	Sean Grant W PTS 6 Hartlepool
01.10.00	Chris Emanuele W PTS 6 Hartlepool
24.11.00	Gary Groves W RSC 2 Darlington
09.12.00	Chris Jickells W PTS 4 Southwark

11.02.01	Paddy Folan W RSC 6 Hartlepool
06.05.01	Anthony Hanna W PTS 4 Hartlepool
04.06.01	Anthony Hanna W PTS 4 Hartlepool
09.09.01	John Barnes W RSC 8 Hartlepool
	(Vacant Northern Area S.Bantamweight Title)
29.11.01	Joel Viney W PTS 6 Hartlepool
26.01.02	Stevie Quinn W CO 2 Dagenham
18.03.02	Marc Callaghan DREW 6 Crawley
18.05.02	Mark Payne W PTS 8 Millwall
18.10.02	Frankie DeMilo W PTS 12 Hartlepool
	(Vacant WBF S. Bantamweight Title)
14.12.02	Anthony Hanna W PTS 8 Newcastle
07.06.03	Afrim Mustafa W RSC 5 Trieste, Italy
26.07.03	Rocky Dean W RSC 1 Plymouth
04.10.03	Nikolai Eremeev W PTS 6 Belfast
08.11.03	Gennadiy Delisandru W PTS 6 Bridgend
16.04.04	Mark Payne W RSC 7 Hartlepool
	(Vacant British S.Bantamweight Title)
02.06.04	Vladimir Borov W PTS 6 Hereford

Career: 20 contests, won 19, drew 1.

Michael Hunter   Les Clark

Nasser Hussain

Bradford. *Born* Bradford, 26 October, 1974
L. Heavyweight. Ht. 6'0"
Manager T. Miller

10.02.03	Ben Ogden L CO 2 Sheffield
01.12.03	Steve Scott L RTD 4 Barnsley

Career: 2 contest, lost 2.

Karim Hussine

Balham. *Born* Tunisia, 22 March, 1970
Welterweight. Ht. 5'9"
Manager K. Sanders

19.04.00	Steve Brumant W PTS 4 Kensington
01.07.00	Leigh Wicks W PTS 6 Southwark
28.09.00	Matthew Ashmole W PTS 4 Kensington
01.04.01	Samuel Figueroa W PTS 4 Reno, Nevada, USA
27.04.01	R.J.Karstens L PTS 6 Lake Tahoe, Nevada, USA
05.06.01	Reggie Davis L PTS 4 Las Vegas, Nevada, USA
21.09.01	Gerald Coleman W PTS 8 Tampa, Florida, USA
22.07.03	Bobby Banghar L PTS 6 Bethnal Green
25.10.03	Kevin McIntyre L PTS 6 Edinburgh

Career: 9 contests, won 5, lost 4.

I J

Egbui Ikeagwo

Luton. *Born* Ibaden, Nigeria, 14 October, 1975
L. Heavyweight. Ht. 6'0½"
Manager Self

12.05.03	Michael Matthewsian W PTS 6 Southampton	
13.06.03	Leigh Alliss L PTS 6 Bristol	
06.02.04	Paul Owen W PTS 4 Sheffield	

Career: 3 contests, won 2, lost 1.

Christian Imaga

Sydenham. *Born* Lagos, Nigeria, 1 January, 1980
S. Middleweight. Ht. 6'0"
Manager B. Baker

07.04.04 Mark Phillips W PTS 6 Leicester
Square

Career: 1 contest, won 1.

Christian Imaga　　　　　Les Clark

David Ingleby

Lancaster. *Born* Lancaster, 14 June, 1980
Heavyweight. Ht. 6'3"
Manager B. Myers

09.06.03 Costi Marin L RSC 1 Bradford
01.12.03 Paul Bonson L PTS 6 Leeds
28.02.04 Paul King L RSC 3 Manchester
01.05.04 Jason Callum L PTS 6 Coventry

Career: 4 contests, lost 4.

Richard Inquieti

Eastwood. *Born* Langley Mill, 19 October, 1968
Welterweight. Ht. 6'3¼"
Manager Self

30.09.96 Peter Varnavas L CO 2 Manchester
20.02.97 Paul Johnson W PTS 6 Mansfield
12.03.97 Tony Smith W RSC 2 Stoke

19.03.97 Andy Peach L RSC 1 Stoke
18.08.97 Jawaid Khaliq L RSC 5 Nottingham
18.09.97 Danny Bell L RSC 1 Alfreton
11.11.97 Trevor Smith L RSC 3 Edgbaston
08.12.97 Danny Bell L RSC 1 Nottingham
07.10.98 Sean O'Sullivan W PTS 6 Stoke
29.10.98 Dean Nicholas L RSC 1 Newcastle
02.12.98 Martyn Thomas L RSC 3 Stoke
25.03.99 Shane Junior L CO 2 Edgbaston
06.03.00 Martyn Bailey W RSC 5 Bradford
28.03.00 David Smales L PTS 6 Hartlepool
05.05.00 Martyn Bailey L PTS 6 Pentre Halkyn
20.11.00 Darren Spencer L RSC 1 Glasgow
04.02.01 Neil Bonner L PTS 6 Queensferry
23.02.01 Dean Nicholas L PTS 6 Irvine
08.03.01 Alan Campbell L PTS 6 Blackpool
01.04.01 Stuart Elwell L PTS 6 Wolverhampton
09.04.01 Gavin Wake L PTS 6 Bradford
20.04.01 Darren Williams L PTS 6 Dublin
03.06.01 Nicky Leech L PTS 6 Hanley
15.09.01 Andrei Ivanov DREW 6 Nottingham
23.09.01 Wayne Shepherd L PTS 6 Shaw
04.10.01 Danny Moir L PTS 6 Sunderland
15.10.01 Danny Parkinson L RSC 1 Bradford
13.11.01 Peter Dunn DREW 6 Leeds
24.11.01 Gavin Wake L PTS 6 Wakefield
06.12.01 John Jackson W RSC 3 Sunderland
08.02.02 Mark Paxford L PTS 6 Preston
18.03.02 Gavin Pearson L PTS 6 Glasgow
22.04.02 Ciaran Duffy L PTS 6 Glasgow
29.04.02 Gavin Pearson L PTS 6 Bradford
09.05.02 Lee Armstrong W RSC 5 Sunderland
03.06.02 Gary Porter L PTS 6 Glasgow
03.08.02 Dean Walker L PTS 6 Derby
28.09.02 Gavin Wake L PTS 6 Wakefield
10.10.02 Mark Paxford L PTS 6 Stoke
18.10.02 Franny Jones L PTS 6 Hartlepool
01.11.02 Michael Jennings L RSC 2 Preston
22.12.02 Danny Moir L RTD 3 Salford
20.01.03 Andy Gibson L RSC 5 Glasgow
14.04.03 Craig Dickson L PTS 4 Glasgow
02.06.03 Jamie Coyle L RSC 2 Glasgow
06.10.03 Ady Clegg L PTS 6 Barnsley
10.02.04 Chris Steele W RSC 4 Barnsley
20.02.04 Brett James L PTS 6 Southampton
15.03.04 Ady Clegg L PTS 6 Bradford
26.04.04 Richard Swallow L RSC 1 Cleethorpes

Career: 50 contests, won 8, drew 2, lost 40.

Andrei Ivanov

Nottingham. *Born* Rostov, Russia, 15 April, 1980
Middleweight. Ht. 6'0"
Manager J. Gill

15.09.01 Richard Inquieti DREW 6 Nottingham
10.10.01 Paddy Martin W RSC 2 Stoke
16.11.01 Peter Jackson L PTS 6 West Bromwich
12.12.01 Wayne Shepherd W PTS 6 Nottingham
17.12.01 Tony Montana DREW 6 Cleethorpes
07.02.02 Chris Steele W PTS 6 Stoke
08.03.02 Tony Byrne L PTS 6 Ellesmere Port
15.03.02 Paul Lomax L PTS 6 Spennymoor
02.06.02 Greg Hadwin W PTS 6 Shaw
05.10.02 Andy Halder L PTS 6 Coventry
17.04.03 Sonny Pollard L PTS 6 Hull
08.05.03 Paul Smith L RSC 2 Widnes
01.12.03 Lee Williamson L RSC 4 Barnsley
27.04.04 Mark Wall W CO 6 Leeds
07.05.04 Raz Harrison L RSC 2 Doncaster
08.06.04 Dean Walker L PTS 6 Sheffield
19.06.04 Colin McNeil L RSC 4 Renfrew

Career: 17 contests, won 4, drew 2, lost 11.

Peter Jackson

Halesowen. *Born* Wordsley, 27 January, 1976
Midlands Area S.Middleweight Champion.
Ht. 5'11"
Manager Self

28.01.01 Harry Butler W PTS 6 Wolverhampton
01.04.01 Jamie Logan W PTS 6 Wolverhampton
20.05.01 Jamie Logan W PTS 6 Wolverhampton
09.09.01 Neil Bonner W PTS 6 Hartlepool
16.11.01 Andrei Ivanov W PTS 6 West
Bromwich
17.02.02 Alan Jones L PTS 6 Wolverhampton
13.04.02 Simon Andrews W PTS 4
Wolverhampton
03.08.02 Jimmy Steel W PTS 4 Blackpool
08.09.02 Mike Duffield W PTS 4
Wolverhampton
02.11.02 Mike Duffield L PTS 10
Wolverhampton
*(Vacant Midlands Area S.Middleweight
Title)*
15.02.03 Simeon Cover L RSC 2 Wolverhampton
17.07.03 Mike Duffield W PTS 10 Walsall
*(Midlands Area S.Middleweight Title
Challenge)*
11.12.03 Ryan Rhodes L PTS 6 Bethnal Green
19.02.04 Patrick Cito DREW 4 Dudley

Career: 14 contests, won 9, drew 1, lost 4.

Hamid Jamali

Birmingham. *Born* Iran, 23 November, 1973
S. Middleweight. Ht. 5'9"
Manager Self

09.12.02 Dale Nixon W CO 1 Birmingham
24.02.03 Harry Butler W PTS 6 Birmingham
06.10.03 Simeon Cover W PTS 6 Birmingham
08.12.03 Gary Ojuederie W PTS 6 Birmingham
08.03.04 Ojay Abrahams W PTS 8 Birmingham
10.05.04 Jason Collins W PTS 8 Birmingham

Career: 6 contests, won 6.

Brett James (Eleftheriou)

St Pancras. *Born* London, 3 November, 1975
Welterweight. Former Southern Area
Welterweight Champion. Ht. 5'8"
Manager E. Maloney

20.01.00 Colin Vidler W PTS 6 Piccadilly
21.02.00 Julian Kacanolli W PTS 4 Southwark
04.07.00 Colin Vidler W PTS 4 Tooting
04.11.00 Matt Scriven W RTD 1 Bethnal Green
20.01.01 Jay Mahoney W PTS 4 Bethnal Green
07.04.01 Paul Denton W PTS 4 Wembley
16.06.01 Karl Taylor DREW 4 Wembley
14.07.01 Lee Williamson W PTS 6 Wembley
29.09.01 Ernie Smith W PTS 6 Southwark
12.02.02 Karl Taylor DREW 4 Bethnal Green
23.06.02 Lee Williamson W PTS 6 Southwark
23.08.02 Brian Coleman W PTS 6 Bethnal
Green
25.10.02 David Walker L RSC 4 Bethnal Green
*(Southern Area Welterweight Title
Challenge)*
15.05.03 Keith Jones W PTS 4 Mayfair
01.08.03 Sammy Smith W PTS 10 Bethnal
Green
*(Vacant Southern Area Welterweight
Title)*

18.11.03 Iain Eldridge W PTS 10 Bethnal Green
(Southern Area Welterweight Title Defence)
20.02.04 Richard Inquieti W PTS 6 Southampton
01.04.04 Michael Jennings L RTD 5 Bethnal Green
(WBU International Welterweight Title Challenge)
25.06.04 Chas Symonds L RSC 4 Bethnal Green
(Southern Area Welterweight Title Defence)
Career: 19 contests, won 14, drew 2, lost 3.

Fred Janes
Cardiff. *Born* Cardiff, 17 December, 1984
Featherweight. Ht. 5'9"
Manager D. Gardiner

23.11.03 Paddy Folan W RSC 5 Rotherham
13.12.03 Steve Bell L PTS 4 Manchester
13.02.04 Michael Graydon DREW 6 Bristol
06.03.04 John Bothwell DREW 4 Renfrew
01.04.04 Martin Power L RSC 2 Bethnal Green
02.06.04 John Simpson L PTS 6 Hereford
Career: 6 contests, won 1, drew 2, lost 3.

Fred Janes　　　　　　Les Clark

Henry Janes
Cardiff. *Born* Cardiff, 24 May, 1983
S. Featherweight. Ht. 5'7"
Manager D. Gardiner

24.05.03 Steve Foster L PTS 6 Bethnal Green
02.06.03 Matt Teague L PTS 6 Cleethorpes
20.06.03 Derry Matthews L RSC 1 Liverpool
07.09.03 Steve Gethin W PTS 4 Shrewsbury
30.10.03 Kevin O'Hara L PTS 6 Belfast
30.11.03 Ian Reid W PTS 6 Swansea
13.12.03 Andy Morris L PTS 4 Manchester
19.01.04 John Simpson L PTS 8 Glasgow
07.02.04 Lee Whyatt W PTS 4 Bethnal Green
06.03.04 Kevin O'Hara L PTS 6 Renfrew
13.03.04 Danny Wallace W PTS 4 Huddersfield
03.04.04 Derry Matthews L PTS 4 Manchester
22.04.04 Barry Hawthorne L PTS 6 Glasgow
19.06.04 Scott Flynn W RSC 4 Renfrew
Career: 14 contests, won 5, lost 9.

Henry Janes　　　　　　Les Clark

(Robin) Rob Jeffries (Jeffrey)
Bexleyheath. *Born* Crayford, 25 June, 1973
Lightweight. Ht. 5'8"
Manager E. Maloney

22.07.03 Jaz Virdee W PTS 6 Bethnal Green
25.09.03 Anthony Hanna W PTS 6 Bethnal Green
18.11.03 Dave Hinds W PTS 6 Bethnal Green
20.02.04 Chris McDonagh W RSC 2 Bethnal Green
25.06.04 Declan English W PTS 6 Bethnal Green
Career: 5 contests, won 5.

Rob Jeffries　　　　　　Les Clark

Michael Jennings
Chorley. *Born* Preston, 9 September, 1977
Welterweight. Former Undefeated WBU Inter-Continental Welterweight Champion. Ht. 5'9¹/₂"
Manager F. Warren/B. Hughes

15.05.99 Tony Smith W RSC 1 Blackpool
11.12.99 Lee Molyneux W PTS 4 Liverpool
29.02.00 Lee Molyneux W PTS 6 Widnes
25.03.00 Brian Coleman W PTS 6 Liverpool
16.05.00 Brian Coleman W PTS 6 Warrington
29.05.00 William Webster W PTS 6 Manchester
08.07.00 Paul Denton W PTS 6 Widnes
04.09.00 Mark Ramsey W PTS 6 Manchester
25.11.00 Ernie Smith W PTS 4 Manchester
11.12.00 Paul Denton W PTS 4 Widnes

10.02.01 Mark Haslam W RSC 2 Widnes
07.07.01 David Kirk W PTS 6 Manchester
15.09.01 Gary Harrison W PTS 6 Manchester
09.02.02 James Paisley W RSC 3 Manchester
01.06.02 Lee Williamson W PTS 4 Manchester
28.09.02 Karl Taylor W RSC 4 Manchester
01.11.02 Richard Inquieti W RSC 2 Preston
18.01.03 Lee Williamson W RTD 4 Preston
08.05.03 Jimmy Gould W RTD 6 Widnes
(Vacant WBU Inter-Continental Welterweight Title)
27.09.03 Sammy Smith W RTD 4 Manchester
(WBU Inter-Continental Welterweight Title Defence)
13.12.03 Peter Dunn W PTS 6 Manchester
01.04.04 Brett James W RTD 5 Bethnal Green
(WBU Inter-Continental Welterweight Title Defence)
22.05.04 Rafal Jackiewicz W PTS 8 Widnes
Career: 23 contests, won 23.

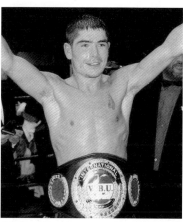

Michael Jennings　　　　　　Les Clark

Carl Johanneson
Leeds. *Born* Leeds, 1 August, 1978
WBF S.Featherweight Champion. Ht. 5'5"
Manager J. Durkin

08.07.00 Calvin Sheppard W PTS 3 North Carolina, USA
15.09.00 Sean Thomassen W RSC 1 Paterson, New Jersey, USA
14.10.00 Hiep Bui W RSC 1 Scranton, Pennsylvania, USA
08.12.00 Walusimbi Kizito W PTS 4 Atlantic City, New Jersey, USA
12.04.01 Efrain Guzman W PTS 4 Melville, New York, USA
04.05.01 Calvin Sheppard W RSC 4 Atlantic City, New Jersey, USA
26.06.01 Joey Figueroa W PTS 6 NYC, New York, USA
26.10.01 Jose Ramon Disla W RSC 5 Atlantic City, New Jersey, USA
14.12.01 Angel Rios W PTS 6 Uncasville, Connecticut, USA
03.03.02 Kema Muse W PTS 6 Scranton, Pennsylvania, USA
02.07.02 James Baker W RSC 4 Washington DC, USA
16.01.03 Juan R. Llopis W RSC 5 Philadelphia, Pennsylvania, USA

05.06.03 Koba Gogoladze L PTS 8 Detroit, Michigan, USA
18.07.03 Reggie Sanders W PTS 6 Dover, Delaware, USA
21.08.03 Steve Trumble W RSC 2 Philadelphia, Pennsylvania, USA
30.01.04 Harold Grey W RSC 5 Philadelphia, Pennsylvania, USA
20.03.04 Carl Greaves W RTD 3 Wembley
(*WBF S.Featherweight Title Challenge*)
08.05.04 Andrew Ferrans W RSC 6 Bristol
(*WBF S.Featherweight Title Defence*)
19.06.04 Alexander Abramenko W RSC 5 Muswell Hill
(*WBF S.Featherweight Title Defence*)
Career: 19 contests, won 18, lost 1.

Carl Johanneson   Les Clark

(Garnet) Chill John
Brighton. *Born* St Vincent, 11 August, 1977
Lightweight. Ht. 5'7"
Manager R. Davies

22.10.00 Paul Philpott W PTS 6 Streatham
03.02.01 Dave Travers W PTS 4 Brighton
25.02.01 Scott Hocking W RSC 4 Streatham
05.05.01 Woody Greenaway W PTS 6 Brighton
04.07.01 Steve Hanley W PTS 4 Bloomsbury
20.10.01 Mark Halstead W PTS 4 Portsmouth
01.12.01 Pete Buckley W PTS 4 Bethnal Green
13.04.02 Jonathan Thaxton L RSC 2 Norwich
12.07.02 Daniel Thorpe W PTS 4 Southampton
22.09.02 Jason Hall L PTS 6 Southwark
12.10.02 Graham Earl L PTS 10 Piccadilly
(*Southern Area Lightweight Title Challenge*)
21.12.02 Lee Meager L RSC 5 Dagenham
02.10.03 Danny Hunt L PTS 10 Liverpool
(*Vacant English Lightweight Title*)
21.02.04 Peter McDonagh L RTD 2 Brighton
Career: 14 contests, won 8, lost 6.

Clint Johnson
Leeds. *Born* Leeds, 13 April, 1974
L. Heavyweight. Ht. 6'2"
Manager Self

11.11.97 Jon Penn W RSC 2 Leeds
04.12.97 John O'Byrne L PTS 6 Sunderland
17.02.98 Rob Galloway W PTS 6 Leeds
20.09.98 Rob Galloway W PTS 6 Sheffield

29.10.98 Mike White L PTS 6 Newcastle
06.11.98 Gerard Zdiarski W PTS 4 Mayfair
07.12.98 Carl Nicholson W PTS 6 Bradford
16.02.99 Danny Southam L RSC 5 Leeds
15.09.99 Steve Loftus W PTS 6 Harrogate
28.03.00 Martin Jolley W PTS 6 Hartlepool
17.04.00 Alex Mason L PTS 6 Birmingham
20.05.00 Jason Barker L RSC 1 Rotherham
23.10.00 Joe Gillon L CO 4 Glasgow
17.05.01 Paul Bonson L PTS 6 Leeds
18.06.01 Mark Brookes L PTS 6 Bradford
13.09.01 Darren Littlewood W PTS 6 Sheffield
03.11.01 Joe Gillon W CO 3 Glasgow
03.12.01 Jimmy Steel DREW 6 Leeds
15.12.01 Mark Brookes L PTS 4 Sheffield
18.02.02 Billy McClung L PTS 6 Glasgow
01.03.02 Billy McClung L PTS 6 Irvine
16.03.02 Clinton Woods L RSC 3 Bethnal Green
08.10.02 Allan Foster L PTS 6 Glasgow
02.12.02 Greg Scott-Briggs W PTS 6 Leeds
08.02.03 Andrew Lowe L PTS 6 Brentford
05.04.03 Darren Corbett L RSC 4 Belfast
12.10.03 Scott Lansdowne L PTS 4 Sheffield
01.12.03 Simeon Cover W PTS 6 Leeds
20.03.04 Courtney Fry L RSC 2 Wembley
Career: 29 contests, won 11, drew 1, lost 17.

Clive Johnson
Basingstoke. *Born* Botswana, 18 October, 1977
L. Middleweight. Ht. 5'10"
Manager Self

18.02.99 Harry Butler W PTS 6 Barking
20.05.99 Joe Skeldon W PTS 6 Barking
07.08.99 Gareth Hogg L PTS 4 Dagenham
09.10.99 Jamie Moore L RSC 3 Manchester
07.04.00 Kevin Lang W RSC 1 Bristol
08.09.00 Chris Henry L PTS 4 Bristol
06.10.00 Colin Vidler L PTS 6 Maidstone
26.03.01 David Baptiste W PTS 6 Peterborough
28.09.01 John Humphrey L PTS 6 Millwall
09.02.02 Darren McInulty L PTS 8 Coventry
18.01.03 Matthew Hall L PTS 4 Preston
27.03.04 Alexander Sipos L PTS 6 Magdeburg, Germany
Career: 12 contests, won 4, lost 8.

Craig Johnson
Clay Cross. *Born* Chesterfield, 10 November, 1980
Lightweight. Ht. 5'7"
Manager H. Rainey

25.04.04 Peter Allen W PTS 6 Nottingham
Career: 1 contest, won 1.

Darren Johnstone
Larkhall. *Born* Motherwell, 30 March, 1982
Lightweight. Ht. 5'9"
Manager T. Gilmour

17.11.03 Jamie Hill W PTS 6 Glasgow
15.03.04 Ian Reid W PTS 6 Glasgow
07.06.04 Joel Viney W PTS 6 Glasgow
Career: 3 contests, won 3.

Alan Jones
Aberystwyth. *Born* Aberystwyth, 6 October, 1976
Middleweight. Ht. 6'1"
Manager T. Gilmour

15.09.01 Martyn Woodward W CO 3 Swansea

21.10.01 Kenny Griffith W RSC 4 Pentre Halkyn
17.02.02 Peter Jackson W PTS 6 Wolverhampton
16.03.02 Allan Foster DREW 6 Northampton
07.10.02 Donovan Smillie W RSC 6 Birmingham
23.02.03 Leigh Wicks W PTS 8 Aberystwyth
06.10.03 Jason Collins W PTS 8 Birmingham
30.10.03 Jim Rock W PTS 8 Belfast
02.06.04 Jason Collins W PTS 6 Hereford
Career: 9 contests, won 8, drew 1.

Davey Jones
Doncaster. *Born* Grimsby, 30 May, 1977
Middleweight. Ht. 5'11"
Manager J. Rushton

23.09.02 William Webster W PTS 6 Cleethorpes
08.11.02 William Webster W PTS 6 Doncaster
30.11.02 Matt Scriven W PTS 6 Newark
16.12.02 Gary Jones W PTS 6 Cleethorpes
21.02.03 Jimi Hendricks W PTS 6 Doncaster
09.05.03 Wayne Shepherd W PTS 6 Doncaster
22.09.03 Steve Brumant L PTS 6 Cleethorpes
26.02.04 Paul Smith L PTS 4 Widnes
06.03.04 Paul Buchanan L PTS 4 Renfrew
Career: 9 contest, won 6, lost 3.

Franny Jones
Darlington. *Born* Burnley, 7 February, 1981
L. Middleweight. Ht. 5'9½"
Manager M. Marsden

05.05.02 Surinder Sekhon W PTS 6 Hartlepool
28.09.02 Martin Scotland W PTS 6 Wakefield
18.10.02 Richard Inquieti W PTS 6 Hartlepool
27.02.03 Danny Moir DREW 6 Sunderland
17.03.03 Gary Porter W PTS 6 Glasgow
11.07.03 Gary Cummings W RSC 2 Darlington
10.10.03 Pedro Thompson W PTS 6 Darlington
13.12.03 Matthew Hatton DREW 6 Manchester
05.03.04 Danny Moir NC 3 Darlington
(*Vacant Northern Area L.Middleweight Title*)
16.04.04 Brian Coleman W PTS 6 Hartlepool
Career: 10 contests, won 7, drew 2, no contest 1.

Gary Jones
Birmingham. *Born* Birmingham, 26 October, 1976
S. Middleweight. Ht. 6'1"
Manager Self

15.07.00 Danny Smith L RSC 1 Norwich
16.09.00 Liam Lathbury L RSC 5 Bethnal Green
11.12.00 Andrew Facey L PTS 6 Cleethorpes
31.01.01 Paul Buchanan L RTD 1 Piccadilly
16.11.01 Tony Byrne L PTS 6 Preston
06.12.01 Danny Moir L PTS 6 Sunderland
26.09.02 Sonny Pollard L PTS 6 Hull
21.10.02 Dave Pearson W RSC 3 Cleethorpes
30.10.02 Mark Thornton L PTS 4 Leicester Square
29.11.02 Danny Grainger L PTS 6 Hull
16.12.02 Davey Jones L PTS 6 Cleethorpes
24.03.03 Ben Ogden L RSC 6 Barnsley
31.05.03 Dave Pearson W RSC 2 Barnsley
06.06.03 Amer Khan L PTS 6 Hull
13.06.03 Darren McDermott L RSC 1 Queensway
05.10.03 Donovan Smillie L CO 2 Bradford
14.02.04 Karl Wheeler L RSC 1 Holborn
Career: 17 contests, won 2, lost 15.

Henry Jones

Pembroke. *Born* Haverfordwest, 23
December, 1975
Lightweight. Ht. 5'0"
Manager M. Goodall

17.06.95	Abdul Mannon W PTS 6 Cardiff	
07.07.95	Harry Woods L PTS 4 Cardiff	
07.10.95	Frankie Slane L PTS 4 Belfast	
28.11.95	Jason Thomas L PTS 4 Cardiff	
20.12.95	Brendan Bryce W PTS 6 Usk	
20.03.96	Danny Lawson W CO 1 Cardiff	
29.05.96	Ian Turner L PTS 6 Ebbw Vale	
02.10.96	Jason Thomas W PTS 4 Cardiff	
26.10.96	Danny Costello L RSC 3 Liverpool	
29.04.97	Tommy Waite L PTS 4 Belfast	
19.05.97	Francky Leroy L RSC 1 Coudekerque, France	
02.12.97	Ian Turner L RSC 8 Swansea *(Vacant Welsh Bantamweight Title)*	
30.10.98	Tiger Singh W CO 4 Peterborough	
05.05.00	Jason Edwards L PTS 6 Pentre Halkyn	
28.11.02	Jon Honney L PTS 4 Finchley	
23.02.03	David Vaughan L PTS 6 Aberystwyth	
10.04.03	Daleboy Rees L PTS 4 Clydach	
07.05.03	Jason Nesbitt W PTS 6 Ellesmere Port	
15.06.03	Dean Lambert L RSC 4 Bradford	
20.04.04	Scott Lawton L PTS 6 Sheffield	
19.06.04	Colin Bain L PTS 4 Renfrew	

Career: 21 contests, won 6, lost 15.

Keith Jones

Cefn Hengoed. *Born* Bradwell, 4
December, 1968
Welterweight. Former Undefeated British
Masters Lightweight Champion. Ht. 5'5¾"
Manager Self

17.05.94	Abdul Mannon L PTS 6 Kettering	
13.06.94	G. G. Goddard L PTS 6 Liverpool	
21.07.94	G. G. Goddard L RSC 1 Battersea	
12.09.94	Marco Fattore L PTS 4 Mayfair	
29.09.94	Marlon Ward L PTS 4 Bethnal Green	
21.10.94	James Murray L CO 3 Glasgow	
27.11.94	Daniel Lutaaya L CO 1 Southwark	
03.09.96	Benny May W RSC 2 Bethnal Green	
18.09.96	Kevin Sheil W PTS 4 Tylorstown	
04.10.96	Andy Ross DREW 6 Pentre Halkyn	
18.10.96	Wayne Jones DREW 6 Barnstaple	
06.11.96	Robert Grubb W PTS 4 Tylorstown	
22.11.96	Tony Mulholland L PTS 4 Liverpool	
03.12.96	Alex Moon L RTD 5 Liverpool	
21.01.97	Greg Upton DREW 6 Bristol	
26.02.97	Greg Upton L PTS 6 Cardiff	
07.03.97	Dean Murdoch L PTS 6 Weston super Mare	
20.03.97	Kevin Sheil DREW 8 Solihull	
04.04.97	Tony Mulholland L PTS 4 Liverpool	
22.05.97	Darrell Easton L PTS 4 Southwark	
02.10.98	Dean Pithie L PTS 8 Cheshunt	
10.10.98	Steve Murray L RSC 4 Bethnal Green	
21.11.98	Mat Zegan L PTS 4 Southwark	
30.11.98	Eddie Nevins L PTS 4 Manchester	
14.12.98	Roy Rutherford L PTS 6 Birmingham	
12.01.99	Richard Evatt L CO 3 Bethnal Green	
23.02.99	Simon Chambers DREW 4 Cardiff	
12.03.99	Maurycy Gojko L PTS 4 Bethnal Green	
09.04.99	Brian Carr L PTS 8 Glasgow	
23.04.99	Dewi Roberts W PTS 6 Clydach	
01.05.99	Steve Murray L RSC 6 Crystal Palace	
04.06.99	Luis Navarro L RSC 5 Malaga, Spain	
02.07.99	Alan Bosworth L PTS 6 Bristol	
15.07.99	Tomas Jansson L PTS 4 Peterborough	
20.08.99	Jason Hall L PTS 6 Bloomsbury	
02.10.99	Jason Dee L RSC 5 Cardiff	
06.11.99	Isaac Sebaduka W PTS 4 Bethnal Green	
14.11.99	Lee Armstrong L PTS 6 Bradford	
04.12.99	Franny Hogg L PTS 4 Manchester	
14.12.99	Roy Rutherford L PTS 4 Coventry	
18.01.00	Carl Greaves L PTS 6 Mansfield	
29.01.00	Steve Murray L PTS 4 Manchester	
27.02.00	Mark McGowan W RSC 7 Plymouth *(British Masters Lightweight Title Challenge)*	
25.03.00	Alex Moon L PTS 6 Liverpool	
12.05.00	Jason Cook L PTS 10 Swansea *(Welsh L. Welterweight Title Challenge)*	
01.07.00	Matty Leonard W RSC 4 Southwark	
25.07.00	Koba Gogoladze L PTS 4 Southwark	
19.08.00	Richard Evatt L PTS 6 Brentwood	
16.09.00	David Walker L PTS 6 Bethnal Green	
21.10.00	Francis Barrett L PTS 4 Wembley	
16.11.00	Jimmy Phelan DREW 6 Hull	
27.11.00	Kevin Bennett L PTS 8 Birmingham	
11.12.00	Steve Saville L PTS 8 Birmingham	
02.01.01	Mark Payne L PTS 6 Coventry	
15.01.01	Matthew Hatton L PTS 4 Manchester	
03.02.01	David Burke L PTS 4 Manchester	
10.02.01	Nigel Wright L PTS 4 Widnes	
23.02.01	Darren Melville L PTS 4 Barking	
29.03.01	Ted Bami L PTS 4 Hammersmith	
10.04.01	Dean Pithie L PTS 4 Wembley	
22.04.01	Brian Gentry L PTS 8 Streatham	
08.05.01	Kevin Bennett L PTS 6 Barnsley	
20.05.01	Jimmy Gould L PTS 6 Wolverhampton	
02.06.01	Mally McIver L PTS 6 Wakefield	
23.06.01	Alan Bosworth L PTS 6 Peterborough	
14.07.01	Wayne Rigby L CO 3 Wembley	
18.08.01	Steve Conway L PTS 8 Dewsbury	
28.09.01	Daniel James L PTS 6 Millwall	
20.10.01	Ronnie Nailen L PTS 4 Glasgow	
10.11.01	Colin Lynes L PTS 6 Wembley	
17.11.01	Willie Limond L PTS 4 Glasgow	
24.11.01	Steve Murray L RSC 4 Bethnal Green	
13.04.02	Jimmy Gould L PTS 8 Wolverhampton	
27.04.02	Lee Armstrong L PTS 6 Huddersfield	
09.05.02	Martin Holgate L PTS 6 Leicester Square	
13.06.02	Ajose Olusegun L PTS 6 Leicester Square	
23.06.02	Ted Bami L RSC 4 Southwark	
15.09.02	Ross McCord W RSC 4 Swansea *(Vacant Welsh Welterweight Title)*	
05.10.02	Tony Conroy W RSC 4 Coventry	
02.11.02	Gary Young L PTS 4 Belfast	
16.11.02	Glenn McClarnon L PTS 6 Nottingham	
09.12.02	Steve Saville L PTS 4 Birmingham	
21.12.02	Francis Barrett L PTS 6 Dagenham	
23.02.03	Jason Williams L PTS 10 Aberystwyth *(Welsh Welterweight Title Defence)*	
08.03.03	Leo O'Reilly L PTS 6 Bethnal Green	
21.03.03	Kevin Bennett L PTS 4 West Bromwich	
05.04.03	Gary Greenwood DREW 8 Coventry	
12.04.03	Barry Morrison L PTS 4 Bethnal Green	
26.04.03	Ajose Olusegun L PTS 6 Brentford	
15.05.03	Brett James L PTS 4 Mayfair	
05.10.03	Ali Nuumembe L PTS 6 Bradford	
24.10.03	Carl Greaves L PTS 6 Bethnal Green	
07.11.03	Bobby Vanzie L PTS 6 Sheffield	
27.11.03	Sammy Smith L PTS 10 Longford *(Vacant British Masters L.Welterweight Title)*	
11.12.03	Lenny Daws L PTS 6 Bethnal Green	
27.03.04	Gary Young L PTS 6 Edinburgh	
07.04.04	John Alldis L PTS 6 Leicester Square	
24.04.04	Tony Doherty L PTS 6 Reading	
02.06.04	Kevin McIntyre L PTS 6 Hereford	

Career: 99 contests, won 9, drew 7, lost 83.

Michael Jones

Liverpool. *Born* Liverpool, 14 November,
1974
L.Middleweight. Former Commonwealth
L.Middleweight Champion. Ht. 6'0¼"
Manager Self

15.11.97	Harry Butler W PTS 4 Bristol	
17.01.98	Martin Cavey W CO 1 Bristol	
07.03.98	Darren McInulty W PTS 4 Reading	
25.04.98	Koba Kulu W RSC 3 Cardiff	
06.06.98	G. L. Booth W RSC 2 Liverpool	
10.10.98	Takaloo W PTS 6 Bethnal Green	
19.12.98	Ojay Abrahams W PTS 6 Liverpool	
26.06.99	Paul King W PTS 6 Glasgow	
11.03.00	Alan Gilbert W RTD 3 Kensington	
02.06.00	Mohammed Boualleg W PTS 8 Ashford	
03.02.01	Howard Clarke W PTS 4 Manchester	
24.04.01	Judicael Bedel W PTS 6 Liverpool	
06.10.01	Delroy Mellis W PTS 8 Manchester	
10.12.01	Piotr Bartnicki W RSC 4 Liverpool	
13.04.02	Mark Richards W RSC 1 Liverpool	
28.05.02	Joshua Onyango W RSC 6 Liverpool *(Commonwealth L. Middleweight Title Challenge)*	
08.02.03	Howard Clarke W PTS 6 Liverpool	
19.04.03	Jamie Moore L PTS 12 Liverpool *(Commonwealth L.Middleweight Title Defence. Vacant British L.Middleweight Title)*	
18.10.03	Ojay Abrahams W PTS 6 Manchester	
13.03.04	Jason Williams W PTS 6 Huddersfield	
10.04.04	Darren Rhodes W RSC 3 Manchester *(Final Elim. British L.Middleweight Title)*	

Career: 21 contests, won 20, lost 1.

(Lee) Taz Jones

Abercynon. *Born* Aberdare, 24 August,
1982
Welterweight. Ht. 5'11"
Manager B. Coleman

15.09.02	David White DREW 4 Swansea	
02.11.02	Gerard McAuley DREW 4 Belfast	
21.12.02	Luke Rudd W RTD 1 Millwall	
08.01.03	Elroy Edwards W PTS 6 Aberdare	
27.09.03	Matthew Hatton L PTS 4 Manchester	
06.12.03	Ernie Smith W PTS 4 Cardiff	
21.02.04	Craig Lynch W PTS 4 Cardiff	
17.04.04	Andy Gibson W PTS 6 Belfast	

Career: 8 contests, won 5, drew 2, lost 1.

(Nathaniel) Nate Joseph

Bradford. *Born* Bradford, 6 June, 1979
Cruiserweight. Ht. 5'10"
Manager C. Aston

20.11.02	Lee Mountford L PTS 6 Leeds	
03.02.03	Gary Thompson W PTS 4 Bradford	
13.04.03	Eamonn Glennon W PTS 6 Bradford	
13.05.03	Lee Mountford W PTS 6 Leeds	
31.05.03	Brian Gascoigne L RTD 1 Barnsley	
07.12.03	Earl Ling DREW 6 Bradford	
16.01.04	Terry Morrill L PTS 6 Bradford	
16.04.04	Michael Pinnock W PTS 4 Bradford	

Career: 8 contests, won 4, drew 1, lost 3.

Marty Kayes

Downpatrick. *Born* Ashton under Lyne, 16 December, 1975
Bantamweight. Ht. 5'5¹/₂"
Manager Self

27.05.01 Darren Cleary L PTS 4 Manchester
07.07.01 Darren Cleary L PTS 4 Manchester
15.10.01 Darren Taylor L PTS 4 Southampton
26.01.02 Lee Georgiou L PTS 6 Bethnal Green
13.03.02 Sunkanmi Ogunbiyi L PTS 4 Mayfair
30.10.02 Sunkanmi Ogunbiyi L PTS 4 Leicester Square
16.12.02 Andy Roberts L PTS 6 Cleethorpes
01.02.03 Stevie Quinn L PTS 4 Belfast
21.02.03 Andy Roberts L PTS 6 Doncaster
05.04.03 Stevie Quinn L RSC 5 Belfast
29.08.03 Derry Matthews L RTD 2 Liverpool
17.10.03 John Bothwell L PTS 6 Glasgow
07.12.03 Sean Hughes L PTS 6 Bradford
13.02.04 Lee Haskins L PTS 6 Bristol
15.03.04 Sandy Bartlett L PTS 6 Glasgow
01.05.04 Ryan Barrett L RSC 2 Gravesend
Career: 16 contests, lost 16.

Gokhan Kazaz

Walthamstow. *Born* Turkey, 21 November, 1977
Middleweight. Ht. 5'9"
Manager F. Maloney

17.07.03 Joel Ani W PTS 4 Dagenham
18.09.03 Jimi Hendricks W PTS 4 Dagenham
06.11.03 Tomas da Silva W PTS 4 Dagenham
07.02.04 Patrick Cito W PTS 4 Bethnal Green
13.05.04 Alan Gilbert W PTS 4 Bethnal Green
Career: 5 contests, won 5.

John Keeton

Sheffield. *Born* Sheffield, 19 May, 1972
Cruiserweight. Former Undefeated WBF & WBO Inter-Continental Cruiserweight Champion. Ht. 6'0"
Manager Self

11.08.93 Tony Colclough W RSC 1 Mansfield
15.09.93 Val Golding L PTS 6 Ashford
27.10.93 Darren McKenna W RSC 3 Stoke
01.12.93 Julius Francis L PTS 4 Bethnal Green
19.01.94 Dennis Bailey W RTD 2 Stoke
17.02.94 Dermot Gascoyne L RSC 1 Dagenham
09.04.94 Eddie Knight W RTD 5 Mansfield
11.05.94 John Rice W RSC 5 Sheffield
02.06.94 Devon Rhooms W RSC 2 Tooting
06.09.94 Mark Walker W RSC 5 Stoke
24.09.94 Dirk Wallyn L CO 3 Middlekerke, Belgium
26.10.94 Lee Archer W PTS 6 Stoke
09.12.94 Bruce Scott L CO 2 Bethnal Green
11.02.95 Rudiger May L PTS 6 Frankfurt, Germany
06.03.95 Simon McDougall W RSC 5 Mayfair
07.07.95 Nicky Piper L RTD 2 Cardiff
15.09.95 Steve Osborne W RSC 4 Mansfield
27.10.95 Nicky Wadman W RSC 1 Brighton
03.11.95 Monty Wright W RSC 4 Dudley
11.11.95 Denzil Browne W RSC 4 Halifax
30.01.96 Cesar Kazadi W RSC 3 Lille, France
11.05.96 Terry Dunstan L RSC 1 Bethnal Green
(*British Cruiserweight Title Challenge*)
14.09.96 John Pierre W PTS 4 Sheffield
14.12.96 Nigel Rafferty W RTD 3 Sheffield
12.04.97 Nigel Rafferty W RSC 6 Sheffield
11.10.97 Kelly Oliver L RSC 8 Sheffield
(*Vacant WBO Inter-Continental Cruiserweight Title*)
16.05.98 Jacob Mofokeng L RTD 4 Hammanskraal, South Africa
18.07.98 Kelly Oliver W RSC 2 Sheffield
23.01.99 Garry Delaney W PTS 12 Cheshunt
(*Vacant WBO Inter-Continental Cruiserweight Title*)
15.05.99 William Barima W RTD 3 Sheffield
29.02.00 Tony Booth W RSC 2 Widnes
16.12.00 Bruce Scott L CO 6 Sheffield
(*Vacant British Cruiserweight Title*)
21.07.01 Radcliffe Green W PTS 4 Sheffield
19.03.02 Butch Lesley W PTS 12 Slough
(*Vacant WBF Cruiserweight Title*)
16.04.04 Paul Bonson W PTS 4 Bradford
Career: 35 contests, won 24, lost 11.

David Kehoe

Northampton. *Born* Northampton, 24 December, 1972
Welterweight. Ht. 5'10¹/₂"
Manager Self

06.02.96 Simon Frailing W CO 1 Basildon
20.04.96 Paul Salmon W PTS 6 Brentwood
12.11.96 Peter Nightingale L PTS 6 Dudley
28.04.97 Craig Kelley L DIS 3 Enfield
18.11.97 Peter Nightingale DREW 4 Mansfield
27.01.98 Paul Miles L PTS 4 Bethnal Green
11.03.98 Trevor Tacy W RTD 1 Bethnal Green
28.03.98 David Thompson W PTS 6 Crystal Palace
26.05.98 Dave Hinds W RSC 5 Mayfair
08.09.98 Marc Smith W PTS 6 Bethnal Green
12.01.99 Gary Flear L PTS 4 Bethnal Green
25.01.99 Roger Sampson L PTS 4 Glasgow
12.03.99 Jamie McKeever L RSC 2 Bethnal Green
02.07.99 Mark McGowan L RSC 3 Bristol
(*Vacant British Masters Lightweight Title*)
13.09.99 Stephen Smith L DIS 2 Bethnal Green
05.10.99 John Humphrey L PTS 4 Bloomsbury
24.10.99 Young Muttley L RTD 1 Wolverhampton
02.12.99 Liam Maltby L PTS 4 Peterborough
19.02.00 Dariusz Snarski DREW 6 Prestwick
10.03.00 Ted Bami L PTS 4 Bethnal Green
17.04.00 Mark Hawthorne L PTS 4 Birmingham
25.07.00 P.J.Gallagher L PTS 6 Southwark
08.09.00 Dariusz Snarski W PTS 4 Hammersmith
27.11.00 Anthony Maynard L RSC 5 Birmingham
16.03.02 Wayne Wheeler DREW 6 Northampton
28.05.02 Ricky Eccleston L RSC 4 Liverpool
14.09.02 Danny Hunt L RSC 3 Bethnal Green
16.11.02 Gwyn Wale L PTS 4 Nottingham
01.02.03 Mark Winters L RSC 2 Belfast
29.10.03 Pete Buckley W PTS 6 Leicester Square
Career: 30 contests, won 8, drew 3, lost 19.

David Keir

Liverpool. *Born* Liverpool, 23 September, 1977
Welterweight. Ht. 5'9¹/₂"
Manager T. Gilmour

10.12.01 Lee Williamson DREW 4 Liverpool
11.02.02 Sammy Smith L PTS 6 Southampton
13.04.02 Lee Williamson W PTS 4 Liverpool
03.06.02 Paul McIlwaine W CO 2 Glasgow
23.09.02 Gary Porter L PTS 8 Glasgow
15.10.02 Costas Katsantonis W PTS 6 Bethnal Green
15.02.03 Matthew Hatton W RSC 4 Wembley
28.04.03 Darrell Grafton L DIS 5 Nottingham
31.05.03 Robert Burton L RSC 9 Barnsley
(*Central Area Welterweight Title Challenge*)
08.05.04 Michael Lomax L RTD 4 Dagenham
Career: 10 contests, won 4, drew 1, lost 5.

David Keir   Les Clark

Damaen Kelly

Belfast. *Born* Belfast, 3 April, 1973
Flyweight. Former Undefeated WBF & IBO Flyweight Champion. Former Undefeated European Flyweight Champion. Former Undefeated WBC International S.Flyweight Champion. Former British & Commonwealth Flyweight Champion. Ht. 5'5"
Manager Self

27.09.97 Chris Thomas W RSC 1 Belfast
22.11.97 Bojidar Ivanov W CO 1 Manchester
20.12.97 Anthony Hanna W PTS 4 Belfast
14.02.98 Hristo Lessov W RSC 2 Southwark
14.03.98 Mark Reynolds W RSC 4 Bethnal Green
02.05.98 Krasimir Tcholakov W RSC 3 Kensington
26.09.98 Mike Thomas W PTS 6 Uncasville, Connecticut, USA
12.12.98 Alfonso Zvenyika W PTS 12 Chester
(*Commonwealth Flyweight Title Challenge*)
13.03.99 Anthony Hanna W PTS 12 Manchester
(*Vacant British Flyweight Title*)

Commonwealth Flyweight Title Defence)

22.05.99 Keith Knox L RTD 6 Belfast
(British & Commonwealth Flyweight Title Defences)
16.10.99 Igor Gerasimov W RSC 4 Belfast
(Vacant WBC International S. Flyweight Title)
12.02.00 Alexander Mahmutov W PTS 12 Sheffield
(European Flyweight Title Challenge)
12.06.00 Jose Antonio Lopez Bueno W PTS 12 Belfast
(European Flyweight Title Defence)
30.09.00 Zolile Mbitye W PTS 12 Peterborough
(IBO Flyweight Title Defence)
17.02.01 Paulino Villabos W PTS 12 Bethnal Green
(IBO Flyweight Title Defence)
31.07.01 Sipho Mantyi W RSC 4 Bethnal Green
18.01.02 Simphewe Xabendini W RSC 1 Coventry
21.05.02 Celso Dangud W PTS 12 Custom House
(Vacant WBF Flyweight Title)
05.10.02 Jovy Oracion W PTS 8 Liverpool
27.09.03 Irene Pacheco L RSC 7 Barranquilla, Colombia,
(IBF Flyweight Title Challenge)
17.04.04 Andrei Kostin W RSC 1 Belfast
26.06.04 Delroy Spencer W RSC 4 Belfast
Career: 22 contests, won 20, lost 2.

Michael Kelly
Dundalk. *Born* Dundalk, 28 April, 1975
Lightweight. Ht. 5'8"
Manager B. Hearn

28.02.04 Carl Allen W PTS 4 Bridgend
17.04.04 Baz Carey W PTS 4 Belfast
26.06.04 Simon Wilson W PTS 4 Belfast
Career: 3 contests, won 3.

Colin Kenna   Les Clark

Colin Kenna
Southampton. *Born* Dublin, 28 July, 1976
Heavyweight. Ht. 6'1"
Manager J. Bishop

25.02.01 Slick Miller W RSC 3 Streatham
22.04.01 Eamonn Glennon W PTS 4 Streatham
15.10.01 Tony Booth W PTS 6 Southampton
11.02.02 Dave Clarke W RSC 4 Southampton
08.04.02 James Gilbert W RSC 1 Southampton
12.07.02 Gary Williams W RSC 3 Southampton
01.11.02 Paul Buttery DREW 6 Preston
17.03.03 Derek McCafferty W PTS 6 Southampton
12.05.03 Paul Bonson W PTS 6 Southampton
01.08.03 Michael Sprott L RSC 1 Bethnal Green
(Southern Area Heavyweight Title Challenge)
26.10.03 Darren Ashton W CO 1 Longford
20.02.04 Paul Bonson W PTS 6 Southampton
30.03.04 Chris Woollas W PTS 6 Southampton
12.05.04 Mark Krence L RTD 3 Reading
Career: 14 contests, won 11, drew 1, lost 2.

Ryan Kerr
Bannockburn. *Born* Falkirk, 19 March, 1982
Northern Area S.Middleweight Champion. Ht. 5'9"
Manager T. Conroy

17.09.01 Pedro Thompson W RSC 1 Glasgow
04.10.01 Colin McCash W PTS 6 Sunderland
03.11.01 Tomas da Silva W PTS 4 Glasgow
21.02.02 Wayne Shepherd W PTS 6 Sunderland
03.10.02 Steve Timms W RSC 1 Sunderland
05.12.02 Martin Thompson W RSC 4 Sunderland
27.02.03 Surinder Sekhon W PTS 6 Sunderland
17.03.03 Lee Molloy W PTS 8 Glasgow
02.10.03 Eddie Haley W PTS 8 Sunderland
26.02.04 Eddie Haley W RSC 5 Sunderland
(Vacant Northern Area S.Middleweight Title)
Career: 10 contests, won 10.

Jawaid Khaliq (Akhtar)
Nottingham. *Born* Reading, 30 July, 1970
IBO Welterweight Champion. Former Undefeated Commonwealth & Midlands Area Welterweight Champion. Former Undefeated Midlands Area & WBF European L. Middleweight Champion. Ht. 5'10½"
Manager T. Gilmour/C. Aston

18.08.97 Richard Inquieti W RSC 5 Nottingham
13.09.97 Martin Holgate W RSC 6 Millwall
13.12.97 Mark Ramsey DREW 4 Sheffield
07.02.98 Takaloo W RSC 4 Cheshunt
07.03.98 Koba Kulu W PTS 4 Reading
05.09.98 Harry Butler W PTS 4 Telford
03.12.98 Frederic Klose L PTS 8 Epernay, France
27.09.99 Lee Murtagh W RSC 5 Leeds
(Vacant WBF European L. Middleweight Title)
14.12.99 Dirk Kaltenbach W CO 2 Telde, Gran Canaria
15.01.00 Lee Bird W RSC 4 Doncaster
27.02.00 Jason Collins W PTS 6 Leeds
21.05.00 Dennis Berry W RSC 6 Derby
(Vacant Midlands Area L. Middleweight Title)

13.08.00 Ernie Smith W RSC 4 Nottingham
(Vacant Midlands Area Welterweight Title)
28.10.00 Trevor Smith W RSC 1 Coventry
27.11.00 Sean Sullivan W PTS 12 Birmingham
(Vacant Commonwealth Welterweight Title)
26.02.01 Howard Clarke W PTS 6 Nottingham
11.06.01 Willy Wise W PTS 12 Nottingham
(IBO Welterweight Title Challenge)
15.09.01 Jacek Bielski W CO 5 Nottingham
(IBO Welterweight Title Defence)
03.11.01 Luther Smith W RSC 3 Glasgow
23.02.02 Maxim Nesterenko W RSC 12 Nottingham
(IBO Welterweight Title Defence)
27.07.02 Jose Rosa W PTS 12 Nottingham
(IBO Welterweight Title Defence)
16.11.02 Roman Dzuman W PTS 12 Nottingham
(IBO Welterweight Title Defence)
01.03.03 Jan Bergman W RSC 7 Carnival City, South Africa
(IBO Welterweight Title Defence)
20.09.03 Maxim Nesterenko W PTS 12 Nottingham
(IBO Welterweight Title Defence)
14.02.04 Ener Julio W PTS 12 Nottingham
(IBO Welterweight Title Defence)
Career: 25 contests, won 23, drew 1, lost 1.

Amer Khan
Sheffield. *Born* Sheffield, 21 February, 1981
L. Heavyweight. Ht. 6'2"
Manager B. Ingle

06.06.03 Gary Jones W PTS 6 Hull
31.07.03 Michael Pinnock W PTS 6 Sheffield
05.09.03 Shpetim Hoti W RTD 4 Sheffield
04.12.03 Terry Morrill W PTS 6 Sunderland
06.02.04 Terry Morrill W PTS 6 Sheffield
03.04.04 Michael Pinnock W PTS 6 Sheffield
17.06.04 Hastings Rasani W PTS 6 Sheffield
Career: 7 contests, won 7.

Amer Khan   Les Clark

Nathan King

Mountain Ash. *Born* Aberdare, 19 March, 1981
L. Heavyweight. Ht. 6'3"
Manager B. Coleman

27.01.01	Tony Oakey L PTS 6 Bethnal Green
28.04.01	Pinky Burton W PTS 4 Cardiff
09.06.01	Michael Pinnock W PTS 4 Bethnal Green
09.10.01	Darren Ashton W PTS 6 Cardiff
24.11.01	Peter Haymer W PTS 4 Bethnal Green
12.02.02	Peter Haymer W PTS 4 Bethnal Green
20.04.02	Radcliffe Green W PTS 6 Cardiff
17.08.02	Valery Odin L PTS 6 Cardiff
14.12.02	Paul Bonson L PTS 4 Newcastle
10.04.03	Ovill McKenzie L PTS 4 Clydach
28.06.03	Varuzhan Davtyan W PTS 4 Cardiff
21.02.04	Daniel Sackey L PTS 4 Cardiff
12.03.04	Elvis Michailenko L PTS 6 Millwall

Career: 13 contests, won 7, lost 6.

Nathan King   Les Clark

Paul King

Sheffield. *Born* Sheffield, 9 August, 1974
Heavyweight. Ht. 6'3"
Manager G. Rhodes

10.02.04	Billy Wilson L PTS 6 Barnsley
28.02.04	David Ingleby W RSC 3 Manchester
12.03.04	Micky Steeds L PTS 6 Millwall
03.04.04	Carl Baker W PTS 6 Sheffield
10.04.04	Albert Sosnowski L PTS 4 Manchester
02.06.04	Scott Gammer L RSC 3 Hereford

Career: 6 contests, won 2, lost 4.

David Kirk

Sutton in Ashfield. *Born* Mansfield, 5 October, 1974
Welterweight. Former Undefeated WBF European Welterweight Champion. Ht. 5'8"
Manager Self

01.11.96	Arv Mittoo W PTS 6 Mansfield
04.12.96	Stuart Rimmer W PTS 6 Stoke
20.02.97	Chris Price W PTS 6 Mansfield
16.03.97	Gary Hibbert L PTS 6 Shaw
25.03.97	Miguel Matthews W PTS 6 Wolverhampton
28.04.97	Mark Breslin L PTS 8 Glasgow
06.10.97	Christian Brady L PTS 6 Birmingham
30.10.97	Trevor Tacy L PTS 6 Newark
08.12.97	Nick Hall L PTS 6 Nottingham
12.01.98	Juha Temonen DREW 6 Helsinki, Finland
24.01.98	Jason Cook L RSC 3 Cardiff
24.02.98	Roy Rutherford L PTS 6 Edgbaston
11.03.98	Patrick Gallagher L PTS 6 Bethnal Green
27.04.98	Tommy Peacock L PTS 6 Manchester
08.05.98	Chris Barnett L PTS 6 Manchester
23.05.98	Graham Earl L PTS 4 Bethnal Green
04.06.98	Mark Richards L PTS 6 Dudley
21.09.98	Steve McLevy L PTS 8 Glasgow
12.10.98	Malcolm Melvin L PTS 10 Birmingham
	(Midlands Area L. Welterweight Title Challenge)
31.10.98	Bernard Paul L PTS 6 Southend
28.11.98	Glenn McClarnon L PTS 4 Belfast
11.12.98	Charlie Kane L PTS 8 Prestwick
20.02.99	Dennis Berry L PTS 10 Thornaby
	(Vacant Continental European Welterweight Title)
09.05.99	Sammy Smith L PTS 6 Bracknell
20.05.99	Steve Brumant W PTS 4 Kensington
05.06.99	Neil Sinclair L PTS 8 Cardiff
11.09.99	Glenn McClarnon L PTS 6 Sheffield
20.10.99	Dave Gibson W PTS 6 Stoke
18.11.99	Adrian Chase W PTS 10 Mayfair
	(Vacant WBF European Welterweight Title)
26.11.99	Gerard Murphy L RTD 3 Hull
25.03.00	Jacek Bielski L PTS 6 Liverpool
29.04.00	Eamonn Magee L RSC 8 Wembley
13.08.00	Ram Singh W PTS 6 Nottingham
09.09.00	Mally McIver L PTS 6 Newark
23.09.00	Steve Murray L PTS 4 Bethnal Green
09.10.00	Steve Saville W PTS 8 Birmingham
19.11.00	Gavin Down L PTS 10 Chesterfield
	(Vacant British Masters L.Welterweight Title)
01.12.00	Alan Bosworth DREW 8 Peterborough
04.02.01	Mark Winters L PTS 6 Queensferry
28.02.01	Ossie Duran L PTS 8 Kensington
	(Vacant WBF European Welterweight Title)
10.03.01	Junior Witter L RSC 2 Bethnal Green
10.04.01	Colin Lynes L PTS 6 Wembley
20.04.01	Mark Winters L PTS 6 Dublin
16.06.01	Oscar Hall L PTS 6 Derby
07.07.01	Michael Jennings L PTS 6 Manchester
28.07.01	Jonathan Thaxton L PTS 4 Wembley
13.09.01	David Walker DREW 8 Sheffield
17.11.01	Kevin McIntyre L PTS 4 Glasgow
24.11.01	Ivan Kirpa L PTS 4 Bethnal Green
08.12.01	Chris Saunders L CO 2 Chesterfield
26.01.02	Colin Lynes L PTS 6 Dagenham
09.02.02	David Barnes L RTD 1 Manchester
11.03.02	Matthew Macklin L PTS 4 Glasgow
25.05.02	Francis Barrett L PTS 6 Portsmouth
08.06.02	Kevin McIntyre L RTD 4 Renfrew
28.09.02	Matthew Hatton W PTS 6 Manchester
22.03.03	Kevin McIntyre L RSC 1 Renfrew
24.05.03	Nigel Wright L PTS 4 Bethnal Green
31.05.03	Sammy Smith L PTS 4 Bethnal Green
08.06.03	Adnan Amar L PTS 6 Nottingham
04.10.03	Francis Barrett L PTS 6 Muswell Hill
10.04.04	Albert Sosnowski L PTS 4 Manchester
07.05.04	Gary Woolcombe L PTS 4 Bethnal Green
19.06.04	Gary Young L PTS 4 Renfrew

Career: 64 contests, won 10, drew 3, lost 51.

Mark Krence

Chesterfield. *Born* Chesterfield, 24 August, 1976
Midlands Area Heavyweight Champion. Ht. 6'5"
Manager D. Hobson

09.04.00	Slick Miller W PTS 6 Alfreton
21.10.00	Neil Kirkwood W PTS 6 Sheffield
11.12.00	Tony Booth W PTS 6 Sheffield
20.01.01	Nigel Rafferty W PTS 4 Bethnal Green
24.03.01	Mark Williams W PTS 4 Sheffield
27.07.01	Shane Woollas W PTS 4 Sheffield
13.09.01	Luke Simpkin W PTS 4 Sheffield
25.09.01	Darren Chubbs W PTS 4 Liverpool
15.12.01	Eamonn Glennon W RSC 2 Sheffield
16.03.02	Neil Kirkwood W RSC 4 Bethnal Green
11.05.02	Gary Williams W PTS 6 Chesterfield
21.05.02	Audley Harrison L PTS 6 Custom House
03.08.02	Tony Booth W PTS 4 Derby
05.10.02	Gary Williams W RSC 4 Chesterfield
24.01.03	Petr Horacek W RSC 4 Sheffield
18.03.03	Paul Bonson W PTS 4 Reading
10.06.03	Luke Simpkin W RTD 8 Sheffield
	(Vacant Midlands Area Heavyweight Title)
01.08.03	Derek McCafferty W PTS 4 Bethnal Green
05.09.03	Collice Mutizwa W CO 2 Sheffield
06.02.04	Mendauga Kulikauskas W PTS 8 Sheffield
12.05.04	Colin Kenna W RTD 3 Reading

Career: 21 contests, won 20, lost 1.

Mark Krence   Les Clark

Kristian Laight

Nuneaton. *Born* Nuneaton, 15 June, 1980
Lightweight. Ht. 5'10"
Manager J. Gill

26.09.03	James Paisley L PTS 6 Millwall
14.11.03	Matt Teague L PTS 6 Hull
05.12.03	Justin Hicks L PTS 6 Bristol
07.02.04	Kevin Mitchell L PTS 4 Bethnal Green
30.03.04	Chris McDonagh L PTS 6 Southampton
08.04.04	Jaz Virdee W PTS 6 Peterborough
20.04.04	Femi Fehintola L PTS 6 Sheffield
04.06.04	Gary Coombes DREW 6 Dudley
19.06.04	Ryan Barrett L PTS 4 Muswell Hill

Career: 9 contests, won 1, drew 1, lost 7.

Kristian Laight Les Clark

Danny Lannigan

Hattersley. *Born* Ashton under Lyne, 27
March, 1983
S. Featherweight. Ht. 5'9"
Manager S. Wood/T. Gilmour

26.06.04 Willie Valentine L PTS 4 Belfast
Career: 1 contest, lost 1.

Scott Lansdowne

Leicester. *Born* Leicester, 11 August, 1972
Midlands Area Cruiserweight Champion.
Former Undefeated WBF European
S.Cruiserweight Champion. Ht. 5'10"
Manager D. Coldwell

15.12.98	Gary Williams W PTS 6 Sheffield
11.09.99	Luke Simpkin W PTS 4 Sheffield
09.12.99	Geoff Hunter W PTS 6 Sheffield
20.05.00	Gary Williams W RSC 1 Leicester
	(Vacant WBF European S. Cruiserweight Title)
21.10.00	Adam Cale W RSC 5 Sheffield
29.01.01	Nigel Rafferty W PTS 4 Peterborough
28.04.02	Tony Booth L RSC 4 Southwark
23.06.02	Paul Bonson L PTS 4 Southwark
30.11.02	Tony Dowling W RSC 2 Newark

(Vacant Midlands Area Cruiserweight Title)
16.03.03	Michael Pinnock W PTS 6 Nottingham
12.10.03	Clint Johnson W PTS 4 Sheffield
11.12.03	Steven Spartacus L RSC 3 Bethnal Green
	(Vacant English L.Heavyweight Title)

Career: 12 contests, won 9, lost 3.

Scott Lansdowne Les Clark

Gareth Lawrence

Sidcup. *Born* Barking, 21 August, 1980
S. Middleweight. Ht. 6'2"
Manager M. Roe

01.05.04 Paul Buchanan L PTS 4 Gravesend
Career: 1 contest, lost 1.

Scott Lawton Les Clark

Scott Lawton

Stoke. *Born* Stoke, 23 September, 1976
Midlands Area Lightweight Champion.
Ht. 5'10"
Manager Self

29.09.01	Dave Hinds W RSC 2 Southwark
08.12.01	Ilias Miah W PTS 4 Dagenham

26.01.02	Pete Buckley W PTS 4 Bethnal Green
26.04.02	Pete Buckley W PTS 4 Coventry
06.09.02	Ben Hudson W PTS 4 Bethnal Green
30.01.03	Dave Stewart L PTS 6 Piccadilly
26.04.03	Chris McDonagh W RSC 2 Brentford
13.06.03	Jason Nesbitt W PTS 6 Queensway
14.11.03	Jimmy Beech W RSC 5 Bethnal Green
20.04.04	Henry Jones W PTS 6 Sheffield
17.06.04	Carl Allen W PTS 10 Sheffield
	(Vacant Midlands Area Lightweight Title)

Career: 11 contests, won 10, lost 1.

Barrie Lee

Arbroath. *Born* Arbroath, 29 March, 1982
L. Middleweight. Ht. 5'8"
Manager A. Morrison

25.10.03	Dave Wakefield W PTS 4 Edinburgh
29.11.03	Brian Coleman W PTS 4 Renfrew
27.03.04	Arv Mittoo W PTS 4 Edinburgh
23.04.04	William Webster W PTS 6 Glasgow
28.05.04	Brian Coleman W PTS 6 Glasgow
19.06.04	Craig Lynch W PTS 6 Renfrew

Career: 6 contests, won 6.

Marcus Lee (Marriott)

Bethnal Green. *Born* London, 13 April,
1972
Cruiserweight. Ht. 6'2"
Manager T. Sims

05.03.03	Paul Bonson L PTS 4 Bethnal Green
03.06.03	Scott Baker W RSC 3 Bethnal Green
26.07.03	Simon Goodwin W PTS 4 Plymouth
11.12.03	Coleman Barrett L PTS 4 Bethnal Green

Career: 4 contests, won 2, lost 2.

Marcus Lee Les Clark

Willie Limond

Glasgow. *Born* Glasgow, 2 February, 1979
European Union S.Featherweight
Champion. Ht. 5'7"
Manager K. Morrison

12.11.99	Lennie Hodgkins W RTD 1 Glasgow
13.12.99	Steve Hanley W PTS 6 Glasgow
24.02.00	Nigel Senior W RSC 6 Glasgow
18.03.00	Phil Lashley W RSC 1 Glasgow
07.04.00	Jimmy Beech W RSC 2 Glasgow

26.05.00	Billy Smith W PTS 4 Glasgow	
24.06.00	Haroon Din W PTS 4 Glasgow	
10.11.00	Danny Connelly W PTS 6 Glasgow	
17.12.00	Billy Smith W PTS 6 Glasgow	
15.02.01	Marcus Portman W PTS 6 Glasgow	
03.04.01	Trevor Smith W PTS 4 Bethnal Green	
27.04.01	Choi Tseveenpurev W PTS 6 Glasgow	
07.09.01	Gary Reid W PTS 8 Glasgow	
03.11.01	Rakhim Mingaleev W PTS 6 Glasgow	
17.11.01	Keith Jones W PTS 4 Glasgow	
11.03.02	Dave Hinds W PTS 6 Glasgow	
06.09.02	Assen Vassilev W RSC 3 Glasgow	
22.03.03	Jimmy Beech W CO 4 Renfrew	
12.07.03	Alex Arthur L RSC 8 Renfrew	

(British S.Featherweight Title Challenge)

01.11.03	Dariusz Snarski W RSC 1 Glasgow	
29.11.03	Anthony Hanna W PTS 4 Renfrew	
06.03.04	Dafydd Carlin W RSC 1 Renfrew	
19.06.04	Youssouf Djibaba W PTS 10 Renfrew	

(Vacant European Union S.Featherweight Title)

Career: 23 contests, won 22, lost 1.

Willie Limond   Les Clark

Earl Ling
Ipswich. *Born* Kings Lynn, 9 March, 1972
Cruiserweight. Ht. 5'10"
Manager Self

08.09.92	Eddie Collins W PTS 6 Norwich
11.05.93	Mark Hale L RSC 2 Norwich
12.12.94	Clinton Woods L RSC 5 Cleethorpes
04.12.95	Jeff Finlayson L PTS 6 Manchester
26.02.96	Peter Waudby L PTS 6 Hull
19.03.96	James Lowther L RSC 4 Leeds
16.05.98	Dean Ashton DREW 6 Chigwell
02.07.98	Dean Ashton L RSC 2 Ipswich
17.09.98	Jimmy Steel DREW 6 Brighton
19.01.99	Israel Khumalo L RSC 1 Ipswich
15.07.00	Mike Duffield W PTS 6 Norwich
04.11.00	Andrew Facey L PTS 6 Derby
16.06.01	Andrew Facey DREW 6 Derby
04.07.01	Calvin Stonestreet L PTS 4 Bloomsbury
13.04.02	Simeon Cover W CO 4 Norwich
25.04.02	Lee Whitehead W PTS 6 Hull
21.11.02	Michael Pinnock W PTS 6 Hull
12.04.03	Ryan Walls L RSC 4 Norwich
07.12.03	Nate Joseph DREW 6 Bradford
21.02.04	Hastings Rasani DREW 6 Norwich

Career: 20 contests, won 5, drew 5, lost 10.

Wayne Llewelyn
Beckenham. *Born* Greenwich, 20 April, 1970
Heavyweight. Ht. 6'3½"
Manager Self

18.01.92	Chris Coughlan W RSC 3 Kensington
30.03.92	Steve Stewart W RSC 4 Eltham
23.04.92	Gary Charlton W RSC 6 Eltham
10.12.92	Gary McCrory W RSC 2 Glasgow
23.05.93	Cordwell Hylton W PTS 6 Brockley
01.12.93	Manny Burgo W PTS 6 Bethnal Green
14.04.94	Vance Idiens W RSC 1 Battersea
22.05.94	Cordwell Hylton W CO 2 Crystal Palace
03.05.95	Mitch Rose W PTS 4 NYC, New York, USA
07.07.95	Vance Idiens W RSC 1 Cardiff
11.08.95	Carlos Monroe W RSC 3 New Orleans, Louisiana, USA
26.04.96	Steve Garber W CO 1 Cardiff
08.06.96	Dermot Gascoyne W RSC 4 Newcastle
22.03.97	Mike Sedillo W CO 2 Wythenshawe
20.09.97	Michael Murray W RTD 4 Aachen, Germany
21.03.98	Everton Davis W PTS 8 Bethnal Green
06.06.98	Pele Reid L CO 1 Liverpool

(Elim. British Heavyweight Title)

18.02.99	Derek Williams W RSC 3 Bossier City, Louisiana, USA
03.06.99	Frankie Swindell L CO 2 Mount Pleasant, Michigan, USA
21.08.99	Terry Veners W RSC 3 Coachella, California, USA
28.11.99	Terry Veners W CO 2 Monterey, California, USA
10.03.00	William Barima W CO 1 Bethnal Green
19.03.00	Augustin Corpus L PTS 8 Tunica, Mississippi, USA
14.10.00	Michael Sprott W RSC 3 Wembley
08.12.00	Alex Vasiliev L RSC 1 Crystal Palace
01.04.01	Luke Simpkin W PTS 6 Southwark
19.01.02	Andreas Simon W CO 1 Berlin, Germany
22.03.02	Ladislav Husarik W PTS 6 Berlin, Germany
07.09.02	Vladislav Druso W PTS 6 Munich, Germany
15.04.04	Jameel McCline L RSC 1 NYC, New York, USA

Career: 30 contests, won 25, lost 5.

Dean Lloyd
Bedworth. *Born* Nuneaton, 25 May, 1974
L. Middleweight. Ht. 5'10"
Manager J. Weaver

13.09.03	Pedro Thompson L RSC 3 Coventry
09.04.04	Mark Wall L PTS 6 Rugby

Career: 2 contests, lost 2.

Robert Lloyd-Taylor (Lloyd)
Hayes. *Born* Perivale, 1 September, 1980
Welterweight. Ht. 5'11¼"
Manager G. Taylor

27.09.02	Wayne Wheeler W PTS 6 Bracknell
25.10.02	Nicky Leech L PTS 6 Cotgrave
20.12.02	Dean Larter W PTS 4 Bracknell
26.04.03	Ben Hudson L PTS 4 Brentford
31.05.03	Aidan Mooney W PTS 4 Bethnal Green
26.10.03	Arv Mittoo W PTS 6 Longford
14.11.03	Michael Lomax L PTS 6 Bethnal Green

07.04.04	Joe Mitchell W RSC 5 Leicester Square
07.05.04	Chas Symonds L RTD 5 Bethnal Green

Career: 9 contests, won 5, lost 4.

Gary Lockett
Cwmbran. *Born* Pontypool, 25 November, 1976
Middleweight. Former WBO Inter-Continental L. Middleweight Champion.
Ht. 5'10"
Manager Self

06.09.96	Ernie Loveridge W PTS 4 Liverpool
26.10.96	Charlie Paine W RSC 4 Liverpool
24.10.98	Lee Bird W RSC 2 Liverpool
27.02.99	Carl Smith W RSC 2 Bethnal Green
15.05.99	Mike Whittaker W RSC 2 Blackpool
19.06.99	Kid Halls W CO 1 Dublin
09.03.00	Kevin Thompson W CO 2 Liverpool
04.11.00	David Baptiste W PTS 4 Bethnal Green
23.01.01	Abdul Mehdi W RSC 2 Crawley
03.03.01	Hussain Osman W CO 2 Wembley
07.04.01	Howard Clarke W RSC 2 Wembley
08.05.01	Mike Algoet W PTS 6 Barnsley
14.07.01	Howard Clarke W CO 1 Wembley
25.09.01	Denny Dalton W RSC 1 Liverpool
24.11.01	Chris Nembhard W RSC 2 Bethnal Green
09.02.02	Kevin Kelly W CO 4 Manchester

(Vacant WBO Inter-Continental L.Middleweight Title)

20.04.02	Youri Tsarenko L PTS 12 Cardiff

(WBO Inter-Continental L.Middleweight Title Defence)

23.11.02	Viktor Fesetchko W PTS 8 Derby
29.03.03	Jason Collins W CO 1 Portsmouth
08.05.03	Yuri Tsarenko W PTS 10 Widnes
28.06.03	Michael Monaghan W PTS 10 Cardiff
21.02.04	Kreshnik Qato W RSC 2 Cardiff
12.06.04	Matt Galer W RSC 4 Manchester

Career: 23 contests, won 22, lost 1.

Gary Logan
Croydon. *Born* Lambeth, 10 October, 1968
L. Middleweight. Former Southern Area Middleweight Champion. Former Undefeated Southern Area Welterweight Champion. Ht. 5'8¾"
Manager Self

05.10.88	Peppy Muire W RTD 3 Wembley
02.11.88	Tony Gibbs W PTS 6 Southwark
07.12.88	Pat Dunne W PTS 6 Piccadilly
12.01.89	Mike Russell W CO 1 Southwark
20.02.89	Dave Griffiths W RSC 5 Mayfair
29.03.89	Ronnie Campbell W PTS 6 Wembley
10.05.89	Tony Britland W CO 1 Kensington
07.06.89	Davey Hughes W CO 1 Wembley
24.08.89	Mike English W CO 2 Tampa, Florida, USA
04.10.89	Simon Eubank W PTS 6 Kensington
12.10.89	Jimmy Thornton W PTS 6 Southwark
08.11.89	Chris Blake L PTS 8 Wembley
10.01.90	Julian Eavis W PTS 8 Kensington
03.03.90	Anthony Joe Travis W CO 5 Wembley
09.05.90	Joseph Alexander W PTS 8 Wembley
13.09.90	Manuel Rojas W PTS 8 Watford
16.01.91	Julian Eavis W RSC 5 Kensington
18.02.91	Gordon Blair W CO 1 Mayfair
25.04.91	Trevor Ambrose W PTS 8 Mayfair
17.10.91	Des Robinson W PTS 8 Southwark
15.10.92	Mick Duncan W PTS 8 Lewisham

17.12.92   Roy Rowland W RSC 4 Wembley
(Vacant Southern Area Welterweight Title)
23.05.93   Glyn Rhodes W CO 3 Brockley
25.06.93   Gordon Blair W RSC 6 Battersea
14.08.93   Paul King W CO 2 Hammersmith
28.11.93   Paul King W CO 4 Southwark
11.12.93   Horace Fleary W PTS 8 Dusseldorf, Germany
09.02.94   Graham Cheney L RSC 10 Bethnal Green
(WBC International Welterweight Title Challenge)
29.09.94   Ojay Abrahams W PTS 10 Bethnal Green
(Southern Area Welterweight Title Defence)
25.10.94   Nick Hall DREW 8 Southwark
02.06.95   Del Bryan L RSC 11 Bethnal Green
(British Welterweight Title Challenge)
21.03.96   Paul Wesley W PTS 6 Southwark
13.04.96   Ensley Bingham L RSC 6 Wythenshawe
(British L. Middleweight Title Challenge)
01.04.01   Adrian Kirkbride W RSC 1 Southwark
03.06.01   Spencer Fearon W RSC 2 Southwark
(Vacant Southern Area Middleweight Title)
28.07.01   Ojay Abrahams W RSC 4 Wembley
28.10.01   Hussain Osman L PTS 10 Southwark
(Southern Area Middleweight Title Defence)
04.05.02   Takaloo L RSC 10 Bethnal Green
(WBU L.Middleweight Title Challenge)
20.07.02   Hussain Osman L PTS 12 Bethnal Green
(Vacant WBO Inter-Continental Middleweight Title)
08.12.02   Wayne Asker W PTS 6 Bethnal Green
18.02.03   Matthew Tait W PTS 8 Bethnal Green
18.10.03   Jamie Moore L CO 5 Manchester
(British & Commonwealth L.Middleweight Title Challenges)
Career: 42 contests, won 33, drew 1, lost 8.

Gary Logan   Philip Sharkey

Michael Lomax

Chingford. *Born* London, 25 September, 1978
Welterweight. Ht. 6'0"
Manager M. Brennan

05.07.03   Ernie Smith W PTS 4 Brentwood
20.09.03   Peter Dunn W PTS 4 Nottingham
14.11.03   Robert Lloyd-Taylor W PTS 6 Bethnal Green
16.01.04   Craig Lynch W PTS 6 Bradford
31.01.04   Steve Brumant W PTS 6 Bethnal Green
08.05.04   David Keir W RTD 4 Dagenham
Career: 6 contests, won 6.

Michael Lomax   Les Clark

Paul Lomax

Sunderland. *Born* Sunderland, 11 May, 1974
Middleweight. Ht. 6'0½"
Manager T. Callighan

23.07.00   Reece McAllister L PTS 6 Hartlepool
10.06.01   Tony Byrne L PTS 6 Ellesmere Port
17.11.01   Oscar Hall L PTS 4 Dewsbury
09.12.01   Tony Byrne L PTS 6 Blackpool
15.03.02   Andrei Ivanov W PTS 6 Spennymoor
29.04.02   Martyn Bailey DREW 6 Bradford
28.05.02   James Davenport W CO 3 Liverpool
07.05.03   Martyn Bailey L RTD 3 Ellesmere Port
(British Masters Middleweight Title Challenge)
12.10.03   Dean Walker L PTS 6 Sheffield
10.02.04   Robert Burton L PTS 6 Barnsley
Career: 10 contests, won 2, drew 1, lost 7.

Chris Long

Calne. *Born* Gloucester, 5 March, 1980
L. Welterweight. Ht. 5'9"
Manager T. Woodward

15.05.03   Darren Goode W RSC 1 Clevedon
21.09.03   Daniel Thorpe L PTS 6 Bristol
17.11.03   Stuart Green L PTS 6 Glasgow
13.02.04   Justin Hicks W RSC 4 Bristol
29.02.04   Gareth Perkins L PTS 6 Bristol
12.03.04   Ivor Bonavic W PTS 6 Millwall
01.05.04   Stuart Phillips W RSC 1 Bridgend
19.06.04   Ceri Hall L PTS 4 Muswell Hill
Career: 8 contests, won 4, lost 4.

Chris Long   Les Clark

Keith Long

Brixton. *Born* Greenwich, 30 July, 1968
Heavyweight. Ht. 5'11½"
Manager D. Williams/F. Warren

15.02.97   Steve Cranston W PTS 4 Tooting
04.02.99   Gordon Minors W PTS 6 Lewisham
24.04.99   Derek McCafferty L PTS 4 Peterborough
07.08.99   Israel Ajose DREW 6 Dagenham
29.11.99   Mark Potter W PTS 8 Wembley
13.04.00   Harry Senior W PTS 10 Holborn
18.11.00   Luke Simpkin W RSC 3 Dagenham
13.09.01   Mike Holden W PTS 10 Sheffield
(Elim.British Heavyweight Title)
08.07.02   Alexei Varakin W RSC 4 Mayfair
17.09.02   Danny Williams L PTS 12 Bethnal Green
(British & Commonwealth Heavyweight Title Challenges)
15.02.03   Slick Miller W RSC 1 Wembley
24.01.04   Denis Bakhtov L PTS 12 Wembley
(WBC International Heavyweight Title Challenge)
Career: 12 contests, won 8, drew 1, lost 3.

Gerard Longdon

Gospel Oak. *Born* London, 16 December, 1980
L. Heavyweight. Ht. 6'0"
Manager F. Maloney

25.06.04   Dave Pearson W PTS 4 Bethnal Green
Career: 1 contest, won 1.

Andrew Lowe

Hackney. *Born* Hackney, 23 June, 1974
Southern Area L. Heavyweight Champion.
Ht. 5'10"
Manager Self

19.05.01	Rob Stevenson W PTS 4 Wembley	
16.06.01	William Webster W RSC 2 Dagenham	
20.10.01	Tom Cannon W PTS 4 Glasgow	
24.11.01	Paul Wesley W PTS 4 Bethnal Green	
15.12.01	Mark Snipe W PTS 4 Chigwell	
12.02.02	Ali Forbes W PTS 4 Bethnal Green	
04.05.02	Radcliffe Green W PTS 4 Bethnal Green	
12.10.02	Paul Bonson W PTS 4 Bethnal Green	
08.02.03	Clint Johnson W PTS 6 Brentford	
29.03.03	Radcliffe Green W PTS 10 Wembley	

(Vacant Southern Area L.Heavyweight Title)

31.05.03	Neil Linford W PTS 10 Bethnal Green	

(Elim. British L. Heavyweight Title)

07.11.03	Radcliffe Green W PTS 6 Sheffield	
20.03.04	Varuzhan Davtyan W PTS 6 Wembley	
12.05.04	Peter Oboh L RTD 10 Reading	

(British & Commonwealth L.Heavyweight Title Challenges)

Career: 14 contests, won 13, lost 1.

Freddie Luke

West Kingsdown. *Born* Dartford, 2
February, 1977
L. Welterweight. Ht. 5'7"
Manager M. Roe

01.05.04 Wayne Wheeler W RSC 1 Gravesend
Career: 1 contest, won 1.

Craig Lynch

Edinburgh. *Born* Edinburgh, 22 July, 1974
L. Middleweight. Ht. 6'1"
Manager A. Bowers

13.05.95	James Clamp DREW 6 Glasgow	
08.06.95	Gary Silvester W RSC 3 Glasgow	
15.09.95	Adam Baldwin W PTS 6 Glasgow	
25.11.95	Jim Rock L PTS 4 Dublin	
02.03.96	Hughie Davey L PTS 4 Newcastle	
08.06.96	Hughie Davey L PTS 4 Newcastle	
24.10.96	Pat Wright L PTS 6 Wembley	
21.02.02	Gary Firby W RSC 3 Sunderland	
26.04.02	Kevin McIntyre L PTS 10 Glasgow	

(Vacant Scottish Welterweight Title)

25.10.02	Joel Ani W PTS 6 Millwall	
23.11.02	Bradley Pryce L CO 4 Derby	
16.01.04	Michael Lomax L PTS 6 Bradford	
30.01.04	Gilbert Eastman L PTS 6 Dagenham	
21.02.04	Taz Jones L PTS 4 Cardiff	
03.04.04	Thomas McDonagh L PTS 6 Manchester	
06.05.04	Matthew Hall L PTS 6 Barnsley	
19.06.04	Barrie Lee L PTS 6 Renfrew	

Career: 17 contests, won 4, drew 1, lost 12.

Colin Lynes

Hornchurch. *Born* Whitechapel, 26
November, 1977
IBO L.Welterweight Champion. Former
IBO Inter-Continental L.Welterweight
Champion. Ht. 5'7¹/₂"
Manager Self

04.06.98	Les Frost W CO 1 Barking	
23.07.98	Ram Singh W CO 1 Barking	
22.10.98	Brian Coleman W RSC 2 Barking	
31.10.98	Marc Smith W PTS 4 Basingstoke	
10.12.98	Trevor Smith W RSC 1 Barking	
25.02.99	Dennis Griffin W PTS 6 Kentish Town	
20.05.99	Mark Haslam W PTS 4 Barking	
18.05.00	Jason Vlasman W RSC 2 Bethnal Green	
16.09.00	Karl Taylor W PTS 6 Bethnal Green	
14.10.00	Brian Coleman W PTS 6 Wembley	
09.12.00	Jimmy Phelan W PTS 6 Southwark	
17.02.01	Mark Ramsey W PTS 6 Bethnal Green	
10.04.01	David Kirk W PTS 6 Wembley	
10.11.01	Keith Jones W PTS 6 Wembley	
01.12.01	Leonti Voronchuk W PTS 6 Bethnal Green	
26.01.02	David Kirk W PTS 6 Dagenham	
23.03.02	Peter Dunn W PTS 4 Southwark	
18.05.02	Kevin Bennett W RSC 4 Millwall	
29.06.02	Ian Smith W RSC 7 Brentwood	
21.09.02	Abdelilah Touil W CO 7 Brentwood	
07.12.02	Richard Kiley W RSC 9 Brentwood	

(Vacant IBO Inter-Continental L.Welterweight Title)

08.03.03	Samuel Malinga L RTD 8 Bethnal Green	

(IBO Inter-Continental L.Welterweight Title Defence)

18.10.03	Brian Coleman W PTS 4 Manchester	
22.11.03	Fabrice Colombel W PTS 6 Belfast	
31.01.04	Cesar Levia W PTS 8 Bethnal Green	
08.05.04	Pablo Sarmiento W PTS 12 Dagenham	

(IBO L.Welterweight Title Challenge)

Career: 26 contests, won 25, lost 1.

Colin Lynes   Les Clark

M

Lee McAllister

Aberdeen. *Born* Aberdeen, 5 October, 1982
L.Welterweight. Former Undefeated British
Masters L.Welterweight Champion.
Ht. 5'9"
Manager B. Ingle/F. Warren

19.10.02 Baz Carey W PTS 4 Renfrew
17.11.02 Arv Mittoo W PTS 6 Bradford
23.02.03 Lee Williamson W PTS 6 Shrewsbury
13.04.03 Ernie Smith W PTS 4 Bradford
12.05.03 Ernie Smith W PTS 6 Birmingham
15.06.03 Brian Coleman W PTS 6 Bradford
11.07.03 John-Paul Ryan W RTD 2 Darlington
17.07.03 Dean Hickman L PTS 6 Walsall
03.08.03 Brian Coleman W PTS 4 Stalybridge
06.09.03 Jeff Thomas W PTS 10 Aberdeen
*(Vacant British Masters
L.Welterweight Title)*
28.11.03 Ernie Smith W PTS 6 Hull
30.01.04 Karl Taylor W PTS 4 Dagenham
08.03.04 Lee Williamson W PTS 6 Birmingham
15.05.04 Martin Hardcastle W PTS 8 Aberdeen

Career: 14 contests, won 13, lost 1.

Lee McAllister   Les Clark

Kevin McBride

Clones. *Born* Monaghan, 10 May, 1973
All-Ireland Heavyweight Champion.
Ht. 6'5"
Manager Self

17.12.92 Gary Charlton DREW 6 Barking
13.02.93 Gary Williams W PTS 4 Manchester
15.09.93 Joey Paladino W CO 2 Bethnal Green
13.10.93 Chris Coughlan W PTS 4 Bethnal
Green
01.12.93 John Harewood W RSC 3 Bethnal
Green
06.05.94 Edgar Turpin W RSC 1 Atlantic City,
New Jersey, USA
04.06.94 Roger Bryant W CO 1 Reno, Nevada,
USA

17.06.94 Stanley Wright W PTS 6 Atlantic City,
New Jersey, USA
26.08.94 James Truesdale W RSC 3 Upper
Marlboro, Maryland, USA
24.09.94 Graham Arnold W RSC 2 Wembley
12.11.94 Dean Storey W RSC 3 Dublin
10.12.94 John Lamphrey W RSC 1 Portland,
Maine, USA
07.02.95 Carl Gaffney W RSC 1 Ipswich
03.03.95 Carl McGrew W RSC 5 Boston, Mass,
USA
22.04.95 Jimmy Harrison W RSC 1 Boston,
Mass, USA
13.05.95 Atelea Kalhea W CO 1 Sacramento,
California, USA
02.07.95 Steve Garber W RSC 7 Dublin
06.11.96 Shane Woollas W RSC 2 Hull
03.12.96 R.F. McKenzie W RSC 6 Liverpool
21.01.97 Tui Toia W RSC 2 Kansas City,
Missouri, USA
07.02.97 Louis Monaco L RSC 5 Las Vegas,
Nevada, USA
28.04.97 Stoyan Stoyanov W RSC 1 Hull
02.06.97 Paul Douglas W RSC 5 Belfast
*(Vacant All-Ireland Heavyweight
Title)*
30.08.97 Axel Schulz L RSC 9 Berlin, Germany
22.11.97 Yuri Yelistratov W RSC 1 Manchester
11.04.98 Michael Murray L RSC 3 Southwark

26.06.99 Domingo Monroe W CO 1 Boston,
Mass, USA
11.08.01 Willie Phillips W PTS 10 Little Rock,
Arkansas, USA
01.11.01 Rodney McSwain W PTS 10 Little
Rock, Arkansas, USA
18.01.02 Davarryl Williamson L RSC 5 Las
Vegas, Nevada, USA
27.05.02 Gary Winmon W RSC 2 Revere, Mass,
USA
26.07.02 Reynaldo Minus W RSC 3 Boston,
Mass, USA
26.10.02 Craig Tomlinson W RSC 3 Revere,
Mass, USA
17.03.03 Najee Shaheed W RSC 7 Brockton,
Mass, USA
09.08.03 Lenzie Morgan W CO 1 Brockton,
Mass, USA
04.12.03 Marcus Rhode W RSC 3 Boston, Mass,
USA

Career: 36 contests, won 31, drew 1, lost 4.

Derek McCafferty

Kettering. *Born* Aberdeen, 10 November,
1968
Heavyweight. Ht. 6'3½"
Manager K. Sanders

22.02.99 Gary Williams W CO 1 Peterborough

Enzo Maccarinelli   Les Clark

24.04.99	Keith Long W PTS 4 Peterborough
15.07.99	Mike Holden L RSC 1 Peterborough
13.09.99	Mark Potter L PTS 6 Bethnal Green
18.12.99	Georgi Kandelaki L PTS 8 Southwark
22.09.01	Audley Harrison L PTS 6 Newcastle
13.12.01	Pele Reid L RSC 3 Leicester Square
26.01.02	Mark Potter L PTS 6 Bethnal Green
25.05.02	Georgie Kandelaki L RTD 5 Portsmouth
10.07.02	Mark Potter L RSC 6 Wembley
06.09.02	Pele Reid DREW 4 Bethnal Green
17.09.02	Michael Sprott L PTS 8 Bethnal Green
20.12.02	Roman Greenberg L PTS 4 Bracknell
15.02.03	John McDermott L PTS 4 Wembley
17.03.03	Colin Kenna L PTS 6 Southampton
29.03.03	Matthew Ellis L PTS 4 Wembley
16.04.03	Herbie Hide L RSC 7 Nottingham
21.06.03	Danny Venter L PTS 4 Manchester
01.08.03	Mark Krence L PTS 4 Bethnal Green
13.09.03	Scott Gammer L PTS 6 Newport

Career: 20 contests, won 2, drew 1, lost 17.

Enzo Maccarinelli

Swansea. *Born* Swansea, 20 August, 1980
WBU Cruiserweight Champion. Ht. 6'4"
Manager F. Warren/C. Pearson

02.10.99	Paul Bonson W PTS 4 Cardiff
11.12.99	Mark Williams W RSC 1 Merthyr
26.02.00	Nigel Rafferty W RSC 3 Swansea
12.05.00	Lee Swaby L CO 3 Swansea
11.12.00	Chris Woollas W PTS 4 Widnes
28.04.01	Darren Ashton W CO 1 Cardiff
09.10.01	Eamonn Glennon W RSC 2 Cardiff
15.12.01	Kevin Barrett W RSC 2 Wembley
12.02.02	James Gilbert W RSC 2 Bethnal Green
20.04.02	Tony Booth W PTS 4 Cardiff
17.08.02	Tony Booth W RTD 2 Cardiff
12.10.02	Dave Clarke W RSC 2 Bethnal Green
18.01.03	Paul Bonson W PTS 4 Preston
29.03.03	Valery Shemishkur W RSC 1 Portsmouth
28.06.03	Bruce Scott W RSC 4 Cardiff *(Vacant WBU Cruiserweight Title)*
13.09.03	Andrei Kiarsten W CO 1 Newport *(WBU Cruiserweight Title Defence)*
06.12.03	Earl Morais W RSC 1 Cardiff *(WBU Cruiserweight Title Defence)*
21.02.04	Garry Delaney W RSC 8 Cardiff *(WBU Cruiserweight Title Defence)*

Career: 18 contests, won 17, lost 1.

Glenn McClarnon

Lurgan. *Born* Carrickfergus, 1 July, 1974
Welterweight. Ht. 5'9"
Manager J. Breen/M. Callahan

20.12.97	Marc Smith W PTS 4 Belfast
21.02.98	Andrew Reed W CO 1 Belfast
28.04.98	Brian Robb W RSC 2 Belfast
18.09.98	Mark Ramsey W PTS 4 Belfast
28.11.98	David Kirk W PTS 4 Belfast
12.01.99	Ram Singh W RSC 1 Bethnal Green
25.01.99	Dean Nicholas W CO 1 Glasgow
12.03.99	Mark Ramsey W PTS 6 Bethnal Green
25.05.99	Steve Tuckett W PTS 4 Mayfair
11.09.99	David Kirk W PTS 6 Sheffield
27.11.99	Chris Barnett L PTS 12 Liverpool *(Vacant IBO International L. Welterweight Title)*
01.04.00	Bernard Paul W RTD 5 Bethnal Green
19.08.00	Brian Coleman W PTS 6 Brentwood

13.10.00	Allan Vester L PTS 12 Aarhus, Denmark *(IBF Inter-Continental L.Welterweight Title Challenge)*
02.12.00	John Ameline L PTS 4 Bethnal Green
03.03.01	Peter Dunn W PTS 4 Wembley
28.04.01	Jacek Bielski L PTS 12 Wroclaw, Poland *(Vacant IBO Inter-Continental Welterweight Title)*
25.09.01	Gary Ryder L PTS 8 Liverpool
10.11.01	Rosalin Nasibulin W PTS 6 Wembley
26.01.02	Kevin Bennett W PTS 8 Dagenham
16.11.02	Keith Jones W PTS 6 Nottingham
22.02.03	Ossie Duran L RSC 2 Huddersfield
30.10.03	Ronnie Nailen W RSC 1 Belfast
03.04.04	David Barnes L PTS 12 Manchester *(British Welterweight Title Challenge)*

Career: 24 contests, won 17, lost 7.

Joe McCluskey

Coventry. *Born* Coventry, 26 November, 1977
L. Welterweight. Ht. 5'9"
Manager O. Delargy

01.05.04	John-Paul Ryan W RTD 2 Coventry

Career: 1 contest, won 1.

Darren McDermott

Dudley. *Born* Dudley, 17 July, 1978
Middleweight. Ht. 6'1"
Manager D. Powell

26.04.03	Leigh Wicks W PTS 4 Brentford
13.06.03	Gary Jones W RSC 1 Queensway
30.10.03	Harry Butler W PTS 4 Dudley
21.02.04	Freddie Yemofio W RSC 3 Cardiff
15.04.04	Mark Phillips W PTS 4 Dudley

Career: 5 contests, won 5.

John McDermott   Les Clark

John McDermott

Horndon. *Born* Basildon, 26 February, 1980
Heavyweight. Ht. 6'3"
Manager J. Branch

23.09.00	Slick Miller W RSC 1 Bethnal Green
21.10.00	Gary Williams W PTS 4 Wembley
13.11.00	Geoff Hunter W RSC 1 Bethnal Green
27.01.01	Eamonn Glennon W RSC 1 Bethnal Green
24.02.01	Alexei Osokin W PTS 4 Bethnal Green
26.03.01	Mal Rice W RSC 2 Wembley
09.06.01	Luke Simpkin W PTS 6 Bethnal Green
22.09.01	Gary Williams W RSC 4 Bethnal Green
24.11.01	Gordon Minors W RSC 3 Bethnal Green
19.01.02	Tony Booth W RSC 1 Bethnal Green
04.05.02	Martin Roothman W RSC 1 Bethnal Green
14.09.02	Alexander Mileiko W RSC 2 Bethnal Green
12.10.02	Mendauga Kulikauskas W PTS 6 Bethnal Green
14.12.02	Jason Brewster W RSC 1 Newcastle
15.02.03	Derek McCafferty W PTS 4 Wembley
08.05.03	Konstantin Prizyuk W PTS 8 Widnes
18.09.03	Nicolai Popov L RSC 2 Dagenham
13.05.04	James Zikic W RSC 4 Bethnal Green

Career: 18 contests, won 17, lost 1.

Chris McDonagh

Maidenhead. *Born* Ascot, 9 July, 1978
Lightweight. Ht. 5'10"
Manager J. Evans

22.11.01	Jason Gonzales W PTS 6 Paddington
26.01.02	Dave Hinds W PTS 4 Bethnal Green
25.02.02	Baz Carey W PTS 6 Slough
19.03.02	Ray Wood W PTS 4 Slough
25.04.02	Vatche Wartanian L PTS 4 Las Vegas, Nevada, USA
21.05.02	Daniel Thorpe W PTS 6 Custom House
12.07.02	Tony Montana L PTS 4 Southampton
27.09.02	Gareth Wiltshaw L RSC 1 Bethnal Green
20.12.02	Jason Nesbitt W PTS 6 Bracknell
26.04.03	Scott Lawton L RSC 2 Brentford
27.11.03	David Vaughan DREW 4 Longford
20.02.04	Rob Jeffries L RSC 2 Bethnal Green
30.03.04	Kristian Laight W PTS 6 Southampton
12.05.04	Anthony Hanna W PTS 4 Reading
05.06.04	Danny Hunt L CO 3 Bethnal Green

Career: 15 contests, won 8, drew 1, lost 6.

Peter McDonagh

Bermondsey. *Born* Galway, 21 December, 1977
Southern Area Lightweight Champion.
Ht. 5'9"
Manager Self

28.04.02	Arv Mittoo W PTS 6 Southwark
23.06.02	Dave Hinds W PTS 6 Southwark
14.09.02	Pete Buckley W PTS 4 Bethnal Green
27.10.02	Ben Hudson L PTS 6 Southwark
18.02.03	Daffyd Carlin L PTS 4 Bethnal Green
08.04.03	Ben Hudson W PTS 4 Bethnal Green
08.11.03	Ceri Hall L PTS 4 Bridgend
22.11.03	James Gorman L PTS 4 Belfast
21.02.04	Chill John W RTD 2 Brighton
06.03.04	Barry Hughes L PTS 6 Renfrew
07.04.04	Jon Honney W PTS 10 Leicester Square *(Vacant Southern Area Lightweight Title)*

Career: 11 contests, won 6, lost 5.

Thomas McDonagh

Manchester. *Born* Manchester, 8 December, 1980
WBU Inter-Continental L.Middleweight Champion. Ht. 6'0"
Manager F. Warren/B. Hughes

09.10.99	Lee Molyneux W PTS 4 Manchester	
06.11.99	Lee Molyneux W PTS 4 Widnes	
11.12.99	Arv Mittoo W RSC 2 Liverpool	
29.01.00	Emmanuel Marcos W PTS 4 Manchester	
29.02.00	William Webster W RTD 2 Widnes	
25.03.00	Lee Molyneux W PTS 6 Liverpool	
16.05.00	Richie Murray W PTS 4 Warrington	
29.05.00	David Baptiste W PTS 6 Manchester	
04.09.00	Colin Vidler W PTS 6 Manchester	
11.12.00	Richie Murray W PTS 6 Widnes	
15.01.01	Kid Halls W RSC 4 Manchester	
10.02.01	Harry Butler W PTS 6 Widnes	
17.03.01	David Baptiste W PTS 4 Manchester	
07.07.01	Paul Denton W PTS 6 Manchester	
15.09.01	Howard Clarke W PTS 6 Manchester	
27.10.01	Mark Richards DREW 4 Manchester	
09.02.02	Tomas da Silva DREW 4 Manchester	
01.06.02	Delroy Mellis W PTS 4 Manchester	
28.09.02	Brian Coleman W RSC 1 Manchester	
18.01.03	Tomas da Silva W PTS 4 Preston	
05.04.03	Paul Wesley W PTS 6 Manchester	
08.05.03	Marcus Portman W PTS 6 Widnes	
27.09.03	Eugenio Monteiro W PTS 12 Manchester *(Vacant WBU Inter-Continental L.Middleweight Title)*	
26.02.04	Bobby Banghar W CO 2 Widnes *(WBU Inter-Continental L.Middleweight Title Defence)*	
03.04.04	Craig Lynch W PTS 6 Manchester	
06.05.04	Bradley Pryce W PTS 12 Barnsley *(WBU Inter-Continental L.Middleweight Title Defence)*	

Career: 26 contests, won 24, drew 2.

Rob MacDonald

Droylsden. *Born* Manchester, 26 July, 1981
L. Middleweight. Ht. 6'0"
Manager W. Barker

28.02.04	Vince Baldassara L PTS 6 Manchester	
20.03.04	Lee Hodgson L RSC 3 Wembley	

Career: 2 contest, lost 2.

Steve McGuire

Glenrothes. *Born* Kirkcaldy, 1 June, 1981
L. Heavyweight. Ht. 6'2"
Manager T. Gilmour

17.11.03	Shane White W CO 2 Glasgow	
22.04.04	Paul Billington W RTD 3 Glasgow	

Career: 2 contests, won 2.

George McIlroy

Stevenston. *Born* Irvine, 12 March, 1984
Welterweight. Ht. 5'10"
Manager T. Gilmour

28.02.03	Paul McIlwaine W PTS 4 Irvine	
14.04.03	Paul Rushton W RSC 1 Glasgow	
20.10.03	Norman Dhalie W PTS 6 Glasgow	

Career: 3 contests, won 3.

Paul McIlwaine

Bangor. *Born* Belfast, 18 June, 1980
Welterweight. Ht. 5'5"
Manager Self

16.11.01	Robert Murray L RSC 6 Dublin	
21.01.02	Tony McPake L RTD 1 Glasgow	
11.03.02	Gary Young L CO 2 Glasgow	
24.04.02	Ross McCord L PTS 4 Dublin	
03.06.02	David Keir L CO 2 Glasgow	
19.10.02	Luke Rudd L RTD 1 Norwich	
08.12.02	Barry Hughes L RSC 2 Glasgow	
28.02.03	George McIlroy L PTS 4 Irvine	
05.04.03	Paul Rushton DREW 4 Belfast	
12.04.03	Kevin Anderson L RSC 2 Bethnal Green	
15.05.03	Gary Woolcombe L RSC 2 Mayfair	
28.06.03	Tony Doherty L RSC 1 Cardiff	
13.09.03	Baz Carey L RTD 2 Coventry	

Career: 13 contests, drew 1, lost 12.

Tyrone McInerney

Huddersfield. *Born* Huddersfield, 24 March, 1978
Welterweight. Ht. 5'6"
Manager D. Coldwell/T. Schofield

08.06.04	Judex Meemea DREW 6 Sheffield	

Career: 1 contest, drew 1.

Conroy McIntosh   Les Clark

Conroy McIntosh

Wolverhampton. *Born* Wolverhampton, 5 December, 1973
Middleweight. Ht. 5'7"
Manager Self

31.01.01	Ross Murray W CO 1 Piccadilly	
23.06.01	Francie Doherty L PTS 4 Peterborough	
22.09.01	Tomas da Silva L PTS 4 Canning Town	
11.02.02	Ty Browne DREW 4 Southampton	
03.03.02	Wayne Shepherd DREW 6 Shaw	
21.05.02	Ty Browne DREW 4 Custom House	
13.07.02	Darren Covill W PTS 4 Wolverhampton	

17.11.02	Gary Dixon W RSC 2 Shaw	
30.11.02	Andy Halder L PTS 4 Coventry	
22.02.03	George Robshaw L PTS 4 Huddersfield	
08.03.03	Andy Halder L PTS 4 Coventry	
20.06.03	Michael Thomas W CO 2 Gatwick	
07.09.03	Roddy Doran L PTS 10 Shrewsbury *(Vacant Midlands Area Middleweight Title)*	
07.11.03	P.J.Maxwell L RSC 4 Sheffield	
07.04.04	Lee Hodgson W RSC 3 Leicester Square	
13.05.04	Ajay Abrahams W RSC 2 Bethnal Green	

Career: 16 contests, won 6, drew 3, lost 7.

David McIntyre

Paisley. *Born* Paisley, 20 June, 1978
Featherweight. Ht. 5'5"
Manager Self

19.10.02	Andy Robinson W PTS 4 Renfrew	
14.03.03	Stuart Sanderson L PTS 6 Glasgow	
22.03.03	Steve Foster L PTS 4 Renfrew	
12.07.03	Steve Foster L RTD 3 Renfrew	

Career: 4 contests, won 1, lost 3.

Kevin McIntyre

Paisley. *Born* Paisley, 5 May, 1978
Scottish Welterweight Champion. Ht. 5'10½"
Manager T. Gilmour

13.11.98	Ray Wood W RSC 4 Glasgow	
18.02.99	Gareth Dooley W RSC 3 Glasgow	
21.05.99	Mohamed Helel W PTS 6 Glasgow	
26.06.99	Karim Bouali L RTD 1 Glasgow	
18.03.00	Chris Hall W RSC 3 Glasgow	
07.04.00	Dave Travers W RSC 4 Glasgow	
26.05.00	Tommy Peacock W RSC 5 Glasgow	
24.06.00	Lee Williamson W PTS 4 Glasgow	
02.10.00	Paul Denton W PTS 6 Glasgow	
10.11.00	Mark Ramsey W RSC 4 Glasgow	
17.12.00	Ernie Smith W PTS 6 Glasgow	
15.02.01	John Humphrey L RSC 4 Glasgow	
27.04.01	Michael Smyth W PTS 4 Glasgow	
17.11.01	David Kirk W PTS 4 Glasgow	
16.12.01	Manzo Smith W PTS 6 Glasgow	
11.03.02	Karl Taylor W PTS 4 Glasgow	
26.04.02	Craig Lynch W PTS 10 Glasgow *(Vacant Scottish Welterweight Title)*	
08.06.02	David Kirk W RTD 5 Renfrew	
19.10.02	Nigel Wright W PTS 6 Renfrew	
22.03.03	David Kirk W RSC 1 Renfrew	
12.07.03	Paul Denton W PTS 4 Renfrew	
25.10.03	Karim Hussine W PTS 6 Edinburgh	
13.12.03	David Barnes L RTD 8 Manchester *(British Welterweight Title Challenge)*	
02.06.04	Keith Jones W PTS 6 Hereford	

Career: 24 contests, won 21, lost 3.

(Malcolm) Mally McIver

Dewsbury. *Born* Dewsbury, 29 January, 1974
Lightweight. Ht. 5'9"
Manager T. Gilmour/C. Aston

12.02.00	Arv Mittoo W PTS 4 Sheffield	
27.05.00	Paul Philpott W PTS 4 Southwark	
09.09.00	David Kirk W PTS 6 Newark	
05.02.01	Alan Kershaw W PTS 4 Hull	
24.03.01	Steve Hanley W PTS 4 Sheffield	
02.06.01	Keith Jones W PTS 6 Wakefield	
18.08.01	Mark Bowen L RSC 1 Dewsbury	

17.11.01	Daniel Thorpe W PTS 6 Dewsbury
03.03.02	Dave Hinds W PTS 6 Shaw
02.06.02	Gary Greenwood L RSC 1 Shaw
09.02.03	Jason Nesbitt W PTS 4 Bradford
31.05.03	Peter Allen W PTS 6 Barnsley
09.06.03	Chris Duggan W RSC 3 Bradford
06.09.03	Nigel Senior W PTS 4 Huddersfield
07.12.03	Daniel Thorpe L PTS 10 Bradford
	(Vacant Central Area Lightweight Title)

Career: 15 contests, won 12, lost 3.

Jason McKay

Banbridge. *Born* Craigavon, NI, 11 October, 1977
S. Middleweight. Ht. 6'1"
Manager Self

18.02.02	Jimmy Steel W PTS 4 Glasgow
11.05.02	Harry Butler W PTS 4 Dagenham
27.07.02	Simon Andrews W RSC 3 Nottingham
08.10.02	Dean Cockburn W PTS 4 Glasgow
08.02.03	William Webster W RSC 1 Liverpool
12.04.03	Marcin Radola W RSC 1 Bethnal Green
17.05.03	Varuzhan Davtyan W PTS 6 Liverpool
04.10.03	Jamie Hearn W PTS 8 Belfast
22.11.03	Ojay Abrahams W PTS 4 Belfast
17.04.04	Alan Gilbert W PTS 6 Belfast
26.06.04	Ciaran Healy W PTS 6 Belfast

Career: 11 contests, won 11.

John Mackay (Mukaya)

Canning Town. *Born* Uganda, 20 October, 1981
S. Bantamweight. Ht. 5'6"
Manager Self

15.06.01	Chris Emanuele L RSC 4 Millwall
22.09.01	Jason Nesbitt W PTS 4 Canning Town
16.11.01	Willie Valentine W RSC 4 Dublin
28.11.01	Jamie Yelland W RSC 6 Bethnal Green
18.01.02	Stephen Chinnock L PTS 4 Coventry
20.04.02	Dazzo Williams W PTS 6 Wembley
02.06.02	Choi Tseveenpurev L RSC 5 Shaw
27.07.02	Chris Hooper W PTS 4 Nottingham
23.11.02	Henry Castle W RTD 8 Derby
22.03.03	Brian Carr W PTS 8 Renfrew
16.01.04	Steve Molitor L PTS 8 Bradford
29.02.04	Choi Tsveenpurev L RSC 3 Shaw
01.05.04	Junior Anderson W CO 2 Gravesend
19.06.04	Mickey Bowden W PTS 8 Muswell Hill

Career: 14 contests, won 9, lost 5.

Jamie McKeever

Birkenhead. *Born* Birkenhead, 7 July, 1979
Featherweight. Former British Featherweight Champion. Former Undefeated Central Area Featherweight Champion. Ht. 5'6½"
Manager Self

12.03.98	Dave Hinds W PTS 4 Liverpool
08.04.98	Kid McAuley W RTD 1 Liverpool
06.06.98	Brian Coleman W PTS 4 Liverpool
21.07.98	Stuart Rimmer W PTS 4 Widnes
31.10.98	John T. Kelly L PTS 6 Southend
22.01.99	Garry Burrell W RSC 2 Carlisle
12.03.99	David Kehoe W RSC 2 Bethnal Green
28.05.99	Arv Mittoo W PTS 6 Liverpool
02.10.99	Lee Armstrong DREW 6 Cardiff
27.11.99	Nigel Leake W RSC 2 Liverpool
01.07.00	Gary Flear L PTS 4 Manchester

09.10.00	Marc Callaghan W PTS 6 Liverpool
20.03.01	Craig Docherty L RSC 3 Glasgow
25.09.01	Sebastian Hart W PTS 4 Liverpool
10.12.01	Andrew Ferrans W PTS 6 Liverpool
09.03.02	James Rooney W PTS 6 Manchester
13.04.02	Barry Hawthorne W PTS 6 Liverpool
07.09.02	Tony Mulholland W PTS 10 Liverpool
	(Vacant Central Area Featherweight Title)
08.02.03	Tony Mulholland W RSC 6 Liverpool
	(Vacant British Featherweight Title)
17.05.03	Roy Rutherford L PTS 12 Liverpool
	(British Featherweight Title Defence)
28.02.04	Dazzo Williams L PTS 12 Bridgend
	(British Featherweight Title Challenge)

Career: 21 contests, won 15, drew 1, lost 5.

Dave McKenna

Port Glasgow. *Born* Greenock, 8 January, 1975
Heavyweight. Ht. 6'3"
Manager T. Gilmour

18.03.02	Leighton Morgan L DIS 3 Glasgow
14.04.03	Costi Marin L DIS 5 Glasgow
07.06.04	Dave Clarke W PTS 6 Glasgow

Career: 3 contests, won 1, lost 2.

Ovill McKenzie

Canning Town. *Born* Jamaica, 26 November, 1979
L. Heavyweight. Ht. 5'9"
Manager A. Bowers

06.03.03	Leigh Alliss W PTS 4 Bristol
10.04.03	Nathan King W PTS 4 Clydach
02.06.03	Pinky Burton L PTS 8 Glasgow
18.09.03	Peter Haymer L PTS 4 Mayfair
24.10.03	Courtney Fry L PTS 4 Bethnal Green
15.11.03	Edwin Cleary W PTS 4 Coventry
30.01.04	Steven Spartacus W PTS 6 Dagenham
12.03.04	Harry Butler W RSC 2 Millwall
03.04.04	Denis Inkin L PTS 8 Manchester

Career: 9 contests, won 5, lost 4.

Ovill McKenzie   Les Clark

Matthew Macklin

Birmingham. *Born* Birmingham, 14 May, 1982
L. Middleweight. Ht. 5'10"
Manager F. Maloney/F. Warren

17.11.01	Ram Singh W RSC 1 Glasgow
15.12.01	Christian Hodorogea W CO 1 Wembley
09.02.02	Dimitri Protkunas W RTD 3 Manchester
11.03.02	David Kirk W PTS 4 Glasgow
20.04.02	Illia Spassov W CO 3 Cardiff
01.06.02	Guy Alton W RSC 3 Manchester
28.09.02	Leonti Voronchuk W RSC 5 Manchester
15.02.03	Ruslan Yakupov W PTS 6 Wembley
24.05.03	Paul Denton W PTS 6 Bethnal Green
06.11.03	Andrew Facey L PTS 10 Dagenham
	(Vacant English L.Middleweight Title)
21.02.04	Dean Walker W CO 1 Cardiff
24.04.04	Scott Dixon W RTD 5 Reading
12.06.04	Ojay Abrahams W PTS 4 Manchester

Career: 13 contests, won 12, lost 1.

Colin McNeil

Fauldhouse. *Born* Lanark, 21 December, 1972
L. Middleweight. Ht. 5'8"
Manager A. Morrison/F. Warren

06.03.04	Arv Mittoo W PTS 4 Renfrew
27.03.04	Lee Williamson W PTS 4 Edinburgh
19.06.04	Andrei Ivanov W RSC 2 Renfrew

Career: 3 contests, won 3.

Brian Magee

Belfast. *Born* Lisburn, 9 June, 1975
S.Middleweight. Former IBO S.Middleweight Champion. Former Undefeated IBO Inter-Continental S.Middleweight Champion. Ht. 6'0"
Manager Self

13.03.99	Dean Ashton W RSC 2 Manchester
22.05.99	Richard Glaysher W RSC 1 Belfast
22.06.99	Chris Howarth W RSC 1 Ipswich
13.09.99	Dennis Doyley W RSC 3 Bethnal Green
16.10.99	Michael Pinnock W RSC 3 Belfast
12.02.00	Terry Morrill W RTD 4 Sheffield
21.02.00	Rob Stevenson W RSC 5 Southwark
20.03.00	Darren Ashton W RTD 5 Mansfield
15.04.00	Pedro Carragher W CO 2 Bethnal Green
12.06.00	Jason Barker W PTS 8 Belfast
11.11.00	Teimouraz Kikelidze W RSC 4 Belfast
29.01.01	Neil Linford W PTS 12 Peterborough
	(Vacant IBO Inter-Continental S. Middleweight Title)
31.07.01	Chris Nembhard W RSC 6 Bethnal Green
10.12.01	Ramon Britez W CO 1 Liverpool
	(IBO S. Middleweight Title Challenge)
18.03.02	Vage Kocharyan W PTS 8 Crawley
15.06.02	Mpush Makambi W RSC 7 Leeds
	(IBO S. Middleweight Title Defence)
09.11.02	Jose Spearman W PTS 12 Altrincham
	(IBO S. Middleweight Title Defence)
22.02.03	Miguel Jimenez W PTS 12 Huddersfield
	(IBO S. Middleweight Title Defence)
21.06.03	Andre Thysse W RSC 10 Manchester
	(IBO S.Middleweight Title Defence)
04.10.03	Omar Eduardo Gonzalez W RSC 1 Belfast
	(IBO S.Middleweight Title Defence)
22.11.03	Hacine Cherifi W RTD 8 Belfast
	(IBO S.Middleweight Title Defence)

17.04.04 Jerry Elliott W PTS 12 Belfast
(IBO S.Middleweight Title Defence)
26.06.04 Robin Reid L PTS 12 Belfast
(IBO S.Middleweight Title Defence)
Career: 23 contests, won 22, lost 1.

Eamonn Magee   Les Clark

Eamonn Magee

Belfast. *Born* Belfast, 13 July, 1971
WBU Welterweight Champion. Former
Undefeated Commonwealth
L.Welterweight Champion. Ht. 5'9"
Manager Self

25.11.95 Pete Roberts W CO 4 Dublin
09.03.96 Steve McGovern W PTS 4 Millstreet
28.05.96 John Stovin W RSC 2 Belfast
03.09.96 Kevin McKillan W RTD 4 Belfast
05.11.96 Shaun Stokes W RSC 2 Belfast
28.01.97 Karl Taylor W PTS 6 Belfast
03.03.97 Troy Townsend W RSC 1 Austin,
Texas, USA
28.03.97 Teddy Reid L PTS 6 Boston, Mass,
USA
29.04.97 Peter Nightingale W RTD 2 Belfast
02.06.97 Kevin McKillan W RSC 3 Belfast
*(Elim. All-Ireland L. Welterweight
Title)*
14.02.98 Dennis Griffin W RSC 2 Southwark
26.09.98 Allan Hall W RSC 7 York
30.11.98 Paul Burke L PTS 12 Manchester
*(Vacant Commonwealth
L. Welterweight Title)*
22.05.99 Alan Temple W CO 3 Belfast
10.07.99 Karl Taylor W RTD 3 Southwark
13.09.99 Paul Burke W RSC 6 Bethnal Green
*(Commonwealth L. Welterweight Title
Challenge)*
16.10.99 Radoslav Gaidev W RSC 1 Belfast
04.03.00 Joseph Miyumo W RSC 1 Peterborough
*(Commonwealth L. Welterweight Title
Defence)*
29.04.00 David Kirk W RSC 8 Wembley
16.09.00 Pavel Melnikov W PTS 8 Bethnal
Green
11.11.00 Shea Neary W PTS 12 Belfast
*(Commonwealth L. Welterweight Title
Defence)*
13.03.01 Alan Bosworth W RSC 5 Plymouth
12.05.01 Harrison Methula W RSC 7 Plymouth
*(Commonwealth L. Welterweight Title
Defence)*

27.10.01 Matthews Zulu W PTS 12 Manchester
*(Commonwealth L.Welterweight Title
Defence)*
09.02.02 Jonathan Thaxton W RSC 6
Manchester
*(Commonwealth L. Welterweight Title
Defence)*
01.06.02 Ricky Hatton L PTS 12 Manchester
(WBU L. Welterweight Title Challenge)
28.09.02 Alan Bosworth W RSC 5 Manchester
14.06.03 Otkay Urkal L PTS 12 Magdeburg,
Germany
*(European L.Welterweight Title
Challenge)*
06.12.03 Jimmy Vincent W PTS 12 Cardiff
(Vacant WBU Welterweight Title)
Career: 29 contests, won 25, lost 4.

(Jason) Jay Mahoney

Peterborough. *Born* Peterborough, 21
September, 1971
L. Welterweight. Ht 5'8"
Manager Self

05.12.94 Shaun O'Neill W PTS 6 Houghton le
Spring
20.02.95 David Thompson W RSC 4 Manchester
08.03.95 Peter Hickenbottom W PTS 6 Solihull
03.04.95 Blue Butterworth W PTS 6 Manchester
02.10.95 Anthony Maynard L PTS 8
Birmingham
17.12.96 Roger Hunte W RSC 5 Bethnal Green
24.02.97 Chris Barnett W PTS 6 Manchester
02.01.01 Andrzej Butowicz L PTS 4 Coventry
20.01.01 Brett James L PTS 4 Bethnal Green
25.02.01 Gavin Down L RSC 1 Derby
23.06.01 Gary Greenwood W PTS 4
Peterborough
29.03.03 Ross Minter L RSC 2 Portsmouth
08.05.03 Matthew Hatton L PTS 6 Widnes
24.05.03 Ross Minter L PTS 6 Bethnal Green
17.07.03 Matthew Hatton L RSC 1 Dagenham
06.09.03 Barry Morrison L RSC 2 Huddersfield
Career: 16 contests, won 7, lost 9.

Jas Malik   Les Clark

(Jasim) Jas Malik

Cardiff. *Born* Cardiff, 4 April, 1973
L. Welterweight. Ht. 5'11¹/₂"
Manager B. Baker

05.03.00 Steve Sharples W RSC 1 Shaw
04.07.00 Dave Travers W PTS 6 Tooting

30.11.00 Jimmy Phelan L RSC 4 Bloomsbury
29.03.01 Darren Melville L RSC 1
Hammersmith
26.09.02 Ben Hudson L CO 3 Fulham
01.08.03 Pete Buckley L PTS 4 Bethnal Green
24.10.03 Lance Hall L RSC 1 Bethnal Green
Career: 7 contests, won 2, lost 5.

Steve Mallett

Thetford. *Born* Bury St Edmonds, 28
December, 1977
Middleweight. Ht. 6'2"
Manager G. Holmes

21.02.04 Jonathan Woollins W PTS 4 Norwich
Career: 1 contest, won 1.

(Constantin) Costi Marin

Huddersfield. *Born* Romania, 11 May, 1970
Heavyweight. Ht. 6'1"
Manager C. Aston

20.11.02 Dave Clarke L RSC 2 Leeds
03.02.03 Steve Tuck W RSC 1 Bradford
26.02.03 Leighton Morgan W RSC 2 Bristol
17.03.03 Dave Clarke L PTS 6 Glasgow
14.04.03 Dave McKenna W DIS 5 Glasgow
28.04.03 Neil Cleaver W RSC 2 Nottingham
02.06.03 Brian Gascoigne L PTS 6 Glasgow
09.06.03 David Ingleby W RSC 1 Bradford
11.10.03 Matt Skelton L RSC 1 Portsmouth
Career: 9 contests, won 5, lost 4.

John Marshall

Glossop. *Born* Australia, 28 May, 1975
Welterweight. Ht. 5'6"
Manager T. Gilmour/S. Wood

07.09.01 Dave Stewart L PTS 6 Glasgow
23.12.01 Arv Mittoo W RSC 1 Salford
21.01.02 Gary Hamilton W PTS 4 Glasgow
17.02.02 Joel Viney W RSC 6 Salford
31.05.02 Tony Montana W PTS 6 Hull
21.07.02 Daniel Thorpe W RSC 1 Salford
02.11.02 Mark Winters L RSC 5 Belfast
28.04.03 Young Muttley L RSC 5 Nottingham
18.09.03 Ross Minter DREW 6 Dagenham
Career: 9 contests, won 5, drew 1, lost 3.

Martin Marshall

Sunderland. *Born* Sunderland, 28 January,
1983
L. Middleweight. Ht. 6'1"
Manager T. Conroy

14.05.04 Richard Mazurek DREW 6 Sunderland
Career: 1 contest, drew 1.

Tommy Marshall

Plymouth. *Born* Aberystwyth, 22 August,
1984
Welterweight. Ht. 6'0"
Manager C. Sanigar

02.04.04 Chris Brophy DREW 6 Plymouth
Career: 1 contest, drew 1.

Derry Matthews

Liverpool. *Born* Liverpool, 23 September,
1983
S. Bantamweight. Ht. 5'8¹/₂"
Manager F. Warren/S. Vaughan

18.01.03	Sergei Tasimov W CO 1 Preston
05.04.03	Jus Wallie W PTS 4 Manchester
08.05.03	Steve Gethin W RSC 3 Widnes
20.06.03	Henry Janes W RSC 1 Liverpool
29.08.03	Marty Kayes W RTD 2 Liverpool
02.10.03	Alexei Volchan W RSC 2 Liverpool
13.12.03	Pete Buckley W PTS 4 Manchester
26.02.04	Gareth Payne W RSC 4 Widnes
03.04.04	Henry Janes W PTS 4 Manchester

Career: 9 contests, won 9.

(Patrick) P.J. Maxwell (Drinkwater)

Manchester. *Born* USA, 20 March, 1979
Middleweight. Ht. 5'8"
Manager Self

17.03.98	Danny Thornton W PTS 6 Sheffield
12.08.00	Matthew Ashmole W RSC 3 Wembley
26.03.01	Jason Collins L PTS 4 Wembley
27.10.01	Prince Kasi Kaihau W CO 4 Manchester
09.02.02	Leigh Wicks W PTS 4 Manchester
09.03.03	Surinder Sekhon W RSC 1 Shaw
10.06.03	Andy Halder W RSC 1 Sheffield
05.09.03	Isidro Gonzalez W RSC 6 Sheffield
07.11.03	Conroy McIntosh W RSC 4 Sheffield
17.06.04	Howard Clarke W RSC 1 Sheffield

Career: 10 contests, won 9, lost 1.

P.J. Maxwell   Les Clark

Anthony Maynard

Birmingham. *Born* Birmingham, 12
January, 1972
Lightweight. Former Undefeated Midlands
Area Lightweight Champion. Ht. 5'8"
Manager Self

17.10.94	Malcolm Thomas W PTS 6 Birmingham
02.11.94	Dean Phillips W PTS 6 Birmingham
25.01.95	Neil Smith L PTS 6 Stoke
07.02.95	Anthony Campbell W PTS 8 Wolverhampton
08.03.95	Scott Walker W PTS 6 Solihull
28.03.95	Kid McAuley W PTS 8 Wolverhampton
11.05.95	Gary Hiscox W RSC 4 Dudley
06.06.95	Richard Swallow L RSC 2 Leicester
02.10.95	Jay Mahoney W PTS 8 Birmingham
26.10.95	Ray Newby W PTS 8 Birmingham

17.01.96	Tom Welsh W RSC 8 Solihull
06.03.96	G. G. Goddard W RSC 3 Solihull
20.03.97	Richard Swallow W PTS 6 Solihull
24.10.97	Brian Coleman W CO 1 Birmingham
27.03.98	Gary Flear W RSC 9 Telford
	(Vacant Midlands Area Lightweight Title)
30.05.98	Michael Ayers W PTS 8 Bristol
21.11.98	Stephen Smith L PTS 10 Southwark
27.11.00	David Kehoe W RSC 5 Birmingham
07.04.01	Alfred Kotey L RTD 6 Wembley
	(Vacant WBF Inter-Continental Lightweight Title)
11.06.01	Woody Greenaway W PTS 4 Nottingham
08.10.01	Bobby Vanzie L RSC 1 Barnsley
	(British Lightweight Title Challenge)
09.03.02	David Burke L PTS 6 Manchester
09.11.02	Chris Barnett W PTS 6 Altrincham
08.02.03	Gary Hibbert DREW 6 Liverpool
18.10.03	Gary Hibbert L PTS 6 Manchester
07.02.04	Danny Hunt L PTS 10 Bethnal Green
	(English Lightweight Title Challenge)

Career: 26 contests, won 17, drew 1, lost 8.

Richard Mazurek

Leamington. *Born* Leamington, 20 January,
1977
L. Middleweight. Ht. 5'10"
Manager O. Delargy

15.11.03	Neil Addis W PTS 6 Coventry
21.02.04	Simon Hopkins W RSC 3 Brighton
01.05.04	Brian Coleman W PTS 6 Coventry
14.05.04	Martin Marshall DREW 6 Sunderland

Career: 4 contests, won 3, drew 1.

Elvis Mbwakongo

Bermondsey. *Born* Zaire, 12 July, 1979
Welterweight. Ht. 5'10"
Manager E. Maloney

27.10.02	James Paisley W RSC 2 Southwark
08.12.02	Arv Mittoo W PTS 6 Bethnal Green
18.02.03	Neil Murray W RSC 1 Bethnal Green
08.04.03	Pedro Thompson W RSC 1 Bethnal Green
03.06.03	Cristian Hodorogea W PTS 4 Bethnal Green
25.09.03	Brian Coleman W PTS 6 Bethnal Green

Career: 6 contests, won 6.

Lee Meager

Salford. *Born* Salford, 18 January, 1978
Lightweight. Ht. 5'8"
Manager Self

16.09.00	Pete Buckley W PTS 4 Bethnal Green
14.10.00	Chris Jickells W PTS 4 Wembley
18.11.00	Billy Smith W RSC 1 Dagenham
09.12.00	Jason Nesbitt W RSC 2 Southwark
05.02.01	Carl Allen DREW 6 Hull
13.03.01	Lennie Hodgkins W RSC 3 Plymouth
12.05.01	Jason White W PTS 4 Plymouth
31.07.01	Steve Hanley W PTS 6 Bethnal Green
13.09.01	Arv Mittoo W PTS 6 Sheffield
16.03.02	Jason Nesbitt W PTS 6 Bethnal Green
10.05.02	Pete Buckley W PTS 6 Bethnal Green
25.10.02	Iain Eldridge W RSC 5 Bethnal Green
21.12.02	Chill John W RSC 5 Dagenham
28.01.03	Carl Allen W PTS 8 Nottingham
28.11.03	Pete Buckley W PTS 4 Derby

11.12.03	Charles Shepherd W RTD 7 Bethnal Green
02.06.04	Michael Muya W PTS 8 Nottingham

Career: 17 contests, won 16, drew 1.

Judex Meemea

Bristol. *Born* Mauritius, 24 November,
1973
Welterweight. Ht. 5'10"
Manager C. Sanigar

21.02.04	Jay Morris DREW 4 Brighton
08.06.04	Tyrone McInerney DREW 6 Sheffield

Career: 2 contests, drew 2.

Delroy Mellis

Brixton. *Born* Jamaica, 7 January, 1971
L. Middleweight. Former Undefeated
Southern Area L. Middleweight Champion.
Ht. 5'8"
Manager B. Baker

27.02.98	Pat Larner L PTS 4 Brighton
16.04.98	Sonny Thind L RTD 5 Mayfair
09.06.98	Darren Christie L PTS 4 Hull
10.09.98	Paul Miles W RSC 3 Acton
03.10.98	Wayne Asker L PTS 6 Crawley
06.11.98	Darren Bruce L RTD 3 Mayfair
21.01.99	Darren Christie L PTS 6 Piccadilly
04.02.99	Sergei Dzindziruk L RSC 3 Lewisham
24.03.99	Martyn Thomas W RSC 3 Bayswater
20.05.99	Daniel James L PTS 4 Barking
02.07.99	Jason Williams L PTS 6 Bristol
30.09.99	Steve Brumant L PTS 4 Kensington
16.10.99	Jacek Bielski L PTS 4 Bethnal Green
18.11.99	Dennis Griffin W RSC 5 Mayfair
29.11.99	George Scott L PTS 6 Wembley
20.03.00	Lance Crosby L PTS 4 Mansfield
01.04.00	Paul Knights W RSC 3 Bethnal Green
15.05.00	Christian Brady W RSC 6 Birmingham
01.07.00	Cham Joof DREW 6 Southwark
22.07.00	Alan Gilbert W RSC 3 Watford
	(Vacant Southern Area L.Middleweight Title)
22.10.00	Allan Gray W RSC 6 Streatham
	(Southern Area L.Middleweight Title Defence)
23.01.01	Alan Gilbert W RSC 3 Crawley
	(Southern Area L. Middleweight Title Defence)
20.04.01	Chris Nembhard W RSC 8 Millwall
	(Southern Area L. Middleweight Title Defence)
07.09.01	Jason Collins L DIS 5 Bethnal Green
06.10.01	Michael Jones L PTS 8 Manchester
13.12.01	Ossie Duran L PTS 10 Leicester Square
	(WBF European Welterweight Title Challenge)
01.06.02	Thomas McDonagh L PTS 4 Manchester
15.06.02	Chardan Ansoula L RTD 4 Tottenham
07.09.02	Jamie Moore L CO 6 Liverpool
06.12.03	Wayne Alexander W RSC 8 Cardiff
16.04.04	Gilbert Eastman L RSC 5 Bradford
	(Southern Area L.Middleweight Title Challenge)

Career: 31 contests, won 10, drew 1, lost 20.

Malcolm Melvin

Birmingham. *Born* Birmingham, 5
February, 1967
Welterweight. Former Undefeated All-

Ireland & Midlands Area L. Welterweight Champion. Ht. 5'7"
Manager Self

28.11.85	Steve Foster DREW 6 Ilkeston
04.12.85	Simon Collins L PTS 6 Stoke
24.03.86	Rocky McGran L PTS 6 Mayfair
10.04.86	Lincoln Pennant W PTS 6 Leicester
21.04.86	Malcolm Davies W PTS 6 Birmingham
07.05.86	Julian Monville W PTS 6 Solihull
19.01.88	Antonio Fernandez L RSC 4 Kings Heath
07.03.88	John Ellis L PTS 6 Piccadilly
03.12.89	Dave Jenkins W PTS 6 Birmingham
05.02.90	Trevor Meikle W PTS 6 Brierley Hill
22.02.90	Chris Saunders L PTS 4 Hull
19.03.90	Barry North W PTS 6 Brierley Hill
30.04.90	Andy Kent W RSC 5 Brierley Hill
04.06.90	Brendan Ryan L RSC 7 Edgbaston
03.09.90	Dave Jenkins W PTS 8 Dudley
13.11.90	Brendan Ryan W PTS 10 Edgbaston
	(Vacant Midlands Area L. Welterweight Title)
18.03.91	Carl Brasier W PTS 6 Piccadilly
17.06.91	Dean Bramhald W PTS 6 Edgbaston
21.05.92	Mark Kelly W PTS 6 Cradley Heath
05.10.92	Ross Hale L PTS 10 Bristol
	(Elim. British L. Welterweight Title)
17.11.92	Tusikoleta Nkalankete DREW 8 Paris, France
16.03.93	Shaun Cogan W PTS 10 Edgbaston
	(Vacant All-Ireland L. Welterweight Title & Midlands Area L. Welterweight Title Defence)
29.06.93	Mark Kelly W PTS 6 Edgbaston
24.11.93	Alan Peacock W PTS 8 Solihull
08.03.94	Julian Eavis W PTS 6 Edgbaston
28.06.94	John Smith W PTS 6 Edgbaston
18.02.95	Ross Hale L PTS 12 Shepton Mallet
	(British & Commonwealth L. Welterweight Title Challenges)
21.05.96	Karl Taylor W PTS 10 Edgbaston
	(Midlands Area L. Welterweight Title Defence)
03.06.96	Jamie Morris W RSC 2 Birmingham
09.06.97	Jimmy Phelan W RSC 2 Birmingham
30.09.97	Wayne Windle W PTS 6 Edgbaston
24.02.98	Ray Newby W PTS 6 Edgbaston
12.10.98	David Kirk W PTS 10 Birmingham
	(Midlands Area L. Welterweight Title Defence)
13.02.99	Junior Witter L RSC 2 Newcastle
	(Vacant WBF L. Welterweight Title)
06.12.99	Harry Butler W PTS 8 Birmingham
13.03.00	Peter Nightingale W PTS 6 Birmingham
14.10.00	Harry Dhami L PTS 12 Wembley
	(British Welterweight Title Challenge)
04.03.02	Harry Butler W PTS 8 Birmingham
08.12.03	Wayne Wheeler W RSC 6 Birmingham

Career: 39 contests, won 27, drew 2, lost 10.

(Elviss) Elvis Michailenko

Beckton. *Born* Jormala, Latvia, 13 September, 1976
European Union L.Heavyweight Champion. Former Undefeated WBF European L.Heavyweight Champion. Former WBA Inter-Continental L.Heavyweight Champion. Ht. 5'11¹/₂"
Manager A. Bowers

18.05.00	Adam Cale W PTS 4 Bethnal Green

21.09.00	Shpetim Hoti W PTS 4 Bloomsbury
09.10.00	Tony Dodson DREW 6 Liverpool
02.11.00	Freddie Yemofio W PTS 6 Kensington
28.02.01	Tommy Matthews W PTS 4 Kensington
09.03.01	Tommy Matthews W PTS 4 Millwall
20.04.01	Dean Ashton W RSC 4 Millwall
16.06.01	Sven Hamer W RSC 6 Wembley
	(Vacant WBF European L. Heavyweight Title)
28.09.01	Paul Bonson W PTS 6 Millwall
23.11.01	Paul Bonson W PTS 6 Bethnal Green
15.03.02	Hastings Rasani W RSC 5 Millwall
29.06.02	Varuzhan Davtyan W PTS 6 Brentwood
03.10.02	Alejandro Lakatus W PTS 12 Madrid, Spain
	(Vacant WBA Inter-Continental L.Heavyweight Title)
24.05.03	Hastings Rasini W RSC 4 Bethnal Green
14.11.03	Peter Oboh L RSC 11 Bethnal Green
	(WBA Inter-Continental L.Heavyweight Title Defence)
12.03.04	Nathan King W PTS 6 Millwall
01.05.04	Tony Booth W RTD 4 Gravesend
11.06.04	Giovanni Alvarez W PTS 10 Copenhagen, Denmark
	(European Union L.Heavyweight Title Challenge)

Career: 18 contests, won 16, drew 1, lost 1.

(Alvin) Slick Miller

Doncaster. *Born* Doncaster, 12 May, 1968
Heavyweight. Ht. 6'2"
Manager Self

28.04.94	Declan Faherty L RSC 2 Hull
06.10.94	Kent Davis L PTS 6 Hull
17.11.94	Graham Wassell L RSC 1 Sheffield
29.09.95	Mark Richardson L PTS 6 Hartlepool
13.01.96	Geoff Hunter DREW 6 Halifax
13.02.96	Danny Williams L RSC 1 Bethnal Green
15.03.96	Tony Booth L PTS 6 Hull
22.03.96	Tony Dowling L RSC 4 Mansfield
26.09.96	Steve Pettit L PTS 6 Walsall
22.11.96	Tony Booth L RSC 5 Hull
17.03.97	Michael Sprott L CO 1 Mayfair
25.04.97	Pele Lawrence L PTS 6 Mere
16.05.97	Edwin Cleary DREW 6 Hull
20.10.97	Neil Simpson L RTD 1 Leicester
16.04.98	Kevin Mitchell L RSC 2 Mayfair
08.06.98	Stevie Pettit W CO 1 Birmingham
30.11.98	Neil Simpson L CO 3 Leicester
23.01.99	Faisal Mohammed L RSC 2 Cheshunt
25.03.99	Nigel Rafferty L PTS 8 Edgbaston
17.04.99	Ahmet Oner L RSC 1 Dublin
24.10.99	Nigel Rafferty W RSC 4 Wolverhampton
25.03.00	Brian Kilbride L RSC 1 Liverpool
09.04.00	Mark Krence L PTS 6 Alfreton
11.06.00	Glenn Williams L PTS 4 Salford
08.07.00	Tony Dowling L PTS 4 Widnes
23.09.00	John McDermott L RSC 1 Bethnal Green
03.02.01	Scott Baker W RSC 4 Brighton
18.02.01	Hughie Robertson W RSC 2 Southwark
25.02.01	Colin Kenna L RSC 3 Streatham
05.05.01	Danny Percival W CO 1 Edmonton
31.07.01	Neil Hosking L RSC 2 Bethnal Green
07.09.01	Jason Brewster L PTS 6 West Bromwich

22.09.01	Dennis Bakhtov L CO 1 Bethnal Green
22.11.01	Petr Horacek L PTS 4 Paddington
26.01.02	Fola Okesela L RSC 1 Dagenham
23.09.02	Tony Booth L PTS 6 Cleethorpes
12.10.02	Matt Legg W RSC 2 Bethnal Green
27.10.02	Matt Skelton L CO 1 Southwark
09.12.02	Paul Butlin L PTS 6 Nottingham
15.02.03	Keith Long L RSC 1 Wembley
18.09.03	Micky Steeds L PTS 4 Mayfair
15.11.03	Jason Callum L PTS 4 Coventry
28.11.03	Carl Baker L CO 1 Hull
25.04.04	Tony Dowling L RSC 2 Nottingham
24.06.04	Simon Francis L PTS 6 Gibraltar

Career: 45 contests, won 7, drew 2, lost 36.

Ross Minter

Crawley. *Born* Crawley, 10 November, 1978
Welterweight. Ht. 5'7³/₄"
Manager Self

26.03.01	Brian Coleman W PTS 4 Wembley
05.05.01	Trevor Smith W RTD 3 Edmonton
28.07.01	Lee Williamson W PTS 4 Wembley
24.11.01	Karl Taylor W PTS 4 Bethnal Green
15.12.01	Ernie Smith W RSC 2 Wembley
02.03.02	Paul Denton W PTS 6 Bethnal Green
25.05.02	Howard Clarke L RSC 2 Portsmouth
12.10.02	Dafydd Carlin W RSC 1 Bethnal Green
15.02.03	Karl Taylor W PTS 6 Wembley
29.03.03	Jay Mahoney W RSC 2 Portsmouth
24.05.03	Jay Mahoney W PTS 6 Bethnal Green
18.09.03	John Marshall DREW 6 Dagenham

Career: 12 contests, won 10, drew 1, lost 1.

Joe Mitchell

Birmingham. *Born* Birmingham, 8 February, 1971
Welterweight. Ht. 5'9"
Manager T. Nerwal

20.02.04	20.02.04 Steve Scott W PTS 6 Doncaster
07.04.04	Robert Lloyd-Taylor L RSC 5 Leicester Square

Career: 2 contests, won 1, lost 1.

Kevin Mitchell

Dagenham. *Born* Dagenham, 29 October, 1984
S. Featherweight. Ht. 5'8"
Manager F. Warren/F. Maloney

17.07.03	Stevie Quinn W CO 1 Dagenham
18.09.03	Csabi Ladanyi W RSC 1 Dagenham
06.11.03	Vlado Varhegyi W RSC 3 Dagenham
24.01.04	Jaz Virdee W RSC 1 Wembley
07.02.04	Kristian Laight W PTS 4 Bethnal Green
24.04.04	Eric Patrac W RSC 1 Reading
13.05.04	Slimane Kebaili W RSC 1 Bethnal Green
05.06.04	Jason Nesbitt W RSC 3 Bethnal Green

Career: 8 contests, won 8.

(Arvill) Arv Mittoo

Birmingham. *Born* Birmingham, 8 July, 1971
L. Middleweight. Ht. 5'8"
Manager Self

31.01.96	Alan Bosworth L PTS 6 Stoke

13.02.96	Tommy Janes L PTS 6 Cardiff	
21.02.96	Danny Lutaaya L PTS 6 Piccadilly	
20.05.96	Terry Whittaker L CO 5 Cleethorpes	
29.06.96	Craig Stanley L PTS 4 Erith	
23.09.96	Thomas Bradley DREW 6 Cleethorpes	
03.10.96	John T. Kelly L PTS 6 Sunderland	
01.11.96	David Kirk L PTS 6 Mansfield	
14.11.96	Thomas Bradley L RSC 4 Sheffield	
22.05.97	Craig Stanley W RSC 3 Southwark	
02.09.97	Trevor Tacy L PTS 6 Manchester	
22.09.97	Steve Conway L PTS 6 Cleethorpes	
09.10.97	Steve Conway L PTS 6 Leeds	
23.10.97	Marco Fattore W PTS 6 Mayfair	
11.11.97	Kevin McCarthy L PTS 6 Bethnal Green	
03.12.97	Marc Smith W PTS 6 Stoke	
31.01.98	Harry Andrews L PTS 4 Edmonton	
06.03.98	Gavin McGill W PTS 6 Hull	
18.03.98	Marc Smith W PTS 6 Stoke	
26.03.98	Danny Lutaaya DREW 6 Piccadilly	
11.04.98	Charlie Rumbol L PTS 4 Southwark	
21.04.98	Adam Spelling W PTS 4 Edmonton	
02.10.98	Sammy Smith L PTS 4 Cheshunt	
16.10.98	Mark Haslam L PTS 6 Salford	
25.11.98	Brian Coleman L PTS 6 Clydach	
27.01.99	Ernie Smith DREW 6 Stoke	
26.02.99	Mark Payne L PTS 4 Coventry	
17.03.99	Marc Smith L PTS 6 Stoke	
20.05.99	John Humphrey L PTS 6 Barking	
28.05.99	Jamie McKeever L PTS 6 Liverpool	
04.06.99	Oscar Hall L PTS 6 Hull	
02.07.99	Wahid Fats L PTS 6 Manchester	
21.07.99	Brian Gentry L RSC 4 Bloomsbury	
20.10.99	Steve Saville L PTS 8 Stoke	
31.10.99	Ross McCord L PTS 6 Raynes Park	
15.11.99	Lee Sharp L PTS 6 Glasgow	
22.11.99	Mohamed Helel L PTS 6 Piccadilly	
29.11.99	Peter Swinney L PTS 4 Wembley	
11.12.99	Thomas McDonagh L RSC 2 Liverpool	
12.02.00	Mally McIver L PTS 4 Sheffield	
10.03.00	Jason Hall W RSC 3 Bethnal Green	
08.04.00	Junior Witter L PTS 4 Bethnal Green	
17.04.00	Gavin Pearson L PTS 6 Glasgow	
13.05.00	Chris Steele W RSC 3 Barnsley	
21.05.00	Gavin Down L PTS 6 Derby	
06.06.00	Casey Brooke W PTS 6 Brierley Hill	
15.07.00	Steve Conway L PTS 6 Norwich	
30.09.00	Mark Florian L PTS 4 Peterborough	
07.10.00	Jesse James Daniel L PTS 4 Doncaster	
16.11.00	Lance Crosby L RSC 3 Hull	
28.01.01	Stuart Elwell L PTS 6 Wolverhampton	
19.02.01	Lee Sharp L PTS 6 Glasgow	
26.02.01	Gavin Wake L PTS 4 Nottingham	
24.03.01	Richard Holden L PTS 6 Newark	
01.04.01	Babatunde Ajayi L PTS 6 Southwark	
20.04.01	Manzo Smith L PTS 4 Millwall	
08.05.01	Robert Burton L PTS 4 Barnsley	
04.06.01	Gary Porter L PTS 6 Glasgow	
16.06.01	Gavin Down L PTS 6 Derby	
14.07.01	Lee Byrne L PTS 4 Wembley	
13.09.01	Lee Meager L PTS 6 Sheffield	
23.09.01	Anthony Christopher DREW 6 Shaw	
28.10.01	Peter Swinney L PTS 4 Southwark	
16.11.01	Terry Ham L PTS 6 Preston	
10.12.01	Lee Armstrong L PTS 6 Bradford	
23.12.01	John Marshall L RSC 1 Salford	
15.04.02	Chris Duggan L PTS 6 Shrewsbury	
28.04.02	Peter McDonagh L PTS 6 Southwark	
10.05.02	Oscar Hall L PTS 4 Bethnal Green	
15.06.02	Chris Saunders L PTS 6 Norwich	
23.06.02	Mark Stupple L PTS 6 Southwark	
17.09.02	Gwyn Wale L PTS 6 Bethnal Green	
05.10.02	Dean Lambert L PTS 4 Huddersfield	

17.11.02	Lee McAllister L PTS 6 Bradford	
30.11.02	Richard Swallow L PTS 4 Coventry	
08.12.02	Elvis Mbwakongo L PTS 6 Bethnal Green	
20.12.02	Nathan Ward L PTS 6 Bracknell	
23.02.03	Adnan Amar L PTS 6 Shrewsbury	
16.03.03	Jonathan Woollins L PTS 4 Nottingham	
08.04.03	Justin Hudson L PTS 4 Bethnal Green	
28.04.03	Barry Morrison L RSC 3 Nottingham	
03.06.03	Chas Symonds L PTS 6 Bethnal Green	
13.06.03	Gary Steadman L PTS 4 Queensway	
22.07.03	Gary Woolcombe L PTS 6 Bethnal Green	
01.08.03	Mark Alexander L PTS 4 Bethnal Green	
26.10.03	Robert Lloyd-Taylor L PTS 6 Longford	
23.11.03	Scott Haywood L PTS 6 Rotherham	
21.02.04	Steve Russell L PTS 6 Norwich	
06.03.04	Colin McNeil L PTS 4 Renfrew	
27.03.04	Barrie Lee L PTS 4 Edinburgh	
16.04.04	Nadeem Siddique L PTS 6 Bradford	
19.06.04	Ashley Theophane L PTS 4 Muswell Hill	

Career: 92 contests, won 9, drew 4, lost 79.

Arv Mittoo   Les Clark

(Qais) Mo (Ariya)
Sheffield. *Born* Kabul, Afghanistan, 15 February, 1979
Middleweight. Ht. 5'9"
Manager H. Rainey

12.07.02	Danny Gwilym L PTS 6 Southampton	
27.09.02	Freddie Yemofio W PTS 4 Bracknell	
09.05.03	Freddie Yemofio W PTS 4 Longford	
12.10.03	Danny Gwilym W PTS 6 Sheffield	
10.02.04	Danny Thornton L PTS 6 Barnsley	

Career: 5 contests, won 3, lost 2.

Colin Moffett
Belfast. *Born* Belfast, 15 April, 1975
Flyweight. Ht. 5'6"
Manager Self

05.11.96	Shane Mallon W RSC 2 Belfast	
28.01.97	Anthony Hanna W PTS 4 Belfast	
29.04.97	Gary Hickman W PTS 4 Belfast	

02.06.97	Jason Thomas L RSC 3 Belfast	
20.12.97	Graham McGrath DREW 4 Belfast	
18.09.98	Anthony Hanna DREW 4 Belfast	
28.11.98	Shaun Norman W PTS 4 Belfast	
31.07.99	Waj Khan W CO 1 Carlisle	
16.10.99	Delroy Spencer L PTS 4 Bethnal Green	
31.03.00	Steffen Norskov L PTS 4 Esbjerg, Denmark	
05.06.00	Keith Knox L RSC 3 Glasgow	
02.12.00	Dale Robinson L PTS 4 Bethnal Green	
15.09.01	Chris Emanuele L RSC 4 Nottingham	
27.04.02	Levi Pattison L RSC 2 Huddersfield	
27.07.02	Jim Betts L RSC 3 Nottingham	
30.10.03	John Bothwell DREW 4 Belfast	
08.05.04	Lee Haskins L RSC 2 Bristol	
19.06.04	Michael Crossan DREW 4 Renfrew	

Career: 18 contests, won 5, drew 4, lost 9.

Danny Moir
Gateshead. *Born* Gateshead, 21 January, 1972
British Masters L.Middleweight Champion. Ht. 5'11"
Manager T. Conroy

04.10.01	Richard Inquieti W PTS 6 Sunderland	
20.10.01	Lee Minter W RSC 1 Portsmouth	
06.12.01	Gary Jones W PTS 6 Sunderland	
08.02.02	Colin McCash W RSC 3 Preston	
08.03.02	Martyn Bailey L PTS 6 Ellesmere Port	
25.03.02	Gavin Pearson L PTS 6 Sunderland	
03.10.02	Andy Gibson L RTD 4 Sunderland	
22.12.02	Richard Inquieti W RTD 3 Salford	
20.01.03	Gary Porter W PTS 6 Glasgow	
27.02.03	Franny Jones DREW 6 Sunderland	
17.03.03	Ciaran Duffy L PTS 6 Glasgow	
29.05.03	Eugenio Monteiro L PTS 6 Sunderland	
09.06.03	Danny Parkinson L PTS 6 Bradford	
02.10.03	Omar Gumati W PTS 6 Sunderland	
20.10.03	Craig Dickson L RSC 3 Glasgow	
04.12.03	Wayne Shepherd W PTS 6 Sunderland	
21.12.03	Geraint Harvey W PTS 6 Bolton	
05.03.04	Franny Jones NC 3 Darlington (Vacant Northern Area L.Middleweight Title)	
12.03.04	Gary Porter DREW 6 Irvine	
25.03.04	Kevin Phelan W PTS 10 Longford (Vacant British Masters L.Middleweight Title)	
27.05.04	Kevin Anderson L RSC 1 Huddersfield	

Career: 21 contests, won 10, drew 2, lost 8, no contest 1..

Michael Monaghan
Nottingham. *Born* Nottingham, 31 May, 1976
Middleweight. Ht. 5'10³/₄"
Manager D. Coldwell

23.09.96	Lee Simpkin W PTS 6 Cleethorpes	
24.10.96	Lee Bird W RSC 6 Lincoln	
09.12.96	Lee Simpkin W PTS 6 Chesterfield	
16.12.96	Carlton Williams W PTS 6 Cleethorpes	
20.03.97	Paul Miles W PTS 6 Newark	
26.04.97	Paul Ryan L RSC 2 Swadlincote	
05.07.97	Ali Khattab W PTS 4 Glasgow	
18.08.97	Trevor Meikle W PTS 6 Nottingham	
12.09.97	Willie Quinn L PTS 6 Glasgow	
19.09.97	Roy Chipperfield W PTS 6 Salford	
30.09.97	George Richards L PTS 6 Edgbaston	
10.03.98	Anthony van Niekirk L RTD 6 Hammanskraal, South Africa	

23.04.98 Darren Sweeney L PTS 10 Edgbaston
*(Midlands Area Middleweight Title
Challenge)*
19.09.98 Jim Rock L PTS 12 Dublin
*(Vacant WAA Inter-Continental
S. Middleweight Title)*
27.11.98 Mark Dawson W PTS 6 Nottingham
07.12.98 Mike Whittaker L PTS 6 Manchester
14.09.02 Paul Billington W RSC 4 Newark
30.11.02 Gary Beardsley W PTS 6 Newark
24.02.03 Jason Collins W PTS 8 Birmingham
16.04.03 Carl Froch L RSC 3 Nottingham
28.06.03 Gary Lockett L PTS 10 Cardiff
13.09.03 Tomas da Silva W PTS 6 Newport
25.04.04 Jason Collins W PTS 6 Nottingham
05.06.04 Wayne Elcock L PTS 4 Bethnal Green
Career: 24 contests, won 14, lost 10.

(Elton) Tony Montana (Gashi)

Sheffield. *Born* Yugoslavia, 5 August, 1982
Central Area L.Welterweight Champion.
Ht. 5'8"
Manager Self

24.11.00 Dave Gibson W PTS 6 Hull
03.12.00 Gary Greenwood DREW 6 Shaw
31.01.01 Pete Buckley W PTS 6 Piccadilly
13.02.01 Barrie Kelley L PTS 6 Brierley Hill
06.03.01 Chris Price W PTS 6 Yarm
18.03.01 Ray Wood DREW 6 Shaw
26.03.01 Francis Barrett L PTS 4 Wembley
24.05.01 Ajose Olusegun L RSC 1 Kensington
07.09.01 Mark Hawthorne L CO 3 Bethnal
Green
16.11.01 Young Muttley L PTS 6 West
Bromwich
30.11.01 Brian Gifford W PTS 6 Hull
17.12.01 Andrei Ivanov DREW 6 Cleethorpes
31.01.02 James Paisley W PTS 6 Piccadilly
11.02.02 Ernie Smith W PTS 6 Shrewsbury
13.04.02 Nicky Leech L PTS 6 Wolverhampton
11.05.02 Robbie Sivyer L PTS 6 Chesterfield
31.05.02 John Marshall L PTS 6 Hull
12.07.02 Chris McDonagh W PTS 4
Southampton
08.09.02 Jimmy Gould W PTS 8
Wolverhampton
21.09.02 Christophe de Busillet L PTS 6
Norwich
02.11.02 Young Muttley L PTS 4
Wolverhampton
22.12.02 Mark Haslam W PTS 6 Salford
28.01.03 Gavin Down L PTS 4 Nottingham
22.03.03 George Telfer W PTS 4 Renfrew
17.07.03 Young Muttley L PTS 4 Walsall
28.11.03 Lenny Daws L PTS 6 Derby
06.02.04 Bobby Vanzie L PTS 6 Sheffield
14.02.04 Gary Hibbert W PTS 6 Nottingham
15.04.04 Dean Hickman L PTS 6 Dudley
23.04.04 Lee Williamson W PTS 6 Leicester
22.05.04 Wayne Rigby W PTS 10 Manchester
*(Vacant Central Area L.Welterweight
Title)*
Career: 31 contests, won 13, drew 3, lost 15.

Eugenio Monteiro

Manchester. *Born* Capo Verde, Portugal, 16
August, 1970
WBU Middleweight Champion. Ht. 5'8"
Manager J. Gill

03.11.00 Gustavo Fernandez L RSC 1 Cordoba,
Spain

24.02.01 Spartak Chincharauli W PTS 4 Olhao,
Portugal
16.11.01 Jaroslaw Klimczuk W RSC 2 Vigo,
Spain
14.12.01 Rafael Perez L PTS 6 Barcelona, Spain
29.01.02 Miguel Angel Dominguez W PTS 6
Estoril, Portugal
15.02.02 Amadeo Pena Lloveras W RSC 4
Barcelona, Spain
22.03.02 Luca Mori W RSC 4 Toscolano
Maderno, Italy
06.04.02 Koren Gevor L PTS 6 Hamburg,
Germany
25.05.02 Ottavio Barone W RSC 5 Spoleto, Italy
05.07.02 Antonio Postigo Lagos W RSC 4
Algarve, Portugal
04.10.02 Ruben Varon Fernandez L PTS 8
Guadalajara, Spain
22.11.02 Lansana Diallo L PTS 8 Ixelles,
Belgium
14.12.02 Ruben Diaz W PTS 6 Zeanuri, Spain
07.02.03 Alvaro Moreno W RSC 6 Algarve,
Portugal
(Vacant TWBA L.Middleweight Title)
29.05.03 Danny Moir W PTS 6 Sunderland
27.09.03 Thomas McDonagh L PTS 12
Manchester
*(Vacant WBU Inter-Continental
L.Middleweight Title)*
28.11.03 Gilbert Eastman W PTS 8 Derby
24.01.04 Takaloo W PTS 8 Wembley
14.05.04 Albert Airapeitian L PTS 8
Torrelodones, Spain
12.06.04 Anthony Farnell W RSC 10
Manchester
(WBU Middleweight Title Challenge)
Career: 20 contests, won 13, lost 7.

Aidan Mooney

Risca. *Born* Newcastle, 7 July, 1980
Welterweight. Ht. 6'0"
Manager H. Holland

08.01.03 Gareth Wiltshaw W PTS 4 Aberdare
31.05.03 Robert Lloyd-Taylor L PTS 4 Bethnal
Green
29.10.03 Chris Brophy W RSC 5 Leicester
Square
Career: 3 contests, won 2, lost 1.

Jamie Moore

Salford. *Born* Salford, 4 November, 1978
British L.Middleweight Champion. Former
Commonwealth L.Middleweight
Champion. Ht. 5'8"
Manager S. Wood/T. Gilmour

09.10.99 Clive Johnson W RSC 3 Manchester
13.11.99 Peter Nightingale W PTS 4 Hull
19.12.99 Paul King W PTS 6 Salford
29.02.00 David Baptiste W RSC 3 Manchester
20.03.00 Harry Butler W RSC 2 Mansfield
14.04.00 Jimmy Steel W PTS 6 Manchester
27.05.00 Koba Kulu W RTD 3 Southwark
07.10.00 Leigh Wicks W PTS 4 Doncaster
12.11.00 Prince Kasi Kaihau W RSC 2
Manchester
25.11.00 Wayne Shepherd W RSC 3 Manchester
17.03.01 Richie Murray W RSC 1 Manchester
27.05.01 Paul Denton W RSC 3 Manchester
07.07.01 Scott Dixon L CO 5 Manchester
*(Vacant WBO Inter-Continental
L.Middleweight Title)*

26.01.02 Harry Butler W RSC 3 Dagenham
09.03.02 Andrzej Butowicz W RSC 5
Manchester
07.09.02 Delroy Mellis W CO 6 Liverpool
08.02.03 Akhmed Oligov W PTS 6 Liverpool
19.04.03 Michael Jones W PTS 12 Liverpool
*(Vacant British L. Middleweight Title.
Commonwealth L. Middleweight Title
Challenge)*
18.10.03 Gary Logan W CO 5 Manchester
*(British & Commonwealth
L.Middleweight Title Defences)*
22.11.03 Andrew Facey W RSC 7 Belfast
*(British & Commonwealth
L.Middleweight Title Defences)*
10.04.04 Adam Katumwa W RSC 5 Manchester
*(Vacant Commonwealth
L.Middleweight Title)*
26.06.04 Ossie Duran L RSC 3 Belfast
*(Commonwealth L.Middleweight Title
Defence)*
Career: 22 contests, won 20, lost 2.

Jamie Moore   Les Clark

Mark Moran

Liverpool. *Born* Liverpool, 16 February,
1982
Bantamweight. Ht. 5'6"
Manager S. Vaughan/F. Warren

02.10.03 Steve Gethin W PTS 4 Liverpool
13.12.03 Delroy Spencer W PTS 4 Manchester
26.02.04 Darren Cleary W PTS 4 Widnes
03.04.04 Neil Read W RSC 2 Manchester
22.05.04 Darren Cleary DREW 4 Widnes
Career: 5 contests, won 4, drew 1.

Tony Moran

Liverpool. *Born* Liverpool, 4 July, 1973
Cruiserweight. Ht. 6'6"
Manager T. Gilmour

26.04.01 Shaun Bowes L PTS 6 Gateshead
13.11.01 Paul Bonson L PTS 6 Leeds
19.03.02 Graham Nolan W PTS 6 Slough
10.05.02 Eamonn Glennon W RTD 1 Preston
03.06.02 Dave Clarke W PTS 6 Glasgow

07.09.02	Adam Cale W PTS 4 Liverpool
05.10.02	Jason Brewster W PTS 4 Liverpool
29.11.02	Adam Cale W RSC 1 Liverpool
08.02.03	Michael Pinnock W PTS 4 Liverpool
17.02.03	Brian Gascoigne W RSC 1 Glasgow
19.04.03	Paul Bonson W PTS 4 Liverpool
17.05.03	Tony Booth W PTS 6 Liverpool
27.10.03	Matthew Ellis W RSC 4 Glasgow
13.03.04	Mark Hobson L RSC 3 Huddersfield
	(British & Commonwealth
	Cruiserweight Title Challenges)

Career: 14 contests, won 11, lost 3.

Terry Morrill

Hull. *Born* Hull, 2 February, 1965
Cruiserweight. Former Central Area L.
Middleweight Champion. Ht. 5'10¼"
Manager Self

10.12.88	Chris Richards W PTS 6 Crystal Palace
08.02.89	Newton Barnett W PTS 6 Kensington
28.03.89	Skip Jackson L RSC 5 Glasgow
27.06.89	Mark Howell W PTS 6 Kensington
10.10.89	Spencer Alton W PTS 6 Hull
15.11.89	Davey Hughes DREW 4 Lewisham
08.12.89	Tony Baker W PTS 6 Doncaster
22.02.90	Mark Holden W RSC 7 Hull
	(Central Area L. Middleweight Title
	Challenge)
10.04.90	Ernie Noble W RSC 7 Doncaster
20.05.90	Jason Rowe L CO 6 Sheffield
	(Central Area L. Middleweight Title
	Defence)
31.10.90	Shaun Cummins L RSC 1 Crystal Palace
14.03.91	Delroy Waul DREW 8 Middleton
28.05.91	Eamonn Loughran L CO 1 Cardiff
16.10.92	Shamus Casey W PTS 6 Hull
16.09.93	Des Robinson W PTS 8 Hull
12.11.93	Shamus Casey W PTS 8 Hull
09.05.96	Lee Simpkin W RSC 5 Hull
06.11.96	Roy Chipperfield W RSC 1 Hull
28.11.96	Jeff Finlayson W PTS 6 Hull
27.02.97	Prince Kasi Kaihau W PTS 6 Hull
21.11.97	Mark Dawson W PTS 6 Hull
28.03.98	Howard Eastman L RTD 4 Hull
09.06.98	Glenn Williams L PTS 4 Hull
30.09.99	Sven Hamer L PTS 6 Kensington
23.10.99	Danilo Haeussler L PTS 8 Telford
13.11.99	Jamie Warters L PTS 8 Hull
12.02.00	Brian Magee L RTD 4 Sheffield
25.07.00	Konstantin Schvets L PTS 6 Southwark
05.05.01	Peter Haymer L PTS 4 Edmonton
21.07.01	Ruben Groenewald L RSC 4 Sheffield
01.11.01	Tony Booth L RSC 7 Hull
14.11.03	Simeon Cover L PTS 6 Hull
04.12.03	Amer Khan L PTS 6 Sunderland
16.01.04	Nate Joseph W PTS 6 Bradford
06.02.04	Amer Khan L PTS 6 Sheffield
25.03.04	Sam Price W RSC 3 Longford
03.04.04	Danny Grainger L RSC 5 Sheffield
02.06.04	Coleman Barrett L PTS 4 Nottingham
14.06.04	Dean Cockburn L RTD 4 Cleethorpes

Career: 39 contests, won 17, drew 2, lost 20.

Andy Morris

Wythenshawe. *Born* Manchester, 10 March,
1983
S. Featherweight. Ht. 5'6½"
Manager F. Warren/F. Maloney

18.01.03	Jason Nesbitt W PTS 4 Preston

05.04.03	Haroon Din W RSC 1 Manchester
08.05.03	Daniel Thorpe W PTS 4 Widnes
06.11.03	Dave Hinds W PTS 4 Dagenham
13.12.03	Henry Janes W PTS 4 Manchester
26.02.04	Daniel Thorpe W RSC 3 Widnes
03.04.04	Carl Allen W PTS 4 Manchester
12.06.04	Jus Wallie W PTS 6 Manchester

Career: 8 contests, won 8.

Jay Morris

Newport, IoW. *Born* Newport, IoW, 8 May,
1978
Welterweight. Ht. 5'7"
Manager R. Davies

21.02.04	Judex Meemea DREW 4 Brighton
30.03.04	Casey Brooke W RSC 1 Southampton

Career: 2 contests, won 1, drew 1.

Barry Morrison

Motherwell. *Born* Bellshill, 8 May, 1980
L.Welterweight. Ht. 5'7"
Manager T. Gilmour

12.04.03	Keith Jones W PTS 4 Bethnal Green
28.04.03	Arv Mittoo W RSC 3 Nottingham
05.07.03	Cristian Hodorogea W RSC 3 Brentwood
06.09.03	Jay Mahoney W RSC 2 Huddersfield
04.10.03	Sergei Starkov W PTS 6 Belfast
01.11.03	Tarik Amrous W PTS 8 Glasgow
28.02.04	Zoltan Surman W RSC 3 Bridgend
22.04.04	Andrei Devyataykin W PTS 8 Glasgow

Career: 8 contests, won 8.

Abdul Mougharbel (Almgharbel)

Dewsbury. *Born* Syria, 10 November, 1975
Bantamweight. Ht. 5'4"
Manager C. Aston

15.03.04	Hussain Nasser W RTD 3 Bradford
19.04.04	Sandy Bartlett W PTS 6 Glasgow

Career: 2 contests, won 2.

Lee Mountford

Pudsey. *Born* Leeds, 1 September, 1972
Heavyweight. Ht. 6'2"
Manager T. O'Neill

19.04.02	Gary Thompson DREW 4 Darlington
24.06.02	Eamonn Glennon L PTS 6 Bradford
20.11.02	Nate Joseph W PTS 6 Leeds
03.02.03	Eamonn Glennon DREW 6 Bradford
28.02.03	Gary Thompson W PTS 6 Irvine
13.05.03	Nate Joseph L PTS 6 Leeds
01.12.03	Dave Clarke W PTS 6 Bradford
15.03.04	Greg Scott-Briggs DREW 6 Bradford
09.04.04	Carl Wright L PTS 4 Rugby
20.04.04	Lee Swaby L RSC 1 Sheffield

Career: 10 contests, won 3, drew 3, lost 4.

Steve Mullin

Liverpool. *Born* Liverpool, 7 July, 1983
S. Featherweight. Ht. 5'7"
Manager S. Vaughan

19.04.03	Daniel Thorpe L RSC 1 Liverpool
20.06.03	Dave Hinds W PTS 4 Liverpool
29.08.03	Peter Allen W PTS 6 Liverpool
08.12.03	Sid Razak W PTS 6 Birmingham
08.03.04	Sid Razak W PTS 6 Birmingham

Career: 5 contests, won 4, lost 1.

Rendall Munroe

Leicester. *Born* Leicester, 1 June, 1980
S. Featherweight. Ht. 5'7"
Manager M. Shinfield

20.09.03	Joel Viney W RTD 3 Nottingham
23.11.03	John-Paul Ryan W PTS 6 Rotherham
14.02.04	Neil Read W RSC 1 Nottingham
09.04.04	Anthony Hanna W PTS 6 Rugby
26.04.04	Baz Carey W PTS 6 Cleethorpes

Career: 5 contests, won 5.

Rendall Munroe   Les Clark

Lawrence Murphy

Uddingston. *Born* Bellshill, 9 February,
1976
Middleweight. Former WBU Middleweight
Champion. Ht. 6'1"
Manager A. Morrison

15.05.98	Mark Owens W RSC 2 Edinburgh
17.09.98	Lee Bird W RSC 3 Glasgow
13.11.98	Ian Toby W PTS 6 Glasgow
18.02.99	Mike Duffield W RSC 2 Glasgow
26.06.99	Harry Butler W RSC 1 Glasgow
17.12.00	Michael Alexander W PTS 6 Glasgow
07.09.01	Chris Nembhard DREW 6 Glasgow
17.11.01	Leigh Wicks W PTS 4 Glasgow
16.12.01	Kreshnik Qato W PTS 6 Glasgow
11.03.02	Rob Stevenson W RSC 1 Glasgow
22.03.03	Leigh Wicks W PTS 4 Renfrew
12.07.03	Jason Collins W PTS 4 Renfrew
25.10.03	Howard Clarke W PTS 6 Edinburgh
29.11.03	Wayne Elcock W CO 1 Renfrew
	(WBU Middleweight Title Challenge)
06.03.04	Anthony Farnell L RSC 3 Renfrew
	(WBU Middleweight Title Defence)

Career: 15 contests, won 13, drew 1, lost 1.

John Murray

Manchester. *Born* Manchester, 20
December, 1984
S. Featherweight. Ht. 5'8"
Manager S. Wood/T. Gilmour

06.09.03	Pete Buckley W PTS 4 Huddersfield
18.10.03	Matthew Burke W RSC 1 Manchester
21.12.03	Jason Nesbitt W PTS 6 Bolton
30.01.04	Norman Dhalie W CO 2 Dagenham
12.03.04	John-Paul Ryan W RSC 1 Nottingham
02.06.04	Anthony Hanna W PTS 4 Nottingham

Career: 6 contests, won 6.

Oneal Murray

Brixton. *Born* Jamaica, 8 March, 1973
Cruiserweight. Ht. 6'0"
Manager D. V. Williams

29.03.01	Oddy Papantoniou L PTS 4 Hammersmith	
04.10.01	Michael Pinnock W PTS 6 Finsbury	
15.10.01	Joe Brame W RSC 2 Southampton	
15.12.01	Steven Spartacus L RSC 4 Chigwell	
27.01.02	Adam Cale W PTS 4 Streatham	
23.02.03	Brodie Pearmaine L PTS 4 Streatham	
13.04.03	Dave Clarke L PTS 4 Streatham	
14.02.04	Tony Booth L PTS 8 Holborn	

Career: 8 contests, won 3, lost 5.

Steve Murray

Harlow. *Born* Harlow, 5 October, 1975
Lightweight. Former WBO Inter-Continental Lightweight Champion. Former Undefeated IBF Inter-Continental Lightweight Champion. Ht. 5'6"
Manager Self

10.10.98	Keith Jones W RSC 4 Bethnal Green
14.11.98	Dave Travers W RSC 2 Cheshunt
23.01.99	Marc Smith W RSC 1 Cheshunt
30.01.99	Dewi Roberts W RSC 1 Bethnal Green
03.04.99	Woody Greenaway W CO 2 Kensington
01.05.99	Keith Jones W RSC 6 Crystal Palace
26.06.99	Brian Coleman W PTS 6 Millwall
07.08.99	Pete Buckley W PTS 6 Dagenham
15.11.99	Karl Taylor W RSC 1 Bethnal Green
29.01.00	Keith Jones W PTS 4 Manchester
19.02.00	Juan Carlos Zummaraga W RSC 1 Dagenham
	(Vacant IBF Inter-Continental Lightweight Title)
29.05.00	Wahid Fats W RSC 3 Manchester
24.06.00	Nono Junior W RSC 4 Glasgow
12.08.00	Alan Temple W RSC 2 Wembley
	(IBF Inter-Continental Lightweight Title Defence. Elim. British Lightweight Title)
23.09.00	David Kirk W PTS 4 Bethnal Green
24.02.01	Sergei Starkov W PTS 8 Bethnal Green
05.05.01	Bobby Vanzie L RSC 7 Edmonton
	(British Lightweight Title Challenge)
22.09.01	Darren Melville W PTS 8 Bethnal Green
24.11.01	Keith Jones W RSC 4 Bethnal Green
15.12.01	Jason Hall W RSC 4 Wembley
	(Elim. British Lightweight Title)
02.03.02	Viktor Baranov W RSC 5 Bethnal Green
	(Vacant WBO Inter-Continental Lightweight Title)
04.05.02	Rosalin Nasibulin W CO 5 Bethnal Green
14.09.02	Yuri Romanov L RSC 10 Bethnal Green
	(WBO Inter-Continental Lightweight Title Defence)
15.02.03	Graham Earl L RSC 2 Wembley
	(Southern Area Lightweight Title Challenge. Final Elim. British Lightweight Title)
24.01.04	Jimmy Beech W RSC 4 Wembley
01.04.04	Martin Watson W PTS 10 Bethnal Green

Career: 26 contests, won 23, lost 3.

Lee Murtagh

Leeds. *Born* Leeds, 30 September, 1973
L.Middleweight. Former British Masters Middleweight Champion. Former British Masters L.Middleweight Champion. Ht. 5'9¼"
Manager J. O'Neill/K. Walker

12.06.95	Dave Curtis W PTS 6 Bradford
25.09.95	Roy Gbasai W PTS 6 Bradford
30.10.95	Cam Raeside L PTS 6 Bradford
11.12.95	Donovan Davey W PTS 6 Bradford
13.01.96	Peter Varnavas W PTS 6 Halifax
05.02.96	Shamus Casey W PTS 6 Bradford
20.05.96	Shaun O'Neill W PTS 6 Bradford
24.06.96	Michael Alexander W PTS 6 Bradford
28.10.96	Jimmy Vincent L RSC 2 Bradford
14.04.97	Lee Simpkin W PTS 6 Bradford
09.10.97	Brian Dunn W PTS 6 Leeds
05.03.98	Wayne Shepherd W PTS 6 Leeds
08.08.98	Alan Gilbert W PTS 4 Scarborough
13.03.99	Keith Palmer DREW 6 Manchester
27.09.99	Jawaid Khaliq L RSC 5 Leeds
	(Vacant WBF European L.Middleweight Title)
27.02.00	Gareth Lovell W PTS 6 Leeds
24.09.00	Jon Foster W PTS 6 Shaw
03.12.00	Michael Alexander W PTS 6 Shaw
17.05.01	Ojay Abrahams L RSC 2 Leeds
	(Vacant British Masters L.Middleweight Title)
03.03.02	Howard Clarke NC 2 Shaw
19.04.02	Neil Bonner W PTS 6 Darlington
21.06.02	Wayne Shepherd W PTS 10 Leeds
	(Vacant British Masters Middleweight Title)
02.12.02	Martyn Bailey L RSC 6 Leeds
	(British Masters Middleweight Title Defence)
10.05.03	Darren Rhodes L PTS 6 Huddersfield
15.09.03	Matt Scriven W DIS 9 Leeds
	(British Masters L.Middleweight Title Challenge)
01.12.03	Gary Beardsley L RSC 6 Leeds
	(British Masters L.Middleweight Title Defence)
08.06.04	Robert Burton L CO 3 Sheffield
	(Vacant Central Area L.Middleweight Title)

Career: 27 contests, won 17, drew 1, lost 8, no contest 1.

(Nikos) Rocky Muscus (Agrapidis Israel)

Chertsey. *Born* Athens, Greece, 5 August, 1983
L. Middleweight. Ht. 5'6½"
Manager J. Evans

12.05.03	Danny Cooper L PTS 6 Southampton
18.09.03	Wayne Wheeler L PTS 6 Mayfair
27.10.03	Graham Delehedy L RSC 2 Glasgow

Career: 3 contests, lost 3.

Farai Musiiwa

Birmingham. *Born* Zimbabwe, 20 March, 1980
S. Middleweight. Ht. 5'11"
Manager Self

18.12.99	Rodgers Mudzihari W RSC 3 Harare, Zimbabwe
29.01.00	Jacob Ndlovu W RSC 2 Harare, Zimbabwe
05.02.00	Richard Natsika W RSC 4 Harare, Zimbabwe
26.02.00	Boxer King W RSC 1 Harare, Zimbabwe
04.03.00	Soul Sibanda W RSC 5 Harare, Zimbabwe
25.03.00	Farai Kachigwanda L RSC 3 Harare, Zimbabwe
24.06.00	Patrick Mulambo W PTS 6 Harare, Zimbabwe
24.03.01	Tapiwa Mapindano L PTS 4 Harare, Zimbabwe
25.05.01	Frank Mutiyaya W PTS 8 Gwaru, Zimbabwe
07.07.01	Jonas Mwale W RSC 3 Gwaru, Zimbabwe
06.10.01	Saidi Kassim W PTS 10 Harare, Zimbabwe
16.02.02	Peter Musundire W CO 1 Harare, Zimbabwe
16.02.02	Richard Hwata W RSC 6 Harare, Zimbabwe
25.05.02	Benny Chilando W RSC 6 Livingstone, Zambia
13.07.02	Gift Chiombela W RSC 3 Harare, Zimbabwe
05.10.02	James Hare L RSC 8 Huddersfield
	(Commonwealth Welterweight Title Challenge)
27.11.02	Joshua Okine L RSC 4 Mayfair
	(Vacant WBF Welterweight Title)
26.07.03	Adrian Stone L CO 4 Plymouth
20.09.03	Mihaly Kotai W PTS 6 Nottingham
19.10.03	Gary Dixon W PTS 6 Shaw
06.12.03	Eric Teymour L PTS 6 Cardiff
07.02.04	Wayne Elcock L PTS 6 Bethnal Green
21.02.04	Bradley Pryce W PTS 6 Cardiff

Career: 23 contests, won 16, lost 7.

(Lee) Young Muttley (Woodley)

West Bromwich. *Born* West Bromwich, 17 May, 1976
English L.Welterweight Champion. Former Undefeated Midlands Area L.Welterweight Champion. Ht. 5'8½"
Manager E. Johnson

03.09.99	Dave Hinds W RSC 4 West Bromwich
24.10.99	David Kehoe W RTD 1 Wolverhampton
22.01.00	Wahid Fats L PTS 4 Birmingham
18.02.00	Stuart Rimmer W RSC 1 West Bromwich
27.11.00	Peter Dunn W RSC 3 Birmingham
07.09.01	Jon Honney W RSC 1 West Bromwich
16.11.01	Tony Montana W PTS 6 West Bromwich
26.11.01	Lee Byrne W RSC 1 Manchester
23.02.02	Brian Coleman W PTS 4 Nottingham
23.03.02	Adam Zadworny W RSC 3 Southwark
02.11.02	Tony Montana W PTS 4 Wolverhampton
21.03.03	Gary Reid W RSC 7 West Bromwich
	(Vacant Midlands Area L.Welterweight Title)
28.04.03	John Marshall W RSC 5 Nottingham
17.07.03	Tony Montana W PTS 4 Walsall
19.02.04	Peter Dunn W PTS 4 Dudley
08.05.04	Sammy Smith W RSC 1 Bristol
	(Vacant English L.Welterweight Title)

Career: 16 contests, won 15, lost 1.

147

Ronnie Nailen

Glasgow. *Born* Belfast, 2 April, 1981
Welterweight. Ht. 5'10"
Manager R. Bannan

24.05.01	David White W PTS 6 Glasgow
20.10.01	Keith Jones W PTS 4 Glasgow
08.06.02	Brian Coleman W PTS 4 Renfrew
30.10.03	Glenn McClarnon L RSC 1 Belfast

Career: 4 contests, won 3, lost 1.

Ian Napa

Hackney. *Born* Zimbabwe, 14 March, 1978
Featherweight. Former Undefeated
Southern Area Flyweight Champion.
Ht. 5'1"
Manager B. Lawrence

06.06.98	Nick Tooley W PTS 6 Liverpool
14.07.98	Nicky Booth W PTS 6 Reading
10.10.98	Sean Green W PTS 6 Bethnal Green
30.01.99	Delroy Spencer W PTS 6 Bethnal Green
15.11.99	Mark Reynolds W PTS 10 Bethnal Green
	(Southern Area Flyweight Title Challenge)
19.02.00	Anthony Hanna W PTS 6 Dagenham
08.04.00	Delroy Spencer W PTS 8 Bethnal Green
15.07.00	Jamie Evans W PTS 4 Millwall
13.11.00	Jason Booth L PTS 12 Bethnal Green
	(British & Commonwealth Flyweight Title Challenges)
24.02.01	Oleg Kiryukhin W PTS 6 Bethnal Green
09.06.01	Peter Culshaw L RSC 8 Bethnal Green
	(WBU Flyweight Title Challenge)
08.05.04	Danny Costello W PTS 4 Dagenham

Career: 12 contests, won 10, lost 2.

Ian Napa   Les Clark

Hussain Nasser

Sheffield. *Born* Yemen, 14 February, 1984
Flyweight. Ht. 5'2"
Manager J. Ingle

17.10.03	Michael Crossan L PTS 6 Glasgow
15.03.04	Abdul Mougharbel L RTD 3 Bradford

Career: 2 contests, lost 2.

Johnny Nelson

Sheffield. *Born* Sheffield, 4 January, 1967
WBO Cruiserweight Champion. Former
Undefeated British & European
Cruiserweight Champion. Former
Undefeated WBU Heavyweight Champion.
Former WBF Heavyweight Champion.
Former WBF Cruiserweight Champion.
Former Undefeated Central Area
Cruiserweight Champion. Ht. 6'2"
Manager J. Ingle

18.03.86	Peter Brown L PTS 6 Hull
15.05.86	Tommy Taylor L PTS 6 Dudley
03.10.86	Magne Havnaa L PTS 4 Copenhagen, Denmark
20.11.86	Chris Little W PTS 6 Bredbury
19.01.87	Gypsy Carman W PTS 6 Mayfair
02.03.87	Doug Young W PTS 6 Huddersfield
10.03.87	Sean Daly W RSC 1 Manchester
28.04.87	Brian Schumacher L PTS 8 Halifax
03.06.87	Byron Pullen W RSC 3 Southwark
14.12.87	Jon McBean W RSC 6 Edgbaston
01.02.88	Dennis Bailey L PTS 8 Northampton
24.02.88	Cordwell Hylton W RSC 1 Sheffield
25.04.88	Kenny Jones W CO 1 Liverpool
04.05.88	Crawford Ashley W PTS 8 Solihull
06.06.88	Lennie Howard W CO 2 Mayfair
31.08.88	Andrew Gerrard W PTS 8 Stoke
26.10.88	Danny Lawford W RSC 2 Sheffield
	(Vacant Central Area Cruiserweight Title)
04.04.89	Steve Mormino W RSC 2 Sheffield
21.05.89	Andy Straughn W CO 8 Finsbury Park
	(British Cruiserweight Title Challenge)
02.10.89	Ian Bulloch W CO 2 Hanley
	(British Cruiserweight Title Defence)
27.01.90	Carlos de Leon DREW 12 Sheffield
	(WBC Cruiserweight Title Challenge)
14.02.90	Dino Homsey W RSC 7 Brentwood
28.03.90	Lou Gent W CO 4 Bethnal Green
	(British Cruiserweight Title Defence)
27.06.90	Arthur Weathers W RSC 2 Kensington
05.09.90	Andre Smith W PTS 8 Brighton
14.12.90	Markus Bott W RSC 12 Karlsruhe, Germany
	(Vacant European Cruiserweight Title)
12.03.91	Yves Monsieur W RTD 8 Mansfield
	(European Cruiserweight Title Defence)
16.05.92	James Warring L PTS 12 Fredericksburg, USA
	(IBF Cruiserweight Title Challenge)
15.08.92	Norbert Ekassi L RSC 3 Ajaccio, France
29.10.92	Corrie Sanders L PTS 10 Morula, South Africa
30.04.93	Dave Russell W RSC 11 Melbourne, Australia
	(WBF Cruiserweight Title Challenge)
11.08.93	Tom Collins W RSC 1 Mansfield
	(WBF Cruiserweight Title Defence)
01.10.93	Francis Wanyama L DIS 10 Waregem, Belgium
	(WBF Cruiserweight Title Defence)
20.11.93	Jimmy Thunder W PTS 12 Auckland, New Zealand
	(WBF Heavyweight Title Challenge)

Hussain Nasser (right column continued)

05.04.94	Henry Akinwande L PTS 10 Bethnal Green
05.11.94	Nikolai Kulpin W PTS 12 Bangkok, Thailand
	(WBF Heavyweight Title Defence)
22.08.95	Adilson Rodrigues L PTS 12 Sao Paulo, Brazil
	(WBF Heavyweight Title Defence)
03.12.95	Adilson Rodrigues L PTS 12 Sao Paulo, Brazil
	(WBF Heavyweight Title Challenge)
20.01.96	Tony Booth W RSC 2 Mansfield
14.12.96	Dennis Andries W RSC 7 Sheffield
	(Vacant British Cruiserweight Title)
22.02.97	Patrice Aouissi W RSC 7 Berck sur Mer, France
	(Vacant European Cruiserweight Title)
19.07.97	Michael Murray W PTS 4 Wembley
11.10.97	Dirk Wallyn W RSC 1 Sheffield
	(European Cruiserweight Title Defence)
18.07.98	Peter Oboh W RTD 6 Sheffield
27.03.99	Carl Thompson W RSC 5 Derby
	(WBO Cruiserweight Title Challenge)
15.05.99	Bruce Scott W PTS 12 Sheffield
	(WBO Cruiserweight Title Defence)
07.08.99	Willard Lewis W RTD 4 Dagenham
	(WBO Cruiserweight Title Defence)
18.09.99	Sione Asipeli W PTS 12 Las Vegas, Nevada, USA
	(WBO Cruiserweight Title Defence)
06.11.99	Christophe Girard W CO 4 Widnes
	(WBO Cruiserweight Title Defence)
08.04.00	Pietro Aurino W RTD 7 Bethnal Green
	(WBO Cruiserweight Title Defence)
07.10.00	Adam Watt W RSC 5 Doncaster
	(WBO Cruiserweight Title Defence)
27.01.01	George Arias W PTS 12 Bethnal Green
	(WBO Cruiserweight Title Defence)
21.07.01	Marcelo Dominguez W PTS 12 Sheffield
	(WBO Cruiserweight Title Defence)
24.11.01	Alex Vasiliev W PTS 12 Bethnal Green
	(Vacant WBU Heavyweight Title)
06.04.02	Ezra Sellers W CO 8 Copenhagen, Denmark
	(WBO Cruiserweight Title Defence)
23.11.02	Guillermo Jones DREW 12 Derby
	(WBO Cruiserweight Title Defence)
15.11.03	Alexander Petkovic W PTS 12 Bayreuth, Germany
	(WBO Cruiserweight Title Defence)

Career: 57 contests, won 43, drew 2, lost 12.

Chris Nembhard

Leytonstone. *Born* Jamaica, 26 December, 1976
S. Middleweight. Ht. 6'1"
Manager Self

29.09.00	Gary Ojuederie W RSC 1 Bethnal Green
02.11.00	Koba Kulu W PTS 6 Kensington
10.11.00	William Webster W RSC 1 Mayfair
15.02.01	Keith Ellwood W RSC 2 Glasgow
23.02.01	David Baptiste W PTS 8 Barking
09.03.01	Rob Stevenson W RSC 2 Millwall
20.04.01	Delroy Mellis L RSC 8 Millwall
	(Southern Area L. Middleweight Title Challenge)
31.07.01	Brian Magee L RSC 6 Bethnal Green
07.09.01	Lawrence Murphy DREW 6 Glasgow
24.11.01	Gary Lockett L RSC 2 Bethnal Green
13.09.02	Mark Graversen W RTD 2 Aarhus, Denmark

20.10.02　Matthew Barney L PTS 10 Southwark
　　　　　(*Southern Area S. Middleweight Title*
　　　　　Challenge)
27.11.03　Denis Inkin L CO 4 Moscow, Russia
　　　　　(*IBF International S.Middleweight*
　　　　　Title Challenge)
Career: 13 contests, won 7, drew 1, lost 5.

Jason Nesbitt

Birmingham. *Born* Birmingham, 15
December, 1973
Lightweight. Ht. 5'9"
Manager Self

06.11.00　Stephen Chinnock L PTS 6
　　　　　Wolverhampton
09.12.00　Lee Meager L RSC 2 Southwark
29.01.01　Henry Castle L CO 6 Peterborough
27.03.01　Billy Smith W PTS 6 Brierley Hill
21.05.01　Sid Razak L PTS 6 Birmingham
04.06.01　Andrew Ferrans L RSC 2 Glasgow
07.07.01　Colin Toohey L PTS 4 Manchester
15.09.01　Colin Toohey L PTS 4 Manchester
22.09.01　John Mackay L PTS 4 Canning Town
01.11.01　Chris Hooper L RSC 6 Hull
16.03.02　Lee Meager L PTS 6 Bethnal Green
27.03.02　Greg Edwards W RSC 5 Mayfair
20.04.02　Henry Castle L PTS 4 Cardiff
04.05.02　Danny Hunt L PTS 4 Bethnal Green
15.06.02　Jesse James Daniel L PTS 4 Leeds
27.07.02　Craig Spacie L PTS 4 Nottingham
23.08.02　Billy Corcoran L PTS 4 Bethnal Green
25.10.02　Billy Corcoran L RSC 2 Bethnal Green
03.12.02　Mark Bowen L PTS 6 Shrewsbury
11.12.02　Matt Teague L PTS 6 Hull
20.12.02　Chris McDonagh L PTS 6 Bracknell
18.01.03　Andy Morris L PTS 4 Preston
09.02.03　Mally McIver L PTS 6 Bradford
09.03.03　Choi Tseveenpurev L PTS 8 Shaw
29.03.03　Kevin O'Hara L RSC 3 Portsmouth
07.05.03　Henry Jones L PTS 6 Ellesmere Port
02.06.03　Stefy Bull L PTS 6 Cleethorpes
13.06.03　Scott Lawton L PTS 6 Queensway
17.07.03　Haider Ali L PTS 4 Dagenham
29.08.03　Gary Thornhill L CO 1 Liverpool
05.10.03　Nadeem Siddique L PTS 6 Bradford
08.11.03　Harry Ramogoadi L PTS 6 Coventry
23.11.03　Amir Ali L PTS 6 Rotherham
10.12.03　Femi Fehintola L PTS 6 Sheffield
21.12.03　John Murray L PTS 6 Bolton
06.02.04　Femi Fehintola L PTS 6 Sheffield
23.02.04　Carl Greaves L PTS 6 Nottingham
05.03.04　Haroon Din L PTS 6 Darlington
12.03.04　Stuart Green L PTS 8 Irvine
03.04.04　Daniel Thorpe L PTS 6 Sheffield
16.04.04　John O'Donnell L PTS 4 Bradford
27.04.04　Jim Betts L PTS 6 Leeds
07.05.04　Jus Halim L PTS 6 Bethnal Green
28.05.04　John Bothwell W RSC 3 Glasgow
05.06.04　Kevin Mitchell L RSC 3 Bethnal Green
Career: 45 contests, won 3, lost 42.

Dean Nicholas

South Shields. *Born* South Shields, 9 May,
1973
Welterweight. Ht. 5'9"
Manager Self

22.09.95　David Thompson W PTS 6 Hull
02.11.95　Paul Scott W PTS 6 Houghton le
　　　　　Spring
20.11.95　Shaun Gledhill W RSC 4 Glasgow
14.02.96　Shaun O'Neill W PTS 6 Sunderland

22.04.96　John Smith W PTS 6 Glasgow
09.05.96　John Docherty L PTS 6 Glasgow
23.09.96　Mark Breslin L PTS 8 Glasgow
01.12.96　C. J. Jackson DREW 6 Shaw
27.02.97　Keith Scott L PTS 6 Sunderland
09.10.97　Donovan Davey W PTS 6 Hull
27.10.97　Ray Newby L PTS 6 Nottingham
30.11.97　Lee Molyneux W PTS 6 Shaw
03.02.98　Leon Cessiron L RSC 4 Pont Audemer,
　　　　　France
07.04.98　Jose Etinoff L CO 1 Epernay, France
29.10.98　Richard Inquieti W RSC 1 Newcastle
25.01.99　Glenn McClarnon L CO 1 Glasgow
29.05.99　Peter Dunn W PTS 6 South Shields
29.06.99　Paul Knights L RSC 4 Bethnal Green
17.04.00　James Docherty L RSC 6 Glasgow
23.10.00　James Hare L RSC 1 Glasgow
24.11.00　Oscar Hall L PTS 6 Darlington
05.02.01　Danny Parkinson L PTS 6 Bradford
23.02.01　Richard Inquieti W PTS 6 Irvine
19.03.01　Darren Spencer L RSC 4 Glasgow
22.09.01　Oscar Hall L DIS 9 Newcastle
　　　　　(*Vacant Northern Area Welterweight*
　　　　　Title)
04.12.03　Danny Parkinson W RSC 4 Huddersfield
19.01.04　Craig Dickson L RSC 5 Glasgow
Career: 27 contests, won 11, drew 1, lost 15.

Lee Nicholson

Doncaster. *Born* Mexborough, 10
November, 1976
L. Heavyweight. Ht. 5'11"
Manager J. Rushton

24.09.01　Jason Brewster L PTS 6 Cleethorpes
17.02.02　Jason Brewster L PTS 6 Wolverhampton
11.05.02　Fola Okesola L RSC 1 Bethnal Green
07.09.03　Stewart West L RSC 2 Shrewsbury
01.12.03　Mike Duffield W PTS 6 Barnsley
15.12.03　Simeon Cover L RSC 4 Cleethorpes
Career: 6 contests, won 1, lost 5.

Dale Nixon

Taunton. *Born* Exeter, 11 May, 1970
L. Heavyweight. Ht. 6'2"
Manager N. Christian

09.03.93　Ian Vokes W RSC 2 Bristol
27.05.93　Chris Nurse W RSC 2 Bristol
26.06.93　Tim Robinson W RSC 2 Keynsham
03.11.93　Jason McNeill W RSC 1 Bristol
10.03.94　Jerry Mortimer DREW 4 Bristol
31.03.94　Steve Thomas DREW 4 Bristol
25.06.94　Robert Peel W PTS 6 Cullompton
07.10.94　Robert Peel W RSC 7 Taunton
06.05.95　Darren Ashton L RSC 4 Shepton Mallet
09.12.02　Hamid Jamali L CO 1 Birmingham
06.03.03　Liam Lathbury L PTS 4 Bristol
17.03.03　Michael Matthewsian DREW 6
　　　　　Southampton
05.04.03　Mark Phillips W PTS 6 Coventry
13.06.03　Darren Dorrington L RSC 5 Bristol
05.12.03　Leigh Alliss L RSC 2 Bristol
13.02.04　Gareth Hogg L RTD 4 Bristol
Career: 16 contest, won 7, drew 3, lost 6.

Danny Norton

Stourbridge. *Born* Wordsley, 8 November,
1969
L. Heavyweight. Ht. 6'0"
Manager Self

07.10.01　Mark Phillips W PTS 6 Wolverhampton

19.04.02　Andy Vickers W CO 2 Darlington
13.07.02　Liam Lathbury W PTS 4
　　　　　Wolverhampton
20.12.02　Jamie Hearn L PTS 4 Bracknell
19.02.04　Shpetim Hoti W PTS 4 Dudley
15.04.04　William Webster W PTS 4 Dudley
04.06.04　Simeon Cover W RSC 3 Dudley
Career: 7 contests, won 6, lost 1.

Robert Norton

Stourbridge. *Born* Dudley, 20 January, 1972
Cruiserweight. Former WBU Cruiserweight
Champion. Ht. 6'2"
Manager J. Weaver

30.09.93　Stuart Fleet W CO 2 Walsall
27.10.93　Kent Davis W PTS 6 West Bromwich
02.12.93　Eddie Pyatt W RSC 2 Walsall
26.01.94　Lennie Howard W PTS 6 Birmingham
17.05.94　Steve Osborne W PTS 6 Kettering
05.10.94　Chris Woollas DREW 6 Wolverhampton
30.11.94　L. A. Williams W RSC 2
　　　　　Wolverhampton
10.02.95　Newby Stevens W RSC 3 Birmingham
22.02.95　Steve Osborne W PTS 6 Telford
21.04.95　Cordwell Hylton W PTS 6 Dudley
25.10.95　Nigel Rafferty W RSC 6 Telford
31.01.96　Gary Williams W RSC 2 Birmingham
25.04.96　Steve Osborne W RSC 5 Mayfair
01.10.96　Andrew Benson W RSC 6 Birmingham
12.11.96　Nigel Rafferty W PTS 8 Dudley
11.02.97　Touami Benhamed W RSC 5 Bethnal
　　　　　Green
16.04.97　Tony Booth W RSC 4 Bethnal Green
20.12.97　Darren Corbett L PTS 12 Belfast
　　　　　(*Commonwealth Cruiserweight Title*
　　　　　Challenge)
03.04.98　Adrian Nicolai W RSC 2 West
　　　　　Bromwich
03.10.98　Tim Brown W CO 3 West Bromwich
01.04.99　Jacob Mofokeng W PTS 12
　　　　　Birmingham
　　　　　(*WBU Cruiserweight Title Challenge*)
24.09.99　Sebastiaan Rothmann L RSC 8 Merthyr
　　　　　(*WBU Cruiserweight Title Defence*)
30.09.00　Tony Booth W RSC 3 Peterborough
18.11.00　Darron Griffiths W PTS 10 Dagenham
　　　　　(*Elim. British Cruiserweight Title*)
05.02.01　Lee Swaby W PTS 8 Hull
30.11.02　Paul Bonson W PTS 6 Coventry
05.09.03　Mark Hobson L PTS 12 Sheffield
　　　　　(*Commonwealth Cruiserweight Title*
　　　　　Challenge. Vacant British
　　　　　Cruiserweight Title)
09.04.04　Greg Scott-Briggs W CO 1 Rugby
Career: 28 contests, won 24, drew 1, lost 3.

(Paulus) Ali Nuumbembe

Glossop. *Born* Oshakati, Namibia, 24 June,
1978
Welterweight. Ht. 5'8¹/₂"
Manager B. Ingle

16.04.03　Dai Bando W PTS 4 Nottingham
15.06.03　Ernie Smith W PTS 4 Bradford
03.08.03　Lee Williamson W PTS 6 Stalybridge
29.08.03　Ernie Smith W PTS 6 Liverpool
05.10.03　Keith Jones W PTS 6 Bradford
07.12.03　Brian Coleman W RTD 2 Bradford
16.01.04　Wayne Wheeler W RSC 1 Bradford
29.02.04　William Webster W RSC 3 Shaw
10.04.04　Peter Dunn W PTS 6 Manchester
Career: 9 contests, won 9.

Tony Oakey

Portsmouth. *Born* Portsmouth, 2 January, 1976
L.Heavyweight. Former WBU L.Heavyweight Champion. Former Undefeated Commonwealth & Southern Area L.Heavyweight Champion. Ht. 5'8"
Manager Self

12.09.98	Smokey Enison W RSC 2 Bethnal Green	
21.11.98	Zak Chelli W RSC 1 Southwark	
16.01.99	Jimmy Steel W PTS 4 Bethnal Green	
06.03.99	Mark Dawson W PTS 4 Southwark	
10.07.99	Jimmy Steel W PTS 4 Southwark	
01.10.99	Michael Pinnock W PTS 4 Bethnal Green	
21.02.00	Darren Ashton W PTS 4 Southwark	
13.03.00	Martin Jolley W PTS 6 Bethnal Green	
21.10.00	Darren Ashton W PTS 4 Wembley	
27.01.01	Nathan King W PTS 6 Bethnal Green	
26.03.01	Butch Lesley W PTS 10 Wembley *(Southern Area L. Heavyweight Title Challenge)*	
08.05.01	Hastings Rasani W RSC 10 Barnsley *(Vacant Commonwealth L. Heavyweight Title)*	
09.09.01	Konstantin Ochrej W RSC 4 Southwark	
20.10.01	Chris Davies W PTS 12 Portsmouth *(Commonwealth L.Heavyweight Title Defence)*	
02.03.02	Konstantin Shvets W PTS 12 Bethnal Green *(Vacant WBU L. Heavyweight Title)*	
25.05.02	Neil Simpson W PTS 12 Portsmouth *(WBU L. Heavyweight Title Defence)*	
12.10.02	Andrei Kaersten W PTS 12 Bethnal Green *(WBU L. Heavyweight Title Defence)*	
29.03.03	Neil Linford W PTS 12 Portsmouth *(WBU L. Heavyweight Title Defence)*	
11.10.03	Matthew Barney L PTS 12 Portsmouth *(WBU L.Heavyweight Title Defence)*	

Career: 19 contests, won 18, lost 1.

Stephen Oates

Fulham. *Born* Leeds, 11 July, 1975
S. Featherweight. Ht. 5'5½"
Manager A. Bowers

29.11.97	Gary Hickman W PTS 4 Norwich	
17.01.98	Chris Emanuele W RSC 4 Bristol	
07.02.98	Stevie Quinn W PTS 4 Cheshunt	
07.03.98	Marty Chestnut W PTS 6 Reading	
16.05.98	Harry Woods W PTS 4 Bethnal Green	
14.07.98	John Matthews L PTS 4 Reading	
10.10.98	Graham McGrath W PTS 4 Bethnal Green	
14.11.98	Chris Jickells W PTS 6 Cheshunt	
13.02.99	Delroy Pryce L PTS 6 Newcastle	
03.04.99	Ross Cassidy W RSC 1 Kensington	
26.06.99	Harry Woods W PTS 6 Millwall	
04.09.99	Danny Ruegg W PTS 6 Bethnal Green	
15.11.99	Jason Thomas W PTS 6 Bethnal Green	
19.02.00	Jason Thomas W PTS 6 Dagenham	
21.10.00	Daniel Ring W RSC 1 Wembley	
16.12.00	Chris Jickells W PTS 4 Sheffield	
17.03.01	Chris Emanuele W PTS 8 Manchester	
09.06.01	Nathan Sting L PTS 8 Bethnal Green	
10.11.01	Kevin Gerowski W PTS 6 Wembley	
23.02.02	Nicky Booth L RSC 7 Nottingham *(British & Commonwealth Bantamweight Title Challenges)*	
24.10.03	Harry Ramogoadi L PTS 6 Bethnal Green	

Career: 21 contests, won 16, lost 5.

Peter Oboh

Brockley. *Born* Nigeria, 6 September, 1968
British, Commonwealth & WBA Inter-Continental L.Heavyweight Champion. Ht. 6'2"
Manager D. Powell

12.05.93	Antonio Russo W RSC 5 Cassino, Italy	
14.01.94	Ridha Soussi W PTS 6 Tagliacozzo, Italy	
13.05.94	Antonio Pasqualino W RSC 2 Avellino, Italy	
16.10.95	Tim Redman W RTD 2 Mayfair	
09.07.96	Yuri Yelistratov W PTS 6 Bethnal Green	
27.08.96	Joe Siluvangi L RSC 6 Windsor	
03.12.96	Andy Lambert W CO 1 Liverpool	
04.03.97	Garry Delaney L DIS 8 Southwark	
01.11.97	Scott Welch L PTS 6 Glasgow	
18.07.98	Johnny Nelson L RTD 6 Sheffield	
26.09.98	Ole Klemetsen W CO 1 York	
21.11.98	Terry Dunstan L PTS 8 Southwark	
18.06.99	Thomas Hansvoll W RSC 2 Vejle, Denmark	
21.07.99	Ray Kane W RSC 2 Bloomsbury	
29.01.01	Chris Davies W RSC 8 Peterborough *(Elim. Commonwealth L. Heavyweight Title)*	
06.09.02	George Adipo W CO 1 Bethnal Green	

Peter Oboh　　　　　　　　　　　Les Clark

(Vacant Commonwealth L.Heavyweight Title)
08.03.03 Neil Simpson W RSC 11 Coventry
(Commonwealth L.Heavyweight Title Defence. Vacant British L.Heavyweight Title)
14.11.03 Elvis Michailenko W RSC 11 Bethnal Green
(WBA Inter-Continental L.Heavyweight Title Challenge)
12.05.04 Andrew Lowe W RTD 10 Reading
(British & Commonwealth L.Heavyweight Title Defences)
Career: 19 contests, won 14, lost 5.

Gary O'Connor
Manchester. *Born* Manchester, 29 August, 1978
L. Welterweight. Ht. 5'10"
Manager S. Wood/T. Gilmour

21.12.03 Chris Brophy W PTS 6 Bolton
29.02.04 Pete Buckley W PTS 6 Shaw
Career: 2 contests, won 2.

Valery Odin
Canning Town. *Born* Guadeloupe, 23 December, 1974
L. Heavyweight. Ht. 6'2¹/₂"
Manager Self

15.06.01 Tom Cannon W PTS 4 Millwall
22.09.01 Mark Brookes W PTS 4 Canning Town
09.10.01 Wayne Ellcock L PTS 4 Cardiff
10.11.01 Tony Dodson L RSC 4 Wembley
13.12.01 Calvin Stonestreet W RSC 2 Leicester Square
10.02.02 Radcliffe Green W PTS 6 Southwark
20.04.02 Toks Owoh W PTS 8 Wembley
21.05.01 Mark Smallwood L RSC 4 Custom House
17.08.02 Nathan King W PTS 6 Cardiff
17.09.02 Charden Ansoula L PTS 6 Bethnal Green
26.10.02 Chris Davies L PTS 6 Maesteg
28.01.03 Carl Froch L RSC 6 Nottingham
06.09.03 Kai Kurzawa L PTS 8 Efurt, Germany
19.06.04 Courtney Fry L PTS 8 Muswell Hill
Career: 14 contests, won 6, lost 8.

John O'Donnell
Shepherds Bush. *Born* Croydon, 13 November, 1985
L. Welterweight. Ht. 5'11"
Manager R. McCracken

16.04.04 Jason Nesbitt W PTS 4 Bradford
02.06.04 Dave Hinds W PTS 4 Nottingham
Career: 2 contests, won 2.

Keiran O'Donnell
Leeds. *Born* Leeds, 10 December, 1974
Cruiserweight. Ht. 6'2"
Manager T. O'Neill

11.11.03 Michael Pinnock W PTS 6 Leeds
Career: 1 contest, won 1.

Kevin O'Hara
Belfast. *Born* Belfast, 21 September, 1981
Featherweight. Ht. 5'6"
Manager M.Callahan/J.Breen/F.Warren

02.11.02 Mike Harrington W RSC 1 Belfast
01.02.03 Jus Wallie W RSC 2 Belfast
29.03.03 Jason Nesbitt W RSC 3 Portsmouth
14.06.03 Piotr Niesporek W PTS 4 Magdeburg, Germany
02.10.03 Vladimir Borov W PTS 6 Liverpool
30.10.03 Henry Janes W PTS 6 Belfast
29.11.03 Gareth Payne W PTS 4 Renfrew
06.03.04 Henry Janes W PTS 6 Renfrew
01.04.04 Buster Dennis W PTS 4 Bethnal Green
06.05.04 Choi Tsveenpurev L PTS 8 Barnsley
Career: 10 contests, won 9, lost 1.

Kevin O'Hara   Les Clark

Gary Ojuederie
Watford. *Born* Watford, 13 September, 1979
S. Middleweight. Ht. 6'0"
Manager Self

29.09.00 Chris Nembhard L RSC 1 Bethnal Green
08.12.03 Hamid Jamali L PTS 6 Birmingham
13.02.04 Jason Samuels L DIS 3 Bristol
28.02.04 Mike Allen W RSC 1 Bridgend
Career: 4 contests, won 1, lost 3.

Gary Ojuederie   Les Clark

Nick Okoth
Battersea. *Born* Camden Town, 19 July, 1973
L. Heavyweight. Ht. 5'11"
Manager J. Rooney

18.09.03 Mark Phillips W PTS 4 Mayfair
28.02.04 Paulie Silva L PTS 6 Manchester
08.04.04 Karl Wheeler L PTS 6 Peterborough
24.04.04 Daniel Sackey L RSC 2 Reading
Career: 4 contests, won 1, lost 3.

Nick Okoth   Les Clark

Kelly Oliver
Lincoln. *Born* Lincoln, 11 November, 1973
Cruiserweight. Former Undefeated WBO Inter-Continental & British Masters Cruiserweight Champion. Ht. 6'3"
Manager C. Sanigar

20.01.96 Steve Osborne W RSC 4 Mansfield
16.03.96 Marvin O'Brien W RSC 2 Glasgow
13.04.96 Andrew Benson W PTS 4 Wythenshawe
06.07.96 John Pierre W PTS 4 Manchester
14.09.96 Tony Booth W RSC 2 Sheffield
30.11.96 Nigel Rafferty W PTS 6 Tylorstown
18.01.97 Tony Booth W RSC 4 Swadlincote
14.03.96 Chris Woollas W PTS 6 Reading
05.06.97 Darren Westover W RTD 1 Bristol
02.08.97 Chris Woollas W RSC 3 Barnsley
11.10.97 John Keeton W RSC 8 Sheffield
(Vacant WBO Inter-Continental Cruiserweight Title)
15.11.97 Sergei Korolev W PTS 12 Bristol
(WBO Inter-Continental Cruiserweight Title Defence)
21.03.98 Brian la Spada W RSC 6 Bethnal Green
(WBO Inter-Continental Cruiserweight Title Defence)
18.04.98 Nigel Rafferty W RSC 4 Manchester
18.07.98 John Keeton L RSC 2 Sheffield
19.06.99 Chris P. Bacon W PTS 8 Dublin
03.12.99 John Wyborn W RSC 2 Peterborough
05.03.00 Lee Swaby W PTS 10 Peterborough
(Vacant British Masters Cruiserweight Title)
17.05.00 John Kiser W PTS 10 NYC, New York, USA
01.09.00 Sebastiaan Rothmann L RSC 10 Brakpan, South Africa
(WBU Cruiserweight Title Challenge)
26.07.03 Tony Booth W PTS 4 Plymouth
Career: 21 contests, won 19, lost 2.

Ajose Olusegun

London. *Born* Nigeria, 6 December, 1979
ABU L.Welterweight Champion. Ht. 5'9"
Manager Self

24.05.01	Tony Montana W RSC 1 Kensington
21.06.01	Woody Greenaway W RSC 1 Earls Court
09.09.01	Sunni Ajayi W PTS 6 Lagos, Nigeria
04.10.01	Stuart Rimmer W RTD 2 Finsbury
13.03.02	Gary Flear W PTS 4 Mayfair
13.06.02	Keith Jones W PTS 6 Leicester Square
30.10.02	Martin Holgate W RSC 7 Leicester Square
27.11.02	Vladimir Kortovski W RSC 1 Tel Aviv, Israel
15.12.02	Adewale Adegbusi W RSC 6 Lagos, Nigeria
20.03.03	Cristian Hodorogea W PTS 4 Queensway
26.04.03	Keith Jones W PTS 6 Brentford
29.10.03	Karl Taylor W PTS 6 Leicester Square
10.04.04	Victor Kpadenue W PTS 12 Carabas, Nigeria
	(ABU L.Welterweight Title Challenge)

Career: 13 contests, won 13.

Hussain Osman

Paddington. *Born* Syria, 25 July, 1973
Middleweight. Former IBO Inter-Continental & Southern Area
S.Middleweight Champion. Former Undefeated WBO Inter-Continental
Southern Area Middleweight Champion. Ht. 5'9¹/₂"
Manager Self

09.05.99	Wayne Asker W PTS 4 Bracknell
20.05.99	Karim Bouali W PTS 4 Barking
15.07.99	Neil Linford W RSC 5 Peterborough
05.10.99	Ojay Abrahams W PTS 4 Bloomsbury
05.02.00	Joey Ainscough W PTS 4 Bethnal Green
01.04.00	George Foreman W PTS 4 Bethnal Green
22.05.00	Steve Timms W RSC 2 Coventry
25.09.00	James Lowther L PTS 8 Barnsley
03.03.01	Gary Lockett L CO 2 Wembley
26.05.01	Lee Molloy W RSC 1 Bethnal Green
04.06.01	Richard Williams L PTS 10 Hartlepool
28.10.01	Gary Logan W PTS 10 Southwark
	(Southern Area Middleweight Title Challenge)
26.01.02	Matthew Barney W RTD 9 Dagenham
	(Vacant IBO Inter-Continental S.Middleweight Title. Southern Area S.Middleweight Title Challenge)
08.04.02	Matthew Barney L PTS 12 Southampton
	(IBO Inter-Continental & Southern Area S. Middleweight Title Defences)
21.05.02	Darren Rhodes W PTS 10 Custom House
20.07.02	Gary Logan W PTS 12 Bethnal Green
	(Vacant WBO Inter-Continental Middleweight Title)
21.12.02	Howard Eastman L RTD 4 Dagenham
31.05.03	Gary Beardsley W RSC 5 Bethnal Green

09.10.03	Scott Dann L PTS 8 Bristol
01.04.04	Eric Teymour L RSC 8 Bethnal Green

Career: 20 contests, won 13, lost 7.

Paul Owen

Sheffield. *Born* Sheffield, 3 October, 1975
S. Middleweight. Ht. 5'10¹/₂"
Manager D. Hobson

05.05.00	Shane Thomas DREW 6 Pentre Halkyn
08.07.00	Chris Crook W RSC 1 Rotherham
05.10.00	Andy Vickers L PTS 6 Sunderland
24.11.00	Reece McAllister L PTS 6 Darlington
07.12.00	Ian Toby L RTD 5 Sunderland
05.02.01	Steve Timms L RSC 1 Bradford
10.05.01	Gary Dixon W RSC 3 Sunderland
21.06.01	Reece McAllister DREW 6 Sheffield
13.09.01	Reece McAllister W RSC 1 Sheffield
08.02.02	Lee Woodruff W RSC 2 Preston
22.09.02	Matthew Barney L CO 7 Southwark
	(Vacant British Masters S.Middleweight Title)
02.12.02	Jimmy Steel W PTS 6 Bradford
14.03.03	Barry Connell L PTS 6 Glasgow
31.07.03	Patrick Cito W PTS 6 Sheffield
07.11.03	Harry Butler W PTS 4 Sheffield
07.12.03	Barry Connell L PTS 6 Glasgow
06.02.04	Egbui Ikeagwo L PTS 4 Sheffield
20.04.04	Darren Stubbs L PTS 6 Sheffield

Career: 18 contests, won 7, drew 2, lost 9.

(Tokunbo) Toks Owoh (Owomoyela)

Camden Town. *Born* Newham, 21 July, 1972
L. Heavyweight. Ht. 5'10½"
Manager H. Holland

24.10.95	Marvin O'Brien W RSC 2 Southwark
08.11.95	Dave Fulton W RSC 1 Bethnal Green
29.11.95	Nicky Wadman W PTS 6 Southwark
19.01.96	Ernie Loveridge W PTS 4 Bracknell
27.03.97	James Branch W RSC 1 Norwich
02.08.97	Peter Vosper W RSC 1 Barnsley
29.11.97	Sven Hamer W PTS 8 Norwich
27.03.98	Darren Ashton W RSC 2 Telford
25.04.98	Omar Sheika L RSC 4 Cardiff
26.09.98	Tony Booth W PTS 6 Norwich
30.01.99	Israel Khumalo W RSC 2 Bethnal Green
03.04.99	Paul Wesley W CO 5 Kensington
26.06.99	Peter Mason W RSC 1 Millwall
23.10.99	Eddie Haley W RSC 3 Telford
29.02.00	Konstantin Okhrej W RTD 4 Widnes
19.06.00	Tony Booth W RSC 3 Burton
23.09.00	Glengoffe Johnson L RSC 6 Bethnal Green
	(Vacant IBF Inter-Continental S.Middleweight Title)
18.01.02	Mondli Mbonambi W PTS 8 Coventry
20.04.02	Valery Odin L PTS 8 Wembley
21.05.02	Erik Teymour L PTS 6 Custom House
08.05.04	Ryan Walls L PTS 6 Bristol

Career: 21 contests, won 16, lost 5.

Toks Owoh   Les Clark

Alan Page (Paige)

Hattersley. *Born* Manchester, 17 April, 1976
S. Middleweight. Ht. 6'0"
Manager Self

01.07.00	William Webster W PTS 4 Manchester
09.09.00	Piotr Bartnicki W PTS 4 Manchester
12.11.00	Dean Ashton W RSC 2 Manchester
22.12.02	Harry Butler W RSC 1 Salford
16.02.03	Darren Ashton W PTS 4 Salford
08.06.03	Patrick Cito W RSC 3 Shaw
21.06.03	Marcin Radola W RSC 2 Manchester
06.09.03	Mark Phillips W PTS 6 Huddersfield
28.11.03	Carl Froch L RSC 7 Derby
	(Vacant English S.Middleweight Title.
	Elim. British S.Middleweight Title)
10.04.04	Darren Stubbs W PTS 4 Manchester

Career: 10 contests, won 9, lost 1.

James Paisley

Mile End. *Born* Ballymena, 4 January 1980
L. Welterweight. Ht. 5'8"
Manager Self

09.09.01	Babatunde Ajayi L PTS 4 Southwark
28.10.01	Carl Walton W PTS 4 Southwark
15.12.01	David Barnes L RTD 2 Wembley
31.01.02	Tony Montana L PTS 6 Piccadilly
09.02.02	Michael Jennings L RSC 3 Manchester
11.03.02	Nigel Wright L PTS 4 Glasgow
23.06.02	Jason Gonzales W PTS 6 Southwark
17.09.02	Dave Stewart L RSC 5 Bethnal Green
20.10.02	Pete Buckley W PTS 4 Southwark
27.10.02	Elvis Mbwakongo L RSC 2 Southwark
22.02.03	Gwyn Wale L RSC 1 Huddersfield
26.09.03	Kristian Laight W PTS 6 Millwall
06.12.03	Tony Doherty L RSC 3 Cardiff
20.02.04	Justin Hudson W PTS 4 Bethnal Green

Career: 14 contests, won 5, lost 9.

Lee Palmer

Pontefract. *Born* Pontefract, 4 June, 1982
Middleweight. Ht. 5'9"
Manager S. Butler

08.12.03	Chris Steele DREW 6 Barnsley

Career: 1 contest, drew 1.

Danny Parkinson

Bradford. *Born* Bradford, 6 August, 1980
Welterweight. Ht. 5'11"
Manager C. Aston

12.06.00	Ram Singh W RSC 3 Bradford
04.12.00	Ram Singh W PTS 6 Bradford
05.02.01	Dean Nicholas W PTS 6 Bradford
19.03.01	Lee Sharp L PTS 6 Glasgow
15.10.01	Richard Inquieti W RSC 1 Bradford
04.03.02	Matt Scriven W PTS 6 Bradford
09.06.03	Danny Moir W PTS 6 Bradford
05.10.03	Wayne Shepherd W RSC 5 Bradford
20.10.03	Pedro Thompson W RSC 3 Bradford
04.12.03	Dean Nicholas L RSC 4 Huddersfield
26.02.04	Gary Porter W PTS 6 Sunderland

Career: 11 contests, won 9, lost 2.

Mark Paxford

Wigan. *Born* Leigh, 18 February, 1979
L. Middleweight. Ht. 5'9¼"
Manager Self

22.09.00	Colin McCash DREW 6 Wrexham
03.12.00	Paddy Martin W RSC 3 Shaw
04.02.01	Matt Scriven W PTS 6 Queensferry
10.12.01	Pedro Thompson W PTS 6 Bradford
08.02.02	Richard Inquieti W PTS 6 Preston
09.05.02	Gavin Pearson L PTS 6 Sunderland
10.10.02	Richard Inquieti W PTS 6 Stoke
26.10.02	Wayne Shepherd W PTS 6 Wigan
19.10.03	Lee Williamson W PTS 6 Shaw
29.02.04	Brian Coleman W PTS 6 Shaw

Career: 10 contests, won 8, drew 1, lost 1.

Gareth Payne

Coventry. *Born* Coventry, 14 April, 1973
British Masters Bantamweight Champion.
Midlands Area S.Bantamweight Champion.
Ht. 5'3"
Manager A. Phillips

12.07.99	Lennie Hodgkins W PTS 4 Coventry
22.10.99	Danny Mulligan W RSC 2 Coventry
14.12.99	Paul Quarmby W PTS 4 Coventry
22.01.00	Sean Grant W RSC 1 Birmingham
22.05.00	Nicky Booth L PTS 4 Coventry
28.10.00	Chris Emanuele W CO 1 Coventry
02.01.01	Danny Lawson W RSC 1 Coventry
19.12.01	Delroy Spencer W PTS 4 Coventry
18.01.02	Delroy Spencer W PTS 4 Coventry
25.02.02	Jamie Yelland L RSC 3 Slough
26.04.02	Chris Emanuele W RSC 3 Coventry
	(British Masters Bantamweight Title
	Challenge)
18.05.02	Jim Betts L PTS 6 Millwall
10.10.02	Jamie Yelland L PTS 10 Stoke
22.03.03	John-Paul Ryan W PTS 4 Coventry
07.06.03	Neil Read W RSC 5 Coventry
	(Vacant Midlands Area
	S.Bantamweight Title)
30.10.03	Steve Gethin L PTS 6 Dudley
08.11.03	Neil Read W PTS 4 Coventry
29.11.03	Kevin O'Hara L PTS 4 Renfrew
26.02.04	Derry Matthews L RSC 4 Widnes

Career: 19 contests, won 11, lost 8.

Mark Payne

Coventry. *Born* Coventry, 29 March, 1976
S. Bantamweight. Ht. 5'6"
Manager O. Delargy

11.05.98	Dave Travers W RTD 3 Leicester
24.09.98	David Jeffrey W RSC 2 Edgbaston
30.11.98	Danny Lawson W RSC 1 Leicester
11.12.98	Stevie Quinn W RSC 2 Cheshunt
26.02.99	Arv Mittoo W PTS 4 Coventry
12.07.99	John Barnes W PTS 4 Coventry
05.10.99	Isaac Sebaduka W PTS 6 Bloomsbury
14.12.99	Harry Woods W PTS 4 Coventry
10.03.00	Vlado Varhegyi W PTS 6 Bethnal Green
08.09.00	Vladimir Borov W PTS 6 Hammersmith
28.10.00	Rakhim Mingaleev W PTS 6 Coventry
02.01.01	Keith Jones W PTS 6 Coventry
19.05.01	Dazzo Williams L PTS 8 Wembley
22.09.01	Rakhim Mingaleev W PTS 6 Newcastle
19.12.01	Stevie Quinn W RTD 2 Coventry
18.05.02	Michael Hunter L PTS 8 Millwall

Mark Paxford

16.04.03	Billy Corcoran DREW 4 Nottingham
05.07.03	Marc Callaghan W PTS 6 Brentwood
16.04.04	Michael Hunter L RSC 7 Hartlepool
	(Vacant British S.Bantamweight Title)

Career: 19 contests, won 15, drew 1, lost 3.

Brodie Pearmaine

Lewes. *Born* London, 3 April, 1967
Heavyweight. Ht. 6'0"
Manager R. Davies

24.02.00	Paul Fiske L PTS 6 Sunderland
11.02.02	Mark Gladwell W RSC 3 Southampton
08.04.02	Joe Brame W RSC 1 Southampton
23.06.02	Tommy Eastwood L PTS 4 Southwark
21.12.02	James Zikic L PTS 4 Millwall
23.02.03	Oneal Murray W PTS 4 Streatham
05.09.03	Lee Swaby L RTD 4 Sheffield
11.11.03	Billy Wilson W PTS 6 Leeds
21.02.04	Micky Steeds L RSC 1 Brighton

Career: 9 contests, won 3, lost 6.

Brodie Pearmaine   Les Clark

Dave Pearson

Middlesbrough. *Born* Middlesbrough, 1 April, 1974
S. Middleweight. Ht. 6'2¾"
Manager M. Shinfield

15.04.02	Ian Thomas L CO 3 Shrewsbury
03.10.02	Gary Firby W CO 3 Sunderland
21.10.02	Gary Jones L RSC 3 Cleethorpes
05.12.02	Chris Steele W PTS 6 Sunderland
24.03.03	Reagan Denton L PTS 6 Barnsley
31.05.03	Gary Jones L RSC 2 Barnsley
11.07.03	Ben Coward L PTS 6 Darlington
16.02.04	Brian Coleman L PTS 6 Scunthorpe
26.02.04	Tony Quigley L RSC 1 Widnes
26.04.04	Mark Phillips L RSC 6 Cleethorpes
25.06.04	Gerard Longdon L PTS 4 Bethnal Green

Career: 11 contests, won 2, lost 9.

David Pereira

Kennington. *Born* Lambeth, 22 May, 1981
S. Featherweight. Ht. 5'8"
Manager A. Booth

17.06.04	Declan English W PTS 6 Sheffield

Career: 1 contest, won 1.

Gareth Perkins

Swansea. *Born* Swansea, 17 December, 1982
L. Welterweight. Ht. 5'5"
Manager N. Hodges

29.02.04 Chris Long W PTS 6 Bristol
Career: 1 contest, won 1.

Kevin Phelan

Slough. *Born* Slough, 11 June, 1977
L. Middleweight. Ht. 6'1"
Manager G. Carmen

27.09.02 Lee Hodgson L RSC 1 Bracknell
21.03.03 Jimi Hendricks W RSC 6 Longford
12.04.03 Steve Russell W PTS 4 Norwich
26.04.03 Dave Wakefield W PTS 4 Brentford
09.05.03 Leigh Wicks W PTS 6 Longford
26.10.03 Brian Coleman W PTS 6 Longford
27.11.03 Dave Wakefield W PTS 6 Longford
25.03.04 Danny Moir L PTS 10 Longford
          *(Vacant British Masters
          L.Middleweight Title)*
02.06.04 David Walker L PTS 6 Nottingham
Career: 9 contests, won 6, lost 3.

Dean Phillips

Llanelli. *Born* Swansea, 1 February, 1976
Lightweight. Ht. 5'6"
Manager Self

10.03.94 Paul Richards L PTS 6 Bristol
23.03.94 Phil Janes W RSC 1 Cardiff
27.08.94 Craig Kelley W RSC 4 Cardiff
21.09.94 Steve Edwards W RTD 4 Cardiff
02.11.94 Anthony Maynard L PTS 6
          Birmingham
04.02.95 Greg Upton W PTS 6 Cardiff
04.03.95 Mike Deveney W PTS 8 Livingston
24.03.95 Bamana Dibateza W PTS 6 Swansea
16.06.95 Danny Luutaya W RSC 2 Southwark
22.07.95 Colin McMillan L PTS 8 Millwall
20.09.95 Mervyn Bennett W PTS 6 Ystrad
16.03.96 Mike Anthony Brown W RSC 6
          Glasgow
26.04.96 Bamana Dibateza W PTS 6 Cardiff
19.09.96 Peter Judson L RSC 10 Manchester
          *(Vacant IBF Inter-Continental
          S. Featherweight Title)*
24.01.98 Jimmy Phelan W PTS 6 Cardiff
25.04.98 Steve Conway L PTS 6 Cardiff
30.11.03 Nigel Senior W CO 1 Swansea
28.02.04 Gary Hibbert W RSC 5 Bridgend
01.05.04 Michael Muya W PTS 8 Bridgend
Career: 19 contests, won 14, lost 5.

Mark Phillips

St Clare's. *Born* Carmarthen, 28 April, 1975
L. Heavyweight. Ht. 6'0"
Manager N. Christian

26.10.00 Shayne Webb W PTS 6 Clydach
12.12.00 Tommy Matthews W PTS 6 Clydach
13.03.01 William Webster W RTD 1 Plymouth
07.10.01 Danny Norton L PTS 6
          Wolverhampton
12.12.01 Simon Andrews W PTS 6 Clydach
25.04.02 Mark Ellwood L PTS 6 Hull
10.05.02 Scott Dann L PTS 6 Bethnal Green
23.06.02 Gareth Hogg L PTS 4 Southwark
10.07.02 Scott Dann L PTS 4 Wembley
03.12.02 Jamie Hearn L PTS 4 Bethnal Green
20.12.02 Ryan Walls L PTS 4 Bracknell
06.03.03 Darren Dorrington L PTS 8 Bristol
21.03.03 Steve Timms L PTS 6 West Bromwich
05.04.03 Dale Nixon L PTS 6 Coventry
13.04.03 Donovan Smillie L PTS 6 Bradford
12.05.03 Leigh Alliss L PTS 6 Southampton
27.05.03 Steven Spartacus L RSC 2 Dagenham
30.06.03 Roddy Doran L PTS 6 Shrewsbury
06.09.03 Alan Page L PTS 6 Huddersfield
18.09.03 Nick Okoth L PTS 4 Mayfair
09.10.03 Leigh Alliss L PTS 4 Bristol
30.11.03 Jimi Hendricks W PTS 6 Swansea
16.01.04 Donovan Smillie L PTS 4 Bradford
07.04.04 Christian Imaga L PTS 6 Leicester
          Square
15.04.04 Darren McDermott L PTS 4 Dudley
26.04.04 Dave Pearson W RSC 6 Cleethorpes
04.06.04 Steve Timms L PTS 6 Dudley
Career: 27 contests, won 6, lost 21.

Stuart Phillips

Port Talbot. *Born* Abergavenny, 24 January, 1981
L. Welterweight. Ht. 5'8"
Manager D. Davies

08.11.03 Lance Hall W PTS 4 Bridgend
30.11.03 Wayne Wheeler W PTS 4 Swansea
01.05.04 Chris Long L RSC 1 Bridgend
Career: 3 contests, won 2, lost 1.

Esham Pickering

Newark. *Born* Newark, 7 August, 1976
European & Commonwealth
S.Bantamweight Champion. Former
Undefeated British Masters Bantamweight
Champion. Ht. 5'5"
Manager J. Ingle

23.09.96 Brendan Bryce W RSC 5 Cleethorpes
24.10.96 Kevin Sheil W PTS 6 Lincoln

Esham Pickering   Les Clark

22.11.96 Amjid Mahmood W RSC 2 Hull
09.12.96 Des Gargano W RTD 2 Chesterfield
16.12.96 Graham McGrath W PTS 6 Cleethorpes
20.03.97 Robert Braddock W RSC 6 Newark
12.04.97 Graham McGrath W PTS 4 Sheffield
26.04.97 Mike Deveney W PTS 4 Swadlincote
16.05.97 Chris Price W PTS 6 Hull
26.06.97 Graham McGrath W PTS 6 Salford
01.11.97 Mike Deveney W RSC 8 Glasgow
 (Elim. British Featherweight Title)
09.05.98 Jonjo Irwin L PTS 12 Sheffield
 (Vacant British Featherweight Title)
11.09.98 Louis Veitch W PTS 6 Newark
15.08.99 Chris Lyons W RSC 2 Derby
23.10.99 Ian Turner W PTS 6 Telford
20.11.99 Marc Smith W PTS 6 Grantham
19.02.00 Kevin Gerowski W PTS 10 Newark
 (Vacant British Masters Bantamweight Title. Elim. British Bantamweight Title)
13.08.00 Lee Williamson W PTS 6 Nottingham
16.12.00 Mauricio Martinez L RSC 1 Sheffield
 (WBO Bantamweight Title Challenge)
15.09.01 Carl Allen W PTS 6 Derby
08.12.01 Carl Allen W PTS 8 Chesterfield
20.04.02 Carl Allen W PTS 6 Derby
24.09.02 Alejandro Monzon L PTS 12 Gran Canaria, Spain
 (Vacant WBA Inter-Continental S.Featherweight Title)
02.12.02 Carl Allen W PTS 6 Leicester
08.02.03 Duncan Karanja W CO 5 Brentford
 (Vacant Commonwealth S.Bantamweight Title)
12.07.03 Brian Carr W RSC 4 Renfrew
 (Vacant British S.Bantamweight Title. Commonwealth S.Bantamweight Title Defence)
24.10.03 Alfred Tetteh W RSC 7 Bethnal Green
 (Commonwealth S.Bantamweight Title Defence)
16.01.04 Vincenzo Gigliotti W CO 10 Bradford
 (Vacant European S.Bantamweight Title)
12.05.04 Juan Garcia Martin W RSC 8 Reading
 (European S.Bantamweight Title Defence)
Career: 29 contests, won 26, lost 3.

Wayne Pinder

Manchester. *Born* Manchester, 15 April, 1978
S.Middleweight. Former WBF Middleweight Champion. Ht. 6'0"
Manager S. Wood/T. Gilmour

27.04.98 C. J. Jackson W PTS 6 Manchester
01.06.98 Carlton Williams W PTS 6 Manchester
26.10.98 Mark Owens DREW 6 Manchester
28.02.99 Lee Bird W RSC 5 Shaw
13.03.99 Paul O'Rourke W RSC 3 Manchester
02.05.99 Carl Smith W RSC 5 Shaw
02.07.99 Donovan Davey W PTS 6 Manchester
19.09.99 Paul King W PTS 6 Shaw
11.06.00 Colin Vidler W PTS 6 Salford
01.07.00 Gary Beardsley W PTS 4 Manchester
09.09.00 Ian Toby W PTS 4 Manchester
12.11.00 James Donoghue W PTS 6 Manchester
17.03.01 Leigh Wicks W PTS 4 Manchester
27.05.01 Dean Ashton W PTS 6 Manchester
07.07.01 Ian Toby W RTD 5 Manchester

26.11.01 Howard Clarke W PTS 6 Manchester
09.03.02 Jimmy Steel W PTS 4 Manchester
21.07.02 Darren Covill W PTS 6 Salford
09.11.02 Darren Rhodes W RSC 4 Altrincham
28.01.03 Damon Hague W RSC 7 Nottingham
 (Vacant WBF Middleweight Title)
16.04.03 Damon Hague L RSC 2 Nottingham
 (WBF Middleweight Title Defence)
21.06.03 Howard Clarke W PTS 4 Manchester
12.03.04 Leigh Wicks W PTS 4 Nottingham
10.04.04 Howard Clarke W PTS 4 Manchester
Career: 24 contests, won 22, drew 1, lost 1.

Michael Pinnock

Birmingham. *Born* Birmingham, 6 June, 1965
Cruiserweight. Ht. 6'0"
Manager Self

19.05.95 David Flowers L PTS 6 Leeds
13.06.95 Mark Snipe L PTS 6 Basildon
20.06.95 Darren Sweeney L PTS 8 Birmingham
06.09.95 Steve Loftus L PTS 6 Stoke
21.09.95 Luan Morena L PTS 4 Battersea
24.10.95 Graham Townsend L PTS 4 Southwark
17.11.95 Graham Townsend L PTS 4 Bethnal Green
03.12.95 Neville Smith L RSC 5 Southwark
23.01.96 Butch Lesley L PTS 4 Bethnal Green
05.03.96 Panayiotis Panayiotiou L PTS 4 Bethnal Green
16.03.96 Mark Hickey L PTS 6 Barnstaple
25.03.96 Lee Simpkin W PTS 6 Birmingham
03.04.96 Jason Hart L PTS 6 Bethnal Green
24.04.96 Gordon Behan L PTS 6 Solihull
03.05.96 David Larkin DREW 6 Sheffield
14.05.96 Mervyn Penniston L RSC 2 Dagenham
19.07.96 Chris Davies L PTS 6 Ystrad
29.07.96 Stuart Fleet L RSC 3 Skegness
04.10.96 Paul Bonson L PTS 6 Wakefield
28.10.96 Zak Goldman DREW 6 Leicester
14.11.96 Paul Bonson DREW 6 Sheffield
21.11.96 Darren Sweeney W RSC 5 Solihull
26.11.96 Mark Smallwood L PTS 6 Wolverhampton
03.02.97 Neil Simpson L PTS 6 Leicester
09.06.97 Mark Hobson L PTS 6 Bradford
05.07.97 Paschal Collins L PTS 6 Glasgow
02.09.97 Mike Gormley L PTS 6 Manchester
18.09.97 Martin Jolley DREW 6 Alfreton
04.10.97 Zoltan Sarossy L PTS 4 Muswell Hill
27.10.97 Johnny Hooks DREW 6 Nottingham
11.11.97 Graham Townsend L PTS 8 Bethnal Green
25.11.97 Barry Thorogood L PTS 8 Wolverhampton
15.12.97 Greg Scott-Briggs L PTS 6 Nottingham
02.02.98 Glenn Williams L CO 5 Manchester
30.04.98 Bobby Banghar L PTS 6 Purfleet
18.05.98 Jon O'Brien L PTS 6 Cleethorpes
22.10.98 Paul Carr L PTS 6 Barking
29.10.98 Paul Carr DREW 6 Bayswater
05.12.98 Dave Stenner W RSC 3 Bristol
03.04.99 Robert Zlotkowski L PTS 4 Carlisle
15.05.99 Damon Hague L PTS 4 Sheffield
05.06.99 Leif Keiski L PTS 6 Cardiff
02.07.99 Mike Gormley L RSC 6 Manchester
01.10.99 Tony Oakey L PTS 4 Bethnal Green
16.10.99 Brian Magee L RSC 3 Belfast
17.04.00 Gordon Behan L PTS 6 Birmingham
15.05.00 Tony Booth L PTS 6 Cleethorpes
25.05.00 Neil Linford L PTS 4 Peterborough

08.09.00 Steven Spartacus L PTS 4 Hammersmith
10.11.00 Tony Griffiths L PTS 4 Mayfair
01.12.00 Allan Foster L PTS 4 Peterborough
29.01.01 Ivan Botton W PTS 4 Peterborough
20.03.01 Joe Gillon L PTS 6 Glasgow
28.03.01 Darren Ashton DREW 4 Piccadilly
09.06.01 Nathan King L PTS 4 Bethnal Green
21.06.01 Paul Bonson L PTS 6 Sheffield
27.07.01 Mark Brookes L PTS 4 Sheffield
15.09.01 Tony Dowling L PTS 6 Derby
04.10.01 Oneal Murray L PTS 6 Finsbury
21.10.01 Peter Merrall DREW 6 Pentre Halkyn
28.10.01 Radcliffe Green L PTS 4 Southwark
24.11.01 Steven Spartacus L PTS 4 Bethnal Green
09.12.01 Andrew Facey L PTS 6 Shaw
16.12.01 Sam Price L PTS 4 Southwark
16.03.02 Carl Froch L RSC 4 Bethnal Green
21.11.02 Earl Ling L PTS 6 Hull
16.12.02 Eamonn Glennon DREW 6 Cleethorpes
08.02.03 Tony Moran L PTS 4 Liverpool
23.02.03 Ryan Walls L PTS 6 Streatham
16.03.03 Scott Lansdowne L PTS 6 Nottingham
24.03.03 Pinky Burton L PTS 4 Barnsley
10.06.03 Mark Brookes L PTS 4 Sheffield
31.07.03 Amer Khan L PTS 6 Sheffield
06.10.03 Reagan Denton L PTS 6 Barnsley
26.10.03 Ryan Walls L PTS 10 Longford
 (Vacant British Masters Cruiserweight Title)
11.11.03 Keiran O'Donnell L PTS 6 Leeds
03.04.04 Amer Khan L PTS 6 Sheffield
16.04.04 Nate Joseph L PTS 4 Bradford
08.05.04 Leigh Alliss L PTS 4 Bristol
07.06.04 Sandy Robb L PTS 6 Glasgow
Career: 80 contests, won 4, drew 9, lost 67.

(Stephen) Sonny Pollard

Hull. *Born* Hull, 3 November, 1976
Middleweight. Ht. 5'9¼"
Manager Self

09.06.98 Shamus Casey W PTS 4 Hull
08.08.98 Harry Butler L RSC 4 Scarborough
04.03.00 Wayne Elcock L RSC 3 Peterborough
26.09.02 Gary Jones W PTS 6 Hull
11.12.02 Martin Scotland W RSC 2 Hull
03.04.03 Wayne Shepherd W PTS 6 Hull
17.04.03 Andrei Ivanov W PTS 6 Hull
25.09.03 Patrick Cito W PTS 6 Hull
14.11.03 Howard Clarke W PTS 6 Hull
Career: 9 contests, won 7, lost 2.

Gary Porter

Glasgow. *Born* Glasgow, 12 September, 1978
L. Middleweight. Ht. 5'9"
Manager Self

04.06.01 Arv Mittoo W PTS 6 Glasgow
17.09.01 Carl Walton W PTS 6 Glasgow
03.11.01 Sam Mottram W PTS 4 Glasgow
22.04.02 Matt Scriven W PTS 6 Glasgow
03.06.02 Richard Inquieti W PTS 6 Glasgow
23.09.02 David Keir W PTS 8 Glasgow
20.01.03 Danny Moir L PTS 6 Glasgow
17.03.03 Franny Jones L PTS 6 Glasgow
26.02.04 Danny Parkinson L PTS 6 Sunderland
12.03.04 Danny Moir DREW 6 Irvine
Career: 10 contests, won 6, drew 1, lost 3.

Marcus Portman

West Bromwich. *Born* West Bromwich, 26 September, 1980
British Masters Welterweight Champion. Ht. 6'0"
Manager D. Bradley

18.02.00	Ray Wood W PTS 6 West Bromwich
28.03.00	Billy Smith W PTS 6 Wolverhampton
10.09.00	Alan Kershaw W RSC 2 Walsall
15.02.01	Willie Limond L PTS 6 Glasgow
01.04.01	Tony Smith W PTS 6 Wolverhampton
20.04.01	Darren Melville L RSC 3 Millwall
07.09.01	Tony Smith W PTS 6 West Bromwich
15.09.01	Matthew Hatton L RSC 3 Manchester
12.12.01	Ross McCord DREW 4 Clydach
18.01.02	Andy Egan W PTS 4 Coventry
25.02.02	Sammy Smith W PTS 6 Slough
27.04.02	Gavin Wake W PTS 4 Huddersfield
08.05.03	Thomas McDonagh L PTS 6 Widnes
17.05.03	Scott Dixon W PTS 6 Liverpool
30.06.03	Wayne Wheeler W RSC 3 Shrewsbury
07.09.03	Jason Williams W PTS 6 Shrewsbury
19.02.04	Richard Swallow W PTS 10 Dudley
	(British Masters Welterweight Title Challenge)
03.04.04	Chris Saunders L RSC 1 Sheffield
	(Vacant English Welterweight Title)

Career: 18 contests, won 12, drew 1, lost 5.

Dean Powell

Peckham. *Born* Salisbury, 4 June, 1970
Middleweight. Ht. 5'9"
Manager Self

17.12.96	Matthew Tait L PTS 6 Bethnal Green
11.02.97	Matthew Tait L RSC 4 Bethnal Green
26.09.98	Brian Knudsen L PTS 4 York
12.12.98	Jeff Mills W RSC 3 Southwark
16.01.99	Neil Linford L RSC 1 Bethnal Green
22.11.01	Darren Covill W PTS 4 Mayfair
15.10.02	Alan Gilbert L PTS 4 Bethnal Green
03.12.02	Tomas da Silva W PTS 4 Bethnal Green
08.02.03	Lee Hodgson L PTS 4 Brentford
13.04.03	Michael Thomas L RSC 1 Streatham
20.06.03	Mark Thornton L PTS 6 Gatwick
04.10.03	Matthew Thirlwall L RSC 2 Muswell Hill

Career: 12 contests, won 3, lost 9.

Martin Power

St Pancras. *Born* London, 14 February, 1980
Bantamweight. Ht. 5'6"
Manager Self

09.06.01	Sean Grant W PTS 4 Bethnal Green
28.07.01	Andrew Greenaway W RSC 3 Wembley
22.09.01	Stevie Quinn W RSC 2 Bethnal Green
24.11.01	Anthony Hanna W PTS 4 Bethnal Green
19.01.02	Gareth Wiltshaw W PTS 4 Bethnal Green
08.07.02	Darren Cleary W PTS 4 Mayfair
12.10.02	Stevie Quinn W RSC 4 Bethnal Green
15.02.03	Stevie Quinn W RTD 1 Wembley
29.03.03	Dave Hinds W PTS 4 Portsmouth
17.07.03	Darren Cleary W PTS 6 Dagenham
06.11.03	Rocky Dean W PTS 6 Dagenham
24.01.04	Delroy Spencer W RTD 1 Wembley
01.04.04	Fred Janes W RSC 2 Bethnal Green
13.05.04	Jean-Marie Codet W PTS 8 Bethnal Green

Career: 14 contests, won 14.

Martin Power Les Clark

Sam Price

Reading. *Born* Hillingdon, 6 July, 1981
L. Heavyweight. Ht. 6'0½"
Manager Self

16.12.01	Michael Pinnock W PTS 4 Southwark
10.02.02	Calvin Stonestreet W PTS 4 Southwark
19.03.02	Jimmy Steel W PTS 4 Slough
21.03.03	Harry Butler W PTS 4 Longford
25.03.04	Terry Morrill L RSC 3 Longford

Career: 5 contests, won 4, lost 1.

Tom Price

Cardiff. *Born* Bristol, 23 November, 1982
Welterweight. Ht. 5'11"
Manager D. Davies

22.09.03	Matt Teague L PTS 6 Cleethorpes
24.04.04	Nathan Graham L RSC 2 Reading

Career: 2 contests, lost 2.

Bradley Pryce (Price)

Newbridge. *Born* Newport, 15 March, 1981
Welterweight. Former Undefeated IBF Inter-Continental L.Welterweight Champion. Former Undefeated WBO Inter-Continental Lightweight Champion. Ht. 5'11"
Manager E. Calzaghe/F. Warren

17.07.99	Dave Hinds W PTS 4 Doncaster
23.10.99	David Jeffrey W RSC 3 Telford
06.11.99	Eddie Nevins W RSC 2 Widnes

Marcus Portman Les Clark

Tom Price Les Clark

29.01.00	Pete Buckley W PTS 4 Manchester
29.02.00	Carl Allen W PTS 4 Widnes
16.05.00	Carl Allen W RSC 3 Warrington
15.07.00	Gary Flear W RSC 1 Millwall
07.10.00	Gary Reid W RSC 5 Doncaster
27.01.01	Joel Viney W RSC 3 Bethnal Green
17.03.01	Brian Coleman W PTS 4 Manchester
28.04.01	Jason Hall W PTS 12 Cardiff
	(Vacant WBO Inter-Continental
	Lightweight Title)
21.07.01	Stuart Patterson W RSC 5 Sheffield
09.10.01	Lucky Sambo W PTS 12 Cardiff
	(WBO Inter-Continental Lightweight
	Title Defence)
12.02.02	Gavin Down W RSC 9 Bethnal Green
	(Vacant IBF Inter-Continental
	L.Welterweight Title)
20.04.02	Dafydd Carlin W RSC 8 Cardiff
08.06.02	Pete Buckley W RSC 1 Renfrew
17.08.02	Ted Bami L RSC 6 Cardiff
23.11.02	Craig Lynch W CO 4 Derby
01.02.03	Neil Sinclair L RSC 8 Belfast
	(British Welterweight Title Challenge)
08.05.03	Ivan Kirpa W PTS 10 Widnes
21.02.04	Farai Musiiwa L PTS 6 Cardiff
06.05.04	Thomas McDonagh L PTS 12 Barnsley
	(WBU International L.Middleweight
	Title Challenge)

Career: 22 contests, won 18, lost 4.

Kreshnik Qato

Wembley. *Born* Albania, 13 August, 1978
Middleweight. Ht. 5'9$^{1}/_{2}$"
Manager Self

28.09.01	Erik Teymour L PTS 6 Millwall
16.12.01	Lawrence Murphy L PTS 6 Glasgow
08.04.02	Ty Browne W PTS 4 Southampton
10.05.02	Paul Jones L PTS 6 Millwall
20.03.03	Jason Collins W PTS 4 Queensway
13.04.03	Mark Thornton W RSC 3 Streatham
13.05.03	Danny Thornton W PTS 6 Leeds
26.07.03	Scott Dann L RSC 2 Plymouth
26.09.03	Joel Ani W PTS 6 Millwall
14.11.03	Steven Bendall L PTS 8 Bethnal Green
21.02.04	Gary Lockett L RSC 2 Cardiff

Career: 11 contests, won 5, lost 6.

Tony Quigley

Liverpool. *Born* Liverpool, 1 October, 1984
S. Middleweight. Ht. 5'10"
Manager F. Warren/D. Powell

26.02.04	Dave Pearson W RSC 1 Widnes
22.05.04	Patrick Cito W PTS 4 Widnes

Career: 2 contests, won 2.

Mickey Quinn (McAllister)

Belfast. *Born* Belfast, 7 January, 1979
Middleweight. Ht. 5'10$^{1}/_{4}$"
Manager J. Breen/M. Callahan

01.06.02	Harry Butler W PTS 4 Manchester
28.09.02	Lee Williamson W RSC 2 Manchester
01.02.03	Joel Ani W PTS 4 Belfast
14.06.03	Vedran Akrap L PTS 4 Magdeburg, Germany
30.10.03	Barry Thorogood W PTS 4 Belfast

Career: 5 contests, won 4, lost 1.

Stevie Quinn

Newtownards. *Born* Newtonards, 14 November, 1969
Bantamweight. Ht. 5'7"
Manager Self

07.02.98	Stephen Oates L PTS 4 Cheshunt
28.04.98	Tommy Waite L RSC 3 Belfast
11.12.98	Mark Payne L RSC 2 Cheshunt
17.04.99	Chris Edwards W RSC 4 Dublin
22.05.99	Ross Cassidy W PTS 4 Belfast
16.10.99	Anthony Hanna L PTS 4 Belfast
19.02.00	Barry Hawthorne W RSC 5 Prestwick
12.06.00	Mickey Coveney L PTS 4 Belfast
20.10.00	Sean Grant W RSC 2 Belfast
11.11.00	Paul Weir W PTS 4 Belfast
27.01.01	Hussein Hussein L RTD 2 Bethnal Green
01.04.01	Richmond Asante W PTS 4 Southwark
28.04.01	Noel Wilders L RTD 6 Cardiff
22.09.01	Martin Power L RSC 2 Bethnal Green
19.12.01	Mark Payne L RTD 2 Coventry
26.01.02	Michael Hunter L CO 2 Dagenham
12.10.02	Martin Power L RSC 4 Bethnal Green
07.12.02	Marc Callaghan W PTS 4 Brentwood
01.02.03	Marty Kayes W PTS 4 Belfast
15.02.03	Martin Power L RTD 1 Wembley
05.04.03	Marty Kayes W RSC 5 Belfast
17.07.03	Kevin Mitchell L CO 1 Dagenham

Career: 22 contests, won 9, lost 13.

Bradley Pryce Les Clark

Furhan Rafiq

Glasgow. *Born* Glasgow, 16 December, 1977
Featherweight. Ht. 5'8"
Manager T. Gilmour

19.04.04 Paddy Folan W PTS 6 Glasgow
Career: 1 contest, won 1.

Harry Ramogoadi

Coventry. *Born* South Africa, 21 March, 1976
S. Featherweight. Ht. 5'6"
Manager J. Weaver/D. Lutaaya

20.11.98 Dan Ngweyna W PTS 4 Thembisa, South Africa
24.01.99 Zachariah Madau W PTS 4 Johannesburg, South Africa
26.03.99 Jan van Rooyen DREW 4 Witbank, South Africa
27.06.99 Kenneth Buhlalu W PTS 4 Durban, South Africa
23.07.99 Bethule Machedi W PTS 4 Johannesburg, South Africa
25.09.99 Malepa Levi W PTS 6 Nelspruit, South Africa
01.12.99 Mandla Mashiane L PTS 6 Johannesburg, South Africa
13.07.00 Martin Mnyandu L PTS 6 Johannesburg, South Africa
28.10.00 Trevor Gouws W PTS 6 Johannesburg, South Africa
18.02.01 Thomas Mashaba DREW 6 Johannesburg, South Africa
15.04.01 Malepa Levi W PTS 8 Johannesburg, South Africa
02.11.01 Malcolm Klaasen W PTS 6 Benoni, South Africa
08.02.02 Takalani Kwinda W PTS 8 Johannesburg, South Africa
09.10.02 Ariel Mathebula W PTS 6 Sandton, South Africa
24.10.03 Stephen Oates W PTS 6 Bethnal Green
08.11.03 Jason Nesbitt W PTS 6 Coventry
09.04.04 Nigel Senior W RSC 1 Rugby
Career: 17 contests, won 13, drew 2, lost 2.

Hastings Rasani

Birmingham. *Born* Zimbabwe, 16 April, 1974
L. Heavyweight. Ht. 6'2"
Manager Self

21.12.97 Elias Chikwanda W RSC 4 Harare, Zimbabwe
28.02.98 Victor Ndebele W CO 1 Harare, Zimbabwe
04.04.98 William Mpoku W PTS 8 Harare, Zimbabwe
03.05.98 Nightshow Mafukidze W CO 3 Harare, Zimbabwe
30.05.98 Frank Mutiyaya W RSC 4 Harare, Zimbabwe
24.07.98 Ambrose Mlilo L RSC 9 Harare, Zimbabwe

13.01.99 Tobia Wede W RSC 4 Harare, Zimbabwe
27.02.99 Ambrose Mlilo L CO 9 Harare, Zimbabwe
17.04.99 Eric Sauti W RSC 2 Harare, Zimbabwe
05.06.99 Gibson Mapfumo W RSC 2 Harare, Zimbabwe
02.01.01 Neil Simpson L CO 4 Coventry
(*Vacant Commonwealth L.Heavyweight Title*)
28.04.01 Arigoma Chiponda W DIS Harare, Zimbabwe
08.05.01 Tony Oakey L RSC 10 Barnsley
(*Vacant Commonwealth L.Heavyweight Title*)
06.10.01 Sipho Moyo L CO 9 Harare, Zimbabwe
15.03.02 Elvis Michailenko L RSC 5 Millwall
24.05.03 Elvis Michailenko L RSC 4 Bethnal Green
31.07.03 Mark Brookes L PTS 6 Sheffield
05.09.03 Carl Thompson L RSC 1 Sheffield
04.10.03 Steven Spartacus L RSC 1 Muswell Hill
11.11.03 Denzil Browne L PTS 6 Leeds
13.02.04 Leigh Alliss L PTS 6 Bristol
21.02.04 Earl Ling DREW 6 Norwich
12.03.04 Simeon Cover W CO 6 Irvine
20.03.04 David Haye L RSC 1 Wembley
12.05.04 Jamie Hearn L RSC 4 Reading
17.06.04 Amer Khan L PTS 6 Sheffield
Career: 26 contests, won 10, drew 1, lost 15.

(Shahid) Sid Razak

Birmingham. *Born* Birmingham, 9 March, 1973
S. Featherweight. Ht. 5'7"
Manager Self

13.02.01 Neil Read W PTS 6 Brierley Hill
27.03.01 Tommy Thomas W RSC 2 Brierley Hill
21.05.01 Jason Nesbitt W PTS 6 Birmingham
08.10.01 Gareth Wiltshaw L PTS 6 Birmingham
14.09.02 J.J.Moore L PTS 6 Newark
26.09.02 Chris Hooper L PTS 6 Hull
08.12.03 Steve Mullin L PTS 6 Birmingham
08.03.04 Steve Mullin L PTS 6 Birmingham
Career: 8 contests, won 3, lost 5.

Neil Read

Bilston. *Born* Wolverhampton, 9 February, 1972
S. Bantamweight. Ht. 5'4"
Manager P. Bowen

08.02.00 Gary Groves W PTS 6 Wolverhampton
10.09.00 Stephen Chinnock L RSC 5 Walsall
30.11.00 Paddy Folan L PTS 6 Blackpool
13.02.01 Sid Razak L PTS 6 Brierley Hill
08.03.01 John-Paul Ryan W PTS 6 Stoke
26.08.01 Lee Holmes L PTS 6 Warrington
06.12.01 Chris Edwards L PTS 8 Stoke
28.01.02 Jamil Hussain L CO 2 Barnsley
13.04.02 Stephen Chinnock L CO 3 Wolverhampton
(*Midlands Area Featherweight Title Challenge*)
29.06.02 Jamie Yelland L PTS 6 Brentwood
03.08.02 Isaac Ward L RSC 1 Blackpool
23.09.02 Andy Roberts L PTS 6 Cleethorpes
10.10.02 Chris Edwards L PTS 6 Stoke
08.11.02 Andy Roberts L PTS 6 Doncaster
02.12.02 Steve Gethin L RTD 3 Leicester

10.02.03 Sean Hughes L PTS 6 Sheffield
17.03.03 Junior Anderson W CO 2 Southampton
07.06.03 Gareth Payne L RSC 5 Coventry
(*Vacant Midlands Area S.Bantamweight Title*)
05.09.03 Andy Roberts L PTS 6 Doncaster
09.10.03 Lee Haskins L PTS 4 Bristol
08.11.03 Gareth Payne L PTS 4 Coventry
14.02.04 Rendall Munroe L RSC 1 Nottingham
03.04.04 Mark Moran L RSC 2 Manchester
14.06.04 Wayne Bloy DREW 6 Cleethorpes
Career: 24 contests, won 3, drew 1, lost 20.

(Dale) Daleboy Rees

Swansea. *Born* Swansea, 7 July, 1979
S. Featherweight. Ht. 5'7"
Manager D. Williams

15.09.02 Greg Edwards W PTS 4 Swansea
08.01.03 Joel Viney W RSC 5 Aberdare
25.01.03 Pavel Potipko W PTS 4 Bridgend
10.04.03 Henry Jones W PTS 4 Clydach
30.11.03 Buster Dennis L PTS 6 Swansea
20.02.04 Henry Castle L RSC 4 Bethnal Green
Career: 6 contests, won 4, lost 2.

Gary Reid

Stoke. *Born* Jamaica, 20 November, 1972
L. Welterweight. Ht. 5'5¹/₂"
Manager Self

09.12.98 Carl Tilley W CO 1 Stoke
11.02.99 Ted Bami L RSC 2 Dudley
23.03.99 Lee Williamson W PTS 6 Wolverhampton
07.10.99 Stuart Rimmer W RSC 2 Mere
19.12.99 No No Junior L PTS 6 Salford
14.04.00 Lee Molyneux W PTS 6 Manchester
18.05.00 Sammy Smith W RSC 1 Bethnal Green
23.07.00 Kevin Bennett L RSC 4 Hartlepool
21.09.00 Karim Bouali L PTS 4 Bloomsbury
07.10.00 Bradley Pryce L RSC 5 Doncaster
07.09.01 Willie Limond L PTS 8 Glasgow
22.09.01 Francis Barrett L PTS 4 Bethnal Green
17.02.02 Richie Caparelli W PTS 6 Salford
02.03.02 Paul Halpin L RSC 3 Bethnal Green
26.04.02 Martin Watson L PTS 6 Glasgow
28.05.02 Gareth Jordan DREW 6 Liverpool
13.07.02 Gary Greenwood L RSC 5 Coventry
05.10.02 Joel Viney W CO 2 Coventry
18.11.02 Martin Watson L RSC 4 Glasgow
21.03.03 Young Muttley L RSC 7 West Bromwich
(*Vacant Midlands Area L.Welterweight Title*)
10.10.03 Oscar Hall W RSC 2 Darlington
Career: 21 contests, won 8, drew 1, lost 12.

Ian Reid

Battersea. *Born* Lambeth, 30 August, 1972
Lightweight. Ht. 5'2"
Manager Self

30.03.93 Russell Rees L PTS 6 Cardiff
31.08.93 Jason Hutson W RSC 6 Croydon
10.11.93 Marcus McCrae L PTS 6 Bethnal Green
09.12.94 Mark Bowers L PTS 6 Bethnal Green
17.05.95 Michael Brodie L RSC 3 Ipswich
30.11.03 Henry Janes L PTS 6 Swansea
07.12.03 John Bothwell L PTS 6 Glasgow
15.03.04 Darren Johnstone L PTS 6 Glasgow
Career: 8 contests, won 1, lost 7.

Robin Reid

Runcorn. Liverpool, 19 February, 1971
IBO S.Middleweight Champion. Former
Undefeated WBF S.Middleweight
Champion. Former WBC S.Middleweight
Champion. Ht. 5'9"
Manager Self

27.02.93	Mark Dawson W RSC 1 Dagenham	
06.03.93	Julian Eavis W RSC 2 Glasgow	
10.04.93	Andrew Furlong W PTS 6 Swansea	
10.09.93	Juan Garcia W PTS 6 San Antonio, Texas, USA	
09.10.93	Ernie Loveridge W PTS 4 Manchester	
18.12.93	Danny Juma DREW 6 Manchester	
09.04.94	Kesem Clayton W RSC 1 Mansfield	
04.06.94	Andrew Furlong W RSC 2 Cardiff	
17.08.94	Andrew Jervis W RSC 1 Sheffield	
19.11.94	Chris Richards W RSC 3 Cardiff	
04.02.95	Bruno Westenberghs W RSC 1 Cardiff	
04.03.95	Marvin O'Brien W RSC 6 Livingston	
06.05.95	Steve Goodwin W CO 1 Shepton Mallet	
10.06.95	Martin Jolley W CO 1 Manchester	
22.07.95	John Duckworth W PTS 8 Millwall	
15.09.95	Trevor Ambrose W CO 5 Mansfield	
10.11.95	Danny Juma W PTS 8 Derby	
26.01.96	Stinger Mason W RSC 2 Brighton	
16.03.96	Andrew Flute W RSC 7 Glasgow	
26.04.96	Hunter Clay W RSC 1 Cardiff	
08.06.96	Mark Dawson W RSC 5 Newcastle	
31.08.96	Don Pendleton W RTD 4 Dublin	
12.10.96	Vincenzo Nardiello W CO 7 Milan, Italy	

(WBC S. Middleweight Title Challenge)

08.02.97	Giovanni Pretorius W RSC 7 Millwall	

(WBC S. Middleweight Title Defence)

03.05.97	Henry Wharton W PTS 12 Manchester	

(WBC S. Middleweight Title Defence)

11.09.97	Hassine Cherifi W PTS 4 Widnes	

(WBC S. Middleweight Title Defence)

19.12.97	Thulani Malinga L PTS 12 Millwall	

(WBC S. Middleweight Title Defence)

18.04.98	Graham Townsend W RSC 6 Manchester	
13.02.99	Joe Calzaghe L PTS 12 Newcastle	

(WBO S. Middleweight Title Challenge)

24.06.00	Silvio Branco L PTS 12 Glasgow	

(WBU S. Middleweight Title Challenge)

08.12.00	Mike Gormley W RSC 1 Crystal Palace	

(Vacant WBF S. Middleweight Title)

19.05.01	Roman Babaev W RSC 3 Wembley	

(WBF S. Middleweight Title Defence)

14.07.01	Soon Botes W RSC 4 Liverpool	

(WBF S.Middleweight TitleDefence)

20.10.01	Jorge Sclarandi W CO 3 Glasgow	

(WBF S. Middleweight Title Defence)

19.12.01	Julio Cesar Vasquez W PTS 12 Coventry	

(WBF S. Middleweight Title Defence)

10.07.02	Francisco Mora W PTS 12 Wembley	

(WBF S. Middleweight Title Defence)

29.11.02	Mondili Mbonambi W RSC 2 Liverpool	
05.04.03	Enrique Carlos Campos W RSC 8 Leipzig, Germany	
04.10.03	Willard Lewis W RSC 6 Zwickau, Germany	
24.10.03	Dmitri Adamovich W CO 4 Bethnal Green	
13.12.03	Sven Ottke L PTS 12 Nuremberg, Germany	

(WBA & IBF S.Middleweight Title Challenges)

26.06.04	Brian Magee W PTS 12 Belfast	

(IBO S.Middleweight Title Challenge)

Career: 42 contests, won 37, drew 1, lost 4.

Michael Rennie

Margate. *Born* Lambeth, 10 September, 1982
L. Middleweight. Ht. 5'10"
Manager A. Gower

08.05.04	Brian Coleman W PTS 4 Dagenham	

Career: 1 contest, won 1.

Michael Rennie Les Clark

Darren Rhodes

Leeds. *Born* Leeds, 16 September, 1975
L. Middleweight. Ht. 5'11"
Manager Self

18.07.98	Andy Kemp W RSC 1 Sheffield	
10.10.98	Perry Ayres W CO 2 Bethnal Green	
27.02.99	Gareth Lovell W PTS 4 Oldham	
01.05.99	Carlton Williams W RSC 4 Crystal Palace	
29.05.99	Sean Pritchard DREW 4 Halifax	
09.10.99	Leigh Wicks W PTS 4 Manchester	
11.12.99	Leigh Wicks W PTS 4 Liverpool	
25.03.00	Leigh Wicks W PTS 4 Liverpool	
29.05.00	Dean Ashton W RSC 3 Manchester	
08.07.00	Jason Collins DREW 4 Widnes	
04.09.00	Jason Collins W PTS 4 Manchester	
11.12.00	Paul Wesley W PTS 4 Widnes	
17.03.01	Andrew Facey W PTS 4 Manchester	
07.07.01	Wayne Elcock L PTS 4 Manchester	
24.11.01	Simeon Cover W RSC 5 Wakefield	
02.03.02	Andrew Facey L RSC 6 Wakefield	

(Vacant Central Area Middleweight Title)

21.05.02	Hussain Osman L PTS 10 Custom House	
15.06.02	Harry Butler W PTS 4 Leeds	
28.09.02	Martin Thompson W PTS 8 Wakefield	
09.11.02	Wayne Pinder L RSC 4 Altrincham	
12.04.03	Mihaly Kotai L PTS 10 Bethnal Green	
10.05.03	Lee Murtagh W PTS 6 Huddersfield	
05.07.03	Darren Bruce W RSC 3 Brentwood	
06.09.03	Scott Dixon DREW 6 Huddersfield	
04.12.03	Steve Roberts W CO 6 Huddersfield	
10.04.04	Michael Jones L RSC 3 Manchester	

(Final Elim. British L.Middleweight Title)

Career: 26 contests, won 16, drew 3, lost 7.

Ryan Rhodes

Sheffield. *Born* Sheffield, 20 November, 1976
Middleweight. Former Undefeated WBO
Inter-Continental Middleweight Champion.
Former Undefeated British & IBF Inter-
Continental L. Middleweight Champion.
Ht. 5'8½"
Manager Self

04.02.95	Lee Crocker W RSC 2 Cardiff	
04.03.95	Shamus Casey W CO 1 Livingston	
06.05.95	Chris Richards W PTS 6 Shepton Mallet	
15.09.95	John Rice W RSC 2 Mansfield	
10.11.95	Mark Dawson W PTS 6 Derby	
20.01.96	John Duckworth W RSC 2 Mansfield	
26.01.96	Martin Jolley W CO 3 Brighton	
11.05.96	Martin Jolley W RSC 2 Bethnal Green	
25.06.96	Roy Chipperfield W RSC 1 Mansfield	
14.09.96	Del Bryan W PTS 6 Sheffield	
14.12.96	Paul Jones W RSC 8 Sheffield	

(Vacant British L. Middleweight Title)

25.02.97	Peter Waudby W CO 1 Sheffield	

(British L. Middleweight Title Defence)

14.03.97	Del Bryan W RSC 7 Reading	

(British L. Middleweight Title Defence)

12.04.97	Lindon Scarlett W RSC 1 Sheffield	

(Vacant IBF Inter-Continental L. Middleweight Title)

02.08.97	Ed Griffin W RSC 2 Barnsley	

(IBF Inter-Continental L. Middleweight Title Defence. Vacant WBO L. Middleweight Title)

11.10.97	Yuri Epifantsev W RSC 2 Sheffield	

(Final Elim. WBO Middleweight Title)

13.12.97	Otis Grant L PTS 12 Sheffield	

(Vacant WBO Middleweight Title)

18.07.98	Lorant Szabo W RSC 8 Sheffield	

(WBO Inter-Continental Middleweight Title Challenge)

28.11.98	Fidel Avendano W RSC 1 Sheffield	

(WBO Inter-Continental Middleweight Title Defence)

27.03.99	Peter Mason W RSC 1 Derby	
17.07.99	Jason Matthews L CO 2 Doncaster	

(Vacant WBO Middleweight Title)

15.01.00	Eddie Haley W RSC 5 Doncaster	
16.05.00	Ojay Abrahams W PTS 6 Warrington	
21.10.00	Michael Alexander W PTS 6 Wembley	
16.12.00	Howard Clarke W PTS 6 Sheffield	
21.07.01	Youri Tsarenko W PTS 6 Sheffield	
27.10.01	Jason Collins W PTS 4 Manchester	
16.03.02	Lee Blundell W RSC 3 Bethnal Green	

(Vacant WBF Inter-Continental Middleweight Title)

16.04.03	Paul Wesley W CO 3 Nottingham	
25.07.03	Alan Gilbert W RSC 5 Norwich	
11.12.03	Peter Jackson W PTS 6 Bethnal Green	
12.03.04	Scott Dixon W PTS 8 Nottingham	
16.04.04	Tomas da Silva W RSC 4 Bradford	

Career: 33 contests, won 30, lost 3.

Wayne Rigby

Manchester. *Born* Manchester, 19 July, 1973
L.Welterweight. Former WBF

L.Welterweight Champion. Former
Undefeated IBO Inter-Continental
Lightweight Champion. Former British
Lightweight Champion. Former Undefeated
Central Area Lightweight Champion.
Ht. 5'6"
Manager Self

27.02.92	Lee Fox L PTS 6 Liverpool
08.06.92	Leo Turner W PTS 6 Bradford
02.07.92	Leo Turner W CO 5 Middleton
05.10.92	Colin Innes W PTS 6 Manchester
01.12.92	John T. Kelly L PTS 6 Hartlepool
02.06.94	Kid McAuley W PTS 6 Middleton
13.06.94	Chris Clarkson W PTS 6 Liverpool
22.09.94	Mark Hargreaves W PTS 6 Bury
06.03.95	Kelton McKenzie L PTS 8 Leicester
18.05.95	John T. Kelly W PTS 6 Middleton
05.06.95	Hugh Collins W RSC 4 Glasgow
17.01.96	Kid McAuley W PTS 6 Solihull
24.03.96	Steve Tuckett W PTS 6 Shaw
27.09.96	Jimmy Phelan W PTS 10 Hull
	(Central Area Lightweight Title Challenge)
07.03.97	Alan Bosworth W RSC 5 Northampton
10.01.98	Tanveer Ahmed W PTS 12 Bethnal Green
	(Vacant British Lightweight Title)
11.04.98	Matt Brown W RTD 8 Southwark
	(British Lightweight Title Defence)
17.10.98	Bobby Vanzie L RSC 10 Manchester
	(British Lightweight Title Defence)
31.07.99	Mark McGowan W RSC 4 Carlisle
11.09.99	Alan Temple L PTS 8 Sheffield
04.12.99	Mark Haslam W CO 3 Peterborough
27.05.00	Dariusz Snarski W RSC 8 Mayfair
	(Vacant IBO Inter-Continental Lightweight Title)
01.07.00	Michael Ayers L RSC 10 Manchester
	(IBO Lightweight Title Challenge)
03.03.01	Michael Ayers L PTS 12 Wembley
	(IBO Lightweight Title Challenge)
14.07.01	Keith Jones W CO 3 Wembley
26.11.01	Antonio Ramirez W PTS 12 Manchester
	(Vacant WBF L.Welterweight Title)
09.03.02	Sedat Puskulla W CO 1 Manchester
	(Vacant WBF L. Welterweight Title)
18.05.02	Colin Dunne L RTD 10 Millwall
	(WBU Lightweight Title Challenge. Vacant WBF Lightweight Title)
09.11.02	Gary Ryder L PTS 12 Altrincham
	(WBF L. Welterweight Title Defence)
22.05.04	Tony Montana L PTS 10 Manchester
	(Vacant Central Area L.Welterweight Title)

Career: 30 contests, won 20, lost 10.

Steve Roache

Shefford. *Born* Camberwell, 8 April, 1973
Middleweight. Ht. 6'0"
Manager P. Rees

18.09.03 Ojay Abrahams L CO 2 Mayfair
Career: 1 contest, lost 1.

(Alexander) Sandy Robb

Nairn. *Born* Irvine, 5 April, 1981
Cruiserweight. Ht. 6'0"
Manager T. Gilmour

07.06.04 Michael Pinnock W PTS 6 Glasgow
Career: 1 contest, won 1.

Andy Roberts

Doncaster. *Born* Doncaster, 4 March, 1976
Bantamweight. Former Undefeated Central
Area Bantamweight Champion. Former
Central Area Flyweight Champion. Ht. 5'3"
Manager J. Rushton

20.10.94	Robert Grubb DREW 6 Walsall
12.12.94	Jason Morris W PTS 6 Doncaster
09.02.95	Robert Grubb DREW 6 Doncaster
22.03.95	Michael Edwards L PTS 6 Stoke
06.04.95	Steve Williams L PTS 6 Sheffield
05.05.95	Jason Morris W PTS 6 Doncaster
22.06.95	Paul Quarmby L PTS 6 Houghton le Spring
30.06.95	Stefy Bull L PTS 4 Doncaster
17.10.95	Robert Grubb L PTS 6 Wolverhampton
08.11.95	Graham McGrath W PTS 6 Scunthorpe
28.11.95	Graham McGrath L PTS 6 Wolverhampton
26.01.96	Darren Greaves W RSC 5 Doncaster
29.03.96	Graham McGrath L PTS 6 Doncaster
20.05.96	Neil Parry L PTS 6 Bradford
24.06.96	Neil Parry L PTS 6 Bradford
12.09.96	Steve Williams L PTS 6 Doncaster
23.09.96	Willie Smith W RSC 4 Bradford
03.10.96	Chip O'Neill W PTS 6 Sunderland
17.12.96	Neil Parry DREW 6 Doncaster
20.03.97	Marcus Duncan W PTS 10 Doncaster
	(Central Area Bantamweight Title Challenge)
10.07.97	David Coldwell W RSC 3 Doncaster
	(Vacant Central Area Flyweight Title)
12.11.97	Louis Veitch L PTS 10 Blackpool
	(Central Area Flyweight Title Defence)
04.12.97	David Coldwell L PTS 6 Doncaster
19.03.98	Anthony Hanna W PTS 6 Doncaster
13.05.98	Graham McGrath DREW 6 Scunthorpe
18.09.98	Barry Waite L RSC 1 Belfast
18.03.99	Terry Gaskin L RSC 8 Doncaster
17.07.99	Chris Emanuele L PTS 4 Doncaster
15.01.00	Terry Gaskin L RSC 8 Doncaster
	(Vacant Central Area Flyweight Title)
21.05.00	Gary Ford DREW 6 Shaw
23.07.00	Mbwana Matumla L RSC 2 Dar es Salaam, Tanzania
	(WBA Inter-Continental S.Flyweight Title Challenge)
07.10.00	Chris Edwards L PTS 4 Doncaster
23.09.02	Neil Read W PTS 6 Cleethorpes
08.11.02	Neil Read W PTS 6 Doncaster
30.11.02	Steve Williams L PTS 6 Newark
16.12.02	Marty Kayes W PTS 6 Cleethorpes
21.02.03	Marty Kayes W PTS 6 Doncaster
05.09.03	Neil Read W PTS 6 Doncaster

Career: 38 contests, won 14, drew 5, lost 19.

Steve Roberts

West Ham. *Born* Newham, 3 December,
1972
L.Middleweight. Former WBF
L.Middleweight Champion. Former
Undefeated WBF S.Middleweight
Champion. Former Undefeated Southern
Area L.Middleweight Champion. Ht. 5'11"
Manager Self

16.03.95	Julian Eavis W PTS 6 Basildon
23.05.95	Andy Peach W RSC 3 Potters Bar
13.06.95	Robbie Dunn W RSC 3 Basildon
20.09.95	Jason Hart W RSC 5 Potters Bar

30.09.95	Dick Hanns-Kat W CO 1 Basildon
25.11.95	Ernie Loveridge W PTS 4 Dagenham
23.01.96	Andrew Jervis W PTS 6 Bethnal Green
20.04.96	Peter Vosper W PTS 6 Brentwood
04.05.96	George Richards W PTS 6 Dagenham
27.09.96	Rob Stevenson W PTS 6 Stevenage
27.11.96	Lindon Scarlett W PTS 6 Bethnal Green
08.03.97	Adan Lugo W CO 4 Brentwood
08.04.97	Gilbert Jackson W PTS 10 Bethnal Green
	(Vacant Southern Area L. Middleweight Title)
30.08.97	Peter Mitchell W PTS 6 Cheshunt
08.10.97	Darren Covill W PTS 6 Poplar
05.06.98	Danny Quacoe W RTD 4 Southend
20.12.99	Mike Whittaker W PTS 6 Bethnal Green
05.02.00	Danny Thornton W PTS 6 Bethnal Green
01.04.00	Chris Crook W RSC 3 Bethnal Green
16.06.00	Mike Algoet W PTS 12 Bloomsbury
	(Vacant WBF S. Middleweight Title)
19.08.00	Scott Dixon W RSC 9 Brentwood
	(Vacant WBF L.Middleweight Title)
02.12.00	Mohammed Hissani W RSC 7 Bethnal Green
	(WBF L. Middleweight Title Defence)
03.03.01	Sergio Acuna W RSC 1 Wembley
	(WBF L. Middleweight Title Defence)
07.04.01	Keith Mullings W RSC 2 Wembley
	(WBF L. Middleweight Title Defence)
26.05.01	William Gare W RSC 9 Bethnal Green
	(WBF L. Middleweight Title Defence)
15.09.01	Andrzej Butowicz W RTD 7 Nottingham
	(WBF L. Middleweight Title)
10.11.01	Ron Weaver W PTS 12 Wembley
	(WBF L. Middleweight Title Defence)
28.01.02	Troy Lowry W RSC 4 Barnsley
	(WBF L. Middleweight Title Defence)
23.03.02	Kirino Garcia W PTS 12 Southwark
	(WBF L. Middleweight Title Defence)
27.07.02	Andre Pestriaev L PTS 12 Nottingham
	(WBF L. Middleweight Title Defence)
09.10.03	Lorant Szabo W PTS 8 Bristol
04.12.03	Darren Rhodes L CO 6 Huddersfield

Career: 32 contests, won 30, lost 2.

Dale Robinson

Huddersfield. *Born* Huddersfield, 9 April,
1980
Commonwealth Flyweight Champion.
Former Undefeated Central Area Flyweight
Champion. Ht. 5'4"
Manager T. Gilmour/C. Aston

25.09.00	John Barnes W PTS 4 Barnsley
28.10.00	Delroy Spencer W RSC 4 Coventry
02.12.00	Colin Moffett W PTS 4 Bethnal Green
26.02.01	Christophe Rodrigues W PTS 6 Nottingham
07.04.01	Andrei Kostin W PTS 6 Wembley
08.05.01	Terry Gaskin W RTD 3 Barnsley
	(Central Area Flyweight Title Challenge)
27.04.02	Jason Thomas W RSC 4 Huddersfield
18.05.02	Sergei Tasimov W RSC 3 Millwall
15.06.02	Kakhar Sabitov W PTS 6 Leeds
05.10.02	Alain Bonnel W PTS 8 Huddersfield
30.11.02	Marc Dummett W RSC 3 Liverpool

22.02.03	Spencer Matsangura W PTS 12 Huddersfield *(Vacant Commonwealth Flyweight Title)*
10.05.03	Zolile Mbityi W PTS 12 Huddersfield *(Commonwealth Flyweight Title Defence)*
09.10.03	Emil Stoica W RSC 3 Bristol
04.12.03	Pavel Kubasov W CO 4 Huddersfield
13.03.04	Jason Booth L PTS 12 Huddersfield *(IBO S.Flyweight Title Challenge)*
27.05.04	Moses Kinyau W PTS 6 Huddersfield

Career: 17 contests, won 16, lost 1.

George Robshaw

Leeds. *Born* Hull, 14 March, 1976
L. Middlewcight. Ht. 6'0"
Manager Self

07.10.00	William Webster W PTS 4 Doncaster
16.12.01	Dean Ashton W RTD 2 Southwark
09.11.02	Piotr Bartnicki W PTS 4 Altrincham
22.02.03	Conroy McIntosh W PTS 4 Huddersfield
10.05.03	Dean Cockburn W PTS 6 Huddersfield
04.10.03	Tommy Tolan W PTS 4 Belfast
04.12.03	Jamie Coyle DREW 6 Huddersfield

Career: 7 contests, won 6, drew 1.

Reggie Robshaw

Leeds. *Born* Wakefield, 10 June, 1977
L. Middleweight. Ht. 5'10"
Manager Self

01.04.01	Jason McElligott W PTS 4 Southwark
24.03.02	Pedro Thompson W PTS 6 Streatham
09.11.02	Martin Scotland W RSC 1 Altrincham
22.02.03	Elroy Edwards W PTS 4 Huddersfield
10.05.03	Michael Thomas L RSC 5 Huddersfield
13.03.04	Steve Brumant L PTS 4 Huddersfield

Career: 6 contests, won 4, lost 2.

Derek Roche

Leeds. *Born* Bedford, 19 July 1972
Welterweight. Former British Welterweight
Champion. Former Undefeated Central
Area Welterweight Champion. Ht. 5'9"
Manager T. Gilmour

26.09.94	Michael Alexander W RSC 6 Bradford
05.12.94	Shamus Casey W PTS 6 Bradford
30.01.95	Carl Smith W RSC 3 Bradford
23.02.95	Charlie Paine W CO 1 Hull
25.03.95	Rob Stevenson W PTS 6 Rothwell
12.06.95	Paul King W PTS 6 Bradford
25.09.95	Hughie Davey W PTS 6 Bradford
11.11.95	Rick North W RSC 2 Halifax

Reggie Robshaw　　　　　　　　Les Clark

11.12.95	Kevin McKenzie W RSC 3 Bradford
13.01.96	Shamus Casey W PTS 6 Halifax
07.03.96	Wayne Shepherd W RSC 3 Bradford
23.09.96	Trevor Meikle W PTS 10 Bradford *(Central Area Welterweight Title Challenge)*
23.10.96	Paul Miles W RSC 2 Halifax
09.12.96	Gary Beardsley W RSC 2 Bradford
17.02.97	Michael Alexander W DIS 4 Bradford
09.06.97	Chris Saunders W RSC 4 Bradford *(Central Area Welterweight Title Defence. Elim. British Welterweight Title)*
13.11.97	Hughie Davey W RSC 3 Bradford
23.02.98	Darren McInulty W PTS 6 Glasgow
06.11.98	Del Bryan W RSC 10 Mayfair *(Vacant IBO Inter-Continental L. Middleweight Title)*
10.04.99	Charlie Kane W RSC 7 Manchester *(Vacant British Welterweight Title)*
31.07.99	Georgie Smith W PTS 12 Carlisle *(British Welterweight Title Defence)*
22.10.99	Scott Dixon W PTS 12 Coventry *(British Welterweight Title Defence)*
27.03.00	Harry Dhami L PTS 12 Barnsley *(British Welterweight Title Defence)*
25.09.00	Brian Coleman W PTS 6 Barnsley
11.11.00	Adrian Stone L RSC 2 Belfast *(IBO L.Middleweight Title Challenge)*
08.05.01	Paul Denton W PTS 6 Barnsley
07.07.01	Zoltan Szili W RSC 4 Amsterdam, Holland
08.10.01	Adam Zadworny W RSC 4 Barnsley
26.01.02	Jan Bergman L PTS 12 Bethnal Green *(WBU Welterweight Title Challenge)*
15.06.02	Neil Sinclair L CO 1 Leeds *(British Welterweight Title Challenge)*
21.09.02	Darren Bruce W PTS 8 Brentwood
10.05.03	Jason Williams W RSC 2 Huddersfield
07.06.03	Silvio Rojas W PTS 6 Trieste, Italy
10.04.04	Mihaly Kotai L RSC 11 Manchester *(WBF L.Middleweight Title Challenge)*

Career: 34 contests, won 29, lost 5.

Jim Rock

Dublin. *Born* Dublin, 12 March, 1972
Middleweight. All-Ireland
S. Middleweight & L. Middleweight
Champion. Former Undefeated WAA Inter-

George Robshaw　　　　　　　　Les Clark

Continental S. Middleweight Champion.
WBF European L. Middleweight
Champion. Ht. 5'11"
Manager M. O'Callaghan

25.11.95	Craig Lynch W PTS 4 Dublin
09.03.96	Peter Mitchell W PTS 6 Millstreet
03.09.96	Rob Stevenson W PTS 6 Belfast
05.11.96	Danny Quacoe W RSC 4 Belfast
28.01.97	Roy Chipperfield W RTD 2 Belfast
12.04.97	George Richards W PTS 6 Sheffield
13.09.97	Robert Njie W CO 3 Millwall
18.04.98	Ensley Bingham L RSC 7 Manchester
19.09.98	Michael Monaghan W PTS 12 Dublin
	(Vacant WAA Inter-Continental
	S. Middleweight Title)
14.12.98	Perry Ayres W RTD 3 Cleethorpes
22.01.99	Jimmy Vincent W PTS 10 Dublin
20.02.99	Pedro Carragher W RSC 3 Thornaby
	(Vacant WBF European
	L. Middleweight Title)
17.04.99	Michael Alexander W RSC 1 Dublin
	(Vacant All-Ireland S. Middleweight
	Title)
19.06.99	Kevin Thompson W PTS 4 Dublin
15.04.00	Allan Gray W PTS 10 Bethnal Green
	(Vacant All-Ireland L. Middleweight
	Title)
12.06.00	Alan Gilbert W PTS 6 Belfast
20.10.00	Brooke Welby W RSC 3 Belfast
11.11.00	David Baptiste W PTS 4 Belfast
08.12.00	Tommy Attardo W PTS 8 Worcester, Mass, USA
24.03.01	Hollister Elliott W CO 6 Worcester, Mass, USA
20.04.01	Jason Collins W PTS 6 Dublin
01.12.01	Ian Cooper L PTS 6 Bethnal Green
24.04.02	Harry Butler W PTS 6 Dublin
01.02.03	Takaloo L RSC 9 Belfast
	(Vacant WBU L. Middleweight Title)
30.10.03	Alan Jones L PTS 8 Belfast

Career: 25 contests, won 21, lost 4.

Jason Rushton

Doncaster. *Born* Doncaster, 15 February, 1983
Middleweight. Ht. 5'10"
Manager J. Rushton/F. Warren

27.10.01	Ram Singh W PTS 6 Manchester
09.02.02	Brian Gifford W RSC 1 Manchester
01.06.02	Tony Smith W PTS 4 Manchester
08.11.02	Gary Hadwin W CO 4 Doncaster
21.02.03	Wayne Shepherd W PTS 6 Doncaster
05.09.03	Harry Butler W PTS 4 Doncaster
27.09.03	Jimi Hendricks W PTS 4 Manchester
06.03.04	Peter Dunn W PTS 6 Renfrew
06.05.04	Peter Dunn W PTS 4 Barnsley

Career: 9 contests, won 9.

Paul Rushton

Barnsley. *Born* Barnsley, 28 February, 1973
L. Welterweight. Ht. 5'9"
Manager T. Schofield

21.10.02	Craig Dickson L RSC 2 Glasgow
10.02.03	Lee Bedell L RSC 3 Sheffield
05.04.03	Paul McIlwaine DREW 4 Belfast
14.04.03	George McIlroy L RSC 1 Glasgow
06.06.03	Dave Hinds L PTS 6 Hull
15.06.03	Martin Hardcastle L RTD 2 Bradford
25.07.03	Jackson Williams L PTS 4 Norwich

Career: 7 contests, drew 1, lost 6.

Paul Rushton   Les Clark

Steve Russell

Norwich. *Born* Norwich, 1 September, 1979
Middleweight. Ht. 5'10"
Manager J. Ingle

12.04.03	Kevin Phelan L PTS 4 Norwich
06.06.03	Jimi Hendricks L PTS 6 Norwich
20.06.03	Carl Wall L PTS 4 Liverpool
21.02.04	Arv Mittoo W PTS 6 Norwich
30.03.04	Dmitry Donetskiy L PTS 6 Southampton

Career: 5 contests, won 1, lost 4.

Steve Russell   Les Clark

Roy Rutherford

Coventry. *Born* Coventry, 4 August, 1973
English S.Featherweight Champion. Former British Featherweight Champion. Ht. 5'6"
Manager P. Lynch

24.02.98	David Kirk W PTS 6 Edgbaston
26.03.98	Vic Broomhead W PTS 6 Solihull

23.04.98	Dave Hinds W RSC 5 Edgbaston
21.05.98	Carl Allen W PTS 6 Solihull
24.09.98	Dean Murdoch W RSC 3 Edgbaston
14.12.98	Keith Jones W PTS 6 Birmingham
08.03.99	Marc Smith W PTS 6 Birmingham
19.06.99	Marc Smith W RTD 2 Dublin
22.10.99	Woody Greenaway W PTS 4 Coventry
14.12.99	Keith Jones W PTS 4 Coventry
22.01.00	Chris Williams W PTS 8 Birmingham
22.05.00	Alexander Tiranov W PTS 6 Coventry
28.10.00	Richard Evatt L PTS 10 Coventry
07.04.01	Nikolai Eremeev DREW 4 Wembley
26.05.01	Marc Callaghan W RSC 3 Bethnal Green
10.12.01	Frederic Bonifai W RSC 4 Liverpool
12.04.03	Dariusz Snarski W RSC 4 Bethnal Green
17.05.03	Jamie McKeever W PTS 12 Liverpool
	(British Featherweight Title Challenge)
22.11.03	Dazzo Williams L PTS 12 Belfast
	(British Featherweight Title Defence)
14.02.04	Stephen Chinnock W RSC 4 Nottingham
	(Vacant English S.Featherweight Title)
02.06.04	Dazzo Williams L PTS 12 Hereford
	(British Featherweight Title Challenge)

Career: 21 contests, won 17, drew 1, lost 3.

John-Paul Ryan

Northampton. *Born* Enfield, 1 April, 1971
L. Welterweight. Ht. 5'5"
Manager Self

07.12.00	Paddy Folan W PTS 6 Stoke
08.03.01	Neil Read L PTS 6 Stoke
28.05.02	Paddy Folan W PTS 6 Leeds
25.06.02	Sean Hughes L PTS 6 Rugby
18.10.02	Isaac Ward L PTS 6 Hartlepool
20.01.03	John Simpson L PTS 6 Glasgow
16.02.03	Simon Chambers L RSC 2 Salford
22.03.03	Gareth Payne L PTS 4 Coventry
24.05.03	Sean Hughes L PTS 6 Sheffield
11.07.03	Lee McAllister L RTD 2 Darlington
13.09.03	Joel Viney L PTS 6 Coventry
26.09.03	Femi Fehintola L PTS 6 Reading
30.10.03	Dean Hickman L PTS 6 Dudley
23.11.03	Rendall Munroe L PTS 6 Rotherham
12.03.04	John Murray L RSC 1 Nottingham
01.05.04	Joe McCluskey L RTD 2 Coventry

Career: 16 contests, won 2, lost 14.

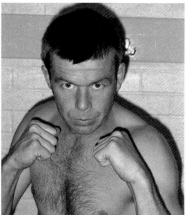

John-Paul Ryan   Les Clark

(Saheed) Silence Saheed (Salawu)

Canning Town. *Born* Ibadan, Nigeria, 1 January, 1978
L. Welterweight. Ht. 5'6"
Manager A. Bowers

28.03.03	Martin Hardcastle W PTS 4 Millwall	
10.04.03	Ceri Hall DREW 4 Clydach	
27.05.03	Francis Barrett W RSC 1 Dagenham	
11.10.03	Wayne Wheeler W RSC 1 Portsmouth	
15.11.03	Gary Greenwood W RTD 1 Coventry	
21.11.03	Jaz Virdee W RSC 2 Millwall	
01.05.04	Alan Temple L DIS 8 Gravesend	
	(Vacant British Masters Lightweight Title)	

Career: 7 contests, won 5, drew 1, lost 1.

Jason Samuels

Cardiff. *Born* Newport, 11 December, 1973
Middleweight. Ht. 6'0"
Manager Self

02.07.99	Luke Clayfield W RSC 1 Bristol	
10.10.00	Steve Brumant W PTS 6 Brierley Hill	
23.09.02	Andy Gibson L PTS 4 Glasgow	
25.01.03	Paul Astley W CO 1 Bridgend	
17.05.03	Geard Ajetovic L PTS 4 Liverpool	
13.02.04	Gary Ojuederie W DIS 3 Bristol	

Career: 6 contests, won 4, lost 2.

Jason Samuels   Les Clark

Chris Saunders

Barnsley. *Born* Barnsley, 15 August, 1969
English Welterweight Champion. Former
British Welterweight Champion. Ht. 5'8"
Manager D. Ingle

22.02.90	Malcolm Melvin W PTS 4 Hull	
10.04.90	Mike Morrison W PTS 6 Doncaster	
20.05.90	Justin Graham W RSC 3 Sheffield	
29.11.90	Ross Hale L PTS 6 Bayswater	
05.03.91	Rocky Ferrari L PTS 4 Glasgow	
19.03.91	Richard Woolgar W RSC 3 Leicester	
26.03.91	Felix Kelly L PTS 6 Bethnal Green	

17.04.91	Billy Schwer L RSC 1 Kensington	
16.05.91	Richard Burton L PTS 6 Liverpool	
06.06.91	Mark Tibbs W RSC 6 Barking	
30.06.91	Billy Schwer L RSC 3 Southwark	
01.08.91	James Jiora W PTS 6 Dewsbury	
03.10.91	Gary Flear L PTS 6 Burton	
24.10.91	Ron Shinkwin W PTS 6 Dunstable	
21.11.91	J. P. Matthews L RSC 4 Burton	
30.01.92	John O. Johnson L PTS 6 Southampton	
11.02.92	Eddie King W RSC 4 Wolverhampton	
27.02.92	Richard Burton L PTS 10 Liverpool	
	(Vacant Central Area L. Welterweight Title)	
09.09.92	John O. Johnson DREW 6 Stoke	
01.10.92	Mark McCreath L RSC 4 Telford	
01.12.92	Shea Neary L PTS 6 Liverpool	
22.02.93	Cham Joof L PTS 4 Eltham	
16.03.93	Mark Elliot L PTS 6 Wolverhampton	
26.04.93	Dean Hollington W RSC 5 Lewisham	
23.10.93	Michael Smyth L PTS 6 Cardiff	
02.12.93	Rob Stewart L PTS 4 Sheffield	
03.03.94	Kevin Lueshing W RSC 4 Ebbw Vale	
04.06.94	Jose Varela W CO 2 Dortmund, Germany	
26.08.94	Julian Eavis W PTS 6 Barnsley	
26.09.94	Julian Eavis W PTS 6 Cleethorpes	
26.10.94	Lindon Scarlett W PTS 6 Leeds	
17.12.94	Roberto Welin W RSC 7 Cagliari, Italy	
15.09.95	Del Bryan W PTS 12 Mansfield	
	(British Welterweight Title Challenge)	
13.02.96	Kevin Lueshing L RSC 3 Bethnal Green	
	(British Welterweight Title Defence)	
25.06.96	Michael Carruth L RSC 10 Mansfield	
09.06.97	Derek Roche L RSC 4 Bradford	
	(Central Area Welterweight Title Challenge. Elim. British Welterweight Title)	
27.02.98	Scott Dixon L PTS 10 Glasgow	
	(Elim. British Welterweight Title)	
17.04.99	Michael Carruth L RSC 5 Dublin	
08.12.01	David Kirk W CO 2 Chesterfield	
15.06.02	Arv Mittoo W PTS 6 Norwich	
24.09.02	Robert Pacuraru W RTD 4 Gran Canaria, Spain	
09.02.03	Richard Swallow W PTS 4 Bradford	
03.04.04	Marcus Portman W RSC 1 Sheffield	
	(Vacant English Welterweight Title)	
19.06.04	Peter Dunn W PTS 4 Muswell Hill	

Career: 44 contests, won 22, drew 1, lost 21.

Bruce Scott

Hackney. *Born* Jamaica, 16 August, 1969
Cruiserweight. Former Undefeated British,
Commonwealth & WBU Inter-Continental
Cruiserweight Champion. Former
Undefeated Southern Area Cruiserweight
Champion. Ht. 5'9½"
Manager F. Warren

25.04.91	Mark Bowen L PTS 6 Mayfair	
16.09.91	Randy B. Powell W RSC 5 Mayfair	
21.11.91	Steve Osborne W PTS 6 Burton	
27.04.92	John Kaighin W CO 4 Mayfair	
07.09.92	Lee Prudden W PTS 6 Bethnal Green	
03.12.92	Mark Pain W RSC 5 Lewisham	
15.02.93	Paul McCarthy W PTS 6 Mayfair	
22.04.93	Sean O'Phoenix W RSC 3 Mayfair	
14.06.93	John Oxenham W RSC 1 Bayswater	
04.10.93	Simon McDougall W PTS 6 Mayfair	
16.12.93	Bobby Mack W RSC 4 Newport	
05.04.94	Steve Osborne W RSC 5 Bethnal Green	
17.10.94	Bobbi Joe Edwards W PTS 8 Mayfair	

09.12.94	John Keeton W CO 2 Bethnal Green	
19.04.95	Nigel Rafferty W RSC 2 Bethnal Green	
19.05.95	Cordwell Hylton W RSC 1 Southwark	
11.11.95	Tony Booth W RSC 3 Halifax	
05.03.96	Nick Manners W RSC 5 Bethnal Green	
13.07.96	Tony Booth W PTS 8 Bethnal Green	
30.11.96	Nicky Piper L RSC 7 Tylorstown	
	(Commonwealth L. Heavyweight Title Challenge)	
15.05.97	Grant Briggs W RSC 2 Reading	
04.10.97	Tony Booth L PTS 8 Muswell Hill	
21.04.98	Dominic Negus W RSC 9 Edmonton	
	(Southern Area Cruiserweight Title Challenge)	
28.11.98	Darren Corbett W RSC 10 Belfast	
	(Commonwealth Cruiserweight Title Challenge. Vacant British Cruiserweight Title)	
15.05.99	Johnny Nelson L PTS 12 Sheffield	
	(WBO Cruiserweight Title Challenge)	
17.07.99	Juan Carlos Gomez L RSC 6 Dusseldorf, Germany	
	(WBC Cruiserweight Title Challenge)	
08.04.00	Chris Woollas W RSC 2 Bethnal Green	
24.06.00	Adam Watt L RSC 4 Glasgow	
	(Vacant Commonwealth Cruiserweight Title)	
16.12.00	John Keeton W CO 6 Sheffield	
	(Vacant British Cruiserweight Title)	
10.03.01	Garry Delaney W RTD 3 Bethnal Green	
	(British Cruiserweight Title Defence. Vacant Commonwealth Cruiserweight Title)	
28.07.01	Rene Janvier W PTS 12 Wembley	
	(Vacant WBU Inter-Continental Cruiserweight Title)	
28.06.03	Enzo Maccarinelli L RSC 4 Cardiff	
	(Vacant WBU Cruiserweight Title)	
07.02.04	Radcliffe Green W PTS 6 Bethnal Green	

Career: 33 contests, won 26, lost 7.

Steve Scott

Doncaster. *Born* Doncaster, 22 October, 1970
Middleweight. Ht. 5'11"
Manager J. Rushton

21.02.03	Martin Thompson DREW 6 Doncaster	
09.05.03	Jimi Hendricks L PTS 6 Doncaster	
02.06.03	Ben Coward DREW 6 Cleethorpes	
05.09.03	Chris Steele DREW 6 Doncaster	
22.09.03	Geraint Harvey L PTS 6 Cleethorpes	
01.12.03	Hussain Nasser W RTD 4 Barnsley	
15.12.03	Jonathan Woollins W PTS 6 Cleethorpes	
20.02.04	Joe Mitchell L PTS 6 Doncaster	

Career: 8 contests, won 2, drew 3, lost 3.

Greg Scott-Briggs

Chesterfield. *Born* Swaziland, 6 February, 1966
Cruiserweight. Ht. 6'1"
Manager M. Shinfield

04.02.92	Mark McBiane W PTS 6 Alfreton	
03.03.92	Tony Colclough W RSC 2 Cradley Heath	
30.03.92	Carl Smallwood L PTS 6 Coventry	
27.04.92	Richard Atkinson L PTS 6 Bradford	
28.05.92	Steve Walton W PTS 6 Gosforth	
04.06.92	Joe Frater L PTS 6 Cleethorpes	

30.09.92	Carl Smallwood L PTS 6 Solihull
17.03.93	Carl Smallwood L PTS 8 Stoke
26.04.93	Tony Colclough W RSC 4 Glasgow
08.06.93	Peter Flint W RSC 1 Derby
07.09.93	Steve Loftus W RSC 2 Stoke
22.09.93	Paul Hanlon W PTS 6 Chesterfield
04.11.93	Lee Archer L PTS 8 Stafford
24.11.93	Tony Colclough W PTS 6 Solihull
08.12.93	Lee Archer W RTD 6 Stoke
08.02.94	Nigel Rafferty L PTS 6 Wolverhampton
17.02.94	Lee Archer L PTS 8 Walsall
11.03.94	Monty Wright L PTS 8 Wolverhampton
26.09.94	Dave Battey W RSC 4 Cleethorpes
11.10.94	Mark Smallwood L PTS 8 Wolverhampton
29.10.94	Mark Smallwood L PTS 6 Cannock
12.11.94	Thomas Hansvoll L PTS 4 Randers, Denmark
30.11.94	Monty Wright L PTS 6 Wolverhampton
06.03.95	Neil Simpson L RTD 5 Leicester
15.09.95	David Flowers L PTS 6 Darlington
29.11.95	Neil Simpson L DIS 7 Solihull
	(Vacant Midlands Area L. Heavyweight Title)
20.03.96	Stinger Mason W PTS 6 Stoke
26.10.96	Danny Peters L PTS 6 Liverpool
13.06.97	Jamie Warters L RSC 5 Leeds
15.12.97	Michael Pinnock W PTS 6 Nottingham
11.05.98	Neil Simpson L PTS 6 Leicester
25.11.98	Sven Hamer L CO 2 Streatham
13.03.99	Ole Klemetsen L CO 4 Manchester
24.04.99	Monty Wright W RSC 3 Peterborough
20.05.99	Sven Hamer W RSC 5 Kensington
03.10.99	Carl Smallwood W PTS 6 Chesterfield
09.04.00	Tony Booth L PTS 10 Alfreton
	(Vacant British Masters L. Heavyweight Title)
15.07.00	Clinton Woods L RSC 3 Millwall
03.08.02	Lee Swaby L RSC 4 Derby
21.10.02	Chris Woollas L PTS 6 Cleethorpes
02.12.02	Clint Johnson L PTS 6 Leeds
01.08.03	David Haye L CO 1 Bethnal Green
31.01.04	Albert Sosnowski L CO 2 Bethnal Green
15.03.04	Lee Mountford DREW 6 Bradford
09.04.04	Robert Norton L CO 1 Rugby
08.06.04	Neil Dawson L RSC 3 Sheffield
	Career: 46 contests, won 15, drew 1, lost 30.

Matt Scriven

Nottingham. *Born* Nottingham, 1 September, 1973
Midlands Area L.Middleweight Champion. Former British Masters L.Middleweight Champion. Ht. 5'10"
Manager T. Harris

26.11.97	Shamus Casey W PTS 6 Stoke
08.12.97	Shane Thomas W PTS 6 Bradford
20.03.98	C. J. Jackson L PTS 6 Ilkeston
15.05.98	Lee Bird W RSC 5 Nottingham
08.10.98	Stevie McCready L RTD 3 Sunderland
01.04.99	Adrian Houldey W PTS 6 Birmingham
25.04.99	Danny Thornton L RSC 4 Leeds
27.06.99	Shane Junior L RSC 2 Alfreton
11.09.99	David Arundel L RTD 1 Sheffield
20.03.00	James Docherty L PTS 8 Glasgow
27.03.00	Matt Mowatt L PTS 4 Barnsley
09.04.00	David Matthews W PTS 6 Alfreton
06.06.00	Jackie Townsley L RSC 3 Motherwell
04.11.00	Brett James RTD 1 Bethnal Green

04.02.01	Mark Paxford L PTS 6 Queensferry
26.02.01	Pedro Thompson W RTD 1 Nottingham
12.03.01	Ernie Smith W PTS 6 Birmingham
20.03.01	James Docherty L RSC 1 Glasgow
21.05.01	Christian Brady L RSC 5 Birmingham
	(Vacant Midlands Area Welterweight Title)
21.10.01	Neil Bonner NC 1 Glasgow
04.03.02	Danny Parkinson L PTS 6 Bradford
22.04.02	Gary Porter L PTS 6 Glasgow
28.05.02	Peter Dunn W PTS 8 Leeds
14.09.02	Ernie Smith W PTS 6 Newark
29.09.02	James Lee L RTD 4 Shrewsbury
30.11.02	Davey Jones L PTS 6 Newark
16.03.03	Lee Williamson W PTS 10 Nottingham
	(Vacant Midlands Area & British Masters L. Middleweight Titles)
08.06.03	Wayne Shepherd W PTS 10 Nottingham
	(British Masters L.Middleweight Title Defence)
15.09.03	Lee Murtagh L DIS 9 Leeds
	(British Masters L.Middleweight Title Defence)
12.03.04	David Walker L RSC 3 Nottingham
12.06.04	Matthew Hatton L RSC 4 Manchester
	Career: 30 contests, won 11, lost 18, no contest 1.

Ebrima Secka

Brighton. *Born* Gambia, 1 March, 1975
Heavyweight. Ht. 6'0"
Manager R. Davies

27.04.04	Paul Butlin L PTS 6 Leeds
	Career: 1 contest, lost 1.

Nigel Senior

Nottingham. *Born* Wallsend, 19 November, 1962
Lightweight. Former British Masters Lightweight Champion. Ht. 5'5"
Manager J. Gill

03.10.85	Mark Needham W RSC 4 Nottingham
14.10.85	Anthony Brown L PTS 6 Leicester
21.10.85	Peter Bowen DREW 6 Sheffield
11.11.85	Sugar Gibiliru L RSC 5 Liverpool
24.03.86	Joe Donohoe L PTS 6 Mayfair
07.04.86	Billy Joe Dee W PTS 6 Nottingham
15.04.86	Wayne Andrews W PTS 6 Merton
23.04.86	Nigel Haddock L PTS 6 Stoke
19.05.86	Nigel Haddock DREW 6 Nottingham
09.06.86	Nigel Crook W PTS 6 Manchester
23.08.86	Tony Graham DREW 6 Manchester
04.09.86	Gary King W PTS 6 Merton
23.09.86	Carl Cleasby W PTS 6 Batley
20.10.86	Gary Maxwell L PTS 8 Nottingham
29.10.86	Nigel Haddock L PTS 6 Ebbw Vale
11.11.86	Darren Connellan L PTS 6 Batley
28.11.86	Ian Honeywood W RSC 5 Peterborough
16.12.86	Paul Timmons L PTS 6 Alfreton
27.01.87	Russell Davison DREW 8 Manchester
09.02.87	Joe Duffy W CO 3 Glasgow
16.02.87	Dean Bramhald W PTS 8 Glasgow
14.03.87	Floyd Havard L RSC 5 Southwark
13.04.87	John Bennie L PTS 6 Glasgow
01.05.87	Gary de Roux L PTS 8 Peterborough
04.06.87	John Feeney L PTS 8 Sunderland
28.09.87	George Jones L PTS 8 Birmingham
09.11.87	Rocky Lawlor L RSC 5 Birmingham
27.01.88	Ronnie Green L PTS 8 Stoke

24.02.88	John Bennie L PTS 6 Glasgow
08.03.88	Billy Joe Dee W PTS 6 Batley
23.03.88	Glyn Rhodes L PTS 8 Sheffield
30.03.88	Paul Gadney L PTS 6 Bethnal Green
17.04.88	Dave Kettlewell W PTS 6 Peterborough
25.04.88	Dean Bramhald L PTS 8 Nottingham
10.09.88	Herve Jacob L PTS 8 Grande-Synthe, France
07.10.88	Daniel Londas L PTS 8 Bordeaux, France
25.01.89	Henry Armstrong L PTS 8 Stoke
14.02.89	John Davison L RSC 8 Sunderland
20.03.89	Wayne Weekes L PTS 6 Nottingham
24.04.89	Ian Honeywood L PTS 4 Nottingham
10.05.89	Nigel Wenton L RSC 2 Kensington
19.04.90	Les Walsh L PTS 8 Oldham
30.04.90	Kruga Hydes W PTS 6 Nottingham
21.05.90	Peter Konyegwachie L RSC 7 Mayfair
07.09.90	Jimmy Owens L PTS 6 Liverpool
18.10.90	Frankie Foster L CO 2 Hartlepool
	(Vacant Northern Area S. Featherweight Title)
03.12.90	Mark Antony L PTS 8 Cleethorpes
10.12.90	Noel Carroll W PTS 6 Nottingham
06.03.91	Richard Joyce L PTS 8 Croydon
01.12.99	Chris Jickells L RSC 2 Stoke
24.02.00	Willie Limond L RSC 2 Glasgow
26.03.00	Steve Brook L PTS 6 Nottingham
17.04.00	Steve Brook L PTS 6 Bradford
11.05.00	John Barnes L PTS 6 Sunderland
20.05.00	Gary Wilson L PTS 6 Rotherham
06.06.00	Barry Hawthorne L PTS 6 Motherwell
10.09.00	Steve Gethin DREW 6 Walsall
22.09.00	Jason Edwards W PTS 6 Wrexham
01.10.00	James Rooney L PTS 6 Hartlepool
09.10.00	Ricky Eccleston L PTS 4 Liverpool
26.10.00	Nigel Leake W PTS 6 Stoke
04.11.00	Marc Callaghan L RSC 4 Bethnal Green
07.12.00	Alex Stewart W PTS 8 Stoke
22.01.01	Craig Docherty L RSC 4 Glasgow
08.03.01	Jason White L PTS 8 Stoke
24.03.01	Carl Greaves L CO 6 Newark
	(Vacant Midlands Area S. Featherweight Title)
18.06.01	Dave Cotterill L PTS 6 Bradford
21.07.01	Gavin Rees L RSC 2 Sheffield
15.09.01	Inderpaul Sandhu L PTS 4 Nottingham
24.09.01	Haroon Din L PTS 6 Cleethorpes
07.10.01	Pete Buckley W PTS 6 Wolverhampton
01.11.01	Anthony Hanna W PTS 6 Hull
17.11.01	Gary Greenwood L PTS 6 Coventry
01.12.01	Marc Callaghan W CO 1 Bethnal Green
09.12.01	Pete Buckley L PTS 6 Shaw
17.12.01	Haroon Din L PTS 6 Cleethorpes
25.02.02	Brian Gentry W RSC 8 Slough
	(British Masters Lightweight Title Challenge)
26.04.02	Dean Pithie L PTS 6 Coventry
28.05.02	Colin Toohey L PTS 4 Liverpool
08.09.02	Stephen Chinnock L PTS 6 Wolverhampton
17.11.02	Charles Shepherd L PTS 6 Shaw
30.11.02	Gary Greenwood L PTS 4 Coventry
22.03.03	Tony McPake L PTS 4 Renfrew
26.04.03	Dave Stewart L RSC 2 Brentford
	(British Masters Lightweight Title Defence)
06.06.03	Jackson Williams L PTS 8 Norwich
15.06.03	Nadeem Siddique L PTS 6 Bradford
06.09.03	Mally McIver L PTS 4 Huddersfield
15.09.03	Martin Hardcastle L PTS 6 Leeds

02.10.03	Nigel Wright L RSC 5 Liverpool	
30.11.03	Dean Phillips L CO 1 Swansea	
21.02.04	Jackson Williams L PTS 6 Norwich	
09.04.04	Harry Ramogoadi L RSC 1 Rugby	
22.05.04	Joel Viney W PTS 6 Manchester	
30.05.04	Robbie Murray L PTS 6 Dublin	
08.06.04	Amir Ali L PTS 6 Sheffield	
19.06.04	Barry Hughes L RSC 3 Renfrew	

Career: 96 contests, won 21, drew 5, lost 70.

Charles Shepherd

Carlisle. *Born* Burnley, 28 June, 1970
Lightweight. Former IBO S.Featherweight
Champion. Former Undefeated British,
Commonwealth & IBO Inter-Continental
S.Featherweight Champion. Ht. 5'4"
Manager J. Doughty

28.10.91	Chris Aston W PTS 6 Leicester
31.01.92	Alan McDowall L RSC 3 Glasgow
18.05.92	Mark Legg W PTS 6 Marton
25.09.92	George Naylor W RSC 4 Liverpool
22.10.92	Didier Hughes L PTS 4 Bethnal Green
13.02.93	Nigel Wenton W PTS 8 Manchester
23.05.93	Cham Joof W PTS 4 Brockley
21.10.93	Karl Taylor W RTD 5 Bayswater
09.02.94	Justin Juuko L RSC 5 Bethnal Green
21.04.94	Tony Foster L PTS 10 Hull
	(Vacant Central Area Lightweight Title)
29.09.94	Frankie Foster W RSC 3 Tynemouth
08.03.95	Bamana Dibateza W PTS 8 Solihull
26.04.95	Kelton McKenzie W RSC 7 Solihull
23.05.95	Michael Ayers L RSC 3 Potters Bar
	(British Lightweight Title Challenge)
14.11.95	John Stovin W RSC 4 Bury
22.04.96	Marc Smith W RSC 2 Crystal Palace
29.06.96	P. J. Gallagher L PTS 12 Erith
	(British S. Featherweight Title Challenge)
28.10.96	Harry Escott W PTS 8 Glasgow
22.09.97	Dave McHale W RSC 10 Glasgow
	(Vacant British S. Featherweight Title)
08.11.97	Matt Brown W PTS 12 Southwark
	(British S. Featherweight Title Defence)
02.05.98	Peter Judson W PTS 12 Kensington
	(British S. Featherweight Title Defence)
22.01.99	Trust Ndlovu W CO 6 Carlisle
	(Vacant Commonwealth S. Featherweight Title)
03.04.99	Smith Odoom W PTS 12 Carlisle
	(Commonwealth S. Featherweight Title Defence)
31.07.99	Tom Johnson W PTS 12 Carlisle
	(Vacant IBO S. Featherweight Title)
26.02.00	Affif Djelti L RSC 6 Carlisle
	(IBO S. Featherweight Title Defence)
05.06.00	Rakhim Mingaleev W PTS 12 Glasgow
	(Vacant IBO Inter-Continental S. Featherweight Title)
18.09.00	James Armah L RTD 9 Glasgow
	(Vacant Commonwealth S. Featherweight Title)
11.11.00	Tontcho Tontchev L PTS 12 Belfast
	(WBA Inter-Continental S.Featherweight Title Challenge)
20.03.01	Alex Moon L PTS 12 Glasgow
	(Vacant Commonwealth S. Featherweight Title)
14.07.01	Isaac Sebaduka L RSC 5 Wembley
17.11.02	Nigel Senior W PTS 6 Shaw

19.10.03	Daniel Thorpe W PTS 6 Shaw
11.12.03	Lee Meager L RTD 7 Bethnal Green
28.05.04	Barry Hughes DREW 12 Glasgow
	(Vacant WBU Inter-Continental Lightweight Title)

Career: 34 contests, won 21, drew 1, lost 12.

Wayne Shepherd

Carlisle. *Born* Whiston, 3 June, 1959
L. Middleweight. Ht. 5'6"
Manager Self

07.10.91	Benji Joseph W PTS 6 Bradford
28.10.91	Noel Henry W PTS 6 Leicester
16.12.91	Dave Maj DREW 6 Manchester
03.02.92	Dave Maj L PTS 6 Manchester
30.03.92	Hughie Davey L PTS 6 Bradford
18.05.92	Dave Whittle W PTS 6 Marton
14.10.92	Richard Swallow L PTS 8 Stoke
31.10.92	George Scott L RSC 6 Earls Court
13.02.93	Delroy Waul L RSC 5 Manchester
31.03.93	Derek Grainger L RSC 4 Barking
11.06.93	Hughie Davey L PTS 6 Gateshead
06.09.93	Shea Neary L RTD 2 Liverpool
26.01.94	James McGee W PTS 6 Stoke
28.02.94	Craig Winter L PTS 6 Manchester
02.03.95	Denny Johnson L PTS 6 Cramlington
06.04.95	Shaun Stokes L PTS 6 Sheffield
22.05.95	Peter Varnavas W PTS 6 Morecambe
01.06.95	Tommy Quinn L PTS 6 Musselburgh
29.07.95	Shaun O'Neill L PTS 4 Whitley Bay
07.10.95	Neil Sinclair L PTS 6 Belfast
30.10.95	John Stronach L PTS 6 Bradford
11.12.95	Shamus Casey L PTS 6 Morecambe
07.03.96	Derek Roche L RSC 3 Bradford
22.04.96	Gilbert Eastman L PTS 4 Crystal Palace
25.06.96	Geoff McCreesh L PTS 4 Stevenage
26.09.96	John Docherty L PTS 6 Glasgow
10.11.96	John Docherty L PTS 6 Glasgow
22.12.96	Chris Barnett L PTS 6 Salford
16.03.97	C. J. Jackson L PTS 6 Shaw
14.10.97	Joe Townsley L PTS 8 Kilmarnock
22.11.97	G. L. Booth L PTS 4 Manchester
05.03.98	Lee Murtagh L PTS 6 Leeds
20.03.98	Wayne Burchell L PTS 6 Leeds
28.04.98	Danny Ryan L DIS 4 Belfast
14.06.98	Matt Mowatt DREW 6 Shaw
20.09.98	Matt Mowatt W PTS 6 Sheffield
12.10.98	Danny Thornton L PTS 6 Bradford
03.12.98	Lee Molloy L PTS 4 Mayfair
22.01.99	Lee Bird W PTS 6 Carlisle
16.02.99	Paul O'Rourke L PTS 6 Leeds
07.08.99	Alan Gilbert DREW 8 Dagenham
	(Vacant British Masters L. Middleweight Title)
28.10.99	Matt Mowatt W PTS 6 Burnley
15.11.99	James Docherty L PTS 8 Glasgow
14.12.99	Joe Townsley L PTS 6 Coventry
26.02.00	Martin Thompson W PTS 4 Carlisle
05.03.00	Jason Collins L PTS 6 Shaw
21.05.00	Andy Vickers L PTS 6 Shaw
23.10.00	Jackie Townsley L PTS 4 Glasgow
25.11.00	Jamie Moore L RSC 3 Manchester
22.01.01	Joe Townsley L PTS 6 Glasgow
20.03.01	Scott Dixon L PTS 6 Glasgow
28.03.01	Andrew Buchanan L RSC 2 Piccadilly
23.09.01	Richard Inquieti W PTS 6 Shaw
21.10.01	Martyn Bailey L PTS 6 Pentre Halkyn
03.11.01	Ciaran Duffy L PTS 6 Glasgow
10.12.01	Andrei Ivanov W PTS 6 Nottingham
09.02.02	Brendan Halford L PTS 6 Coventry
21.02.02	Ryan Kerr L PTS 6 Sunderland
03.03.02	Conroy McIntosh DREW 6 Shaw

02.06.02	Dean Walker L PTS 6 Shaw
21.06.02	Lee Murtagh L PTS 10 Leeds
	(Vacant British Masters Middleweight Title)
06.10.02	Neil Bonner L PTS 6 Rhyl
26.10.02	Mark Paxford L PTS 6 Wigan
17.11.02	Sam Gorman W PTS 6 Shaw
21.02.03	Jason Rushton L PTS 6 Doncaster
09.03.03	Brian Coleman W PTS 6 Shaw
03.04.03	Sonny Pollard L PTS 6 Hull
09.05.03	Davey Jones L PTS 6 Doncaster
08.06.03	Matt Scriven L PTS 6 Nottingham
	(British Masters L.Middleweight Title Challenge)
13.09.03	Peter Dunn L PTS 6 Wakefield
05.10.03	Danny Parkinson L RSC 5 Bradford
04.12.03	Danny Moir L PTS 6 Sunderland
23.02.04	Adnan Amar L RSC 5 Nottingham

Career: 73 contests, won 13, drew 4, lost 56.

Nadeem Siddique

Bradford. *Born* Bradford, 28 October, 1977
L. Welterweight. Ht. 5'8"
Manager J. Ingle

17.11.02	Daniel Thorpe W PTS 4 Bradford
09.02.03	Norman Dhalie W PTS 4 Bradford
13.04.03	Dave Hinds W PTS 4 Bradford
15.06.03	Nigel Senior W PTS 6 Bradford
05.10.03	Jason Nesbitt W PTS 6 Bradford
27.10.03	Daniel Thorpe W PTS 6 Glasgow
07.12.03	Chris Duggan W RSC 2 Bradford
16.01.04	Pete Buckley W PTS 6 Bradford
16.04.04	Arv Mittoo W PTS 6 Bradford
15.05.04	Joel Viney W PTS 6 Aberdeen

Career: 10 contests, won 10.

(Paulino) Paulie Silva

Droylsden. *Born* Almada, Portugal, 29
April, 1978
L. Heavyweight. Ht. 5'10"
Manager W. Barker

28.02.04	Nick Okoth W PTS 6 Manchester
02.04.04	Courtney Fry L PTS 4 Plymouth

Career: 2 contests, won 1, lost 1.

Luke Simpkin

Swadlincote. *Born* Derby, 5 May, 1979
Heavyweight. Ht. 6'2"
Manager Self

24.09.98	Simon Taylor W CO 3 Edgbaston
16.10.98	Chris P. Bacon L PTS 6 Salford
10.12.98	Jason Flisher W RSC 5 Barking
04.02.99	Danny Watts L CO 3 Lewisham
28.05.99	Tommy Bannister W RSC 4 Liverpool
07.08.99	Owen Beck L PTS 4 Dagenham
11.09.99	Scott Lansdowne L PTS 4 Sheffield
11.03.00	Albert Sosnowski L PTS 4 Kensington
27.03.00	Mark Hobson L PTS 4 Barnsley
29.04.00	Johan Thorbjoernsson L PTS 4 Wembley
23.09.00	Mark Potter L PTS 6 Bethnal Green
30.09.00	Gordon Minors DREW 4 Peterborough
18.11.00	Keith Long L RSC 3 Dagenham
03.02.01	Paul Buttery W RSC 1 Manchester
01.04.01	Wayne Llewelyn L PTS 6 Southwark
24.04.01	Darren Chubbs L PTS 6 Liverpool
06.05.01	Billy Bessey L PTS 6 Hartlepool
09.06.01	John McDermott L PTS 6 Bethnal Green
13.09.01	Mark Krence L PTS 4 Sheffield

165

10.12.01	Mark Hobson L RTD 3 Liverpool
27,.01.02	Pele Reid DREW 4 Streatham
15.03.02	Mike Holden L PTS 6 Millwall
13.04.02	Fola Okesola W PTS 4 Liverpool
10.05.02	Julius Francis DREW 6 Millwall
23.08.02	Mark Potter L PTS 6 Bethnal Green
10.06.03	Mark Krence L RTD 8 Sheffield
	(Vacant Midlands Area Heavyweight Title)
05.09.03	Roman Greenberg L RTD 4 Sheffield
25.04.04	Dave Clarke W RSC 2 Nottingham

Career: 28 contests, won 6, drew 3, lost 19.

John Simpson

Greenock. *Born* Greenock, 26 July, 1983
Featherweight. Ht. 5'7"
Manager T. Gilmour

23.09.02	Simon Chambers W RSC 1 Glasgow
06.10.02	Lee Holmes L PTS 6 Rhyl
07.12.02	Matthew Burke W PTS 4 Brentwood
20.01.03	John-Paul Ryan W PTS 6 Glasgow
17.02.03	Joel Viney W RTD 1 Glasgow
14.04.03	Simon Chambers W PTS 6 Glasgow
20.10.03	Steve Gethin W PTS 8 Glasgow
01.11.03	Mark Alexander W PTS 4 Glasgow
19.01.04	Henry Janes W PTS 8 Glasgow
31.01.04	Gennadiy Delisandru W PTS 4 Bethnal Green
22.04.04	Jus Wallie W PTS 6 Glasgow
02.06.04	Fred Janes W PTS 6 Hereford

Career: 12 contests, won 11, lost 1.

Neil Simpson

Coventry. *Born* London, 5 July, 1970
L.Heavyweight. Former Undefeated British
& Commonwealth L.Heavyweight
Champion. Former Midlands Area
L.Heavyweight Champion. Ht. 6'2"
Manager Self

04.10.94	Kenny Nevers W PTS 4 Mayfair
20.10.94	Johnny Hooks W RSC 2 Walsall
05.12.94	Chris Woollas L PTS 6 Cleethorpes
15.12.94	Paul Murray W PTS 6 Walsall
06.03.95	Greg Scott-Briggs W RTD 5 Leicester
17.03.95	Thomas Hansvold L PTS 4 Copenhagen, Denmark
26.04.95	Craig Joseph L PTS 6 Solihull
11.05.95	Andy McVeigh L CO 2 Dudley
24.06.95	Dave Owens W RSC 1 Cleethorpes
25.09.95	Tony Booth L PTS 8 Cleethorpes
11.10.95	Darren Ashton W RSC 3 Solihull
29.11.95	Greg Scott-Briggs W DIS 7 Solihull
	(Vacant Midlands Area L. Heavyweight Title)
19.02.96	Stephen Wilson L PTS 6 Glasgow
27.03.96	Tony Booth W PTS 6 Whitwick
26.04.96	Dean Francis L RSC 3 Cardiff
02.10.96	Chris Davies W PTS 4 Cardiff
28.10.96	Nigel Rafferty W PTS 8 Leicester
03.12.96	Danny Peters L PTS 6 Liverpool
03.02.97	Michael Pinnock W PTS 6 Leicester
25.04.97	Stuart Fleet L PTS 10 Cleethorpes
	(Midlands Area L. Heavyweight Title Defence)
20.10.97	Slick Miller W RTD 1 Leicester
15.12.97	Chris Woollas L PTS 6 Cleethorpes
11.05.98	Greg Scott-Briggs W PTS 6 Leicester
30.11.98	Slick Miller W CO 3 Leicester
26.02.99	Adam Cale W RSC 3 Coventry
12.07.99	Tony Booth W PTS 10 Coventry
	(Elim. British L. Heavyweight Title)

14.12.99	Darren Corbett L PTS 12 Coventry
	(Vacant IBO Inter-Continental L. Heavyweight Title)
22.05.00	Mark Baker W PTS 12 Coventry
	(Vacant British & Commonwealth L. Heavyweight Titles)
18.11.00	Mark Delaney W RSC 1 Dagenham
	(British L. Heavyweight Title Defence)
02.01.01	Hastings Rasani W CO 4 Coventry
	(Vacant Commonwealth L. Heavyweight Title)
06.04.01	Yawe Davis L RSC 3 Grosseto, Italy
	(Vacant European L. Heavyweight Title)
25.05.02	Tony Oakey L PTS 12 Portsmouth
	(WBU L. Heavyweight Title Challenge)
08.03.03	Peter Oboh L RSC 11 Coventry
	(Commonwealth L.Heavyweight Title Challenge. Vacant British L.Heavyweight Title)
20.04.04	Mark Brookes L PTS 10 Sheffield
	(Elim. British L.Heavyweight Title)

Career: 34 contests, won 19, lost 15.

Matt Skelton

Bedford. *Born* Bedford, 23 January, 1968
British & Commonwealth Heavyweight
Champion. Former Undefeated English
Heavyweight Champion. Ht. 6'3"
Manager K. Sanders/F. Maloney

22.09.02	Gifford Shillingford W RSC 2 Southwark
27.10.02	Slick Miller W CO 1 Southwark
08.12.02	Neil Kirkwood W RSC 1 Bethnal Green
18.02.03	Jacklord Jacobs W RSC 4 Bethnal Green
08.04.03	Alexei Varakin W CO 2 Bethnal Green
15.05.03	Dave Clarke W RSC 1 Mayfair
17.07.03	Antoine Palatis W RSC 4 Dagenham
18.09.03	Mike Holden W RSC 6 Dagenham
	(Vacant English Heavyweight Title)
11.10.03	Costi Marin W RSC 1 Portsmouth
25.10.03	Ratko Draskovic W RSC 3 Edinburgh
15.11.03	Patriche Costel W CO 1 Bayreuth, Germany

Matt Skelton   Les Clark

07.02.04 Julius Francis W PTS 10 Bethnal Green
(English Heavyweight Title Defence)
24.04.04 Michael Sprott W CO 12 Reading
(British & Commonwealth Heavyweight Title Challenges)
05.06.04 Bob Mirovic W RTD 4 Bethnal Green
(Commonwealth Heavyweight Title Defence)
Career: 14 contests, won 14.

Anthony Small
Deptford. *Born* London, 28 June, 1981
Welterweight. Ht. 5'9"
Manager A. Booth

12.05.04 Lance Hall W RSC 1 Reading
Career: 1 contest, won 1.

Donovan Smillie
Bradford. *Born* Bradford, 9 August, 1975
British Masters S.Middleweight Champion.
Ht. 5'10½"
Manager J. Ingle

10.04.99 Sean Pritchard W RSC 1 Manchester
02.05.99 Mark Dawson W PTS 6 Shaw
04.12.99 Mark Dawson W PTS 4 Manchester
14.04.00 Dennis Doyley W PTS 4 Manchester
25.11.00 Ojay Abrahams L RSC 2 Manchester
30.11.01 Rob Stevenson W PTS 6 Hull
17.12.01 Mark Chesters W PTS 6 Cleethorpes
17.02.02 William Webster W PTS 6 Salford
20.04.02 Mike Duffield L PTS 4 Derby
15.06.02 Wayne Asker DREW 6 Norwich
07.10.02 Alan Jones L RSC 6 Birmingham
17.11.02 William Webster W PTS 6 Bradford
09.02.03 Robert Burton W PTS 6 Bradford
13.04.03 Mark Phillips W PTS 6 Bradford
15.06.03 Mike Duffield W RSC 3 Bradford
(Vacant British Masters S.Middleweight Title)
03.08.03 William Webster W RSC 4 Stalybridge
05.10.03 Gary Jones W CO 2 Bradford
07.12.03 Patrick Cito W PTS 6 Bradford
16.01.04 Mark Phillips W PTS 4 Bradford
16.04.04 Patrick Cito W RSC 3 Bradford
Career: 20 contests, won 16, drew 1, lost 3.

Danny Smith
Lowestoft. *Born* Great Yarmouth, 6 October, 1979
Middleweight. Ht. 6'0"
Manager Self

15.07.00 Gary Jones W RSC 1 Norwich
04.11.00 Rob Stevenson DREW 6 Derby
28.03.01 Simeon Cover W PTS 6 Piccadilly
08.06.01 Rob Stevenson W PTS 6 Hull
13.04.02 Freddie Yemofio W PTS 6 Norwich
15.06.02 William Webster W PTS 6 Norwich
21.09.02 Mike Duffield W PTS 6 Norwich
12.04.03 Simeon Cover W CO 5 Norwich
06.06.03 Gary Cummings W PTS 6 Norwich
25.07.03 William Webster W PTS 4 Norwich
21.02.04 Lee Williamson W PTS 6 Norwich
Career: 11 contests, won 10, drew 1.

Ernie Smith
Stourport. *Born* Kidderminster, 10 June, 1978
Welterweight. Ht. 5'8"
Manager Self

24.11.98 Woody Greenaway L PTS 6 Wolverhampton
05.12.98 Gavin Rees L PTS 4 Bristol
27.01.99 Arv Mittoo DREW 6 Stoke
11.02.99 Tony Smith W PTS 6 Dudley
22.02.99 Liam Maltby W PTS 4 Peterborough
08.03.99 Wayne Jones W PTS 6 Birmingham
18.03.99 Carl Greaves L PTS 6 Doncaster
25.03.99 Brian Coleman L PTS 6 Edgbaston
27.05.99 Brian Coleman W PTS 6 Edgbaston
14.06.99 Dave Gibson W PTS 6 Birmingham
22.06.99 Koba Gogoladze L RSC 1 Ipswich
03.10.99 Gavin Down L RSC 1 Chesterfield
30.11.99 Brian Coleman L PTS 8 Wolverhampton
13.12.99 Richie Murray L RSC 5 Cleethorpes
24.02.00 Brian Coleman L PTS 6 Edgbaston
02.03.00 Oscar Hall L PTS 6 Birkenhead
10.03.00 John Tiftik L PTS 4 Chigwell
18.03.00 Biagio Falcone L PTS 4 Glasgow
07.04.00 Barry Connell L PTS 6 Glasgow
14.04.00 Jose Luis Castro L PTS 6 Madrid, Spain
06.05.00 Matthew Barr L PTS 4 Southwark
15.05.00 Harry Butler L PTS 6 Birmingham
26.05.00 Biagio Falcone L PTS 4 Glasgow
06.06.00 Chris Henry L PTS 8 Brierley Hill
08.07.00 Takaloo L RSC 4 Widnes
13.08.00 Jawaid Khaliq L RSC 4 Nottingham
(Vacant Midlands Area Welterweight Title)
24.09.00 Shaun Horsfall L PTS 6 Shaw
09.10.00 Dave Gibson W PTS 6 Birmingham
22.10.00 Matthew Barr L PTS 4 Streatham
06.11.00 Stuart Elwell L PTS 6 Wolverhampton
25.11.00 Michael Jennings L PTS 4 Manchester
03.12.00 Shaun Horsfall L PTS 6 Shaw
17.12.00 Kevin McIntyre L PTS 6 Glasgow
20.01.01 David Walker L RTD 1 Bethnal Green
12.03.01 Matt Scriven L PTS 6 Birmingham
24.03.01 Bobby Banghar L PTS 4 Chigwell
12.05.01 Jon Harrison L PTS 4 Plymouth
21.05.01 Brian Coleman W PTS 6 Birmingham
03.06.01 Babatunde Ajayi L PTS 4 Southwark
16.06.01 Bobby Banghar L PTS 4 Dagenham
26.07.01 Andy Abrol L PTS 6 Blackpool
13.09.01 Leo O'Reilly L PTS 6 Sheffield
29.09.01 Brett James L PTS 6 Southwark
01.11.01 Lance Crosby L PTS 6 Hull
17.11.01 Nigel Wright L PTS 4 Glasgow
15.12.01 Ross Minter L RSC 2 Wembley
11.02.02 Tony Montana L PTS 6 Shrewsbury
13.05.02 Martin Scotland W RTD 2 Birmingham
15.06.02 Gavin Wake L PTS 4 Leeds
08.07.02 Gavin Rees L RSC 5 Mayfair
06.09.02 Ricky Burns L PTS 6 Glasgow
14.09.02 Matt Scriven L PTS 6 Newark
29.09.02 Anthony Christopher L PTS 6 Shrewsbury
18.11.02 Craig Dickson L PTS 6 Glasgow
03.12.02 Anthony Christopher W PTS 6 Shrewsbury
23.02.03 Gary Greenwood L PTS 4 Shrewsbury
24.03.03 Darrell Grafton L PTS 6 Barnsley
13.04.03 Lee McAllister L PTS 4 Bradford
28.04.03 Adnan Amar L PTS 6 Cleethorpes
12.05.03 Lee McAllister L PTS 6 Birmingham
31.05.03 Robbie Sivyer L PTS 6 Barnsley
08.06.03 Jonathan Woollins W PTS 4 Nottingham
15.06.03 Ali Nuumembe L PTS 4 Bradford
05.07.03 Michael Lomax L PTS 4 Brentwood
29.08.03 Ali Nuumembe L PTS 6 Liverpool
04.10.03 Lenny Daws L PTS 4 Muswell Hill

18.11.03 Chas Symonds L PTS 6 Bethnal Green
28.11.03 Lee McAllister L PTS 6 Hull
06.12.03 Taz Jones L PTS 4 Cardiff
07.02.04 Gary Woolcombe L PTS 4 Bethnal Green
09.04.04 Richard Swallow L PTS 4 Rugby
19.04.04 Craig Dickson L PTS 6 Glasgow
10.05.04 Adnan Amar L PTS 6 Birmingham
27.05.04 Graham Delehedy L RSC 3 Huddersfield
Career: 74 contests, won 10, drew 1, lost 63.

Paul Smith
Liverpool. *Born* Liverpool, 6 October, 1982
Middleweight. Ht. 5'11"
Manager F. Warren

05.04.03 Howard Clarke W PTS 4 Manchester
08.05.03 Andrei Ivanov W RSC 2 Widnes
20.06.03 Elroy Edwards W RSC 2 Liverpool
29.08.03 Patrick Cito W PTS 4 Liverpool
02.10.03 Mike Duffield W RSC 1 Liverpool
13.12.03 Joel Ani W PTS 4 Manchester
26.02.04 Davey Jones W PTS 4 Widnes
03.04.04 Howard Clarke W PTS 4 Manchester
12.06.04 Steve Timms W RSC 1 Manchester
Career: 9 contests, won 9.

Sammy Smith
Bracknell. *Born* Chichester, 12 May, 1978
Welterweight. Former Undefeated British Masters L.Welterweight Champion.
Ht. 5'6"
Manager G. Carmen

26.03.98 Shaba Edwards W PTS 6 Acton
28.04.98 Les Frost W CO 2 Brentford
02.10.98 Arv Mittoo W PTS 4 Cheshunt
27.10.98 Rudy Valentino W PTS 6 Brentford
07.12.98 Ross McCord W RSC 5 Acton
25.02.99 Trevor Smith W RSC 2 Kentish Town
08.03.99 Brian Coleman L PTS 8 Birmingham
09.05.99 David Kirk W PTS 6 Bracknell
09.04.00 Gavin Down L PTS 6 Alfreton
18.05.00 Gary Reid L RSC 1 Bethnal Green
11.02.02 David Keir W PTS 6 Southampton
25.02.02 Marcus Portman L PTS 4 Slough
09.05.03 Brian Coleman W PTS 6 Longford
31.05.03 David Kirk W PTS 4 Bethnal Green
01.08.03 Brett James L PTS 10 Bethnal Green
(Vacant Southern Area Welterweight Title)
27.09.03 Michael Jennings L RTD 4 Manchester
(WBU Inter-Continental Welterweight Title Challenge)
27.11.03 Keith Jones W PTS 10 Longford
(Vacant British Masters L.Welterweight Title)
08.05.04 Young Muttley L RSC 1 Bristol
(Vacant English L.Welterweight Title)
Career: 18 contests, won 11, lost 7.

Stephen Smith
Kentish Town. *Born* Hammersmith, 18 July, 1973
L.Welterweight. Former Undefeated IBC L.Welterweight Champion. Former Undefeated IBF Inter-Continental Lightweight Champion. Former Undefeated German International S.Featherweight Champion. Ht. 5'8"
Manager A. Booth

17.09.94	Marty Chestnut W RSC 5 Leverkusen, Germany
08.10.94	Jason Lepre W RSC 1 Halle, Germany
11.02.95	Fred Reeve W CO 1 Frankfurt, Germany
25.03.95	Pascal Ragaut W PTS 6 Dusseldorf, Germany
27.05.95	Vladimir Komarov W RSC 5 Dortmund, Germany
09.09.95	Juan Leiva W RSC 6 Bielfield, Germany
14.10.95	Abdul Mannon W RSC 3 Munich, Germany
17.02.96	Kid McAuley W RSC 4 Dortmund, Germany
20.04.96	Senturk Ozdemir W PTS 10 Dusseldorf, Germany (German International S. Featherweight Title Challenge)
25.05.96	Chris Jickells W RSC 3 Leipzig, Germany
22.06.96	Brian Robb W RSC 4 Dortmund, Germany
31.08.96	Angel Vasilev W PTS 8 Palma de Mallorca
23.11.96	Manny Santiago W PTS 8 Munich, Germany
15.02.97	Ullises Chong W RSC 2 Vienna, Austria
13.04.97	Peter Feher W CO 1 Cologne, Germany
01.06.97	Emmanuel Burton W DIS 3 Riesa, Germany
05.10.97	Bruno Rabanales W RSC 7 Gera, Germany
08.11.97	Rudy Valentino W PTS 8 Southwark
11.04.98	Ervine Blake W RTD 4 Southwark
30.05.98	Ferenc Szakallas W RSC 3 Riesa, Germany
21.11.98	Anthony Maynard W PTS 10 Southwark
06.03.99	Gary Flear W RTD 7 Southwark (Vacant IBF Inter-Continental Lightweight Title)
08.05.99	Ivo Golakov W RSC 3 Bethnal Green (IBF Inter-Continental Lightweight Title Defence)
13.09.99	David Kehoe W DIS 2 Bethnal Green
21.02.00	Bobby Vanzie L RSC 9 Southwark (British & Commonwealth Lightweight Title Challenges)
27.05.00	Michael Davies W PTS 10 Southwark
13.07.00	Assen Vassilev W RSC 1 Bethnal Green
18.11.00	Leonti Voronchuk W PTS 6 Dagenham
10.04.01	Zoltan Kalocsai W PTS 12 Wembley (Vacant IBC L. Welterweight Title)
22.09.01	Melikhaya August W CO 4 Newcastle (IBC L. Welterweight Title Defence)
28.11.01	Victor Hugo Paz W PTS 12 Bethnal Green (IBC L. Welterweight Title Defence)
20.04.02	Rocky Martinez W PTS 12 Wembley (IBC L. Welterweight Title Defence)
28.09.02	Ricky Hatton L DIS 2 Manchester (WBU L.Welterweight Challenge)
27.05.03	Jon Honney W PTS 8 Dagenham
11.12.03	Alan Bosworth L PTS 10 Bethnal Green (Vacant English L.Welterweight Title)

Career: 35 contests, won 32, lost 3.

Tony Smith

Rotherham. *Born* Sheffield, 15 August, 1967
L. Middleweight. Ht. 5'8"
Manager Self

12.03.97	Richard Inquieti L RSC 2 Stoke
25.04.97	Dean Bramhald L PTS 6 Cleethorpes
03.05.97	Anas Oweida L RSC 1 Manchester
09.06.97	Christian Brady L RSC 4 Birmingham
10.07.97	Mark Allen L PTS 6 Doncaster
08.10.97	Marc Smith L PTS 6 Stoke
20.11.97	Marc Smith W PTS 6 Solihull
04.12.97	Dean Bramhald L PTS 6 Doncaster
15.01.98	Marc Smith L PTS 6 Solihull
13.05.98	Chris Price W PTS 6 Scunthorpe
21.05.98	Marc Smith L PTS 6 Solihull
21.09.98	Dave Gibson L RSC 6 Cleethorpes
09.12.98	Sean O'Sullivan L PTS 6 Stoke
11.02.99	Ernie Smith L PTS 6 Dudley
18.03.99	Rene Grayel DREW 6 Doncaster
15.05.99	Michael Jennings L RSC 1 Blackpool
04.10.99	Barry Hughes L RSC 5 Glasgow
30.11.99	Craig Clayton L PTS 6 Wolverhampton
08.12.99	Craig Clayton L PTS 6 Stoke
21.05.00	Shaun Horsfall L RSC 4 Shaw
03.02.01	Danny Wray L RSC 1 Brighton
12.03.01	Casey Brooke W PTS 6 Birmingham
01.04.01	Marcus Portman L PTS 6 Wolverhampton
03.06.01	Sam Mottram L PTS 6 Hanley
07.09.01	Marcus Portman L PTS 6 West Bromwich
15.09.01	Ross McCord L PTS 6 Swansea
10.10.01	Jamie Logan L PTS 6 Stoke
10.12.01	Sam Mottram L PTS 6 Nottingham
09.02.02	Andy Egan L PTS 4 Coventry
01.06.02	Jason Rushton L PTS 4 Manchester
20.02.04	Casey Brooke W PTS 6 Doncaster

Career: 31 contests, won 4, drew 1, lost 26.

Craig Spacie

Chesterfield. *Born* Chesterfield, 13 March, 1976
S. Featherweight. Ht. 5'5½"
Manager M. Shinfield

Steven Spartacus   Les Clark

18.09.97	Robert Braddock W RSC 6 Alfreton
03.12.97	Dave Travers W RSC 3 Stoke
16.05.98	Michael Gomez L RSC 3 Bethnal Green
14.10.98	Chris Williams W PTS 6 Stoke
02.12.98	David Morris DREW 6 Stoke
17.03.99	Carl Allen L PTS 8 Stoke
03.10.99	Dean Murdoch W RSC 5 Chesterfield
28.11.99	Andy Green W PTS 6 Chesterfield
18.01.00	Marco Fattore W RTD 1 Mansfield
29.02.00	Alex Moon W PTS 6 Widnes
20.03.00	Chris Williams L PTS 6 Mansfield
11.05.00	Pete Buckley W PTS 4 Newark
25.02.01	J.J.Moore W PTS 4 Derby
06.03.01	J.J.Moore W PTS 6 Yarm
17.04.02	Mark Bowen L PTS 8 Stoke
11.05.02	Dave Hinds W PTS 6 Chesterfield
27.07.02	Jason Nesbitt W PTS 4 Nottingham
16.11.02	Richard Evatt W RSC 2 Nottingham
28.04.03	Andrew Ferrans W PTS 6 Nottingham
20.09.03	Eric Odumasi L PTS 6 Nottingham
14.02.04	Dariusz Snarski L RSC 5 Nottingham

Career: 21 contests, won 14, drew 1, lost 6.

Steven Spartacus (Smith)

Ipswich. *Born* Bury St Edmunds, 3
November, 1976
English & British Masters L.Heavyweight
Champion. Ht. 5'10½"
Manager Self

08.09.00	Michael Pinnock W PTS 4 Hammersmith
30.09.00	Martin Jolley W PTS 6 Chigwell
24.03.01	Calvin Stonestreet W PTS 4 Chigwell
16.06.01	Kevin Burton W RSC 1 Dagenham
07.09.01	Rob Stevenson W RSC 4 Bethnal Green
27.10.01	Darren Ashton W PTS 4 Manchester
24.11.01	Michael Pinnock W PTS 4 Bethnal Green
15.12.01	Oneal Murray W RSC 4 Chigwell
19.01.02	Darren Ashton W PTS 4 Bethnal Green
14.09.02	Calvin Stonestreet W RSC 3 Bethnal Green
08.02.03	Paul Bonson W PTS 6 Norwich
27.05.03	Mark Phillips W RSC 2 Dagenham
25.07.03	Simeon Cover W CO 3 Norwich
	(Vacant British Masters L.Heavyweight Title)
04.10.03	Hastings Rasani W RSC 1 Muswell Hill
11.12.03	Scott Lansdowne W RSC 3 Bethnal Green
	(Vacant English L.Heavyweight Title)
30.01.04	Ovill McKenzie L PTS 6 Dagenham
02.06.04	Varuzhan Davtyan W RSC 1 Nottingham

Career: 17 contests, won 16, lost 1.

Delroy Spencer

Walsall. *Born* Walsall, 25 July, 1968
British Masters Flyweight Champion.
Ht. 5'4"
Manager D. Poston

30.10.98	Gwyn Evans L PTS 4 Peterborough
21.11.98	Jamie Evans W PTS 4 Southwark
30.01.99	Ian Napa L PTS 6 Bethnal Green
26.02.99	Chris Edwards W PTS 6 West Bromwich
30.04.99	Nicky Booth L PTS 6 Scunthorpe
06.06.99	Nicky Booth L PTS 4 Nottingham
19.06.99	Willie Valentine L PTS 4 Dublin

16.10.99	Colin Moffett W PTS 4 Bethnal Green
31.10.99	Shane Mallon W PTS 6 Raynes Park
29.11.99	Lee Georgiou L PTS 4 Wembley
19.02.00	Steffen Norskov L PTS 4 Aalborg, Denmark
08.04.00	Ian Napa L PTS 8 Bethnal Green
15.04.00	Lee Georgiou L PTS 4 Bethnal Green
04.07.00	Ankar Miah W RSC 3 Tooting
13.07.00	Darren Hayde W PTS 4 Bethnal Green
30.09.00	Paul Weir L PTS 8 Chigwell
28.10.00	Dale Robinson L RSC 4 Coventry
02.12.00	Keith Knox W PTS 6 Bethnal Green
08.05.01	Levi Pattison L PTS 4 Barnsley
22.05.01	Mimoun Chent L DIS 5 Telde, Gran Canaria
16.06.01	Sunkanmi Ogunbiyi L PTS 4 Wembley
22.11.01	Darren Taylor W PTS 8 Paddington
	(Vacant British Masters Flyweight Title)
09.12.01	Shinny Bayaar L PTS 4 Shaw
19.12.01	Gareth Payne L PTS 4 Coventry
18.01.02	Gareth Payne W PTS 4 Coventry
28.01.02	Levi Pattison L RSC 5 Barnsley
19.10.03	Shinny Bayaar L PTS 6 Shaw
13.12.03	Mark Moran L PTS 4 Manchester
24.01.04	Martin Power L RTD 1 Wembley
23.04.04	Chris Edwards DREW 6 Leicester
26.06.04	Damaen Kelly L RSC 4 Belfast

Career: 31 contests, won 9, drew 1, lost 21.

Michael Sprott

Reading. *Born* Reading, 16 January, 1975
Heavyweight. Former British &
Commonwealth Heavyweight Champion.
Former Undefeated Southern Area & WBF
European Heavyweight Champion.
Ht. 6'0¾"
Manager D. Powell/F. Warren

20.11.96	Geoff Hunter W RSC 1 Wembley
19.02.97	Johnny Davison W CO 2 Acton
17.03.97	Slick Miller W CO 1 Mayfair
16.04.97	Tim Redman W CO 2 Bethnal Green
20.05.97	Waldeck Fransas W PTS 6 Edmonton
02.09.97	Gary Williams W PTS 6 Southwark
08.11.97	Darren Fearn W PTS 6 Southwark
06.12.97	Nick Howard W RSC 1 Wembley
10.01.98	Johnny Davison W RSC 2 Bethnal Green
14.02.98	Ray Kane W RTD 1 Southwark
14.03.98	Michael Murray W PTS 6 Bethnal Green
12.09.98	Harry Senior L RSC 6 Bethnal Green
	(Vacant Southern Area Heavyweight Title)
16.01.99	Gary Williams W PTS 6 Bethnal Green
10.07.99	Chris Woollas W RTD 4 Southwark
18.01.00	Tony Booth W PTS 6 Mansfield
14.10.00	Wayne Llewelyn L RSC 3 Wembley
17.02.01	Timo Hoffmann W PTS 8 Bethnal Green
24.03.01	Timo Hoffmann L PTS 8 Magdeburg, Germany
03.11.01	Corrie Sanders L RSC 1 Brakpan, South Africa
20.12.01	Jermell Lamar Barnes W PTS 8 Rotterdam, Holland
12.02.02	Danny Williams L RTD 8 Bethnal Green
	(British & Commonwealth Heavyweight Title Challenges)
09.05.02	Pele Reid W RSC 7 Leicester Square
	(Vacant WBF European Heavyweight Title)

10.07.02	Garing Lane W PTS 6 Wembley
17.09.02	Derek McCafferty W PTS 8 Bethnal Green
12.12.02	Tamas Feheri W RSC 2 Leicester Square
24.01.03	Mike Holden W RSC 4 Sheffield
18.03.03	Mark Potter W RSC 3 Reading
	(Southern Area Heavyweight Title Challenge. Elim. British Heavyweight Title)
10.06.03	Petr Horacek W CO 1 Sheffield
01.08.03	Colin Kenna W RSC 1 Bethnal Green
	(Southern Area Heavyweight Title Defence)
26.09.03	Danny Williams L RSC 5 Reading
	(British & Commonwealth Heavyweight Title Challenges)
24.01.04	Danny Williams W PTS 12 Wembley
	(British & Commonwealth Heavyweight Title Challenges)
24.04.04	Matt Skelton L CO 12 Reading
	(British & Commonwealth Heavyweight Title Defences)

Career: 32 contests, won 25, lost 7.

Michael Sprott   Les Clark

Micky Steeds

Isle of Dogs. *Born* London, 14 September,
1983
Heavyweight. Ht. 6'0"
Manager J. Rooney

18.09.03	Slick Miller W PTS 4 Mayfair
21.02.04	Brodie Pearmaine W RSC 1 Brighton
12.03.04	Paul King W PTS 6 Millwall

Career: 3 contests, won 3.

Chris Steele

Dodworth. *Born* Barnsley, 28 March, 1980
Middleweight. Ht. 6'0"
Manager Self

14.11.99	Gavin Pearson L PTS 6 Bradford
02.03.00	Elias Boswell W RSC 4 Blackpool
13.05.00	Arv Mittoo L RSC 3 Barnsley

05.12.00	Colin McCash L RSC 4 Nottingham
08.03.01	Andy Abrol L RSC 6 Blackpool
08.04.01	David Smales L PTS 6 Wrexham
26.04.01	Sam Mottram L PTS 6 Gateshead
10.05.01	Sam Mottram L PTS 6 Sunderland
11.06.01	Darrell Grafton L RSC 1 Nottingham
07.02.02	Andrei Ivanov L PTS 6 Stoke
17.02.02	James Davenport L PTS 6 Salford
22.04.02	Scott Millar L PTS 6 Glasgow
11.05.02	Nicky Leech L PTS 6 Newark
05.12.02	Dave Pearson L PTS 6 Sunderland
08.01.03	Paul Astley L PTS 4 Aberdare
24.01.03	Andy Halder L PTS 4 Sheffield
05.09.03	Steve Scott DREW 6 Doncaster
08.12.03	Lee Palmer DREW 6 Barnsley
10.02.04	Richard Inquieti L RSC 4 Barnsley

Career: 19 contests, won 1, drew 2, lost 16.

Dave Stewart

Ayr. *Born* Irvine, 5 September, 1975
Lightweight. Former Undefeated British
Masters Lightweight Champion. Ht. 6'0¼"
Manager A. Sims

15.02.01	Danny Connelly W PTS 6 Glasgow
27.04.01	Woody Greenaway W PTS 6 Glasgow
07.09.01	John Marshall W PTS 6 Glasgow
15.06.02	Dave Hinds W PTS 6 Tottenham
06.09.02	Pete Buckley W PTS 6 Bethnal Green
17.09.02	James Paisley W RSC 5 Bethnal Green
30.01.03	Scott Lawton W PTS 6 Piccadilly
26.04.03	Nigel Senior W RSC 2 Brentford
	(British Masters Lightweight Title Challenge)
27.05.03	Pete Buckley W PTS 4 Dagenham
01.08.03	Norman Dhalie W RTD 2 Bethnal Green
26.09.03	Jimmy Beech W RTD 2 Reading
14.11.03	Pete Buckley W PTS 4 Bethnal Green
16.04.04	Carl Allen W PTS 6 Bradford

Career: 13 contests, won 13.

Dave Stewart   Les Clark

Adrian Stone

Bristol. *Born* Bristol, 19 July, 1971
Welterweight. Former Undefeated IBO
L.Middleweight Champion. Former
Undefeated IBO Inter-Continental
Welterweight Champion. Ht. 5'7"
Manager C. Sanigar

06.02.93	Sean Daughtry W PTS 6 NYC, New York, USA
16.04.93	James Crosby T. DRAW 2 Hamilton, New Jersey, USA
08.05.93	Rey Robinson W PTS 4 East Mahanoy Junction, Pennsylvania, USA
28.05.93	Nate Reynolds W RSC 4 Hamilton, New Jersey, USA
10.07.93	George Mitchell W RSC 2 Bushkill, Pennsylvania, USA
10.11.93	Ernest Stroman W PTS 4 Atlantic City, New Jersey, USA
23.01.94	Sylvie Furlong W CO 1 Boston, Mass, USA
20.02.94	Robert West W CO 2 Biloxi, Mississippi, USA
21.04.94	Victor Perez W PTS 8 Ledyard, Connecticut, USA
22.07.94	John Jester W CO 3 Robinsonville, Mississippi, USA
18.08.94	Wayne Richards W CO 5 Melville, New York, USA
19.10.94	Curtis Peoples W RSC 7 Catskill, New York, USA
14.12.94	Israel Figueroa W RSC 2 Boston, Mass, USA
17.02.95	Ross Thompson W DIS 7 Atlantic City, New Jersey, USA
07.04.95	James Hughes L RSC 10 Salem, Mass, USA
	(USBA Welterweight Title Challenge)
21.07.95	John Duplessis W RSC 5 New Orleans, Louisiana, USA
10.11.95	Roger Turner W RSC 9 Atlantic City, New Jersey, USA
03.02.96	Darryl Lattimore W RSC 1 Liverpool
01.04.96	Mroslav Gregoriev W CO 1 Den Bosch, Holland
14.05.96	Skipper Kelp L PTS 10 Ledyard, Connecticut, USA
18.10.96	Gilberto Flores T. DRAW 5 NYC, New York, USA
15.11.96	Otilio Villareal W PTS 10 Somerset, New Jersey, USA
12.12.96	Johar Lashlin W CO 2 Vancouver, Canada
	(Vacant IBO Inter-Continental Welterweight Title)
27.03.97	John-John Pacquing W RSC 6 Edmonton, Canada
29.07.97	Greg Johnson W RSC 4 NYC, New York, USA
12.12.97	Bobby Butters W RSC 2 Mason City, Iowa, USA
25.04.98	Desi Ford W CO 4 Biloxi, Mississippi, USA
18.08.98	Vernon Forrest L RSC 11 Tunica, Mississippi, USA
	(Vacant NABF Welterweight Title)
18.02.99	Darren Covill W RSC 2 Barking
28.08.99	Benji Singleton W RSC 3 Secaucus, New Jersey, USA
14.01.00	Michael Corleone W RSC 3 Long Island, New York, USA
15.04.00	Michael Carruth W RTD 5 Bethnal Green
	(Vacant IBO L. Middleweight Title)
15.07.00	Geoff McCreesh W RSC 6 Millwall
	(IBO L.Middleweight Title Defence)
11.11.00	Derek Roche W RSC 2 Belfast
	(IBO L. Middleweight Title Defence)
13.03.01	Joe Townsley W PTS 12 Plymouth
	(IBO L. Middleweight Title Defence)

21.07.01	Shane Mosley L RSC 3 Las Vegas, Nevada, USA
	(WBC Welterweight Title Challenge)
08.02.03	Sultan Dondon W RSC 4 Brentford
29.03.03	Carlito Brozas W RSC 2 Wembley
26.07.03	Farai Musiiwa W CO 4 Plymouth
09.10.03	Sergio Martinez L RSC 12 Bristol
	(IBO L.Middleweight Title Challenge)

Career: 40 contests, won 33, drew 2, lost 5.

Darren Stubbs

Oldham. *Born* Manchester, 16 October, 1971
S. Middleweight. Ht. 5'10"
Manager J. Doughty

02.06.02	Adam Cale W RSC 6 Shaw
21.06.02	Dean Cockburn L RSC 1 Leeds
17.11.02	Shpetim Hoti W RTD 2 Shaw
29.11.02	Jamie Wilson W PTS 6 Hull
09.03.03	Martin Thompson W RSC 3 Shaw
18.03.03	Jamie Hearn W RSC 3 Reading
08.06.03	Danny Grainger L RSC 2 Shaw
19.10.03	Paul Wesley W PTS 6 Shaw
29.02.04	Patrick Cito W PTS 6 Shaw
10.04.04	Alan Page L PTS 4 Manchester
20.04.04	Paul Owen W PTS 6 Sheffield

Career: 11 contests, won 8, lost 3.

Mark Stupple

Bermondsey. *Born* Bermondsey, 23
September, 1970
L. Middleweight. Ht. 5'8"
Manager E. Maloney

28.04.02	Pedro Thompson L RSC 4 Southwark
23.06.02	Arv Mittoo W PTS 6 Southwark
18.11.03	Brian Coleman W PTS 6 Bethnal Green

Career: 3 contests, won 2, lost 1.

Mark Stupple   Les Clark

Lee Swaby

Lincoln. *Born* Lincoln, 14 May, 1976
Cruiserweight. Former Undefeated British
Masters Cruiserweight Champion. Ht. 6'2"
Manager D. Hobson

29.04.97	Naveed Anwar W PTS 6 Manchester
19.06.97	Liam Richardson W RSC 4 Scunthorpe
30.10.97	Phil Ball W RSC 3 Newark
17.11.97	L. A. Williams W PTS 6 Manchester
02.02.98	Tim Redman L PTS 6 Manchester
27.02.98	John Wilson W CO 3 Glasgow
07.03.98	Phill Day L PTS 4 Reading
08.05.98	Chris P. Bacon L RSC 3 Manchester
17.07.98	Chris P. Bacon L PTS 6 Mere
19.09.98	Cathal O'Grady L RSC 1 Dublin
20.12.98	Mark Levy L RTD 5 Salford
23.06.99	Lee Archer W PTS 6 West Bromwich
04.09.99	Garry Delaney L PTS 8 Bethnal Green
03.10.99	Brian Gascoigne DREW 6 Chesterfield
11.12.99	Owen Beck L PTS 4 Liverpool
05.03.00	Kelly Oliver L PTS 10 Peterborough *(Vacant British Masters Cruiserweight Title)*
15.04.00	Mark Levy W PTS 4 Bethnal Green
12.05.00	Enzo Maccarinelli W CO 3 Swansea
26.05.00	Steffen Nielsen L PTS 4 Holbaek, Denmark
09.09.00	Tony Dowling W RSC 9 Newark *(Vacant British Masters Cruiserweight Title)*
05.02.01	Robert Norton L PTS 8 Hull
24.03.01	Crawford Ashley L PTS 8 Sheffield
30.04.01	Eamonn Glennon W PTS 6 Glasgow
02.06.01	Denzil Browne DREW 8 Wakefield
31.07.01	Stephane Allouane W PTS 4 Bethnal Green
13.09.01	Kevin Barrett W PTS 4 Sheffield
15.12.01	Chris Woollas W RSC 4 Sheffield
27.04.02	Mark Hobson L PTS 10 Huddersfield *(Final Elim. British Cruiserweight Title)*
03.08.02	Greg Scott-Briggs W RSC 4 Derby
05.12.02	Eamonn Glennon W PTS 4 Sheffield
24.01.03	Tommy Eastwood W PTS 6 Sheffield
10.06.03	Paul Bonson W PTS 4 Sheffield
05.09.03	Brodie Pearmaine W RTD 4 Sheffield
20.04.04	Lee Mountford W RSC 1 Sheffield
27.05.04	Mark Hobson L RSC 6 Huddersfield *(British & Commonwealth Cruiserweight Title Challenges)*

Career: 35 contests, won 19, drew 2, lost 14.

Richard Swallow

Northampton. *Born* Northampton, 10 February, 1970
Welterweight. Former British Masters Welterweight Champion. Ht. 5'8"
Manager Self

15.10.90	Richard O'Brien L RTD 1 Kettering
14.02.91	Dave Fallon W RSC 4 Southampton
06.03.91	Carl Brasier W PTS 6 Croydon
02.05.91	Mike Morrison W PTS 6 Northampton
24.03.92	Dean Bramhald W PTS 8 Wolverhampton
06.04.92	Dean Bramhald W PTS 6 Northampton
29.04.92	Chris Aston W RSC 3 Solihull
14.10.92	Wayne Shepherd W PTS 8 Stoke
24.11.92	Chris Mulcahy W PTS 6 Wolverhampton
20.01.93	Ray Newby W PTS 8 Solihull
03.03.93	Ray Newby L PTS 8 Solihull
11.06.93	Soren Sondergaard L RTD 3 Randers, Denmark
08.02.94	Billy McDougall W PTS 6 Wolverhampton
30.09.94	Bernard Paul W PTS 8 Bethnal Green

31.10.94	Carl Wright L PTS 6 Liverpool
09.12.94	Jason Rowland L RSC 2 Bethnal Green
14.02.95	Jason Beard L PTS 6 Bethnal Green
17.03.95	Frank Olsen L RSC 1 Copenhagen, Denmark
06.06.95	Anthony Maynard W RSC 2 Leicester
23.10.95	Shaun Stokes L PTS 6 Leicester
22.11.95	Gary Beardsley DREW 6 Sheffield
17.01.96	Shaun Stokes W PTS 6 Solihull
12.02.96	Nicky Bardle W RSC 4 Heathrow
28.10.96	Bobby Vanzie L PTS 6 Bradford
20.03.97	Anthony Maynard L PTS 6 Solihull
12.05.97	Nigel Bradley W PTS 6 Leicester
16.11.02	Lee Williamson W PTS 4 Coventry
30.11.02	Arv Mittoo W PTS 4 Coventry
09.12.02	Jon Hilton W PTS 6 Nottingham
09.02.03	Chris Saunders L PTS 4 Bradford
07.06.03	Tony Conroy L RSC 5 Coventry *(Vacant Midlands Area Welterweight Title)*
30.10.03	Jimmy Gould W PTS 10 Dudley *(Vacant British Masters Welterweight Title)*
19.02.04	Marcus Portman L PTS 10 Dudley *(British Masters Welterweight Title Defence)*

09.04.04	Ernie Smith W PTS 4 Rugby
26.04.04	Richard Inquieti W RSC 1 Cleethorpes

Career: 35 contests, won 21, drew 1, lost 13.

Chas Symonds

Croydon. *Born* Croydon, 8 July, 1982
Southern Area Welterweight Champion.
Ht. 5'6"
Manager E. Maloney

18.02.03	Darren Goode W RSC 2 Bethnal Green
08.04.03	Lee Bedell W PTS 4 Bethnal Green
03.06.03	Arv Mittoo W PTS 6 Bethnal Green
22.07.03	Pete Buckley W PTS 6 Bethnal Green
25.09.03	Ben Hudson W PTS 6 Bethnal Green
18.11.03	Ernie Smith W PTS 6 Bethnal Green
20.02.04	Dave Wakefield W RSC 5 Bethnal Green
24.04.04	Geraint Harvey W PTS 4 Reading
07.05.04	Robert Lloyd-Taylor W RTD 5 Bethnal Green
25.06.04	Brett James W RSC 4 Bethnal Green *(Southern Area Welterweight Title Challenge)*

Career: 10 contests, won 10.

Chas Symonds

Les Clark

Gavin Tait

Carmarthen. *Born* Carmarthen, 2 March, 1976
L. Welterweight. Ht. 5'7"
Manager N. Hodges

07.06.04 Stuart Green L PTS 6 Glasgow
Career: 1 contest, lost 1.

Matthew Tait

Harrow. *Born* Hillingdon, 15 April, 1973
L. Middleweight. Ht. 5'10½"
Manager Self

17.12.96 Dean Powell W PTS 6 Bethnal Green
29.01.97 Paul Webb W RTD 1 Bethnal Green
11.02.97 Dean Powell W RSC 4 Bethnal Green
12.07.97 Lee Bird W PTS 6 Earls Court
09.09.97 Chris Pollock W RSC 5 Bethnal Green
28.11.97 Mark Sawyers W PTS 6 Bethnal Green
11.03.98 Vince Rose W PTS 6 Bethnal Green
28.04.98 Freddie Yemofio W PTS 6 Brentford
14.05.98 Delroy Leslie W PTS 6 Acton
17.02.01 William Webster W PTS 4 Bethnal Green
24.03.01 Andrew Facey L PTS 4 Chigwell
27.10.02 Tomas da Silva W PTS 6 Southwark
08.12.02 Howard Clarke W PTS 6 Bethnal Green
18.02.03 Gary Logan L PTS 8 Bethnal Green
03.06.03 Wayne Asker W RSC 7 Bethnal Green
18.11.03 Tomas da Silva W PTS 8 Bethnal Green
20.02.04 Allan Gray L PTS 10 Bethnal Green
(Southern Area Middleweight Title Challenge)
Career: 17 contests, won 14, lost 3.

(Mehrdud) Takaloo (Takalobigashi)

Margate. *Born* Iran, 23 September, 1975
L.Middleweight. Former Undefeated WBU
L.Middleweight Champion. Former
Undefeated IBF Inter-Continental
L.Middleweight Champion. Ht. 5'9"
Manager F. Warren

19.07.97 Harry Butler W RSC 1 Wembley
13.09.97 Michael Alexander W PTS 4 Millwall
15.11.97 Koba Kulu W RSC 3 Bristol
19.12.97 Mark Sawyers W PTS 4 Millwall
07.02.98 Jawaid Khaliq L RSC 4 Cheshunt
16.05.98 Anas Oweida W RSC 1 Bethnal Green
10.10.98 Michael Jones L PTS 6 Bethnal Green
30.01.99 Darren McInulty W RSC 5 Bethnal Green
03.04.99 Gareth Lovell W RSC 6 Kensington
26.06.99 Leigh Wicks W CO 3 Millwall
04.09.99 Carlton Williams W RSC 4 Bethnal Green
23.10.99 Prince Kasi Kaihau W RSC 3 Telford
29.01.00 Paul King W RSC 2 Manchester
08.04.00 Biagio Falcone W RTD 4 Bethnal Green
08.07.00 Ernie Smith W RSC 4 Widnes
12.08.00 Howard Clarke W PTS 12 Wembley

(Vacant IBF Inter-Continental L.Middleweight Title)
13.11.00 Jason Collins W RSC 2 Bethnal Green
24.02.01 James Lowther W PTS 12 Bethnal Green
(IBF Inter-Continental L.Middleweight Title Defence)
07.07.01 Anthony Farnell W RSC 1 Manchester
(Vacant WBU L.Middleweight Title)
22.09.01 Scott Dixon W CO 1 Bethnal Green
(WBU L. Middleweight Title Defence)
04.05.02 Gary Logan W RSC 10 Bethnal Green
(WBU L. Middleweight Title Defence)
17.08.02 Daniel Santos L PTS 12 Cardiff
(WBO L.Middleweight Title Challenge. WBU L.Middleweight Title Defence)
01.02.03 Jim Rock W RSC 9 Belfast
(Vacant WBU L. Middleweight Title)
24.05.03 Jose Rosa W PTS 12 Bethnal Green
(WBU L.Middleweight Title Defence)
13.09.03 Vladimir Borovski W CO 3 Newport
24.01.04 Eugenio Monteiro L PTS 8 Wembley
Career: 26 contests, won 22, lost 4.

Karl Taylor

Birmingham. *Born* Birmingham, 5 January, 1966
Welterweight. Former Undefeated
Midlands Area Lightweight Champion. Ht. 5'5"
Manager Self

18.03.87 Steve Brown W PTS 6 Stoke
06.04.87 Paul Taylor L PTS 6 Southampton
12.06.87 Mark Begley W RSC 1 Leamington
18.11.87 Colin Lynch W RSC 4 Solihull
29.02.88 Peter Bradley L PTS 8 Birmingham
04.10.89 Mark Antony W CO 2 Stafford
30.10.89 Tony Feliciello L PTS 8 Birmingham
06.12.89 John Davison L PTS 8 Leicester
23.12.89 Regilio Tuur L RTD 1 Hoogvliet, Holland
22.02.90 Mark Ramsey L RSC 4 Hull
29.10.90 Steve Walker DREW 6 Birmingham
10.12.90 Elvis Parsley L PTS 6 Birmingham
16.01.91 Wayne Windle W PTS 8 Stoke
02.05.91 Billy Schwer L RSC 2 Northampton
25.07.91 Peter Till L RSC 4 Dudley
(Midlands Area Lightweight Title Challenge)
24.02.92 Charlie Kane L PTS 8 Glasgow
28.04.92 Richard Woolgar W PTS 6 Wolverhampton
29.05.92 Alan McDowall L PTS 6 Glasgow
25.07.92 Michael Armstrong L RSC 3 Manchester
02.11.92 Hugh Forde L PTS 6 Wolverhampton
23.11.92 Dave McHale L PTS 8 Glasgow
22.12.92 Patrick Gallagher L RSC 3 Mayfair
13.02.93 Craig Dermody L RSC 5 Manchester
31.03.93 Craig Dermody W PTS 6 Barking
07.06.93 Mark Geraghty W PTS 8 Glasgow
13.08.93 Giorgio Campanella L CO 6 Arezzo, Italy
05.10.93 Paul Harvey W PTS 6 Mayfair
21.10.93 Charles Shepherd L RTD 5 Bayswater
21.12.93 Patrick Gallagher L PTS 6 Mayfair
09.02.94 Alan Levene W RSC 2 Brentwood
01.03.94 Shaun Cogan L PTS 6 Dudley
15.03.94 Patrick Gallagher L PTS 6 Mayfair
18.04.94 Peter Till W PTS 10 Walsall
(Midlands Area Lightweight Title Challenge)

24.05.94 Michael Ayers DREW 8 Sunderland
12.11.94 P. J. Gallagher L PTS 6 Dublin
29.11.94 Dingaan Thobela W PTS 8 Cannock
31.03.95 Michael Ayers L RSC 8 Crystal Palace
(British Lightweight Title Challenge)
06.05.95 Cham Joof W PTS 8 Shepton Mallet
23.06.95 Poli Diaz L PTS 8 Madrid, Spain
02.09.95 Paul Ryan L RSC 3 Wembley
04.11.95 Carl Wright L PTS 6 Liverpool
15.12.95 Peter Richardson L PTS 8 Bethnal Green
23.01.96 Paul Knights DREW 6 Bethnal Green
05.03.96 Andy Holligan L PTS 6 Barrow
20.03.96 Mervyn Bennett W PTS 8 Cardiff
21.05.96 Malcolm Melvin L PTS 10 Edgbaston
(Midlands Area L. Welterweight Title Challenge)
07.10.96 Joshua Clottey L RSC 2 Lewisham
20.12.96 Anatoly Alexandrov L RSC 7 Bilbao, Spain
28.01.97 Eamonn Magee L PTS 6 Belfast
28.02.97 Mark Breslin L RSC 6 Kilmarnock
30.08.97 Gilbert Eastman L PTS 4 Cheshunt
25.10.97 Tontcho Tontchev L PTS 4 Queensferry
22.11.97 Bobby Vanzie L PTS 6 Manchester
18.04.98 Ricky Hatton L RSC 1 Manchester
18.07.98 James Hare L PTS 4 Sheffield
26.09.98 Oktay Urkal L PTS 8 Norwich
28.11.98 Junior Witter L PTS 4 Sheffield
06.03.99 George Scott L RSC 4 Southwark
15.05.99 Jon Thaxton L PTS 6 Sheffield
10.07.99 Eamonn Magee L RTD 3 Southwark
06.11.99 Alan Sebire W PTS 6 Widnes
15.11.99 Steve Murray L RSC 1 Bethnal Green
19.08.00 Iain Eldridge L PTS 4 Brentwood
04.09.00 Tomas Jansson L PTS 6 Manchester
16.09.00 Colin Lynes L PTS 6 Bethnal Green
09.12.00 David Walker L PTS 6 Southwark
10.02.01 Matthew Hatton L PTS 4 Widnes
10.03.01 Francis Barrett L RSC 3 Bethnal Green
10.04.01 Costas Katsantonis L PTS 4 Wembley
16.06.01 Brett James DREW 4 Wembley
15.09.01 David Barnes L PTS 4 Manchester
28.10.01 Babatunde Ajayi L PTS 4 Southwark
24.11.01 Ross Minter L PTS 4 Bethnal Green
15.12.01 Alexandra Vetoux L PTS 4 Wembley
12.02.02 Brett James DREW 4 Bethnal Green
11.03.02 Kevin McIntyre L PTS 4 Glasgow
04.05.02 Matthew Hatton L RSC 3 Bethnal Green
25.06.02 Rimell Taylor DREW 6 Rugby
20.07.02 Matthew Hatton L RTD 2 Bethnal Green
28.09.02 Michael Jennings L RSC 4 Manchester
16.11.02 Gavin Wake L PTS 4 Nottingham
30.11.02 Tony Conroy L PTS 4 Coventry
14.12.02 Alexander Vetoux L RTD 3 Newcastle
15.02.03 Ross Minter L PTS 6 Wembley
29.03.03 Alexander Vetoux L RSC 1 Portsmouth
08.05.03 Tony Doherty L PTS 4 Widnes
25.07.03 Lenny Daws L RTD 2 Norwich
06.10.03 Jonathan Woollins W PTS 6 Birmingham
29.10.03 Ajose Olusegun L PTS 6 Leicester Square
29.11.03 Gary Young L RSC 3 Renfrew
30.01.04 Lee McAllister L PTS 4 Dagenham
05.03.04 Oscar Hall L PTS 6 Darlington
27.03.04 Jamie Arthur L PTS 6 Edinburgh
06.05.04 Ashley Theophane L PTS 4 Barnsley
22.05.04 Tony Doherty L RTD 2 Widnes
Career: 95 contests, won 16, drew 6, lost 73.

Luke Teague

Hull. *Born* Grimsby, 7 December, 1972
L. Middleweight. Ht. 6'1"
Manager S. Fleet/S. Pollard

22.09.03 Lance Hall W RSC 1 Cleethorpes
14.11.03 William Webster W PTS 6 Hull
15.12.03 Simon Hopkins DREW 6 Cleethorpes
Career: 3 contests, won 2, drew 1.

Matt Teague

Grimsby. *Born* Grimsby, 14 July, 1980
Featherweight. Ht. 5'9"
Manager S. Fleet/S. Pollard

21.11.02 Andy Robinson W RTD 3 Hull
11.12.02 Jason Nesbitt W PTS 6 Hull
17.04.03 Martin Hardcastle L PTS 6 Hull
02.06.03 Henry Janes W PTS 6 Cleethorpes
22.09.03 Tom Price W PTS 6 Cleethorpes
14.11.03 Kristian Laight W PTS 6 Hull
15.12.03 Dave Hinds W PTS 6 Cleethorpes
14.06.04 Dean Ward W PTS 6 Cleethorpes
Career: 8 contests, won 7, lost 1.

Daniel Teasdale

Rotherham. *Born* Rotherham, 4 September, 1982
S. Middleweight. Ht. 6'1"
Manager T. Gilmour/G. Rhodes

23.11.03 Patrick Cito NC 1 Rotherham
10.02.04 Ojay Abrahams W PTS 6 Barnsley
01.04.04 Tomas da Silva W PTS 4 Bethnal Green
06.05.04 Ojay Abrahams W PTS 4 Barnsley
Career: 4 contests, won 3, no contest 1.

Daniel Teasdale   Les Clark

George Telfer

Hawick. *Born* Hawick, 26 May, 1979
L. Welterweight. Ht. 5'7"
Manager K. Morrison

14.03.03 Vince Baldassara W PTS 4 Glasgow
22.03.03 Tony Montana L PTS 4 Renfrew
12.07.03 Pete Buckley W PTS 4 Renfrew
25.10.03 James Gorman W PTS 4 Edinburgh
07.12.03 Dave Hill W RSC 4 Glasgow
06.03.04 Nigel Wright L RSC 3 Renfrew
Career: 6 contests, won 4, lost 2.

Alan Temple

Hartlepool. *Born* Hartlepool, 21 October, 1972
British Masters Lightweight Champion. Ht. 5'8"
Manager Self

29.09.94 Stevie Bolt W CO 2 Bethnal Green
22.11.94 Phil Found W PTS 6 Bristol
07.02.95 Brian Coleman W PTS 6 Ipswich
27.04.95 Everald Williams L PTS 6 Bethnal Green
29.09.95 Kevin McKillan W PTS 6 Hartlepool
23.11.95 Rudy Valentino L RSC 3 Marton
02.03.96 Tony Foster W PTS 6 Newcastle
08.06.96 Micky Hall W RSC 2 Newcastle
20.09.96 Scott Dixon L PTS 4 Glasgow
24.10.96 Billy Schwer L PTS 8 Wembley
04.12.96 Harry Escott W PTS 8 Hartlepool
12.02.97 Tanveer Ahmed L RSC 8 Glasgow
    (Elim. British Lightweight Title)
13.02.98 Bobby Vanzie L CO 3 Seaham
    (Elim. British Lightweight Title)
21.03.98 Michael Ayers L RSC 2 Bethnal Green
31.10.98 Alan Bosworth W PTS 6 Basingstoke
20.02.99 Ivan Walker W PTS 4 Thornaby
05.03.99 David Burke L PTS 8 Liverpool
01.05.99 Jason Rowland L PTS 6 Crystal Palace
22.05.99 Eamonn Magee L CO 3 Belfast
26.06.99 Steve McLevy W RSC 6 Glasgow
11.09.99 Wayne Rigby W PTS 8 Sheffield
02.11.99 Souleymane M'Baye L RTD 7 Ciudad Real, Spain
12.08.00 Steve Murray L RSC 2 Wembley
    (IBF Inter-Continental Lightweight Title Challenge. Elim. British Lightweight Title)
26.03.01 Jonathan Thaxton L PTS 4 Wembley
04.06.01 Gary Hibbert W PTS 6 Hartlepool
21.07.01 Junior Witter L CO 5 Sheffield
10.11.01 Colin Dunne L RSC 7 Wembley
09.03.02 Gary Hibbert L RSC 1 Manchester
26.10.02 Leo O'Reilly W RSC 4 Maesteg
21.12.02 Darren Melville L PTS 8 Millwall
01.05.04 Silence Saheed W DIS 8 Gravesend
    (Vacant British Masters Lightweight Title)
Career: 31 contests, won 14, lost 17.

(Eranos) Erik Teymour (Teymurazov)

Canning Town. *Born* Moscow, Russia, 1 March, 1979
S. Middleweight. Ht. 5'8¹/₂"
Manager Self

14.07.01 Dean Ashton W RSC 2 Liverpool
31.07.01 Leigh Wicks W RSC 1 Bethnal Green
28.09.01 Kreshnik Qato W PTS 6 Millwall
23.11.01 Harry Butler W RSC 2 Bethnal Green
16.12.01 Howard Clarke W PTS 6 Southwark
15.03.02 Darren Littlewood W RSC 1 Millwall
26.04.02 Sam Soliman L PTS 8 Glasgow
21.05.02 Toks Owoh W PTS 6 Custom House
25.10.02 Donatas Bondarevas W RSC 3 Millwall
30.11.02 Varuzhan Davtyan W PTS 6 Liverpool
08.02.03 Radcliffe Green W RTD 1 Norwich
28.03.03 Paul Bonson W PTS 6 Millwall
24.05.03 Varuzhan Davtyan W PTS 4 Bethnal Green
13.09.03 Vage Kocharyan W PTS 4 Newport
06.12.03 Farai Musiiwa W PTS 6 Cardiff

01.04.04 Hussain Osman W RSC 8 Bethnal Green
Career: 16 contests, won 15, lost 1.

Ashley Theophane

Kilburn. *Born* London, 20 August, 1980
L. Welterweight. Ht. 5'7"
Manager I. Akay/D. Coldwell

03.06.03 Lee Bedell W RSC 4 Bethnal Green
22.07.03 Brian Coleman W PTS 6 Bethnal Green
25.04.04 David Kirk W PTS 6 Nottingham
06.05.04 Karl Taylor W PTS 4 Barnsley
05.06.04 Chris Brophy W RSC 3 Bethnal Green
19.06.04 Arv Mittoo W PTS 4 Muswell Hill
Career: 6 contests, won 6.

Matthew Thirlwall

Bermondsey. *Born* Middlesbrough, 28 November, 1980
Middleweight. Ht. 5'9¹/₂"
Manager Self

16.03.02 William Webster W RSC 1 Bethnal Green
10.05.02 Leigh Wicks W PTS 4 Bethnal Green
23.08.02 Harry Butler W RSC 3 Bethnal Green
25.10.02 Jason Collins W RSC 5 Bethnal Green
21.12.02 Howard Clarke W PTS 6 Dagenham
28.01.03 Gary Beardsley L PTS 6 Nottingham
16.04.03 Gary Beardsley W PTS 6 Nottingham
27.05.03 Leigh Wicks W PTS 6 Dagenham
04.10.03 Dean Powell W RSC 2 Muswell Hill
11.12.03 Harry Butler W PTS 6 Bethnal Green
12.03.04 Patrick Cito W RSC 3 Nottingham
Career: 11 contests, won 10, lost 1.

Matthew Thirlwall   Les Clark

Jason Thomas

Merthyr Tydfill. *Born* Pontypridd, 7 October, 1976
Bantamweight. Ht. 5'6"
Manager Self

28.11.95 Henry Jones W PTS 4 Cardiff

08.12.95	John Sillo L PTS 6 Liverpool
13.01.96	Paul Griffin L RSC 2 Manchester
02.10.96	Henry Jones L PTS 4 Cardiff
23.10.96	Noel Wilders L PTS 6 Halifax
27.11.96	Jason Booth L PTS 4 Swansea
02.06.97	Colin Moffett W RSC 3 Belfast
02.08.97	Peter Culshaw L PTS 8 Barnsley
14.10.97	Graham McGrath W PTS 6 Wolverhampton
25.10.97	Keith Knox W PTS 8 Queensferry
04.12.97	Sean Green DREW 4 Doncaster
13.02.98	Nick Tooley W PTS 6 Weston super Mare
18.04.98	Hector Orozco DREW 4 Manchester
14.05.98	John Matthews L PTS 6 Acton
03.10.98	Michael Alldis L PTS 6 Crawley
06.02.99	Noel Wilders L PTS 10 Halifax *(Elim. British Bantamweight Title)*
15.05.99	Alex Moon L PTS 8 Blackpool
24.09.99	Frankie DeMilo W RSC 2 Merthyr
15.11.99	Stephen Oates L PTS 6 Bethnal Green
19.02.00	Stephen Oates L PTS 6 Dagenham
29.03.00	Frankie DeMilo L RSC 8 Piccadilly *(Vacant British Masters S. Bantamweight Title)*
06.10.00	Takalani Ndlovu L RSC 2 Maidstone
05.12.00	Kevin Gerowski L PTS 8 Nottingham
24.05.01	Stuart Sanderson DREW 6 Glasgow
08.06.01	Karim Quibir L CO 4 Orense, Spain
17.11.01	Chris Emanuele L RSC 1 Coventry
23.02.02	Jason Booth L PTS 6 Nottingham
27.04.02	Dale Robinson L RSC 4 Huddersfield
05.10.02	Gary Davis L RSC 5 Liverpool
24.03.03	Chris Emanuele W PTS 4 Barnsley
05.12.03	Lee Haskins L PTS 6 Bristol
29.02.04	Riaz Durgahed L RSC 1 Bristol

Career: 32 contests, won 7, drew 3, lost 22.

Jeff Thomas

St Annes. *Born* Holland, 30 October, 1981
Lightweight. Ht. 5'10"
Manager L. Veitch

09.12.01	Peter Allen W PTS 6 Blackpool
20.07.02	Pete Buckley W PTS 4 Bethnal Green
03.08.02	Gareth Wiltshaw W DIS 2 Blackpool
26.10.02	Dave Curran W RSC 6 Wigan
28.04.03	Daniel Thorpe W PTS 6 Cleethorpes
09.05.03	Carl Allen DREW 6 Doncaster
08.06.03	Norman Dhalie W PTS 6 Shaw
06.09.03	Lee McAllister L PTS 10 Aberdeen *(Vacant British Masters L.Welterweight Title)*
07.12.03	Martin Hardcastle L PTS 10 Bradford *(Vacant British Masters S.Featherweight Title)*

Career: 9 contests, won 6, drew 1, lost 2.

Michael Thomas

Brighton. *Born* Nigeria, 14 September, 1971
Middleweight. Ht. 6'1"
Manager J. Pyle

04.04.97	Jimmy Steel W PTS 6 Brighton
23.02.03	Joel Ani L DIS 1 Streatham
13.04.03	Dean Powell W RSC 1 Streatham
10.05.03	Reggie Robshaw W RSC 5 Huddersfield
20.06.03	Conroy McIntosh L CO 2 Gatwick
21.02.04	Andy Halder L RSC 3 Brighton

Career: 6 contests, won 3, lost 3.

(Adrian) Carl Thompson

Manchester. *Born* Manchester, 26 May, 1964
IBO Cruiserweight Champion. Former WBO Cruiserweight Champion. Former Undefeated European, British & WBC International Cruiserweight Champion. Ht. 6'0"
Manager Self

06.06.88	Darren McKenna W RSC 2 Manchester
11.10.88	Paul Sheldon W PTS 6 Wolverhampton
13.02.89	Steve Osborne W PTS 6 Manchester
07.03.89	Sean O'Phoenix W RSC 4 Manchester
04.04.89	Keith Halliwell W RSC 1 Manchester
04.05.89	Tenko Ernie W CO 4 Mayfair
12.06.89	Steve Osborne W PTS 8 Manchester
11.07.89	Peter Brown W RSC 5 Batley
31.10.89	Crawford Ashley L RSC 6 Manchester *(Vacant Central Area L. Heavyweight Title)*
21.04.90	Francis Wanyama L PTS 6 St Amandsberg, Belgium
07.03.91	Terry Dixon W PTS 8 Basildon
01.04.91	Yawe Davis L RSC 2 Monaco, Monte Carlo
04.09.91	Nicky Piper W RSC 3 Bethnal Green

04.06.92	Steve Lewsam W RSC 8 Cleethorpes *(Vacant British Cruiserweight Title)*
17.02.93	Arthur Weathers W CO 2 Bethnal Green *(Vacant WBC International Cruiserweight Title)*
31.03.93	Steve Harvey W CO 1 Bethnal Green
25.07.93	Willie Jake W CO 3 Oldham
02.02.94	Massimiliano Duran W CO 8 Ferrara, Italy *(European Cruiserweight Title Challenge)*
14.06.94	Akim Tafer W RSC 6 Epernay, France *(European Cruiserweight Title Defence)*
10.09.94	Dionisio Lazario W RSC 1 Birmingham
13.10.94	Tim Knight W RSC 5 Paris, France
10.06.95	Ralf Rocchigiani L RSC 11 Manchester *(Vacant WBO Cruiserweight Title)*
13.04.96	Albert Call W RTD 4 Wythenshawe
09.11.96	Jason Nicholson W PTS 8 Manchester
26.04.97	Keith McMurray W RSC 4 Zurich, Switzerland
04.10.97	Ralf Rocchigiani W PTS 12 Hannover, Germany *(WBO Cruiserweight Title Challenge)*
18.04.98	Chris Eubank W PTS 12 Manchester *(WBO Cruiserweight Title Defence)*

Carl Thompson   Les Clark

18.07.98 Chris Eubank W RSC 9 Sheffield
(WBO Cruiserweight Title Defence)
27.03.99 Johnny Nelson L RSC 5 Derby
(WBO Cruiserweight Title Defence)
03.12.99 Terry Dunstan W CO 12 Peterborough
(Vacant British Cruiserweight Title)
13.05.00 Alain Simon W RSC 6 Barnsley
(Vacant European Cruiserweight Title)
25.09.00 Alexei Illiin W RSC 2 Barnsley
(European Cruiserweight Title Defence)
03.02.01 Uriah Grant W RSC 5 Manchester
(IBO Cruiserweight Title Challenge)
26.11.01 Ezra Sellers L RSC 4 Manchester
(IBO Cruiserweight Title Defence)
10.06.03 Phill Day W CO 4 Sheffield
05.09.03 Hastings Rasani W RSC 1 Sheffield
07.11.03 Paul Bonson W PTS 6 Sheffield
06.02.04 Sebastiaan Rothmann W RSC 9 Sheffield
(IBO Cruiserweight Title Challenge)
Career: 38 contests, won 32, lost 6.

Gary Thompson

Lancaster. *Born* Darwen, 22 June, 1981
Cruiserweight. Ht. 5'9"
Manager Self

22.09.01 Michael Thompson L RSC 3 Newcastle
16.11.01 Adam Cale W PTS 6 Preston
10.12.01 Rob Galloway W PTS 6 Bradford
23.12.01 Lee Whitehead L PTS 4 Salford
08.02.02 Shane White DREW 6 Preston
17.02.02 Lee Whitehead L DREW 6 Salford
19.04.02 Lee Mountford DREW 4 Darlington
11.05.02 Tony Dowling L RSC 3 Newark
18.10.02 Michael Thompson L PTS 4 Hartlepool
26.10.02 Paul Richardson DREW 6 Wigan
02.12.02 Danny Thornton L PTS 6 Leeds
03.02.03 Nate Joseph L PTS 4 Bradford
28.02.03 Lee Mountford L PTS 6 Irvine
07.06.03 Carl Wright L RTD 2 Coventry
06.05.04 Simon Francis L PTS 4 Barnsley
15.05.04 Simeon Cover L PTS 6 Aberdeen
08.06.04 Simon Francis L RTD 2 Sheffield
Career: 17 contests, won 2, drew 4, lost 11.

(Patrick) Pedro Thompson

Birmingham. *Born* Birmingham, 27 July, 1962
L. Middleweight. Ht. 5'9½"
Manager Self

03.10.98 Joe Skeldon W RSC 5 West Bromwich
25.11.98 Ross McCord L RSC 2 Clydach
22.04.99 Craig Clayton W PTS 6 Dudley
15.05.99 Reagan Denton L PTS 4 Sheffield
20.09.99 Sergei Dziniruk L RTD 2 Peterborough
02.12.99 Julian Kacanolli W PTS 6 Peterborough
12.12.99 Darren Boys L PTS 6 Chigwell
24.02.00 Martin Scotland W RSC 4 Edgbaston
23.03.00 Ojay Abrahams DREW 6 Bloomsbury
25.05.00 Brendan Rollinson L RSC 2 Hull
02.10.00 Keith Ellwood L RSC 3 Glasgow
28.11.00 Simon Sherrington L RSC 5 Brierley Hill
04.02.01 Martyn Bailey L PTS 6 Queensferry
26.02.01 Matt Scriven L RTD 1 Nottingham
17.09.01 Ryan Kerr L RSC 1 Glasgow
13.12.01 Ciaran Duffy L PTS 6 Leeds
10.12.01 Mark Paxford L PTS 6 Bradford
04.03.02 Lee Williamson L PTS 6 Bradford

24.03.02 Reggie Robshaw L PTS 6 Streatham
28.04.02 Mark Stupple W RSC 4 Southwark
10.05.02 David Walker L RSC 3 Bethnal Green
25.06.02 Sam Gorman L PTS 6 Rugby
13.07.02 Darren McInulty DREW 6 Coventry
28.09.02 Matthew Hall L RSC 1 Manchester
14.12.02 Matthew Hall L PTS 4 Newcastle
21.12.02 Gilbert Eastman L RSC 2 Dagenham
22.03.03 Tony Conroy L PTS 6 Coventry
08.04.03 Elvis Mbwakongo L RSC 1 Bethnal Green
12.05.03 Adnan Amar L RSC 4 Birmingham
13.09.03 Dean Lloyd W RSC 3 Coventry
10.10.03 Franny Jones L PTS 6 Darlington
20.10.03 Danny Parkinson L RSC 3 Bradford
Career: 32 contests, won 6, drew 2, lost 24.

Gary Thornhill

Liverpool. *Born* Liverpool, 11 February, 1968
Featherweight. Former Undefeated British Featherweight Champion. Former Undefeated WBO Inter-Continental & Central Area S. Featherweight Champion. Ht. 5'6½"
Manager S. Vaughan

27.02.93 Brian Hickey W CO 4 Ellesmere Port
02.07.93 Dougie Fox W CO 1 Liverpool
30.10.93 Miguel Matthews W PTS 6 Chester
01.12.93 Wayne Windle W PTS 6 Stoke
25.02.94 Edward Lloyd DREW 6 Chester

06.05.94 Derek Amory W RSC 1 Liverpool
25.03.95 Craig Kelley W PTS 6 Chester
20.04.95 Michael Hermon W RSC 6 Liverpool
30.06.95 Chip O'Neill W RTD 3 Liverpool
04.11.95 Kid McAuley W PTS 6 Liverpool
08.12.95 Des Gargano W RTD 2 Liverpool
(Vacant Central Area S. Featherweight Title)
13.04.96 Dominic McGuigan W RSC 3 Liverpool
25.06.96 Chris Jickells W PTS 6 Stevenage
11.12.96 Justin Juuko L RSC 8 Southwark
(Commonwealth S. Featherweight Title Challenge)
13.12.97 Pete Buckley W PTS 6 Sheffield
06.06.98 Dean Pithie W CO 8 Liverpool
(WBO Inter-Continental S. Featherweight Title Challenge)
19.12.98 Steve Conway W RSC 9 Liverpool
(WBO Inter-Continental S. Featherweight Title Defence)
07.08.99 Chris Jickells W RSC 4 Dagenham
04.09.99 Michael Gomez L RSC 2 Bethnal Green
(Vacant British S. Featherweight Title)
06.11.99 Marc Smith W PTS 6 Widnes
11.12.99 Pete Buckley W PTS 6 Liverpool
29.02.00 Benny Jones W PTS 6 Widnes
16.05.00 Richie Wenton W RTD 8 Warrington
(Vacant British Featherweight Title)
09.06.01 Pete Buckley W PTS 4 Bethnal Green
15.09.01 Scott Harrison L RSC 5 Manchester
(British & Commonwealth Featherweight Title Challenges)

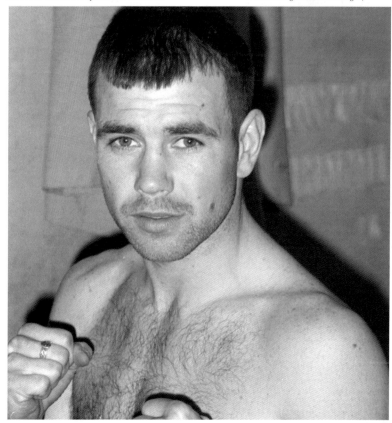

Gary Thornhill   Les Clark

175

06.09.02 Rakhim Mingaleev W PTS 6 Glasgow
05.10.02 Nicky Cook L RSC 7 Liverpool
          (WBF Inter-Continental
          S.Featherweight Title Challenge)
29.08.03 Jason Nesbitt W CO 1 Liverpool
22.05.04 Daniel Thorpe W RSC 4 Manchester
Career: 29 contests, won 24, drew 1, lost 4.

Danny Thornton

Leeds. *Born* Leeds, 20 July, 1978
Central Area Middleweight Champion.
Ht. 5'10"
Manager Self

06.10.97 Pedro Carragher L PTS 6 Bradford
13.11.97 Shaun O'Neill DREW 6 Bradford
08.12.97 Shaun O'Neill DREW 6 Bradford
09.02.98 Roy Chipperfield W RSC 4 Bradford
17.03.98 P. J. Maxwell L PTS 6 Sheffield
30.03.98 Mark Owens W PTS 6 Bradford
15.05.98 Danny Bell W PTS 6 Nottingham
15.06.98 Jimmy Hawk W PTS 6 Bradford
12.10.98 Wayne Shepherd W PTS 6 Bradford
21.02.99 Shaun O'Neill W RSC 5 Bradford
25.04.99 Matt Scriven W RSC 4 Leeds
14.06.99 Martin Thompson W PTS 6 Bradford
18.10.99 Paul Henry W PTS 4 Bradford
14.11.99 Dean Ashton W PTS 4 Bradford
06.12.99 Lee Blundell L PTS 6 Bradford
05.02.00 Steve Roberts L PTS 6 Bethnal Green
25.03.00 Lee Molloy W RSC 2 Liverpool
06.06.00 Joe Townsley L RSC 7 Motherwell
          (IBO Inter-Continental
          L. Middleweight Title Challenge)
30.11.00 Lee Blundell L RSC 8 Blackpool
          (Vacant Central Area L. Middleweight
          Title)
20.03.01 Ian Toby W PTS 8 Leeds
13.11.01 Matt Galer L RSC 4 Leeds
02.12.02 Gary Thompson W PTS 6 Leeds
13.05.03 Kreshnik Qato L PTS 6 Leeds
06.06.03 Jason Collins W PTS 10 Hull
          (Vacant Central Area Middleweight
          Title)
28.11.03 Jason Collins W PTS 10 Hull
          (Central Area Middleweight Title
          Defence)
10.02.04 Mo W PTS 6 Barnsley
08.05.04 Scott Dann L RSC 3 Bristol
          (Vacant English Middleweight Title)
Career: 27 contests, won 16, drew 2, lost 9.

Barry Thorogood

Cardiff. *Born* Cardiff, 1 December, 1972
L.Middleweight. Former Undefeated Welsh
Middleweight Champion. Ht. 6'0"
Manager P. Boyce

28.10.92 Robert Peel W PTS 6 Cardiff
14.12.92 James Campbell W RSC 4 Cardiff
27.01.93 Russell Washer W PTS 6 Cardiff
24.03.93 Darren McInulty W PTS 6 Cardiff
28.04.93 Stuart Dunn L RSC 2 Solihull
13.09.93 Glenn Catley L PTS 4 Bristol
23.10.93 Mark Atkins W PTS 4 Cardiff
10.11.93 Robert Peel W PTS 6 Ystrad
29.01.94 Darren Dorrington DREW 6 Cardiff
02.03.94 Darren Pilling W PTS 6 Solihull
12.03.94 Geoff McCreesh L PTS 6 Cardiff
27.04.94 Dave Johnson DREW 8 Solihull
20.05.94 Andrew Furlong L RSC 4 Acton
17.10.94 Howard Eastman L RSC 6 Mayfair
29.11.94 Robert Peel W PTS 10 Cardiff
          (Vacant Welsh Middleweight Title)

08.03.95 Paul Matthews W PTS 4 Cardiff
12.04.95 Robert Peel W RSC 8 Llanelli
          (Welsh Middleweight Title Defence)
07.07.95 Cornelius Carr L RSC 6 Cardiff
28.11.95 Paul Busby L PTS 8 Cardiff
25.11.97 Michael Pinnock W PTS 8
          Wolverhampton
21.01.98 Michael Alexander W PTS 8 Stoke
10.02.98 Phil Epton L PTS 8 Wolverhampton
26.03.98 Peter Waudby W PTS 8 Solihull
14.12.98 Kevin Burton W PTS 8 Birmingham
27.01.99 Phil Epton W PTS 8 Stoke
17.03.03 Dean Cockburn L PTS 4 Southampton
30.10.03 Mickey Quinn L PTS 4 Belfast
Career: 27 contests, won 15, drew 2, lost 10.

Daniel Thorpe

Sheffield. *Born* Sheffield, 24 September,
1977
Lightweight. Former Central Area
Lightweight Champion. Ht. 5'7½"
Manager J. Ingle

07.09.01 Brian Gifford DREW 4 Bethnal Green
24.09.01 Ram Singh W RSC 4 Cleethorpes
17.11.01 Mally McIver L PTS 6 Dewsbury
10.12.01 Jason Gonzales W RSC 2 Birmingham
17.12.01 Joel Viney L RSC 2 Cleethorpes
11.02.02 Gareth Wiltshaw L PTS 6 Shrewsbury
04.03.02 Dave Travers W PTS 6 Birmingham
13.04.02 Jackson Williams L PTS 6 Norwich
11.05.02 Dean Scott W RSC 1 Chesterfield
21.05.02 Chris McDonagh L PTS 6 Custom
          House
08.06.02 Gary Young L RSC 1 Renfrew
12.07.02 Chill John L PTS 4 Southampton
21.07.02 John Marshall L RSC 1 Salford
22.09.02 Albi Hunt L PTS 6 Southwark
05.10.02 Gavin Down L RSC 2 Chesterfield
17.11.02 Nadeem Siddique L PTS 4 Bradford
29.11.02 Pete Buckley W PTS 6 Hull
21.12.02 Billy Corcoran L CO 2 Dagenham
16.02.03 Eddie Nevins L RSC 8 Salford
          (Vacant Central Area S.Featherweight
          Title)
22.03.03 Jamie Arthur L PTS 4 Renfrew
29.03.03 Danny Hunt L PTS 6 Portsmouth
12.04.03 Jackson Williams L PTS 6 Norwich
19.04.03 Steve Mullin W RSC 1 Liverpool
28.04.03 Jeff Thomas L PTS 6 Cleethorpes
08.05.03 Andy Morris L PTS 4 Widnes
08.06.03 Choi Tsveenpurev L PTS 8 Shaw
20.06.03 Colin Toohey L PTS 6 Liverpool
28.06.03 Gavin Rees L RSC 1 Cardiff
03.08.03 Joel Viney L PTS 6 Stalybridge
06.09.03 Joel Viney W PTS 6 Aberdeen
13.09.03 Sean Hughes L PTS 6 Wakefield
21.09.03 Chris Long W PTS 6 Bristol
12.10.03 Baz Carey DREW 6 Sheffield
19.10.03 Charles Shepherd L PTS 6 Shaw
27.10.03 Nadeem Siddique L PTS 6 Glasgow
06.11.03 Lee Beavis L PTS 4 Dagenham
07.12.03 Mally McIver W PTS 10 Bradford
          (Vacant Central Area Lightweight
          Title)
21.12.03 Pete Buckley W PTS 6 Bolton
26.02.04 Andy Morris L RSC 3 Widnes
03.04.04 Jason Nesbitt W PTS 6 Sheffield
23.04.04 Dave Hinds W PTS 6 Leicester
07.05.04 Stefy Bull L PTS 10 Doncaster
          (Central Area Lightweight Title
          Defence)
22.05.04 Gary Thornhill L RSC 4 Manchester
Career: 43 contests, won 12, drew 2, lost 29.

Steve Timms

West Bromwich. *Born* West Bromwich, 10
December, 1974
S. Middleweight. Ht. 5'11"
Manager Self

30.04.99 Matthew Pepper W RSC 3 Scunthorpe
02.07.99 Paul O'Rourke W RSC 2 Manchester
03.09.99 William Webster W RSC 4 West
          Bromwich
03.12.99 Allan Foster L RSC 4 Peterborough
22.01.00 Pedro Carragher DREW 4
          Birmingham
02.03.00 Pedro Carragher W PTS 6 Blackpool
28.03.00 Andy Vickers W RSC 4 Hartlepool
22.05.00 Hussain Osman L RSC 2 Coventry
05.02.01 Paul Owen W RSC 1 Bradford
26.04.01 Andrew Buchanan L RSC 4 Gateshead
03.10.02 Ryan Kerr L RSC 1 Sunderland
21.03.03 Mark Phillips W PTS 6 West
          Bromwich
04.06.04 Mark Phillips W PTS 6 Dudley
12.06.04 Paul Smith L RSC 1 Manchester
Career: 14 contests, won 8, drew 1, lost 5.

Choi Tseveenpurev

Oldham. *Born* Mongolia, 6 October, 1971
British Masters Featherweight Champion.
Ht. 5'5¾"
Manager J. Doughty

22.11.96 Jeun-Tae Kim W CO 8 Seoul, South
          Korea
01.05.99 Bulan Bugiarso L PTS 12 Kalimanton,
          Indonesia
12.08.99 Jiao Hasabayar W RSC 4 Ulan-Bator,
          Mongolia
22.08.99 Con Roksa W CO 3 Seinyeng, China
21.05.00 David Jeffrey W RSC 2 Shaw
24.09.00 Billy Smith W RTD 2 Shaw
03.12.00 Chris Williams W PTS 4 Shaw
27.04.01 Willie Limond L PTS 6 Glasgow
23.09.01 Steve Hanley W PTS 6 Shaw
06.10.01 Livinson Ruiz W PTS 4 Manchester
09.12.01 Kevin Gerowski W RSC 5 Shaw
          (Vacant British Masters Featherweight
          Title)
22.03.02 Chris Emanuele W PTS 4 Coventry
02.06.02 John Mackay W RSC 5 Shaw
17.11.02 Peter Allen W RSC 4 Shaw
09.03.03 Jason Nesbitt W PTS 8 Shaw
08.06.03 Daniel Thorpe W PTS 8 Shaw
29.02.04 John Mackay W RSC 3 Shaw
13.03.04 Lehlohonolo Ledwaba L PTS 8
          Copenhagen, Denmark
06.05.04 Kevin O'Hara W PTS 8 Barnsley
Career: 19 contests, won 16, lost 3.

(Jeremy) Jed Tytler

Hartlepool. *Born* Beverley, 8 September,
1972
L. Middleweight. Ht. 5'9¼"
Manager T. O'Neill/D. Coldwell

16.03.01 James Lee L RSC 3 Portsmouth
24.05.01 Charden Ansoula L RSC 2 Kensington
20.10.03 Jamie Coyle L RSC 2 Glasgow
08.12.03 Robert Burton L PTS 6 Barnsley
07.02.04 Martin Concepcion L RSC 2 Bethnal
          Green
Career: 5 contests, lost 5.

Bobby Vanzie

Bradford. *Born* Bradford, 11 January, 1974
Lightweight. Former British &
Commonwealth Lightweight Champion.
Former Undefeated Central Area
Lightweight Champion. Ht. 5'5"
Manager J. Doughty

22.05.95	Alan Peacock W RSC 1 Morecambe
29.10.95	Steve Tuckett W RSC 2 Shaw
14.11.95	John Smith W PTS 6 Bury
07.03.96	John Smith W PTS 6 Bradford
02.06.96	Anthony Campbell W PTS 6 Shaw
28.10.96	Richard Swallow W PTS 6 Bradford
24.02.97	Mark Ramsey DREW 8 Glasgow
08.06.97	C. J. Jackson W RSC 3 Shaw
23.10.97	Stuart Rimmer W RTD 8 Mayfair
	(Vacant Central Area Lightweight Title)
22.11.97	Karl Taylor W PTS 6 Manchester
13.02.98	Alan Temple W CO 3 Seaham
	(Elim. British Lightweight Title)
01.06.98	Gary Flear W PTS 6 Manchester
17.10.98	Wayne Rigby W RSC 10 Manchester
	(British Lightweight Title Challenge)
01.04.99	Anthony Campbell W PTS 12 Birmingham
	(British Lightweight Title Defence)
28.05.99	Athanus Nzau W RSC 10 Liverpool
	(Vacant Commonwealth Lightweight Title)
13.09.99	Brian Coleman W PTS 6 Bethnal Green
04.12.99	Vincent Howard W PTS 12 Manchester
	(Commonwealth Lightweight Title Defence)
21.02.00	Stephen Smith W RSC 9 Southwark
	(British & Commonwealth Lightweight Title Defences)
17.04.00	Paul Kaoma W RSC 2 Birmingham
	(Commonwealth Lightweight Title Defence)
09.09.00	Joseph Charles W RSC 6 Manchester
	(Commonwealth Lightweight Title Defence)
09.10.00	Laatekwei Hammond W RSC 8 Liverpool
	(Commonwealth Lightweight Title Defence)
03.02.01	James Armah L PTS 12 Manchester
	(Commonwealth Lightweight Title Defence)
05.05.01	Steve Murray W RSC 7 Edmonton
	(British Lightweight Title Defence)
08.10.01	Anthony Maynard W RSC 1 Barnsley
	(British Lightweight Title Defence)
01.06.02	Viktor Baranov W PTS 8 Manchester
12.10.02	Andrei Devyataykin W PTS 8 Bethnal Green
18.01.03	Yuri Romanov L RSC 8 Preston
	(WBO Inter-Continental Lightweight Title Challenge)
17.07.03	Graham Earl L PTS 12 Dagenham
	(British Lightweight Title Defence)
07.11.03	Keith Jones W PTS 6 Sheffield
06.02.04	Tony Montana W PTS 6 Sheffield
05.06.04	Graham Earl L PTS 12 Bethnal Green
	(Vacant British Lightweight Title)

Career: 31 contests, won 26, drew 1, lost 4.

David Vaughan

Blackwood. *Born* Caerphilly, 12 April, 1978
L. Welterweight. Ht. 5'8"
Manager D. Gardiner

23.02.03	Henry Jones W PTS 6 Aberystwyth
08.03.03	Ryan Barrett DREW 4 Bethnal Green
21.03.03	Dean Hickman L PTS 6 West Bromwich
10.05.03	Gwyn Wale DREW 4 Huddersfield
27.11.03	Chris McDonagh DREW 4 Longford

Career: 5 contests, won 1, drew 3, lost 1.

Jimmy Vincent

Birmingham. *Born* Barnet, 5 June, 1969
Welterweight. Former Undefeated British
Masters L Middleweight Champion.
Ht. 5'8"
Manager Self

19.10.87	Roy Williams W PTS 6 Birmingham
11.11.87	Mick Greenwood W PTS 6 Stafford
19.11.87	Darryl Pettit W RSC 6 Ilkeston
24.11.87	Roy Williams W PTS 6 Wolverhampton
14.02.88	Niel Leggett L PTS 6 Peterborough
29.02.88	Billy Cawley W CO 1 Birmingham
13.04.88	Dave Croft W PTS 6 Wolverhampton
16.05.88	Barry North W PTS 6 Wolverhampton
14.06.88	Dean Dickinson W PTS 6 Birmingham
20.09.88	Henry Armstrong L PTS 6 Stoke
10.10.88	Henry Armstrong L PTS 6 Manchester

Bobby Vanzie   Les Clark

177

17.10.88	Dean Dickinson W PTS 6 Birmingham
14.11.88	Peter Gabbitus L PTS 6 Stratford upon Avon
22.11.88	Barry North W RSC 4 Wolverhampton
12.12.88	Tony Feliciello L PTS 8 Birmingham
09.09.92	Mark Dawson L PTS 6 Stoke
23.09.92	Mark Epton W RSC 6 Leeds
17.12.92	Jason Rowland L PTS 6 Wembley
06.03.93	Mark Tibbs W PTS 6 Glasgow
27.08.96	Geoff McCreesh L RSC 1 Windsor
26.09.96	David Bain W RSC 3 Walsall
28.10.96	Lee Murtagh W RSC 2 Bradford
18.01.97	Tommy Quinn W RSC 1 Swadlincote
25.02.97	Kevin Adamson W PTS 6 Sheffield
25.03.97	Gary Jacobs L RSC 1 Lewisham
25.10.97	Ahmed Dottuev L PTS 6 Queensferry
29.01.98	Craig Winter L PTS 6 Pentre Halkyn
28.03.98	Zoltan Sarossy DREW 6 Hull
18.09.98	Danny Ryan L PTS 12 Belfast
	(Vacant IBO Inter-Continental S. Middleweight Title)
24.10.98	Darren Dorrington DREW 6 Bristol
25.11.98	Cornelius Carr L PTS 6 Streatham
05.12.98	Wayne Alexander L RSC 3 Bristol
22.01.99	Jim Rock L PTS 10 Dublin
29.04.99	Anthony McFadden L PTS 6 Bethnal Green
11.12.00	Harry Butler W PTS 6 Birmingham
31.10.01	Jason Williams W PTS 10 Birmingham

	(Vacant British Masters L.Middleweight Title)
10.12.01	Ojay Abrahams W PTS 10 Birmingham
	(British Masters L.Middleweight Title Defence)
26.04.02	Darren McInulty W CO 6 Coventry
	(British Masters L. Middleweight Title Defence)
21.12.02	David Walker W RSC 8 Dagenham
	(Final Elim. British Welterweight Title)
17.07.03	David Barnes L PTS 12 Dagenham
	(Vacant British Welterweight Title)
06.12.03	Eamonn Magee L PTS 12 Cardiff
	(Vacant WBU Welterweight Title)

Career: 41 contests, won 21, drew 2, lost 18.

Joel Viney

Blackpool. *Born* Manchester, 25 September, 1973
Lightweight. Ht. 5'7¾"
Manager Self

02.03.00	Duncan Armstrong W PTS 6 Blackpool
09.06.00	Gareth Wiltshaw W PTS 6 Blackpool
30.11.00	Dave Cotterill L RSC 1 Blackpool
27.01.01	Bradley Pryce L RSC 3 Bethnal Green
10.03.01	Kevin Lear L RSC 2 Bethnal Green

04.06.01	Barry Hawthorne L PTS 8 Glasgow
11.06.01	Inderpaul Sandhu L PTS 4 Nottingham
26.07.01	Mark Winters L RSC 4 Blackpool
15.10.01	Tasawar Khan L PTS 6 Bradford
29.11.01	Michael Hunter L PTS 6 Hartlepool
09.12.01	Paddy Folan W PTS 6 Blackpool
17.12.01	Daniel Thorpe W RSC 2 Cleethorpes
21.01.02	Andrew Ferrans L PTS 8 Glasgow
17.02.02	John Marshall L RSC 6 Salford
18.03.02	Craig Docherty L CO 1 Glasgow
05.05.02	Andy McLean L PTS 6 Hartlepool
28.05.02	Tony McPake L RSC 1 Liverpool
29.06.02	Matthew Burke L PTS 4 Brentwood
17.08.02	Henry Castle L RSC 1 Cardiff
23.09.02	Sean Green L PTS 6 Cleethorpes
05.10.02	Gary Reid L CO 2 Coventry
09.11.02	Darryn Walton L PTS 6 Altrincham
18.11.02	Andrew Ferrans L PTS 6 Glasgow
02.12.02	Gareth Wiltshaw W PTS 6 Bradford
16.12.02	Pete Buckley W PTS 6 Cleethorpes
08.01.03	Daleboy Rees L RSC 5 Aberdare
08.02.03	Jackson Williams L PTS 4 Norwich
17.02.03	John Simpson L RTD 1 Glasgow
22.03.03	Martin Watson L RSC 2 Renfrew
09.05.03	Stefy Bull L RTD 3 Doncaster
07.06.03	Baz Carey L PTS 6 Coventry
03.08.03	Daniel Thorpe W PTS 6 Stalybridge
06.09.03	Daniel Thorpe L PTS 6 Aberdeen
13.09.03	John-Paul Ryan W PTS 6 Coventry
20.09.03	Rendall Munroe L RTD 3 Nottingham
20.10.03	Pete Buckley L PTS 6 Bradford
27.10.03	Barry Hawthorne L RSC 1 Glasgow
15.05.04	Nadeem Siddique L PTS 6 Aberdeen
22.05.04	Nigel Senior L PTS 6 Manchester
07.06.04	Darren Johnstone L PTS 6 Glasgow

Career: 40 contests, won 8, lost 32.

Jimmy Vincent   Les Clark

Joel Viney   Les Clark

(Jaspreet) Jaz Virdee

Peterborough. *Born* London, 26 March, 1979
Lightweight. Ht. 5'9"
Manager I. Pauly

22.07.03	Rob Jeffries L PTS 6 Bethnal Green
27.09.03	Steve Bell L RSC 1 Manchester
21.11.03	Silence Saheed L RSC 2 Millwall
24.01.04	Kevin Mitchell L RSC 1 Wembley
08.04.04	Kristian Laight L PTS 6 Peterborough

Career: 5 contests, lost 5.

Dave Wakefield

Tooting. *Born* London, 8 January, 1979
L. Middleweight. Ht. 5'11"
Manager D. Powell

12.12.02	Mark Thornton L PTS 4 Leicester Square
13.04.03	Jon Hilton W PTS 4 Streatham
26.04.03	Kevin Phelan L PTS 4 Brentford
03.06.03	Justin Hudson L PTS 4 Bethnal Green
13.06.03	William Webster DREW 6 Queensway
25.10.03	Barrie Lee L PTS 4 Edinburgh
27.11.03	Kevin Phelan L PTS 6 Longford
20.02.04	Chas Symonds L RSC 5 Bethnal Green
15.05.04	Alan Campbell DREW 6 Aberdeen

Career: 9 contests, won 1, drew 2, lost 6.

Gwyn Wale

Mexborough. *Born* Barnsley, 24 August, 1984
L. Welterweight. Ht. 5'8"
Manager T. Gilmour/C. Aston

17.09.02	Arv Mittoo W PTS 6 Bethnal Green
05.10.02	Martin Hardcastle W PTS 4 Huddersfield
16.11.02	David Kehoe W PTS 4 Nottingham
22.02.03	James Paisley W RSC 1 Huddersfield
10.05.03	David Vaughan DREW 4 Huddersfield
13.09.03	Gary Cummings L PTS 6 Wakefield

Career: 6 contests, won 4, drew 1, lost 1.

David Walker

Bermondsey. *Born* Bromley, 17 June, 1976
L.Middleweight. Former Undefeated Southern Area L.Middleweight Champion. Former Undefeated Southern Area Welterweight Champion. Ht. 5'10"
Manager Self

29.04.00	Dave Fallon W RSC 1 Wembley
27.05.00	Stuart Rimmer W RSC 2 Southwark
15.07.00	Billy Smith W RTD 2 Millwall
16.09.00	Keith Jones W PTS 6 Bethnal Green
14.10.00	Jason Vlasman W RSC 1 Wembley
18.11.00	Gary Flear W PTS 4 Dagenham
09.12.00	Karl Taylor W PTS 6 Southwark
20.01.01	Ernie Smith W RTD 1 Bethnal Green
17.02.01	Paul Denton W PTS 4 Bethnal Green
19.05.01	Mark Ramsey W PTS 4 Wembley
14.07.01	David White W PTS 4 Liverpool
13.09.01	David Kirk DREW 8 Sheffield
16.03.02	Paul Dyer W RSC 6 Bethnal Green *(Vacant Southern Area Welterweight Title)*
10.05.02	Pedro Thompson W RSC 3 Bethnal Green
23.08.02	Robert Burton W RSC 2 Bethnal Green
25.10.02	Brett James W RSC 4 Bethnal Green *(Southern Area Welterweight Title Defence)*
21.12.02	Jimmy Vincent L RSC 8 Dagenham *(Final Elim. British Welterweight Title)*
05.03.03	Ojay Abrahams W PTS 6 Bethnal Green
16.04.03	Leigh Wicks W PTS 6 Nottingham
27.05.03	John Humphrey W CO 2 Dagenham *(Southern Area L.Middleweight Title Challenge. Elim. British L.Middleweight Title)*
25.07.03	Spencer Fearon W RSC 4 Norwich *(Southern Area L.Middleweight Title Defence)*
04.10.03	Roman Karmazin L RTD 3 Muswell Hill *(European L.Middleweight Title Challenge)*
12.03.04	Matt Scriven W RSC 3 Nottingham
02.06.04	Kevin Phelan W PTS 6 Nottingham

Career: 24 contests, won 21, drew 1, lost 2.

Dean Walker

Sheffield. *Born* Sheffield, 25 April, 1979
L. Middleweight. Ht. 5'11"
Manager D. Coldwell

21.10.00	Colin McCash DREW 6 Sheffield
11.12.00	James Lee L PTS 6 Sheffield
27.07.01	Chris Duggan W RSC 4 Sheffield
15.12.01	William Webster W PTS 6 Sheffield
03.03.02	Shaun Horsfall W PTS 6 Shaw
02.06.02	Wayne Shepherd W PTS 6 Shaw
03.08.02	Richard Inquieti W PTS 6 Derby
05.10.02	Martin Scotland W PTS 6 Chesterfield
24.05.03	Neil Bonner W PTS 6 Sheffield
12.10.03	Paul Lomax W PTS 6 Sheffield
10.02.04	Neil Addis W PTS 6 Barnsley
21.02.04	Matthew Macklin L CO 1 Cardiff
08.06.04	Andrei Ivanov W PTS 6 Sheffield

Career: 13 contests, won 10, drew 1, lost 2.

Carl Wall

Liverpool. *Born* Liverpool, 29 July, 1976
Middleweight. Ht. 5'10³/₄"
Manager Self

11.12.00	Rob Stevenson W PTS 4 Widnes
10.02.01	Brian Coleman W RSC 1 Widnes
20.06.03	Steve Russell W PTS 4 Liverpool
29.08.03	Jimi Hendricks W PTS 6 Liverpool
02.10.03	Tomas da Silva DREW 4 Liverpool

Career: 5 contest, won 4, drew 1.

Mark Wall

Dudley. *Born* Sandwell, 1 September, 1978
Middleweight. Ht. 5'8"
Manager N. Nobbs

09.04.04	Dean Lloyd W PTS 6 Rugby
27.04.04	Andrei Ivanov L CO 6 Leeds
25.06.04	Jake Guntert L CO 1 Bethnal Green

Career: 3 contests, won 1, lost 2.

Danny Wallace

Leeds. *Born* Leeds, 12 July, 1980
S. Bantamweight. Ht. 5'7"
Manager M. Marsden

24.08.01	Roger Glover W PTS 4 Atlantic City, USA
12.04.02	Michael Weaver DREW 4 Philadelphia, USA
22.02.03	Jamil Hussain W RSC 1 Huddersfield
12.04.03	Ian Turner W RSC 4 Bethnal Green
10.05.03	Marcel Kasimov L RSC 3 Huddersfield
06.09.03	Alexei Volchan W PTS 4 Huddersfield
31.01.04	Jamie Yelland W PTS 6 Bethnal Green
13.03.04	Henry Janes L PTS 4 Huddersfield

Career: 8 contests, won 5, drew 1, lost 2.

(Walisundra) Jus Wallie (Mudiyanselage)

Balham. *Born* Sri Lanka, 14 May, 1976
S. Featherweight. Ht. 5'5"
Manager E. Maloney

01.02.03	Kevin O'Hara L RSC 2 Belfast
29.03.03	Henry Castle W RSC 2 Portsmouth
05.04.03	Derry Matthews L PTS 4 Manchester
08.05.03	Steve Bell DREW 4 Widnes
31.05.03	J.J.Moore W RSC 1 Bethnal Green
29.11.03	Haider Ali L PTS 4 Renfrew
06.12.03	Jamie Arthur L PTS 6 Cardiff
21.02.04	Samuel Kebede L PTS 8 Cardiff
22.04.04	John Simpson L PTS 6 Glasgow
07.05.04	Jason Nesbitt W PTS 6 Bethnal Green
12.06.04	Andy Morris L PTS 6 Manchester
19.06.04	Martin Watson L PTS 6 Renfrew

Career: 12 contests, won 3, drew 1, lost 8.

Jus Wallie   Les Clark

Ryan Walls

Slough. *Born* Reading, 29 January, 1979
L.Heavyweight. Former British Masters Cruiserweight Champion. Ht. 6'0¹/₂"
Manager G. Carmen

20.12.02	Mark Phillips W PTS 4 Bracknell
23.02.03	Michael Pinnock W PTS 6 Streatham
21.03.03	Jimmy Steel W PTS 6 Longford
12.04.03	Earl Ling W RSC 4 Norwich
09.05.03	Darren Ashton W PTS 6 Longford
01.08.03	Darren Ashton W PTS 4 Bethnal Green
26.10.03	Michael Pinnock W PTS 10 Longford *(Vacant British Masters Cruiserweight Title)*
25.03.04	Pinky Burton L PTS 10 Longford *(British Masters Cruiserweight Title Defence)*
08.05.04	Toks Owoh W PTS 6 Bristol

Career: 9 contests, won 8, lost 1.

Dean Ward

Birmingham. *Born* Birmingham, 12 August, 1975
Featherweight. Ht. 5'6"
Manager N. Nobbs

23.04.04	Michael Crossan L PTS 6 Glasgow

07.05.04 David Bailey L PTS 6 Bethnal Green
14.06.04 Matt Teague L PTS 6 Cleethorpes
Career: 3 contests, lost 3.

Dean Ward   Les Clark

Isaac Ward

Darlington. *Born* Darlington, 7 April, 1977
Featherweight. Ht. 5'5"
Manager M. Marsden

03.08.02 Neil Read W RSC 1 Blackpool
18.10.02 John-Paul Ryan W PTS 6 Hartlepool
14.12.02 Steve Gethin W PTS 4 Newcastle
11.07.03 Rocky Dean DREW 4 Darlington
13.09.03 Pete Buckley W PTS 6 Wakefield
10.10.03 Rocky Dean W PTS 6 Darlington
04.12.03 Jamie Yelland W PTS 6 Huddersfield
05.03.04 Steve Gethin W PTS 6 Darlington
16.04.04 Pete Buckley W PTS 6 Hartlepool
Career: 9 contests, won 8, drew 1.

Nathan Ward

Reading. *Born* Reading, 19 July, 1979
L. Welterweight. Ht. 5'10"
Manager Self

27.09.02 Darren Goode W RSC 1 Bracknell
03.12.02 Dean Larter W PTS 4 Bethnal Green
20.12.02 Arv Mittoo W PTS 4 Bracknell
18.03.03 Pete Buckley W PTS 4 Reading
26.04.03 Cristian Hodorogea L RSC 1 Brentford
26.09.03 Casey Brooke W RSC 1 Reading
26.11.03 Lance Hall L PTS 4 Mayfair
12.05.04 Dave Hinds W PTS 4 Reading
Career: 8 contests, won 6, lost 2.

Martin Watson

Coatbridge. *Born* Bellshill, 12 May, 1981
Scottish Lightweight Champion. Ht. 5'8"
Manager R. Bannon/A. Morrison

24.05.01 Shaune Danskin W RSC 3 Glasgow
20.10.01 Jon Honney W RSC 3 Glasgow
16.12.01 Richie Caparelli W PTS 6 Glasgow
11.03.02 Pete Buckley W PTS 4 Glasgow
26.04.02 Gary Reid W PTS 6 Glasgow
08.06.02 Scott Miller W RSC 2 Renfrew
18.11.02 Gary Reid W RSC 4 Glasgow
22.03.03 Joel Viney W RSC 2 Renfrew
16.05.03 Barry Hughes W RTD 8 Glasgow
              (Vacant Scottish Lightweight Title)
30.10.03 Mark Winters DREW 8 Belfast

01.04.04 Steve Murray L PTS 10 Bethnal Green
19.06.04 Jus Wallie W PTS 6 Renfrew
Career: 12 contests, won 10, drew 1, lost 1.

William Webster

Birmingham. *Born* Birmingham, 14 March,
1970
Middleweight. Ht. 6'0"
Manager Self

05.06.99 Brian Knudsen L RSC 4 Cardiff
15.08.99 Edwin Cleary L PTS 6 Derby
03.09.99 Steve Timms L RSC 4 West Bromwich
12.11.99 Biagio Falcone L PTS 6 Glasgow
20.11.99 Gary Beardsley L PTS 6 Grantham
02.12.99 Wayne Elcock L PTS 6 Peterborough
13.12.99 Biagio Falcone L RSC 1 Glasgow
21.02.00 Scott Millar L PTS 6 Glasgow
29.02.00 Thomas McDonagh L RTD 2 Widnes
28.03.00 Peter McCormack L PTS 6
              Wolverhampton
13.04.00 Steve Ryan L PTS 4 Holborn
15.05.00 Mike Duffield W PTS 6 Birmingham
29.05.00 Michael Jennings L PTS 6 Manchester
19.06.00 Damon Hague L PTS 4 Burton
01.07.00 Alan Page L PTS 4 Manchester
25.09.00 Reagan Denton L PTS 4 Barnsley
07.10.00 George Robshaw L PTS 4 Doncaster
10.11.00 Chris Nembhard L RSC 1 Mayfair
28.01.01 Peter Nightingale L PTS 6
              Wolverhampton
17.02.01 Matthew Tait L PTS 4 Bethnal Green
25.02.01 Gary Beardsley L PTS 6 Derby
13.03.01 Mark Phillips L RTD 1 Plymouth
16.06.01 Andrew Lowe L RSC 2 Dagenham
15.12.01 Dean Walker L PTS 6 Sheffield
23.12.01 James Davenport L RSC 5 Salford
17.02.02 Donovan Smillie L PTS 6 Salford
03.03.02 Gary Dixon L PTS 6 Shaw
16.03.02 Matthew Thirlwall L RSC 1 Bethnal
              Green
15.04.02 Roddy Doran L PTS 8 Shrewsbury
15.06.02 Danny Smith L PTS 6 Norwich
23.09.02 Davey Jones L PTS 6 Cleethorpes
10.10.02 Kenroy Lambert W PTS 6 Piccadilly
25.10.02 Andrew Facey L PTS 4 Cotgrave
08.11.02 Davey Jones L PTS 6 Doncaster
17.11.02 Donovan Smillie L PTS 6 Bradford
11.12.02 Mark Ellwood L PTS 6 Hull
21.12.02 Darren Covill W PTS 4 Dagenham
08.02.03 Jason McKay L RSC 1 Liverpool
13.06.03 Dave Wakefield DREW 6 Queensway
11.07.03 Oscar Hall L PTS 8 Darlington
25.07.03 Danny Smith L PTS 4 Norwich
03.08.03 Donovan Smillie L RSC 4 Stalybridge
14.11.03 Luke Teague L PTS 6 Hull
08.12.03 Reagan Denton L RSC 6 Barnsley
29.02.04 Ali Nuumembe L RSC 3 Shaw
15.04.04 Danny Norton L PTS 4 Dudley
23.04.04 Barrie Lee L PTS 6 Glasgow
01.05.04 Mike Allen L CO 2 Bridgend
05.06.04 Martin Concepcion L RSC 1 Bethnal
              Green
Career: 49 contests, won 3, drew 1, lost 45.

Paul Wesley

Birmingham. *Born* Birmingham, 2 May,
1962
S. Middleweight. Ht. 5'9"
Manager Self

20.02.87 B. K. Bennett L PTS 6 Maidenhead
18.03.87 Darryl Ritchie DREW 4 Stoke

08.04.87 Dean Murray W PTS 6 Evesham
29.04.87 John Wright W PTS 4 Loughborough
12.06.87 Leon Thomas W RSC 2 Leamington
16.11.87 Steve McCarthy L CO 8 Southampton
25.01.88 Paul Murray W PTS 8 Birmingham
29.02.88 Paul Murray DREW 8 Birmingham
15.03.88 Johnny Williamson W CO 2
              Bournemouth
09.04.88 Joe McKenzie W RSC 6 Bristol
10.05.88 Tony Meszaros W PTS 8 Edgbaston
21.03.89 Carlton Warren L CO 2 Wandsworth
10.05.89 Rod Douglas L CO 1 Kensington
24.10.89 Nigel Rafferty L PTS 6
              Wolverhampton
22.11.89 Nigel Rafferty L PTS 8 Stafford
28.11.89 Nigel Rafferty L PTS 6
              Wolverhampton
05.12.89 Ian Strudwick L PTS 6 Catford
24.01.90 Rocky Feliciello W PTS 6 Solihull
19.02.90 Nigel Rafferty L PTS 8 Birmingham
22.03.90 John Ashton L PTS 10 Wolverhampton
              *(Midlands Area Middleweight Title
              Challenge)*
17.04.90 Winston May DREW 8 Millwall
09.05.90 Alan Richards W PTS 8 Solihull
04.06.90 Julian Eavis W PTS 8 Birmingham
18.09.90 Shaun Cummins L RSC 1
              Wolverhampton
17.10.90 Julian Eavis W PTS 6 Stoke
23.01.91 Wally Swift Jnr L PTS 10 Solihull
              *(Midlands Area L. Middleweight Title
              Challenge)*
20.03.91 Horace Fleary L RSC 5 Solihull
16.05.91 Delroy Waul L RSC 7 Liverpool
04.07.91 Neville Brown W RSC 1 Alfreton
31.07.91 Francesco dell'Aquila L PTS 8 Casella,
              Italy
03.10.91 Neville Brown L PTS 8 Burton
29.10.91 Tony Collins DREW 8 Kensington
03.03.92 Antonio Fernandez L PTS 10 Cradley
              Heath
              *(Vacant Midlands Area Middleweight
              Title)*
10.04.92 Jean-Charles Meuret L PTS 8 Geneva,
              Switzerland
03.06.92 Sumbu Kalambay L PTS 10 Salice
              Terme, Italy
29.10.92 Ian Strudwick W RSC 1 Bayswater
14.11.92 Paul Busby L PTS 8 Cardiff
24.11.92 Paul Jones W RSC 2 Doncaster
16.03.93 Chris Pyatt L PTS 10 Mayfair
04.06.93 Jacques le Blanc L PTS 10 Moncton,
              Canada
28.07.93 Antonio Fernandez L RSC 3 Brixton
              *(Midlands Area Middleweight Title
              Challenge)*
09.10.93 Warren Stowe W PTS 10 Manchester
              (Elim. British L. Middleweight Title)
09.02.94 Steve Collins L PTS 8 Brentwood
10.02.95 Robert McCracken L PTS 12
              Birmingham
              *(British L. Middleweight Title
              Challenge)*
24.02.95 Scott Doyle W PTS 8 Weston super
              Mare
18.03.95 Crisanto Espana L PTS 6 Millstreet
21.04.95 Gilbert Jackson L RSC 6 Dudley
              (Elim. British L. Middleweight Title)
31.01.96 Howard Eastman L RSC 1 Birmingham
21.03.96 Gary Logan L PTS 6 Southwark
13.04.96 Harry Simon L RTD 4 Wythenshawe
26.09.96 Nigel Rafferty DREW 6 Walsall
19.10.96 Glenn Catley L RSC 7 Bristol

25.03.97 Chris Johnson L CO 2 Lewisham
07.02.98 Paul Carr L PTS 6 Cheshunt
07.03.98 Omar Sheika L RTD 4 Reading
23.09.98 Lester Jacobs L CO 4 Bloomsbury
13.02.99 Geoff McCreesh L PTS 8 Newcastle
03.04.99 Toks Owoh L CO 5 Kensington
23.03.00 Lester Jacobs L PTS 6 Bloomsbury
13.04.00 Sam Soliman L PTS 6 Holborn
19.08.00 Adrian Dodson L PTS 4 Brentwood
18.11.00 Paul Bowen L PTS 4 Dagenham
11.12.00 Darren Rhodes L PTS 4 Widnes
08.03.01 Lee Blundell L RSC 3 Blackpool
25.09.01 Tony Dodson L PTS 6 Liverpool
17.11.01 Dean Cockburn L PTS 4 Glasgow
24.11.01 Andrew Lowe L PTS 4 Bethnal Green
08.12.01 David Starie L CO 1 Dagenham
05.04.03 Thomas McDonagh L PTS 6
         Manchester
16.04.03 Ryan Rhodes L CO 3 Nottingham
19.10.03 Darren Stubbs L PTS 6 Shaw
Career: 71 contests, won 16, drew 5, lost 50.

Stewart West

Birmingham. *Born* Birmingham, 28
September, 1974
L. Heavyweight. Ht. 6'0"
Manager D. Bradley

07.09.03 Lee Nicholson W RSC 2 Shrewsbury
13.09.03 Danny Berwick W RSC 3 Coventry
26.11.03 James Zikic L RSC 3 Mayfair
Career: 3 contests, won 2, lost 1.

Karl Wheeler

Peterborough. *Born* Peterborough, 30 May,
1982
L. Heavyweight. Ht. 6'3"
Manager I. Pauly

07.05.03 Martin Thompson W PTS 6 Ellesmere
         Port
29.05.03 Paul Billington W PTS 6 Sunderland
14.02.04 Gary Jones W RSC 1 Holborn
08.04.04 Nick Okoth W PTS 6 Peterborough
Career: 4 contests, won 4.

Wayne Wheeler

Plymouth. *Born* Plymouth, 24 February,
1970
Welterweight. Ht. 5'8"
Manager Self

24.03.01 J.J. Moore L RSC 4 Newark
12.05.01 Byron Pryce L RSC 2 Plymouth
16.12.01 Danny Gwilym W RSC 2 Bristol
17.02.02 Dean Hickman DREW 6
         Wolverhampton
16.03.02 David Kehoe DREW 6 Northampton
13.04.02 Dean Hickman L PTS 6
         Wolverhampton
11.05.02 Carl Greaves L RSC 1 Newark
13.07.02 Steve Saville L RSC 2 Wolverhampton
27.09.02 Robert Lloyd-Taylor L PTS 6
         Bracknell
05.10.02 Abdul Mannon W RSC 2 Liverpool
15.10.02 Iain Eldridge DREW 4 Bethnal Green
26.10.02 Justin Parsons W CO 2 Maesteg
30.11.02 Andy Egan L RSC 1 Coventry
08.02.03 Luke Rudd L RSC 2 Norwich
13.06.03 Nathan Wyatt W PTS 6 Bristol
30.06.03 Marcus Portman L RSC 3 Shrewsbury
18.09.03 Rocky Muscus W PTS 6 Mayfair
11.10.03 Silence Saheed L RSC 1 Portsmouth

30.11.03 Stuart Phillips L PTS 4 Swansea
08.12.03 Malcolm Melvin L RSC 6 Birmingham
16.01.04 Ali Nuumembe L RSC 1 Bradford
01.05.04 Freddie Luke L RSC 1 Gravesend
Career: 22 contests, won 5, drew 3, lost 14.

Shane White

Wells. *Born* Bristol, 27 January, 1972
L. Heavyweight. Ht. 5'9"
Manager Self

08.02.02 Gary Thompson DREW 6 Preston
18.03.02 Billy McClung W RTD 4 Glasgow
21.09.03 Paul Billington DREW 6 Bristol
17.11.03 Steve McGuire L CO 2 Glasgow
21.12.03 Paul Billington W RSC 2 Bristol
29.02.04 Harry Butler W PTS 6 Bristol
Career: 6 contests, won 3, drew 2, lost 1.

Lee Whyatt

Morden. *Born* Croydon, 16 September,
1977
S. Bantamweight. Ht. 5'7"
Manager D. Williams/F. Warren

07.02.04 Henry Janes L PTS 4 Bethnal Green
Career: 1 contest, lost 1.

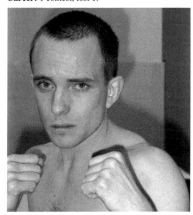

Lee Whyatt   Les Clark

Leigh Wicks

Brighton. *Born* Worthing, 29 July, 1965
S. Middleweight. Ht. 5'6¼"
Manager Self

29.04.87 Fidel Castro W PTS 6 Hastings
26.09.87 Jason Rowe W PTS 6 Hastings
18.11.87 Lou Ayres W PTS 6 Holborn
26.01.88 Theo Marius L PTS 8 Hove
15.02.88 Shamus Casey W PTS 6 Copthorne
26.04.88 Franki Moro DREW 8 Hove
04.05.88 Tony Britton W PTS 8 Wembley
18.05.88 Mark Howell W RSC 8 Portsmouth
25.05.88 Newton Barnett DREW 8 Hastings
22.11.88 Roy Callaghan L PTS 8 Basildon
16.03.89 Tony Britland W PTS 8 Southwark
12.10.89 Tony Gibbs W CO 2 Southwark
08.02.90 Ernie Noble W PTS 8 Southwark
26.04.90 Julian Eavis DREW 8 Mayfair
06.11.90 Gordon Blair W PTS 8 Mayfair
10.01.91 Barry Messam W PTS 6 Wandsworth
14.02.91 Kevin Thompson W PTS 8
         Southampton

21.10.91 Tony Britland W RSC 3 Mayfair
20.02.92 Mick Duncan L PTS 8 Glasgow
30.04.92 Darren Morris DREW 6 Mayfair
19.10.92 Bozon Haule W PTS 8 Mayfair
20.01.93 Robert McCracken L PTS 8
         Wolverhampton
17.02.93 Kevin Lueshing L PTS 6 Bethnal
         Green
22.04.93 Warren Stowe L PTS 6 Bury
27.10.95 Danny Quacoe W RSC 4 Brighton
18.11.95 Gary Jacobs L RTD 3 Glasgow
26.01.96 Wayne Appleton L PTS 6 Brighton
05.03.96 Kevin Thompson L PTS 6 Bethnal
         Green
24.03.97 Ross Hale L PTS 6 Bristol
08.04.97 Ahmet Dottuev L RSC 1 Bethnal
         Green
29.05.97 Nicky Thurbin L PTS 8 Mayfair
11.07.97 Darren Covill L RSC 2 Brighton
27.11.97 Lester Jacobs L PTS 6 Bloomsbury
06.12.97 Rhoshi Wells L PTS 4 Wembley
21.02.98 Neil Sinclair L RSC 1 Belfast
24.03.98 Ojay Abrahams L PTS 6 Bethnal Green
05.06.98 Darren Bruce L PTS 6 Southend
25.11.98 Darren Covill W PTS 4 Streatham
22.02.99 Neil Linford L PTS 4 Peterborough
26.06.99 Takaloo L CO 3 Millwall
09.10.99 Darren Rhodes L PTS 4 Manchester
27.11.99 Geoff McCreesh L PTS 6 Lubeck,
         Germany
11.12.99 Darren Rhodes L PTS 4 Liverpool
21.02.00 Sergei Dzinziruk L RSC 2 Southwark
25.03.00 Darren Rhodes L PTS 4 Liverpool
08.04.00 Spencer Fearon L PTS 4 Bethnal Green
02.06.00 Allan Foster L PTS 4 Ashford
24.06.00 Scott Dixon L PTS 4 Glasgow
01.07.00 Karim Hussine L PTS 6 Southwark
30.09.00 Bobby Banghar L PTS 4 Peterborough
07.10.00 Jamie Moore L PTS 4 Doncaster
11.11.00 Brian Knudsen L RSC 5 Belfast
17.03.01 Wayne Pinder L PTS 4 Manchester
29.03.01 Lester Jacobs L PTS 6 Hammersmith
05.05.01 Ty Browne L PTS 6 Brighton
08.06.01 Jason Collins L PTS 4 Hull
21.07.01 Damon Hague L PTS 4 Sheffield
31.07.01 Erik Teymour L RSC 1 Bethnal Green
30.09.01 Liam Lathbury L PTS 4 Bristol
09.10.01 Ruben Groenewald L PTS 6 Cardiff
28.10.01 Allan Gray L PTS 4 Southwark
17.11.01 Lawrence Murphy L PTS 4 Glasgow
08.12.01 Wayne Asker L PTS 4 Dagenham
16.12.01 Allan Gray L PTS 4 Southwark
31.01.02 Freddie Yemofio W PTS 6 Piccadilly
09.02.02 P.J. Maxwell L PTS 4 Manchester
13.04.02 Andrew Facey L PTS 6 Norwich
10.05.02 Matthew Thirlwall L PTS 4 Bethnal
         Green
17.09.02 Kenroy Lambert L PTS 6 Bethnal
         Green
23.11.02 Damon Hague L PTS 6 Derby
03.12.02 Lee Hodgson L PTS 4 Bethnal Green
08.02.03 Spencer Fearon L PTS 6 Brentford
23.02.03 Alan Jones L PTS 8 Aberystwyth
22.03.03 Lawrence Murphy L PTS 4 Renfrew
16.04.03 David Walker L PTS 6 Nottingham
26.04.03 Darren McDermott L PTS 4 Brentford
09.05.03 Kevin Phelan L PTS 6 Longford
27.05.03 Matthew Thirlwall L PTS 4 Dagenham
20.06.03 Alan Gilbert L PTS 4 Gatwick
25.07.03 Daniel Cadman L PTS 4 Norwich
27.11.03 Matthew Barr L PTS 4 Longford
21.02.04 Alan Gilbert L PTS 4 Brighton
12.03.04 Wayne Pinder L PTS 4 Nottingham
Career: 83 contests, won 17, drew 4, lost 62.

Noel Wilders

Castleford. *Born* Castleford, 4 January, 1975
Bantamweight. Former European
Bantamweight Champion. Former
Undefeated IBO, British & Central Area
Bantamweight Champion. Ht. 5'5"
Manager T. Callighan

16.03.96	Neil Parry W RTD 4 Sheffield
04.06.96	Graham McGrath W PTS 6 York
04.10.96	Tiger Singh W PTS 6 Wakefield
23.10.96	Jason Thomas W PTS 6 Halifax
12.03.97	John Matthews W PTS 6 Stoke
20.04.97	Shaun Anderson W PTS 6 Leeds
13.11.97	Anthony Hanna W PTS 6 Bradford
06.02.98	Marcus Duncan W RSC 6 Wakefield
	(Vacant Central Area Bantamweight Title)
21.05.98	Matthew Harris W PTS 6 Bradford
18.07.98	Sean Grant W RSC 4 Sheffield
23.10.98	Fondil Madani W DIS 7 Wakefield
28.11.98	Ross Cassidy W PTS 8 Sheffield
06.02.99	Jason Thomas W PTS 10 Halifax
	(Elim. British Bantamweight Title)
24.04.99	Anthony Hanna W PTS 6 Peterborough
22.06.99	Ady Lewis W RSC 6 Ipswich
	(Final Elim. British Bantamweight Title)
30.10.99	Francis Ampofo W PTS 12 Peterlee
	(Vacant British Bantamweight Title)
18.01.00	Steve Williams W RTD 11 Mansfield
	(British Bantamweight Title Defence)
20.03.00	Kamel Guerfi W PTS 12 Mansfield
	(Vacant IBO Bantamweight Title)
15.07.00	Paul Lloyd W PTS 12 Millwall
	(IBO Bantamweight Title Defence)
28.04.01	Stevie Quinn W RTD 6 Cardiff
21.07.01	Chris Emanuele W PTS 6 Sheffield
15.06.02	Sean Grant W RSC 3 Leeds
28.01.03	Fabien Guillerme W PTS 12 Nice, France
	(Vacant European Bantamweight Title)
18.03.03	Frederic Patrac DREW 4 Reading
	(European Bantamweight Title Defence)
10.06.03	David Guerault L RSC 7 Sheffield
	(European Bantamweight Title Defence)
06.02.04	Vladimir Borov W PTS 4 Sheffield

Career: 26 contests, won 24, drew 1, lost 1.

Danny Williams

Brixton. *Born* London, 13 July, 1973
WBU Inter-Continental Heavyweight
Champion. Former British &
Commonwealth Heavyweight Champion.
Former Undefeated WBO Inter-Continental
Heavyweight Champion. Ht. 6'3"
Manager Self

21.10.95	Vance Idiens W CO 2 Bethnal Green
09.12.95	Joey Paladino W RSC 1 Bethnal Green
13.02.96	Slick Miller W RSC 1 Bethnal Green
09.03.96	James Wilder W PTS 4 Millstreet
13.07.96	John Pierre W PTS 4 Bethnal Green
31.08.96	Andy Lambert W RSC 2 Dublin
09.11.96	Michael Murray W CO 1 Manchester
08.02.97	Shane Woollas W RSC 2 Millwall
03.05.97	Albert Call W RSC 4 Manchester
19.07.97	R. F. McKenzie W RSC 2 Wembley
15.11.97	Bruce Douglas W RSC 2 Bristol
19.12.97	Derek Amos W RSC 4 NYC, New York, USA

21.02.98	Shane Woollas W RSC 2 Belfast
16.05.98	Antonio Diaz W CO 3 Bethnal Green
10.10.98	Antoine Palatis W PTS 12 Bethnal Green
	(Vacant WBO Inter-Continental Heavyweight Title)
03.04.99	Julius Francis L PTS 12 Kensington
	(British & Commonwealth Heavyweight Title Challenges)
02.10.99	Ferenc Deak W RTD 1 Namur, Belgium
18.12.99	Harry Senior W PTS 12 Southwark
	(Vacant Commonwealth Heavyweight Title)
19.02.00	Anton Nel W CO 5 Dagenham
06.05.00	Michael Murray W RSC 6 Frankfurt, Germany
24.06.00	Craig Bowen-Price W CO 1 Glasgow
23.09.00	Quinn Navarre W RSC 6 Bethnal Green
21.10.00	Mark Potter W RSC 6 Wembley
	(Commonwealth & WBO Inter-Continental Heavyweight Title Defences. Vacant British Heavyweight Title)
09.06.01	Kali Meehan W RSC 1 Bethnal Green
	(Commonwealth Heavyweight Title Defence)
28.07.01	Julius Francis W CO 4 Wembley
	(British & Commonwealth Heavyweight Title Defences)
15.12.01	Shawn Robinson W RSC 2 Mashantucket Connecticut, USA
12.02.02	Michael Sprott W RTD 7 Bethnal Green
	(British & Commonwealth Heavyweight Title Defences)
17.09.02	Keith Long W PTS 12 Bethnal Green
	(British & Commonwealth Heavyweight Title Defences)
08.02.03	Sinan Samil Sam L RSC 6 Berlin, Germany
	(European Heavyweight Title Challenge)
26.04.03	Bob Mirovic W RSC 4 Brentford
	(Commonwealth Heavyweight Title Defence)
26.09.03	Michael Sprott W RSC 5 Reading
	(British & Commonwealth Heavyweight Title Defences)
24.01.04	Michael Sprott L PTS 12 Wembley
	(British & Commonwealth Heavyweight Title Defences)
01.04.04	Ratko Draskovic W RSC 1 Bethnal Green
13.05.04	Augustin N'Gou W RTD 3 Bethnal Green
	(Vacant WBU Inter-Continental Heavyweight Title)

Career: 34 contests, won 31, lost 3.

Dazzo Williams   Les Clark

(Darren) Dazzo Williams

Hereford. *Born* Lambeth, 19 March, 1974
British Featherweight Champion. Ht. 5'8"
Manager T. Gilmour

24.02.01	Mickey Coveney W CO 1 Bethnal Green
19.05.01	Mark Payne W PTS 8 Wembley
14.07.01	Dimitri Gorodetsky W RSC 3 Liverpool
19.12.01	Mark Alexander W PTS 6 Coventry
18.01.02	Zolani Msolo W RSC 2 Coventry
20.04.02	John Mackay L PTS 6 Wembley
26.10.02	Carl Allen L RSC 2 Maesteg
25.01.03	Vladimir Borov W PTS 6 Bridgend
08.03.03	Marc Callaghan W PTS 8 Bethnal Green
17.05.03	Stephen Chinnock W PTS 10 Liverpool *(Elim. British Featherweight Title)*
22.11.03	Roy Rutherford W PTS 12 Belfast *(British Featherweight Title Challenge)*
28.02.04	Jamie McKeever W PTS 12 Bridgend *(British Featherweight Title Defence)*
02.06.04	Roy Rutherford W PTS 12 Hereford *(British Featherweight Title Defence)*

Career: 13 contests, won 11, lost 2.

Jackson Williams

Norwich. *Born* Norwich, 19 June, 1981
Lightweight. Ht. 5'6^{1}/2"
Manager J. Ingle

13.04.02	Daniel Thorpe W PTS 6 Norwich
15.06.02	Jason Gonzales W PTS 6 Norwich
21.09.02	Baz Carey W PTS 6 Norwich
10.10.02	Jason Gonzales W PTS 4 Piccadilly
08.02.03	Joel Viney W PTS 4 Norwich
24.02.03	Anthony Hanna L PTS 6 Birmingham
12.04.03	Daniel Thorpe W PTS 6 Norwich
06.06.03	Nigel Senior W PTS 8 Norwich
25.07.03	Paul Rushton W PTS 4 Norwich
21.02.04	Nigel Senior W PTS 6 Norwich
14.05.04	Haroon Din L RSC 5 Sunderland *(Vacant British Masters L.Welterweight Title)*

Career: 11 contests, won 9, lost 2.

(Leon) Jason Williams

Swansea. *Born* Swansea, 11 July, 1974
Welterweight. Former Undefeated Welsh
Welterweight Champion. Ht. 5'11"
Manager Self

19.04.97	Jon Harrison L PTS 6 Plymouth
21.06.97	Dewi Roberts W RSC 1 Cardiff
26.09.97	Darren Covill W PTS 6 Port Talbot
15.11.97	Peter Federenko W PTS 4 Bristol
24.01.98	Danny Quacoe W PTS 4 Cardiff
23.02.98	Adrian Chase W PTS 4 Windsor
30.03.98	Rob Pitters W RSC 3 Tenerife
30.05.98	Prince Kasi Kaihau W CO 2 Bristol
14.07.98	Jon Harrison W RTD 2 Reading
05.12.98	Mark Ramsey W PTS 6 Bristol
23.04.99	Harry Butler W RSC 7 Clydach
05.06.99	Paul Miles W RSC 2 Cardiff
02.07.99	Delroy Mellis W PTS 6 Bristol
24.09.99	Michael Smyth L RSC 3 Merthyr *(Vacant Welsh Welterweight Title)*
07.04.00	David Baptiste W PTS 6 Bristol
08.09.00	Karim Bouali L RSC 5 Bristol
03.11.00	Mark Ramsey L CO 6 Ebbw Vale
15.09.01	Mark Richards W PTS 6 Swansea
31.10.01	Jimmy Vincent L PTS 10 Birmingham

(Vacant British Masters L.Middleweight Title)

16.03.02	Charden Ansoula L RSC 5 Northampton
23.02.03	Keith Jones W PTS 10 Aberystwyth *(Welsh Welterweight Title Challenge)*
10.05.03	Derek Roche L RSC 2 Huddersfield
07.09.03	Marcus Portman L PTS 6 Shrewsbury
13.03.04	Michael Jones L PTS 6 Huddersfield
01.05.04	James Hare L RSC 2 Bridgend

Career: 25 contests, won 15, lost 10.

Mark Williams

Birmingham. *Born* Birmingham, 16
September, 1969
Heavyweight. Ht. 6'1"
Manager Self

18.09.98	Mark Levy L PTS 6 Manchester
26.09.98	Faisal Mohammed L RSC 2 Norwich
10.12.98	Anthony Wright W PTS 6 Barking
19.01.99	Cliff Elden W PTS 6 Ipswich
24.03.99	Kenny Gayle DREW 6 Bayswater
29.04.99	Frode Stenasham L RSC 4 Bethnal Green
23.06.99	Jason Brewster DREW 6 West Bromwich
11.12.99	Enzo Maccarinelli L RSC 1 Merthyr
20.03.00	Michael Thompson L PTS 4 Mansfield
04.07.00	Kenny Gayle L PTS 4 Tooting

Richard Williams

Stockwell. *Born* London, 9 May, 1971
L.Middleweight. Former IBO
L.Middleweight Champion. Former
Undefeated Commonwealth & WBF
L.Middleweight Champion. Ht. 5'9^{1}/2"
Manager B. Hearn

08.03.97	Marty Duke W RSC 3 Brentwood
30.06.97	Danny Quacoe W PTS 4 Bethnal Green
02.09.97	Michael Alexander L PTS 4 Southwark
16.10.99	Pedro Carragher W RSC 2 Bethnal Green
06.11.99	Lee Bird W RSC 4 Bethnal Green
20.12.99	Harry Butler W RSC 1 Bethnal Green
17.04.00	Kevin Thompson W CO 1 Birmingham
16.06.00	Piotr Bartnicki W RSC 3 Bloomsbury
08.09.00	Dean Ashton W RSC 1 Hammersmith
04.11.00	Howard Clarke W CO 4 Bethnal Green
02.12.00	Aziz Daari W RSC 2 Bethnal Green
23.01.01	Tony Badea W RSC 3 Crawley
29.09.00	Paul Maskell W RSC 2 Bethnal Green
20.01.01	Faisal Mohammed L RSC 3 Bethnal Green
24.03.01	Mark Krence L PTS 4 Sheffield
21.06.01	Ali Forbes L PTS 4 Earls Court
07.09.01	Chris Davies L RSC 4 Bethnal Green
30.05.04	Joe Egan L RTD 5 Dublin

Career: 16 contests, won 3, drew 2, lost 11.

Richard Williams   Les Clark

(Commonwealth L. Middleweight Title Challenge)
04.06.01 Hussain Osman W PTS 10 Hartlepool
25.09.01 Andrew Murray W RSC 3 Liverpool
(Commonwealth L. Middleweight Title Defence)
20.10.01 Viktor Fesetchko W RSC 6 Portsmouth
01.12.01 Shannan Taylor W RSC 4 Bethnal Green
(Commonwealth L. Middleweight Title Defence. Vacant IBO L. Middleweight Title)
29.06.02 Paul Samuels T DRAW 3 Brentwood
(IBO L. Middleweight Title Defence)
07.12.02 Paul Samuels W RSC 10 Brentwood
(IBO L. Middleweight Title Defence)
08.03.03 Andrei Pestriaev W PTS 12 Bethnal Green
(IBO L. Middleweight Title Defence. WBF L. Middleweight Title Challenge)
21.06.03 Sergio Martinez L PTS 12 Manchester
(IBO L.Middleweight Title Defence)
31.01.04 Ayittey Powers W RSC 7 Bethnal Green
(Vacant Commonwealth L.Middleweight Title)
17.04.04 Sergio Martinez L RTD 9 Belfast
(IBO L.Middleweight Title Challenge)
Career: 22 contests, won 18, drew 1, lost 3.

Lee Williamson

Worcester. *Born* Worcester, 3 February, 1974
L. Middleweight. Ht. 5'9"
Manager Self

26.10.98 Trevor Tacy L PTS 6 Manchester
26.11.98 David Smales W PTS 6 Bradford
16.01.99 Graham Earl L RSC 4 Bethnal Green
23.03.99 Gary Reid L PTS 6 Wolverhampton
22.04.99 Brian Gifford W PTS 6 Dudley
15.05.99 James Hare L RSC 2 Sheffield
11.10.99 Carl Allen W PTS 6 Birmingham
28.10.99 Mark Hargreaves L PTS 6 Burnley
30.11.99 Marc Smith W PTS 6 Wolverhampton
11.12.99 Brian Carr DREW 6 Liverpool
24.01.00 Craig Docherty L PTS 6 Glasgow
08.02.00 Carl Allen L PTS 8 Wolverhampton
19.02.00 Kevin Lear L PTS 4 Dagenham
04.03.00 Liam Maltby L PTS 6 Peterborough
28.03.00 Carl Allen L PTS 8 Wolverhampton
06.06.00 Dave Travers W PTS 6 Brierley Hill
24.06.00 Kevin McIntyre L PTS 4 Glasgow
08.07.00 Tony Mulholland L PTS 8 Widnes
13.08.00 Esham Pickering L PTS 6 Nottingham
29.09.00 Darren Melville L RSC 4 Bethnal Green
21.10.00 Graham Earl L RSC 3 Wembley
24.11.00 Pete Buckley W PTS 6 Hull
09.12.00 Terry Butwell L PTS 4 Southwark
27.01.01 Danny Hunt W RSC 2 Bethnal Green
10.02.01 Geir Inge Jorgensen L RSC 3 Widnes
20.03.01 James Rooney L PTS 4 Glasgow
26.03.01 Liam Maltby L PTS 6 Peterborough
03.04.01 Danny Hunt L PTS 4 Bethnal Green
06.05.01 James Rooney L PTS 6 Hartlepool
21.06.01 Gavin Wake L PTS 6 Sheffield
14.07.01 Brett James L PTS 6 Wembley
28.07.01 Ross Minter L PTS 4 Wembley
15.09.01 Gavin Down L PTS 6 Derby
10.12.01 David Keir DREW 4 Liverpool
04.03.02 Pedro Thompson W PTS 6 Bradford
13.04.02 David Keir L PTS 4 Liverpool
13.05.02 Chris Duggan W RSC 3 Birmingham

01.06.02 Michael Jennings L PTS 4 Manchester
23.06.02 Brett James L PTS 6 Southwark
28.09.02 Mickey Quinn L RSC 2 Manchester
16.11.02 Richard Swallow L PTS 4 Coventry
30.11.02 Mark Dillon W PTS 4 Liverpool
18.01.03 Michael Jennings L RTD 4 Preston
23.02.03 Lee McAllister L PTS 6 Shrewsbury
16.03.03 Matt Scriven L PTS 10 Nottingham
(Vacant Midlands Area & British Masters L. Middleweight Titles)
07.06.03 Andy Egan L PTS 6 Coventry
12.07.03 Gary Young L PTS 4 Renfrew
03.08.03 Ali Nuumembe L PTS 6 Stalybridge
13.09.03 Andy Halder L PTS 6 Coventry
19.10.03 Mark Paxford L PTS 6 Shaw
08.11.03 Andy Halder L PTS 6 Coventry
21.11.03 Darren Covill W PTS 6 Millwall
01.12.03 Andrei Ivanov W RSC 4 Barnsley
14.02.04 Gary Woolcombe L PTS 6 Holborn
21.02.04 Danny Smith L PTS 6 Norwich
08.03.04 Lee McAllister L PTS 6 Birmingham
27.03.04 Colin McNeil L PTS 4 Edinburgh
23.04.04 Tony Montana L PTS 6 Leicester
07.05.04 Jake Guntert L PTS 6 Bethnal Green
04.06.04 Oscar Hall L PTS 6 Hull
Career: 60 contests, won 12, drew 2, lost 46.

Billy Wilson

York. *Born* York, 28 December, 1980
Heavyweight. Ht. 6'6"
Manager T. O'Neill

15.09.03 Carl Baker L RSC 2 Leeds
11.11.03 Brodie Pearmaine W PTS 6 Leeds
10.02.04 Paul King W PTS 6 Barnsley
Career: 3 contests, won 2, lost 1.

Simon Wilson

Belfast. *Born* Carrickfergus, 2 June, 1970
Lightweight. Ht. 5'7"
Manager A. Wilton

26.06.04 Michael Kelly L PTS 4 Belfast
Career: 1 contest, lost 1.

Gareth Wiltshaw

Stoke. *Born* Stoke, 22 August, 1980
L. Welterweight. Ht. 5'7"
Manager Self

17.04.00 John Meade W PTS 6 Bradford
09.06.00 Joel Viney L PTS 6 Blackpool
08.07.00 Kevin England DREW 6 Rotherham
20.11.00 Al Garrett L PTS 6 Glasgow
30.11.00 Mickey Coveney L PTS 4 Peterborough
18.02.01 Richmond Asante L PTS 4 Southwark
08.04.01 Jason Edwards L PTS 6 Wrexham
20.05.01 Stephen Chinnock L PTS 6 Wolverhampton
03.06.01 Mickey Coveney L PTS 4 Southwark
08.10.01 Sid Razak W PTS 6 Birmingham
27.10.01 Steve Foster L PTS 4 Manchester
19.01.02 Martin Power L PTS 4 Bethnal Green
11.02.02 Daniel Thorpe W PTS 6 Shrewsbury
02.03.02 Jesse James Daniel L RSC 3 Wakefield
20.04.02 Haroon Din L PTS 6 Derby
04.05.02 Steve Foster L PTS 4 Bethnal Green
13.06.02 Ryan Barrett L PTS 4 Leicester Square
03.08.02 Jeff Thomas L DIS 2 Blackpool
27.09.02 Chris McDonagh W RSC 1 Bracknell
07.10.02 Steve Saville L RSC 3 Birmingham
09.11.02 Eddie Nevins L PTS 4 Altrincham
17.11.02 Haroon Din L PTS 6 Bradford

02.12.02 Joel Viney L PTS 6 Bradford
08.01.03 Aidan Mooney L PTS 4 Aberdare
15.02.03 Dean Hickman L PTS 6 Wolverhampton
16.03.03 Adnan Amar L PTS 6 Nottingham
12.07.03 Colin Bain L PTS 4 Renfrew
23.11.03 Steve Conway L RSC 5 Rotherham
Career: 28 contests, won 4, drew 1, lost 23.

Juliette Winter

Derby. *Born* Whitehaven, 21 February, 1973
Bantamweight. Ht. 5'6"
Manager Self

16.06.01 Sara Hall L RTD 4 Derby
20.09.01 Claire Cooper L RSC 4 Blackfriars
20.03.03 Cathy Brown W PTS 4 Queensway
24.01.04 Esther Schouten L RTD 3 Amsterdam, Holland
Career: 4 contests, won 1, lost 3.

Mark Winters

Antrim. *Born* Antrim, 29 December, 1971
Lightweight. Former British L. Welterweight Champion. Ht. 5'8"
Manager Self

04.03.95 Trevor Smith W PTS 6 Livingston
10.06.95 Mark McGowan W PTS 6 Manchester
09.09.95 Anthony Campbell W PTS 4 Cork
25.11.95 John O. Johnson W RSC 2 Dublin
13.01.96 Rick North W PTS 4 Manchester
09.03.96 Danny Quacoe W RSC 2 Millstreet
08.06.96 Brian Coleman W PTS 4 Newcastle
31.08.96 John Smith W PTS 4 Dublin
30.11.96 Paul Dyer W PTS 6 Tylorstown
14.03.97 Paul Denton W PTS 8 Reading
03.05.97 Jimmy Phelan W PTS 4 Manchester
11.10.97 Carl Wright W PTS 12 Sheffield
(Vacant British L. Welterweight Title)
21.02.98 Bernard Paul W PTS 12 Belfast
(British L. Welterweight Title Defence)
16.05.98 Jason Rowland L PTS 12 Bethnal Green
(British L. Welterweight Title Defence)
05.09.98 Junior Witter L PTS 8 Telford
23.10.99 James Hare DREW 6 Telford
11.12.99 Ricky Hatton L RSC 4 Liverpool
(WBO Inter-Continental L. Welterweight Title Challenge)
04.02.01 David Kirk W PTS 6 Queensferry
20.04.01 David Kirk W PTS 6 Dublin
26.07.01 Joel Viney W RSC 4 Blackpool
15.12.01 Graham Earl L PTS 10 Wembley
(Elim. British Lightweight Title)
02.11.02 John Marshall W RSC 5 Belfast
01.02.03 David Kehoe W RSC 2 Belfast
30.10.03 Martin Watson DREW 8 Belfast
Career: 24 contests, won 18, drew 2, lost 4.

Junior Witter

Bradford. *Born* Bradford, 10 March, 1974
British, Commonwealth & European L.Welterweight Champion. Former Undefeated European Union, WBU Inter-Continental & WBF L.Welterweight Champion. Ht. 5'7"
Manager J. Ingle

18.01.97 Cam Raeside DREW 6 Swadlincote
04.03.97 John Green W PTS 6 Yarm
20.03.97 Lee Molyneux W RSC 6 Salford

25.04.97	Trevor Meikle W PTS 6 Mere	
15.05.97	Andreas Panayi W RSC 5 Reading	
02.08.97	Brian Coleman W PTS 4 Barnsley	
04.10.97	Michael Alexander W PTS 4 Hannover, Germany	
07.02.98	Mark Ramsey DREW 6 Cheshunt	
05.03.98	Brian Coleman W PTS 6 Leeds	
18.04.98	Jan Bergman W PTS 6 Manchester	
05.09.98	Mark Winters W PTS 8 Telford	
28.11.98	Karl Taylor W PTS 4 Sheffield	
13.02.99	Malcolm Melvin W RSC 2 Newcastle *(Vacant WBF L. Welterweight Title)*	
17.07.99	Isaac Cruz W PTS 8 Doncaster	
06.11.99	Harry Butler W PTS 6 Widnes	
21.03.00	Mrhai Iourgh W RSC 1 Telde, Gran Canaria	
08.04.00	Arv Mittoo W PTS 4 Bethnal Green	
24.06.00	Zab Judah L PTS 12 Glasgow *(IBF L. Welterweight Title Challenge)*	
20.10.00	Steve Conway W RTD 4 Belfast	
25.11.00	Chris Henry W RSC 3 Manchester	
10.03.01	David Kirk W RSC 2 Bethnal Green	
22.05.01	Fabrice Faradji W RSC 1 Telde, Gran Canaria	
21.07.01	Alan Temple W CO 5 Sheffield	
27.10.01	Colin Mayisela W RSC 2 Manchester *(Vacant WBU Inter-Continental L.Welterweight Title)*	
16.03.02	Alan Bosworth W RSC 3 Northampton *(Vacant British L.Welterweight Title)*	
08.07.02	Laatekwi Hammond W RSC 2 Mayfair *(Vacant Commonwealth L.Welterweight Title)*	
19.10.02	Lucky Samba W RSC 2 Renfrew	
23.11.02	Giuseppe Lauri W RSC 2 Derby *(Final Elim. WBO L. Welterweight Title)*	
05.04.03	Jurgen Haeck W RTD 4 Manchester *(Vacant European Union L.Welterweight Title)*	
27.09.03	Fred Kinuthia W RSC 2 Manchester *(Commonwealth L.Welterweight Title Defence)*	
16.04.04	Oscar Hall W RSC 3 Bradford	
02.06.04	Salvatore Battaglia W RSC 2 Nottingham *(Vacant European L.Welterweight Title)*	

Career: 32 contests, won 29, drew 2, lost 1.

Lee Woodruff

Lancaster. *Born* Lancaster, 27 February, 1980
S. Middleweight. Ht. 5'11"
Manager Self

18.03.01	Tommy Matthews W RSC 2 Shaw	
26.04.01	Paul Buchanan L PTS 6 Gateshead	
26.07.01	Paul Martin W RSC 1 Blackpool	
23.09.01	Louis Swales W RSC 4 Shaw	
08.02.02	Paul Owen L RSC 2 Preston	
19.06.04	Tom Cannon L PTS 4 Renfrew	

Career: 6 contests, won 3, lost 3.

Clinton Woods

Sheffield. *Born* Sheffield, 1 May, 1972
L.Heavyweight. Former Undefeated British, European, WBC International & Commonwealth L.Heavyweight Champion. Former Commonwealth S.Middleweight Champion. Former Undefeated Central Area S.Middleweight Champion. Ht. 6'2"
Manager D. Hobson

17.11.94	Dave Proctor W PTS 6 Sheffield	
12.12.94	Earl Ling W RSC 5 Cleethorpes	
23.02.95	Paul Clarkson W RSC 1 Hull	
06.04.95	Japhet Hans W RSC 3 Sheffield	
16.05.95	Kevin Burton W PTS 6 Cleethorpes	
14.06.95	Kevin Burton W RSC 6 Batley	
21.09.95	Paul Murray W PTS 6 Sheffield	
20.10.95	Phil Ball W RSC 4 Mansfield	
22.11.95	Andy Ewen W RSC 3 Sheffield	
05.02.96	Chris Walker W RSC 6 Bradford	
16.03.96	John Duckworth W PTS 8 Sheffield	
13.06.96	Ernie Loveridge W PTS 6 Sheffield	
14.11.96	Craig Joseph W PTS 10 Sheffield *(Vacant Central Area S. Middleweight Title)*	
20.02.97	Rocky Shelly W RSC 2 Mansfield	
10.04.97	Darren Littlewood W RSC 6 Sheffield *(Central Area S. Middleweight Title Defence)*	
26.06.97	Darren Ashton W PTS 6 Sheffield	
25.10.97	Danny Juma W PTS 8 Queensferry	
26.11.97	Jeff Finlayson W PTS 8 Sheffield	
06.12.97	Mark Baker W PTS 12 Wembley *(Vacant Commonwealth S.Middleweight Title)*	
28.03.98	David Starie L PTS 12 Hull *(Commonwealth S. Middleweight Title Defence)*	
18.06.98	Peter Mason W RTD 4 Sheffield	
30.11.98	Mark Smallwood W RSC 7 Manchester	
13.03.99	Crawford Ashley W RSC 8 Manchester *(British, Commonwealth & European L. Heavyweight Title Challenges)*	
10.07.99	Sam Leuii W RSC 6 Southwark *(Commonwealth L. Heavyweight Title Defence)*	
11.09.99	Lenox Lewis W RSC 10 Sheffield *(Commonwealth L. Heavyweight Title Defence)*	
10.12.99	Terry Ford W RTD 4 Warsaw, Poland	
12.02.00	Juan Perez Nelongo W PTS 12 Sheffield *(European L. Heavyweight Title Defence)*	
29.04.00	Ole Klemetsen W RSC 9 Wembley *(European L. Heavyweight Title Defence)*	
15.07.00	Greg Scott-Briggs W RSC 3 Millwall	
24.03.01	Ali Forbes W RTD 10 Sheffield *(Vacant WBC International L. Heavyweight Title)*	
27.07.01	Paul Bonson W PTS 6 Sheffield	
13.09.01	Yawe Davis W PTS 12 Sheffield *(Final Elim.WBC L.Heavyweight Title)*	
16.03.02	Clint Johnson W RSC 3 Bethnal Green	
07.09.02	Roy Jones L RSC 6 Portland, Oregon, USA *(WBC, WBA & IBF L.Heavyweight Title Challenges)*	
24.01.03	Sergio Martin Beaz W RSC 3 Sheffield	
18.03.03	Arturo Rivera W RSC 2 Reading	
10.06.03	Demetrius Jenkins W RSC 7 Sheffield	
07.11.03	Glengoffe Johnson DREW 12 Sheffield *(Vacant IBF L.Heavyweight Title)*	
06.02.04	Glengoffe Johnson L PTS 12 Sheffield *(Vacant IBF L.Heavyweight Title)*	

Career: 39 contests, won 35, drew 1, lost 3.

Gary Woolcombe

Welling. *Born* London, 4 August, 1982
Welterweight. Ht. 5'10³/₄"
Manager E. Maloney

15.05.03	Paul McIlwaine W RSC 2 Mayfair	
22.07.03	Arv Mittoo W PTS 6 Bethnal Green	
25.09.03	Pete Buckley W PTS 6 Bethnal Green	
18.11.03	John Butler W PTS 4 Bethnal Green	
07.02.04	Ernie Smith W PTS 4 Bethnal Green	
14.02.04	Lee Williamson W PTS 6 Holborn	
07.05.04	David Kirk W PTS 4 Bethnal Green	
05.06.04	Ivor Bonavic W PTS 4 Bethnal Green	

Career: 8 contests, won 8.

Gary Woolcombe   Les Clark

Chris Woollas

Epworth. *Born* Scunthorpe, 22 November, 1973
Heavyweight. Former Undefeated Midlands Area Cruiserweight Champion. Ht. 5'11"
Manager M. Shinfield

17.08.94	Darren Littlewood W RSC 4 Sheffield	
05.10.94	Robert Norton DREW 6 Wolverhampton	
05.12.94	Neil Simpson W PTS 6 Cleethorpes	
10.02.95	Monty Wright L RSC 4 Birmingham	
30.06.95	Kenny Nevers L RSC 2 Doncaster	
25.09.95	Cliff Elden DREW 6 Cleethorpes	
08.11.95	Stevie Pettit W PTS 6 Walsall	
17.11.95	Markku Salminen L PTS 6 Helsinki, Finland	
11.12.95	Cliff Elden DREW 6 Cleethorpes	
15.02.96	Pele Lawrence W RSC 6 Sheffield	
29.02.96	John Pierre DREW 6 Scunthorpe	
16.03.96	David Jules W PTS 6 Sheffield	
22.04.96	Jacklord Jacobs DREW 4 Crystal Palace	
30.05.96	Martin Langtry L RSC 6 Lincoln *(Midlands Area Cruiserweight Title Challenge)*	
03.09.96	Darren Corbett L RSC 7 Belfast	
02.10.96	Rocky Shelly W RSC 6 Stoke	
09.10.96	Nigel Rafferty W PTS 6 Stoke	
28.10.96	Colin Brown L PTS 8 Glasgow	
10.11.96	Michael Gale DREW 6 Glasgow	
25.11.96	Albert Call L PTS 6 Cleethorpes	
17.12.96	Darren Corbett L RSC 1 Doncaster	
16.01.97	Mark Smallwood L PTS 8 Solihull	
31.01.97	Tim Redman L PTS 6 Pentre Halkyn	
14.03.97	Kelly Oliver L PTS 6 Reading	
24.03.97	Mikael Lindblad L RSC 7 Helsinki, Finland	
19.06.97	Ian Henry W PTS 6 Scunthorpe	
02.08.97	Kelly Oliver L RSC 3 Barnsley	
15.12.97	Neil Simpson W PTS 6 Cleethorpes	
26.01.98	Colin Brown W PTS 6 Glasgow	
26.03.98	Cliff Elden L PTS 4 Scunthorpe	

06.05.98	Simon McDougall W PTS 6 Blackpool
21.07.98	Matthew Ellis L RSC 5 Widnes
11.09.98	Lennox Williams W PTS 6 Cleethorpes
12.03.99	Albert Sosnowski L PTS 4 Bethnal Green
27.05.99	Nigel Rafferty W PTS 10 Edgbaston
	(Midlands Area Cruiserweight Title Challenge)
10.07.99	Michael Sprott L RTD 4 Southwark
13.09.99	Dominic Negus L PTS 10 Bethnal Green
	(Elim. British Cruiserweight Title)
09.10.99	Chris P. Bacon L PTS 4 Manchester
30.10.99	Terry Dunstan L RSC 1 Southwark
08.04.00	Bruce Scott L RSC 2 Bethnal Green
13.07.00	Firat Aslan L RSC 2 Bethnal Green
08.09.00	Petr Horacek L PTS 4 Hammersmith
21.10.00	Danny Percival L PTS 4 Wembley
18.11.00	Matthew Ellis L PTS 4 Dagenham
11.12.00	Enzo Maccarinelli L PTS 4 Widnes
15.12.01	Lee Swaby L RSC 4 Sheffield
21.10.02	Greg Scott-Briggs W PTS 6 Cleethorpes
01.11.02	Spencer Wilding DREW 6 Preston
28.04.03	Eamonn Glennon W PTS 6 Cleethorpes
22.11.03	Albert Sosnowski L RSC 1 Belfast
16.02.04	Dave Clarke W PTS 6 Scunthorpe
30.03.04	Colin Kenna L PTS 6 Southampton

Career: 52 contests, won 16, drew 7, lost 29.

Jonathan Woollins

Selston. *Born* Mansfield, 14 May, 1983
L. Middleweight. Ht. 6'1"
Manager J. Ingle

16.03.03	Arv Mittoo W PTS 4 Nottingham
08.06.03	Ernie Smith L PTS 4 Nottingham
03.08.03	Chris Duggan W RSC 1 Stalybridge
06.10.03	Karl Taylor L PTS 6 Birmingham
15.12.03	Steve Scott L PTS 6 Cleethorpes
21.02.04	Steve Mallett L PTS 4 Norwich

Career: 6 contests, won 2, lost 4.

Carl Wright

Rugby. *Born* Rugby, 26 April, 1978
Cruiserweight. Ht. 6'1¼"
Manager J. Weaver

25.06.02	Dave Clarke W PTS 6 Rugby
05.10.02	Adam Cale W PTS 6 Coventry
16.11.02	Jimmy Steel W PTS 6 Coventry
08.03.03	Gary Williams W PTS 6 Coventry
16.03.03	Darren Ashton DREW 6 Nottingham
07.06.03	Gary Thompson W RTD 2 Coventry
13.09.03	Darren Ashton W PTS 4 Coventry
09.04.04	Lee Mountford W PTS 4 Rugby
01.05.04	Paul Bonson W PTS 6 Coventry

Career: 9 contests, won 8, drew 1.

Nigel Wright

Crook. *Born* Bishop Auckland, 22 June, 1979
L. Welterweight. Ht. 5'9"
Manager G. Robinson

10.02.01	Keith Jones W PTS 4 Widnes
15.09.01	Tommy Peacock W RSC 1 Manchester
17.11.01	Ernie Smith W PTS 4 Glasgow
19.01.02	Woody Greenaway W CO 2 Bethnal Green
11.03.02	James Paisley W PTS 4 Glasgow
19.10.02	Kevin McIntyre L PTS 6 Renfrew
29.03.03	Darren Melville W PTS 6 Portsmouth

24.05.03	David Kirk W PTS 4 Bethnal Green
02.10.03	Nigel Senior W RSC 5 Liverpool
29.11.03	Jason Hall W PTS 6 Renfrew
06.03.04	George Telfer W RSC 3 Renfrew
22.05.04	Jon Honney W RSC 2 Widnes

Career: 12 contests, won 11, lost 1.

Nathan Wyatt

Gloucester. *Born* Gloucester, 4 May, 1979
Middleweight. Ht. 5'8"
Manager C. Sanigar

13.06.03	Wayne Wheeler L PTS 6 Bristol
02.04.04	Jon Harrison L PTS 6 Plymouth

Career: 2 contests, lost 2.

Jamie Yelland

Finchley. *Born* London, 5 March, 1975
Bantamweight. Ht. 5'5"
Manager P. Rees

11.03.00	Chris Emanuele W PTS 4 Kensington
22.07.00	Daniel Ring W PTS 4 Watford
06.10.00	Simon Stowell DREW 4 Maidstone
31.10.00	John Barnes W PTS 4 Hammersmith
07.04.01	John Barnes W PTS 4 Wembley
31.07.01	Paddy Folan W RSC 5 Bethnal Green
28.11.01	John Mackay L RSC 6 Bethnal Green
25.02.02	Gareth Payne W RSC 3 Slough
29.06.02	Neil Read W PTS 6 Brentwood
10.10.02	Gareth Payne W PTS 10 Stoke
28.04.03	Nicky Booth L PTS 12 Nottingham
	(British Bantamweight Title Challenge)
04.12.03	Isaac Ward L PTS 6 Huddersfield
31.01.04	Danny Wallace L PTS 6 Bethnal Green

Career: 13 contests, won 8, drew 1, lost 4.

Jamie Yelland   Les Clark

Freddie Yemofio

Hayes. *Born* London, 15 July, 1969
S. Middleweight. Ht. 5'10"
Manager D. Currivan

31.08.93	Lee Sara L PTS 6 Croydon
30.09.93	Martin Rosamond L PTS 6 Hayes
20.05.94	Lee Blundell L RSC 6 Acton
30.09.94	Jason Hart L PTS 6 Bethnal Green
26.05.95	Robert Harper W PTS 6 Norwich
28.04.98	Matthew Tait L PTS 6 Brentford

14.05.98	Matt Galer L RSC 4 Acton
07.12.98	Matthew Barney L PTS 4 Acton
12.08.00	Spencer Fearon L RSC 4 Wembley
02.11.00	Elvis Michailenko L PTS 6 Kensington
09.12.00	Liam Lathbury L PTS 4 Southwark
29.01.01	Francie Doherty L RSC 4 Peterborough
05.05.01	Danny Wray L PTS 6 Brighton
12.05.01	Simon Andrews L PTS 4 Plymouth
31.01.02	Leigh Wicks L PTS 6 Piccadilly
11.02.02	Roddy Doran L PTS 8 Shrewsbury
27.03.02	Kenroy Lambert L PTS 6 Mayfair
13.04.02	Danny Smith L PTS 6 Norwich
27.09.02	Mo L PTS 4 Bracknell
10.10.02	Darren Covill W PTS 4 Piccadilly
29.11.02	Lee Molloy L PTS 4 Liverpool
23.02.03	Mark Thornton L RSC 1 Streatham
09.05.03	Mo L PTS 4 Longford
08.11.03	Mike Allen L RSC 4 Bridgend
21.02.04	Darren McDermott L RSC 3 Cardiff

Career: 25 contests, won 2, lost 23.

Gary Young

Edinburgh. *Born* Edinburgh, 23 May, 1983
Welterweight. Ht. 5'7"
Manager F. Maloney

11.03.02	Paul McIlwaine W CO 2 Glasgow
08.06.02	Daniel Thorpe W RSC 1 Renfrew
02.11.02	Keith Jones W PTS 4 Belfast
22.03.03	Dean Larter W RSC 2 Renfrew
12.07.03	Lee Williamson W PTS 4 Renfrew
25.10.03	Peter Dunn W PTS 6 Edinburgh
29.11.03	Karl Taylor W RSC 3 Renfrew
06.03.04	Anthony Christopher W CO 1 Renfrew
27.03.04	Keith Jones W PTS 6 Edinburgh
19.06.04	David Kirk W PTS 4 Renfrew

Career: 10 contests, won 10.

James Zikic

Watford. *Born* Harrow, 31 March, 1977
Heavyweight. Ht. 6'2"
Manager A. Bowers

19.10.02	Tony Booth W PTS 4 Norwich
21.12.02	Brodie Pearmaine W PTS 4 Millwall
26.11.03	Stewart West W RSC 3 Mayfair
28.02.04	Scott Gammer L PTS 6 Bridgend
13.05.04	John McDermott L RSC 4 Bethnal Green

Career: 5 contests, won 3, lost 2.

James Zikic   Les Clark

British Area Title Bouts During 2003-2004

Central Area

Titleholders at 30 June 2004

Fly: *vacant.* **Bantam:** *vacant.* **S.Bantam:** Sean Hughes. **Feather:** *vacant.* **S.Feather:** Eddie Nevins. **Light:** Stefy Bull. **L.Welter:** Tony Montana. **Welter:** Matthew Hatton. **L.Middle:** Robert Burton. **Middle:** Danny Thornton. **S.Middle:** *vacant.* **L.Heavy:** *vacant.* **Cruiser:** Denzil Browne. **Heavy:** *vacant.*

5 October	Sean Hughes W RSC 4 Paddy Folan, Bradford (Vacant S.Bantamweight Title)
28 November	Danny Thornton W PTS 10 Jason Collins, Hull (Middleweight Title Defence)
7 December	Daniel Thorpe W PTS 10 Mally McIver, Bradford (Vacant Lightweight Title)
6 May	Robert Burton L PTS 10 Matthew Hatton, Barnsley (Welterweight Title Defence)
7 May	Daniel Thorpe L PTS 10 Stefy Bull, Doncaster (Lightweight Title Defence)
22 May	Tony Montana W PTS 10 Wayne Rigby, Manchester (Vacant L.Welterweight Title)
8 June	Robert Burton W CO 3 Lee Murtagh, Sheffield (Vacant L.Middleweight Title)

Between 1 July 2003 and 30 June 2004, Gary Hibbert (light), Lee Armstrong (L.Middle) and Tony Dodson (S.Middle) all relinquished their titles.

Midlands Area

Titleholders at 30 June 2004

Fly: *vacant.* **Bantam:** *vacant.* **S.Bantam:** Gareth Payne. **Feather:** Stephen Chinnock. **S.Feather:** *vacant.* **Light:** Scott Lawton. **L.Welter:** Dean Hickman. **Welter:** Tony Conroy. **L.Middle:** Matt Scriven. **Middle:** *vacant.* **S.Middle:** Peter Jackson. **L.Heavy:** *vacant.* **Cruiser:** Scott Lansdowne. **Heavy:** Mark Krence.

17 July	Mike Duffield L PTS 10 Peter Jackson, Walsall (S.Middleweight Title Defence)
7 September	Roddy Doran W PTS 10 Conroy McIntosh, Shrewsbury (Vacant Middleweight Title)
4 June	Dean Hickman W RSC 8 Adnan Amar, Dudley (Vacant L.Welterweight Title)
17 June	Scott Lawton W PTS 10 Carl Allen, Sheffield (Vacant Lightweight Title)

Between 1 July 2003 and 30 June 2004, Anthony Maynard (Light) and Young Muttley (L.Welter) both relinquished their titles, while Roddy Duran (Middle) forfeited his on being suspended from boxing for six months.

Northern Area

Titleholders at 30 June 2004

Fly: *vacant.* **Bantam:** *vacant.* **S.Bantam:** *vacant.* **Feather:** *vacant.* **S.Feather:** *vacant.* **Light:** *vacant.* **L.Welter:** *vacant.* **Welter:** Oscar Hall. **L.Middle:** *vacant.* **Middle:** Eddie Haley. **S.Middle:** Ryan Kerr. **L.Heavy:** *vacant.* **Cruiser:** *vacant.* **Heavy:** *vacant.*

| 26 February | Ryan Kerr W RSC 5 Eddie Haley, Sunderland (Vacant S.Middleweight Title) |
| 5 March | Franny Jones NC 3 Danny Moir, Darlington (Vacant L.Middleweight Title) |

Between 1 July 2003 and 30 June 2004, Michael Hunter (S.Bantam) relinquished his title.

Northern Ireland Area

Titleholders at 30 June 2004

Fly: *vacant.* **Bantam:** *vacant.* **S.Bantam:** *vacant.* **Feather:** *vacant.* **S.Feather:** *vacant.* **Light:** Dafydd Carlin. **L.Welter:** *vacant.* **Welter:** *vacant.* **L.Middle:** *vacant.* **Middle:** *vacant.* **S.Middle:** *vacant.* **L.Heavy:** *vacant.* **Cruiser:** *vacant.* **Heavy:** *vacant.*

There were no title bouts held during 2003-2004.

Scottish Area

Titleholders at 30 June 2004

Fly: *vacant.* **Bantam:** *vacant.* **S.Bantam:** *vacant.* **Feather:** Brian Carr. **S.Feather:** *vacant.* **Light:** Martin Watson. **L.Welter:** *vacant.* **Welter:** Kevin McIntyre. **L.Middle:** *vacant.* **Middle:** *vacant.* **S.Middle:** *vacant.* **L.Heavy:** *vacant.* **Cruiser:** *vacant.* **Heavy:** *vacant.*

There were no title bouts held during 2003-2004

Southern Area

Titleholders at 30 June 2004

Fly: *vacant.* **Bantam:** *vacant.* **S.Bantam:** *vacant.* **Feather:** *vacant.* **S.Feather:** *vacant.* **Light:** Peter McDonagh. **L.Welter:** Francis Barrett. **Welter:** Chas Symonds. **L.Middle:** Gilbert Eastman. **Middle:** Allan Gray. **S.Middle:** *vacant.* **L.Heavy:** Andrew Lowe. **Cruiser:** Garry Delaney. **Heavy:** *vacant.*

| 25 July | David Walker W RSC 4 Spencer Fearon, Norwich (L.Middleweight Title Defence) |

1 August	Brett James W PTS 10 Sammy Smith, Bethnal Green (Vacant Welterweight Title)
1 August	Michael Sprott W RSC 1 Colin Kenna, Bethnal Green (Heavyweight Title Defence)
4 October	Gilbert Eastman W RSC 4 Spencer Fearon, Muswell Hill (Vacant L.Middleweight Title)
18 November	Brett James W PTS 10 Iain Eldridge, Bethnal Green (Welterweight Title Defence)
20 February	Allan Gray W PTS 10 Matthew Tait, Bethnal Green (Middleweight Title Defence)
7 April	Peter McDonagh W PTS 10 Jon Honney, Leicester Square (Vacant Lightweight Title)
16 April	Gilbert Eastman W RSC 5 Delroy Mellis, Bradford (L.Middleweight Title Defence)
25 June	Brett James L RSC 4 Chas Symonds, Bethnal Green (Welterweight Title Defence)

Between 1 July 2003 and 30 June 2004, Ian Napa (Fly), Graham Earl (Light) and Michael Sprott (Heavy) all relinquished their titles.

Welsh Area

Titleholders at 30 June 2004

Fly: *vacant.* **Bantam:** *vacant.* **S.Bantam:** *vacant.* **Feather:** *vacant.* **S.Feather:** *vacant.* **Light:** *vacant.* **L.Welter:** *vacant.* **Welter:** *vacant.* **L.Middle:** *vacant.* **Middle:** *vacant.* **S.Middle:** *vacant.* **L.Heavy:** *vacant.* **Cruiser:** *vacant.* **Heavy:** *vacant.*

Between 1 July 2003 and 30 June 2004, Jason Cook (L.Welter) and Jason Williams (Welter) both relinquished their titles. There were no title bouts held during 2003-2004.

Western Area

Titleholders at 30 June 2004

Fly: *vacant.* **Bantam:** *vacant.* **S.Bantam:** *vacant.* **Feather:** *vacant.* **S.Feather:** *vacant.* **Light:** *vacant.* **L.Welter:** *vacant.* **Welter:** *vacant.* **L.Middle:** *vacant.* **Middle:** *vacant.* **S.Middle:** Darren Dorrington. **L.Heavy:** *vacant.* **Cruiser:** *vacant.* **Heavy:** *vacant.*

Between 1 July 2003 and 30 June 2004, Frankie DeMilo (S.Bantam) forfeited his title due to moving his base outside the country. There were no title bouts held during 2003-2004

Prior to losing his Southern Area welterweight title to Chas Symonds, Brett James (right) made a successful defence when outpointing Sammy Smith   Les Clark

English Title Bouts During 2003-2004

Due to the fact that there is often a dearth of competition for certain weights at Area level, the BBBoC had long felt the need for an English title and, having taken the necessary steps, Matt Skelton and Mike Holden were matched to contest the innuagural English title contest on 18 September 2003. In addition, the Board, at the last AGM, introduced Celtic championships to accommodate boxers from Northern Ireland, Scotland and Wales.

Titleholders at 30 June 2004

Fly: *vacant.* **Bantam:** *vacant.* **S.Bantam:** *vacant.* **Feather:** Steve Foster. **S.Feather:** Roy Rutherford. **Light:** Danny Hunt. **L.Welter:** Young Muttley. **Welter:** Chris Saunders. **L.Middle:** Andrew Facey. **Middle:** Scott Dann. **S.Middle:** *vacant.* **L.Heavy:** Steven Spartacus. **Cruiser:** *vacant.* **Heavy:** *vacant.*

18 September	Matt Skelton W RSC 6 Mike Holden, Dagenham (Vacant Heavyweight Title)
2 October	Danny Hunt W PTS 10 Chill John, Liverpool (Vacant Lightweight Title)
6 November	Andrew Facey W PTS 10 Matthew Macklin, Dagenham (Vacant L.Middleweight Title)
14 November	David Haye W RSC 1 Tony Dowling, Bethnal Green (Vacant Cruiserweight Title). Haye relinquished title
28 November	Carl Froch W RSC 7 Alan Page, Derby (Vacant S.Middleweight Title). Froch relinquished title
11 December	Alan Bosworth W PTS 10 Stephen Smith, Bethnal Green (Vacant L.Welterweight Title). Bosworth relinquished title
11 December	Steven Spartacus W RSC 3 Scott Lansdowne, Bethnal Green (Vacant L.Heavyweight Title)
7 February	Matt Skelton W PTS 10 Julius Francis, Bethnal Green (Heavyweight Title Defence). Skelton relinquished title
7 February	Danny Hunt W PTS 10 Anthony Maynard, Bethnal Green (Lightweight Title Defence)
14 February	Roy Rutherford W RSC 4 Stephen Chinnock, Nottingham (Vacant S.Featherweight Title)
26 February	Steve Foster W RSC 6 Sean Hughes, Widnes (Vacant Featherweight Title)
3 April	Chris Saunders W RSC 1 Marcus Portman, Sheffield (Vacant Welterweight Title)
8 May	Scott Dann W RSC 3 Danny Thornton, Bristol (Vacant Middleweight Title)
8 May	Young Muttley W RSC 1 Sammy Smith, Bristol (Vacant L.Welterweight Title)

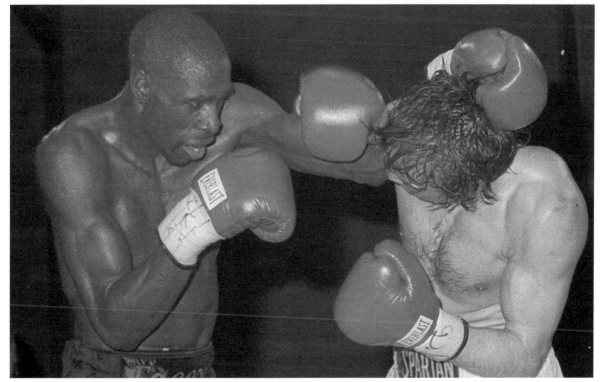

Andrew Facey (left) surprised many when outpointing the highly-touted Matthew Macklin to land the innaugural English light-middleweight title

Les Clark

British Title Bouts During 2003-2004

All of last season's title bouts are shown in date order within their weight divisions and give the contestants' respective weights, along with the scorecard if going to a decision. Every contest is summarised briefly and all referees are named.

Flyweight

Jason Booth (England) relinquished in December 2003 after winning the IBO championship on 20 September and deciding to concentrate on defending that title.

Bantamweight

Nicky Booth (England) forfeited in June 2004 after being convicted for criminal offences outside the ring.

S. Bantamweight

12 July 2003   Esham Pickering 8.10 (England) W RSC 4 Brian Carr 8.10 (Scotland), Braehead Arena, Renfrew. Referee: Howard Foster. Billed for the vacant title after Michael Alldis (England) retired in December 2002 following a car accident, Pickering ended the career of Carr, who announced his retirement after the contest. Pickering was also defending his Commonwealth crown. The game Scot had been outspeeded and outboxed before being dropped by a right cross in the third and then rescued by the referee on the 1.30 mark after Pickering had cut loose yet again. Pickering vacated in February 2004 to concentrate on the Commonwealth and European crowns.

16 April 2004   Michael Hunter 8.9 (England) W RSC 7 Mark Payne 8.8 (England), Borough Hall, Hartlepool. Referee: Mickey Vann. A new champion was crowned after Payne had been rescued by the referee at 2.08 of the seventh round, having come under intense pressure and was reeling around the ring defenceless. According to Simon Block, the BBBoC's General Secretary, it was one of the best fights he'd seen throughout the season, but was unfortunately not covered by television. Tit-for-tat for six rounds, it was after Payne had given his all that Hunter got on top, but it had been a great little battle.

Featherweight

22 November 2003   Roy Rutherford 8.13 (England) L PTS 12 Dazzo Williams 8.13½ (Wales), King's Hall, Belfast. Referee: Paul Thomas 114-115. In what was an extremely close contest, the referee plumped for Williams, while many others saw the champion retaining his title after appearing to control the pace. The men were certainly evenly matched and there would never be much between them. While the cleaner work came from Rutherford, picking his punches carefully, Williams matched it with aggression and spirited flurries, which obviously caught the eye of the referee.

28 February 2004   Dazzo Williams 8.13¼ (Wales) W PTS 12 Jamie McKeever 9.0 (England), The Recreation Centre, Bridgend. Referee: Ian John-Lewis 116-113.

Looking to regain the title, the unfortunate McKeever had his right eye almost closed shut from the second round on and finished the fight with much facial damage after bravely making it through to the final bell. Although unable to pick up many of the punches coming his way, the challenger was always looking to set up attacks, but the better quality came from Williams, who pressured his rival throughout.

2 June 2004   Dazzo Williams 8.13½ (Wales) W PTS 12 Roy Rutherford 8.13 (England), The Leisure Centre, Hereford. Referee: Richie Davies 117-112. Although he had to survive a few difficult moments during the middle of the contest, Williams had the better of Rutherford this time round, but both men could be congratulated for putting up a tremendous battle in what was rightly recognised as one of the 'Contests of the Year'. Both men suffered bouts of tiredness as they gave it their all, but neither wavered in their pursuit of the decision, which, ultimately, went to Williams by dint of quality shots landed, especially the right uppercut.

S. Featherweight

12 July 2003   Alex Arthur 9.4 (Scotland) W RSC 8 Willie Limond 9.3¾ (Scotland), Braehead Arena, Renfrew. Referee: Richie Davies. Limond started well, but the third round saw him staggered after being caught by heavy rights and he was never really in the contest after that, although showing his left-hand skills on a number of occasions. The damage had been done and although Arthur often left himself open the challenger, who was cut on the left eye in the fifth, lacked the power to take advantage. From then on the end was in sight and, whilst not being decked, Limond was being overpowered in the eighth to such a degree that the referee was forced to rescue him on the 1.51 mark.

25 October 2003   Alex Arthur 9.4 (Scotland) L RSC 5 Michael Gomez 9.4 (England), Meadowbank Stadium, Edinburgh. Referee: John Coyle. Arthur, who took three attempts to make the weight, never really got going in this one and was hurt early on before slumping to one of British boxing's biggest upsets at the hand of Gomez, thought by many to be past it. How wrong they were. Both men received eye damage in the third and it was noticeable that Gomez, looking to get to close quarters, was having no trouble finding the champion. In the fifth session, Gomez, despite having been hurt himself, dropped Arthur with a cracking left hook for three and then landed two tremendous rights that put the champion down again for another count of three, before the referee came to Arthur's rescue just as another right hand decked him yet again.

Lightweight

17 July 2003   Bobby Vanzie 9.9 (England) L PTS 12 Graham Earl 9.9 (England), Goresbrook Leisure Centre, Dagenham. Referee: Paul Thomas 114-116. Sticking to his game plan, Earl boxed exceedingly well and never really let Vanzie get set with damaging punches that could have turned the fight. At the final bell it was still too close for comfort, but Earl, despite being cut over the right eye in the ninth, had negated much of the champion's better work by getting into a rhythm from the halfway stage to pick up points from both hands and not allowing his rival any respite. Earl was stripped in mid-May 2004 after twice pulling out of a mandated rematch against Vanzie, but when Steve Murray, chosen to meet Vanzie for the vacant title, also pulled out, Earl readily obliged.

5 June 2004   Graham Earl 9.8¼ (England) W PTS 12 Bobby Vanzie 9.9 (England), York Hall, Bethnal Green, London, London. Referee: Terry O'Connor 115-114. Once again it was extremely tight, with Vanzie's work easier on the eye, but the result was the same. Right from the start, Earl, punching accurately with the knuckle part of the glove, busied himself, while Vanzie often posed, but the last three rounds all appeared to go the latter's way and no one would have complained had he received the decision. It was that tight.

L. Welterweight

Junior Witter (England) failed to defend during the period.

Welterweight

17 July 2003   David Barnes 10.4¾ (England) W PTS 12 Jimmy Vincent 10.6½ (England), Goresbrook Leisure Centre, Dagenham. Referee: John Keane 115-114. Billed for the vacant title after Neil Sinclair (Ireland) relinquished his belt in April 2003 in order to concentrate on getting a world championship opportunity, there were many who felt that the wrong man picked up the belt on the result. Certainly, Vincent, the underdog, was the busier of the two and for the first two thirds had carried the fight to Barnes, never giving him much chance to find a rhythm, and getting through to head and body with hurtful rights. Although Barnes, a southpaw, got himself back into the fight from the ninth onwards, it looked as though he had left it too late, but, following the decision, the word was that much of his early countering had been effective and that was the reason for the decision being in his favour.

13 December 2003   David Barnes 10.6½ (England) W RTD 8 Kevin McIntyre 10.5½ (Scotland), MEN Arena, Manchester. Referee: Larry O'Connell. Making the fight from the opening bell, McIntyre, also a southpaw, was going reasonably well for five rounds, despite being cut on

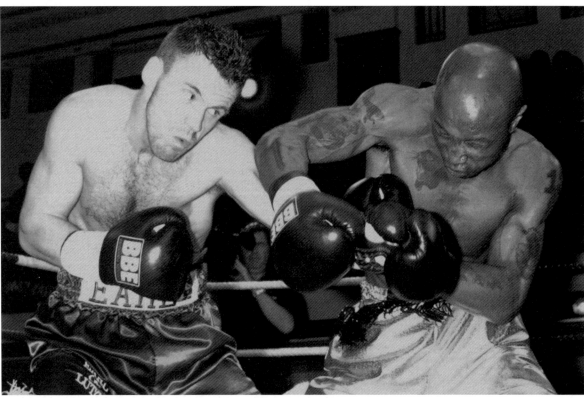

In their return contest, as in their first encounter involving the British lightweight title, it was the cleaner punching Earl (left) who impressed the referee

Les Clark

the left eye in the fourth, but in the sixth it became clear that Barnes had his challenger's measure. Right-lefts were doing the damage and, in the eighth, Barnes opened up to put his rival down for four before chopping him down again a few moments later, which resulted in the towel being thrown in on the 60 second mark.

3 April 2004   David Barnes 10.7 (England) W PTS 12 Glenn McClarnon 10.5$^{1}/_{4}$ (Northern Ireland), MEN Arena, Manchester. Referee: Paul Thomas 118-111. Surprisingly competititve, the challenger gave Barnes a real test, never taking a backward step and looking to make the latter fight every step of the way. However, by the ninth round Barnes had begun to pull away, targeting the body and making McClarnon miss. Although there were still some good exchanges, it was clear that the Irishman had begun to run out of ideas and the decision surprised no one.

L. Middleweight

18 October 2003   Jamie Moore 10.13$^{3}/_{4}$ (England) W CO 5 Gary Logan 10.13$^{1}/_{4}$ (England), MEN Arena, Manchester. Referee: Ian John-Lewis. Always in a position to get his southpaw punches off, Moore handed out a systematic beating, putting his rival down in both the second and the third, the latter knockdown being deemed to have gone low, for which a point was docked. At a later date, video evidence would show the punch to have been legal. Badly cut on the right eye in the fourth, it was just a matter of time before the brave Logan wilted and, with just 16 seconds of the fifth session remaining, he was counted out after being decked from a big left hook, following a battery of blows to head and body. This was also a defence of Moore's Commonwealth title.

22 November 2003   Jamie Moore 10.13$^{1}/_{2}$ (England) W RSC 7 Andrew Facey 10.13$^{3}/_{4}$ (England), King's Hall, Belfast. Referee: Dave Parris. Down twice in the second, once in the fifth, once in the sixth and yet again a round later, the referee came to Facey's rescue at 1.24 of the seventh after he was taking punches without reply and looking disorganised. Defending both the British and Commonwealth belts, Moore himself went down in the sixth, but got up to dominate once more as the challenger's leaky defence continued to let him down.

Middleweight

Howard Eastman (England) relinquished in May 2004 to concentrate on his European crown and securing a world title shot.

S. Middleweight

22 November 2003   Tony Dodson 11.12$^{1}/_{4}$ (England) W RSC 11 Allan Foster 11.13 (Scotland), King's Hall, Belfast. Referee: John Coyle. Dodson and Foster were matched to contest the vacant title after Matthew Barney (England) relinquished on winning the WBU light-heavyweight crown on 11 October 2003. Cut over the right eye in the first minute, didn't deter Foster and he did good work, especially on the inside, and proved worthy of the

challenge despite the fact that he had never travelled beyond six rounds. Dodson, who was also cut when a head clash in the third left him with damage on the left eye, eventually found his way through what had become a battle of attrition. In the 11th, after a big left hook, followed up by a whole range of punches, sent Foster down for an eight count, he was quickly rescued by the referee on the 0.57 marker when it was apparent that he couldn't defend himself.

L. Heavyweight

12 May 2004   Peter Oboh 12.4 (England, via Nigeria) W RTD 10 Andrew Lowe 12.5 (England), Rivermead Leisure Centre, Reading. Referee: Mark Green. It didn't take long for the southpaw champion to work Lowe out, his longer reach and punching power giving him a big edge. Cut over the left eye in the fourth, taking a sustained beating from head to body, the brave Lowe tried in vain, but was put down before the round ended. Battling away to get into the eighth, Lowe was cut over the other eye and knocked down by a left uppercut, but he came out for the ninth, only to be floored again. Somehow he got through the tenth, but that was it for the night as his corner wisely retired him on his stool. This was also a defence of Oboh's Commonwealth title.

Cruiserweight

5 September 2003   Mark Hobson 13.7$^{3}/_{4}$ (England) W PTS 12 Robert Norton 13.7$^{3}/_{4}$ (England), Ponds Forge Arena, Sheffield. Referee: Marcus McDonnell 118-110. Hobson and Norton were matched to contest the vacant title as well as Hobson's Commonwealth crown after Bruce Scott (England) was stripped in April 2003, having failed to defend within the expected period. With height and reach over his southpaw opponent, Hobson put his man down in the second and sixth rounds and generally held sway, despite being badly hurt on a few occasions by the dangerous Norton and badly cut by the left eye in the eighth. With the cut worsening, Norton's big chance came in the latter stages, but he was unable to take advantage and Hobson was given the verdict by a clear margin.

13 March 2004   Mark Hobson 13.8 (England) W RSC 3 Tony Moran 13.6$^{1}/_{4}$ (England), The Leisure Centre, Huddersfield, Referee: John Keane. With both the Commonwealth and British titles on the line, this was Moran's big chance, but, despite his excellent win over Matthew Ellis, he had never been beyond six rounds and was ultimately proved to be out of his league, being floored at the end of the first and second before being flattened in the third. To his credit, Moran was always in Hobson's face and, while the final punch was chilling (the referee didn't take up the count, stopping the fight on the 2.10 mark), he can take pride from the fact that he hurt the champion on more than one occasion.

27 May 2004   Mark Hobson 13.8 (England) W RSC 6 Lee Swaby 13.7$^{3}/_{4}$ (England), The Leisure Centre, Huddersfield. Referee: Terry O'Connor. Contested for the

British and Commonwealth titles, the southpaw Swaby, who had twice put Hobson down in a losing eliminator two years earlier, was expected to go close. Unfortunately, for him, revenge was not around the corner and he went down to a stoppage defeat at 1.02 of the sixth when he was under pressure and not fighting back. This would be the final British cruiserweight title fight held at 13 stone, eight pounds as the BBBoC are raising the limit to 14 stone, four pounds to fall into line with the rest of the world.

Heavyweight

26 September 2003 Danny Williams 18.3$\frac{1}{2}$ (England) W RSC 5 Michael Sprott 16.4$\frac{3}{4}$ (England), Rivermead Leisure Centre, Reading. Referee: Terry O'Connor. Outboxed for close on four rounds, Williams let loose a low blow for which he received a warning, before landing heavily in the nether regions and then putting Sprott down for six from smashing right hand to the jaw prior to the bell ending the fourth. Having been warned to keep his punches up at the start of the fifth, Williams again went low and while Sprott was looking to the referee for help the champion landed a big left hook, putting Sprott down heavily. The referee immediately called the fight off with 19 seconds of the round having lapsed, leaving the crowd incensed when Williams was announced as the winner and not disqualified. Both the British and Commonwealth titles were on the line.

24 January 2004 Danny Williams 18.12 (England) L PTS 12 Michael Sprott 17.1 (England), The Conference Centre, Wembley. Referee: Dave Parris 114-115. An extremely controversial verdict saw Williams lose his British and Commonwealth titles to his arch-rival, Sprott, in what was a rematch, following the uproar over their previous contest. This time, it was almost uneventful, with neither man doing an awful lot, although Sprott, whose left eye swelled up in the 11th, landed the better shots, in the seventh and eighth rounds, but then switched off the last three sessions when he should have been looking to make sure of the win.

24 April 2004 Michael Sprott 16.9 (England) L CO 12 Matt Skelton 17.12 (England), Rivermead Leisure Centre, Reading. Referee: Richie Davies. Defending his British and Commonwealth titles, Sprott was up against a tough newcomer in Skelton, but made a fair start and kept going, at times giving the challenger a boxing lesson. There had been no knockdowns, but Skelton had forced the fight and the referee had him four rounds ahead coming up to the final round. Then it all happened. Straight from the bell, Sprott was battered to the canvas as punch after punch rained in and he was counted out on the 56 second mark, in the act of rising as Skelton became champion after less than two years of boxing professionally – a record.

Danny Williams, who controversially lost his British and Commonwealth titles to Michael Sprott (left) last January, has since redeemed himself with a marvellous win over Mike Tyson   Les Clark

Lord Lonsdale Challenge Belts: Outright Winners

Outright Winners of the National Sporting Club's Challenge Belt, 1909-1935 (21)

Under pressure from other promoters with bigger venues, and in an effort to sustain their monopoly – having controlled championship fights in Britain up until that point in time – the National Sporting Club launched the belt in 1909. They did so on the proviso that there should be eight weight divisions – fly, bantam, feather, light, welter, middle, light-heavy, and heavy – and that to win a belt outright a champion must score three title-match victories at the same weight, but not necessarily consecutively. Worth a substantial amount of money, and carrying a £1 a week pension from the age of 50, the President of the NSC, Lord Lonsdale, donated the first of 22 belts struck. Known as the Lonsdale Belt, despite the inscription reading: 'The National Sporting Club's Challenge Belt', the first man to put a notch on a belt was Freddie Welsh, who outpointed Johnny Summers for the lightweight title on 8 November 1909, while Jim Driscoll became the first man to win one outright. The record time for winning the belt is held by Jim Higgins (279 days).

FLYWEIGHT	Jimmy Wilde; Jackie Brown
BANTAMWEIGHT	Digger Stanley; Joe Fox; Jim Higgins; Johnny Brown; Dick Corbett; Johnny King
FEATHERWEIGHT	Jim Driscoll; Tancy Lee; Johnny Cuthbert; Nel Tarleton
LIGHTWEIGHT	Freddie Welsh
WELTERWEIGHT	Johnny Basham; Jack Hood
MIDDLEWEIGHT	Pat O'Keefe; Len Harvey; Jock McAvoy
L. HEAVYWEIGHT	Dick Smith
HEAVYWEIGHT	Bombardier Billy Wells; Jack Petersen

Note: Both Dick Corbett and Johnny King – with one notch apiece on the 'special' British Empire Lonsdale Belt that was struck in 1933 and later presented to the winner of the Tommy Farr v Joe Louis fight – were allowed to keep their Lonsdale Belts with just two notches secured; Freddie Welsh, also with two notches, was awarded a belt due to his inability to defend because of the First World War; the first bantam belt came back into circulation and was awarded to Johnny Brown; Al Foreman, with just one notch on the second lightweight belt, took it back to Canada with him without the consent of the BBBoC; while the second light-heavy belt was awarded to Jack Smith of Worcester for winning a novices heavyweight competition. Having emigrated to New Zealand, Smith later presented the visiting Her Majesty The Queen with the belt and it now hangs in the BBBoC's offices.

Outright Winners of the BBBoC Lord Lonsdale Challenge Belt, 1936-2004 (110)

Re-introduced by the British Boxing Board of Control as the Lord Lonsdale Challenge Belt, but of less intrinsic value – Benny Lynch's eight-round win over Pat Palmer (16 September 1936 at Shawfield Park, Glasgow) got the new version underway – Eric Boon became the first man to win one outright, in 1939, following victories over Dave Crowley (2) and Arthur Danahar. Since those early days, six further weight divisions have been added and, following on from Henry Cooper's feat of winning three Lonsdale Belts outright, on 10 June 1981 the BBBoC's rules and regulations were amended to read that no boxer shall receive more than one belt as his own property, in any one weight division. From 1 September 1999, any boxer putting a notch on a Lonsdale Belt for the first time will require three more notches at the same weight before he can call the belt his own. However, men who already have a notch on the Lonsdale Belt prior to 1 September 1999 can contest it under the former ruling of three winning championship contests at the same weight. Incidentally, the fastest of the modern belt winners is Ryan Rhodes (90 days), while Chris and Kevin Finnegan are the only brothers to have each won a belt outright.

FLYWEIGHT	Jackie Paterson; Terry Allen; Walter McGowan; John McCluskey; Hugh Russell; Charlie Magri; Pat Clinton; Robbie Regan; Francis Ampofo; Ady Lewis
BANTAMWEIGHT	Johnny King; Peter Keenan (2); Freddie Gilroy; Alan Rudkin; Johnny Owen; Billy Hardy; Drew Docherty; Nicky Booth
S. BANTAMWEIGHT	Richie Wenton; Michael Brodie; Michael Alldis
FEATHERWEIGHT	Nel Tarleton; Ronnie Clayton (2); Charlie Hill; Howard Winstone (2); Evan Armstrong; Pat Cowdell; Robert Dickie; Paul Hodkinson; Colin McMillan; Sean Murphy; Jonjo Irwin
S. FEATHERWEIGHT	Jimmy Anderson; John Doherty; Floyd Havard; Charles Shepherd; Michael Gomez
LIGHTWEIGHT	Eric Boon; Billy Thompson; Joe Lucy; Dave Charnley; Maurice Cullen; Ken Buchanan; Jim Watt; George Feeney; Tony Willis; Carl Crook; Billy Schwer; Michael Ayers; Bobby Vanzie

L. WELTERWEIGHT	Joey Singleton; Colin Power; Clinton McKenzie; Lloyd Christie; Andy Holligan; Ross Hale
WELTERWEIGHT	Ernie Roderick; Wally Thom; Brian Curvis (2); Ralph Charles; Colin Jones; Lloyd Honeyghan; Kirkland Laing; Del Bryan; Geoff McCreesh; Derek Roche; Neil Sinclair
L. MIDDLEWEIGHT	Maurice Hope; Jimmy Batten; Pat Thomas; Prince Rodney; Andy Till; Robert McCracken; Ryan Rhodes; Ensley Bingham
MIDDLEWEIGHT	Pat McAteer; Terry Downes; Johnny Pritchett; Bunny Sterling; Alan Minter; Kevin Finnegan; Roy Gumbs; Tony Sibson; Herol Graham; Neville Brown; Howard Eastman
S. MIDDLEWEIGHT	Sammy Storey; David Starie
L. HEAVYWEIGHT	Randy Turpin; Chic Calderwood; Chris Finnegan; Bunny Johnson; Tom Collins; Dennis Andries; Tony Wilson; Crawford Ashley
CRUISERWEIGHT	Johnny Nelson; Terry Dunstan; Bruce Scott
HEAVYWEIGHT	Henry Cooper (3); Horace Notice; Lennox Lewis; Julius Francis; Danny Williams

Note: Walter McGowan and Charlie Magri, with one notch apiece, kept their belts under the three years/no available challengers' ruling, while Johnny King, with two notches, was awarded the belt on the grounds that the Second World War stopped him from making further defences. Incidentally, King and Nel Tarleton are the only men to have won both the NSC and BBBoC belts outright.

Howard Eastman (right), the latest outright winner of the Lonsdale middleweight belt, is seen here on his way to putting a notch on a second belt by beating Scott Dann in April 2003   Les Clark

British Champions Since Gloves, 1878-2004

The listings below show the tenure of all British champions at each weight since gloves (two ounces or more) were introduced to British rings under Queensberry Rules. Although Charley Davis (147 lbs) had beaten Ted Napper (140 lbs) with gloves in 1873, we start with Denny Harrington, who defeated George Rooke for both the English and world middleweight titles in London on 12 March 1878. We also make a point of ignoring competition winners, apart from Anthony Diamond who beat Dido Plumb for the middles title over 12 rounds, basically because full championship conditions or finish fights of three-minute rounds were not applied. Another point worth bearing in mind, is that prior to the 1880s there were only five weights – heavy, middle, light, feather and bantam. Anything above 154 lbs, the middleweight limit, was classified a heavyweight contest, whereas lightweight, feather and bantamweight poundages were much looser. Therefore, to put things into current perspective, in many cases we have had to ascertain the actual poundage of fighters concerned and relate them to the modern weight classes. Another point worth remembering is that men born outside Britain who won international titles in this country, are not recorded for fear of added confusion and, although many of the champions or claimants listed before 1909 were no more than English titleholders, having fought for the 'championship of England', for our purposes they carry the 'British' label.

Prior to 1909, the year that the Lord Lonsdale Challenge Belt was introduced and weight classes subsequently standardised, poundages within divisions could vary quite substantially, thus enabling men fighting at different weights to claim the same 'title' at the same time. A brief history of the weight fluctuations between 1891 and 1909, shows:

Bantamweight With the coming of gloves, the division did not really take off until Nunc Wallace established himself at 112 lbs on beating (small) Bill Goode after nine rounds in London on 12 March 1889. Later, with Wallace fighting above the weight, Billy Plimmer was generally recognised as the country's leading eight stoner, following victories over Charles Mansford and Jem Stevens, and became accepted as world champion when George Dixon, the number one in America's eyes, gradually increased his weight. In 1895, Pedlar Palmer took the British title at 112 lbs, but by 1900 he had developed into a 114 pounder. Between 1902 and 1904, Joe Bowker defended regularly at 116 lbs and in 1909 the NSC standardised the weight at 118 lbs, even though the USA continued for a short while to accept only 116 lbs.

Featherweight Between 1886 and 1895, one of the most prestigious championship belts in this country was fought for at 126 lbs and, although George Dixon was recognised in the USA as world featherweight champion – gradually moving from 114 to 122 lbs – no major international contests took place in Britain during the above period at his weight. It was only in 1895, when Fred Johnson took the British title at 120 lbs, losing it to Ben Jordan two years later, that we came into line with the USA. Ben Jordan became an outstanding champion who, between 1898 and 1899, was seen by the NSC as world champion at 120 lbs. However, first Harry Greenfield, then Jabez White and Will Curley, continued to claim the 126 lbs version of the British title and it was only in 1900, when Jack Roberts beat Curley, that the weight limit was finally standardised at nine stone.

Lightweight Outstanding champions often carried their weights as they grew in size. A perfect example of this was Dick Burge, the British lightweight champion from 1891-1901, who gradually increased from 134 to 144 lbs, while still maintaining his right to the title. It was not until 1902 that Jabez White brought the division into line with the USA. Later, both White, and then Goldswain, carried their weight up to 140 lbs and it was left to Johnny Summers to set the current limit of 135 lbs.

Welterweight The presence of Dick Burge fighting from 134 to 144 lbs plus up until 1900, explains quite adequately why the welterweight division, although very popular in the USA, did not take off in this country until 1902. The championship was contested between 142 and 146 lbs in those days and was not really supported by the NSC, but by 1909 with their backing it finally became established at 147 lbs.

On 8 September 1970, Bunny Sterling became the first immigrant to win a British title under the ten-year residential ruling, while earlier, on 28 June 1948, Dick Turpin won the British middleweight title and, in doing so, became the first coloured fighter to win the title, thus breaking down the so-called 'colour bar'.

Note that the Lonsdale Belt notches (title bout wins) relate to NSC, 1909-1935, and BBBoC, 1936-2004.

Champions in **bold** are accorded national recognition.

*Undefeated champions (Does not include men who forfeited titles).

Title Holder	Lonsdale Belt Notches	Tenure	Title Holder	Lonsdale Belt Notches	Tenure	Title Holder	Lonsdale Belt Notches	Tenure
Flyweight (112 lbs)			**Percy Jones**	1	1914	**Joe Symonds**	1	1915-1916
Sid Smith		1911	Joe Symonds		1914	**Jimmy Wilde***	3	1916-1923
Sid Smith	1	1911-1913	**Tancy Lee**	1	1914-1915	**Elky Clark***	2	1924-1927
Bill Ladbury		1913-1914	Jimmy Wilde		1914-1915	**Johnny Hill***	1	1927-1929

Title Holder	Lonsdale Belt Notches	Tenure	Title Holder	Lonsdale Belt Notches	Tenure	Title Holder	Lonsdale Belt Notches	Tenure
Jackie Brown		1929-1930	Jackie Paterson	2	1947-1949	George McKenzie	2	1924-1925
Bert Kirby	1	1930-1931	Stan Rowan*	1	1949	Johnny Curley	2	1925-1927
Jackie Brown	3	1931-1935	Danny O'Sullivan	1	1949-1951	Johnny Cuthbert	1	1927-1928
Benny Lynch*	2	1935-1938	Peter Keenan	3	1951-1953	Harry Corbett	1	1928-1929
Jackie Paterson	4	1939-1948	John Kelly	1	1953-1954	Johnny Cuthbert	2	1929-1931
Rinty Monaghan*	1	1948-1950	Peter Keenan	3	1954-1959	Nel Tarleton	1	1931-1932
Terry Allen	1	1951-1952	Freddie Gilroy*	4	1959-1963	Seaman Tommy Watson	2	1932-1934
Teddy Gardner*	1	1952	Johnny Caldwell	1	1964-1965	Nel Tarleton	2	1934-1936
Terry Allen	2	1952-1954	Alan Rudkin	1	1965-1966	Johnny McGrory	1	1936-1938
Dai Dower*	1	1955-1957	Walter McGowan	1	1966-1968	Jim Spider Kelly	1	1938-1939
Frankie Jones	2	1957-1960	Alan Rudkin*	4	1968-1972	Johnny Cusick	1	1939-1940
Johnny Caldwell*	1	1960-1961	Johnny Clark*	1	1973-1974	Nel Tarleton*	3	1940-1947
Jackie Brown	1	1962-1963	Dave Needham	1	1974-1975	Ronnie Clayton	6	1947-1954
Walter McGowan*	1	1963-1966	Paddy Maguire	1	1975-1977	Sammy McCarthy	1	1954-1955
John McCluskey*	3	1967-1977	Johnny Owen*	4	1977-1980	Billy Spider Kelly	1	1955-1956
Charlie Magri*	1	1977-1981	John Feeney	1	1981-1983	Charlie Hill	3	1956-1959
Kelvin Smart	1	1982-1984	Hugh Russell	1	1983	Bobby Neill	1	1959-1960
Hugh Russell*	3	1984-1985	Davy Larmour	1	1983	Terry Spinks	2	1960-1961
Duke McKenzie*	2	1985-1986	John Feeney	1	1983-1985	Howard Winstone*	7	1961-1969
Dave Boy McAuley*	1	1986-1988	Ray Gilbody	2	1985-1987	Jimmy Revie	2	1969-1971
Pat Clinton*	3	1988-1991	Billy Hardy*	5	1987-1991	Evan Armstrong	2	1971-1972
Robbie Regan	1	1991	Joe Kelly	1	1992	Tommy Glencross	1	1972-1973
Francis Ampofo	1	1991	Drew Docherty	4	1992-1997	Evan Armstrong*	2	1973-1975
Robbie Regan*	2	1991-1992	Paul Lloyd	2	1997-1999	Vernon Sollas	1	1975-1977
Francis Ampofo	3	1992-1996	Noel Wilders*	2	1999-2000	Alan Richardson	2	1977-1978
Mickey Cantwell*	1	1996-1997	Ady Lewis	1	2000	Dave Needham	2	1978-1979
Ady Lewis*	3	1997-1998	Tommy Waite	1	2000	Pat Cowdell*	3	1979-1982
Damaen Kelly	1	1999	Nicky Booth	5	2000-2004	Steve Sims*	1	1982-1983
Keith Knox	1	1999				Barry McGuigan*	2	1983-1986
Jason Booth	2	1999-	**S. Bantamweight (122 lbs)**			Robert Dickie	3	1986-1988
			Richie Wenton*	3	1994-1996	Peter Harris	1	1988
Bantamweight (118 lbs)			Michael Brodie*	3	1997-1999	Paul Hodkinson*	3	1988-1990
Nunc Wallace*		1889-1891	Patrick Mullings	1	1999	Sean Murphy	2	1990-1991
Billy Plimmer		1891-1895	Drew Docherty*	1	1999	Gary de Roux	1	1991
Tom Gardner		1892	Michael Alldis	3	1999-2001	Colin McMillan*	3	1991-1992
Willie Smith		1892-1896	Patrick Mullings	1	2001	John Davison*	1	1992-1993
Nunc Wallace		1893-1895	Michael Alldis*	1	2002	Sean Murphy	1	1993
George Corfield		1893-1896	Esham Pickering*	1	2003-2004	Duke McKenzie*	1	1993-1994
Pedlar Palmer		1895-1900	Michael Hunter	1	2004-	Billy Hardy*	1	1994
Billy Plimmer		1896-1898				Michael Deveney	1	1995
Harry Ware		1899-1900	**Featherweight (126 lbs)**			Jonjo Irwin	2	1995-1996
Harry Ware		1900-1902	Bill Baxter		1884-1891	Colin McMillan	1	1996-1997
Andrew Tokell		1901-1902	Harry Overton		1890-1891	Paul Ingle*	3	1997-1998
Jim Williams		1902	Billy Reader		1891-1892	Jonjo Irwin*	2	1998-1999
Andrew Tokell		1902	Fred Johnson		1891-1895	Gary Thornhill	1	2000
Harry Ware		1902	Harry Spurden		1892-1895	Scott Harrison*	3	2001-2002
Joe Bowker		1902-1910	Jack Fitzpatrick		1895-1897	Jamie McKeever	1	2003
Owen Moran		1905-1907	Fred Johnson		1895-1897	Roy Rutherford	1	2003
Digger Stanley		1906-1910	Harry Greenfield		1896-1899	Dazzo Williams	3	2003-
Digger Stanley	2	1910-1913	Ben Jordan*		1897-1900			
Bill Beynon	1	1913	Jabez White		1899-1900	**S. Featherweight (130 lbs)**		
Digger Stanley	1	1913-1914	Will Curley		1900-1901	Jimmy Anderson*	3	1968-1970
Curley Walker*	1	1914-1915	Jack Roberts		1901-1902	John Doherty	1	1986
Joe Fox*	3	1915-1917	Will Curley		1902-1903	Pat Cowdell	1	1986
Tommy Noble	1	1918-1919	Ben Jordan*		1902-1905	Najib Daho	1	1986-1987
Walter Ross*	1	1919-1920	Joe Bowker		1905	Pat Cowdell	1	1987-1988
Jim Higgins	3	1920-1922	Johnny Summers		1906	Floyd Havard	1	1988-1989
Tommy Harrison		1922-1923	Joe Bowker		1905-1906	John Doherty	1	1989-1990
Bugler Harry Lake	1	1923	Jim Driscoll		1906-1907	Joey Jacobs	1	1990
Johnny Brown	3	1923-1928	Spike Robson		1906-1907	Hugh Forde	1	1990
Alf Pattenden	2	1928-1929	Jim Driscoll*	3	1907-1913	Kevin Pritchard	1	1990-1991
Johnny Brown		1928	Spike Robson		1907-1910	Robert Dickie	1	1991
Teddy Baldock		1928-1929	Ted Kid Lewis*	1	1913-1914	Sugar Gibiliru	1	1991
Teddy Baldock*	1	1929-1931	Llew Edwards*	1	1915-1917	John Doherty	1	1991-1992
Dick Corbett	1	1931-1932	Charlie Hardcastle	1	1917	Michael Armstrong	1	1992
Johnny King	1	1932-1934	Tancy Lee*	3	1917-1919	Neil Haddock	2	1992-1994
Dick Corbett*	1	1934	Mike Honeyman	2	1920-1921	Floyd Havard*	3	1994-1995
Johnny King	1+2	1935-1947	Joe Fox*	1	1921-1922	P. J. Gallagher	2	1996-1997

Title Holder	Lonsdale Belt Notches	Tenure
Charles Shepherd	3	1997-1999
Michael Gomez*	5	1999-2002
Alex Arthur	3	2002-2003
Michael Gomez	1	2003-

Lightweight (135 lbs)

Title Holder	Lonsdale Belt Notches	Tenure
Dick Burge		1891-1897
Harry Nickless		1891-1894
Tom Causer		1894-1897
Tom Causer		1897
Dick Burge*		1897-1901
Jabez White		1902-1906
Jack Goldswain		1906-1908
Johnny Summers		1908-1909
Freddie Welsh	1	1909-1911
Matt Wells	1	1911-1912
Freddie Welsh*	1	1912-1919
Bob Marriott*	1	1919-1920
Ernie Rice	1	1921-1922
Seaman Nobby Hall		1922-1923
Harry Mason		1923-1924
Ernie Izzard	2	1924-1925
Harry Mason		1924-1925
Harry Mason*	1	1925-1928
Sam Steward		1928-1929
Fred Webster		1929-1930
Al Foreman*	1	1930-1932
Johnny Cuthbert		1932-1934
Harry Mizler		1934
Jackie Kid Berg		1934-1936
Jimmy Walsh	1	1936-1938
Dave Crowley	1	1938
Eric Boon	3	1938-1944
Ronnie James*	1	1944-1947
Billy Thompson	3	1947-1951
Tommy McGovern	1	1951-1952
Frank Johnson	1	1952-1953
Joe Lucy	1	1953-1955
Frank Johnson	1	1955-1956
Joe Lucy	2	1956-1957
Dave Charnley*	3	1957-1965
Maurice Cullen	4	1965-1968
Ken Buchanan*	2	1968-1971
Willie Reilly*	1	1972
Jim Watt	1	1972-1973
Ken Buchanan*	1	1973-1974
Jim Watt*	2	1975-1977
Charlie Nash*	1	1978-1979
Ray Cattouse	2	1980-1982
George Feeney*	3	1982-1985
Tony Willis	3	1985-1987
Alex Dickson	1	1987-1988
Steve Boyle	2	1988-1990
Carl Crook	5	1990-1992
Billy Schwer	1	1992-1993
Paul Burke	1	1993
Billy Schwer*	2	1993-1995
Michael Ayers*	5	1995-1997
Wayne Rigby	2	1998
Bobby Vanzie	5	1998-2003
Graham Earl	1	2003-2004
Graham Earl	1	2004-

L. Welterweight (140 lbs)

Title Holder	Lonsdale Belt Notches	Tenure
Des Rea	1	1968-1969
Vic Andreetti*	2	1969-1970
Des Morrison	1	1973-1974
Pat McCormack	1	1974
Joey Singleton	3	1974-1976
Dave Boy Green*	1	1976-1977
Colin Power*	2	1977-1978
Clinton McKenzie	1	1978-1979
Colin Power	1	1979
Clinton McKenzie	5	1979-1984
Terry Marsh*	1	1984-1986
Tony Laing*	1	1986
Tony McKenzie	2	1986-1987
Lloyd Christie	3	1987-1989
Clinton McKenzie*	1	1989
Pat Barrett*	2	1989-1990
Tony Ekubia	1	1990-1991
Andy Holligan	3	1991-1994
Ross Hale	4	1994-1995
Paul Ryan	1	1995-1996
Andy Holligan*	1	1996-1997
Mark Winters	2	1997-1998
Jason Rowland*	2	1998-2000
Ricky Hatton*	1	2000-2001
Junior Witter	1	2002-

Welterweight (147 lbs)

Title Holder	Lonsdale Belt Notches	Tenure
Charlie Allum		1903-1904
Charlie Knock		1904-1906
Curly Watson		1906-1910
Young Joseph		1908-1910
Young Joseph	1	1910-1911
Arthur Evernden		1911-1912
Johnny Summers		1912
Johnny Summers	2	1912-1914
Tom McCormick		1914
Matt Wells		1914
Johnny Basham	3	1914-1920
Matt Wells		1914-1919
Ted Kid Lewis		1920-1924
Tommy Milligan*		1924-1925
Hamilton Johnny Brown		1925
Harry Mason		1925-1926
Jack Hood*	3	1926-1934
Harry Mason		1934
Pat Butler*		1934-1936
Dave McCleave		1936
Jake Kilrain	1	1936-1939
Ernie Roderick	5	1939-1948
Henry Hall	1	1948-1949
Eddie Thomas	2	1949-1951
Wally Thom	1	1951-1952
Cliff Curvis*	1	1952-1953
Wally Thom	2	1953-1956
Peter Waterman*	2	1956-1958
Tommy Molloy	2	1958-1960
Wally Swift	1	1960
Brian Curvis*	7	1960-1966
Johnny Cooke	2	1967-1968
Ralph Charles*	3	1968-1972
Bobby Arthur	1	1972-1973
John H. Stracey*	1	1973-1975
Pat Thomas	2	1975-1976
Henry Rhiney	2	1976-1979
Kirkland Laing	1	1979-1980
Colin Jones*	3	1980-1982
Lloyd Honeyghan*	2	1983-1985
Kostas Petrou	1	1985
Sylvester Mittee	1	1985
Lloyd Honeyghan*	1	1985-1986
Kirkland Laing	4	1987-1991
Del Bryan	2	1991-1992
Gary Jacobs*	2	1992-1993
Del Bryan	4	1993-1995
Chris Saunders	1	1995-1996
Kevin Lueshing	1	1996-1997
Geoff McCreesh*	4	1997-1999
Derek Roche	3	1999-2000
Harry Dhami	3	2000-2001
Neil Sinclair*	4	2001-2003
David Barnes	3	2003-

L. Middleweight (154 lbs)

Title Holder	Lonsdale Belt Notches	Tenure
Larry Paul	2	1973-1974
Maurice Hope*	3	1974-1977
Jimmy Batten	3	1977-1979
Pat Thomas	3	1979-1981
Herol Graham*	2	1981-1983
Prince Rodney*	1	1983-1984
Jimmy Cable	2	1984-1985
Prince Rodney	2	1985-1986
Chris Pyatt*	1	1986
Lloyd Hibbert*	1	1987
Gary Cooper	1	1988
Gary Stretch	2	1988-1990
Wally Swift Jnr	2	1991-1992
Andy Till	3	1992-1994
Robert McCracken*	3	1994-1995
Ensley Bingham*	2	1996
Ryan Rhodes*	3	1996-1997
Ensley Bingham	3	1997-1999
Wayne Alexander*	2	2000-2003
Jamie Moore	3	2003-

Middleweight (160 lbs)

Title Holder	Lonsdale Belt Notches	Tenure
Denny Harrington		1878-1880
William Sheriff*		1880-1883
Bill Goode		1887-1890
Toff Wall*		1890
Ted Pritchard		1890-1895
Ted White		1893-1895
Ted White*		1895-1896
Anthony Diamond*		1898
Dick Burge*		1898-1900
Jack Palmer		1902-1903
Charlie Allum		1905-1906
Pat O'Keefe		1906
Tom Thomas	1	1906-1910
Jim Sullivan*	1	1910-1912
Jack Harrison*	1	1912-1913
Pat O'Keefe	2	1914-1916
Bandsman Jack Blake	1	1916-1918
Pat O'Keefe*	1	1918-1919
Ted Kid Lewis		1920-1921
Tom Gummer	1	1920-1921
Gus Platts		1921
Johnny Basham		1921
Ted Kid Lewis	2	1921-1923
Johnny Basham		1921
Roland Todd		1923-1925
Roland Todd		1925-1927
Tommy Milligan	1	1926-1928
Frank Moody		1927-1928
Alex Ireland		1928-1929
Len Harvey	5	1929-1933
Jock McAvoy	3+2	1933-1944
Ernie Roderick	1	1945-1946
Vince Hawkins	1	1946-1948
Dick Turpin	2	1948-1950
Albert Finch	1	1950

Title Holder	Lonsdale Belt Notches	Tenure
Randy Turpin*	1	1950-1954
Johnny Sullivan	1	1954-1955
Pat McAteer*	3	1955-1958
Terry Downes	1	1958-1959
John Cowboy McCormack	1	1959
Terry Downes	2	1959-1962
George Aldridge	1	1962-1963
Mick Leahy	1	1963-1964
Wally Swift	1	1964-1965
Johnny Pritchett*	4	1965-1969
Les McAteer	1	1969-1970
Mark Rowe	1	1970
Bunny Sterling	4	1970-1974
Kevin Finnegan*	1	1974
Bunny Sterling*	1	1975
Alan Minter	3	1975-1977
Kevin Finnegan	1	1977
Alan Minter*	1	1977-1978
Tony Sibson	1	1979
Kevin Finnegan*	1	1979-1980
Roy Gumbs	3	1981-1983
Mark Kaylor	1	1983-1984
Tony Sibson*	1	1984
Herol Graham*	1	1985-1986
Brian Anderson	1	1986-1987
Tony Sibson*	1	1987-1988
Herol Graham	4	1988-1992
Frank Grant	2	1992-1993
Neville Brown	6	1993-1998
Glenn Catley*	1	1998
Howard Eastman*	4	1998-2004

S. Middleweight (168 lbs)

Title Holder	Lonsdale Belt Notches	Tenure
Sammy Storey	2	1989-1990
James Cook*	1	1990-1991
Fidel Castro	2	1991-1992
Henry Wharton*	1	1992-1993
James Cook	1	1993-1994
Cornelius Carr*	1	1994
Ali Forbes	1	1995
Sammy Storey*	1	1995
Joe Calzaghe*	2	1995-1997
David Starie	1	1997
Dean Francis*	2	1997-1998
David Starie*	5	1998-2003
Matthew Barney*	1	2003
Tony Dodson	1	2003-

L. Heavyweight (175lbs)

Title Holder	Lonsdale Belt Notches	Tenure
Dennis Haugh		1913-1914
Dick Smith	2	1914-1916
Harry Reeve*	1	1916-1917
Dick Smith*	1	1918-1919
Boy McCormick*	1	1919-1921
Jack Bloomfield*	1	1922-1924
Tom Berry	1	1925-1927
Gipsy Daniels*	1	1927
Frank Moody	1	1927-1929
Harry Crossley	1	1929-1932
Jack Petersen*	1	1932
Len Harvey*	1	1933-1934
Eddie Phillips		1935-1937
Jock McAvoy	1	1937-1938
Len Harvey	2	1938-1942
Freddie Mills*	1	1942-1950
Don Cockell	2	1950-1952
Randy Turpin*	1	1952
Dennis Powell	1	1953
Alex Buxton	2	1953-1955
Randy Turpin*	1	1955
Ron Barton*	1	1956
Randy Turpin*	2	1956-1958
Chic Calderwood	3	1960-1963
Chic Calderwood*	1	1964-1966
Young John McCormack	2	1967-1969
Eddie Avoth	2	1969-1971
Chris Finnegan	2	1971-1973
John Conteh*	2	1973-1974
Johnny Frankham	1	1975
Chris Finnegan	1	1975-1976
Tim Wood	1	1976-1977
Bunny Johnson*	3	1977-1981
Tom Collins	3	1982-1984
Dennis Andries*	5	1984-1986
Tom Collins*	1	1987
Tony Wilson	3	1987-1989
Tom Collins*	1	1989-1990
Steve McCarthy	1	1990-1991
Crawford Ashley*	3	1991-1992
Maurice Core*	2	1992-1994
Crawford Ashley	3	1994-1999
Clinton Woods*	1	1999-2000
Neil Simpson*	2	2000-2002
Peter Oboh	2	2003-

Cruiserweight (190 lbs)

Title Holder	Lonsdale Belt Notches	Tenure
Sam Reeson*	1	1985-1986
Andy Straughn	1	1986-1987
Roy Smith	1	1987
Tee Jay	1	1987-1988
Glenn McCrory*	2	1988
Andy Straughn	1	1988-1989
Johnny Nelson*	3	1989-1991
Derek Angol*	2	1991-1992
Carl Thompson*	1	1992-1994
Dennis Andries	1	1995
Terry Dunstan*	3	1995-1996
Johnny Nelson*	1	1996-1998
Bruce Scott	1	1998-1999
Carl Thompson*	1	1999-2000
Bruce Scott	2	2000-2003
Mark Hobson	3	2003-

Heavyweight (190 lbs +)

Title Holder	Lonsdale Belt Notches	Tenure
Tom Allen*		1878-1882
Charlie Mitchell*		1882-1894
Jem Smith		1889-1891
Ted Pritchard		1891-1895
Jem Smith		1895-1896
George Chrisp		1901
Jack Scales		1901-1902
Jack Palmer		1903-1906
Gunner Moir		1906-1909
Iron Hague		1909-1910
P.O. Curran		1910-1911
Iron Hague		1910-1911
Bombardier Billy Wells	3	1911-1919
Joe Beckett		1919
Frank Goddard	1	1919
Joe Beckett*	1	1919-1923
Frank Goddard		1923-1926
Phil Scott*		1926-1931
Reggie Meen		1931-1932
Jack Petersen	3	1932-1933
Len Harvey		1933-1934
Jack Petersen		1934-1936
Ben Foord		1936-1937
Tommy Farr*	1	1937-1938
Len Harvey*	1	1938-1942
Jack London	1	1944-1945
Bruce Woodcock	2	1945-1950
Jack Gardner	1	1950-1952
Johnny Williams	1	1952-1953
Don Cockell*	1	1953-1956
Joe Erskine	2	1956-1958
Brian London	1	1958-1959
Henry Cooper*	9	1959-1969
Jack Bodell	1	1969-1970
Henry Cooper	1	1970-1971
Joe Bugner	1	1971
Jack Bodell	1	1971-1972
Danny McAlinden	1	1972-1975
Bunny Johnson	1	1975
Richard Dunn	2	1975-1976
Joe Bugner*	1	1976-1977
John L. Gardner*	2	1978-1980
Gordon Ferris	1	1981
Neville Meade	1	1981-1983
David Pearce*	1	1983-1985
Hughroy Currie	1	1985-1986
Horace Notice*	4	1986-1988
Gary Mason	2	1989-1991
Lennox Lewis*	3	1991-1993
Herbie Hide*	1	1993-1994
James Oyebola	1	1994-1995
Scott Welch*	1	1995-1996
Julius Francis	4	1997-2000
Mike Holden*	1	2000
Danny Williams	5	2000-2004
Michael Sprott	1	2004
Matt Skelton	1	2004-

Henry Cooper, the former British, British Empire and European heavyweight champion, seen recently visiting the International Boxing Hall of Fame in America
Les Clark

Retired or Inactive Post-War British Champions: Career Summary

Includes all British champions, along with British boxers who have won major international titles since 1945, who had retired by July 2003 or have been inactive since that date. The section does not include champions still active (for their records see under Active British-Based Boxers), while undefeated champions are those who relinquished their titles, not forfeited them.

George Aldridge British Middleweight Champion, 1962-1963. *Born* 01.02.36. *From* Market Harborough. *Pro Career* 1956-1963 (52 contests, won 36, drew 2, lost 14).

Michael Alldis British S. Bantamweight Champion, 1999-2001. Undefeated British and Commonwealth S. Bantamweight Champion, 2002. *Born* 25.05.68. *From* Crawley. *Pro Career* 1992-2002 (21 contests, won 24, lost 8).

Terry Allen British Flyweight Champion, 1951-1952. Undefeated British Flyweight Champion, 1952-1954. European and World Flyweight Champion, 1950. *Born* 18.06.24. *From* Islington. *Birthname* Edward Govier. *Deceased* 1987. *Pro Career* 1942-1954 (74 contests, won 60, drew 1, lost 13).

Francis Ampofo British Flyweight Champion, 1991. Undefeated British Flyweight Champion, 1992-1996. Undefeated Commonwealth Flyweight Champion, 1993. Commonwealth Flyweight Champion, 1994-1995. *Born* Ghana 05.06.67. *From* Bethnal Green. *Pro Career* 1990-2002 (28 contests, won 17, lost 11).

Brian Anderson British Middleweight Champion, 1986-1987. *Born* 09.07.61. *From* Sheffield. *Pro Career* 1980-1987 (39 contests, won 27, drew 3, lost 9).

Jimmy Anderson Undefeated British S. Featherweight Champion, 1968-1970. *Born* 01.10.42. *From* Waltham Cross. *Pro Career* 1964-1971 (37 contests, won 27, drew 1, lost 9).

Vic Andreetti Undefeated British L. Welterweight Champion, 1969-1970. *Born* 29.01.42. *From* Hoxton. *Pro Career* 1961-1969 (67 contests, won 51, drew 3, lost 13).

Dennis Andries Undefeated British L. Heavyweight Champion, 1984-86. World L. Heavyweight Champion (WBC version), 1986-1987, 1989, and 1990-1991. British Cruiserweight Champion, 1995. *Born* Guyana 05.11.53. *From* Hackney. *Pro Career* 1978-1996 (65 contests, won 49, drew 2, lost 14).

Derek Angol Undefeated British Cruiserweight Champion, 1991-1992. Undefeated Commonwealth Cruiserweight Champion, 1989-1993. *Born* 28.11.64. *From* Camberwell. *Pro Career* 1986-1996 (31 contests, won 28, lost 3).

Evan Armstrong British Featherweight Champion, 1971-1972. Undefeated British Featherweight Champion, 1973-1975. Commonwealth Featherweight Champion, 1974. *Born* 15.02.43. *From* Ayr. *Pro Career* 1963-1974 (54 contests, won 39, drew 1, lost 14).

Michael Armstrong British S. Featherweight Champion, 1992. *Born* 18.12.68. *From* Moston. *Birthname* Morris. *Pro Career* 1987-1994 (26 contests, won 18, drew 1, lost 7).

Bobby Arthur British Welterweight Champion, 1972-1973. *Born* 25.07.47. *From* Coventry. *Pro Career* 1967-1976 (41 contests, won 26, lost 15).

Crawford Ashley Undefeated British L. Heavyweight Champion, 1991-1992. British L. Heavyweight Champion, 1994-1999. European L. Heavyweight Champion, 1997 and 1998-1999. Commonwealth L. Heavyweight Champion, 1998-1999. *Born* 20.05.64. *From* Leeds. *Birthname* Gary Crawford. *Pro Career* 1987-2001 (44 contests, won 33, drew 1, lost 10).

Eddie Avoth British L. Heavyweight Champion, 1969-1971. Commonwealth L. Heavyweight Champion, 1970-1971. *Born* 02.05.45. *From* Cardiff. *Pro Career* 1963-1972 (53 contests, won 44, lost 9).

Pat Barrett Undefeated British L. Welterweight Champion, 1989-1990. European L. Welterweight Champion, 1990-1992. *Born* 22.07.67. *From* Manchester. *Pro Career* 1987-1994 (42 contests, won 37, drew 1, lost 4).

Ron Barton Undefeated British L. Heavyweight Champion, 1956. *Born* 25.02.33. *From* West Ham. *Pro Career* 1954-1961 (31 contests, won 26, lost 5).

Jimmy Batten British L. Middleweight Champion, 1977-1979. *Born* 07.11.55. *From* Millwall. *Pro Career* 1974-1983 (49 contests, won 40, lost 9).

Nigel Benn Commonwealth Middleweight Champion, 1988-1989. World Middleweight Champion (WBO version), 1990. World S. Middleweight Champion (WBC version), 1992-1996. *Born* 22.01.64. *From* Ilford. *Pro Career* 1987-1996 (48 contests, won 42, drew 1, lost 5).

Ensley Bingham Undefeated British L. Middleweight Champion, 1996. British L. Middleweight Champion, 1997-1999. *Born* 27.05.63. *From* Manchester. *Pro Career* 1986-1999 (28 contests, won 20, lost 8).

Jack Bodell British Heavyweight Champion, 1969-1970 and 1971-1972. Commonwealth Heavyweight Champion, 1971-1972. European Heavyweight Champion, 1971. *Born* 11.08.40. *From* Swadlincote. *Pro Career* 1962-1972 (71 contests, won 58, lost 13).

Steve Boyle British Lightweight Champion, 1988-1990. *Born* 28.11.62. *From* Glasgow. *Pro Career* 1983-1993 (33 contests, won 25, drew 2, lost 6).

Cornelius Boza-Edwards Undefeated European S. Featherweight Champion, 1982. World S. Featherweight Champion, 1981 (WBC version). *Born* Uganda, 27.05.56. *From* London. *Pro Career* 1976-1987 (53 contests, won 45, drew 1, lost 7).

Jim Brady British Empire Bantamweight Championship Claimant, 1941-1945. *From* Dundee. *Deceased* 1980. *Pro Career* 1932-1947 (169 contests, won 104, drew 15, lost 50).

Jackie Brown British and British Empire Flyweight Champion, 1962-1963. *Born* 02.03.35. *From* Edinburgh. *Pro Career* 1958-1966 (44 contests, won 32, drew 1, lost 10, no contest 1).

Neville Brown British Middleweight Champion, 1993-1998. *Born* 26.02.66. *From* Burton. *Pro Career* 1989-2000 (40 contests, won 32, lost 8).

Frank Bruno Undefeated European Heavyweight Champion, 1985-1986. World Heavyweight Champion (WBC version), 1995-96. *Born* 16.11.61. *From* Wandsworth. *Pro Career* 1982-1996 (45 contests, won 40, lost 5).

Del Bryan British Welterweight Champion, 1991-1992 and 1993-1995. *Born* 16.04.1967. *From* Birmingham. *Pro Career* 1986-1998 (52 contests, won 32, drew 1, lost 19).

Ken Buchanan Undefeated British Lightweight Champion, 1968-1971, and 1973-1974. Undefeated European Lightweight Champion, 1974-1975. World Lightweight Champion, 1970-1971. World Lightweight Champion, (WBA version), 1971-1972. *Born* 28.06.45. *From* Edinburgh. *Pro Career* 1965-1982 (69 contests, won 61, lost 8).

Joe Bugner British, Commonwealth and European Heavyweight Champion, 1971. Undefeated European Heavyweight Champion, 1972-1975. European Heavyweight Champion, 1976-1977. Undefeated British and Commonwealth Heavyweight Champion, 1976-1977. *Born* Hungary, 13.03.50. *From* Bedford. *Pro Career* 1967-1999 (83 contests, won 69, drew 1, lost 13).

David Burke Undefeated Commonwealth Lightweight Champion, 2002. *Born* 03.02.75. *From* Liverpool. *Pro Career* 1997-2003 (24 contests, won 22, lost 2).

Paul Burke British and Commonwealth Lightweight Champion, 1993. Commonwealth L. Welterweight Champion, 1997 and 1998-1999. *Born* 25.07.66. *From* Preston. *Pro Career* 1987-1999 (43 contests, won 28, drew 2, lost 13).

Alex Buxton British L. Heavyweight Champion, 1953-1955. *Born* 10.05.25. *From* Watford. *Pro Career* 1942-1963 (125 contests, won 78, drew 4, lost 43).

Jimmy Cable British L. Middleweight Champion, 1984-1985. European L. Middleweight Champion, 1984. *Born* 07.09.57. *From* Crawley. *Pro Career* 1980-1988 (41 contests, won 30, drew 2, lost 9).

Chic Calderwood British and British Empire L. Heavyweight Champion, 1960-1963. Undefeated British L. Heavyweight Champion, 1964-1966. *Born* 09.01.37. *From* Craigneuk. *Birthname* Charles Calderwood. *Deceased* 1966. *Pro Career* 1957-1966 (55 contests, won 44, drew 1, lost 9, no contest 1).

Johnny Caldwell Undefeated British Flyweight Champion, 1960-1961. British and British Empire Bantamweight Champion, 1964-1965. World Bantamweight Champion (EBU version), 1961-1962. *Born* 07.05.38. *From* Belfast. *Pro Career* 1958-1965 (35 contests, won 29, drew 1, lost 5).

Mickey Cantwell Undefeated British Flyweight Champion, 1996-1997. *Born* 23.11.64. *From* Eltham. *Pro Career* 1991-2001 (22 contests, won 14, drew 1, lost 7).

Cornelius Carr Undefeated British S. Middleweight Champion, 1994. *Born* 09.04.69. *From* Middlesbrough. *Pro Career* 1987-2001 (38 contests, won 34, lost 4).

Fidel Castro British S. Middleweight Champion, 1991-1992. *Born* 17.04.63. *From* Nottingham. *Birthname* Smith. *Pro Career* 1987-1995 (30 contests, won 22, lost 8).

Glenn Catley Undefeated British Middleweight Champion, 1998. World S. Middleweight Champion (WBC version), 2000. *Born* 15.03.72. *From* Bristol. *Pro Career* 1993-2003 (34 contests, won 27, lost 7).

Ray Cattouse British Lightweight Champion, 1980-1982. *Born* 24.07.52. *From* Balham. *Pro Career* 1975-1983 (31 contests, won 26, drew 3, lost 2).

Ralph Charles Undefeated British and British Empire/Commonwealth Welterweight Champion, 1968-1972. European Welterweight Champion, 1970-1971. *Born* 05.02.43. *From* West Ham. *Pro Career* 1963-1972 (43 contests, won 39, lost 4).

Dave Charnley Undefeated British Lightweight Champion, 1957-1965. British Empire Lightweight Champion, 1959-1962. European Lightweight Champion, 1960-1963. *Born* 10.10.35. *From* Dartford. *Pro Career* 1954-1964 (61 contests, won 48, drew 1, lost 12).

Lloyd Christie British L. Welterweight Champion, 1987-1989. *Born* 28.02.62. *From* Wolverhampton. *Pro Career* 1981-1989 (46 contests, won 24, drew 1, lost 21).

Johnny Clark Undefeated British and European Bantamweight Champion, 1973-1974. *Born* 10.09.47. *From* Walworth. *Pro Career* 1966-1974 (43 contests, won 39, drew 1, lost 3).

Ronnie Clayton British Featherweight Champion, 1947-1954. British Empire Featherweight Championship Claimant, 1947-1951. European Featherweight Champion, 1947-1948. *Born* 09.02.23. *From* Blackpool. *Deceased* 1999. *Pro Career* 1941-1954 (113 contests, won 79, drew 8, lost 26).

Pat Clinton Undefeated British Flyweight Champion, 1988-1991. Undefeated European Flyweight Champion, 1990-1991. World Flyweight Champion (WBO version), 1992-1993. *Born* 04.04.64. *From* Croy. *Pro Career* 1985-1991 (23 contests, won 20, lost 3).

Ray Close Undefeated European S. Middleweight Champion, 1993. *Born* 20.01.69. *From* Belfast. *Pro Career* 1988-1997 (29 contests, won 25, drew 1, lost 3).

Don Cockell British L. Heavyweight Champion, 1950-1952. Undefeated European L. Heavyweight Champion, 1951-1952. Undefeated British Heavyweight Champion, 1953-1956. British Empire Heavyweight Championship Claimant, 1953-1954. Undefeated British Empire Heavyweight Champion, 1954-1956. *Born* 22.09.28. *From* Battersea. *Deceased* 1983. *Pro Career* 1946-1956 (80 contests, won 65, drew 1, lost 14).

Steve Collins Undefeated World Middleweight Champion (WBO version),

1994-1995. Undefeated World S. Middleweight Champion (WBO version), 1995-1997. *Born* 21.07.64. *From* Dublin. *Pro Career* 1986-1997 (39 contests, won 36, lost 3).

Tom Collins British L. Heavyweight Champion, 1982-1984. Undefeated British L. Heavyweight Champion, 1987 and 1989-1990. European L. Heavyweight Champion, 1987-1988 and 1990-1991. *Born* Curacao, 01.07.55. *From* Leeds. *Pro Career* 1977-1993 (50 contests, won 26, drew 2, lost 22).

John Conteh Undefeated British, Commonwealth and European L. Heavyweight Champion, 1973-1974. World L. Heavyweight Champion (WBC version), 1974-1977. *Born* 27.05.51. *From* Liverpool. *Pro Career* 1971-1980 (39 contests, won 34, drew 1, lost 4).

James Cook Undefeated British S. Middleweight Champion, 1990-1991. British S. Middleweight Champion, 1993-1994. European S. Middleweight Champion, 1991-1992. *Born* Jamaica, 17.05.59. *From* Peckham. *Pro Career* 1982-1994 (35 contests, won 25, lost 10).

Johnny Cooke British and British Empire Welterweight Champion, 1967-1968. *Born* 17.12.34. *From* Bootle. *Pro Career* 1960-1971 (93 contests, won 52, drew 7, lost 34).

Gary Cooper British L. Middleweight Champion, 1988. *Born* 31.05.57. *From* Lymington. *Pro Career* 1978-1989 (27 contests, won 16, drew 2, lost 9).

Henry Cooper Undefeated British Heavyweight Champion, 1959-1969. British Heavyweight Champion, 1970-1971. British Empire/Commonwealth Heavyweight Champion, 1959-1971. Undefeated European Heavyweight Champion, 1964 and 1968-1969. European Heavyweight Champion, 1970-1971. *Born* 03.05.34. *From* Bellingham. *Pro Career* 1954-1971 (55 contests, won 40, drew 1, lost 14).

Maurice Core Undefeated British L. Heavyweight Champion, 1992-1994. *Born* 22.06.65. *From* Manchester. *Birthname* Maurice Coore. *Pro Career* 1990-1996 (18 contests, won 15, drew 1, lost 2).

Pat Cowdell Undefeated British Featherweight Champion, 1979-1982. Undefeated European Featherweight Champion, 1982-1983. British S. Featherweight Champion, 1986 and 1987-1988. European S. Featherweight Champion, 1984-1985. *Born* 18.08.53. *From* Warley. *Pro Career* 1977-1988 (42 contests, won 36, lost 6).

Carl Crook British and Commonwealth Lightweight Champion, 1990-1992. *Born* 10.11.63. *From* Chorley. *Pro Career* 1985-1993 (31 contests, won 26, drew 1, lost 4).

Maurice Cullen British Lightweight Champion, 1965-1968. *Born* 30.12.37. *From* Shotton. *Deceased* 2001. *Pro Career* 1959-1970 (55 contests, won 45, drew 2, lost 8).

Hughroy Currie British Heavyweight Champion, 1985-1986. *Born* Jamaica, 09.02.59. *From* Catford. *Pro Career* 1981-1989 (29 contests, won 17, drew 1, lost 11).

Brian Curvis Undefeated British and British Empire Welterweight Champion, 1960-1966. *Born* 14.08.37. *From* Swansea. *Birthname* Brian Nancurvis. *Pro Career* 1959-1966 (41 contests, won 37, lost 4).

Cliff Curvis Undefeated British Welterweight Champion, 1952-1953. British Empire Welterweight Championship Claimant, 1952. *Born* 02.11.27. *From* Swansea. *Birthname* Cliff Nancurvis. *Pro Career* 1944-1953 (55 contests, won 42, drew 1, lost 12).

Najib Daho British S. Featherweight Champion, 1986-1987. Commonwealth Lightweight Champion, 1989-1990. *Born* Morocco, 13.01.59. *From* Manchester. *Deceased* 1993. *Pro Career* 1977-1991 (60 contests, won 34, drew 1, lost 25).

John Davison Undefeated British Featherweight Champion, 1992-1993. *Born* 30.09.58. *From* Newcastle. *Pro Career* 1988-1993 (20 contests, won 15, lost 5).

Gary DeRoux British Featherweight Champion, 1991. *Born* 04.11.62. *From* Peterborough. *Pro Career* 1986-1993 (22 contests, won 13, drew 1, lost 8).

Mike Deveney British Featherweight Champion, 1995. *Born* 14.12.65.

From Paisley. *Pro Career* 1991-1998 (42 contests, won 22, drew 1, lost 19).

Robert Dickie British Featherweight Champion, 1986-1988. British S. Featherweight Champion, 1991. *Born* 23.06.64. *From* Swansea. *Pro Career* 1983-1993 (28 contests, won 22, drew 2, lost 4).

Alex Dickson British Lightweight Champion, 1987-1988. *Born* 01.10.62. *From* Larkhall. *Pro Career* 1985-1989 (22 contests, won 18, drew 1, lost 3).

Drew Docherty Undefeated British S. Bantamweight Champion, 1999. British Bantamweight Champion, 1992-1997. *Born* 29.11.65. *From* Condorrat. *Pro Career* 1989-2000 (24 contests, won 16, drew 1, lost 7).

John Doherty British S. Featherweight Champion, 1986, 1989-1990, and 1991-1992. *Born* 17.07.62. *From* Bradford. *Pro Career* 1982-1992 (39 contests, won 28, drew 3, lost 8).

Pat Doherty Commonwealth Lightweight Champion, 1989. *Born* 12.04.62. *From* Croydon. *Pro Career* 1981-1989 (32 contests, won 18, drew 3, lost 11).

Dai Dower Undefeated British Flyweight Champion, 1955-1957. Undefeated British Empire Flyweight Champion, 1954-1957. European Flyweight Champion, 1955. *Born* 26.06.33. *From* Abercynon. *Pro Career* 1953-1958 (37 contests, won 34, lost 3).

Terry Downes British Middleweight Champion, 1958-1959 and 1959-1962. World Middleweight Champion (NY/EBU version), 1961-1962. *Born* 09.05.36. *From* Paddington. *Pro Career* 1957-1964 (44 contests, won 35, lost 9).

Richard Dunn British and Commonwealth Heavyweight Champion, 1975-1976. European Heavyweight Champion, 1976. *Born* 19.01.45. *From* Bradford. *Pro Career* 1969-1977 (45 contests, won 33, lost 12).

Terry Dunstan Undefeated British Cruiserweight Champion, 1995-1996. Undefeated European Cruiserweight Champion, 1998. *Born* 21.10.68. *From* Vauxhall. *Pro Career* 1992-1999 (21 contests, won 19, lost 2).

Tony Ekubia British L. Welterweight Champion, 1990-1991. Commonwealth L. Welterweight Champion, 1989-1991. *Born* Nigeria, 06.03.60. *From* Manchester. *Pro Career* 1986-1993 (25 contests, won 21, lost 4).

Joe Erskine British Heavyweight Champion, 1956-1958. British Empire Heavyweight Champion, 1957-1958. *Born* 26.01.34. *From* Cardiff. *Deceased* 1990. *Pro Career* 1954-1964 (54 contests, won 45, drew 1, lost 8).

Chris Eubank Undefeated WBO Middleweight Champion, 1990-1991. WBO S. Middleweight Title, 1991-1995. *Born* 08.08.1966. *From* Brighton. *Pro Career* 1985-1998 (52 contests, won 45, drew 2, lost 5).

George Feeney Undefeated British Lightweight Champion, 1982-1985. *Born* 09.02.57. *From* West Hartlepool. *Pro Career* 1977-1984 (29 contests, won 19, lost 10).

John Feeney British Bantamweight Champion, 1981-1983 and 1983-1985. *Born* 15.05.58. *From* West Hartlepool. *Pro Career* 1977-1987 (48 contests, won 35, lost 13).

Gordon Ferris British Heavyweight Champion, 1981. *Born* 21.11.52. *From* Enniskillen. *Pro Career* 1977-1982 (26 contests, won 20, lost 6).

Darren Fifield Commonwealth Flyweight Champion, 1993-1994. *Born* 09.10.69. *From* Henley. *Pro Career* 1992-1996 (13 contests, won 7, drew 2, lost 4).

Albert Finch British Middleweight Champion, 1950. *Born* 16.05.26. *From* Croydon. *Pro Career* 1945-1958 (103 contests, won 72, drew 9, lost 21, no contest 1).

Chris Finnegan British L. Heavyweight Champion, 1971-1973. Undefeated British L. Heavyweight Champion, 1975-1976. Commonwealth L. Heavyweight Champion, 1971-1973. European L. Heavyweight Champion, 1972. *Born* 05.06.44. *From* Iver. *Pro Career* 1968-1975 (37 contests, won 29, drew 1, lost 7).

Kevin Finnegan British Middleweight Champion, 1977. Undefeated British Middleweight Champion, 1974 and 1979-1980. European Middleweight

Champion, 1974-1975 and 1980. *Born* 18.04.48. *From* Iver. *Pro Career* 1970-1980 (47 contests, won 35, drew 1, lost 11).

Ali Forbes British S. Middleweight Champion, 1995. *Born* 07.03.61. *From* Sydenham. *Pro Career* 1989-2002 (25 contests, won 14, drew 1, lost 10).

Hugh Forde British S. Featherweight Champion, 1990. Commonwealth S. Featherweight Champion, 1991. *Born* 07.05.64. *From* Birmingham. *Pro Career* 1986-1995 (31 contests, won 24, lost 7).

Steve Foster Commonwealth L. Middleweight Champion, 1996-1997. *Born* 28.12.60. *From* Salford. *Pro Career* 1981-1999 (39 contests, won 20, drew 2, lost 17).

Dean Francis Undefeated British and European S.Middleweight Champion, 1997-1998. *Born* 23.01.74. *From* Basingstoke. *Pro Career* 1994-2003 (25 contests, won 22, lost 3).

Johnny Frankham British L. Heavyweight Champion, 1975. *Born* 06.06.48. *From* Reading. *Pro Career* 1970-1976 (40 contests, won 28, drew 1, lost 11).

P.J. Gallagher British S. Featherweight Champion, 1996-1997. *Born* 14.02.73. *From* Wood Green. *Pro Career* 1993-2000 (20 contests, won 19, lost 1).

Jack Gardner British Heavyweight Champion, 1950-1952. British Empire Heavyweight Championship Claimant, 1950-1952. European Heavyweight Champion, 1951. *Born* 06.11.26. *From* Market Harborough. *Deceased* 1978. *Pro Career* 1948-1956 (34 contests, won 28, lost 6).

John L. Gardner Undefeated British Heavyweight Champion, 1978-1980. Undefeated Commonwealth Heavyweight Champion, 1978-1981. Undefeated European Heavyweight Champion, 1980-1981. *Born* 19.03.53. *From* Hackney. *Pro Career* 1973-1983 (39 contests, won 35, lost 4).

Teddy Gardner Undefeated British and European Flyweight Champion, 1952. British Empire Flyweight Championship Claimant, 1952. *Born* 27.01.22. *From* West Hartlepool. *Deceased* 1977. *Pro Career* 1938-1952 (66 contests, won 55, drew 3, lost 8).

Sugar Gibiliru British S. Featherweight Champion, 1991. *Born* 13.07.66. *From* Liverpool. *Pro Career* 1984-1995 (55 contests, won 16, drew 7, lost 32).

Ray Gilbody British Bantamweight Champion, 1985-1987. *Born* 21.03.60. *From* Warrington. *Pro Career* 1983-1987 (16 contests, won 11, drew 1, lost 4).

Freddie Gilroy Undefeated British and British Empire Bantamweight Champion, 1959-1963. European Bantamweight Champion, 1959-1960. *Born* 07.03.36. *From* Belfast. *Pro Career* 1957-1962 (31 contests, won 28, lost 3).

Tommy Glencross British Featherweight Champion, 1972-1973. *Born* 31.07.47. *From* Glasgow. *Pro Career* 1967-1978 (48 contests, won 31, drew 1, lost 16).

Herol Graham Undefeated British L. Middleweight Champion, 1981-1983. Undefeated Commonwealth L. Middleweight Champion, 1981-1984. Undefeated European L. Middleweight Champion, 1983-1984. Undefeated British Middleweight Champion, 1985-1986. British Middleweight Champion, 1988-1992. European Middleweight Champion, 1986-1987. *Born* 13.09.59. *From* Sheffield. *Pro Career* 1978-1998 (54 contests, won 48, lost 6).

Frank Grant British Middleweight Champion, 1992-1993. *Born* 22.05.65. *From* Bradford. *Pro Career* 1986-1993 (26 contests, won 22, lost 4).

Dave Boy Green Undefeated British and European L. Welterweight Champion, 1976-1977. European Welterweight Champion, 1979. *Born* 02.06.53. *From* Chatteris. *Pro Career* 1974-1981 (41 contests, won 37, lost 4).

Roy Gumbs British Middleweight Champion, 1981-1983. Commonwealth Middleweight Champion, 1983. *Born* St Kitts, 05.09.54. *From* Tottenham. *Pro Career* 1976-1985 (40 contests, won 26, drew 3, lost 11).

Neil Haddock British S. Featherweight Champion, 1992-1994. *Born*

22.06.64. *From* Llanelli. *Pro Career* 1987-1994 (26 contests, won 14, drew 1, lost 11).

Ross Hale British and Commonwealth L. Welterweight Champion, 1994-1995. *Born* 28.02.1967. *From* Bristol. *Pro Career* 1989-1998 (33 contests, won 29, lost 4).

Henry Hall British Welterweight Champion, 1948-1949. *Born* 06.09.22. *From* Sheffield. *Deceased* 1979. *Pro Career* 1945-1952 (66 contests, won 43, drew 3, lost 20).

Prince Naseem Hamed Undefeated European Bantamweight Champion, 1994-1995. Undefeated WBO Featherweight Champion, 1997-2000. Undefeated IBF Featherweight Champion, 1997. WBC Featherweight Champion, 1999-2000. *Born* 12.02.74. *From* Sheffield. *Pro Career* 1992-2002 (37 contests, won 36, lost 1).

Billy Hardy Undefeated British Bantamweight Champion, 1987-1991. Undefeated British Featherweight Champion, 1994. Undefeated Commonwealth Featherweight Champion, 1992-1996. European Featherweight Champion, 1995-1998. *Born* 05.09.1964. *From* Sunderland. *Pro Career* 1983-1998 (48 contests, won 37, drew 2, lost 9).

Peter Harris British Featherweight Champion, 1988. *Born* 23.08.62. *From* Swansea. *Pro Career* 1983-1996 (33 contests, won 16, drew 2, lost 15).

Paul Harvey Commonwealth S. Featherweight Champion, 1991-1992. *Born* 10.11.64. *From* Ilford. *Pro Career* 1989-1994 (22 contests, won 16, drew 1, lost 5).

Floyd Havard British S. Featherweight Champion, 1988-1989. Undefeated British S. Featherweight Champion, 1994-1995. *Born* 16.10.65. *From* Swansea. *Pro Career* 1985-1996 (36 contests, won 34, lost 2).

Vince Hawkins British Middleweight Champion, 1946-1948. *Born* 15.04.23. *From* Eastleigh. *Pro Career* 1940-1950 (86 contests, won 75, drew 1, lost 10).

Lloyd Hibbert Undefeated British L. Middleweight Champion, 1987. Commonwealth L. Middleweight Champion, 1987. *Born* 29.06.59. *From* Birmingham. *Pro Career* 1979-1987 (23 contests, won 19, lost 4).

Charlie Hill British Featherweight Champion, 1956-1959. *Born* 20.06.30. *From* Cambuslang. *Pro Career* 1953-1959 (36 contests, won 31, lost 5).

Paul Hodkinson Undefeated British Featherweight Champion, 1988-1990. Undefeated European Featherweight Champion, 1989-1991. World Featherweight Champion, 1991-1993 (WBC version). *Born* 14.09.65. *From* Liverpool. *Pro Career* 1986-1994 (26 contests, won 22, drew 1, lost 3).

Andy Holligan British and Commonwealth L. Welterweight Champion, 1991-1994 and 1996-1997. *Born* 06.06.67. *From* Liverpool. *Pro Career* 1987-1998 (30 contests, won 27, lost 3).

Lloyd Honeyghan Undefeated British Welterweight Champion, 1983-1985 and 1985-1986. Undefeated Commonwealth & European Champion, 1985-1986. World Welterweight Champion, 1986. World Welterweight Champion (WBC version), 1986-1987 and 1988-1989. World Welterweight Champion (IBF version), 1986-1987. Commonwealth L. Middleweight Champion, 1993-1994. *Born* 22.04.60, Jamaica. *From* Bermondsey. *Pro Career* 1980-1995 (48 contests, won 43, lost 5).

Maurice Hope Undefeated British L. Middleweight Champion, 1974-1977. Undefeated Commonwealth L. Middleweight Champion, 1976-1979. Undefeated European L. Middleweight Champion, 1976-1978. World L. Middleweight Champion (WBC version), 1979-1981. *Born* Antigua, 06.12.51. *From* Hackney. *Pro Career* 1973-1982 (35 contests, won 30, drew 1, lost 4).

Mickey Hughes Commonwealth L. Middleweight Champion, 1992-1993. *Born* 13.06.62. *From* St Pancras. *Pro Career* 1985-1993 (31 contests, won 24, lost 7).

Mo Hussein Commonwealth Lightweight Champion, 1987-1989. *Born* 17.11.62. *From* West Ham. *Pro Career* 1982-1989 (27 contests, won 23, lost 4).

Paul Ingle World Featherweight Champion (IBF Version), 1999-2000. Undefeated British Featherweight Champion, 1997-1998. Undefeated

Commonwealth and European Champion, 1997-1999. *Born* 22.06.72. *From* Scarborough. *Pro Career* (25 contests, won 23, lost 2).

Jonjo Irwin British Featherweight Champion, 1995-1996. Undefeated British Featherweight Champion, 1998-1999. Commonwealth Featherweight Champion, 1996-1997. *Born* 31.05.69. *From* Doncaster. *Pro Career* 1992-1999 (24 contests, won 19, lost 5).

Gary Jacobs Undefeated British Welterweight Champion, 1992-1993. Commonwealth Welterweight Champion, 1988-1989. European Welterweight Champion, 1993-1994. *Born* 10.12.65. *From* Glasgow. *Pro Career* 1985-1997 (53 contests, won 45, lost 8).

Joey Jacobs British S. Featherweight Champion, 1990. *Born* 01.10.60. *From* Manchester. *Pro Career* 1986-1991 (15 contests, won 10, lost 5).

Ronnie James Undefeated British Lightweight Champion, 1944-1947. *Born* 08.10.17. *From* Swansea. *Deceased* 1977. *Pro Career* 1933-1947 (119 contests, won 98, drew 5, lost 16).

Tee Jay British Cruiserweight Champion, 1987-1988. *Born* Ghana, 21.01.62. *Birthname* Taju Akay. *From* Notting Hill. *Pro Career* 1985-1991 (19 contests, won 14, drew 1, lost 4).

Bunny Johnson British and Commonwealth Heavyweight Champion, 1975. Undefeated British L. Heavyweight Champion, 1977-1981. *Born* Jamaica, 10.05.47. *From* Birmingham. *Birthname* Fitzroy Johnson. *Pro Career* 1968-1981 (73 contests, won 55, drew 1, lost 17).

Frank Johnson British Lightweight Champion, 1952-1953 and 1955-1956. British Empire Lightweight Championship Claimant, 1953. *Born* 27.11.28. *From* Manchester. *Birthname* Frank Williamson. *Deceased* 1970. *Pro Career* 1946-1957 (58 contests, won 47, lost 11).

Barry Jones Undefeated WBO S. Featherweight Champion, 1997-1998. *Born* 03.05.74. *From* Cardiff. *Pro Career* 1992-2000 (20 contests, won 18, drew 1, lost 1).

Colin Jones Undefeated British Welterweight Champion, 1980-1982. Undefeated Commonwealth Welterweight Champion, 1981-1984. Undefeated European Welterweight Champion, 1982-1983. *Born* 21.03.59. *From* Gorseinon. *Pro Career* 1977-1985 (30 contests, won 26, drew 1, lost 3).

Frankie Jones British Flyweight Champion, 1957-1960. British Empire Flyweight Champion, 1957. *Born* 12.02.33. *From* Plean. *Deceased* 1991. *Pro Career* 1955-1960 (25 contests, won 17, lost 8).

Paul Jones Commonwealth Middleweight Champion, 1998-1999. *Born* 19.11.66. *From* Sheffield. *Pro Career* 1986-2002 (44 contests, won 31, drew 1, lost 12).

Peter Kane Undefeated World Flyweight Champion, 1938-1939. European Bantamweight Champion, 1947-1948. *Born* 28.04.18. *From* Golborne. *Birthname* Peter Cain. *Deceased* 1991. *Pro Career* 1934-1948 (102 contests, won 92, drew 2, lost 7, no contest 1).

Mark Kaylor British and Commonwealth Middleweight Champion, 1983-1984. *Born* 11.05.61. *From* West Ham. *Pro Career* 1980-1991 (48 contests, won 40, drew 1, lost 7).

Peter Keenan British Bantamweight Champion, 1951-1953 and 1954-1959. British Empire Bantamweight Champion, 1955-1959. European Bantamweight Champion, 1951-1952 and 1953. *Born* 08.08.28. *From* Glasgow. *Deceased* 2000. *Pro Career* 1948-1959 (66 contests, won 54, drew 1, lost 11).

Billy Spider Kelly British Featherweight Champion, 1955-1956. British Empire Featherweight Championship Claimant, 1954. British Empire Featherweight Champion, 1954-1955. *Born* 21.04.32. *From* Londonderry. *Pro Career* 1950-1962 (83 contests, won 56, drew 4, lost 23).

Joe Kelly British Bantamweight Champion, 1992. *Born* 18.05.64. *From* Glasgow. *Pro Career* 1985-1992 (27 contests, won 18, drew 2, lost 7).

John Kelly British and European Bantamweight Champion, 1953-1954. *Born* 17.01.32. *From* Belfast. *Pro Career* 1951-1957 (28 contests, won 24, lost 4).

Johnny King British Bantamweight Champion, 1932-1934 and 1935-1947.

British Empire Bantamweight Championship Claimant, 1932-1934. *Born* 08.01.12. *From* Manchester. *Deceased* 1963. *Pro Career* 1926-1947 (222 contests, won 158, drew 15, lost 48, no contest 1).

Keith Knox British and Commonwealth Flyweight Champion, 1999. *Born* 20.06.67. *From* Bonnyrigg. *Pro Career* 1994-2001 (23 contests, won 13, drew 2, lost 8).

Kirkland Laing British Welterweight Champion, 1987-1991. European Welterweight Champion, 1990. *Born* 20.06.54, Jamaica. *From* Nottingham. *Pro Career* 1975-1994 (56 contests, won 43, drew 1, lost 12).

Tony Laing Undefeated British L. Welterweight Champion, 1986. Commonwealth L. Welterweight Champion, 1987-1988. *Born* 22.09.57. *From* Nottingham. *Pro Career* 1977-1988 (18 contests, won 13, drew 1, lost 4).

Davy Larmour British Bantamweight Champion, 1983. *Born* 02.04.52. *From* Belfast. *Pro Career* 1977-1983 (18 contests, won 11, lost 7).

Mick Leahy British Middleweight Champion, 1963-1964. *Born* Cork, 12.03.35. *From* Coventry. *Pro Career* 1956-1965 (72 contests, won 46, drew 7, lost 19).

Ady Lewis Undefeated British and Commonwealth Flyweight Champion, 1997-1998. British and Commonwealth Bantamweight Champion, 2000. *Born* 31.05.75. *From* Bury. *Pro Career* 1994-2001 (25 contests, won 19, drew 1, lost 5).

Lennox Lewis Undefeated British Heavyweight Champion, 1991-1993. Undefeated Commonwealth Heavyweight Champion, 1992-1993. Undefeated European Heavyweight Champion, 1990-1992. World Heavyweight Champion (WBC version), 1992-1994 and 1997-2001. Undefeated World Heavyweight Champion (IBF version), 2001-2002. Undefeated World Heavyweight Champion (WBA version), 1999-2000. Undefeated World Heavyweight Champion (WBC version), 2001-2004. *Born* 02.09.65. *From* London. *Pro Career* 1989-2004 (44 contests, won 41, drew 1, lost 2).

Stewart Lithgo Commonwealth Cruiserweight Champion, 1984. *Born* 02.06.57. *From* West Hartlepool. *Pro Career* 1977-1987 (30 contests, won 16, drew 2, lost 12).

Paul Lloyd British Bantamweight Champion, 1997-1999. Undefeated Commonwealth Bantamweight Champion, 1996-2000. Undefeated European Bantamweight Champion, 1998-1999. *Born* 07.12.68. *From* Ellesmere Port. *Pro Career* 1992-2000 (27 contests, won 20, lost 7).

Brian London British and British Empire Heavyweight Champion, 1958-1959. *Born* 19.06.34. *From* Blackpool. *Birthname* Brian Harper. *Pro Career* 1955-1970 (58 contests, won 37, drew 1, lost 20).

Jack London British Heavyweight Champion, 1944-1945. British Empire Heavyweight Championship Claimant, 1944-1945. *Born* 23.06.13. *From* West Hartlepool. *Birthname* Jack Harper. *Deceased* 1964. *Pro Career* 1931-1949 (141 contests, won 95, drew 5, lost 39, no contests 2).

Eamonn Loughran Undefeated Commonwealth Welterweight Champion, 1992-1993. WBO Welterweight Champion, 1993-1996. *Born* 05.06.70. *Fron* Ballymena. *Pro Career* 1987-1996 (30 contests, won 26, drew 1, lost 2, no contest 1).

Joe Lucy British Lightweight Champion, 1953-1955 and 1956-1957. *Born* 09.02.30. *From* Mile End. *Deceased* 1991. *Pro Career* 1950-1957 (37 contests, won 27, lost 10).

Kevin Lueshing British Welterweight Champion, 1996-1997. *Born* 17.04.1968. *From* Beckenham. *Pro Career* 1991-1999 (25 contests, won 21, lost 4).

Danny McAlinden British and Commonwealth Heavyweight Champion, 1972-1975. *Born* Newry, 01.06.47. *From* Coventry. *Pro Career* 1969-1981 (45 contests, won 31, drew 2, lost 12).

Les McAteer British and British Empire Middleweight Champion, 1969-1970. *Born* 19.08.45. *From* Birkenhead. *Pro Career* 1965-1979 (39 contests, won 27, drew 2, lost 10).

Pat McAteer Undefeated British Middleweight Champion, 1955-1958.

British Empire Middleweight Champion, 1955-1958. *Born* 17.03.32. *From* Birkenhead. *Pro Career* 1952-1958 (57 contests, won 49, drew 2, lost 6).

Dave McAuley Undefeated British Flyweight Champion, 1986-1988. World Flyweight Champion (IBF version), 1989-1992. *Born* 15.06.61. *From* Larne. *Pro Career* 1983-1992 (23 contests, won 18, drew 2, lost 3).

Sammy McCarthy British Featherweight Champion, 1954-1955. *Born* 05.11.31. *From* Stepney. *Pro Career* 1951-1957 (53 contests, won 44, drew 1, lost 8).

Steve McCarthy British L. Heavyweight Champion, 1990-1991. *Born* 30.07.62. *From* Southampton. *Pro Career* 1987-1994 (17 contests, won 12, drew 1, lost 4).

John McCluskey Undefeated British Flyweight Champion, 1967-1977. Commonwealth Flyweight Champion, 1970-1971. *Born* 23.01.44. *From* Hamilton. *Pro Career* 1965-1975 (38 contests, won 23, lost 15).

John Cowboy McCormack British Middleweight Champion, 1959. European Middleweight Champion, 1961-1962. *Born* 09.01.35. *From* Maryhill. *Pro Career* 1957-1966 (45 contests, won 38, lost 7).

Young John McCormack British L. Heavyweight Champion, 1967-1969. *Born* Dublin, 11.12.44. *From* Brixton. *Pro Career* 1963-1970 (42 contests, won 33, drew 1, lost 8).

Pat McCormack British L. Welterweight Champion, 1974. *Born* Dublin, 28.04.46. *From* Brixton. *Pro Career* 1968-1975 (49 contests, won 30, drew 1, lost 18).

Robert McCracken Undefeated British L. Middleweight Champion, 1994-1995. Commonwealth Middleweight Champion, 1995-1997. *Born* 31.05.68. *From* Birmingham. *Pro Career* 1991-2001 (35 contests, won 33, lost 2).

Geoff McCreesh Undefeated British Welterweight Champion, 1997-1999. *Born* 12.06.70. *From* Bracknell. *Pro Career* 1994-2001 (30 contests, won 23, lost 7).

Glenn McCrory Undefeated British Cruiserweight Champion, 1988. Undefeated Commonwealth Cruiserweight Champion, 1987-1989. World Cruiserweight Champion (IBF version), 1989-1990. *Born* 23.09.64. *From* Annfield Plain. *Pro Career* 1984-1993 (39 contests, won 30, drew 1, lost 8).

Wayne McCullough World Bantamweight Champion (WBC version), 1995-1997. *Born* 07.07.70. *From* Belfast. *Pro Career* 1993-2003 (30 contests, won 26, lost 4).

Jim McDonnell Undefeated European Featherweight Champion, 1985-1987. *Born* 12.09.60. *From* Camden Town. *Pro Career* 1983-1998 (30 contests, won 26, lost 4).

Tommy McGovern British Lightweight Champion, 1951-1952. *Born* 05.02.24. *From* Bermondsey. *Deceased* 1989. *Pro Career* 1947-1953 (66 contests, won 45, drew 4, lost 17).

Walter McGowan Undefeated British Flyweight Champion, 1963-1966. Undefeated British Empire Flyweight Champion, 1963-1969. World Flyweight Champion (WBC version), 1966. British and British Empire Bantamweight Champion, 1966-1968. *Born* 13.10.42. *From* Hamilton. *Pro Career* 1961-1969 (40 contests, won 32, drew 1, lost 7).

Barry McGuigan Undefeated British Featherweight Champion, 1983-1986. Undefeated European Featherweight Champion, 1983-1985. World Featherweight Champion (WBA version), 1985-1986. *Born* 28.02.61. *From* Clones. *Pro Career* 1981-1989 (35 contests, won 32, lost 3).

Clinton McKenzie British L. Welterweight Champion, 1978-1979 and 1979-1984. Undefeated British L. Welterweight Champion, 1989. European L. Welterweight Champion, 1981-1982. *Born* 15.09.55. *From* Croydon. *Pro Career* 1976-1989 (50 contests, won 36, lost 14).

Duke McKenzie Undefeated British Flyweight Champion, 1985-1986. Undefeated European Flyweight Champion, 1986-1988. World Flyweight Champion (IBF version), 1988-1989. World Bantamweight Champion (WBO version), 1991-1992. World S. Bantamweight Champion (WBO version), 1992-1993. Undefeated British Featherweight Champion, 1993-1994. *Born* 05.05.63. *From* Croydon. *Pro Career* 1982-1998 (46 contests, won 39, lost 7).

Tony McKenzie British L. Welterweight Champion, 1986-1987. *Born* 04.03.63. *From* Leicester. *Pro Career* 1983-1993 (34 contests, won 26, drew 1, lost 7).

Ian McLeod Undefeated Commonwealth S. Featherweight Champion, 2000. *Born* 11.06.69. *From* Kilmarnock. *Pro Career* 1992-2000 (14 contests, won 11, drew 1, lost 2).

Colin McMillan Undefeated British Featherweight Champion, 1991-1992. British Featherweight Champion, 1996-1997. Undefeated Commonwealth Featherweight Champion, 1992. World Featherweight Champion (WBO version), 1992. *Born* 12.02.66. *From* Barking. *Pro Career* 1988-1997 (35 contests, won 31, lost 4).

Noel Magee Commonwealth L. Heavyweight Champion, 1995. *Born* 16.12.65. *From* Belfast. *Pro Career* 1985-1997 (37 contests, won 27, drew 2, lost 8).

Charlie Magri Undefeated British Flyweight Champion, 1977-1981. Undefeated European Flyweight Champion, 1979-1983 and 1984-1985. European Flyweight Champion, 1985-1986. World Flyweight Champion (WBC version), 1983. *Born* Tunisia, 20.07.56. *From* Stepney. *Pro Career* 1977-1986 (35 contests, won 30, lost 5).

Paddy Maguire British Bantamweight Champion, 1975-1977. *Born* 26.09.48. *From* Belfast. *Pro Career* 1969-1977 (35 contests, won 26, drew 1, lost 8).

Terry Marsh Undefeated British L. Welterweight Champion, 1984-1986. European L. Welterweight Champion, 1985-1986. Undefeated World L. Welterweight Champion (IBF version), 1987. *Born* 07.02.58. *From* Basildon. *Pro Career* 1981-1987 (27 contests, won 26, drew 1).

Gary Mason British Heavyweight Champion, 1989-1991. *Born* Jamaica, 15.12.62. *From* Wandsworth. *Pro Career* 1984-1991 (36 contests, won 35, lost 1).

Jason Matthews Undefeated Commonwealth Middleweight Champion, 1999. WBO Middleweight Champion, 1999. *Born* 20.07.70. *From* Hackney. *Pro Career* 1995-1999 (23 contests, won 21, lost 2).

Neville Meade British Heavyweight Champion, 1981-1983. *Born* Jamaica, 12.09.48. *From* Swansea. *Pro Career* 1974-1983 (34 contests, won 20, drew 1, lost 13).

Freddie Mills Undefeated British L. Heavyweight Champion, 1942-1950. British Empire L. Heavyweight Championship Claimant, 1942-1950. Undefeated European L. Heavyweight Champion, 1947-1950. World L. Heavyweight Champion (GB version), 1942-1946. World L. Heavyweight Champion, 1948-1950. *Born* 26.06.19. *From* Bournemouth. *Deceased* 1965. *Pro Career* 1936-1950 (101 contests, won 77, drew 6, lost 18).

Alan Minter British Middleweight Champion, 1975-1977. Undefeated British Middleweight Champion, 1977-1978. European Middleweight Champion, 1977. Undefeated European Middleweight Champion, 1978-1979. World Middleweight Champion, 1980. *Born* 17.08.51. *From* Crawley. *Pro Career* 1972-1981 (49 contests, won 39, lost 9, no contest 1).

Sylvester Mittee British Welterweight Champion, 1985. Commonwealth Welterweight Champion, 1984-1985. *Born* St Lucia, 29.10.56. *From* Bethnal Green. *Pro Career* 1977-1988 (33 contests, won 28, lost 5).

Tommy Molloy British Welterweight Champion, 1958-1960. *Born* 02.02.34. *From* Birkenhead. *Pro Career* 1955-1963 (43 contests, won 34, drew 2, lost 6, no contest 1).

Rinty Monaghan Undefeated British and World Flyweight Champion, 1948-1950. British Empire Flyweight Championship Claimant, 1948-1950. Undefeated European Flyweight Champion, 1949-1950. World Flyweight Champion (NBA version), 1947-1948. *Born* 21.08.20. *From* Belfast. *Birthname* John Monaghan. *Deceased* 1984. *Pro Career* 1934-1949 (66 contests, won 51, drew 6, lost 9).

Alex Moon Commonwealth S. Featherweight Champion, 2001-2002. *Born* 17.11.71. *From* Liverpool. *Pro Career* 1995-2003 (27 contests, won 19, drew 2, lost 6).

Des Morrison British L. Welterweight Champion, 1973-1974. *Born* Jamaica, 01.02.50. *From* Bedford. *Pro Career* 1970-1982 (50 contests, won 36, drew 2, lost 12).

Patrick Mullings British S. Bantamweight Champion, 1999 and 2001. Commonwealth Featherweight Champion, 1999-2000. *Born* 19.10.70. *From* Harlesden. *Pro Career* 1994-2001 (30 contests, won 24, lost 6).

Sean Murphy British Featherweight Champion, 1990-1991 and 1993. *Born* 01.12.64. *From* St Albans. *Pro Career* 1986-1994 (27 contests, won 22, lost 5).

Charlie Nash Undefeated British Lightweight Champion, 1978-1979. Undefeated European Lightweight Champion, 1979-1980. European Lightweight Champion, 1980-1981. *Born* 10.05.51. *From* Derry. *Pro Career* 1975-1983 (30 contests, won 25, lost 5).

Dave Needham British Bantamweight Champion, 1974-1975. British Featherweight Champion, 1978-1979. *Born* 15.08.51. *From* Nottingham. *Pro Career* 1971-1980 (39 contests, won 30, drew 1, lost 8).

Bobby Neill British Featherweight Champion, 1959-1960. *Born* 10.10.33. *From* Edinburgh. *Pro Career* 1955-1960 (35 contests, won 28, lost 7).

Horace Notice Undefeated British and Commonwealth Heavyweight Champion, 1986-1988. *Born* 07.08.57. *From* Birmingham. *Pro Career* 1983-1988 (16 contests, won 16).

John O'Brien British Empire Featherweight Champion, 1967. *Born* 20.02.37. *From* Glasgow. *Deceased* 1979. *Pro Career* 1956-1971 (47 contests, won 30, lost 17).

Chris Okoh Commonwealth Cruiserweight Champion, 1995-1997. *Born* 18.04.69. *From* Croydon. *Pro Career* 1993-1999 (16 contests, won 14, lost 2).

Spencer Oliver European S. Bantamweight Champion, 1997-1998. *Born* 27.03.75. *From* Barnet. *Pro Career* 1995-1998 (15 contests, won 14, lost 1).

Danny O'Sullivan British Bantamweight Champion, 1949-1951. *Born* 06.01.23. *From* Finsbury Park. *Deceased* 1990. *Pro Career* 1947-1951 (43 contests, won 33, drew 1, lost 9).

Johnny Owen Undefeated British Bantamweight Champion, 1977-1980. Undefeated Commonwealth Bantamweight Champion, 1978-1980. Undefeated European Bantamweight Champion, 1980. *Born* 07.01.56. *From* Merthyr. *Deceased* 1980. *Pro Career* 1976-1980 (28 contests, won 25, drew 1, lost 2).

James Oyebola British Heavyweight Champion, 1994-1995. *Born* Nigeria 10.06.61. *From* Paddington. *Pro Career* 1987-1996 (23 contests, won 18, drew 1, lost 4).

Jackie Paterson British Flyweight Champion, 1939-1948. British Empire Flyweight Championship Claimant, 1940-1948. World Flyweight Champion, 1943-1947. World Flyweight Champion (GB/NY version), 1947-1948. British Bantamweight Champion, 1947-1949. British Empire Bantamweight Championship Claimant, 1945-1949. European Bantamweight Champion, 1946. *Born* 05.09.20. *From* Springfield. *Deceased* 1966. *Pro Career* 1938-1950 (92 contests, won 64, drew 3, lost 25).

Bernard Paul Commonwealth L. Welterweight Champion, 1997-1999. *Born* 22.20.65. *From* Tottenham. *Pro Career* 1991-2000 (35 contests, won 21, drew 4, lost 10).

Larry Paul British L. Middleweight Champion, 1973-1974. *Born* 19.04.52. *From* Wolverhampton. *Pro Career* 1973-1978 (40 contests, won 30, drew 1, lost 9).

David Pearce Undefeated British Heavyweight Champion, 1983-1985. *Born* 08.05.59. *From* Newport. *Deceased* 2000. *Pro Career* 1978-1984 (21 contests, won 17, drew 1, lost 3).

Kostas Petrou British Welterweight Champion, 1985. *Born* 17.04.59. *From* Birmingham. *Pro Career* 1981-1988 (37 contests, won 30, lost 7).

Tiger Al Phillips European Featherweight Champion, 1947. British Empire Featherweight Championship Claimant, 1947. *Born* 25.01.20. *From* Aldgate. *Deceased* 1999. *Pro Career* 1938-1951 (89 contests, won 72, drew 3, lost 14).

Nicky Piper Undefeated Commonwealth L. Heavyweight Champion, 1995-1997. *Born* 05.05.66. *From* Cardiff. *Pro Career* 1989-1997 (33 contests, won 26, drew 2, lost 5).

Dean Pithie Commonwealth S. Featherweight Champion, 2002-2003. *Born* 18.01.74. *From* Coventry. *Pro Career* 1995-2003 (32 contests, won 25, drew 2, lost 5).

Dennis Powell British L. Heavyweight Champion, 1953. *Born* 12.12.24. *From* Four Crosses. *Deceased* 1993. *Pro Career* 1947-1954 (68 contests, won 42, drew 4, lost 22).

Colin Power Undefeated British L. Welterweight Champion, 1977-1978. British L. Welterweight Champion, 1979. European L. Welterweight Champion, 1978. *Born* 02.02.56. *From* Paddington. *Pro Career* 1975-1983 (34 contests, won 28, drew 1, lost 5).

Kevin Pritchard British S. Featherweight Champion, 1990-1991. *Born* 26.09.61. *From* Liverpool. *Pro Career* 1981-1991 (48 contests, won 23, drew 3, lost 22).

Johnny Pritchett Undefeated British Middleweight Champion, 1965-1969. Undefeated British Empire Middleweight Champion, 1967-1969. *Born* 15.02.43. *From* Bingham. *Pro Career* 1963-1969 (34 contests, won 32, drew 1, lost 1).

Chris Pyatt Undefeated British L. Middleweight Champion, 1986. European L. Middleweight Champion, 1986-1987. Undefeated Commonwealth L. Middleweight Champion, 1991-1992. Commonwealth L. Middleweight Champion, 1995-1996. World Middleweight Champion (WBO version), 1993-1994. *Born* 03.07.63. *From* Leicester. *Pro Career* 1983-1997 (51 contests, won 46, lost 5).

Des Rea British L. Welterweight Champion, 1968-1969. *Born* 09.01.44. *From* Belfast. *Pro Career* 1964-1974 (69 contests, won 28, drew 5, lost 36).

Mark Reefer Undefeated Commonwealth S. Featherweight Champion, 1989-1990. *Born* 16.03.64. *Birthname* Mark Thompson. *From* Dagenham. *Pro Career* 1983-1992 (32 contests, won 23, drew 1, lost 8).

Sam Reeson Undefeated British Cruiserweight Champion, 1985-1986. Undefeated European Cruiserweight Champion, 1987-1988. *Born* 05.01.63. *From* Battersea. *Pro Career* 1983-1989 (26 contests, won 24, lost 2).

Robbie Regan Undefeated World Bantamweight Champion (WBO version), 1996-1997. British Flyweight Champion, 1991. Undefeated British Flyweight Champion, 1991-1992. Undefeated European Flyweight Champion, 1992-1993 and 1994-1995. *Born* 30.08.68. *From* Cefn Forest. *Pro Career* 1989-1996 (22 contests, won 17, drew 3, lost 2).

Willie Reilly Undefeated British Lightweight Champion, 1972. *Born* 25.03.47. *From* Glasgow. *Pro Career* 1968-1972 (23 contests, won 13, drew 3, lost 7).

Jimmy Revie British Featherweight Champion, 1969-1971. *Born* 08.07.47. *From* Stockwell. *Pro Career* 1966-1976 (48 contests, won 38, drew 1, lost 9).

Henry Rhiney British Welterweight Champion, 1976-1979. European Welterweight Champion, 1978-1979. *Born* Jamaica, 28.11.51. *From* Luton. *Pro Career* 1973-1980 (57 contests, won 32, drew 6, lost 19).

Alan Richardson British Featherweight Champion, 1977-1978. *Born* 04.11.48. *From* Fitzwilliam. *Pro Career* 1971-1978 (27 contests, won 17, drew 1, lost 9).

Dick Richardson European Heavyweight Champion, 1960-1962. *Born* 01.06.34. *From* Newport. *Deceased* 1999. *Pro Career* 1954-1963 (47 contests, won 31, drew 2, lost 14).

Steve Robinson European Featherweight Champion, 1999-2000. WBO Featherweight Champion, 1993-1995. *Born* 13.12.68. *From* Cardiff. *Pro Career* 1989-2002 (51 contests, won 32, drew 2, lost 17).

Ernie Roderick British Welterweight Champion, 1939-1948. European Welterweight Champion, 1946-1947. British Middleweight Champion, 1945-1946. *Born* 25.01.14. *From* Liverpool. *Deceased* 1986. *Pro Career* 1931-1950 (142 contests, won 114, drew 4, lost 24).

Prince Rodney Undefeated British L. Middleweight Champion, 1983-1984. British L. Middleweight Champion, 1985-1986. *Born* 31.10.58. *From* Huddersfield. *Pro Career* 1977-1990 (41 contests, won 31, drew 1, lost 9).

Stan Rowan Undefeated British Bantamweight Champion, 1949. British Empire Bantamweight Championship Claimant, 1949. *Born* 06.09.24. *From* Liverpool. *Deceased* 1997. *Pro Career* 1942-1953 (67 contests, won 46, drew 5, lost 16).

Mark Rowe British and Commonwealth Middleweight Champion, 1970. *Born* 12.07.47. *Born* 12.07.47. *From* Camberwell. *Pro Career* 1966-1973 (47 contests, won 38, drew 1, lost 8).

Jason Rowland Undefeated British L. Welterweight Champion, 1998-2000. *Born* 06.08.70. *From* West Ham. *Pro Career* 1989-2003 (28 contests, won 26, lost 2).

Alan Rudkin British Bantamweight Champion, 1965-1966. Undefeated British Bantamweight Champion, 1968-1972. British Empire Bantamweight Champion, 1965-1966 and 1968-1969. European Bantamweight Champion, 1971. Undefeated Commonwealth Bantamweight Champion, 1970-1972. *Born* 18.11.41. *From* Liverpool. *Pro Career* 1962-1972 (50 contests, won 42, lost 8).

Hugh Russell Undefeated British Flyweight Champion, 1984-1985. British Bantamweight Champion, 1983. *Born* 15.12.59. *From* Belfast. *Pro Career* 1981-1985 (19 contests, won 17, lost 2).

Paul Ryan British and Commonwealth L. Welterweight Champion, 1995-1996. *Born* 02.02.65. *From* Hackney. *Pro Career* 1991-1997 (28 contests, won 25, lost 3).

Billy Schwer British Lightweight Champion, 1992-1993. Undefeated British Lightweight Champion, 1993-1995. Commonwealth Lightweight Champion, 1992-1993 and 1993-1995. Undefeated European Lightweight Champion, 1997-1999. *Born* 12.04.69. *From* Luton. *Pro Career* 1990-2001 (45 contests, won 39, lost 6).

Tony Sibson British Middleweight Champion, 1979. Undefeated British Middleweight Champion, 1984 and 1987-1988. Undefeated Commonwealth Middleweight Champion, 1980-1983 and 1984-1988. Undefeated European Middleweight Champion, 1980-1982. European Middleweight Champion, 1984-1985. *Born* 09.04.58. *From* Leicester. *Pro Career* 1976-1988 (63 contests, won 55, drew 1, lost 7).

Steve Sims Undefeated British Featherweight Champion, 1982-1983. *Born* 10.10.58. *From* Newport. *Pro Career* 1977-1987 (29 contests, won 14, drew 1, lost 14).

Neil Sinclair Undefeated British Welterweight Champion, 2001-2003. *Born* 23.02.74. *From* Belfast. *Pro Career* 1995-2003 (30 contests, won 27, lost 3).

Joey Singleton British L. Welterweight Champion, 1974-1976. *Born* 06.06.51. *From* Kirkby. *Pro Career* 1973-1982 (40 contests, won 27, drew 2, lost 11).

Kelvin Smart British Flyweight Champion, 1982-1984. *Born* 18.12.60. *From* Caerphilly. *Pro Career* 1979-1987 (29 contests, won 17, drew 2, lost 10).

Roy Smith British Cruiserweight Champion, 1987. *Born* 31.08.61. *From* Nottingham. *Pro Career* 1985-1991 (26 contests, won 18, lost 8).

Vernon Sollas British Featherweight Champion, 1975-1977. *Born* 14.08.54. *From* Edinburgh. *Pro Career* 1973-1977 (33 contests, won 25, drew 1, lost 7).

Terry Spinks British Featherweight Champion, 1960-1961. *Born* 28.02.38. *From* Canning Town. *Pro Career* 1957-1962 (49 contests, won 41, drew 1, lost 7).

David Starie British S. Middleweight Champion, 1997. Undefeated British S. Middleweight Champion, 1998-2003. Commonwealth S. Middleweight Champion, 1998-2003. *Born* 11.06.74. *From* Bury St Edmunds. *Pro Career* 1994-2003 (35 contests, won 31, lost 4).

Bunny Sterling British Middleweight Champion, 1970-1974. Undefeated British Middleweight Champion, 1975. Commonwealth Middleweight Champion, 1970-1972. European Middleweight Champion, 1976. *Born* Jamaica, 04.04.48. *From* Finsbury Park. *Pro Career* 1966-1977 (57 contests, won 35, drew 4, lost 18).

Sammy Storey British S. Middleweight Champion, 1989-1990. Undefeated British S. Middleweight Champion, 1995. *Born* 09.08.63. *From* Belfast. *Pro Career* 1985-1997 (31 contests, won 25, lost 6).

John H. Stracey Undefeated British Welterweight Champion, 1973-1975. Undefeated European Welterweight Champion, 1974-1975. World Welterweight Champion (WBC version), 1975-1976. *Born* 22.09.50. *From* Bethnal Green. *Pro Career* 1969-1978 (51 contests, won 45, drew 1, lost 5).

Andy Straughn British Cruiserweight Champion, 1986-1987 and 1988-1989. *Born* Barbados, 25.12.59. *From* Hitchin. *Pro Career* 1982-1990 (27 contests, won 18, drew 2, lost 7).

Gary Stretch British L. Middleweight Champion, 1988-1990. *Born* 04.11.65. *From* St Helens. *Pro Career* 1985-1993 (25 contests, won 23, lost 2).

Johnny Sullivan British Empire Middleweight Championship Claimant, 1954. British and British Empire Middleweight Champion, 1954-1955. *Born* 19.12.32. *From* Preston. *Birthname* John Hallmark. *Pro Career* 1948-1960 (97 contests, won 68, drew 3, lost 26).

Neil Swain Undefeated Commonwealth S. Bantamweight Champion, 1995 and 1996-1997. *Born* 04.09.71. *From* Gilfach Goch. *Pro Career* 1993-1997 (24 contests, won 17, lost 7).

Wally Swift British Welterweight Champion, 1960. British Middleweight Champion, 1964-1965. *Born* 10.08.36. *From* Nottingham. *Pro Career* 1957-1969 (88 contests, won 68, drew 3, lost 17).

Wally Swift Jnr British L. Middleweight Champion, 1991-1992. *Born* 17.02.66. *From* Birmingham. *Pro Career* 1985-1994 (38 contests, won 26, drew 1, lost 11).

Nel Tarleton British Featherweight Champion, 1931-1932 and 1934-1936. Undefeated British Featherweight Champion, 1940-1947. Undefeated British Empire Featherweight Championship Claimant, 1940-1947. *Born* 14.01.06. *From* Liverpool. *Deceased* 1956. *Pro Career* 1926-1945 (144 contests, won 116, drew 8, lost 20).

Wally Thom British Welterweight Champion, 1951-1952 and 1953-1956. British Empire Welterweight Championship Claimant, 1951-1952. European Welterweight Champion, 1954-1955. *Born* 14.06.26. *From* Birkenhead. *Deceased* 1980. *Pro Career* 1949-1956 (54 contests, won 42, drew 1, lost 11).

Eddie Thomas British Welterweight Champion, 1949-1951. European Welterweight Champion, 1951. British Empire Welterweight Championship Claimant, 1951. *Born* 27.07.26. *From* Merthyr. *Deceased* 1997. *Pro Career* 1946-1954 (48 contests, won 40, drew 2, lost 6).

Pat Thomas British Welterweight Champion, 1975-1976. British L. Middleweight Champion, 1979-1981. *Born* St Kitts, 05.05.50. *From* Cardiff. *Pro Career* 1970-1984 (57 contests, won 35, drew 3, lost 18, no contest 1).

Billy Thompson British Lightweight Champion, 1947-1951. European Lightweight Champion, 1948-1949. *Born* 20.12.25. *From* Hickleton Main. *Pro Career* 1945-1953 (63 contests, won 46, drew 4, lost 13).

Andy Till British L. Middleweight Champion, 1992-1994. *Born* 22.08.63. *From* Northolt. *Pro Career* 1986-1995 (24 contests, won 19, lost 5).

Dick Turpin British Middleweight Champion, 1948-1950. British Empire Middleweight Championship Claimant, 1948-1949. *Born* 26.11.20. *From* Leamington Spa. *Deceased* 1990. *Pro Career* 1937-1950 (103 contests, won 76, drew 6, lost 20, no contest 1).

Randy Turpin Undefeated British Middleweight Champion, 1950-1954. British Empire Middleweight Championship Claimant, 1952-1954. European Middleweight Champion, 1951-1954. World Middleweight Champion, 1951. World Middleweight Champion (EBU version), 1953. Undefeated British L. Heavyweight Champion, 1952, 1955, and 1956-1958. British Empire L. Heavyweight Championship Claimant, 1952-1954. Undefeated British Empire L. Heavyweight Champion, 1954-1955. *Born* 07.06.28. *From* Leamington Spa. *Deceased* 1966. *Pro Career* 1946-1958 (73 contests, won 64, drew 1, lost 8).

Tommy Waite British and Commonwealth Bantamweight Champion, 2000. *Born* 11.03.72. *From* Belfast. *Pro Career* 1996-2001 (15 contests, won 11, lost 4).

Keith Wallace Undefeated Commonwealth Flyweight Champion, 1983-1984. *Born* 29.03.61. *From* Liverpool. *Deceased* 2000. *Pro Career* 1982-1990 (25 contests, won 20, lost 5).

Peter Waterman Undefeated British Welterweight Champion, 1956-1958. Undefeated European Welterweight Champion, 1958. *Born* 08.12.34. *From* Clapham. *Deceased* 1986. *Pro Career* 1952-1958 (46 contests, won 41, drew 2, lost 3).

Michael Watson Undefeated Commonwealth Middleweight Champion, 1989-1991. *Born* 15.03.65. *From* Islington. *Pro Career* 1984-1991 (30 contests, won 25, drew 1, lost 4).

Jim Watt British Lightweight Champion, 1972-1973. Undefeated British Lightweight Champion, 1975-1977. Undefeated European Lightweight Champion, 1977-1979. World Lightweight Champion (WBC version), 1979-1981. *Born* 18.07.48. *From* Glasgow. *Pro Career* 1968-1981 (46 contests, won 38, lost 8).

Paul Weir Undefeated WBO M. Flyweight Champion, 1993-1994. WBO L. Flyweight Champion, 1994-1995. *Born* 16.09.67. *From* Irvine. *Pro Career* 1992-2000 (20 contests, won 14, lost 6).

Scott Welch Undefeated British Heavyweight Champion, 1995-1996. Commonwealth Heavyweight Champion, 1995-1997. *Born* 21.04.1968. *From* Shoreham. *Pro Career* 1992-1999 (26 contests, won 22, lost 4).

Richie Wenton Undefeated British S. Bantamweight Champion, 1994-1996. *Born* 28.10.67. *From* Liverpool. *Pro Career* 1988-2001 (30 contests, won 24, lost 6).

Henry Wharton Undefeated British S. Middleweight Champion, 1992-1993. Undefeated Commonwealth Champion, 1991-1997. Undefeated European S. Middleweight Champion, 1995-1996. *Born* 23.11.1967. *From* York. *Pro Career* 1989-1998 (31 contests, won 27, drew 1, lost 3).

Derek Williams Commonwealth Heavyweight Champion, 1988-1992. European Heavyweight Champion, 1989-1992. *Born* 11.03.65. *From* Peckham. *Pro Career* 1984-1999 (35 contests, won 22, lost 13).

Johnny Williams British Heavyweight Champion, 1952-1953. British Empire Heavyweight Championship Claimant, 1952-1953. *Born* 25.12.26. *From* Rugby. *Pro Career* 1946-1956 (75 contests, won 60, drew 4, lost 11).

Tony Willis British Lightweight Champion, 1985-1987. *Born* 17.06.60. *From* Liverpool. *Pro Career* 1981-1989 (29 contests, won 25, lost 4).

Nick Wilshire Commonwealth L. Middleweight Champion, 1985-1987. *Born* 03.11.61. *From* Bristol. *Pro Career* 1981-1987 (40 contests, won 36, lost 4).

Tony Wilson British L. Heavyweight Champion, 1987-1989. *Born* 25.04.64. *From* Wolverhampton. *Pro Career* 1985-1993 (29 contests, won 20, drew 1, lost 8).

Howard Winstone Undefeated British Featherweight Champion, 1961-1969. European Featherweight Champion, 1963-1967. World Featherweight Champion (WBC version), 1968. *Born* 15.04.39. *From* Merthyr. *Deceased* 2000. *Pro Career* 1959-1968 (67 contests, won 61, lost 6).

Tim Wood British L. Heavyweight Champion, 1976-1977. *Born* 10.08.51. *From* Leicester. *Pro Career* 1972-1979 (31 contests, won 19, drew 1, lost 11).

Bruce Woodcock British Heavyweight Champion, 1945-1950. British Empire Heavyweight Championship Claimant, 1945-1950. European Heavyweight Champion, 1946-1949. *Born* 18.01.21. *From* Doncaster. *Deceased* 1997. *Pro Career* 1942-1950 (39 contests, won 35, lost 4).

Richie Woodhall WBC S. Middleweight Champion, 1998-1999. Commonwealth Middleweight Champion, 1992-1995. Undefeated European Middleweight Champion, 1995-1996. *Born* 17.04.68. *From* Telford. *Pro Career* 1990-2000 (29 contests, won 26, lost 3).

Commonwealth Title Bouts During 2003-2004

All of last season's title bouts are shown in date order within their weight divisions and give the contestants' respective weights, along with the scorecard if going to a decision. Every contest involving a British fighter is summarised briefly and all British officials are named.

Flyweight
Dale Robinson (England) failed to defend during the period.

Bantamweight
Steve Molitor (Canada) forfeited the title in April 2004 after failing to meet the deadlines for a defence.

S. Bantamweight
12 July 2003 Esham Pickering 8.10 (England) W RSC 4 Brian Carr 8.10 (Scotland), Braehead Arena, Renfrew, Scotland. Referee: Howard Foster. For a summary, see under British Title Bouts During 2003-2004

24 October 2003 Esham Pickering 8.10 (England) W RSC 7 Alfred Tetteh 8.9½ (Ghana), York Hall, Bethnal Green, London, England. Referee: Mark Green. Despite making a poor start, by the third round Pickering had put that behind him and was jabbing and moving to pick up the points, although the challenger remained dangerous. Into the seventh, with it still looking a hard night's work for the champion, he suddenly uncorked a tremendous right uppercut to the jaw that felled Tetteh. Although up at seven, the Ghanaian was deemed by the referee to be in no position to defend himself and the fight was stopped.

Featherweight
24 October 2003 Nicky Cook 8.13¾ (England) W PTS 12 Anyetei Laryea 9.0 (Ghana), York Hall, Bethnal Green, London, England. Referee: Richie Davies 119-110. Showing that he could go the distance at a hard pace, Cook had all the tools to stop the Ghanaian inside the distance, but was unable to halt a man who proved to be as tough as they make them. Outscored in virtually every round, Laryea still made the champion aware that he was a dangerous opponent and got a big round of applause at the finish for his game performance.

S. Featherweight
1 November 2003 Craig Docherty 9.3¼ (Scotland) W PTS 12 Abdul Malik Jabir 9.2½ (Ghana), Bellahouston Sports Centre, Glasgow, Scotland. Referee: Ian John-Lewis 117-114. Badly cut over the left eye in the first round, Docherty somehow survived to keep his fight plan together against a tough opponent, who, despite lacking a heavy dig, was always dangerous. Ignoring the wound, Docherty got the jab going to box his way back into the contest and, although the pace got a little frantic at times, he was always in control, the only real danger being whether the eye damage would worsen. Due to a cool head and excellent corner work, Docherty fully deserved the verdict, despite it being seen as closer in some quarters.

22 April 2004 Craig Docherty 9.4 (Scotland) W RSC 6 Kpakpo Allotey 9.3¾ (Ghana), Kelvin Hall, Glasgow, Scotland. Referee: John Keane. Continuing to show marked improvement, Docherty pressured the counter-punching Allotey at every opportunity, cutting the ring down and giving the challenger limited space to work in. Gradually, Allotey came apart and, in the fifth round, under pressure on the ropes, he was cut over the left eye. In the next session, with punches bouncing off Allotey's head, at the 0.46 mark, the referee brought matters to an end even though the latter was trying to fight back.

Lightweight
8 November 2003 Michael Muya 9.8½ (Kenya) L PTS 12 Kevin Bennett 9.8½ (England), The Recreation Centre, Bridgend, Wales. Referee: John Keane 113-116. In a fight that could have gone either way, the former soldier made an early start against the fragile looking champion, who, despite having quick hands, lacked power. But, into the latter rounds, Bennett, suffering with a bloody nose, began to struggle and it became touch and go as to whether he would make it to the final bell. Muya was now well on top, but lacked the power to finish the job and Bennett, cheered on by his supporters, somehow made it to be rewarded with the decision, prior to receiving oxygen on his stool. Bennett relinquished his title in April 2004 to concentrate on an IBO championship challenge against Jason Cook.

L. Welterweight
27 September 2003 Junior Witter 9.13½ (England) W RSC 2 Fred Kinuthia 9.12½ (Kenya), MEN Arena, Manchester, England. Referee: Larry O'Connell. This one didn't last too long as the unfortunate Kinuthia came apart at the seams to be rescued by the referee after 2.51 of the second round. Although the first session went without a knockdown, Witter came out in the second punching more forcefully and began to hurt his man with solid hooks to the head before going to work on the body. Having already touched down, Kinuthia was then put down by heavy rights and lefts and, although rising at the count of two, was rescued by the referee when it was clear that he was in no position to defend himself.

Welterweight
26 December 2003 Ossie Duran (Ghana) W PTS 12

Joshua Okine (Ghana), Accra, Ghana. Contested for the vacant championship after James Hare (England) gave up his belt on winning the WBF championship on 21 June 2003, Duran later vacated the title on winning the welter crown on 26 June 2004.

L. Middleweight

18 October 2003 Jamie Moore 11.0 (England) W CO 5 Gary Logan 10.13$^{1}/_{4}$ (England), MEN Arena, Manchester, England. Referee: Ian John-Lewis. For a summary, see under British Title Bouts During 2003-2004

22 November 2003 Jamie Moore 10.13$^{1}/_{2}$ (England) W RSC 7 Andrew Facey 10.13$^{3}/_{4}$ (England), King's Hall, Belfast, Northern Ireland. Referee: Dave Parris. For a summary, see under British Title Bouts During 2003-2004. Moore relinquished the title in January 2004 and stepped aside to allow his promotional stablemate, Richard Williams, to contest the vacancy

31 January 2004 Richard Williams 11.0 (England) W RSC 7 Ayittey Powers 10.12$^{1}/_{2}$ (Ghana), York Hall, Bethnal Green, London, England. Referee: Howard Foster. Once Williams got down to work and concentrated on the body against a limited, cuffing, but hard-hitting

opponent, it was clear to see that the fight would not last too long. By the fifth, the Ghanaian looked sold out as body punches took their toll and, in the seventh, fading fast and covering up in a corner without response, the referee had seen enough, calling a halt on the 2.54 mark. Williams relinquished the title in March 2004 to concentrate on a crack at the IBO crown held by Sergio Martinez

10 April 2004 Jamie Moore 11.0 (England) W RSC 5 Adam Katumwa 10.11 (Uganda), MEN Arena, Manchester, England. Referee: Terry O'Connor. Giving it everything after losing the opening three rounds, the southpaw Ugandan came back strongly to win the fourth session before Moore, who had become ragged, came on strongly to reassert his authority in the fifth. Sensing that he needed to get back into the contest, Moore went to work, throwing heavy punches from both hands, and although Katumwa didn't take a count he was under severe pressure when rescued by the referee on the 2.18 mark.

26 June 2004 Jamie Moore 11.0 (England) L RSC 3 Ossie Duran 10.10$^{1}/_{4}$ (Ghana), King's Hall, Belfast, Northern Ireland. Referee: Richie Davies. Carrying a

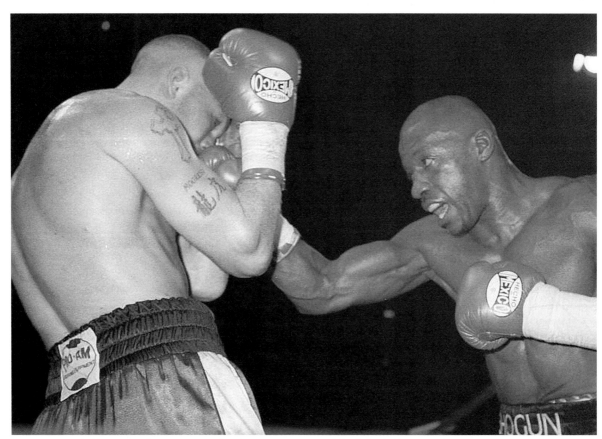

Jamie Moore (left), seen on the receiving end in this picture, successfully defended his British and Commonwealth light-middleweight titles when knocking out Gary Logan in the fifth round last October   Les Clark

damaged hip into the ring (although some said it went in the second round) did Moore no favours at all and once Duran realised that all wasn't well he got down to business. Having won the exploratory first round, the Ghanaian picked up the pace, threading in jabs, and began to slam in rights over the top. In the third, it was apparent that Moore was not going to survive for much longer and after taking a heavy left to the jaw and crashing over he was rescued by the referee, who dispensed with the count, on the 1.06 mark.

Middleweight

Howard Eastman (England) relinquished the championship in May 2004 in order to concentrate on the European title and securing a world title shot.

S. Middleweight

1 August 2003   Charles Adamu 11.12 (Ghana) W PTS 12 Matthew Barney 11.13$^{1}/_{2}$ (England), York Hall, Bethnal Green, London, England. Referee: Terry O'Connor 116-114. Billed for the vacant crown after Andre Thysse (South Africa) automatically forfeited the championship on losing an IBO title challenge to the Irishman, Brian Magee, on 21 June 2003, Barney lost the opportunity of winning the title when outscore over 12 awful rounds. In a contest of holding and mauling, with very little boxing, Barney's workrate was non existant, while the awkward, clumsy Adamu at least produced a few punches to catch the eye of the referee.

12 March 2004   Charles Adamu 11.10 (Ghana) L PTS 12 Carl Froch 11.13$^{3}/_{4}$ (England), The Ice Arena, Nottingham, England. Referee: Marcus McDonnell 116-113. It took Froch several rounds to get going, especially after having difficulty in avoiding the tough champion's long rights over the top. However, by the sixth, Froch was beginning to pick his punches better and floored Adamu with a great right hand in the eighth, but it remained close and only a good last round by the challenger secured the title. It had been close and proved that the promising Froch still has a long way to go before attaining world class.

2 June 2004   Carl Froch 11.13 (England) W RSC 11 Mark Woolnough 11.13$^{3}/_{4}$ (Canada, via England), The Ice Arena, Nottingham, England. Referee: Dave Parris. Another competitive match for Froch, saw him pick his punches well against the busier Woolnough, who certainly came to fight and for six rounds did well. However, by the eighth, the champion had warmed to the task with snappy punches to head and body and, despite being unable to put Woolnough down, was beginning to wear his man down. Although the pace dropped in the latter stages, Froch was beginning to cut loose more and more and it was no surprise when the referee came to the Canadian southpaw's aid at 1.47 of the 11th after he had retreated to the ropes without hitting back.

L. Heavyweight

12 May 2004   Peter Oboh 12.4 (England, via Nigeria) W RTD 10 Andrew Lowe 12.5 (England), Rivermead Leisure Centre, Reading, England. Referee: Mark Green. For a summary, see under British Title Bouts During 2003-2004.

Cruiserweight

5 September 2003   Mark Hobson 13.7$^{3}/_{4}$ (England) W PTS 12 Robert Norton 13.7$^{3}/_{4}$ (England), Ponds Forge Arena, Sheffield, England. Referee: Marcus McDonnell 118-110. For a summary, see under British Title Bouts During 2003-2004

13 March 2004   Mark Hobson 13.8 (England) W RSC 3 Tony Moran 13.6$^{1}/_{4}$ (England), The Leisure Centre, Huddersfield, England. Referee: John Keane. For a summary, see under British Title Bouts During 2003-2004

27 May 2004   Mark Hobson 13.8 (England) W RSC 6 Lee Swaby 13.7$^{3}/_{4}$ (England), The Leisure Centre, Huddersfield, England. Referee: Terry O'Connor. For a summary, see under British Title Bouts During 2003-2004.

Heavyweight

26 September 2003   Danny Williams 18.3$^{1}/_{2}$ (England) W RSC 5 Michael Sprott 16.4$^{3}/_{4}$ (England), Rivermead Leisure Centre, Reading, England. Referee: Terry O'Connor. For a summary, see under British Title Bouts During 2003-2004

24 January 2004   Danny Williams 18.12 (England) L PTS 12 Michael Sprott 17.1 (England), Conference Centre, Wembley, England. Referee: Dave Parris 114-115. For a summary, see under British Title Bouts During 2003-2004

24 April 2004   Michael Sprott 16.9 (England) L CO 12 Matt Skelton 17.12 (England), Rivermead Leisure Centre, Reading, England. Referee: Richie Davies. For a summary, see under British Title Bouts During 2003-2004

5 June 2004   Matt Skelton 17.13$^{3}/_{4}$ (England) W RTD 4 Bob Mirovic 19.3 (Australia), York Hall, Bethnal Green, London, England. Referee: Paul Thomas. Showing raw aggression and total commitment, Skelton crashed his way through the battle-hardened Mirovic, who, after giving the champion more than a scare or two, eventually came apart. Having floored the Australian heavily in the first, Skelton then found his right eye closing midway through the second and also had to endure some hard whacks himself as the challenger occasionally found the target with heavy rights and lefts. Both men appeared dead tired in the third, but again Skelton dumped his rival heavily with a right-left to the head. Up at seven, somehow Mirovic survived to get through the fourth before retiring on his stool at the end of the session when all in.

PROFESSIONAL BOXING PROMOTERS' ASSOCIATION

PRESENTS

THE BRITISH MASTERS CHAMPIONS

UNDER BBB OF C RULES

HEAVY:	VACANT
CRUISER:	PINKY BURTON
LIGHT-HEAVY:	STEVEN SPARTACUS
SUPER-MIDDLE:	DONOVAN SMILLIE
MIDDLE:	MARTYN BAILEY
LIGHT-MIDDLE:	DANNY MOIR
WELTER:	MARCUS PORTMAN
LIGHT-WELTER:	HAROON DIN
LIGHTWEIGHT:	ALAN TEMPLE
SUPER-FEATHER:	ANDREW FERRANS
FEATHER:	CHOI TSEVEENPUREV
SUPER-BANTAM:	VACANT
BANTAM:	GARETH PAYNE
FLYWEIGHT:	DELROY SPENCER

THE ONLY ALLCOMERS TITLE OPERATING IN BRITISH BOXING. OUR CHAMPIONS HAVE TO DEFEND WHEN A VALID CHALLENGE IS MADE WITH MORE THAN 30 DAYS NOTICE. TO CHALLENGE FOR OUR TITLE, PROMOTERS SHOULD APPLY TO:

THE PBPA	TEL: 020 7592 0102
P O BOX 25188	FAX: 020 7592 0087
LONDON	EMAIL: bdbaker@tinyworld.co.uk
SW1V 3WL	

CHAIRMAN: Bruce Baker
GENERAL SECRETARY: Greg Steene
DIRECTORS: B. Baker, G. Steene, P. Brogan, J. Gill, J. Evans, R. Cameron

MEMBERSHIP OPEN TO ALL SMALL HALL PROMOTERS

Commonwealth Champions, 1887-2004

Since the 1997 edition, Harold Alderman's magnificent research into Imperial British Empire title fights has introduced many more claimants/champions than were shown previously. Prior to 12 October 1954, the date that the British Commonwealth and Empire Boxing Championships Committee was formed, there was no official body as such and the Australian and British promoters virtually ran the show, with other members of the British Empire mainly out in the cold. We have also listed Canadian representatives, despite championship boxing in that country being contested over ten or 12 rounds at most, but they are not accorded the same kind of recognition that their British and Australian counterparts are. On 8 September 1970, Bunny Sterling became the first immigrant to win a British title under the ten-year residential ruling and from that date on champions are recorded by domicile rather than by birthplace. Reconstituted as the British Commonwealth Boxing Championships Committee on 22 November 1972, and with a current membership that includes Australia, Bahama, Ghana, Guyana, Jamaica, Kenya, New Zealand, Nigeria, South Africa, Tanzania, Trinidad and Tobago, Zambia, and Zimbabwe, in 1989 the 'British' tag was dropped.

COMMONWEALTH COUNTRY CODE

A = Australia; BAH = Bahamas; BAR = Barbados; BER = Bermuda; C = Canada; E = England; F = Fiji; GH = Ghana; GU = Guyana; I = Ireland; J = Jamaica; K = Kenya; N = Nigeria; NZ = New Zealand; NI = Northern Ireland; PNG = Papua New Guinea; SA = South Africa; SAM = Samoa; S = Scotland; T = Tonga; TR = Trinidad; U = Uganda; W = Wales; ZA = Zambia; ZI = Zimbabwe.

Champions in **bold** denote those recognised by the British Commonwealth and Empire Boxing Championships Committee (1954 to date) and, prior to that, those with the best claims

*Undefeated champions (Does not include men who forfeited titles)

Title Holder	Birthplace/ Domicile	Tenure	Title Holder	Birthplace/ Domicile	Tenure	Title Holder	Birthplace/ Domicile	Tenure
Flyweight (112 lbs)			**Bantamweight (118 lbs)**			Ray Minus*	BAH	1986-1991
Elky Clark*	S	1924-1927	**Digger Stanley**	E	1904-1905	John Armour*	E	1992-1996
Harry Hill	E	1929	**Owen Moran**	E	1905	Paul Lloyd*	E	1996-2000
Frenchy Belanger	C	1929	**Ted Green**	A	1905-1911	Ady Lewis	E	2000
Vic White	A	1929-1930	**Charlie Simpson***	A	1911-1912	Tommy Waite	NI	2000
Teddy Green	A	1930-1931	**Jim Higgins**	S	1920-1922	Nicky Booth	E	2000-2002
Jackie Paterson	S	1940-1948	**Tommy Harrison**	E	1922-1923	Steve Molitor	C	2002-2004
Rinty Monaghan*	NI	1948-1950	**Bugler Harry Lake**	E	1923			
Teddy Gardner	E	1952	**Johnny Brown**	E	1923-1928	**S. Bantamweight (122 lbs)**		
Jake Tuli	SA	1952-1954	Billy McAllister	A	1928-1930	Neil Swain	W	1995
Dai Dower*	W	1954-1957	**Teddy Baldock***	E	1928-1930	Neil Swain	W	1996-1997
Frankie Jones	S	1957	Johnny Peters	E	1930	Michael Brodie	E	1997-1999
Dennis Adams*	SA	1957-1962	**Dick Corbett**	E	1930-1932	Nedal Hussein*	A	2000-2001
Jackie Brown	S	1962-1963	**Johnny King**	E	1932-1934	Brian Carr	S	2001-2002
Walter McGowan*	S	1963-1969	**Dick Corbett**	E	1934	Michael Alldis	E	2002
John McCluskey	S	1970-1971	Frankie Martin	C	1935-1937	Esham Pickering	E	2003-
Henry Nissen	A	1971-1974	Baby Yack	C	1937			
Big Jim West*	A	1974-1975	Johnny Gaudes	C	1937-1939	**Featherweight (126 lbs)**		
Patrick Mambwe	ZA	1976-1979	Lefty Gwynn	C	1939	**Jim Driscoll***	W	1908-1913
Ray Amoo	N	1980	Baby Yack	C	1939-1940	**Llew Edwards**	W	1915-1916
Steve Muchoki	K	1980-1983	**Jim Brady**	S	1941-1945	**Charlie Simpson***	A	1916
Keith Wallace*	E	1983-1984	**Jackie Paterson**	S	1945-1949	Tommy Noble	E	1919-1921
Richard Clarke	J	1986-1987	**Stan Rowan**	E	1949	**Bert Spargo**	A	1921-1922
Nana Yaw Konadu*	GH	1987-1989	**Vic Toweel**	SA	1949-1952	**Bert McCarthy**	A	1922
Alfred Kotey*	GH	1989-1993	**Jimmy Carruthers***	A	1952-1954	**Bert Spargo**	A	1922-1923
Francis Ampofo*	E	1993	**Peter Keenan**	S	1955-1959	**Billy Grime**	A	1923
Daren Fifield	E	1993-1994	**Freddie Gilroy***	NI	1959-1963	**Ernie Baxter**	A	1923
Francis Ampofo	E	1994-1995	**Johnny Caldwell**	NI	1964-1965	Leo Kid Roy	C	1923
Danny Ward	SA	1995-1996	**Alan Rudkin**	E	1965-1966	**Bert Ristuccia**	A	1923-1924
Peter Culshaw	E	1996-1997	**Walter McGowan**	S	1966-1968	Barney Wilshur	C	1923
Ady Lewis*	E	1997-1998	**Alan Rudkin**	E	1968-1969	Benny Gould	C	1923-1924
Alfonso Zvenyika	ZI	1998	**Lionel Rose***	A	1969	**Billy Grime**	A	1924
Damaen Kelly	NI	1998-1999	**Alan Rudkin***	E	1970-1972	Leo Kid Roy	C	1924-1932
Keith Knox	S	1999	**Paul Ferreri**	A	1972-1977	**Johnny McGrory**	S	1936-1938
Jason Booth*	E	1999-2003	**Sulley Shittu**	GH	1977-1978	**Jim Spider Kelly**	NI	1938-1939
Dale Robinson	E	2003-	**Johnny Owen***	W	1978-1980	**Johnny Cusick**	E	1939-1940
			Paul Ferreri	A	1981-1986	**Nel Tarleton**	E	1940-1947

Title Holder	Birthplace/ Domicile	Tenure	Title Holder	Birthplace/ Domicile	Tenure	Title Holder	Birthplace/ Domicile	Tenure
Tiger Al Phillips	E	1947	**S. Featherweight (130 lbs)**			Dick Burge*	E	1894-1895
Ronnie Clayton	E	1947-1951	Billy Moeller	A	1975-1977	Jim Murphy*	NZ	1894-1897
Roy Ankrah	GH	1951-1954	Johnny Aba*	PNG	1977-1982	Eddie Connolly*	C	1896-1897
Billy Spider Kelly	NI	1954-1955	Langton Tinago	ZI	1983-1984	Jack Goldswain	E	1906-1908
Hogan Kid Bassey*	N	1955-1957	John Sichula	ZA	1984	Jack McGowan	A	1909
Percy Lewis	TR	1957-1960	Lester Ellis*	A	1984-1985	Hughie Mehegan	A	1909-1910
Floyd Robertson	GH	1960-1967	John Sichula	ZA	1985-1986	Johnny Summers*	E	1910
John O'Brien	S	1967	Sam Akromah	GH	1986-1987	Hughie Mehegan	A	1911
Johnny Famechon*	A	1967-1969	John Sichula	ZA	1987-1989	Freddie Welsh*	W	1912-1914
Toro George	NZ	1970-1972	Mark Reefer*	E	1989-1990	Ernie Izzard	E	1928
Bobby Dunne	A	1972-1974	Thunder Aryeh	GH	1990-1991	Tommy Fairhall	A	1928-1930
Evan Armstrong	S	1974	Hugh Forde	E	1991	Al Foreman	E	1930-1933
David Kotey*	GH	1974-1975	Paul Harvey	E	1991-1992	Jimmy Kelso	A	1933
Eddie Ndukwu	N	1977-1980	Tony Pep	C	1992-1995	Al Foreman*	E	1933-1934
Pat Ford*	GU	1980-1981	Justin Juuko*	U	1995-1998	Laurie Stevens*	SA	1936-1937
Azumah Nelson*	GH	1981-1985	Charles Shepherd*	E	1999	Dave Crowley	E	1938
Tyrone Downes	BAR	1986-1988	Mick O'Malley	A	1999-2000	Eric Boon	E	1938-1944
Thunder Aryeh	GH	1988-1989	Ian McLeod*	S	2000	Ronnie James*	W	1944-1947
Oblitey Commey	GH	1989-1990	James Armah*	GH	2000-2001	Arthur King	C	1948-1951
Modest Napunyi	K	1990-1991	Alex Moon	E	2001-2002	Frank Johnson	E	1953
Barrington Francis*	C	1991	Dean Pithie	E	2002-2003	Pat Ford	A	1953-1954
Colin McMillan*	E	1992	Craig Docherty	S	2003-	Ivor Germain	BAR	1954
Billy Hardy*	E	1992-1996				Pat Ford	A	1954-1955
Jonjo Irwin	E	1996-1997	**Lightweight (135 lbs)**			Johnny van Rensburg	SA	1955-1956
Paul Ingle*	E	1997-1999	Jim Burge	A	1890	Willie Toweel	SA	1956-1959
Patrick Mullings	E	1999-2000	George Dawson*	A	1890	Dave Charnley	E	1959-1962
Scott Harrison*	S	2000-2002	Harry Nickless	E	1892-1894	Bunny Grant	J	1962-1967
Nicky Cook	E	2003-	Arthur Valentine	E	1894-1895	Manny Santos*	NZ	1967

Nicky Cook (left) looked good when successfully defending the Commonwealth featherweight title last October against the dangerous Ghanaian, Anyetei Laryea

Les Clark

Title Holder	Birthplace/ Domicile	Tenure
Love Allotey	GH	1967-1968
Percy Hayles	J	1968-1975
Jonathan Dele	N	1975-1977
Lennox Blackmore	GU	1977-1978
Hogan Jimoh	N	1978-1980
Langton Tinago	ZI	1980-1981
Barry Michael	A	1981-1982
Claude Noel	T	1982-1984
Graeme Brooke	A	1984-1985
Barry Michael*	A	1985-1986
Langton Tinago	ZI	1986-1987
Mo Hussein	E	1987-1989
Pat Doherty	E	1989
Najib Daho	E	1989-1990
Carl Crook	E	1990-1992
Billy Schwer	E	1992-1993
Paul Burke	E	1993
Billy Schwer	E	1993-1995
David Tetteh	GH	1995-1997
Billy Irwin	C	1997
David Tetteh	GH	1997-1999
Bobby Vanzie	E	1999-2001
James Armah*	GH	2001-2002
David Burke*	E	2002
Michael Muya	K	2003
Kevin Bennett*	E	2003-2004

L. Welterweight (140 lbs)

Title Holder	Birthplace/ Domicile	Tenure
Joe Tetteh	GH	1972-1973
Hector Thompson	A	1973-1977
Baby Cassius Austin	A	1977-1978
Jeff Malcolm	A	1978-1979
Obisia Nwankpa	N	1979-1983
Billy Famous	N	1983-1986
Tony Laing	E	1987-1988
Lester Ellis	A	1988-1989
Steve Larrimore	BAH	1989
Tony Ekubia	E	1989-1991
Andy Holligan	E	1991-1994
Ross Hale	E	1994-1995
Paul Ryan	E	1995-1996
Andy Holligan	E	1996-1997
Bernard Paul	E	1997-1999
Eamonn Magee	NI	1999-
Paul Burke	E	1997
Felix Bwalya*	ZA	1997
Paul Burke	E	1998-1999
Eamonn Magee*	NI	1999-2002
Junior Witter	E	2002-

Welterweight (147 lbs)

Title Holder	Birthplace/ Domicile	Tenure
Tom Williams	A	1892-1895
Dick Burge	E	1895-1897
Eddie Connelly*	C	1903-1905
Joe White*	C	1907-1909
Johnny Summers	E	1912-1914
Tom McCormick	I	1914
Matt Wells	E	1914-1919
Fred Kay	A	1915
Tommy Uren	A	1915-1916
Fritz Holland	A	1916
Tommy Uren	A	1916-1919
Fred Kay	A	1919-1920
Johnny Basham	W	1919-1920
Bermondsey Billy Wells	E	1922

Title Holder	Birthplace/ Domicile	Tenure
Ted Kid Lewis	E	1920-1924
Tommy Milligan*	S	1924-1925
Jack Carroll	A	1928
Charlie Purdie	A	1928-1929
Wally Hancock	A	1929-1930
Tommy Fairhall*	A	1930
Jack Carroll	A	1934-1938
Eddie Thomas	W	1951
Wally Thom	E	1951-1952
Cliff Curvis	W	1952
Gerald Dreyer	SA	1952-1954
Barry Brown	NZ	1954
George Barnes	A	1954-1956
Darby Brown	A	1956
George Barnes	A	1956-1958
Johnny van Rensburg	SA	1958
George Barnes	A	1958-1960
Brian Curvis*	W	1960-1966
Johnny Cooke	E	1967-1968
Ralph Charles	E	1968-1972
Clyde Gray	C	1973-1979
Chris Clarke	C	1979
Clyde Gray*	C	1979-1980
Colin Jones	W	1981-1984
Sylvester Mittee	E	1984-1985
Lloyd Honeyghan*	E	1985-1986
Brian Janssen	A	1987
Wilf Gentzen	A	1987-1988
Gary Jacobs	S	1988-1989
Donovan Boucher	C	1989-1992
Eamonn Loughran*	NI	1992-1993
Andrew Murray*	GU	1993-1997
Kofi Jantuah*	GH	1997-2000
Scott Dixon*	S	2000
Jawaid Khaliq*	E	2000-2001
Julian Holland	A	2001-2002
James Hare*	E	2002-2003
Ossie Duran*	GH	2003-2004

L. Middleweight (154 lbs)

Title Holder	Birthplace/ Domicile	Tenure
Charkey Ramon*	A	1972-1975
Maurice Hope*	E	1976-1979
Kenny Bristol	GU	1979-1981
Herol Graham*	E	1981-1984
Ken Salisbury	A	1984-1985
Nick Wilshire	E	1985-1987
Lloyd Hibbert	E	1987
Troy Waters*	A	1987-1991
Chris Pyatt*	E	1991-1992
Mickey Hughes	E	1992-1993
Lloyd Honeyghan	E	1993-1994
Leo Young	A	1994-1995
Kevin Kelly	A	1995
Chris Pyatt	E	1995-1996
Steve Foster	E	1996-1997
Kevin Kelly	A	1997-1999
Tony Badea	C	1999-2001
Richard Williams*	E	2001
Joshua Onyango	K	2002
Michael Jones	E	2002-2003
Jamie Moore*	E	2003-2004
Richard Williams*	E	2004
Jamie Moore	E	2004
Ossie Duran	GH	2004-

Middleweight (160 lbs)

Title Holder	Birthplace/ Domicile	Tenure
Chesterfield Goode	E	1887-1890
Toff Wall	E	1890-1891
Jim Hall	A	1892-1893
Bill Heffernan	NZ	1894-1896
Bill Doherty	A	1896-1897
Billy Edwards	A	1897-1898
Dido Plumb*	E	1898-1901
Tom Duggan	A	1901-1903
Jack Palmer*	E	1902-1904
Jewey Cooke	E	1903-1904
Tom Dingey	C	1904-1905
Jack Lalor	SA	1905
Ted Nelson	A	1905
Tom Dingey	C	1905
Sam Langford*	C	1907-1911
Ed Williams	A	1908-1910
Arthur Cripps	A	1910
Dave Smith	A	1910-1911
Jerry Jerome	A	1913
Arthur Evernden	E	1913-1914
Mick King	A	1914-1915
Les Darcy*	A	1915-1917
Ted Kid Lewis	E	1922-1923
Roland Todd	E	1923-1926
Len Johnson	E	1926-1928
Tommy Milligan	S	1926-1928
Alex Ireland	S	1928-1929
Len Harvey	E	1929-1933
Del Fontaine	C	1931
Ted Moore	E	1931
Jock McAvoy	E	1933-1939
Ron Richards*	A	1940
Ron Richards*	A	1941-1942
Bos Murphy	NZ	1948
Dick Turpin	E	1948-1949
Dave Sands*	A	1949-1952
Randy Turpin	E	1952-1954
Al Bourke	A	1952-1954
Johnny Sullivan	E	1954-1955
Pat McAteer	E	1955-1958
Dick Tiger	N	1958-1960
Wilf Greaves	C	1960
Dick Tiger*	N	1960-1962
Gomeo Brennan	BAH	1963-1964
Tuna Scanlon*	NZ	1964
Gomeo Brennan	BAH	1964-1966
Blair Richardson*	C	1966-1967
Milo Calhoun	J	1967
Johnny Pritchett*	E	1967-1969
Les McAteer	E	1969-1970
Mark Rowe	E	1970
Bunny Sterling	E	1970-1972
Tony Mundine*	A	1972-1975
Monty Betham	NZ	1975-1978
Al Korovou	A	1978
Ayub Kalule	U	1978-1980
Tony Sibson*	E	1980-1983
Roy Gumbs	E	1983
Mark Kaylor	E	1983-1984
Tony Sibson*	E	1984-1988
Nigel Benn	E	1988-1989
Michael Watson*	E	1989-1991
Richie Woodhall	E	1992-1995
Robert McCracken	E	1995-1997

Title Holder	Birthplace/ Domicile	Tenure
Johnson Tshuma	SA	1997-1998
Paul Jones	E	1998-1999
Jason Matthews*	E	1999
Alain Bonnamie*	C	1999-2000
Sam Soliman	A	2000
Howard Eastman*	E	2000-2004

S. Middleweight (168 lbs)

Title Holder	Birthplace/ Domicile	Tenure
Rod Carr	A	1989-1990
Lou Cafaro	A	1990-1991
Henry Wharton*	E	1991-1997
Clinton Woods	E	1997-1998
David Starie	E	1998-2003
Andre Thysse	SA	2003
Charles Adamu	GH	2003-2004
Carl Froch	E	2004-

L. Heavyweight (175 lbs)

Title Holder	Birthplace/ Domicile	Tenure
Dave Smith*	A	1911-1915
Jack Bloomfield*	E	1923-1924
Tom Berry	E	1927
Gipsy Daniels*	W	1927
Len Harvey	E	1939-1942

Title Holder	Birthplace/ Domicile	Tenure
Freddie Mills*	E	1942-1950
Randy Turpin*	E	1952-1955
Gordon Wallace	C	1956-1957
Yvon Durelle*	C	1957-1959
Chic Calderwood	S	1960-1963
Bob Dunlop*	A	1968-1970
Eddie Avoth	W	1970-1971
Chris Finnegan	E	1971-1973
John Conteh*	E	1973-1974
Steve Aczel	A	1975
Tony Mundine	A	1975-1978
Gary Summerhays	C	1978-1979
Lottie Mwale	ZA	1979-1985
Leslie Stewart*	TR	1985-1987
Willie Featherstone	C	1987-1989
Guy Waters*	A	1989-1993
Brent Kosolofski	C	1993-1994
Garry Delaney	E	1994-1995
Noel Magee	I	1995
Nicky Piper*	W	1995-1997
Crawford Ashley	E	1998-1999
Clinton Woods*	E	1999-2000
Neil Simpson	E	2001

Title Holder	Birthplace/ Domicile	Tenure
Tony Oakey*	E	2001-2002
Peter Oboh	E	2002-

Cruiserweight (190 lbs)

Title Holder	Birthplace/ Domicile	Tenure
Stewart Lithgo	E	1984
Chisanda Mutti	ZA	1984-1987
Glenn McCrory*	E	1987-1989
Apollo Sweet	A	1989
Derek Angol*	E	1989-1993
Francis Wanyama	U	1994-1995
Chris Okoh	E	1995-1997
Darren Corbett	NI	1997-1998
Bruce Scott	E	1998-1999
Adam Watt*	A	2000-2001
Bruce Scott*	E	2001-2003
Mark Hobson	E	2003-

Heavyweight (190 lbs +)

Title Holder	Birthplace/ Domicile	Tenure
Peter Jackson*	A	1889-1901
Dan Creedon	NZ	1896-1903
Billy McColl	A	1902-1905
Tim Murphy	A	1905-1906
Bill Squires	A	1906-1909
Bill Lang	A	1909-1910
Tommy Burns*	C	1910-1911
P.O. Curran	I	1911
Dan Flynn	I	1911
Bombardier Billy Wells	E	1911-1919
Bill Lang	A	1911-1913
Dave Smith	A	1913-1917
Joe Beckett*	E	1919-1923
Phil Scott	E	1926-1931
Larry Gains	C	1931-1934
Len Harvey	E	1934
Jack Petersen	W	1934-1936
Ben Foord	SA	1936-1937
Tommy Farr	W	1937
Len Harvey*	E	1939-1942
Jack London	E	1944-1945
Bruce Woodcock	E	1945-1950
Jack Gardner	E	1950-1952
Johnny Williams	W	1952-1953
Don Cockell	E	1953-1956
Joe Bygraves	J	1956-1957
Joe Erskine	W	1957-1958
Brian London	E	1958-1959
Henry Cooper	E	1959-1971
Joe Bugner	E	1971
Jack Bodell	E	1971-1972
Danny McAlinden	NI	1972-1975
Bunny Johnson	E	1975
Richard Dunn	E	1975-1976
Joe Bugner*	E	1976-1977
John L. Gardner*	E	1978-1981
Trevor Berbick	C	1981-1986
Horace Notice*	E	1986-1988
Derek Williams	E	1988-1992
Lennox Lewis*	E	1992-1993
Henry Akinwande	E	1993-1995
Scott Welch	E	1995-1997
Julius Francis*	E	1997-1999
Danny Williams	E	1999-2004
Michael Sprott	E	2004
Matt Skelton	E	2004-

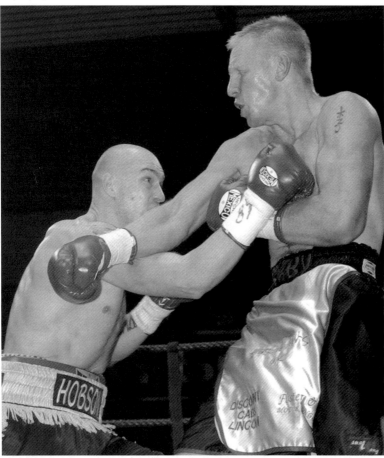

In scoring a good win over the tough Lee Swaby, Mark Hobson (left) kept hold of his Commonwealth light-heavyweight title as well as putting a third notch on a Lonsdale Belt   Les Clark

European Title Bouts During 2003-2004

All of last season's title bouts are shown in date order within their weight divisions and give the boxers respective weights, along with the scorecard if going to a decision. There is also a short summary of any bout that involved a British contestant and British officials are listed where applicable.

Flyweight
14 November 2003   Brahim Asloum 7.13$\frac{1}{4}$ (France) W PTS 12 Jose Antonio Bueno 7.13$\frac{1}{4}$ (Spain), Levallois-Perret, France. Scorecards: 119-110, Larry O'Connell 117-111, Paul Thomas 114-114. Billed for the vacant title after Russia's Alexander Mahmutov vacated in September in order to prepare for a crack at the WBO champion, Omar Narvaez, on the same bill.

29 April 2004   Brahim Asloum 8.0 (France) W PTS 12 Ivan Pozo 7.13$\frac{1}{2}$ (Spain), Levallois-Perret, France. Scorecards: 116-112, Dave Parris 115-113, 115-113.

Bantamweight
11 June 2004   David Guerault 8.4$\frac{3}{4}$ (France) L RSC 1 Frederic Patrac 8.3 (France), Nancy, France.

S. Bantamweight
16 January 2004   Esham Pickering 8.10 (England) W CO 10 Vincenzo Gigliotti 8.8$\frac{3}{4}$ (Italy), Pennington's Nightclub, Bradford, England. Billed for the vacant title after the champion, Mahyar Monshipour (France), handed back his belt in July 2003 on winning the WBA championship, Pickering made a good start and was out in front until the rugged Italian came back into it during the middle rounds. However, in the eighth, the British and Commonwealth champion picked up the pace again with right uppercuts and left hooks to the body. The finish was now in sight and, following a head clash that unsettled Gigliotti in the tenth, he sank to the canvas to be counted out at 2.20 of the session after being hit by a short left to the temple.

12 May 2004   Esham Pickering 8.9$\frac{1}{2}$ (England) W RSC 8 Juan Garcia Martin 8.7 (Spain), Rivermead Leisure Centre, Reading, England. In what turned out to be an extremely competitive fight, the Spaniard looking dangerous with the right and Pickering bouncing in and out to score points, it looked as though it would go the distance until Martin turned away in the eighth, holding his right elbow. It was apparent that he didn't want to continue and following a standing count, the referee called it off on the 2.19 mark.

Featherweight
20 March 2004   Cyril Thomas 8.13$\frac{3}{4}$ (France) L CO 9 Nicky Cook 9.0 (England), The Arena, Wembley, England. A clash of unbeaten fighters saw the Frenchman's left jab pitted against the rugged power of the body-punching Englishman, who simply wouldn't take no for an answer. Although many shots seemed borderline, Cook was

Esham Pickering (left) made a successful defence of his European super-bantam title when stopping Spain's Juan Garcia Martin last May

Les Clark

allowed to continue and eventually Thomas crumbled. Dropped twice towards the end of the seventh, body punches again doing the damage, the champion made it through the eighth before being dropped by a left hook to the side and being counted out at 1.09 of the ninth, while in the act of rising.

S. Featherweight
4 October 2003   Affif Djelta 9.2 (France) L RSC 10 Boris Sinitsin 9.2$^{1}/_{2}$ (Russia), Rouen, France.
7 February 2004   Boris Sinitsin 9.3$^{3}/_{4}$ (Russia) W PTS 12 Joao Antonio Bento 9.3$^{3}/_{4}$ (Portugal), Algarve, Portugal.
29 April 2004   Boris Sinitsin 9.3$^{1}/_{2}$ (Russia) W PTS 12 Ali Oubaali 9.1$^{1}/_{2}$ (France), Levallois-Perret, France. Scorecards: 116-113, 116-113, 113-116. Referee: Dave Parris.

Lightweight
14 November 2003   Stefano Zoff 9.6$^{3}/_{4}$ (Italy) W RSC 7 Christophe de Busellet 9.8$^{1}/_{2}$ (France), Levallois-Perret, France. Referee: Larry O'Connell. Judge: Paul Thomas.
13 March 2004   Stefano Zoff 9.7$^{1}/_{2}$ (Italy) W PTS 12 Laszlo Komjathi 9.9$^{1}/_{4}$ (Hungary), Manerba del Garda, Italy. Scorecards: 119-109, 119-110, Paul Thomas 118-112.

L. Welterweight
24 November 2003   Oktay Urkal 9.13$^{1}/_{4}$ (Germany) W PTS 12 Krzysztof Bienias 9.13 (Poland), Riesa, Germany. Scorecards: 120-108, 120-108, 120-107. Urkal vacated during November 2003 to concentrate on a world title shot against the WBA secondary champion, Vivien Harris.
2 June 2004   Junior Witter 9.13$^{1}/_{2}$ (England) W RSC 2 Salvatore Battaglia 9.13 (Italy), The Ice Arena, Nottingham, England. Giving an expert display in how to hit without being hit himself, Witter quickly opened up the Italian with speed and accuracy and it was no surprise when a right hook dropped Battaglia in the opening session. The end was already in sight, with Battaglia cut under the right eye, and the second round saw more of the same. Twice dropped heavily, a left to the temple doing instant damage, the challenger was rescued by the referee on the 1.18 mark.

Welterweight
Frederic Klose (France) failed to make a defence during the period.

L. Middleweight
4 October 2003   Roman Karmazin 10.13$^{3}/_{4}$ (Russia) W RTD 3 David Walker 10.13$^{1}/_{2}$ (England), Alexandra Palace Grand Hall, Muswell Hill, London, England. Referee: Mickey Vann. Judges: Richie Davies, Larry O'Connell, Ian John-Lewis. Given a crack at the title, the brave Walker unfortunately found himself out of his depth and was dropped in the second and twice in the third before being rescued by the referee after his corner threw the towel in. The champion's reach made life impossible, the jab going in, followed by hooks to the body opening Walker up throughout and although Karmazin picked up a cut left eye the end was always in sight. The finish, which came at 2.07 of round three, was clinical and although Walker wanted to continue it was over. Karmazin vacated in April 2004 to concentrate on other options he had in the pipeline.

Middleweight
25 July 2003   Howard Eastman 11.6 (England) W RTD 8 Hacine Cherifi 11.5$^{1}/_{2}$ (France), Sports Village, Norwich, England. Boxing well within himself, Eastman was in cruise control by the fifth and was beginning to pick Cherifi, who was cut on the left eye during that session, apart as he constantly upped the pressure. After handing out continual punishment during the next three rounds, it came as no surprise when Cherifi retired himself at the end of the eighth after the contest had become too one sided.
30 January 2004   Howard Eastman (England) 11.5$^{1}/_{2}$ W PTS 12 Sergei Tatevosyan 11.5$^{1}/_{4}$ (Russia), Goresbrook Leisure Centre, Dagenham, England. Scorecards: 116-113, 117-112, 120-109. By Eastman's standards this was a disappointing performance and, at times, he was made to look 'plodding' by the tricky Russian southpaw, who often embarrassed the champion by his movement and fleet of foot. However, while at no time did Eastman look likely to lose to the light-punching challenger, who finished with a cut left eye, he was unable to set his man up and, ultimately, had to settle for the points win.

S. Middleweight
4 October 2003   Danilo Haeussler 11.13$^{1}/_{2}$ (Germany) L PTS 12 Mads Larsen 11.13$^{3}/_{4}$ (Denmark), Zwickau, Germany. Scorecards: 108-120, 112-116, 112-116. Referee: Paul Thomas. Larsen relinquished the title in June 2004, due to medical problems to his neck making him unavailable to defend within the required period.

L. Heavyweight
12 July 2003   Stipe Drews 12.6$^{1}/_{4}$ (Croatia) W PTS 12 Kamel Amrane 12.4$^{3}/_{4}$ (France), Leverkusen, Germany. Scorecards: 116-112, 116-112, 120-109. Referee: Dave Parris.
18 November 2003   Stipe Drews 12.6$^{1}/_{2}$ (Croatia) W RSC 6 Olivier Beard 12.4$^{1}/_{2}$ (France), Hamburg, Germany. Referee: Mickey Vann.
8 May 2004   Stipe Drews 12.6$^{1}/_{2}$ (Croatia) W PTS 12 Konstantin Shvets 12.6$^{1}/_{4}$ (Ukraine), Dortmund, Germany. Scorecards: 120-108, 120-102, 120-108. Referee: Mickey Vann. Drews relinquished the title towards the end of June 2004 to pursue other opportunities.

Cruiserweight
27 March 2004   Vincenzo Canatore 14.0$^{1}/_{4}$ (Italy) W PTS 12 Ismael Abdoul 13.7$^{3}/_{4}$ (Belgium, Rome, Italy. Scorecards: 119-109, 117-111, 117-112. Referee: Ian John-Lewis. Originally intended to be a fight to decide the championship between Canatore and Alexander Gurov, after Pietro Aurino relinquished the title in November 2003 rather than face the latter, Abdoul was a replacement for Gurov, who cried off injured.
5 June 2004   Vincenzo Canatore 14.3 (Italy) DREW 12 Rudiger May 14.2$^{3}/_{4}$ (Germany), Chemnitz, Germany. Scorecards: 115-114, 114-115, 115-115.

Heavyweight
14 February 2004   Sinan Samil Sam 17.0 (Turkey) L PTS 12 Luan Krasniqi 16.7$^{1}/_{2}$ (Germany), Stuttgart, Germany. Scorecards: 113-115, 113-116, 114-114. Referee: Richie Davies.

European Champions, 1909-2004

Prior to 1946, the championship was contested under the auspices of the International Boxing Union, re-named that year as the European Boxing Union (EBU). The IBU had come into being when Victor Breyer, a Paris-based journalist and boxing referee who later edited the Annuaire du Ring (first edition in 1910), warmed to the idea of an organisation that controlled boxing right across Europe, regarding rules and championship fights between the champions of the respective countries. He first came to London at the end of 1909 to discuss the subject with the NSC, but went away disappointed. However, at a meeting between officials from Switzerland and France in March 1912, the IBU was initially formed and, by June of that year, had published their first ratings. By April 1914, Belgium had also joined the organisation, although it would not be until the war was over that the IBU really took off. Many of the early champions shown on the listings were the result of promoters, especially the NSC, billing their own championship fights. Although the (French dominated) IBU recognised certain champions, prior to being re-formed in May 1920, they did not find their administrative 'feet' fully until other countries such as Italy (1922), Holland (1923), and Spain (1924), produced challengers for titles. Later in the 1920s, Germany (1926), Denmark (1928), Portugal (1929) and Romania (1929) also joined the fold. Unfortunately, for Britain, its representatives (Although the BBBoC, as we know it today, was formed in 1929, an earlier attempt to form a Board of Control had been initiated in April 1918 by the NSC and it was that body who were involved here) failed to reach agreement on the three judges' ruling, following several meetings with the IBU early in 1920 and, apart from Elky Clark (fly), Ernie Rice and Alf Howard (light), and Jack Hood (welter), who conformed to that stipulation, fighters from these shores would not be officially recognised as champions until the EBU was formed in 1946. This led to British fighters claiming the title after beating IBU titleholders, or their successors, under championship conditions in this country. The only men who did not come into this category were Kid Nicholson (bantam), and Ted Kid Lewis and Tommy Milligan (welter), who defeated men not recognised by the IBU. For the record, the first men recognised and authorised, respectively, as being champions of their weight classes by the IBU were: Sid Smith and Michel Montreuil (fly), Charles Ledoux (bantam), Jim Driscoll and Louis de Ponthieu (feather), Freddie Welsh and Georges Papin (light), Georges Carpentier and Albert Badoud (welter), Georges Carpentier and Ercole Balzac (middle), Georges Carpentier and Battling Siki (light-heavy and heavy).

EUROPEAN COUNTRY CODE

AU = Austria; BEL = Belgium; BUL = Bulgaria; CRO = Croatia; CZ = Czechoslovakia; DEN = Denmark; E = England; FIN = Finland; FR = France; GER = Germany; GRE = Greece; HOL = Holland; HUN = Hungary; ITA = Italy; KAZ = Kazakhstan; LUX = Luxembourg; NI = Northern Ireland; NOR = Norway; POL = Poland; POR = Portugal; ROM = Romania; RUS = Russia; S = Scotland; SP = Spain; SWE = Sweden; SWI = Switzerland; TU = Turkey; UK = Ukraine; W = Wales; YUG = Yugoslavia.

Champions in **bold** denote those recognised by the IBU/EBU

*Undefeated champions (Does not include men who may have forfeited titles)

Title Holder	Birthplace/ Domicile	Tenure
Flyweight (112 lbs)		
Sid Smith	E	1913
Bill Ladbury	E	1913-1914
Percy Jones	W	1914
Joe Symonds	E	1914
Tancy Lee	S	1914-1916
Jimmy Wilde	W	1914-1915
Jimmy Wilde*	W	1916-1923
Michel Montreuil	BEL	1923-1925
Elky Clark*	S	1925-1927
Victor Ferrand	SP	1927
Emile Pladner	FR	1928-1929
Johnny Hill	S	1928-1929
Eugene Huat	FR	1929
Emile Degand	BEL	1929-1930
Kid Oliva	FR	1930
Lucien Popescu	ROM	1930-1931
Jackie Brown	E	1931-1935
Praxile Gyde	FR	1932-1935
Benny Lynch	S	1935-1938
Kid David*	BEL	1935-1936
Ernst Weiss	AU	1936
Valentin Angelmann*	FR	1936-1938
Enrico Urbinati*	ITA	1938-1943
Raoul Degryse	BEL	1946-1947
Maurice Sandeyron	FR	1947-1949
Rinty Monaghan*	NI	1949-1950
Terry Allen	E	1950
Jean Sneyers*	BEL	1950-1951
Teddy Gardner*	E	1952
Louis Skena*	FR	1953-1954
Nazzareno Giannelli	ITA	1954-1955
Dai Dower	W	1955
Young Martin	SP	1955-1959
Risto Luukkonen	FIN	1959-1961
Salvatore Burruni*	ITA	1961-1965
Rene Libeer	FR	1965-1966
Fernando Atzori	ITA	1967-1972
Fritz Chervet	SWI	1972-1973
Fernando Atzori	ITA	1973
Fritz Chervet*	SWI	1973-1974
Franco Udella	ITA	1974-1979
Charlie Magri*	E	1979-1983
Antoine Montero	FR	1983-1984
Charlie Magri*	E	1984-1985
Franco Cherchi	ITA	1985
Charlie Magri	E	1985-1986
Duke McKenzie*	E	1986-1988
Eyup Can*	TU	1989-1990
Pat Clinton*	S	1990-1991
Salvatore Fanni	ITA	1991-1992
Robbie Regan*	W	1992-1993
Luigi Camputaro	ITA	1993-1994
Robbie Regan*	W	1994-1995
Luigi Camputaro*	ITA	1995-1996
Jesper Jensen	DEN	1996-1997
David Guerault*	FR	1997-1999
Alexander Mahmutov	RUS	1999-2000
Damaen Kelly*	NI	2000
Alexander Mahmutov	RUS	2000-2002
Mimoun Chent	FR	2002-2003
Alexander Mahmutov*	RUS	2003
Brahim Asloum	FR	2003-
Bantamweight (118 lbs)		
Joe Bowker	E	1910
Digger Stanley	E	1910-1912
Charles Ledoux	FR	1912-1921
Bill Beynon	W	1913
Tommy Harrison	E	1921-1922
Charles Ledoux	FR	1922-1923
Bugler Harry Lake	E	1923
Johnny Brown	E	1923-1928
Henry Scillie*	BEL	1925-1928
Kid Nicholson	E	1928
Teddy Baldock	E	1928-1931
Domenico Bernasconi	ITA	1929
Carlos Flix	SP	1929-1931
Lucien Popescu	ROM	1931-1932
Domenico Bernasconi	ITA	1932
Nicholas Biquet	BEL	1932-1935
Maurice Dubois	SWI	1935-1936
Joseph Decico	FR	1936
Aurel Toma	ROM	1936-1937
Nicholas Biquet	BEL	1937-1938
Aurel Toma	ROM	1938-1939
Ernst Weiss	AU	1939
Gino Cattaneo	ITA	1939-1941
Gino Bondavilli*	ITA	1941-1943
Jackie Paterson	S	1946
Theo Medina	FR	1946-1947
Peter Kane	E	1947-1948
Guido Ferracin	ITA	1948-1949

Title Holder	Birthplace/Domicile	Tenure
Luis Romero	SP	1949-1951
Peter Keenan	S	1951-1952
Jean Sneyers*	BEL	1952-1953
Peter Keenan	S	1953
John Kelly	NI	1953-1954
Robert Cohen*	FR	1954-1955
Mario D'Agata	ITA	1955-1958
Piero Rollo	ITA	1958-1959
Freddie Gilroy	NI	1959-1960
Pierre Cossemyns	BEL	1961-1962
Piero Rollo	ITA	1962
Alphonse Halimi	FR	1962
Piero Rollo	ITA	1962-1963
Mimoun Ben Ali	SP	1963
Risto Luukkonen	FIN	1963-1964
Mimoun Ben Ali	SP	1965
Tommaso Galli	ITA	1965-1966
Mimoun Ben Ali	SP	1966-1968
Salvatore Burruni*	ITA	1968-1969
Franco Zurlo	ITA	1969-1971
Alan Rudkin	E	1971
Agustin Senin*	SP	1971-1973
Johnny Clark*	E	1973-1974
Bob Allotey	SP	1974-1975
Daniel Trioulaire	FR	1975-1976
Salvatore Fabrizio	ITA	1976-1977
Franco Zurlo	ITA	1977-1978
Juan Francisco Rodriguez	SP	1978-1980
Johnny Owen*	W	1980
Valerio Nati	ITA	1980-1982
Giuseppe Fossati	ITA	1982-1983
Walter Giorgetti	ITA	1983-1984
Ciro de Leva*	ITA	1984-1986
Antoine Montero	FR	1986-1987
Louis Gomis*	FR	1987-1988
Fabrice Benichou	FR	1988
Vincenzo Belcastro*	ITA	1988-1990
Thierry Jacob*	FR	1990-1992
Johnny Bredahl*	DEN	1992
Vincenzo Belcastro	ITA	1993-1994
Prince Naseem Hamed*	E	1994-1995
John Armour*	E	1995-1996
Johnny Bredahl	DEN	1996-1998
Paul Lloyd*	E	1998-1999
Johnny Bredahl*	DEN	1999-2000
Luigi Castiglione	ITA	2000-2001
Fabien Guillerme	FR	2001
Alex Yagupov	RUS	2001
Spend Abazi	SWE	2001-2002
Noel Wilders	E	2003
David Guerault	FR	2003-2004
Frederic Patrac	FR	2004-

S. Bantamweight (122 lbs)

Title Holder	Birthplace/Domicile	Tenure
Vincenzo Belcastro	ITA	1995-1996
Salim Medjkoune	FR	1996
Martin Krastev	BUL	1996-1997
Spencer Oliver	E	1997-1998
Sergei Devakov	UK	1998-1999
Michael Brodie*	E	1999-2000
Vladislav Antonov	RUS	2000-2001
Salim Medjkoune*	FR	2001-2002
Mahyar Monshipour*	FR	2002-2003
Esham Pickering	E	2003-

Featherweight (126 lbs)

Title Holder	Birthplace/Domicile	Tenure
Young Joey Smith	E	1911
Jean Poesy	FR	1911-1912
Jim Driscoll*	W	1912-1913
Ted Kid Lewis*	E	1913-1914
Louis de Ponthieu*	FR	1919-1920
Arthur Wyns	BEL	1920-1922
Billy Matthews	E	1922

Title Holder	Birthplace/Domicile	Tenure
Eugene Criqui*	FR	1922-1923
Edouard Mascart	FR	1923-1924
Charles Ledoux	FR	1924
Henri Hebrans	BEL	1924-1925
Antonio Ruiz	SP	1925-1928
Luigi Quadrini	ITA	1928-1929
Knud Larsen	DEN	1929
Jose Girones	SP	1929-1934
Maurice Holtzer*	FR	1935-1938
Phil Dolhem	BEL	1938-1939
Lucien Popescu	ROM	1939-1941
Ernst Weiss	AU	1941
Gino Bondavilli	ITA	1941-1945
Ermanno Bonetti*	ITA	1945-1946
Tiger Al Phillips	E	1947
Ronnie Clayton	E	1947-1948
Ray Famechon	FR	1948-1953
Jean Sneyers	BEL	1953-1954
Ray Famechon	FR	1954-1955
Fred Galiana*	SP	1955-1956
Cherif Hamia	FR	1957-1958
Sergio Caprari	ITA	1958-1959
Gracieux Lamperti	FR	1959-1962
Alberto Serti	ITA	1962-1963
Howard Winstone	W	1963-1967
Jose Legra*	SP	1967-1968
Manuel Calvo	SP	1968-1969
Tommaso Galli	ITA	1969-1970
Jose Legra*	SP	1970-1972
Gitano Jiminez	SP	1973-1975
Elio Cotena	ITA	1975-1976
Nino Jimenez	SP	1976-1977
Manuel Masso	SP	1977
Roberto Castanon*	SP	1977-1981
Salvatore Melluzzo	ITA	1981-1982
Pat Cowdell*	E	1982-1983
Loris Stecca*	ITA	1983
Barry McGuigan*	NI	1983-1985
Jim McDonnell*	E	1985-1987
Valerio Nati*	ITA	1987
Jean-Marc Renard*	BEL	1988-1989
Paul Hodkinson*	E	1989-1991
Fabrice Benichou	FR	1991-1992
Maurizio Stecca	ITA	1992-1993
Herve Jacob	FR	1993
Maurizio Stecca	ITA	1993
Stephane Haccoun	FR	1993-1994
Stefano Zoff	ITA	1994
Medhi Labdouni	FR	1994-1995
Billy Hardy	E	1995-1998
Paul Ingle*	E	1998-1999
Steve Robinson	W	1999-2000
Istvan Kovacs*	HUN	2000-2001
Manuel Calvo*	SP	2001-2002
Cyril Thomas	FR	2002-2004
Nicky Cook	E	2004-

S. Featherweight (130 lbs)

Title Holder	Birthplace/Domicile	Tenure
Tommaso Galli	ITA	1971-1972
Domenico Chiloiro	ITA	1972
Lothar Abend	GER	1972-1974
Sven-Erik Paulsen*	NOR	1974-1976
Roland Cazeaux	FR	1976
Natale Vezzoli	ITA	1976-1979
Carlos Hernandez	SP	1979
Rodolfo Sanchez	SP	1979
Carlos Hernandez	SP	1979-1982
Cornelius Boza-Edwards*	E	1982
Roberto Castanon	SP	1982-1983
Alfredo Raininger	ITA	1983-1984
Jean-Marc Renard	BEL	1984
Pat Cowdell	E	1984-1985
Jean-Marc Renard*	BEL	1986-1987

Title Holder	Birthplace/Domicile	Tenure
Salvatore Curcetti	ITA	1987-1988
Piero Morello	ITA	1988
Lars Lund Jensen	DEN	1988
Racheed Lawal	DEN	1988-1989
Daniel Londas*	FR	1989-1991
Jimmy Bredahl*	DEN	1992
Regilio Tuur	HOL	1992-1993
Jacobin Yoma	FR	1993-1995
Anatoly Alexandrov*	KAZ	1995-1996
Julian Lorcy*	FR	1996
Djamel Lifa	FR	1997-1998
Anatoly Alexandrov*	RUS	1998
Dennis Holbaek Pedersen	DEN	1999-2000
Boris Sinitsin	RUS	2000
Dennis Holbaek Pedersen*	DEN	2000
Tontcho Tontchev*	BUL	2001
Boris Sinitsin	RUS	2001-2002
Pedro Oscar Miranda	SP	2002
Affif Djelti	FR	2002-2003
Boris Sinitsin	RUS	2003-

Lightweight (135 lbs)

Title Holder	Birthplace/Domicile	Tenure
Freddie Welsh	W	1909-1911
Matt Wells	E	1911-1912
Freddie Welsh*	W	1912-1914
Georges Papin	FR	1920-1921
Ernie Rice	E	1921-1922
Seaman Nobby Hall	E	1922-1923
Harry Mason	E	1923-1926
Fred Bretonnel	FR	1924
Lucien Vinez	FR	1924-1927
Luis Rayo*	SP	1927-1928
Aime Raphael	FR	1928-1929
Francois Sybille	BEL	1929-1930
Alf Howard	E	1930
Harry Corbett	E	1930-1931
Francois Sybille	BEL	1930-1931
Bep van Klaveren	HOL	1931-1932
Cleto Locatelli	ITA	1932
Francois Sybille	BEL	1932-1933
Cleto Locatelli*	ITA	1933
Francois Sybille	BEL	1934
Carlo Orlandi*	ITA	1934-1935
Enrico Venturi*	ITA	1935-1936
Vittorio Tamagnini	ITA	1936-1937
Maurice Arnault	FR	1937
Gustave Humery	FR	1937-1938
Aldo Spoldi*	ITA	1938-1939
Karl Blaho	AU	1940-1941
Bruno Bisterzo	ITA	1941
Ascenzo Botta	ITA	1941
Bruno Bisterzo	ITA	1941-1942
Ascenzo Botta	ITA	1942
Roberto Proietti	ITA	1942-1943
Bruno Bisterzo	ITA	1943-1946
Roberto Proietti*	ITA	1946
Emile Dicristo	FR	1946-1947
Kid Dussart	BEL	1947
Roberto Proietti	ITA	1947-1948
Billy Thompson	E	1948-1949
Kid Dussart	BEL	1949
Roberto Proietti*	ITA	1949-1950
Pierre Montane	FR	1951
Elis Ask	FIN	1951-1952
Jorgen Johansen	DEN	1952-1954
Duilio Loi*	ITA	1954-1959
Mario Vecchiatto	ITA	1959-1960
Dave Charnley	E	1960-1963
Conny Rudhof*	GER	1963-1964
Willi Quatuor*	GER	1964-1965
Franco Brondi	ITA	1965
Maurice Tavant	FR	1965-1966
Borge Krogh	DEN	1966-1967
Pedro Carrasco*	SP	1967-1969

Title Holder	Birthplace/Domicile	Tenure
Miguel Velazquez	SP	1970-1971
Antonio Puddu	ITA	1971-1974
Ken Buchanan*	S	1974-1975
Fernand Roelandts	BEL	1976
Perico Fernandez*	SP	1976-1977
Jim Watt*	S	1977-1979
Charlie Nash*	NI	1979-1980
Francisco Leon	SP	1980
Charlie Nash	NI	1980-1981
Joey Gibilisco	ITA	1981-1983
Lucio Cusma	ITA	1983-1984
Rene Weller	GER	1984-1986
Gert Bo Jacobsen	DEN	1986-1988
Rene Weller*	GER	1988
Policarpo Diaz*	SP	1988-1990
Antonio Renzo	ITA	1991-1992
Jean-Baptiste Mendy*	FR	1992-1994
Racheed Lawal	DEN	1994
Jean-Baptiste Mendy*	FR	1994-1995
Angel Mona	FR	1995-1997
Manuel Carlos Fernandes	FR	1997
Oscar Garcia Cano	SP	1997
Billy Schwer*	E	1997-1999
Oscar Garcia Cano	SP	1999-2000
Lucien Lorcy*	FR	2000-2001
Stefano Zoff*	ITA	2001-2002
Jason Cook	W	2002-2003
Stefano Zoff	ITA	2003-

L. Welterweight (140 lbs)

Title Holder	Birthplace/Domicile	Tenure
Olli Maki	FIN	1964-1965
Juan Sombrita-Albornoz	SP	1965
Willi Quatuor*	GER	1965-1966
Conny Rudhof	GER	1967
Johann Orsolics	AU	1967-1968
Bruno Arcari*	ITA	1968-1970
Rene Roque	FR	1970-1971
Pedro Carrasco*	SP	1971-1972
Roger Zami	FR	1972
Cemal Kamaci	TU	1972-1973
Toni Ortiz	SP	1973-1974
Perico Fernandez*	SP	1974
Jose Ramon Gomez-Fouz	SP	1975
Cemal Kamaci*	TU	1975-1976
Dave Boy Green*	E	1976-1977
Primo Bandini	ITA	1977
Jean-Baptiste Piedvache	FR	1977-1978
Colin Power	E	1978
Fernando Sanchez	SP	1978-1979
Jose Luis Heredia	SP	1979
Jo Kimpuani	FR	1979-1980
Giuseppe Martinese	ITA	1980
Antonio Guinaldo	SP	1980-1981
Clinton McKenzie	E	1981-1982
Robert Gambini	FR	1982-1983
Patrizio Oliva*	ITA	1983-1985
Terry Marsh	E	1985-1986
Tusikoleta Nkalankete	FR	1987-1989
Efren Calamati	ITA	1989-1990
Pat Barrett	E	1990-1992
Valery Kayumba	ITA	1992-1993
Christian Merle	FR	1993-1994
Valery Kayumba	FR	1994
Khalid Rahilou*	FR	1994-1996
Soren Sondergaard*	DEN	1996-1998
Thomas Damgaard*	DEN	1998-2000
Oktay Urkal*	GER	2000-2001
Gianluca Branco*	ITA	2001-2002
Oktay Urkal*	GER	2002-2003
Junior Witter	E	2004-

Welterweight (147 lbs)

Title Holder	Birthplace/Domicile	Tenure
Young Joseph	E	1910-1911
Georges Carpentier*	FR	1911-1912
Albert Badoud*	SWI	1915-1921
Johnny Basham	W	1919-1920
Ted Kid Lewis	E	1920-1924
Piet Hobin	BEL	1921-1925
Billy Mack	E	1923
Tommy Milligan	S	1924-1925
Mario Bosisio*	ITA	1925-1928
Leo Darton	BEL	1928
Alf Genon	BEL	1928-1929
Gustave Roth	BEL	1929-1932
Adrien Aneet	BEL	1932-1933
Jack Hood*	E	1933
Gustav Eder	GER	1934-1936
Felix Wouters	BEL	1936-1938
Saverio Turiello	ITA	1938-1939
Marcel Cerdan*	FR	1939-1942
Ernie Roderick	E	1946-1947
Robert Villemain*	FR	1947-1948
Livio Minelli	ITA	1949-1950
Michele Palermo	ITA	1950-1951
Eddie Thomas	W	1951
Charles Humez*	FR	1951-1952
Gilbert Lavoine	FR	1953-1954
Wally Thom	E	1954-1955
Idrissa Dione	FR	1955-1956
Emilio Marconi	ITA	1956-1958
Peter Waterman*	E	1958
Emilio Marconi	ITA	1958-1959
Duilio Loi*	ITA	1959-1963
Fortunato Manca*	ITA	1964-1965
Jean Josselin	FR	1966-1967
Carmelo Bossi	ITA	1967-1968
Fighting Mack	HOL	1968-1969
Silvano Bertini	ITA	1969
Jean Josselin	FR	1969
Johann Orsolics	AU	1969-1970
Ralph Charles	E	1970-1971
Roger Menetrey	FR	1971-1974
John H. Stracey*	E	1974-1975
Marco Scano	ITA	1976-1977
Jorgen Hansen	DEN	1977
Jorg Eipel	GER	1977
Alain Marion	FR	1977-1978
Jorgen Hansen	DEN	1978
Josef Pachler	AU	1978
Henry Rhiney	E	1978-1979
Dave Boy Green	E	1979
Jorgen Hansen*	DEN	1979-1981
Hans-Henrik Palm	DEN	1982
Colin Jones*	W	1982-1983
Gilles Elbilia	FR	1983-1984
Gianfranco Rosi	ITA	1984-1985
Lloyd Honeyghan*	E	1985-1986
Jose Varela	GER	1986-1987
Alfonso Redondo	SP	1987
Mauro Martelli*	SWI	1987-1988
Nino la Rocca	ITA	1989
Antoine Fernandez	FR	1989-1990
Kirkland Laing	E	1990
Patrizio Oliva*	ITA	1990-1992
Ludovic Proto	FR	1992-1993
Gary Jacobs*	S	1993-1994
Jose Luis Navarro	SP	1994-1995
Valery Kayumba	FR	1995
Patrick Charpentier*	FR	1995-1996
Andrei Pestriaev*	RUS	1997
Michele Piccirillo*	ITA	1997-1998
Maxim Nesterenko	RUS	1998-1999
Alessandro Duran	ITA	1999
Andrei Pestriaev	RUS	1999-2000
Alessandro Duran	ITA	2000
Thomas Damgaard	DEN	2000-2001
Alessandro Duran	ITA	2001-2002
Christian Bladt	DEN	2002
Michel Trabant*	GER	2002-2003
Frederic Klose	FR	2003-

L. Middleweight (154 lbs)

Title Holder	Birthplace/Domicile	Tenure
Bruno Visintin	ITA	1964-1966
Bo Hogberg	SWE	1966
Yolande Leveque	FR	1966
Sandro Mazzinghi*	ITA	1966-1968
Remo Golfarini	ITA	1968-1969
Gerhard Piaskowy	GER	1969-1970
Jose Hernandez	SP	1970-1972
Juan Carlos Duran	ITA	1972-1973
Jacques Kechichian	FR	1973-1974
Jose Duran	SP	1974-1975
Eckhard Dagge	GER	1975-1976
Vito Antuofermo	ITA	1976
Maurice Hope*	E	1976-1978
Gilbert Cohen	FR	1978-1979
Marijan Benes	YUG	1979-1981
Louis Acaries	FR	1981
Luigi Minchillo*	ITA	1981-1983
Herol Graham*	E	1983-1984
Jimmy Cable	E	1984
Georg Steinherr	GER	1984-1985
Said Skouma*	FR	1985-1986
Chris Pyatt	E	1986-1987
Gianfranco Rosi*	ITA	1987
Rene Jacquot*	FR	1988-1989
Edip Secovic	AU	1989
Giuseppe Leto	ITA	1989
Gilbert Dele*	FR	1989-1990
Said Skouma	FR	1991
Mourad Louati	HOL	1991
Jean-Claude Fontana	FR	1991-1992
Laurent Boudouani	FR	1992-1993
Bernard Razzano	FR	1993-1994
Javier Castillejos	SP	1994-1995
Laurent Boudouani*	FR	1995-1996
Faouzi Hattab	FR	1996
Davide Ciarlante*	ITA	1996-1997
Javier Castillejo*	SP	1998
Mamadou Thiam*	FR	1998-2000
Roman Karmazin*	RUS	2000
Mamadou Thiam*	FR	2001
Wayne Alexander*	E	2002
Roman Karmazin*	RUS	2003-2004

Middleweight (160 lbs)

Title Holder	Birthplace/Domicile	Tenure
Georges Carpentier*	FR	1912-1918
Ercole Balzac	FR	1920-1921
Gus Platts	E	1921
Willem Westbroek	HOL	1921
Johnny Basham	W	1921
Ted Kid Lewis	E	1921-1923
Roland Todd	E	1923-1924
Ted Kid Lewis	E	1924-1925
Bruno Frattini	ITA	1924-1925
Tommy Milligan	S	1925-1928
Rene Devos	BEL	1926-1927
Barthelemy Molina	FR	1928
Alex Ireland	S	1928-1929
Mario Bosisio	ITA	1928
Leone Jacovacci	ITA	1928-1929
Len Johnson	E	1928-1929
Marcel Thil	FR	1929-1930
Mario Bosisio	ITA	1930-1931
Poldi Steinbach	AU	1931
Hein Domgoergen	GER	1931-1932
Ignacio Ara	SP	1932-1933
Gustave Roth	BEL	1933-1934
Marcel Thil*	FR	1934-1938
Edouard Tenet	FR	1938
Bep van Klaveren	HOL	1938
Anton Christoforidis	GRE	1938-1939
Edouard Tenet	FR	1939
Josef Besselmann*	GER	1942-1943
Marcel Cerdan	FR	1947-1948

221

Title Holder	Birthplace/ Domicile	Tenure
Cyrille Delannoit	BEL	1948
Marcel Cerdan*	FR	1948
Cyrille Delannoit	BEL	1948-1949
Tiberio Mitri*	ITA	1949-1950
Randy Turpin	E	1951-1954
Tiberio Mitri	ITA	1954
Charles Humez	FR	1954-1958
Gustav Scholz*	GER	1958-1961
John Cowboy McCormack	S	1961-1962
Chris Christensen	DEN	1962
Laszlo Papp*	HUN	1962-1965
Nino Benvenuti*	ITA	1965-1967
Juan Carlos Duran	ITA	1967-1969
Tom Bogs	DEN	1969-1970
Juan Carlos Duran	ITA	1970-1971
Jean-Claude Bouttier	FR	1971-1972
Tom Bogs*	DEN	1973
Elio Calcabrini	ITA	1973-1974
Jean-Claude Bouttier	FR	1974
Kevin Finnegan	E	1974-1975
Gratien Tonna*	FR	1975
Bunny Sterling	E	1976
Angelo Jacopucci	ITA	1976
Germano Valsecchi	ITA	1976-1977
Alan Minter	E	1977
Gratien Tonna	FR	1977-1978
Alan Minter*	E	1978-1979
Kevin Finnegan	E	1980
Matteo Salvemini	ITA	1980
Tony Sibson*	E	1980-1982
Louis Acaries	FR	1982-1984
Tony Sibson	E	1984-1985
Ayub Kalule	DEN	1985-1986
Herol Graham	E	1986-1987
Sumbu Kalambay*	ITA	1987
Pierre Joly	FR	1987-1988
Christophe Tiozzo*	FR	1988-1989
Francesco dell' Aquila	ITA	1989-1990
Sumbu Kalambay*	ITA	1990-1993
Agostino Cardamone*	ITA	1993-1994
Richie Woodhall*	E	1995-1996
Alexandre Zaitsev	RUS	1996
Hassine Cherifi*	FR	1996-1998
Agostino Cardamone*	ITA	1998
Erland Betare*	FR	1999-2000
Howard Eastman*	E	2001
Christian Sanavia	ITA	2001-2002
Morrade Hakkar*	FR	2002
Howard Eastman	E	2003-

S. Middleweight (168 lbs)

Title Holder	Birthplace/ Domicile	Tenure
Mauro Galvano*	ITA	1990-1991
James Cook	E	1991-1992
Franck Nicotra*	FR	1992
Vincenzo Nardiello	ITA	1992-1993
Ray Close*	NI	1993
Vinzenzo Nardiello	ITA	1993-1994
Frederic Seillier*	FR	1994-1995
Henry Wharton*	E	1995-1996
Frederic Seillier*	FR	1996
Andrei Shkalikov*	RUS	1997
Dean Francis*	E	1997-1998
Bruno Girard*	FR	1999
Andrei Shkalikov	RUS	2000-2001
Danilo Haeussler	GER	2001-2003
Mads Larsen*	DEN	2003-2004

L. Heavyweight (175 lbs)

Title Holder	Birthplace/ Domicile	Tenure
Georges Carpentier	FR	1913-1922
Battling Siki	FR	1922-1923
Emile Morelle	FR	1923
Raymond Bonnel	FR	1923-1924
Louis Clement	SWI	1924-1926
Herman van T'Hof	HOL	1926
Fernand Delarge	BEL	1926-1927
Max Schmeling*	GER	1927-1928
Michele Bonaglia*	ITA	1929-1930
Ernst Pistulla*	GER	1931-1932
Adolf Heuser	GER	1932
John Andersson	SWE	1933
Martinez de Alfara	SP	1934
Marcel Thil	FR	1934-1935
Merlo Preciso	ITA	1935
Hein Lazek	AU	1935-1936
Gustave Roth	BEL	1936-1938
Adolf Heuser*	GER	1938-1939
Luigi Musina*	ITA	1942-1943
Freddie Mills*	E	1947-1950
Albert Yvel	FR	1950-1951
Don Cockell*	E	1951-1952
Conny Rux*	GER	1952
Jacques Hairabedian	FR	1953-1954
Gerhard Hecht	GER	1954-1955
Willi Hoepner	GER	1955
Gerhard Hecht	GER	1955-1957
Artemio Calzavara	ITA	1957-1958
Willi Hoepner	GER	1958
Erich Schoeppner	GER	1958-1962
Giulio Rinaldi	ITA	1962-1964
Gustav Scholz*	GER	1964-1965
Giulio Rinaldi	ITA	1965-1966
Piero del Papa	ITA	1966-1967
Lothar Stengel	GER	1967-1968
Tom Bogs*	DEN	1968-1969
Yvan Prebeg	YUG	1969-1970
Piero del Papa	ITA	1970-1971
Conny Velensek	GER	1971-1972
Chris Finnegan	E	1972
Rudiger Schmidtke	GER	1972-1973
John Conteh*	E	1973-1974
Domenico Adinolfi	ITA	1974-1976
Mate Parlov*	YUG	1976-1977
Aldo Traversaro	ITA	1977-1979
Rudi Koopmans	HOL	1979-1984
Richard Caramonolis	FR	1984
Alex Blanchard	HOL	1984-1987
Tom Collins	E	1987-1988
Pedro van Raamsdonk	HOL	1988
Jan Lefeber	HOL	1988-1989
Eric Nicoletta	FR	1989-1990
Tom Collins	E	1990-1991
Graciano Rocchigiani*	GER	1991-1992
Eddie Smulders	HOL	1993-1994
Fabrice Tiozzo*	FR	1994-1995
Eddy Smulders	HOL	1995-1996
Crawford Ashley	E	1997
Ole Klemetsen*	NOR	1997-1998
Crawford Ashley	E	1998-1999
Clinton Woods*	E	1999-2000
Yawe Davis	ITA	2001-2002
Thomas Ulrich*	GER	2002-2003
Stipe Drews*	CRO	2003-2004

Cruiserweight (190 lbs)

Title Holder	Birthplace/ Domicile	Tenure
Sam Reeson*	E	1987-1988
Angelo Rottoli	ITA	1989
Anaclet Wamba*	FR	1989-1990
Johnny Nelson*	E	1990-1992
Akim Tafer*	FR	1992-1993
Massimiliano Duran	ITA	1993-1994
Carl Thompson	E	1994
Alexander Gurov	UK	1995
Patrice Aouissi	FR	1995
Alexander Gurov*	UK	1995-1996
Akim Tafer*	FR	1996-1997
Johnny Nelson	E	1997-1998
Terry Dunstan*	E	1998
Alexei Iliin	RUS	1999
Torsten May*	GER	1999-2000
Carl Thompson*	E	2000-2001
Alexander Gurov*	UK	2001-2002
Pietro Aurino*	ITA	2002-2003
Vincenzo Canatore	ITA	2004-

Heavyweight (190 lbs +)

Title Holder	Birthplace/ Domicile	Tenure
Georges Carpentier	FR	1913-1922
Battling Siki	FR	1922-1923
Erminio Spalla	ITA	1923-1926
Paolino Uzcudun	SP	1926-1928
Harry Persson	SWE	1926
Phil Scott	E	1927
Pierre Charles	BEL	1929-1931
Hein Muller	GER	1931-1932
Pierre Charles	BEL	1932-1933
Paolino Uzcudun	SP	1933
Primo Carnera	ITA	1933-1935
Pierre Charles	BEL	1935-1937
Arno Kolblin	GER	1937-1938
Hein Lazek	AU	1938-1939
Adolf Heuser	GER	1939
Max Schmeling*	GER	1939-1941
Olle Tandberg	SWE	1943
Karel Sys*	BEL	1943-1946
Bruce Woodcock	E	1946-1949
Joe Weidin	AU	1950-1951
Jack Gardner	E	1951
Hein Ten Hoff	GER	1951-1952
Karel Sys	BEL	1952
Heinz Neuhaus	GER	1952-1955
Franco Cavicchi	ITA	1955-1956
Ingemar Johansson*	SWE	1956-1959
Dick Richardson	W	1960-1962
Ingemar Johansson*	SWE	1962-1963
Henry Cooper*	E	1964
Karl Mildenberger	GER	1964-1968
Henry Cooper*	E	1968-1969
Peter Weiland	GER	1969-1970
Jose Urtain	SP	1970
Henry Cooper	E	1970-1971
Joe Bugner	E	1971
Jack Bodell	E	1971
Jose Urtain	SP	1971-1972
Jurgen Blin	GER	1972
Joe Bugner*	E	1972-1975
Richard Dunn	E	1976
Joe Bugner	E	1976-1977
Jean-Pierre Coopman	BEL	1977
Lucien Rodriguez	FR	1977
Alfredo Evangelista	SP	1977-1979
Lorenzo Zanon	SP	1979-1980
John L. Gardner*	E	1980-1981
Lucien Rodriguez	FR	1981-1984
Steffen Tangstad	NOR	1984-1985
Anders Eklund	SWE	1985
Frank Bruno*	E	1985-1986
Steffen Tangstad	NOR	1986
Alfredo Evangelista	SP	1987
Anders Eklund	SWE	1987
Francesco Damiani	ITA	1987-1989
Derek Williams	E	1989-1990
Jean Chanet	FR	1990
Lennox Lewis*	E	1990-1992
Henry Akinwande*	E	1993-1995
Zeljko Mavrovic*	CRO	1995-1998
Vitali Klitschko*	UK	1998-1999
Vladimir Klitschko*	UK	1999-2000
Vitali Klitschko*	UK	2000-2001
Luan Krasniqi	GER	2002
Przemyslaw Saleta	POL	2002
Sinan Samil Sam	TU	2002-2004
Luan Krasniqi	GER	2004-

A-Z of Current World Champions

by Eric Armit

Shows the record since 1 July 2003, plus career summary and pen portrait, of all men holding IBF, WBA, WBC and WBO titles as at 30 June 2004. The author has also produced the same data for those who first won titles between 1 July 2003 and 30 June 2004, but were no longer champions at the end of the period in question. Incidentally, the place name given is the respective boxer's domicile and may not necessarily be his birthplace, while all nicknames are shown where applicable in brackets. Not included are British fighters, Joe Calzaghe (WBO super-middleweight champion), Johnny Nelson (WBO cruiserweight champion) and Scott Harrison (WBO featherweight champion). Their full records can be found among the Active British-Based Boxers: Career Records' section.

Eagle Akakura

Pichit, Thailand. *Born*: 4 December, 1978
WBC M. Flyweight Champion

Major Amateur Honours: None known
Turned Pro: January 2000
Significant Results: Nico Thomas W CO 3, Noel Tunacao W PTS 10, Elmer Gejon W PTS 8
Type/Style: Short, sturdy, orthodox and a good boxer, he is not a puncher
Points of Interest: Real name is Den Junlaphan. He has also boxed as Den Sorjaturong and Eagle Okuda, but is now fighting under the name of his new sponsor 'Kyowa' after falling out with 'Akakura'. Turned pro in Thailand but moved his base to Japan after only five contests, having been fighting over ten rounds by his third fight. Is married to a former female boxer and has won five fights by stoppage or kayo

10.01.04	Jose Antonio Aguirre W PTS 12 Tokyo *(WBC M.Flyweight Title Challenge)*
28.06.04	Satoshi Kogumazaka W TD 8 Yokohama *(WBC M.Flyweight Title Defence)*
Career: 13 contests, won 13.	

Rosendo (Buffalo) Alvarez

Managua, Nicaragua. *Born* 6 May, 1970
WBA L.Flyweight Champion. Former WBA M.Flyweight Champion

Major Amateur Honours: Competed in the 1991 Pan-American Games and claims 66 wins in 78 fights
Turned Pro: December 1992
Significant Results: José Bonilla W PTS 12 and W CO 11, Chana Porpaoin W PTS 12, Kermin Guardia W CO 3, Eric Chavez W PTS 12, Songkram Porpaoin W RSC 11, Ricardo Lopez T Draw 7 and L PTS 12, Beibis Mendoza L DIS 7 and W PTS 12, Pitchitnoi Chor Siriwat W RSC 12
Type/Style: A fine boxer, who is both skilful and fast, he is also a good in-fighter with a fair punch. However, he has poor discipline
Points of Interest: 5'5" tall. Has 21 wins inside the distance under his belt and has beaten both of the Porpaoin twins. Made five defences of his WBA mini-flyweight title before losing it when he failed to make the weight for his second fight with Ricardo Lopez. Lost for the vacant title to Beibis Mendoza in August 2000, but outpointed him in March 2001 to become champion again and has made three defences. Has had problems with drink and drugs

13.12.03	Jose Victor Burgos DREW 12 Atlantic City *(WBA L.Flyweight Title Defence. IBF L.Flyweight Title Challenge)*
Career: 36 contests, won 32, drew 2, lost 2.	

Noel (El Verdugo) Arambulet

Churuguara, Venezuela. *Born* 18 May, 1974
WBA M.Flyweight Champion

Major Amateur Honours: A former Venezuelan national champion, he claims 128 wins in 144 fights
Turned Pro: November 1996
Significant Results: Jose Garcia L PTS 12 and W PTS 12, Jomo Gamboa W PTS 12 and L PTS 12, Keitaro Hoshino W PTS 12 (twice)
Type/Style: Busy and clever he is a hit-and-run type, but lacks a big punch
Points of Interest: First won the WBA title in October 1999 by beating Joma Gamboa, before losing it to the same man in his second defence. Regained the title with a points win over Keitaro Hoshino in July 2002 and defended successfully against Hoshino in December 2002. Has made only one defence in 19 months due to injuries and is rumoured to be having weight problems. Is married and has two children

12.07.03	Yutaka Niida W PTS 12 Yokohama *(WBA M.Flyweight Title Defence)*
Career: 24 contests, won 20, drew 1, lost 2, no contest 1.	

Jorge (Travieso) Arce

Los Mochis, Mexico. *Born* 27 July, 1979
WBC L.Flyweight Champion. Former WBO L.Flyweight Champion

Major Amateur Honours: None known, but claims 37 wins in 40 bouts
Turned Pro: January 1996
Significant Results: Jose Victor Burgos L PTS 12, Miguel Martinez W CO 2, Juan Domingo Cordoba W PTS 12, Salvatore Fanni W RSC 6, Michael Carbajal L RSC 11, Juanito Rubillar W PTS 12, Melchor Cob Castro W TD 6, Yo-Sam Choi W RSC 6, Augustin Luna W RSC 3, Ernesto Castro W CO 1
Type/Style: Tall and slim, he is a stylish fighter with good speed and power and seems to be growing in stature
Points of Interest: 5'7" tall. Won the WBO title in December 1998 but lost the crown in his second defence in July 1999 to Michael Carbajal. Became the interim WBC titleholder in October 2001, outpointing Juanito Rubillar, won the full title in July 2002 when halting Yosam Choi in Seoul, and has made five defences. Collapsed after beating Cob Castro in a title defence in May 2003, seemingly due to the effort of making the weight, but has made a full recovery. Is a stablemate to the Morales brothers, Erik and Diego, and has 27 wins by stoppage or kayo

10.01.04	Jomo Gamboa W CO 2 Mexico City
	(WBC L.Flyweight Title Defence)
24.04.04	Melchor Cob Castro W CO 5 Tuxtla Gutierrez
	(WBC L.Flyweight Title Defence)
Career: 40 contest, won 36, drew 1, lost 3.	

Wayne (Big Truck) Braithwaite

Plaisience, Guyana. *Born* 9 August, 1975

WBC Cruiserweight Champion. Former Undefeated Guyanan L.Heavyweight Champion

Major Amateur Honours: A four-time Guyanan champion, he competed in the 1996 South American Olympic trials and claims 57 wins in 60 amateur fights
Turned Pro: February 1997
Significant Results: Wayne Harris W CO 7, Adam Watt W RSC 1, Dale Brown W RSC 8, Louis Azile W RSC 12, Vincenzo Cantatore W RSC 10, Ravea Springs W RSC 4
Type/Style: Is a pressure fighter and big-punching southpaw who often switches guards
Points of Interest: 6'4" tall. Won the vacant WBC title by halting Vincenzo Cantatore in October 2002 and has made three defences. Now based in New York, he has 17 wins inside the distance

13.12.03	Luis Andres Pineda W RSC 1 Atlantic City
	(WBC Cruiserweight Title Defence)
17.04.04	Louis Azille W PTS 12 New York City
	(WBC Cruiserweight Title Defence)
Career: 21 contests, won 21.	

Silvio Branco

Civitavecchia, Italy. *Born* 26 August, 1966

Former WBA L.Heavyweight Champion. Former Undefeated Italian Middleweight Champion. Former WBA L.Heavyweight Champion

Major Amateur Honours: None known, but claims 30 fights with only one defeat
Turned Pro: July 1988
Significant Results: Agostino Cardamone L PTS 12 (twice) and L CO 10, Richie Woodhall L RSC 9,

Rodney Toney DREW 12, Thomas Tate W PTS 12, Verno Phillips W PTS 12, Glengoffe Johnson W PTS 12, Robin Reid W PTS 12, Sven Ottke L PTS 12, Stipe Drews L PTS 12
Type/Style: Is a strong, orthodox boxer with a sound chin and good stamina
Points of Interest: 6'0" tall. Following in the family tradition, his father and two brothers all boxed professionally, he failed in challenges for the European middleweight and light-heavyweight titles and IBF super-middleweight title before beating Mehdi Sahnoune for the WBA title. Has 30 wins inside the distance

22.07.03	Raul Barreto W RSC 6 Pavia
10.10.03	Mehdi Sahnoune W RSC 11 Marseilles
	(WBA L.Heavyweight Title Challenge)
20.03.04	Fabrice Tiozzo L PTS 12 Lyon
	(WBA L.Heavyweight Title Defence)
Career: 59 contests, won 49, drew 2, lost 8.	

Johnny Bredahl

Copenhagen, Denmark. *Born* 27 August, 1968

WBA Bantamweight Champion. Former Undefeated WBO S.Flyweight Champion. Former Undefeated European Bantamweight Champion

Major Amateur Honours: A bronze medallist in the 1986 European Youth Championships and 1987 Senior Championships, and a Scandinavian and Danish champion, he competed in the 1988 Olympics
Turned Pro: December 1988
Significant Results: Jose Quirino W PTS 12, Rafael Caban W PTS 12, Wayne McCullough L RSC 8, Efrain Pintor W RSC 2, Alex Yagupov W PTS 12 (twice), Paul Lloyd W RSC 1, Paulie Ayala L PTS 12, Eidy Moya W CO 9, Silvio Gamez W PTS 12
Type/Style: Stylish, upright boxer with an excellent jab and sharp puncher. Good stamina
Points of Interest: 5'8" tall. Real name Johnny Bredahl Johansen. Failed in bids to win WBC and WBA titles before finding success against Moya in April 2002. since when he has defended his title three times. Was unbeaten in eight European title fights. 26 wins by stoppage or knockout

24.10.03	David Guerault W PTS 12 Copenhagen
	(WBA Bantamweight Title Defence)
13.03.04	Nobuaki Naka W PTS 12 Copenhagen
	(WBA Bantamweight Title Defence)
Career: 57 contests, won 55, lost 2.	

Lamon (Relentless) Brewster

Indianapolis, USA. *Born* 5 June, 1973
WBO Heavyweight Champion

Major Amateur Honours: The Californian State Golden Gloves champion in 1992 and 1993, he won a silver medal in the 1995 Pan-American Games. Also won a bronze medal in the 1994 US Championships and a gold medal 1995 US Championships
Turned Pro: November 1996
Significant Results: Clifford Etienne L PTS 10, Charles Shufford L PTS 10, Nate Jones W RSC 3, Tommy Martin W RSC 3
Type/Style: Is powerful with a relaxed style, good hand speed and a hard punch
Points of Interest: 6'1" tall. Devoutly religious and a former High School graduate, he was inactive for 13 months before climbing off the floor to beat Vladimir Klitschko. Has 27 wins inside the distance on his record

10.04.04	Vladimir Klitschko W RSC 5 Las Vegas
	(Vacant WBO Heavyweight Title)
Career: 32 contests, won 30, drew 2, lost 2.	

Jose Victor Burgos

Puebla, Mexico. *Born* 10 April, 1974
IBF L. Flyweight Champion. Former Undefeated Mexican L. Flyweight Champion

Major Amateur Honours: None known
Turned Pro: February 1993
Significant Results: Edgar Cardenas W PTS 12, Jorge Arce W PTS 12, Jacob Matlala L TD 8, Eric Morel L PTS 12, Jesper Jensen L PTS 12, Roberto Leyva L RSC 8, Juan Keb-Baas W PTS 10, Alex Sanchez L PTS 12, DREW 12 and W RSC 12
Type/Style: A flashy fighter, he has a good jab and fast hands
Points of Interest: 5'3" tall. Won the WBO title in his second try by stopping Alex Sanchez in February

2003, having lost and drawn with him in previous efforts. For a long time considered to be only a journeyman, losing his first four pro fights, which included two first-round stoppages, he has lost only one of his last 14 fights. Has 22 wins inside the distance to his name and has made two defences of his title

13.12.03	Rosendo Alvarez DREW 12 Atlantic City *(IBF L.Flyweight Title Defence. WBA L.Flyweight Title Challenge)*
15.05.04	Fahlan Sakkreerin W RSC 6 Las Vegas *(IBF L.Flyweight Title Defence)*
Career: 53 contests, won 37, drew 3, lost 13.	

Chris (Rapid Fire) Byrd

Flint, Michigan, USA. *Born* 15 August, 1970
IBF Heavyweight Champion. Former WBO Heavyweight Champion

Major Amateur Honours: The US champion in 1989 at 156lbs and in 1991 and 1992 at 165 lbs, he won a silver medal in the 1992 Olympic Games
Turned Pro: January 1993
Significant Results: Arthur Williams W PTS 10, Phil Jackson W PTS 12, Lionel Butler W RSC 8, Uriah Grant W PTS 10, Ike Ibeabuchi L RSC 5, Vitali Klitschko W RTD 9, Vladimir Klitschko L PTS 12, David Tua W PTS 12, Evander Holyfield W PTS 12
Type/Style: Is a slick, fast moving southpaw
Points of Interest: Comes from a family of boxers, his Father being head coach for the US amateur team and other members of his family, including a sister, have also fought as professionals. Won the WBO title by beating Vitali Klitschko in April 2000, but lost in his first defence six months later to Vladimir Klitschko. He went on to win the vacant IBF title in December 2002, outpointing Evander Holyfield, and has made two defences. Has had only three fights in two years

20.09.03	Fres Oquendo W PTS 12 Uncasville *(IBF Heavyweight Title Defence)*
17.04.04	Andrew Golota DREW 12 New York *(IBF Heavyweight Title Defence)*
Career: 40 contests, won 37, drew 1, lost 2.	

Chris Byrd   Les Clark

Ivan (Iron Boy) Calderon

Guaynabo, Puerto Rico. *Born* 7 January, 1975
WBO M.Flyweight Champion

Major Amateur Honours: A bronze medallist in the 1999 Pan-American Games, he competed in the World Championships that year. Won a silver medal in the 1999 Central American Games, before competing in the 2000 Olympic Games. Claims 110 wins in 130 bouts
Turned Pro: February 2001
Significant Results: Jorge Romero W RTD 4, Alejandro Moreno W PTS 10, Eduardo Marquez W TD 9
Type/Style: Southpaw. Good counter-puncher but lacks power
Points of Interest: 5'0" tall. Won the WBO title with a technical verdict over Eduardo Marquez in May last year and has two defences, which would have been three if Edgar Cardenas had made the weight for a prospective defence in March. An extrovert, who is tremendously popular in Puerto Rico, he has only four wins by stoppage or kayo

05.09.03	Lorenzo Trejo W PTS 12 Caguas *(WBO M.Flyweight Title Defence)*
06.12.03	Alex Sanchez W PTS 12 Bayamon *(WBO M.Flyweight Title Defence)*
20.03.04	Edgar Cardenas W CO 11 Guaynabo
Career: 19 contests, won 19.	

Jose Luis Castillo

Empalme, Mexico. *Born* December 14,1973
WBC Lightweight Champion. Former Undefeated Mexican Featherweight Champion

Major Amateur Honours: None, but claims 30 wins in 33 fights
Turned Pro: May 1990
Significant Results: Cesar Soto L RSC 2, Javier Jauregui L RSC 10 (twice), Rafael Olvera W RSC 7, Hector Marquez W RSC 10, Javier Alvarez L RSC 11, Sandro Marcos W RSC 6, Jorge Paez W RSC 5, Steve Johnston W PTS 12 and DREW 12, Cesar Bazan W RSC 6, Sung-Ho Yuh W RSC 1, Floyd Mayweather L PTS 12 (twice)
Type/Style: A tight, compact boxer and a sharp puncher, who likes to work inside, he has a strong left jab, a good chin and great stamina, but is prone to cuts
Points of Interest: 5'9" tall. His father was also a pro and fought for the Mexican lightweight title. José Luis, who turned pro when just 16, is a former sparring partner to Julio Cesar Chavez and has 45 wins inside the distance on his record. Although he has lost six times, three of his defeats have been due to cuts. After winning the WBC title by beating Steve Johnston in June 2000, he lost it to Floyd Mayweather in his fourth defence in April 2002. He then failed in a challenge against Mayweather in December 2002, but regained the title by beating Juan Lazcano after Mayweather relinquished the title

10.10.03	Saul Duran W RSC 8 Brownsville
13.02.04	Derrick Parks W RSC 2 Laughlin
05.06.04	Juan Lazcano W PTS 12 Las Vegas *(Vacant WBC Lightweight Title)*
Career: 57 contests, won 50, drew 1, lost 6.	

Jesus (El Matador) Chavez

Parral. Mexico. *Born* 12 November, 1972
Former WBC S.Featherweight Champion

Major Amateur Honours: None known
Turned Pro: August 1994
Significant Results: Carlos Gerena L PTS 8 and W RSC 6, Javier Jauregui W PTS 12, Julio Alvarez W PTS 12,

225

Daryl Pinckney W RSC 6, Tom Johnson W RTD 7, Floyd Mayweather L RTD 9

Type/Style: A tough pressure fighter who wears the opposition down, he has a strong chin and good stamina

Points of Interest: 5'5" tall with a 65" reach. From a boxing family, his father fought as a pro, he served three-and-half years in jail for assault and was deported from the USA twice as an illegal immigrant. Trained by Ronnie Shields, an ex boxer, he lost his fifth fight to Carlos Gerena and then won 31 in a row before losing to Floyd Mayweather in a challenge for the WBC title in November 2001. Suffering a torn rotator cuff early in his fight against Erik Morales, but lasting the distance, he has stopped or kayoed 28 opponents

15.08.03	Sirimongkol Singmanasak W PTS 12 Austin *(WBC S.Featherweight Title Challenge)*
28.02.04	Erik Morales L PTS 12 Las Vegas *(WBC S.Featherweight Title Defence)*
Career: 43 contests, won 40, lost 3.	

In-Jin Chi

Seoul, South Korea. *Born* 18 July, 1973
WBC Featherweight Champion.
Former Undefeated Korean
Bantamweight Champion

Major Amateur Honours: None known
Turned Pro: November 1991
Significant Results: Jesse Maca W PTS 10 and W PTS 12, Baby Lorona W PTS 10, Erik Morales L PTS 12, Sammy Duran W RSC 3
Type/Style: Tough, raw and aggressive, he is a good body puncher with a strong chin
Points of Interest: 5'7" tall with a 67" reach. Although he lost his first paid fight, since then only Erik Morales has beaten him and he now boasts 17 wins inside the distance

02.07.03	Thongcharoen Mahasap Condo W RSC 4 Inchon
18.10.03	Michael Brodie DREW 12 Manchester *(Vacant WBC Featherweight Title)*
10.04.04	Michael Brodie W CO 7 Manchester *(Vacant WBC Featherweight Title)*
Career: 31 contests, won 28, drew 1, lost 2.	

In-Jin Chi Les Clark

Diego (Chico) Corrales

Columbia,USA. *Born* 25 August,1977
WBO S.Featherweight Champion.
Former IBF S.Featherweight
Champion

Major Amateur Honours: Won a silver medal in the US Junior and Senior Championships in 1994 and a bronze Medal in the 1995 Pan-American Games
Turned Pro: March 1996
Significant Results: Steve Quinones W RSC 4, Rafael Meran W CO 2, Hector Arroyo W RSC 5, Gary St Clair W PTS 12, Roberto Garcia W RSC 7, John Brown W PTS 12, Derrick Gainer W RSC 3, Justin Juuko W RSC 10, Angel Manfredy W RSC 3, Floyd Mayweather L RSC 10
Type/Style: Is a strong, heavy hitter and a good combination puncher, he is occasionally let down by a suspect defence
Points of Interest: 5'11" tall with a 73" reach. His Father was a pro and it was no surprise when Diego started boxing at the age of 12. Won the IBF title in October 1999, stopping Roberto Garcia, and made four defences before relinquishing his belt and being on the floor five times

when losing to Floyd Mayweather in a challenge for the WBC title in January 2001. Was jailed in 2001 for spousal assault and was inactive for two years. Has stopped or knocked out 31 opponents

04.10.03	Joel Casamayor L RSC 6 Las Vegas
06.03.04	Joel Casamayor W PTS 12 Uncasville *(Vacant WBO S.Featherweight Title)*
Career: 40 contests, won 38, lost 2.	

Diego Corrales

Kelvin (Koncrete) Davis

Natchez, USA. *Born* 26 May, 1978
IBF Cruiserweight Champion

Major Amateur Honours: None known
Turned Pro: October 1999
Significant Results: David Vedder DREW 6, Arthur Williams W PTS 12, Ravea Springs L PTS 10, Rogerio Lobo W RSC 1, O'Neil Bell L RSC 11
Type/Style: Small, compact and focused, he is a hard puncher, although limited
Points of Interest: Only 5'7" tall, he is trained and managed by his brother Kelly, having been a wrestler in High School. With 15 wins inside the distance on his record, he is similar in style to Mike Tyson and also sports a facial tattoo

24.11.03	Louis Azille W PTS 12 Bushkill
01.05.04	Ezra Sellers W RSC 8 Miami *(Vacant IBF Cruiserweight Title)*
Career: 24 contests, won 21, drew 1, lost 2.	

Oscar (Golden Boy) de la Hoya

Montebello, USA. *Born* 4 February, 1973
WBO Middleweight Champion. Former WBC & WBA L. Middleweight Champion. Former WBC Welterweight Champion. Former Undefeated WBC L.Welterweight Champion. Former Undefeated IBF & WBO Lightweight Champion. Former Undefeated WBO S.Featherweight Champion

Major Amateur Honours: The US champion in 1990/91, he won gold at the 1992 Olympics. Was also the national Golden Gloves champion in 1989
Turned Pro: November 1992
Significant Results: Genaro Hernandez W RSC 6, James Leija W RSC 2, Julio Cesar Chavez W RSC 4 and W RTD 8, Miguel Gonzalez W PTS 12, Pernell Whitaker W PTS 12, Hector Camacho W PTS 12, Ike Quartey W PTS 12, Oba Carr W RSC 11, Felix Trinidad L PTS 12, Derrell Coley W RSC 7, Shane Mosley L PTS 12, Arturo Gatti W RSC 5, Javier Castillejo W RSC 12, Fernando Vargas W RSC 11, Yori Boy Campas W RSC 7
Type/Style: Is a smooth,classy boxer who is a fast and accurate puncher
Points of Interest: 5'11" tall. While winning seven versions of world titles in six divisions, he has beaten 15 world or former world champions, with 29 of his wins coming inside the distance. Boxing since the age of six, he lost the WBC welterweight title to Felix Trinidad, but defeated Derrell Coley in an eliminator and was declared WBC champion again after Trinidad moved up a division. Having lost the title to Shane Mosley in June 2000, Oscar moved up to light-middleweight and won the WBC crown when beating Javier Castillejo in June 2001, only to lose his title on a seemingly unjust decision, to Mosley. Has since won the WBO middleweight title when defeating Felix Sturm in another tough call

13.09.03	Shane Mosley L PTS 12 Las Vegas *(WBC & WBA L.Middleweight Title Defences)*
05.06.04	Felix Sturm W PTS 12 Las Vegas *(WBO Middleweight Title Challenge)*
Career: 40 contests, won 37, lost 3.	

Oscar de la Hoya

Julio (The Kid) Diaz

Huiquilpan, Mexico. *Born* 24 December, 1979
IBF Lightweight Champion

Major Amateur Honours: Won a silver medal in the 1995 US Junior Olympics and competed in the 1998 US Championships
Turned Pro: December 1999
Significant Results: Justo Sencion W CO 9, Dario Esalas W CO 4, Angel Manfredy L PTS 12, Juan Valenzuela L CO 1, James Crayton W PTS 10, Ernesto Zepeda W RSC 7, Miguel Angel Huerta W RSC 8
Type/Style: A skinny, long limbed boxer with excellent left jab and punching power, he also switches. While making excellent progress there are still question marks over his chin
Points of Interest: 5'9" tall with a 70" reach. From a boxing family, his elder brother, Antonio, lost in challenges for the WBC and WBO welterweight titles and two other brothers also boxed as pros. Points deductions for low blows cost him decision against Angel Manfredy and after that loss and another to Juan Valenzuela, Julio almost gave up boxing to become a construction worker. Has 22 wins inside the distance

19.03.04	Courtney Burton W RSC 11 El Cajon
13.05.04	Javier Jauregui W PTS 12 San Diego *(IBF Lightweight Title Challenge)*
Career: 32 contests, won 30, lost 2.	

Nelson (Fueguete) Dieppa

Vieques, Puerto Rico. *Born* 25 February, 1971
WBO L. Flyweight Champion

Major Amateur Honours: Won a bronze medal in the 1991 World Championships, a bronze medal in the 1991 Pan-American Games and competed in the 1992 Olympic Games
Turned Pro: February 1993
Significant Results: Pablo Tiznado W CO 6, Carlos Murillo L PTS 10, Ramon Hurtado W CO 3, Will Grigsby L PTS 12, Julio Coronel W PTS 10, Andy Tabanas W RSC 11, Falan Sakkririn W PTS 12, Jhon Molina T DRAW 2
Type/Style: Is a clever, slick boxer with a solid right-hand punch
Points of Interest: Trained by Felix Trinidad (senior), he has 12 wins inside the distance. Although he lost to Will Grigsby for the WBO title in July 2000, when Grigsby failed a drugs test and was stripped, he won the vacant crown by beating Andy Tabanas in April 2001. Has made only three defences in three years due to contract problems

20.03.04	Kermin Guardia W CO 1 Guaynabo *(WBO L.Flyweight Title Defence)*
Career: 24 contests, won 20, drew 2, lost 2.	

Zsolt (Fire) Erdei

Budapest, Hungary. *Born* 31 May, 1974
WBO L.Heavyweight Champion

Major Amateur Honours: The European Junior champion in 1992, he competed in the 1995 World Championships, won a gold medal in the 1997 championships. In the European Championships, he won silver in 1996 and gold in 1998 and 2000. He also competed in the 1996 and 2000 Olympics, winning a bronze medal in the latter event
Turned Pro: December 2000
Significant Results: Jim Murray W CO 5, Juan Carlos Gimenez W RSC 8, Massimiliano Saiani W RSC 7
Type/Style: Is an excellent technical craftsman and a quick combination puncher with a strong, accurate jab
Points of Interest: 5'10" tall with a 72" reach. Based in Germany, he was floored twice in early fights, but brought the WBO title back to his stable after

227

fellow Universum fighter, Dariusz Michalczewski, had lost to Julio Gonzalez. Has 13 wins inside the distance

17.01.04	Julio Gonzalez W PTS 12 Karlsruhe (WBO L.Heavyweight Title Challenge)
08.05.04	Hugo Herman Garay W PTS 12 Dortmund (WBO L.Heavyweight Title Defence)
Career: 20 contests, won 20.	

Acelino (Popo) Freitas   Les Clark

Acelino (Popo) Freitas
Salvador de Bahia, Brazil. *Born* 21 September, 1975
WBO Lightweight Champion. Former Undefeated WBO & WBA S.Featherweight Champion. Former Brazilian Lightweight Champion

Major Amateur Honours: Won a silver medal in the 1995 Pan-American Games and claims 72 wins in 74 fights
Turned Pro: July 1995
Significant Results: Anatoly Alexandrov W CO 1, Claudio Martinet W CO 3, Barry Jones W RSC 8, Javier Jauregui W RSC 1, Lemuel Nelson W RSC 2, Carlos Rios W RSC 9, Orlando Soto W RSC 4, Alfred Kotey W PTS 10, Joel Casamayor W PTS 12, Daniel

Attah W PTS 12, Juan Carlos Ramirez W RSC 4
Type/Style: Strong and aggressive, he has fast hands, is a quick starter and has crushing puncher with his right hand. On the downside, he can be careless
Points of Interest: 5'7" tall. The member of yet another boxing family, Luiz Carlos, his brother, is also a pro and double Brazilian champion, Acelino won his first 29 fights inside the distance, 22 of them coming within the first three rounds. Has 12 first-round finishes and made ten defences of his WBO super-featherweight title, including the double title victory over Joel Casamayor, and three defences of his combined title before relinquishing in order to move up to lightweight

09.08.03	Jorge Barrios W RSC 12 Miami (WBO & WBA S.Featherweight Title Defences)
03.01.04	Artur Grigorian W PTS 12 Uncasville (WBO Lightweight Title Challenge)
Career: 35 contests, won 35.	

Julio Gonzalez
Guerrero Negro, Mexico. *Born* 30 July, 1976
Former WBO L.Heavyweight Champion

Major Amateur Honours: Lost to Vassily Jirov in the quarter-finals of the 1996 Olympics
Turned Pro: April 1997
Significant Results: Jorge Amparo W RSC 5, Julian Letterlough W PTS 12, Roy Jones L PTS 12, Joseph Kiwanuka W RSC 8, Glengoffe Johnson W PTS 10
Type/Style: Is a tough, aggressive and busy battler
Points of Interest: 6'2" tall. The first Mexican to win a version of the world title at light-heavyweight, he was down three times against Julian Letterlough and had Letterlough down twice. Having lost to Roy Jones in July 2001, in a challenge for the WBC, WBA and IBF titles, he was given little chance of beating Dariusz Michalczewski, who was unbeaten in 48 fights. Has 22 wins inside the distance on his record

18.10.03	Dariusz Michalczewski W PTS 12 Hamburg (WBO L.Heavyweight Title Challenge)
17.01.04	Zsolt Erdei L PTS 12 Karlsruhe (WBO L.Heavyweight Title Defence)
21.05.04	Orlando Rivera W PTS 10 Corpus Christi
Career: 38 contests, won 36, lost 2.	

Joan (Little Tyson) Guzman
Santo Domingo, Dominican Republic. *Born* 1 May, 1976
WBO S.Bantamweight Champion. Former Undefeated Dominican Featherweight & S. Bantamweight Champion

Major Amateur Honours: Competing in the 1995 Pan-American Games and 1996 Olympics, he was a three-time Central American Champion
Turned Pro: September 1997
Significant Results: Francisco DeLeon W CO 11, Hector Avila W CO 2, Edgar Ruiz W PTS 12, Fabio Oliva W CO 3
Type/Style: A compact, powerful, short-armed fighter with good movement and a strong body puncher, he could be a star of the future
Points of Interest: 5'7" tall. Having won the vacant WBO title in Cardiff in August 2002, knocking out Fabio Oliva, contract problems and post-ponements meant he was inactive for 11 months before beating Jorge Monsalvo. With 17 wins inside the distance, he is now managed by Sycuan Native American group

28.07.03	Jorge Monsalvo W CO 1 Santo Domingo
29.08.03	Alfaro Gonzalez W CO 1 Panama City
26.02.04	Agapito Sanchez W RSC 7 San Diego (WBO S.Bantamweight Title Defence)
Career: 21 contests, won 21.	

Vivian (Magnificent) Harris
Georgetown, Guyana. *Born* 17 June, 1978
WBA L. Welterweight Champion

Major Amateur Honours: Was the New York Golden Gloves champion in 1996
Turned Pro: November 1997

Significant Results: Hector Arroyo W RTD 2, Gary St Clair W PTS 10, Ray Oliveira L PTS 10, Ivan Robinson DREW 10, Golden Johnson W RTD 5, Mike Clark W PTS 12, Ubaldo Hernandez W PTS 12, Diobelis Hurtado W RSC 2

Type/Style: Is a fast handed, classy boxer with an excellent jab

Points of Interest: 5'11" tall. His elder brother, Wayne, was also a pro, losing to Reggie Johnson for the WBA middleweight title in 1993, while his trainer is Lennox Blackmoore, who lost to Aaron Pryor for the WBA light-welterweight title in 1981. Stabbed in the stomach in a mugging in 2000, he originally won the 'WBA' title by beating Diobelis Hurtado in October 2002, but did not become full champion until the WBA stripped 'super champion', Kostya Tszyu, in June 2004. Has 16 wins inside the distance and made two defences of his 'WBA' title

12.07.03	Souleymane Mbaye W PTS 12 Las Vegas *(WBA Secondary L.Welterweight Title defence)*
17.04.04	Oktay Urkal W PTS 12 Berlin *(WBA Secondary L. Welterweight Title Defence)*
Career: 26 contests, won 24, drew 1, lost 1.	

Carlos (Famoso) Hernandez

Bellflower, California, USA. *Born* 23 January, 1971

IBF S.Featherweight Champion

Major Amateur Honours: None, but claims 21 wins in 25 fights

Turned Pro: January 1992

Significant Results: Gregorio Vargas W PTS 10, Genaro Hernandez L PTS 12, Floyd Mayweather L PTS 12, Justin Juuko W PTS 10, Mark Burse W PTS 10, David Santos W TD 8, Moises Pedroza W CO 2

Type/Style: Bullish and strong, with an aggressive, crude style, he has a good left hook and a good chin

Points of Interest: Although his parents are from El Salvador, Carlos was born in California and counts scuba diving and rock climbing among his hobbies. Having failed against Genaro Hernandez in 1997 and Floyd Mayweather in 2001 in previous attempts to win a version of the title, he then beat David Santos in February

2003 for the vacant crown and has made just the one defence. Has 24 stoppage or kayo wins

| 04.10.03 | Steve Forbes W TD 10 Los Angeles *(IBF S. Featherweight Title Defence)* |
| **Career:** 44 contests, won 40, drew 1, lost 3. | |

Bernard (The Executioner) Hopkins

Philadelphia, USA. *Born* 15 January, 1965

WBC, WBA and IBF Middleweight Champion

Major Amateur Honours: None, but claims 95 wins in 99 fights

Turned Pro: October 1988

Significant Results: Roy Jones L PTS 12, Lupe Aquino W PTS 12, Segundo Mercado DREW 12 and W PTS 12, Robert Allen NC 4 and W RSC 7, Antwun Echols W PTS 12 and W RSC 10, Syd Vanderpool W PTS 12, Keith Holmes W PTS 12, Felix Trinidad W RSC 12, Carl Daniels W RTD 10, Morrade Hakkar W RTD 8

Type/Style: Strong if mechanical, he is a powerful puncher with fast hands

Points of Interest: 6'0" tall with a 71" reach. The nephew of former pro Art McCloud, he spent five years in jail. Entering the ring wearing an executioners mask and a cape, and despite losing his first paid fight, he can now boast of 28 wins inside the distance. Lost to Roy Jones in his first attempt to win the IBF title and drew with Segundo Mercado for the vacant title before beating Mercado in a return in April 1995. Has made 15 title defences of his IBF title and carried off the WBC title by outpointing Keith Holmes in April 2001 and then the WBA title when halting Felix Trinidad in September 2001. Injured his ankle in first fight with Robert Allen when he was pushed out of the ring and bout was declared a no contest. Has 31 wins inside the distance and has taken part in 20 world title fights

13.12.03	William Joppy W PTS 12 Atlantic City *(IBF,WBA & WBC Middleweight Title Defences)*
05.06.04	Robert Allen W PTS 12 Las Vegas *(IBF,WBA & WBC Middleweight Title Defences)*
Career: 48 contests, won 44, drew 1, lost 2, no contest 1.	

Bernard Hopkins

Javier (Chatito) Jauregui

Guadalajara, Mexico. *Born* 5 September, 1973

Former IBF Lightweight Champion. Former Mexican Featherweight Champion

Major Amateur Honours: None known

Turned Pro: February 1988

Significant Results: Raul Martinez L RSC 9 and W RSC 8, Jose Luis Castillo W RSC 10 (twice), Jesus Chavez L PTS 12, Agapito Sanchez L PTS 10, Jose Badillo W PTS 12, Acelino Freitas L CO 1, Miguel Castillas W RSC 6, Alex Trujillo W PTS 12, Juan Gomez Trinidad W CO 4

Type/Style: Is a tough, rugged pressure fighter with an unorthodox crouching style

Points of Interest: 5'6" tall. Turned pro at the age of 15 and had been campaigning for 15 years before becoming IBF champion, having made eight defences of his Mexican title. The two wins over the current WBC lightweight champion, Jose Luis Castillo, were both due to cuts. Has 34 wins inside the distance

22.11.03	Leavander Johnson W RSC 11 Los Angeles *(Vacant IBF Lightweight Title)*
13.05.04	Julio Diaz L PTS 12 San Diego *(IBF Lightweight Title Defence)*
Career: 60 contests, won 47, drew 2, lost 11.	

Glengoffe (Gentleman) Johnson

Miami, USA. *Born* Clarendon, Jamaica, 2 January 1969

IBF L.Heavyweight Champion

Major Amateur Honours: Competed in the 1992 US National Golden Gloves at 165lbs
Turned Pro: March 1993
Significant Results: Barnard Hopkins L RSC 11, Merqui Sosa L PTS 10, Joseph Kiwanuka L PTS 10, Sven Ottke L PTS 12, Syd Vanderpool L PTS 10, Silvio Branco L PTS 12, Omar Sheika L PTS 10, Toks Owoh W RSC 6, Thomas Ulrich W CO 6, Derrick Harmon L PTS 10, Julio Gonzalez L PTS 10, Daniel Judah DREW 10, Eric Harding W PTS 12
Type/Style: Although a good, solid experienced technician, he sometimes does not put enough effort in to convince the judges
Points of Interest: 5'10" tall. Moved to the USA in 1984 and is now a US citizen. At one time managed by Sugar Ray Leonard, he lost to Bernard Hopkins for the IBF middleweight title in 1997, the only time he has been stopped, and to Sven Ottke for the IBF super-middleweight title in 1999. At one stage he had a run of only two wins in nine bouts, but many of his losses have been disputed or were close verdicts in the other man's backyard. Has 27 wins inside the distance

07.11.03	Clinton Woods DREW 12 Sheffield	
	(Vacant IBF L.Heavyweight Title)	
06.02.04	Clinton Woods W PTS 12 Sheffield	
	(Vacant IBF L.Heavyweight Title)	
Career: 51 contests, won 40, drew 2, lost 9.		

Glengoffe Johnson   Les Clark

Mark (Too Sharp) Johnson
Washington, USA. *Born* 13 August 1971
WBO S. Flyweight Champion. Former Undefeated IBF S.Flyweight & Flyweight Champion

Major Amateur Honours: Was the 1986 US Junior Olympic champion and the 1988 National Golden Gloves champion
Turned Pro: February 1990
Significant Results: Richie Wenton L PTS 4, Alberto Jimenez W PTS 12, Ancee Gedeon W PTS 10, Francisco Tejedor W CO 1, Alex Montiel W PTS 12, Ratanchai Sor Vorapin W PTS 12, Jorge Lacierva W RTD 8, Raul Juarez NC 4, Rafael Marquez L PTS 10 and L RSC 8
Type/Style: Is a strong, aggressive fast-handed puncher
Points of Interest: 5'3" tall. Won the IBF flyweight title in may 1996 and made seven defences before moving up to win the IBF super-flyweight title in 1999. He then made two defences before being stripped of the title after being jailed for breaking his wife's jaw in an assault. Inactive for 18 months, he has put together 28 wins by stoppage or kayo

16.08.03	Fernando Montiel W PTS 12 Uncasville	
	(WBO S.Flyweight Title Challenge)	
06.03.04	Luis Bolano W RSC 4 Uncasville	
	(WBO S.Flyweight Title Defence)	
Career: 47 contests, won 43, lost 3, no decision 1.		

Roy Jones
Pensacola, USA. *Born* 16 January, 1969
WBA Heavyweight Champion. Former WBC L.Heavyweight Champion. Former Undefeated WBA Heavyweight Champion. Former Undefeated WBC, WBA and IBF L.Heavyweight Champion. Former Undefeated IBF S. Middleweight Champion

Major Amateur Honours: Won a silver medal in the 1988 Olympics, having been the National Golden Gloves champion in 1986 and 1987
Turned Pro: May 1989
Significant Results: Bernard Hopkins W PTS 12, James Toney W PTS 12, Mike McCallum W PTS 12, Montell Griffin L DIS 9 and W RSC 1, Virgil

Hill W CO 4, Louis Del Valle W PTS 12, Reggie Johnson W PTS 12, David Telesco W PTS 12, Richard Hall W RSC 11, Eric Harding W RTD 10, Derrick Harding W RTD 10, Julio Gonzalez W PTS 12, Glen Kelly W CO 7, Clinton Woods W RSC 6, John Ruiz W PTS 12
Type/Style: A brilliant boxer, who is fast, skilful, possesses lightning reflexes, and has a kayo punch in either hand
Points of Interest: 5'11" tall. Originally trained and managed by his father, Roy, he also plays basketball to a high standard and has appeared in films. With 38 wins inside the distance, he was only a welterweight when he won the Golden Gloves. Making eight defences of his IBF super-middleweight title before relinquishing, he lost his WBC light-heavyweight title to Montell Griffin in March 1997 but won it back just four months later. Became the first former world middleweight champion to win a version of the heavyweight title when he beat John Ruiz in March 2003 and then moved back down to light-heavyweight to regain the WBC title on defeating Antonio Tarver. In his last contest, Tarver took the title back when knocking him out inside a round

08.11.03	Antonio Tarver W PTS 12 Las Vegas	
	(WBC L.Heavyweight Title Challenge)	
15.05.04	Antonio Tarver L RSC 2 Las Vegas	
	(WBC L.Heavyweight Title Defence)	
Career: 51 contests, won 49, lost 2.		

Roy Jones

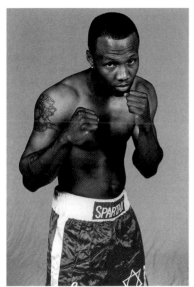

Zab Judah

Zab Judah

New York, USA. *Born* 27
October,1977
Former Undefeated WBO
L.Welterweight Champion. Former
IBF L.Welterweight Champion

Major Amateur Honours: A three-
times New York Golden Gloves
champion, he won a bronze medal in
the 1995 National Golden Gloves and
was a reserve for the United States
team at the 1996 Olympic Games.
Claims 110 wins in 115 fights
Turned Pro: September 1996
Significant Results: Mickey Ward W
PTS 12, Darryl Tyson W RSC 11,
Wilfredo Negron W RSC 4, Jan
Bergman W CO 4, Junior Witter W
PTS 12, Terron Millett W RSC 4,
Hector Quiroz W RSC 8, Reggie
Green W RSC 10, Allan Vester W
RSC 3, Kostya Tszyu L RSC 2, Omar
Weiss W PTS 10
Type/Style: Is a stylish, classy, very
fast and flashy southpaw, who has
tremendous talent but is brash and
arrogant
Points of Interest: 5'7" tall. From a
boxing family, Dad Yoel was former
world kickboxing champion and
trained Zab, who started boxing at the
age of six, at the Judah Brothers Gym.
Earlier known as 'Pernell Whitaker
(junior)', because of the time he spent
sparring with the former world

champion, two of his brothers also
won New York Golden Gloves titles
and Daniel is now a world-rated
cruiserweight. Won the IBF interim title
in January 1999 by beating Wilfredo
Negron and the vacant title by beating
Jan Bergman in February 2000. Made
five defences of his IBF title before
losing to Kostya Tszyu in a unification
match for the WBC, WBA and IBF
titles in 2001. Moved up to welterweight to challenge Cory Spinks and
relinquished the light-welter title in
June 2004 after beating Rafael Pineda
and being promised a rematch with the
former. Has 22 wins inside the distance
on his record

12.07.03	DeMarcus Corley W PTS 12 Las Vegas *(WBO L.Welterweight Title Challenge)*
13.12.03	Jamie Rangel W CO 1 Atlantic City *(WBO L.Welterweight Title Defence)*
10.04.04	Cory Spinks L PTS 12 Las Vegas *(IBF, WBC & WBA Welterweight Titles Challenge)*
15.05.04	Rafael Pineda W PTS 12 Las Vegas *(Vacant WBO Inter-Continental Welterweight Title)*

Career: 34 contests, won 31, lost 2, no contest 1.

Katsushige Kawashima

Chiba, Japan. *Born* 6 October, 1974
WBC S.Flyweight Champion. Former
Undefeated Japanese S.Flyweight
Champion

Major Amateur Honours: None known
Turned Pro: February 1997
Significant Results: Samuth
Sithnarupol W CO 2, Jess Maca L PTS
12, Yokthai Sith-Oar W PTS 10,
Shingo Sasaki W PTS 10, Masamori
Tokuyama L PTS 12
Type/Style: Is a game, aggressive banger
with a hard punch in his right hand
Points of Interest: Managed and
promoted by the former WBC and
WBA mini-flyweight champion,
Hideyuki Ohashi, he was runner-up in
the Japanese novice championships in
1997. Moved up to bantamweight to
challenge Jess Maca for the OPBF
title, then back down to his natural
weight, losing to Masamori Tokuyama
in a challenge for the WBC title in
June last year, which he put down to a
back injury. Has since beaten
Tokuyama for the title and has 18 wins
inside the distance

18.10.03	Hosup Noh W PTS 10 Tokyo
15.01.04	Dent Sithsopha W CO 2 Yokohama
28.06.04	Masamori Tokuyama W RSC 1 Yokohama *(WBC S.Flyweight Title Challenge)*

Career: 29 contests, won 26, lost 3.

Vitali Klitschko   Les Clark

Vitali (Iron Fist) Klitschko

Belovodsk, Ukraine. *Born* 19
February,1971
WBC Heavyweight Champion. Former
WBO Heavyweight Champion.
Former Undefeated European
Heavyweight Champion

Major Amateur Honours: The
European Junior Champion in 1993, a
silver medallist in the 1995 World
championships and the World Military
champion in the same year, he claims
195 wins in 210 fights
Turned Pro: November 1996
Significant Results: Julius Francis W
RSC 2, Mario Schiesser W CO 2,
Herbie Hide W CO 2, Obed Sullivan
W RSC 9, Chris Byrd L RTD 9, Timo
Hoffman W PTS 12, Orlin Norris W
RTD 1, Ross Puritty W RSC 11,
Vaughan Bean W RSC 11, Larry
Donald W RSC 10, Lennox Lewis L
RSC 6
Type/Style: Is a tall, upright fighter
with a heavy punch in his right hand
Points of Interest: 6'7" tall with an 80"
reach. The brother of an Olympic gold
medal winner and also a former WBO
champion, Vladimir, he has stopped
each of the fighters, Ross Puritty and
Corrie Sanders, who have beaten his
brother. Won the WBO title in June
1999 by beating Herbie Hide and made
three defences before losing to Chris

Byrd in April 2000, when he suffered a torn rotator cuff. Apart from the Timo Hoffman contest every other fight has ended inside the distance and the judges had him ahead against Lennox Lewis when cuts forced the stoppage. Has 33 wins inside the distance

06.12.03	Kirk Johnson W RSC 2 New York
24.04.04	Corrie Sanders W RSC 8 Los Angeles
	(Vacant WBC Heavyweight Title)
Career: 36 contests, won 34, lost 2.	

Oscar (Chololo) Larios

Guadalajara, Mexico. *Born* 1 November, 1976
WBC S.Bantamweight Champion.
Former Undefeated Mexican S.Bantamweight Champion

Major Amateur Honours: None known, but claims 48 wins in 50 fights
Turned Pro: January 1994
Significant Results: Agapito Sanchez L RSC 5, Cesar Soto W PTS 12, Guillermo Jorrin L PTS 12 and W RSC 1, John Lowey W PTS 10, Angel Chacon W PTS 12, Israel Vazquez L RSC 1 and W CO 12, Marcos Licona W PTS 10, Shigeru Nakazato W PTS 12
Type/Style: Tall and skinny, he is a (fast) jab and move fighter
Points of Interest: 5'7" tall. Trained at one time by former WBC featherweight champion, Marcos Villasana, he once worked as a stonemason and made seven defences of his Mexican title before moving into world class. Was the WBC interim champion from May 2002 until beating Willie Jorrin for the full title in November 2002 and has made four defences, all in Japan and all against fighters from the Far East, suffering a broken jaw against Shigeru Nakazato in April 2003. Has 35 wins inside the distance

24.08.02	Manabu Fukushima W RSC 8 Tokyo
07.09.03	Kozo Ishii W RSC 2 Nagoya
	(WBC S.Bantamweight Title Defence)
22.11.03	Napapol Kiatisakchokchai W RSC 10 Los Angeles
	(WBC S.Bantamweight Title Defence)
06.03.04	Shigeru Nakazato W PTS 12 Saitama
	(WBC S.Bantamweight Title Defence)
11.06.04	Jesus Perez W PTS 10 Fort Worth
Career: 56 contests, won 52, drew 1, lost 3.	

Antonio Margarito

Tijuana, Mexico. *Born* 18 March, 1978
WBO Welterweight Champion

Major Amateur Honours: None known
Turned Pro: January 1994
Significant Results: Larry Dixon L PTS 10, Rodney Jones L PTS 10, Alfred Ankamah W CO 4, Danny Perez W PTS 8 and W PTS 12, David Kamau W CO 2, Frankie Randall W RSC 4, Daniel Santos NC 1, Antonio Diaz W RSC 10, Andrew Lewis W RSC 2
Type/Style: Is a tall, aggressive banger, although a bit one paced, and has a good jab and a strong chin
Points of Interest: 5'10" tall with a 73" reach. Turned pro at the age of 15 and suffered three early defeats, but is unbeaten in his last 22 bouts, with 21 wins inside the distance. His fight with Daniel Santos for the WBO title was stopped and declared a no contest due to Antonio suffering a bad cut, prior to him winning the vacant title by beating Antonio Diaz in March 2002. Has made three defences

17.10.03	Maurice Bentley W RSC 2 Phoenix
31.01.04	Hercules Kyvelos W RSC 2 Phoenix
	(WBO Welterweight Title Defence)
Career: 34 contests, won 30, lost 3, no contest 1.	

Juan Manuel (Dinamita) Marquez

Mexico City, Mexico. *Born* 23 August, 1973
IBF & WBA Featherweight Champion

Major Amateur Honours: None known, but claims 32 wins in 33 bouts
Turned Pro: May 1993
Significant Results: Julian Wheeler W RSC 10, Julio Gervacio W CO 10, Agapito Sanchez W PTS 12, Alfred Kotey W PTS 12, Freddy Norwood L PTS 12, Daniel Jimenez W RTD 7, Julio Gamboa W RTD 6, Robbie Peden W RSC 10, Manuel Medina W RSC 7
Type/Style: A solid, compact stylist, he is also a hard puncher with either hand
Points of Interest: 5'7" tall. Despite studying to be an accountant, having been an amateur since the age of 12 he took up pro boxing, following in the footsteps of his father, who had boxed as a pro. Although boxing was in his

blood, his brother being the IBF bantamweight champion, Rafael Marquez, he lost his first pro fight on a disqualification. Lost to Freddy Norwood in a challenge for the WBA title in September 1999, then won the IBF title by beating Manuel Medina in February 2003. In his last fight, he was floored three times in the first round of his fight with Manny Pacquiao, but got up to retain his titles on a drawn verdict. Has 33 wins by stoppage or kayo on his record

16.08.03	Marcos Licona W RSC 9 Uncasville
01.11.03	Derrick Gainer W TD 7 Grand Rapids
	(IBF Featherweight Title Defence. WBA Featherweight Title Challenge)
08.05.04	Manny Pacquiao DREW 12 Las Vegas
	(IBF & WBA Featherweight title Defences)
Career: 45 contests, won 42, drew 1, lost 2.	

Rafael Marquez

Mexico City, Mexico. *Born* 25 March, 1975
IBF Bantamweight Champion

Major Amateur Honours: None known
Turned Pro: September 1995
Significant Results: Victor Rabanales L CO 8, Francisco Mateos L RSC 3, Tomas Rivera W CO 2, Genaro Garcia L RSC 2, Aquilies Guzman W RSC 7, Gerardo Espinoza W RSC 4, Mark Johnson W PTS 10 and W RSC 8, Tim Austin W RSC 8
Type/Style: Although being compact and solid, and a big puncher with the right hand, his defence sometimes lets him down
Points of Interest: 5'5" tall. Lost his first pro fight against Victor Rabanales, who was a former WBC bantamweight champion with more than 50 fights to his name at the time. His time came when he won the IBF title by stopping Tim Austin in February 2003 just two weeks after his brother, Juan Manuel Marquez, won the IBF featherweight title. His father, also Rafael, was a pro in the 1950s. Has 28 wins inside the distance and all of his losses have come inside the distance

04.10.03	Mauricio Pastrana W PTS 12 Los Angeles
	(IBF Bantamweight Title Defence)
31.01.04	Pete Frissina W RSC 2 Phoenix
	(IBF Bantamweight Title Defence)

Career: 34 contests, won 31, lost 3.

Manuel Medina

Tijuana, Mexico. *Born* 30 March,1971
Former WBO and IBF Featherweight Champion. Former WBC Featherweight Champion. Former Undefeated NABF Featherweight Champion

Major Amateur Honours: None and had only four fights
Turned Pro: October 1985
Significant Results: Troy Dorsey W PTS 12, Tom Johnson W TD 9 and L PTS 12 (twice), Alejandro Gonzalez W PTS 12, Luisito Espinosa L PTS 12, Prince Naseem Hamed L RSC 11, Paul Ingle L PTS 12, Frankie Toledo W PTS 10 and W RSC 6, Johnny Tapia L PTS 12, Juan Manuel Marquez L RSC 7
Type/Style: An awkward, busy fighter with a good jab and limitless stamina, he can give any fighter problems but lacks punching power
Points of Interest: 5'9" tall with a 71" reach. Turned pro at the age of 14 and lied about his age. Won the IBF title on three separate occasions, having first become champion in 1991, and was the WBC champion for only three months. Has taken part in 21 world title fights

12.07.03	Scott Harrison W PTS 12 Renfrew
	(WBO Featherweight Title Challenge)
29.11.03	Scott Harrison L RSC 11 Renfrew
	(WBO Featherweight Title Defence)

Career: 77 contests, won 63, lost 14.

Mahyar (Little Tyson) Monshipour

Poitiers, France. *Born* Tehran, Iran, 21 March, 1975
WBA S.Bantamweight Champion. Former Undefeated French & European S.Bantamweight Champion

Major Amateur Honours: None known
Turned Pro: October 1996
Significant Results: Sandor Koczak L RSC 3, German Guartos DREW 6 and W RSC 3, Turkay Kaya W PTS 8 and W RSC 6, Michael Alldis W PTS 8, Salim Bouaita W RSC 9, Mustapha Hame W RSC 6
Type/Style: Although a crude brawler at times, he is an extremely strong all-action fighter
Points of Interest: 5'5" tall. Despite two losses, one of them against Sandor Koczak on cuts, he won the European title by stopping Turkay Kaya in July 2002 and made two defences prior to winning the WBA super-bantam crown on beating Salim Medjkoune in July 2003. Has 16 wins inside the distance. Is now also promoting fights

04.07.03	Salim Medjkoune W CO 12 Poitiers
	(WBA S.Bantamweight Title Challenge)
16.12.03	Jairo Tagliaferro W RTD 7 Levallois-Perret
	(WBA S.Bantamweight Title Defence)
27.05.04	Salim Medjkoune W RSC 8 Clermont-Ferrand
	(WBA S.Bantamweight Title Defence)

Career: 29 contests, won 25, drew 2, lost 2.

Erik (The Terrible) Morales

Tijuana, Mexico. *Born* 1 September,1976
WBC Featherweight Champion. Former Undefeated WBC S.Bantamweight Champion. Former Undefeated WBO S.Bantamweight Champion. Former Undefeated Mexican S.Bantamweight Champion

Major Amateur Honours: None, but claims 108 wins in 114 fights
Turned Pro: March 1993
Significant Results: Daniel Zaragoza W CO 11, Jose Luis Bueno W CO 2, Hector Acero Sanchez W PTS 12, Junior Jones W RSC 4, Angel Chacon W RSC 2, Juan Carlos Ramirez W RSC 9, Reynante Jamili W RSC 6, Wayne McCullough W PTS 12, Marco Antonio Barrera W PTS 12 and L PTS 12, Guty Espadas W PTS 12, In-Jin Chi W PTS 12, Paulie Ayala W PTS 12
Type/Style: Is a cool, upright, pressure fighter who can bang hard with both hands
Points of Interest: 5'8" tall. From a boxing background, his dad fought Orlando Canizales as a pro and his brother, Diego, is a former WBO super-flyweight champion. Turning

pro at the age of 16, he has 34 wins inside the distance. Made nine defences of his WBC super-bantamweight title before relinquishing and after beating Marco Antonio Barrera for the WBO title on a hotly disputed decision he also relinquished that title. Won the WBC title by decisioning Guty Espadas in February 2001, but lost it to Barrera in a return bout in June 2002. He then regained the title by outpointing Paulie Ayala in November 2002 and made two defences before moving up to super-featherweight. Has taken part in 17 WBC title fights

04.10.03	Guty Espadas W RSC 3 Los Angeles
28.02.04	Jesus Chavez W PTS 12 Las Vegas
	(WBC S.Featherweight Title Challenge)

Career: 47 contests, won 46, lost 1.

Erik Morales

Jean-Marc Mormeck

Pointe-A-Pitre, Guadeloupe. *Born* 3 June, 1972
WBA Cruiserweight Champion. Former Undefeated French L.Heavyweight Champion

Major Amateur Honours: None, but claims 13 wins in 15 fights
Turned Pro: March 1995
Significant Results: Lee Manuel Osie L PTS 4, Alain Simon W PTS 10, Pascual Warusfel W PTS 10, Valery

Vikhor W RSC 3, Virgil Hill W RTD 8, Dale Brown W RSC 8, Alexander Gurov W RSC 8

Type/Style: Although a strong, stocky, aggressive pressure fighter with a hard, clubbing right hand, he is not a devastating puncher

Points of Interest: 6'0" tall. Only took up boxing after being injured at football when 15 and later worked as a security guard at McDonalds. Although suffering from injuries, having had three operations on his right hand, he won the WBA title by beating Virgil Hill in February 2002 and has made three defences. Now based in the USA with Don King as his promoter, he has 21 wins by stoppage or kayo

22.05.04	Virgil Hill W PTS 12 Brakpan
	(WBA Cruiserweight Title Defence)
Career: 32 contests, won 30, lost 2.	

Shane (Sugar) Mosley

Lynwood, USA. *Born* 7 September, 1971
Former WBC & WBA L.Middleweight Champion. Former WBC Welterweight Champion. Former Undefeated IBF Lightweight Champion

Major Amateur Honours: In 1989-90 and 1992 he was the US champion, winning a silver medal in the 1989 World Junior Championships. Interestingly, he lost in the finals of the US Olympic trials to Vernon Forrest

Turned Pro: February 1993

Significant Results: Phillip Holiday W PTS 12, Juan Molina W RSC 8, James Leija W RTD 9, Golden Johnson W CO 7, John Brown W RSC 8, Oscar de la Hoya W PTS 12, Antonio Diaz W RSC 6, Shannan Taylor W RTD 5, Adrian Stone W RSC 3, Vernon Forrest L PTS 12 (twice), Raul Marquez T Draw 3

Type/Style: Is a slick, smooth, fast-handed stylist with quick reflexes and good mobility, who can also punch with power

Points of Interest: 5'9" tall with a 74" reach. Started boxing at eight years old, being trained by his father, he beat Oscar de la Hoya as an amateur. Made eight defences of the IBF lightweight title before moving up to win the

welterweight crown, defeating de la Hoya in June 2000, and defended the WBC welterweight title three times before losing it to Vernon Forrest in January 2002. Has 35 wins inside the distance

13.09.03	Oscar De La Hoya W PTS 12 Las Vegas
	(WBC & WBA L. Middleweight Title Challenges)
13.03.04	Ronald Wright L PTS 12 Las Vegas
	(WBC & WBA L.Middleweight title Defences. IBF L.Middleweight Title Challenge)
Career: 43 contests, won 39, lost 3, no decision 1.	

Shane Mosley   Les Clark

Anthony Mundine

Sydney, Australia. *Born* 21 May, 1975
Former WBA S.Middleweight Champion. Former Unbeaten Australian S. Middleweight Champion

Major Amateur Honours: None

Turned Pro: July 2000

Significant Results: Marc Bargero W RSC 6, Sam Soliman W PTS 12, Guy Waters W CO 2, Sven Ottke L CO 10, Darren Obah W RSC 6, Lester Ellis W RSC 3, Rick Thornberry W RSC 11, Sean Sullivan W PTS 12

Type/Style: Clever and quick, with a good brain, he is also a sharp puncher

Points of Interest: A former top rugby league player, his father, Tony, was a top pro who lost to Carlos Monzon for the world middleweight title in 1974, was Australian champion at middle-

weight, light-heavyweight and heavyweight and the Commonwealth champion at middleweight and light-heavyweight. Anthony won the Australian super-middleweight title in only his fifth fight before eventually losing to Sven Ottke in challenge for the IBF title in December 2001. Became the 'WBA champion' by beating Antwun Echols, but was only recognised as a full champion after Ottke, the WBA 'super champion', retired at the end of March 2004. A strong speaker for Aboriginal rights, he has 15 wins by stoppage or kayo to his name

03.09.03	Antwun Echols W PTS 12 Sydney
	(Vacant WBA Secondary S.Middleweight Title)
19.01.04	Yoshinori Nishizawa W RSC 5 Wollongong
	(WBA Secondary S.Middleweight Title Defence)
05.05.04	Manny Siaca L PTS 12 Sydney
	(WBA S.Middleweight Title Defence)
Career: 22 contests, won 20, lost 2.	

Alexander (Explosivo) Munoz

Miranda, Venezuela. *Born* 8 February, 1979
WBA S. Flyweight Champion

Major Amateur Honours: An outstanding amateur who claims 129 wins in 158 fights, he competed in the World Junior Championships in 1997 and won a silver medal in the Americas Championships the same year

Turned Pro: March 1998

Significant Results: Ramon Games W RSC 10, Sornpichai Kratchingdaeng W RSC 5, Shoji Kobayashi W RSC 8, Eiji Kojima W CO 2

Type/Style: Has an all-out aggressive style with a punch to match and is deadly with the left hook

Points of Interest: 5'5" tall with a 68" reach. Holds the record for the most consecutive inside the distance wins by a Venezuelan fighter after winning his first 23 fights by kayo or stoppage. Had Shoji Kobayashi on the floor five times when winning the WBA title in March 2002, but following the Eiji Kojima fight in July of that year was injured by a street mugging, which contributed to his inactivity

| 04.10.03 | Hidenobu Honda W PTS 12 Tokyo *(WBA S.Flyweight Title Defence)* |
| 03.01.04 | Eiji Kojima W RSC 10 Osaka *(WBA S.Flyweight Title Defence)* |

Career: 25 contests, won 25.

Omar (Huracan) Narvaez

Trelew, Argentina. *Born* 7 October, 1975
WBO Flyweight Champion

Major Amateur Honours: Won a bronze medal in the 1997 World Championships, a silver medal in the 1999 World Championships, a gold medal in the 1999 Pan-American Games and competed in the 1996 and 2000 Olympics
Turned Pro: December 2000
Significant Results: Carlos Montiveros DREW 4, Wellington Vicente W PTS 10, Marcos Obregon W PTS 10, Adonis Rivas W PTS 12, Luis Lazarate W DIS 10, Andrea Sarritzu W PTS 12, Everardo Morales W RSC 5
Type/Style: A stocky and aggressive southpaw, he has fast hands
Points of Interest: Trained by the Cuban, Sarbelio Fuentes, he became the first of the 2000 Olympians to win a version of a world title, having beaten the current WBO super-bantamweight champion, Joan Guzman, in the 1996 Olympics. Won the WBO title in only his 12th fight by beating Adonis Rivas in July 2002 and has made six defences. Has ten wins inside the distance on his record

09.08.03	Andrea Sarritzu DREW 12 Villasimius *(WBO Flyweight Title Defence)*
14.11.03	Alexander Mahmutov W TD 10 Levallois-Perret *(WBO Flyweight Title Defence)*
06.03.04	Reginaldo Martins W RSC 3 Buenos Aires *(WBO Flyweight Title Defence)*

Career: 18 contests, won 16, drew 2.

Irene (Mambaco) Pacheco

San Juan de Uraba, Colombia. *Born* 26 March, 1971
IBF Flyweight Champion

Major Amateur Honours: None known
Turned Pro: November 1993
Significant Results: Luis Cox W RSC 9, Ferid Ben Jeddu W RSC 4, Pedro Pena W CO 11, Masibuleke Makepula W PTS 12, Mike Trejo W RSC 4, Alex Montiel W PTS 12
Type/Style: A clever boxer, he is an awkward, spidery southpaw, who can switch. Is also a good body puncher
Points of Interest: 5'6" tall. Never fighting for any other major title before becoming the IBF champion, he has stopped or knocked out 22 of his opponents and has only been taken the distance seven times. Has made six title defences since winning the vacant IBF title, beating Luis Cox in April 1999, but has suffered from a brittle right hand and has made only two defences since November 2001

| 27.09.03 | Damaen Kelly W RTD 6 Barranquilla *(IBF Flyweight Title Defence)* |

Career: 29 contests, won 29.

Lorenzo (Lencho) Parra

Aragua, Venezuela. *Born* 19 August, 1978
WBA Flyweight Champion

Major Amateur Honours: Competed in the 1996 World Junior Championships and claims 268 wins in 278 fights
Turned Pro: March 1999
Significant Results: Edicson Torres W RSC 12, Jose Lopez W CO 11, Edgar Velazquez W PTS 12
Type/Style: A stringy little fighter, who is clever and has excellent movement, he also possesses a sharp punch
Points of Interest: 5'5" tall. Trained by Pedro Gamarro, who won a silver medal in the 1976 Olympics, he was fighting ten rounders in only his sixth bout. Has 17 wins by stoppage or kayo

12.07.03	Jose Luis Martinez W RSC 2 Isla Margarita
06.12.03	Eric Morel W PTS 12 Bayamon *(WBA Flyweight Title Challenge)*
04.06.04	Takefumi Sakata W PTS 12 Tokyo *(WBA Flyweight Title Defence)*

Career: 23 contests, won 23.

Luis (Dinamita) Perez

Managua, Nicaragua. *Born* 6 April, 1978
IBF S.Flyweight Champion

Major Amateur Honours: None known
Turned Pro: November 1996

Significant Results: Leon Salazar W RSC 4, Justo Zuniga W CO 1, Vernie Torres L PTS 12, Moises Castro W PTS 10, Edicson Torres W PTS 12 (twice), Felix Machado W PTS 12
Type/Style: Is a skinny, skilful southpaw with a strong jab who lacks a big punch
Points of Interest: 5'5" tall with a 67" reach. Managed by Anna Alvarez, the wife of Resendo Alvarez, the WBA light-flyweight champion, he had only five days notice of the first fight with Felix Machado in January 2003 when winning the IBF title. Has 14 wins inside the distance

| 13.12.03 | Felix Machado W PTS 12 Atlantic City *(IBF S.Flyweight Title Defence)* |

Career: 23 contests, won 22, lost 1.

Verno Phillips

Troy, USA. *Born* 29 November, 1969
IBF L. Middleweight Champion. Former WBO L. Middleweight Champion

Major Amateur Honours: None known
Turned Pro: January 1988
Significant Results: Larry Barnes L PTS 10, Hector Vilte W RSC 4, Lupe Aquino W RSC 7, Santos Cardona W PTS 12 (twice), Gianfranco Rosi L PTS 12 and W PTS 12, Paul Jones L PTS 12, Godfrey Nyakana W CO 11, Julian Jackson W CO 9, Kassim Ouma L PTS 10, Bronco McKart W PTS 10
Type/Style: Although a slick boxer with a real kayo punch, he can be lazy at times
Points of Interest: 5'8" tall. Was an ordinary club fighter in New York State with a 10-4 record before moving his base to Argentina, where he established a winning run which took him to a victory over Lupe Aquino in 1993 for the WBO title. Having lost his title to Gianfranco Rosi in 1995 in his fourth defence, he looked jaded in losing to Paul Jones in a challenge for the WBO title in November 1995 and was an in-and-out performer until beating Bronco McKart in April 2003. Winning the vacant IBF title in June 2004, after Ronnie Wright was stripped, he now has 20 wins by stoppage or kayo to his name

235

05.09.03	Michael Lerma W PTS 10 Las Vegas
05.03.04	Julio Garcia W RSC 1 San Diego
05.06.04	Carlos Bojorquez W RTD 6 Joplin
	(Vacant IBF L.Middleweight Title)
Career: 48 contests, won 38, drew 1, lost 9.	

Daniel Reyes

Maria La Baja, Colombia. *Born* 5 May, 1972
IBF M.Flyweight Champion. Former Undefeated Colombian M. Flyweight Champion

Major Amateur Honours: Competed in the 1993 Pan-American Games and reached the quarter-finals of the Games in 1995, before being a quarter-finalist in the 1996 Olympic Games. Claims over 60 wins in 80 contests
Turned Pro: December 1996
Significant Results: Edgar Velasquez W PTS 10, Roberto Levya L PTS 12, Ever Bolanos W RSC 2
Type/Style: Is an orthodox boxer with a fast, hard jab and quick hands
Points of Interest: 5'4" tall. Previously trained by the former WBC bantam-weight champion, Miguel Lora, he won his first 24 fights. In his first fight outside Colombia he lost to Roberto Levya in New York in 2001 for the vacant IBF title, before turning the tables on Levya last April. Has 29 wins inside the distance

04.10.03	Edgar Cardenas W RSC 6 Los Angeles
	(IBF M.Flyweight Title Challenge)
10.04.04	Roberto Levya W RSC 3 Cartagena
	(IBF M.Flyweight Title Defence)
Career: 35 contests, won 34, drew 1, lost 1.	

John (The Quite Man) Ruiz

Chelsea, USA. *Born* 4 January, 1972
WBA Heavyweight Champion
IBF M.Flyweight Champion. Former Undefeated Colombian M. Flyweight Champion

Major Amateur Honours: Competed in the 1991 World Championships and won a gold medal in the 1991 Olympic Festival, prior to losing in the 1992 Olympic trials
Turned Pro: August 1992
Significant Results: Sergei Kobozev L PTS 10, Julius Francis W CO 4, Danell Nicholson L PTS 12, Boris Powell W PTS 10, David Tua L RSC 1, Tony

Tucker W RSC 11, Jerry Ballard W RSC 4, Evander Holyfield L PTS 12, W PTS 12, and DREW 12, Kirk Johnson W DIS 10, Roy Jones L PTS 12
Type/Style: Is strong with an awkward forward leaning style and a solid jab
Points of Interest: 6'2" tall. Named after John Kennedy and the first boxer of Puerto Rican origins to win the heavyweight title, when he outpointed Evander Holyfield in March 2001, he made two defences, including a draw with Holyfield, before losing the title to Roy Jones in March 2003. Won the WBA interim title by beating Hasim Rahman in December 2003 and became a full champion when Jones moved back down to light-heavy-weight. Unfortunate to be plagued by hand problems, he was voted Puerto Rican Fighter of the Year in 2002 and has 28 wins by stoppage or kayo

13.12.03	Hasim Rahman W PTS 12 Atlantic City
	(Vacant WBA Interim Heavyweight Title)
17.04.04	Fres Oquendo W RSC 9 New York City
	(WBA Heavyweight Title Defence)
Career: 46 contests, won 40, drew 1, lost 5.	

John Ruiz   Les Clark

Veeraphol (Death Mask) Sahaprom

Nakhon Ratchaseema, Thailand. *Born* 16 November, 1968
WBC Bantamweight Champion.
Former WBA Bantamweight Champion

Major Amateur Honours: None
Turned Pro: December 1994
Significant Results: Daourang Chuwatana W PTS 12, Nana Yaw Konadu L RSC 2, Rolando Pascua W PTS 10, Joichiro Tatsuyoshi W CO 6, Adan Vargas W PTS 12, Toshiaki Nishioka W PTS 12 and DREW 12, Oscar Arciniega W RSC 5, Julio Coronel W PTS 12, Hugo Dianzo W PTS 12
Type/Style: A flat-footed, classy stalker with a high, tight guard, he is also a big right-hand puncher
Points of Interest: 5'4" tall. Came out of kickboxing to professional boxing, winning the WBC International title in his first fight and the WBA title in his fourth. His real name is Veerapol Sumranklang, but he now fights as Veeraphol Sahaprom, getting his nickname from his stony expression when fighting. Held the WBA title for only four months, but has made 13 defences of his WBC crown. Interestingly, his fight with Julio Coronel was the first world title fight held on a bridge. Has 31 wins by stoppage or kayo

04.10.03	Toshiaki Nishioka DREW 12 Tokyo
	(WBC Bantamweight Title Defence)
06.03.04	Toshiaki Nishioka W PTS 12 Saitama
	(WBC Bantamweight Title Defence)
01.05.04	Julio Cesar Avila W RSC 12 Nongkai
	(WBC Bantamweight Title Defence)
26.06.04	Rajabu Mahoja W RTD 5 Chiangmai
Career: 47 contests, won 44, drew 2, lost 1.	

Cristian Sanavia

Piove Di Sacco, Italy. *Born* 27 February, 1975
WBC S. Middleweight Champion. Former European Middleweight Champion. Former Undefeated Italian Middleweight Champion

Major Amateur Honours: Won the Italian title in 1996
Turned Pro: October 1997
Significant Results: Marco Dell'Uomo W PTS 10, Alessandro Filippo W RTD 7, Jerry Elliott W PTS 12, Ramon

Moyano W RSC 12, Morrade Hakkar W PTS 12 and L RSC 7

Type/Style: Small for a middleweight, he has a stiff southpaw right jab and a good technique, but is not a puncher

Points of Interest: 5'7" tall. Won the Italian title by beating Marco Dell'Uomo in 1999 and the European title by defeating Morrade Hakkar in December 2001, before losing it to Hakkar in his first defence in May 2002. Was in line to fight Howard Eastman in an eliminator for the WBC middleweight title when he was given the shot at Markus Beyer, which saw him land the super-middleweight title in June 2004. Has only 12 wins inside the distance

14.10.03	Sebe Mugurel W PTS 6 Milan	
13.12.03	Didier Nkuku Mupeko W PTS 8 Padua	
10.02.04	Mike Algoet W PTS 8 Padua	
05.06.04	Markus Beyer W PTS 12 Chemnitz *(WBC S. Middleweight Title Challenge)*	

Career: 34 contests, won 33, lost 1.

Daniel Santos

San Juan, Puerto Rico. *Born* 10 October, 1975

WBO L. Middleweight Champion. Former Undefeated WBO Welterweight Champion

Major Amateur Honours: Won a bronze medal in the 1992 World Junior Championships, competed in the 1993 World Championship and the 1994 Goodwill Games, won a silver medal in the 1995 Pan-American Games, competed in the 1995 World Championships and won a bronze medal in the 1996 Olympic Games

Turned Pro: September 1996

Significant Results: Luis Verdugo T DRAW 1, William Ruiz W RSC 3, Ray Lovato W RSC 2, Kofi Jantuah L RSC 5, Ahmed Katajev L PTS 12 and W CO 5, Giovanni Parisi W RSC 4, Neil Sinclair W CO 2, Antonio Margarito NC 1, Yori Boy Campas W RSC 11, Takaloo W PTS 12, Fulgencio Zuniga W PTS 12

Type/Style: Is a fast, clever, flashy southpaw, who carries a heavy left-hand punch, but his chin is questionable and so is stamina

Points of Interest: 6'0" tall. Lost to David Reid in the Pan-American Games as an amateur before going unbeaten in his first 21 fights as a pro. Having lost a disputed decision to Ahmed Katajev in his first challenge for the WBO welterweight title, the WBO ordered a rematch, which he won in May 2000. Defending the title three times before relinquishing and winning the vacant light-middleweight championship, beating Yori Boy Campas in March 2002, he has now made three defences. Has 20 wins inside the distance to his credit

17.04.04	Michael Lerma W PTS 12 Tampa *(WBO L.Middleweight Title Defence)*	

Career: 32 contests, won 28, drew 1, lost 2, no contest 1.

Manny Siaca

Toa Baja, Puerto Rico. Born: 21 November, 1975

WBA S.Middleweight Champion

Major Amateur Honours: None known

Turned Pro: April 1997

Significant Results: Danny Garcia W RSC 2, Bruno Girard L PTS 12, Byron Mitchell L CO 12 and L PTS 12

Type/Style: Tall, with a relaxed style and a nice long jab

Points of Interest: Managed by his father, Manny (senior), he has fought mainly as a light-heavyweight and even as high as cruiserweight. Lost to Bruno Girard in a challenge for the WBA super-middleweight title in September 2000 and to Byron Mitchell for the vacant title in March 2001 after Girard was stripped on the morning of the show for refusing to fight Manny. He then lost again to Mitchell in a challenge for the title in September of the same year. Had only two fights in 31 months before beating Anthony Mundine, who had become champion after the retirement of Sven Ottke. Has 16 wins inside the distance

20.09.03	Demetrius Jenkins W RTD 4 Uncasville	
05.05.04	Anthony Mundine W PTS 12 Sydney *(WBA S.Middleweight Title Challenge)*	

Career: 22 contests, won 18, lost 4.

Lakva Sim

Ulan Bator, Mongolia. *Born* 10 March, 1971

WBA Lightweight Champion. Former WBA S.Featherweight Champion

Major Amateur Honours: A gold medallist in the 1995 King's Cup, he claims only 12 losses in 164 fights

Turned Pro: December 1995

Significant Results: Noree Jockygym W CO 6, Gilberto Gonzalez W RSC 6, Yong-Soo Choi L PTS 12, Takanori Hatakeyama W RSC 5, Yodesnan Sornontachai L PTS 12, Jong-Kwon Baek L PTS 12, Luis Villalta W RSC 4

Type/Style: Is a tough and aggressive hustler, who carries a strong right-hand punch

Points of Interest: His real name is Lkhagva Dugarbaatar and he became the first fighter from Mongolia to win a world title when he won the WBA super-featherweight title on beating Takenori Hatakeyama in 1999. Having been based in both Korea and Thailand, he fought and won inside the distance in a scheduled 12-round title fight in his pro debut and in only his sixth fight lost to Yong-Soo Choi in a challenge for the WBA super-featherweight title. After winning the WBA super-featherweight title, he lost it in his first defence in October 1999 to Jong-Kwon Baek and failed in a challenge for the same title in 2002, losing to Yodesnan Sornontachai. Multi-lingual and married to a university professor, he has 16 wins by stoppage or kayo

06.12.03	Bert Navarez W CO 3 Seoul	
10.04.04	Miguel Callist W RSC 5 Las Vegas *(Vacant WBA Lightweight Title)*	

Career: 23 contests, won 19, drew 1, lost 3.

Yodesnan Sornontachai

Srisaket , Thailand. *Born* 12 August 19, 1974.

WBA S. Featherweight Champion

Major Amateur Honours: None known

Turned Pro: November 1993

Significant Results: German Cuello W RSC 1, Fernando Montilla W CO 4, Jesus Zatarin W RSC 9, Lakva Sim W PTS 12, Lamont Pearson W RSC 9

Type/Style: Is a sturdy southpaw who is a good body puncher and has a strong chin

Points of Interest: 5'6" tall. Named Teera Pongwan, he has also fought as

Nanthachai 3K Battery, being unbeaten in 35 fights since his last defeat, in1994. Won the vacant 'WBA' title by beating Lavka Sim in April 2002 after Acelino Freitas beat the reigning champion, Joel Casamayor, to become the 'super champion' and made two defences of his title before becoming the full champion when Freitas moved up to lightweight in January 2004. Has made one defence of his title and has 35 wins by stoppage or kayo to his name

15.08.03	Larry Pelonia W RSC 2 Bangkok
05.12.03	Farik Debour W RSC 6 Bangkok
08.02.04	Ryuhei Sugita W RSC 7 Gifu
	(WBA S.Featherweight Title Defence)
Career: 45 contests, won 42, drew 1, lost 1.	

Ratanchai Sowvoraphin

Korat, Thailand. *Born* 1 November, 1976
WBO Bantamweight Champion.
Former Thai L.Flyweight Champion.
Former Undefeated Thai S.Flyweight Champion

Major Amateur Honours: None known
Turned Pro: April 1992
Significant Results: Abdi Pohan W PTS 12 and L TD 4, Somsak Singchachawan W PTS 10, Mark Johnson L PTS 12, Gerry Penalosa L RSC 6, Yoddamrong Sithyodthong L PTS 10, Danny Romero W PTS 10, Tim Austin L PTS 12, Chris John L PTS 10
Type/Style: A southpaw and a counter puncher, he is tough but limited
Points of Interest: 5'5" tall. Christened Chaiya Phothong, his younger brother, Ratanapol, was the IBF mini-flyweight champion and made 20 title defences. Ratanchai won the Thai light-flyweight title in his sixth fight before losing to Mark Johnson for the vacant IBF super-flyweight title in 1999 and then to Tim Austin for the IBF bantamweight title in 2001. On winning the world title he became first Thai fighter to win a WBO crown in the first WBO championship fight held in Thailand

11.07.03	Andre Talabessy W CO 2 Ratanathibeth
04.09.03	Eldred Romero W RSC 6 Sukhothai
03.10.03	Dimitri Atonov W PTS 12 Korat
26.12.03	Obote Amene W CO 3 Rayong
07.05.04	Cruz Carbajal W PTS 12 Nakornrachasima
	(WBO Bantamweight Title Challenge)
Career: 62 contests, won 54, lost 8.	

Cory (The Next Generation) Spinks

St Louis, Missouri, USA. *Born* 20 February, 1978
WBA, WBC & IBF Welterweight Champion

Major Amateur Honours: Won a gold medal in the 1997 Police Athletic League Championships and claims 78 wins in 81 contests
Turned Pro: November 1997
Significant Results: Antonio Diaz L PTS 12, Jorge Vaca W RSC 7, Edgar Ruiz W PTS 10, Larry Marks W PTS 12, Michele Piccirillo L PTS 12 and W PTS 12, Rafael Pineda W TD 7
Type/Style: A tall, upright southpaw, he has good speed and is a fine combination puncher
Points of Interest: 5'10" tall. The son of the former world heavyweight champion, Leon Spinks, and the nephew of Michael Spinks, his loss to Michele Piccirillo for the vacant IBF title in April 2002 was controversial and led to the return fight in March last year which saw Cory win on points. Has only 11 wins by stoppage or kayo

13.12.03	Ricardo Mayorga W PTS 12 Atlantic City
	(IBF Welterweight Title Defence. WBA & WBC Welterweight Title Challenges)
10.04.04	Zab Judah W PTS 12 Las Vegas
	(IBF, WBA & WBC Welterweight Title Defences)
Career: 35 contests, won 33, lost 2.	

Felix (Storm) Sturm

Leverkusen, Germany. *Born* 31 January, 1979
WBO Middleweight Champion

Major Amateur Honours: The German champion in 1995, 1998 and 1999, he won a gold medal in the 1997 European Junior Championships, was a quarter-finalist in the 1999 World Championships, won a gold medal in the 2000 European Championships and was a quarter-finalist in the 2000 Olympics. Claims 113 wins in 122 fights
Turned Pro: January 2001
Significant Results: Lorant Szabo W PTS 8, Tshepo Mashego W PTS 10

Cory Spinks   Les Clark

Type/Style: Tall, strong and a technically sound box-puncher with a strong jab, he is not not a big puncher
Points of Interest: 5'11" tall. Fought in the amateurs under his real name, Adnan Catic, but took the name Sturm, which means storm in German, as a pro. Has only nine wins inside the distance

12.07.03	Roberto Vecchio W RSC 5 Leverkusen
13.09.03	Hector Javier Velazco W PTS 12 Berlin (WBO Middleweight Title Challenge)
20.12.03	Ruben Varon W PTS 12 Kiel (WBO Middleweight Title Defence)
05.06.04	Oscar de la Hoya L PTS 12 Las Vegas (WBO Middleweight Title Defence)
Career: 21 contests, won 20, lost 1.	

Antonio (The Magic Man) Tarver

Orlando, Florida, USA. *Born* 21 November, 1968
WBC L.Heavyweight Champion. Former Undefeated IBF L.Heavyweight Champion

Major Amateur Honours: The US champion in 1993 and 1995 and the national Golden Gloves champion in 1994, he won gold medals in both the 1995 Pan-American Games and World Championships before winning a bronze medal in the 1996 Olympic Games
Turned Pro: February 1997
Significant Results: Mohamed Ben Guesima W RSC 9, Ernest Mateen W RSC 1, Eric Harding L PTS 12 and W RSC 5, Chris Johnson W RSC 10, Reggie Johnson W PTS 12, Montell Griffin W PTS 12
Type/Style: A tall, skinny southpaw with a good jab, he is also a fair puncher
Points of Interest: 6'2" tall. Trained by Buddy McGirt, and known to wear a top hat and cape into the ring, he was awarded the keys to the City of Orlando for his exploits as an amateur. Won the vacant IBF and WBC titles by beating Montell Griffin in April 2003, but was stripped of the IBF title for fighting Roy Jones instead of giving Griffin a return bout. He later declared himself bankrupt just before the second fight with Jones. Has 18 wins inside the distance

08.11.03	Roy Jones L PTS12 Las Vegas (*WBC L.Heavyweight Title Defence*)
15.05.04	Roy Jones W RSC 2 Las Vegas (*WBC L.Heavyweight Title Challenge*)
Career: 24 contests, won 22, lost 2.	

Antonio Tarver   Les Clark

Fabrice Tiozzo

Saint Denis, France. *Born* 8 May,1969
WBA L.Heavyweight Champion. Former WBA Cruiserweight Champion. Former Undefeated WBC L.Heavyweight Champion. Former Undefeated European & French L.Heavyweight Champion

Major Amateur Honours: Won silver medals in the 1987 World Junior Championships and World Military Championships, prior to becoming the French champion in 1988
Turned Pro: November 1988
Significant Results: Virgil Hill L PTS 12 and L RSC 1, Mike McCallum W PTS 12, Eddy Smulders W RSC 7, Maurice Core W RSC 4, Nate Miller W PTS 10
Type/Style: Has an upright style and is strong and skilful with a solid chin
Points of Interest: 6'1" tall. From a boxing family, his brother, Christophe, was the WBA super-middleweight champion, he made only two defences of his WBC title before weight problems forced him to move up to cruiserweight. Won the WBA title by beating Nate Miller in 1997 and made four defences before losing to Virgil Hill in December 2000. He then had only one fight in 27 months before

returning in March 2003, prior to winning the WBA light-heavyweight title in March 2004. Has 30 wins inside the distance

04.07.03	Joey De Grandis W RSC 4 Poitiers
20.03.04	Silvio Branco W PTS 12 Lyon (*WBA L.Heavyweight Title Challenge*)
Career: 48 contests, won 46, lost 2.	

Kostya Tszyu

Australia. *Born* Serov, Russia, 19 September, 1969
WBC and IBF L.Welterweight Champion. Former Undefeated WBA Champion.

Major Amateur Honours: Won a gold medal in the European Junior Championships in 1986, a silver medal in the World Junior Championships in 1987, a gold medal in the European Championships in 1989 and 1991, a bronze medal in the 1989 World Championships and a gold medal in the 1991 World Championships
Turned Pro: March 1992
Significant Results: Jake Rodriguez W RSC 6, Roger Mayweather W PTS 12, Hugo Pineda W RSC 11, Jan Bergman W CO 6, Vince Phillips L RSC 10, Rafael Ruelas W RSC 8, Diosbelys Hurtado W RSC 5, Miguel Gonzalez W RSC 10, Julio Cesar Chavez W RSC 6, Sharmba Mitchell W RTD 7, Oktay Urkal W PTS 12, Zab Judah W RSC 2, Ben Tackie W PTS 12
Type/Style: Is an aggressive, two-fisted fighter and a dangerous puncher with both hands
Points of Interest: 5'7" tall. Born in Russia, but now based in Australia, he made six defences of the IBF title before being stopped by Vince Phillips in May 1997. He then won the vacant WBC title by halting Miguel Gonzalez in August 1999, the WBA title by retiring Sharmba Mitchell in February 2001, and became a triple champion following his win over Zab Judah in November 2001. Inactive since January 2003 due to an injury, he forfeited the WBA version of the title in June 2004. Has 24 wins inside the distance

INACTIVE DURING 2003-2004
Career: 32 contests, won 30, drew 1, lost 1.

239

Israel (Magnifico) Vazquez

Mexico City, Mexico. *Born* 25 December, 1977
IBF S.Bantamweight Champion

Major Amateur Honours: None known, although he claims 58 wins
Turned Pro: March 1995
Significant Results: Marcos Licona L PTS 12, Eddy Saenz W CO 3, Ever Beleno W CO 2, Osvaldo Guerrero W PTS 10, Oscar Larios L CO 12, Jorge Julio W RSC 10
Type/Style: Is quick, but upright, with a high, tight guard and a hard punch
Points of Interest: 5'6" tall with a 66" reach. Gave up karate to concentrate on boxing, his inspiration being the great Ruben Olivares. Lost to Oscar Larios for the vacant WBC interim super-bantamweight title in May 2002 before winning the vacant IBF super-bantam crown in March 2004. Has 27 wins inside the distance

19.09.03	Trinidad Mendoza W CO 7 Bakersfield
25.03.04	Jose Luis Valbuena W RSC 12 Los Angeles
	(Vacant IBF S.Bantamweight Title)
Career: 39 contests, won 36, lost 3.	

Hector Javier (Artillero) Velazco

Villa Gesell, Argentine. *Born* 20 May, 1973
Former WBO Middleweight Champion

Major Amateur Honours: None known, but boasts an amateur record of 31 wins, 11 losses and nine draws
Turned Pro: September 1996
Significant Results: Jorge Arias L DIS 1, Ariel Arrieta L CO 4, Hugo Sclarandi W PTS 8 and W PTS 12, Rogerio Cacciatore W CO 8, Juan Italo Meza W RSC 7, Andras Galfi W RSC 7
Type/Style: Has an upright style described as 'Monzon-like' but that flatters him. Is a hard puncher, though
Points of Interest: Was originally only recognised as the interim champion after beating Andras Galfi in May 2003, but was given full recognition early in July 2003 when it became apparent that the champion, Harry Simon, would be inactive for a long period. Has 14 wins inside the distance

13.09.03	Felix Sturm L PTS 12 Berlin
	(WBO Middleweight Title Defence)
06.03.04	Ramon Britez W PTS 8 Buenos Aires
19.06.04	Mariano Carrera L RSC 10 Buenos Aires
Career: 35 contests, won 30, drew 1, lost 4.	

Pongsaklek Wonjongkam

Nakhornatchaseema, Thailand. *Born* 11 August, 1977
WBC Flyweight Champion

Major Amateur Honours: None
Turned Pro: December 1994
Significant Results: Randy Mangubat W CO 3, Mzukisi Sikali W RSC 1, Juanito Rubillar W PTS 10, Malcolm Tunacao W RSC 1, Daisuke Naito W CO 1, Jesus Martinez W PTS 12, Hidenobu Honda W PTS 12
Type/Style: A tough, aggressive pressure fighter, he is also a southpaw with a wicked right hook
Points of Interest: 5'1" tall. Christened Dongskorn Wonjongkan, previously boxing under the names of Nakornthong Parkview and Sithkanongsak, his last loss was in December 1995 and he is unbeaten in his last 40 bouts. Won the WBC title by halting Malcolm Tunacao in March 2001 and has made nine defences, putting Daisuke Naito away in just 34 seconds, but being floored by Ronnie Canate last time out. Has 27 wins by stoppage or kayo

14.11.03	Hussein Hussein W PTS 12 Bangkok
	(WBC Flyweight Title Defence)
03.01.04	Masaki Nakanuma W PTS 12 Yokohama
	(WBC Flyweight Title Defence)
30.04.04	Ronnie Canate W RSC 3 Nakornrachasima
Career: 53 contests, won 51, lost 2.	

Ronald (Winkie) Wright

St Petersburg, USA. *Born* 26 November, 1971
WBA & WBC L.Middleweight Champion. Former Undefeated IBF L.Middleweight Champion, Former WBO L.Middleweight Champion

Major Amateur Honours: Won a gold medal in the 1990 Olympic Festival, was a quarter-finalist in the 1989 Golden Gloves and was an amateur International at the age of 18
Turned Pro: October 1990
Significant Results: Julio Cesar Vasquez L PTS 12, Tony Marshall W PTS 12, Bronco McKart W PTS 12 (twice) and W DIS 8, Ensley Bingham W PTS 12, Steve Foster W RSC 6, Adrian Dodson W RSC 6, Harry Simon L PTS 12, Fernando Vargas L PTS 12 Keith Mulling W PTS 12, Robert Frazier W PTS 12, Jason Papillion W RSC 5, Juan Carlos Candelo W PTS 12
Type/Style: Is a slick and clever southpaw
Points of Interest: 5'10" tall. Floored six times by Julio Cesar Vasquez in an unsuccessful challenge for the WBA title in 1994, he beat Bronco McKart for the WBO title May 1996, but lost it to Harry Simon in August 1998. Lost to Fernando Vargas in a challenge for the IBF title in December 1999, but then won the vacant IBF title by beating Robert Frazier in October 2001. Made four defences of the IBF title before beating Shane Mosley to add the WBA and WBC titles to his collection, but was ultimately stripped of the IBF title for fighting Mosley. Has 25 wins by stoppage or kayo

08.11.03	Angel Hernandez W PTS 12 Las Vegas
	(IBF L.Middleweight Title Defence)
13.03.04	Shane Mosley W PTS 12 Las Vegas
	(IBF L.Middleweight Title Defence. WBC & WBA L.Middleweight title Challenges)
Career: 50 contests, won 47, lost 3.	

Ronald Wright   Les Clark

World Title Bouts During 2003-2004

by Bob Yalen

All of last season's title bouts for the IBF, WBA, WBC and WBO are shown in date order within their weight division and give the boxers' respective weights, along with the scorecard if going to a decision. There is also a short summary of every bout that involved a British contestant, and British officials, where applicable, are listed. Yet again there were no WORLD TITLE FIGHTS as such – even if you allow for Cory Spinks (Welter) and Bernard Hopkins (Middle), who hold three of the four major titles – just a proliferation of champions recognised by the above four commissions and spread over 17 weight divisions. Below the premier league, come other commissions such as the WBU, IBO, IBC and WBF, etc, etc, which would devalue the world championships even further if one recognised their champions as being the best in the world. Right now, the WBA have decided to continue recognising their champions who move on to claim other commissions' titles as super champions – despite vacating the title and creating a new champion, who, for our purposes, will be classified as a secondary champion – which if taken up in general could eventually lead to the best man at his weight being recognised universally as a world champion if the fights can be made. The WBC have since followed suit by naming their titleholders who unify titles as 'emeritus' champions.

M. Flyweight

IBF

4 October 2003   Edgar Cardenas 7.7 (Mexico) L RSC 6 Daniel Reyes 7.6½ (Colombia), Los Angeles, California, USA.

10 April 2004   Daniel Reyes 7.7 (Colombia) W RSC 3 Roberto Levya 7.7 (Mexico), Cartagena, Colombia.

WBA

12 July 2003   Noel Arambulet 7.7 (Venezuela) W PTS 12 Yutaka Niida 7.6½ (Japan), Yokohama, Japan. Scorecards: 115-114, 115-114, 114-116. On 31 January 2004, Venezuela's Juan Landaeta won the interim title on outpointing Chana Porpaoin (Thailand) over 12 rounds in Caracas, Venezuela and successfully defended it against the same man, on points over 12 rounds, in Bangkok, Thailand on 5 May 2004.

WBC

10 January 2004   Jose Antonio Aguirre 7.7 (Mexico) L PTS 12 Eagle Akakura 7.7 (Thailand), Tokyo, Japan. Scorecards: 107-120, 108-119, 110-117.

28 June 2004   Eagle Akakura 7.6¾ (Thailand) W TD 8 Satoshi Kogomazaka 7.6¾ (Japan), Yokohama, Japan. Scorecards: 80-71, 80-71, 80-73.

WBO

5 September 2003   Ivan Calderon 7.7 (Puerto Rico) W PTS 12 Lorenzo Trejo 7.6½ (Mexico), Caguas, Puerto Rico. Scorecards: 118-119, 119-112, 117-111.

6 December 2003   Ivan Calderon 7.7 (Puerto Rico) W PTS 12 Alex Sanchez 7.7 (Puerto Rico), Bayamon, Puerto Rico. Scorecards: 118-110, 117-111, 116-112.

L. Flyweight

IBF

13 December 2003   Jose Victor Burgos 7.10 (Mexico) DREW 12 Rosendo Alvarez 7.10 (Nicaragua), Atlantic City, New Jersey, USA. Scorecards: 112-116, 116-113, 114-114.

15 May 2004   Jose Victor Burgos 7.10 (Mexico) W RSC 6 Fahlan Sakkeerin 7.9 (Thailand), Las Vegas, Nevada, USA.

WBA

13 December 2003   Rosendo Alvarez 7.10 (Nicaragua) DREW 12 Jose Victor Burgos 7.10 (Mexico), Atlantic City, New Jersey, USA . Scorecards: 116-112, 113-116, 114-114. On 15 November, in Yeosu City, South Korea, Colombia's Beibis Mendoza had earlier outpointed the local, Yo-Sam Choi over 12 rounds to win the interim title.

WBC

10 January 2004   Jorge Arce 7.9 (Mexico) W CO 2 Jomo Gamboa 7.10 (Philippines), Mexico City, Mexico.

24 April 2004   Jorge Arce 7.7 3/4 (Mexico) W CO 5 Melchor Cob Castro 7.7¾ (Mexico), Tuxtla Gutierrez, Mexico.

WBO

20 March 2004   Nelson Dieppa 7.10 (Puerto Rico) W CO 1 Kermin Guardia 7.10 (Colombia), Guaynabo, Puerto Rico. Prior to the contest, Guardia had won the interim title when outpointing Jhon Molina over 12 rounds in Barranquilla, Colombia on 11 July 2003.

Flyweight

IBF

27 September 2003   Irene Pacheco 7.13¾ (Colombia) W RTD 6 Damaen Kelly 7.13¾ (Ireland), Barranquilla, Colombia. Judge: Dave Parris. Following a feeling out period, Pacheco soon picked up the pace and by the third round was beginning to get through Kelly's defences. In the next session, the champion again upped the pace and right through to the end of the fifth session totally dominated proceedings, winging in punches to head and body. Down at the start of the sixth from a body punch and down twice more in the same round, also from body punches, Kelly retired on his stool prior to the seventh getting underway.

WBA

6 December 2003   Eric Morel 8.0 (USA) L PTS 12 Lorenzo Parra 7.13¾ (Venezuela), Bayamon, Puerto Rico. Scorecards: 111-116, 111-116, 112-115.

4 June 2004   Lorenzo Parra 8.0 (Venezuela) W PTS 12 Takefumi Sakata 8.0 (Japan), Tokyo, Japan. Scorecards: 115-113, 117-111, 114-114. Referee: John Coyle.

WBC

14 November 2003   Pongsaklek Wonjongkam 8.0 (Thailand) W PTS 12 Hussein Hussein 7.13½ (Australia), Bangkok, Thailand. Scorecards: 117-111, 117-113, 116-111.

3 January 2004   Pongsaklek Wonjongkam 8.0 (Thailand) W PTS 12 Masaki Nakanuma 8.0 (Japan), Yokohama, Japan. Scorecards: 116-112, 116-113, 115-113.

WBO

9 August 2003   Omar Narvaez 7.12¼ (Argentina) DREW 12 Andrea Sarritzu 7.11¼ (Italy), Villasimius, Sardinia. Scorecards: 116-112, Roy Francis 113-115, 114-114.

14 November 2003   Omar Narvaez 8.0 (Argentina) W RTD 10 Alexander Mahmutov 7.13½ (Russia), Levallois-Perret, France. Judge: Paul Thomas.

6 March 2004   Omar Narvaez 7.13½ (Argentina) W RSC 3 Reginaldo Martins 7.11 (Brazil), Buenos Aires, Argentina.

S. Flyweight

IBF

13 December 2003   Luis Perez 8.2 (Nicaragua) W PTS 12 Felix Machado 8.3 (Venezuela), Atlantic City, New Jersey, USA. Scorecards: 115-113, 117-111, 119-109.

WBA

4 October 2003   Alexander Munoz 8.3 (Venezuela) W PTS 12 Hidenobu Honda 8.3 (Japan), Tokyo, Japan. Scorecards: 116-112, 118-110, 119-109. Referee: John Coyle.

3 January 2004   Alexander Munoz 8.2¾ (Venezuela) W RSC 10 Eiji Kojima 8.3 (Japan), Osaka, Japan. On 16 May 2004, in Gifu, Japan, Mexico's Martin Castillo won the interim title when stopping Hideyasu Ishihara (Japan) in the 11th round.

WBC

3 January 2004   Masamori Tokuyama 8.3 (Japan) W PTS 12 Dmitri Kirilov 8.2½ (Russia), Osaka, Japan. Scorecards: 117-111, 117-112, 116-112.

28 June 2004   Masamori Tokuyama 8.3 (Japan) L RSC 1 Katsushige Kawashima 8.3 (Japan), Yokohama, Japan.

WBO

16 August 2003   Fernando Montiel 8.3 (Mexico) L PTS 12 Mark Johnson 8.3 (USA), Uncasville, Connecticut, USA. Scorecards: 112-115, 110-117, 114-114.

6 March 2004   Mark Johnson 8.3 (USA) W RSC 4 Luis Bolano 8.3 (Colombia), Uncasville, Connecticut, USA.

Bantamweight

IBF

4 October 2003   Rafael Marquez 8.5 (Mexico) W PTS 12 Mauricio Pastrana 8.4½ (Panama), Los Angeles, California, USA. Scorecards: 118-110, 118-110, 117-111.

31 January 2004   Rafael Marquez 8.5¾ (Mexico) W RSC 2 Pete Frissina 8.6 (USA), Phoenix, Arizona, USA.

WBA

24 October 2003   Johnny Bredahl 8.6 (Denmark) W PTS 12 David Guerault 8.5¾ (France), Copenhagen, Denmark. Scorecards: 114-113, 118-111, Paul Thomas 117-110. Earlier, on 4 October, in Tokyo, Japan, Hideki Todaka (Japan) acquired the interim title when outpointing Venezuela's Silvio Gamez over 12 rounds, but later lost it to Mexico's Julio Zarate (l pts 12 in Saitama, Japan on 6 March 2004).

13 March 2004   Johnny Bredahl 8.6 (Denmark) W PTS 12 Nobuaki Naka 8.6 (Japan), Copenhagen, Denmark. Scorecards: 117-112, 118-109, 117-111.

WBC

4 October 2003   Veeraphol Sahaprom 8.6 (Thailand) DREW 12 Toshiaki Nishioka 8.5½ (Japan), Tokyo, Japan. Scorecards: Mark Green 116-112, 113-114, 115-115

6 March 2004   Veeraphol Sahaprom 8.6 (Thailand) W PTS 12 Toshiaki Nishioka 8.6 (Japan), Saitama, Japan. Scorecards: 118-109, 117-109, 116-110.

1 May 2004   Veeraphol Sahaprom 8.6 (Thailand) W RSC 12 Julio Cesar Avila 8.5½ (Mexico), Nongkai, Thailand.

WBO

4 October 2003   Cruz Carbajal 8.6 (Mexico) W RSC 8 Gerardo Espinoza 8.6 (Mexico), Las Vegas, Nevada, USA.

7 May 2004   Cruz Carbajal 8.5 (Mexico) L PTS 12 Ratanchai Sowvoraphin 8.5½ (Thailand), Nakornrachasima, Thailand. Scorecards: 109-118, 110-116, 111-116.

S. Bantamweight

IBF

26 July 2003   Manny Pacquiao 8.8 (Philippines) W RSC 3 Emmanuel Lucero 8.9¼ (Mexico), Los Angeles, California, USA. Pacquiao vacated the title following his 11th round retirement win over Marco Antonio Barerra at feather-weight in San Antonio, Texas, USA on 15 November 2003.

25 March 2004   Israel Vazquez 8.9 (Mexico) W RSC 12 Jose Luis Valbuena 8.10 (Venezuela), Los Angeles, California, USA.

WBA

4 July 2003   Salim Medjkoune 8.8½ (France) L CO 12 Mahyar Monshipour 8.7 (France), Poitiers, France.

16 December 2003   Mahyar Monshipour 8.7¾ (France) W RTD 7 Jairo Tagliaferro 8.10 (Venezuela), Levallois-Perret, France.

27 May 2004   Mahyar Monshipour 8.9½ (France) W RSC 8 Salim Medjkoune 8.9¼ (France), Clermont-Ferrand, France.

WBC

7 September 2003   Oscar Larios 8.9¾ (Mexico) W RSC 2 Kozo Ishii 8.10 (Japan), Nagoya, Japan. Referee: Richie Davies.

22 November 2003   Oscar Larios 8.10 (Mexico) W RSC 10 Napapol Kiatisakchokchai 8.10 (Thailand), Los Angeles, California, USA.

6 March 2004   Oscar Larios 8.10 (Mexico) W PTS 12

Shigeru Nakazato 8.9½ (Japan), Saitama, Japan. Scorecards: 118-109, 120-107, 116-112. Referee: Richie Davies.

WBO

26 February 2004   Joan Guzman 8.9¾ (Dominican Republic) W RSC 7 Agapito Sanchez 8.9¾ (Dominican Republic), San Diego, California, USA.

Featherweight

IBF

1 November 2003   Juan Manuel Marquez 8.13¾ (Mexico) W TD 7 Derrick Gainer 9.0 (USA), Grand Rapids, Michigan, USA. Scorecards: 73-60, 73-60, 69-64.

8 May 2004   Juan Manuel Marquez 8.13 (Mexico) DREW 12 Manny Pacquiao 8.13 (Philippines), Las Vegas, Nevada, USA. Scorecards: 115-110, 110-115, 113-113.

WBA

1 November 2003   Derrick Gainer 9.0 (USA) L TD 7 Juan Manuel Marquez 8.13¾ (Mexico), Grand Rapids, Michigan, USA. Scorecards: 69-64, 60-73, 60-73. Earlier, on 26 September 2003, in Bali, Indonesia, Chris John (Indonesia) outpointed Oscar Leon (Colombia) over 12 rounds to win the 'secondary' title.

8 May 2004   Juan Manuel Marquez 8.13 (Mexico) DREW 12 Manny Pacquiao 8.13 (Philippines), Las Vegas, Nevada, USA. Scorecards: 115-110, 110-115, 113-113. Not long after, on 4 June 2004, Indonesia's Chris John outscored Osamu Sato (Japan) over 12 rounds in Tokyo, Japan to retain the 'secondary' title.

WBC

18 October 2003   In-Jin Chi 8.13¾ (South Korea) DREW 12 Michael Brodie 9.0 (England), MEN Arena, Manchester, England. Scorecards: 114-112, 113-113, 113-113. This one was billed for the vacant title after Erik Morales moved up a division, having knocked out Guty Espadas inside three rounds in Los Angeles, California, USA on 4 October 2003, in a WBC super-featherweight eliminator. Initially, the WBC announced that they were calling Morales their 'emeritus' featherweight champion, but that came to nothing after Morales stated that he would never box at nine stone again, thus Brodie v Chi would decide the championship. After appearing to be a good winner, Chi was later told that one of the cards had been

Following their wonderful first contest, the return match, again for the vacant WBC featherweight title, saw In-Jin Chi (right) run out a convincing winner over Manchester's Michael Brodie   Les Clark

incorrectly added up and the result was a majority draw, due to a mistake over points deductions on the head-clash ruling. The fight itself was superb, with both men giving everything, and more, Brodie virtually finishing with both eyes shut and Chi cut above and below the left eye. Brodie was down in the second round and, at times, looked like being overwhelmed, but came back magnificently, while Chi also proved to be a fighting man, who wouldn't take no for an answer.

10 April 2004   In-Jin Chi 8.13³/₄ (South Korea) W CO 7 Michael Brodie 9.0 (England), MEN Arena, Manchester, England. Using his reach advantage to great effect, Chi never allowed Brodie, who looked to move in and out, to settle as he fired in long, raking punches to head and body. Having learned the lessons of their first fight, Chi put the Englishman down inside two minutes and from then on dominated, despite being cut on the left eye in the fourth, before landing a tremendous left hook that put Brodie down to be counted out on the 2.48 marker. The finishing punch appeared to land on Brodie's already suspected broken nose and there was no way back from that.

WBO

12 July 2003   Scott Harrison 8.13³/₄ (Scotland) L PTS 12 Manuel Medina 8.13³/₄ (Mexico), Braehead Arena, Refrew, Scotland. Scorecards: Roy Francis 113-118, 112-116, 115-113. Referee: Mickey Vann. In what was quite an upset, Harrison was outworked by the Mexican veteran, who prodded and poked away with both hands all night, without ever looking to do any damage. Meanwhile, the champion, unable to pin his rival down for long and cut on the left eye in the eighth, landed the better quality blows but there were fewer of them and, at times, he appeared one paced. While there were no doubts that it was close, Medina proved that he was still a difficult man to beat on this performance.

29 November 2003   Manuel Medina 8.13¹/₂ (Mexico) L RSC 11 Scott Harrison 8.13³/₄ (Scotland), Braehead Arena, Refrew, Scotland. Judge: Roy Francis. Making an early start, Harrison made his mind up not to allow Medina to find his gears this time round and had his rival on the floor in the first from an accumulation of punches. However, Medina is a rough, tough fighter of the old school and the champion was cut over the left eye in the fourth before the Mexican was also cut, over the right eye, as the fight turned this way and that, becoming messy right through to the tenth session when Harrison took control again. Put down for six, then again prior to the bell, Medina was unravelling and, in the 11th, the end came when he was smashed to the canvas by a right to the temple and rescued by the referee.

6 March 2004   Scott Harrison 8.13¹/₂ (Scotland) W RSC 5 Walter Estrada 8.13¹/₄ (Colombia), Braehead Arena, Renfrew, Scotland. Judge: Mickey Vann. Coming in as a replacement for William Abelyan, the tall southpaw from Colombia caused Harrison quite a few problems during the first three rounds, especially when throwing punches from peculiar angles, but by the fourth session the champion had settled. Moving up a gear, Harrison began to pressure Estrada, who was cut above the left eye, and put him on the floor for an eight count before setting about him big-time in the

the sixth and knocking him down twice more to bring about the referee's intervention on the 1.03 mark.

19 June 2004   Scott Harrison 8.13 (Scotland) W RSC 3 William Abelyan 8.13³/₄ (Armenia), Braehead Arena, Renfrew, Scotland. Judge: John Coyle. Although this was considered to be a difficult defence against a wily southpaw opponent, Harrison showed he was genuine world class when he dumped Abelyan twice in the third to force a a stoppage at 1.45 of the round. There was no doubting the challenger's class, but he was dismissed by a champion of supreme confidence and one who realised he was about to make his mark on the division when it comes to making unification matches.

S. Featherweight
IBF

4 October 2003   Carlos Hernandez 9.2¹/₂ (USA) W TD 10 Steve Forbes 9.3¹/₄ (USA), Los Angeles, California, USA. Scorecards: 97-93, 97-94, 98-92.

WBA

9 August 2003   Acelino Freitas 9.4 (Brazil) W RSC 12 Jorge Barrios 9.3 (Argentina), Miami, Florida, USA. Thailand's Yodesnan Sornontachai (formerly known as Nanthachai), the interim champion, was given full championship status when Freitas moved up to lightweight after winning the WBO crown on 3 January 2004.

8 February 2004   Yodesnan Sornontachai 9.4 (Thailand) W RSC 7 Ryuhei Sugita 9.3¹/₂ (Japan), Gifu. Japan.

WBC

15 August 2003   Sirimongkol Singmanasak 9.4 (Thailand) L PTS 12 Jesus Chavez 9.4 (Mexico), Austin, Texas, USA. Scorecards: 110-118, John Keane 111-117, 111-117.

28 February 2004   Jesus Chavez 9.4 (Mexico) L PTS 12 Erik Morales 9.4 (Mexico), Las Vegas, Nevada, USA. Scorecards: 108-118, 109-117, John Keane 112-115.

WBO

9 August 2003   Acelino Freitas 9.4 (Brazil) W RSC 12 Jorge Barrios 9.3 (Argentina), Miami, Florida, USA. Freitas relinquished the title when moving up a division in January 2004, on winning the WBO lightweight crown.

6 March 2004   Diego Corrales 9.4 (USA) W PTS 12 Joel Casamayor 9.4 (Cuba), Uncasville, Connecticut, USA. Scorecards: 115-112, 115-112, 113-114.

Lightweight
IBF

22 November 2003   Javier Jauregui 9.9 (Mexico) W RSC 11 Leavander Johnson 9.9 (USA), Los Angeles, California, USA. Billed for the vacant title after Paul Spadafora (USA) had relinquished the championship belt in June 2003 in order to fight in a higher weight division.

13 May 2004   Javier Jauregui 9.8 (Mexico) L PTS 12 Julio Diaz 9.8³/₄ (Mexico), San Diego, California, USA. Scorecards: 110-118, 110-118, 117-117.

WBA

10 April 2004   Lakva Sim 9.7¹/₂ (Mongolia) W RSC 5

Miguel Callist 9.9 (Panama), Las Vegas, Nevada, USA. This match for the vacant championship came about after Leonardo Dorin (Romania) forfeited his title on the scales on 25 October 2003 when due to defend against Callist in Bucharest, Romania.

WBC

1 November 2003   Floyd Mayweather 9.9 (USA) W RSC 7 Philip Ndou 9.8¹/₂ (South Africa), Grand Rapids, Michigan, USA. Floyd Mayweather vacated the title when he moved up a division after defeating DeMarcus Corley (w pts12 in Atlantic City, New Jersey, USA on 22 May 2004) in a WBC light-welterweight championship eliminator.

5 June 2004   Jose Luis Castillo 9.8¹/₂ (Mexico) W PTS 12 Juan Lazcano 9.9 (USA), Las Vegas, Nevada, USA. Scorecards: 115-113, 116-112, 117-111.

WBO

3 January 2004   Artur Grigorian 9.8 (Uzbekistan) L PTS 12 Acelino Freitas 9.9 (Brazil), Uncasville, Connecticut, USA. Scorecards: 107-116, 107-116, 108-11.

L. Welterweight
IBF

While Kostya Tszyu (Russia) remained inactive during the period due to injury, America's Sharmba Mitchell outscored Lovemore Ndou (South Africa) over 12 rounds in Atlantic City, New Jersey, USA on 7 February 2004, to win the vacant interim title and successfully defended it against the American, Mike Stewart (w pts 12 in Manchester, England, on 3 April 2004).

WBA

Kostya Tszyu (Russia), the WBA 'super' champion, forfeited the title in June 2004 and Vivien Harris, who had twice successfully defended the 'secondary' crown, against Souleymane Mbaye (w pts 12 in Las Vegas, Nevada, USA on 12 July 2003) and Oktay Urkal (w pts 12 in Berlin, Germany on 17 April 2004), was declared champion.

WBC

Although inactive throughout 2003-2004, Kostya Tszyu (Russia) remained the WBC 'emeritus' champion, while Canada's Arturo Gatti won the 'interim/secondary' title when outpointing Gianluca Branco (Italy) over 12 rounds in Atlantic City, New Jersey, USA on 24 January 2004.

WBO

12 July 2003   DeMarcus Corley 9.13¹/₂ (USA) L PTS 12 Zab Judah 10.0 (USA), Las Vegas, Nevada, USA. Scorecards: 115-112, 112-115, 112-115.

13 December 2003   Zab Judah 10.0 (USA) W CO 1 Jamie Rangel 10.0 (Colombia), Atlantic City, New Jersey, USA. Judah vacated the title in June 2004 after beating Rafael Pineda for the WBO Inter-Continental crown on 15 May.

Welterweight
IBF

13 December 2003   Cory Spinks 10.6 (USA) W PTS 12 Ricardo Mayorga 10.6 (Nicaragua), Atlantic City, New

Jersey, USA. Scorecards: John Keane 117-110, 114-112, 114-114.

10 April 2004   Cory Spinks 10.7 (USA) W PTS 12 Zab Judah 10.6 (USA), Las Vegas, Nevada, USA. Scorecards: 116-111, 114-112, 114-112.

WBA

13 December 2003   Ricardo Mayorga 10.6 (Nicaragua) L PTS 12 Cory Spinks 10.6 (USA), Atlantic City, New Jersey, USA. Scorecards: John Keane 110-117, 112-114, 114-114. Earlier, a contest for the vacant 'secondary' title saw Jose Antonio Rivera (Puerto Rico) beat Germany's Michael Trabant (w pts 12 in Berlin, Germany on 13 September 2003).

10 April 2004   Cory Spinks 10.7 (USA) W PTS 12 Zab Judah 10.6 (USA), Las Vegas, Nevada, USA. Scorecards: 116-111, 114-112, 114-112.

WBC

13 December 2003   Ricardo Mayorga 10.6 (Nicaragua) L PTS 12 Cory Spinks 10.6 (USA), Atlantic City, New Jersey, USA. Scorecards: John Keane 110-117, 112-114, 114-114.

10 April 2004   Cory Spinks 10.7 (USA) W PTS 12 Zab Judah 10.6 (USA), Las Vegas, Nevada, USA. Scorecards: 116-111, 114-112, 114-112.

WBO

31 January 2004   Antonio Margarito 10.6¹/₂ (Mexico) W PTS 12 Danny Perez 10.5¹/₂ (USA), Anaheim, California, USA. Scorecards: 120-108, 118-110, 120-108.

8 February 2004   Antonio Margarito 10.6³/₄ (Mexico) W RSC 2 Hercules Kyvelos 10.7 (Canada), Phoenix, Arizona, USA.

L. Middleweight
IBF

8 November 2003   Ronald Wright 11.0 (USA) W PTS 12 Angel Hernandez 11.0 (USA), Las Vegas, Nevada, USA. Scorecards: 119-109, 118-110, 118-111.

13 March 2004   Ronald Wright 11.0 (USA) W PTS 12 Shane Mosley 11.0 (USA), Las Vegas, Nevada, USA. Scorecards: 117-111, 117-111, 116-112. Wright was stripped of the title in April 2004 when unable to meet his number-one challenger due to contractual commitments.

5 June 2004   Verno Phillips 10.13¹/₂ (USA) W RTD 6 Carlos Bojorquez 11.0 (Mexico), Joplin, Missouri, USA.

WBA

13 September 2003   Oscar de la Hoya 11.0 (USA) L PTS 12 Shane Mosley 11.0 (USA), Las Vegas, Nevada, USA. Scorecards: 113-115, 113-115, 113-115. On 20 September 2003, in Uncasville, Connecticut, USA, Mexico's Alejandro Garcia retained the 'secondary' title when retiring Rhoshii Wells in the tenth round, but was parted from the so-called title when crushed by the American, Travis Simms (l co 5 in Atlantic City, New Jersey, USA on 13 December 2003).

13 March 2004   Shane Mosley 11.0 (USA) L PTS 12 Ronald Wright 11.0 (USA), Las Vegas, Nevada, USA. Scorecards: 111-117, 111-117, 112-116.

WBC

13 September 2003   Oscar de la Hoya 11.0 (USA) L PTS 12 Shane Mosley 11.0 (USA), Las Vegas, Nevada, USA. Scorecards: 113-115, 113-115, 113-115.

13 March 2004   Shane Mosley 11.0 (USA) L PTS 12 Ronald Wright 11.0 (USA), Las Vegas, Nevada, USA. Scorecards: 111-117, 111-117, 112-116.

WBO

17 April 2004   Daniel Santos 10.13^{1}/$_2$ (Puerto Rico) W PTS 12 Michael Lerma 10.13 1/4 (USA), Tampa, Florida, USA. Scorecards: 120-107, 120-107, 118-110.

Middleweight

IBF

13 December 2003   Bernard Hopkins 11.6 (USA) W PTS 12 William Joppy 11.5 (USA), Atlantic City, New Jersey, USA. Scorecards: 119-108, 119-109, 118-109.

5 June 2004   Bernard Hopkins 11.5 (USA) W PTS 12 Robert Allen 11.6 (USA), Las Vegas, Nevada, USA. Scorecards: 119-107, 119-107, 117-109.

WBA

13 December 2003   Bernard Hopkins 11.6 (USA) W PTS 12 William Joppy 11.5 (USA), Atlantic City, New Jersey, USA. Scorecards: 119-108, 119-109, 118-109. On 1 May 2004, in Miami, Florida, Australia's Maselino Masoe stopped Evans Ashira (Kenya) inside two rounds to win the 'secondary' title.

5 June 2004   Bernard Hopkins 11.5 (USA) W PTS 12 Robert Allen 11.6 (USA), Las Vegas, Nevada, USA. Scorecards: 119-107, 119-107, 117-109.

WBC

13 December 2003   Bernard Hopkins 11.6 (USA) W PTS 12 William Joppy 11.5 (USA), Atlantic City, New Jersey, USA. Scorecards: 119-108, 119-109, 118-109.

5 June 2004   Bernard Hopkins 11.5 (USA) W PTS 12 Robert Allen 11.6 (USA), Las Vegas, Nevada, USA. Scorecards: 119-107, 119-107, 117-109.

WBO

13 September 2003   Hector Javier Velazco 11.5^{1}/$_4$ (Argentina) L PTS 12 Felix Sturm 11.4^{3}/$_4$ (Germany), Berlin, Germany. Scorecards: 113-115, 112-116, 115-113. Velazco, the interim champ, was making his first defence, having been appointed as champion after Harry Simon was stripped in early July 2003. The decision was taken after it was recognised that Simon had not fully recovered from injuries sustained in a serious car accident and had legal issues still to be sorted out.

20 December 2003   Felix Sturm 11.5^{3}/$_4$ (Germany) W PTS 12 Ruben Varon 11.4^{3}/$_4$ (Spain), Kiel, Germany. Scorecards: Paul Thomas 120-108, 120-108, 118-110.

5 June 2004   Felix Sturm 11.6 (Germany) L PTS 12

In his only defence of the WBO super-middleweight title during the season, Joe Calzaghe (right) scored a comfortable stoppage win over the Armenian, Mger Mkrtchian

Les Clark

Oscar de la Hoya 11.6 (USA), Las Vegas, Nevada, USA. Scorecards: 113-115, 113-115, 113-115.

S. Middleweight
IBF

6 September 2003   Sven Ottke 12.0 (Germany) W PTS 12 Mads Larsen 11.13½ (Denmark), Erfurt, Germany. Scorecards: 115-113, 115-113, 114-114

13 December 2003   Sven Ottke 12.0 (Germany) W PTS 12 Robin Reid 12.0 (England), Nuremburg, Germany. Scorecards: 116-113, 115-112, 116-111. Yet again Ottke successfully defended his title on home turf when all seemed lost, this time against the unlucky Reid. With the referee taking centre stage virtually throughout, warning Reid continuously and ignoring what seemed to be a perfectly good knockdown when Ottke was sent down, it turned into an untidy affair. It also suited a man who lacked the workrate of a champion and was clearly near the end of his reign according to most experts present.

27 March 2004   Sven Ottke 11.13½ (Germany) W PTS 12 Armand Krajnc 11.12½ (Slovenia), Magdeburg, Germany. Scorecards: 120-108, 120-110, 119-109. Ottke announced his retirement from boxing immediately following the contest.

WBA

6 September 2003   Sven Ottke 12.0 (Germany) W PTS 12 Mads Larsen 11.13½ (Denmark), Erfurt, Germany. Scorecards: 115-113, 115-113, 114-114. Three days earlier, on 3 September, in Sydney, Australia, Australia's Anthony Mundine outscored the American, Antwun Echols, over 12 rounds to win the vacant 'secondary' title.

13 December 2003   Sven Ottke 12.0 (Germany) W PTS 12 Robin Reid 12.0 (England), Nuremburg, Germany. Scorecards: 116-113, 115-112, 116-111. For a summary, see under IBF title fights. On 19 January 2004, Anthony Mundine (Australia) retained the 'secondary' title with a fifth-round stoppage win over Yoshinori Nishizawa (Japan) in Wollongong, Australia.

27 March 2004   Sven Ottke 11.13½ (Germany) W PTS 12 Armand Krajnc 11.12½ (Slovenia), Magdeburg, Germany. Scorecards: 120-108, 120-110, 119-109. Ottke announced his retirement immediately after the contest, leaving Anthony Mundine as the fully recognised WBA champion.

5 May 2004   Anthony Mundine 11.13¼ (Australia) L PTS 12 Manny Siaca 11.13½ (Puerto Rico), Sydney, Australia. Scorecards: 114-113, 113-115, 113-115.

WBC

16 August 2003   Markus Beyer 11.13½ (Germany) W DIS 5 Danny Green 11.13½ (Australia), Nuremburg, Germany. On 20 December 2003, in Montreal, Canada, Green stopped Canada's Eric Lucas in the sixth round and thus won the interim title in doing so.

28 February 2004   Markus Beyer 11.12¾ (Germany) W PTS 12 Andre Thysse 11.13¼ (South Africa), Dresden, Germany. Scorecards: 119-109, 117-111, 117-112. Referee: Larry O'Connell.

5 June 2004   Markus Beyer 11.13½ (Germany) L PTS 12 Cristian Sanavia 11.12½ (Italy), Chemnitz, Germany. Scorecards: Larry O'Connell 115-114, 115-116, 113-116. Referee: Mark Green.

WBO

21 February 2004   Joe Calzaghe 11.13¾ (Wales) W RSC 7 Mger Mkrtchian 11.13 (Armenia), The Ice Rink, Cardiff, Wales. Referee: Paul Thomas. Defending for the 14th time, Calzaghe took his time to deal with the tough Mkrtchian, who was not overawed in the least, but by the fifth one could see that the challenger was gradually being worn down. Although the brave Armenian was still willing to trade, the seventh saw him hit with a barrage of punches, the last two being heavy lefts which sent him down. Up before being counted out, he didn't look like a man who could last much longer and the referee called it off on the 1.05 mark. On 8 May 2004, in Dortmund, Germany, Germany's Mario Veit outpointed Kabary Salem (Egypt) over 12 rounds to win the vacant interim title.

L. Heavyweight
IBF

7 November 2003   Glengoffe Johnson 12.6 (Jamaica) DREW 12 Clinton Woods 12.5¾ (England), Hillsborough Leisure Centre, Sheffield, England. Scorecards: 116-112, 113-115, Howard Foster 114-114. Referee: Ian John-Lewis. In a match that was originally intended to be an eliminator, it assumed full title status at the end of October 2003 when Antonio Tarver opted to return his belt ahead of a WBC title showdown with Roy Jones on 8 November.

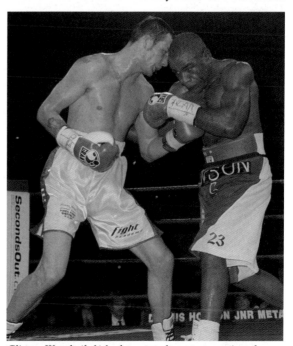

Clinton Woods (left) had two tough contests against the seasoned Glengoffe Johnson for the vacant IBF light-heavyweight title, drawing the first and losing the second on points

Les Clark

Although the American appeared to win handily it was more to do with him winning rounds on the judges' cards with plenty to spare, whereas Woods edged or nicked his winning rounds. Contested under the ten-point 'must' system, because there were no knockdowns all winning rounds were scored 10-9. To be fair, Johnson looked to be the better craftsman of the two, but Woods, who damaged his left hand, well warranted a rematch for his dogged persistence.

6 February 2004   Glengoffe Johnson 12.6 (Jamaica) W PTS 12 Clinton Woods 12.6½ (England), Ponds Forge Leisure Centre, Sheffield, England. Scorecards: 116-112, 115-113, Ian John-Lewis 115-113. Referee: Dave Parris. Once again it was closely contested, but this time Johnson did just enough to ensure that he won enough rounds on the judges' scorecards to land the vacant title in his 35th year. Both men were all-in at the final bell, in what again had been a hard battle, despite a lack of knockdowns and injuries, and Johnson was looking forward to some good pay days.

WBA

10 October 2003   Mehdi Sahnoune 12.7 (France) L RSC 11 Silvio Branco 12.7 (Italy), Marseilles, France.

20 March 2004   Silvio Branco 12.5¾ (Italy) L PTS 12 Fabrice Tiozzo 12.7 (France), Lyon, France. Scorecards: 112-114, 112-114, 113-113. Immediately prior to Roy Jones meeting Antonio Tarver for the WBC title on 15 May 2004, the WBA announced that they had appointed Jones as their 'super' champion, which would have left Tiozzo as the 'secondary' champion. However, that decision was later rescinded, possibly in the wake of the Graciano Rocchigiani legal stand against the WBC, and Tiozzo remained the champion.

WBC

8 November 2003   Antonio Tarver 12.7 (USA) L PTS 12 Roy Jones 12.7 (USA), Las Vegas, Nevada, USA. Scorecards: 112-116, 111-117, 114-114.

15 May 2004   Roy Jones 12.6 (USA) L RSC 2 Antonio Tarver 12.7 (USA), Las Vegas, Nevada, USA.

WBO

18 October 2003   Dariusz Michalczewski 12.6¼ (Poland) L PTS 12 Julio Gonzalez 12.6¼ (Mexico), Hamburg, Germany. Scorecards: 112-116, 115-113, 112-116.

17 January 2004   Julio Gonzalez 12.4½ (Mexico) L PTS 12 Zsolt Erdei 12.4 (Hungary), Karlsruhe, Germany. Scorecards: 110-118, 110-118, 111-117. Referee: John Coyle.

8 May 2004   Zsolt Erdei 12.5¾ (Hungary) W PTS 12 Hugo Herman Garay 12.6¾ (Argentina), Dortmund, Germany. Scorecards: 115-113, 116-112, 114-114.

Cruiserweight

IBF

1 May 2004   Kelvin Davis 13.8 (USA) W RSC 8 Ezra Sellers 13.8 (USA), Miami, Florida, USA. Contested for the vacant title after James Toney handed in his belt in January 2004 to concentrate on the heavyweight division.

WBA

22 May 2004   Jean-Marc Mormeck 13.4¼ (Guadeloupe) W PTS 12 Virgil Hill 13.2¾ (USA), Brakpan, South Africa. Scorecards: 115-114, 115-113, 115-113.

WBC

13 December 2003   Wayne Braithwaite 13.7 (Guyana) W RSC 1 Luis Andres Pineda 14.3 (Panama), Atlantic City, New Jersey, USA.

17 April 2004   Wayne Braithwaite 13.6 (Guyana) W PTS 12 Louis Azille 13.11¾ (Dominican Republic), NYC, New York, USA. Scorecards: 119-108, 120-107, 118-107.

WBO

15 November 2003   Johnny Nelson 13.7½ (England) W PTS 12 Alexander Petkovic 13.6¾ (Russia), Bayreuth, Germany. Scorecards: 115-113, 115-113, 114-114. Geared up for his number-one contender, Nelson gave very few chances to Petkovic, while controlling the fight with the jab and looking sharp. There were no knockdowns and, while it was clear that the challenger would be a tough nut to crack, it was also clear that he had no idea as to how to break the champion's defences down, merely following him around and swinging punches in the vain hope that they might connect. What was surprising was not that Nelson won, convincingly if you like, but the scoring of the three judges, who must have awarded rounds to Petkovic merely on the grounds of coming forward rather than landing scoring punches.

Heavyweight

IBF

20 September 2003   Chris Byrd 15.1¾ (USA) W PTS 12 Fres Oquendo 16.0 (Puerto Rico), Uncasville, Connecticut, USA. Scorecards: 115-113, 116-112, 117-111.

17 April 2004   Chris Byrd 15.0½ (USA) DREW 12 Andrew Golota 16.13½ (Poland), NYC, New York, USA. Scorecards: 113-115, 115-113, 114-114.

WBA

17 April 2004   John Ruiz 17.2 (Puerto Rico) W RSC 9 Fres Oquendo 15.12½ (Puerto Rico), NYC, New York, USA. Ruiz had won the interim title on 13 December 2003, beating Hasim Rahman on points over 12 rounds in Atlantic City, New Jersey, and was appointed champion in February 2004 after Roy Jones had moved back down to light-heavyweight.

WBC

24 April 2004   Vitali Klitschko 17.7 (Ukraine) W RSC 8 Corrie Sanders 16.11 (South Africa), Los Angeles, California, USA. Billed for the vacant title after Lennox Lewis (England) announced his retirement in February 2004.

WBO

10 April 2004   Lamon Brewster 16.2 (USA) W RSC 5 Vladimir Klitschko 17.5 (Ukraine), Las Vegas, Nevada, USA. Judge: Paul Thomas. Brewster got his chance to win the vacant title after South Africa's Corrie Sanders handed his belt back early in October 2003, prior to meeting the American in Germany on 18 October.

World Champions Since Gloves, 1889-2004

Since I began to carry out extensive research into world championship boxing from the very beginnings of gloved action, I discovered much that needed to be amended regarding the historical listings as we know them, especially prior to the 1920s. Although yet to finalise my researches, despite making considerable changes, the listings are the most comprehensive ever published. Bearing all that in mind, and using a wide range of American newspapers, the aim has been to discover just who had claims, valid or otherwise. Studying the records of all the recognised champions, supplied by Professor Luckett Davis and his team, fights against all opposition have been analysed to produce the ultimate data. Because there were no boxing commissions as such in America prior to the 1920s, the yardstick used to determine valid claims were victories over the leading fighters of the day and recognition given within the newspapers. Only where that criteria has been met have I adjusted previous information.

Championship Status Code:

AU = Austria; AUST = Australia; CALIF = California; CAN = Canada; CLE = Cleveland Boxing Commission; EBU = European Boxing Union; FL = Florida; FR = France; GB = Great Britain; GEO = Georgia; H = Hawaii; IBF = International Boxing Federation; IBU = International Boxing Union; ILL = Illinois; LOUIS = Louisiana; MARY = Maryland; MASS = Massachusetts; MICH = Michigan; NBA = National Boxing Association; NC = North Carolina; NY = New York; PEN = Pennsylvania; SA = South Africa; TBC = Territorial Boxing Commission; USA = United States; WBA = World Boxing Association; WBC = World Boxing Council; WBO = World Boxing Organisation.

Champions in **bold** are accorded universal recognition.

*Undefeated champions (Only relates to universally recognised champions prior to 1962 and thereafter WBA/WBC/IBF/WBO champions. Does not include men who forfeited titles).

Title Holder	Birthplace	Tenure	Status
M. Flyweight (105 lbs)			
Kyung-Yung Lee*	S Korea	1987	IBF
Hiroki Ioka	Japan	1987-1988	WBC
Silvio Gamez*	Venezuela	1988-1989	WBA
Samuth Sithnaruepol	Thailand	1988-1989	IBF
Napa Kiatwanchai	Thailand	1988-1989	WBC
Bong-Jun Kim	S Korea	1989-1991	WBA
Nico Thomas	Indonesia	1989	IBF
Rafael Torres	Dom Republic	1989-1992	WBO
Eric Chavez	Philippines	1989-1990	IBF
Jum-Hwan Choi	S Korea	1989-1990	WBC
Hideyuki Ohashi	Japan	1990	WBC
Fahlan Lukmingkwan	Thailand	1990-1992	IBF
Ricardo Lopez*	Mexico	1990-1997	WBC
Hi-Yon Choi	S Korea	1991-1992	WBA
Manny Melchor	Philippines	1992	IBF
Hideyuki Ohashi	Japan	1992-1993	WBA
Ratanapol Sowvoraphin	Thailand	1992-1996	IBF
Chana Porpaoin	Thailand	1993-1995	WBA
Paul Weir*	Scotland	1993-1994	WBO
Alex Sanchez	Puerto Rico	1993-1997	WBO
Rosendo Alvarez	Nicaragua	1995-1998	WBA
Ratanapol Sowvoraphin	Thailand	1996-1997	IBF
Ricardo Lopez*	Mexico	1997-1998	WBC/WBO
Zolani Petelo*	S Africa	1997-2000	IBF
Ricardo Lopez*	Mexico	1998	WBC
Eric Jamili	Philippines	1998	WBO
Kermin Guardia*	Colombia	1998-2002	WBO
Ricardo Lopez*	Mexico	1998-1999	WBA/WBC
Wandee Chor Chareon	Thailand	1999-2000	WBC
Noel Arambulet	Venezuela	1999-2000	WBA
Jose Antonio Aguirre	Mexico	2000-2004	WBC
Jomo Gamboa	Philippines	2000	WBA
Keitaro Hoshino	Japan	2000-2001	WBA
Chana Porpaoin	Thailand	2001	WBA
Roberto Levya	Mexico	2001-2003	IBF
Yutaka Niida*	Japan	2001	WBA
Keitaro Hoshino	Japan	2002	WBA
Jorge Mata	Spain	2002-2003	WBO
Noel Arambulet	Venezuela	2002-	WBA
Miguel Barrera	Colombia	2002-2003	IBF
Eduardo Marquez	Nicaragua	2003	WBO
Ivan Calderon	Puerto Rico	2003-	WBO
Edgar Cardenas	Mexico	2003	IBF
Daniel Reyes	Colombia	2003-	IBF
Eagle Akakura	Thailand	2004-	WBC
L. Flyweight (108 lbs)			
Franco Udella	Italy	1975	WBC
Jaime Rios	Panama	1975-1976	WBA
Luis Estaba	Venezuela	1975-1978	WBC
Juan Guzman	Dom Republic	1976	WBA
Yoko Gushiken	Japan	1976-1981	WBA
Freddie Castillo	Mexico	1978	WBC
Sor Vorasingh	Thailand	1978	WBC
Sun-Jun Kim	S Korea	1978-1980	WBC
Shigeo Nakajima	Japan	1980	WBC
Hilario Zapata	Panama	1980-1982	WBC
Pedro Flores	Mexico	1981	WBA
Hwan-Jin Kim	S Korea	1981	WBA
Katsuo Tokashiki	Japan	1981-1983	WBA
Amado Ursua	Mexico	1982	WBC
Tadashi Tomori	Japan	1982	WBC
Hilario Zapata	Panama	1982-1983	WBC
Jung-Koo Chang*	S Korea	1983-1988	WBC
Lupe Madera	Mexico	1983-1984	WBA
Dodie Penalosa	Philippines	1983-1986	IBF
Francisco Quiroz	Dom Republic	1984-1985	WBA
Joey Olivo	USA	1985	WBA
Myung-Woo Yuh	S Korea	1985-1991	WBA
Jum-Hwan Choi	S Korea	1986-1988	IBF
Tacy Macalos	Philippines	1988-1989	IBF
German Torres	Mexico	1988-1989	WBC
Yul-Woo Lee	S Korea	1989	WBC
Muangchai Kitikasem	Thailand	1989-1990	IBF
Jose de Jesus	Puerto Rico	1989-1992	WBO
Humberto Gonzalez	Mexico	1989-1990	WBC
Michael Carbajal*	USA	1990-1993	IBF
Rolando Pascua	Philippines	1990-1991	WBC
Melchor Cob Castro	Mexico	1991	WBC
Humberto Gonzalez	Mexico	1991-1993	WBC
Hiroki Ioka	Japan	1991-1992	WBA

WORLD CHAMPIONS SINCE GLOVES, 1889-2004

Title Holder	Birthplace	Tenure	Status	Title Holder	Birthplace	Tenure	Status
Josue Camacho	Puerto Rico	1992-1994	WBO	**Pone Kingpetch**	Thailand	1960-1962	
Myung-Woo Yuh*	S Korea	1992-1993	WBA	**Fighting Harada**	Japan	1962-1963	
Michael Carbajal	USA	1993-1994	IBF/WBC	**Pone Kingpetch**	Thailand	1963	
Silvio Gamez	Venezuela	1993-1995	WBA	**Hiroyuki Ebihara**	Japan	1963-1964	
Humberto Gonzalez	Mexico	1994-1995	WBC/IBF	**Pone Kingpetch**	Thailand	1964-1965	
Michael Carbajal*	USA	1994	WBO	**Salvatore Burruni**	Italy	1965	
Paul Weir	Scotland	1994-1995	WBO	Salvatore Burruni	Italy	1965-1966	WBC
Hi-Yong Choi	S Korea	1995-1996	WBA	Horacio Accavallo*	Argentina	1966-1968	WBA
Saman Sorjaturong*	Thailand	1995	WBC/IBF	Walter McGowan	Scotland	1966	WBC
Jacob Matlala*	South Africa	1995-1997	WBO	Chartchai Chionoi	Thailand	1966-1969	WBC
Saman Sorjaturong	Thailand	1995-1999	WBC	Efren Torres	Mexico	1969-1970	WBC
Carlos Murillo	Panama	1996	WBA	Hiroyuki Ebihara	Japan	1969	WBA
Michael Carbajal	USA	1996-1997	IBF	Bernabe Villacampo	Philippines	1969-1970	WBA
Keiji Yamaguchi	Japan	1996	WBA	Chartchai Chionoi	Thailand	1970	WBC
Pichitnoi Chor Siriwat	Thailand	1996-2000	WBA	Berkrerk Chartvanchai	Thailand	1970	WBA
Mauricio Pastrana	Colombia	1997-1998	IBF	Masao Ohba*	Japan	1970-1973	WBA
Jesus Chong	Mexico	1997	WBO	Erbito Salavarria	Philippines	1970-1971	WBC
Melchor Cob Castro	Mexico	1997-1998	WBO	Betulio Gonzalez	Venezuela	1971-1972	WBC
Mauricio Pastrana	Colombia	1997-1998	IBF	Venice Borkorsor*	Thailand	1972-1973	WBC
Juan Domingo Cordoba	Argentina	1998	WBO	Chartchai Chionoi	Thailand	1973-1974	WBA
Jorge Arce	Mexico	1998-1999	WBO	Betulio Gonzalez	Venezuela	1973-1974	WBC
Will Grigsby	USA	1998-1999	IBF	Shoji Oguma	Japan	1974-1975	WBC
Michael Carbajal*	USA	1999-2000	WBO	Susumu Hanagata	Japan	1974-1975	WBA
Ricardo Lopez*	Mexico	1999-2002	IBF	Miguel Canto	Mexico	1975-1979	WBC
Yo-Sam Choi	S Korea	1999-2002	WBC	Erbito Salavarria	Philippines	1975-1976	WBA
Masibuleke Makepula*	S Africa	2000	WBO	Alfonso Lopez	Panama	1976	WBA
Will Grigsby	USA	2000	WBO	Guty Espadas	Mexico	1976-1978	WBA
Beibis Mendoza	Colombia	2000-2001	WBA	Betulio Gonzalez	Venezuela	1978-1979	WBA
Rosendo Alvarez	Nicaragua	2001-	WBA	Chan-Hee Park	S Korea	1979-1980	WBC
Nelson Dieppa	Puerto Rico	2001-	WBO	Luis Ibarra	Panama	1979-1980	WBA
Jorge Arce	Mexico	2002-	WBC	Tae-Shik Kim	S Korea	1980	WBA
Jose Victor Burgos	Mexico	2003-	IBF	Shoji Oguma	Japan	1980-1981	WBC
				Peter Mathebula	S Africa	1980-1981	WBA
Flyweight (112 lbs)				Santos Laciar	Argentina	1981	WBA
Johnny Coulon	Canada	1910	USA	Antonio Avelar	Mexico	1981-1982	WBC
Sid Smith	England	1911-1913	GB	Luis Ibarra	Panama	1981	WBA
Sid Smith	England	1913	GB/IBU	Juan Herrera	Mexico	1981-1982	WBA
Bill Ladbury	England	1913-1914	GB/IBU	Prudencio Cardona	Colombia	1982	WBC
Percy Jones	Wales	1914	GB/IBU	Santos Laciar*	Argentina	1982-1985	WBA
Tancy Lee	Scotland	1915	GB/IBU	Freddie Castillo	Mexico	1982	WBC
Joe Symonds	England	1915-1916	GB/IBU	Eleonicio Mercedes	Dom Republic	1982-1983	WBC
Jimmy Wilde	Wales	1916	GB/IBU	Charlie Magri	Tunisia	1983	WBC
Jimmy Wilde	Wales	1916-1923		Frank Cedeno	Philippines	1983-1984	WBC
Pancho Villa*	Philippines	1923-1925		Soon-Chun Kwon	S Korea	1983-1985	IBF
Fidel la Barba	USA	1925-1927	NBA/CALIF	Koji Kobayashi	Japan	1984	WBC
Fidel la Barba*	USA	1927		Gabriel Bernal	Mexico	1984	WBC
Johnny McCoy	USA	1927-1928	CALIF	Sot Chitalada	Thailand	1984-1988	WBC
Izzy Schwartz	USA	1927-1929	NY	Hilario Zapata	Panama	1985-1987	WBA
Frenchy Belanger	Canada	1927-1928	NBA	Chong-Kwan Chung	S Korea	1985-1986	IBF
Newsboy Brown	Russia	1928	CALIF	Bi-Won Chung	S Korea	1986	IBF
Frankie Genaro	USA	1928-1929	NBA	Hi-Sup Shin	S Korea	1986-1987	IBF
Emile Pladner	France	1929	NBA/IBU	Fidel Bassa	Colombia	1987-1989	WBA
Frankie Genaro	USA	1929-1931	NBA/IBU	Dodie Penalosa	Philippines	1987	IBF
Midget Wolgast	USA	1930-1935	NY	Chang-Ho Choi	S Korea	1987-1988	IBF
Young Perez	Tunisia	1931-1932	NBA/IBU	Rolando Bohol	Philippines	1988	IBF
Jackie Brown	England	1932-1935	NBA/IBU	Yong-Kang Kim	S Korea	1988-1989	WBC
Jackie Brown	England	1935	GB/IBU	Duke McKenzie	England	1988-1989	IBF
Benny Lynch	Scotland	1935-1937	GB/NBA	Elvis Alvarez*	Colombia	1989	WBO
Small Montana	Philippines	1935-1937	NY/CALIF	Sot Chitalada	Thailand	1989-1991	WBC
Valentin Angelmann	France	1936-1938	IBU	Dave McAuley	Ireland	1989-1992	IBF
Peter Kane*	England	1938-1939	NBA/NY/GB/IBU	Jesus Rojas	Venezuela	1989-1990	WBA
Little Dado	Philippines	1938-1939	CALIF	Yukihito Tamakuma	Japan	1990-1991	WBA
Little Dado	Philippines	1939-1943	NBA/CALIF	Isidro Perez	Mexico	1990-1992	WBO
Jackie Paterson	Scotland	1943-1947		Yul-Woo Lee	S Korea	1990	WBA
Jackie Paterson	Scotland	1947-1948	GB/NY	Muangchai Kitikasem	Thailand	1991-1992	WBC
Rinty Monaghan	Ireland	1947-1948	NBA	Elvis Alvarez	Colombia	1991	WBA
Rinty Monaghan*	Ireland	1948-1950		Yong-Kang Kim	S Korea	1991-1992	WBA
Terry Allen	England	1950		Pat Clinton	Scotland	1992-1993	WBO
Dado Marino	Hawaii	1950-1952		Rodolfo Blanco	Colombia	1992	IBF
Yoshio Shirai	Japan	1952-1954		Yuri Arbachakov	Russia	1992-1997	WBC
Pascual Perez	Argentina	1954-1960		Aquiles Guzman	Venezuela	1992	WBA

250

Title Holder	Birthplace	Tenure	Status
Pichit Sitbangprachan*	Thailand	1992-1994	IBF
David Griman	Venezuela	1992-1994	WBA
Jacob Matlala	S Africa	1993-1995	WBO
Saen Sorploenchit	Thailand	1994-1996	WBA
Alberto Jimenez	Mexico	1995-1996	WBO
Francisco Tejedor	Colombia	1995	IBF
Danny Romero*	USA	1995-1996	IBF
Mark Johnson*	USA	1996-1998	IBF
Jose Bonilla	Venezuela	1996-1998	WBA
Carlos Salazar	Argentina	1996-1998	WBO
Chatchai Sasakul	Thailand	1997-1998	WBC
Hugo Soto	Argentina	1998-1999	WBA
Ruben Sanchez	Mexico	1998-1999	WBO
Manny Pacquiao	Philippines	1998-1999	WBC
Silvio Gamez	Venezuela	1999	WBA
Irene Pacheco	Colombia	1999-	IBF
Jose Antonio Lopez	Spain	1999	WBO
Sornpichai Pisanurachan	Thailand	1999-2000	WBA
Medgoen Singsurat	Thailand	1999-2000	WBC
Isidro Garcia	Mexico	1999-2000	WBO
Malcolm Tunacao	Philippines	2000-2001	WBC
Eric Morel	USA	2000-2003	WBA
Fernando Montiel*	Mexico	2000-2002	WBO
Pongsaklek Wonjongkam	Thailand	2001-	WBC
Adonis Rivas	Nicaragua	2002	WBO
Omar Narvaez	Argentina	2002-	WBO
Lorenzo Parra	Venezuela	2003-	WBA

S. Flyweight (115 lbs)

Title Holder	Birthplace	Tenure	Status
Rafael Orono	Venezuela	1980-1981	WBC
Chul-Ho Kim	S Korea	1981-1982	WBC
Gustavo Ballas	Argentina	1981	WBA
Rafael Pedroza	Panama	1981-1982	WBA
Jiro Watanabe	Japan	1982-1984	WBA
Rafael Orono	Venezuela	1982-1983	WBC
Payao Poontarat	Thailand	1983-1984	WBC
Joo-Do Chun	S Korea	1983-1985	IBF
Jiro Watanabe	Japan	1984-1986	WBC
Kaosai Galaxy*	Thailand	1984-1992	WBA
Elly Pical	Indonesia	1985-1986	IBF
Cesar Polanco	Dom Republic	1986	IBF
Gilberto Roman	Mexico	1986-1987	WBC
Elly Pical	Indonesia	1986-1987	IBF
Santos Laciar	Argentina	1987	WBC
Tae-Il Chang	S Korea	1987	IBF
Jesus Rojas	Colombia	1987-1988	WBC
Elly Pical	Indonesia	1987-1989	IBF
Gilberto Roman	Mexico	1988-1989	WBC
Jose Ruiz	Puerto Rico	1989-1992	WBO
Juan Polo Perez	Colombia	1989-1990	IBF
Nana Yaw Konadu	Ghana	1989-1990	WBC
Sung-Il Moon	S Korea	1990-1993	WBC
Robert Quiroga	USA	1990-1993	IBF
Jose Quirino	Mexico	1992	WBO
Katsuya Onizuka	Japan	1992-1994	WBA
Johnny Bredahl	Denmark	1992-1994	WBO
Julio Cesar Borboa	Mexico	1993-1994	IBF
Jose Luis Bueno	Mexico	1993-1994	WBC
Hiroshi Kawashima	Japan	1994-1997	WBC
Harold Grey	Colombia	1994-1995	IBF
Hyung-Chul Lee	S Korea	1994-1995	WBA
Johnny Tapia*	USA	1994-1997	WBO
Alimi Goitia	Venezuela	1995-1996	WBA
Carlos Salazar	Argentina	1995-1996	IBF
Harold Grey	Colombia	1996	IBF
Yokthai Sith-Oar	Thailand	1996-1997	WBA
Danny Romero	USA	1996-1997	IBF
Gerry Penalosa	Philippines	1997-1998	WBC
Johnny Tapia*	USA	1997-1998	IBF/WBO
Satoshi Iida	Japan	1997-1998	WBA
In-Joo Cho	S Korea	1998-2000	WBC

Title Holder	Birthplace	Tenure	Status
Victor Godoi	Argentina	1998-1999	WBO
Jesus Rojas	Venezuela	1998-1999	WBA
Mark Johnson	USA	1999-2000	IBF
Diego Morales	Mexico	1999	WBO
Hideki Todaka	Japan	1999-2000	WBA
Adonis Rivas	Nicaragua	1999-2001	WBO
Felix Machado	Venezuela	2000-2003	IBF
Masamori Tokuyama	Japan	2000-2004	WBC
Silvio Gamez	Venezuela	2000-2001	WBA
Celes Kobayashi	Japan	2001-2002	WBA
Pedro Alcazar	Panama	2001-2002	WBO
Alexander Munoz	Venezuela	2002-	WBA
Fernando Montiel	Mexico	2002-2003	WBO
Luis Perez	Nicaragua	2003-	IBF
Mark Johnson	USA	2003-	WBO
Katsushige Kawashima	Japan	2004-	WBC

Bantamweight (118 lbs)

Title Holder	Birthplace	Tenure	Status
Tommy Kelly	USA	1889	
George Dixon	Canada	1889-1890	
Chappie Moran	England	1889-1890	
Tommy Kelly	USA	1890-1892	
Billy Plimmer	England	1892-1895	
Pedlar Palmer	England	1895-1899	
Terry McGovern	USA	1899	USA
Pedlar Palmer	England	1899-1900	GB
Terry McGovern*	USA	1899-1900	
Clarence Forbes	USA	1900	
Johnny Reagan	USA	1900-1902	
Harry Ware	England	1900-1902	GB
Harry Harris	USA	1901	
Harry Forbes	USA	1901-1902	
Kid McFadden	USA	1901	
Dan Dougherty	USA	1901	
Andrew Tokell	England	1902	GB
Harry Ware	England	1902	GB
Harry Forbes	USA	1902-1903	USA
Joe Bowker	England	1902-1904	GB
Frankie Neil	USA	1903-1904	USA
Joe Bowker*	England	1904-1905	
Frankie Neil	USA	1905	USA
Digger Stanley	England	1905-1907	
Owen Moran	England	1905-1907	
Jimmy Walsh	USA	1905-1908	USA
Owen Moran	England	1907	GB
Monte Attell	USA	1908-1910	
Jimmy Walsh	USA	1908-1911	
Digger Stanley	England	1909-1912	GB
Frankie Conley	Italy	1910-1911	
Johnny Coulon	Canada	1910-1911	
Monte Attell	USA	1910-1911	
Johnny Coulon	Canada	1911-1913	USA
Charles Ledoux	France	1912-1913	GB/IBU
Eddie Campi	USA	1913-1914	
Johnny Coulon	Canada	1913-1914	
Kid Williams	Denmark	1913-1914	
Kid Williams	Denmark	1914-1915	
Kid Williams	Denmark	1915-1917	
Johnny Ertle	USA	1915-1918	
Pete Herman	USA	1917-1919	
Pal Moore	USA	1918-1919	
Pete Herman	USA	1919-1920	
Joe Lynch	USA	1920-1921	
Pete Herman	USA	1921	
Johnny Buff	USA	1921-1922	
Joe Lynch	USA	1922-1923	
Joe Lynch	USA	1923-1924	NBA
Joe Burman	England	1923	NY
Abe Goldstein	USA	1923-1924	NY
Joe Lynch	USA	1924	
Abe Goldstein	USA	1924	

Title Holder	Birthplace	Tenure	Status
Eddie Martin	USA	1924-1925	
Charley Rosenberg	USA	1925-1926	
Charley Rosenberg	USA	1926-1927	NY
Bud Taylor*	USA	1926-1928	NBA
Bushy Graham*	Italy	1928-1929	NY
Al Brown	Panama	1929-1931	
Al Brown	Panama	1931	NY/IBU
Pete Sanstol	Norway	1931	CAN
Al Brown	Panama	1931-1933	
Al Brown	Panama	1933-1934	NY/NBA/IBU
Speedy Dado	Philippines	1933	CALIF
Baby Casanova	Mexico	1933-1934	CALIF
Sixto Escobar	Puerto Rico	1934	CAN
Sixto Escobar	Puerto Rico	1934-1935	NBA
Al Brown	Panama	1934-1935	NY/IBU
Lou Salica	USA	1935	CALIF
Baltazar Sangchilli	Spain	1935-1938	IBU
Lou Salica	USA	1935	NBA/NY
Sixto Escobar	Puerto Rico	1935-1937	NBA/NY
Harry Jeffra	USA	1937-1938	NY/NBA
Sixto Escobar	Puerto Rico	1938-1939	NY/NBA
Al Brown	Panama	1938	IBU
Sixto Escobar	Puerto Rico	1939	
George Pace	USA	1939-1940	NBA
Lou Salica	USA	1939	CALIF
Tony Olivera	USA	1939-1940	CALIF
Little Dado	Philippines	1940	CALIF
Lou Salica	USA	1940-1941	
Kenny Lindsay	Canada	1941	CAN
Lou Salica	USA	1942	NY
David Kui Kong Young	Hawaii	1941-1943	TBC
Lou Salica	USA	1941-1942	NY/NBA
Manuel Ortiz	USA	1942-1943	NBA
Manuel Ortiz	USA	1943-1945	NY/NBA
David Kui Kong Young	Hawaii	1943	TBC
Rush Dalma	Philippines	1943-1945	TBC
Manuel Ortiz	USA	1945-1947	
Harold Dade	USA	1947	
Manuel Ortiz	USA	1947-1950	
Vic Toweel	S Africa	1950-1952	
Jimmy Carruthers*	Australia	1952-1954	
Robert Cohen	Algeria	1954	
Robert Cohen	Algeria	1954-1956	NY/EBU
Raton Macias	Mexico	1955-1957	NBA
Mario D'Agata	Italy	1956-1957	NY/EBU
Alphonse Halimi	Algeria	1957	NY/EBU
Alphonse Halimi	Algeria	1957-1959	
Joe Becerra*	Mexico	1959-1960	
Alphonse Halimi	Algeria	1960-1961	EBU
Eder Jofre	Brazil	1960-1962	NBA
Johnny Caldwell	Ireland	1961-1962	EBU
Eder Jofre	Brazil	1962-1965	
Fighting Harada	Japan	1965-1968	
Lionel Rose	Australia	1968-1969	
Ruben Olivares	Mexico	1969-1970	
Chuchu Castillo	Mexico	1970-1971	
Ruben Olivares	Mexico	1971-1972	
Rafael Herrera	Mexico	1972	
Enrique Pinder	Panama	1972	
Enrique Pinder	Panama	1972-1973	WBC
Romeo Anaya	Mexico	1973	WBA
Rafael Herrera	Mexico	1973-1974	WBC
Arnold Taylor	S Africa	1973-1974	WBA
Soo-Hwan Hong	S Korea	1974-1975	WBA
Rodolfo Martinez	Mexico	1974-1976	WBC
Alfonso Zamora	Mexico	1975-1977	WBA
Carlos Zarate	Mexico	1976-1979	WBC
Jorge Lujan	Panama	1977-1980	WBA
Lupe Pintor*	Mexico	1979-1983	WBC
Julian Solis	Puerto Rico	1980	WBA
Jeff Chandler	USA	1980-1984	WBA
Albert Davila	USA	1983-1985	WBC
Richard Sandoval	USA	1984-1986	WBA
Satoshi Shingaki	Japan	1984-1985	IBF
Jeff Fenech*	Australia	1985-1987	IBF
Daniel Zaragoza	Mexico	1985	WBC
Miguel Lora	Colombia	1985-1988	WBC
Gaby Canizales	USA	1986	WBA
Bernardo Pinango*	Venezuela	1986-1987	WBA
Takuya Muguruma	Japan	1987	WBA
Kelvin Seabrooks	USA	1987-1988	IBF
Chang-Yung Park	S Korea	1987	WBA
Wilfredo Vasquez	Puerto Rico	1987-1988	WBA
Kaokor Galaxy	Thailand	1988	WBA
Orlando Canizales*	USA	1988-1994	IBF
Sung-Il Moon	S Korea	1988-1989	WBA
Raul Perez	Mexico	1988-1991	WBC
Israel Contrerras*	Venezuela	1989-1991	WBO
Kaokor Galaxy	Thailand	1989	WBA
Luisito Espinosa	Philippines	1989-1991	WBA
Greg Richardson	USA	1991	WBC
Gaby Canizales	USA	1991	WBO
Duke McKenzie	England	1991-1992	WBO
Joichiro Tatsuyushi*	Japan	1991-1992	WBC
Israel Contrerras	Venezuela	1991-1992	WBA
Eddie Cook	USA	1992	WBA
Victor Rabanales	Mexico	1992-1993	WBC
Rafael del Valle	Puerto Rico	1992-1994	WBO
Jorge Elicier Julio	Colombia	1992-1993	WBA
Il-Jung Byun	S Korea	1993	WBC
Junior Jones	USA	1993-1994	WBA
Yasuei Yakushiji	Japan	1993-1995	WBC
John Michael Johnson	USA	1994	WBA
Daorung Chuwatana	Thailand	1994-1995	WBA
Alfred Kotey	Ghana	1994-1995	WBO
Harold Mestre	Colombia	1995	IBF
Mbulelo Botile	S Africa	1995-1997	IBF
Wayne McCullough	Ireland	1995-1997	WBC
Veeraphol Sahaprom	Thailand	1995-1996	WBA
Daniel Jimenez	Puerto Rico	1995-1996	WBO
Nana Yaw Konadu	Ghana	1996	WBA
Robbie Regan*	Wales	1996-1998	WBO
Daorung Chuwatana	Thailand	1996-1997	WBA
Sirimongkol Singmanassak	Thailand	1997	WBC
Nana Yaw Konadu	Ghana	1997-1998	WBA
Tim Austin	USA	1997-2003	IBF
Joichiro Tatsuyoshi	Japan	1997-1998	WBC
Jorge Elicier Julio	Colombia	1998-2000	WBO
Johnny Tapia	USA	1998-1999	WBA
Veeraphol Sahaprom	Thailand	1998-	WBC
Paulie Ayala	USA	1999-2001	WBA
Johnny Tapia*	USA	2000	WBO
Mauricio Martinez	Panama	2000-2002	WBO
Eidy Moya	Venezuela	2001-2002	WBA
Cruz Carbajal	Mexico	2002-2004	WBO
Johnny Bredahl	Denmark	2002-	WBA
Rafael Marquez	Mexico	2003-	IBF
Ratanchai Sowvoraphin	Thailand	2004-	WBO

S. Bantamweight (122 lbs)

Title Holder	Birthplace	Tenure	Status
Rigoberto Riasco	Panama	1976	WBC
Royal Kobayashi	Japan	1976	WBC
Dong-Kyun Yum	S Korea	1976-1977	WBC
Wilfredo Gomez*	Puerto Rico	1977-1983	WBC
Soo-Hwan Hong	S Korea	1977-1978	WBA
Ricardo Cardona	Colombia	1978-1980	WBA
Leo Randolph	USA	1980	WBA
Sergio Palma	Argentina	1980-1982	WBA
Leonardo Cruz	Dom Republic	1982-1984	WBA
Jaime Garza	USA	1983-1984	WBC
Bobby Berna	Philippines	1983-1984	IBF
Loris Stecca	Italy	1984	WBA

Title Holder	Birthplace	Tenure	Status	Title Holder	Birthplace	Tenure	Status
Seung-In Suh	S Korea	1984-1985	IBF	George Dixon	Canada	1896-1900	
Victor Callejas	Puerto Rico	1984-1986	WBA	Harry Greenfield	England	1897-1899	
Juan Meza	Mexico	1984-1985	WBC	Ben Jordan	England	1897-1899	
Ji-Won Kim*	S Korea	1985-1986	IBF	Will Curley	England	1897-1899	
Lupe Pintor	Mexico	1985-1986	WBC	Dave Sullivan	Ireland	1898	
Samart Payakarun	Thailand	1986-1987	WBC	Ben Jordan	England	1899-1905	GB
Louie Espinosa	USA	1987	WBA	Eddie Santry	USA	1899-1900	
Seung-Hoon Lee*	S Korea	1987-1988	IBF	Terry McGovern	USA	1900	
Jeff Fenech*	Australia	1987-1988	WBC	Terry McGovern	USA	1900-1901	USA
Julio Gervacio	Dom Republic	1987-1988	WBA	Young Corbett II	USA	1901-1903	USA
Bernardo Pinango	Venezuela	1988	WBA	Eddie Hanlon	USA	1903	
Daniel Zaragoza	Mexico	1988-1990	WBC	Young Corbett II	USA	1903-1904	
Jose Sanabria	Venezuela	1988-1989	IBF	Abe Attell	USA	1903-1904	
Juan J. Estrada	Mexico	1988-1989	WBA	Abe Attell	USA	1904-1911	USA
Fabrice Benichou	Spain	1989 1990	IBF	Joe Bowker	England	1905-1907	GB
Kenny Mitchell	USA	1989	WBO	Jim Driscoll	Wales	1907-1912	GB
Valerio Nati	Italy	1989-1990	WBO	Abe Attell	USA	1911-1912	
Jesus Salud	USA	1989-1990	WBA	Joe Coster	USA	1911	
Welcome Ncita	S Africa	1990-1992	IBF	Joe Rivers	Mexico	1911	
Paul Banke	USA	1990	WBC	Johnny Kilbane	USA	1911-1912	
Orlando Fernandez	Puerto Rico	1990-1991	WBO	Jim Driscoll*	Wales	1912-1913	GB/IBU
Luis Mendoza	Colombia	1990-1991	WBA	Johnny Kilbane	USA	1912-1922	USA
Pedro Decima	Argentina	1990-1991	WBC	Johnny Kilbane	USA	1922-1923	NBA
Kiyoshi Hatanaka	Japan	1991	WBC	Johnny Dundee	Italy	1922-1923	NY
Jesse Benavides	USA	1991-1992	WBO	**Eugene Criqui**	France	1923	
Daniel Zaragoza	Mexico	1991-1992	WBC	**Johnny Dundee***	Italy	1923-1924	
Raul Perez	Mexico	1991-1992	WBA	Kid Kaplan	Russia	1925	NY
Thierry Jacob	France	1992	WBC	**Kid Kaplan***	Russia	1925-1926	
Wilfredo Vasquez	Puerto Rico	1992-1995	WBA	Honeyboy Finnegan	USA	1926-1927	MASS
Tracy Harris Patterson	USA	1992-1994	WBC	Benny Bass	Russia	1927-1928	NBA
Duke McKenzie	England	1992-1993	WBO	**Tony Canzoneri**	USA	1928	
Kennedy McKinney	USA	1992-1994	IBF	**Andre Routis**	France	1928-1929	
Daniel Jimenez	Puerto Rico	1993-1995	WBO	**Bat Battalino**	USA	1929-1932	
Vuyani Bungu *	S Africa	1994-1999	IBF	Bat Battalino	USA	1932	NBA
Hector Acero-Sanchez	Dom Republic	1994-1995	WBC	Tommy Paul	USA	1932-1933	NBA
Marco Antonio Barrera	Mexico	1995-1996	WBO	Kid Chocolate*	Cuba	1932-1934	NY
Antonio Cermeno *	Venezuela	1995-1997	WBA	Baby Arizmendi	Mexico	1932-1933	CALIF
Daniel Zaragoza	Mexico	1995-1997	WBC	Freddie Miller	USA	1933-1936	NBA
Junior Jones	USA	1996-1997	WBO	Baby Arizmendi	Mexico	1934-1935	NY
Erik Morales*	Mexico	1997-2000	WBC	Baby Arizmendi	Mexico	1935-1936	NY/MEX
Kennedy McKinney*	USA	1997-1998	WBO	Baby Arizmendi	Mexico	1936	MEX
Enrique Sanchez	Mexico	1998	WBA	Petey Sarron	USA	1936-1937	NBA
Marco Antonio Barrera	Mexico	1998-2000	WBO	Henry Armstrong	USA	1936-1937	CALIF/MEX
Nestor Garza	Mexico	1998-2000	WBA	Mike Belloise	USA	1936	NY
Lehlohonolo Ledwaba	S Africa	1999-2001	IBF	Maurice Holtzer	France	1937-1938	IBU
Erik Morales	Mexico	2000	WBC/WBO	Henry Armstrong*	USA	1937-1938	NBA/NY
Erik Morales*	Mexico	2000	WBC	Leo Rodak	USA	1938	MARY
Marco Antonio Barrera*	Mexico	2000-2001	WBO	Joey Archibald	USA	1938-1939	NY
Clarence Adams	USA	2000-2001	WBA	Leo Rodak	USA	1938-1939	NBA
Willie Jorrin	USA	2000-2002	WBC	**Joey Archibald**	USA	1939-1940	
Manny Pacquiao*	Philippines	2001-2003	IBF	Joey Archibald	USA	1940	NY
Agapito Sanchez*	Dom Republic	2001-2002	WBO	Petey Scalzo	USA	1940-1941	NBA
Yober Ortega	Venezuela	2001-2002	WBA	Jimmy Perrin	USA	1940	LOUIS
Yoddamrong Sithyodthong	Thailand	2002	WBA	Harry Jeffra	USA	1940-1941	NY/MARY
Osamu Sato	Japan	2002	WBA	Joey Archibald	USA	1941	NY/MARY
Joan Guzman	Dom Republic	2002-	WBO	Richie Lemos	USA	1941	NBA
Salim Medjkoune	France	2002-2003	WBA	Chalky Wright	Mexico	1941-1942	NY/MARY
Oscar Larios	Mexico	2002-	WBC	Jackie Wilson	USA	1941-1943	NBA
Mahyar Monshipour	France	2003-	WBA	Willie Pep	USA	1942-1946	NY
Israel Vazquez	Mexico	2004-	IBF	Jackie Callura	Canada	1943	NBA
				Phil Terranova	USA	1943-1944	NBA
Featherweight (126 lbs)				Sal Bartolo	USA	1944-1946	NBA
Ike Weir	Ireland	1889-1890		**Willie Pep**	USA	1946-1948	
Billy Murphy	New Zealand	1890-1893		**Sandy Saddler**	USA	1948-1949	
George Dixon	Canada	1890-1893		**Willie Pep**	USA	1949-1950	
Young Griffo	Australia	1890-1893		**Sandy Saddler***	USA	1950-1957	
Johnny Griffin	USA	1891-1893		**Hogan Kid Bassey**	Nigeria	1957-1959	
Solly Smith	USA	1893		**Davey Moore**	USA	1959-1963	
George Dixon	Canada	1893-1896		**Sugar Ramos**	Cuba	1963-1964	
Solly Smith	USA	1896-1898		**Vicente Saldivar***	Mexico	1964-1967	
Frank Erne	USA	1896-1897		Raul Rojas	USA	1967	CALIF

253

Title Holder	Birthplace	Tenure	Status
Howard Winstone	Wales	1968	WBC
Raul Rojas	USA	1968	WBA
Johnny Famechon	France	1968-1969	AUST
Jose Legra	Cuba	1968-1969	WBC
Shozo Saijyo	Japan	1968-1971	WBA
Johnny Famechon	France	1969-1970	WBC
Vicente Saldivar	Mexico	1970	WBC
Kuniaki Shibata	Japan	1970-1972	WBC
Antonio Gomez	Venezuela	1971-1972	WBA
Clemente Sanchez	Mexico	1972	WBC
Ernesto Marcel*	Panama	1972-1974	WBA
Jose Legra	Cuba	1972-1973	WBC
Eder Jofre	Brazil	1973-1974	WBC
Ruben Olivares	Mexico	1974	WBA
Bobby Chacon	USA	1974-1975	WBC
Alexis Arguello*	Nicaragua	1974-1977	WBA
Ruben Olivares	Mexico	1975	WBC
David Kotey	Ghana	1975-1976	WBC
Danny Lopez	USA	1976-1980	WBC
Rafael Ortega	Panama	1977	WBA
Cecilio Lastra	Spain	1977-1978	WBA
Eusebio Pedroza	Panama	1978-1985	WBA
Salvador Sanchez*	Mexico	1980-1982	WBC
Juan Laporte	Puerto Rico	1982-1984	WBC
Min-Keun Oh	S Korea	1984-1985	IBF
Wilfredo Gomez	Puerto Rico	1984	WBC
Azumah Nelson*	Ghana	1984-1988	WBC
Barry McGuigan	Ireland	1985-1986	WBA
Ki-Yung Chung	S Korea	1985-1986	IBF
Steve Cruz	USA	1986-1987	WBA
Antonio Rivera	Puerto Rico	1986-1988	IBF
Antonio Esparragoza	Venezuela	1987-1991	WBA
Calvin Grove	USA	1988	IBF
Jeff Fenech*	Australia	1988-1989	WBC
Jorge Paez*	Mexico	1988-1990	IBF
Maurizio Stecca	Italy	1989	WBO
Louie Espinosa	USA	1989-1990	WBO
Jorge Paez*	Mexico	1990-1991	IBF/WBO
Marcos Villasana	Mexico	1990-1991	WBC
Kyun-Yung Park	S Korea	1991-1993	WBA
Troy Dorsey	USA	1991	IBF
Maurizio Stecca	Italy	1991-1992	WBO
Manuel Medina	Mexico	1991-1993	IBF
Paul Hodkinson	England	1991-1993	WBC
Colin McMillan	England	1992	WBO
Ruben Palacio	Colombia	1992-1993	WBO
Tom Johnson	USA	1993-1997	IBF
Steve Robinson	Wales	1993-1995	WBO
Gregorio Vargas	Mexico	1993	WBC
Kevin Kelley	USA	1993-1995	WBC
Eloy Rojas	Venezuela	1993-1996	WBA
Alejandro Gonzalez	Mexico	1995	WBC
Manuel Medina	Mexico	1995	WBC
Prince Naseem Hamed*	England	1995-1997	WBO
Luisito Espinosa	Philippines	1995-1999	WBC
Wilfredo Vasquez	Puerto Rico	1996-1998	WBA
Prince Naseem Hamed *	England	1997	WBO/IBF
Prince Naseem Hamed*	England	1997-1999	WBO
Hector Lizarraga	Mexico	1997-1998	IBF
Freddie Norwood	USA	1998	WBA
Manuel Medina	Mexico	1998-1999	IBF
Antonio Cermeno	Venezuela	1998-1999	WBA
Cesar Soto	Mexico	1999	WBC
Freddie Norwood	USA	1999-2000	WBA
Prince Naseem Hamed	England	1999-2000	WBC/WBO
Paul Ingle	England	1999-2000	IBF
Prince Naseem Hamed*	England	2000	WBO
Gustavo Espadas	Mexico	2000-2001	WBC
Derrick Gainer	USA	2000-2003	WBA
Mbulelo Botile	S Africa	2000-2001	IBF
Istvan Kovacs	Hungary	2001	WBO

Title Holder	Birthplace	Tenure	Status
Erik Morales	Mexico	2001-2002	WBC
Frankie Toledo	USA	2001	IBF
Julio Pablo Chacon	Argentina	2001-2002	WBO
Manuel Medina	Mexico	2001-2002	IBF
Johnny Tapia	USA	2002	IBF
Marco Antonio Barrera*	Mexico	2002	WBC
Scott Harrison	Scotland	2002-	WBO
Erik Morales*	Mexico	2002-2003	WBC
Juan Manuel Marquez*	Mexico	2003	IBF
Juan Manuel Marquez	Mexico	2003-	IBF/WBA
In-Jin Chi	South Korea	2004-	WBC

S. Featherweight (130 lbs)

Title Holder	Birthplace	Tenure	Status
Johnny Dundee	Italy	1921-1923	NY
Jack Bernstein	USA	1923	NY
Jack Bernstein	USA	1923	NBA/NY
Johnny Dundee	Italy	1923-1924	NBA/NY
Kid Sullivan	USA	1924-1925	NBA/NY
Mike Ballerino	USA	1925	NBA/NY
Tod Morgan	USA	1925-1929	NBA/NY
Benny Bass	Russia	1929-1930	NBA/NY
Benny Bass	Russia	1930-1931	NBA
Kid Chocolate	Cuba	1931-1933	NBA
Frankie Klick	USA	1933-1934	NBA
Sandy Saddler	USA	1949-1950	NBA
Sandy Saddler	USA	1950-1951	CLE
Harold Gomes	USA	1959-1960	NBA
Flash Elorde	Philippines	1960-1962	NBA
Flash Elorde	Philippines	1962-1967	WBA
Raul Rojas	USA	1967	CALIF
Yoshiaki Numata	Japan	1967	WBA
Hiroshi Kobayashi	Japan	1967-1971	WBA
Rene Barrientos	Philippines	1969-1970	WBC
Yoshiaki Numata	Japan	1970-1971	WBC
Alfredo Marcano	Venezuela	1971-1972	WBA
Ricardo Arredondo	Mexico	1971-1974	WBC
Ben Villaflor	Philippines	1972-1973	WBA
Kuniaki Shibata	Japan	1973	WBA
Ben Villaflor	Philippines	1973-1976	WBA
Kuniaki Shibata	Japan	1974-1975	WBC
Alfredo Escalera	Puerto Rico	1975-1978	WBC
Sam Serrano	Puerto Rico	1976-1980	WBA
Alexis Arguello*	Nicaragua	1978-1980	WBC
Yasutsune Uehara	Japan	1980-1981	WBA
Rafael Limon	Mexico	1980-1981	WBC
Cornelius Boza-Edwards	Uganda	1981	WBC
Sam Serrano	Puerto Rico	1981-1983	WBA
Rolando Navarrete	Philippines	1981-1982	WBC
Rafael Limon	Mexico	1982	WBC
Bobby Chacon	USA	1982-1983	WBC
Roger Mayweather	USA	1983-1984	WBA
Hector Camacho*	Puerto Rico	1983-1984	WBC
Rocky Lockridge	USA	1984-1985	WBA
Hwan-Kil Yuh	S Korea	1984-1985	IBF
Julio Cesar Chavez*	Mexico	1984-1987	WBC
Lester Ellis	England	1985	IBF
Wilfredo Gomez	Puerto Rico	1985-1986	WBA
Barry Michael	England	1985-1987	IBF
Alfredo Layne	Panama	1986	WBA
Brian Mitchell*	S Africa	1986-1991	WBA
Rocky Lockridge	USA	1987-1988	IBF
Azumah Nelson	Ghana	1988-1994	WBC
Tony Lopez	USA	1988-1989	IBF
Juan Molina*	Puerto Rico	1989	WBO
Juan Molina	Puerto Rico	1989-1990	WBO
Kamel Bou Ali	Tunisia	1989-1992	WBO
Tony Lopez	USA	1990-1991	IBF
Joey Gamache*	USA	1991	WBA
Brian Mitchell*	S Africa	1991-1992	IBF
Genaro Hernandez	USA	1991-1995	WBA
Juan Molina*	Puerto Rico	1992-1995	IBF

Title Holder	Birthplace	Tenure	Status
Daniel Londas	France	1992	WBO
Jimmy Bredahl	Denmark	1992-1994	WBO
Oscar de la Hoya*	USA	1994	WBO
James Leija	USA	1994	WBC
Gabriel Ruelas	USA	1994-1995	WBC
Regilio Tuur*	Surinam	1994-1997	WBO
Eddie Hopson	USA	1995	IBF
Tracy Harris Patterson	USA	1995	IBF
Yong-Soo Choi	S Korea	1995-1998	WBA
Arturo Gatti*	Canada	1995-1997	IBF
Azumah Nelson	Ghana	1996-1997	WBC
Genaro Hernandez	USA	1997-1998	WBC
Barry Jones*	Wales	1997-1998	WBO
Roberto Garcia	USA	1998-1999	IBF
Anatoly Alexandrov	Kazakhstan	1998-1999	WBO
Takenori Hatakeyama	Japan	1998-1999	WBA
Floyd Mayweather*	USA	1998-2002	WBC
Lakva Sim	Mongolia	1999	WBA
Acelino Freitas*	Brazil	1999-2002	WBO
Diego Corrales*	USA	1999-2000	IBF
Jong-Kwon Baek	S Korea	1999-2000	WBA
Joel Casamayor	Cuba	2000-2002	WBA
Steve Forbes	USA	2000-2002	IBF
Acelino Freitas*	Brazil	2002-2004	WBO/WBA
Sirimongkol Singmanassak	Thailand	2002-2003	WBC
Carlos Hernandez	USA	2003-	IBF
Jesus Chavez	Mexico	2003-2004	WBC
Yodesnan Sornontachai	Thailand	2004-	WBA
Erik Morales	Mexico	2004-	WBC
Diego Corrales	USA	2004-	WBO

Lightweight (135 lbs)

Title Holder	Birthplace	Tenure	Status
Jack McAuliffe	Ireland	1889-1894	USA
Jem Carney	England	1889-1891	
Jimmy Carroll	England	1889-1891	
Dick Burge	England	1891-1896	GB
George Lavigne	USA	1894-1896	USA
George Lavigne	USA	1896	
George Lavigne	USA	1896-1897	
Eddie Connolly	Canada	1896-1897	
George Lavigne	USA	1897-1899	
Frank Erne	Switzerland	1899-1902	
Joe Gans	USA	1902	
Joe Gans	USA	1902-1906	
Jabez White	England	1902-1905	GB
Jimmy Britt	USA	1902-1905	
Battling Nelson	Denmark	1905-1907	
Joe Gans	USA	1906-1908	
Battling Nelson	Denmark	1908-1910	
Ad Wolgast	USA	1910-1912	
Willie Ritchie	USA	1912	
Freddie Welsh	Wales	1912-1914	GB
Willie Ritchie	USA	1912-1914	USA
Freddie Welsh	Wales	1914-1917	
Benny Leonard*	USA	1917-1925	
Jimmy Goodrich	USA	1925	NY
Rocky Kansas	USA	1925-1926	
Sammy Mandell	USA	1926-1930	
Al Singer	USA	1930	
Tony Canzoneri	USA	1930-1933	
Barney Ross*	USA	1933-1935	
Tony Canzoneri	USA	1935-1936	
Lou Ambers	USA	1936-1938	
Henry Armstrong	USA	1938-1939	
Lou Ambers	USA	1939-1940	
Sammy Angott	USA	1940-1941	NBA
Lew Jenkins	USA	1940-1941	NY
Sammy Angott*	USA	1941-1942	
Beau Jack	USA	1942-1943	NY
Slugger White	USA	1943	MARY
Bob Montgomery	USA	1943	NY

Title Holder	Birthplace	Tenure	Status
Sammy Angott	USA	1943-1944	NBA
Beau Jack	USA	1943-1944	NY
Bob Montgomery	USA	1944-1947	NY
Juan Zurita	Mexico	1944-1945	NBA
Ike Williams	USA	1945-1947	NBA
Ike Williams	USA	1947-1951	
Jimmy Carter	USA	1951-1952	
Lauro Salas	Mexico	1952	
Jimmy Carter	USA	1952-1954	
Paddy de Marco	USA	1954	
Jimmy Carter	USA	1954-1955	
Wallace Bud Smith	USA	1955-1956	
Joe Brown	USA	1956-1962	
Carlos Ortiz	Puerto Rico	1962-1963	
Carlos Ortiz*	Puerto Rico	1963-1964	WBA/WBC
Kenny Lane	USA	1963-1964	MICH
Carlos Ortiz	Puerto Rico	1964-1965	
Ismael Laguna	Panama	1965	
Carlos Ortiz	Puerto Rico	1965-1966	
Carlos Ortiz*	Puerto Rico	1966-1967	WBA
Carlos Ortiz	Puerto Rico	1967-1968	
Carlos Teo Cruz	Dom Republic	1968-1969	
Mando Ramos	USA	1969-1970	
Ismael Laguna	Panama	1970	
Ismael Laguna	Panama	1970	WBA
Ken Buchanan*	Scotland	1970-1971	WBA
Ken Buchanan	Scotland	1971	
Ken Buchanan	Scotland	1971-1972	WBA
Pedro Carrasco	Spain	1971-1972	WBC
Mando Ramos	USA	1972	WBC
Roberto Duran*	Panama	1972-1978	WBA
Chango Carmona	Mexico	1972	WBC
Rodolfo Gonzalez	Mexico	1972-1974	WBC
Guts Ishimatsu	Japan	1974-1976	WBC
Esteban de Jesus	Puerto Rico	1976-1978	WBC
Roberto Duran*	Panama	1978-1979	
Jim Watt	Scotland	1979-1981	WBC
Ernesto Espana	Venezuela	1979-1980	WBA
Hilmer Kenty	USA	1980-1981	WBA
Sean O'Grady	USA	1981	WBA
Alexis Arguello*	Nicaragua	1981-1983	WBC
Claude Noel	Trinidad	1981	WBA
Arturo Frias	USA	1981-1982	WBA
Ray Mancini	USA	1982-1984	WBA
Edwin Rosario	Puerto Rico	1983-1984	WBC
Charlie Choo Choo Brown	USA	1984	IBF
Harry Arroyo	USA	1984-1985	IBF
Livingstone Bramble	USA	1984-1986	WBA
Jose Luis Ramirez	Mexico	1984-1985	WBC
Jimmy Paul	USA	1985-1986	IBF
Hector Camacho*	Puerto Rico	1985-1987	WBC
Edwin Rosario	Puerto Rico	1986-1987	WBA
Greg Haugen	USA	1986-1987	IBF
Vinny Pazienza	USA	1987-1988	IBF
Jose Luis Ramirez	Mexico	1987-1988	WBC
Julio Cesar Chavez*	Mexico	1987-1988	WBA
Greg Haugen	USA	1988-1989	IBF
Julio Cesar Chavez*	Mexico	1988-1989	WBA/WBC
Mauricio Aceves	Mexico	1989-1990	WBO
Pernell Whitaker*	USA	1989	IBF
Edwin Rosario	Puerto Rico	1989-1990	WBA
Pernell Whitaker*	USA	1989-1990	IBF/WBC
Juan Nazario	Puerto Rico	1990	WBA
Pernell Whitaker*	USA	1990-1992	IBF/WBC/WBA
Dingaan Thobela*	S Africa	1990-1992	WBO
Joey Gamache	USA	1992	WBA
Miguel Gonzalez*	Mexico	1992-1996	WBC
Giovanni Parisi*	Italy	1992-1994	WBO
Tony Lopez	USA	1992-1993	WBA
Fred Pendleton	USA	1993-1994	IBF
Dingaan Thobela	S Africa	1993	WBA

255

Title Holder	Birthplace	Tenure	Status	Title Holder	Birthplace	Tenure	Status
Orzubek Nazarov	Kyrghyzstan	1993-1998	WBA	Mushy Callahan	USA	1926-1927	NBA
Rafael Ruelas	USA	1994-1995	IBF	Mushy Callahan	USA	1927-1930	NBA/NY
Oscar de la Hoya*	USA	1994-1995	WBO	Mushy Callahan	USA	1930	NBA
Oscar de la Hoya*	USA	1995	WBO/IBF	Jackie Kid Berg	England	1930-1931	NBA
Oscar de la Hoya*	USA	1995-1996	WBO	Tony Canzoneri	USA	1931-1932	NBA
Phillip Holiday	S Africa	1995-1997	IBF	Johnny Jadick	USA	1932	NBA
Jean-Baptiste Mendy	France	1996-1997	WBC	Johnny Jadick	USA	1932-1933	PEN
Artur Grigorian	Uzbekistan	1996-2004	WBO	Battling Shaw	Mexico	1933	LOUIS
Steve Johnston	USA	1997-1998	WBC	Tony Canzoneri	USA	1933	LOUIS
Shane Mosley*	USA	1997-1999	IBF	Barney Ross*	USA	1933-1935	ILL
Jean-Baptiste Mendy	France	1998-1999	WBA	Maxie Berger	Canada	1939	CAN
Cesar Bazan	Mexico	1998-1999	WBC	Harry Weekly	USA	1941-1942	LOUIS
Steve Johnston	USA	1999-2000	WBC	Tippy Larkin	USA	1946-1947	NY/NBA
Julien Lorcy	France	1999	WBA	Carlos Ortiz	Puerto Rico	1959-1960	NBA
Stefano Zoff	Italy	1999	WBA	Duilio Loi	Italy	1960-1962	NBA
Paul Spadafora*	USA	1999-2003	IBF	Duilio Loi	Italy	1962	WBA
Gilberto Serrano	Venezuela	1999-2000	WBA	Eddie Perkins	USA	1962	WBA
Takanori Hatakeyama	Japan	2000-2001	WBA	Duilio Loi*	Italy	1962-1963	WBA
Jose Luis Castillo	Mexico	2000-2002	WBC	Roberto Cruz	Philippines	1963	WBA
Julien Lorcy	France	2001	WBA	Eddie Perkins	USA	1963-1965	WBA
Raul Balbi	Argentina	2001-2002	WBA	Carlos Hernandez	Venezuela	1965-1966	WBA
Leonardo Dorin	Romania	2002-2003	WBA	Sandro Lopopolo	Italy	1966-1967	WBA
Floyd Mayweather*	USA	2002-2004	WBC	Paul Fujii	Hawaii	1967-1968	WBA
Javier Jauregui	Mexico	2003-2004	IBF	Nicolino Loche	Argentina	1968-1972	WBA
Acelino Freitas	Brazil	2004-	WBO	Pedro Adigue	Philippines	1968-1970	WBC
Lakva Sim	Mongolia	2004-	WBA	Bruno Arcari*	Italy	1970-1974	WBC
Julio Diaz	Mexico	2004-	IBF	Alfonso Frazer	Panama	1972	WBA
Jose Luis Castillo	Mexico	2004-	WBC	Antonio Cervantes	Colombia	1972-1976	WBA
				Perico Fernandez	Spain	1974-1975	WBC
				Saensak Muangsurin	Thailand	1975-1976	WBC

L. Welterweight (140 lbs)

Title Holder	Birthplace	Tenure	Status
Pinkey Mitchell	USA	1922-1926	NBA
Wilfred Benitez	USA	1976	WBA

Pryor seen retaining his WBA light-welter title on 9 September 1983, having knocked our Alexis Arguello in the tenth round

Title Holder	Birthplace	Tenure	Status	Title Holder	Birthplace	Tenure	Status
Miguel Velasquez	Spain	1976	WBC	Mysterious Billy Smith	USA	1892-1894	
Saensak Muangsurin	Thailand	1976-1978	WBC	Tommy Ryan	USA	1894-1897	USA
Antonio Cervantes	Colombia	1977-1980	WBA	Tommy Ryan	USA	1897-1899	
Wilfred Benitez*	USA	1977-1978	NY	Dick Burge	GB	1897	
Sang-Hyun Kim	S Korea	1978-1980	WBC	George Green	USA	1897	
Saoul Mamby	USA	1980-1982	WBC	Tom Causer	GB	1897	
Aaron Pryor*	USA	1980-1984	WBA	Joe Walcott	Barbados	1897	
Leroy Haley	USA	1982-1983	WBC	George Lavigne	USA	1897-1899	
Bruce Curry	USA	1983-1984	WBC	Dick Burge	GB	1897-1898	
Johnny Bumphus	USA	1984	WBA	Mysterious Billy Smith	USA	1898-1900	
Bill Costello	USA	1984-1985	WBC	Bobby Dobbs	USA	1898-1902	
Gene Hatcher	USA	1984-1985	WBA	Rube Ferns	USA	1900	
Aaron Pryor	USA	1984-1985	IBF	Matty Matthews	USA	1900	
Ubaldo Sacco	Argentina	1985-1986	WBA	Eddie Connolly	Canada	1900	
Lonnie Smith	USA	1985-1986	WBC	Matty Matthews	USA	1900-1901	
Patrizio Oliva	Italy	1986-1987	WBA	Rube Ferns	USA	1901	
Gary Hinton	USA	1986	IBF	Joe Walcott	Barbados	1901-1906	
Rene Arredondo	Mexico	1986	WBC	Eddie Connolly	Canada	1902-1903	GB
Tsuyoshi Hamada	Japan	1986-1987	WBC	Matty Matthews	USA	1902-1903	
Joe Manley	USA	1986-1987	IBF	Rube Ferns	USA	1903	
Terry Marsh*	England	1987	IBF	Martin Duffy	USA	1903-1904	
Juan M. Coggi	Argentina	1987-1990	WBA	Honey Mellody	USA	1904	
Rene Arredondo	Mexico	1987	WBC	Jack Clancy	USA	1904-1905	GB
Roger Mayweather	USA	1987-1989	WBC	Dixie Kid	USA	1904-1905	
James McGirt	USA	1988	IBF	Buddy Ryan	USA	1904-1905	
Meldrick Taylor	USA	1988-1990	IBF	Sam Langford	Canada	1904-1905	
Hector Camacho	Puerto Rico	1989-1991	WBO	George Petersen	USA	1905	
Julio Cesar Chavez*	Mexico	1989-1990	WBC	Jimmy Gardner	USA	1905	
Julio Cesar Chavez*	Mexico	1990-1991	IBF/WBC	Mike Twin Sullivan	USA	1905-1906	
Loreto Garza	USA	1990-1991	WBA	Joe Gans	USA	1906	
Greg Haugen	USA	1991	WBO	Joe Walcott	Barbados	1906	USA
Hector Camacho	Puerto Rico	1991-1992	WBO	Honey Mellody	USA	1906	USA
Edwin Rosario	Puerto Rico	1991-1992	WBA	Honey Mellody	USA	1906-1907	
Julio Cesar Chavez	Mexico	1991-1992	WBC	Joe Thomas	USA	1906-1907	
Rafael Pineda	Colombia	1991-1992	IBF	Mike Twin Sullivan	USA	1907-1911	
Akinobu Hiranaka	Japan	1992	WBA	Jimmy Gardner	USA	1907-1908	
Carlos Gonzalez	Mexico	1992-1993	WBO	Frank Mantell	USA	1907-1908	
Pernell Whitaker*	USA	1992-1993	IBF	Harry Lewis	USA	1908-1910	
Morris East	Philippines	1992-1993	WBA	Jack Blackburn	USA	1908	
Juan M. Coggi	Argentina	1993-1994	WBA	Jimmy Gardner	USA	1908-1909	
Charles Murray	USA	1993-1994	IBF	Willie Lewis	USA	1909-1910	
Zack Padilla*	USA	1993-1994	WBO	Harry Lewis	USA	1910-1911	GB/FR
Frankie Randall	USA	1994	WBC	Jimmy Clabby	USA	1910-1911	
Jake Rodriguez	USA	1994-1995	IBF	Dixie Kid	USA	1911-1912	GB/FR
Julio Cesar Chavez	Mexico	1994-1996	WBC	Ray Bronson	USA	1911-1914	
Frankie Randall	USA	1994-1996	WBA	Marcel Thomas	France	1912-1913	FR
Konstantin Tszyu	Russia	1995-1997	IBF	Wildcat Ferns	USA	1912-1913	
Sammy Fuentes	Puerto Rico	1995-1996	WBO	Spike Kelly	USA	1913-1914	
Juan M. Coggi	Argentina	1996	WBA	Mike Glover	USA	1913-1915	
Giovanni Parisi	Italy	1996-1998	WBO	Mike Gibbons	USA	1913-1914	
Oscar de la Hoya*	USA	1996-1997	WBC	Waldemar Holberg	Denmark	1914	
Frankie Randall	USA	1996-1997	WBA	Tom McCormick	Ireland	1914	
Khalid Rahilou	France	1997-1998	WBA	Matt Wells	England	1914-1915	AUSTR
Vince Phillips	USA	1997-1999	IBF	Kid Graves	USA	1914-1917	
Carlos Gonzalez	Mexico	1998-1999	WBO	Jack Britton	USA	1915	
Sharmba Mitchell	USA	1998-2001	WBA	Ted Kid Lewis	England	1915-1916	
Terron Millett	USA	1999	IBF	Jack Britton	USA	1916-1917	
Randall Bailey	USA	1999-2000	WBO	Ted Kid Lewis	England	1917	
Kostya Tszyu*	Russia	1999-2001	WBC	**Ted Kid Lewis**	England	1917-1919	
Zab Judah	USA	2000-2001	IBF	**Jack Britton**	USA	1919-1922	
Ener Julio	Colombia	2000-2001	WBO	**Mickey Walker**	USA	1922-1923	
Kostya Tszyu*	Russia	2001	WBA/WBC	Mickey Walker	USA	1923-1924	NBA
DeMarcus Corley	USA	2001-2003	WBO	Dave Shade	USA	1923	NY
Kostya Tszyu	Russia	2001-2004	WBA/WBC/IBF	Jimmy Jones	USA	1923	NY/MASS
Zab Judah*	USA	2003-2004	WBO	**Mickey Walker**	USA	1924-1926	
Kostya Tszyu	Russia	2004	WBC/IBF	**Pete Latzo**	USA	1926-1927	
Vivien Harris	Guyana	2004-	WBA	**Joe Dundee**	Italy	1927-1928	
				Joe Dundee	Italy	1928-1929	NY
Welterweight (147 lbs)				Jackie Fields	USA	1929	NBA
Paddy Duffy	USA	1889-1890		**Jackie Fields**	USA	1929-1930	
Tommy Ryan	USA	1891-1894		**Young Jack Thompson**	USA	1930	

Title Holder	Birthplace	Tenure	Status
Tommy Freeman	USA	1930-1931	
Young Jack Thompson	USA	1930	
Lou Brouillard	Canada	1931-1932	
Jackie Fields	USA	1932-1933	
Young Corbett III	Italy	1933	
Jimmy McLarnin	Ireland	1933-1934	
Barney Ross	USA	1934	
Jimmy McLarnin	Ireland	1934-1935	
Barney Ross	USA	1935-1938	
Barney Ross	USA	1938	NY/NBA
Felix Wouters	Belgium	1938	IBU
Henry Armstrong	USA	1938-1940	
Fritzie Zivic	USA	1940	
Fritzie Zivic	USA	1940-1941	NY/NBA
Izzy Jannazzo	USA	1940-1942	MARY
Red Cochrane	USA	1941-1942	NY/NBA
Red Cochrane	USA	1942-1946	
Marty Servo	USA	1946	
Sugar Ray Robinson*	USA	1946-1951	
Johnny Bratton	USA	1951	NBA
Kid Gavilan	Cuba	1951-1952	NBA/NY
Kid Gavilan	Cuba	1952-1954	
Johnny Saxton	USA	1954-1955	
Tony de Marco	USA	1955	
Carmen Basilio	USA	1955-1956	
Johnny Saxton	USA	1956	
Carmen Basilio*	USA	1956-1957	
Virgil Akins	USA	1957-1958	MASS
Virgil Akins	USA	1958	
Don Jordan	Dom Republic	1958-1960	
Benny Kid Paret	Cuba	1960-1961	
Emile Griffith	Virgin Islands	1961	
Benny Kid Paret	Cuba	1961-1962	
Emile Griffith	Virgin Islands	1962-1963	
Luis Rodriguez	Cuba	1963	
Emile Griffith*	Virgin Islands	1963-1966	
Willie Ludick	S Africa	1966-1968	SA
Curtis Cokes*	USA	1966	WBA
Curtis Cokes*	USA	1966-1967	WBA/WBC
Charley Shipes	USA	1966-1967	CALIF
Curtis Cokes	USA	1968-1969	
Jose Napoles	Cuba	1969-1970	
Billy Backus	USA	1970-1971	
Jose Napoles	Cuba	1971-1972	
Jose Napoles*	Cuba	1972-1974	WBA/WBC
Hedgemon Lewis	USA	1972-1974	NY
Jose Napoles	Cuba	1974-1975	
Jose Napoles	Cuba	1975	WBC
Angel Espada	Puerto Rico	1975-1976	WBA
John H. Stracey	England	1975-1976	WBC
Carlos Palomino	Mexico	1976-1979	WBC
Pipino Cuevas	Mexico	1976-1980	WBA
Wilfred Benitez	USA	1979	WBC
Sugar Ray Leonard	USA	1979-1980	WBC
Roberto Duran	Panama	1980	WBC
Thomas Hearns	USA	1980-1981	WBA
Sugar Ray Leonard	USA	1980-1981	WBC
Sugar Ray Leonard*	USA	1981-1982	
Don Curry*	USA	1983-1984	WBA
Milton McCrory	USA	1983-1985	WBC
Don Curry*	USA	1984-1985	WBA/IBF
Don Curry	USA	1985-1986	
Lloyd Honeyghan	Jamaica	1986	
Lloyd Honeyghan	Jamaica	1986-1987	WBC/IBF
Mark Breland	USA	1987	WBA
Marlon Starling	USA	1987-1988	WBA
Jorge Vaca	Mexico	1987-1988	WBC
Lloyd Honeyghan	Jamaica	1988-1989	WBC
Simon Brown*	Jamaica	1988-1991	IBF
Tomas Molinares	Colombia	1988-1989	WBA
Mark Breland	USA	1989-1990	WBA
Marlon Starling	USA	1989-1990	WBC
Genaro Leon*	Mexico	1989	WBO
Manning Galloway	USA	1989-1993	WBO
Aaron Davis	USA	1990-1991	WBA
Maurice Blocker	USA	1990-1991	WBC
Meldrick Taylor	USA	1991-1992	WBA
Simon Brown*	Jamaica	1991	WBC/IBF
Simon Brown	Jamaica	1991	WBC
Maurice Blocker	USA	1991-1993	IBF
James McGirt	USA	1991-1993	WBC
Crisanto Espana	Venezuela	1992-1994	WBA
Gert Bo Jacobsen*	Denmark	1993	WBO
Pernell Whitaker	USA	1993-1997	WBC
Felix Trinidad*	Puerto Rico	1993-2000	IBF
Eamonn Loughran	Ireland	1993-1996	WBO
Ike Quartey	Ghana	1994-1998	WBA
Jose Luis Lopez	Mexico	1996-1997	WBO
Michael Loewe*	Romania	1997-1998	WBO
Oscar de la Hoya	USA	1997-1999	WBC
Ahmed Kotiev	Russia	1998-2000	WBO
James Page	USA	1998-2000	WBA
Oscar de la Hoya	USA	2000	WBC
Daniel Santos*	Puerto Rico	2000-2002	WBO
Shane Mosley	USA	2000-2002	WBC
Andrew Lewis	Guyana	2001-2002	WBA
Vernon Forrest	USA	2001	IBF
Vernon Forrest	USA	2002-2003	WBC
Antonio Margarito	Mexico	2002-	WBO
Ricardo Mayorga*	Nicaragua	2002-2003	WBA
Michele Piccirillo	Italy	2002-2003	IBF
Ricardo Mayorga	Nicaragua	2003	WBA/WBC
Cory Spinks*	USA	2003-	IBF
Cory Spinks	USA	2003-	IBF/WBA/WBC

L. Middleweight (154 lbs)

Title Holder	Birthplace	Tenure	Status
Emile Griffith*	USA	1962-1963	AU
Denny Moyer	USA	1962-1963	WBA
Ralph Dupas	USA	1963	WBA
Sandro Mazzinghi	Italy	1963-1965	WBA
Nino Benvenuti	Italy	1965-1966	WBA
Ki-Soo Kim	S Korea	1966-1968	WBA
Sandro Mazzinghi	Italy	1968-1969	WBA
Freddie Little	USA	1969-1970	WBA
Carmelo Bossi	Italy	1970-1971	WBA
Koichi Wajima	Japan	1971-1974	WBA
Oscar Albarado	USA	1974-1975	WBA
Koichi Wajima	Japan	1975	WBA
Miguel de Oliveira	Brazil	1975	WBC
Jae-Do Yuh	S Korea	1975-1976	WBA
Elisha Obed	Bahamas	1975-1976	WBC
Koichi Wajima	Japan	1976	WBA
Jose Duran	Spain	1976	WBA
Eckhard Dagge	Germany	1976-1977	WBC
Miguel Castellini	Argentina	1976-1977	WBA
Eddie Gazo	Nicaragua	1977-1978	WBA
Rocky Mattioli	Italy	1977-1979	WBC
Masashi Kudo	Japan	1978-1979	WBA
Maurice Hope	Antigua	1979-1981	WBC
Ayub Kalule	Uganda	1979-1981	WBA
Wilfred Benitez	USA	1981-1982	WBC
Sugar Ray Leonard*	USA	1981	WBA
Tadashi Mihara	Japan	1981-1982	WBA
Davey Moore	USA	1982-1983	WBA
Thomas Hearns*	USA	1982-1986	WBC
Roberto Duran*	Panama	1983-1984	WBA
Mark Medal	USA	1984	IBF
Mike McCallum*	Jamaica	1984-1987	WBA
Carlos Santos	Puerto Rico	1984-1986	IBF
Buster Drayton	USA	1986-1987	IBF
Duane Thomas	USA	1986-1987	WBC
Matthew Hilton	Canada	1987-1988	IBF

Title Holder	Birthplace	Tenure	Status
Lupe Aquino	Mexico	1987	WBC
Gianfranco Rosi	Italy	1987-1988	WBC
Julian Jackson*	Virgin Islands	1987-1990	WBA
Don Curry	USA	1988-1989	WBC
Robert Hines	USA	1988-1989	IBF
John David Jackson*	USA	1988-1993	WBO
Darrin van Horn	USA	1989	IBF
Rene Jacqot	France	1989	WBC
John Mugabi	Uganda	1989-1990	WBC
Gianfranco Rosi	Italy	1989-1994	IBF
Terry Norris	USA	1990-1993	WBC
Gilbert Dele	France	1991	WBA
Vinny Pazienza*	USA	1991-1992	WBA
Julio Cesar Vasquez	Argentina	1992-1995	WBA
Verno Phillips	USA	1993-1995	WBO
Simon Brown	USA	1993-1994	WBC
Terry Norris	USA	1994	WBC
Vince Pettway	USA	1994-1995	IBF
Luis Santana	Dom Republic	1994-1995	WBC
Pernell Whitaker*	USA	1995	WBA
Gianfranco Rosi	Italy	1995	WBO
Carl Daniels	USA	1995	WBA
Verno Phillips	USA	1995	WBO
Paul Vaden	USA	1995	IBF
Terry Norris*	USA	1995	WBC
Paul Jones	England	1995-1996	WBO
Terry Norris	USA	1995-1997	IBF/WBC
Julio Cesar Vasquez	Argentina	1995-1996	WBA
Bronco McKart	USA	1996	WBO
Ronald Wright	USA	1996-1998	WBO
Laurent Boudouani	France	1996-1999	WBA
Terry Norris	USA	1997	WBC
Raul Marquez	USA	1997	IBF
Luis Campas	Mexico	1997-1998	IBF
Keith Mullings	USA	1997-1999	WBC
Harry Simon*	Namibia	1998-2001	WBO
Fernando Vargas	USA	1998-2000	IBF
Javier Castillejo	Spain	1999-2001	WBC
David Reid	USA	1999-2000	WBA
Felix Trinidad*	Puerto Rico	2000	WBA
Felix Trinidad*	Puerto Rico	2000-2001	IBF/WBA
Oscar de la Hoya*	USA	2001-2002	WBC
Fernando Vargas	USA	2001-2002	WBA
Ronald Wright*	USA	2001-2004	IBF
Daniel Santos	Puerto Rico	2002-	WBO
Oscar de la Hoya	USA	2002-	WBA/WBC
Shane Mosley	USA	2003-2004	WBA/WBC
Ronald Wright	USA	2004-	IBF/WBA/WBC
Ronald Wright	USA	2004-	WBA/WBC
Verno Phillips	USA	2004-	IBF

Middleweight (160 lbs)

Title Holder	Birthplace	Tenure	Status
Nonpareil Jack Dempsey	Ireland	1889-1891	USA
Bob Fitzsimmons	England	1891-1893	USA
Jim Hall	Australia	1892-1893	GB
Bob Fitzsimmons	England	1893-1894	
Bob Fitzsimmons	England	1894-1899	
Frank Craig	USA	1894-1895	GB
Dan Creedon	New Zealand	1895-1897	GB
Tommy Ryan	USA	1895-1896	
Kid McCoy	USA	1896-1898	
Tommy Ryan	USA	1898-1905	
Charley McKeever	USA	1900-1902	
George Gardner	USA	1901-1902	
Jack O'Brien	USA	1901-1905	
George Green	USA	1901-1902	
Jack Palmer	England	1902-1903	GB
Hugo Kelly	USA	1905-1908	
Jack Twin Sullivan	USA	1905-1908	
Sam Langford	Canada	1907-1911	
Billy Papke	USA	1908	

Title Holder	Birthplace	Tenure	Status
Stanley Ketchel	USA	1908	
Billy Papke	USA	1908	
Stanley Ketchel	USA	1908-1910	
Billy Papke	USA	1910-1913	
Stanley Ketchel*	USA	1910	
Hugo Kelly	USA	1910-1912	
Cyclone Johnny Thompson	USA	1911-1912	
Harry Lewis	USA	1911	
Leo Houck	USA	1911-1912	
Georges Carpentier	France	1911-1912	
Jack Dillon	USA	1912	
Frank Mantell	USA	1912-1913	
Frank Klaus	USA	1912-1913	
Georges Carpentier	France	1912	IBU
Jack Dillon	USA	1912-1915	
Eddie McGoorty	USA	1912-1913	
Frank Klaus	USA	1913	IBU
Jimmy Clabby	USA	1913-1914	
George Chip	USA	1913-1914	
Joe Borrell	USA	1913-1914	
Jeff Smith	USA	1913-1914	
Eddie McGoorty	USA	1914	AUSTR
Jeff Smith	USA	1914	AUSTR
Al McCoy	USA	1914-1917	
Jimmy Clabby	USA	1914-1915	
Mick King	Australia	1914	AUSTR
Jeff Smith	USA	1914-1915	AUSTR
Young Ahearn	England	1915-1916	
Les Darcy*	Australia	1915-1917	AUSTR
Mike Gibbons	USA	1916-1917	
Mike O'Dowd	USA	1917-1920	
Johnny Wilson	USA	1920-1921	
Johnny Wilson	USA	1921-1922	NBA/NY
Bryan Downey	USA	1921-1922	OHIO
Johnny Wilson	USA	1922-1923	NBA
Dave Rosenberg	USA	1922	NY
Jock Malone	USA	1922-1923	OHIO
Mike O'Dowd	USA	1922-1923	NY
Johnny Wilson	USA	1923	
Harry Greb	USA	1923-1926	
Tiger Flowers	USA	1926	
Mickey Walker	USA	1926-1931	
Gorilla Jones	USA	1932	NBA
Marcel Thil	France	1932-1933	NBA/IBU
Marcel Thil	France	1933-1937	IBU
Ben Jeby	USA	1933	NY
Lou Brouillard	Canada	1933	NY
Lou Brouillard	Canada	1933	NY/NBA
Vearl Whitehead	USA	1933	CALIF
Teddy Yarosz	USA	1933-1934	PEN
Vince Dundee	USA	1933-1934	NY/NBA
Teddy Yarosz	USA	1934-1935	NY/NBA
Babe Risko	USA	1935-1936	NY/NBA
Freddie Steele	USA	1936-1938	NY/NBA
Fred Apostoli	USA	1937-1938	IBU
Edouard Tenet	France	1938	IBU
Young Corbett III	Italy	1938	CALIF
Freddie Steele	USA	1938	NBA
Al Hostak	USA	1938	NBA
Solly Krieger	USA	1938-1939	NBA
Fred Apostoli	USA	1938-1939	NY
Al Hostak	USA	1939-1940	NBA
Ceferino Garcia	Philippines	1939-1940	NY
Ken Overlin	USA	1940-1941	NY
Tony Zale	USA	1940-1941	NBA
Billy Soose	USA	1941	NY
Tony Zale	USA	1941-1947	
Rocky Graziano	USA	1947-1948	
Tony Zale	USA	1948	
Marcel Cerdan	Algeria	1948-1949	
Jake la Motta	USA	1949-1950	

Title Holder	Birthplace	Tenure	Status
Jake la Motta	USA	1950-1951	NY/NBA
Sugar Ray Robinson	USA	1950-1951	PEN
Sugar Ray Robinson	USA	1951	
Randy Turpin	England	1951	
Sugar Ray Robinson*	USA	1951-1952	
Randy Turpin	England	1953	GB/EBU
Carl Bobo Olson	Hawaii	1953-1955	
Sugar Ray Robinson	USA	1955-1957	
Gene Fullmer	USA	1957	
Sugar Ray Robinson	USA	1957	
Carmen Basilio	USA	1957-1958	
Sugar Ray Robinson	USA	1958-1959	
Sugar Ray Robinson	USA	1959-1960	NY/EBU
Gene Fullmer	USA	1959-1962	NBA
Paul Pender	USA	1960-1961	NY/EBU
Terry Downes	England	1961-1962	NY/EBU
Paul Pender	USA	1962	NY/EBU
Dick Tiger	Nigeria	1962-1963	NBA
Dick Tiger	Nigeria	1963	
Joey Giardello	USA	1963-1965	
Dick Tiger	Nigeria	1965-1966	
Emile Griffith	Virgin Islands	1966-1967	
Nino Benvenuti	Italy	1967	
Emile Griffith	Virgin Islands	1967-1968	
Nino Benvenuti	Italy	1968-1970	
Carlos Monzon	Argentina	1970-1974	
Carlos Monzon*	Argentina	1974-1976	WBA
Rodrigo Valdez	Colombia	1974-1976	WBC
Carlos Monzon*	Argentina	1976-1977	
Rodrigo Valdez	Colombia	1977-1978	
Hugo Corro	Argentina	1978-1979	
Vito Antuofermo	Italy	1979-1980	
Alan Minter	England	1980	
Marvin Hagler	USA	1980-1987	
Marvin Hagler	USA	1987	WBC/IBF
Sugar Ray Leonard	USA	1987	WBC
Frank Tate	USA	1987-1988	IBF
Sumbu Kalambay	Zaire	1987-1989	WBA
Thomas Hearns	USA	1987-1988	WBC
Iran Barkley	USA	1988-1989	WBC
Michael Nunn	USA	1988-1991	IBF
Roberto Duran	Panama	1989-1990	WBC
Doug de Witt	USA	1989-1990	WBO
Mike McCallum	Jamaica	1989-1991	WBA
Nigel Benn	England	1990	WBO
Chris Eubank*	England	1990-1991	WBO
Julian Jackson	Virgin Islands	1990-1993	WBC
James Toney*	USA	1991-1993	IBF
Gerald McClellan*	USA	1991-1993	WBO
Reggie Johnson	USA	1992-1993	WBA
Gerald McClellan*	USA	1993-1995	WBC
Chris Pyatt	England	1993-1994	WBO
Roy Jones*	USA	1993-1994	IBF
John David Jackson	USA	1993-1994	WBA
Steve Collins*	Ireland	1994-1995	WBO
Jorge Castro	Argentina	1994	WBA
Julian Jackson	Virgin Islands	1995	WBC
Bernard Hopkins*	USA	1995-2001	IBF
Lonnie Bradley*	USA	1995-1998	WBO
Quincy Taylor	USA	1995-1996	WBC
Shinji Takehara	Japan	1995-1996	WBA
Keith Holmes	USA	1996-1998	WBC
William Joppy	USA	1996-1997	WBA
Julio Cesar Green	Dom Republic	1997-1998	WBA
William Joppy	USA	1998-2001	WBA
Hassine Cherifi	France	1998-1999	WBC
Otis Grant*	Canada	1998	WBO
Bert Schenk	Germany	1999	WBO
Keith Holmes	USA	1999-2001	WBC
Jason Matthews	England	1999	WBO
Armand Krajnc	Slovenia	1999-2002	WBO

Title Holder	Birthplace	Tenure	Status
Bernard Hopkins*	USA	2001	WBC/IBF
Felix Trinidad	Puerto Rico	2001	WBA
Bernard Hopkins	USA	2001-	WBC/WBA/IBF
Harry Simon	Namibia	2002-2003	WBO
Hector Javier Velazco	Argentina	2003	WBO
Felix Sturm	Germany	2003-2004	WBO
Oscar de la Hoya	USA	2004-	WBO

S. Middleweight (168 lbs)

Title Holder	Birthplace	Tenure	Status
Murray Sutherland	Scotland	1984	IBF
Chong-Pal Park*	S Korea	1984-1987	IBF
Chong-Pal Park	S Korea	1987-1988	WBA
Graciano Rocchigiani*	Germany	1988-1989	IBF
Fully Obelmejias	Venezuela	1988-1989	WBA
Sugar Ray Leonard*	USA	1988-1990	WBC
Thomas Hearns*	USA	1988-1991	WBO
In-Chul Baek	S Korea	1989-1990	WBA
Lindell Holmes	USA	1990-1991	IBF
Christophe Tiozzo	France	1990-1991	WBA
Mauro Galvano	Italy	1990-1992	WBC
Victor Cordoba	Panama	1991-1992	WBA
Darrin van Horn	USA	1991-1992	IBF
Chris Eubank	England	1991-1995	WBO
Iran Barkley	USA	1992-1993	IBF
Michael Nunn	USA	1992-1994	WBA
Nigel Benn	England	1992-1996	WBC
James Toney	USA	1993-1994	IBF
Steve Little	USA	1994	WBA
Frank Liles	USA	1994-1999	WBA
Roy Jones*	USA	1994-1997	IBF
Steve Collins*	Ireland	1995-1997	WBO
Thulani Malinga	S Africa	1996	WBC
Vincenzo Nardiello	Italy	1996	WBC
Robin Reid	England	1996-1997	WBC
Charles Brewer	USA	1997-1998	IBF
Joe Calzaghe	Wales	1997-	WBO
Thulani Malinga	S Africa	1997-1998	WBC
Richie Woodhall	England	1998-1999	WBC
Sven Ottke*	Germany	1998-2003	IBF
Byron Mitchell	USA	1999-2000	WBA
Markus Beyer	Germany	1999-2000	WBC
Bruno Girard	France	2000-2001	WBA
Glenn Catley	England	2000	WBC
Dingaan Thobela	S Africa	2000	WBC
Dave Hilton	Canada	2000-2001	WBC
Byron Mitchell	USA	2001-2003	WBA
Eric Lucas	Canada	2001-2003	WBC
Sven Ottke*	Germany	2003-2004	IBF/WBA
Markus Beyer	Germany	2003-2004	WBC
Anthony Mundine	Australia	2004	WBA
Manny Sica	Puerto Rico	2004-	WBA
Cristian Sanavia	Italy	2004-	WBC

L. Heavyweight (175 lbs)

Title Holder	Birthplace	Tenure	Status
Jack Root	Austria	1903	
George Gardner	Ireland	1903	
George Gardner	Ireland	1903	USA
Bob Fitzsimmons	England	1903-1905	USA
Jack O'Brien	USA	1905-1911	
Sam Langford	Canada	1911-1913	
Georges Carpentier	France	1913-1920	IBU
Jack Dillon	USA	1914-1916	USA
Battling Levinsky	USA	1916-1920	USA
Georges Carpentier	France	1920-1922	
Battling Siki	Senegal	1922-1923	
Mike McTigue	Ireland	1923-1925	
Paul Berlenbach	USA	1925-1926	
Jack Delaney*	Canada	1926-1927	
Jimmy Slattery	USA	1927	NBA
Tommy Loughran	USA	1927	NY
Tommy Loughran*	USA	1927-1929	

Title Holder	Birthplace	Tenure	Status	Title Holder	Birthplace	Tenure	Status
Jimmy Slattery	USA	1930	NY	Iran Barkley*	USA	1992	WBA
Maxie Rosenbloom	USA	1930-1931		Virgil Hill*	USA	1992-1996	WBA
Maxie Rosenbloom	USA	1931-1933	NY	Henry Maske	Germany	1993-1996	IBF
George Nichols	USA	1932	NBA	Mike McCallum	Jamaica	1994-1995	WBC
Bob Godwin	USA	1933	NBA	Dariusz Michalczewski*	Poland	1994-1997	WBO
Maxie Rosenbloom	USA	1933-1934		Fabrice Tiozzo	France	1995-1997	WBC
Maxie Rosenbloom	USA	1934	NY	Virgil Hill	USA	1996-1997	IBF/WBA
Joe Knight	USA	1934-1935	FL/NC/GEO	Roy Jones	USA	1997	WBC
Bob Olin	USA	1934-1935	NY	Montell Griffin	USA	1997	WBC
Al McCoy	Canada	1935	CAN	Dariusz Michalczewski*	Poland	1997	WBO/IBF/WBA
Bob Olin	USA	1935	NY/NBA	Dariusz Michalczewski	Poland	1997-2003	WBO
John Henry Lewis	USA	1935-1938	NY/NBA	William Guthrie	USA	1997-1998	IBF
Gustav Roth	Belgium	1936-1938	IBU	Roy Jones*	USA	1997-1998	WBC
Ad Heuser	Germany	1938	IBU	Lou del Valle	USA	1997-1998	WBA
John Henry Lewis	USA	1938		Reggie Johnson	USA	1998-1999	IBF
John Henry Lewis	USA	1938-1939	NBA	Roy Jones*	USA	1998-1999	WBC/WBA
Melio Bettina	USA	1939	NY	Roy Jones*	USA	1999-2002	WBC/WBA/IBF
Len Harvey	England	1939-1942	GB	Roy Jones*	USA	2002-2003	WBA/WBC
Billy Conn	USA	1939-1940	NY/NBA	Mehdi Sahnoune	France	2003	WBA
Anton Christoforidis	Greece	1941	NBA	Antonio Tarver*	USA	2003-	IBF/WBC
Gus Lesnevich	USA	1941	NBA	Silvio Branco	Italy	2003-2004	WBA
Gus Lesnevich	USA	1941-1946	NY/NBA	Julio Gonzalez	Mexico	2003-2004	WBO
Freddie Mills	England	1942-1946	GB	Antonio Tarver	USA	2003-	WBC
Gus Lesnevich	USA	1946-1948		Zsolt Erdei	Hungary	2004-	WBO
Freddie Mills	England	1948-1950		Glengoffe Johnson	Jamaica	2004-	IBF
Joey Maxim	USA	1950-1952		Fabrice Tiozzo	France	2004-	WBA
Archie Moore	USA	1952-1960					
Archie Moore	USA	1960-1962	NY/EBU	**Cruiserweight (190 lbs)**			
Harold Johnson	USA	1961-1962	NBA	Marvin Camel	USA	1979-1980	WBC
Harold Johnson	USA	1962-1963		Carlos de Leon	Puerto Rico	1980-1982	WBC
Willie Pastrano	USA	1963		Ossie Ocasio	Puerto Rico	1982-1984	WBA
Willie Pastrano*	USA	1963-1964	WBA/WBC	S. T. Gordon	USA	1982-1983	WBC
Eddie Cotton	USA	1963-1964	MICH	Marvin Camel	USA	1983-1984	IBF
Willie Pastrano	USA	1964-1965		Carlos de Leon	Puerto Rico	1983-1985	WBC
Jose Torres	Puerto Rico	1965-1966		Lee Roy Murphy	USA	1984-1986	IBF
Dick Tiger	Nigeria	1966-1968		Piet Crous	S Africa	1984-1985	WBA
Bob Foster	USA	1968-1970		Alfonso Ratliff	USA	1985	WBC
Bob Foster*	USA	1970-1972	WBC	Dwight Muhammad Qawi	USA	1985-1986	WBA
Vicente Rondon	Venezuela	1971-1972	WBA	Bernard Benton	USA	1985-1986	WBC
Bob Foster*	USA	1972-1974		Carlos de Leon	Puerto Rico	1986-1988	WBC
John Conteh	England	1974-1977	WBC	Evander Holyfield*	USA	1986-1987	WBA
Victor Galindez	Argentina	1974-1978	WBA	Rickey Parkey	USA	1986-1987	IBF
Miguel Cuello	Argentina	1977-1978	WBC	Evander Holyfield*	USA	1987-1988	WBA/IBF
Mate Parlov	Yugoslavia	1978	WBC	**Evander Holyfield***	USA	1988	
Mike Rossman	USA	1978-1979	WBA	Taoufik Belbouli*	France	1989	WBA
Marvin Johnson	USA	1978-1979	WBC	Carlos de Leon	Puerto Rico	1989-1990	WBC
Victor Galindez	Argentina	1979	WBA	Glenn McCrory	England	1989-1990	IBF
Matt Saad Muhammad	USA	1979-1981	WBC	Robert Daniels	USA	1989-1991	WBA
Marvin Johnson	USA	1979-1980	WBA	Boone Pultz	USA	1989-1990	WBO
Mustafa Muhammad	USA	1980-1981	WBA	Jeff Lampkin*	USA	1990-1991	IBF
Michael Spinks*	USA	1981-1983	WBA	Magne Havnaa*	Norway	1990-1992	WBO
Dwight Muhammad Qawi	USA	1981-1983	WBC	Masimilliano Duran	Italy	1990-1991	WBC
Michael Spinks*	USA	1983-1985		Bobby Czyz	USA	1991-1993	WBA
J. B. Williamson	USA	1985-1986	WBC	Anaclet Wamba	Congo	1991-1995	WBC
Slobodan Kacar	Yugoslavia	1985-1986	IBF	James Warring	USA	1991-1992	IBF
Marvin Johnson	USA	1986-1987	WBA	Tyrone Booze	USA	1992-1993	WBO
Dennis Andries	Guyana	1986-1987	WBC	Al Cole*	USA	1992-1996	IBF
Bobby Czyz	USA	1986-1987	IBF	Marcus Bott	Germany	1993	WBO
Thomas Hearns*	USA	1987	WBC	Nestor Giovannini	Argentina	1993-1994	WBO
Leslie Stewart	Trinidad	1987	WBA	Orlin Norris	USA	1993-1995	WBA
Virgil Hill	USA	1987-1991	WBA	Dariusz Michalczewski*	Poland	1994-1995	WBO
Charles Williams	USA	1987-1993	IBF	Ralf Rocchigiani	Germany	1995-1997	WBO
Don Lalonde	Canada	1987-1988	WBC	Nate Miller	USA	1995-1997	WBA
Sugar Ray Leonard*	USA	1988	WBC	Marcelo Dominguez	Argentina	1995-1998	WBC
Michael Moorer*	USA	1988-1991	WBO	Adolpho Washington	USA	1996-1997	IBF
Dennis Andries	Guyana	1989	WBC	Uriah Grant	USA	1997	IBF
Jeff Harding	Australia	1989-1990	WBC	Carl Thompson	England	1997-1999	WBO
Dennis Andries	Guyana	1990-1991	WBC	Imamu Mayfield	USA	1997-1998	IBF
Leonzer Barber	USA	1991-1994	WBO	Fabrice Tiozzo	France	1997-2000	WBA
Thomas Hearns	USA	1991-1992	WBA	Juan Carlos Gomez*	Cuba	1998-2002	WBC
Jeff Harding	Australia	1991-1994	WBC	Arthur Williams	USA	1998-1999	IBF

Name	Country	Years	Org
Johnny Nelson	England	1999-	WBO
Vassily Jirov	Kazakhstan	1999-2003	IBF
Virgil Hill	USA	2000-2002	WBA
Jean-Marc Mormeck	Guadeloupe	2002-	WBA
Wayne Braithwaite	Guyana	2002-	WBC
James Toney*	USA	2003-2004	IBF
Kelvin Davis	USA	2004-	IBF

Heavyweight (190 lbs+)

Name	Country	Years	Org
John L. Sullivan	USA	1889-1892	USA
Peter Jackson	Australia	1889-1892	
Frank Slavin	Australia	1890-1892	GB/AUST
Peter Jackson	Australia	1892-1893	GB/AUST
James J. Corbett	USA	1892-1894	USA
James J. Corbett	USA	1894-1895	
James J. Corbett	USA	1895-1897	
Peter Maher	Ireland	1895-1896	
Bob Fitzsimmons	England	1896-1897	
Bob Fitzsimmons	England	1897-1899	
James J. Jeffries	USA	1899-1902	
James J. Jeffries	USA	1902-1905	
Denver Ed Martin	USA	1902-1903	
Jack Johnson	USA	1902-1908	
Bob Fitzsimmons	England	1905	
Marvin Hart	USA	1905-1906	
Jack O'Brien	USA	1905-1906	
Tommy Burns	Canada	1906-1908	
Jack Johnson	USA	1908-1909	
Jack Johnson	USA	1909-1915	
Sam Langford	USA	1909-1911	
Sam McVey	USA	1911-1912	
Sam Langford	USA	1912-1914	
Luther McCarty	USA	1913	
Arthur Pelkey	Canada	1913-1914	
Gunboat Smith	USA	1914	
Harry Wills	USA	1914	
Georges Carpentier	France	1914	
Sam Langford	USA	1914-1915	
Jess Willard	USA	1915-1919	
Joe Jeannette	USA	1915	
Sam McVey	USA	1915	
Harry Wills	USA	1915-1916	
Sam Langford	USA	1916-1917	
Bill Tate	USA	1917	
Sam Langford	USA	1917-1918	
Harry Wills	USA	1918-1926	
Jack Dempsey	USA	1919-1926	
Gene Tunney*	USA	1926-1928	
Max Schmeling	Germany	1930-1932	
Jack Sharkey	USA	1932-1933	
Primo Carnera	Italy	1933-1934	
Max Baer	USA	1934-1935	
James J. Braddock	USA	1935	
James J. Braddock	USA	1935-1936	NY/NBA
George Godfrey	USA	1935-1936	IBU
James J. Braddock	USA	1936-1937	
Joe Louis*	USA	1937-1949	
Ezzard Charles	USA	1949-1950	NBA
Lee Savold	USA	1950-1951	GB/EBU
Ezzard Charles	USA	1950-1951	NY/NBA
Joe Louis	USA	1951	GB/EBU
Jersey Joe Walcott	USA	1951	NY/NBA
Jersey Joe Walcott	USA	1951-1952	
Rocky Marciano*	USA	1952-1956	
Floyd Patterson	USA	1956-1959	
Ingemar Johansson	Sweden	1959-1960	
Floyd Patterson	USA	1960-1962	
Sonny Liston	USA	1962-1964	
Muhammad Ali	USA	1964	
Muhammad Ali*	USA	1964-1967	WBC
Ernie Terrell	USA	1965-1967	WBA
Muhammad Ali	USA	1967	
Muhammad Ali	USA	1967-1968	WBC
Joe Frazier*	USA	1968-1970	NY/MASS
Jimmy Ellis	USA	1968-1970	WBA
Joe Frazier	USA	1970-1973	
George Foreman	USA	1973-1974	
Muhammad Ali	USA	1974-1978	
Leon Spinks	USA	1978	
Leon Spinks	USA	1978	WBA
Larry Holmes*	USA	1978-1983	WBC
Muhammad Ali*	USA	1978-1979	WBA
John Tate	USA	1979-1980	WBA
Mike Weaver	USA	1980-1982	WBA
Michael Dokes	USA	1982-1983	WBA
Gerrie Coetzee	S Africa	1983-1984	WBA
Larry Holmes	USA	1983-1985	IBF
Tim Witherspoon	USA	1984	WBC
Pinklon Thomas	USA	1984-1986	WBC
Greg Page	USA	1984-1985	WBA
Tony Tubbs	USA	1985-1986	WBA
Michael Spinks	USA	1985-1987	IBF
Tim Witherspoon	USA	1986	WBA
Trevor Berbick	Jamaica	1986	WBC
Mike Tyson*	USA	1986-1987	WBC
James Smith	USA	1986-1987	WBA
Mike Tyson*	USA	1987	WBA/WBC
Tony Tucker	USA	1987	IBF
Mike Tyson	USA	1987-1989	
Mike Tyson	USA	1989-1990	IBF/WBA/WBC
Francesco Damiani	Italy	1989-1991	WBO
James Douglas	USA	1990	IBF/WBA/WBC
Evander Holyfield	USA	1990-1992	IBF/WBA/WBC
Ray Mercer	USA	1991-1992	WBO
Michael Moorer*	USA	1992-1993	WBO
Riddick Bowe	USA	1992	IBF/WBA/WBC
Riddick Bowe	USA	1992-1993	IBF/WBA
Lennox Lewis	England	1992-1994	WBC
Tommy Morrison	USA	1993	WBO
Michael Bentt	England	1993-1994	WBO
Evander Holyfield	USA	1993-1994	WBA/IBF
Herbie Hide	England	1994-1995	WBO
Michael Moorer	USA	1994	WBA/IBF
Oliver McCall	USA	1994-1995	WBC
George Foreman	USA	1994-1995	WBA/IBF
Riddick Bowe*	USA	1995-1996	WBO
George Foreman*	USA	1995	IBF
Bruce Seldon	USA	1995-1996	WBA
Frank Bruno	England	1995-1996	WBC
Frans Botha	S Africa	1995-1996	IBF
Mike Tyson	USA	1996	
Michael Moorer	USA	1996-1997	IBF
Henry Akinwande*	England	1996-1997	WBO
Mike Tyson	USA	1996	WBA
Evander Holyfield*	USA	1996-1997	WBA
Lennox Lewis*	England	1997-1999	WBC
Herbie Hide	England	1997-1999	WBO
Evander Holyfield	USA	1997-1999	IBF/WBA
Vitali Klitschko	Ukraine	1999-2000	WBO
Lennox Lewis*	England	1999-2000	IBF/WBA/WBC
Chris Byrd	USA	2000	WBO
Lennox Lewis	England	2000-2001	IBF/WBC
Evander Holyfield	USA	2000-2001	WBA
Vladimir Klitschko	Ukraine	2000-2003	WBO
John Ruiz	USA	2001-2003	WBA
Hasim Rahman	USA	2001	WBC/IBF
Lennox Lewis*	England	2001-2002	WBC/IBF
Lennox Lewis*	England	2002-2004	WBC
Chris Byrd	USA	2002-	IBF
Roy Jones*	USA	2003	WBA
Corrie Sanders*	S Africa	2003	WBO
Lamon Brewster	USA	2004-	WBO
John Ruiz	Puerto Rico	2004-	WBA
Vitali Klitschko	Ukraine	2004-	WBC

Early Gloved Championship Boxing: The 'True' Facts (Part 6)

by Harold Alderman

Following on from our previous exploration of how the weight classes came into being in the early days of gloved boxing, this time round we examine 152 to 170lbs, which includes major bouts contested at catchweights. Recognising that many fights listed by weight divisions prior to the advent of the named-weight divisions and weight limits announced by the National Sporting Club on 11 February 1909 did not add up, I started my research in the early 1960s, using world-wide newspaper reports, which included a thorough examination of the Sporting Life, Bells Life, Mirror of Life, Sportsman, and Police Gazette, etc. It did not take long to discover that the vast majority of fights, certainly in this country, were made at every two pounds, plus or minus two pounds. This is how it was as boxing transferred from the bare-knuckle days to gloves, passing through phases of driving gloves, kid gloves, and two-ounce gloves to what we have today and takes us through to 1909.

152lbs to 154lbs (10 Stone 12 lbs to 11 stone)

1871

11 November 'Bat' Mullins w pts 3 E.Whyman, 'The Jolly Butchers', Camden Town, London. The final of a silver cup competition for men 'under' 154lbs, which was open to the world.

14 November 'Bat' Mullins w pts 3 Ben Bendoff, 'The Garden Arms', Castle Street, Leicester Square, London. Known as 'Langhams' after it's late owner, Nat Langham, the famous bare-knuckle middleweight who had died on 1 September, aged 51, this was the final of a silver cup catchweight competition, billed as being 'open to the world'. Note that just three entered, Mullins beating Parkinson (Birmingham), while Bendoff beat T. Mullins. No weights were given.

12 December 'Bat' Mullins w pts 3 John Edward 'Plantagenet' Green, 'The Garden Arms', Castle Street, Leicester Square, London. The final of a silver cup catchweight competition that was open to the world, in the previous round Mullins beat Danny Cronin, while Green drew the bye.

1872

16 April Bill Brooks (Mile End) w pts 5 James Stewart (Glasgow), The Prince of Wales Running Grounds, Bow, London. The final of a 154lbs (limit) middleweight competition for a £50 silver championship cup. Named the Bow Cup, the competition had started on Easter Monday, 1 April (postponed from Good Friday, 29 March) with rounds held on 2 and 15 April. In the previous round, Brooks (real surname Biggs) beat W. McGrechan, while Stewart beat T. Buffalo. The other winner, George Charles, injured himself beating J. Pardew (Parden also given) and had to withdraw. There was lots of confusion over this competition, which was also called a 'heavyweight' competition for all over 154lbs, while the 128lbs competition was called a 'middleweight' competition and Stewart, with a given weight of 155lbs, was stated to be one pound overweight in some reports.

20 April James Stewart challenges Bill Brooks to a return for the Bow Cup and 154lbs 'heavyweight' championship for £25 a-side. In the same issue of *Bells Life*, Brooks was also challenged by J. Sheppard (London) and Ted Napper (London).

27 April Brooks accepted the challenge of Ted Napper – *Bells Life*.

6 July As Bill Brooks and James Stewart cannot come to terms, 'Professor' Alf Austin challenges Brooks to a bout for the 154lbs 'heavyweight' Bow Cup and the championship for £5 a-side, and left a £1 deposit. Later on, Austin is given as Albert 'Ted' Austin – *Bells Life*.

9 November The154lbs Bow Cup championship match has been made for 2 December between the holder, Bill Brooks, and 'Professor' Alf Austin. Charley Davis (Stepney), the 161lbs middleweight champion, challenged the winner at catchweights, £50 a-side. Earlier, on 13 May, Davis had trained down to win a 144lbs (limit) competition - *Bells Life*.

23 November Brooks versus Austin put back to 11 December and changed from five rounds to three rounds - *Bells Life*.

30 November The Brooks versus Austin match is brought forward from 11 December to 9 December and the distance put back to the original five rounds of three minutes each for £10 a-side at the Metropolitan Swimming Baths, Ashley Crescent, City Road, near 'The Eagle' - *Bells Life*. Austin is now called the holder of the Bow Cup and 154lbs championship, Brooks having forfeited to him. However, it was pointed out by the sponsors of the Bow Cups that these couldn't be won by forfeit and that Brooks was still the rightful owner.

2 December Brooks versus Austin was called off on production of a doctor's certificate, stating that Brooks was too ill to box and confined to bed with a fever, rheumatism and delirium. The referee, Mr Leverell, of *Bells Life*, then visited both the doctor and Brooks to check that the story was true, which it was, and so declared a forfeit on part of Brooks. Austin received the money (£10) at the *Bells Life* office on Friday 6 December. However, Austin didn't receive the Bow Cup, as that could not be won by forfeit, but had to be fought for and had to be won four times in succession to become the property of the individual concerned.

11 December William Brooks, the holder of the 154lbs Bow Cup, died at his residence, 156 Jubilee Street, Mile End Road, of rheumatic fever, Aged 23.

14 December 'Professor' Alf Austin must now meet Charley Davis for the 154lbs Bow Cup and championship or one of the other 'Big Guns' and beat them before he can claim the 154lbs trophy - *Bells Life*.

28 December A letter from the donators of the Bow Cup, C. Parnell, W. Preston, Bill Richardson and R. Lewis, states that 'Professor' Alf Austin has no right in claiming the 154lbs championship and Bow Cup, as those trophies could not be won on a forfeit, or walk-over and, although Austin had made a match with Brooks for same, he would have no chance with such men as Charley Davis, the 161lbs middleweight champion, James Stewart, Abe Daultry, Ted Napper, the 140lbs lightweight champion, Jack Baldock or John McConnell (Glasgow), the last named now matched to box Charley Davis for the 154lbs championship and Bow Cup with gloves for endurance - £50 a-side - *Bells Life*. Davis currently held claims to both the 144lbs (limit) and 161lbs (limit) titles, which was possible due to the scarcity of men at these higher weights. It was felt that anyone just below or around 140lbs could put on weight and if, half decent, win the various competitions held at the higher weights, which normally only had three or four entries.

1873

7 January Charley Davis w co 14 John 'Scotty' McConnell, Albert Austin's Rooms, 10 Bloomfield Street, (between Liverpool Street and Finsbury Circus), London. Scheduled for a finish, the fight had been given billing as being for the 154lbs (limit) championship and Bow Cup, but Davis was six pounds over the weight, thus, in reality, turning the bout into one at catchweights. Despite that, Davis laid claim to the 154lbs (limit) title and Bow Cup with nothing said, although all the sporting press had commented on his being overweight.

18 January Ted Napper put down a £10 deposit with *Bells Life* for a bout with the holder, Charley Davis, for the 154lbs championship and Bow Cup - *Bells Life*.

25 January Charley Davis accepted the above challenge - *Bells Life*.

21 April Charley Davis w rtd 25 Ted Napper, The Grafton Hall, Grafton Street, Soho, London. Davis (147lbs) was much younger than Napper (140lbs), being in his 24th year, and was too good. Billed for the 154lbs (limit) championship and

Bow Cup over three-minute rounds, *Bells Life* complained that various journals were not represented at the fight printed sensational accounts of the bout when, in fact, both men were at the races in the days following, fit and well.

28 April   At 'The Earl of Warwick' Mile End Gate Road, Davis was presented with the 154lbs Bow Cup by Mr Mulders.

1874

9 May   Charley Davis is the 154lbs middleweight champion. This was repeated throughout the year – *Bells Life*.

1875

9 January   Charley Davis continues to be seen as the 154lbs middleweight champion. Again, this was repeated throughout the year and well into 1876 in all sporting papers, but, apart from the odd exhibition, he did nothing boxing wise.

1876

5 August   George Rooke (USA, born Ireland) sailed from New York bound for the UK, bringing with him his silver engraved five-inch-wide championship belt, composed of five plates hinged together that was presented to him by his New York friends. He arrived on 2 September.

22 November   Charley Davis withdrew from a proposed exhibition on this date due to illness, having boxed exhibitions on 14 and 18 November, and it was announced that he was retiring from boxing and giving up his 154lbs championship. Although the 19 December issue of *Bells Life* still called him the 154lbs champion, by this time the Bow Cup seemed to have been forgotten.

1877

17 November   George Rooke, who lived for a time in Birmingham, England, challenges the world at 152lbs, give or take two pounds, for the world middleweight title and a £50 or £100 cup under MoQ Rules, with gloves. He had made three attempts to make a match against Denny Harrington, but all had fallen through, Harrington's backer, Ted Napper, refusing the terms offered – *Sporting Life*.

24 November   Rooke, now calling himself the 154lbs champion of America and England, repeated the above challenge, but at 154lbs, Denny Harrington preferred – *Sporting Life*.

29 December   The proposed Rooke v Harrington bout has ended in a forfeit paid by Harrington – *Sporting Life*.

1878

12 January   George Rooke challenges All-England up to 154lbs, £100 or £200 a-side, and left £10 deposit – *Bells Life*. This was repeated on 19 January, but for £50 or £100 a-side – *Bells Life*.

19 January   Denny Harrington challenges George Rooke on the same terms as before - *Bells Life*.

12 March   Denny Harrington (London, born Ireland) w co 6 George Rooke, The Royal Surrey Gardens, Camberwell, London. Referee: Charlie Conquest. Note that *Bells Life* says the venue was in Walworth. Billed for the world 154lbs (limit) middleweight title and a 100 guinea (£105) cup, to a finish under MoQ Rules with gloves. *Bells Life* also differed to the *Sporting Life* with weights, giving Harrington at 153¹/₂ and Rooke 150¹/₂, but all reports agreed it was a terrible bout, all tugging and hugging.

16 March   Denny Harrington challenges the world at 154lbs, £100 a-side, Alf Greenfield (Birmingham) or Jim Highland (Birmingham), sometimes known as Ireland, preferred. He repeated this to Greenfield on 12 and 19 June, but at 152lbs – *Sporting Life*.

23 March   The 'Young Prussian', whose real name was William Sheriff (Leicester), weighing 144lbs, accepted above if Harrington laid £50 to his £40 – *Sporting Life*. In the same issue, Highland accepted if at catchweights, while Greenfield stated he was surprised at Harrington challenging him at 154lbs. Harrington, knowing that Greenfield is only a 140lbs man, would box him at 147 or 148lbs (later 146 to 147 was given), £50 a-side. On 26 July, in the *Sporting Life*, Greenfield stated that he failed to see how Harrington could be the 154lbs middleweight champion if he won't box outside of London.

17 July   Alf Greenfield is called the 154lbs middleweight champion, although still challenging at 148lbs – *Sporting Life*.

7 September   Florie Barnett (London), in reply to Alf Greenfield, stated that he couldn't box at 148lbs, but would box him at 152lbs – *Sporting Life*.

1879

15 February   Alf Greenfield is called the self-styled middleweight champion, without any weights being mentioned – *Sporting Life*.

13 August   Alf Greenfield forfeited £40 already down for bout against Denny Harrington, by not putting down his next deposit, which was due – *Sporting Life*.

15 August   Alf Greenfield stated that it was Harrington who hadn't placed any money at all – *Sporting Life*.

23 August   Denny Harrington stated that he did stake £80 and bout only fell through because Alf Greenfield's backers refused to go on – *Sporting Life*.

17 November   George Rooke challenges the world at 152lbs, give or take two pounds – *Sporting Life*.

27 November   Denny Harrington w disq 18 Alf Greenfield (Birmingham), Lambeth Baths Gym, Westminster Bridge Road, London. Referee: Charlie Conquest. Originally billed for the 154lbs (limit) middleweight title and championship belt, but with Harrington (168lbs) overweight by 1 stone the bout went on at catchweights. Harrington had once again cheated on his training, being fat and untrained, while Greenfield (154lbs) was on top throughout. If Greenfield had been patient he would have won and was extremely unlucky to lose. Harrington, having been knocked back onto the ropes, was laying backwards on them and was hit twice by Greenfield, after which Harrington's people appealed for a foul. The foul was given, which was surprising because the act of hitting a man who was on the ropes had never previously been considered to be a foul.

1880

3 February   Mike Donovan stated that George Rooke, who was claiming the American 154lbs middleweight title (158lbs was also given), couldn't claim this as he had been a resident in Birmingham, England for the last three years. Rooke had challenged Donovan for $1000 and the American 154lbs title. Again, 158lbs was also given, as Rooke couldn't get under 154lbs – *The Sportsman*.

18 February   Jem Brock w pts 3 'Young' Dyer (Birmingham), Mr Sullivan's, 'The Somerset Arms', New Road, Whitechapel, London. The final of a middleweight competition, no weights were mentioned, only that Dyer, who was 28lbs heavier, looked an easy winner. Just four turned up, Brock beating 'Young' Donovan and Dyer beating 'Young' Trickett.

15 February   The death of Charley Davis (real first name Michael), aged 30, at his home in 29 Well Street, Whitechapel is announced. He was buried at Bow Cemetery, Grove Road.

24 February   Articles were signed for a bout involving the world 154lbs middleweight title between the holder, Denny Harrington, and Joe Collins, alias 'Tug Wilson', of Leicester. It was to be contested under MoQ Rules, with gloves, to a finish for £200 a-side, plus a £400 trophy.

4 May   The Denny Harrington v Joe Collins bout at Detling, Kent was prevented by the police after it had been moved from Rainham, Kent. An attempt to bring the bout off on 5 May also failed and at a meeting arranged for 6 May, Wilson's people didn't turn up. Following that, Harrington formally claimed the stakes. The bout, originally set for MoQ Rules and gloves had been changed to London Prize Ring Rules (bare-knuckles).

7 August   Joe Collins challenges the world at 154lbs – *Sporting Life*.

18 August   William Sheriff challenges Denny Harrington for the 154lbs middleweight title – *Sporting Life*.

28 August   Denny Harrington challenges all at 154lbs – *Sporting Life*.

8 September   William Sheriff challenges the world at 154lbs, £50 up to £100 a-side, 'Bat' Mullins or Denny Harrington preferred – *Sporting Life*.

17 December   William Sheriff (Leicester) w rtd 11 Denny Harrington, Lapsworth, near Kingswood, Warwickshire. Referee: Charles Bedford. Scheduled for a finish, Sheriff, aged 33, took the world 154lbs middleweight title and a £200 trophy under MoQ Rules with gloves. The fight was made at 154lbs, give or take two pounds. After the ring was broken in Harrington's corner, the referee ordered them to 'The Bell' at Marston Green where another ring was formed. Although Sheriff was willing to resume, Harrington refused as the police were present. All parties returned for a meeting which was held that evening. At the meeting, the referee ordered them to continue the bout the following morning, but Harrington's party would not agree and the bout was awarded to Sheriff.

1881

3 August   Joe Collins (Leicester) challenges All-England at 154lbs, £50 or £100 a-side – *Sporting Life*.

7 September   Joe Collins is the 154lbs English middleweight champion – *Sporting Life*.

1 December George Rooke w rtd 4 William McClellan (New York), Kelly and Bliss Pool Room, Hunters Point, Long Island, New York, USA. Referee: William Muldoon. Billed for the American middleweight title, $1,00 a-side, with no weights given or stipulated, although Rooke claimed never to have weighed more than 155lbs in his career.

19 December George Say (Haggerston) w co 1 (two minutes, ten seconds) George 'Yorkie' Cashley (Leeds), 'The Spread Eagle', Kingsland Road, Shoreditch, London. Referee: Charles Bedford. The final of a 154lbs 'pro' competition for a silver cup donated by W.J. Francis, only four entries turned up. Say, a well-known walker, beat 'Lumpy' Hughes (w rtd 2), while Cashley outpointed Obe Atterbury (w pts 3). The room was used as the HQ of the Kingsland School of Arms.

1882

8 March Joe Collins challenges the world at 154lbs, £100 up to £500 a side – *Sporting Life*.

22 March Denny Harrington challenges the world at 154lbs – *Sporting Life*. Harrington had, in fact, already fought the final bout of his career on 17 December 1880.

25 March William Sheriff, who had won the world 154lbs (limit) middleweight title from Denny Harrington has now retired, but will meet Joe Collins (Leicester) for same – *Sporting Life*.

7 October William Sheriff is now going to the USA, where he challenges any middleweight in the world at 154lbs for the world title, $500 a-side, which he still holds - *Sporting Life*.

7 November Bill Springhall (Battersea, late Brighton) w co 3 Jack Massey (Bloomsbury), Walter Watson's and Bob Habbijam's West End School of Arms, 74 Newman Street, off Oxford Street, London. The final of Bob Habbijam's 154lbs English championship competition, in previous rounds Springhall, also given as Springall, beat Bill Natty and Tom Longer, while Massey beat Pat Condon and 'Young' Johnny Walker (real surname Badman). Massey was a head taller and 14lbs heavier than Springhall. The *Sporting Life* report, which was all mixed up, gave the result in the final as 'w co 1' and stated that Springhall had won a similar competition some years ago at Bow, but no trace of that could be found.

15 November John Pollock Clow (West Denver, USA) w co 17 William H. Cush (Pittsburgh, Pennsylvania, USA), Tern Hall, West Denver, Colorado, USA. Billed for the Colorado middleweight championship and J.K.Fox's *Police Gazette* Championship Medal, but no weights were given or stipulated. Clow's opponent's surname was also given as Cash and the report does not make clear as to whether the bout was with gloves or bare-knuckles, although thought to be the latter.

5 December Bill Springhall is the English 154lbs (limit) middleweight champion – *Sporting Life*.

23 December 'Bat' Mullins is the middleweight champion – *Sporting Life*. Note that the veteran, Mullins, was aged between 33 and 37, there being a debate as to his actual year of birth - 1845 or 1849.

30 December Jim Goode (Mile End New Town) challenges 'Bat' Mullins at 154lbs – *Sporting Life*. In the same issue it was reported that Bill Springhall, the English 154lbs champion from Birmingham, won Billy Madden's heavyweight competition, but no weights were stipulated.

1883

13 January Bill Springhall is the English 154lbs (limit) champion, which was repeated in the 17 January and 24 January issues, after which he withdrew his £10 deposit, as it hadn't been covered – *Sporting Life*.

27 January A proposed Jim Goode v 'Bat' Mullins bout for the 154lbs title fell through as Goode wanted 'endurance', while Mullins insisted on only three or four rounds – *Sporting Life*.

3 February Tom Longer (Clerkenwell) w pts 3 Arthur Cooper, 'The Bell', Red Lion Market, London. Referee: Mr W. Reardon. The final of an All-England 154lbs (limit) competition, there were only four entries. In the previous round, Longer, sometimes given as 'Longman', beat his brother Sam Longer, while Cooper beat J. Smith.

14 February Jack Burke (Brixton) w pts 4 (extra round) Jack Massey (Bloomsbury), Bob Habbijam's West End School of Arms, 74 Newman Street, London. The final of Bob Habbijam's £40 English 154lbs (limit) silver cup competition, Burke, in previous rounds of the competition, which had started on 8 February, beat 'Lumpy' Hughes, drew a bye, then beat William 'Coddy' Middings in the semi-final, while the veteran, Massey, beat Harry Arnold, J. Sheehy (given as

Spledy in the first series) and drew the bye in the semi-final. The weight of this competition was not given in the majority of reports, just stating it was an all-comers competition, although Middings was considered a 157lbs man.

21 February Bill Springhall put down a deposit to cover a bout with Jack Burge – *Sporting Life*.

19 April William 'Coddy' Middings, a 157lbs man, was the winner of Tom Symonds' £20 middleweight (no weights given) competition – *Sporting Life*.

26 May Bill Springhall is still the English 157lbs (limit) champion – *Sporting Life*.

16 June William Sheriff, the world 154lbs middleweight champion, sails for the USA on 21 June aboard 'The Lord Gough' and will meet anybody in the world and in the USA for his world 154lbs title. Sheriff was, by this time, coming up for his 36th birthday and there was some doubt that he could get down to that weight – *Sporting Life*.

1884

7 June Bill Springhall, the winner of an All-England 154lbs (limit) championship competition, is now back in the UK – *Sporting Life*.

16 August Bill 'Chesterfield' Goode (Shadwell), the younger brother of Jim Goode, challenges Woolf Bendoff at 154lbs, £50 or £100 a-side. In reply, Bendoff said that he couldn't make 154lbs, but would box at catchweights – *Sporting Life*.

26 August Jim Smith (Hoxton) challenges Bill Springhall to decide just who is the English 154lbs champion under MoQ Rules with gloves, for up to £100 a-side – *Sporting Life*.

1 September Bill Springhall stated that his business paid too well to box for such a small sum as £50 a-side, but would box Smith in six weeks time for the English 154lbs (limit), title if for £100 a-side – *Sporting Life*.

2 September Jim Smith's backers offered to match Bill 'Chesterfield' Goode with Bill Springhall, the English 154lbs (limit) champion at that weight, £100 a-side – *Sporting Life*. But in the 5 September edition of the *Sporting Life*, Goode said he didn't challenge Springhall.

10 November Bill Springhall, the winner of the world 154lbs championship competition, has now arranged to go to the USA at the end of November, which was later put back to 31 December – *Sporting Life*.

26 November Bill Springhall is the English 154lbs (limit) champion, which was repeated on 16 and 27 December – *Sporting Life*.

1885

8 January Put back from 31 December, Bill Springhall, the English 154lbs (limit) champion, left for New York on the White Star Liner, 'Britannic'.

23 February Bill Springhall drew 1 Joe Denning (Brooklyn, NYC, New York, USA), Clarendon Hall, Philadelphia, USA. The bout lasted just 65 seconds, the Police entering the ring and stopping it, leaving the decision to be given as a draw, although Springhall claimed it as a one round win for him. Denning, stated to be the ex-American amateur heavyweight champion, was a substitute for Alf Greenfield (Birmingham, England). No weights were given or stipulated.

2 March Bill Springhall no decision 4 Billy Gabic (Pittsburgh), Philadelphia, Pennsylvania, USA. Gabic (Gabey also given), who was known for just standing and taking it until opponent tired, was slammed from pillar to post by Springhall. However, Springhall failed to get the decision, some reports showing the result to be a points win for Gabic, as Springhall had failed to stop him inside the four rounds. The result was also given as Gabic (w co 4). No weights were given or stipulated.

11 May Bill Springhall w rtd 3 George Rooke, Yurn Hall, Eastforth Street, New York, USA. No weights were given or stipulated and the bout turned out to be the last one in Bill Springhall's career.

6 July Bill Springhall arrived back in Liverpool aboard 'The Britannic', having had just three bouts in the USA. He beat Denning in 65 seconds, then 'smothered' Gabic in four rounds but didn't get the verdict, and then caused George Rooke to retire in three rounds, Disappointingly, he couldn't get any of the top American middleweights to meet him.

7 July Bill Springhall challenges 'Nonpareil' Jack Dempsey (real name John Kelly), the claimant of the American 154lbs (limit) middleweight title, to a bout for the world 154lbs (limit) title for £1000 a-side, either in the UK or USA – *Sportsman*

3 October Bill Springhall took over 'The Queens' in Wandsworth Road, Battersea and retired from boxing.

1886

23 January The self-styled English middleweight champion (no weights given), Dick Collier, accepted the challenge of Alf Kilbride (Bradford) to a bout with gloves for £25 or £50 a-side. Note that the veteran Collier was known only as a bare-knuckle fighter – *Sporting Life*.

14 April 'Nonpareil' Jack Dempsey will box Joe Ellingsworth for the American middleweight championship belt, but no weights were given – *Sporting Life*.

24 July Charlie 'Toff' Wall (Hackney) is the 154lbs (limit) middleweight champion. This was a real surprise as Wall had been boxing at 144lbs and then 148lb – *Sporting Life*.

18 August Jim Young (Mile End) challenges both 'Toff' Wall and Charlie Mitchell (Birmingham), but no weights were mentioned – *Sporting Life*.

21 August Charlie 'Toff' Wall accepts the challenge of Jim Young, £100 up to £200 a-side – *Sporting Life*.

21 December England's boxing talent is comparable to any in the world, with England undoubtedly having the world champion at the 154lbs (limit) – *Sporting Life*.

1887

14 February Bill Natty w pts 12 Pat Condon (Haggerston), The Lambeth School of Arms, Lambeth Walk, Paradise Street, Lambeth, London. Contested for the English 154lbs (limit) championship, which was a certain misprint for the 10-6 (limit) silver championship belt presented by Jack Nanson, along with £20.

23 July Charlie 'Toff' Wall is the English 154lbs champion – *Sporting Life*.

11 September Bill 'Chesterfield' Goode, 'The City Pet', is the English 154lbs (limit) champion – *Sporting Life*.

13 December 'Nonpareil' Jack Dempsey w rtd 45 Johnny Reagan (NYC, New York), Manhasset, New York, USA. Contested in two rings to a finish it involved the American 154lbs title and American championship belt.

1888

21 January Jack Hickey (Birmingham, born Ireland) challenges Bill 'Chesterfield' Goode at 154lbs and states that if the challenge is refused he will formally claim the English title at the weight – *Sporting Life*. On 24 January, Goode accepted Hickey.

29 January Mike Jennett (Leicester) challenges Bill 'Chesterfield' Goode or Jack Hickey at 154lbs, using two-ounce gloves for £50 or £100 a-side – *Sportsman*.

3 March Jack Hickey challenges Charlie 'Toff' Wall to a bout for the English 154lbs (limit) middleweight title – *Sporting Life*.

5 March The *Sporting Life* stated that if Charlie 'Toff' Wall is not going to the USA he should accept Jack Hickey's challenge to a bout for the English 154lbs (limit) middleweight title.

14 March Bill 'Chesterfield' Goode challenges Jack Hickey to a bout for the English 154lbs (limit) middleweight title – *Sporting Life*. In the same issue, it stated that four men were now claiming the English 154lbs (limit) title in Charlie 'Toff' Wall, Bill 'Chesterfield' Goode, Jack Hickey and Mike Jennett.

23 May Jack Hickey challenges anyone at 154lbs (limit), £100 a-side – *Sporting Life*.

16 May Bill 'Chesterfield' Goode challenges all at 152lbs to 154lbs, £100 a-side and a deposit – *Sporting Life*. This was repeated on 24 May.

3 August 'California' Jack Dempsey, real name Bill Lurney, the Pacific Coast lightweight champion, must not be confused with the famous 'Nonpariel' Jack Dempsey, the American 154lbs middleweight champion – *Sportsman*.

19 August Jack Hickey is the English 154lbs champion – *Sporting Life*.

9 September 'Nonpariel' Jack Dempsey challenges Charlie Mitchell in order to settle who is the world middleweight champion. No weight was given – *Sportsman*.

14 October Jack Hickey challenges any man in England for the English 154lbs (limit) title, £100 up to £500 a-side, and the winner of the forthcoming Bill 'Chesterfield' Goode v Arthur Bobbett bout preferred. On 5 December, the *Sporting Life* stated that Goode was preferred, which was accepted on 8 December – *Sporting Life*.

23 November Bill 'Chesterfield' Goode w pts 12 Arthur Bobbett (Fulham), The Grand Circus, Peter Street, Manchester. Reported as being for the English 152lbs title, but when the bout was first made on 22 July it was articled as for the English 154lbs (limit) title, with Goode staking £250 to Bobbett's £200.

8 December Alec Burns (Battersea) w pts 4 Jem Burchell (Shoreditch),

Westminster Aquarium Theatre, London. The final of Frank Hindes' 154lbs (limit) English championship competition, in previous rounds Burns beat Patsy Mann and Jim Porter, while Burchell beat James Monroe and Pat Condon.

1889

24 January Alf Mitchell (Kingsland, London, late Cardiff) challenges all at 154lbs, Charlie 'Toff' Wall preferred, for a Pelican Club £200 purse – *Sporting Life*.

9 March Charlie 'Toff' Wall is the English 154lbs (limit) champion – *Sporting Life*.

16 March Jem Burchell w pts 5 (extra round) Arthur Bobbett, The Royal Agricultural Hall, Islington. The final of a 154lbs (limit) English championship competition, promoted by Charley Smith and Jack Baldock, in previous rounds Burchell beat Charlie Parish and Bill Husband, while Bobbett beat J.Andrews and Jim Portex (Portea also given).

27 April Ted White (Clerkenwell) w pts 4 'Bat' Mullins, Royal Agricultural Hall, Islington, London. The final of a 154lbs English championship competition, in previous rounds White beat Jem Burchell and 'Young' Jones, while Mullins beat Lachie Thomson and Arthur Bobbett.

8 May In Cork, Ireland, Jack Hickey, the ex-claimant of the English 154lbs (limit) middleweight title, who was working at Cork races as a bookmaker, was arrested and charged with the manslaughter of A. Mahoney. After giving Hickey much aggravation, Mahoney had struck the ex-fighter with his whip, whereupon Hickey hit him, his fist breaking his jaw, and Mahoney died two days later in the infirmary. Hickey was discharged on 4 July, but was ordered to come for judgement when called upon.

10 July Bill 'Chesterfield' Goode is the English 154lbs middleweight champion, not Ted Pritchard, who can only win that title by beating Goode for it – *Sporting Life*.

14 December Alf Ball (Deptford) challenges any 154lbs middleweight in England for the English title. If no takers, Ball would automatically claim the title – *Sporting Life*.

1890

13 January Alf Ball is the English 154lbs (limit) middleweight champion, having claimed the title as no one had accepted his challenge. Within weeks, however, Ball was boxing at 156lbs and later even heavier. In fact, Ball, first and foremost a boxing booth owner, never got below that weight again – *Sportsman*.

18 February 'Nonpareil' Jack Dempsey w rsf 28 'Australian' Billy McCarthy (Australia, born Poplar, London, England), San Francisco, California, USA. Made at catchweights, but reported as being for the world 154lbs (limit) middleweight title with five-ounce gloves, Dempsey weighed 147¹/₂ to McCarthy's 152¹/₂.

20 February 'Young' Mitchell (San Francisco) w co 13 (12 also given) George LaBlanche, San Francisco, California, USA. Reported as being for the North American/world 154lbs title, with seemingly no grounds for same, it was regarded in some quarters as a 'fake' fight, due mainly to LaBlanche's character and reputation. Mitchell, real name John L. Herget, carried the reputation of being a very honest man throughout his life, so if it was a 'fix' it was most likely to be on LaBlanche's part. Going on the form of both men, Mitchell was much the better of the two and the most likely winner in any case, being among the top two or three in the weight class throughout his career, although, now, all but forgotten.

21 March Jem Burchell w pts 20 Bill Husband, The Pelican Club, London. Referee: Bernard J. Angle. Articled for a £100 purse, no weights were given or stipulated and no title billing was attached. It was called a return, as a few weeks earlier Husband had outpointed Burchell over 12 rounds at this same venue.

4 May Jack Welland challenges All-England at 154lbs, Alf Ball preferred – *Sporting Life*.

10 May Ted White challenges any of the so-called 154lbs middleweight champions for the title, Ted Pritchard preferred, over 12 rounds and a £100 purse – *Sporting Life*. On 13 May, Arthur Bobbett accepted, but for 'endurance' and a £100 purse – *Sporting Life*.

14 May Alf Mitchell challenges Bill 'Chesterfield' Goode or Charlie 'Toff' Wall for the English 154lbs (limit) title. He also challenged any man in world for the world title at the same weight, £200 up to £500 a-side, 'Nonpareil' Jack Dempsey preferred, and will willingly box him in the USA at the California Athletic Club – *Sporting Life*.

23 May	Mitchell repeated this, but was now calling himself the English 154lbs champion and any bout for the world title must be to a finish and bare-knuckles. Note this claim to the English title pertaining to bare-knuckles under London Prize Ring Rules, stemmed from his win over Alf Ball in this style on 18 April. Winning on a 64th round retirement, it didn't belong in a history of MoQ (glove) bouts. On 3 September, Mitchell was still signing himself as the 154lbs middleweight champion – *Sporting Life*.
19 June	Arthur Bobbett challenges All-England at 154lbs and was accepted by Jim Richardson (Wood Green) a day later – *Sporting Life*.
8 July	Jack Burke (Lambeth, London, England), 'The Irish Lad', challenges 'Nonpareil' Jack Dempsey for the world 154lbs middleweight title – *Sporting Life*.
12 July	Bob Fitzsimmons (Australia, late of New Zealand, born Helston, Cornwall, England, now of the USA) challenges the world at 154lbs – *Sporting Life*.
14 July	Fitzsimmons is accepted by Charlie 'Toff' Wall – *Sporting Life*.
22 August	Ted White challenges Arthur Bobbett at 154lbs – *Sporting Life*.
30 August	'Nonpareil' Jack Dempsey (USA), in reply to Jack Burke, stated that he wouldn't box over 154lbs – *Sporting Life*.
6 September	Jack Burke agreed to accept 'Nonpareil' Jack Dempsey's terms and box at a limit of 154lbs, £2000 a-side and best purse, but the bout has to be in England with Dempsey allowed £100 for expenses. If Dempsey refuses to accept, Burke challenges any middleweight in the world at the weight – *Sporting Life*.
10 September	'Nonpareil' Jack Dempsey repeated what he had said on 30 August, that he wouldn't box Jack Burke at the 154lbs (limit), seemingly ignoring what Burke had said on 6 September, and now hopes to meet Bob Fitzsimmons at 154lbs in New Orleans – *Sporting Life*.
13 September	Jack Burke again stated he would get down to 154lbs for a bout against 'Nonpareil' Jack Dempsey, £1000 or £2000 a-side and best purse, and on Dempsey's acceptance, Burke would put down a £500 deposit and the bout could take place in the USA – *Sporting Life*.
14 October	Alf Mitchell stated that as Bill 'Chesterfield' Goode had failed to turn up on 13 October to make a match for the English 154lbs (limit) middleweight title, he would box Charlie 'Toff' Wall, who styled himself the English 154lbs (limit) middleweight champion. For this title or any 154lbs middleweight in the world, Mitchell would back himself for £1000 to £800 or £500 to £400 – *Sporting Life*.
15 October	'Young' Mitchell challenges All-England at either 150lbs or 154lbs (limit) for £200 a-side in England or USA, Ted Pritchard or Charlie 'Toff' Wall preferred – *Sporting Life*.
15 October	Ted Pritchard (Lambeth, born South Wales) accepted the challenge of Alf Mitchell at 154lbs, £200 a-side and sent in a £50 deposit as his match of 4 October against 'Australian' Billy McCarthy at the 154lbs (limit) had been called off after McCarthy weighed in at 161lbs, seven pounds overweight – *Sporting Life*. In the same issue, John O'Brien (Cardiff) also accepted the challenge of Alf Mitchell, £100 or £200 a-side, at the 154lbs (limit), or any other middleweight at that weight in England.
15 October	The *Sporting Life* stated that the winner of the forthcoming 28 October bout between Danny Kelleher and Martin Harris (Minneapolis), 'The Black Pearl', at the Twin City AC, Minneapolis, can be matched with Charlie 'Toff' Wall, England's 154lbs (limit) middleweight champion.
3 December	Jim Richardson challenges all at 154lbs and a day later was accepted by Ted Ashwick (Camberwell) – *Sporting Life*.
1891	
14 January	Bob Fitzsimmons w ko 3 'Nonpareil' Jack Dempsey, New Orleans, USA. Billed as being for the American/world 154lbs (limit) middleweight title, both were under 151lbs, with Dempsey stated to be a sick man and, on 16 January, he publicly announced his retirement from boxing.
12 March	Ted Pritchard w co 3 Jack Burke, The Albany Club, Holloway, London. Referee: George Vize. Billed as for the English 154lbs (limit) title, £500 a-side and £200 purse (total £1,200), both were said to be inside at the 3pm weigh-in. It was stated that Burke was, in fact, born in Lambeth, London, England on 10 September 1861 of Irish parents and not in Killarney, Ireland as claimed.
14 March	Arthur Bobbett w pts 4 Bill Husbands (Knightsbridge), The Pelican Club, Gerard Street, Soho, London. The final of a
	154lbs (limit), £25 middleweight competition, in previous rounds, Bobbett beat Felix Scott and Bill Cheese, while Husband beat J. Donoghue and Jim Kendrick.
7 April	Ted Pritchard is the world 154lbs (limit) champion and, on 10 April, he was presented with an 154lbs middleweight championship belt – *The Sportsman*.
19 October	'Australian' Billy McCarthy w co 12 Arthur Bobbett, NSC, Covent Garden, London. Made at catchweights, Bobbett was a last-minute substitute for Charlie 'Toff' Wall, who had been down to box McCarthy on the same terms over 20 three-minute rounds, but failed to turn up. This 'run-out', one of many by the multi-talented Wall, in effect, finished his career. Content with his pipe and a pint, he seemingly had no interest in money whatsoever and just seemed to please himself as to turn up for a bout or not. He was happy with his job of hauling coal, which kept him in beer and 'bacca', and ultimately proved to be such a waste of a supreme talent. He was a man with no ambitions beyond his daily need and yet it was freely acknowledged that none, irrespective of weight, could live with him in a boxing ring.
15 December	Ted Pritchard w co 4 Alf Mitchell, Bob Habbijam's West End School of Arms, Newman Street, London. Billed for the English/world 154lbs (limit) middleweight title.
30 December	Arthur Akers (Leicester) challenges Alf Hanlon (Manchester) at 154lbs – *Sporting Life*.
1892	
30 January	John O'Brien, who in the 13 January edition of the *Sporting Life* had challenged world at the 154lbs (limit), was stated to have now challenged the world at the 154lbs (limit). However, three days later in the same paper, he stated that his challenge was at the 158lbs (limit), which was the top middleweight class.
5 October	Arthur Bobbett is coming back after long rest and, now that Ted Pritchard has moved up to the 158lbs (limit) class, challenges all England at 154lbs – *Sporting Life*.
6 October	Bobbett's challenge is accepted by Jim Richardson – *Sporting Life*.
22 December	Jack Birch (Aldershot) challenges any of the many English 154lb champions – *Sporting Life*.
24 December	Fred Greenbank stated that if Jack (Fred also given) Birch couldn't get a bout with any of the 154lbs champions he would meet him at that weight – *Sporting Life*.
1893	
10 January	Jack Hart (Liverpool) challenges any 154lbs man in London, Jack Welland preferred – *Sporting Life*.
24 April	Ted White w pts 3 George Chrisp (Newcastle), NSC, Covent Garden, London. Referee: B.J. Angle. Scheduled for 20 three-minute rounds at 154lbs, £100 a-side, but with no title billing, White had won a championship competition at this weight on 27 April 1889 and had challenged at this weight on and off ever since.
27 April	Jim Richardson challenges any 154lbs (limit) middleweight in England, Ted White preferred – *Sporting Life*.
6 November	'Dido' Plumb (Balls Pond Road), accepted the challenge of Jack Hart at 154lbs and one night later won a Frank Hindes' 158lbs competition. A month later, Plumb challenged all 148 to 150lbs – *Sporting Life*.
1894	
16 March	Frank Craig (Harlem) w rsf 9 Fred Morris, Long Island, New York, USA. A private show held at the 'Morrisania', both men were coloured and known as 'The Coffee Cooler' and 'Muldoon's Cyclone', respectively. No weights were given or stipulated in a match thought to have been made at 154lbs.
1895	
6 July	Anthony Diamond accepted a challenge made to him at 154lbs by John Jackson (Crewe) – *Sporting Life*.
10 September	'Dido' Plumb challenges All-England at either 150lbs or 154lbs – *Sporting Life*.
1896	
2 March	Charles 'Kid' McCoy w co 15 Tommy Ryan, The Empire AC, Long Island, New York, USA. Billed as being for the American/world 154lbs (limit) title, with the *Sporting Life* and *Philadelphia Item* reporting that both men weighed 154lbs. However, the *Brooklyn Eagle* stated that McCoy came in at 155lbs, one pound overweight, with the bout going on at catchweights. Ryan was billed as the world 148lbs (limit) welterweight champion and, although a loser in this one, if McCoy was overweight that would have given Ryan a claim to the 154lbs title by forfeit.
18 March	Charles 'Kid' McCoy w disq 6 'Mysterious' Billy Smith,

Boston, Mass, USA. Billed for the American/world 154lbs title.

14 October Ted White is the English 154lbs (limit) champion. However, White's bout of 1 June 1896 for the English 158lbs (limit) title, was, in fact, the final bout of his career – *Sporting Life*.

1897

27 February 'Dido' Plumb challenges the world at 154lbs, no one barred. This was repeated throughout the year – *Sporting Life*.

1 September 'Dido' Plumb is the world 154lbs (limit) champion – *Mirror of Life*.

28 September 'Young' Bill England (Hackney) challenges All-England at 150 up to 154lbs – *Sporting Life*.

4 October Pat Daley/Daly (London, born Ireland, late New York), the English 140lbs champion, challenges 'Dido' Plumb, the world and English 154lbs (limit) champion, at 152lbs, £100 or £200 a-side – *Sporting Life*.

10 November J. Brady (Stratford) challenges All-England at 154lbs for an NSC purse – *Sporting Life*.

1898

5 January 'Dido' Plumb is the English 154lbs (limit) champion – *Mirror of Life*.

5 January 'Paddy' Purtell (USA) challenges All-England at 154lbs – *Sporting Life*.

9 February Albury Clifford (Tasmania) challenges All-England at 154lbs, Arthur Akers and Jim Richardson preferred, £200 a-side and an NSC purse. This was repeated on 6 October and 3 November – *Sporting Life*.

25 February Anthony Diamond (Birmingham) w pts 12 'Dido' Plumb, The Olympic Club, Berwick Street, Birmingham. The final of a 154lbs (limit) championship belt competition, with the winner also getting £75, in previous rounds Diamond, whose comeback this was, beat John Jackson then drew the bye, while Plumb, who went into this competition billed as the reigning English 154lbs champion, drew the bye and beat Jim Richardson in the semi-final. This was the only one in the whole series of these competitions not criticized for the poor class of the competitors, Diamond and Plumb being acknowledged as the best two men at the weight in the country, hence the low number of entries. Twelve rounds was the lowest number of rounds allowed for a major championship bout at this time. Following this win, Diamond promptly announced his retirement from boxing.

23 May 'Dido' Plumb w co 4 'Australian' Billy Edwards, NSC, Covent Garden , London. Scheduled for 20 three-minute rounds in a 17 foot square ring, the mythical Imperial Empire 154lbs (limit) title was also on the line. Edwards was 'walking' it and was 10 to 1 to win with Plumb on the verge of a kayo defeat, but Edwards, on rushing in to finish it, walked on to a punch and was himself knocked out.

6 September Anthony Diamond confirmed that he was now retired from boxing for good – *Sporting Life*.

12 September 'Dido' Plumb is the English 154lbs (limit) champion, having reclaimed the title on the retirement of Anthony Diamond – *Sporting Life*. This was repeated throughout the rest of the year and in the 10 November issue of the *Sporting Life* he challenged the world at the weight.

29 November Bill Heffernan (South Africa, late New Zealand, born Scotland) challenges the world at 154lbs, Jim Richardson (Newcastle), 'Dido' Plumb, George Chrisp and Dan Creedon (New Zealand) preferred, for £50 or £100 a-side, and put down a £10 deposit – *Sporting Life*.

1899

18 January 'Dido' Plumb is the English 154lbs (limit) middleweight champion. This was repeated throughout the year — *Mirror of Life*.

15 March Harry Neumier (Stepney) challenges All-England at 154lbs – *Sporting Life*.

1 May 'Dido' Plumb w co 9 Bill Heffernan, NSC, Covent Garden, London. Referee: J.H.Douglas. Being born in Scotland qualified Heffernan (151lbs) to box for an English title and this one was given world title billing in some reports, as well as being billed for both the English and Imperial Empire 154lbs (limit) middleweight title, £100 a-side and a £150 purse. This was one of the first English and Imperial Empire title bouts, although not all reports list Imperial billing.

13 May 'Dido' Plumb is the world 154lbs (limit) champion – *Sporting Life*. A misprint in a June issue of the *Sporting Life* gave Tom Woodley (Fulham) as the English 154lbs champion, but it was the 146lbs title that he claimed.

12 December George Gardiner (Lowell, Mass, USA) w rsf 7 (broke left

arm) Jack Moffatt (Chicago, Illinois, USA), The Broadway AC, NYC, New York, USA. Referee: Charlie White. Scheduled for 20 rounds at 154lbs, no weights were given and no title billing was attached.

1900

13 February Harry Neumier w pts 15 Dave Peters (Treorchy), Aldgate Baths, Goulstone Street, London. Referee: Sydney Rushton. Scheduled for 15 three-minute rounds at 154lbs, no weights were given and no title billing was attached. On 6 April, in the *Sporting Life*, Peters challenged Neumier to a return at 158lbs.

19 March 'Dido' Plumb w co 8 'Australian' Jim Ryan, NSC, Covent Garden, London. Scheduled for 15 three-minute rounds and billed for the Imperial British Empire 154lbs (limit) title. The world title was also given, as was English, even though Ryan was not eligible to contest the English title. Six-ounce gloves were used and the weigh-in was held two days prior to the bout, on Saturday, 17 March, which was an old prize ring rule revised in the early days of gloved boxing.

5 April 'Dido' Plumb is the English 154lbs (limit) champion. This was repeated throughout year – *Sporting Life*.

5 July Pat Daley/Daly, who has now put on a lot of weight, challenges 'Dido' Plumb to a bout at catchweights over 20 three-minute rounds, £100 a-side and best purse – *Sporting Life*.

12 October Efforts were made to match Pat Daley/Daly at 154lbs with the American, George Gardner, over 20 three-minute rounds, £100 a-side and £150 purse, with a 4pm weigh-in. Daley/Daly had already accepted, but on 2 November Gardner sailed for South Africa so the bout fell through – *Sporting Life*.

1901

22 March 'Dido' Plumb is the English 154lbs (limit) middleweight champion – *Sporting Life*.

24 June Jack Palmer (Benwell) w co 5 Lachie Thomson (Glasgow), Ginnett's Circus, Newcastle. Referee: George T. Dunning, the Editor of *The Sportsman*. Scheduled for 20 three-minute rounds, it was a catchweight bout, with Palmer restricted to 154lbs, while Thomson could be any weight. Thomson's weight was not given and no title billing was attached, but in later years Palmer's claims to the English middleweight title was seen as stemming from this bout.

3 July 'Dido' Plumb challenges 'Philadelphia' Jack O'Brien (USA) at the 154lbs (limit) for the world title, £100 or £200 a-side – *Mirror of Life*. On 31 July, the *Sporting Life* reported that a match had been made between them for the world 154lbs (limit) middleweight title.

'Philadelphia' Jack O'Brien

19 August 'Philadelphia' Jack O'Brien w ko 6 'Dido' Plumb, Ginnett's Circus, Newcastle. Referee: Ed Plummer. Scheduled for 15 three-minute rounds and billed for the world 154lbs (limit) title, £200 a-side and £250 purse (total £650), a 10am weigh-in and using four-ounce gloves. Some reports, as par for the course, also gave it as being for the English title, but O'Brien (real name James Francis Hagen) was not eligible.

25 November 'Dido' Plumb, the ex-English 154lbs (limit) middleweight champion states that he has retired from boxing following his 19 August loss to 'Philadelphia' Jack O'Brien for the world 154lbs middleweight title – *Sporting Life*. Plumb did more or less stay retired, having just two more bouts, an eight-round draw in 1902 and another draw in 1910, over six rounds. Plumb was first and foremost a booth boxer.

29 November Harry Neumier challenges All-England at 148 to 154lbs, Tom Woodley or 'Jewey' Cook (Bloomsbury and Hammersmith) preferred. He would also be happy to meet 'Philadelphia' Jack O'Brien at 154lbs, 2pm weigh-in, £100 a-side and best purse – *Sporting Life*.

1902

16 January In list of world champions given by actual weights, not named divisions, the American, George Gardner, is given as being the 154lbs (limit) champion – *Sporting Life*.

27 January 'Philadelphia' Jack O'Brien w disq 3 Charley McKeever (Philadelphia, Pennsylvania, USA), The Country AC, Leeds. Scheduled for 15 three-minute rounds at 154lbs and originally billed for the world title at that weight, O'Brien came in at 157½lbs at the 3pm weigh-in and paid forfeit. The bout then went on at catchweights, £200 a-side and purse.

23 May 'Dido' Plumb is the English 154lbs (limit) middleweight champion – *Sporting Life*.

8 December Dick Jordan (Woolwich) challenges All-England at 154lbs – *Sporting Life*.

1903

16 April 'Dido' Plumb is still claiming to be the English 154lbs (limit) middleweight champion, while Jack Palmer is the English 158lbs middleweight champion – *Sporting Life*. However, Plumb, to all intents and purposes, had retired.

1904

1 February Charlie Knock (Stratford) w pts 12 Charlie Allum (Notting Hill), Wonderland, Whitechapel Road, London. Referee: J.T.Hulls. Articled for 12 two-minute rounds at catchweights for £275 and Mr Jones' silver cup – *Sporting Life*.

2 March Charlie Allum, who had been getting billed as the English 144lbs (limit) champion, challenges All-England at 154lbs, Peter Brown (Woolwich) or Charlie Knock preferred. He also challenged the world at 154lbs, Jack Clancy (USA), Arthur Cripps (Australia) or Dan Sinclair (Canada) preferred – *Sporting Life*.

3 March 'Dido' Plumb challenges the world at 154lbs – *Sporting Life*.

16 March Jim Courtney (Barry Island, born London) w pts 15 Pat O'Keefe (Canning Town), The South Wales NSC, Queens Street Hall Arcade, Cardiff. Scheduled for 15 three-minute rounds, no weights were given or stipulated and no title billing was attached. This one was almost certainly a catchweights bout.

2 May Jim Courtney w ko 10 Pat O'Keefe, The South Wales NSC, Queens Street Hall Arcade, Cardiff. Scheduled for 15 three-minute rounds, for £75, with no weights given or stipulated and no title billing, yet again it was almost certainly a catchweight bout.

23 May Jim Courtney w ko 11 Pat O'Keefe, The South Wales NSC, Queens Street Hall Arcade, Cardiff. The third fight between the pair over 15 three-minute rounds, this time for £80, no weights were given or stipulated and, yet again, it would almost certainly have been a catchweight bout. O'Keefe was a substitute for Peter Brown (Woolwich).

3 October Jim Courtney w pts 10 Jim Styles (Marylebone, London), The South Wales NSC, The Queens Street Hall Arcade, Cardiff. The final of an international 154lbs (limit) championship competition, in previous rounds Courtney beat Jack Meekins and Andrew Jeptha, the coloured South African, while Styles beat Pat O'Keefe, Jack Costello and Harry Fowler.

1905

1 February Joe Platford (Tottenham) challenges All-England at 154lbs, which was repeated in the 18 February issue of the *Sporting Life* and immediately accepted by Bill Curzon.

8 April Charlie Allum challenges All-England at 150 to 154lbs – *Sporting Life*.

Jack 'Twin' Sullivan

17 October Jack 'Twin' Sullivan (Cambridge, Mass, USA) w pts 20 Tommy Burns (Canada), Los Angeles, California, USA. Made at catchweights, but given in some reports as being for a world 154lbs (limit) title, Burns came in at 163lbs. Also stated to have been for the world 158lbs (limit) title. No weights were given for Sullivan.

6 November Charlie Allum challenges All-England at 154lbs, £200 up to £500 a-side, for the English title. This was repeated in the 21 November issue of the *Sporting Life* and accepted by Harry Neumier, who had just returned from the USA – *Sporting Life*.

28 November Mike Crawley (Limehouse) challenges Harry Shearing (Walthamstow) at 154lbs, £100 up to £200 a-side, but in the 1 December issue of the *Sporting Life* Shearing stated that he couldn't get below 168lbs.

9 December Mike Crawley challenges All-England at 154lbs – *Sporting Life*.

1906

5 January Pat O'Keefe challenges All-England at 154lbs, Jack Palmer, Jack Kingsland (Paddington), Charlie Allum or Charlie Knock preferred – *Sporting Life*.

23 February Charlie Allum w pts 10 Billy Huggins (Higgins also given), Civil Engineers School Avenue, 3 Athans, Paris, France. Referee: Lovell Graham. Given billing as a French 154lbs (limit) title fight, but neither man eligible. Allum was injured during the bout and at the end of ten rounds, the referee stopped the action and declared Allum the winner on points. No weights were given.

21 April Pat Daley/Daly, while announcing that 147lbs was his best weight, went on to challenge All-England at 154lbs, £50 up to £100 a-side, over 15 or 20 rounds and a 2pm weigh-in, Pat O'Keefe, Charlie Allum or Tom Thomas (Penycraig, South Wales) preferred – *Sporting Life*.

2 May Charlie Allum challenges All-England between 150 and 154lbs – *Sporting Life*.

9 May Joe Platford accepted Charlie Allum – *Sporting Life*.

17 May Mike Crawley challenges All-England at 148lbs up to 154lbs – *Sporting Life*.

5 October Maurice Greenfield (Birmingham) w rsf 10 Jack Costello (Birmingham), The Odd Fellows Hall, Nechells, Birmingham. Billed for the 154lbs championship (almost certainly 'Midlands' title meant), during the third round a spectator called 'time' and Greenfield walked to his corner and sat down. When the time keeper called for them to box on,

269

Greenfield was still sitting down and Costello hit him with a terrific punch on the jaw, almost finishing him. A foul was claimed but refused, the referee (not named) ordering a rest of about three minutes after which the bout was resumed.

19 December Mike Crawley challenges Tom Lancaster (Spennymoor) at 154lbs – *Sporting Life*.

1907

6 April Charlie Allum, the English 150lbs (limit) champion, challenges Tom Lancaster at 154lbs over 15 or 20 rounds, £50 or £100 a-side – *Sporting Life*. This was repeated on 2 October.

3 August Arthur Daley (London) challenges All-England, 148lbs up to 154lbs – *Mirror of Life*.

9 August Joe Platford challenges any 154lbs man in England or Wales for the best purse – *Sporting Life*.

30 December Hugo Kelly drew 10 Billy Papke, Milwaukee, Wisconsin, USA. Reported as being for the American 154lbs (limit) middleweight title with a 3pm weigh-in, although the men were top class it was not contested over a recognized championship distance. No weight was given for Papke, but Kelly weighed 151lbs.

1908

1 January Sid Doyle (Islington) challenges All-England at 154lbs – *Sporting Life*.

9 January Mike Crawley challenges All-England between 150 and 154lbs, Tom Lancaster preferred – *Sporting Life*.

22 February Stanley Ketchel (USA) w co 1 Mike 'Twin' Sullivan (Cambridge, Mass, USA), Milwaukee, USA. Although reported variously as being contested at 149lbs, 151lbs and 154lbs, in some quarters it was considered to involve the American 154lbs (limit) title.

30 May Charlie Allum challenges All-England at 154lbs over 15 or 20 rounds – *Sporting Life*.

14 July Jack Kingsland challenges All-England at 154lbs, Jack Costello or Steve Smith (London) preferred. He also sent out challenges to Bart Connelly (USA) and Herbert Synnott (Australia) on the same terms – *Sporting Life*.

1909

18 January Sid Doyle (Islington) is the English 154lbs (limit) champion – *Sporting Life*. This was repeated on 17 February.

11 February On this day, the NSC introduced eight-named 'spread-weight' divisions, effectively ending champions at every two pounds. On 26 June, Charlie Allum challenged All-England between 150 and 154lbs in the *Mirror of Life*, but that was basically it until the weight class was revived in the 1960s.

154lbs to 156lbs (11 Stone to 11 Stone 2 lbs)

1884

19 July Mike Cleary (USA) w rtd 1 Jim Goode (London, England), Chicago, USA. Made at catchweights, no weights were given and there was no title billing. The bout itself lasted just two minutes, Goode suffering a broken jaw.

30 July 'Nonpariel' Jack Dempsey (New York, born Ireland) w rtd 22 George Fulljames (Canada, born London, England), Seguins Point (Great Kill Point also given), Princes Bay, Staten Island, New York, USA. Referee: Ned Mallahan. Made at catchweights, contested under London Prize Ring rules, using kid gloves, and with no title involvement are the only true hard facts of this bout. In spite of all that has been written about it over the years, all the varying weights given in the different reports don't help, such as Dempsey being 137, 140 and 145lbs to Fulljames' 124 and 126lbs. In the American papers, which invariably reported it as involving the world middleweight title, in spite of it being at catchweights, how such differences in the weights given remain a mystery. Dempsey weighing 140lbs to Fulljames' 126lbs seems the most likely weight for the bout, which was possibly called a middleweight contest. Something like the 1872 Bow Cup 128lbs event being classified as a 'middleweight' go in some reports. It should be put down to reporters' mistakes which were never corrected.

1886

4 March 'Nonpareil' Jack Dempsey w ko13 George LaBlanche (Canada), West Chester Shore, Larchmont Sound, Long Island, New York, USA. Contested at catchweights under MoQ Rules, using kid driving gloves, with no title involvement, Dempsey weighing 149lbs to LaBlanche's 155, the *New York Herald* reported it as being for the American catchweight/ middleweight title and over the years this was

used in various record books. For the record, it was attended by nine selected people.

1887

13 July Jem Mace will back Tom Lees (Australia) with any one in the world at 154lbs, give or take two pounds – *Sporting Life*.

1888

18 August George LaBlanche w ko 3 Jack Varley (London, England), Near Yonkers, 30 miles from New York City, USA. Contested in two-ounce gloves and to a finish, both were arrested afterwards. There was no title billing given and LaBlanche weighed 155lbs to Varley's 154.

1890

21 January The *Sporting Life* reported a match being made involving the English 156lbs middleweight title between Ted Pritchard and Alf Mitchell for Friday, 12 March. Articled for 12 rounds, a 6pm weigh-in and £100 a-side, it was called off when Pritchard was taken ill. Mitchell then challenged the world at 154lbs to 156, nobody barred.

28 February Alf Ball (Deptford) w ko 12 Jack Welland (Hackney), The Goodwin Club, Kingsland Road, Shoreditch, London. Scheduled for 12 rounds, Ball weighing 156lbs to Welland's 153¼, there was no title billing and Ball weighed in wearing a sweater. However, he would base his claim to the English 156lbs middleweight title on this win.

21 August Alf Mitchell (Cardiff), the 154lbs middleweight champion, challenges the world, 'bare-knuckles' or gloves, with bare-knuckles preferred. He had won the 154lbs middleweight title in a bare-knuckle bout on 8 April 1889 by beating Alf Ball – *Sporting Life*.

1 October Alf Mitchell challenges the world, £200 or £500 a-side, Charlie 'Toff' Wall or Bill 'Chesterfield' Goode preferred. Mitchell signed himself as the world middleweight champion – *Sporting Life*.

1893

10 May Alf Mitchell is the former 154 to 156lbs middleweight champion – *Sporting Life*.

1895

18 February Jerry Driscoll (London, late Royal Navy) w pts 20 George Chrisp (Newcastle), NSC, Covent Garden, London. Referee: B.J.Angle. Made at 154lbs, give or take two pounds, £50 a-side and a £75 purse totalling £175, there was no title billing and Driscoll announced that win, lose or draw he would retire after this bout as he was getting married. Driscoll scaled 155lbs to Chrisp's 154.

1896

5 September Bill Doherty (Melbourne, Australia) w ko 18 Bill Heffernan (Australia, late New Zealand. Born Scotland), The Amphitheatre, Johannesburg, South Africa. Referee: Jack Marshall. Scheduled for 20 rounds and billed a for the Imperial Empire 156lbs title, it was also reported as being for the South African middleweight title. Doherty weighed 155lbs to Heffernan's 156.

13 November 'Dido' Plumb (Balls Pond Road, London) challenges All-England at 154lbs, give or take two pounds, to 156lbs – *Sporting Life*.

1897

15 April George Chrisp stated that he would box Harry Neumier (Stepney), but at 156lbs not 152lbs, for £50 a-side, over 20 three-minute rounds, wearing four-ounce gloves – *Sporting Life*.

11 December 'Paddy' Purtell (USA) challenges All-England at 154 to 156lbs, George Chrisp preferred for £100 a-side – *Sporting Life*.

1900

15 February Harry Neumier w pts 15 Dave Peters (Treorchy), Aldgate Baths, Goulstone Street, London. Referee: Sydney Rushton. No weights were given or stipulated and it was almost certainly a catchweights contest. Following the bout, Peters challenged Neumier to a return at 158lbs.

1901

18 October Jack Bennett (USA) w pts 15 Charlie McKeever (Philadelphia, Pennsylvania, USA), Delaware, USA. Made at 155lbs, but no weights were given and no title billing announced.

9 December Jack Palmer (Benwell) no contest 2 Charlie McKeever, Ginnett's Circus, Newcastle. Referee: Mr Plummer. Scheduled for 15 three-minute rounds, it was stopped by the police before it really got going. Articled as a catchweight bout, with McKeever being restricted to 154lbs, Palmer to be any weight, McKeever was two pounds overweight at 156lbs. Contested in four-ounce gloves, it carried £100 a-side and a £125 purse, totalling £325.

1902

4 July	'Dido' Plumb challenges All-England at 154 to 158lbs – *Sporting Life*. A piece in the *Toronto Daily Mail* during the year on the poorness of British boxers, called Plumb, who was primarily a booth boxer, 'The Biggest Dub of them All'.
27 August	'Dido' Plumb challenges Jack Palmer at 156lbs over 15 rounds of three minutes - *Sporting Life*.
30 August	Jack Palmer challenges All-England at 156lbs, over 15 or 20 rounds at £25 or £50 a-side, 'Dido' Plumb preferred – *Sporting Life*. This was repeated in the 26 November issue.
4 November	Tom Woodley (Fulham) challenges any middleweight in England, no weight stipulated. In the same issue of the *Sporting Life* it states, Charlie Wilson (Notting Hill) is the English middleweight champion. Again no was weight stipulated.
19 December	Tom Woodley challenges Jack Palmer, 'Dido' Plumb and Charlie Wilson to a 'handicap' bout, Woodley to be 146lbs and the other three restricted to 156lbs – *Sporting Life*.

1906

23 April	Pat O'Keefe (Canning Town) w ko 6 Charlie Allum (Notting Hill), NSC, Covent Garden, London. Referee: Tom Scott. Scheduled for 15 three-minute rounds and billed for the English 156lbs middleweight championship, O'Keefe weighed 156lbs to Allum's 153¹/₂. On 19 March of that year, O'Keefe had won a bout billed as being for the English 158lbs title.
29 August	Tom Lancaster (Spennymoor) challenges Peter Brown (Woolwich) at 154lbs to 156lbs, £25 or £50 a-side – *Sporting Life*.

1907

12 December	Stanley Ketchel (Grand Rapids, Michigan, USA) w pts 20 Joe Thomas (Beverly, Mass, USA), San Francisco, California, USA. Made at 155lbs, no weights were given and no title billing was claimed in the *San Francisco Chronicle*, while the Spoting Life reported that it was contested in Oakland.

1908

7 January	Tom Lancaster challenges all at 154lbs to 156lbs over 20 three-minute rounds and £50 a-side, Andrew Jeptha (Cape Town) and Jim Styles (Marylebone) preferred.
24 February	Tom Lancaster w pts 20 Andrew Jeptha (South Africa), Ginnett's Circus, Newcastle. Referee: Robert P. Watson. Made at 149 to 156lbs (limit), £50 a-side and a £125 purse, totalling £225, there was no title billing given and Lancaster weighed 156lbs.
28 February	Jack Kingsland (Paddington) challenges Tom Lancaster at 156lbs, £50 a-side and the best purse – *Sporting Life*.
9 May	Stanley Ketchel w ko 20 Jack 'Twin' Sullivan (Cambridge, Mass, USA), San Francisco, California, USA. Made at 156lbs, with both men claiming the American/world title at 154lbs, no weights were given. It was scheduled for 35 rounds.
16 June	Tom Lancaster challenges Joe White (Cardiff, born Canada), at 154lbs to 156lbs, 1pm weigh-in, using four-ounce gloves, £25 or £50 a-side and a best purse – *Sporting Life*.

1909

11 February	The National Sporting Club in London introduced eight-named 'spread-weight' divisions, which effectively ended the 'every two-pounds' class of champions and English titles were in future to be known as British titles. With Tom Lancaster still claiming the English title at the weight, he beat Mexborough's Tom Stokes (w disq 10 in Hull on 26 June) in a fight billed as being for the English Pitmens' title, but following that the weight class died out.

156lbs to 158lbs (11 Stone 2 lbs To 11 stone 4 lbs)

1877

26 October	James 'Jem' Goode (Drury Lane) drew 29 Mickey Rees (Spitalfields), Saddlers Wells Theatre, Clerkenwell, London. Referee: Mr. Robert Watson. Scheduled for a finish and billed as being for the English 158lbs middleweight championship and a £100 cup according to both *Bells Life* and the *Sportsman*, it was not reported as such in the *Sporting Life*. On the police stopping the bout, which was called the greatest glove action seen up to this time by both *Bells Life* and the *Sporting Life*, the referee arranged to meet the men next day when, after debate, the decision was given as a draw. Rees was given £5 to agree to this, as he had certainly had the best of it due to Goode having broken his right arm against the ring post in the second round (first

round also given) and fighting on for another 27 rounds with just one arm. The veteran of several bare-knuckle bouts, Rees, aged 35, was making his debut with gloves. *The Sportsman's* reporter once again hammered glove boxing, being the third man that he had seen and all had been poor adverts for what he termed as a 'so-called' sport.

3 December	'Young' Posh Price w ko 28 Harry Skates, Jack Baldock's East London Gym, Number One Railway Arch, Station Place, Dean Street, off Commercial Road, Shadwell, London. Referee: Mr Robert Watson officiated from inside the ring as he always did, being the only man to do so at this time. Articled for a finish, Price scaling 156lbs to Skates' 158, and made at the 158lbs (limit) for a £25 cup under MoQ Rules with gloves, there was no title billing. *The Sportsman* gave Price's weight as 164lbs, which would have made him six pounds overweight, but am certain this was a misprint as there was no mention of his being overweight.

1879

7 April	J.Bryan (Brian and Bryant also given) w pts 3 Max Kirby, 'The White Bear', Long Walk, Bermondsey, London. Judge: M.Rees. The final of a middleweight competition, when it started on 31 March it was called a heavyweight tournament. With three men entered, Bryan beat 'Young' Marshall, with Kirby getting the bye.

1881

18 May	Jack Burke (Lambeth), 'The Irish Lad', challenges Charlie Mitchell (Birmingham) at any style, £25 or £50 a-side, but no weights stipulated. Mitchell accepted on 24 May and they agreed to meet at the *Sporting Life* office to make the match, which eventually took place on 16 June with bare-knuckles under London Prize Ring Rules, the police calling a halt after 77 minutes.
30 August	Denny Harrington (London, born Ireland) challenges Charlie Mitchell, £100 a-side – *Sporting Life*.

1885

18 March	Bill Springhall (Battersea, England), now in the USA, challenges the world at 158lbs, backed by John Clark (Philadelphia). However, following Springhall's bout with Billy Gabic in Philadelphia, Clark dropped Springhall 'like a hot potato' and withdrew all his backing.
11 May	Bill Springhall w ko 3 George Rooke (New York, USA, born Ireland). No weights were given or stipulated and there was no title billing.
6 July	Bill Springhall is now back from the USA, where all the top men refused to fight him and challenges 'Nonpareil' Jack Dempsey (USA, born Ireland), £100 a-side, no weights given, in either UK or USA – *Sporting Life*.

1887

30 August	Bill 'Chesterfield' Goode (Shadwell) w rtd 15 Tom Lees (Australia), Lambeth School Of Arms, Lambeth Walk, Paradise Street, Lambeth, London. Referee: B.J. Angle. Scheduled for a finish, Goode scaling 149lbs to Lees 156¹/₂, it was made at the156lbs (limit) and, as a gimmick, billed for the English 158lbs title before it was pointed out that only someone born in the British Isles could contest an English title, Lees not being eligible. Lees, a former heavyweight champion of Australia, was badly weakened by getting down to 158lbs, far below his natural weight, and showed nothing like his true form.
15 October	Tom Lees (Australia) w disq 5 (low blow) Bill 'Chesterfield' Goode, Waites Rooms, Brewer Street, Golden Square, Soho, London. Referee: J.T. Hulls. Made at catchweights, Lees (164lbs) was dropped by low blow, which caused an uproar, and the referee left the ring and the building too scared to give his decision while in the building. At first it was thought that a draw had been given, but it wasn't until later that Mr Hulls gave his decision as a disqualification win for Lees.
24 December	Jack Burke, now in Australia, challenges Charlie Mitchell with gloves for £50 a-side. No weights were stipulated, however – *Sporting Mirror*.
28 December	A real effort is being made to match England's Charlie 'Toff' Wall against 'Nonpareil' Jack Dempsey, the 158lbs American champion, in order to decide the true world 158lbs middleweight champion. However, Dempsey, a married man, wouldn't leave his family and America to go to England and, in spite of many efforts to get Wall to the USA, he was scared of the water, so would not sail - a phobia handed down to some of his descendants to this day - so the match never happened.

1888

1 August	It was stated that when the former policeman, Tom Lees, first

went to the USA he challenged and was matched with 'Nonpareil' Jack Dempsey, but backed out of the arranged bout. He then got matched with Jimmy Carroll in New York for 23 August, but has now ducked out of that one – *Sporting Mirror*.

1889

30 January   Teddy O'Neil (Liverpool) challenges All-England at 158lbs, Alf Mitchell (Late Cardiff) preferred. This was repeated in the 12 March issue of the *Sporting Life*.

15 October   Both Bill 'Chesterfield' Goode and Charlie 'Toff' Wall are signing themselves as the English 158lbs (limit) middleweight champion, while efforts are being made to match them. This was to go on for several weeks and 'Sportsman' of *Sporting Life* in the 23 October issue carried a letter from an ex boxer, signing himself LBJ, stating that the Wall v Goode bout should be held in public over 12 rounds, as private shows, with limited numbers of fans allowed to either side, were 'all bosh' and nearly always led to trouble and disputed endings. It's the public that makes boxing and all shows should be held in public and over 12 rounds, as 12 rounds are the ideal number of rounds to settle who's the best man. This sort of show would make glove boxing one of the top sports – *Sporting Life*.

29 November   Both Charlie 'Toff' Wall and Jim Young (Fulham) are claiming to be the English 158lbs champion – *Sporting Life*.

29 November   Alf Ball (Deptford) challenges any 158lbs middleweight in the world, £100 up to £200 a-side. This was repeated in the 24 December issue of the *Sporting Life*, when Ball added that if there was no acceptance to his challenge by various claimants of the English 158lbs (limit) title, such as Bill 'Chesterfield' Goode, Charlie 'Toff' Wall, Alf Mitchell and Jim Young, he would automatically claim the title, as proposed bouts with Alf Mitchell and Jim Young had both fallen through – *Sporting Life*.

1890

6 February   James Richardson (Wood Green, London) drew 4 Jack Martin (Hull), Hengler's Circus, Hull. The final of Mr Shelley's 158lbs (limit) All-England competition, £20 to the winner and £5 to the runner-up, in previous rounds Richardson beat Joe Wilson (Leicester) and 'Barney' Lambert, while Martin beat Jack Rawlins(Hull) and Alf Bailey (Salford). It was not reported as a championship competition.

7 February   Charlie 'Toff' Wall (Hackney) w pts 12 Bill 'Chesterfield' Goode, The Pelican Club, Gerrard Street, Soho, London. Billed for the English 158lbs (limit) middleweight title, with a 1-2pm weigh in place, a £225 purse and £500 a-side (total £1225), Wall scaled 157lbs to Goode's 156. This was, in fact, the final bout of Wall's career, other than exhibitions.

13 February   'Nonpareil' Jack Dempsey w rtd 28 Billy McCarthy (Melbourne, Australia, born Poplar, London, England), The California AC, San Francisco, California, USA. Given billing as a world 158lbs (limit) middleweight title fight, Dempsey scaling 157^{1}/$_{2}$lbs to McCarthy's 151^{1}/$_{2}$lbs, it was contested in small gloves for a $1,800 purse.

19 February   John O'Brien (Roath) w ko 3 Felix Scott (Liverpool, born Barbados), The Lyceum Theatre, Pembroke Place, Liverpool. Scott (144lbs), a coloured fighter, who was just out of prison after doing 18 months, broke his arm in the first round and from then on was at the mercy of O'Brien (158lbs). Made at catchweights for a £50 purse (£40 to winner, £10 to loser), it was scheduled for 20 rounds.

14 March   Charlie 'Toff' Wall is the 158lbs champion – *Sporting Life*.

27 August   Jack Burke challenges 'Nonpareil' Jack Dempsey at 156 to 158lbs, £1000 up to £2000 a-side. This was repeated in 2 September issue of the *Sporting Life*, even after Dempsey had stated he wouldn't box over 154lbs on 30 August.

3 September   Charlie 'Toff' Wall is still signing himself the English 158lbs champion – *Sporting Life*. In the same issue, the ex-guardsman, Alf Mitchell (late of Cardiff), is also signing himself off as the English middleweight champion.

17 November   George Kessler (Montana, late of England) w disq 13 George LaBlanche (Canada), Butte City, Montana, USA. No weights were given or stipulated and no title billing was reported, but LaBlanche, the so-called middleweight champion, was being well beaten when disqualified for kicking his man in the groin. LaBlanche was so exhausted that he had to be carried to his corner, while Kessler, an English peddler out of Montana, jumped over the top rope to leave the ring.

25 November   Ted Bryant (Chelsea) w ko 1 John O'Brien, Bob Habbijam's West End School of Boxing, Newman Street, off Oxford Street, London. Made at catchweights, it was felt that O'Brien was a dead certainty to win as he was over 14lbs heavier than Bryant (148lbs). The *Sporting Life* gave the time of contest as being 37 seconds, including the count, but the *Sporting Mirror* gave it as 47 seconds, the kayo being a pure fluke. O'Brien challenged Bryant to return and stated that he would back himself for £600 to Bryant's £200. In the 28 November issue of the *Sporting Life*, Bryant stated that he would only give O'Brien a return if at 147lbs.

1891

10 January   Arthur Akers (Leicester) w pts 3 Alf Suffolk (Lambeth, London), Rowland's Circus, Carr Lane, Hull. The final night of Mr J.H. Shelley's week-long 158lbs All-England competition for £20, in previous rounds Akers received a bye and then beat Jack Welland, while Suffolk beat Fred Greenbank and George Chrisp.

14 January   Bob Fitzsimmons (Now a US citizen, but late Australia and New Zealand, born England) w ko 13 'Nonpareil' Jack Dempsey. Billed for the American/world middleweight championship, reports as to the exact stipulated weight vary from 152lbs, 154lbs, 156lbs and 158lbs. For the record, Fitzsimmons scaled 150^{1}/$_{2}$ to Dempsey's 147^{1}/$_{2}$.

24 February   Bob Fitzsimmons, the holder of the American 158lbs (limit) middleweight title, challenges anyone in the UK, Ted Pritchard, Charlie 'Toff' Wall preferred, to meet him for the undisputed world 158lbs (limit) title as he proposed a UK trip – *Sporting Mirror*.

25 February   Charlie 'Toff' Wall, the English 158lbs (limit) champion, accepted Fitzsimmons' challenge, but would box any 158lbs man in the world for the title. However, Wall, a great fighter that he undoubtedly was, had, in fact, fought the last serious bout of his career, as other than exhibitions he never boxed again after 7 February 1890. His complete lack of interest in money, being content to have just a few shillings, a few pints and a skittle alley for his services, plus a dislike of training, led to him being very unreliable in going through with proposed matches and, coupled with an inborn fear of water which caused him to refuse to cross the pond, plus the fact that most boxers avoided him if at all possible, saw him ultimately walk away from boxing. His failure to turn up for his 19 October 1891 bout against 'Australian' Billy McCarthy, being 'the straw that broke the camels back' and no one would touch him after that. However, the only comment he would make was that he would go back to his work, hauling coals. Just happy to live from day to day with a 'tomorrow could look after itself' attitude, he was one of the most wasted talents ever.

12 September   John O'Brien, now claiming the English 158lbs (limit) title, challenges the world at that weight – *Sporting Life*.

23 September   Ted Pritchard (Lambeth, born Wales), the English 154lbs (limit) champion, asked what right had John O'Brien to claim the English 158lbs (limit) title and challenged O'Brien at 158lbs for the English title, £500 a-side and best purse and winner take all – *Sporting Life*.

17 November   Bob Fitzsimmons challenges Ted Pritchard to settle the dispute over just who was the world 158lbs (limit) middleweight champion. He said that if the NSC would put up a £1,000 purse, he would come to the UK – *Sporting Life*.

18 November   Ted Pritchard accepted Fitzsimmons' challenge, but, in the same issue, the NSC seemed to ignore Pritchard's claims to the English or world 158lbs (limit) title by matching Jack O'Brien against Alf Mitchell for the English 158lbs (limit) middleweight title. Pritchard, in July, had won a claim to the English heavyweight title, but stated that he wouldn't press that claim as he was not big enough – *Sporting Life*.

21 December   John O'Brien w ko 8 Alf Mitchell, NSC, Covent Garden, London. Scheduled for 20 three-minute rounds and given billing as being for the English 158lbs (limit) middleweight championship and belt, O'Brien weighed in at 157lbs to Mitchell's 158.

1892

13 January   John O'Brien challenges the world for the 158lbs middleweight championship and belt, plus an NSC purse of £500, no one barred, Ted Pritchard, Bob Fitzsimmons and Jimmy Carroll (USA, born England) for choice. O'Brien had a £100 deposit at the *Sporting Life* office for three months to bind the match. On 30 January, the *Sporting Life* gave the challenge at 154lbs and, on 3 February, in the same paper, O'Brien stated that his challenge was at 158lbs, the top middleweight class.

4 March   On this date, a Pritchard v O'Brien bout was made for the

English 158lbs (limit) title, with only the venue still to be settled. The NSC offered a £550 purse and not a penny more, plus a championship belt, but both the Bolingbroke Club and the Temple Club in Fleet Street offered an £800 purse. However, the bout fell through as O'Brien refused to box anywhere other than the NSC, even though its purse offer was much smaller. Pritchard, already the English 154lbs (limit) middleweight champion, then claimed the English 158lbs (limit) middleweight title also after O'Brien's refusal to fight and was offered a bout in the USA with Bob Fitzsimmons to find the true world 158lbs middleweight champion. Due to take place on 5 September at the Olympic Club in New Orleans for a £5,000 purse, Pritchard having signed the contract on 4 May, unfortunately, on 11 May, Fitzsimmons refused to go ahead with the match, stating that Pritchard had signed to meet John O'Brien instead, which he hadn't. The Bolingbroke Club, London then made an offer of a £1,200 purse for the Pritchard v Fitzsimmons bout, plus £2000 a-side, totalling £5,200, but Fitzsimmons signed for the Olympic Club, New Orleans. Articles were then sent to London on 25 May, but Pritchard refused to sign as the Olympic Club had dropped their original purse offer from £5,000 to $1,200, so this bout also fell through.

8 March   Ted Pritchard is now formally claiming the English 158lbs (limit) title – *Sporting Life*.

4 June   George Chrisp (Newcastle) w ko 2 Jack Hart (Smithfield), Central Hall, Holborn, London. The final of an All-England 158lbs (limit) competition over four rounds, in previous heats Chrisp beat Frank Ring and Jim Richardson, while Hart beat 'Barney' Lambert and H. Manning.

19 August   Jim Hall (Australia) w ko 4 Ted Pritchard in a fight held on the Sussex Downs at the training grounds of a racing stable, about four miles from Brighton. Scheduled for a finish, both men weighing 157lbs, it was billed as being for the world 158lbs (limit) title, claimed by Pritchard. It was also given English title billing, ignoring fact that, as an Australian, Hall was ineligible to box for an English title. To do so, one had to be born in the British Isles of British parents. The bout was actually made at 158lbs, give or take two pounds, so it really belonged to the 160lbs weight class, but with both under 158lbs it was given credence as being for that title, which automatically created a dispute as, in America, Bob Fitzsimmons was being billed as the American and world 158lbs (limit) champion.

30 November Jim Hall is the world 158lbs champion, 154 to 160lbs was also given – *Sporting Life*.

7 December   Alf Bowman (Mile End), the former ABA heavyweight champion, challenges All-England at 158lbs for an NSC purse – *Sporting Life*. On 10 December, Charlie Bartlett, 'The Meat Market Black', accepted the challenge.

1893

11 January   Jim Young is the undefeated English 158lbs champion – *Sporting Life*.

6 March   Ted White (Walthamstow) w pts 4 Alf Bowman, NSC, Covent Garden, London. Referee: B.J.Angle. The final of an NSC 158lbs (limit) English middleweight championship belt competition, in previous rounds White beat Harry Holdsworth and George Chrisp, while Bowman beat George Mason (Exeter) and Jerry (given as Jim) Driscoll, the champion of the Navy. The belt, valued at £100, which was presented to White by Sir George Chetwynd, had originally been intended for the winner of a Ted Pritchard v 'Australian' Bill McCarthy bout.

20 September Alfred Pearce (London) is calling himself the 'coloured' 158lbs (limit) middleweight champion of England – *Sporting Life*.

7 October   Arthur Akers w pts 4 George Chrisp, The Coliseum, Leeds. The final of J.H.Shelley's English 158lbs (limit) championship competition, in previous rounds Akers beat Alf Bowman and Jack Hughes, while Chrisp picked up a bye before beating Victor Layton.

6 December   Fred Bryant (Briant also given), the English middleweight champion, is to meet 'Dido' Plumb in a finish bout in Paris, France during the middle of December. No weights were mentioned. This was almost certainly Ted Bryant (Chelsea) and there was no record of the bout ever coming off – *Sporting Life*.

13 December Arthur Akers is the English 158lbs (limit) middleweight champion – *Sporting Life*.

20 December Ted Pritchard challenges the world at 158lbs, £500 a-side – *Sporting Life*.

1894

21 April   London George Chrisp w ko 1 Ted Rich (Victoria), St Andrews Hall, Newman Street, off Oxford Street, London. Contested over four rounds, this was the final night of Frank Hindes' English 158lbs championship competition, which had been a week-long tournament. Hindes boasted that he had made more champions than anybody else. In previous rounds, Chrisp beat J. Dorling and 'Nobby' Peterson, while Rich beat Arthur Morris and J. Brian.

25 May   Arthur Akers challenges all at 158lbs – *Sporting Life*. Reported in the papers around this time, but with no date given, was a contest in Sydney, Australia between Tom Duggan (Melbourne) and Pat O'Toole (Sydney, born Ireland) for the vacant Australian 158lbs middleweight title. Tom Duggan, weighing 157lbs, forced O'Toole, weighing 156¹/₂lbs, to retire in nine rounds.

5 June   Ted Rich w rtd 3 Alfred Pearce, Paris, France. Made at 158lbs, no weights were given and no title billing was attached.

22 August   Jim Johnson, the 'coloured' middleweight champion of the North-West States of America, challenges Ted Pritchard at 158lbs, £200 a-side and an NSC purse – *Sporting Life*.

26 September Bob Fitzsimmons w ko 2 Dan Creedon (New Zealand), New Orleans, Louisiana, USA. Billed for the world 158lbs (limit) title, some comments were passed as to the correctness of the weights given as it was known that Fitzsimmons, at the time, was having trouble getting down to 158lbs, no matter what he said to the contrary, and 156lbs for him was looked on as being a bit doubtful. Creedon weighed 157lbs.

8 October   Frank Craig (Harlem, New York) w ko 2 John O'Brien, NSC, Covent Garden, London. Referee: B.J. Angle. Scheduled for a finish, Craig weighing 157lbs to O'Brien's 158, it was billed for the world 158lbs (limit) middleweight title and carried a £150 purse. O'Brien, who had been ill in bed with sciatica just 14 days prior to the bout, had weakened himself getting down to 158lbs, as he was a natural 160lbs man, and was down four times prior to the knockout. In fact, he should never have been allowed to box by NSC doctor. Craig was the 'coloured' world champion at 158lbs.

10 November Ted Pritchard is the English 158lbs (limit) champion. This was repeated in the 18 December issue of the *Sporting Life*.

17 November 'Dido' Plumb (Kingsland) w ko 2 Alec Young (Peckham), Central Hall, Holborn, London. Scheduled for four rounds, this was the final of Frank Hindes' English 158lbs (limit) championship competition. In previous rounds, Plumb beat A. Edwards and Bill Husbands, while Young beat Steve Merry and H. Oliver.

23 November Frank Craig exhibition 3 Bill Miles (Somers Town), The Eden Palace of Varieties, Great Queen Street, Holborn, London. Records of Craig nearly all carry a w ko 2 bout with Alf Mitchell on this date at the NSC, when, in fact, there's no record of any such bout taking place at 158lbs or any other weight.

26 November Ted Pritchard w ko 2 Dick Burge (Newcastle), The Eden Palace of Varieties, Great Queen Street, Holborn, London. Referee: Joe Steers. Made at catchweights, on the proviso that Pritchard wasn't to exceed 160lbs, no weigh-in took place, no weights were given, and it was over a non-championship course of ten rounds. Stated to be for £300 a-side, with the *Mirror of Life* reporting it as a defence of Pritchard's 158lbs middleweight title, prior to the bout they argued for more than an hour over the appointment of a referee, until Joe Steers was agreed on. Burge, after 'walking' the first round, was floored in the second by a punch to the jaw, but Pritchard, instead of retiring to his corner as per the rules, stood over his man and, while Burge was on his knees, hit him twice. The second punch that landed turned Burge right over, his head hitting the canvas with a thud, and he was counted out. Strangely, Pritchard was returned the winner, instead of being disqualified as he should have been.

6 December   Jerry Driscoll, the Navy champion, challenges George Chrisp or Arthur Akers, claimants of the English 158lbs title, and was accepted by Akers four days later – *Sporting Life*.

17 December Frank Craig w ko 1 Ted Pritchard, Central Hall, Holborn, London. Referee: J. C. Calder. Although over three rounds, hardly a recognised championship course, it was billed as involving the world 158lbs (limit) middleweight title by the *Mirror of Life*, but no weights were given out at the 2pm weigh-in. In a bout lasting one minute, 46 seconds, Pritchard, the slight favourite in the betting, was seconded by Charlie

Mitchell and like all bouts involving Mitchell, in which he wasn't a participant, it was believed to be a 'fix', but nothing could be proved.

18 December Ted Pritchard, the English 158lbs (limit) champion, stated that his bout with Frank Craig, the world 158lbs (limit) championship claimant, had no title involvement, being just an international match over the non-championship course of ten rounds.

1895

11 February On this day it was announced that 'Nonpareil' Jack Dempsey had been pronounced insane and advised to be put into an insane asylum – *Sporting Life*.

8 April Anthony Diamond (Birmingham) w pts 12 Jack Varley (Birmingham), The Curzon Hall, Suffolk Street, Birmingham. Billed as catchweight bout, with Diamond scaling 154lbs to Varley's 158, at a later date it was reported as having been for the English 158lbs (limit) title.

2 September Charlie Johnson (St Paul, Minnesota, USA) w rtd 17 George Chrisp, Ginnett's Circus, Newcastle. Scheduled for 20 rounds at catchweight, no weights given and no title billing attached, Chrisp retired at end of the 17th round.

14 September George LaBlanche, 'The Marine', challenges All-England at 158lbs – *Sporting Life*.

14 October Dan Creedon w pts 20 Frank Craig, NSC, Covent Garden, London. Reported in the majority of papers as being a world 158lbs middleweight title fight, Creedon scaled 156lbs to Craig's 157.

1896

11 January Dan Creedon is listed as the Australian 158lbs middleweight champion – *Mirror of Life*.

1 June Ted White w rsf 16 'Dido' Plumb, NSC, Covent Garden, London. Scheduled for 20 three-minute rounds and billed for the English 158lbs (limit) middleweight title, it was the final bout of White's career.

26 December Charles 'Kid' McCoy (USA) w ko 9 Bill Doherty (Australia), The Amphitheatre, Johannesburg, South Africa. Referee: Mr Maturin. Given billing for the world 158lbs middleweight title, claimed by McCoy (156lbs), Doherty weighed 158lbs.

1897

2 February Fred Morris (New York), 'Muldoons Cyclone', challenges all at 158lbs, Frank Craig preferred. This was repeated in the 4 February issue of the *Sporting Life*. In response, Craig stated he couldn't box under 160lbs.

19 March Ted White is the English 158lbs (limit) middleweight champion – *Sporting Life*.

24 March Frank Craig, 'The Coffee Cooler', challenges Bob Fitzsimmons for the world 158lbs (limit) middleweight title, £500 a-side. However, Fitzsimmons had long been unable to get down to 158lbs and had just won the world heavyweight title. Regardless, Craig stated that if the challenge was not accepted he would claim the world 158lbs title – *Mirror of Life*. Craig had lost his claim to this title on 14 October 1895 and just eight weeks previously had stated he was no longer able to get below 160lbs, so it was difficult to see where his claim was coming from.

7 April E.W. Rollins, 'Starlight', of Australia, aged 46, challenges the world at the 158lbs limit for the world title, Bob Fitzsimmons barred – *Sporting Life*.

23 June George Chrisp w disq 12 'Starlight', Ginnett's Circus, Newcastle. Referee: E.A. Humphreys of the *Sporting Life*. Scheduled for 20 three-minute rounds, Chrisp scaling 158lbs to 'Starlight's' 157, the match was made at the 160lbs (limit), but no title billing was attached.

23 October Dick O'Brien (Boston, Mass, USA, born St John, Canada) w rsf 2 Frank Craig, The Olympic Club, Berwick Street, Birmingham. Referee: John S. Barnes. Billed for the world and American 158lbs (limit) middleweight title (claimed by Craig) and scheduled for 20 three-minute rounds, this was O'Brien's debut in UK, but once again some reports give the same old bunk about it being for the English title, for which neither man was eligible. The *Sporting Life* gave the result as O'Brien, stated incorrectly to be born in Ireland, w ko 2.

17 December Charles 'Kid' McCoy w rtd 15 Dan Creedon, The Long Island City AC, New York, USA. Scheduled for 25 rounds, McCoy weighing 155½lbs to Creedon's 157, it was billed for the world 158lbs (limit) middleweight title, claimed by McCoy, with Creedon badly weakened by getting down to the weight. The fight was also reported to be at catchweights, with the given weight for Creedon being manufactured.

1898

9 February Bill 'Chesterfield' Goode, who is to come back after eight years, challenges anyone in England for the English 158lbs (limit) title. When Goode did come back it was in a bout made at 166lbs – *Sporting Life*.

9 February 'Australian' Billy Edwards challenges all England at 158lbs, £200 a-side and an NSC purse, Jim Richardson, Arthur Akers and George Chrisp preferred – *Sporting Life*.

25 February Tommy Ryan (Syracuse) w ko 18 George Green (USA), San Francisco, California, USA. Made at catchweights, it was also stated to be at 158lbs and have American/world title billing, but Green ''Young Corbett'', was reckoned to be seven pounds heavier. Ten months later, in a bout against Dan Creedon, Green weighed 152lbs.

14 March Dick Guthrie is the middleweight champion of Canada – *Mirror of Life*.

11 April George Chrisp w ko 8 Jim Richardson (Honolulu, late Wood Green), The Standard Theatre, Gateshead. Referee: Ed Plummer of the *Sporting Life*. Scheduled for 20 three-minute rounds and billed as for the English middleweight title at 160lbs, both men came in at 158lbs. At various times, however, it was stated to be for the 158lbs title, but was not given title billing in all reports. Richardson, although billed from Honolulu, was a born-and-bred Londoner who had gone to Honolulu a year or so previous, either to work or as a seaman.

2 August Tommy Ryan challenges Arthur Akers at the 158lbs (limit) for the world middleweight title at that weight – *Sporting Life*.

12 September Jack Bonner (Philadelphia, USA) w ko 2 Dan Creedon, Coney Island, New York, USA. With no weights given or stipulated and no title billing, it was almost certainly a catchweight bout, but some hinted that it was made at 158lbs and gave Bonner, 158lbs, a title claim at the weight.

14 September Jim Richardson challenges all England at 158lbs, £50 a-side – *Mirror of Life*.

24 October Tommy Ryan w pts 20 Jack Bonner, Coney Island AC (Greater New York AC), NYC, New York, USA. With Ryan weighing 149lbs to Bonner's 158, in a bout billed as both at catchweights bout and for the American/world 158lbs (limit) middleweight title, Ryan increased his claim at the weight.

23 November Tommy Ryan w rtd 9 Johnny Gorman (USA), Syracuse, New York, USA. Given as both a catchweight bout and one involving the American/world 158lbs (limit) middleweight title, Ryan weighed 149lbs to Gorman's 157½lbs.

28 November Dan Creedon challenges the world at 158lbs, up to £1000 a-side, no one barred and Jack Bonner, Tommy Ryan, Charles 'Kid' McCoy, Frank Craig, all of the USA, and Bill Heffernan (South Africa and New Zealand, born Scotland) and George Chrisp and 'Dido' Plumb, both from England, preferred *Sporting Life*.

23 December Tommy Ryan w ko 14 Dick O'Brien, Hartford, Connecticut, USA. Given as both at catchweights and for the American/world 158lbs middleweight title, Ryan scaled 148lbs to O'Brien's 158.

30 December George Green w pts 20 Dan Creedon, Woodwards Pavilion, San Francisco, California, USA. The *Sporting Life* reports this as being for the world 158lbs middleweight title, but it is also given as a catchweight bout, with doubts raised as to Creedon's ability to still get to 158lbs and the truth of his given weight.

1899

18 January The ex-ABA middleweight champion in 1895 and 1898 and the ex-ABA heavyweight champion in 1897 and 1898, G.L. Townsend (Greenwich), challenges 'Dido' Plumb, the 154lbs champion, at 158lbs *Mirror of Life*.

19 May Joe Walcott (New York, born Barbados) w ko 14 Dick O'Brien, The Broadway AC, NYC, New York, USA. Scheduled for 20 rounds, it was variously reported to be a 158lbs title fight or at catchweights, with O'Brien restricted to 158lbs. For the record, Walcott scaled 140lbs to O'Brien's 151lbs.

8 July Contracts have been signed for a world 158lbs middleweight title bout during September between Charles 'Kid' McCoy and Bob Fitzsimmons, who, now that he had lost the world heavyweight title, was trying to reclaim his old crown, which McCoy also claimed. However, it was common knowledge that Fitzsimmons couldn't get down to 158lbs – *Sporting Life*.

5 September Charles 'Kid' McCoy w ko 3 Jeff Thorne (Greenwich,

England), The Broadway AC, NYC, New York, USA. Made at 158lbs without title billing, the former amateur, Thorne, real name G.L. Townsend, was just a 'novice' as a pro, but if both were inside 158 then McCoy's statement that it was a defence of his title claim at the weight was correct. It was scheduled for 20 three-minute rounds.

9 September Danny Erasmus (South Africa) w disq 2 Jim Holloway (Pretoria, South Africa), Kimberley, South Africa. Articled for the South African 158lbs (limit) middleweight title over 20 rounds, Erasmus weighing 158lbs to Holloway's 138lbs, the latter was well on top, having Erasmus down three times in the first round and again in the second, whereupon Erasmus just kept dropping down to avoid being hit. Holloway then hit him on one of those occasions, for which he was then disqualified.

13 September Jim Holloway w ko 1 Danny Erasmus, Kimberley, South Africa. In a return for the South African 158lbs (limit) middleweight title, no admission fee was charged and Erasmus' reign of just four days was a record for the shortest tenure of any major titleholder making a defence.

18 September Tommy Ryan w rsf 10 Frank Craig, Brooklyn, New York, USA. Originally made at 158lbs for the American/world middleweight title to be decided over 20 rounds, Craig was unable to get down to that weight, so it went on at catchweights.

22 November George England (Hackney) challenges All-England at 158lbs – *Sporting Life*.

18 December Jack Thompson (Newcastle) w rsf 5 Jim Richardson, The Standard Theatre, Gateshead. Referee: Tom Gamble. Scheduled for 20 rounds, both men scaling 157lbs, it was later given as an English title fight at 158lbs, £50 purse and £50 a-side, although it was more likely to have involved the Northern title over 20 rounds.

1900

10 January 'Dido' Plumb is the English 158lbs middleweight champion – *Mirror of Life*.

15 February Harry Neumier (Stepney) w pts 15 Dave Peters (Treorchy), Aldgate Baths, Goulstone Street, London. Referee: Sydney Rushton. Made at catchweights with no title billing given, in the 6 April issue of the *Sporting Life* Peters challenged Neumier to a return at 158lbs.

18 May Charles 'Kid' McCoy w rsc 6 Dan Creedon, NYC, New York, USA. Made at 158lbs, catchweights also given, there was no title billing attached or weights mentioned in newspaper reports of the fight.

1 June Charles 'Kid' McCoy w ko 13 Jack Bonner, NYC, New York, USA. Stated to be for the American/world 158lbs title over 25 rounds, but no weights were given.

27 November Tommy Ryan w pts 6 'Kid' Carter, Chicago, Illinois, USA. Made at 158lbs, with both men inside, but not over a recognised championship distance and no weights given. To involve a major title bout there had to be 12 rounds or more contested over three minutes duration and for a certain monetary value, which these American six rounders were not. This was an American idea of trying to pass six-round bouts off as genuine title bouts by stating that they were made at a stipulated poundage. And, with the advent of the no-decision bout in the USA, it was to become used more and more, with lots of reporters going along with it.

1901

29 January Dick Burge no contest 2 Jerry Driscoll, The Standard Theatre, Gateshead. Referee: Ed Plummer of the *Sporting Life* Given billing as an English 158lbs middleweight title fight in some quarters and made at 156lbs, give or take two pounds, £200 a-side for a £150 purse (total £550), it was scheduled for 15 three-minute rounds. Like the majority of Burge's bouts, it came to light that it was a 'fix' and that prior to the bout both had agreed to split the purse and that each retain their stake money, so there was no need to fight for the money. The first round was all hugging and wrestling, with both men falling repeatedly, and in the second the referee entered the ring and declared the bout off after both had again gone down together. The referee, Plummer, then left the ring and soon after left the building, before there was an attempt to carry on with a new referee, Jack Haggerty. However, both men refused to box for a purse only and matters were concluded. Burge and Driscoll escaped unpunished, as they were both paid and each had his stake money returned after splitting the purse as agreed at £75 each. Following this, Burge again announced his retirement from boxing and he never boxed again, thanks mainly to a

little help from the law as, on 22 February 1902 after spending three months inside on remand, he got ten years for fraud.

4 March Tommy Ryan w rtd 17 Tommy West (Chicago, born Cardiff), Louisville, Kentucky, USA. Given American/world 158lbs title billing and scheduled for 20 rounds, but with no weights given.

29 March Dave Peters challenges Jerry Driscoll at 158lbs, £100 a-side and an NSC purse – *Sporting Life*.

22 April Jack Palmer (Benwell) w ko 4 Andrew 'Cock' Robin (Glasgow, late of Belfast), Ginnett's Circus, Newcastle. Referee: Ed Plummer. Scheduled for 20 three-minute rounds and made at 158lbs, £25 a-side and £65 purse, it was not a large enough monetary sum for a major title and no title billing was given.

4 July George Gardner (Lowell, Mass, USA) w rsf 3 Jack Moffatt (USA), San Francisco, California, USA. Billed as being for the American/world 158lbs title, Gardner scaling 158lbs to Moffatt's 156, 159lbs was also given. It was also reported as a Californian State title bout.

7 August Mike Flynn (Islington) challenges any 158lbs middleweight in England at £100 a-side – *Sporting Life*.

24 August Jack Palmer w pts 10 Harry Barrett (Clerkenwell, London), Ginnett's Circus, Newcastle. Made at catchweights over a non-championship distance, no weights were given and no title billing was attached.

10 October George Green w disq 6 Tommy Ryan, Kansas City, Missouri, USA. Made at catchweights, with Ryan limited to 158lbs and Green (147lbs) to be any weight, it was also given at 158lbs. No weight was given for Ryan, who was disqualified for using his knee. It was not a billed title bout as it was not over a recognised title distance.

21 November Tommy West challenges 'Dido' Plumb, the English 154lbs champion, to a bout at 158lbs (154lbs also given) over ten or 15 rounds, £100 or £200 a-side – *Sporting Life*. Plumb had, in fact, more or less retired after 19 August 1901 bout.

13 December Dave Peters challenges Jack Palmer or Charley McKeever (Philadelphia, Pennsylvania, USA), the claimant of the world 152lbs title, £50 or £100 a-side – *Sporting Life*.

1902

10 January Tommy West challenges All-England at 158lbs, £100 a-side – *Sporting Life*.

27 January 'Philadelphia' Jack O'Brien (USA) w disq 3 Charley McKeever, The County AC, Leeds. Made at catchweights for £200 a-side and purse, the match had originally been made at 154lbs, but at the 3pm weigh-in O'Brien came in at 157½lbs and had to pay forfeit. The bout then went on at catchweights, although some reports gave it 158lbs world title billing, with some trying to tag it as an English title bout between two Americans.

30 January Tommy Ryan w ko 7 George Green, Kansas City, Missouri, USA. Made at 158lbs for the American/world title, no weights were given.

25 March Jack Palmer, 'The Pitmens' champion', real surname Liddell, wanted to know why George Chrisp, after challenging All-England, would not accept Palmer's challenge to a match from 152lbs up to 170lbs, £20 a-side upwards. Interestingly, Chrisp, aged 30, the claimant to the English heavyweight title, hadn't boxed since May 1901 and was considered retired – *Mirror of Life*.

12 April Jack Palmer w ko 11 Joe White (Cardiff, born Canada), Ginnett's Circus, Newcastle. Referee: J.R. Smoult. Scheduled for 20 three-minute rounds, Palmer scaling 156lbs to White's 154¼lbs, it was a catchweight handicap match with Palmer restricted to 158lbs and White allowed to be any weight for £200 a-side and purse. There was no title billing, although Palmer was claiming the English 158lbs (limit) title, and White, with a real name of Jack Robinson, was claiming to be the Canadian champion, prior to moving to the UK. In the 16 April issue of the *Sporting Life*, Palmer was challenged by Jack Scales (Bethnal Green) at catchweights.

26 May Tommy Ryan w ko 4 Jimmy Handler, Kansas City, Missouri, USA. With no weights or title billing given, it was possibly contested at catchweights, with Handler claiming to be inside 158lbs.

23 June Jack Palmer w ko 7 Dave Peters, Prince of Wales Circus, Merthyr. Referee: Tom Davies (Pontypridd). Billed as being for the English 158lbs title, give or take two pounds, but no weights given, the *Mirror of Life* called Palmer the acknowledged English 158lbs middleweight champion, while the *Cardiff Evening Express* (which gave the result as w ko

8) reported the bout as an eliminator for the English 160lbs (limit) middleweight title. However, two-minute rounds automatically ruled it out as a major title bout. Peters, billed as the Welsh champion, fell over the ropes and was counted out, further enraging the crowd, which had been giving out cries of 'foul' against Palmer throughout and the referee had to make his escape to 'The Vanguard Inn'.

24 June Tommy Ryan w ko 3 Johnny Gorman, NSC, Covent Garden, London. Billed as being for the world 158lbs title, but reported as a catchweight bout, Ryan weighed 151lbs to Gorman's 158lbs.

2 July Joe White challenges the world at 158lbs – *Sporting Life*.

4 July 'Dido' Plumb challenges All-England at 154 to 158lbs. An item in the *Toronto Daily Mail* this year on the poorness of British boxers, called 'Dido' Plumb, 'The Biggest Dub of Them All' – *Sporting Life*.

15 September Tommy Ryan w ko 6 'Kid' Carter, Fort Erie, Canada. Reported as an American/world 158lbs title, with both inside, no actual weights were given.

1 October Jack Palmer challenges 'Dido' Plumb at 158lbs over 15 or 20 rounds of three-minutes duration, £100 a-side and best purse, using four-ounce gloves to decide the English middleweight title – *Sporting Life*. Two days later, the challenge is accepted by Tom Smith (London) and the pair are matched for a title bout on 23 October.

23 October Jack Palmer w ko 2 Tom Smith, The National AC, 241 Marylebone Road, London. Referee: Professor Murray. Scheduled for ten three-minute rounds and billed for the English 158lbs (limit) title for £50 a-side and purse, it really wasn't over a recognised championship distance, with the monetary reward also not large enough for a major title bout. Smith, a pupil of 'Professor' A.J. Newton, was but a novice, while it was Palmer's London debut.

5 November Tom Woodley (Fulham) challenges any middleweight in England, although no weight is mentioned. In the same issue of the *Sporting Life*, Charlie Wilson (Notting Hill) is called the English middleweight champion, but again no weight was given.

24 November Jack Palmer w pts 15 Eddie Connolly (USA, born Canada). NSC, Covent Garden, London. Referee: J.H. Douglas. A catchweight handicap match, with Palmer restricted to 158lbs and Connolly allowed to be any weight, the actual weights were not given. The *Mirror of Life* gave it English 158lbs title billing, but Connolly was not eligible to box for the English title. Strangely, the *Mirror of Life* were often printing in the 'Editorials' that only British-born citizens of British parents could box for an English title, yet often billed international bouts as being for English titles. However, they were not alone in this.

1903

31 January Jack Palmer challenges All-England for the English 158lbs middleweight title, but if there are no acceptances he will go to the USA in February – *Sporting Life*.

10 February 'Soldier' Jack Thompson (Australia) w 6 'Snowy' Sturgeon (Australia), The Sydney NSC, Australia. Scheduled for 20 rounds and billed as being for the Australian middleweight title, no weights were given or stipulated. The 24 February issue of the *Sporting Life* reported that Thompson (155½lbs) defended his Australian middleweight title with a three-round stoppage win over Jim Richardson (Late Honolulu) at the Sydney NSC. Although it was reported as a fight scheduled for 20 rounds, no date was given.

20 April 'Philadelphia' Jack O'Brien drew 10 Joe Walcott, Boston, Mass, USA. A catchweight bout, although no weights and title billing were given it was felt that both men were inside 158lbs, with Walcott, one of the outstanding coloured men of the day, announced as the recognised 142lbs class champion of America.

22 April Jack Palmer is the English 158lbs champion – *Sporting Life*. He was also given as the 154lbs champion, which was certainly a misprint.

25 May Jack 'Twin' Sullivan (USA) drew 15 Jack Palmer, NSC, Covent Garden, London. Billed for the world 158lbs title and once again given English title billing, despite Sullivan (153lbs) being an American, 156lbs was also given as the articled poundage. Palmer weighed 156lbs.

17 September Fred Higgins (Birmingham, late London) challenges All-England at 158lbs, Charlie Wilson preferred. This was repeated in the 24 October issue of the *Sporting Life*.

12 December 'Philadelphia' Jack O'Brien w pts 15 Jack 'Twin' Sullivan, Boston, Mass, USA. With no weights given or stipulated and

no title billing reported, O'Brien scaled 158lbs to Sullivan's 153, strengthening his claim at the weight.

14 December Jack Palmer w rtd 2 (end of round) Sgt T. Harris (Essex Regiment), The Standard Theatre, Gateshead. Referee: Bert Dorman. When the match was made on 25 November, it was stated to be for the English 158lbs (limit) title over 15 rounds, with a 2am weigh-in and reported as such in both the *Newcastle-on-Tyne Chronicle* and the *Sporting Man*. That aside, no title was mentioned in the *Sporting Life* report, which also gave result as 'w rtd 3'. However, most reports stated that Harris was put down at the end of the second round and was saved by the bell and that the towel was thrown in during interval.

29 December 'Philadelphia' Jack O'Brien drew 10 Hugo Kelly, Kansas City, Missouri, USA. Articled at 158lbs, both men were inside but no weights were given and no title billing was mentioned.

1904

27 January Tommy Ryan no decision 6 'Philadelphia' Jack O'Brien, Philadelphia, Pennsylvania, USA. Stated to be at 158lbs, with both inside, no weights were reported and O'Brien was thought by the press to have had the better of it.

27 February Charlie Wilson is called the English 158lbs champion. This was repeated in the 9 April issue of the *Sporting Life* and the 29 June *Mirror of Life*.

2 March Jack Palmer, the English 158lbs champion, accepted the challenge of Arthur Cripps (Australia) at 158lbs, with £50 a-side and best purse, and the next day Cripps put down a £25 deposit to bind a match with Palmer, Charlie Knock or Charlie Allum at 158lbs over 15 or 20 three-minute rounds, using four-ounce gloves, £50 a-side and the best purse *Sporting Life*.

12 March Jack Palmer, the English 158lbs champion, has left for South Africa – *Sporting Life*.

6 April Jack 'Twin' Sullivan w pts 20 Hugo Kelly, Kansas City, Missouri, USA. No weights were given or stipulated and no title billing reported, but it was thought to have been contested around the 158lbs mark.

14 April 'Philadelphia' Jack O'Brien w ko 3 Jack 'Twin' Sullivan, St Louis, Missouri, USA. Made at 158lbs, although no weights were given and no title billing was reported, the contest had a bearing on the championship at that weight.

7 May Jack Palmer w pts 20 Jack Lalor, The Wanderers Club, Johannesburg, South Africa. Billed as being for the South African middleweight title, it really just an international bout, although Imperial British Empire title billing would not have been out of place. All international bouts in South Africa invariably got called as being for the 'South African' title, which not only cheapened that country's title, but created several champions at the same weight.

1905

4 January Jack Palmer is the English 158lbs champion. This was repeated in the 15 March issue of the *Mirror of Life*, when it was stated that Palmer was ill with an intestinal disorder.

10 January 'Philadelphia' Jack O'Brien challenges the world to decide the 158lbs (limit) title, Bob Fitzsimmons or Tommy Ryan preferred – *Sporting Life*.

24 March 'Philadelphia' Jack O'Brien w disq 2 'Young' Peter Jackson, Baltimore, Maryland, USA. Billed as involving the American/world 158lbs title, Jackson, real name Sim Thompkins, weighed 152lbs, but no weight was given for O'Brien. Jackson was one of the leading negro fighters of the day.

7 April 'Philadelphia' Jack O'Brien w pts 10 'Young' Peter Jackson, Baltimore, Maryland, USA. Made at 158lbs, but not over the recognised distance, both men came in at 154lbs.

25 April Hugo Kelly w pts 10 'Philadelphia' Jack O'Brien, Indianapolis, Indiana, USA. Made at 158lbs, no weights were given and it was not over a recognised title course.

27 April Pat O'Keefe (Canning Town) challenges any other claimant of the English 158lbs (limit) title, £100 a-side. In the same issue of the *Sporting Life*, Charlie Wilson challenged All-England at 158 to 172lbs.

7 June Hugo Kelly drew 10 Tommy Burns (Canada), Detroit, Michigan, USA. Made at 158lbs, no weights were given, but Kelly's claim would have almost certainly been on the line against Burns, real name Noah Brusso.

21 June Charlie Allum challenges Jack Palmer for the English 158lbs (limit) title over 15 or 20 rounds – *Sporting Life*.

5 August Charlie Wilson challenges Jack Palmer or Charlie Allum to a bout for the English 158lbs title over 20 three-minute rounds, £100 a-side and an NSC purse. The title was being claimed by all three reported the *Sporting Life* on 16 August.

8 August Charlie Allum accepted Charlie Wilson's challenge and, on 19 August, insisted on a ringside weigh-in, as he could easily do 150lbs let alone 158lbs, and to meet that day to make the match. Wilson turned up, but Allum didn't and Wilson repeated his challenge to All-England at 158lbs with a 2pm weigh-in. He repeated this again on 6 September, when it was announced that Jack Palmer was giving up his claim to the English 158lbs title in order to box as a heavyweight – *Sporting Life*.

11 September Charlie Allum again challenges Charlie Wilson at 158lbs – *Sporting Life*.

17 October Jack 'Twin' Sullivan w pts 20 Tommy Burns, Los Angeles, California, USA. Made at catchweights, with Burns well above 158lbs, Sullivan laid claim to the American/world 158lbs title, reputedly on strength of this win.

25 November Bob Brown (Belfast) challenges any middleweight in the British Isles, £50 or £100 a-side. No weight was stipulated, though – *Sporting Life*.

11 December Hugo Kelly drew 10 'Young' Mahoney, Indianapolis, Indiana, USA. In defence of his claim at 158lbs, Kelly contested this one at that poundage, but no weights were given and it was not over a recognised title distance.

Tommy Burns

1906

17 January Geoff Thorne challenges the world at 158lbs, £100 or £200, Jack Palmer preferred – *Sporting Life*.

27 January Tom Lancaster (Spennymoor) w ko 11 George Chrisp, Ginnett's Circus, Newcastle. Scheduled for 20 rounds at catchweights, no weights were given and no title billing was attached, but was thought to be at around 158lbs. This was a comeback for Chrisp after nearly three years out of the ring.

4 February Jack Kingsland (Paddington, London) w ko 6 Tom Lancaster, Ginnett's Circus, Newcastle. Made at catchweights and scheduled for 20 three-minute rounds, no weights were given but Lancaster was said to be about ten pounds heavier.

9 March Hugo Kelly drew 20 Jack 'Twin' Sullivan, Los Angeles, California, USA. Billed for the American/world 158lbs middleweight title, both were said to be inside but no actual weights were given.

19 March Pat O'Keefe (Canning Town) w pts 15 Mike Crawley (Limehouse), NSC, Covent Garden, London. Billed for the English 158lbs title, £50 a-side and purse, both men weighed 157½lbs.

31 March Tom Lancaster w ko 6 Bombardier Davis (Canning Town), Ginnett's Circus, Newcastle. Made at 158 lbs over 20 three-minute rounds, £25 a-side.

23 April Pat O'Keefe w ko 6 Charlie Allum, NSC, Covent Garden, London. Referee: Tom Scott. Scheduled for 15 three-minute rounds and billed for the English 156lbs championship, it was also thought to also involve the 158lbs title. O'Keefe weighed 156lbs to Allum's 153½lbs.

27 April Pat O'Keefe will defend his English 158lbs title against anyone – *Sporting Life*.

30 April 'Jewey' Cook (Hammersmith), real name Abe Cohen, accepted O'Keefe's challenge – *Sporting Life*.

28 May Tom Thomas (Penycraig) w pts 15 Pat O'Keefe, NSC, Covent Garden, London. Referee: J.H. Douglas. Billed for the English 158lbs middleweight title, Thomas weighed 156lbs to O'Keefe's 155½lbs.

23 June Tom Lancaster w ko 18 Jack Kingsland, Ginnett's Circus, Newcastle. Made at 158lbs and scheduled for 20 rounds, no weights were given and there was no title billing attached.

25 June Hugo Kelly w ko 3 'Young' Mahoney, Indianapolis, Indiana, USA. Reported as an American/world 158lbs title fight, no actual weights were given.

14 August 'Bombardier' Davis challenges All-England at 158lbs, Tom Lancaster or Peter Brown (Woolwich) preferred – *Sporting Life*.

18 August Tom Lancaster w ko 4 Alf Rogers, The Running Grounds, Durham. Scheduled for 20 rounds, no weights were given and no title billing was mentioned. The *Mirror of Life* gave Rogers as the opponent, but the *Sporting Life*'s 1910 Record Book stated that Lancaster's opponent was 'Bombardier' Davis.

24 August Hugo Kelly w ko 6 Tony Caponi, Leavenworth, Kansas, USA. Billed for the American/world 158lbs title.

4 December Tom Lancaster w ko 7 'Bombardier' Davis, Ginnett's Circus, Newcastle. Referee: J.R. Smoult. Scheduled for 20 rounds for £200, Lancaster scaled 158lbs to Davis' 154. There was no title billing given.

1907

9 February Bobby Dobbs (Cardiff, late USA), a negro aged 48, challenges Tom Thomas at 158lbs – *Mirror of Life*. Thomas refused the challenge as he wouldn't box a coloured man.

11 February Tom Lancaster w ko14 Jack Kingsland, Ginnett's Circus, Newcastle. Scheduled for 20 rounds, with no weights stipulated and no title billing attached, it was thought to involve Lancater's 158lbs English title claim.

11 February Pat O'Keefe w rsf 2 Joe Scott (Stoke Newington), NSC, Covent Garden, London. Referee: J.H. Douglas. Scheduled for 15 rounds, no weights were given or stipulated and no title billing was reported, but it was thought to involve O'Keefe's English title claim at 158lbs.

1 March Pat O'Keefe w ko 7 Charlie Allum, Salle Wagram, Paris, France. Referee: William 'Brummy' Meadows. Scheduled for 20 rounds, with no weights given or stipulated and no title billing reported, it was for a £200 purse (£140 to winner - £60 to loser) and thought to involve O'Keefe's 158lbs English title claim.

2 March Pat O'Keefe challenges Robert 'Curly' Watson at 158lbs, £50 a-side – *Sporting Life*.

25 March Tom Lancaster w pts 20 Mike Crawley, Ginnett's Circus, Newcastle. Referee: J.R.Smoult. Made at 156 to 158lbs, £25 a-side and £150 purse, with no weights given and no title billing reported, it was a bad decision, Crawley looking to be a good winner.

22 April Sam Langford (Boston, born Canada) w ko 4 James 'Tiger' Smith (Merthyr), NSC, Covent Garden, London. Billed as being for the world 158lbs title, it was also given English title billing, for which Langford was not eligible. However, the Imperial British Empire title would have been in order. Langford, a negro, weighed 154lbs and Smith, a southpaw with a surname of Addis, 151lbs.

4 May Pat O'Keefe challenges Sam Langford over 20 three-minute rounds at 158lbs – *Mirror of Life*.

10 May Hugo Kelly drew 20 Jack 'Twin' Sullivan, Los Angeles, California, USA. Made at 158lbs, no weights were given and no title billing was attached, despite it involving Kelly's claim at the weight.

3 June Tom Lancaster w pts 15 Seaman Fred Broadbent (Maidenhead), NSC, Covent Garden, London. Referee: J.H. Douglas. Made at 158lbs, Lancaster scaling 157lbs to Broadbent's 155, the former defended his claim at the weight despite a lack of title billing.

11 June Tom Thomas challenges any 'white' man in England at 158lbs, up to £100 a-side – *Sporting Life*.

15 June Pat O'Keefe challenges any 158lbs man in England, Tom Thomas, Tom Lancaster or Jack Costello preferred – *Sporting Life*.

27 August Sam Langford w pts 10 Larry Temple (USA), Chelsea, Mass, USA. Billed for the world 'coloured' 158lbs title, but not over a recognised championship distance.

26 October	Pat Daley/Daly (London, born Ireland) challenges Tom Lancaster at 158lbs over 15 or 20 rounds of three minutes, £25 up to £100 a-side – *Mirror of Life*.
12 November	Sam Langford w pts 20 'Young' Peter Jackson (Baltimore), Los Angeles, California, USA. Billed for the world 'coloured' 158lbs title.
14 November	James 'Tiger' Smith w ko 1 Charlie Allum, National AC, Merthyr. Made at 158lbs and scheduled for 20 rounds, individual weights were not given and no title billing was attached. The following day, Smith challenged All-England at the weight, £50 or £100 a-side. This was repeated in the 23 November issue of the *Sporting Life*.
9 December	Articles were signed for a bout over 20 three-minute rounds between Pat Daley/Daly and Tom Lancaster at 156 to 158lbs, to take place within three weeks from 16 December. The bout fell through on the stakes being withdrawn on 2 January 1908.
9 December	Jack Costello (Birmingham) w rtd 6 Charley Knock, The Drill Hall, Sheffield. Made at 158lbs, £50 a-side and £65 purse, Knock was forced to retire with a fractured forearm.
23 December	Tom Lancaster w pts 20 Mike Crawley, Ginnett's Circus, Newcastle. Referee: Robert Watson. Made at 156 to 158lbs, £25 a-side and £150 purse, Lancaster scaling 156½lbs to Crawley's 153½, there was no title billing attached despite Lancaster's claim at the weight.

1908

4 January	Tom Woodley challenges All-England at 150 up to 158lbs, over 15 or 20 rounds, £25 or £50 a-side – *Sporting Life*.
9 January	Jack Palmer (Plumstead, London) w pts 20 Bobby Dobbs (USA), The Gymnastic Club, Christian Street, Liverpool. Made at catchweights and contested over two-minute rounds, £26 a-side and purse, although no weights were given it was thought to be around the 158lbs limit. Note that this Jack Palmer was a different man from Jack Palmer from Benwell, although both were around the same weight.
27 January	James 'Tiger' Smith w ko 11 Jack Costello, The Drill Hall, Norfolk Road, Birmingham. Referee: Robert Watson. Contested over 20 three-minute rounds at 158lbs, a noon weigh-in, £100 a-side and £100 purse, there was no title billing despite both men claiming the English championship at the weight
3 February	Pat O'Keefe, now back from the USA, challenges All-England at 158lbs, Tom Lancaster and James 'Tiger' Smith preferred. Although currently weighing 170lbs, due to having malaria while in USA, O'Keefe can get down to 158lbs – *Sporting Life*.
11 March	Sam Langford w pts 8 Larry Temple, Boston, Mass, USA. Made at 158lbs, but not over a championship distance, no weights were given although Langford was stated to be over the prescribed weight, while Temple was inside the weight.
16 March	Billy Papke (USA) w pts 10 Hugo Kelly, Milwaukee, Wisconsin, USA. Made at 158lbs and given American/world title billing, although not over a recognised title course, Kelly had insisted this return had to be at 158lbs as he had weakened himself by getting down to 154lbs. In fact, Kelly had over done it by getting down to 151lbs and lost his claim to Papke.
13 April	Pat Daley/Daly no contest 7 (not trying) Charlie Knock, The Drill Hall, Norfolk Road, Sheffield. Referee: Tom Gamble. Scheduled for 20 two-minute rounds at 158lbs, £100 a-side and £80 purse, neither man should have been boxing as both were unfit. Daley/Daly had just two days previously lost on a seventh-round ko in a bout in Paris, which he had taken as a three-day substitute, while Knock had still not fully recovered from a broken arm.
30 April	Tom Thomas, the claimant to the English 158lbs title, is to come back after nearly two years out of the ring, having been laid up with rheumatic fever – *Sporting Life*.
7 May	Fred Broadbent challenges all at 158lbs, Pat Daley/Daly preferred – *Sporting Life*.
20 May	On this day, a 20-round bout between James 'Tiger' Smith and Steve Smith (Canning Town) arranged to be held in Paris, France at The Casino, was cancelled after an official ran off with the takings. Both men were then offered £80 to go on with a six-round bout, but refused.
1 June	Tom Thomas w ko 4 James 'Tiger' Smith, NSC, Covent Garden, London. Billed for the English and Welsh 158lbs title, £100 a-side, Thomas weighed 157lbs to Smith's 154.
4 June	Stanley Ketchel w pts 10 Billy Papke, Milwaukee, Wisconsin, USA. Although given American/world 158lbs

	title billing, it was not over a recognised championship course.
6 June	Tom Lancaster challenges Tom Thomas for the English/British 158 lbs title, £50 or £100 a-side – *Sporting Life*.
20 June	Tom Lancaster w ko 8 'Bombardier' Davis, The Running Grounds, Durham. Referee: Charlie Beadling. Scheduled for 15 rounds and made at 158lbs, Lancaster's claim at the weight was on the line in this one, despite a lack of billing.
31 July	Stanley Ketchel w ko 3 Hugo Kelly, The Coliseum, San Francisco, California, USA. Reported as an American/world 156 to 158lbs title fight, both men inside the weight, but no actual weights were given. The 30 September issue of the *Sporting Life* reported that, at the 6pm weigh-in, it was announced as being at 156lbs, give or take two pounds.
7 September	Billy Papke w rsf 12 Stanley Ketchel, Los Angeles, California, USA. Billed for the American/world 158lbs title, although no weights were given, Ketchel had, in fact, signed to meet 'Young' Peter Jackson in a title defence on this date at Goldfield, Nevada, but then withdrew after refusing to box a negro and took the bout with Papke instead.
17 October	Tom Thomas w ko 6 Jack Costello, Ivor AC, Swansea. Referee: Robert Watson. Scheduled for 20 two-minute rounds at catchweights for a purse only, no weights were given, but on 10 October Costello was 160lbs and stated that he would be 158lbs on fight night. The *Sporting Life* report stated that Thomas should now meet Tom Lancaster to settle who is the English 158lbs champion.
19 October	Tom Lancaster w ko 3 Fred Wilmott (Sunderland), Ginnett's Circus, Newcastle. Referee: J.T. Hulls. Contested at 158lbs, both men scaling 157½lbs, there was no title billing given in a match made for £25 a-side and 60% of gate. The *Sporting Life* report stated that Lancaster v Tom Thomas should now be made.
7 November	In the USA, Billy Papke refused to box Sam Langford, stating that he wouldn't box a coloured man under any circumstances – *Mirror of Life*.
9 November	Tom Lancaster challenges All-England at 158lbs over 20 three-minute rounds, £100 or £200 a-side, an NSC purse, a ringside weigh-in and using four-ounce gloves – *Sporting Life*.
26 November	Stanley Ketchel w ko 11 Billy Papke, San Francisco, California, USA. Billed for the American/world 158lbs title, no weights were given.

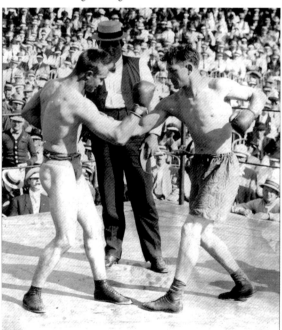

Stanley Ketchel (right) squares off against Billy Papke prior to regaining the 158lbs title

28 November Tom Lancaster w ko 6 Harry Croxon (West Drayton, London), The Newcastle SC, Elswick. No weights were given or stipulated and no title billing accorded, but it was thought to involve Lancaster's 158lbs English title claim.

17 December Tom Thomas w pts 20 Bart Connolly (USA, The Gymnastic Club, Christian Street, Liverpool. Referee: J.T. Hulls. Made at catchweights, £100 a-side and £300 purse, Thomas was ten pounds heavier than Connolly, but no weights were given and following the bout, Connolly challenged Thomas to a return at 158lbs, £200 up to £500 a-side.

1909
5 January Sam Langford challenges Stanley Ketchel for the world 158lbs middleweight title, Ketchel to make any terms he liked, with Langford stating that if he failed to stop Ketchel inside ten rounds then Ketchel could have the entire purse – *Sporting Life*.

8 February On this day in London, the NSC introduced eight-named 'spread-weight' divisions and stipulated that English titles would, in future, be known as British titles. While the introduction of the new weight scales effectively 'killed' off the every two-pound class champions, the middleweight limit being set at 160lbs, the 158lbs class went on, at least in the in USA, more or less undisturbed for several more years.

158lbs to 160lbs (11 stone 4 lbs to 11 stone 6 lbs)
1872
3 February Jack Hicks w pts 3 Charley Davis (Stepney), 'The Beavers Arms', Bakers Row, Whitechapel Road, London. Interestingly, 'The Beavers Arms' adjoined the 'Pavilion Theatre'. The final of a silver cup middleweight competition, which was open to the world, in the previous round Hicks beat the veteran, Joe Rowe, while Davis beat Obe Atterbury. Both Hicks and Atterbury weighed about 132/133lbs, with Davis believed to be about 144lbs. At this period of time, anyone under 126lbs was considered as a lightweight – featherweight was also used – and from 126lbs up to 144lbs men were considered as middleweights. Anybody weighing above that was seen to be a heavyweight, depending who the reporter was.

13 July An article in *Bells Life* reported Charley Davis as the 161lbs middleweight champion, which was possibly a misprint for 147lbs.

1873
7 January Charley Davis w ko 14 John 'Scotty' McConnell (Glasgow, born Ireland), 'Professor' Albert Austin's Rooms, 10 Bloomfield Street, London. Scheduled for a finish, Davis weighing 160lbs to McConnell's 154lbs, the prize was the 154lbs Bow Cup and English championship, Strangely, the Bow Cup rules of five rounds, four of three minutes and a final round of four minutes, were ignored, as was the fact that Davis was badly out of condition and over the weight.

21 April Charley Davis w rtd 25 Ted Napper (Shoreditch), Grafton Street Hall, Soho, London. Articled to a finish for the 154lbs (limit) Bow Cup and English championship, Davis, weighing 147lbs, was billed as the English 160lbs champion. Napper weighed 141lbs.

6 December Charley Davis is the middleweight champion – *Bells Life*.
1875
12 January Jack Madden w pts 3 George Hope, The Hall of Science, St Lukes, Old Street, London. The final of a 160lbs (limit) heavyweight competition, in previous rounds, held on 26 and 28 December 1874, Madden, the son of the ex-boxer, Mike Madden, had beaten E. Burns and W. Watson, while Hope beat J.Reid before drawing the bye.

26 July 'Young' Griffiths w pts 3 Florrie Barnett, The Running Grounds, Hackney Wick, London. The final of a 160lbs (limit) heavyweight competition for a silver cup saw just three men entered. In the only semi-final, Barnett beat 'Young' Hope, while Griffiths drew the bye.

1876
22 January Joe Goss (Northampton) is the self-styled world middleweight champion, which almost certainly pertained to bare knuckles – *Bells Life*.

1880
28 August Denny Harrington challenges anyone at 154lbs to 160lbs – *Sporting Life*.
1887
26 October Jim Kendrick (Lambeth, born Ireland) w pts 3 Alf Mitchell (London, late Cardiff), 'Professor' Waites' Rooms, 1 Brewer Street, Golden Square, Soho, London. There were just three entries for Jem Mace's 160lbs middleweight competition and to reach the final Kendrick drew the bye, while Mitchell beat Tom Avis.

12 December Jim Young (Fulham) should be billed as the English 160lbs champion – *Sporting Life*.

1889
9 February Alf Ball (Deptford) is calling himself the English 160lbs middleweight champion – *The Sportsman*. However, both Ball and the ex-Guardsman, Alf Mitchell, were overweight for the 23 February 160lbs world championship competition.

23 February Charlie Bartlett (Canning Town) w rtd 1 (cut eye) Josh Alexander (South Woolwich), The Royal Aquarium, Westminster, London. The final of Frank Hindes' 160lbs world championship competition contested over four rounds, in previous legs Bartlett, 'The Meat Market Black', had a bye, then beat Ernie 'Smokey' Bishop, while Alexander beat Charlie Parish and J. Fenton. The *Sporting Life* commented on the really poor class of entrants for this competition, which made a mockery of the whole thing.

2 March Teddy O'Neil (Liverpool) challenges the world at 158 to 160lbs over 12 rounds, £50 or £100 a-side – *Sporting Mirror*.

16 March Alf Mitchell w pts 4 Charlie Bartlett, Royal Agricultural Hall, Islington, London. This was the last day of a six-day show, which was promoted by Charley White, 'The Dukes Motto', Charley Smith and Jack Baldock. The final of a catchweight competition, in previous rounds Mitchell beat Jim Richardson and Ted Burchell, while Bartlett beat two big men in Jack 'Baby' Partridge and Bob Wallis, both of whom had nothing but size.

1890
17 March Alf Ball drew 10 Harry Downie (Australia, born Edinburgh), The Ormande Club, Walworth Road, London. Made at 158 to 159lbs, 3pm weigh-in, for £200 and carrying no title billing, prior to the bout an agreement was made that if it went the distance it would be called a draw, which is what happened. Ball weighed 158lbs to Downie's 152.

3 December John O'Brien (Roath), the Welsh champion, challenges any man in England between 158lbs and 160lbs for £100 or £200 a-side – *Sporting Life*.

1891
3 January Alf Ball is the English 159lbs middleweight champion – *Sporting Life*.

7 March John O'Brien w ko 9 Ted White (Walthamstow), The Pelican Club, Gerrard Street, Soho, London. Referee: George Vize. Scheduled for 15 three-minute rounds at 160lbs for a £90 purse and using four-ounce gloves, while there was actual title billing, it was considered by the majority to involve the English 160lbs (limit) title and O'Brien's claim to this following his win over White (151lbs) was largely upheld. O'Brien weighed 159lbs.

28 May John O'Brien w ko 7 Alf Ball, The Pelican Club, Gerrard Street, Soho, London. This one was stipulated for a finish at catchweights with no title billing, but as both men had been claiming the 160lbs English title and although Ball, known as 'The Gypsy', weighed 167¾lbs, in what was final bout of his career, it seemed natural that O'Brien (156lbs) would press his claim to the English 160lbs title. This was in spite of, what for him, was the low weight of being two pounds under 158lbs and it was that weight class that he set his sights on. On 21 December of this same year, he won a 158lbs (limit) title bout.

1892
5 January Ted Fenton (Wood Green) challenges All-England at 160lbs to decide the English 160lbs (limit) championship, John O'Brien preferred – *Sporting Life*.

20 August Jim Hall (Sydney, Australia) w ko 4 Ted Pritchard (Lambeth) in a fight held on the Race Horse Training Ground, on the Sussex Downs, about four miles from Brighton. Brought forward from 22 August, scheduled for a finish, and billed for the world 158lbs title and although English title billing, which Hall (157lbs) was not eligible for. It could have only involved the Imperial British Empire title, which was unofficial. Pritchard also weighed 157lbs.

8 November Jim Hall is the world 158 to 160lbs middleweight champion according to the *Sporting Life*. This was repeated on 30 November. On 27 November, the paper stated that Hall and Bob Fitzsimmons (USA, late Australia and New Zealand, born England) were to meet to decide just who was world 158 to 160lbs champion for 40,000 dollars purse, winner take all.

30 November Arthur Akers (Leicester) challenges T. Gamble (Manchester) at 158 to 160lbs, £100 or £200 a-side and any number of rounds – *Sporting Life*.

30 November Ted Pritchard is the English 160lbs (limit) champion reported the *Sporting Life*. In the same issue, it states that Charlie 'Toff' Wall is the retired English middleweight champion.

22 December In the USA, the Bob Fitzsimmons v Jim Hall world 160lbs (limit) middleweight title bout is now set for 8 March 1893, but Fitzsimmons, who two weeks ago agreed to the bout being for the 160lbs (class) title, now wants it to be at 158lbs or catchweights. The pair reached an agreement to contest the bout at catchweights in five-ounce gloves, as Hall couldn't get down to 160lbs anymore. It was also agreed on a 40,000 dollars purse, 2500 dollars to the loser, the rest to winner – *Sporting Life*.

30 December Due to illness, John O'Brien has had to forfeit all of his 158 to 160lb engagements and may never box again – *Sporting Mirror*.

1893

4 January Bob Florrie challenges any middleweight in England for an NSC purse, Ted Fenton preferred – *Sporting Life*.

8 March Bob Fitzsimmons w ko 4 Jim Hall, The Crescent City AC, New Orleans, Louisiana, USA. Referee: 'Proffesor' Duffy. Scheduled for a finish at catchweights, it had originally been intended to be for the world 160lbs (limit) middleweight title. But, on it being found that neither man could make that weight, Fitzsimmons scaling 165lbs to Hall's 175, a catchweights bout was agreed. Yet, many newspapers still reported it as being for the world 160lbs title. It was later claimed that the bout was 'fixed' for Hall to lose and that might explain why he was so heavy, as he hadn't bothered to train.

21 November Ted Pritchard challenges All-England, £200 up to £500 a-side – *Sporting Life*. However, in the 5 December issue, it had been changed to All-England at catchweights and any middleweight in the world, bar Bob Fitzsimmons and Jim Hall. Then, in the 20 December issue, he was challenging the world at 158lbs, £500 a-side, and a contest against the heavyweight, Frank 'Paddy' Slavin (Australia).

1894

2 May John O'Brien challenges any middleweight in England up to the 160lbs (limit), £100 or £200 a-side, which was repeated in the 10 July issue of the *Sporting Life*.

22 May Ted Pritchard stated in the *Sporting Life* that he was not interested in boxing until the racing season was over, so John O'Brien can claim the English 160lbs (limit) title if he wants and he (Pritchard) will box him for it once the racing season is finished.

23 May John O'Brien stated that as Ted Pritchard had ignored his repeated challenges he was formally claiming the English 160lbs (limit) title and would defend it against anyone – *Sporting Life*.

19 June Ted Pritchard is the English 160lbs (limit) champion – *Sporting Life*.

28 June Ted Pritchard is the ex-English 160lbs (limit) champion – *Sporting Life*.

3 August Martin 'Buffalo' Costello (Australia, born USA) challenges Ted Pritchard or any 160lbs middleweight in England – *Sporting Life*. Interestingly, on 13 December 1893, Costello had got two years in prison for engaging in a prize fight in Roby, Indiana, USA, so one can only assume that he had been released.

26 November Ted Pritchard w ko 2 Dick Burge (Newcastle), The Eden Palace (formerly The Novelty Theatre), Great Queen Street, Holborn, London. Referee: Joe Steers, the ex-ABA heavyweight champion. Made at catchweights over ten rounds, but with a clause that Pritchard should not exceed 160lbs and Burge could be any weight, no weights were given. Agreed at £300 a-side, the men had argued for more than an hour over the choice of referee, until Joe Steers was agreed on. Burge 'walked' the first round, but was put down in the second and Pritchard, standing over him, hit him twice while down. The second time he was hit, Burge turned completely over and his head cracked the boards with a thud. Steers, instead of disqualifying Pritchard, counted Burge out, thus giving Pritchard the win. The bout was strongly suspected of being 'fixed' in order to bring off a betting coup, as so many of Burge's bouts seemed to be.

15 December 'Dido' Plumb (Balls Pond Road) w rsf 2 Jack Bryan (Drury Lane), Central Hall, Holborn, London. Referee: Robert Watson. Contested over four rounds, this was the final of Frank Hindes' English 160lbs (limit) championship competition. In previous rounds, Plumb beat Sid Robinson and Jack Hart, while Bryan beat Alf Perkins and 'Nobby' Peterson.

1895

2 February Ted Rich (Walworth) w ko 1 (90 seconds) Fred Greenbank (Hounslow), Central Hall, Holborn, London. Referee: B.J.Angle. The final of Frank Hindes' All-England 160lbs (limit) competition, contested over four sessions, in previous rounds Rich beat 'Paddy' Ryan (also in 90 seconds) and drew the bye, while Greenbank beat Jack Hart and Arthur Morris.

13 April Frank Craig (Harlem, NYC, New York) w rtd 1 John O'Brien, Central Hall, Holborn, London. Scheduled for 20 two-minute rounds, Craig was to have met Ted Pritchard over four three-minute rounds at 158lbs, but Pritchard was taken ill and O'Brien was drafted in as a last-minute substitute to box at catchweights. Unfortunately, O'Brien, who had been drinking in a pub, from which he had to be fetched, entered the ring blind drunk and had a job standing up before somehow getting through the first round, only to retire at the end of it. It was called the most disgraceful conduct ever seen by a boxer and would finish O'Brien's career, at least as far as London was concerned. This, to all intents and purposes, proved to be true. The 22 February issue of the *Mirror of Life* stated that O'Brien had lost his Welsh heavyweight title to Tom James (Aberaman) following the above bout with Frank Craig, but the James contest has not been traced.

10 September 'Sailor' Brown (USA) challenges Frank Craig, 'The Coffee Cooler', Dan Creedon (New Zealand), or any middleweight in England. Brown's full name was Charles Brown – *Sporting Life*.

9 October Ted Fenton w rsc 4 'Sailor' Brown, The Greyhound Hotel, Newmarket. Scheduled for 12 rounds, no weights were given or stipulated and there was no title billing. Brown, just weeks away from his 32nd birthday, had up to the last two to three years put together a creditable record in the USA, but was now past his best.

1896

23 October Dan Creedon w pts 20 Harry Baker (Chicago), Maspeth, NYC, New York, USA. Billed for the world 160lbs middleweight title, with both men spot on the weight, Creedon was down in first and saved by the bell at the count of five.

11 December Dan Creedon w rsc 9 Dick O'Brien, The Broadway AC, NYC, New York, USA. Referee: Dick Roche. Scheduled for 20 rounds and billed as a catchweight contest, O'Brien weighed 158lbs, but no weight was given for Creedon. Although O'Brien was inside 160lbs, the title Creedon was claiming, it was even advertised as non-title catchweight bout. One report stated that O'Brien had once again been training on ale. O'Brien was a notorious boozer, who just couldn't leave it alone, but in spite of this he was still a top-class fighter.

1897

12 January Dan Creedon w rsf 4 Jim Williams (USA), Albany, New York, USA. Billed as being for the world 160lbs title over 20 rounds, Creedon weighed 159lbs to Williams' 158.

22 March The *Sporting Mirror* reported that Dan Creedon was now boxing at 165lbs, with it being freely stated that he could no longer get down to 160lbs. However, he proved that statement wrong when, on 17 December of that year, he got down to 157lbs for a 158lbs title bout, but weakened himself in doing so.

23 June George Chrisp (Newcastle) w disq 12 'Starlight' (Australia), Ginnett's Circus, Newcastle. Referee: E.A.Humphrey. Made at 160lbs and scheduled for 20 rounds, E.W.Rollins, a negro boxing as 'Starlight', was disqualified for persistent holding. Chrisp weighed 158lbs.

22 September 'Starlight', the Australian negro, aged 46, challenges All-England at weights between 157 and 160lbs. In the same issue of the *Sporting Life*, Canning Town's Jack Welch (Welsh also given) challenged All-England at 160lbs, £5 a-side, but in the 13 December issue, the challenge was to George Chrisp or 'Paddy' Purtell (USA) at 160lbs, £50 or £100 a-side.

1898

2 January Jack Walsh challenges All-England at 160lbs over 10 or 20 rounds – *Sporting Life*.

16 March Dick Guthrie is the middleweight champion of Canada – *Mirror of Life*

23 March Dan Creedon is to retire as the result of an arm injury, but ruined himself with years of wine and women – *Mirror of Life*.

11 April George Chrisp, the English 160lbs (limit) champion, challenges the north of England at 160lbs, £500 or £100 a-side – *Sporting Life*.

11 April George Chrisp w ko 8 Jim Richardson (Honolulu, late Wood Green, London), The Standard Theatre, Gateshead. Billed in some reports as being for the English 160lbs (limit) title, both men came in at 158lbs

29 October Dick Burge challenges any 160lbs middleweight in England, £1000 a-side and best purse over 20 rounds. Burge had to go for a best purse as, since his 31 May 1897 bout with Tom Causer at the NSC, he was, in effect, barred from there because of his reputation for 'fight fixing', along with Charlie Mitchell – *Sporting Life*.

24 November Frank Craig w ko 12 George Chrisp, Ginnett's Circus, Newcastle. Referee: J.T.Hulls. Reported as being for the world 160lbs title over 20 rounds, with English title billing also given, for which Craig was not eligible. With neither man any longer considered to be in forefront of the world 160lbs division, it was, in reality, just an international bout. Craig scaled 158¹/₂lbs to Chrisp's 158.

1899

21 February Frank Craig, 'The Harlem Coffee Cooler', challenges any middleweight in the world, £100 a-side, Jack Bonner (Philadelphia) preferred – *Sporting Life*.

18 September Tommy Ryan (Syracuse, New York) w rsf 10 Frank Craig, Brooklyn, NYC, New York, USA. Scheduled for 20 rounds and made at 158lbs for the world title, Craig was unable to make that weight so it went on at catchweights. It is not certain whether both men were under 160lbs, but if they were Craig's flimsy claim at that weight would have passed to Ryan.

1901

19 March Pat Daley/Daly, the English 140lbs champion and winner of the English heavyweight championship competition, challenges Jack Scales (Bethnal Green) over 15 three-minute or 20 two-minute rounds, £100 or £200 a-side. Daley/Daly to be confined to 146lbs and Scales to 160 – *Sporting Life*.

22 April Harry Neumier (Stepney) w ko 4 Jack Scales, Wonderland, Whitechapel Road, London. Scheduled for six rounds, Scales being a claimant to the English heavyweight title, it was contested at catchweights. Both were about 160lbs, although Scales was possibly nearer 162lbs – *Sporting Life*. The *Mirror of Life* gave the result as Neumier winning by a first-round knockout.

27 April Harry Neumier challenges any 160lbs (limit) middleweight, 'Philadelphia' Jack O'Brien preferred, £50 a-side upwards – *Sporting Life*.

1902

31 January Jack Root w disq 7 George Gardner (Lowell, Mass, USA, born County Clare, Ireland), San Francisco, California, USA. Although made at catchweights, with no weights given or stipulated, the *Chicago Tribune* reported it as being for the American/world 160lbs title. Both were said to be over 158lbs, but again no actual weights were given.

25 March Jack Palmer (Benwell), 'The Pitmens' Champion', wanted to know why George Chrisp, after challenging All-England wouldn't accept his challenge from 156lbs up to 162, £20 a-side upwards. Chrisp, the claimant to the English heavyweight title and 30 years of age, hadn't fought since May 1901 and to all intents and purposes was retired – *Sporting Life*.

23 June Jack Palmer w ko 7 Dave Peters (Treorchy), Prince of Wales Circus, Merthyr. Referee: Tom Davis (Pontypridd). Billed for the English 158 to 160lbs (limit) title (158lbs limit also given), it was scheduled for 20 two-minute rounds. Although both the *South Wales Echo* and the *Western Mail* reported it as being an eliminator for the 160lbs (limit) title, the *Cardiff Evening Express*, which gave the result as w ko 8, called it a 160lbs (limit) title bout. However, it should be ruled out as a title bout as only two-minute rounds applied. In the seventh, Peters fell over the top rope and was counted out, which enraged the crowd who had been giving out cries of foul against Palmer throughout. Following that, the referee had to make his escape through 'The Vanguard Inn'.

1903

21 April Arthur Cripps (Brisbane, Australia) w pts 20 'Soldier' Jack Thompson, NSC, Sydney, Australia. Billed for the Australian

middleweight title held by Thompson, no weights were given or stipulated.

1905

27 April Charlie Wilson (Notting Hill) challenges All-England at 158lbs up to 172 – *Sporting Life*.

1906

12 September Pat O'Keefe (Canning Town) is the English 160lbs (limit) champion – *Sporting Life*.

10 November Charlie Wilson claims the English 160lbs title and was billed as such in the 28 November issue of the *Sporting Life*.

1907

6 April 'Young' Peter Jackson (USA) challenges the world at 158lbs upwards, £50 up to £200 a-side, Sam Langford preferred – *Sporting Life*.

1908

3 March Sam Langford w pts 8 Larry Temple, Boston, Mass, USA. Made at 158lbs and not over a title distance, it was noted because of the quality of the contestants. Although Langford was overweight, Temple was inside 158lbs.

19 June Jack Costello (Birmingham) challenges All-England at 160lbs – *Sporting Life*. The challenge was accepted by Charlie Allum (Notting Hill) on 11 July.

Jack Root

19 August An American article discusses 'The side stepping of Sam Langford' with Stanley Ketchel, Billy Papke, Jack 'Twin' Sullivan and Hugo Kelly all refusing to box him. While in England, Tom Thomas and Charlie Wilson both refuse to box a coloured man, but the truth of the matter was that Langford was far too good for any of them.

1909

11 February On this day in London, the NSC introduced eight-named 'spread-weight' divisions, which, in effect, ended the every two-pound classes, with 160lbs being named as the middleweight limit, the spread being from 147lbs. From hereon, English titles officially became British titles.

160lbs to 162lbs (11 stone 6 lbs to 11 stone 8 lbs)
1872

1 February Charley Davis (Stepney) w pts 3 'Bat' Mullins, Alec Keen's 'Victoria Tavern', Kilburn, London. The final of a 161lbs open competition for a £20 silver cup. With just four entries, in the previous round Davis beat Abe Daultry (w rtd 2), while Mullins forced Jim Gollagher (not Gallagher) to retire in the second round. This was stated to be only the second-ever glove competition held and the first at middleweight.

13 July Charley Davis is the 161lbs (limit) middleweight champion – *Bells Life.*

1882

26 April Joe Collins (Leicester), alias 'Tug Wilson', the English 161lbs middleweight champion, challenges any 161lbs man in the world. Collins also challenged Alf Greenfield for English heavyweight title – *Bells Life.*

1884

31 May Jack Massey challenges All-England at 162lbs, £50 or £100 a-side, or Jem Smith, Jack Kniveton and Bill Coddy at catchweights. All of the last three named accepted the challenge on 2 June, Kniveton beating Massey in a bare-knuckle catchweight bout on 10 July - *Sporting Life.*

1889

16 March Alf Mitchell (Kingsland, late Cardiff) w pts 4 Charlie Bartlett (Canning Town), Royal Agricultural Hall, Islington, London. The final of a catchweights competition, in previous rounds Mitchell beat Jim Richardson and Ted Burchell, while Bartlett, 'The Meat Market Black', beat two big men in Jack 'Baby' Partridge and Bob Wallis, both of whom had little but size. Both Mitchell and Bartlett were stated to be about 160 to 162lbs.

1 April Jim Haines (Lambeth) w rtd 1 (80 seconds) Jack Welland (Hackney), The Pelican Club, Denman Street, Soho, London. Contested over four rounds, this was the final of a catchweights competition. In previous rounds, Haines beat Elijah Ball and M.Moore, while Welland beat D. Tackrell and Jack 'Baby' Partridge. Prior to entering this competition, Wellard was a complete novice, having had just four boxing lessons from Charlie 'Toff' Wall. Haines weighed 162lbs.

27 April Bill 'Chesterfield' Goode (Shadwell) w pts 4 Teddy O'Neil (Liverpool), Royal Agricultural Hall, Islington, London. The final of a Ben Hyams' catchweight championship competition, in previous rounds Goode beat James Stewart (Glasgow) and Ted Burchell, while O'Neil beat Jack Davenport, 'The Black', and Josh Cosnett (Birmingham).

30 May Jim Haines w pts 4 Alf Bowman (Mile End), Her Majesty's Theatre, The Haymarket, London. The final of a Frank Hindes' catchweight championship competition with just four entries. In the previous round, Haines beat Charlie Bartlett and Bowman, the ABA heavyweight champion of 1889, beat Jim Richardson. Haines, a coloured man, weighed 162lbs.

8 June Jim Haines w pts 3 Jack Welland, The Pelican Club, Denman Street, Soho, London. Referee: Bob Watson. The final of a catchweights compeition, in previous rounds Haines beat Arthur Cooper and Harry Nickless, while Welland had the bye prior to beating Jack Watson. Haines weighed 162lbs. This was the Pelican Club's final show on these premises before moving to Gerrard Street.

27 August George LaBlanche (Canada) w ko 32 'Nonpariel' Jack Dempsey (USA, born Ireland), The California AC, San Francisco, California, USA. Made at catchweights under MoQ Rules and using five-ounce gloves, despite there being no title billing, LaBlanche (161lbs), 'The Marine', claimed the middleweight title after knocking Dempsey (151lbs) out. However, his claim was ignored by the California AC, who stated that as the bout was at catchweights, with LaBlanche seven pounds over the recognised middleweight limit of

154lbs, he had not won any such title. Also, there was much controversy over the winning blow, which came to be known a the 'pivot punch' because, after missing his opponent, the elbow came back with full force on the jaw and was considered illegal by just about everyone in the sport.

14 December Jack Welland w pts 4 Jim Richardson (Wood Green), Saddlers Wells Theatre, Clerkenwell, London. The final of a catchweight championship competition, in previous rounds Welland beat Charlie Bartlett and Elijah Ball, while Richardson beat Tom Longer, a 170lbs man, and Arthur Cooper.

1890

12 September Jim Haines, the 'coloured' champion of England, challenges all at 162lbs, no one barred – *Sporting Life.*

1891

4 April Jack Welland w pts 6 Jim Haines, Her Majesty's Theatre, The Haymarket, London. Referee: George Vize. The final of a catchweight competition, in previous rounds Welland beat 'Barney' Lambert and Charlie Bartlett, while Haines beat Jack 'Baby' Partridge and drew the bye.

1894

16 May The death of Jim Haines in the Middlesex Hospital, Tottenham Court Road, of cancer after lingering and painful illness was reported on this day. He was buried on Tuesday, 27 May in the Kensal Green Cemetery.

1 November Arthur Bobbett (Fulham) challenges All-England at 162lbs – *Sporting Life.* Four days later the challenge was accepted by Jack Welland. In the same issue of the *Sporting Life*, Bobbett's challenge was also accepted by two long-retired veterans in Charlie 'Toff' Wall and the ex-guardsman, Alf Mitchell.

1898

8 January George Chrisp (Newcastle) challenges Arthur Akers (Leicester) at 160 to 162lbs – *Sporting Life.* On 11 January, Chrisp was accepted.

8 October Jack Walsh (Canning Town) challenges All-England at 162lbs at the NSC or New Olympic Club, Berwick Street, Birmingham over 20 rounds – *Sporting Life*

1899

27 May Jack Welsh challenges the English 160lbs champion, George Chrisp, at 162lbs – *Sporting Life.*

29 August Joe Choynski (San Francisco, California, USA) w pts 20 'Australian' Jim Ryan, The Dubuque AC, Dubuque, Iowa, USA. Made at catchweights, with no stipulated weight, it was given billing as being for the world light-heavyweight championship – the first time this term had been used. However, as the bout was a substitution, it lost any credibility it may have had, if any. The promoter of the show, Lou Houseman, later became famous for creating the light-heavyweight division, but, in reality, he invented a new name for a division which in its early days was no more than another name for catchweights - bouts between men above 160lbs. Choynski weighed 158lbs to Ryan's 162.

1901

30 October Jack Root (Chicago) w ko 2 'Australian' Jim Ryan, Louisville, Kentucky, USA. Scheduled for 20 rounds and billed as being for the middleweight championship of the western States, both men were believed to be about 162lbs or over.

1902

25 March It was reported in the *Sporting Life* and *Mirror of Life* that Jack Palmer (Benwell), 'The Pitmens' champion', wanted to know why George Chrisp, after challenging All-England, refused to accept his challenge from 156 to 162lbs for £20 a-side upwards. Chrisp, 30 years old and a claimant to the English heavyweight title, hadn't fought since 20 May 1901 and was, to all intents and purposes, retired, although he later made comebacks in both 1903 and 1906. This was the last recorded challenge at 162lbs as men of this weight always seemed to be boxing at catchweights, thus making it almost impossible to record a true picture of the various classes above 160lbs. There were so few men marginally above that weight that the best of them tended to go for the heavyweight title.

162lbs to 164lbs (11 Stone 8 lbs to 11 stone 10 lbs)
1879

26 May Denny Harrington (London, born Ireland) w disq 2 'Florie' Barnett. Held in a railway arch near Snowfields, Bermondsey Street, The Borough, London. Referee: J.J. Enn. Using a ring measuring 13 foot by 16 foot, Harrington weighing 163lbs to Barnett's 161, it was billed as being for the 'United Kingdom' (First and last time this term was used for an actual report on a championship bout) 164lbs middleweight title. Catchweights was also given and it was reported to be for £50 a-side in the *Sporting Mirror* and £25 in the *Sporting Life*. Injured in training, Barnett, who entered the ring with a dislocated right shoulder which was bound up, was put down in the second round and his seconds entered the ring, thus getting him disqualified. In truth, he was down and out, but should never have been allowed to box with such an injury.

1886

3 December Jack Burke (London, England), known as 'The Irish Lad', is called the best 164lbs man in the USA by John L. Sullivan – *Sporting Mirror*.

1888

23 December In Australia, Jack Burke wrote a letter to the Melbourne *Sportsman* announcing his retirement from boxing.

1889

25 June Jim Hynds/Haines (Lambeth), the 'coloured' 163lbs champion of England, challenges All-England at that weight, £100 a-side, no one barred – *Sporting Life*.

14 August Ching Ghook (Shoreditch), the coloured scrapper, accepted Haines' challenge, but only if over eight rounds. The bout was arranged but fell through after Haines was stabbed in Battersea.

28 November Jim Haines claims to be the 'black' middleweight champion – *Sporting Life*.

1890

16 July Ted Fenton (Wood Green) w pts 12 Jim Burchell, The Greyhound Hotel, Newmarket. No weights were given or stipulated in a catchweight bout, where both were said to be 160 to 164lbs.

12 September Jim Haines, the coloured champion of England, challenges all at 162lbs, no one barred – *Sporting Life*.

1894

12 March Jerry Driscoll w disq 8 Ted Fenton, NSC, Covent Garden, London. Scheduled for 20 rounds at catchweights, Driscoll was said to be 157lbs, while no weight was given for Fenton.

16 May The death of Jim Haines, the coloured fighter, in the Middlesex Hospital, Tottenham Court Road of cancer was announced today. He had been in hospital for 11 weeks and had several operations. Haines was buried on 27 May at Kensal Green Cemetery.

11 October John O'Brien (Roath) challenges the world at 164lbs, Ted Pritchard or Frank Craig (New York) preferred – *Sporting Life*.

1898

23 May Arthur Akers (Leicester) w rsc 2 Bill 'Chesterfield' Goode (Shadwell), NSC, Covent Garden, London. Scheduled for 20 rounds at catchweights, Akers weighing 162½ to Goode's 162, it was made at 162lbs with no title billing and both were inside 164lbs.

5 September 5 Dick Burge (Newcastle) w ko 1 (1.05 seconds) Arthur Akers, The New Adelphi Club, Maiden Lane, The Strand, London. Referee: George T.Dunning of the *Sportsman*. Scheduled for 20 rounds at catchweights, no weights were given, but Akers was said to be over 14lbs heavier. With no title billing, it was stated to be a blatant 'fix', arranged by Burge and Charlie Mitchell (Birmingham), who seconded Burge. Mitchell was alleged to 'fix' almost every bout he touched and had also corrupted Burge, who, prior to the above fight, had been touring with the Harry Cullis Booth, as was Akers. It was reported that if Burge and Mitchell were allowed to continue as they were, the public would lose faith in boxing, of which the large majority of bouts were genuine.

1900

24 February Joe Walcott (NYC, born Barbados) w rsc 7 Joe Choynski (USA), The Broadway AC, NYC, New York, USA. Referee: Johnny White. Made at catchweights, Choynski (163lbs), the 5 to 1 on favourite, was down five times in the first round before being eventually stopped, having suffered a broken rib. Walcott weighed 140lbs. There was no title billing, but many years later it was stated that Walcott had claimed the world light-heavyweight title following this win, which he hadn't.

1905

27 April Charlie Wilson (Notting Hill) challenges All-England at 158lbs up to 172lbs – *Sporting Life*.

1906

27 April 'Seaman' E. Kelley (HMS Jupiter, Portsmouth) challenges

All-England at a limit of 164lbs, £10 a-side and best purse. Kelley had been boxing less than a year – *Sporting Life*.

26 May James 'Tiger' Smith (Merthyr) w ko 1 (2 minutes, 42 seconds) 'Seaman' E. Kelley, NSC, Covent Garden, London. Referee: J.H.Douglas. Scheduled for 20 rounds at catchweights, with no weights given, the inexperienced Kelley was proved to be woefully limited.

1909

11 February On this day in London, the NSC introduced the eight-named 'spread-weight' divisions, thus doing away with the various weight classes at every two pounds that went to make up the various English division. At the same time, English titles were renamed 'British'. This weight, like most above 160lbs, were mainly covered in the catchweight list as there were so few men above 160lbs who didn't fall into the heavyweight class and the few there were seemed content to box each other. The last big fight at the weight came on 28 April, in Brisbane Stadium, Australia, when Dave Smith (New Zealand), weighing 160lbs, outpointed Pat O'Keefe (Canning Town), weighing 164lbs, over 20 rounds. No weights were stipulated and no title billing was given.

164lbs to 166lbs (11 stone 10 lbs to 11 stone 12 lbs)

1890

3 October Jack Welland (Hackney) is now boxing in the 164 to 166lbs class, but will box Ted White (Walthamstow) at catchweights. The next day, White stated he was only 150lbs, but would meet Welland at 164lbs, £100 a-side – *Sporting Life*.

1891

4 April Jack Welland w pts 6 Jim Haines (Lambeth), Her Majesty's Theatre, The Haymarket, Westminster, London. The final night of Frank Hindes' seven-night catchweights competition, in previous rounds Welland beat 'Barney' Lambert and Charlie Bartlett, while Haines, who was coloured, beat Jack 'Baby' Partridge and drew the bye.

5 December Jack Welland w pts 7 Alf Bowman (Mile End), The Goodwin Club, Kingsland Road, Shoreditch, London. The final night of Ben Hyams' six-night competition tournament, in previous rounds Welland beat Ted Burchell and drew the bye', while Bowman, the 1889 ABA heavyweight champion, drew the bye, before beating Bob Baldwin.

1897

22 March Dan Creedon (New Zealand) w ko 4 Charley Strong (New York), The New Arena AC, 42nd Street, off Broadway, NYC, New York, USA. Referee: Walter DeBaun. Made at 165lbs, there was no title billing and it was freely stated that Creedon, the claimant of the world 160lbs title, could no longer get down to that weight.

15 April Arthur Akers (Leicester) accepted the challenge of Woolf Bendoff (London), but at 164lbs not 168lbs – *Sporting Life*.

1898

23 May Arthur Akers w rsc 2 Bill 'Chesterfield' Goode (Shadwell), NSC, Covent Garden, London. Contested over 20 rounds in a 17 foot ring, in a match made at 166lbs, Akers weighed 162lbs. Although no title billing was given, the £200 a-side (£20 also given) and a £200 purse totalling £600, proved it to be an important fight. It was Goode's comeback after eight years out of the ring.

1899

8 October The sudden death of Arthur Akers, aged 30, was announced, following a bout of pneumonia. He had been travelling with the booth of Harry Cullis and was thought to have caught a chill while on the booth. Besides being a top-class boxer, for the last seven years he had been a regular forward for Leicester rugby club. Akers left a widow, but no children.

1902

18 August George Gardner (Lowell, Mass, USA) w ko 17 Jack Root (USA), Salt Lake City, Utah, USA. Made at 165lbs, there was no title billing, but both were stated to be inside the weight.

1903

4 July George Gardner w ko 12 Jack Root, Fort Erie, Canada. Billed as being for the American/world 165lbs title, with both reported to be inside the weight. Gardner was also recognised as the 170lbs (limit) champion.

1905

27 April Charlie Wilson (Notting Hill) challenges All-England at 158lbs, up to 172lbs – *Sporting Life*.

20 December 'Philadelphia' Jack O'Brien w rtd 13 Bob Fitzsimmons, San

Francisco, California, USA. Scheduled for 20 rounds and billed as eliminator for the world heavyweight (catchweight also given) title, Fitzsimmons was the 170lbs champion. Despite winning, O'Brien never laid claim to either the 165lb or 170lb titles and within a year fought for the world heavyweight championship. However, years after his retirement from boxing O'Brien would claim to be the ex-world light-heavyweight champion and, indeed, appears in all the record books as a former 175lbs champion, which was the limit given to this division when the NSC formed the eight-named 'spread-weight' divisions in February 1909. The last two big fights at 166lbs appear to be those in Sydney, Australia between 'Cyclone' Johnny Thompson (USA) and Billy Papke (USA) in Sydney, Australia on 11 February 1911 and Papke against Dave Smith (Australia, born New Zealand) on 11 March 1911. With both scheduled for 20 rounds, Thompson, weighing 158lbs, stopped the 165lbs' Papke, while the latter knocked out Smith inside seven rounds. In 1912, the newly formed New York State Athletic Commission stated that it would recognize a 165lbs light-heavyweight division and Fireman Jim Flynn stated he was claiming same, but there is no record of any attempt by Flynn to defend this claim and the weight class finally died out.

166lbs to 168lbs (11 stone 12 lbs to 12 stone)
1879
27 November Denny Harrington (London, born Ireland) w disq18 Alf Greenfield (Birmingham), Lambeth Baths, London. With Harrington weighing 168lbs to Greenfield's 159, it was a catchweights bout but with no title billing and no weights stipulated. It was later stated to have carried world and English middleweight status.

1888
21 July Tom Longer (Clerkenwell) challenges All-England at 168lbs, £50 or £100 a-side – *The Sportsman*.

31 December Alf Mitchell (London, late Cardiff) w pts 12 Teddy O'Neil (Liverpool), Lyceum Theatre, Pembroke Street, Liverpool. With Mitchell weighing 161lbs to O'Neil's 168, it was variously billed as being for the 168lbs catchweight championship of England, the heavyweight championship of Lancashire and the catchweight 12 stone championship of Lancashire, despite Mitchell not being eligible to contest the championship of Lancashire as he was not resident there and not born there.

1891
27 January John O'Brien (Roath), the Welsh champion, challenges anyone in the world inside 168lbs, £100 or £200 a-side – *Sporting Life*.

1897
14 April Woolf Bendoff, weighing 168lbs, is now back in Britain and challenges All-England at the weight, no one barred, with Arthur Akers and George Chrisp preferred – *Sporting Life*. A day later, Akers accepted Bendoff's challenge, but at 164lbs.

30 April Walter Johnson (Boston, Mass, USA), a coloured man, challenges All-England at 168lbs – *Sporting Life*.

23 September James 'Tut' Ryan (Australia) challenges the world at 168lbs – *Sporting Life*.

1899
25 September Joe Choynski (San Francisco, California, USA) w ko 3 Jim Hall (Australia), The Nonpareil AC, Louisville, Kentucky, USA. Scheduled for 20 rounds, Choynski weighed 160lbs to Hall's 168lbs. Made at catchweights with no weight stipulated, it was also given world light-heavyweight title billing, but again with no weights given. One fight report stated that the kayo looked like a dive. A previous catchweight bout of Choynski's on 29 August 1899, when neither man was over 162lbs, also gave the same billing for what it was worth and that it was a substitute bout.

1900
12 January Charles 'Kid' McCoy (USA) w ko 4 Joe Choynski, NYC, New York, USA. Made at catchweights, with no weights given and no title billing.

11 October Joe Choynski announced his retirement from boxing, but was boxing again on 2 November and continued until 1904.

1901
23 January Jack Scales (Bethnal Green) challenges George Chrisp at 168lbs, £200 or £500 a-side, 15 or 20 rounds, for an NSC purse – *Sporting Life*.

1 October Pat Daley/Daly (London, born Ireland) challenges Jack Scales over 15 or 20 rounds, £50 or £100 a-side, at 168lbs – *Sporting Life*. A day later, Scales accepted the challenge.

1905
20 February Charlie Wilson (Notting Hill) challenges All-England up to 168lbs or Jack Scales at catchweights. This was repeated in the 27 April edition of the *Sporting Life*, but as 158lbs up to 172lbs.

1 December Harry Shearing (Walthamstow, late Canada) challenges All-England at 168lbs or over, as he can't get down below 168lbs – *Sporting Life*.

1906
14 November Harry Shearing challenges All-England at 154lbs up to 168lbs, no one barred. It is almost certain that 154lbs is a misprint – *Sporting Life*.

1908
9 June Herbert Synnott (Australia) challenges all at 168lbs – *Sporting Life*.

1909
11 February On this day in London, the NSC introduced eight-named 'spread-weight' divisions, in effect killing off the every two-pound classes. Also English titles were to be renamed 'British' titles. This division then lay dormant until revived in 1967 as the super-middleweight division.

168lbs to 170lbs (12 stone to 12 stone 2 lbs)
1881
1 December George Rooke (USA, born Ireland) w rtd 3 (sponge/towel) William McClellan (USA), Hunter's Point, Long Island Sound, New York, USA. Contested under London Prize Ring Rules, although called a catchweight bout the very same report stated that the American middleweight title was at stake. *The Sportsman* gave the result as w ko 3, while the *Sporting Life* reported it as w rtd 4. McClellan weighed 153lbs, while Rooke was 12lbs over the top middleweight class of 158lbs.

1887
19 July John F. Clow (Denver, Colorado, USA) challenges any 170lbs man in American, no one barred – *Sporting Life*.

14 November John F. Clow drew Frank Glover (Chicago, Illinois, USA) at about 170lbs, but no weights, venue, or number of rounds contested are known.

1889
27 January Joe Choynski (San Francisco, California, USA) w ko 14 Frank Glover, California AC, San Francisco, California, USA. With this win, Choynski, who was said to be making his pro debut despite having at least two recorded bouts prior to this, can be matched against any 170lbs man in American according to newspaper reports.

1891
28 February Owen Sullivan w rtd 22 Herbert Goddard, Melbourne AC, Australia. Both men scaled 170lbs with a £100 purse involved.

1892
1 February George Chrisp (Newcastle) w ko 4 Harry Downie (Edinburgh), Old Gaiety Theatre of Varieties, Nelson Street, Newcastle. Refereee: Dick Burge. Made at 170lbs for £25 a-side and a £30 purse, both men were inside, but actual weights were not given. There was no title billing attached for this 12 rounder.

1899
24 March Charles 'Kid' McCoy w pts 20 Joe Choynski, Mechanics Pavilion, San Francisco, California, USA. Referee: Jim Kennedy, a substitute for John L.Sullivan. Made at catchweights with no title billing, McCoy scaled 158lbs to Choynski's 169.

20 October Joe Choynski w ko 7 'Australian' Jim Ryan, NYC, New York, USA. Choynski scaled 169lbs to Ryan's 165.

23 October Joe Choynski w ko 3 Dick Moore, St Louis, Missouri, USA. Made at catchweights, no weights were given and no title billing was attached.

1900
17 December George Chrisp w ko 14 Harry Smith (Birmingham), Ginnett's Circus, Newcastle. Referee: T.W.Gale. Scheduled for 20 rounds at catchweights, it was also given English heavyweight title billing for £50 a-side and £60 purse (total £150). However, the stakes were not high enough for it to be a major title bout at this weight, £200 being minimum amount allowed in the rules. Chrisp weighed 170lbs to Smith's 163.

1901
20 May 'Philadelphia' Jack O'Brien w ko 11 George Chrisp,

Ginnett's Circus, Newcastle. Referee: George Dunning. Scheduled for 20 rounds, this was an international bout at catchweights for £855 in side stakes and £300 purse, with O'Brien (154lbs) betting £50 that he would beat Chrisp (170lbs) inside ten rounds. He also bet £75 to £50 that he would win inside the distance.

24 May   Marvin Hart (Louisville, Kentucky, USA) w ko 7 Dan Creedon (New Zealand). Made at catchweights, with Hart weighing 170lbs to Creedon's 169, following the fight the winner was claiming the American 170lbs title.

7 October   Marvin Hart challenges the world at 170lbs – *Sporting Life.*

1 November   Marvin Hart w ko 10 Jack Beauscholte (USA), Empire AC, Louisville, Kentucky, USA. Scheduled for 20 rounds, although there was no title billing given it was thought that both men were inside 170lbs, thus putting Hart's claim at risk.

17 December   'Wild' Bill Hanrahan (Louisville, late Brooklyn, born Ottawa, Canada) w rtd 5 Marvin Hart, Louisville, Kentucky, USA. Scheduled fo 25 rounds and involving the American/world 170lbs(12-2) title, Hanrahan took over Hart's claim at the weight on winning.

1902

16 January   The *Sporting Life* published a list of present day world champions and gave the 170lbs champion as 'Wild' Bill Hanrahan.

7 March   Joe Choynski w ko 5 'Wild' Bill Hanrahan, The Empire AC, Louisville, Kentucky, USA. With both men inside 170lbs, Choynski reclaimed the title at the weight.

24 March   'Kid' Carter (Brooklyn, NYC, New York, USA) w ko 1 Joe Choynski, Chicago, Illinois, USA. Despite being a mere six rounder at 165lbs, Carter took over Choynski's 170lbs title claim on the result.

18 April   The death of 'Wild' Bill Hanrahan from pneumonia in the County Hospital, Chicago, aged 20/21, was reported on this day. He had been about to enter the ring, when a doctor discovered he had temperature of 102 and had been in the hospital several days prior to his death.

3 May   Marvin Hart w ko 9 'Kid' Carter, Empire AC, Louisville, Kentucky, USA. Carter, whose real name was Edward Blaswick, lost his 170lbs American title claim in this one, with both men thought to be inside the weight.

1903

13 May   George Gardner (Lowell, Mass, USA) w pts 12 Marvin Hart, Louisville, Kentucky, USA. Billed as for the American/world 170lbs title, Hart, the holder, was six pounds over the weight so it went on at catchweights, but didn't stop Gardner (168lbs) from claiming the title.

25 November   Bob Fitzsimmons w pts 20 George Gardner, Mechanics Pavilion, San Francisco, California, USA. Billed for the world 170lbs (limit) light-heavyweight title, and made at 168lbs, give or take two pounds, Gardner lost his claim to Fitzsimmons, who stated that he broke the knuckles of both hands early on. The referee, Ed Graney, called it the worst fight he'd every seen as the crowd hissed and booed throughout. Gardner didn't seem to want to win and suffered knock downs in the fifth, 13th and 14th rounds, which cost him the fight.

Bob Fitzsimmons (right) poses with George Gardner before boxing his way to a 20-round points victory and winning the 170lbs title

1905

27 April   Charlie Wilson (Notting Hill) challenges All-England at 158 up to 172lbs – *Sporting Life*

1 December   Harry Shearing challenges All-England at 168lbs or over, as he can't get below that weight – *Sporting Life.*

20 December   'Philadelphia' Jack O'Brien w rtd 13 Bob Fitzsimmons, Mechanic's Pavilion, San Francisco, California, USA. Billed as an eliminator for the world heavyweight (catchweight also given) title - and indeed Bob Fitzsimmons (164lbs) fought for that title within a year – there was no mention of the 170lbs title held by Fitzsimmons (165lbs) being involved despite both men being inside that weight.

1909

11 February   The NSC in London, England introduced eight-named 'spread-weight' divisions on this day and the 170lbs class was absorbed into the 175lbs light-heavyweight division. In June 1912, the newly formed French-based IBU (International Boxing Union) recognised Sam Langford as the 170lbs (limit) light-heavyweight champion, with his five-round stoppage win over Jack O'Brien (166lbs) in NYC, New York on 15 August 1911, being the basis for recognition. Although Langford was the outstanding man around, he had weighed 173lbs for his fight with O'Brien, but, easy going, he never pushed any of his very strong title claims and the 170lbs weight class passed into the history books.

Catchweights

This term when used for men over 158lbs was, to all intents and purposes, just another word for heavyweights, but because, at least prior to 1905, so many men between 146 and 170lbs seemed to engage in catchweight bouts and because these men were not recognised as bona-fide heavyweights, it seems only fair to try and record their 'doings' and various title claims, etc, in this section. This invariably means repeating bouts that appear in other lists, but needs to be done in order to try and paint a clearer picture of just what was happening at the time. Note that light-heavyweights are also incorporated into this list.

1879

27 November   Denny Harrington (London, born Ireland) w disq 18 Alf Greenfield (Birmingham, born Northampton), Lambeth Baths, London. Made at catchweights with ordinary gloves under MoQ Rules and no weight stipulation, there was no title billing in the majority of reports. However, it was later stated to have carried world and English middleweight title billing, but with a difference of 18lbs between them and Harrington ten pounds over the recognised top-class of 158lbs for middleweight it doesn't really check out. Greenfield weighed 150lbs.

1881

1 December   George Rooke (USA, born Ireland) w rtd 3 (sponge/towel) William McClellan (USA), Hunters Point, Long Island Sound, New York, USA. Made at catchweights, with hard gloves and contested under London Prize Ring Rules, although called a catchweight bout, the very same reports state it to be for the Amercan middleweight title. *The Sportsman* gave the result as w ko 3, the *Sporting Life* says w rtd 4 and Rooke was 12lbs over the middleweight class of 158lbs, whilc McClellan weighed 153lbs.

1888

14 April   Bill 'Chesterfield' Goode (Shadwell) w pts 4 Ted Burchell (Shoreditch), Royal Agricultural Hall, Islington High Street, London. The final of Ben Hyams' English catchweight championship competition, in previous rounds Goode, reported to be a bit over 168lbs, beat Charlie Paris and 'Baby' Jack Partridge, while Burchell beat Sam Breeze and Mike Tanner.

4 June   Alf Mitchell (Kingsland, late Cardiff) w pts 4 (extra round) Alf Ball (Deptford), The Pelican Club, Denman Street, Soho, London. The final of a catchweight competition, there were only four entries, Mitchell beating Charley Hudson and Ball beating Josh Alexander in the semis.

27 June   Felix Scott (Liverpool) w pts 10 Jack Davenport, The Pelican Club, Denman Street, Soho, London. Billed for the English 'coloured' championship, no weights were given or stipulated. Scott was reported as the holder, while Davenport looked fully a stone (14lbs) heavier.

11 July   Albert Pearce (Newcastle) challenges Felix Scott, £25 (£50 also given) a-side, to a finish for the English 'coloured' 152lbs title. On 7 July in Liverpool, Scott won a 140lbs championship competition before being arrested for assault on a policeman some time previously and, on 1 August, Scott got 18 months in prison – *Sporting Mirror*.

8 December Charlie 'Toff' Wall (Hackney) w pts 4 Alf Mitchell, The Aquarium Theatre, Westminster, London. The final of Frank Hindes' English catchweights competition, in previous rounds Wall beat Ted Burchell and Mike Moore, while Mitchell beat Josh Cosnett and Jack Massey.

15 December Ted Burchell w pts 4 Alf Mitchell, Her Majesty's Theatre, The Haymarket, London. The final of a six-night Pelican Club English championship competition run by E. Wells and John Fleming, in previous rounds Burchell beat Joe Stubbins and drew the bye, while Mitchell beat Jim Young and T. Callaghan. Immediately following the competition, Mitchell accepted the challenge of Teddy O'Neil (Liverpool, born Ireland) to All-England at catchweights.

31 December Alf Mitchell w pts 12 Teddy O'Neil, The Lyceum Theatre, Pembroke Street, Liverpool. Billed for the catchweights championship of Lancashire, Mitchell, weighing 161lbs, was not a resident and therefore not eligible. O'Neil weighed 168lbs.

1889

16 March Alf Mitchell w pts 4 Charlie Bartlett (Canning Town), The Royal Agricultural Hall, Islington, London. The final of an English catchweights championship competition, in previous rounds Mitchell beat Jim Richardson and Ted Burchell, while Bartlett, 'The Meat Market Black', beat 'Baby' Jack Partridge and Bob Wallis. Mitchell and Bartlett were both about 160/162lbs, while Partridge was close to 168lbs and Wallis was around 182lbs. The last two named had little going for them other than size.

1 April Jim Haines (Lambeth) w rtd 1 (80 seconds) Jack Welland (Hackney), The Pelican Club, Denman Street, Soho, London. The final of a catchweight competition contested over four rounds, in previous rounds Haines (162lbs) beat Elijah Ball and Mick Moore, while Welland beat D. Tackrell and 'Baby' Jack Partridge. It was said that Welland was just a raw novice, who, prior to this competition, had received just four boxing lessons from Charlie 'Toff' Wall.

27 April Bill 'Chesterfield' Goode w pts 4 Teddy O'Neil, The Royal Agricultural Hall, Islington, London. The final day of Ben Hyams' six-day championship tournament, in previous rounds Goode beat James Stewart (Glasgow) and Ted Burchell, while O'Neil beat Jack Davenport, a coloured fighter, and Josh Coshnett (Birmingham).

30 May Jim Haines w pts 4 Alf Bowman (Mile End), Her Majesty's Theatre, The Haymarket, London. The final day of Frank Hindes' seven-day English catchweights championship competition, in previous round Haines beat Charlie Bartlett, a coloured fighter, while Bowman, the 1889 ABA heavyweight champion, beat Jim Richardson (Wood Green).

8 June Jim Haines w pts 3 Jack Welland, The Pelican Club, Denman Street, Soho, London. This was the club's last show of the season and their last show in Denman Street before moving into new premises. Referee: Robert Watson. In previous rounds, Haines beat Arthur Cooper and Harry Nickless, while Welland drew the bye and beat Jack Watson.

14 December Jack Welland w pts 4 Jim Richardson, Saddlers Wells Theatre, Clerkenwell, London. The final of an English catchweight championship competition, in previous rounds Welland beat Charlie Bartlett and Elijah Ball, while Richardson beat Tom Longer, a 170lbs man, and Arthur Cooper.

1890

21 April Jack Wannop (New Cross) w rtd 12 Josh Coshnett, The Ormonde Club, Walworth Road, London. This one was scheduled for a finish at catchweights with no weights given or stipulated and no title billing. Interestingly, the 36-year-old Wannop was more famous as a wrestler.

26 May Joe Choynski (San Francisco, California, USA) w ko 9 Jack Davis (Omaha, Nebraska, USA), San Francisco, California, USA. For $1,500 at catchweights, Choynski scaled 165lbs to Davis' 172lbs. There was no title billing given.

3 October Jack Welland is now boxing in the 164 to 166lbs division, but will meet Ted White (Walthamstow) at catchweights – *Sporting Life*.

1891

1 January Charlie Bartlett, the coloured middleweight, who is generally known as 'The Meat Market Black' or 'Meat Market Charlie' and, who has boxed in many catchweight competitions, has

now been ill for several months and is unable to follow his occupation – *Sporting Life*. Note that there was also another man of the same name and he also came from Canning Town, but fought at 112lbs.

4 April Jack Welland w pts 6 Jim Haines, Her Majesty's Theatre, The Haymarket, London. Referee: George Vize. The final night of Frank Hindes' seven-day championship competition, in previous rounds Welland beat 'Barney' Lambert and Charlie Bartlett, while Haines beat Jack 'Baby' Partridge and drew the bye.

5 December Jack Welland w pts 7 Alf Bowman, The Goodwin Club, Kingsland Road, Shoreditch, London. The final of Ben Hyams' catchweight competition, in previous rounds Welland beat Ted Burchell and drew the bye, while Bowman drew a bye before beating Bob Baldwin in the semi-final.

1893

8 March Bob Fitzsimmons (USA, formerly Australia and New Zealand, born England) w ko 4 Jim Hall (Sydney, Australia), The Crescent City AC, New Orleans, Louisiana, USA. Referee: 'Professor' Duffy. Scheduled for a finish, Fitzsimmons weighing 165lbs to Hall's 175lbs. Hall was also given as being 163$\frac{1}{2}$lbs. Made at catchweights, having originally been made for the world 160lbs middleweight title until both admitted they couldn't make the weight. Hall stated that he couldn't get anywhere near 160lbs, so a catchweight bout was agreed on. However, some reports still gave it as being for the world 160lbs title.

29 May Jim Hall w ko 7 Frank 'Paddy' Slavin (Australia), NSC, Covent Garden, London. Referee: George Vize. Made at catchweights, Hall's weight was given out as being 159$\frac{1}{2}$lbs, but was felt to be well above that. It later came to light that the bout was an out-and-out 'fix', arranged by Charlie Mitchell, the Birmingham middle-cum-heavyweight who was a friend of both men. The referee was far too lenient and should have nipped the whole sorry affair in the bud at an early stage. Charlie Mitchell, during the late 1880s into the early 1900s gained the reputation as a 'King of the Fixers' and gang leader. Any bouts in which Mitchell had dealings were, more often than not, considered to be 'shady' and it was Mitchell who was stated to have led Dick Burge off the straight and narrow when Burge joined up with him in the fixing of fights. Burge himself, engaged in several fixed bouts, but Mitchell, strangely enough, never did, although taking every advantage possible.

5 December Ted Pritchard (Lambeth) challenges All-England at catchweights – *Sporting Life*

20 December Ted Pritchard challenges Frank 'Paddy' Slavin at catchweights, £500 a-side – *Sporting Life*.

1894

16 May Jim Haines died on this day, from cancer, in the Middlesex Hospital, Tottenham Court Road, London, following a lingering and painful illness in which he spent 11 weeks in hospital undergoing several operations. He was buried at Kensal Green on 27 May – *Sporting Life*.

20 October Ted Fenton (Wood Green) w pts 4 Arthur Morris (Fulham), The Central Hall, Holborn, London. Referee: J.T. Hulls. The final of Frank Hindes' catchweight competition, in previous rounds Fenton beat Mike Moran and Charlie Hensley, while Morris beat W. Durling and C. Marney.

1897

14 April Woolf Bendoff (London), weighing 168lbs, is now back in the UK and challenges All-England at catchweights, no one barred – *Sporting Life*.

30 November Arthur Akers (Leicester) w disq 1 'Paddy' Purtell (Kansas City, Missouri, USA), The Olympic Club, Berwick Street, Birmingham. Referee: J.S.Barnes. Scheduled for 20 rounds, Akers weighing 170lbs to Purtell's 160, it was made at catchweights, £500 a-side and a £200 purse, with no title billing attached. Purtell, blind drunk and taking a beating, was rescued when his seconds threw in the towel, then climbed into the ring, thus getting their man disqualified. This bout finished Purtell as a fighter as far as England was concerned and, just like Dick O'Brien (Canada), he was a good class fighter who just couldn't lay off the 'booze', which ruined his career.

17 December Charles 'Kid' McCoy (USA) w rtd 15 Dan Creedon (New Zealand), Long Island, New York, USA. Made at catchweights, with given weights stated to have been manufactured in order to give the bout credence as a world 158lbs (limit) middleweight title bout, the weights of the men were announced as McCoy 155$\frac{1}{2}$lbs and Creedon 157lbs. In reality, McCoy came in at 160lbs to Creedon's 165. It was later stated that if Creedon had got down to the given weight for him, he would have badly weakened.

1898

5 September Dick Burge (Newcastle) w ko 1 Arthur Akers, The New Adelphi Club (formerly The Old Cyder Cellers), Maiden Lane, The Strand, London. Referee: George T. Dunning. Scheduled for 20 rounds and made at catchweights for £1000, Akers, over a stone (14lbs) heavier, was beaten in just 105 seconds. In the aftermath, this was stated to be a blatant 'fix' arranged by Dick Burge and Charlie Mitchell, a man who was alleged to 'fix' every bout he touched. Mitchell had acted as a second to Burge, who had been travelling with Harry Cullis' booth, as had Akers. The papers openly reported that if Mitchell and Burge were allowed to continue as they were, the public would lose faith in boxing, of which the large majority of bouts were genuine. This was later stated to be only time Akers ever took part in a 'fixed' bout, other than 'gee' bouts on the booths.

1899

24 March Charles 'Kid' McCoy w pts 20 Joe Choynski, Mechanics Pavilion, San Francisco, California, USA. Referee: Jim Kennedy, a substitute for John L. Sullivan. Made at catchweights, McCoy weighed 158lbs to Choynski's 169.

18 August Jack McCormick (Philadelphia, Pennsylvania, USA) w ko 1 Charles 'Kid' McCoy, Chicago, Illinois, USA. A six rounder at catchweights, McCoy was caught cold by a 'sucker' punch. McCormick was thought to weigh about 175lbs, but no weights were given out.

14 September Jack Scales (Bethnal Green) challenges All-England at catchweights, four-ounce gloves, £25 up to £100 a-side, an NSC purse and over 15 or 20 rounds, George Chrisp preferred – *Sporting Life*.

27 September Charles 'Kid' McCoy w disq 8 Jack McCormick, The Lennox AC, NYC, New York, USA. Scheduled for 20 rounds at catchweights, McCoy gave McCormick a brutal beating and could have knocked him out any time he wished, choosing instead to prolong McCormick's suffering, which was the reason McCoy was so unpopular with the fight fans. In the eighth round, McCormick, in a bad way, went down without being hit and was disqualified. The ending was also given as a technical knock-out and a referee's stoppage.

29 September Jack Walsh (Canning Town) challenges All-England at catchweights, ten up to 20 rounds and an NSC purse – *Sporting Life*. Note that this was a different man from Jack Walsh (Brentwood).

1900

11 February Dick Burge challenges All-England at catchweights – *Sporting Life*.

10 March Pat Daley/Daly challenges All-England at catchweights, £200 a-side and no one barred – *Sporting Life*.

5 July Pat Daley/Daly, who is now on tour with Arthur Cannon's booth, has put on a lot of weight so challenges 'Dido' Plumb or Jerry Driscoll at catchweights over 20 rounds, £100 a-side and an NSC purse – *Sporting Life*.

11 October Joe Choynski announces his retirement from boxing, despite boxing again on 2 November – *Sporting Life*.

12 November George Chrisp challenges any man in the north at catchweights, Harry Smith (Birmingham, born Stoke) preferred, over 20 three-minute rounds and £25 a-side – *Sporting Life*.

17 December George Chrisp w ko 14 Harry Smith, Ginnett's Circus, Newcastle. Referee: T.W. Gale. Scheduled for 20 three-minute rounds, Chrisp weighing 170lbs to Smith's 163, it was contested at catchweights, £50 a-side and a £60 purse. It was also given English heavyweight title billing, which Chrisp had a claim to, but the money involved was not high enough for a major title bout.

1901

22 April Harry Neumier (Stepney) w ko 4 Jack Scales, Wonderland, Whitechapel Road, London. Contested over six rounds at catchweights, Scales was, at this time, one of several men claiming the English heavyweight title.

20 May 'Philadelphia' Jack O'Brien (USA) w ko 11 George Chrisp, Ginnett's Circus, Newcastle. Referee: George T. Dunning of the *Sportsman*. Scheduled for 20 rounds, O'Brien weighing 154lbs to Chrisp's 170, it was an international bout at catchweights, £825 in side stakes plus £300 purse. O'Brien had also bet £50 that he would win inside ten rounds and £25 to £50 that he would win inside the distance.

25 June 'Philadelphia' Jack O'Brien w ko 6 Harry Neumier, Ginnett's Circus, Newcastle. Scheduled for 20 three-minute rounds, it was an international bout at catchweights with no weights given.

23 September Jack Scales w ko 11 Jack Palmer (Benwell), Ginnett's Circus, Newcastle. Referee: George T Dunning. Scheduled for 20 rounds, Scales weighing 175lbs to Palmer's 164, and made at catchweights, £50 a-side and £70 purse, there was an objection lodged by Palmer's backer that the count was only five seconds. However, the referee's verdict stood.

4 October Dave Peters (Treorchy), the Welsh champion, challenges the winner of the Jack Palmer v Harry Smith bout at catchweights, £25 or £50 a-side – *Sporting Life*.

7 October Jack Palmer w ko 7 Harry Smith, The County AC, Leeds. Referee and promoter: Jack Haggerty. Scheduled for 12 rounds at catchweights, it was for £25 a-side and a £40 purse.

23 October Pat Daley/Daly challenges all, no one barred – *Sporting Life*.

11 November Jack Palmer w ko 11 Jim Styles (Marylebone, London), Ginnett's Circus, Newcastle. Referee: J. Smoult. Scheduled for 20 three-minute rounds at catchweights, £25 a-side and £70 purse, and contested in four-ounce gloves, no weights were given but reports state that Palmer was 12lbs heavier.

14 November Harry Smith w rsf 4 Dick Moore (Philadelphia, Pennsylvania, USA, born Tipperary, Ireland), The Gymnastic Club, Dale Street, Liverpool. Referee: Tom Gamble. Scheduled for 20 two-minute rounds, it was an international catchweight bout for £25 a-side and £40 purse, but no weights were given. Moore, another top American fighter renowned for his drinking habits, was stated to be drunk before he entered the ring. Ruined by drink, it was Moore's 11th loss by stoppage in his last 16 bouts, 13 of which he'd lost.

1902

31 January Jack Root (Chicago, born Austria) w disq 7 George Gardner (USA, born Ireland). Made at catchweights and billed for the American/world catchweight title, with no weights given or stipulated, even though it was reported as a title bout. Both men were over 158lbs.

16 April Jack Scales challenges Jack Palmer at catchweights, £25 or £50 a-side – *Sporting Life*.

18 August George Gardner w rsf 17 Jack Root, Salt Lake City, Utah, USA. Made at catchweights, no weights were announced.

1903

23 February Jack Mullen (Wrekenton) w ko 11 George Chrisp, Ginnett's Circus, Newcastle. Referee: J.A. Smith. Articled for 15 rounds at catchweights, £50 a-side (£25 also given), plus an £80 purse. Although both were around 172lbs, no actual weights were given. It was the comeback of Chrisp, who, prior to his retirement, had a claim to the English heavyweight title.

22 April Jack Root w pts 10 Charles 'Kid' McCoy, Light Guard Armoury, Detroit, Michigan, USA. Referee: Bat Materson of 'Wild West' fame. Despite being billed for the American/world 175lbs light-heavyweight title, McCoy weighing 173lbs to Root's 168, it was not over a recognised championship course.

4 July George Gardner w ko 12 Jack Root, The International AC, Fort Erie, Ontario, Canada. Scheduled for 20 rounds and given billing as involving the world 175lbs title, in the first report published it was misprinted as 165lbs.

1905

20 February Charlie Wilson (Notting Hill) challenges Jack Scales at catchweights or for an All-England 168lbs title – *Sporting Life*.

1906

14 February 'Philadelphia' Jack O'Brien is the world light-heavyweight champion at 163lbs – *Sporting Life*

19 December Jack Palmer challenges all at 176lbs – *Sporting Life*.

1908

18 August Stanley Ketchel (Grand Rapids, Michigan, USA) w ko 2 Joe Thomas (USA), San Francisco, California, USA. Made at catchweights, Thomas was believed to have been restricted to 172lbs, while Ketchel came in at 168.

1909

11 February On this day in London, the NSC introduced eight-named 'spread-weight' divisions, one of them being the light-heavyweight division, which started at 160lbs and ran to 175lbs, a spread of 15lbs. This decision would, in effect, bring an end to catchweight bouts having a major influence on a wide spread of weight classes.

Highlights from the 2003-2004 Amateur Season

by Chris Kempson

It was another good season overall, both domestically and also on the international stage. A teenage lightweight, Amir Khan, stole all the headlines in this country by becoming the sole Briton to qualify for the Olympic Games in Athens in August. Similarly, a young Irishman, southpaw middleweight, Andy Lee, did likewise for the Emerald Isle. An extremely difficult task to win through to Athens, it will be even harder for them once they both start to box there, but all credit to them and the amazing potential they each have. We will follow their progress with considerable interest, but first please join me as we look at all the other fine boxers who made this season one to remember.

JULY

England once again covered themselves in medal glory at the annual International Junior Olympics at the Louisiana Convention Center in Alexandria, Louisiana in the United States, from 23 June-8 July. The 12-strong team came home with four golds, a silver and seven bronze. One of England's gold medallists for 15/16 year-olds was the teenage sensation from Bury ABC, Amir Khan, but there is so much more about him to follow.

At senior level there were no medals for Britain or Ireland at the 12th World Championships held in Bangkok, Thailand from 6-12 July. The chasm between most of the British and Irish boxers and the rest of the world is huge, but England's Darren Barker at welterweight and Ireland's light-heavyweight, Kenneth Egan, fell just short of a medal, both being eliminated in their quarter-finals.

Ireland defeated Canada 6-4 in a junior international at the Ringside Club in Dublin on 16 July in the middle of a heatwave.

England rounded the month off in fine style, claiming six medals from their eight-strong team at the Brandenburg Cup under-19 multi-nations in Frankfurt/Oder in Germany from 17-20 July. England secured two silvers and four bronze in what was the eighth staging of this tournament, with boxers from 16 countries competing.

AUGUST

The successful run of Bury's brilliant Amir Khan continued with a gold medal success at lightweight (60 kgs) in the European Cadet (under-17) Championships in Kaunas, Lithuania from 1-9 August. Khan beat four Eastern Europeans for gold and also won the 'Best Boxer of the Championship' award and the prestigious Ahmert Comert Cup for the 'Most Outstanding Performance'. He is clearly a young man to watch.

On the domestic front, Scotland announced a new Championship for 17 to 19 year-olds.

Success was distributed well in the third Common-wealth Federation Championships, staged at the Titiwangsa Stadium in Kuala Lumpur, Malaysia from 25 August – 1 September. For England, their super-heavyweight, David Price (Salisbury), won gold, Don Broadhurst of Birmingham Irish and Mick O'Connell (Marines) each secured silver, at fly and heavy, respectively, while light-flyweight James Fowl (Haileybury), middleweight Neil Perkins (Kirkdale) and light-heavyweight Tony Davies (Army) each took bronze. Northern Ireland fared well too, with silvers for Martin Lindsay at feather and Eamonn O'Kane at middle, and a bronze for Paul Baker at flyweight. Scotland weighed in with a bronze from their super-heavyweight, Ian Millarvie; while Repton's Tony Cesay won a bronze for Sierra Leone in the light-welterweight division, which was the West African nation's first boxing medal at a major international championship.

While back in Europe, England's juniors acquitted themselves very well indeed, winning four bronze medals at the European Junior Championships in Warsaw, Poland from 23-31 August. England's medals came from Stephen Smith (bantam), Frankie Gavin (feather), John O'Donnell (light) and Tony Jeffries (middle). Once again the Eastern European nations dominated the medal table.

SEPTEMBER

This month proved to be a quiet one in terms of competitive action, as clubs at home were preparing for their new domestic season. On the international front a short rest period was being taken after several months of hectic competitive action, although Scottish boxers were in action at the Nationen Cup in Neustad, Austria from 26-28 September. This was a low-key tournament where, curiously, Craig McEwan won gold at 71kgs, a weight abolished on 1 January 2003. Ian McCabe gained silver at flyweight, while junior prospect, Willie Bilan, took silver in the under-19 category at lightweight.

OCTOBER

Ireland made the trip to France where they met with defeat in both their international matches. First of all they went down 6-4 in Bastia on the island of Corsica on 3 October and then narrowly lost 5-4 (plus one bout void) at Toulon three days later. Later in the month, on 27 October, Ireland drew 3-3 with Holland in Rotterdam.

The preliminary stages of the Irish under-21 championships took place on 10 and 11 October, with the finals staged at the National Stadium on 17 October.

At the 24th Tammer multi-nations tournament held in Tampere, Finland from 16-19 October, the Welsh heavyweight, Kevin Evans, and England's light-heavyweight, Tony Davies, both won gold. Wales also lifted two bronze, via the fists of Darren Edwards (feather) and Matthew Edmonds (fly), respectively, while England's super-heavyweight, David Price, also got a bronze as did Scotland's Mark Hastie at lightweight. In all, 91 boxers from 19 nations boxed in Tampere.

NOVEMBER

In Trondheim, Norway, on 1 November, an experimental England team were just edged out by four bouts to three by the host nation, in a match which contained one junior contest and six senior bouts.

The United States team came to London town on 3 November. To be precise they visited the York Hall at Bethnal Green, which was the first open-show international against the USA to take place in London since 1961. Much credit for this imaginative action was due to the London ABA and, in particular, to its Honorary Secretary, Keith Walters. England won the day 6-4 and then proceeded to thump their American visitors 9-0 at the Everton Park Sports Centre on Merseyside three days later.

Ireland performed well in the multi-nations tournament held at the Rochester Park Hotel in Cork from 4-7 November, winning three golds, seven silver and three bronze. Eight countries took part, including the United States.

Bury's incredible Amir Khan won gold in the inaugural European Student Championships for boxers aged 16, in Rome from 10-15 November, in the lightweight division. England also won four other medals, via Tom McDonagh with a silver at 70kgs, and three bronzes which went to Joseph Murray (46kgs), Luke Campbell (48kgs) and James McElvaney (54kgs). Ireland, too, did well at this tournament, gaining a total of six medals. Gold went to David Joyce who beat Tom McDonagh on countback in the 70 kilos final, while Carl Frampton collected silver at 50kgs and bronzes went to Joe Joyce at 52 kilos, David Oliver Joyce at 54 kilos, John McDonagh at 57 kilos and Keith Boyle at 66 kilos.

Wales defeated Norway 5-3 in their opening international foray of the season on 15 November at the Penyrheol Leisure Centre in Swansea.

The early rounds of the Ulster Senior Championships were boxed off on 18 and 20 November, with the finals taking place on 24 November before a large Ulster Hall audience.

England middleweight, Ricardo Samms, won a bronze medal at the Copenhagen Cup event in Denmark from 26-29 November, while Fitzroy Lodge's Scott McDonald was eliminated at the 48kgs quarter-final stage on his senior England debut.

At Ipswich, on 26 November, Ireland won 7-6 over their English hosts in a schoolboy international.

DECEMBER

Not content with having beaten their Australian counterparts in the Rugby Union World Cup Final 'Down Under', England's amateurs thumped the Aussies twice in three days in mixed bouts in London on 1 and 4 December, respectively. On the first occasion at the Wembley Conference Centre, England triumphed 9-3 in a junior/senior match and followed this up with a 9-2 success in a junior/youth/senior encounter at the National Sports Centre Gym at Crystal Palace. The only disappointment being the abysmally small attendances at each venue.

Once again this month saw the finals of the NACYP Championships. The Class 'A' finals took place at Retford Town Hall, Nottingham on 4 December, the Class 'C' finals followed on 10 December at the Royal Lancaster Hotel in London, while the Class 'B' finals were boxed off at the Adelphi Hotel in Liverpool on 17 December, on a Vauxhall Motors ABC-organised dinner show.

The finals of the Irish Senior Championships were held at the National Stadium in Dublin on 19 December, the earlier rounds having taken place on 5,6,12 and 13 December.

The finals of the National Novice Championships were held at their now traditional home at Knottingley Leisure Centre in West Yorkshire on 20 December.

JANUARY

As soon as the New Year had been ushered in, attention began to focus clearly on the difficult qualifying process for the Athens' Olympic Games in August. There were to be four international qualifying tournaments for boxers from Europe.

England triumphed in a schoolboy international over Ireland 8-5 at Westport, County Mayo on 7 January, to get their year off to a flying start.

There was medal success for English, Scottish and Irish boxers in the Norway Box Cup held in Oslo from 9-11 January. Birtley Police Boys middleweight, Gary Barr, landed silver for England and there were bronzes at welterweight for Tom Coward (Wombwell and Dearne) and at heavyweight for Sam Sexton. Scotland's Kenneth Anderson took gold in the light-heavyweight division, while fellow Scot, Mark Hastie, won silver at lightweight. Two other Scots, James Ancliff (feather) and James Cusick (light-welter), each took bronze. Ireland's Fergus Turner won silver in the welterweight category and Katie Taylor clinched gold for the Emerald Isle in the Women's 60kgs final.

Once more Bury ABC's Amir Khan, who lives in Bolton, stole the international headlines when he won another gold medal, on this occasion at the Adidas Box Gala in Germany from 9-11 January.

Khan, who turned 17 last December, is too young to enter the ABA Senior Championships, but is old enough for international competition, including the Olympics. In what was his first taste of senior competition, Khan was named, not surprisingly, 'Best Technical English Boxer'. Such an award was made to each country. Other medals were distributed as follows: Fisher's bustling welterweight, Sam Webb, got a gold, while the Army's Tony Davies and Ireland's Marvin Lee had a share of gold in the light-heavyweight class. Cleckheaton Academy featherweight, Gary Sykes, also did well in this tournament, winning two out of three bouts in a round-robin tournament that also involved boxers from Germany and Lithuania.

Craig Lyon was England's only representative in the 48th Istvan Bocksai Memorial multi-nations event in Debrecen, Hungary from 14-17 January. The Wigan light-flyweight was a narrow loser in the quarter-finals to the eventual gold medallist, Viacheslav Gojan, from Moldova.

Next up was the Gee Bee multi-nations tournament in Helsinki, Finland from 17-19 January and it was a competition in which Irish and Scottish boxers really excelled. There were golds for Ireland's Eric Donovan and Kenneth Egan at 54kgs and 81kgs, respectively, and also one for Scotland's Craig McEwan at 69 kgs. Silver went to Ireland's Paul Hyland at 51kgs, with Scotland's James Ancliff doing likewise at 54kgs. Stewart Langley got England's only medal, a bronze at 51kgs, while Ireland's Andrew Murray captured a bronze at 60kgs, with two Scots, James Cusick and Kenneth Anderson, also securing a bronze each at 64kgs and 81kgs, respectively.

In an international match on 18 January, comprising juniors and cadets, Ireland were beaten 6-3 by France at Dublin's National Stadium.

The finals of the Welsh ABA Senior Championships were staged at the Ebbw Vale Leisure Centre on 31 January, the preliminaries having taken place at the Newport Centre on 10 and 11 January.

FEBRUARY

Ireland had a 'win double' over Scotland on 20 and 22 February, respectively. On the first date, at the National Stadium in Dublin, they triumphed 7-3, while on the second occasion, at the Brandon House Hotel in New Ross, Wexford, the score was 5-3 in their favour. England Under-19s also scored their own double triumph, with victories over their German counterparts, firstly by 8-2 at Lowestoft on 18 February and then following a scoreline of 6-2 in Basingstoke, two days later.

The 35th European Senior Championships in Pula, Croatia from 19-29 February – our first Olympic qualifying tournament – produced a magnificent bronze medal for the Irish middleweight, Andy Lee, from the St Francis' club in Limerick. It provided the very talented southpaw, a former Repton club member in his early days in London, with entry to the Athens Olympics. The 19-year-old Lee won three times to reach the last four and guaranteed himself an automatic trip to Greece.

The Irish Intermediate Championships culminated with finals night at the National Stadium in Dublin on 27 February, earlier rounds having been boxed-off on 6,7,13, 14 and 21 of that month.

MARCH

England Under-19s did not fare so well in their return engagement with Germany, losing the first match 8-4 in Duren on 5 March, but improving somewhat two days later in Schriesheim to win four bouts, as did their German hosts, with one bout given as a draw.

The annual Scottish ABA Senior finals went ahead at the Monklands Time Capsule in Coatbridge on 26 March. Twenty-four hours later, the ABA Senior finals took place at the Wembley Conference Centre before a very small audience. This did nothing to fortify the status of this event, which seems to be diminishing in prominence year by year; not least by the non-participation of a number of top prospects, often due to international duties and the like. Their absence from the ABA Senior Championship is worrying and, in many respects, almost falsifies the credentials of some who win the national title in a substantially limited field.

The London ABA polled five champions. Scott McDonald (Fitzroy Lodge) at 48kgs; Stewart Langley (Hollington) at 51kgs; Matthew Marsh (West Ham) at 54kgs; Murtala Abdusalem (St Pancras Kronk) at 81kgs and, finally, 'Mighty' Joe Young (Repton) at 91kgs+, a former sparring partner of no less than 2000 Olympic gold medallist, Audley Harrison, MBE, also once of Repton fame.

On 27 and 28 March, also staged in London, at the Goresbrook Leisure Centre in Dagenham, the 57th National Schoolboy Championships were boxed-off.

APRIL

The finals of the Senior Four Nations tournament took place in Glasgow's Kelvin Hall on 3 April, the semi-finals being held there the previous day. England topped the medal table with five golds, followed by Ireland with four, with one each for the hosts, Scotland, and Wales.

Seventeen-year-old Amir Khan ensured Britain will have a boxer at August's Olympic Games in Athens, when he unbelievably struck gold at the Strandja Cup qualifying tournament in Plovdiv, Bulgaria from 30 March - 4 April. Khan avenged his European Senior Championships loss to Georgia's Kashia Avtandil, stopping Armenia's Bagrat Avoyan and then clinched his Athens place with a semi-final victory over Romania's Adrian Alexandru, all finalists qualifying for the Olympics. He got his gold medal on a walkover when his opponent from Azerbaijan, Rovshan Husynov, withdrew. The college student who is too young to box in the ABA Senior Championships also received the Strandja Cup prize for 'Best Boxer'.

The two remaining Olympic qualifying tournaments in Gothenburg, Sweden from 20-25 April and in Baku, Azerbaijan from 27 April – 2 May were not fruitful for British and Irish boxers, although the Irish heavyweight, Alan Reynolds, went close in Gothenburg and Darran Langley (light-flyweight) and Neil Perkins (welterweight) were also unlucky, for England, in the latter tournament.

England's five-man team at the junior multi-nations event in Wloclawek, Poland from 26 April-2 May, all came home with a medal. Gold went to South Durham's Bradley Saunders in the 57kgs category and also to Danny Price (Westway Eastfield) at 81kgs. The two silvers were claimed by Rotunda's Stephen Smith at 54kgs and Dale Youth's James Degale in the 75kgs category. Bronze went to welterweight, Joe Selkirk, from Rotunda.

In an international match held in Austria, on 23 April, Scotland defeated their hosts 5-3, with one contest given as a draw.

MAY

The Scottish Cadets Championships (for boxers born 1988-89) took place on 1 May at the Town Hall in Grangemouth.

The month was indeed a busy one, with three prestigious international tournaments taking place within ten days. First up was the President's Cup multi-nations for cadets (under-17) in Baku, Azerbaijan from 7-10 May. England scooped four medals, a gold and three bronze. Travis Dickenson (66kgs) from Birtley Police Boys won gold, while Paddy Jones (48kgs), Aaron Fletcher (63kgs) and George Groves (75kgs) each gleaned bronze.

Three bronze medals amounted to England's spoils at the eighth Algiras Socikas multi-nations in Kaunas, Lithuania from 13-16 May. John Watson (Higherside Police) at light-welter, Sam Webb (Fisher) at welter and Ricardo Samms (Bilborough Police) at middleweight, being the recipients of those medals.

The ninth Brandenburg Cup proved to be a lucrative medal ground for three English boxers and one Irishman. This Under-19 multi-nations took place in Frankfurt/Oder, Germany from 13-16 May. England's two bronzes fell to Bradley Saunders (South Durham) at feather and Joe Selkirk the Rotunda welter, while Dale Youth's James Degale, at middleweight, went one better to land silver. Ireland's Darren O'Neill got a bronze at 81kgs.

The Irish Junior Championships took place on 14 and 15 May, with the finals being concluded at the National Stadium on 21 May. It was a triumph for the Joyce family. Brothers, John-Joe and David, and cousins, David Oliver and David Anthony, were all winners, with John Joe winning his seventh national title – six in Boys and Youth Championships.

Amir Khan, who went to Athens for the Acropolis Cup multi-nations from 26 -30 May, found himself up against the world number-one, Mario Kindelan, of Cuba, in his opening bout and, not surprisingly, was outpointed by the southpaw master in the Peristeri Boxing Hall, which will host the sport in the Athens Olympics. Kindelan is the reigning Olympic and World Senior champion at lightweight and will be a big threat to Amir and all the others in this weight division.

The end of the month saw the Junior ABA finals, along with three Women's National Championship finals take place at Huddersfield Town Hall on 29 May. Also around this time, the Welsh ABA Cadet/Youth Championships encompassed finals at three venues.

Ireland finished top of the medals table when they hosted the Cadets Four Nations tournament at Ballybunion in County Kerry on 28 and 29 May, while England were in second spot, Wales in third and Scotland in fourth place.

JUNE

In a sport whose personnel seldom get the recognition they deserve, it was very pleasing to learn that an MBE was being awarded to Scotland's John McDermott, the Blantyre Miners coach. John was a Commonwealth Games gold medallist at featherweight in Perth, Australia in 1962.

The annual Four Nations Schoolboys tournament was held at the Everton Park Sports Centre on Merseyside on 4 and 5 June, England securing 15 gold, four silver and four bronze medals to dominate the event. One youngster who grabbed gold for England was Haroon Khan (Bury), in the under 36kgs in Class 'A'. Haroon's elder brother is, of course, Amir Khan, Britain's sole representative in the boxing ring at the Athens' Olympics.

The second annual Six Nations Junior tournament was held in the open air in Rome on 5 and 6 June and involved boxers from Ireland, Scotland, England, Italy, Russia and Switzerland. At 51kgs, Ireland's Terence Doheny outpointed Paul Edwards of England in the final; at 54kgs, John Joyce of Ireland stopped Giuseppe Picardi of Italy in the final, while Scotland's Jason Hastie clinched the third/fourth place box-off when outscoring England's Connell Farrelly; at 57kgs, David Anthony Joyce, from Ireland, outpointed Scotland's Joseph Kelso in the final; at 60kgs, in the final, Scotland's David Appleby was outscored by the Russian, Ruslan Birzhanov; at 64kgs, Manuel Ernesti from Italy took the main honours when Scotland's Willie Bilan was disqualified in the second round of their final encounter, while Ireland's David Joyce was outpointed by Anton Buzolin from Italy in the third/fourth place box-off and, up at 75kgs, England's Paddy Wright was stopped in the final by Ivano del Monte from Italy. All in all it was a successful trip for British and Irish contestants.

Throughout the season it seemed that a major international event meant a gold medal for Amir Khan and once again it proved to be the case at the World Junior (Under-19) Championships in Jeju, South Korea from 10-20 June. The amazing teenager won five times, with only one day off, to hit the gold standard once again, as opponents from Taiwan, Cuba, Kazakhstan, France and, finally, Uzbekistan were left in his wake. Amir also won the 'Best Boxer of the Tournament' trophy and now he heads for Athens with the hopes of Britain's boxing fans riding on his young shoulders. He will not be phased in the least.

Also, in South Korea, there was a magnificent bronze medal in the light-heavyweight category for Daniel Price, from the Westway club in Scarborough, who lost in the semi-finals to the eventual gold medallist from Cuba, Ismaikel Perez. England's combined efforts hoisted them to fourth place in the medal table and to fifth place in the official nation standings, where the number of wins, not just medals, are taken into account. This is encouraging news indeed for the younger elements within our sport and let us hope that they will remain in boxing and go on to achieve much success in the senior ranks.

Back home, England ended up with ten golds when the Four Nations Junior tournament was held in Aberavon in Wales on 18 and 19 June. Ireland were in second place with six golds, Scotland third with three golds and the host nation in fourth spot with two golds.

In the European Union Championships, held in Madrid from 20-26 June, Ireland's Olympic middleweight representative, Andy Lee, won a silver medal, while bronzes were clinched for England by David Mulholland at lightweight, Neil Parsons at welterweight and Tony Jeffries up at light-heavyweight.

To end for a change on an administrative note, the ABAE Executive decided on 26 June to launch, next season, the 'Goldenboy Championships' for novice-level schoolboys, the innovative championships being for those of school age with under ten bouts at the time of entry. Hopefully, this will do much to eradicate the sort of mismatches which occur in the current schools event.

My own personal plea for the coming season is to ask all true amateur boxing supporters to come out in force and make their presence known and felt at national championships and at international matches staged here. Our boxers deserve your support, which will not only benefit them but the sport as well.

ABA National Championships, 2003-2004

Note: Only men who actually fought are included.

Combined Services v Western Counties

Combined Services
The Nelson Barracks Gymnasium, Portsmouth – 12 February
L.Fly: no entries. **Fly:** *final:* D.Barriball (Army) wo. **Bantam:** *final:* C.Sagar (Army) w pts A.Boyle (RN). **Feather:** *final:* A.Urrutia (RN) w rsc 3 P.Murray (Army). **Light:** *final:* C.Pacy (Army) w rsc 4 A.Lancey (RN). **L.Welter:** *final:* K.Green (RN) w pts S.Patterson (Army). **Welter:** *final:* S.Briggs (Army) w pts S.Elwell (RN). **Middle:** *final:* S.McDonald (RN) w pts D.Frost (Army). **L.Heavy:** *semi-finals:* I.Aldridge (RAF) wo, L.Spare (Army) w pts S.Tighe (RN); *final:* L.Spare w pts I.Aldridge. **Heavy:** *final:* M.O'Connell (RN) w pts J.Toal (Army). **S.Heavy:** *final:* N.Suku (RN) w pts J.Tuiauta (Army).

Western Counties
Northern Division   Riverside Leisure Centre, Bristol – 14 February & The Football Ground, Frome – 20 February
L.Fly: no entries. **Fly:** no entries. **Bantam:** no entries. **Feather:** no entries. **Light:** *final:* J.Nicholas (Southmead) w pts S.Hussain (Walcot). **L.Welter:** *final:* E.Hedges (Southmead) w pts J.Bickham (Taunton). **Welter:** *semi-finals:* A.Berkley (Synwell) wo, C.Thomas (Taunton) w pts A.Woodward (Watchet); *final:* C.Thomas w pts A.Berkley. **Middle:** *semi-finals:* D.Devane (Weston super Mare) wo, D.Guthrie (Yeovil & Reckleford) w pts C.Woods (Penhill RBL); *final:* D.Guthrie w rsc 3 D.Devane. **L.Heavy:** *final:* P.Smyth (Synwell) wo. **Heavy:** *final:* S.Davey (Weston super Mare) wo. **S.Heavy:** *final:* H.Smith (Frome) w pts B.Harding (Penhill RBL).

Southern Division   The Guildhall, Devonport – 14 February
L.Fly: no entries. **Fly:** no entries. **Bantam:** no entries. **Feather:** *semi-finals:* B.Burns (Pilgrim) wo, A.Afsharian (Exeter) w pts L.Bulpin (Leonis); *final:* B.Burns w pts A.Afsharian. **Light:** *final:* D.O'Connor (Devonport) wo. **L.Welter:** *final:* S.Yates (Torbay) w pts A.Cole (Camborne). **Welter:** *semi-finals:* P.Young (Leonis) w rtd 4 T.Houston (Weymouth), A.Kennedy (Devonport) w rsc 4 R.Fearnley (Truro); *final:* P.Young w rsc 1 A.Kennedy. **Middle:** *final:* L.Whane (Apollo) w pts J.Orchard (Poole). **L.Heavy:** no entries. **Heavy:** *final:* N.Hosking (Devonport) wo. **S.Heavy:** *final:* M.Elkins (Barnstaple) w pts D.Lund (Leonis).

Western Counties Finals   Ashton Gate Assembly Rooms, Bristol – 28 February
L.Fly: no entries. **Fly:** no entries. **Bantam:** no entries. **Feather:** B.Burns (Pilgrim) wo. **Light:** J.Nicholas (Southmead) w pts D.O'Connor (Devonport). **L.Welter:** S.Yates (Torbay) w rsc 2 E.Hedges (Southmead). **Welter:** C.Thomas (Taunton) w pts P.Young (Leonis). **Middle:** D.Guthrie (Yeovil & Reckleford) w pts L.Whane (Apollo). **L.Heavy:** P.Smyth (Synwell) wo. **Heavy:** N.Hosking (Devonport) w rsc 3 S.Davey (Weston super Mare). **S.Heavy:** H.Smith (Frome) w pts M.Elkins (Barnstaple).

Combined Services v Western Counties   The Maida Gymnasium, Aldershot – 13 March
L.Fly: no entries. **Fly:** D.Barriball (Army) wo. **Bantam:** C.Sagar (Army) wo. **Feather:** P.Murray (Army) – replaced A.Urrutia (RN)

- wo B.Burns (Pilgrim). **Light:** C.Pacy (Army) w rsc 1 J.Nicholas (Southmead). **L.Welter:** K.Green (RN) w pts S.Yates (Torbay). **Welter:** S.Briggs (Army) w rsc 3 C.Thomas (Taunton). **Middle:** D.Guthrie (Yeovil & Reckleford) w rsc 2 S.McDonald (RN). **L.Heavy:** L.Spare (Army) w pts P.Smyth (Synwell). **Heavy:** M.O'Connell (RN) wo N.Hosking (Devonport). **S.Heavy:** N.Suku (RN) w rsc 3 H.Smith (Frome).

Midland Counties v London

Midland Counties
Northern Zone   The Jungle Club, Leicester – 19 February, The Town Hall, Retford – 27 February & The Regency Suite, Ilkeston – 29 February
L.Fly: *final:* U.Ahmed (Merlin Youth) w pts J.Mulhern (Triumph). **Fly:** no entries. **Bantam:** *final:* P.Walkman (Chadd) w pts A.Brennan (Triumph). **Feather:** *final:* J.Spring (Terry Allen Unique) wo. **Light:** *final:* R.Bennett (Belgrave) wo. **L.Welter:** *quarter-finals:* L.Lothian (Kingsthorpe) wo, J.McCluskey (Bulkington) wo, A.Hill (South Normanton) wo, J.Flinn (Triumph) w rsc 3 N.McQuade (Kettering SoB); *semi-finals:* L.Lothian w pts A.Hill, J.Flinn w pts J.McCluskey; *final:* L.Lothian w pts J.Flinn. **Welter:** *quarter-finals:* C.Johnson (Terry Allen Unique) wo, C.Smith (Kettering SoB) wo, R.Coleman (Grimsby) wo, J.Elliott (South Normanton) w pts D.McClellan (Chesterfield); *semi-finals:* C.Johnson w pts C.Smith, J.Elliott w pts R.Coleman; *final:* C.Johnson w pts J.Elliott. **Middle:** *semi-finals:* A.Blackett (Grimsby) wo, A.Farrell (Triumph) w rsc 3 J.Hockenhull (Belgrave); *final:* A.Blackett w pts A.Farrell. **L.Heavy:** *final:* V.Petkovic (One Nation) wo. **Heavy:** *final:* L.Robinson (Trinity) w pts E.Dube (One Nation). **S.Heavy:** *final:* J.Neil (Triumph) wo.

Southern Zone   The Yew Tree, Walsall – 6 February, Saddlers Nightclub, Walsall – 19 February & St Anne's WMC, Birmingham – 26 February
L.Fly: *final:* M.Gallett (Pleck) wo. **Fly:** no entries. **Bantam:** *final:* A.Odud (Birminghan City) wo. **Feather:** *final:* N.Marston (Shrewsbury & Severnside) w pts S.Walton (Donnington Ex-Servicemen). **Light:** *quarter-finals:* C.Truman (Aston) wo, A.Campbell (Hulton Abbey) wo, M.Gethin (Wednesbury) wo, D.Harrison (Wolverhampton) w pts R.Wyatt (Lye); *semi-finals:* C.Truman w pts A.Campbell, M.Gethin w pts D.Harrison; *final:* C.Truman w pts M.Gethin. **L.Welter:** *final:* M.Gordon (Lions) wo. **Welter:** *semi-final:* D.Johnson (Queensberry Police) w pts D.Gethin (Wednesbury), L.English (Burton) w pts M.Barney (Tamworth); *final:* D.Johnson w pts L.English. **Middle:** *semi-finals:* S.Myatt (Donnington Ex-Servicemen) w pts L.Hough (Pleck), P.Murphy w pts K.Smith (Heathtown); *final:* P.Murphy w pts S.Myatt. **L.Heavy:** *final:* J.Finnegan (Burton) wo. **Heavy:** *final:* J.Boyd (Donninton Ex-Servicemen) wo. **S.Heavy:** *final:* D.Smith (Donnington Ex-Servicemen) w pts C.Elliott (Donnington Ex-Servicemen).

Midland Counties Finals   The Jungle Club, Leicester – 6 March
L.Fly: U.Ahmed (Merlin Youth) w pts M.Gallett (Pleck). **Fly:** no entries. **Bantam:** A.Odud (Birmingham City) w pts P.Walkman (Chadd). **Feather:** N.Marston (Shrewsbury & Severnside) w pts J.Spring (Terry Allen Unique). **Light:** C.Truman (Aston) w pts

R.Bennett (Belgrave). **L.Welter:** L.Lothian (Kingsthorpe) w pts M.Gordon (Lions). **Welter:** C.Johnson (Terry Allen Unique) w pts D.Johnson (Queensberry Police). **Middle:** A.Blackett (Grimsby) w pts P.Murphy (Aston). **L.Heavy:** J.Finnegan (Burton) w pts V.Petkovic (One Nation). **Heavy:** J.Boyd (Donnington Ex-Servicemen) w rsc 1 L.Robinson (Trinity). **S.Heavy:** D.Smith (Donnington Ex-Servicemen) w rsc 1 J.Neil (Triumph).

London
North-East Division   York Hall, Bethnal Green – 5 February
L.Fly: no entries. **Fly:** *final:* T.Joyett (West Ham) wo. **Bantam:** *final:* M.Marsh (West Ham) wo. **Feather:** *semi-finals:* I.Kargbo (Monteagle) wo, L.Ballard (Repton) w pts D.Smith (Dagenham); *final:* L.Ballard w pts I.Kargbo. **Light:** *semi-finals:* I.Mohammed (Repton) wo, A.Wallace (Repton) w pts A.Williams (Repton); *final:* A.Wallace w rsc 2 I.Mohammed. **L.Welter:** *semi-finals:* J.Baker (Repton) w pts R.Richards (Repton), C.McDonagh (Dagenham) w pts I.Sheikh (Repton); *final:* J.Baker w pts C.McDonagh. **Welter:** *final:* L.Calvert (Dagenham) wo. **Middle:** *final:* E.Matthews (Repton) w rsc 2 U.Ali (County). **L.Heavy:** *semi-finals:* M.Yousaf (Monteagle) wo, D.Orwell (Dagenham) w pts E.Monteith (West Ham); *final:* M.Yousaf w rsc 1 D.Orwell. **Heavy:** no entries. **S.Heavy:** *final:* J.Young (Repton) w rtd 1 D.Campbell (Repton).

North-East Division   Brent Town Hall, Wembley – 5 February & Earlsfield ABC, Wandsworth – 13 February
L.Fly: no entries. **Fly:** no entries. **Bantam:** no entries. **Feather:** *semi-final:* P.Liggins (Trojan) wo, M.Mehmet (Finchley) w pts J.Jaworski (Haringey Police); *final:* M.Mehmet w pts P.Liggins. **Light:** *final:* M.Grant (Haringey Police) wo. **L.Welter:** *final:* F.Madoti (St Pancras Kronk) w pts M.Sazish (Hanwell). **Welter:** *quarter-finals:* Jamal Morrison (All Stars) wo, B.Doughty (Angel) wo, Jamie Morrison (All Stars) w O.Ekundayo (St Pancras Kronk), G.Hillyard (St Pancras Kronk) w pts D.Barrett (Trojan); *semi-finals:* Jamie Morrison w pts B.Doughty, Jamal Morrison w pts G.Hillyard; *final:* Jamie Morrison w pts Jamal Morrison. **Middle:** *semi-finals:* G.Barton (Finchley) w pts Y.Doumbia (All Stars), V.Antanavicius (All Stars)w pts A.Haliti (St Pancras Kronk); *final:* G.Barton w pts V.Antanavicius. **L.Heavy:** *semi-finals:* D.Mohseni (All Stars) w pts N.Mirza (Haringey Police), M.Abdusalem (St Pancras Kronk) w pts J.Barrett (Trojan); *final:* M.Abdusalem w pts D.Mohseni. **Heavy:** *semi-finals:* D.Cunnage (Northolt) wo, A.Al-Sady (All Stars) w rtd 3 R.Faustino (All Stars); *final:* D.Cunnage w pts A.Al-Sady. **S.Heavy:** *final:* P.Pierson (Trojan) wo.

South-East Division   National Sports Centre, Crystal Palace – 12 February
L.Fly: *final:* S.McDonald (Fitzroy Lodge) wo. **Fly:** *final:* S.Langley (Hollington) wo. **Bantam:** *final:* C.Brahmbhatt (Bexley) w pts S.Gregory (Samuel Montagu). **Feather:** *final:* A.Bhattia (Eltham) wo. **Light:** *final:* D.Davies (Fitzroy Lodge) w pts R.Flynn (Marvels Lane). **L.Welter:** *quarter-finals:* J.Chambers (Samuel Montagu) wo, D.Richards (Hollington) wo, A.Ideh (Honor Oak) wo, D.Gregory (Fitzroy Lodge) w rsc 3 N.Weise (Eltham); *semi-finals:* A.Ideh w pts D.Richards, J.Chambers w pts D.Gregory; *final:* J.Chambers w pts A.Ideh. **Welter:** *semi-finals:* A.Small (Fitzroy Lodge) w pts M.Olwale (Honor Oak), S.Webb (Fisher) w pts M.Reigate (Fitzroy Lodge); *final:* S.Webb w pts A.Small. **Middle:** *semi-finals:* U.Caramba-Coker (Lynn) w co 3 M.Thirlwall (Fisher), I.Ssenyange (New Addington) w rsc 2 D.Woodhouse (Fitzroy Lodge); *final:* I.Ssenyange w rtd 2 U.Caramba-Coker. **L.Heavy:** *final:* M.McDonagh (Hollington) w

pts D.Johnson (Lynn). **Heavy:** *final:* J.McDonald (Fitzroy Lodge) wo. **S.Heavy:** *semi-finals:* D.Kaufman (Marvels Lane) wo, I.Lewison (Miguel's) w pts D.Akinlade (Fitzroy Lodge); *final:* I.Lewison w pts D.Kaufman.

South-West Division   Earlsfield ABC, Wandsworth – 6 February
L.Fly: no entries. **Fly:** no entries. **Bantam:** no entries. **Feather:** no entries. **Light:** no entries. **L.Welter:** *final:* D.Khan (Earlsfield) wo. **Welter:** no entries. **Middle:** no entries. **L.Heavy:** no entries. **Heavy:** no entries. **S.Heavy:** no entries.

London Semi-Final & Finals   York Hall, Bethnal Green – 19 February & 26 February
L.Fly: *final:* S.McDonald (Fitzroy Lodge) wo. **Fly:** *final:* S.Langley (Hollington) w rtd 1 T.Joyett (West Ham). **Bantam:** *final:* M.Marsh (West Ham) w pts C.Brahmbhatt (Bexley). **Feather:** *semi-finals:* M.Mehmet (Finchley) wo, A.Bhattia (Eltham) w pts L.Ballard (Repton); *final:* A.Bhattia w rsc 1 M.Mehmet. **Light:** *semi-finals:* A.Wallace (Repton) wo, M.Grant (Haringey Police) w pts D.Davies (Fitzroy Lodge); *final:* M.Grant w pts A.Wallace. **L.Welter:** *semi-finals:* F.Madoti (St Pacras Kronk) w pts J.Chambers (Samuel Montagu), D.Khan (Earlsfield) w pts J.Baker (Repton); *final:* F.Madoti w rsc 4 D.Khan. **Welter:** *semi-finals:* S.Webb (Fisher) wo, Jamie Morrison (All Stars) w pts L.Calvert (Dagenham); *final:* S.Webb w pts Jamie Morrison. **Middle:** *semi-finals:* E.Matthews (Repton) wo, I.Ssenyange (New Addington) w rsc 2 G.Barton (Finchley); *final:* E.Matthews w pts I.Ssenyange. **L.Heavy:** *semi-finals:* M.McDonagh (Hollington) wo, M.Abdusalem (St Pancras Kronk) w rsc 2 M.Yousaf (Monteagle); *final:* M.Abdusalem w pts M.McDonagh. **Heavy:** *final:* J.McDonald (Fitzroy Lodge) w pts D.Cunnage (Northolt). **S.Heavy:** *semi-finals:* J.Young (Repton) wo, I.Lewison (Miguel's) w pts P.Pierson (Trojan); *final:* J.Young w pts I.Lewison.

Midland Counties v London   Tile Hill Social Club, Coventry – 13 March
L.Fly: S.McDonald (Fitzroy Lodge) w pts U.Ahmed (Merlin Youth). **Fly:** S.Langley (Hollington) wo. **Bantam:** M.Marsh (West Ham) w pts A.Odud (Birmingham City). **Feather:** A.Bhattia (Eltham) w pts N.Marston (Shrewsbury & Severnside). **Light:** M.Grant (Haringey Police) w pts C.Truman (Aston). **L.Welter:** F.Madoti (St Pancras Kronk) w pts L.Lothian (Kingsthorpe). **Welter:** C.Johnson (Terry Allen Unique) w pts S.Webb (Fisher). **Middle:** A.Blackett (Grimsby) w pts E.Matthews (Repton). **L.Heavy:** M.Abdusalem (St Pancras Kronk) w pts J.Finnegan (Burton). **Heavy:** J.Boyd (Donnington Ex-Servicemen) w pts J.McDonald (Fitzroy Lodge). **S.Heavy:** J.Young (Repton) w pts D.Smith (Donnington Ex-Servicemen).

North-West Counties v Home Counties/ Eastern Counties

Eastern Counties
Essex   The Tute WMC, Tilbury – 30 January
L.Fly: no entries. **Fly:** no entries. **Bantam:** no entries. **Feather:** no entries. **Light:** no entries. **L.Welter:** *final:* A.Ball (Tilbury Dockers) wo. **Welter:** *final:* D.Keston (Clacton) w rsc 1 J.Martin (Canvey). **Middle:** *semi-finals:* B.Harris (Berry Boys) wo, J.Cullinane (Southend) w rsc 2 J.Veal (Rayleigh Mill); *final:*

J.Cullinane w pts B.Harris. **L.Heavy:** no entries. **Heavy:** *final:* H.Mahdavian (Southend) w rsc 3 C.Mitchell (Chadwell & Corringham). **S.Heavy:** no entries.

Mid-Anglia   Campol ABC, Huntingdon – 30 January
L.Fly: no entries. **Fly:** no entries. **Bantam:** no entries. **Feather:** no entries. **Light:** no entries. **L.Welter:** no entries. **Welter:** no entries. **Middle:** *final:* D.Brown (March) wo. **L.Heavy:** no entries. **Heavy:** no entries. **S.Heavy:** no entries.

Norfolk   Ocean Rooms, Gorleston – 24 January
L.Fly: no entries. **Fly:** no entries. **Bantam:** *final:* M.Walsh (Kingfisher) wo. **Feather:** no entries. **Light:** no entries. **L.Welter:** no entries. **Welter:** *final:* S.Crompton (Kingfisher) wo. **Middle:** *final:* W.Green (Aylesham) w pts L.Pizey (Kingfisher). **L.Heavy:** *final:* J.Carrara (Kingfisher) wo. **Heavy:** *final:* S.Sexton (Norwich Lads) wo. **S.Heavy:** no entries.

Suffolk   Pontins Holiday Camp, Pakefield – 6 February
L.Fly: no entries. **Fly:** no entries. **Bantam:** no entries. **Feather:** *final:* R.Mitchell (New Astley) wo. **Light:** *final:* C.Allen (Eastgate) wo. **L.Welter:** no entries. **Welter:** *final:* K.Jackson (Haverhill) wo. **Middle:** no entries. **L.Heavy:** *final:* P.Davies (Lowestoft) wo. **Heavy:** *final:* N.Crawford (Hurstlea) wo. **S.Heavy:** no entries.

Eastern Counties Semi-Finals & Finals   The Braza Centre, March – 20 February
L.Fly: no entries. **Fly:** no entries. **Bantam:** *final:* M.Walsh (Kingfisher) wo. **Feather:** *final:* R.Mitchell (New Astley) wo. **Light:** *final:* C.Allen (Eastgate) wo. **L.Welter:** *final:* A.Ball (Tilbury Dockers) wo. **Welter:** *semi-finals:* S.Crompton (Kingfisher), K.Jackson (Haverhill) w pts D.Keston (Clacton); **final:** K.Jackson w rtd 2 S.Crompton (Kingfisher). **Middle:** *semi-finals:* W.Green (Aylsham) wo, J.Cullinane (Southend) w pts D.Brown (March); *final:* W.Green w pts J.Cullinane. **L.Heavy:** *final:* J.Carrara (Kingfisher) w pts P.Davies (Lowestoft). **Heavy:** *semi-finals:* H.Mahdavian (Southend) wo, S.Sexton (Norwich Lads) w rsc 2 N.Crawford (Hurstlea); *final:* S.Sexton w rsc 3 H.Mahdavian. **S.Heavy:** no entries.

––––––––––––––––

Home Counties   The University, Reading – 5 February & Langdale Hall, Witney – 20 February
L.Fly: *final:* J.Fowl (Haileybury). **Fly:** *final:* D.Culling (Stevenage) wo. **Bantam:** *final:* L.Lewis (Wolvercote) wo. **Feather:** no entries. **Light:** *final:* A.Lever (Bedford) wo. **L.Welter:** *semi-finals:* D.Phillips (Luton Shamrock) wo, P.Stedman (Wolvercote) w pts B.Crotty (Cheshunt); *final:* D.Phillips w pts P.Stedman. **Welter:** *final:* M.Douglas (Bulmershe) w pts L.Cristoe (Bedford). **Middle:** *semi-finals:* T.Sullivan (Cheshunt) wo, S.Mullins (Wolvercote) w pts A.Dennis (Stevenage); *final:* S.Mullins w rsc 1 T.Sullivan. **L.Heavy:** *final:* D.Edwards (Thame) wo. **Heavy:** *final:* C.Goldhawk (Cheshunt) wo. **S.Heavy:** L.Howkins (Pinewood Starr) wo.

––––––––––––––––

Eastern Counties v Home Counties   The Civic Hall, Grays – 5 March
L.Fly: J.Fowl (Haileybury) wo. **Fly:** D.Culling (Stevenage) wo. **Bantam:** L.Lewis (Wolvercote) w pts M.Walsh (Kingfisher). **Feather:** R.Mitchell (New Astley) wo. **Light:** A.Lever (Bedford) w pts C.Allen (Eastgate). **L.Welter:** D.Phillips (Luton Shamrock) w pts A.Ball (Tilbury Dockers). **Welter:** M.Douglas (Bulmershe)

wo K.Jackson (Haverhill). **Middle:** S.Mullins (Wolvercote) w pts W.Green (Aylsham). **L.Heavy:** J.Carrara (Kingfisher) w pts D.Edwards (Thame). **Heavy:** S.Sexton (Norwich Lads) w pts C.Goldhawk (Cheshunt). **S.Heavy:** L.Howkins (Pinewood Starr) wo.

––––––––––––––––

North-West Counties
East Lancs & Cheshire Division   The Larches Social Club, Preston – 16 & 23 February
L.Fly: no entries. **Fly:** no entries. **Bantam:** no entries. **Feather:** *semi-finals:* S.McFadden (Sandygate) wo, J.Kays (Nichols Police) w pts D.Wolfenden (Macclesfield); *final:* S.McFadden w rsc 1 J.Kays. **Light:** *semi-finals:* D.Watson (Bolton Lads) w pts A.Gribben (Ardwick Lads), L.Dorrian (Arrow) w pts D.Boone (Pool of Life); *final:* L.Dorrian w pts D.Watson. **L.Welter:** *semi-finals:* L.Graves (Chorley) wo, D.Askew (Workington) w pts C.Watson (Northside); *final:* D.Askew w pts L.Graves. **Welter:** *semi-finals:* B.Rose (Blackpool & Fylde) w pts M.King (Cleator Moor), D.Vassell (Fox) w pts J.Hussey (Tonge); *final:* B.Rose w pts D.Vassell. **Middle:** *semi-finals:* P.Owen (Olympic) wo, N.Travis (Tonge) w rsc 3 K.Turner (Barton); *final:* P.Owen w pts N.Travis. **L.Heavy:** *final:* P.Trott (Altrincham) w pts L.Kellett (Bolton Lads). **Heavy:** no entries. **S.Heavy:** no entries.

West Lancs & Cheshire Division   Everton Park Sports Centre, Liverpool – 13, 20 & 21 February
L.Fly: *final:* C.Lyon (Wigan) wo. **Fly:** *final:* M.Gerrard (Huyton) w pts M.Sedgwick (Wigan). **Bantam:** *semi-finals:* D.Swanson (Tower Hill) wo, J.Donnelly (Croxteth) w pts M.Robinson (Tower Hill); *final:* J.Donnelly w pts D.Swanson. **Feather:** *final:* D.Mulholland (Salisbury) wo. **Light:** *final:* S.Jennings (Tower Hill) w pts R.Jockings (Rotunda). **L.Welter:** *quarter-finals:* D.Angus (Salisbury) wo, E.Roberts (Gemini) wo, J.Watson (Higherside) wo, S.Williams (Avalon) w pts R.Shearer (Tower Hill); *semi-finals:* D.Angus w pts E.Roberts, J.Watson w pts S.Williams; *final:* J.Watson w pts D.Angus. **Welter:** *semi-finals:* S.Falmer (Kirkwood) wo, M.Murray (St Helen's Town) w rsc 3 L.Kempster (Halewood); *final:* M.Murray w rsc 2 S.Falmer. **Middle:** *final:* S.Birch St Helen's Town) w rsc 3 W.Pauline (Rotunda). **L.Heavy:** *final:* P.Keir (Rotunda) wo. **Heavy:** *semi-finals:* T.Bellew (Rotunda) wo, M.Carroll (Kirkdale) w pts M.Stafford (Kirkby); *final:* T.Bellew w pts M.Carroll. **S.Heavy:** no entries.

North-West Counties Finals   Everton Park Sports Centre, Liverpool – 27 February
L.Fly: C.Lyon (Wigan) wo. **Fly:** M.Gerrard (Huyton) wo. **Bantam:** J.Donnelly (Croxteth) wo. **Feather:** D.Mulholland (Salisbury) w pts S.McFadden (Sandygate). **Light:** L.Dorrian (Arrow) w pts S.Jennings (Tower Hill). **L.Welter:** J.Watson (Higherside) w rsc 3 D.Askew (Workington). **Welter:** M.Murray (St Helen's Town) w pts B.Rose (Blackpool & Fylde). **Middle:** S.Birch (St Helen's Town) w pts P.Owen (Olympic). **L.Heavy:** P.Keir (Rotunda) w pts P.Trott (Altrincham). **Heavy:** T.Bellew (Rotunda) wo. **S.Heavy:** no entries.

––––––––––––––––

North-West Counties v Eastern Counties/Home Counties   Everton Park Sports Centre, Liverpool – 12 March
L.Fly: J.Fowl (Haileybury) wo. **Fly:** M.Gerrard (Huyton) w pts D.Culling (Stevenage). **Bantam:** J.Donnelly (Croxteth) w pts L.Lewis (Wolvercote). **Feather:** D.Mulholland (Salisbury) w pts R.Mitchell (New Astley). **Light:** L.Dorrian (Arrow) w pts A.Lever

(Bedford). **L.Welter:** J.Watson (Higherside) w rsc 3 D.Phillips (Luton Shamrock). **Welter:** M.Murray (St Helen's Town) w rsc 3 M.Douglas (Bulmershe). **Middle:** S.Mullins (Wolvercote) w rsc 1 S.Birch (St Helen's Town). **L.Heavy:** P.Keir (Rotunda) w pts J.Carrara (Norwich Lads). **Heavy:** T.Bellew (Rotunda) w pts S.Sexton (Norwich Lads). **S.Heavy:** L.Howkins (Pinewood Starr) wo.

Southern Counties v North-East Counties

Southern Counties   Gang-Warily Leisure Centre, Fawley – 21 & 28 February
L.Fly: no entries. **Fly:** no entries. **Bantam:** no entries. **Feather:** *final:* D.Goff (St Mary's) w rsc 2 J.Bousquet (St Mary's). **Light:** *semi-finals:* L.Cook (Foley) w pts B.Jones (Crawley), M.Tew (Southampton) w pts W.Dunkley (Swanley; *final:* L.Cook w pts M.Tew. **L.Welter:** *semi-finals:* J.Berry (Sandwich), S.Watson (Lawrence) w pts S.Tobias (Woking); *final:* S.Watson w rsc 4 J.Berry. **Welter:** *semi-finals:* S.Woolford (The Grange) w pts B.Madgewick (City of Portsmouth), M.Welsh (Swanley) w pts A.Martin (Foley); *final:* S.Woolford w pts M.Welsh. **Middle:** *quarter-finals:* A.Watson (Crawley), L.Goddard (Bordon) wo, A.Young (Crawley) wo, P.Morbey (Bognor) w pts S.Ede (Southampton); *semi-finals:* A.Young w rsc 4 P.Morbey, A.Watson w pts L.Goddard; *final:* A.Young w pts A.Watson. **L.Heavy:** *final:* A.Morris (Margate) wo. **Heavy:** *semi-finals:* A.Rose (Newport) w pts S.Reid (White Hawk), G.Potter (The Grange) w rsc 2 F.Booker (Hove); *final:* A.Rose w pts G.Potter; **S.Heavy:** no entries.

North-East Counties
Tyne, Tees & Wear Division   Marton Country Club, Middlesbrough – 3 & 12 February
L.Fly: no entries. **Fly:** no entries. **Bantam:** *final:* S.Hall (Albert Hill) wo. **Feather:** *final:* J.Watson (Romany Way) w pts P.Younger (Sunderland). **Light:** *final:* S.Donkin (Lambton Street) w pts S.Zaman (Middlesbrough). **L.Welter:** *quarter-finals:* G.Roberts (Hartlepool Catholic) wo, J.Donkin (Lambton Street) w pts P.Boyle (Halfpenny), S.Kennedy (Sunderland) w pts G.Fox (South Durham), G.Gallone (Spennymoor BA) w pts J.Haghkar (Bedlington); *semi-finals:* J.Donkin w rsc 4 G.Roberts, S.Kennedy w pts G.Gallone; *final:* S.Kennedy w rtd 2 J.Donkin. **Welter:** *semi-finals:* N.Gittus (East Durham Academy) wo, P.Holborn (Sunderland) w dis 2 M.Marshall (Plains Farm); *final:* N.Gittus w rsc P.Holborn. **Middle:** *semi-finals:* G.Barr (Birtley) wo, M.Denton (Headland) w rsc 4 S.McCrone (Spennymoor BA); *final:* M.Denton w pts G.Barr. **L.Heavy:** *final:* T.Jeffries (Sunderland) w pts W.Scott (Aycliffe). **Heavy:** *final:* C.Clift (Lambton Street) w rsc 3 J.Robinson (Plains Farm). **S.Heavy:** *semi-finals:* C.Burton (Headland) wo, B.Robinon (South Durham) w pts P.Malcolm (Headland); *final:* C.Burton w pts B.Robinson.

Yorkshire & Humberside Division   The Metrodome, Barnsley – 6 February & Birdwell Workingmens' Club, Barnsley – 9 February
L.Fly: no entries. **Bantam:** *final:* E.Heagney (Cleckheaton) wo. **Feather:** no entries. **Light:** *final:* J.Dyer (Burmantofts) wo. **L.Welter:** *final:* J.Fewkes (Sheffield Boxing Centre) wo. **Welter:** *quarter-finals:* T.Coward (Wombwell & Dearne) wo, A.Butlin (Rawthorpe) wo, J.Fletcher (Karmand) wo, R.Ashworth (Scarborough) w pts D.Reynolds (Star); *semi-finals:* T.Coward w pts A.Butlin, J.Fletcher w pts R.Ashworth; *final:* T.Coward w pts

J.Fletcher. **Middle:** *final:* A.Ainger (Handsworth Police) w rsc 1 G.Connelly (Unity). **L.Heavy:** *final:* J.Ibbotson (Handsworth Police) w rsc 3 R.Grant (Unity). **Heavy:** *semi-finals:* N.McGarry (Doncaster Plant) wo, J.Anthony (Rotherham) w pts D.Slaney (Conisborough); *final:* J.Anthony w rsc 3 N.McGarry. **S.Heavy:** no entries.

North-East Counties Finals   The High Pit Entertainment Centre, Cramlington – 19 February
L.Fly: no entries. **Fly:** no entries. **Bantam:** S.Hall (Albert Hill) w pts E.Heagney (Cleckheaton). **Feather:** J.Watson (Romany Way) wo. **Light:** S.Donkin (Lambton Street) w pts J.Dyer (Burmantofts). **L.Welter:** S.Kennedy (Sunderland) w pts J.Fewkes (Sheffield Boxing Centre). **Welter:** T.Coward (Wombwell & Dearne) w pts N.Gittus (East Durham Academy). **Middle:** A.Ainger (Handsworth Police) w pts M.Denton (Headland). **L.Heavy:** T.Jeffries (Sunderland) w pts J.Ibbotson (Handsworth Police). **Heavy:** J.Anthony (Rotherham) w pts C.Clift (Lambton Street). **S.Heavy:** C.Burton (Headland) wo.

Southern Counties v North-East Counties   The Sports Centre, Strood – 6 March
L.Fly: no entries. **Fly:** no entries, **Bantam:** S.Hall (Albert Hill) wo. **Feather:** J.Watson (Romany Way) w pts D.Goff (St Mary's). **Light:** S.Donkin (Lambton Street) w pts L.Cook (Foley). **L.Welter:** S.Kennedy (Sunderland) w pts S.Watson (Lawrence). **Welter:** S.Woolford (The Grange) w rsc 1 T.Coward (Wombwell & Dearne). **Middle:** A.Ainger (Handsworth Police) w pts A.Young (Crawley). **L.Heavy:** T.Jeffries (Sunderland) w co 1 A.Morris (Margate). **Heavy:** J.Anthony (Rotherham) w rsc 4 A.Rose (Newport). **S.Heavy:** C.Burton (Headland) wo.

English ABA Semi-Finals & Finals

L.Fly: *final:* S.McDonald w rsc 3 J.Fowl (Haileybury). **Fly:** *semi-finals:* M.Gerrard (Huyton) wo, S.Langley (Hollington) w pts D.Barriball (Army); *final:* S.Langley w pts M.Gerrard. **Bantam:** *semi-finals:* M.Marsh (West Ham) w pts S.Hill (Albert Hall), J.Donnelly (Croxteth) w pts C.Sagar (Army); *final:* M.Marsh w pts J.Donnelly. **Feather:** *semi-finals:* D.Mulholland (Salisbury) w pts A.Bhattia (Eltham), J.Watson (Romany Way) w pts P.Murray (Army); *final:* D.Mulholland w pts J.Watson. **Light:** *semi-finals:* M.Grant (Haringey Police) w pts L.Dorrian (Arrow), C.Pacy (Army) w pts S.Donkin (Lambton Street); *final:* C.Pacy w pts M.Grant. **L.Welter:** *semi-finals:* F.Madoti (St Pancras Kronk) w pts K.Green (RN), J.Watson (Higherside) w pts S.Kennedy (Sunderland); *final:* J.Watson w pts F.Maditi. **Welter:** *semi-finals:* M.Murray (St Helen's Town) w pts C.Johnson (Terry Allen Unique), S.Briggs (Army) w pts S.Woolford (The Grange); *final:* M.Murray w pts S.Briggs. **Middle:** *semi-finals:* A.Blackett (Grimsby) w pts S.Mullins (Wolvercote), D.Guthrie (Yeovil & Reckleford) w pts A.Ainger (Handsworth Police); *final:* D.Guthrie w rsc 3 A.Blackett. **L.Heavy:** *semi-finals:* M.Abdusalem (St Pancras Kronk) w pts T.Jeffries (Sunderland), L.Spare (Army) w pts P.Keir (Rotunda); *final:* M.Abdusalem w rsc 2 L.Spare. **Heavy:** *semi-finals:* M.O'Connell (RN) w rsc 3 J.Anthony (Rotherham), T.Bellew (Rotunda) w pts J.McDonald (Fitzroy Lodge) – replaced J.Boyd (Donnington Ex-Servicemen). **S.Heavy:** *semi-finals:* J.Young (Repton) w pts N.Suku (RN), L.Howkins (Pinewood Starr) w rsc 4 C.Burton (Headland); *final:* J.Young w rsc 3 L.Howkins.

Irish Championships, 2003-2004

Senior Tournament

The National Stadium, Dublin – 5, 6, 12, 13 & 19 December
L. Fly: *: quarter-finals:* C. Ahern (Baldoyle, Dublin) wo, R. Hickey (Grangecon, Kildare) w pts D. McArdle (Dealgan, Louth); *semi-finals:* C. Ahern w rsc 1 D. Thorpe (St. Aidan's, Wexford), R. Hickey w pts J. Conlon (St. John Bosco, Belfast); *final:* C. Ahern w pts R. Hickey. **Fly:** *semi-finals:* Paul Hyland (Golden Cobra, Dublin) wo, T. Lee (Oughterard, Galway) w pts S. McKim (Abbey, Antrim); *final:* Paul Hyland w pts T. Lee. **Bantam:** *semi-finals:* B. Gillen (Holy Trinity, Belfast) wo, E. Donovan (St. Michael's, Athy) w rsc 2 J. Linden (East Coast, Down); *final:* E. Donovan w pts B. Gillen. **Feather:** *quarter-finals:* M. Lindsey (Immaculata, Belfast) wo, D.A. Joyce (St. Michael's, Athy) w pts D. Sweetman (Golden Corba, Dublin), E. Touhey (Moate, Westmeath) w pts Patrick Hyland (Golden Cobra, Dublin), D. Lawlor (St. Fiach's/Carlow) w pts R. Kane (Bishop Kelly, Tyrone); *semi-finals:* M. Lindsey w rsc 3 D.A. Joyce, E. Touhey w pts D. Lawlor; *final:* M. Lindsey w pts E. Touhey. **Light:** *quarter-finals:* A. Murray (Cavan) w pts E. McEneaney (Dealgan, Louth), E. Hyland (Golden Cobra, Dublin) w pts K. Crawley (Glasnevin, Dublin), S. Ormond (St. Matthew's, Dublin) w pts A. Sadlier (Holy Family, Drogheda), N. Monteith (Dockers, Belfast) w pts G. Dunne (Neilstown, Dublin); *semi-finals:* A. Murray w pts E. Hyland, N. Monteith w pts S. Ormond; *final:* A. Murray w pts N. Monteith. **L. Welter:** *prelims:* P. McCloskey (St. Canice's, Derry) wo, T. Carlyle (Crumlin, Dublin) wo, R. Sheahan (St. Michael's, Athy) wo, M. Wickham (St. Anthony's/St. Patrick's, Wexford) wo, M. Kelly (Dealgan, Louth) wo, T. O'Neill (Mount Tallant, Dublin) wo, D. Hamill (All Saints, Belfast) wo, J. McDonagh (Brosna, Offaly) w pts A. Carlyle (Golden Cobra, Dublin); *quarter-finals:* P. McCloskey w rsc 3 T. Carlyle, R. Sheahan w rsc 3 M. Wickham, M. Kelly w pts T. O'Neill, J. McDonagh w pts D. Hamill; *semi-finals:* P. McCloskey w pts R. Sheahan, M. Kelly w pts J. McDonagh; *final:* P. McCloskey w pts M. Kelly. **Welter:** *prelims:* J. Moore (Arklow, Wicklow) wo, R. Lawless (Portlaoise, Laois) wo, F. Turner (St. Ibar's/ St. Joseph's, Wexford) wo, P. Jennings (St. Matthew's, Dublin) wo, T. Hamill (All Saints, Belfast) wo, S. Jordan (Star, Belfast) wo, J. Dowling (Paulstown, Kilkenny) wo, H. Coyle (Geesala, Mayo) w pts D. Conlon (Crumlin, Dublin); *quarter-finals:* J. Moore w rsc 1 R. Lawless, F. Turner w pts P. Jennings, T. Hamill w pts S. Jordan, H. Coyle w pts J. Dowling; *semi-finals:* J. Moore w pts F. Turner, H. Coyle w pts T. Hamill; *final:* H. Coyle w pts J. Moore. **Middle:** *quarter-finals:* A. Lee (St. Francis, Limerick) wo, E. O'Kane (St. Canice's, Derry) wo, P. Murray (St. Matthew's, Dublin) wo, E. Healy (Portlaoise, Laois) w pts H. Joyce (St. Michael's, Athy); *semi-finals:* A. Lee w pts E. O'Kane, P. Murray w pts E. Healy; *final:* A. Lee w rsc 4 P. Murray. **L. Heavy:** *quarter-finals:* K. Egan (Neilstown, Dublin) wo, S. Dalton (Sunnyside, Cork) wo, M. Lee (Oughterard, Galway) wo, P. Smyth (St. Patrick's, Armagh) w pts

J. Waldron (Castlebar, Mayo); *semi-finals:* K. Egan w rsc 3 S. Dalton, M. Lee w rsc 4 P. Smyth; *final:* K. Egan w pts M. Lee. **Heavy:** *semi-finals:* A. Reynolds (St. Joseph's, Sligo) wo, M. McDonagh (Brosna, Offaly) w rsc 3 T. Donnelly (Mark Heagney, Tyrone); *final:* A Reynolds w rsc 2 M. McDonagh. **S. Heavy:** *semi-finals:* M. Rogan (Immaculata, Belfast) w rsc 4 S. Power (Tramore, Waterford), J. Upton (Crumlin, Dublin) w pts G. Riggs (West Finglas, Dublin); *final:* M. Rogan w rsc 2 J. Upton.

Intermediate Finals

The National Stadium, Dublin – 27 February
L. Fly: F. Campbell (South Meath) w pts N. Muldowney (Midfield, Mayo). **Fly:** T.J. Doheny (Portlaoise, Laoise) w pts P. Lyons (Carrick-on-Suir, Tipperary). **Bantam:** B. Harkin (Twin Towns, Donegal) w pts A. Hopkins (Corinthians, Dublin). **Feather:** W. Casey (Southill, Limerick) w pts T. Dillon (Drimnagh, Dublin). **Light:** J. Quinn (St. Saviour's, Dublin) w pts T. Dwyer (St. Aidan's, Wexford). **L. Welter:** D. O'Sullivan (Fr. Horgan's, Cork) w pts M. McLoughlin (Carndonagh, Donegal). **Welter:** K. Brabazon (St. Saviour's, Dublin) w pts C. Moran (Phibsboro, Dublin). **Middle:** G. Gallagher (Dunfanaghy, Donegal) w pts S. Edgeworth (Edenmore, Dublin). **L. Heavy:** D. O'Neill (Paulstown, Kilkenny) w pts J. Barrett (Olympic, Galway). **Heavy:** G. Smith (Cabra Panthers, Dublin) w pts C. Quigley (Twin Towns, Donegal). **S. Heavy:** T. Smith (Ring, Derry) w rsc 2 A. Vedernikov (Neilstown, Dublin).

Junior Finals

The National Stadium, Dublin – 21 May
L. Fly: K. Fennessy (Clonmel, Tipperary) w pts J. Conlon (St John Bosco, Belfast. **Fly:** D.O. Joyce (St. Michael's, Athy) w pts R. Hickey (Grangecon, Kildare). **Bantam:** J.J. Joyce (St. Michael's, Athy) w pts J. Cooley (St. Joseph's, Derry). **Feather:** J.P. McDonagh (St. Paul's, Waterford) w pts D.A. Joyce (St. Michael's, Athy). **Light:** T. Dwyer (St. Aidan's, Dublin) w pts D. Nevin (Cavan). **L. Welter:** D. Joyce (St. Michael's, Athy) w pts G. McBride (Dunfanaghy, Donegal). **Welter:** J. Sweeney (Drimnagh, Dublin) w pts M. O'Neill (Shamrock, Tyrone). **Middle:** D. Joyce (Moate, Westmeath) w pts E. Walsh (St. Anne's, Westport). **L. Heavy:** M. Stokes (Crumlin, Dublin) w rsc 3 P. Walsh (Claremorris, Mayo). **Heavy:** A. Crampton (St. Broughan's, Offaly) w pts D. Hanley (Loughglynn, Roscommon).

Scottish and Welsh Senior Championships, 2003-2004

Scotland ABA

The Time Capsule, Coatbridge - 6 March & 26 March, Pettycur Bay Centre, Kinghorn – 12 March & The Tree Tops Hotel, Aberdeen – 19 March

L.Fly: *final:* U.Hussain (Kinross) wo. **Fly:** *final:* I.McCabe (Lesmahagow) wo. **Bantam:** *final:* J.Ancliff (Granite City) w rsc 1 G.Nelson (Orbiston). **Feather:** *semi-finals:* N.Bonnini (Hawick) w pts S.Carroll (Granite City), D.Ross (Kincorth) w pts J.McGregory (Four Isles); *final:* N.Bonnini w pts D.Ross. **Light:** *semi-finals:* M.Hastie (Forgewood) w pts M.Prince (Broadwood), G.Izzat (Clovenstone) w pts R.Park (Blantyre); *final:* M.Hastie w pts G.Izzat. **L.Welter:** *prelims:* L.Burnett (Kincorth) wo, A.McKelvie (Orbiston) wo, M.Cittadini (Dennistoun) wo, R.Scott (Springhill) wo, R.Brown (Perth Railways) wo, M.Reid (Sparta) wo, G.McArthur (Clydebank) w rsc 3 F.Monkhouse (Greenock), P.King (Forgewood) w pts J.Cusick (Cardenden); *quarter-finals:* L.Burnett w pts A.McKelvie, M.Cittadini w pts R.Scott, P.King w pts R.Brown, G.McArthur w rsc 3 M.Reid; *semi-finals:* G.McArthur w pts P.King, L.Burnett w pts M.Cittadini; *final:* G.McArthur w pts L.Burnett. **Welter:** *quarter-finals:* J.Carlin (Gilmerton) w pts G.Mathieson (Aberdeen), F.Mahura (Sparta) w pts G.Clarke (Gilmerton), A.Montgomery (Forgewood) w pts T.Moran (Sparta), D.Campbell (Denbeath) w pts P.Burns (Forgewood); *semi-finals:* A.Montgomery w pts D.Campbell, F.Mahura w rtd 4 J.Carlin; *final:* F.Mahura w pts A.Montgomery. **Middle:** *quarter-finals:* B.Moore (Perth Railways) w co 1 J.Cooper (Arbroath), K.Anderson Craigmillar) w rsc 4 M.Sinclair (Kingdom), C.Black (Barn) w pts W.Blackwood (Garnock Valley), P.Warner (Springhill) w pts A.Will (Sparta); *semi-finals:* K.Anderson w rsc 3 B.Moore, C.Black w pts P.Warner; *final:* C.Black wo K.Anderson. **L.Heavy:** *quarter-finals:* E.Latyshev (Aberdeen) wo, G.Brennan (Sparta) w pts C.Greig (Drumchapel), K.Reynolds (Barn) w pts M.Loughlin (Barn), M.Warner (Springhill) w pts M.Donald (Kincorth); *semi-finals:* E.Latyshev w rsc 4 G.Brennan, M.Warner w pts K.Reynolds; *final:* M.Warner w pts E.Latyshev. **Heavy:** *semi-finals:* C.McClung (Discovery) wo, S.Simmons (Leith Victoria) w rsc 3 S.Robb (Inverness); *final:* S.Simmons w rsc 3 C.McClung. **S.Heavy:** *quarter-finals:* I.Millarvie (Lesmahagow) wo, W.Fowler (Kincorth) wo, J.Perry (Larkhall) w pts A.Boyle (Raploch), A.Hughes (Lochside) w pts A.Martin (Leith Victoria); *semi-finals:* I.Millarvie wo W.Fowler, J.Perry wo A.Hughes; *final:* I.Millarvie w pts J.Perry.

Wales ABA

The Leisure Centre, Newport – 10 & 11 January & The Leisure Centre, Ebbw Vale – 31 January

L.Fly: *final:* M.Nasir (St Joseph's) wo, **Fly:** *final:* M.Edmonds (St Joseph's East) w rsc 3 D.Jameson (Trelewis). **Bantam:** *semi-finals:* R.Owen (Gwent) wo, N.Probert (Pembroke) w pts L.Fortt (Jim Driscoll's); *final:* R.Owen w pts N.Probert. **Feather:** *final:* D.Davies (Merthyr) w pts D.Edwards (Cwmavon Hornets). **Light:** *quarter-finals:* A.Urrutia (RN) w pts D.Fortt (Jim Driscoll's), G.Couch (Thame) w pts D.Harty (Heads of the Valley), P.Ashton (Cwmavon Hornets) w pts J.Creese (Prince of Wales), C.O'Sullivan (Fishguard) w pts D.Owen (Portmead); *semi-finals:* G.Couch w pts A.Urrutia, P.Ashton w pts C.O'Sullivan; *final:* P.Ashton w pts G.Couch. **L.Welter:** *prelims:* R.James (Merthyr Ex-Servicemen) wo, A.Lancey (RN) wo, G.Perkins (Premier) wo, N.Burchett (Army) wo, B.Jones (Ferndale) wo, C.Goodridge (Llansamlet) wo, K.Parkinson (Torfaen Warriers) w pts H.Evans (Carmarthen), T.Davies (Kyber Colts) w pts G.Tate (Carmarthen); *quarter-finals:* R.James w pts A.Lancey, G.Perkins w pts N.Burchett, B.Jones w rsc 3 C.Goodridge, T.Davies w pts K.Parkinson; *semi-finals:* R.James w pts G.Perkins, B.Jones w pts T.Davies; *final:* B.Jones w pts R.James. **Welter:** *prelims:* C.Morgan (Llanharan) w pts J.Clark (Clwyd). Morgan withdrew injured, leaving all the other prelims as quarter-final contests. *quarter-finals:* J.Phillips (Gwent) w pts B.Stewart (Berinsfield), W.Lukins (Splott Adventure) w pts C.Ambridge (Rhoose), C.Morgan (Llanharan) w pts J.Clark (Clwyd), J.Way (Cwmcarn) w pts L.Chapman (Victoria Park), A.Thomas (Clwyd) w pts L.Trott (Towy); *semi-finals:* W.Lukins w pts J.Phillips, A.Thomas w pts J.Way; *final:* A.Thomas w pts W.Lukins. **Middle:** *prelims:* L.Owen (Portmead) wo, W.O'Sullivan (Cardigan) wo, J.Edmonds (St Joseph's) wo, K.Hope (Merthyr) wo, L.Goodridge (Llansamlet) wo, F.Borg (Prince of Wales) wo, T.Jones (Cwmgorse) wo, S.Hughes (Red Dragon) w pts S.Goody (Victoria Park); *quarter-finals:* L.Owen w rsc 2 J.Edmonds, K.Hope w pts L.Goodridge, F.Borg w pts T.Jones, W.O'Sullivan w rsc 2 S.Hughes; *semi-finals:* L.Owen w pts K.Hope, W.O'Sullivan w pts F.Borg; *final:* L.Owen w pts W.O'Sullivan. **L.Heavy:** *quarter-finals:* J.Hughes (Newport) w pts J.McCourt (Barry East End), J.Whitfield (Army) w pts M.Davies (Penyrheol), J.Jones (Clwyd) w rtd 4 J.Walters (Prince of Wales), I.Aldridge (RAF) w rsc 3 E.Reynolds (Wilson's); *semi-finals:* J.Jones w pts I.Aldridge, J.Whitfield w rsc 3 J.Hughes; *final:* J.Whitfield w pts J.Jones. **Heavy:** *final:* K.Evans (Carmarthen) w rsc 2 O.Harries (Trostre). **S.Heavy:** *final:* D.Morgan (Bonymaen) wo.

Four Nations Tournament, 2004

Kelvin Hall, Glasgow   2 & 3 April

L. Fly: *semi-finals:* S.McDonald (England) w pts U.Hussain (Scotland), J.Conlon (Ireland) w pts M.Nasir (Wales); *final:* S.McDonald w pts J.Conlon. *Box-off:* M.Nasir w pts U.Hussain. **Fly:** *semi-finals:* S.Langley (England) w pts I.McCabe (Scotland), R.Hickey (Ireland) w pts L.Fortt (Wales; *final:* S.Langley w pts R.Hickey. *Box-off:* L.Fortt w pts I.McCabe. **Bantam:** *semi-finals:* J.Donnelly (England) w pts J.Ancliff (Scotland), N.Probert (Wales) w pts B.Harkin (Ireland); *final:* J.Donnelly w rsc 3 N.Probert. *Box-off:* J.Ancliff w pts B.Harkin. **Feather:** *semi-finals:* D.Joyce (Ireland) w pts D.Davies (Wales), J.Watson (England) w pts N.Bonnini (Scotland); *final:* D.Joyce w pts J.Watson. *Box-off:* D.Davies w pts N.Bonnini. **Light:** *semi-finals:* P.Ashton (Wales) w pts E.Hyland (Ireland), M.Hastie (Scotland) w pts C.Pacy (England); *final:* M.Hastie w pts P.Ashton. *Box-off:* E.Hyland w pts C.Pacy. **L.Welter:** *semi-finals:* G.McArthur (Scotland) w pts J.Crees (Wales), R.Sheahan (Ireland) w pts J.Watson (England); *final:* R.Sheahan w pts G.McArthur. *Box-off:* J.Watson wo J.Crees. **Welter:** *semi-finals:* J.Moore (Ireland) w pts S.Briggs (England), F.Mahura (Scotland) w pts A.Thomas (Wales); *final:* J.Moore w pts F.Mahura. *Box-off:* S.Briggs w pts A.Thomas. **Middle:** *semi-finals:* D.Guthrie (England) wo, E.O'Kane (Ireland) w pts L.Owen (Wales); *final:* E.O'Kane w pts D.Guthrie. *Box-off:* L.Owen wo. **L.Heavy:** *semi-finals:* T.Abdusalem (England) w pts E.Latyshev (Scotland), P.Smyth (Ireland) w pts F.Borg (Wales); *final:* T.Abdusalem w rsc 3 P.Smyth. *Box-off:* F.Borg w pts E.Latyshev. **Heavy:** *semi-finals:* T.Bellew (England) wo, S.Simmons (Scotland) w pts G.Smith (Ireland); *final:* T. Bellew w rsc 3 S.Simmons. *Box-off:* G.Smith wo. **S.Heavy:** *semi-finals:* D.Morgan (Wales) w pts J.Young (England), T.Smith (Ireland) w pts J.Perry (Scotland); *final:* D.Morgan w co 1 T.Smith. *Box-off:* J.Young wo J.Perry.

Note: The following national champions were replaced prior to the tournament.

England: M.Marsh (Bantam), D.Mulholland (Feather), M.Murray (Welter).
Ireland: C.Ahern (L.Fly), P.Hyland (Fly), E.Donovan (Bantam), M.Lindsey (Feather), E.Hyland (Light), P.McCloskey (L.Welter), H.Coyle (Welter), A.Lee (Middle), K.Egan (L.Heavy), A.Reynolds (Heavy), M.Rogan (S.Heavy).
Scotland: C.Black (Middle), M.Warner (L.Heavy), I.Millarvie (S.Heavy).
Wales: M.Edmonds (Fly), R.Owen (Bantam), B.Jones (L.Welter), J.Whitfield (L.Heavy), K.Evans (Heavy).

Stuart Langley, England's Four Nations winner at flyweight, is seen here beating Repton's Tony Joyett in the London ABA final

Les Clark

British and Irish International Matches, 2003-2004

Does not include Multi-nation or championship tournaments, despite them being recognised as international appearances, merely because space will not allow. British and Irish interest in the major tournaments can be found within the pages of Chris Kempson's 'Highlights from the 2003-2004 Amateur Season' elsewhere in the book. We apologise if any international matches have been missed, but we have covered all those we have been made aware of.

Young Ireland (6) v Young Canada (4)   Ringside Club, Dublin – 16 July
(Irish names first): **L. Fly:** R. Molloy w pts I. Shiba. **Bantam:** C. Bates l pts B. Brooks. **Feather:** A. Hopkins l pts S. Boyle. **Light:** J. Quinn w pts P. Kranitz, D. Murphy w pts A. Georges. **L. Welter:** K. Boyle w pts D. Wally, A. Fitzgerald l pts S. Louati. **Middle:** A. Hussain w pts C. Bigras, S. Boyle l pts C. Hannah. **L. Heavy:** G. Hussey w pts M. Reid.

Ireland (4) v France (6)   Bastia, Corsica – 3 October
(Irish names first): **L. Fly:** C. Ahern l pts R. Asloum. **Fly:** T. Lee l pts J. Thomas. **Bantam:** E. Donovan l pts A. Hallab. **Light:** A. Murray w pts M. Boulakhras. **L.Welter:** P. McCloskey l pts W. Blain, M. Kelly w pts R. Lakhlifi. **Welter:** R. Sheahan w pts K. Bettaibi. **Middle:** E. O'Kane l pts M. Diambang. **L.Heavy:** K. Egan l pts J. Dovi. **Heavy:** A. Reynolds w co 1 C. Dettinger.

Ireland (3) v France (5)   Toulon, France – 6 October
(Irish names first): **L. Fly:** C. Ahern l pts S. Takoucht. **Fly:** T. Lee l pts J. Thomas. **Bantam:** E. Donovan l pts A. Hallab. **Light:** A. Murray w pts M. Boulakhras. **L.Welter:** M. Kelly w pts K. Bettaibi. **Welter:** R. Sheahan l pts W. Blain. **Middle:** E. O'Kane w pts J.T. Borges. **L.Heavy:** K. Egan l pts J. Dovi.

Ireland (3) v Holland (3)   Rotterdam, Holland – 27 October
(Irish names first): **Bantam:** K. Bates w pts M. Steenbakkers. **Feather:** R. Kane w pts R. Nokhai. **Light:** G. Dunne l pts H. Kocabas, J. Quinn l pts M. Harutunjan. **L.Welter:** D. Nevin l pts R. Harutunjan. **Welter:** L. McMillan w pts S. Weiss. Note that bouts involving Bates, Quinn, Nevin and McMillan were at junior level.

England (3) v Norway (4)   Trondheim, Norway – 1 November
(English names first): **L.Welter:** A.Fletcher w pts D.Chagula, N.Wray l pts M.Massoudy. **Welter:** R.Ashworth w co 3 S.Bojtsov. **Middle:** D.Frost l rsc 4 K-J Jensen. **L.Heavy:** S.McDonald w pts J.Saether. **S.Heavy:** N.Suku l pts D.Peretiako, M.O'Connell l co 4 A.Barkhall. Note that the bout involving Fletcher was at junior level.

England (6) v USA (4)   York Hall, Bethnal Green, London – 3 November
(English names first): **L.Fly:** S.Langley w pts J.Lester. **Fly:** D. Broadhurst w pts C.Huerta. **Bantam:** L.Otte l pts K.Hudgins. **Feather:** D.Mulholland l pts J.Perez. **L.Welter:** S.Jennings l pts D.Alexander. **Welter:** S.Webb w pts N.Casal. **Middle:** G.Barr w pts D.Livingston, R.Samms w pts J.Greene. **Heavy:** D.Dolan l pts M.Godfrey. **S.Heavy:** D.Price w rsc 3 T.Kauffman.

England (9) v USA (0)   Everton Park Sports Centre, Liverpool – 6 November
(English names first): **L.Fly:** S.Langley w pts J.Lester. **Fly:** D. Broadhurst w pts C.Huerta. **Bantam:** S.Smith w pts R.Valenzuela, N.McDonald w pts K.Hudgins. **Feather:** D.Mulholland w pts J.Perez. **Middle:** R. Samms w pts D. Livingston, G. Barr w pts J. Greene.

Heavy: D. Dolan w pts M. Godfrey. **S.Heavy:** D. Price w rsc 3 T.Kauffman.

Wales (5) v Norway (3)   The Penyrheol Leisure Centre, Swansea – 15 November
(Welsh names first): **Feather:** L.Ford w pts A.Evenson. **L.Welter:** R.Pearce l rsc 4 N.Dubunin, B.Jones w rsc 3 T.Ostad. **Welter:** J.Way l pts K.Tverberg, A.Thomas w pts A.Johnsen. **Middle:** F.Borg w pts K-J.Jensen. **L.Heavy:** J.Jones l pts N-A.Morka. **S.Heavy:** D.Morgan w rsc 2 A.Barkhall.

England (9) v Australia (3)   The Conference Centre, Wembley – 1 December
(English names first): **Bantam:** N.McDonald w pts J.Brunker, J.McElvaney w pts L.Zappivigna. **Feather:** D.Mulholland w pts R.Langham, G.Barker w pts S.Parsons. **Light:** L.Shinkwin w pts G.Gran, B.Skeete w pts A.Hann. **L.Welter:** D.Byrnes l rsc 3 T.Kidd, T.Jacobs w pts M.Hatwell. **Welter:** R.Pickard w rsc 2 S.McArdle, S.Webb l pts D.Geale. **Heavy:** D.Dolan l pts A.Forsyth. **S.Heavy:** D.Price w pts J.Whitehead. Note that bouts involving McElvaney, Barker, Shinkwin, Skeete, Jacobs and Pickard were at junior level.

England (9) v Australia (2)   The National Sports Centre, Crystal Palace – 4 December
(English names first): **Bantam:** S. Langley w pts J. Brunker, J. McElvaney w pts L. Zappivigna. **Feather:** G. Sykes w rsc 4 R.Langham, M.Poston w pts S.Parsons. **Light:** L Shinkwin w pts G.Gran, B.Skeete w pts A.Hann. **L.Welter:** T.Coward l pts T.Kidd, R.Pickard w pts S.McArdle. **Middle:** G.Barr w pts D.Geale. **Heavy:** S.Sexton l rsc 2 A.Forsyth. **S.Heavy:** I.Lewison w pts J.Whitehead. Note that McElvaney, Poston, Shinkwin, Skeete and Pickard were at junior level.

Young England (7) v Young Germany (2)   Waveney Sports Centre, Lowestoft – 18 February
(English names first): **L.Fly:** J.McDonnell w pts R.Beblik. **Fly:** P.Dixon l pts D.Makarow. **Feather:** M.Poston w pts E.Burhard, S.Smith w rsc 3 M.Herfurth, B.Saunders l pts C.Bauer. **Light:** J.O'Donnell w pts S.Westphal. **Welter:** J.Selkirk w pts T.Kruger, R.Pickard w pts K.Buga. **Middle:** J.Degale w pts R.Kress. There was also a cadet contest between the two countries, won by England.

Young England (6) v Young Germany (2)   Basingstoke – 20 February
(English names first): **Fly:** P.Dixon l pts D.Makarow. **Feather:** J.McElvaney w pts E.Burhard, S.Smith w pts C.Bauer, B.Saunders w pts M.Herfurth. **L.Welter:** J.O'Donnell w pts S.Westphal. **Welter:** R.Pickard w pts T.Kruger, J.Selkirk l pts K.Buga. **Middle:** T.Hill w pts R.Kress.

Ireland (7) v Scotland (3)   National Stadium, Dublin – 20 February
(Irish names first): **L.Fly:** R. Hickey w pts U. Hussain. **Bantam:** D.A. Joyce w pts P. Appleby. **Feather:** M. Lindsey w rsc 3 J. Ancliff.

Light: E. Hyland l pts M. Prince. **L.Welter:** R. Sheahan w pts G. McArthur, K. Boyle w pts W. Bilan. **Welter:** J. Moore w pts F. Mahura, S. Davitt l pts E. Finney. **L.Heavy:** P. Smyth w pts M. Warner. **S.Heavy:** M. Rogan l pts I. Millarvie. Note that bouts involving Joyce, Boyle and Davitt were at junior level.

Ireland (5) v Scotland (3)   Brandon House Hotel, New Ross, Co. Wexford – 22 February
(Irish names first): **L.Fly:** J. Conlon w pts U. Hussain. Bantam: J. McDonogh l pts P. Appleby. **Feather:** E. Touhey w rsc 2 J. Ancliff. **Light:** N. Monteith l pts M. Prince. **L.Welter:** P. Reilly l pts W. Bilan. **Welter:** F. Turner w pts F. Mahura, S. Davitt w pts E. Finney. **L.Heavy:** S. O'Grady w pts M. Warner. Note that bouts involving McDonough, Reilly and Davitt were at junior level.

Young England (4) v Young Germany (8)   Duren, Germany – 5 March
(English names first): **L.Fly:** J.Murray w pts R.Beblik. **Fly:** J.McDonnell l pts D.Makarow. **Bantam:** J.Mcelvaney l pts M.Schneider. **Feather:** B.Saunders w pts M.Abramowski. **Light:** F.Gavin l rsc 3 D.Dohl. **L.Welter:** A.Fletcher l pts D.Manulenko.

Welter: J.Fewkes l pts S.Westphal, J.Selkirk w pts T.Vorrath. **Middle:** J.Smyth w pts T.Trollenberg. **L.Heavy:** D.Sadler l rsc 2 A.Hofmeister. **Heavy:** J-L Dickensen l pts R.Krause. **S.Heavy:** B.Smith l pts C.Laarz.

Young England (4) v Young Germany (4)   Schriesheim, Germany – 7 March
(English names first): **L.Fly:** J.Murray w pts H.Bouji. **Bantam:** J.McElvaney w pts J.Fuchs. **Feather:** B.Saunders w pts M.Herfurth. **L.Welter:** J.Fewkes l pts A.Butz, A.Fletcher l rsc 2 A.Miller. **L.Heavy:** D.Sadler l rsc 2 R.Krause, J-L Dickensen l pts B.Schmidt. **Heavy:** T.Dallas w pts M.Bandura. At flyweight, J.McDonnell drew with M.Mieirdierks.

Scotland (5) v Austria (3) - 23 April   Innsbruck, Austria – 23 April
(Scottish names first): **L.Fly:** U.Hussain l pts A.Walti. **Bantam:** J.Hastie w pts N.Kacha. **Feather:** J.Ancliff w pts A.Wanusch. **Light:** M.Prince w pts M.Tamesebired. **L.Welter:** S.Reid w pts l.Enbacher. **Welter:** S.Kynoch l co 1 O.Benjamin. **Middle:** C.Black w pts F.Kolbauer, B.Nisbet l pts O.Obradovic. At lightweight, J.Kelso drew with A.Harlander.

Sam Webb (right), seen here beating America's Nicholas Casal, was one of England's six winners at the York Hall, Bethnal Green last November

Les Clark

British Junior Championship Finals, 2003-2004

National Association of Clubs for Young People (NACYP)

The Town Hall, Retford – 4 December

Class A: 46 kg: P.Jones (Stevenage) w pts M.Ward (Birtley). 48 kg: A.Dainty (Canvey) w pts D.Toohey (Cleckheaton). 50 kg: K.Cosgrove (Hartlepool Catholic) w pts D.Burrell (Samuel Montagu). 52 kg: M.Fagan (Vauxhall Motors) w pts A.Deex (Harwich). 54 kg: N.Hepper (Darlington) L.Gray (Stevenage). 57 kg: J.Wale (Mexborough) L.Jones (Reading). 60 kg: R.Garvey (Earlsfield) w pts M.Docherty (Barn). 63 kg: P.Nugent (West Ham) w pts B.McGivern (Barn). 66 kg: A.Agogo (Triple A) w pts S.Reid (Aberdeen). 70 kg: M.Shinkwin (Bushey) w rsc 3 D.Parkinson (Kirkdale).

The Adelphi Hotel, Liverpool – 17 December

Class B: 48 kg: J.Radford (Newham) w rsc 2 J.Dolan (Birtley). 51 kg: V.Mitchell (West Ham) w pts S.Russell (Paisley YMCA). 54 kg: P.Appleby (Sparta) w rsc 2 C.Duffield (West Ham). 57 kg: M.Murnane (Chalvedon) w pts M.Ungi (Golden Gloves). 60 kg: K.Kirkham (Blackpool & Fylde) w pts R.Giles (Onslow Lions). 64 kg: N.Cain (Dale Youth) w pts P.Fellows (Glasgow Noble Art). 69 kg: T.Carthy (Sunderland) w pts J.Begley (Canvey). 75 kg: T.Saunders (Cheshunt) w pts S.Brookes (Wombwell & Dearne). 81 kg: R.Boardman (King Alfred) w co 1 I.Askew (Lambton Street).

The Royal Lancaster Hotel, Bayswater – 10 December

Class C: 48 kg: P.Jamison (Transport) w pts M.Nasir (St Joseph's East). 51 kg: A.Bridge (Golden Gloves) w pts L.Fortt (Jim Driscoll's). 54 kg: G.Buckland (St Joseph's East) w pts C.Breen (Barn). 57 kg: B.Saunders (South Durham) w pts M.Graydon (Broad Plain). 60 kg: R.Brawley (Springside) w pts T.Thornby (St Mary's). 64 kg: E.Brook (Unity) w pts W.Goddard (Bordon). 69 kg: C.Johnson (Terry Allen Unique) w rsc 3 R.Mahoney (Canvey). 75 kg: J.Degale (Dale Youth) w rsc 3 P.Ward (Birtley). 81 kg: J-L. Dickensen (Birtley) w rsc 1 J.Weston (Eastleigh).

Schools

Goresbrook Leisure Centre, Dagenham – 27 & 28 March

Class 1: 32 kg: C.Hoy (Cheshunt) w pts D.Slater (Birtley). 34 kg: M.Ward (Repton) w pts J.Varey (Burton). 36 kg: G.Langley (Repton) w pts H.Khan (Bury). 39 kg: J.Day (Newham) w pts A.Fowler (Golden Gloves). 42 kg: S.Barnes (Unity) w pts J.Baker (Repton). 45: T.Collins (Middlesbrough) w pts J.Kerr (West Ham). 48 kg: C.Oliver (Kettering) w pts B.Ray (Cheshunt). 51 kg: T.Shaw (Burton) w pts J.Donohue (Southampton). 54 kg: R.Aston (Priory Park) w pts J.Coyle (Foley). 57 kg: J.Cetaj (Walcot) w pts J.Childs (Enfield). 60 kg: J.Williams (Kirkby) w dis 3 C.Moses (Aylesham).

Class 2: 36 kg: S.Sutherland (Stevenage) w pts D.Arnold (Wednesbury). 39 kg: S.Thewlis (Karmand) w pts I.Weaver (Golden Ring). 42 kg: R.Heffron (Boarshaw) w pts C.Fox (Eltham). 45 kg: M.Tallon (Salisbury) w pts A.Morris (Cheshunt). 48 kg: D.Phillips (South Bank) w pts D.Docherty (Bushey). 51 kg: R.Rose (St Mary's) w pts K.Spencer (Lions). 54 kg: W.Claydon (Onslow Lions) w pts D.Boswell (Bolton). 57 kg: S.Cardle (Mill Farm) w pts S.Osmond (Canterbury). 60 kg: C.Briscoe (Hoyle Mill) w pts J.Hancock (Ferry Street).

63 kg: M.Nugent (West Ham) w pts A.White (Langold). 66 kg: J.Grimes (Halewood) wo. 69 kg: M.Hallisey (Pleck) w pts D.Londers (Elm Park).

Class 3: 39 kg: S.Macklin (Heartlands) w pts B.Evans (Stevenage). 42 kg: M.Rooney (Heartlands) w pts S.Upton (Dagenham). 45 kg: M.McGuire (Kettering SoB) w rtd 3 L.Unsworth (Bexley). 48 kg: P.Jones (Stevenage) w pts K.D'eath (Northside). 51 kg: S.Henty (Eltham) w pts G.Hancock (Hartlepool Catholic). 54 kg: S.Vincent (Woking) w pts C.Kelly (St Theresa's). 57 kg: C.Wallace (Durham College) w pts F.Holmes (Stevenage). 60 kg: B-J. Saunders (Cheshunt) w pts F.Connelly (Rotunda). 63 kg: H.Burton (Northside) w pts J.Gosling (Southend). 66 kg: A.Agogo (Triple A) w pts L.Holland (Altrincham). 69 kg: D.Gardner (Cheshunt) w pts L.Bullock (Old Robin Hood). 72 kg: S.Griffiths (Donnington Ex-Servicemen) wo G.Chekorishuilli (All Stars).

Class 4: 42 kg: C.Williamson (Farley) w pts K.Newell (Radford Boys). 45 kg: C.Higgs (Lydney) w pts G.Cullen (Stockbridge). 48 kg: M.Ward (Birtley) w pts A.Dainty (Canvey). 51 kg: C.Duffield (West Ham) w pts D.Curran (Grainger Park). 54 kg: L.Gray (Stevenage) w pts D.Rogers Kettering SoB). 57 kg: B.Henty (Eltham) w rsc 3 J.Wale (Mexborough). 60 kg: K.Kirkham (Blackpool & Fylde) w pts B.Skeete (Earlsfield). 63.5 kg: P.Nugent (West Ham) w pts G.Foot (Marley Potts). 67 kg: T.Dickensen (Birtley) w rsc 3 P.Waites (West Ham). D.Gardner (Cheshunt) w pts R.Lovell (Chester). 75 kg: G.Groves (Dale Youth) w rsc 1 J.Edmonds (Heart of England). 81 kg: D.Kent (Golden Ring) w pts J.Turner (Shildon).

ABA Youth

The Town Hall, Huddersfield – 29 May

Class 5 (born 1987): 48kg: J.Murray (Boarshaw) w pts J.Cole (Dagenham). 51 kg: L.Campbell (St Paul's) w pts K.Hogkinson (Kirkby). 54 kg: C.Smith (Pinewood Starr) w pts M.Chappell (Hard & Fast). 57 kg: D.Watson (Shildon) w pts C.Webb (Haileybury). 60 kg: A.Anwar (Bateson's) w pts M.Ungi (Golden Gloves). 64 kg: J.Creamer (City of Portsmouth) w pts N.Cain (Dale Youth). 69 kg: C.Donoghue (St Aloysius) w pts T.McDonagh (South Norwood & Victory). 75 kg: S.Brookes (Wombwell & Dearne) w pts M.Stanton (Kirkby). 81 kg: M.Fielding (Salisbury) w pts R.Boardman (King Alfred). 91 kg: M.Churcher (Thames Valley) w pts P.Godfrey (Skelmersdale). 91+ kg: no entries.

Class 6 (born 1986): 48 kg: A.Smith (Stockbridge) w pts S.King (Ironworks). 51 kg: J.McDonnell (Wombwell & Dearne) w pts R.Walsh (Kingfisher). 54 kg: L.Walsh (Kingfisher) w pts T.Mills (Repton). 57 kg: M.Bailey (Birmingham City) w pts R.Smart (Southampton). 60 kg: N.Smedley (Steel City) w rsc 1 S.Hart (West Ham). 64 kg: E.Brook (Unity) wo J.Keenan (Ardwick Lads). 69 kg: C.Bunn (Northside) w pts J.Broomfield (New Astley). 75 kg: T.Hill (Golden Ring) wo J.Brazil (Haileybury). 81 kg: J-L Dickensen (Birtley) w rsc 3 S.Kehoe (Gemini). 91 kg: L.Hartley (Halfpenny) w pts C.Snell (Taunton). 91+ kg: E.Jegeni (Haringey Police) wo C.Smith (Pinewood Starr).

ABA Champions, 1881-2004

L. Flyweight
1971 M. Abrams
1972 M. Abrams
1973 M. Abrams
1974 C. Magri
1975 M. Lawless
1976 P. Fletcher
1977 P. Fletcher
1978 J. Dawson
1979 J. Dawson
1980 T. Barker
1981 J. Lyon
1982 J. Lyon
1983 J. Lyon
1984 J. Lyon
1985 M. Epton
1986 M. Epton
1987 M. Epton
1988 M. Cantwell
1989 M. Cantwell
1990 N. Tooley
1991 P. Culshaw
1992 D. Fifield
1993 M. Hughes
1994 G. Jones
1995 D. Fox
1996 R. Mercer
1997 I. Napa
1998 J. Evans
1999 G. Jones
2000 J. Mulherne
2001 C. Lyon
2002 D. Langley
2003 C. Lyon
2004 S. McDonald

Flyweight
1920 H. Groves
1921 W. Cuthbertson
1922 E. Warwick
1923 L. Tarrant
1924 E. Warwick
1925 E. Warwick
1926 J. Hill
1927 J. Roland
1928 C. Taylor
1929 T. Pardoe
1930 T. Pardoe
1931 T. Pardoe
1932 T. Pardoe
1933 T. Pardoe
1934 P. Palmer
1935 G. Fayaud
1936 G. Fayaud
1937 P. O'Donaghue
1938 A. Russell
1939 D. McKay
1944 J. Clinton
1945 J. Bryce
1946 R. Gallacher
1947 J. Clinton
1948 H. Carpenter
1949 H. Riley
1950 A. Jones
1951 G. John
1952 D. Dower
1953 R. Currie
1954 R. Currie

1955 D. Lloyd
1956 T. Spinks
1957 R. Davies
1958 J. Brown
1959 M. Gushlow
1960 D. Lee
1961 W. McGowan
1962 M. Pye
1963 M. Laud
1964 J. McCluskey
1965 J. McCluskey
1966 P. Maguire
1967 S. Curtis
1968 J. McGonigle
1969 D. Needham
1970 D. Needham
1971 P. Wakefield
1972 M. O'Sullivan
1973 R. Hilton
1974 M. O'Sullivan
1975 C. Magri
1976 C. Magri
1977 C. Magri
1978 G. Nickels
1979 R. Gilbody
1980 K. Wallace
1981 K. Wallace
1982 J. Kelly
1983 S. Nolan
1984 P. Clinton
1985 P. Clinton
1986 J. Lyon
1987 J. Lyon
1988 J. Lyon
1989 J. Lyon
1990 J. Armour
1991 P. Ingle
1992 K. Knox
1993 P. Ingle
1994 D. Costello
1995 D. Costello
1996 D. Costello
1997 M. Hunter
1998 J. Hegney
1999 D. Robinson
2000 D. Robinson
2001 M. Marsh
2002 D. Barriball
2003 D. Broadhurst
2004 S. Langley

Bantamweight
1884 A. Woodward
1885 A. Woodward
1886 T. Isley
1887 T. Isley
1888 H. Oakman
1889 H. Brown
1890 J. Rowe
1891 E. Moore
1892 F. Godbold
1893 E. Watson
1894 P. Jones
1895 P. Jones
1896 P. Jones
1897 C. Lamb
1898 F. Herring
1899 A. Avent

1900 J. Freeman
1901 W. Morgan
1902 A. Miner
1903 H. Perry
1904 H. Perry
1905 W. Webb
1906 T. Ringer
1907 E. Adams
1908 H. Thomas
1909 J. Condon
1910 W. Webb
1911 W. Allen
1912 W. Allen
1913 A. Wye
1914 W. Allen
1919 W. Allen
1920 G. McKenzie
1921 L. Tarrant
1922 W. Boulding
1923 A. Smith
1924 L. Tarrant
1925 A. Goom
1926 F. Webster
1927 E. Warwick
1928 J. Garland
1929 F. Bennett
1930 H. Mizler
1931 F. Bennett
1932 L. Treadaway
1933 G. Johnston
1934 A. Barnes
1935 L. Case
1936 A. Barnes
1937 A. Barnes
1938 J. Pottinger
1939 R. Watson
1944 R. Bissell
1945 P. Brander
1946 C. Squire
1947 D. O'Sullivan
1948 T. Profitt
1949 T. Miller
1950 T. Nicholls
1951 T. Nicholls
1952 T. Nicholls
1953 J. Smillie
1954 J. Smillie
1955 G. Dormer
1956 O. Reilly
1957 J. Morrissey
1958 H. Winstone
1959 D. Weller
1960 F. Taylor
1961 P. Benneyworth
1962 P. Benneyworth
1963 B. Packer
1964 B. Packer
1965 R. Mallon
1966 J. Clark
1967 M. Carter
1968 M. Carter
1969 M. Piner
1970 A. Oxley
1971 G. Turpin
1972 G. Turpin
1973 P. Cowdell
1974 S. Ogilvie
1975 S. Ogilvie

1976 J. Bambrick
1977 J. Turner
1978 J. Turner
1979 R. Ashton
1980 R. Gilbody
1981 P. Jones
1982 R. Gilbody
1983 J. Hyland
1984 J. Hyland
1985 S. Murphy
1986 S. Murphy
1987 J. Sillitoe
1988 K. Howlett
1989 K. Howlett
1990 P. Lloyd
1991 D. Hardie
1992 P. Mullings
1993 R. Evatt
1994 S. Oliver
1995 N. Wilders
1996 L. Eedle
1997 S. Oates
1998 L. Pattison
1999 M. Hunter
2000 S. Foster
2001 S. Foster
2002 D. Matthews
2003 N. McDonald
2004 M. Marsh

Featherweight
1881 T. Hill
1882 T. Hill
1883 T. Hill
1884 E. Hutchings
1885 J. Pennell
1886 T. McNeil
1887 J. Pennell
1888 J. Taylor
1889 G. Belsey
1890 G. Belsey
1891 F. Curtis
1892 F. Curtis
1893 T. Davidson
1894 R. Gunn
1895 R. Gunn
1896 R. Gunn
1897 N. Smith
1898 P. Lunn
1899 J. Scholes
1900 R. Lee
1901 C. Clarke
1902 C. Clarke
1903 J. Godfrey
1904 C. Morris
1905 H. Holmes
1906 A. Miner
1907 C. Morris
1908 T. Ringer
1909 A. Lambert
1910 C. Houghton
1911 H. Bowers
1912 G. Baker
1913 G. Baker
1914 G. Baker
1919 G. Baker
1920 J. Fleming
1921 G. Baker

1922 E. Swash
1923 E. Swash
1924 A. Beavis
1925 A. Beavis
1926 R. Minshull
1927 F. Webster
1928 F. Meachem
1929 F. Meachem
1930 J. Duffield
1931 B. Caplan
1932 H. Mizler
1933 J. Walters
1934 J. Treadaway
1935 E. Ryan
1936 J. Treadaway
1937 A. Harper
1938 C. Gallie
1939 C. Gallie
1944 D. Sullivan
1945 J. Carter
1946 P. Brander
1947 S. Evans
1948 P. Brander
1949 H. Gilliland
1950 P. Brander
1951 J. Travers
1952 P. Lewis
1953 P. Lewis
1954 D. Charnley
1955 T. Nicholls
1956 T. Nicholls
1957 M. Collins
1958 M. Collins
1959 G. Judge
1960 P. Lundgren
1961 P. Cheevers
1962 B. Wilson
1963 A. Riley
1964 R. Smith
1965 K. Buchanan
1966 H. Baxter
1967 K. Cooper
1968 J. Cheshire
1969 A. Richardson
1970 D. Polak
1971 T. Wright
1972 K. Laing
1973 J. Lynch
1974 G. Gilbody
1975 R. Beaumont
1976 P. Cowdell
1977 P. Cowdell
1978 M. O'Brien
1979 P. Hanlon
1980 M. Hanif
1981 P. Hanlon
1982 H. Henry
1983 P. Bradley
1984 K. Taylor
1985 F. Havard
1986 P. Hodkinson
1987 P. English
1988 D. Anderson
1989 P. Richardson
1990 B. Carr
1991 J. Irwin
1992 A. Temple
1993 J. Cook

1994 D. Pithie	1898 H. Marks	1932 F. Meachem	1966 J. Head	1996 K. Wing
1995 D. Burrows	1899 H. Brewer	1933 H. Mizler	1967 T. Waller	1997 M. Hawthorne
1996 T. Mulholland	1900 G. Humphries	1934 J. Rolland	1968 J. Watt	1998 A. McLean
1997 S. Bell	1901 A. Warner	1935 F. Frost	1969 H. Hayes	1999 S. Burke
1998 D. Williams	1902 A. Warner	1936 F. Simpson	1970 N. Cole	2000 A. McLean
1999 S. Miller	1903 H. Fergus	1937 A. Danahar	1971 J. Singleton	2001 S. Burke
2000 H. Castle	1904 M. Wells	1938 T. McGrath	1972 N. Cole	2002 A. Morris
2001 S. Bell	1905 M. Wells	1939 H. Groves	1973 T. Dunn	2003 S. Burke
2002 D. Mulholland	1906 M. Wells	1944 W. Thompson	1974 J. Lynch	2004 C. Pacy
2003 K. Mitchell	1907 M. Wells	1945 J. Williamson	1975 P. Cowdell	
2004 D. Mulholland	1908 H. Holmes	1946 E. Thomas	1976 S. Mittee	**L. Welterweight**
	1909 F. Grace	1947 C. Morrissey	1977 G. Gilbody	1951 W. Connor
Lightweight	1910 T. Tees	1948 R. Cooper	1978 T. Marsh	1952 P. Waterman
1881 F. Hobday	1911 A. Spenceley	1949 A. Smith	1979 G. Gilbody	1953 D. Hughes
1882 A. Bettinson	1912 R. Marriott	1950 R. Latham	1980 G. Gilbody	1954 G. Martin
1883 A. Diamond	1913 R. Grace	1951 R. Hinson	1981 G. Gilbody	1955 F. McQuillan
1884 A. Diamond	1914 R. Marriott	1952 F. Reardon	1982 J. McDonnell	1956 D. Stone
1885 A. Diamond	1919 F. Grace	1953 D. Hinson	1983 K. Willis	1957 D. Stone
1886 G. Roberts	1920 F. Grace	1954 G. Whelan	1984 A. Dickson	1958 R. Kane
1887 J. Hair	1921 G. Shorter	1955 S. Coffey	1985 E. McAuley	1959 R. Kane
1888 A. Newton	1922 G. Renouf	1956 R. McTaggart	1986 J. Jacobs	1960 R. Day
1889 W. Neale	1923 G. Shorter	1957 J. Kidd	1987 M. Ayers	1961 B. Brazier
1890 A. Newton	1924 W. White	1958 R. McTaggart	1988 C. Kane	1962 B. Brazier
1891 E. Dettmer	1925 E. Viney	1959 P. Warwick	1989 M. Ramsey	1963 R. McTaggart
1892 E. Dettmer	1926 T. Slater	1960 R. McTaggart	1990 P. Gallagher	1964 R. Taylor
1893 W. Campbell	1927 W. Hunt	1961 P. Warwick	1991 P. Ramsey	1965 R. McTaggart
1894 W. Campbell	1928 F. Webster	1962 B. Whelan	1992 D. Amory	1966 W. Hiatt
1895 A. Randall	1929 W. Hunt	1963 B. O'Sullivan	1993 B. Welsh	1967 B. Hudspeth
1896 A. Vanderhout	1930 J. Waples	1964 J. Dunne	1994 A. Green	1968 E. Cole
1897 A. Vanderhout	1931 D. McCleave	1965 A. White	1995 R. Rutherford	1969 J. Stracey

Salisbury's David Mulholland (left) won the ABA featherweight title for the second time on outpointing John Watson (Higherside) this year

Les Clark

1970 D. Davies
1971 M. Kingwell
1972 T. Waller
1973 N. Cole
1974 P. Kelly
1975 J. Zeraschi
1976 C. McKenzie
1977 J. Douglas
1978 D. Williams
1979 E. Copeland
1980 A. Willis
1981 A. Willis
1982 A. Adams
1983 D. Dent
1984 D. Griffiths
1985 I. Mustafa
1986 J. Alsop
1987 A. Holligan
1988 A. Hall
1989 A. Hall
1990 J. Pender
1991 J. Matthews
1992 D. McCarrick
1993 P. Richardson
1994 A. Temple
1995 A. Vaughan
1996 C. Wall
1997 R. Hatton
1998 N. Wright
1999 D. Happe
2000 N. Wright
2001 G. Smith
2002 L. Daws
2003 L. Beavis
2004 J. Watson

Welterweight
1920 F. Whitbread
1921 A. Ireland
1922 E. White
1923 P. Green
1924 P. O'Hanrahan
1925 P. O'Hanrahan
1926 B. Marshall
1927 H. Dunn
1928 H. Bone
1929 T. Wigmore
1930 F. Brooman
1931 J. Barry
1932 D. McCleave
1933 P. Peters
1934 D. McCleave
1935 D. Lynch
1936 W. Pack
1937 D. Lynch
1938 C. Webster
1939 R. Thomas
1944 H. Hall
1945 R. Turpin
1946 J. Ryan
1947 J. Ryan
1948 M. Shacklady
1949 A. Buxton
1950 T. Ratcliffe
1951 J. Maloney
1952 J. Maloney
1953 L. Morgan
1954 N. Gargano
1955 N. Gargano
1956 N. Gargano
1957 R. Warnes

1958 B. Nancurvis
1959 J. McGrail
1960 C. Humphries
1961 A. Lewis
1962 J. Pritchett
1963 J. Pritchett
1964 M. Varley
1965 P. Henderson
1966 P. Cragg
1967 D. Cranswick
1968 A. Tottoh
1969 T. Henderson
1970 T. Waller
1971 D. Davies
1972 T. Francis
1973 T. Waller
1974 T. Waller
1975 W. Bennett
1976 C. Jones
1977 C. Jones
1978 E. Byrne
1979 J. Frost
1980 T. Marsh
1981 T. Marsh
1982 C. Pyatt
1983 R. McKenley
1984 M. Hughes
1985 E. McDonald
1986 D. Dyer
1987 M. Elliot
1988 M. McCreath
1989 M. Elliot
1990 A. Carew
1991 J. Calzaghe
1992 M. Santini
1993 C. Bessey
1994 K. Short
1995 M. Hall
1996 J. Khaliq
1997 F. Barrett
1998 D. Walker
1999 A. Cesay
2000 F. Doherty
2001 M. Macklin
2002 M. Lomax
2003 D. Happe
2004 M. Murray

L. Middleweight
1951 A. Lay
1952 B. Foster
1953 B. Wells
1954 B. Wells
1955 B. Foster
1956 J. McCormack
1957 J. Cunningham
1958 S. Pearson
1959 S. Pearson
1960 W. Fisher
1961 J. Gamble
1962 J. Lloyd
1963 A. Wyper
1964 W. Robinson
1965 P. Dwyer
1966 T. Imrie
1967 A. Edwards
1968 E. Blake
1969 T. Imrie
1970 D. Simmonds
1971 A. Edwards
1972 L. Paul

1973 R. Maxwell
1974 R. Maxwell
1975 A. Harrison
1976 W. Lauder
1977 C. Malarkey
1978 E. Henderson
1979 D. Brewster
1980 J. Price
1981 E. Christie
1982 D. Milligan
1983 R. Douglas
1984 R. Douglas
1985 R. Douglas
1986 T. Velinor
1987 N. Brown
1988 W. Ellis
1989 N. Brown
1990 T. Taylor
1991 T. Taylor
1992 J. Calzaghe
1993 D. Starie
1994 W. Alexander
1995 C. Bessey
1996 S. Dann
1997 C. Bessey
1998 C. Bessey
1999 C. Bessey
2000 C. Bessey
2001 M. Thirwall
2002 P. Smith

Middleweight
1881 T. Bellhouse
1882 A. H. Curnick
1883 A. J. Curnick
1884 W. Brown
1885 M. Salmon
1886 W. King
1887 R. Hair
1888 R. Hair
1889 G. Sykes
1890 J. Hoare
1891 J. Steers
1892 J. Steers
1893 J. Steers
1894 W. Sykes
1895 G. Townsend
1896 W. Ross
1897 W. Dees
1898 G. Townsend
1899 R. Warnes
1900 E. Mann
1901 R. Warnes
1902 E. Mann
1903 R. Warnes
1904 E. Mann
1905 J. Douglas
1906 A. Murdock
1907 R. Warnes
1908 W. Child
1909 W. Child
1910 R. Warnes
1911 W. Child
1912 E. Chandler
1913 W. Bradley
1914 H. Brown
1919 H. Mallin
1920 H. Mallin
1921 H. Mallin
1922 H. Mallin
1923 H. Mallin

1924 J. Elliot
1925 J. Elliot
1926 F. P. Crawley
1927 F. P. Crawley
1928 F. Mallin
1929 F. Mallin
1930 F. Mallin
1931 F. Mallin
1932 F. Mallin
1933 A. Shawyer
1934 J. Magill
1935 J. Magill
1936 A. Harrington
1937 M. Dennis
1938 H. Tiller
1939 H. Davies
1944 J. Hockley
1945 R. Parker
1946 R. Turpin
1947 R. Agland
1948 J. Wright
1949 S. Lewis
1950 P. Longo
1951 E. Ludlam
1952 T. Gooding
1953 R. Barton
1954 K. Phillips
1955 F. Hope
1956 R. Redrup
1957 P. Burke
1958 P. Hill
1959 F. Elderfield
1960 R. Addison
1961 J. Caiger
1962 A. Matthews
1963 A. Matthews
1964 W. Stack
1965 W. Robinson
1966 C. Finnegan
1967 A. Ball
1968 P. McCann
1969 D. Wallington
1970 J. Conteh
1971 A. Minter
1972 F. Lucas
1973 F. Lucas
1974 D. Odwell
1975 D. Odwell
1976 E. Burke
1977 R. Davies
1978 H. Graham
1979 N. Wilshire
1980 M. Kaylor
1981 B. Schumacher
1982 J. Price
1983 T. Forbes
1984 B. Schumacher
1985 D. Cronin
1986 N. Benn
1987 R. Douglas
1988 M. Edwards
1989 S. Johnson
1990 S. Wilson
1991 M. Edwards
1992 L. Woolcock
1993 J. Calzaghe
1994 D. Starie
1995 J. Matthews
1996 J. Pearce
1997 I. Cooper
1998 J. Pearce

1999 C. Froch
2000 S. Swales
2001 C. Froch
2002 N. Perkins
2003 N. Perkins
2004 D. Guthrie

L. Heavyweight
1920 H. Franks
1921 L. Collett
1922 H. Mitchell
1923 H. Mitchell
1924 H. Mitchell
1925 H. Mitchell
1926 D. McCorkindale
1927 A. Jackson
1928 A. Jackson
1929 J. Goyder
1930 J. Murphy
1931 J. Petersen
1932 J. Goyder
1933 G. Brennan
1934 G. Brennan
1935 R. Hearns
1936 J. Magill
1937 J. Wilby
1938 A. S. Brown
1939 B. Woodcock
1944 E. Shackleton
1945 A. Watson
1946 J. Taylor
1947 A. Watson
1948 D. Scott
1949 *Declared no contest*
1950 P. Messervy
1951 G. Walker
1952 H. Cooper
1953 H. Cooper
1954 A. Madigan
1955 D. Rent
1956 D. Mooney
1957 T. Green
1958 J. Leeming
1959 J. Ould
1960 J. Ould
1961 J. Bodell
1962 J. Hendrickson
1963 P. Murphy
1964 J. Fisher
1965 E. Whistler
1966 R. Tighe
1967 M. Smith
1968 R. Brittle
1969 J. Frankham
1970 J. Rafferty
1971 J. Conteh
1972 W. Knight
1973 W. Knight
1974 W. Knight
1975 M. Heath
1976 G. Evans
1977 C. Lawson
1978 V. Smith
1979 A. Straughn
1980 A. Straughn
1981 A. Straughn
1982 G. Crawford
1983 A. Wilson
1984 A. Wilson
1985 J. Beckles
1986 J. Moran

1987 J. Beckles
1988 H. Lawson
1989 N. Piper
1990 J. McCluskey
1991 A. Todd
1992 K. Oliver
1993 K. Oliver
1994 K. Oliver
1995 K. Oliver
1996 C. Fry
1997 P. Rogers
1998 C. Fry
1999 J. Ainscough
2000 P. Haymer
2001 C. Fry
2002 T. Marsden
2003 J. Boyd
2004 M. Abdusalem

Cruiserweight
1998 T. Oakey
1999 M. Krence
2000 J. Dolan
2001 J. Dolan
2002 J. Dolan

Heavyweight
1881 R. Frost-Smith
1882 H. Dearsley
1883 H. Dearsley
1884 H. Dearsley
1885 W. West
1886 A. Diamond
1887 E. White

1888 W. King
1889 A. Bowman
1890 J. Steers
1891 V. Barker
1892 J. Steers
1893 J. Steers
1894 H. King
1895 W. E. Johnstone
1896 W. E. Johnstone
1897 G. Townsend
1898 G. Townsend
1899 F. Parks
1900 W. Dees
1901 F. Parks
1902 F. Parks
1903 F. Dickson
1904 A. Horner
1905 F. Parks
1906 F. Parks
1907 H. Brewer
1908 S. Evans
1909 C. Brown
1910 F. Storbeck
1911 W. Hazell
1912 R. Smith
1913 R. Smith
1914 E. Chandler
1919 H. Brown
1920 R. Rawson
1921 R. Rawson
1922 T. Evans
1923 E. Eagan
1924 A. Clifton
1925 D. Lister

1926 T. Petersen
1927 C. Capper
1928 J. L. Driscoll
1929 P. Floyd
1930 V. Stuart
1931 M. Flanagan
1932 V. Stuart
1933 C. O'Grady
1934 P. Floyd
1935 P. Floyd
1936 V. Stuart
1937 V. Stuart
1938 G. Preston
1939 A. Porter
1944 M. Hart
1945 D. Scott
1946 P. Floyd
1947 G. Scriven
1948 J. Gardner
1949 A. Worrall
1950 P. Toch
1951 A. Halsey
1952 E. Hearn
1953 J. Erskine
1954 B. Harper
1955 D. Rowe
1956 D. Rent
1957 D. Thomas
1958 D. Thomas
1959 D. Thomas
1960 L. Hobbs
1961 W. Walker
1962 R. Dryden
1963 R. Sanders

1964 C. Woodhouse
1965 W. Wells
1966 A. Brogan
1967 P. Boddington
1968 W. Wells
1969 A. Burton
1970 J. Gilmour
1971 L. Stevens
1972 T. Wood
1973 G. McEwan
1974 N. Meade
1975 G. McEwan
1976 J. Rafferty
1977 G. Adair
1978 J. Awome
1979 A. Palmer
1980 F. Bruno
1981 A. Elliott
1982 H. Hylton
1983 H. Notice
1984 D. Young
1985 H. Hylton
1986 E. Cardouza
1987 J. Moran
1988 H. Akinwande
1989 H. Akinwande
1990 K. Inglis
1991 P. Lawson
1992 S. Welch
1993 P. Lawson
1994 S. Burford
1995 M. Ellis
1996 T. Oakey

1997 B. Stevens
1998 N. Hosking
1999 S. St John
2000 D. Dolan
2001 D. Dolan
2002 D. Dolan
2003 M. O'Connell
2004 A. Bellew

S. Heavyweight
1982 A. Elliott
1983 K. Ferdinand
1984 R. Wells
1985 G. Williamson
1986 J. Oyebola
1987 J. Oyebola
1988 K. McCormack
1989 P. Passley
1990 K. McCormack
1991 K. McCormack
1992 M. Hopper
1993 M. McKenzie
1994 D. Watts
1995 R. Allen
1996 D. Watts
1997 A. Harrison
1998 A. Harrison
1999 W. Bessey
2000 J. McDermott
2001 M. Grainger
2002 M. Grainger
2003 D. Price
2004 J. Young

Murtala Abdusalem (left) from the St Pancras Kronk club, won the 2004 ABA light-heavyweight title when stopping the Army's Lee Spare

Les Clark

International Amateur Champions, 1904-2004

Shows all Olympic, World, European & Commonwealth champions since 1904. British silver and bronze medal winners are shown throughout, where applicable.

Country Code

ALG = Algeria; ARG = Argentina; ARM = Armenia; AUS = Australia; AUT = Austria; AZE = Azerbaijan; BE = Belarus; BEL = Belgium; BUL = Bulgaria; CAN = Canada; CEY = Ceylon (now Sri Lanka); CI = Channel Islands; CUB = Cuba; DEN = Denmark; DOM = Dominican Republic; ENG = England; ESP = Spain; EST = Estonia; FIJ = Fiji Islands; FIN = Finland; FRA = France; GBR = United Kingdom; GDR = German Democratic Republic; GEO = Georgia; GER = Germany (but West Germany only from 1968-1990); GHA = Ghana; GUY = Guyana; HOL = Netherlands; HUN = Hungary; IND = India; IRL = Ireland; ITA = Italy; JAM = Jamaica; JPN = Japan; KAZ = Kazakhstan; KEN = Kenya; LIT = Lithuania; MAS = Malaysia; MEX = Mexico; MRI = Mauritius; NKO = North Korea; NIG = Nigeria; NIR = Northern Ireland; NOR = Norway; NZL = New Zealand; PAK = Pakistan; POL = Poland; PUR = Puerto Rico; ROM = Romania; RUS = Russia; SAF = South Africa; SCO = Scotland; SKO = South Korea; SR = Southern Rhodesia; STV = St Vincent; SWE = Sweden; TCH = Czechoslovakia; THA = Thailand; TUR = Turkey; UGA = Uganda; UKR = Ukraine; URS = USSR; USA = United States of America; UZB = Uzbekistan; VEN = Venezuela; WAL = Wales; YUG = Yugoslavia; ZAM = Zambia.

Olympic Champions, 1904-2004

St Louis, USA - 1904
Fly: G. Finnegan (USA). **Bantam:** O. Kirk (USA). **Feather:** O. Kirk (USA). **Light:** H. Spangler (USA). **Welter:** A. Young (USA). **Middle:** C. May (USA). **Heavy:** S. Berger (USA).

London, England - 1908
Bantam: H. Thomas (GBR). **Feather:** R. Gunn (GBR). **Light:** F. Grace (GBR). **Middle:** J.W.H.T. Douglas (GBR). **Heavy:** A. Oldman (GBR).
Silver medals: J. Condon (GBR), C. Morris (GBR), F. Spiller (GBR), S. Evans (GBR).
Bronze medals: W. Webb (GBR), H. Rodding (GBR), T. Ringer (GBR), H. Johnson (GBR), R. Warnes (GBR), W. Philo (GBR), F. Parks (GBR).

Antwerp, Belgium - 1920
Fly: F. Genaro (USA). **Bantam:** C. Walker (SAF). **Feather:** R. Fritsch (FRA). **Light:** S. Mossberg (USA). **Welter:** T. Schneider (CAN). **Middle:** H. Mallin (GBR). **L. Heavy:** E. Eagan (USA). **Heavy:** R. Rawson (GBR).
Silver medal: A. Ireland (GBR).
Bronze medals: W. Cuthbertson (GBR), G. McKenzie (GBR), H. Franks (GBR).

Paris, France - 1924
Fly: F. la Barba (USA). **Bantam:** W. Smith (SAF). **Feather:** J. Fields (USA). **Light:** H. Nielson (DEN). **Welter:** J. Delarge (BEL). **Middle:** H. Mallin (GBR). **L. Heavy:** H. Mitchell (GBR). **Heavy:** O. von Porat (NOR).
Silver medals: J. McKenzie (GBR), J. Elliot (GBR).

Amsterdam, Holland - 1928
Fly: A. Kocsis (HUN). **Bantam:** V. Tamagnini (ITA). **Feather:** B. van Klaveren (HOL). **Light:** C. Orlando (ITA). **Welter:** E. Morgan (NZL). **Middle:** P. Toscani (ITA). **L. Heavy:** V. Avendano (ARG). **Heavy:** A. Rodriguez Jurado (ARG).

Los Angeles, USA - 1932
Fly: I. Enekes (HUN). **Bantam:** H. Gwynne (CAN). **Feather:** C. Robledo (ARG). **Light:** L. Stevens (SAF). **Welter:** E. Flynn (USA). **Middle:** C. Barth (USA). **L. Heavy:** D. Carstens (SAF). **Heavy:** A. Lovell (ARG).

Berlin, West Germany - 1936
Fly: W. Kaiser (GER). **Bantam:** U. Sergo (ITA). **Feather:** O. Casanova (ARG). **Light:** I. Harangi (HUN). **Welter:** S. Suvio (FIN). **Middle:** J. Despeaux (FRA). **L. Heavy:** R. Michelot (FRA). **Heavy:** H. Runge (GER).

London, England - 1948
Fly: P. Perez (ARG). **Bantam:** T. Csik (HUN). **Feather:** E. Formenti (ITA). **Light:** G. Dreyer (SAF). **Welter:** J. Torma (TCH). **Middle:** L. Papp (HUN). **L. Heavy:** G. Hunter (SAF). **Heavy:** R. Iglesas (ARG).
Silver medals: J. Wright (GBR), D. Scott (GBR).

Helsinki, Finland - 1952
Fly: N. Brooks (USA). **Bantam:** P. Hamalainen (FIN). **Feather:** J. Zachara (TCH). **Light:** A. Bolognesi (ITA). **L. Welter:** C. Adkins (USA). **Welter:** Z. Chychla (POL). **Middle:** L. Papp (HUN). **L. Middle:** F. Patterson (USA). **L. Heavy:** N. Lee (USA). **Heavy:** E. Sanders (USA).
Silver medal: J. McNally (IRL).

Melbourne, Australia - 1956
Fly: T. Spinks (GBR). **Bantam:** W. Behrendt (GER). **Feather:** V. Safronov (URS). **Light:** R. McTaggart (GBR). **L. Welter:** V. Jengibarian (URS). **Welter:** N. Linca (ROM). **L. Middle:** L. Papp (HUN). **Middle:** G. Schatkov (URS). **L.**
Heavy: J. Boyd (USA). **Heavy:** P. Rademacher (USA).
Silver medals: T. Nicholls (GBR), F. Tiedt (IRL).
Bronze medals: J. Caldwell (IRL), F. Gilroy (IRL), A. Bryne (IRL), N. Gargano (GBR), J. McCormack (GBR).

Rome, Italy - 1960
Fly: G. Torok (HUN). **Bantam:** O. Grigoryev (URS). **Feather:** F. Musso (ITA). **Light:** K. Pazdzior (POL). **L. Welter:** B. Nemecek (TCH). **Welter:** N. Benvenuti (ITA). **L. Middle:** W. McClure (USA). **Middle:** E. Crook (USA). **L. Heavy:** C. Clay (USA). **Heavy:** F. de Piccoli (ITA).
Bronze medals: R. McTaggart (GBR), J. Lloyd (GBR), W. Fisher (GBR).

Tokyo, Japan - 1964
Fly: F. Atzori (ITA). **Bantam:** T. Sakurai (JPN). **Feather:** S. Stepashkin (URS). **Light:** J. Grudzien (POL). **L. Welter:** J. Kulej (POL). **Welter:** M. Kasprzyk (POL). **L. Middle:** B. Lagutin (URS). **Middle:** V. Popenchenko (URS). **L. Heavy:** C. Pinto (ITA). **Heavy:** J. Frazier (USA).
Bronze medal: J. McCourt (IRL).

Mexico City, Mexico - 1968
L. Fly: F. Rodriguez (VEN). **Fly:** R. Delgado (MEX). **Bantam:** V. Sokolov (URS). **Feather:** A. Roldan (MEX). **Light:** R. Harris (USA). **L. Welter:** J. Kulej (POL). **Welter:** M. Wolke (GDR). **L. Middle:** B. Lagutin (URS). **Middle:** C. Finnegan (GBR). **L. Heavy:** D. Poznyak (URS). **Heavy:** G. Foreman (USA).

Munich, West Germany - 1972
L. Fly: G. Gedo (HUN). **Fly:** G. Kostadinov (BUL). **Bantam:** O. Martinez (CUB). **Feather:** B. Kusnetsov (URS). **Light:** J. Szczepanski (POL). **L. Welter:** R. Seales (USA). **Welter:** E. Correa (CUB). **L. Middle:** D. Kottysch (GER). **Middle:** V. Lemeschev (URS). **L. Heavy:** M. Parlov (YUG). **Heavy:** T. Stevenson (CUB).
Bronze medals: R. Evans (GBR), G. Turpin (GBR), A. Minter (GBR).

Montreal, Canada - 1976
L. Fly: J. Hernandez (CUB). **Fly:** L. Randolph (USA). **Bantam:** Y-J. Gu (NKO). **Feather:** A. Herrera (CUB). **Light:** H. Davis (USA). **L. Welter:** R. Leonard (USA). **Welter:** J. Bachfield (GDR). **L. Middle:** J. Rybicki (POL). **Middle:** M. Spinks (USA). **L. Heavy:** L. Spinks (USA). **Heavy:** T. Stevenson (CUB).
Bronze medal: P. Cowdell (GBR).

Moscow, USSR - 1980
L. Fly: S. Sabirov (URS). **Fly:** P. Lessov (BUL). **Bantam:** J. Hernandez (CUB). **Feather:** R. Fink (GDR). **Light:** A. Herrera (CUB). **L. Welter:** P. Oliva (ITA). **Welter:** A. Aldama (CUB). **L. Middle:** A. Martinez (CUB). **Middle:** J. Gomez (CUB). **L. Heavy:** S. Kacar (YUG). **Heavy:** T. Stevenson (CUB).
Bronze medals: H. Russell (IRL), A. Willis (GBR).

Los Angeles, USA - 1984
L. Fly: P. Gonzalez (USA). **Fly:** S. McCrory (USA). **Bantam:** M. Stecca (ITA). **Feather:** M. Taylor (USA). **Light:** P. Whitaker (USA). **L. Welter:** J. Page (USA). **Welter:** M. Breland (USA). **L. Middle:** F. Tate (USA). **Middle:** J-S. Shin (SKO). **L. Heavy:** A. Josipovic (YUG). **Heavy:** H. Tillman (USA). **S. Heavy:** T. Biggs (USA).
Bronze medal: B. Wells (GBR).

Seoul, South Korea - 1988
L. Fly: I. Mustafov (BUL). **Fly:** H-S. Kim (SKO). **Bantam:** K. McKinney (USA). **Feather:** G. Parisi (ITA). **Light:** A. Zuelow (GDR). **L. Welter:** V. Yanovsky (URS). **Welter:** R. Wangila (KEN). **L. Middle:** S-H. Park (SKO). **Middle:** H. Maske (GDR). **L. Heavy:** A. Maynard (USA). **Heavy:** R. Mercer (USA). **S. Heavy:** L. Lewis (CAN).
Bronze medal: R. Woodhall (GBR).

Barcelona, Spain - 1992
L. Fly: R. Marcelo (CUB). **Fly:** C-C. Su (NKO). **Bantam:** J. Casamayor (CUB). **Feather:** A. Tews (GER). **Light:** O. de la Hoya (USA). **L. Welter:** H. Vinent (CUB). **Welter:** M. Carruth (IRL). **L. Middle:** J. Lemus (CUB). **Middle:** A. Hernandez (CUB). **L. Heavy:** T. May (GER). **Heavy:** F. Savon (CUB). **S. Heavy:** R. Balado (CUB).
Silver medal: W. McCullough (IRL).
Bronze medal: R. Reid (GBR).

Atlanta, USA - 1996
L. Fly: D. Petrov (BUL). **Fly:** M. Romero (CUB). **Bantam:** I. Kovaks (HUN). **Feather:** S. Kamsing (THA). **Light:** H. Soltani (ALG). **L. Welter:** H. Vinent (CUB). **Welter:** O. Saitov (RUS). **L. Middle:** D. Reid (USA). **Middle:** A. Hernandez (CUB). **L. Heavy:** V. Jirov (KAZ). **Heavy:** F. Savon (CUB). **S. Heavy:** Vladimir Klitschko (UKR).

Sydney, Australia - 2000
L. Fly: B. Aslom (FRA). **Fly:** W. Ponlid (THA). **Bantam:** G. Rigondeaux (CUB). **Feather:** B. Sattarkhanov (KAZ). **Light:** M. Kindelan (CUB). **L. Welter:** M. Abdullaev (UZB). **Welter:** O. Saitov (RUS). **L. Middle:** Y. Ibraimov (KAZ). **Middle:** J. Gutierrez Espinosa (CUB). **L. Heavy:** A. Lebziak (RUS). **Heavy:** F. Savon (CUB). **S. Heavy:** A. Harrison (ENG).

Athens, Greece - 2004
L. Fly: Y. Bartelemi (CUB). **Fly:** Y. Gamboa (CUB). **Bantam:** G. Rigondeaux (CUB). **Feather:** A. Tichtchenko (RUS). **Light:** M. Kindelan (CUB). **L. Welter:** M. Boonjumnong (THA). **Welter:** B. Artayev (KAZ). **Middle:** G. Gaiderbekov (RUS). **L. Heavy:** A. Ward (USA). **Heavy:** O. Solis (CUB). **S. Heavy:** A. Povetkin (RUS).
Silver medal: A. Khan (ENG).

World Champions, 1974-2003

Havana, Cuba - 1974
L. Fly: J. Hernandez (CUB). **Fly:** D. Rodriguez (CUB). **Bantam:** W. Gomez (PUR). **Feather:** H. Davis (USA). **Light:** V. Solomin (URS). **L. Welter:** A. Kalule (UGA). **Welter:** E. Correa (CUB). **L. Middle:** R. Garbey (CUB). **Middle:** R. Riskiev (URS). **L. Heavy:** M. Parlov (YUG). **Heavy:** T. Stevenson (CUB).

Belgrade, Yugoslavia - 1978
L. Fly: S. Muchoki (KEN). **Fly:** H. Strednicki (POL). **Bantam:** A. Horta (CUB). **Feather:** A. Herrera (CUB). **Light:** D. Andeh (NIG). **L. Welter:** V. Lvov (URS). **Welter:** V. Rachkov (URS). **L. Middle:** V. Savchenko (URS). **Middle:** J. Gomez (CUB). **L. Heavy:** S. Soria (CUB). **Heavy:** T. Stevenson (CUB).

Munich, West Germany - 1982
L. Fly: I. Mustafov (BUL). **Fly:** Y. Alexandrov (URS). **Bantam:** F. Favors (USA). **Feather:** A. Horta (CUB). **Light:** A. Herrera (CUB). **L. Welter:** C. Garcia (CUB). **Welter:** M. Breland (USA). **L. Middle:** A. Koshkin (URS). **Middle:** B. Comas (CUB). **L. Heavy:** P. Romero (CUB). **Heavy:** A. Jagubkin (URS). **S. Heavy:** T. Biggs (USA).
Bronze medal: T. Corr (IRL).

Reno, USA - 1986
L. Fly: J. Odelin (CUB). **Fly:** P. Reyes (CUB). **Bantam:** S-I. Moon (SKO). **Feather:** K. Banks (USA). **Light:** A. Horta (CUB). **L. Welter:** V. Shishov (URS). **Welter:** K. Gould (USA). **L. Middle:** A. Espinosa (CUB). **Middle:** D. Allen (USA). **L. Heavy:** P. Romero (CUB). **Heavy:** F. Savon (CUB). **S. Heavy:** T. Stevenson (CUB).

Moscow, USSR - 1989
L. Fly: E. Griffin (USA). **Feather:** A. Khamatov (URS). **Light:** J. Gonzalez (CUB). **L. Welter:** I. Ruzinkov (URS). **Welter:** F. Vastag (Rom). **L. Middle:** I. Akopokhian (URS). **Middle:** A. Kurniavka (URS). **L. Heavy:** H. Maske (GDR). **Heavy:** F. Savon (CUB). **S. Heavy:** R. Balado (CUB).
Bronze medal: M. Carruth (IRL).

Sydney, Australia - 1991
L. Fly: E. Griffin (USA). **Fly:** I. Kovacs (HUN). **Bantam:** S. Todorov (BUL). **Feather:** K. Kirkorov (BUL). **Light:** M. Rudolph (GER). **L. Welter:** K. Tsziu (URS). **Welter:** J. Hernandez (CUB). **L. Middle:** J. Lemus (CUB). **Middle:** T. Russo (ITA). **L. Heavy:** T. May (GER). **Heavy:** F. Savon (CUB). **S. Heavy:** R. Balado (CUB).

Tampere, Finland - 1993
L. Fly: N. Munchian (ARM). **Fly:** W. Font (CUB). **Bantam:** A. Christov (BUL). **Feather:** S. Todorov (BUL). **Light:** D. Austin (CUB). **L. Welter:** H. Vinent (CUB). **Welter:** J. Hernandez (CUB). **L. Middle:** F. Vastag (ROM). **Middle:** A. Hernandez (CUB). **L. Heavy:** R. Garbey (CUB). **Heavy:** F. Savon (CUB). **S. Heavy:** R. Balado (CUB).
Bronze medal: D. Kelly (IRL).

Berlin, Germany - 1995
L. Fly: D. Petrov (BUL). **Fly:** Z. Lunka (GER). **Bantam:** R. Malachbekov (RUS). **Feather:** S. Todorov (BUL). **Light:** L. Doroftel (ROM). **L. Welter:** H. Vinent (CUB). **Welter:** J. Hernandez (CUB). **L. Middle:** F. Vastag (ROM). **Middle:** A. Hernandez (CUB). **L. Heavy:** A. Tarver (USA). **Heavy:** F. Savon (CUB). **S. Heavy:** A. Lezin (RUS).

Budapest, Hungary - 1997
L. Fly: M. Romero (CUB). **Fly:** M. Mantilla (CUB). **Bantam:** R Malakhbekov (RUS). **Feather:** I. Kovacs (HUN). **Light:** A. Maletin (RUS). **L. Welter:** D. Simion (ROM). **Welter:** O. Saitov (RUS). **L. Middle:** A. Duvergel (CUB). **Middle:** Z. Erdei (HUN). **L. Heavy:** A. Lebsiak (RUS). **Heavy:** F. Savon (CUB). **S. Heavy:** G. Kandelaki (GEO).
Bronze medal: S. Kirk (IRL).

Houston, USA - 1999
L. Fly: B. Viloria (USA). **Fly:** B. Jumadilov (KAZ). **Bantam:** R. Crinu (ROM). **Feather:** R. Juarez (USA). **Light:** M. Kindelan (CUB). **L. Welter:** M. Abdullaev (UZB). **Welter:** J. Hernandez (CUB). **L. Middle:** M. Simion (ROM). **Middle:** U. Haydarov (UZB). **L. Heavy:** M. Simms (USA). **Heavy:** M. Bennett (USA). **S. Heavy:** S. Samilsan (TUR).
Bronze medal: K. Evans (WAL).

Belfast, Northern Ireland - 2001
L. Fly: Y. Bartelemi (CUB). **Fly:** J. Thomas (FRA). **Bantam:** G. Rigondeaux (CUB). **Feather:** R. Palyani (TUR). **Light:** M. Kindelan (CUB). **L. Welter:** D. Luna Martinez (CUB). **Welter:** L. Aragon (CUB). **L. Middle:** D. Austin (CUB). **Middle:** A. Gogolev (RUS). **L. Heavy:** Y. Makarenko (RUS). **Heavy:** O. Solis (CUB). **S. Heavy:** R. Chagaev (UZB).
Silver medal: D. Haye (ENG).
Bronze medals: J. Moore (IRL), C. Froch (ENG).

Bangkok, Thailand - 2003
L. Fly: S. Karazov (RUS). **Fly:** S. Jongjohor (THA). **Bantam:** A. Mamedov (AZE). **Feather:** G. Jafarov (KAZ). **Light:** M. Kindelan (CUB). **L. Welter:** W. Blain (FRA). **Welter:** L. Aragon (CUB). **Middle:** G. Golovkin (KAZ). **L. Heavy:** Y. Makarenko (RUS). **Heavy:** O. Solis (CUB). **S. Heavy:** A. Povetkin (RUS).

World Junior Champions, 1979-2004

Yokohama, Japan - 1979
L. Fly: R. Shannon (USA). **Fly:** P. Lessov (BUL). **Bantam:** P-K. Choi (SKO). **Feather:** Y. Gladychev (URS). **Light:** R. Blake (USA). **L. Welter:** I. Akopokhian (URS). **Welter:** M. McCrory (USA). **L. Middle:** A. Mayes (USA). **Middle:** A. Milov (URS). **L. Heavy:** A. Lebedev (URS). **Heavy:** M. Frazier (USA).
Silver medals: N. Wilshire (ENG), D. Cross (ENG).
Bronze medal: I. Scott (SCO).

Santo Domingo, Dominican Republic - 1983
L. Fly: M. Herrera (DOM). **Fly:** J. Gonzalez (CUB). **Bantam:** J. Molina (PUR). **Feather:** A. Miesses (DOM). **Light:** A. Beltre (DOM). **L. Welter:** A. Espinoza (CUB). **Welter:** M. Watkins (USA). **L. Middle:** U. Castillo (CUB). **Middle:** R. Batista (CUB). **L. Heavy:** O. Pought (USA). **Heavy:** A. Williams (USA). **S. Heavy:** L. Lewis (CAN).

Bucharest, Romania - 1985
L. Fly: R-S. Hwang (SKO). **Fly:** T. Marcelica (ROM). **Bantam:** R. Diaz (CUB). **Feather:** D. Maeran (ROM). **Light:** J. Teiche (GDR). **L. Welter:** W. Saeger (GDR). **Welter:** A. Stoianov (BUL). **L. Middle:** M. Franek (TCH). **Middle:** O. Zahalotskih (URS). **L. Heavy:** B. Riddick (USA). **Heavy:** F. Savon (CUB). **S. Heavy:** A. Prianichnikov (URS).

Havana, Cuba - 1987
L. Fly: E. Paisan (CUB). **Fly:** C. Daniels (USA). **Bantam:** A. Moya (CUB). **Feather:** G. Iliyasov (URS). **Light:** J. Hernandez (CUB). **L. Welter:** L. Mihai (ROM). **Welter:** F. Vastag (ROM). **L. Middle:** A. Lobsyak (URS). **Middle:** W. Martinez (CUB). **L. Heavy:** D. Yeliseyev (URS). **Heavy:** R. Balado (CUB). **S. Heavy:** L. Martinez (CUB).
Silver medal: E. Loughran (IRL).
Bronze medal: D. Galvin (IRL).

San Juan, Puerto Rico - 1989
L. Fly: D. Petrov (BUL). **Fly:** N. Monchai (FRA). **Bantam:** J. Casamayor (CUB). **Feather:** C. Febres (PUR). **Light:** A. Acevedo (PUR). **L. Welter:** E. Berger (GDR). **Welter:** A. Hernandez (CUB). **L. Middle:** L. Bedey (CUB). **Middle:** R. Garbey (CUB). **L. Heavy:** R. Alvarez (CUB). **Heavy:** K. Johnson (CAN). **S. Heavy:** A. Burdiantz (URS).
Silver medals: E. Magee (IRL), R. Reid (ENG), S. Wilson (SCO).

Lima, Peru - 1990
L. Fly: D. Alicea (PUR). **Fly:** K. Pielert (GDR). **Bantam:** K. Baravi (URS). **Feather:** A. Vaughan (ENG). **Light:** J. Mendez (CUB). **L. Welter:** H. Vinent (CUB). **Welter:** A. Hernandez (CUB). **L. Middle:** A. Kakauridze (URS).

Middle: J. Gomez (CUB). **L. Heavy:** B. Torsten (GDR). **Heavy:** I. Andreev (URS). **S. Heavy:** J. Quesada (CUB).
Bronze medal: P. Ingle (ENG).

Montreal, Canada - 1992
L. Fly: W. Font (CUB). **Fly:** J. Oragon (CUB). **Bantam:** N. Machado (CUB). **Feather:** M. Stewart (CAN). **Light:** D. Austin (CUB). **L. Welter:** O. Saitov (RUS). **Welter:** L. Brors (GER). **L. Middle:** J. Acosta (CUB). **Middle:** I. Arsangaliev (RUS). **L. Heavy:** S. Samilsan (TUR). **Heavy:** G. Kandeliaki (GEO). **S. Heavy:** M. Porchnev (RUS).
Bronze medal: N. Sinclair (IRL).

Istanbul, Turkey - 1994
L. Fly: J. Turunen (FIN). **Fly:** A. Jimenez (CUB). **Bantam:** J. Despaigne (CUB). **Feather:** D. Simion (ROM). **Light:** L. Diogenes (CUB). **L. Welter:** V. Romero (CUB). **Welter:** E. Aslan (TUR). **L. Middle:** G. Ledsvanys (CUB). **Middle:** M. Genc (TUR). **L. Heavy:** P. Aurino (ITA). **Heavy:** M. Lopez (CUB). **S. Heavy:** P. Carrion (CUB).

Havana, Cuba - 1996
L. Fly: L. Hernandez (CUB). **Fly:** L. Cabrera (CUB). **Bantam:** P. Miradal (CUB). **Feather:** E. Rodriguez (CUB). **Light:** R. Vaillan (CUB). **L. Welter:** T. Mergadze (RUS). **Welter:** J. Brahmer (GER). **L. Middle:** L. Mezquia (CUB). **Middle:** V. Pletniov (RUS). **L. Heavy:** O. Simon (CUB). **Heavy:** A. Yatsenko (UKR). **S. Heavy:** S. Fabre (CUB).
Bronze medal: R. Hatton (ENG).

Buenos Aires, Argentina - 1998
L. Fly: S. Tanasie (ROM). **Fly:** S. Yeledov (KAZ). **Bantam:** S. Suleymanov (UKR). **Feather:** I. Perez (ARG). **Light:** A. Solopov (RUS). **L. Welter:** Y. Tomashov (UKR). **Welter:** K. Oustarkhanov (RUS). **L. Middle:** S. Kostenko (UKR). **Middle:** M. Kempe (GER). **L. Heavy:** H. Yohanson Martinez (CUB). **Heavy:** O. Solis Fonte (CUB). **S. Heavy:** B. Ohanyan (ARM).
Silver medal: H. Cunningham (IRL).
Bronze medal: D. Campbell (IRL).

Budapest, Hungary - 2000
L. Fly: Y. Leon Alarcon (CUB). **Fly:** O. Franco Vaszquez (CUB). **Bantam:** V. Tajbert (GER). **Feather:** G. Kate (HUN). **Light:** F. Adzsanalov (AZE). **L. Welter:** G. Galovkin (KAZ). **Welter:** S. Ustunel (TUR). **L. Middle:** D. Chernysh (RUS). **Middle:** F. Sullivan Barrera (CUB). **L. Heavy:** A. Shekmourov (RUS). **Heavy:** D. Medzhydov (UKR). **S. Heavy:** A. Dmitrienko (RUS).
Bronze medal: C. Barrett (IRL).

Santiago, Cuba - 2002
L. Fly: D. Acripitian (RUS). **Fly:** Y. Fabregas (CUB). **Bantam:** S. Bahodirijan (UZB). **Feather:** A. Tichtchenko (RUS). **Light:** S. Mendez (CUB). **L. Welter:** K. Iliyasov (KAZ). **Welter:** J. McPherson (USA). **L. Middle:** V. Diaz (CUB). **Middle:** A. Duarte (CUB). **L. Heavy:** R. Zavalnyuyk (UKR). **Heavy:** Y. P. Hernandez (CUB). **S. Heavy:** P. Portal (CUB).
Silver medal: A. Lee (IRL).
Bronze medal: N. Brough (ENG).

Jeju Island, South Korea - 2004
L. Fly: P. Bedak (Hun). **Fly:** I. Rahimov (UZB). **Bantam:** A. Abdimomunov (KAZ). **Feather:** E. Ambartsumyan (RUS). **Light:** A. Khan (ENG). **L. Welter:** C. Banteur (CUB). **Welter:** E. Rasulov (UZB). **Middle:** D. Tchudinov (RUS). **L. Heavy:** I. Perez (CUB). **Heavy:** E. Romanov (RUS). **S.Heavy:** D. Boytsov (RUS).
Bronze medal: D. Price (ENG).

European Champions, 1924-2004

Paris, France - 1924
Fly: J. McKenzie (GBR). **Bantam:** J. Ces (FRA). **Feather:** R. de Vergnie (BEL). **Light:** N. Nielsen (DEN). **Welter:** J. Delarge (BEL). **Middle:** H. Mallin (GBR). **L. Heavy:** H. Mitchell (GBR). **Heavy:** O. von Porat (NOR).

Stockholm, Sweden - 1925
Fly: E. Pladner (FRA). **Bantam:** A. Rule (GBR). **Feather:** P. Andren (SWE). **Light:** S. Johanssen (SWE). **Welter:** H. Nielsen (DEN). **Middle:** F. Crawley (GBR). **L. Heavy:** T. Petersen (DEN). **Heavy:** B. Persson (SWE).
Silver medals: J. James (GBR), E. Viney (GBR), D. Lister (GBR).

Berlin, Germany - 1927
Fly: L. Boman (SWE). **Bantam:** K. Dalchow (GER). **Feather:** F. Dubbers (GER). **Light:** H. Domgoergen (GER). **Welter:** R. Caneva (ITA). **Middle:** J. Christensen (NOR). **L. Heavy:** H. Muller (GER). **Heavy:** N. Ramm (SWE).

Amsterdam, Holland - 1928
Fly: A. Kocsis (HUN). **Bantam:** V. Tamagnini (ITA). **Feather:** B. van Klaveren (HOL). **Light:** C. Orlandi (ITA). **Welter:** R. Galataud (FRA). **Middle:** P. Toscani (ITA). **L. Heavy:** E. Pistulla (GER). **Heavy:** N. Ramm (SWE).

Budapest, Hungary - 1930
Fly: I. Enekes (HUN). **Bantam:** J. Szeles (HUN). **Feather:** G. Szabo (HUN). **Light:** M. Bianchini (ITA). **Welter:** J. Besselmann (GER). **Middle:** C. Meroni (ITA). **L. Heavy:** T. Petersen (DEN). **Heavy:** J. Michaelson (DEN).

Los Angeles, USA - 1932
Fly: I. Enekes (HUN). **Bantam:** H. Ziglarski (GER). **Feather:** J. Schleinkofer (GER). **Light:** T. Ahlqvist (SWE). **Welter:** E. Campe (GER). **Middle:** R. Michelot (FRA). **L. Heavy:** G. Rossi (ITA). **Heavy:** L. Rovati (ITA).

Budapest, Hungary - 1934
Fly: P. Palmer (GBR). **Bantam:** I. Enekes (HUN). **Feather:** O. Kaestner GER). **Light:** E. Facchini (ITA). **Welter:** D. McCleave (GBR). **Middle:** S. Szigetti (HUN). **L. Heavy:** P. Zehetmayer (AUT). **Heavy:** G. Baerlund (FIN).
Bronze medal: P. Floyd (GBR).

Milan, Italy - 1937
Fly: I. Enekes (HUN). **Bantam:** U. Sergo (ITA). **Feather:** A. Polus (POL). **Light:** H. Nuremberg (GER). **Welter:** M. Murach (GER). **Middle:** H. Chmielewski (POL). **L. Heavy:** S. Szigetti (HUN). **Heavy:** O. Tandberg (SWE).

Dublin, Eire - 1939
Fly: J. Ingle (IRL). **Bantam:** U. Sergo (ITA). **Feather:** P. Dowdall (IRL). **Light:** H. Nuremberg (GER). **Welter:** A. Kolczyski (POL). **Middle:** A. Raadik (EST). **L. Heavy:** L. Musina (ITA). **Heavy:** O. Tandberg (SWE).
Bronze medal: C. Evenden (IRL).

Dublin, Eire - 1947
Fly: L. Martinez (ESP). **Bantam:** L. Bogacs (HUN). **Feather:** K. Kreuger (SWE). **Light:** J. Vissers (BEL). **Welter:** J. Ryan (ENG). **Middle:** A. Escudie (FRA). **L. Heavy:** H. Quentemeyer (HOL). **Heavy:** G. O'Colmain (IRL).
Silver medals: J. Clinton (SCO), P. Maguire (IRL), W. Thom (ENG), G. Scriven (ENG).
Bronze medals: J. Dwyer (SCO), A. Sanderson (ENG), W. Frith (SCO), E. Cantwell (IRL), K. Wyatt (ENG).

Oslo, Norway - 1949
Fly: J. Kasperczak (POL). **Bantam:** G. Zuddas (ITA). **Feather:** J. Bataille (FRA). **Light:** M. McCullagh (IRL). **Welter:** J. Torma (TCH). **Middle:** L. Papp (HUN). **L. Heavy:** G. di Segni (ITA). **Heavy:** L. Bene (HUN).
Bronze medal: D. Connell (IRL).

Milan, Italy - 1951
Fly: A. Pozzali (ITA). **Bantam:** V. Dall'Osso (ITA). **Feather:** J. Ventaja (FRA). **Light:** B. Visintin (ITA). **L. Welter:** H. Schelling (GER). **Welter:** Z. Chychla (POL). **L. Middle:** L. Papp (HUN). **Middle:** S. Sjolin (SWE). **L. Heavy:** M. Limage (BEL). **Heavy:** G. di Segni (ITA).
Silver medal: J. Kelly (IRL).
Bronze medals: D. Connell (IRL), T. Milligan (IRL), A. Lay (ENG).

Warsaw, Poland - 1953
Fly: H. Kukier (POL). **Bantam:** Z. Stefaniuk (POL). **Feather:** J. Kruza (POL). **Light:** V. Jengibarian (URS). **L. Welter:** L. Drogosz (POL). **Welter:** Z. Chychla (POL). **L. Middle:** B. Wells (ENG). **Middle:** D. Wemhoner (GER). **L. Heavy:** U. Nietchke (GER). **Heavy:** A. Schotzikas (URS).
Silver medal: T. Milligan (IRL).
Bronze medals: J. McNally (IRL), R. Barton (ENG).

Berlin, West Germany - 1955
Fly: E. Basel (GER). **Bantam:** Z. Stefaniuk (POL). **Feather:** T. Nicholls (ENG). **Light:** H. Kurschat (GER). **L. Welter:** L. Drogosz (POL). **Welter:** N. Gargano (ENG). **L. Middle:** Z. Pietrzykowski (POL). **Middle:** G. Schatkov (URS). **L. Heavy:** E. Schoeppner (GER). **Heavy:** A. Schotzikas (URS).

Prague, Czechoslovakia - 1957
Fly: M. Homberg (GER). **Bantam:** O. Grigoryev (URS). **Feather:** D. Venilov (BUL). **Light:** K. Pazdzior (POL). **L. Welter:** V. Jengibarian (URS). **Welter:** M. Graus (GER). **L. Middle:** N. Benvenuti (ITA). **Middle:** Z. Pietrzykowski (POL). **L. Heavy:** G. Negrea (ROM). **Heavy:** A. Abramov (URS).
Bronze medals: R. Davies (WAL), J. Morrissey (SCO), J. Kidd (SCO), F. Teidt (IRL).

Lucerne, Switzerland - 1959
Fly: M. Homberg (GER). **Bantam:** H. Rascher (GER). **Feather:** J. Adamski (POL). **Light:** O. Maki (FIN). **L. Welter:** V. Jengibarian (URS). **Welter:** L. Drogosz (POL). **L. Middle:** N. Benvenuti (ITA). **Middle:** G. Schatkov (URS). **L. Heavy:** Z. Pietrzykowski (POL). **Heavy:** A. Abramov (URS).
Silver medal: D. Thomas (ENG).
Bronze medals: A. McClean (IRL), H. Perry (IRL), C. McCoy (IRL), H. Scott (ENG).

Belgrade, Yugoslavia - 1961
Fly: P. Vacca (ITA). **Bantam:** S. Sivko (URS). **Feather:** F. Taylor (ENG). **Light:** R. McTaggart (SCO). **L. Welter:** A. Tamulis (URS). **Welter:** R. Tamulis

309

(URS). **L. Middle:** B. Lagutin (URS). **Middle:** T. Walasek (POL). **L. Heavy:** G. Saraudi (ITA). **Heavy:** A. Abramov (URS).
Bronze medals: P. Warwick (ENG), I. McKenzie (SCO), J. Bodell (ENG).

Moscow, USSR - 1963
Fly: V. Bystrov (URS). **Bantam:** O. Grigoryev (URS). **Feather:** S. Stepashkin (URS). **Light:** J. Kajdi (HUN). **L. Welter:** J. Kulej (POL). **Welter:** R. Tamulis (URS). **L. Middle:** B. Lagutin (URS). **Middle:** V. Popenchenko (URS). **L. Heavy:** Z. Pietrzykowski (POL). **Heavy:** J. Nemec (TCH).
Silver medal: A. Wyper (SCO).

Berlin, East Germany - 1965
Fly: H. Freisdadt (GER). **Bantam:** O. Grigoryev (URS). **Feather:** S. Stepashkin (URS). **Light:** V. Barranikov (URS). **L. Welter:** J. Kulej (POL). **Welter:** R. Tamulis (URS). **L. Middle:** V. Ageyev (URS). **Middle:** V. Popenchenko (URS). **L. Heavy:** D. Poznyak (URS). **Heavy:** A. Isosimov (URS).
Silver medal: B. Robinson (ENG).
Bronze medals: J. McCluskey (SCO), K. Buchanan (SCO), J. McCourt (IRL).

Rome, Italy - 1967
Fly: H. Skrzyczak (POL). **Bantam:** N. Giju (ROM). **Feather:** R. Petek (POL). **Light:** J. Grudzien (POL). **L. Welter:** V. Frolov (URS). **Welter:** B. Nemecek (TCH). **L. Middle:** V. Ageyev (URS). **Middle:** M. Casati (ITA). **L. Heavy:** D. Poznyak (URS). **Heavy:** M. Baruzzi (ITA).
Silver medal: P. Boddington (ENG).

Bucharest, Romania - 1969
L. Fly: G. Gedo (HUN). **Fly:** C. Ciuca (ROM). **Bantam:** A. Dumitrescu (ROM). **Feather:** I. Orban (HUN). **Light:** S. Cutov (ROM). **L. Welter:** V. Frolov (URS). **Welter:** G. Meier (GER). **L. Middle:** V. Tregubov (URS). **Middle:** V. Tarasenkov (URS). **L. Heavy:** D. Poznyak (URS). **Heavy:** I. Alexe (ROM).
Bronze medals: M. Dowling (IRL), M. Piner (ENG), A. Richardson (ENG), T. Imrie (SCO).

Madrid, Spain - 1971
L. Fly: G. Gedo (HUN). **Fly:** J. Rodriguez (ESP). **Bantam:** T. Badar (HUN). **Feather:** R. Tomczyk (POL). **Light:** J. Szczepanski (POL). **L. Welter:** U. Beyer (GDR). **Welter:** J. Kajdi (HUN). **L. Middle:** V. Tregubov (URS). **Middle:** J. Juotsiavitchus (URS). **L. Heavy:** M. Parlov (YUG). **Heavy:** V. Tchernishev (URS).
Bronze medals: N. McLaughlin (IRL), M. Dowling (IRL), B. McCarthy (IRL), M. Kingwell (ENG), L. Stevens (ENG).

Belgrade, Yugoslavia - 1973
L. Fly: V. Zasypko (URS). **Fly:** C. Gruescu (ROM). **Bantam:** A. Cosentino (FRA). **Feather:** S. Forster (GDR). **Light:** S. Cutov (ROM). **L. Welter:** M. Benes (YUG). **Welter:** S. Csjef (HUN). **L. Middle:** A. Klimanov (URS). **Middle:** V. Lemechev (URS). **L. Heavy:** M. Parlov (YUG). **Heavy:** V. Ulyanich (URS).
Bronze medal: J. Bambrick (SCO).

Katowice, Poland - 1975
L. Fly: A. Tkachenko (URS). **Fly:** V. Zasypko (URS). **Bantam:** V. Rybakov (URS). **Feather:** T. Badari (URS). **Light:** S. Cutov (ROM). **L. Welter:** V. Limasov (URS). **Welter:** K. Marjaama (FIN). **L. Middle:** W. Rudnowski (POL). **Middle:** V. Lemechev (URS). **L. Heavy:** A. Klimanov (URS). **Heavy:** A. Biegalski (POL).
Bronze medals: C. Magri (ENG), P. Cowdell (ENG), G. McEwan (ENG).

Halle, East Germany - 1977
L. Fly: H. Srednicki (POL). **Fly:** L. Blazynski (POL). **Bantam:** S. Forster (GDR). **Feather:** R. Nowakowski (GDR). **Light:** A. Rusevski (YUG). **L. Welter:** B. Gajda (POL). **Welter:** V. Limasov (URS). **L. Middle:** V. Saychenko (URS). **Middle:** I. Shaposhnikov (URS). **L. Heavy:** D. Kvachadze (URS). **Heavy:** E. Gorstkov (URS).
Bronze medal: P. Sutcliffe (IRL).

Cologne, West Germany - 1979
L. Fly: S. Sabirov (URS). **Fly:** H. Strednicki (POL). **Bantam:** N. Khrapzov (URS). **Feather:** V. Rybakov (URS). **Light.** V. Demianenko (URS). **L. Welter:** S. Konakbaev (URS). **Welter:** E. Muller (GER). **L. Middle:** M. Perunovic (YUG). **Middle:** T. Uusiverta (FIN). **L. Heavy:** A. Nikolyan (URS). **Heavy:** E. Gorstkov (URS). **S. Heavy:** P. Hussing (GER).
Bronze medal: P. Sutcliffe (IRL).

Tampere, Finland - 1981
L. Fly: I. Mustafov (BUL). **Fly:** P. Lessov (BUL). **Bantam:** V. Miroschnichenko (URS). **Feather:** R. Nowakowski (GDR). **Light:** V. Rybakov (URS). **L. Welter:** V. Shisov (URS). **Welter:** S. Konakvbaev (URS). **L. Middle:** A. Koshkin (URS). **Middle:** J. Torbek (URS). **L. Heavy:** A Krupin (URS). **Heavy:** A. Jagupkin (URS). **S. Heavy:** F. Damiani (ITA).
Bronze medal: G. Hawkins (IRL).

Varna, Bulgaria - 1983
L. Fly: I. Mustafov (BUL). **Fly:** P. Lessov (BUL). **Bantam:** Y. Alexandrov

(URS). **Feather:** S. Nurkazov (URS). **Light:** E. Chuprenski (BUL). **L. Welter:** V. Shishov (URS). **Welter:** P. Galkin (URS). **L. Middle:** V. Laptev (URS). **Middle:** V. Melnik (URS). **L. Heavy:** V. Kokhanovski (URS). **Heavy:** A. Jagubkin (URS). **S. Heavy:** F. Damiani (ITA).
Bronze medal: K. Joyce (IRL).

Budapest, Hungary - 1985
L. Fly: R. Breitbarth (GDR). **Fly:** D. Berg (GDR). **Bantam:** L. Simic (YUG). **Feather:** S. Khachatrian (URS). **Light:** E. Chuprenski (BUL). **L. Welter:** S. Mehnert (GDR). **Welter:** I. Akopokhian (URS). **L. Middle:** M. Timm (GDR). **Middle:** H. Maske (GDR). **L. Heavy:** N. Shanavasov (URS). **Heavy:** A. Jagubkin (URS). **S. Heavy:** F. Somodi (HUN).
Bronze medals: S. Casey (IRL), J. Beckles (ENG).

Turin, Italy - 1987
L. Fly: N. Munchyan (URS). **Fly:** A. Tews (GDR). **Bantam:** A. Hristov (BUL). **Feather:** M. Kazaryan (URS). **Light:** O. Nazarov (URS). **L. Welter:** B. Abadjier (BUL). **Welter:** V. Shishov (URS). **L. Middle:** E. Richter (GDR). **Middle:** H. Maske (GDR). **L. Heavy:** Y. Vaulin (URS). **Heavy:** A. Vanderlijde (HOL). **S. Heavy:** U. Kaden (GDR).
Bronze medal: N. Brown (ENG).

Athens, Greece - 1989
L. Fly: I.Mustafov (BUL). **Fly:** Y. Arbachakov (URS). **Bantam:** S. Todorov (BUL). **Feather:** K. Kirkorov (BUL). **Light:** V. Nistor (URS). **L. Welter:** I. Ruznikov (URS). **Welter:** S. Mehnert (GDR). **L. Middle:** I. Akopokhian (URS). **Middle:** H. Maske (GDR). **L. Heavy:** S. Lange (GDR). **Heavy:** A. Vanderlijde (HOL). **S. Heavy:** U. Kaden (GDR).
Bronze Medal: D. Anderson (SCO).

Gothenburg, Sweden - 1991
L. Fly: I. Marinov (BUL). **Fly:** I. Kovacs (HUN). **Bantam:** S. Todorov (BUL). **Feather:** P. Griffin (IRL). **Light:** V. Nistor (ROM). **L. Welter:** K. Tsziu (URS). **Welter:** R. Welin (SWE). **L. Middle:** I. Akopokhian (URS). **Middle:** S. Otke (GER). **L. Heavy:** D. Michalczewski (GER). **Heavy:** A. Vanderlijde (HOL). **S. Heavy:** E. Beloussov (URS).
Bronze medals: P. Weir (SCO), A. Vaughan (ENG).

Bursa, Turkey - 1993
L. Fly: D. Petrov (BUL). **Fly:** R. Husseinov (AZE). **Bantam:** R. Malakhbetov (RUS). **Feather:** S. Todorov (BUL). **Light:** J. Bielski (POL). **L. Welter:** N. Suleymanogiu (TUR). **Welter:** V. Karpaclauskas (LIT). **L. Middle:** F. Vastag (ROM). **Middle:** D. Eigenbrodt (GER). **L. Heavy:** I. Kshinin (RUS). **Heavy:** G. Kandelaki (GEO). **S. Heavy:** S. Rusinov (BUL).
Bronze medals: P. Griffin (IRL), D. Williams (ENG), K. McCormack (WAL).

Vejle, Denmark - 1996
L. Fly: D. Petrov (BUL). **Fly:** A. Pakeev (RUS). **Bantam:** I. Kovacs (HUN). **Feather:** R. Paliani (RUS). **Light:** L. Doroftei (ROM). **L. Welter:** O. Urkal (GER). **Welter:** H. Al (DEN). **L. Middle:** F. Vastag (ROM). **Middle:** S. Ottke (GER). **L. Heavy:** P. Aurino (ITA). **Heavy:** L. Krasniqi (GER). **S. Heavy:** A. Lezin (RUS).
Bronze medals: S. Harrison (SCO), D. Burke (ENG), D. Kelly (IRL).

Minsk, Belarus - 1998
L. Fly: S. Kazakov (RUS). **Fly:** V. Sidorenko (UKR). **Bantam:** S. Danilchenko (UKR). **Feather:** R. Paliani (TUR). **Light:** K. Huste (GER). **L. Welter:** D. Simion (ROM). **Welter:** O. Saitov (RUS). **L. Middle:** F. Esther (FRA). **Middle:** Z. Erdei (HUN). **L. Heavy:** A. Lebsiak (RUS). **Heavy:** G. Fragomeni (ITA). **S. Heavy:** A. Lezin (RUS).
Silver Medals: B. Magee (IRL), C. Fry (ENG).
Bronze medal: C. Bessey (ENG).

Tampere, Finland - 2000
L. Fly: Valeri Sidorenko (UKR). **Fly:** Vladimir Sidorenko (UKR). **Bantam:** A. Agagueloglu (TUR). **Feather:** R. Paliani (TUR). **Light:** A. Maletin (RUS). **L. Welter:** A. Leonev (RUS). **Welter:** B. Ueluesoy (TUR). **L. Middle:** A. Catic (GER). **Middle:** Z. Erdei (HUN). **L. Heavy:** A. Lebsiak (RUS). **Heavy:** J. Chanet (FRA). **S. Heavy:** A. Lezin (RUS).

Perm, Russia - 2002
L. Fly: S. Kazakov (RUS). **Fly:** G. Balakshin (RUS). **Bantam:** K. Khatsygov (BE). **Feather:** R. Malakhbekov (RUS). **Light:** A. Maletin (RUS). **L. Welter:** D. Panayotov (BUL). **Welter:** T. Gaidalov (RUS). **L. Middle:** A. Mishin (RUS). **Middle:** O. Mashkin (UKR). **L. Heavy:** M. Gala (RUS). **Heavy:** E. Makarenko (RUS). **S. Heavy:** A. Povetkin (RUS).

Pula, Croatia - 2004
L. Fly: S. Kazakov (RUS). **Fly:** G. Balakchine (RUS). **Bantam:** G. Kovalev (RUS). **Feather:** V. Tajbert (GER). **Light:** D. Stilianov (BUL). **L. Welter:** A. Maletin (RUS). **Welter:** O. Saitov (RUS). **Middle:** G. Gaiderbekov (RUS). **L.**

Heavy: E. Makarenko (RUS). **Heavy:** A. Alekseev (RUS). **S. Heavy:** A. Povetkin (RUS).
Bronze medal: A. Lee (IRL).

Note: Gold medals were awarded to the Europeans who went the furthest in the Olympic Games of 1924, 1928 & 1932.

European Junior Champions, 1970-2003

Miskolc, Hungary - 1970
L. Fly: Gluck (HUN). **Fly:** Z. Kismeneth (HUN). **Bantam:** A. Levitschev (URS). **Feather:** Andrianov (URS). **Light:** L. Juhasz (HUN). **L. Welter:** K. Nemec (HUN). **Welter:** Davidov (URS). **L. Middle:** A. Lemeschev (URS). **Middle:** N. Anfimov (URS). **L. Heavy:** O. Sasche (GDR). **Heavy:** J. Reder (HUN).
Bronze medals: D. Needham (ENG), R. Barlow (ENG), L. Stevens (ENG).

Bucharest, Romania - 1972
L. Fly: A. Turei (ROM). **Fly:** Condurat (ROM). **Bantam:** V. Solomin (URS). **Feather:** V. Lvov (URS). **Light:** S. Cutov (ROM). **L. Welter:** K. Pierwieniecki (POL). **Welter:** Zorov (URS). **L. Middle:** Babescu (ROM). **Middle:** V. Lemeschev (URS). **L. Heavy:** Mirounik (URS). **Heavy:** Subutin (URS).
Bronze medals: J. Gale (ENG), R. Maxwell (ENG), D. Odwell (ENG).

Kiev, Russia - 1974
L. Fly: A. Tkachenko (URS). **Fly:** V. Rybakov (URS). **Bantam:** C. Andreikovski (BUL). **Feather:** V. Sorokin (URS). **Light:** V. Limasov (URS). **L. Welter:** N. Sigov (URS). **Welter:** M. Bychkov (URS). **L. Middle:** V. Danshin (URS). **Middle:** D. Jende (GDR). **L. Heavy:** K. Dafinoiu (ROM). **Heavy:** K. Mashev (BUL).
Silver medal: C. Magri (ENG).
Bronze medals: G. Gilbody (ENG), K. Laing (ENG).

Izmir, Turkey - 1976
L. Fly: C. Seican (ROM). **Fly:** G. Khratsov (URS). **Bantam:** M. Navros (URS). **Feather:** V. Demoianeko (URS). **Light:** M. Puzovic (YUG). **L. Welter:** V. Zverev (URS). **Welter:** K. Ozoglouz (TUR). **L. Middle:** W. Lauder (SCO). **Middle:** H. Lenhart (GER). **L. Heavy:** I. Yantchauskas (URS). **Heavy:** B. Enjenyan (URS).
Silver medal: J. Decker (ENG).
Bronze medals: I. McLeod (SCO), N. Croombes (ENG).

Dublin, Ireland - 1978
L. Fly: R. Marx (GDR). **Fly:** D. Radu (ROM). **Bantam:** S. Khatchatrian (URS). **Feather:** H. Loukmanov (URS). **Light:** P. Oliva (ITA). **L. Welter:** V. Laptiev (URS). **Welter:** R. Filimanov (URS). **L. Middle:** A. Beliave (URS). **Middle:** G. Zinkovitch (URS). **L. Heavy:** I. Jolta (ROM). **Heavy:** P. Stoimenov (BUL).
Silver medals: M. Holmes (IRL), P. Hanlon (ENG), M. Courtney (ENG).
Bronze medals: T. Thompson (IRL), J. Turner (ENG), M. Bennett (WAL), J. McAllister (SCO), C. Devine (ENG).

Rimini, Italy - 1980
L. Fly: A. Mikoulin (URS). **Fly:** J. Varadi (HUN). **Bantam:** F. Rauschning (GDR). **Feather:** J. Gladychev (URS). **Light:** V. Shishov (URS). **L. Welter:** R. Lomski (BUL). **Welter:** T. Holonics (GDR). **L. Middle:** N. Wilshire (ENG). **Middle:** S. Laptiev (URS). **L. Heavy:** V. Dolgoun (URS). **Heavy:** V. Tioumentsev (URS). **S. Heavy:** S. Kormihtsine (URS).
Bronze medals: N. Potter (ENG), B. McGuigan (IRL), M. Brereton (IRL), D. Cross (ENG).

Schwerin, East Germany - 1982
L. Fly: R. Kabirov (URS). **Fly:** I. Filchev (BUL). **Bantam:** M. Stecca (ITA). **Feather:** B. Blagoev (BUL). **Light:** E. Chakimov (URS). **L. Welter:** S. Mehnert (GDR). **Welter:** T. Schmitz (GDR). **L. Middle:** B. Shararov (URS). **Middle:** E. Christie (ENG). **L. Heavy:** Y. Waulin (URS). **Heavy:** A. Popov (URS). **S. Heavy:** V. Aldoshin (URS).
Silver medal: D. Kenny (ENG).
Bronze medal: O. Jones (ENG).

Tampere, Finland - 1984
L. Fly: R. Breitbart (GDR). **Fly:** D. Berg (GDR). **Bantam:** K. Khdrian (URS). **Feather:** O. Nazarov (URS). **Light:** C. Furnikov (BUL). **L. Welter:** W. Schmidt (GDR). **Welter:** K. Doinov (BUL). **L. Middle:** O. Volkov (URS). **Middle:** R. Ryll (GDR). **L. Heavy:** G. Peskov (URS). **Heavy:** R. Draskovic (YUG). **S. Heavy:** L. Kamenov (BUL).
Bronze medals: J. Lowey (IRL), F. Harding (ENG), N. Moore (ENG).

Copenhagen, Denmark - 1986
L. Fly: S. Todorov (BUL). **Fly:** S. Galotian (URS). **Bantam:** D. Drumm (GDR). **Feather:** K. Tsziu (URS). **Light:** G. Akopkhian (URS). **L. Welter:** F. Vastag (ROM). **Welter:** S. Karavayev (URS). **L. Middle:** E. Elibaev (URS). **Middle:** A.

Kurnabka (URS). **L. Heavy:** A. Schultz (GDR). **Heavy:** A. Golota (POL). **S. Heavy:** A. Prianichnikov (URS).

Gdansk, Poland - 1988
L. Fly: I. Kovacs (HUN). **Fly:** M. Beyer (GDR). **Bantam:** M. Aitzanov (URS). **Feather:** M. Rudolph (GDR). **Light:** M. Shaburov (URS). **L. Welter:** G. Campanella (ITA). **Welter:** D. Konsun (URS). **L. Middle:** K. Kiselev (URS). **Middle:** A. Rudenko (URS). **L. Heavy:** O. Velikanov (URS). **Heavy:** A. Ter-Okopian (URS). **S. Heavy:** E. Belusov (URS).
Bronze medals: P. Ramsey (ENG), M. Smyth (WAL).

Usti Nad Labem, Czechoslovakia - 1990
L. Fly: Z. Paliani (URS). **Fly:** K. Pielert (GDR). **Bantam:** K. Baravi (URS). **Feather:** P. Gvasalia (URS). **Light:** J. Hildenbrandt (GDR). **L. Welter:** N. Smanov (URS). **Welter:** A. Preda (ROM). **L. Middle:** A. Kakauridze (URS). **Middle:** J. Schwank (GDR). **L. Heavy:** Iljin (URS). **Heavy:** I. Andrejev (URS). **S. Heavy:** W. Fischer (GDR).
Silver medal: A. Todd (ENG).
Bronze medal: P. Craig (ENG).

Edinburgh, Scotland - 1992
L. Fly: M. Ismailov (URS). **Fly:** F. Brennfuhrer (GER). **Bantam:** S. Kuchler (GER). **Feather:** M. Silantiev (URS). **Light:** S. Shcherbakov (URS). **L. Welter:** O. Saitov (URS). **Welter:** H. Kurlumaz (TUR). **L. Middle:** Z. Erdie (HUN). **Middle:** V. Zhirov (URS). **L. Heavy:** D. Gorbachev (URS). **Heavy:** L. Achkasov (URS). **S. Heavy:** A. Mamedov (URS).
Silver medals: M. Hall (ENG), B. Jones (WAL).
Bronze medals: F. Slane (IRL), G. Stephens (IRL), C. Davies (WAL).

Salonika, Greece - 1993
L. Fly: O. Kiroukhine (UKR). **Fly:** R. Husseinov (AZE). **Bantam:** M. Kulbe (GER). **Feather:** E. Zakharov (RUS). **Light:** O. Sergeev (RUS). **L. Welter:** A. Selihanov (RUS). **Welter:** O. Kudinov (UKR). **L. Middle:** E. Makarenko (RUS). **Middle:** D. Droukovski (RUS). **L. Heavy:** A. Voida (RUS). **Heavy:** Vladimir Klitschko (UKR). **S. Heavy:** A. Moiseev (RUS).
Bronze medal: D. Costello (ENG).

Sifok, Hungary - 1995
L. Fly: D. Gaissine (RUS). **Fly:** A. Kotelnik (UKR). **Bantam:** A. Loutsenko (UKR). **Feather:** S. Harrison (SCO). **Light:** D. Simon (ROM). **L. Welter:** B. Ulusoy (TUR). **Welter:** O. Bouts (UKR). **L. Middle:** O. Bukalo (UKR). **Middle:** V. Plettnev (RUS). **L. Heavy:** A. Derevtsov (RUS). **Heavy:** C. O'Grady (IRL). **S. Heavy:** D. Savvine (RUS).
Silver medal: G. Murphy (SCO).
Bronze medal: N. Linford (ENG).

Birmingham, England - 1997
L. Fly: G. Balakshine (RUS). **Fly:** K. Dzhamoloudinov (RUS). **Bantam:** A. Shaiduline (RUS). **Feather:** D. Marciukaitis (LIT). **Light:** D. Baranov (RUS). **L. Welter:** A. Mishine (RUS). **Welter:** D. Yuldashev (UKR). **L. Middle:** A. Catic (GER). **Middle:** D. Lebedev (RUS). **L. Heavy:** V. Uzelkov (UKR). **Heavy:** S. Koeber (GER). **S. Heavy:** D. Pirozhenko (RUS).
Silver medal: S. Miller (ENG).
Bronze medals: S. Burke (ENG), M. Dean (ENG), P. Pierson (ENG), M. Lee (IRE).

Rijeka, Croatia - 1999
L. Fly: Kibalyuk (UKR). **Fly:** A. Bakhtin (RUS). **Bantam:** V. Simion (ROM). **Feather:** Kiutkhukow (BUL). **Light:** Pontilov (RUS). **L. Welter:** G. Ajetovic (YUG). **Welter:** S. Nouaouria (FRA). **L. Middle:** S. Kazantsev (RUS) **Middle:** D. Tsariouk (RUS). **L. Heavy:** Alexeev (RUS). **Heavy:** Alborov (RUS). **S. Heavy:** Soukhoverkov (RUS).
Bronze medal: S. Birch (ENG).

Sarejevo, Croatia - 2001
L. Fly: A. Taratokin (RUS). **Fly:** E. Abzalimov (RUS). **Bantam:** G. Kovaljov (RUS). **Feather:** M. Hratcev (RUS). **Light:** S. Aydin (TUR). **L. Welter:** D. Mikulin (RUS). **Welter:** O. Bokalo (UKR). **L. Middle:** M. Korobov (RUS). **Middle:** I. Bogdanov (UKR). **L. Heavy:** R. Kahkijev (RUS). **Heavy:** V. Zuyev (BE). **S. Heavy:** I. Timurziejev (RUS).
Bronze medal: K. Anderson (SCO).

Warsaw, Poland - 2003
L. Fly: P. Bedak (HUN). **Fly:** A. Ganev (RUS). **Bantam:** M. Tretiak (UKR). **Feather:** A. Alexandru (ROM). **Light:** A. Aleksiev (RUS). **L. Welter:** T. Tabotadze (UKR). **Welter:** Z. Baisangurov (RUS). **Middle:** J. Machoncev (RUS). **L. Heavy:** I. Michalkin (RUS). **Heavy:** Y. Romanov (RUS). **S. Heavy:** D. Arshba (RUS).
Bronze medal: S. Smith (E), F. Gavin (E), J. O'Donnell (E), T. Jeffries (E).

Note: The age limit for the championships were reduced from 21 to 19 in 1976.

Commonwealth Champions, 1930-2002

Hamilton, Canada - 1930
Fly: W. Smith (SAF). **Bantam:** H. Mizler (ENG). **Feather:** F. Meacham (ENG). **Light:** J. Rolland (SCO). **Welter:** L. Hall (SAF). **Middle:** F. Mallin (ENG). **L. Heavy:** J. Goyder (ENG). **Heavy:** V. Stuart (ENG).
Silver medals: T. Pardoe (ENG), T. Holt (SCO).
Bronze medals: A. Lyons (SCO), A. Love (ENG), F. Breeman (ENG).

Wembley, England - 1934
Fly: P. Palmer (ENG). **Bantam:** F. Ryan (ENG). **Feather:** C. Cattarall (SAF). **Light:** L. Cook (AUS). **Welter:** D. McCleave (ENG). **Middle:** A. Shawyer (ENG). **L. Heavy:** G. Brennan (ENG). **Heavy:** P. Floyd (ENG).
Silver medals: A. Barnes (WAL), J. Jones (WAL), F. Taylor (WAL), J. Holton (SCO).
Bronze medals: J. Pottinger (WAL), T. Wells (SCO), H. Moy (ENG), W. Duncan (NIR), J. Magill (NIR), Lord D. Douglas-Hamilton (SCO).

Melbourne, Australia - 1938
Fly: J. Joubert (SAF). **Bantam:** W. Butler (ENG). **Feather:** A. Henricus (CEY). **Light:** H. Groves (ENG). **Welter:** W. Smith (AUS). **Middle:** D. Reardon (WAL). **L. Heavy:** N. Wolmarans (SAF). **Heavy:** T. Osborne (CAN).
Silver medals: J. Watson (SCO), M. Dennis (ENG).
Bronze medals: H. Cameron (SCO), J. Wilby (ENG).

Auckland, New Zealand - 1950
Fly: H. Riley (SCO). **Bantam:** J. van Rensburg (SAF). **Feather:** H. Gilliland (SCO). **Light:** R. Latham (ENG). **Welter:** T. Ratcliffe (ENG). **Middle:** T. van Schalkwyk (SAF). **L. Heavy:** D. Scott (ENG). **Heavy:** F. Creagh (NZL).
Bronze medal: P. Brander (ENG).

Vancouver, Canada - 1954
Fly: R. Currie (SCO). **Bantam:** J. Smillie (SCO). **Feather:** L. Leisching (SAF). **Light:** P. van Staden (SR). **L. Welter:** M. Bergin (CAN). **Welter:** N. Gargano (ENG). **L. Middle:** W. Greaves (CAN). **Middle:** J. van de Kolff (SAF). **L. Heavy:** P. van Vuuren (SAF). **Heavy:** B. Harper (ENG).
Silver medals: M. Collins (WAL), F. McQuillan (SCO).
Bronze medals: D. Charnley (ENG), B. Wells (ENG).

Cardiff, Wales - 1958
Fly: J. Brown (SCO). **Bantam:** H. Winstone (WAL). **Feather:** W. Taylor (AUS). **Light:** R. McTaggart (SCO). **L. Welter:** H. Loubscher (SAF). **Welter:** J. Greyling (SAF). **L. Middle:** G. Webster (SAF). **Middle:** T. Milligan (NIR). **L. Heavy:** A. Madigan (AUS). **Heavy:** D. Bekker (SAF).
Silver medals: T. Bache (ENG), M. Collins (WAL), J. Jordan (NIR), R. Kane (SCO), S. Pearson (ENG), A. Higgins (WAL), D. Thomas (ENG).
Bronze medals: P. Lavery (NIR), D. Braithwaite (WAL), R. Hanna (NIR), A. Owen (SCO), J. McClory (NIR), J. Cooke (ENG), J. Jacobs (ENG), B. Nancurvis (ENG), R. Scott (SCO), W. Brown (WAL), J. Caiger (ENG), W. Bannon (SCO), R. Pleace (WAL).

Perth, Australia - 1962
Fly: R. Mallon (SCO). **Bantam:** J. Dynevor (AUS). **Feather:** J. McDermott (SCO). **Light:** E. Blay (GHA). **L. Welter:** C. Quartey (GHA). **Welter:** W. Coe (NZL). **L. Middle:** H. Mann (CAN). **Middle:** M. Calhoun (JAM). **L. Heavy:** A. Madigan (AUS). **Heavy:** G. Oywello (UGA).
Silver medals: R. McTaggart (SCO), J. Pritchett (ENG).
Bronze medals: M. Pye (ENG), P. Benneyworth (ENG), B. Whelan (ENG), B. Brazier (ENG), C. Rice (NIR), T. Menzies (SCO), H. Christie (NIR), A. Turmel (CI).

Kingston, Jamaica - 1966
Fly: S. Shittu (GHA). **Bantam:** E. Ndukwu (NIG). **Feather:** P. Waruinge (KEN). **Light:** A. Andeh (NIG). **L. Welter:** J. McCourt (NIR). **Welter:** E. Blay (GHA). **L. Middle:** M. Rowe (ENG). **Middle:** J. Darkey (GHA). **L. Heavy:** R. Tighe (ENG). **Heavy:** W. Kini (NZL).
Silver medals: P. Maguire (NIR), R. Thurston (ENG), R. Arthur (ENG), T. Imrie (SCO).
Bronze medals: S. Lockhart (NIR), A. Peace (SCO), F. Young (NIR), J. Turpin (ENG), D. McAlinden (NIR).

Edinburgh, Scotland - 1970
L. Fly: J. Odwori (UGA). **Fly:** D. Needham (ENG). **Bantam:** S. Shittu (GHA). **Feather:** P. Waruinge (KEN). **Light:** A. Adeyemi (NIG). **L. Welter:** M. Muruli (UGA). **Welter:** E. Ankudey (GHA). **L. Middle:** T. Imrie (SCO). **Middle:** J. Conteh (ENG). **L. Heavy:** F. Ayinla (NIG). **Heavy:** B. Masanda (UGA).
Silver medals: T. Davies (WAL), J. Gillan (SCO), D. Davies (WAL), J. McKinty (NIR).
Bronze medals: M. Abrams (ENG), A. McHugh (SCO), D. Larmour (NIR), S. Oglivie (SCO), A. Richardson (ENG), T. Joyce (SCO), P. Doherty (NIR), J. Rafferty (SCO), L. Stevens (ENG).

Christchurch, New Zealand - 1974
L. Fly: S. Muchoki (KEN). **Fly:** D. Larmour (NIR). **Bantam:** P. Cowdell (ENG). **Feather:** E. Ndukwu (NIG). **Light:** A. Kalule (UGA). **L. Welter:** O. Nwankpa (NIG). **Welter:** M. Muruli (UGA). **L. Middle:** L. Mwale (ZAM). **Middle:** F. Lucas (STV). **L. Heavy:** W. Knight (ENG). **Heavy:** N. Meade (ENG).
Silver medals: E. McKenzie (WAL), A. Harrison (SCO).
Bronze medals: J. Bambrick (SCO), J. Douglas (SCO), J. Rodgers (NIR), S. Cooney (SCO), R. Davies (ENG), C. Speare (ENG), G. Ferris (NIR).

Edmonton, Canada - 1978
L. Fly: S. Muchoki (KEN). **Fly:** M. Irungu (KEN). **Bantam:** B. McGuigan (NIR). **Feather:** A. Nelson (GHA). **Light:** G. Hamill (NIR). **L. Welter:** W. Braithwaite (GUY). **Welter:** M. McCallum (JAM). **L. Middle:** K. Perlette (CAN). **Middle:** P. McElwaine (AUS). **L. Heavy:** R. Fortin (CAN). **Heavy:** J. Awome (ENG).
Silver medals: J. Douglas (SCO), K. Beattie (NIR), D. Parkes (ENG), V. Smith (ENG).
Bronze medals: H. Russell (NIR), M. O'Brien (ENG), J. McAllister (SCO), T. Feal (WAL).

Brisbane, Australia - 1982
L. Fly: A. Wachire (KEN). **Fly:** M. Mutua (KEN). **Bantam:** J. Orewa (NIG). **Feather:** P. Konyegwachie (NIG). **Light:** H. Khalili (KEN). **L. Welter:** C. Ossai (NIG). **Welter:** C. Pyatt (ENG). **L. Middle:** S. O'Sullivan (CAN). **Middle:** J. Price (ENG). **L. Heavy:** F. Sani (FIJ). **Heavy:** W. de Wit (CAN).
Silver medals: J. Lyon (ENG), J. Kelly (SCO), R. Webb (NIR), P. Hanlon (ENG), J. McDonnell (ENG), N. Croombes (ENG), H. Hylton (ENG).
Bronze medals: R. Gilbody (ENG), C. McIntosh (ENG), R. Corr (NIR).

Edinburgh, Scotland - 1986
L. Fly: S. Olson (CAN). **Fly:** J. Lyon (ENG). **Bantam:** S. Murphy (ENG). **Feather:** B. Downey (CAN). **Light:** A. Dar (CAN). **L. Welter:** H. Grant (CAN). **Welter:** D. Dyer (ENG). **L. Middle:** D. Sherry (CAN). **Middle:** R. Douglas (ENG). **L. Heavy:** J. Moran (ENG). **Heavy:** J. Peau (NZL). **S. Heavy:** L. Lewis (CAN).
Silver medals: M. Epton (ENG), R. Nash (NIR), P. English (ENG), N. Haddock (WAL), J. McAlister (SCO), H. Lawson (SCO), D. Young (SCO), A. Evans (WAL).
Bronze medals: W. Docherty (SCO), J. Todd (NIR), K. Webber (WAL), G. Brooks (SCO), J. Wallace (SCO), C. Carleton (NIR), J. Jacobs (ENG), B. Lowe (NIR), D. Denny (NIR), G. Thomas (WAL), A. Mullen (SCO), G. Ferrie (SCO), P. Tinney (NIR), B. Pullen (WAL), E. Cardouza (ENG), J. Oyebola (ENG), J. Sillitoe (CI).

Auckland, New Zealand - 1990
L. Fly: J. Juuko (UGA). **Fly:** W. McCullough (NIR). **Bantam:** S. Mohammed (NIG). **Feather:** J. Irwin (ENG). **Light:** G. Nyakana (UGA). **L. Welter:** C. Kane (SCO). **Welter:** D. Defiagbon (NIG). **L. Middle:** R. Woodhall (ENG). **Middle:** C. Johnson (CAN). **L. Heavy:** J. Akhasamba (KEN). **Heavy:** G. Onyango (KEN). **S. Heavy:** M. Kenny (NZL).
Bronze medals: D. Anderson (SCO), M. Edwards (ENG), P. Douglas (NIR).

Victoria, Canada - 1994
L. Fly: H. Ramadhani (KEN). **Fly:** P. Shepherd (SCO). **Bantam:** R. Peden (AUS). **Feather:** C. Patton (CAN). **Light:** M. Strange (CAN). **L. Welter:** P. Richardson (ENG). **Welter:** N. Sinclair (NIR). **L. Middle:** J. Webb (NIR). **Middle:** R. Donaldson (CAN). **L. Heavy:** D. Brown (CAN). **Heavy:** O. Ahmed (KEN). **S. Heavy:** D. Dokiwari (NIG).
Silver medals: S. Oliver (ENG), J. Cook (WAL), M. Renaghan (NIR), M. Winters (NIR), J. Wilson (SCO).
Bronze medals: D. Costello (ENG), J. Townsley (SCO), D. Williams (ENG).

Kuala Lumpar, Malaysia - 1998
L. Fly: S. Biki (MAS). **Fly:** R. Sunee (MRI). **Bantam:** M. Yomba (TAN). **Feather:** A. Arthur (SCO). **Light:** R. Narh (GHA). **L. Welter:** M. Strange (CAN). **Welter:** J. Molitor (CAN). **L. Middle:** C. Bessey (ENG). **Middle:** J. Pearce (ENG). **L. Heavy:** C. Fry (ENG). **Heavy:** M. Simmons (CAN). **S. Heavy:** A. Harrison (ENG).
Silver medal: L. Cunningham (NIR).
Bronze medals: G. Jones (ENG), A. McLean (ENG), C. McNeil (SCO), J. Townsley (SCO), B. Magee (NIR), K. Evans (WAL).

Manchester, England - 2002
L. Fly: M. Ali Qamar (IND). **Fly:** K. Kanyanta (ZAM). **Bantam:** J. Kane (AUS). **Feather:** H. Ali (PAK). **Light:** J. Arthur (WAL). **L. Welter:** D. Barker (ENG). **Welter:** D. Geale (AUS). **L. Middle:** J. Pascal (CAN). **Middle:** P. Miller (AUS). **L. Heavy:** J. Albert (NIG). **Heavy:** J. Douglas (CAN). **S. Heavy:** D. Dolan (ENG).
Silver medals: D. Langley (ENG), P. Smith (ENG), S. Birch (ENG).
Bronze medals: M. Moran (ENG), A. Morris (ENG), C. McEwan (SCO), A. Young (SCO), K. Evans (WAL).

The Triple Hitters' Boxing Quiz (Part 9)

Compiled by Ralph Oates

QUESTIONS

1. On 28 March 1917, Willie Meehan outpointed a future world heavyweight champion over four rounds. Name the opponent?
   A. Gene Tunney.   B. Jack Dempsey.
   C. Jack Sharkey.

2. On 23 September 1929, Battling Battalino won the world featherweight title when he outpointed the holder, Andre Routis, over 15 rounds. Who refereed this contest?
   A. Eddie Forbes.   B. Bill Conway.   C. Dave Barry.

3. John Henry Lewis retained his world light-heavyweight championship on 13 March 1936 when outpointing Jock McAvoy over 15 rounds. In which country did this contest take place?
   A. England.   B. France.   C. America.

4. Bruce Woodcock won the vacant European heavyweight title on 29 July 1946 when he knocked out Albert Renet. In which round was the kayo administered?
   A. Five.   B. Six.   C. Seven.

5. Future British, European and Empire lightweight champion, Dave Charnley, stopped Pat McCoy in the sixth round on 7 December 1954. At this stage of his career, Charnley was undefeated, but how many professional contests had he participated in?
   A. Three.   B. Four.   C. Five.

6. Dai Corp outpointed Eddie France over six rounds on 27 March 1961. Where did the contest take place?
   A. Cardiff.   B. London.   C. Glasgow.

7. On 12 May 1964, Howard Winstone retained his European featherweight title when the challenger, Lino Mastellaro, retired. Name the final round?
   A. Six.   B. Seven.   C. Eight.

8. On 31 March 1966, Billy Walker stopped Lars Norling in the fourth round. At that point, how many professional contests had Walker taken part in?
   A. 22.   B. 23.   C. 24.

9. Over how many rounds did the future world light-weight champion, Ken Buchanan, outpoint Tommy Garrison on 14 February 1967?
   A. Six.   B. Eight.   C. Ten.

10. In which round did the future world welterweight champion, John H. Stracey, stop Tei Dovi on 10 February 1970?
    A. One.   B. Two.   C. Three.

11. On 27 August 1970, Chris Finnegan lost a 15-round points decision to Tom Bogs when challenging for the European middleweight championship. In which country did this contest take place?
    A. Denmark.   B. France.   C. England.

12. On 7 December 1974, Evan Armstrong lost his Commonwealth featherweight title in Ghana to David Kotey when stopped in round ten. Which version of the world featherweight title did Kotey go on to win?
    A. WBA.   B. WBC.   C. IBF.

13. Jim Watt regained the British lightweight title on 27 January 1975 when he stopped Johnny Cheshire in round seven of a contest for the vacant crown. In which part of Scotland did the bout take place?
    A. Edinburgh.   B. Glasgow.   C. Hamilton.

14. Maurice Hope won the European light-middleweight title on 1 October 1976 when he stopped the defending champion, Vito Antuofermo, in round 15. In which country did this contest take place?
    A. Germany.   B. Italy.   C. England.

15. Enrique Castro was stopped in the first round on 14 October 1980 by future WBC world flyweight champion, Charlie Magri. Up until then, how many of his bouts had Magri won in the opening round?
    A. One.   B. Two.   C. Three.

16. On 17 July 1981, the former British light-welter-weight champion, Joey Singleton, boxed Frankie Decaestecker over eight rounds in Belgium. What was the result?

A. Draw. B. Points win for Singleton.
C. Points win for Decaestecker.

17. Sylvester Mittee won the vacant Commonwealth welterweight title on 10 October 1984 when he stopped Fighting Romanus. In which round?
A. Ten. B. 11. C. 12.

18. Sam Reeson made the first defence of his European cruiserweight title on 28 November 1987 when he knocked out Luigi Ricci in round seven. In which country did this contest take place?
A. Italy. B. France. C. England.

19. Pat Clinton failed to win the vacant European flyweight championship in Denmark on 16 February 1989. By which method did Eyup Can defeat him?
A. Five-round stoppage. B. Eight-round knockout.
C. 12-round points decision.

20. On 31 May 1989, the former European featherweight champion, Jim McDonnell, stopped the former WBA world featherweight title holder, Barry McGuigan, in round four. Where did this contest take place?
A. London. B. Manchester. C. Liverpool.

21. Glenn McCrory won the vacant IBF cruiserweight title on 3 June 1989 when he outpointed Patrick Lumumba over 12 rounds. At that time, how many professional contests had McCrory taken part in?
A. 29. B. 30. C. 31.

22. Henry Akinwande stopped Young Joe Louis in round three on 28 February 1992. In which country did this contest take place?
A. England. B. France. C. Germany.

23. How many contests did the former Commonwealth light-heavyweight champion, Nicky Piper, have during his professional career?
A. 32. B. 33. C. 34.

24. On 10 June 1995, Robin Reid knocked out Martin Jolley in the first round. At this stage of his career, how many of his professional contests had Reid won in the opening round?
A. Four. B. Five. C. Six.

25. Roy Jones retained his IBF super-middleweight title on 15 June 1996 when he stopped Eric Lucas. In which round?
A. Nine. B. Ten. C. 11.

26. Paul Lloyd retained his Commonwealth bantamweight title on 18 February 1997 when he knocked out Lybo Nkoko in the first round. Who was the referee for this contest?
A. John Coyle. B. Richie Davies. C. Mickey Vann.

27. By which method did Sven Ottke retain his IBF super-middleweight title on 8 May 1999 against Gabriel Hernandez?
A. Five-round stoppage. B. Eight-round knockout.
C. 12-round points decision.

28. In which round did Anthony Farnell stop John Long on 29 May 1999 to capture the vacant WBO Inter-Continental light-middleweight title?
A. Four. B. Five. C. Six.

29. Which boxer is nick-named 'The Executioner'?
A. Joe Calzaghe. B. Bernard Hopkins.
C. Markus Beyer.

30. Junior Witter failed to win the IBF light-welterweight title on 24 June 2000 when outpointed over 12 rounds by the title holder, Zab Judah. Where did this contest take place?
A. Glasgow. B. Cardiff. C. Manchester.

31. Which lady boxer was born in the year 1977?
A. Cathy Brown. B. Jane Couch. C. Laila Ali.

32. How many contests did Brian Coleman take part in during the year 2000?
A. 13. B. 14. C. 15.

33. Find the correct christian names to go with the following referees' surnames. 1. Jones. 2. Green. 3. Hinds.
A. Jeff. B. Wynford. C. Mark.

34. Over how many rounds did Enzo Maccarinelli outpoint Chris Woollas on 11 December 2000?
A. Four. B. Six. C. Eight.

35. On 24 November 2001, John McDermott stopped Gordon Minors in the third round. At that point of his career, how many professional contests was McDermott undefeated in?
A. Seven. B. Eight. C. Nine.

36. On 13 March 2002, Cathy Brown outpointed Svetla Taskova. How many rounds were contested?
A. Four. B. Six. C. Eight.

37. Which one of the following boxers did not box in the paid ranks?
A. Graham Moughton.   B. Tom Imrie.   C. Eric Blake.

38. On 28 May 2002, Michael Jones won the Commonwealth light-middleweight crown when he stopped the holder, Joshua Onyango, in round six. Who was the last holder of the title prior to Onyango?
A. Kevin Kelly. B. Richard Williams. C. Tony Badea.

39. On 1 June 2002, Ricky Hatton retained his WBU light-welterweight title when he defeated Eamonn Magee. Name the method of victory?
A. Five-round stoppage.   B. Eight-round knockout.
C. 12-round points decision.

40. In defence of his IBO welterweight title on 27 July 2002, Jawaid Khaliq defeated Jose Rosa on points over 12 rounds to retain his crown. Where did this contest take place?
A. Birmingham.   B. Derby.   C. Nottingham.

41. Nicky Cook retained his WBF Inter-Continental super-featherweight title on 5 October 2002 when he stopped Gary Thornhill in round seven. At this stage of his career, how many professional contests was Cook undefeated in?
A. 17.   B. 18.   C. 19.

42. On 7 December 2002, Colin Lynes won the vacant IBO Inter-Continental light-welterweight crown when he stopped Richard Kiley. In which round?
A. Eight.   B. Nine.   C. Ten.

43. On 14 December 2002, Chris Byrd won the vacant IBF heavyweight championship, when he outpointed Evander Holyfield over 12 rounds. Which version of the world heavyweight title did Byrd previously hold?
A. WBC.   B. WBA.   C. WBO.

44. How many contests did the former British super-featherweight champion, Neil Haddock, have during his professional career?
A. 24.   B. 26.   C. 27.

45. How many times did Joe Calzaghe defend his WBO super-middleweight title during the year of 2002?
A. Once.   B. Twice.   C. Three.

46. During his professional career, which featherweight title did Steve Robinson not hold?
A. World.   B. British.   C. European.

47. Over how many rounds did Jane Couch outpoint Larisa Berezenko on 15 May 2003?
A. Four.   B. Six.   C. Eight.

48. In which round did Joe Calzaghe stop Byron Mitchell on 28 June 2003, in defence of his WBO super-middleweight title?
A. One.   B. Two.   C. Three.

49. On 21 June 2003, Lennox Lewis retained his WBC and IBO heavyweight titles against Vitali Klitschko on a sixth-round stoppage. In which part of America did this contest take place?
A. New York.   B. Las Vegas.   C. Los Angeles.

50. On 18 September 2003, Matt Skelton won the inaugural English heavyweight title when he stopped the former British champion, Mike Holden, in round six. Who was the referee for this contest?
A. Larry O'Connell.   B. Mickey Vann.
C. Mark Green.

315

Shakespeare Boxing Promotions

Invite all unattached professionals and serious amateurs to their superb facilities in Warwickshire

Facilities include:

Saunas, weights and full-size ring

Promotion, Management and Training Provided

Licensed by the British Boxing Board of Control

Contact Jack Weaver on:
01788-574030 & 07774-855767
2-6 Upton Road, Rugby. CV22 7DL

YOUR FUTURE IS IN SAFE HANDS

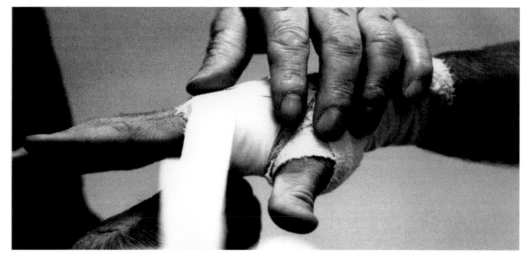

Directory of Ex-Boxers' Associations

by Ron Olver

BOURNEMOUTH Founded 1980. HQ: Fiveways Hotel, Charminster Road, Bournemouth. Dai Dower (P); Percy Singer (T); Dave Fry (VC); Doug Mitchell (S); Peter Fay (C), 24 Monkswell Green, Purewell, Christchurch, Dorset BH23 1MN.

CORK Founded 1973. HQ: Glen Boxing Club, Blackpool, Cork. William O'Leary (P & C); John Martin (S); Phil Murray (VC); John Donovan (T).

CORNWALL Founded 1989. HQ: Fitzsimmons Arms, Coinage Hall Street, Helston. Salvo Nucciforo (C); Eric Bradshaw (S); Stan Cullis (P & PRO), Upper Tolcarne House, Burras Wendron, Nr. Helston TR13 0JD.

CROYDON Founded 1982. HQ: Ivy House Club, Campbell Road, West Croydon. Derek O'Dell (C); Richard Evans (PRO & S); Barry Penny (VC); Gilbert Allnutt (P), 37 Braemar Avenue, Thornton Heath, Croydon CR9 7RJ.

EASTERN AREA Founded 1973. HQ: Norfolk Dumpling, Cattle Market, Hall Road, Norwich. Brian Fitzmaurice (P); Ron Springall (C); Len Cooke (S & T); Clive Campling (VC), 57 Northfields, Norwich NR4 7ES.

HULL & EAST YORKSHIRE Founded 1996. HQ: Tigers Lair, Anlaby Road, Hull. Don Harrison (C); Geoff Rymer (PRO & S); Bert Smith (T), 54 St Aidan Road, Bridlington, E. Yorks.

IPSWICH Founded 1970. HQ: Loco Club, Ipswich. Alby Kingham (P); Vic Thurlow (C & T); Michael Thurlow (S), 147 Clapgate Lane, Ipswich IP3 0RF.

IRISH Founded 1973. HQ: National Boxing Stadium, South Circular Road, Dublin. Val Harris (P); Tommy Bruce (C); Tommy Butler (T); Paddy O'Reilly (VC); Willie Duggan (S), 175 Kimmage Road West, Dublin 6W.

KENT Founded 1997. HQ: RAFA Club, Chatham. Jocko Pett (P); Harry Doherty (C); Paul Nihill, MBE (S & T), 5 Acre Close, Rochester, Kent ME1 2RE.

LEEDS Founded 1952. HQ: North Leeds WMC, Lincoln Green, Leeds 9. Alan Richardson (P); Kevin Cunningham (C & S); Alan Alster (T); Frank Johnson (PRO), Franwyn, 7 Allenby Drive, Leeds LS11 5RP.

LEICESTER Founded 1972. HQ: The Jungle Club, Checketts Road, Leicester. Mick Greaves (P & C); Fred Roberts (T), 138 Aylestone Drive, Leicester LE2 8SA.

LONDON Founded 1971. HQ: The Queen Mary College, Bancroft Road, Mile End, London E1. Stephen Powell (P); Micky O'Sullivan (C); Ron Olver (PRO); Ray Caulfield (T); Mrs Mary Powell (S), 36 St Peters Street, Islington, London N1 8JT.

MANCHESTER Founded 1968. HQ: Hat & Feathers Pub, Ancoats, Manchester. Tommy Proffitt (LP); Jack Edwards (P); Kenny Baker (T); Jimmy Lewis (C); Eddie Copeland (S), 9 Lakeside, Hadfield, Glossop, Derby SK13 1HW.

MERSEYSIDE (Liverpool) Founded 1973. HQ: Arriva Club, Hockenhall Alley, Liverpool. Johnny Cooke (P); Terry Carson (C); Jim Boyd (VC); Jim Jenkinson (S & T), 13 Brooklands Avenue, Waterloo, Liverpool L22 3XY.

MIDLANDS EBA Founded 2002. HQ: The Portland Pavilions, Portland Road, Edgbaston, Birmingham. Richie Woodhall (P); Barry DeLacy (C); Martin Florey (VC); Les Potts (T); Jerry Hjelter (S), 67 Abberley Avenue, Stourport on Severn, Worcs DY13 0LY.

NORTHAMPTON DISTRICT Founded 2001. HQ: Northampton Boys Club, Towcester Road, Northampton. Jeff Tite (P); Keith Hall (C); Sid Green (S & T), 8 Friars Close, Delapre, Northampton NN4 8PU.

NORTHAMPTONSHIRE Founded 1981. HQ: Cue Club, Bridge Street, Northampton. Dick Rogers (P); Gil Wilson (C); George Ward (VC); Peter Cripps (T); Mrs Pam Ward (S), 6 Derwent Close, Kings Heath, Northampton.

NORTHERN FEDERATION Founded 1974. Several member EBAs. Annual Gala. Eddie Copeland (S), 9 Lakeside, Hadfield, Glossop, Derbyshire SK13 1HW.

NORTHERN IRELAND Founded 1970. HQ: Ulster Sports Club, High Street, Belfast. Gerry Hassett (P); H. Hanna (C); S. Thompson (T); George O'Neill (PRO); Al Gibson (S), 900 Crumlin Road, Belfast.

NORTH STAFFS & SOUTH CHESHIRE Founded 1969. HQ: The Saggar Makers Bottom Knocker, Market Place, Burslem, Stoke on Trent. Roy Simms (VC); Les Dean (S); John Greatbach (T); Billy Tudor (C & PRO), 133 Springbank Road, Chell Heath, Stoke on Trent, Staffs ST6 6HW.

NORWICH Founded 1990. HQ: West End Retreat, Brown Street, Norwich. Les King (P); John Pipe (C); Jack Wakefield (T); Albert Howe (S), 15 Grange Close, Hoveton, Norwich NR2 8EA.

NOTTINGHAM Founded 1979. HQ: The Wheatsheaf, Sneinton Road, Nottingham. Len Chorley (P); Walter Spencer (C); Walter Thomas (VC); Gary Rooksby (T); John Kinsella (PRO); Graham Rooksby (S), 42 Spinney Road, Keyworth, Notts NG12 5LN.

PLYMOUTH Founded 1982. HQ: Stoke Social Club, Devonport Road, Plymouth. Tom Pryce-Davies (C); Doug Halliday (S); Tony Penprase (VC); Arthur Willis (T); Buck Taylor (P & PRO), 15 Greenbank Avenue, St Judes, Plymouth PL4 9BT.

PRESTON Founded 1973. HQ: Barney's Piano Bar, Church Street, Preston. John Allen (P & C); Tommy Smith (T); Peter Osborne (S), 39 Prospect Place, Ashton, Preston PR2 1DL.

ST HELENS Founded 1983. HQ: Royal Naval Association, Volunteer Street, St Helens. Johnny Molloy (P); Ray Britch (C); Tommy McNamara (T); Paul Britch (S), 16 Oxley Street, Sutton, St Helens WA9 3PE

SCOTTISH Founded 1997. HQ: Iron Horse Public House, Nile Street, Glasgow. John McCluskey (P); Andy Grant (C); Al Hutcheon (VC); Frank O'Donnell (LP); Peter Baines (T); Liam McColgan (S), 25 Dalton Avenue, Linnvale, Clydebank G81 2SH.

SHEFFIELD Founded 1974. Reformed 2002. HQ: Springwood Hotel, Sheffield. Billy Calvert (P); Harry Carnall (C); John Redfern (S & PRO), 33 Birch Avenue, Chapeltown, Sheffield S35 1RQ.

SQUARE RING Founded 1978. HQ: Snooty Fox Hotel, St Marychurch. George Pook (P); Johnny Mudge (S); Jim Banks (T); Paul King (C), 10 Pine Court Apartments, Middle Warberry Road, Torquay.

SUNDERLAND Founded 1959. HQ: River Wear Social Club, Sunderland. George Martin (P); Teddy Lynn (C); Les Simm (T & S), 21 Orchard Street, Pallion, Sunderland SR4 6QL.

SUSSEX Founded 1974. Reformed 2003. HQ: The Conservative Club, Hove. Tommy Mellis (P); John McNeil (C); Ernie Price (PRO & S), 132 Amberley Drive, Hove, Sussex BN3 8JQ.

SWANSEA & SOUTH WEST WALES Founded 1983. HQ: The Conservative Club, Swansea. Cliff Curvis (P); Gordon Pape (C); Ernie Wallis (T); Len Smith (S), 105 Cockett Road, Swansea SA2 0FG.

TYNESIDE Founded 1970. HQ: Pelaw Social Club, Heworth. Billy Charlton (P); Maxie Walsh (C); Harry Greenwood (VC); Malcolm Dinning (T); Alan Gordon (S), 16 Dove Court, Birtley, Chester le Street, Durham PH3 1HB.

WELSH Founded 1976. HQ: Rhydyfelin Labour Club, Pontypridd. Wynford Jones (P); Ron Bruzas (T); John Floyd (C); Don James (S), 28 Woodfield Road, Talbot Green, Pontyclun, Mid-Glamorgan. Patron - Lord Brooks.

WIRRAL Founded 1973. Reformed 2003. HQ: RNA Club, Birkenhead. Frank Johnson (P); Alan Crowther (S); Pat Garry (T); Terry Carson (C), 14 Spruce Close, Birkenhead, Merseyside CH42 0PG.

The above information is set at the time of going to press and no responsibility can be taken for any changes in officers or addresses of HQs that may happen between then and publication or changes that have not been notified to me.

ABBREVIATIONS
P - President. HP - Honorary President. LP - Life President. AP - Acting President. C - Chairman. VC - Vice Chairman. T - Treasurer. S - Secretary. PRO - Public Relations Officer and/or Press Officer.

LEBA Vice President & PRO, Ron Olver (left), with LEBA President, Stephen Powell, who is wearing his Chain of Office

Obituaries

by Derek O'Dell

It is impossible to list everyone, but I have again done my best to include final tributes for as many of the well-known boxers and other familiar names within the sport who have passed away since the 2004 Yearbook was published. We honour them and remember them.

ADAMS Ansel *From* Trinidad. *Died* October 2003, aged 79. A heavyweight, Ansel began boxing in the West Indies back in 1945 before journeying to England to pursue his career. He registered a four-round win over Reg Andrews of Deal and then stopped the useful Gerry McDermott and ran up eight wins against one defeat, beating Paddy Slavin, Lloyd Barnett, Johnny Arthur of South Africa and that dangerous puncher, Frank Bell, who failed to see out the first round. Two months later Ansel aimed too high and was comfortably outpointed by Johnny Williams. He twice beat Simon Templar, but his career then went into decline, all his defeats coming at the hands of 'name' fighters: Karel Sys, Franco Cavicchi, Ingemar Johansson and Joe Erskine. He did redeem himself by holding Peter Bates to a draw, but his dream of boxing for the Empire title never materialised, Jack Gardner beating him in a ten-round eliminator in 1954. After that came a period in Joe Plant's booth before he hung up the gloves for good.

Ansel Adams

ALONGI Tony *From* Pasaic, New Jersey. *Died* 27 November 2003, aged 64. Two defeats in 46 contests is a good scoresheet, especially when fighting against world-class opposition. Tony came through the ranks quickly and was unbeaten going into 1962, which was his fourth year of punching for pay. He had outpointed Billy Stephan, Jefferson Davis and George Logan before stopping Houston's rising star, Tod Herring. It was then that Rodolfo Diaz stopped him in ten rounds. Tony had grit and bounced back to beat Joe DiGrazio. Billy Daniels beat him in 1963, but that was his last defeat and in the next four years, handled by the astute Charlie Goldman, he knocked out Don Warner, fought draws with George Chuvalo and Jerry Quarry (twice), and trimmed Chip Johnson, Levi Forte and Prentice Snipes. He ended his career in 1967 with a knockout victory over Charlie Hall in Las Vegas.

ARMSTRONG Gene 'Ace' *From* Elizabeth, New Jersey. *Died* August 2004, aged 72. The middleweight division was bursting with talent right throughout Gene's career and he played a prominent role as a contender. He had only four bouts before outpointing Otis Woodward, who, like him, was on the way up at that time, only Gene's rise was quicker. That was his last four-rounder and a brief and successful incursion into the six-round class followed before he got top-of-the-bill ten rounders. He then proved that his pedigree was sound by beating Randy Sandy, Charley Joseph, Rory Calhoun, Italo Scortichini and Henry Hank, but stumbled against a future world champion, Dick Tiger, who beat him twice. When Luis Rodriguez beat him on a stoppage, his top rating dropped, but he remained a dangerous foe at world level.

BARTON Frank *From* Salford. *Died* May 2004, aged 92. Frank's career went back to the 1930s, his record running from 1930 to January 1938. During this time he squeezed in 76 contests for 64 wins and two draws, having started as a flyweight hopeful and contesting the important battles as a lightweight and welterweight. In 1936 he got a shot at the Northern Area championship at 9st 9lbs, but Liverpool's Jimmy Stewart got the better of him. Frank was a strong puncher who beat, among others, Nick Lucas, Jimmy Vaughan, Battling Sullivan, Billy Quinlan, Hal Cartwright, Frank Meacham, Les McCarthy, Len 'Tiger' Smith and Chris Benson by the short route with 38 of his 64 wins coming inside the scheduled distance. Before losing the important one to Stewart, he had stopped five men in a row. There were some good points wins too over men such as Billy Sheldon, Bill Hardy, Len Wickwar, Albert Jamsin,

Tony Butcher (twice), Jimmy Walsh, Tommy Hyams and Bert Cantor. He also drew with the ubiquitous Arnold 'Kid' Sheppard. Early in 1938, at the tail-end of a hard career, he got another shot at the Northern Area championship but suffered a rare knockout defeat by Jack Carrick, who had done the same thing almost exactly a year earlier. This was too much for Frank's pride and he announced his retirement. He never had a soft-touch as an opponent and was good enough to lick most of them clearly.

BLIN Knut *From* Hamburg, Germany. *Died* 10 June 2004, aged 35. Undefeated in a brief pro career of nine bouts, the son of Jurgen Blin was considered to have a future in the game, but was the victim of mental illness. After a period in a mental institution, he underwent a bout of depression before he committed suicide. The record books credit him with eight stoppage victories and one win on points.

BRILL Ben *From* Amsterdam. *Died* September 2003, aged 91. Known by current followers of boxing as an international class referee and judge, he officiated in several important fights in Britain. His style of refereeing always had a strong strain of amateur experience and the professionals often found him to be over-fussy, yet he was firm and fair in his duties. His involvement in boxing can be traced back to 1928 when he finished fifth in the flyweight class at the Amsterdam Olympics. He was already the Dutch flyweight champion and that is going back 76 years when he was 15 years old! During the 1939-45 conflict he was deported to Germany because of his connections with the Nazi party, but he and his wife were Jewish and both were interred in the notorious Belsen Prison Camp. However, they survived and later returned to Holland. Brill was an official at the Olympics when Joe Frazier, George Foreman and Teofilo Stevenson won gold medals and was involved in boxing to within a few years of his death.

BROADBENT Johnny *From* Finsbury Park. *Died* 12 January 2004. I saw Johnny box just once, on an open-air show at Weybridge, where he outpointed Leyson Thomas after coming from behind to do so. A capable professional fighter, having drawn with Harry Legge in his third paid outing in 1949, he had won his debut against Jackie Self in the same venue – High Wycombe Town Hall – where Don Cockell started out. Jamaica's Laurie Henry from the Nat Sellar stable was the first to beat him, but Johnny came back with a win over Arthur Fricker. After losing to Johnny Fish, his quality of opposition gradually increased and he notched up wins over Peter Indaco, Jimmy Blackburn, Denny Sewell and Tommy Organ before Jack Solomons gave him a chance to shine at one of his big shows at Harringay. Unfortunately, Maurice 'Mosh' Mancini was a little too ringwise for him, which was hardly surprising since the man in opposite corner was a stable-mate of Randolph Turpin and a dyed-in-the-wool professional, but Johnny was far from disgraced. Retiring in 1954, he was a popular eight-round fighter in a time when boxing was on par with football for coverage in the papers' sports' pages.

Manny Burgo

BURGO Manny *From* North Shields. *Died* November 2003, aged 69. At just under 14 stone, Manny was the ideal weight for a heavyweight boxer of the 1950s era, having about a dozen amateur contests, losing just one, and winning the National Coal Board title in 1954. The following year, he threw his hat into the paid ring and kicked off his career with a win over Johnny Zedd, who took so much stick that he held on to Manny like a leech and was disqualified in the second round. Within six months of his fistic baptism, he was good enough to challenge Garnett Denny, who put him down heavily in round four. Manny showed courage and determination to get off the deck to win on points. Then, in a match that should never have been made, he was thrown to the lions when he was put in with Tonga's Kitione Lave, who could also punch a bit, and was stopped in round one. Despite this set-back, he was considered good enough to be listed as an outstanding prospect by *'Boxing News'*. Another disappointment followed when Tony Lord stopped him, but Manny was made of stern stuff and it was two years before he again tasted defeat. During this period he knocked out top-rated Frank Bell and stopped George Nuttall, Jim

Cooper and Cliff Purnell. He won a Jack Solomons' Heavyweight Competition in 1957 then knocked out Albert Scott and the former middleweight champion, Albert Finch. Jim Cooper asked for a return and got it. Result? Same as the last time. A lot of engagements were falling through at this time and feeling disenchanted with his luck, Manny boxed below form and lost to Joey Armstrong in six rounds. Offered a match with Sam Langford, who withdrew at short notice, another Tongan, Sifa Kivalu, stepped in and ended his career by a first-round stoppage. It was a sudden end to such a promising career and handled better, Manny could have gone all the way.

BURRUNI Salvatore *From* Alghero, Sardina. *Died* 30 March 2004, aged 70. Salvatore will be remembered as one of the better flyweights to come out of Europe since World War II. He was, at 23, rather late in turning professional, but justified his ambition by winning the Italian title in his second year of boxing. After defending his crown on several occasions he was thrown in with European titleholder, Risto Luukkonen, and surprised his supporters by wearing the Finn down and taking his title, via a 15-rounds points decision. Unbeaten over the next three years, he was a fighting champion who defended against Derek Lloyd, Walter McGowan, Rene Libeer and the Moroccan, Mimoun Ben Ali. With the world title in sight, he relinquished his European championship to challenge Pone Kingpetch, who had twice beaten the great Argentinian, Pascual Perez. Kingpetch was a tall, competent and skilled champion, but the Italian was too strong for him and ran out a clear winner after 15 gruelling rounds. He was 32, rather too old for a flyweight, and increasingly struggling to make the weight, having to shed his gold necklace after weighing in against Australia's Rocky Gattellari, although still strong enough to knock out his man in the 13th round. The WBA had by this time stripped him of their piece of the world title, but he was still clearly the best man at his weight. Unfortunately, his best weight was somewhere between 114-116lbs and, against Britain's Walter McGowan, losing five pounds to make the required limit weakened him. In a cracking contest, he faded in the home stretch and left his world title in Scottish hands. He moved up to bantam and was never beaten at that weight, winning the European title in 1968 by outpointing Ben Ali before ending a fine career, still champion, when knocking out Pierre Vetroff in nine rounds in 1969.

BUXTON Bert *From* Norwich. *Died* 24 April 2004. When World War II ended, Bert took off his amateur vest and turned his fistic intentions to the professional side of the game. He was a stiff puncher and ran up four quick wins before losing to Arthur Harvey, having beaten Kingston's Ernie Ward in his third outing. Ward was nearing the end of his career, but had a wealth of experience. Bert, in the end, proved to be too strong for him. By 1949, Bert had beaten Harry Brooks, Eric Hall, Al Binney, Bobby Fordham and Morley Nightingale. He'd drawn with Arthur Fricker, although quick defeats by Teddy Lee and Stan Davis did much to dampen his progress, but he ended with a respectable record and was Eastern Area welterweight champion in his prime years. In retirement, he was a member of Norwich Ex-Boxers' Association for many years before his death.

CARKIDO Joey *From* Youngstown, Ohio. *Died* 7 June 2004, aged 75. A tough and relentless fighter of the 1940s and early 50s, Joey met four world champions in Paddy DeMarco, Lew Jenkins, Beau Jack and Johnny Saxton. He acquitted himself well and can count Beau Jack as one of his victims. Then there was Charlie Fusari who got the points decision, but had to fight him all the way. Joey began in 1945 and had an impressive score of 47 wins in 50 outings until DeMarco stopped him at the end of 1947. Having previously won against Jimmy Warren, Ray Sales and Al Pennino, he moved into the ten-round class and his good record became spotty thereafter. Willie Beltram drew with him and then beat him thrice, but Joey still had enough left to force Dennis Pat Brady to a draw in 1949. By now, his career had passed its peak and after the Jack and Fusari contests came a downhill slide in which he won only three of his 16 contests. He didn't choose mugs though, the names of Lester Felton, Chuck Taylor and Elmer Beltz on his record show that he was still a respected force and a difficult man to beat.

Eddie Carson

CARSON Eddie *From* Edinburgh. *Died* 9 September 2003, aged 81. A Scottish bantamweight, Eddie – born Willie Marshall – was a busy fighter in those early post-war years when the flyweight and bantamweight ranks were brim-full of young hopefuls. From the off, Eddie showed promise and in his fourth outing he forced Dan McGoldrick to a ten-round draw. Bobby Boland, Jackie Briers, Ike Weir, Max Brady, Richie McCulloch and Willie Myles all crossed gloves with him on his way to his title shot against Charlie Kerr. Of that sextet, only Boland beat him. Eddie knocked out Kerr to win the Scottish title in 1949 before losing it to Norman Tennant, but two years later, the belt was back around his waist after he outpointed Jim Dwyer. He lost it to Billy Taylor, but came back for a third crack at the title and won it by beating Hugh Riley. He'd beaten some of Britain's best men, but his case for a shot at the national title was weakened by successive defeats at the hands of Peter Keenan and the future world champion, Robert Cohen. His old title was vacant again in 1956 and he once again faced Riley, hoping for further honours. Disappointingly, the men knew each other's style so well that it became a maul and after six rounds of wrestling and holding, referee Frank Wilson threw them out. Eddie, who would have got a match with Keenan had he won, never fought again.

Bill Cayton

CAYTON Bill *From* New York. *Died* October 2003, aged 85. In partnership with the late Jimmy Jacobs, Bill will be remembered mostly for his guidance of Mike Tyson towards the undisputed heavyweight championship. The relationship with Tyson soured after Jacobs' death in 1988, with Don King eventually prising the young champion away from Bill in 1992 when their contract expired. Under his guidance, Tyson's financial future was secure, shrewd financial decisions ensuring that he would have a good income for life. All this was thrown away when Bill and Mike split. Bill had plans for Mike's benefit in the years following his retirement and it was sad to see good financial planning come to nothing. Owning the world's best collection of fight films, he and Jacobs scoured the world for old-time fight footage and it is them we must thank for being able to watch fights of the past on the TV monitor. Boxing was his life and he was involved in the game right up to the time that he lost his fight with lung-cancer.

CHAVEZ Eddie *From* San Jose, California. *Died* 22 February 2003, aged 73. Eddie is remembered for being one of Willie Pep's opponents back in 1951 when Willie was virtually unbeatable until Sandy Saddler came along, and gave him a good workout. He had a credible record against former and would-be titleholders, beating Harold Dade, Manuel Ortiz (twice), Paddy DeMarco and Jimmy Carter. There were top-rated men too, who had to bow to the clever Californian - Jock Leslie, Jackie McCoy, Maxie Docusen, Enrique Bolanos, Chu-Chu Jiminez, Glen Flanagan (twice), Jesse Underwood, Armand Savoie and Arthur King. Eddie was a class act and didn't lose many, those beating him were usually very good men like Cisco Andrade and Teddy 'Red Top' Davis. In 1954, service in the army took the edge off his career when he was at his peak, but he boxed on for another three years with only three defeats during that time.

CHAVEZ Fabela *From* Hollywood. *Died* 1 October 2003, aged 73. A classy lightweight, Fabela, born Alexander Chavez in Alburqueue, had a record that ran from 1945 to 1955 and which was studded with names of the 'iron' of the division. He was extremely popular in Californian rings, starting out as a 16-year-old, losing and winning to Art Aragon when he was still a teenager and beating Mario Trigo (twice), Alfredo Escobar and Dave Hernandez. As in most careers, he hit a rough patch, going through 1948 devoid of a victory in only four contests just after Escobar beat him in a return. He then lost to old adversary, Trigo, Tote Martinez and Roberto Takeshita of Honolula. Regrouping in 1950, and now a 20-year-old, he got through the year with a solitary loss to George Araujo, before which he scored a knockout over Tommy Collins. Chavez won the Californian featherweight title from Lauro Salas in 1952 after previously having held the Mexican to a draw, before the latter, en-route to a world title, regained it. Fabela had beaten Harold Dade in June of 1951, but after he beat his namesake, Eddie Chavez, Chico Rosa and Baby Guiterrez, his career went into decline and only one win came prior to August 1955, Teddy 'Red Top' Davis, Armand Savoie, Gil Cadilli, Willie Pep and Charlie Riley all being too good for him. He had four children, 11 grandchildren and two great grandchildren.

CLAPTON Freddie *From* Islington, London. *Died* April 2004, aged 70. A former amateur opponent of Henry

Cooper and an Army champion at light-heavyweight, Freddie had a brief professional career from 1958-1961, running up 17 fights, of which he won 11. His first outing came against Danny Wall, who took the count in six rounds, and wins followed over Jim McDonagh, Laci Tomaczi, Johnny Veron and Alby Albano. He dropped decisions twice to both Brian Whiting and Johnny Gleed and couldn't get past Dennis Harmon until he fought him at Kingston. Harman won two out of three, but there were further wins over Morrie Russell, Derek Kilburn and Eric Ludlam bringing an end to a respectable pro record following a long amateur career.

CRIMMINS Terry *From* Cardiff. *Died* July 2004, aged 63. Terry turned professional just before his 19th birthday and surprised Mark Quinn by knocking him out in the second round. For the first two years of his career, he made steady progress in the six-round class and, on the way, beat Don Cosheril (twice), Tommy Burgoyne and Eddie O'Connor. Although a disqualification loss to Don Weller blotted his record, it didn't stop him from moving into the eight-round class, where he was unbeaten for two years. He got revenge over Weller by taking a well-earned decision in Cardiff in May 1962 and followed up with a good win against that very good boxer from the midlands in Brian Cartwright. In 1963, he campaigned in Australia, but struggled to find his best form and was very disappointing against the little-known Kid Oliva, being stopped in the third of a 12-rounder. He redeemed himself by outpointing Melbourne-based Italian, Gilberto Brondi, but lost the return match in the first round. Returning home, he was inactive for 18 months and while his comeback looked promising when he beat West Ham's Bobby Davis and drew with Scotland's John McDermott, a points defeat by his old foe, Cartwright, convinced him that it was time to retire.

FERNANDEZ Frankie *From* Hawaii. *Died* April 2004, aged 85. Frankie was a classy welterweight, who fought outside his native Hawaii just four times in a distinguished career in which he beat Tommy Bell, Beau Jack, Charlie Salas, Philip 'Wildcat' Kim and Livio Minelli. He'd had only seven fights before winning the Hawaiian lightweight title over ten rounds against Ray Powell, having begun professionally in 1944 and fighting on for five years with but a single defeat – to Frankie Moore. By this time he was a world-class performer and it was May 1949 before he dropped a decision to the talented Bernard Docusen. The 'uncrowned lightweight champion', Freddie Dawson, twice beat Frankie in back-to-back contests in 1951, forcing him to take a year out to consider his future. He came back in 1953 with good performances against Mario Trigo and Joe Fisher, before stopping his fellow countryman, Kim, and although his best days were gone he continued to box at world level with wins over Henry Davis and Minelli. However, a run of defeats by Ramon Fuentes, Chico Varona and Luther Rawlings persuaded him to hang up his gloves.

Frankie Fernandez

FISHER Reg *From* Leyton. *Died* 20 February 2004, aged 73. After a boxing apprenticeship as an amateur, Reg spent a couple of years in the army before turning pro in 1952. He began with a points win over Jack Kofi and settled down quickly, stopping that dangerous puncher, Vic Auguste, and going on to beat Albert Carroll before giving Auguste a return. Vic either knocked them out or got clobbered himself and got to Reg first in the second fight. It taught Reg a lesson and he was a better man for it. Good wins came over Frank O'Brien (twice), Billy Kiernan and Eddie Quill, but when O'Brien beat him in a third match he packed it in for a couple of years. Coming back, he fought in good company against men such as Terry Burnett, Ron Warnes, Paddy O'Callaghan, Leo Maloney and Terry Gill, etc. However, he bit off more than he could chew by fighting Brian Curvis at Wembley Pool and finished boxing in 1960 after a loss to welterweight title-challenger, Tony Mancini.

FLANAGAN Del *From* Minnesota. *Died* 26 December 2003, aged 76. One of two boxing brothers, and a superb, smart-boxing welterweight, Del and his brother Glen racked up 250 fights between them. Both were clever and defensively capable and were destined for long careers, neither showing visual signs of their profession. They were capable, elusive and gifted. Del, who died of a heart-attack, was slightly the more active of the two and in his prime he fought many men who were, or who became, world champions such as Sandy Saddler, Beau Jack, Ralph Dupas, Jimmy Carter, Johnny Bratton, Willie Pastrano, Johnny Saxton, Gene Fullmer, Kid Gavilan, Virgil Akins and Joey Giardello. Some of the other big names on his record are Teddy 'Red Top' Davis, Arthur King, Gert van Heerden, Gil Turner, Ralph 'Tiger' Jones, Ramon Fuentes, Carlos Chavez, Jackie Graves and Lester Felton. He drew with Tommy Campbell and dropped decisions to Yama Bahama, Willie Troy, Juan Padilla and George Araujo. This was, surely, one of the great welterweight craftsmen of the 20th century.

FOSSEY Ernie *From* Islington. *Died* 2 September 2003, aged 73. We had been so accustomed to seeing Ernie as a cornerman on television that it is not surprising that many viewers were unaware that he was a capable fighter in his day and also a successful promoter who put on some marvellous shows at Hornsey Town Hall. He knew boxing inside out and was perhaps the best matchmaker since the days of Mickey Duff. Ernie was a bright and breezy character who took up boxing in the 1950s, beginning with a knockout win over none other than Paddy Byrne in a crowd-pleaser at Hoxton Baths. He went through to mid 1952 and 23 fights before tasting defeat. Although Bill Sliney beat him, Ernie got his revenge twice before the year was over. A bad patch followed, even the best fighters have them, and he went through to 1955 before another win appeared on his account – a victory over Peter Fay. Wins followed over Dave Croll, Johnny Mann and Johnny Miller, but once he lost to Ron Hinson for the vacant Southern Area lightweight championship, his ambition

faded and further losses against the Lambeth taxi-driver, Barney Beale, and Peter Heath persuaded him to bow out. History shows that his future with boxing from that point on was intense and beneficial to the game in so many ways.

Ernie Fossey

GAVIN Al *From* New York. *Died* 9 July 2004, aged 70. One of the world's best cornerman, who worked with name-fighters like William Joppy, Danny Lalonde, Lennox Lewis and Kevin Kelley, etc, passed away following a stroke. Al was one of the quiet, unsung men of boxing, respected by everyone in the trade and one of America's most experienced seconds.

GOLDSTEIN Ski *From* San Diego, California. *Died* August 2003, aged 63. Ski was a heavyweight of the 1960s whose star seemed to shine brightly, before disappointing his fans by losing to the awkward southpaw, Jack Bodell, in three rounds. Prior to fighting in Britain he had beaten Manuel Ramos in Los Angeles after scoring eight stoppage wins against one loss to a respected heavyweight in Billy Stephan. He ran up four more wins against moderate opposition after his British debut before ambitiously taking on the capable Argentinian, Eduardo Corletti, in Rome.

Corletti was far too good for him and talk of Ski as being a prospect ceased thereafter.

GORMAN Dave *From* Fort Worth, Texas. *Died* April 2004, aged 61. Dave was one of the successful managers of the 1980s, and one who handled Don Curry and took him to the brink of greatness before Lloyd Honeyghan burst the bubble. He certainly had no luck with his fighters when opposing Honeyghan, his charge, Gene Hatcher, being bombed out in round one. Steve Cruz was another in his stable and Dave was his handler when Cruz won the WBA featherweight title from Ireland's Barry McGuigan.

GOULD Tony *From* Canterbury. *Died* July 2004. Harold Alderman reported the death of Tony Gould, a lightweight of the 1930s and 40s eras, who, being of Italian extraction, was born Antonio Alzapiedi. His professional career began in 1938 and followed a successful start in the simon-pure ranks. Up to the outbreak of war he was a busy fighter with wins over Young Anthony, Jim Uden, Tich Cuthbert, Seth Phillips, Charlie Hall, Jim Pattison, Billy Marsh and Tommy Allen. After two wins over Peter McGrath, he repeated his victory over Cuthbert and licked Reggie Tofield and Ronnie Davis, who later held him to a draw. Points losses came via Croydon's George Willoughby, Pat Crawford, Jeff Cowans and Willie McCairn. Tony saw wartime service in army uniform and spent a long time as a prisoner of war in one of the notorious prison camps. On returning to civvy street, his best days had gone, but he still had enough skills to beat Bobby Jones of Bow and draw twice with that experienced lightweight, Harry Legge. Tony then lost to Billy Caldicott and a young Mickey Duff. Croydon's Kenny Green became the first man to stop Tony, cut eyes forcing him to haul down the flag in three rounds and when a further stoppage loss came at the fists of Welshman, Dave Harnett, he retired from the game.

GRAY Charlie *From* Sunderland. *Died* May 2004. Charlie, a preliminary lightweight boxer and former shipbuilder fought entirely in the Northern counties in 1952 and 1953. In 17 fights he won ten and drew two, beating Teddy Jones, George Henderson, Charlie MacReady, Johnny Brown, Tommy Duffy and Len Slater, but stepping up in class he dropped a decision to Jackie Butler. Charlie was rated in the one-star class by 'Boxing News' throughout his career.

GREEN Jimmy *From* Warrington. *Died* 19 October 2003, aged 77. One of six brothers, four of whom fought professionally, Jimmy was boxing as a five-stone schoolboy and in his career that followed he never weighed above nine stone. Making steady progress with wins over Al Kenny, Jimmy Webster (twice), Jim Campbell, Sammy Reynolds, Johnny Boom and the future flyweight champion, Teddy Gardner, in 1949 he was involved in a car accident that would have ended the boxing aspirations of most but not one with his spirit. He returned to beat Tommy Proffitt and Peter Fay before making the long

journey to Australia, only to be defeated by Bluey Wilkins and Ray French. Disappointed with this loss of form, he returned home never to fight again. Jimmy had been in there with both Danny and Mickey O'Sullivan and also Frank Johnson. He had also lost a return with Proffitt when the Central Area was at stake. No better fighter ever came from the town of Warrington.

Jimmy Green

GUISSEPPI Fitzroy *From* Trinidad. *Died* March 2004, aged 55. A former world-title challenger, Fitzroy died of a heart attack whilst working as a cornerman at a tournament in Jamaica. As a fighter, he had a record of 52 wins in nearly 80 contests, during which he journeyed to South Korea to challenge Sang-Hyun Kim for the WBC light-welterweight title. Despite flooring Kim twice, Fitzroy saw the verdict go against him. Having beaten Percy Hayles in 1974, he then won the Trinidad lightweight title by stopping Mike Drayton, but was twice beaten by Claude Noel. He also dropped a decision to Carlton Bowers, before turning the tables on Bowers in a return to win the Belize welterweight title. Apart from two sorties into South Korea and Mexico City, he confined his fistic activities to Trinidad and Belize.

HANK Henry *From* Mississippi. *Died* July 2004, aged 69. Born Joe Harrison in 1935, Henry turned pro in 1953 as a fledgling welterweight and stopped his first 18 opponents. Then, in his first eight-rounder, he dropped a decision to Virgil Akins, who was an experienced campaigner with the scalps of Joe Brown, Wallace 'Bud' Smith, Freddie Dawson and Tommy Campbell under his belt. Akins was three and a half years away from winning the world title. Henry, who came back to knock out Chuck Coleman, could sock with both hands and as a middleweight he established himself as a force. Two stoppage victories came over Charlie Cotton who had previously outpointed him and by 1959 he'd beaten Jimmy Beecham, Willie Vaughan, Holly Mims, George Benton and Jesse Bowdry. He was not averse to tackling light-heavies and in 1963 got a crack at Eddie Cotton in a 15 rounder recognised by the Michigan State Commission as being for the world crown. Cotton edged him out and that other great light-heavy, Bob Foster, became the only man to stop him inside the distance, while Joey Giardello, Rory Calhoun, Randy Sandy, Victor Zalazar, Jerry Luedee and Alan Harmon all fell before the fists of 'Hammering Henry' as he was often dubbed. A sole appearance in Scotland saw him floor 'Cowboy' John McCormack three times, only to see the decision go against him. It was a really tough scrap that delighted the fans. A year later the biggest win of Henry's career came when he outpointed the future heavyweight king, Jimmy Ellis. Other notable names on his record are Dick Tiger, Johnny Persol, Roger Rouse, Gordon Wallace, Eddie 'Bossman' Jones, Hal Carroll and Andy Kendall. Henry never got stiffs, facing 'em all in a tough, competitive era.

HART Garnett 'Sugar' *From* Philadelphia. *Died* 15 October 2003, aged 65. Ironically, for a man nicknamed 'Sugar', Garnett died in hospital of diabetes. He was a superb amateur, winning AAU titles at lightweight and welterweight in 1954 before turning professional at 18. He could hit and hit hard. In his first 23 outings, of which he lost two, he went home early 19 times. He'd matured into a class welterweight by his 22nd birthday, drawing with Charlie Cotton, beating Larry Baker, but losing to Virgil Akins and it was a stoppage win over Charlie 'Tombstone' Smith that catapulted him into the top echelon. He forced a draw with Gil Turner and beat both Ralph Dupas and Isaac Logart, all top men. A knockout defeat by Charlie Scott came when his best days were over, but he did manage to score a prestigious win over Rocky Kalingo. However, when Benny Paret and Ted Wright beat him he pulled the plug on his career.

HARTLEY Bob *From* Billingborough. *Died* January 2004, aged 89. A quiet, modest and self-educated man, Bob Hartley was in his later years the author of two boxing books, a book dealer and a contributor to the 'Southern Ex-Boxer'. He was an ex-booth fighter with a good professional record in the Lincolnshire area back in the 1930s. Sid Green, who saw Bob box, called him the best of local boxers of that time. His fights got scant publicity in the trade paper because fights from that part of the country often had no reporter at ringside and it was only in recent years that it was discovered that Bob had forced a draw with Dick Turpin in 1938 at Rugby. This was a fact of which Bob must have been aware, but he never admitted it until a press-cutting was unearthed with details of the promotion. By then, Bob was living in Rugby and fighting on the booths with his friend, Sam Minto. He spoke highly of the Hardy brothers of Leicester, having fought the youngest of that clan three times. Bob shared lodgings with Johnny Williams back at the beginning of Johnny's boxing activities, before moving to Wembley and on to Harrow in his retirement years. His book-dealing was a thriving business and he made many friends. Among them was Fred Snelling, then sales-room manager at Sothebys, who urged Bob to produce the 'History of Boxing Books'. They remained friends until Fred's death in 2001. Bob's health suffered in later years and a back complaint put him in a wheelchair, but he still wrote articles for 'Southern Ex-Boxer' and was mid-way through a series on Pat Daly when he was admitted to hospital. It was pneumonia, that deadly opponent, which ultimately got him.

HAVNAA Magne *From* Norway. *Died* May 2004, aged 40. The former WBO cruiserweight champion, Magne died from a boating accident in his native Norway. He boxed up to 1993 when Roger McKenzie beat him in five rounds. In a career that started in 1986, he beat David Jaco, Alfonzo Ratliff and Johnny Nelson, among others. He won the WBO title on 17 May 1990, stopping Boone Pultz in five rounds and made successful defences against Daniel Netto and Tyrone Booze before handing in his belt in February 1992 due to increasing weight problems.

HAYES Alvin *From* Detroit. *Died* 19 January 2004, aged 44. Still boxing when a drug overdose killed him, at 44 his best days long gone, but he had been a world-rated lightweight at his peak. He was beaten three times in 33 fights and was undefeated in his first 22 outings before Jimmy Paul knocked him out. Alvin was a big puncher himself and 26 of his wins came via the short route, although his three losses were also inside the distance. Two spells in prison interrupted what could have been a brilliant career – a sad saga of talent going to waste.

HOMBURG Willem von *From* Germany. *Died* 10 March 2004, aged 64. Born Norbert Grupe in Berlin, but fighting out of Los Angeles, he had a respectable record against Europe's best and against some good American opposition. He beat Monroe Ratcliff in 1963 – his second year as a pro - and later, when campaigning in Europe, first drew with, then stopped that old warhorse, Archie McBride. Piero Tomasoni outpointed him in Dortmund, but he came back to stop Ulli Ritter and Holland's Bas van Duivenbode and forced credible draws with Erich Schoeppner, Ray Patterson and Gerhard Zech. Guilio Rinaldi beat him twice and he was unfortunate to be disqualified in 11 rounds against Piero del Papa when the European light-heavyweight title was at stake, before stepping out of his class against Oscar Bonavena and being beaten in three rounds. That contest eliminated him as a serious title contender, but he finished with a respectable record of 43 bouts, with 23 wins, seven draws and 11 losses, all but one of his victories coming within the scheduled distance. The son of Richard Grupe, a German heavyweight who met men such as Paco Bueno, Heinz Neuhaus, Elkins Brothers and Al Hoosman in the early post-war years, he later established himself as a Hollywood film star and his face was seen often on television.

JACKSON David *From* Scotland. *Died* May 2004, aged 74. Jackson was an experienced amateur whose career spanned ten years and encompassed nearly 200 fights between 1942 and 1952. His enthusiasm for his chosen sport never faltered and, after his last outing in 1952, he offered his services in the capacity of referee and judge. He also coached and promoted. A referee at the Moscow Olympics in 1980, later becoming a life-member of the World Amateur Boxing Association, David was also a marvellous fund-raiser and charity worker. He never lost his love of the game, even when, in the last eight years of his life, he suffered from cancer, which eventually killed him.

JENKINS Jackie *From* Gisborne, New Zealand. *Died* August 2003, aged 75. Johnny Hanks reported the death of one of the cleverest of New Zealand boxers, who made such an impression in his three fights in this country. Jenkins was a brilliant amateur – a champion at two weight divisions whose exclusion from the 1948 Olympics upset so many of his fans that funds were raised to send him to England to commence a professional career. He started off sensationally by forcing the Welsh champion, Warren Kendall, to retire in six rounds before having a terrific contest with Billy McDonald at Liverpool. McDonald put him down twice for six, but Jenkins got up to force the fight and run out a winner after eight tremendous rounds. He took on Emmett Kenny next and once more was in the best fight of the night, but the experienced Kenny just nicked it on points. Homesickness and English food-rationing saw Jenkins return home and in 1950 he knocked out Francis Joseph in Palmerston prior to drawing with Clem Sands in Auckland. Sands, a very strong fighter, and an experienced one, got on top in the return and forced a stoppage in ten rounds. Jenkins record after that is still being traced.

JONES Davey *From* Wrexham. *Died* January 2004, aged 72. Davey was a familiar face at the ringside, especially at Mickey Duff promotions. For years he was box-office manager, PRO and agent for Duff and in that capacity he had to meet incoming foreign fighters, arrange their accommodation and gymnasium facilities. He got to know all the big names over the years and was a discreet and loyal servant to boxing, gathering up a fine collection of programmes, photos and boxing books, many of them rare. After retiring from his duties, he contracted Parkinson's disease, which he fought with rare courage before succumbing on New Year's day.

KNELL Stan *From* Canterbury. *Died* 30 July 2004, aged 83. Born in 1921 and a war-service veteran, Stan formed the Canterbury Amateur Boxing Club in 1958. Some excellent amateur talent went through his hands, one of them being Ricky Bushell who later turned professional. Several of the men he trained went far in the ABA championships and many were divisional champions and Southern Counties' champs, including Ginger Rice, Robbie Xavier, Roy Williams, Dave Kennard, Steve Ransley, Ron Parry, Dave Smith and Frank Bruno's old foe, Laurie Palmer. At his funeral many of the boys he trained turned up to pay their respects, proving that Stan was regarded highly. He leaves a widow.

LEES Sid *From* Widnes. *Died* May 2003, aged 88. John Sinnott reported that with the death of Sid, whose birthname was Mark Chatterton, Widnes lost another boxer of the 1930s who earned the town such a reputation in the fight game. Mark was one of the top welterweights of his generation, fighting in rings all over the north and in the midlands. So far, only 32 contests for him have been traced, but it is obvious that many unrecorded fights have yet to be found. He fought from 1934 to 1946 and one of his most satisfying wins was in beating Chick Duggan on Christmas day 1938, having lost to Duggan twice by wafer-thin margins. In 1939 he drew with fellow townsman, Bert Chambers, in a local derby before beating Al Gamage at Runcorn Baths. Then, with war looming, five years of inactivity followed and he was 30 before he fought once more. In 1946 he lost to veteran, Chuck Seddon, on points and retired with the distinction of never having been beaten inside the distance.

LOGSDON Blaine *From* Warrington. *Died* April 2004, aged 41. A former challenger for the British light-heavyweight title, he was found dead by his wife. Blaine was born Alan Wheate in the USA, but retained British citizenship through his parents' nationality. A heavy puncher, he had knockout wins over Bert Myrie, Jimmy Ellis, Sean O'Phoenix, Glazz Campbell, Slobadan Kacar and, in the USA, Lavell Stanley. He also recorded knockouts over Crawford Ashley and a stoppage against Gypsy Carmen. Logsdon ran out of luck in his challenge for the vacant British title, Tony Wilson beating him, as did Lou Gent, Alex Romeo and Eddie Smith. Blaine performed well in foreign rings, with two stoppages in the USA, one in France and one in Italy, against a single loss to Yawe Davis in Italy.

LOPEZ Juan Antonio *From* Mexico. *Died* June 2004, aged 52. Juan Antonio was a world-class junior featherweight, who was active from 1973 to 1992 and who started fighting in ten-rounders from the start of his 85-fight career. Up until his abortive challenge to Wilfredo Gomez for the WBC super-bantamweight title in 1978, he had enjoyed good progress with only two losses on his account – one of them being to the great Eder Jofre, then at the end of his career but still a very formidable fighter. Gomez repeated his win in 1982, with the WBC junior bantamweight title at stake, but between those two defeats Juan Antonio had a run of 15 wins, all but one by stoppages, Roberto Torres being the only opponent to last the course. Shuzo Yoshida, Miguel Hernandez, Jesus Pitalua and Abel Torres were among those who found the Mexican's punches too much. Defeats sprinkled his record after that and although he stopped Antonio Beccera and Manuel Torres, a series of losses, terminating in a one round defeat by Marco Antonio Barrera, brought down the curtain on his career.

LOUBET Nat *From* New York. *Died* 25 March 2004, aged 86. The son-in-law of Nat Fleischer, he promised to produce the Ring Record Book when Fleischer died in 1972. This he did from 1972 to 1979, after which Bert Sugar took hold of the reins at 'The Ring' editorial office. Nat then took, or was forced into, a back seat. An extremely modest man, looking at those record books you'll find no blurb on the dust covers that publicise his role, the end papers being blank. Nat shunned the limelight yet his input into the recording of boxing history was immense. Also he was a war-hero, but details of his courage when in uniform had to be dragged out of him. Like his father-in-law, Nat lived to a good age.

McMURDIE Harry *From* Edgware. *Died* 26 November 2003, aged 78. Harry, the most successful of three boxing brothers, boxed as a lightweight from 1947 to 1951, beating Dick Levers, Maurice 'Mosh' Mancini, Hyman Williams, Tony Brazil and Bob Anderson. Harry would go anywhere for a fight, but the nearest he got to fighting before his home crowd was when beating Bob Anderson at Hendon. Al Wilburn spoiled his attempts at a double by outpointing Harry at the same venue one month later. He also fought twice at the Albert Hall, stopping Ken Seeley and losing on points to South Africa's Jackie Soloman. An opponent of the legendary Hal Bagwell, dropping an eight round points verdict in 1948, he fought at Belfast, Portsmouth, Epsom, Dover, Canterbury, Newbury, Hove, Cambridge, Birmingham, Falkirk, Bath and Maidstone. His main losses were against Harry Hughes, Laurie Buxton and Ralph Moss, but he is credited with a draw against Johnny Carrington over eight rounds in distant Southsea. Truly a travelling fighter, he was fit and full of life when a tragic car accident, for which he was not to blame, took his life.

Harry McMurdie

Lenny Mancini

MANCINI Lenny 'Boom Boom' *From* Youngstown, Ohio. *Died* 29 November 2003, aged 84. Modern fans who know of Ray Mancini's rise to title status as WBA champion in 1982, may not realise that his father, Lenny, was a good scrapper too and very popular in New York rings where he did the bulk of his fighting. He fought in the welterweight class and at an early stage in his career, he forced the future champion, Marty Servo, to a draw. Before going into the US Army in 1945, he'd had 36 fights with six losses, having beaten crowd-pleasing Terry Young, Chief Crazy Horse, Abie Kaufman and Irving Eldridge, with losses to Leo Rodak, Sammy Angott and Pete Lello. Wartime activity was sparse, but he managed to fight seven times in 1946 without a loss, one of his victims being Welshman, Cyril Gallie, who succumbed in the first round. Moving up to middleweight he twice took on Rocky Castellani, who was too good for him, but as he always did when losing, Lennie lasted the full distance. He was a tough, all-action fighter and in 57 contests, won 43, drew 3 and lost 11.

MORDEY Bill *From* Australia. *Died* April 2004, aged 67. Perhaps Australia's best boxing promoter since Hugh D. Mackintosh, Bill started as a journalist and took up promoting in 1985. He was instrumental in bringing Jeff Fenech into the world limelight and promoted the superbly organised return with Azumah Nelson in 1992. He also had Kosta Tszyu, Joe Bugner and Jeff Harding leading his shows. His skills and ambition gave these men the opportunity to earn big bucks and his death leaves a gap in the sport of Australian boxing, which is so much poorer for his passing.

MOSES Antonius *From* Jakarta. *Died* January 2004, aged 20. Tragedy struck 20-year-old light-flyweight Moses when he lost his life in an Indonesian hospital from head injuries received when Kaichon Sor Vorapin, of Thailand, knocked him out in round eight. Going into his fight with Vorapin he had an unblemished record of 14 wins and one draw.

NICHOL Cyclone Bob *From* Hebburn. *Died* October 2003, aged 89. Maxie Walsh describes Bob Nichol as being a 'promoter's dream', often standing in as a late substitute at short notice, and often giving away a lot of weight. His known record starts in 1930 and he went on for seven years with 68 fights against some strong opposition. Bob knocked out Con Tansey in 1933, which was a year in which he had an unbeaten run of 11 contests before Jack Rossiter upset him. He won two out of three against Bob Ainsley, but couldn't get past Lynemouth's Pat O'Keefe, who beat him four times. Successes came against Billy Graham, Jack Doyle of North Shields, Jack Rose, Jack Vickers and, in his sole appearance in London, against Joe Harvey. Bob went in with some good scrappers and typical of an old-timer, had five wins in August 1933, four in July, four in October and three in September. They bred 'em hard in his day.

NOTO Masanao *From* Japan. *Died* 2 April 2004, aged 24. After dropping a ten-round verdict to Keisuke Ayukawa, the young super-bantamweight was admitted to hospital 24 hours later, but failed to recover from brain surgery. He was a top-of-bill fighter with a good record.

NUNEZ Danny *From* Dominica. *Died* January 2004, aged 34. A fairly recent world flyweight contender, losing a world-title challenger to then WBA champion, Saen Sor Ploenchit, who was one of only three men to beat him, he had a record of 27 wins and three losses between 1988 and 1994. Living in poverty, and during an extremely cold snap, the unfortunate Danny died of hypothermia.

PALACIO Ruben Dario *From* Colombia. *Died* November 2003, aged 40. A Colombian featherweight, Ruben won a world-title in England, returned to defend it, failed an HIV test and died from the virus nine years later. It is a tragic tale of a man on the verge of riches, suddenly losing everything and, eventually, his life. Born in 1962, he ran up a series of impressive wins before annexing the Colombian bantamweight title, which he defended a month later. However, he soon put on weight and moving up a division won the vacant IBF junior-featherweight title by licking Ji-Won Kim in Korea. Later outpointed by Valero Nati before losing to Jim McDonnell in London, the latter confirmed that the Colombian was a tough and dangerous fighter. He just failed to win the WBA super-bantamweight title by boxing a draw with Luis Mendoza, but was luckier against Colin McMillan with the WBO featherweight crown at stake. Behind on points, but coming on strongly in a bruising fight, Ruben won when McMillan dislocated his shoulder. It was the Colombian's last fight as HIV ate away at him.

PAPP Laszlo *From* Budapest, Hungary. *Died* 16 October 2003, aged 77. Was Laszlo the world's greatest ever amateur? Few would dispute it. Consider his credentials: Gold medals in three Olympic Games, with amateur victories over Ellsworth 'Spider' Webb, Jose Torres, and Ivano Fontana. Getting on in years when he won his last Olympic medal, he decided to turn pro at 31, an age when his contemporaries were close to hanging up their gloves. Apart from his age, physical odds were stacked against him, being short for a middleweight and usually giving away some inches in reach. He started with three un-ambitious wins in Germany then knocked out Hugo Kohler and Francois Anewy to prove that his professional intentions were serious. He went on to beat Sauveur Chiocca, Peter Muller and Ralph 'Tiger' Jones and by 1962 he was the European middleweight champion. After further wins against Luis Folledo, Mick Leahy and Harry Scott, his attentions were on the world title. Although nearly 40, plans were made for him to fight the world champion, Joey Giardello, but the communist government of Hungary pulled the plug and ended his career. Following that, the boxing world was left wondering if he could have achieved his ambition. He left an indelible imprint on the world scene and 'retired' unbeaten.

Laszlo Papp

PARRIS Eric *From* Sussex. *Died* June 2004. A long-serving ABA official and referee, Eric passed away after a short illness. He was a respected referee who never put a boxer at risk, was firm, impartial and always in control.

PHILLIPS Jack *From* Tredegar. *Died* December 2003, aged 89. You have to go back nearly 70 years to be around when Jack started boxing. A real old-timer who could look after himself against the best, he was a workman-like performer, evasive and durable, his best performance coming in 1937 when he held George 'Panther' Purchase to a draw. Strange to say, that after hitting that high spot, he lost his next seven fights – all on points. However, he got back to winning ways by stopping Birmingham's George Willis in ten rounds and twice outpointing Tom Kennedy. It was 1942 before he boxed in London rings and he stopped Rory O'Connor before returning to force a draw against Billy Hawkins. Reg Hoblyn, who beat him in 1946, always spoke highly of Jack. "He was a fine craftsman", said Reg, who insisted that they met twice, although only

one fight got into the record books. Good names crop up throughout Jack's career – Jack Lewis, Eric Dolby, Jake Kilrain, Curly Edwards, Ric Sanders (three times), Paddy Roche, Len Wickwar, Ivor Pickens, who was knocked out in three, Frank Meacham, Walter Redit (twice), Frank Duffy, Henry Hall, Jim Wellard, Gordon Ashun, Stan Hawthorne, Harry Lazar, Eddie Thomas, Willie Whyte, Alf Danahar and Eddie Cardew. In his only fight outside this island, Jack lost to Jan de Bruin on points in Rotterdam. He finished on a winning note, stopping Sanders in 1949 and, after 15 years of ring activity and a good reputation, he lived to a ripe old age.

QUIROGA Robert *From* San Antonio, Texas, USA. *Died* 16 August 2004, aged 34. Turned pro at the age of 17 in March 1987 and soon proved himself to be a tireless fighter with a high workrate. He soon made his mark and having run up wins over fighters such as Joey Olivo and Ray Medel, and, unbeaten he came to England to challenge the Colombian, Juan Polo Perez, for the IBF super-flyweight title. A good winner, he defended the title five times against Vuyani Nene, Vincenzo Belcastro, Akeem Anifowashe, Carlos Mercedo and Jose Ruiz before losing to Julio Cesar Borboa in January 1993. Retiring in 1995, he finished with 20-2 record and will be best remembered for his unforgettable contest against Anifowoshe, which has been recognized by many boxing experts as not only a 'Fight of the Year', but a one of the best fights ever in the super flyweight division. According to local news reports, he was found dying by his vehicle on the Interstate 10 in his hometown of San Antonio, due to multiple stab wounds and died on the way to the hospital. Robert was known as 'Pikin' or 'Little Hot Pepper' for his scrappiness in the ring.

RAMSEY Bob *From* Stepney. *Died* March 2004, aged 84. Although the Second World War slowed down his boxing activity, Bob managed to keep busy and in 1944 went to the well 19 times. Up to then he'd lost only a few – most of them to the best around, Dave Crawley, Hal Cartwright and Harry Lazar coming to mind. Although a smart boxer, but not a big puncher, Bob could look after himself, having 89 fights and never taking the count. He had a strong east-end following and seldom let them down until 1945 came and his reflexes lost their edge. Going into that post-war era, he had beaten Jack Gubbins, Frank Phayer, Ronnie Lush, Bob Lamb, Jimmy Bitmead, Jim Wellard, Ivor Thomas, Jackie Rankin, Dave Finn and Tommy Foxall, but his losses then started to outnumber his victories. In 1945, he registered only five wins in 18 outings, with two draws, but he did beat his arch-rival, Harry 'Kid' Silver, in the last of four attempts and he also turned the tables on Warren Kendall and Danny Webb, both of whom had previously beaten him. Although past his best, Bob still had a lot to offer, but after the future British champion, Eddie Thomas, took a points win off him in 1946, his career petered out in South Africa, where he was twice disqualified against Alf James.

Bob Ramsey

REGAN Ken *From* Blackpool. *Died* June 2004, aged 72. London fans never got the chance to see Ken Regan box as he confined most of his fistic activity to the Blackpool Area. The furthest south he got was to Great Yarmouth, which proved to be an unlucky arena when Leo Maloney outpointed him over eight rounds in November 1955. A big puncher, Ken started boxing in 1949 and only one of his first seven contests went the distance. By 1954, he was fighting in good company, beating Harry Warner, Jimmy O'Connell, Eric Billington, Jimmy Croll, Ken Bebbington (three times), Dave Underwood and Bobby Johnson. On the debit side, however, he lost to Peter King and Albert Carroll, which was no disgrace as they were established and noted fighters. He hit a bad patch in 1955 when he lost to Attu Clottey, Tommy Molloy and Croll and his last contest was the loss to Leo Maloney. But even if his peak days had gone, he still opened the year with a credible draw with Gordon Goodman. In 62 contests, he won 43 and boxed three draws, with 29 of his wins being scored inside the distance.

ROBINSON Jon *From* Hackney. *Died* 14 April 2004, aged 62. My first contact with John was when we were both reporting fights in London and its environs. He was the boxing reporter for the 'Hackney Gazette' and his talented reports and summaries made it respected as the best of London papers for boxing. He gave the amateurs, the life – blood of the game, in-depth coverage and I recognised him as the best man at that job since the days of Walter Bartleman. A real boxing man, he was always helpful and obliging when we cross-checked details and compared notes. Whenever I went to a London show I looked out for him and, more often than not, he was at ringside with his pen and notepad. Jon drifted away from boxing for a few years before re-surfacing as an official with the IBF. Disenchanted with the organisation's politics he resigned to form the WBU, an organisation to which he became passionately dedicated. He was a big man – at one time the biggest in Great Britain – and sometimes took up two seats at ringside. Often outspoken and sometimes controversial, he fought hard for what he considered to be right. Jon was a loyal friend whose life was ended by a stroke and the WBU will find it very difficult to fill the gap he has left behind.

ROOD Joe *From* Aldgate. *Died* 24 October 2003, aged 74. As an amateur and boxing for Eton Manor ABC, Joe was a divisional champion in 1945 before turning pro late in 1946 and getting his career off to a good start by stopping Frank Baldwin of British Honduras in four rounds. Although he saw Army service in 1947-48 as a PTI, he went through 1947 with only one loss in 13 starts and established himself as a top-of-bill fighter when outpointing Wakefield's Johnny McGowan. Other achievements were a draw with Bert Hyland and victories over Johnny Boyd, Jimmy Bray, Tommy Caswell and Gene Fowler. There was also a knockout win over Gordon Griffiths, who was Randolph Turpin's first opponent. The former Empire champion, Bos Murphy, beat Johnny in 1950 and Alex Buxton, Ron Grogan and Alby Hollister were a shade too smart for him. Retiring in 1953, often billed out of Hackney, he was a decent middleweight with a large following.

ROSI Paoli *From* Rieti, Italy. *Died* January 2004, aged 76. A former world lightweight title challenger Paoli, a transplanted Italian from New York, began his career in Italy and had only one loss before emigrating to the USA in 1952. It was two years before this tough scrapper lost in front of American fans and it took the world-class Orlando Zulueta to turn the trick. Wins over Lulu Perez, Joey Lopez, Johnny Gonsalves, Bobby Scanlon, Johnny Busso, Flash Elorde and Frankie Ryff got him a shot at Joe Brown's lightweight title in 1959 but 'Old Bones' was too crafty, too slick and a shade too good that day. Paolo, however, gave him stern opposition before being stopped in round nine. He got another chance to fight Brown, but had to get past Carlos Ortiz first and much to his disappointment Ortiz outpointed him to get the title shot. Wins over Tommy

Tibbs and Lennie Matthews had kept him in contention, but when a loss to Carlos Hernandez followed the Ortiz defeat, he realised that his chance of another title-shot had gone and retired.

SCOTT Bertie *From* Glasgow. *Died* 5 February 2004, aged 71. Brian Donald reported the demise of Bertie Scott, a former Scottish amateur ring star, who boxed for the Glasgow Transport Club from the late 1940s until the early 1960s and went through every weight division before becoming an official. He started as a teenage flyweight with a very orthodox style and no small amount of talent to go with it and went on to represent Scotland many times, notably in the 1958 Commonwealth Games where he was eventually beaten by Brian Nancurvis, who later fought for the world welterweight title under his abbreviated name of Curvis. Bertie fought all the good 'uns in the unpaid ranks, including Charlie Hill, Bobbie Keddie, Jack Dormer and, at heavyweight, Bill Sutherley. He devoted his life to boxing as a boxer, referee, judge and official and, as a result, he was very respected by the fistic fraternity. As a boxer he won titles at nearly every weight.

SEVERINI Piero *From* Italy. *Died* March 2004, aged 35. Suffering a heart-attack when in the prime of life sadly cut down this former light-middleweight from Italy, who boxed from 1989 to 1997. He took just one round to stop Britain's Adrian Riley at the end of 1991 and challenged for the Italian title twice without success, but had a good points win over the top-notch Frenchman, Martin Camara, to put his ability at European level in perspective.

Paolo Rosi (left) on his way to defeat against Carlos Ortiz

SHERRER Jimmy *From* Milwaukee. *Died* 3 August 2003, aged 79. Fighting from 1944 to 1951, following wins over O'Neill Bell and Izzy Janazzo there were indications that Jimmy might make the grade, but he continually hovered around world-class without quite making it into the ratings. His respectable record shows wins over Ralph Zanelli, Cocoa Kid and Jackie Keough and there were two draws with Danny Womber in 1950, but he was then past his best. Losses to Keough and Jesse Turner, both of whom he'd previously beaten, showed him that title dreams would never materialise. Looking at his record shows that he fought in good company, usually without success, but while men such as Chuck Hunter Jose Basora, Anton Raadik and Vince Turpin beat him, there was a fine knockout win over Sammy Secreet and decisions over Zanelli, Keough and Lester Felton. He twice beat Jimmy Welch, but lost a couple of important matches to Walter Cartier. Win or lose he always put up a good fight.

Yoshio Shirai

SHIRAI Yoshio *From* Tokyo, Japan. *Died* 27 December 2003, aged 80. It was Yoshio who brought about the emergence of Japan as a major boxing nation. Until he won the world flyweight championship from Dado Marino in 1952 his country had a limited boxing history at world level. From Yoshio onwards, Japan emerged as a nation which would soon dominate the lower weight divisions. Having one year with the amateurs before turning professional in 1943, he won, lost and re-won national titles at flyweight and bantamweight four times. He lost a ten-round decision to Marino in 1951, then stopped him in seven rounds, the rubber match being for the title. To rub it in he gave Marino another shot but nothing changed and he later defended against Terry Allen, Leo Espinosa and Tanny Campo. Scotland's Vic Herman fought him in a non-title go before Allen got his chance, but Vic, a strong fighter, lost in the tenth. After holding the undefeated Argentinian, Pascual Perez, to a draw, a fight in which he became the first to halt the hard-punching Perez's winning streak, he agreed to a return with the title at stake. While Perez began his climb to greatness by winning over the championship course of 15 rounds, Shirai should have taken a couple of warm up contests to have prepared himself better. Instead, he went straight back in with Perez, who knocked him out in five rounds. It was the Japanese hero's last fight.

SONGKITRAT Chamrern *From* Roicet, Thailand. *Died* 2003, aged 75. Born Samroeng Simadi, the effects of a stroke, which had disabled him some years previously, caused the death of Chamrern who, at 25, was his country's first world-title challenger. He got his shot at the world bantamweight title against Jimmy Carruthers after good wins over Pappy Gault and Kevin James. It was a 12-rounder, an unusual distance for a title fight in 1954, and what a fight it was! The entire 12 rounds took place in the open air during a typhoon. Both fought barefoot on a flooded ring canvas and while Chamrern, a former kick-boxer, was accustomed to that, the ring was littered with broken light-bulbs and had to be swept frequently amidst atrocious conditions. Nat Fleischer, who had been reporting boxing since the days of Jack Johnson, never forgot his incursion into Bangkok and wrote-up the fight enthusiastically in his 'Ring' magazine. Although the Thai boxer had contested very few professional fights, his championship status was undoubted, having won the Orient lightweight title in his third fight and followed up with wins over Britain's Vic Herman and Jimmy Pearce, which indicated that he could get down to the 8st 6lb limit comfortably. He challenged for the title again after Carruthers retired, but was on the losing end to Robert Cohen and had but a single win (against Danny Kid) before quitting the ring in 1955. In 13 outings he won seven drew one and lost five. His bona fides as a title contender cannot be refuted, he was world-class with no argument.

SOO Jimmy *From* Philadelphia. *Died* 5 October 2003, aged 73. Born James Bark, Jimmy turned pro in 1953. He never got into the big money, despite being a very popular fighter, but lost only four of 45 contests, all by stoppages, and in most of them was ahead on points when the end came. Jimmy supplemented his ring earnings with a variety of jobs, including bar-tender, taxi-driver and construction-site worker and got such a steady living from these activities that he dropped out of boxing from 1957 to 1960, following losses to Baby Vasquez and Gene Toran. He came back with determination to make good, stopping Steve Haywood, outpointing Ray Lancaster and grabbing another couple of wins before the big one came – a ten-rounder with Lennie Matthews in 1961. Going into round eight, an upset looked imminent as Jimmy, a big outsider, continued to nick the points until a big left hook took him apart. A loss to J.D. Ellis followed and Jimmy knew it was time to go, but he was never disgraced, often fighting uphill battles and winning the hard way.

TANSEY Jack *From* Liverpool. *Died* February 2004, aged 88. Jack's influence on Merseyside amateur boxing went back to the 1930s before he lost to Johnny Taylor in the 1946 ABA semi-finals, prior to winning the Northern Counties' heavyweight title the following year. After his fighting days were over, he maintained his interest in amateur boxing when becoming an instructor and a very vocal campaigner for the re-introduction of boxing into the schools' curriculum.

Chamrern Songkitrat (right) in action against Jimmy Carruthers

THOMAS Eddie *From* Durban, South Africa. *Died* 9 December 2003, aged 72. Apart from being a hard, uncompromising boxer, Eddie was one of middleweights' hardest punchers, often taking opponents out with a single shot. Many a victim took the count Palooka-fashion and completely unconscious. He banged out Dave Fourie, who greatly outweighed him, with a thudding left hook and later did the same to Mike Holtenhausen, who boxed as plain Mike Holt. In two return matches with Holt, he couldn't repeat that win, but they were hard brutal contests that took a toll on both fighters. As an amateur he won several South African titles but just missed out, rather unfairly, on selection for the 1948 and 1952 Olympics. In disgust, he joined the punch-for-pay ranks and won the national welterweight title after three fights by beating Pat Patrick. He had to beat Pat again to satisfy the National Board that he was the title-holder as the board recognised Peter Galleymore as rightful contender so Eddie flattened him and then took out Patrick in a return. In the UK, he showed good form by drawing with Les Allen in his debut, beating Lew Lazar, Vincent O'Kine and Kit Pompey, before the rising-star, Billy Ellaway, proved a shade too good for him. He returned home, but had lost his ambition and never trained again. In Kitwe he knocked out Howard Fraser and Tony Liversage before retiring at 26 after 32 fights, having knocked out light-heavies, while claiming to have never weighed above the welterweight limit.

THOMSEN Hasse *From* Sweden. *Died* 26 April 2004, aged 62. Thomsen was a bronze-medal winner in the 1972 Olympics at Munich, just missing a contest with Teofilo Stevenson after losing to Ion Alexe in semi-finals. He did briefly turn pro, but realised he had made a mistake and was re-admitted to the amateurs where he had over 100 contests.

WALKER Billy *From* Bethnal Green. *Died* January 2004, aged 86. It was not unusual for a boxer of Billy's time to chalk up over 100 contests as opposition was plentiful and men served long fistic apprenticeships before being considered for title contention. His career started in 1925 and finished in 1930 – five years almost to the month - with 103 outings on his sheet, having proved to be a clever boxer with most wins coming via the distance route. There were also quite a few draws – 17 in all – sprinkling his record, two of them being against the legendary Sam Minto. At that marvellous palace of Sock, Premierland, he appeared 52 times and in his first six months of activity there he lost only one of 22 fights, George Swinbourne of Maidstone being one of his victims along with Plymouth's Kid Kelly. He continued his run of wins with victories over Mark Wembourne, Dave Danahar, Alf Howard of Liverpool, Billy Streets, Billy Handley, Jim Blake (brother of Archie Sexton), Alec Thake, etc, while there were draws with Red Pullen, Josh Laxton and Curley Merritt interspersed with occasional losses to men such as George Rose, Harry Fenn, Sid Cannon (twice) and Seaman Chadwick. It speaks volumes of how the game has changed since 1930, when a man like Billy, who had won over such good opposition, never got within distance of a title shot.

WALKER Scott *From* Arizona. *Died* 7 February 2004, aged 34. A clever welterweight who failed the big test against Julio Cesar Chavez, Scott was found dead in his home. He beat Alexis Arguello when Arguello was making an abortive comeback, but the upset against Chavez jolted his confidence and although boxing to 1991, he never made an impact at world level.

WARNER Harry *From* Dagenham. *Died* June 2004, aged 76. A busy fighter and a product of the boxing booths, Harry boxed as a licensed pro from 1948 to 1954 and had a distinction almost unique in British boxing rings. When he fought Johnny McDonald, both were counted out, but Harry got the decision as he was ahead on points. Interestingly, he had already beaten the same man earlier in the week. Harry was a willing eight-round scrapper who stepped in with many of the good welters and middleweights of his day, beating Harry Legge, Charlie Kray, Eric Skidmore, Santos Martins, Eric Billington, Sammy Hamilton, Gerry Smythe, Jack Thornbury and Dave Brandon, among others. Some who beat him were Kay Kalio, Rod Deamer, Billy Ambrose, Lew Lazar, Bunty Adamson, Bob Foster, Johnny Fish and Gerry Hassett. Towards the end of his career losses slightly outnumbered wins, but he never refused a fight and always gave value for money. After retiring, he went on to become an 'A' Class referee from 1978 and later undertook the appointment of secretary of the Central Area Council.

WHALLEY Tut *From* Hanley. *Died* July 2004, aged 90. John Thomas Whalley, known as 'Tut', boxed from 1930-1941 at a time when there were dozens of flyweights active in all parts of the British Isles. This is highlighted by his 150 known fights and he once knocked out the great Benny Lynch, before being disqualified when the referee decided that his body attack had strayed low. Tut, a southpaw, was 20 at the time but a veteran in experience, having started at 16. His manager, Jack Fitzgerald, kept him busy and Tut beat men such as Snowball Reynolds, Tommy Rogers, Harry Edwards, Percy Dexter, George Marsden and Freddie Webb. There were prestigious draws with Syd Parker, Ken Barrett and Willie Sharkey too. What a host of names to grace a boxing record! After the Lynch debacle, his busiest period came. Wins over Peter Miller, Fred Bebbington, Jim Brady, Pat Warburton, Katsumi Morioka, Tommy Pardoe, Benny Jones, Frank Bonser and Pierce Ellis established his class. Phil Milligan knocked him out in 1936 in a contest for the Northern Area flyweight championship, as did Paddy Ryan three years later. Milligan had narrowly beaten Tut in 1934 and in those days, many fights were over 15 rounds. He then fought his stable-mate, Tiny

Bostock, of Leek, in the open air on a rain-soaked night in Hanley. Bostock was favoured, having beaten Valentin Anglemann and Small Montana, both world-class men. It was a local derby that drew a huge crowd and Tut won it clearly by going inside and using a strong body attack. It was three months before he returned to beat Pat McStravick. Then war loomed and when he lost a return match with Jackie Paterson – they had previously drawn – Tut was convinced that his glory days were over when he lost in under three minutes and that was it.

Tut Whalley

WILLIAMS Ted *From* Huddersfield. *Died* October 2003, aged 65. A former Central Area, light-heavyweight title holder, Ted fought from 1954 to 1960 and had a record of slightly better than 50-50. He had a six fight series with

Jack London, son of the former heavyweight champion, but could win only once. Ted beat Peter Aldridge twice against one loss and twice beat Joe Walcott and Johnny Williamson, while Fred Jackson of Custom House was too good for him, as were Len Mullen and Ken Rowlands. Ted stepped out of his league in 1958, losing to Redvers Sangoe and Chic Calderwood, although he did force Calderwood to go the full route in what was a credible performance. Two wins came over Don McCall, but the world-rated Johnny Halafihi of Tonga beat him in 1957. Ted's best year was his last – 1960 – he gained a good win over Gerry McNally, then stopped Alan Peacock in one of his better performances to win the Central Area title. Flushed with success he took on Yolande Pompey, who beat him in two rounds, but still being the Central Area champion, Ted decided to retire.

Ted Williams

A Boxing Quiz with a Few Below the Belt (Part 9)

Compiled by Les Clark

QUESTIONS

1. Can you name a former boxer who wrote PENNY A PUNCH and A FEW PUNCHES MORE?

2. Maurice Hope took part in six world title fights. How many did he lose and to whom did he lose to?

3. Who took the British heavyweight title from Gordon Ferris?

4. Can you name the first boxer to beat Cornelius Boza Edwards as a professional?

5. Max Baer (junior), son of the former heavyweight champion of the same name, acted in a well-known TV series. Can you name it?

6. What have Roy Jones and Michael Spinks got in common?

7. Which former champion, who clocked up 122 bouts, was known as the 'Cincinnati Cobra'?

8. Who directed Robert DeNiro as Jake LaMotta in THE RAGING BULL?

9. Can you name the only woman elected into the International Boxing Hall of Fame?

10. Who did Barry McGuigan face in a final eliminator before fighting for the vacant British featherweight title?

11. Mike Barrett's first promotion was in December 1962 and his 150th promotion was at the Albert Hall. Do you know who topped the bill in the latter?

12. Cassius Clay was taken the distance in his first pro bout. How many more times was he taken the distance before winning the world title?

13. Chris Eubank was born in Dulwich, south London. Can you name the amateur club he boxed for?

14. Do you know what American, Kevin Perry's claim to fame is?

15. Who was the first British fighter Jake Matala fought?

16. How many major titles did Kostya Tszyu win before turning to the paid ranks?

17. Michael Watson took the Commonwealth middleweight title from Nigel Benn. Against whom was his first defence, and where?

18. Alan Minter was involved in 12 Championship fights, all at middleweight. How many were for vacant titles?

19. Two former world heavyweight champions fought each other on the undercard of the second Andrew Golota v Riddick Bowe fight in Atlantic City. Who were they?

20. Can you name the fighter who ended Miguel Angel Gonzalez's 41-fight unbeaten run?

21. Former world heavyweight champion, Ingemar Johannson, retired from the ring in 1963. Who was his last opponent?

22. This former Southern Area bantamweight champion was a three-times loser; Charlie Magri beat him in a vacant British flyweight contest, Johnny Owen beat him in a challenge for the British and Commonwealth bantamweight titles, and John Feeney defeated him for the vacant British bantamweight title. Can you name him?

23. Can you name a former British light-heavyweight champion who beat 'Baby Boy' Rolle, Dennis Avoth and Boston Blackie, but lost to Les Stevens and Richard Dunn?

24. Humphrey Bogart's last motion picture was a 'boxing' movie. Can you name it?

25. Can you name the first British title fight that John Coyle controlled as referee?

26. Wally Swift (senior) contested either British, British Empire or European titles on no less than nine occasions. How many did he win?

27. How many Swiss boxers have won a European title among the professionals?

28. Can you name the first Australian 'southpaw' heavyweight champion?

29. Brian London's last fight was against Joe Bugner in 1970. Can you name the three Americans he fought and lost to in 1969?

30. When was the ABA formed?

31. When Miguel Angel Gonzalez gave up his WBC lightweight title to move up a weight, who was his first opponent at that higher weight?

32. Can you name a Welsh boxer who beat Johnny Frankham in a final eliminator, but lost to Chris Finnegan on points over 15 rounds for the British and Commonwealth light-heavyweight titles?

33. Joe Erskine was the British heavyweight champion in 1957. Who was rated the number-one challenger to him in the Boxing News annual ratings on the 31st December of that year?

34. What year did the last 20-round bout take place and between whom?

35. How many times did Dennis Andries contest the Southern Area light-heavyweight title?

36. Can you name a boxer who was unbeaten in 44 fights, winning 36 inside the distance before being stopped in three rounds by Ruben Olivares? The boxer in question became a world champion at a later date.

37. Who was the first fighter to take Mike Tyson the distance. Was it James 'Bonecrusher' Smith, James 'Quick' Tillis or Mitch 'Blood' Green?

38. Joey Singleton took the British light-welterweight crown from Pat McCormack at The Stadium in Liverpool. At what venue did he make his first defence?

39. How many fighters did Joe Frazier fight twice during his career?

40. Jerry Quarry fought Brian London twice in the USA. How many times did Jerry come to Britain to fight?

41. How many times did Carl 'Bobo' Olsen fight 'Sugar' Ray Robinson?

42. Larry Paul was the first British light-middleweight champion. Who did he beat for the title?

43. After only eight professional fights, Sean Murphy fought for the Commonwealth bantamweight title. Who did he face?

44. How many times did Billy Hardy fight for and win a British title?

45. At the present time, George Foreman's record stands at 81 fights, with 76 wins and only five losses. Can you name the guys who beat him?

46. Mike Tyson's first 19 fights were all stoppage wins. How many were first-round wins?

47. Who was Chris Finnegan's last opponent?

48. These two fighters both fought Mike Tyson and Herbie Hide. Can you name them?

49. Can you name the third man in the ring for the return fights between Roy Jones v Antonio Tarver, Roy Jones v John Ruiz and Roy Jones v Clinton Woods?

50. How many medals did Britain win in the Commonwealth games in Manchester?

Leading BBBoC License Holders: Names and Addresses

Licensed Promoters

A Force Promotions
Suite 205
18 Soho Square
London
W1D 3QL
0207 025 8384

Bruce Baker
The Garden Flat
38 Lupus Street
London
SW1V 3EB
0207 592 0102

Jack Bishop
76 Gordon Road
Fareham
Hants
PO16 7SS
0132 928 4708

David Bradley
Aston Hall
Aston Lane
Claverley
Nr Wolverhampton
WV5 7DZ
0174 671 0287

Pat Brogan
112 Crewe Road
Haslington
Crewe
Cheshire
0127 087 4825

**Tony Burns
(TBS Promotions)**
67 Peel Place
Woodford Green
Essex
IG5 0PT
0208 550 8911

**Callahan & Breen
Promotions**
Cedar Lodge
589 Antrim Road
Belfast
BT15 4DX
0289 077 0238

David Casey
424 Barking Road
London
E13 8HJ
0207 377 6333

**Tony Celebanski
(Yorkshire Executive
Sporting Club)**
5 Ling Park Avenue
Wilsden
Bradford
BD15 0NE
0127 482 4015

**Dave Coldwell
(Koncrete Promotions)**
Castle Court
2 St John's Road
Sheffield S2 5JX
0114 275 0303

**Annette Conroy
(North East Sporting
Club)**
144 High Street East
Sunderland
Tyne and Wear
SR1 2BL
0191 567 6871

Jane Couch
Spaniorum Farm Gym
Berwick Lane
Bristol
BS35 5RX
0778 073 8096

**Coventry Sporting
Club**
Les Allen/Paul Carpenter
180 Longford Road
Longford
Coventry
0247 636 4237

Pat Cowdell
129a Moat Road
Oldbury, Warley
West Midlands
0121 552 8082

David Currivan
15 Northolt Avenue
South Ruislip
Middlesex HA4 6SS
0208 841 9933

Christine Dalton
12 Ladysmith Road
Grimsby
Lincolnshire
DN32 9EF
0147 231 0288

Wally Dixon
Littlemoss House
1 Wayne Close
Littlemoss
Droylesden
Manchester
M43 7LQ
0161 301 5606

**Jack Doughty
(Tara Promotions)**
Lanc End Cottage
Golden Street
Off Buckstone Road
Shaw
Oldham OL1 8LY
01706 845753

Matthew Ellis
24 Brough Avenue
Blackpool
Lancashire
FY2 0PY
0778 866 1683

**Evans-Waterman
Promotions**
Abgah
88 Windsor Road
Bray
Berkshire
SL6 2DJ
0162 862 3640

**Neil Featherby
(Sportslink
Promotions)**
Unit 6
Drayton Business Park
Taversham
Drayton
Norwich
NR8 6RL
0160 386 8606

Joe Frater
The Cottage
Main Road
Grainthorpe
Louth,
Lincolnshire
0147 234 3194

Dave Garside
33 Lowthian Road
Hartlepool
Cleveland
TS26 8AL
0142 929 1611
07973 792588

**Tommy Gilmour
(St Andrew's Sporting
Club)**
Holiday Inn
Bothwell Street
Glasgow
G2 7EN
0141 248 5461

Johnny Griffin
0116 2262 9287
07989 215287

Jess Harding
c/o UK Industrial Pallets
Ltd
Travellers Lane
Industrial Estate
Travellers Lane
Welham Green
Hatfield
Herts
AL9 7HF
0170 727 0440

**Mick Hennessy
(Hennessy Sports)**
12 Invicta Road
Dartford
Kent
DA2 6AZ
0208 815 4027

**Barry Hearn
(Matchroom)**
10 Western Road
Romford
Essex RM1 3JT
0170 878 2200

Dennis Hobson
130 Handsworth Road
Sheffield
South Yorkshire
S9 4AE
0114 256 0555
07836 252429

**Dennis Hobson Snr
(DVSA Promotions)**
73 Darnall Road
Don Valley
Sheffield
S9 5AH
0114 264 3067

Harry Holland
12 Kendall Close
Feltham
Middlesex
0208 867 0435

**Hull & District
Sporting Club**
Mick Toomey
25 Purton Grove
Bransholme
Hull HU7 4QD
0148 282 4476

Alma Ingle
26 Newman Road
Wincobank
Sheffield S9 1LP
0114 281 1277

John Ingle
20 Rockmount Road
Wincobank
Sheffield
S9 1NF
0114 261 7934

Lion Promotions
The Sport Entertainment
Media Group
Lennox Lewis
98 Cockfosters Road
Barnet
Hertfordshire
EN4 0DP
0208 447 4250

Patrick Loftus
117 Rutland Road
West Bridgeford
Nottingham NG2 5DY
0115 981 0982

Malcolm McKillop
14 Springfield Road
Mangotsfield
Bristol
0117 957 3567

Eugene Maloney
The Lord Clyde Public
House, 9 Wotton Road
Deptford
London SE8 5TQ
0208 692 6313

Frank Maloney
Tara, Lower Camden
Chislehurst
Kent BR7 5JA
0776 869 8358

**John Merton
(John Merton
Promotions)**
Merton Technologies Ltd
38 Delaune Street
London
SE17 3UR
0207 582 5200

Alex Morrison
197 Swanston Street
Laird Business Park
Dalmarnock
Glasgow G40 4HW
0141 554 7777

Katherine Morrison
197 Swanston Street
Laird Business Park
Dalmarnock
Glasgow G40 4HW
0141 554 7777

Steve Pollard
899 Beverley High
Road
Hull HU6 9NJ
0148 280 9455

Joe Pyle
36 Manship Road
Mitcham
Surrey CR4 2AZ
0208 646 7793

**Mark Roe
(AMPRO Promotions)**
48 Westbrooke Road
Sidcup
Kent
DA15 7PH
0208 309 9396

Christine Rushton
20 Alverley Lane
Balby, Doncaster
Yorkshire DN4 9AS
0130 231 0919

Kevin Sanders
135 Coneygree Road
Standground
Peterborough
Cambridgeshire
PE2 8LQ
0173 355 5916

Chris Sanigar
Bristol Boxing Gym
40 Thomas Street
St Agnes
Bristol
Avon BS2 9LL
0117 949 6699

Jamie Sanigar
Bristol Boxing Gym
40 Thomas Street
St Agnes
Bristol
Avon
BS2 9LL
0117 949 6699

**Matt Scriven
(The Robin Hood
Executive Sporting
Club)**
5A The Capes
Nottingham
NG13 9AZ
0115 959 9288
0775 927 1511

**Shakespeare
Promotions
Jack Weaver/Jason
Hollier**
301 Coventry Road
Hinckley
Leicestershire
LE10 0NE
0145 561 9066

Mike Shinfield
126 Birchwood Lane
Somercotes
Derbyshire DE55 4NF
0177 360 3124

Kevin Spratt
8 Springfield Road
Guisley
Leeds LS20 8AL
0194 387 6229

Louis Veitch
80 Sherborne Road
North Shore
Blackpool FY1 2PQ
0125 362 8943

Keith Walker
Wayside Bungalow
Selby Road
Eggborough
DN14 0LN
0197 766 2616

**Frank Warren
(Sports Network)**
Centurion House
Bircherley Green
Hertford
Hertfordshire
SG14 1AP
0199 250 5550

Geraldine Williams
Pendeen
Bodiniel Road
Bodmin
Cornwall PL31 2PE
0120 872 575

Philip Williams
2 Bryn Edwin Corris
Powys
SY20 9SH
0789 014 8537

**Stephen Wood
(Viking Promotions)**
Edward Street
Cambridge Industrial
Area
Salford
Manchester M7 1RL
0161 834 9496

Licensed Managers

Sam Adair
Ashfield Cottage
Barnstaple
Devon
EX31 4DB
0123 747 4989

Isola Akay
129 Portnall Road
Paddington
London W9 3BN
0208 960 7724

Chris Aston
54/56 May Street
Crosland Moor
Huddersfield
West Yorkshire
HD4 5DG
0148 432 9616

Andy Ayling
Centurion House
Bircherley Green
Hertford
Hertfordshire
SG14 1AP
0199250 5550

Bruce Baker
Garden Flat
38 Lupus Street
Pimlico
London
SW1 U3EB
0207 592 0102

Robert Bannan
1c Thornton Street
Townhead, Coatbridge
North Lanarkshire
ML5 2NZ
0123 660 6736

Wayne Barker
34 Hampton Road
Failsworth
Manchester
M35 9HT
0161 681 7088

Jack Bishop
76 Gordon Road
Fareham
Hants
PO16 7SS
0132 928 4708

Adam Booth
57 Jackson Road
Bromley
Kent
BR2 8NT
0793 295 2666

Gerald Boustead
46 Coombe Lane
St Marychurch
Torquay
Devon
TQ2 8DY
0180 332 5195

Peter Bowen
50 Newman Avenue
Lanesfield
Wolverhampton
West Midlands
WV4 6BZ
0190 282 8159

Jackie Bowers
36 Drew Road
Silvertown
London
E16
0796 188 3654

Tony Bowers
3 The Green Walk
Chingford
London
E4
0208 523 8113

Paul Boyce
Winstones
Church Street
Briton Ferry
Neath
West Glamorgan
SA11 2GJ
0163 981 3723

David Bradley
The Dovecote
Aston Hall
Claverley
WV5 7DZ
0174 671 0287

John Branch
44 Hill Way
Holly Lodge Estate
London
NE6 4EP

John Breen
Cedar Lodge
589 Antrim Road
Belfast
BT15
0289 077 0238

Mike Brennan
2 Canon Avenue
Chadwell Heath
Romford
Essex
0208 599 4588

Steve Butler
107 Cambridge Street
Normanton
West Yorkshire
WF6 1ES
0192 489 1097

Trevor Callighan
Apartment 9
Deph Brow
Skircoat Moor Road
Halifax
West Yorkshire
HX3 0GZ
0142 232 2592

George Carman
5 Mansion Lane
Mobile Home Site
Iver
Bucks S10 9RQ
0175 365 3096

John Celebanski
5 Ling Park Avenue
Wilsden
Bradford
BD15 0NE
0127 482 4015

Nigel Christian
89 Oaklands Park
Polperro Road
Looe
Cornwall
PL13 2JS
0150 326 4176

David Coldwell
Castle Court
2 St John's Road
Sheffield
0179 945 6400

Brian Coleman
31 Gwernifor Street
Mountain Ash
Mid-Glamorgan
CF45 3NA
0144 347 8910

William Connelly
72 Clincart Road
Mount Florida
Glasgow
G42
0141 632 5818

Tommy Conroy
144 High Street East
Sunderland
Tyne and Wear
0191 567 6871

Dave Currivan
15 Northolt Avenue
South Ruislip
Middlesex
0208 841 9933

David Davies
10 Bryngelli
Carmel
Llanelli
Dyfed
SA14 7TL
0126 984 3204

John Davies
Unit 14
Rectors Yard
Rectors Lane
Penre Sandycroft
Deeside
Flintshire
CH5 2DH
0124 453 8984

Ronnie Davies
3 Vallensdean Cottages
Hangleton Lane
Portslade
Sussex
0127 341 6497

Owen Delargy
Birchley Farm
Brinklow
Coventry
CV3 2AB
0797 010 2553

Jack Doughty
Lane End Cottage
Golden Street
Off Buckstones Road
Shaw
Oldham OL2 8LY
01706 845753

Mickey Duff
c/o Mrs E Allen
16 Herga Court
Harrow on the Hill
Middlesex HA1 3RS
0208 423 6763

Paul Dykes
Boxing Network
International
Suites 1, 2 & 3, Lord
Lonsdale Chambers
10 Furlong Passage
Burslem
Stoke on Trent
ST6 3AY
0783 177 7310

Jim Evans
88 Windsor Road
Maidenhead
Berkshire SL6 2DJ
0162 862 3640

Stuart Fleet
Dairy Farm Cottage
Old Road
Great Coates
Grimsby
DN37 9NX
0147 231 3764

Tania Follett
123 Calfridus Way
Bracknell
Berkshire
RG12 3HD
07930 904303

Philippe Fondu
1b, Nursery Gardens
Birch Cottage
Chislehurst
Kent BR7 5BW
0208 295 3598

Steve Foster
62 Overdale
Swinton
Salford M27 5WE
0161 794 1723

Dai Gardiner
13 Hengoed Hall Drive
Cefn Hengoed
Mid Glamorgan
CF8 7JW
0144 381 2971

Dave Garside
33 Lowthian Road
Hartlepool
Cleveland TS26 8AL
0142 929 1611

Jimmy Gill
69a Inham Road
Chilwell
Nottingham NG9 4GT
0115 913 5482

Tommy Gilmour
St Andrew's Sporting
Club
Holiday Inn
Bothwell Street
Glasgow G2 7EN
0141 248 5461

Mike Goodall
Ringcraft
Unit 21
Briars Close Business
Park
Evesham
Worcestershire
WR11 4JT
0138 644 2118

Alex Gower
22 Norwood Avenue
Rush Green
Romford
Essex RM7 0QH
0170 875 3474

Lee Graham
28 Smeaton Court
50 Rockingham Street
London SE1 6PF
0207 357 6648

Carl Gunns
14 Whiles Lane
Birstall
Leicester LE4 4EE
0116 267 1494

Jess Harding
c/o UK Industrial Pallets
Ltd
Travellers Lane
Industrial Estate
Travellers Lane
Welham Green
Hatfield
Herts AL9 7HF
0170 727 0440

Tony Harris
237 Stapleford Road
Trowell
Nottingham
NG9 3QE
0115 913 6564

Pat Healy
1 Cranley Buildings
Brookes Market
Holborn
London EC1
0207 242 8121

Barry Hearn
Matchroom
10 Western Road
Romford
Essex RM1 3JT
0170 878 2200

Michael Helliet
Flat 1
Lower Ground Floor
102 Whitfield Street
London
W1T 5EB
0207 387 4314

Martin Herdman
24a Crown Road
St Margarets
Twickenham
Middlesex
TW1 3EE
0208 891 6040

Mick Hill
35 Shenstone House
Aldrington Road
Streatham
London SW16
0208 769 2218

Dennis Hobson
Promotions
130 Handsworth Road
Sheffield
S9 4AE
0114 256 0555

Nicholas Hodges
Llys-y-Deryn
Cilcennin
Lampeter
Ceredigion
West Wales
SA48 8RR
0157 047 0452

Harry Holland
12 Kendall Close
Feltham
Middlesex
0208 867 0435

Gordon Holmes
15 Robert Andrew
Close
Morley St Botolph
Wymondham
Norfolk
NR18 9AA
0195 360 7887

Lloyd Honeyghan
PO Box 17216
London
SE17 1ZU
07956 405007

Brian Hughes
41 Fold Green
Chadderton
Lancashire
OL9 9DX
0161 620 2916

Geoff Hunter
6 Hawkshead Way
Winsford
Cheshire CW7 2SZ
0160 686 2162

Dominic Ingle
26 Newman Road
Sheffield S9 1LP
0114 281 1277

John Ingle
20 Rockmount Road
Wincobank
Sheffield S9
0114 261 7934

Steve James
117 Main Street
Little Harrowden
Wellingborough
Northants
NN9 5BA
0193 322 2241

Errol Johnson
36 Newton Street
West Bromwich
West Midlands
B71 3RQ
0121 532 6118

Thomas Jones
13 Planetree Road
Hale
Cheshire WA15 9JL
0161 980 2661

Brian Lawrence
15 Selan Gardens
Hayes
Middlesex
UB4 0EA
0208 723 0182

Buddy Lee
The Walnuts
Roman Bank
Leverington, Wisbech
Cambridgeshire
PE13 5AR
0194 558 3266

Daniel Lutaaya
3 Knebworth House
Union Grove
London SW8 2RS
07751 262037

Pat Lynch
Gotherington
68 Kelsey Lane
Balsall Common
Near Coventry
CV7 7GL
0167 633374

Paul McCausland
1 Prospect Heights
Carrickfergus
Northern Ireland
BT38 8QY
0289 336 5942

Robert McCracken
16 Dusard Way
Droitwich
Worcestershire
WR9 8UX
0190 579 8976

Jim McDonnell
2 Meadway
Hillside Avenue
Woodford Green
Essex
IG8 7RF
07860 770006

Owen McMahon
3 Atlantic Avenue
Belfast BT15
0289 074 3535

Colin McMillan
60 Billet Road
Chadwell Heath
Romford
Essex
RM6 5SU
0208 597 4464

Eugene Maloney
The Lord Clyde Public
House
9 Wotton Road
Deptford
London
SE8 5TQ
0208 692 6313

Frank Maloney
Tara
Lower Camden
Chislehurst
Kent
BR7 5JA
0199 250 5550

Dennie Mancini
16 Rosedew Road
Off Fulham Palace Road
London
W6 9ET
0208 748 2571

Michael Marsden
1 North View
Roydes Lane
Rothwell
Leeds
LS26 0BQ
0113 282 5565

Terry Marsh
60 Gaynesford
Basildon
Essex
SS16 5SG
0207 0152207

Tommy Miller
128 Clapton Mount
King Cross Road
Halifax
West Yorkshire
0142 236 1147

Clifton Mitchell
42 Wiltshire Road
Derby DE21 6EX
01332 295380

Alex Morrison
197 Swanston Street
Laird Business Park
Dalmarnock
Glasgow G40 4HW
0141 554 7777

Katherine Morrison
197 Swanston Street
Laird Business Park
Dalmarnock
Glasgow
G40 4HW
0141 554 7777

James Murray
87 Spean Street
Glasgow
G44 4DS
0141 637 7926

Bert Myers
8 Thornhill Street
Burnley
Lancashire
BB12 6LU
0781 696 6742

Trevor Nerwal
Wayside Cottage
64 Vicarage Lane
Water Orton
Birmingham
B46 1RU
0121 730 1546

Paul Newman
12 Edgehill Way
Portslade
Brighton
BN41 2PU
0127 341 9777

Norman Nobbs
364 Kings Road
Kingstanding
Birmingham
B44 0UG
0121 355 5341

Stewart Nubley
94 Richmond Road
Kirkby in Ashfield
Nottinghamshire
NG17 7PW
0162 343 2357

James Oyebola
1 Mulgrave Road
London
NW10 1BS
07931 370039

Mark O'Callaghan
1 Keel Gardens
Southborough
Tunbridge Wells
Kent TN4 0JQ
0189 268 9979

Terry O'Neill
48 Kirkfield View
Colton Village
Leeds LS15 9DX
0113 225 6140

James Oyebola
194 Portnall Road
London W9
0208 930 9685

Ian Pauly
1202 Lincoln Road
Peterborough
PE4 6LA
0173 331 1266

Charles Pearson
3 Moordale Road
Grangetown
Cardiff
CF11 7DU
0292 063 9425

Steve Pollard
899 Beverley High Road
Hull
HU6 9NJ
0148 280 9455

David Poston
2 Whitegate Road
Daisy Bank
Bliston
West Midlands
WV14 8UY
0190 249 3040

Brian Powell
138 Laurel Road
Bassaleg
Newport
Gwent
NP10 8PT
0163 389 2165

Dean Powell
Sports Network
Centurion House
Bircherley Green
Hertfordshire
07956 905741

Joe Pyle
36 Manship Road
Mitcham
Surrey
CR4 2AZ
0208 395 6907

Michael Quinn
64 Warren Road
Wanstead
London
E11 2NA
0208 989 0082

Howard Rainey
9 Castlebeck Drive
Sheffield
S2 1NP
0114 264 4106

Paul Rees
11 Abbots Park
London Road
St Albans
Herts AL1 1TW
0172 776 3160

Glyn Rhodes
166 Oldfield Road
Stannington
Sheffield S6 6DY
0114 232 6513

Gus Robinson, MBE
Stranton House
Westview Road
Hartlepool
TS24 0BB
0142 923 4221

Mark Roe
48 Westbrooke Road
Sidcup
Kent
DA15 7PH
0208 309 9396

John Rooney
6 Coach House Mews
217 Long Lane
London SE1 4PP
0788 407 7024

John Rushton
20 Alverley Lane
Balby
Doncaster
DN4 9AS
0130 231 0919

Kevin Sanders
135 Coneygree Road
Peterborough
Cambridgeshire
PE1 8LQ
0173 355 5916

Chris Sanigar
Bristol Boxing Gym
40 Thomas Street
St Agnes
Bristol
BS2 9LL
0117 949 6699

Trevor Schofield
234 Doncaster Road
Barnsley
South Yorkshire
S70 1UQ
0122 629 7376

Matthew Scriven
5a The Capes
Aslockton
Nottingham
NG13 9AZ

Mike Shinfield
126 Birchwood Lane
Somercotes
Derbyshire
DE55 4NE
0177 360 3124

Tony Sims
67 Peel Place
Clayhall
Ilford
Essex
IG5 0PT
0208 550 8911

Les Southey
Oakhouse
Park Way
Hillingdon
Middlesex
0189 525 4719

Gerald Storey
41 Willowbank
Gardens
Belfast
BT15 5AJ
0123 275 3819

Wally Swift
12 Garden Close
Knowle
Solihull
West Midlands
B93 92F
0156 477 5140

Glenroy Taylor
73 Aspen Lane
Northolt
Middlesex
U35 6XH
0795 645 3787

Jack Trickett
Acton Court Hotel
187 Buxton Road
Stockport
Cheshire
SK2 7AB
0161 483 6172

Louis Veitch
80 Sherborne Road
North Shore
Blackpool
FY1 2PQ
0125 362 8943

Keith Walker
Walkers Boxing
Promotions
Headland House
Suite 21-35
Spawd Bone Lane
Knottingley
West Yorkshire
WF11 0HY
0197 760 7888

Frank Warren
Centurion House
Bircherley Green
Hertford
Hertfordshire
SG14 1AP
0199 250 5550

Robert Watt
32 Dowanhill Street
Glasgow G11
0141 334 7465

Jack Weaver
301 Coventry Road
Hinckley
Leicestershire
LE10 0NE
0145 561 9066

Lee Wicks
22a Stone Close
Worthing
West Sussex
BN13 2AU
0190 369 1936

Derek V. Williams
65 Virginia Road
Surrey
CR7 8EN
0208 765 0492

Derek Williams
Pendeen
Bodiniel Road
Bodmin
Cornwall
PL31 2PE
0777 633 0516

John Williams
3a Langham Road
Tottenham
London N15 3QX
0794 933 5787

Alan Wilton
The Bridge
42 Derryboy Road
Crossgar BT30 9LH
0289 754 2195

Barry Winter
9 McNeill Avenue
Linnvale
Clydebank G81 2TB
0141 952 9942

Stephen Wood
Viking Promotions
Edward Street
Cambridge Industrial
Area, Salford
Manchester
M7 1RL
0161 834 9496

Tex Woodward
Spaniorum Farm
Compton Greenfield
Bristol BS12 3RX
0145 463 2448

Licensed Matchmakers

John Ashton
1 Charter Close
Kirby in Ashfield
Nottinghamshire
NG17 8PF
0162 372 1278

Neil Bowers
59 Carson Road
Canning Town
London E16 4BD
0207 473 5631

Nigel Christian
89 Oaklands Park
Polperro Road, Looe
Cornwall PL13 2JS

Jim Evans
88 Windsor Road
Bray, Maidenhead
Berks SL6 2DJ
0162 862 3640

John Gaynor
7 Westhorne Fold
Counthill Drive
Brooklands Road
Crumpsall
Manchester M8 4JN
0161 740 6993

Jimmy Gill
69a Inham Road
Chilwell
Nottingham NG9 4GT
0775 955 7551

Tommy Gilmour
St Andrew's SC
Holiday Inn
Bothwell Street
Glasgow G2 7EN
0141 248 5461

Roy Hilder
2 Farrington Place
Chislehurst
Kent BR7 6BE
0208 325 6156

John Ingle
20 Rockmount Road
Wincobank
Sheffield S9 1LP
0114 261 7934

Stevie James
117 Main Street
Little Harrowden
Wellingbrough
Northamptonshire
NN9 5BA
0193 322 2241

Dennie Mancini
16 Rosedew Road
Off Fulham Palace Road
Hammersmith
London W6 9ET
0208 748 2571

Ken Morton
3 St Quintin Mount
'Bradway'
Sheffield S17 4PQ
0114 262 1829

Dean Powell
Sports Network
Centurion House
Bircherley Green
Hertfordshire
SG14 1AP
0199 250 5550

Richard Poxon
148 Cliffefield Road
Sheffield
S8 9BS
0114 225 7856

John Rushton
20 Averley Lane
Balby
Doncaster
South Yorkshire
0130 231 0919

Chris Sanigar
Bristol Boxing Gym
40 Thomas Street
St Agnes
Bristol BS2 9LL
07831 359978

Tony Sims
67 Peel Place
Clayhall Avenue
Ilford
Essex IG5 0PT
0773 961 7830

Ian Watson
120 York Street
Jarrow
Tyne & Wear
NE32 5RY
07850 779773

John Wilson
1 Shenley Hill
Radlett
Herts WD7 3AS
0192 385 7874

Kristian Laight (right) became the first man to go the distance with the brilliant Dagenham super-featherweight, Kevin Mitchell, when losing on points at the York Hall, Bethnal Green on 7 February

Les Clark

Licensed BBBoC Referees, Timekeepers, Ringwhips and Inspectors

Licensed Referees

Class 'B'
Dean Bramhald	Midland Area
Mark Curry	Northern Area
Seamus Dunne	Southern Area
Christopher Kelly	Central Area
Shaun Messer	Midlands Area
David Morgan	Welsh Area
Kenneth Pringle	Scottish Area
Andrew Wright	Northern Area

Class 'A'
Terence Cole	Northern Area
Lee Cook	Southern Area
Kenneth Curtis	Southern Area
Philip Edwards	Central Area
Roddy Evans	Welsh Area
Keith Garner	Central Area
Paul Graham	Scottish Area
Michael Heatherwick	Welsh Area
Jeff Hinds	Southern Area
Al Hutcheon	Scottish Area
David Irving	Northern Ireland
Wynford Jones	Welsh Area
Victor Loughin	Scottish Area
Grant Wallis	Western Area

Class 'A' Star
Richie Davies	Southern Area
Howard Foster	Central Area
Mark Green	Southern Area
Ian John-Lewis	Southern Area
John Keane	Midlands Area
Marcus McDonnell	Southern Area
Terry O'Connor	Midlands Area
Dave Parris	Southern Area
Paul Thomas	Midlands Area
Mickey Vann	Central Area

Licensed Timekeepers

Michael Alexander	Central Area
Arnold Bryson	Northern Area
Neil Burder	Welsh Area
Richard Clark	Southern Area
Anthony Dunkerley	Midlands Area
Robert Edgeworth	Southern Area
Dale Elliott	Northern Ireland
Harry Foxall	Midlands Area
Eric Gilmour	Scottish Area
Gary Grennan	Central Area
Brian Heath	Midlands Area
Greg Hue	Southern Area
Jon Lee	Western Area
Michael McCann	Southern Area
Peter McCann	Southern Area
Norman Maddox	Midlands Area
Barry Pinder	Central Area
Raymond Rice	Southern Area
Colin Roberts	Central Area
James Russell	Scottish Area
David Walters	Welsh Area
Kevin Walters	Northern Area
Paul Webster	Central Area
Nick White	Southern Area

Licensed Ringwhips

Lester Arthur	Western Area
Michael Burke	Scottish Area
Steve Butler	Central Area
Ernie Draper	Southern Area
Simon Goodall	Midlands Area
Mark Currivan	Southern Area
Lee Gostolo	Central Area
Denzil Lewis	Western Area
Stuart Lithgo	Northern Area
James McCormick	Northern Ireland
Tommy Miller (Jnr)	Central Area
Tommy Rice	Southern Area
Sandy Risley	Southern Area
Stephen Sidebottom	Central Area
Gary Stanford	Southern Area
James Wallace	Scottish Area

Inspectors

Herold Adams	Southern Area
Alan Alster	Central Area
William Ball	Southern Area
Richard Barber	Southern Area
Michael Barnett	Central Area
Don Bartlett	Midlands Area
Ivor Bassett	Welsh Area
David Boulter	Midlands Area
Geoff Boulter	Central Area
Fred Breyer	Southern Area
David Brown	Western Area
Walter Campbell	Northern Ireland
Harry Carroll	Welsh Area
Geoff Collier	Midlands Area
Michael Collier	Southern Area
Julian Courtney	Welsh Area
Robert Curry	Northern Area
Jaswinder Dhaliwal	Midlands Area
Christopher Dolman	Midlands Area
Kevin Fulthorpe	Welsh Area
Bob Galloway	Southern Area
Paul Gooding	Northern Area
Eddie Higgins	Scottish Area
Michael Hills	Northern Area
Alan Honnibal	Western Area
David Hughes	Welsh Area
Francis Keenan	Northern Ireland
James Kirkwood	Scottish Area
Nicholas Laidman	Southern Area
Kevin Leafe	Central Area
Eddie Lillis	Central Area
Fred Little	Western Area
Reginald Long	Northern Area
Bob Lonkhurst	Southern Area
Paul McAllister	Northern Ireland
Sam McAughtry	Northern Ireland
Dave McAuley	Northern Ireland
Liam McColgan	Scottish Area
Billy McCrory	Northern Ireland
Gerry McGinley	Scottish Area
Paul McKeown	Northern Ireland
Neil McLean	Scottish Area
Pat Magee	Northern Ireland
Andy Morris	Central Area
Ron Pavett	Welsh Area
Richard Peers	Central Area
Dave Porter	Southern Area
Fred Potter	Northern Area
Les Potts	Midlands Area
Suzanne Potts	Midlands Area
Steve Ray	Central Area
Bob Rice	Midlands Area
Hugh Russell	Northern Ireland
Charlie Sexton	Scottish Area
Neil Sinclair	Southern Area
Bert Smith	Central Area
Nigel Underwood	Midlands Area
David Venn	Northern Area
Phil Waites	Midlands Area
Ron Warburton	Central Area
Mark Warner	Welsh Area
Danny Wells	Southern Area
Andrew Whitehall	Midlands Area
Trevor Williams	Midlands Area
Barney Wilson	Northern Ireland
Robert Wilson	Scottish Area
Fred Wright	Central Area

Roy Francis, the former Class 'A' Star referee who recently retired   Les Clark

PEACOCK GYMNASIUM

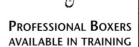

PROMOTER/MANAGER:	TONY BOWERS
AGENT/MATCHMAKER:	ROY HILDER
TRAINERS:	MARTIN BOWERS/JACKIE BOWERS/ALI FORBES/
	JOHN BOSCOE/JOHN HUMPHREY SNR
SECRETARY:	ALAN RITCHINGS

PROFESSIONAL BOXERS
AVAILABLE IN TRAINING

WE ARE VERY PROUD TO BOTH PROMOTE AND MANAGE
THE FOLLOWING LIST OF PROFESSIONAL BOXERS:

JULIUS FRANCIS	HEAVY	EX BRITISH & COMMONWEALTH CHAMPION	23-18-1
GARRY DELANEY	CRUISER	SOUTHERN AREA CHAMPION	31-7-1
ELVIS MICHAILENKO	LIGHT-HEAVY	EUROPEAN UNION CHAMPION	16-1-1
OVILL McKENZIE	LIGHT-HEAVY		5-4-0
ERIK TEYMOUR	SUPER-MIDDLE		15-1-0
THOMAS DA SILVA	LIGHT-MIDDLE		4-15-2
CRAIG LYNCH	LIGHT-MIDDLE		4-12-1
OSCAR MILKITAS	LIGHT-WELTER		4-0-0
SILENCE SAHEED	LIGHT-WELTER		5-1-1
BUSTER DENNIS	FEATHER		4-5-0
JOHN MACKAY	SUPER-BANTAM		9-5-0
ROCKY DEAN	SUPER-BANTAM		7-5-2
JOSEPH AGBEKO	BANTAM	WBF WORLD CHAMPION	21-1-0

READY, WILLING AND ABLE
ANYTIME, ANYPLACE, ANYWHERE

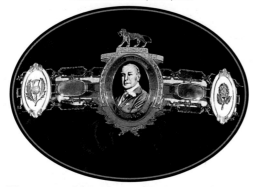

Boxers' Record Index